Suddenly Silver

Other *For Better or For Worse®* Collections

Reality Check
With This Ring
Family Business
Graduation: A Time for Change
The Big 5-0
Sunshine and Shadow
Middle Age Spread
Growing Like a Weed
Love Just Screws Everything Up
Starting from Scratch
"There Goes My Baby!"
Things Are Looking Up . . .
What, Me Pregnant?
If This Is a Lecture, How Long Will It Be?
Pushing 40
It's All Downhill from Here
Keep the Home Fries Burning
The Last Straw
Just One More Hug
"It Must Be Nice to Be Little"
Is This "One of Those Days," Daddy?
I've Got the One-More-Washload Blues . . .

Retrospectives

All About April
The Lives Behind the Lines: 20 Years of For Better or For Worse®
Remembering Farley: A Tribute to the Life of Our Favorite Cartoon Dog
It's the Thought That Counts . . . Fifteenth Anniversary Collection
A Look Inside . . . For Better or For Worse: The 10th Anniversary Collection

Little Books

Isn't He Beautiful?
Isn't She Beautiful?
Wags and Kisses
A Perfect Christmas
Graduation: Just the Beginning!

With Andie Parton

Leaving Home

Suddenly Silver

CELEBRATING 25 YEARS OF FOR BETTER OR FOR WORSE

by Lynn Johnston

Andrews McMeel
Publishing

Kansas City

For Better or For Worse® is distributed by Universal Press Syndicate.

Suddenly Silver copyright © 2004 by Lynn Johnston Productions, Inc. All rights reserved. Printed in the United States of America. No part of this book may be used or reproduced in any manner whatsoever without written permission except in the case of reprints in the context of reviews. For permission information, write EnterCom Canada Inc., 353 MacPherson Drive, Corbeil, Ontario, Canada P0H 1K0.

06 07 08 BAM 10 9 8 7 6 5 4 3 2

ISBN-13: 978-0-7407-4739-7
ISBN-10: 0-7407-4739-8

Library of Congress Control Number: 2004106081

www.FBorFW.com

Contents

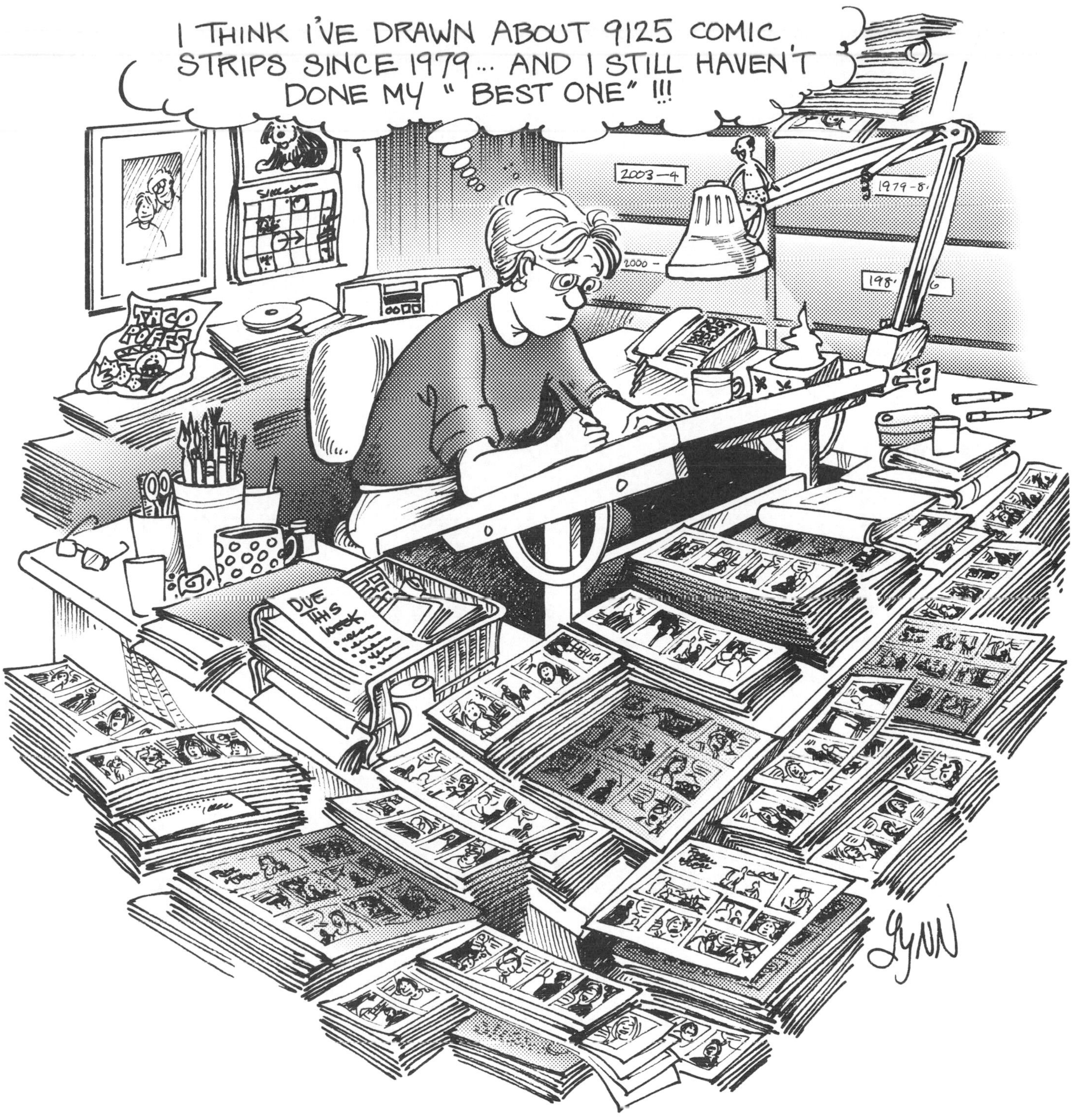
I THINK I'VE DRAWN ABOUT 9125 COMIC STRIPS SINCE 1979... AND I STILL HAVEN'T DONE MY " BEST ONE" !!!
2003–4
TACO PUFFS
DUE THIS WEEK
LYNN

Introduction

I rarely read introductions, especially long-winded ones written by the author who must know, for heaven's sake that he/she is writing largely for an audience who will flip right past it to the good parts. Hoping there ARE any. So, this is a letter to me and perhaps other cartoonists who identify with me and might be compelled to think about their own art in a reflective sort of way.

This is my 25th year of doing the syndicated comic strip *For Better or For Worse*. I look at my work every day and wish it was funnier, better drawn, more meaningful—but it's the best I can do and it's part of me. It's a story that's grown from rough sketches and four-panel gags to something beyond my control. I'm no longer a writer or an artist, but the conduit for a gaggle of characters who love, laugh, fight, flirt, work, worry, and support one another. They have careers and families, live in homes and apartments whose walls, windows, and furnishings I know well.

I enter the home of John and Elly Patterson and I know how many footsteps there are to the kitchen, what pictures are on the walls, which way the cupboards open, and what's inside. I know that their upstairs bathroom needs repairing, the wallpaper needs to be replaced, and there are stains on the hall rugs. I have moved with their now adult children, Michael and Elizabeth, from home to dormitories to crude apartments and houses with landlords, roommates, and furnishings that don't quite fit. They have balanced their freedom with the financial woes that follow, always keeping in touch with home. Always knowing support was there.

In 1979, these story lines began simply enough, but like a pebble tossed into a pond, the initial "plop" became an ever-widening and more complicated overlapping series of circles: events into which new characters were drawn—literally. (I want to say "the *plop* thickened.") The original four family members became five—with pets and neighbors, classmates, business associates, teachers, and incidental characters coming into my head uninvited. Who wants to work so hard? Who needs to design a new face, create a new personality, invent a new story just for them? I didn't.

New characters did this themselves, appearing out of nowhere—first as ghosts in penciled outlines, then inked, visible and alive. Michael Patterson sat next to an odd-looking guy during a university lecture and Josef Weeder happened. I didn't put him there, he just "showed up"—and his name had already been assigned.

"Weed" became Michael's close friend and collaborator. When both graduated from university they continued to work together and at present are living in neighboring row houses on the outskirts of Toronto. I know both of their apartments well—but I've never seen Weed's bedroom.

I have tried to describe this abstract host of people and places that share my mind, but only writers, cartoonists, and serious daydreamers understand. By all means, I should be a shrink's showpiece but I don't upset anyone (or myself) unless I'm very late on a deadline and become unpleasant to live with.

Rod Johnston, who's lived with me now for 29 years, would agree that my two realities make cohabitation a challenge —and if it wasn't for his great sense of humor, his patience, objectivity, and the ability to regress into his own imaginary universe, we'd likely "just be friends."

Despite the fact that new characters enter the strip uninvited, I am every one of them. I am baby Meredith, 13-year-old April, newlyweds Mike and Deanna, Grandpa Jim, and even the pets.

You have to BE a dog to draw a dog! You have to feel what it's like to walk on all fours, scratch with your hind leg, and eat from a dish on the floor. It's not a bad life, actually, because other than food, sex, and hanging around outside, there's not much to think about (sort of like being a teenaged boy, perhaps—but there's a limit to what we can show in the paper).

I am close to 90 when Jim Richards speaks, holds his cane for balance, hugs his second wife, and relives his part in World War II with emotion and cruel clarity. I was his wife, Marian, as she grew frail and died, following her into the peaceful space she gracefully entered, promising to watch over her family as she left them.

I am John Patterson—husband, father, grandpa, dentist, and hobbyist whose stability and strength of character are definitely patterned after the man who has loved me through 25 years of deadlines and weighty self-doubt.

I am Elly Patterson. Elly is me. I draw her the way I feel—her long hair (once a trademark of mine) pulled tightly back in a bun with bangs askew, her posture, her shape, her expressions, thoughts, and character—for better or for worse, are me. Like a mirror image, she looks up from the page. I watch myself dissect a problem, embrace my family, confront my shortcomings, and try to accept the onset of middle age. "Why do you draw Elly Patterson so ugly?" people ask. Even our son, Aaron, asked, "How come she has an inflatable nose, Ma? One day you draw her with a regular-sized schnozz and then, it's blown up like a spud!!!!—How come?" The answer lies somewhere between the two worlds I live in: goofy and genuine, silly and serious, impossible and painfully real. The inflatable nose has helped suppress an inflatable ego, which is equally unattractive and should be made fun of as often as possible!

Twenty-five years ago, I was offered a job that would both challenge and identify me. It has profoundly affected everyone in our family. My husband has been my guide through the pitfalls of celebrity. Our children have enjoyed the laughter, respected my work, and have striven to separate themselves from the cartoon characters, Michael and Elizabeth, who are not Aaron and Kate, but figments of my imagination. I have explored their personalities without exposing them. It would be unthinkable to do so.

The only person you will truly know through my work is me—and I'm still not sure who I am . . . even though Elly Patterson and I have been "working on it" for 25 years!

Welcome to our 25th anniversary collection.

Lynn

September, 2004

The Early Years

Come September (book-flogging season) it will have been 25 years since I signed the contract with Universal Press Syndicate to produce the comic strip, *For Better or For Worse*. I sat at a rosewood table, watched my hand form my signature, and instead of celebrating with the folks who would be my coworkers for perhaps one-third of my life . . . I went back to my Kansas City hotel room and was sick. I called my husband, Rod. "Do I say congratulations," he asked, or "Do you want sympathy?" It took awhile for us to conclude (nervously) that I really could do this, it would be OK. I went home to Dundas, Ontario, looking profoundly confused, insecure, and more pregnant than when I'd left.

Rod was trying to finish dental school, build his own office furniture (in an unheated garage), and get his pilot's license upgraded to floatplane rating. Money was worse than tight and we had our four-year-old son, Aaron, buzzing about on a constant flight plan of his own—which left us sleepless, tense, and busy. We lived in a sort of controlled chaos that pulled us from one day to the next. When I found myself trying to make rudimentary comic strips at the kitchen table while counting contractions, it seemed not at all out of the ordinary. Fortunately, I had asked for a six-month reprieve from a launch date, so these were practice pieces, a time to learn just how to draw the characters I modeled after us, how to time a three- or four-panel gag, and how to time myself. There was so much to do.

Kate was born in December and Rod graduated that spring. We sold our house, I turned my freelance clients over to friends, and we packed everything we had and drove to Lynn Lake, Manitoba—"home" to Rod and "the middle of nowhere" to me.

The strip had not yet started to run. I kept a steady flow of work going to Kansas, using a temperamental fax machine at the dental office, which was a 10-minute walk from the house. Make that an hour. I had to take the kids along. Fortunately, Rod's parents lived en route to downtown, so it was easy to drop them off with his mom, Ruth, and run around on my own. Rod's parents were a godsend and the reason I agreed to take the plunge with my flying dentist. I had met his family and I wanted them. I wanted to be enveloped by their warmth and acceptance and positive attitude.

When the strip debuted in September 1979, I thought I was ready. The regular faxes to Lee Salem (my editor in Kansas City) had set me up with a routine, a style, and a few weeks "in the bank," which was a safety net before the crush of real deadlines began. Strangely enough, I had no problem digging material out of the normal day-to-day stuff that went on around us. The practice and parenthood provided an endless wellspring of grumbling which became gags. I was really good at grumbling!

The strip was like a sounding board, someone I could talk to about how I really felt. When I look back at the earliest efforts, I see such negativity hidden beneath the humor. While Lynn Lake's rugged northern atmosphere was friendly, it was not what I was used to. On the outside, I tried to appear content, controlled, and connected. On the inside, I was lonely for the friends I'd known in the south and missed the amenities and the (imagined) excitement of the city. Having grown up in Vancouver, the adjustment to Ontario had been hard for me. Now I was so far north, literally at the end of the road. Hundreds of miles of wilderness surrounded our little community, and the nearest neighboring town lay 60 miles of muskeg and moose trails away. We had two channels on TV, and one radio station; the paper came a day late because it came by bus. There were two grocery stores and one restaurant you'd willingly trust with your health. The theater was about to be condemned, yet we were so hungry for a taste of "outside" that movies were still shown and we went to them all, making sure our shoes were laced so they wouldn't be glued to the years of gum, Coke, and popcorn embedded in the floor.

My first lesson in small-town etiquette happened when, newly settled in, I happened to make a rude remark about a woman to another woman I had met at the grocery store. By the time I got home the phone was ringing. It was the woman about whom I'd made the mean remark, asking for an apology. I admitted to the remark, humbly asked for her forgiveness, and she let me go, saying, "You're not in the city now, Lynn, here we all know each other."

For Better or For Worse began with hesitant lines, disjointed ideas, and a rather dour attitude, but it was funny. It became part of our lives, like a guest who takes up permanent residency. It really was like having another member of the family move in, or more accurately, a whole bunch of them!

Like a real child, the comic strip hovered constantly on the edge of my consciousness, nudging itself to the forefront even when I was doing something entirely unrelated. My in-laws adopted it too and it seemed natural to have serious discussions about the Pattersons over coffee, just as we would about real family members. Ruth gave me parenting tips regarding Michael and Lizzie, we discussed Elly's '60s hairstyle, wondering if it connected her too much to myself—but then, she and I are one in the same—and that was my *coif de jour*.

The tiny community of Lynn Lake provided great living resources when I needed auxiliary characters. The philandering, chauvinistic Ted was a composite of two men I knew, and Elly's neighbor, Annie, became more and more like my friend Nancy, with whom I shared both the out-post blues and the challenge of raising two small kids who were indoors much of the time, due to the harsh winters we endured.

It was not unusual for the temperature to go down to -40 and below, so indoor activities were creatively organized and a visit to a neighbor's house was both an adventure and a diversion. Nancy and I became dependent on each other, and when she left town, I was devastated. The character Annie then had to fly on her own until I could find another personality to suit her! She was later a composite of two other women, but the relationship diminished, and I focused more on "Connie," Elly's other neighbor. I've always based characters on real people, and the stories are part truth, part fiction. I like to research the material so that situations, if not true, are at least believable. Once, my veterinarian sis-in-law and I talked on the phone for a full hour about Farley's upset stomach, finally pinning the symptoms down to "garbage gastritis" and coming up with a suitable prognosis and treatment.

The earliest strips were drawn tentatively. When I look at it now, the work seems so amateur-ish and the characters rather generic in many ways. Elly could have been any harassed housewife, John any bemused young father, and the kids any kids. It took about a year before their personalities jelled and they began to set about leading their lives as if I were an observer. There were times

4

when I've felt that they were the writers. Ideas and story lines I wanted to explore were not permitted and the work flowed more naturally if I just sat back on the couch with a notepad on my lap, closed my eyes, and let them take me where they wanted to go!

As the characters took over the strip, the artwork sharpened and their features and behavior patterns became more distinctive. Usually, I was able to chronicle their lives working from nine until noon. I could write a week of dailies in a morning, then pencil and ink them the next day. Afternoons, I was free to be mother, community rep for northern touring performers, lead on our curling team, and a fairly good cook.

Those first few years were a wonderful time creatively. The ideas seemed to come so easily, but I had lots of material to draw from. Our children, Aaron and Kate, were the same age as Michael and Elizabeth in FBorFW. And I could find stuff to laugh or complain about every time I turned around! It soon became evident, however, that their close connection to the strip would be a problem. As Aaron's friends at school began to read and discuss the strip it became an uncomfortable intrusion into our children's lives.

The Patterson family was aging and developing in real time, much against my own wishes. They were going to follow us chronologically whether I liked it or not! Rod and I made a conscious decision then to keep the comic strip family static for three years, to allow a separation to occur. Out of respect for our kids' privacy I did not put actual family occurrences into the stories, but despite the three-year gap, they were still teased and identified with the characters, which was not a good thing. The one great benefit was in being able to look at chaos in retrospect. I was a much better parent when I was dealing with imaginary kids three years younger than our own!

For Better or For Worse went into syndication with 150 papers, and the number increased rapidly. With the growing success of the feature came an enlargement of my hat size. I was interviewed by all kinds of people and asked to do public-service announcements, to accept speaking engagements, and eventually go on promotional tours to sell the "collection" books that were published annually. I loved playing celebrity. It got me out of Lynn Lake, away from family and responsibility. I enjoyed the talk shows, the book signings, and interviews. It was all about me!

Americans were especially fun to talk to. Being a woman cartoonist was a novelty, as was my Canadian citizenship, but when it came to talking about where I lived, I could say just about anything and get away with it. I remember one lovely, leggy young thing (her first break as a talk-show host) asking me, "If you live so far north, how do you get your work all the way to Kansas City on time?"

"Dog team," I replied, expecting a laugh.

"Really?" she squealed. "How interesting!!!"

(I knew I had her.) "Yes," I continued. "The dogs run daily over the lakes, which are completely frozen, and we are advised not to cook bacon when the mail goes out, because the dogs will often get distracted, pull toward the smell and tangle all the harnesses."

"Oh, I had no idea!" she gushed, putting her hand over her chest and blinking into the camera.

I couldn't believe she had been so easily hooked, so I let her off, saying, "I'm kidding! We send our stuff by courier like everyone else!"

She was furious, the interview ended abruptly, and as the commercial break went in, she turned to me and said, "How DARE you make me look like such an idiot?" My guess was she wouldn't last long in television.

I got pretty good at looking like an idiot myself. I would do as many interviews as I could, often doing such a ham-up job, I'd lie in my hotel bed later wishing for all the world that I could erase the tape or rewrite the article that would be out there for everyone to see. I watched every show I was on, saw what worked and what didn't, and eventually became quite at home with lights, camera, action.

Meanwhile, back at the ranch, my family was getting past enjoying the kudos. The disadvantages of a mother and wife who came equipped with an invisible crown were becoming obvious. My willingness to play with my new role as celebrity was clearly pointed out by Aaron who, seeing me packing for another trip, said, "Do you have to turn into Lynn Johnston again?" There was also a long talk with Rod, who asked me what I really wanted, and was I aware of how much I was changing, and not for the better.

When I look back now, I realize that, much as it grated at the time, living in a remote mining community was the best thing that could have happened to me. Without the commonsense grounding a small town offers, I might have lost everything—my husband, family, my job, everything!

Art and affection are so easily destroyed by arrogance.

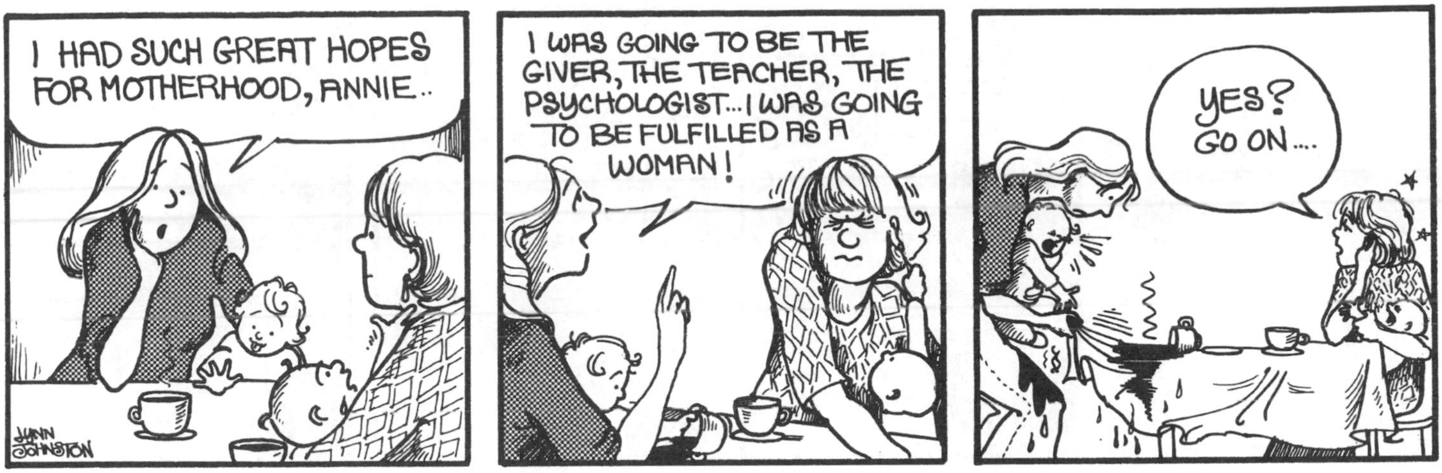
I HAD SUCH GREAT HOPES FOR MOTHERHOOD, ANNIE..
LYNN JOHNSTON
I WAS GOING TO BE THE GIVER, THE TEACHER, THE PSYCHOLOGIST...I WAS GOING TO BE FULFILLED AS A WOMAN!
YES? GO ON....

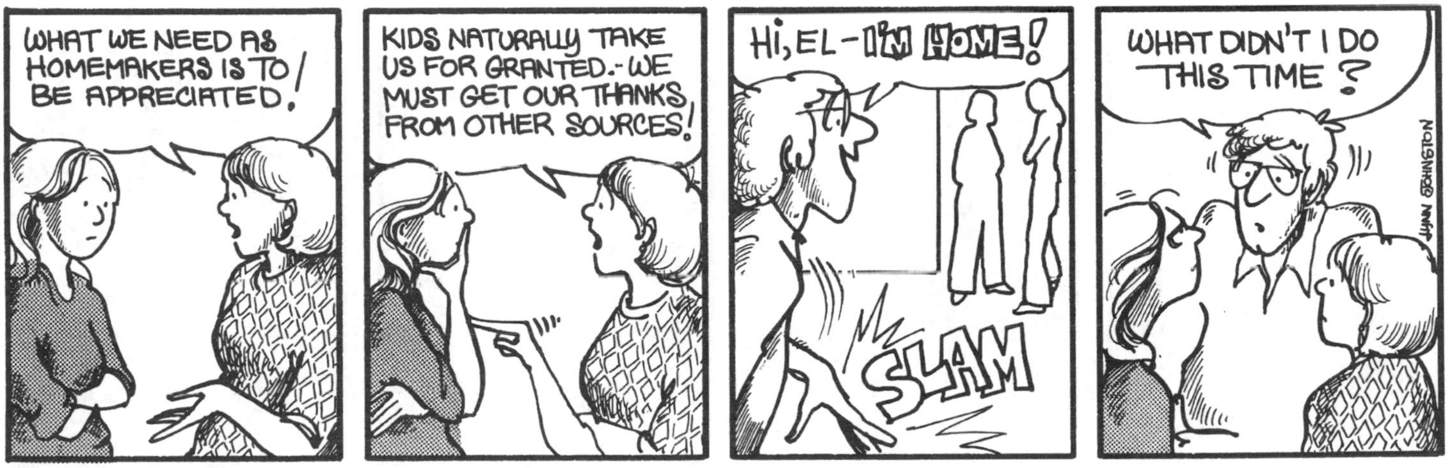
WHAT WE NEED AS HOMEMAKERS IS TO BE APPRECIATED!
KIDS NATURALLY TAKE US FOR GRANTED.- WE MUST GET OUR THANKS FROM OTHER SOURCES!
HI, EL - I'M HOME!
SLAM
WHAT DIDN'T I DO THIS TIME?
LYNN JOHNSTON

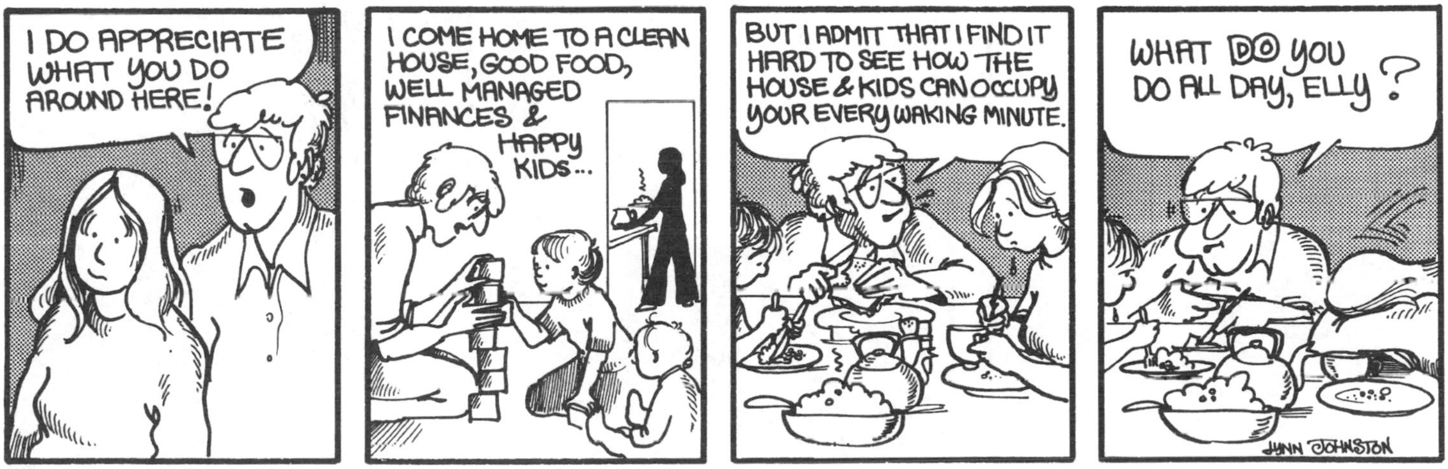
I DO APPRECIATE WHAT YOU DO AROUND HERE!
I COME HOME TO A CLEAN HOUSE, GOOD FOOD, WELL MANAGED FINANCES & HAPPY KIDS...
BUT I ADMIT THAT I FIND IT HARD TO SEE HOW THE HOUSE & KIDS CAN OCCUPY YOUR EVERY WAKING MINUTE.
WHAT DO YOU DO ALL DAY, ELLY?
LYNN JOHNSTON

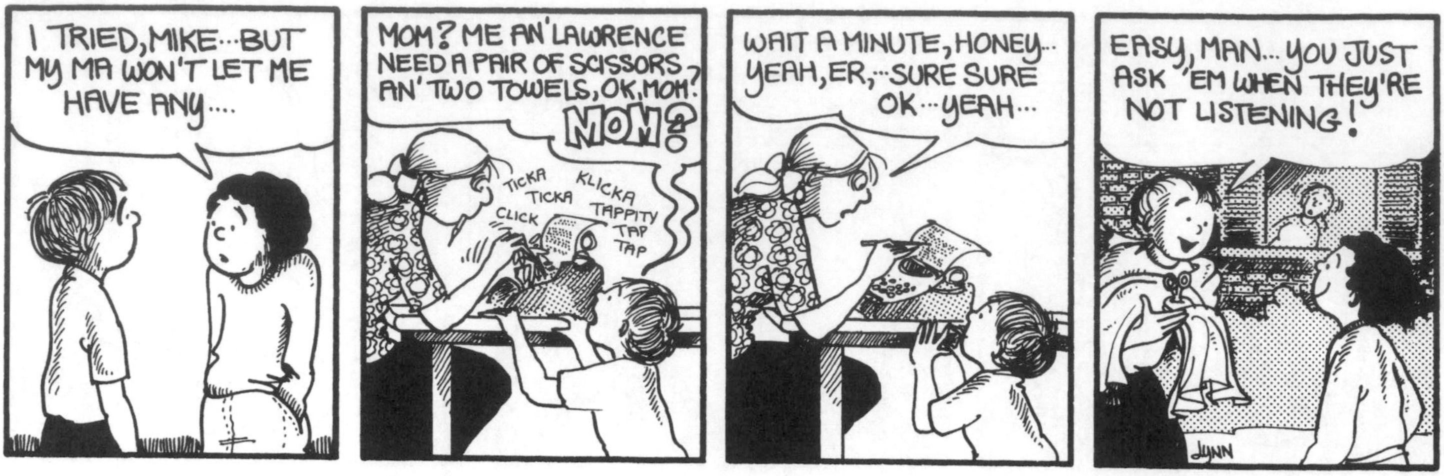
I TRIED, MIKE...BUT MY MA WON'T LET ME HAVE ANY....
MOM? ME AN' LAWRENCE NEED A PAIR OF SCISSORS AN' TWO TOWELS, OK, MOM?
MOM?
TICKA TICKA KLICKA CLICK TAPPITY TAP TAP
WAIT A MINUTE, HONEY... YEAH, ER,...SURE SURE OK...YEAH...
EASY, MAN... YOU JUST ASK 'EM WHEN THEY'RE NOT LISTENING!
LYNN

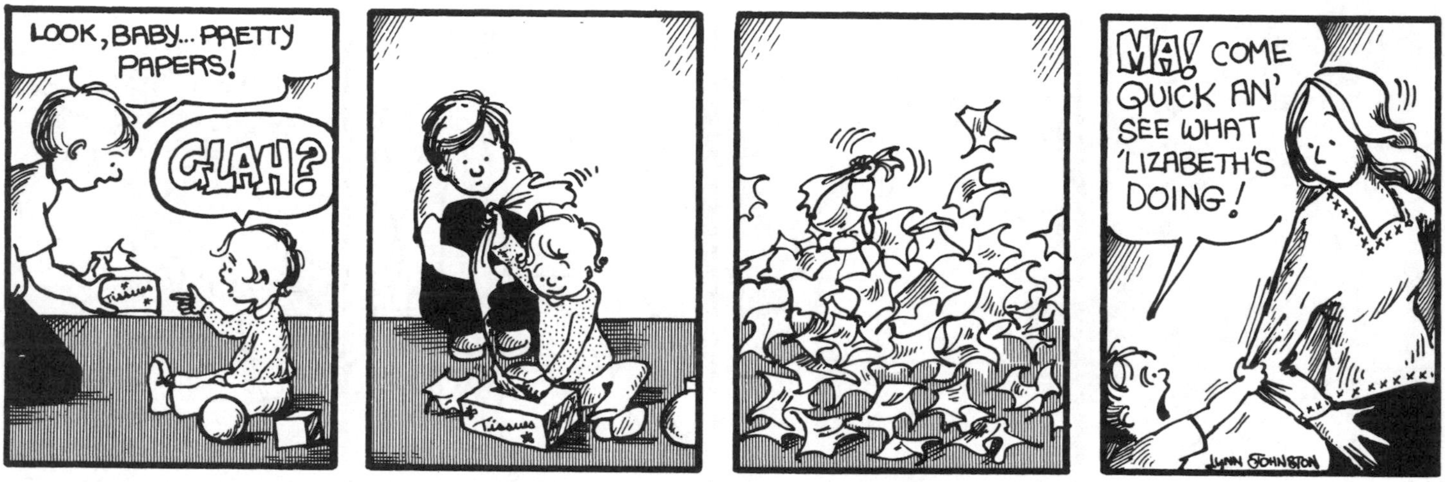
LOOK, BABY... PRETTY PAPERS!
GLAH?
MA! COME QUICK AN' SEE WHAT 'LIZABETH'S DOING!
LYNN JOHNSTON

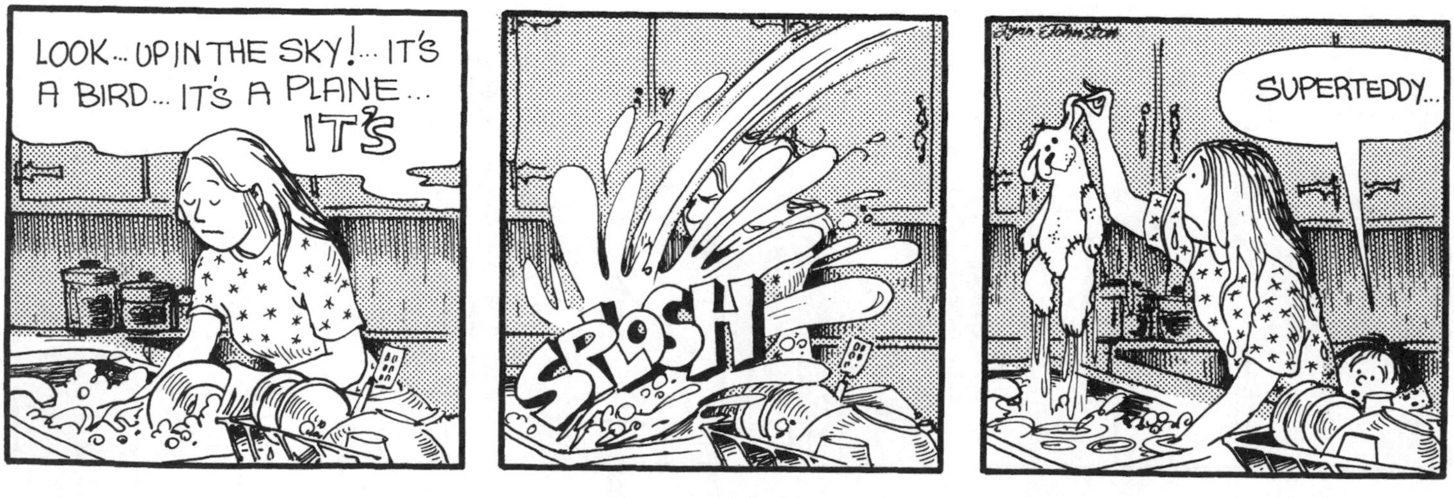
LOOK... UP IN THE SKY!... IT'S A BIRD... IT'S A PLANE... IT'S
SPLOSH
SUPERTEDDY...

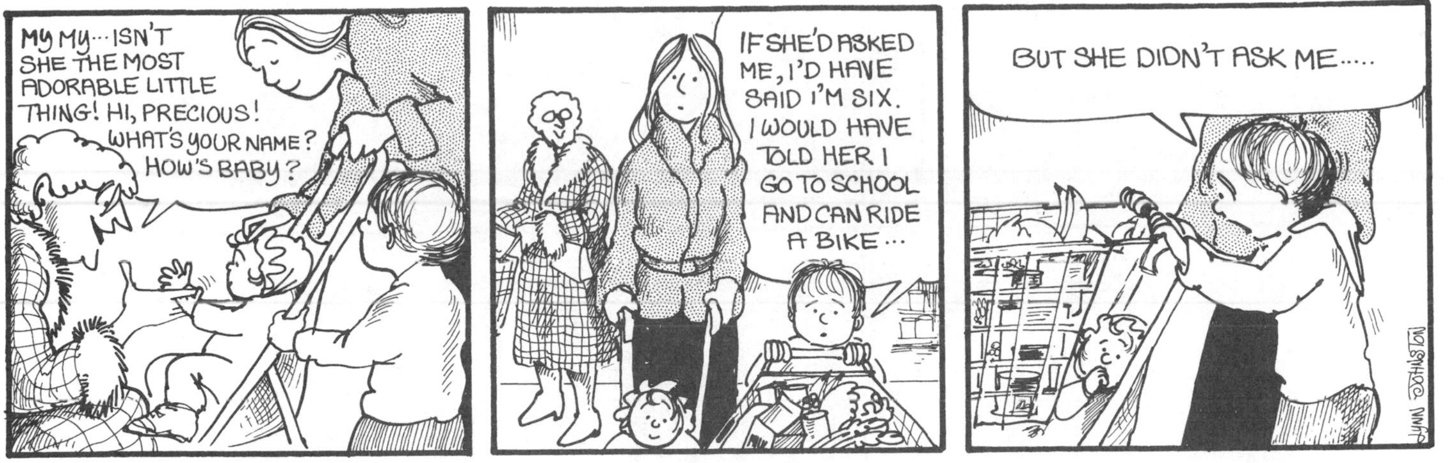
MY MY… ISN'T SHE THE MOST ADORABLE LITTLE THING! HI, PRECIOUS! WHAT'S YOUR NAME? HOW'S BABY?
IF SHE'D ASKED ME, I'D HAVE SAID I'M SIX. I WOULD HAVE TOLD HER I GO TO SCHOOL AND CAN RIDE A BIKE…
BUT SHE DIDN'T ASK ME…..

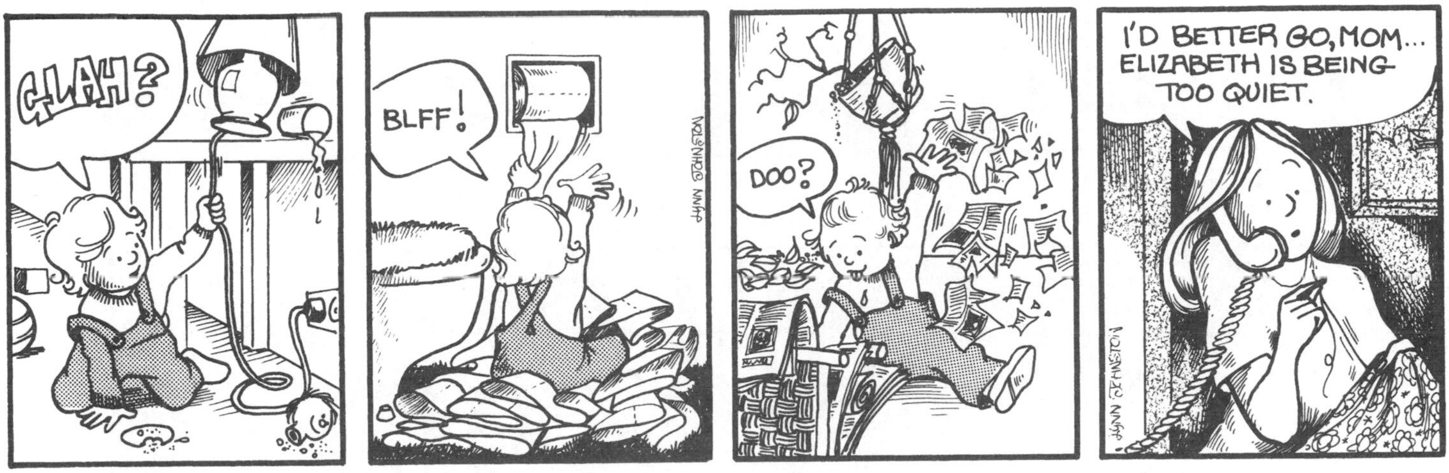
GLAH?
BLFF!
DOO?
I'D BETTER GO, MOM… ELIZABETH IS BEING TOO QUIET.

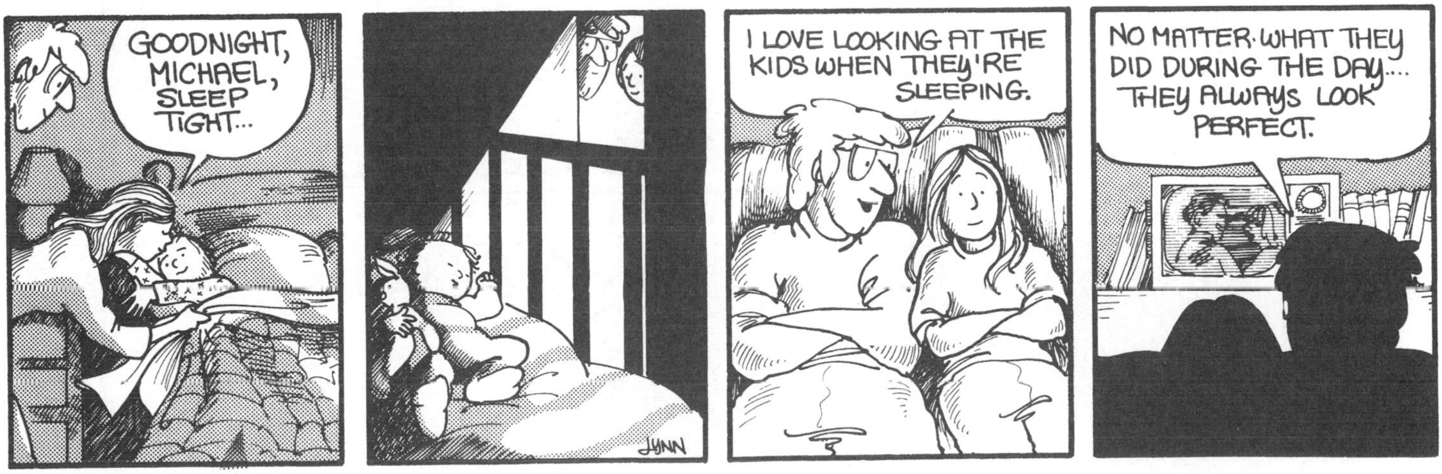
GOODNIGHT, MICHAEL, SLEEP TIGHT…
I LOVE LOOKING AT THE KIDS WHEN THEY'RE SLEEPING.
NO MATTER WHAT THEY DID DURING THE DAY…. THEY ALWAYS LOOK PERFECT.

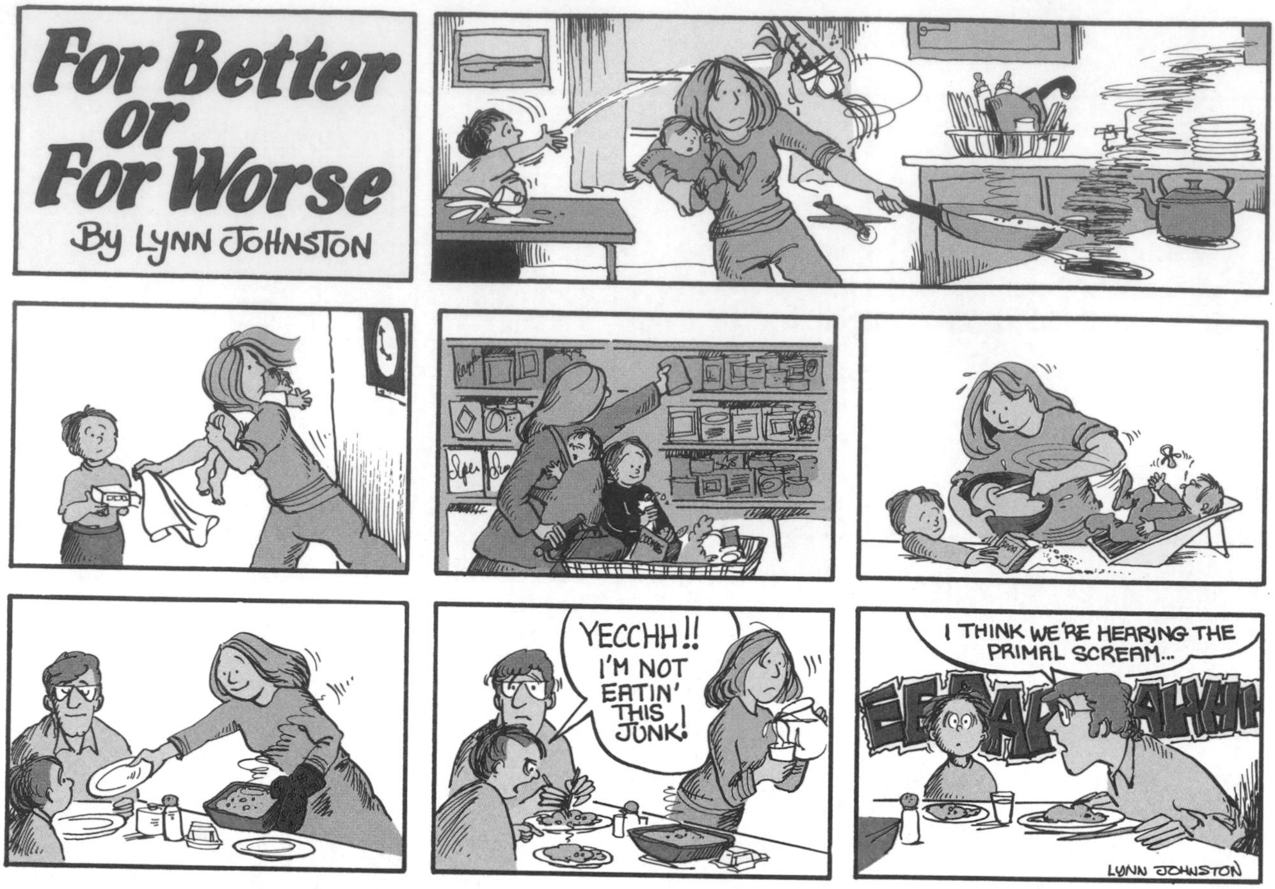
For Better or For Worse
By Lynn Johnston
YECCHH!! I'M NOT EATIN' THIS JUNK!
I THINK WE'RE HEARING THE PRIMAL SCREAM...
LYNN JOHNSTON

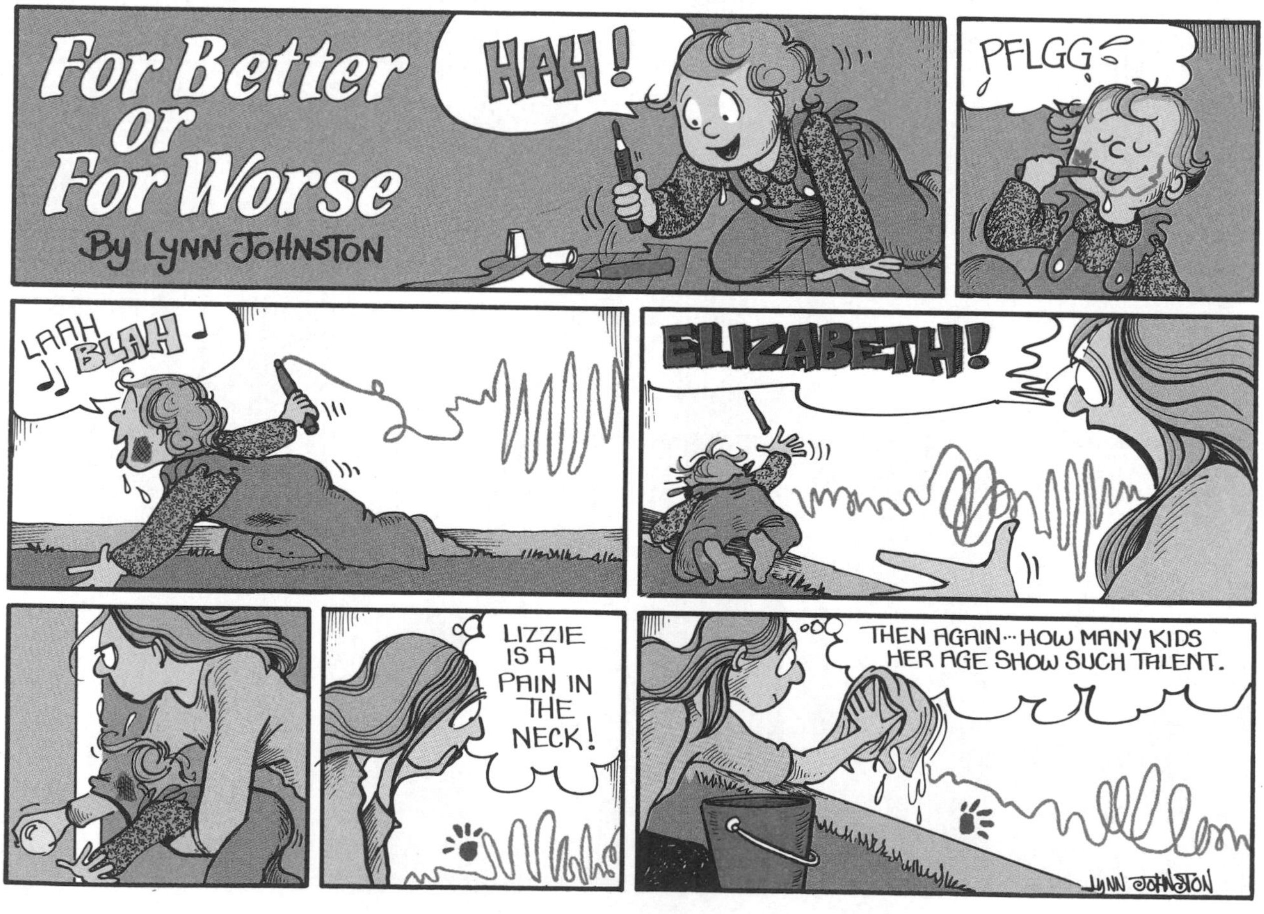
For Better or For Worse
By Lynn Johnston
HAH!
PFLGG
LAAH BLAH
ELIZABETH!
LIZZIE IS A PAIN IN THE NECK!
THEN AGAIN... HOW MANY KIDS HER AGE SHOW SUCH TALENT.
LYNN JOHNSTON

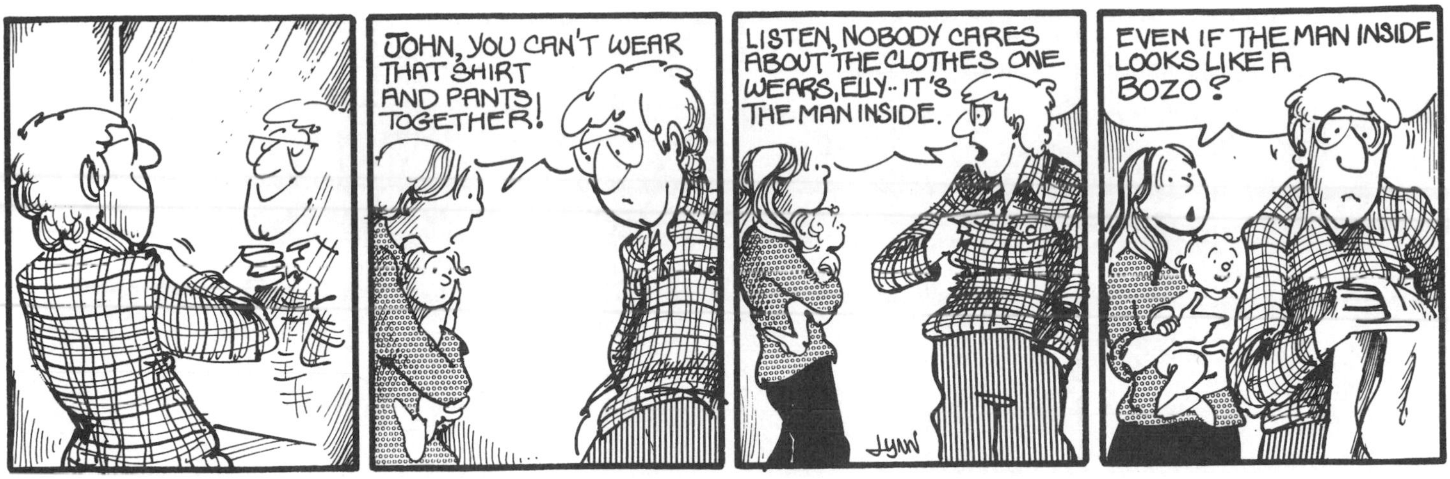
JOHN, YOU CAN'T WEAR THAT SHIRT AND PANTS TOGETHER!
LISTEN, NOBODY CARES ABOUT THE CLOTHES ONE WEARS, ELLY.. IT'S THE MAN INSIDE.
LYNN
EVEN IF THE MAN INSIDE LOOKS LIKE A BOZO?

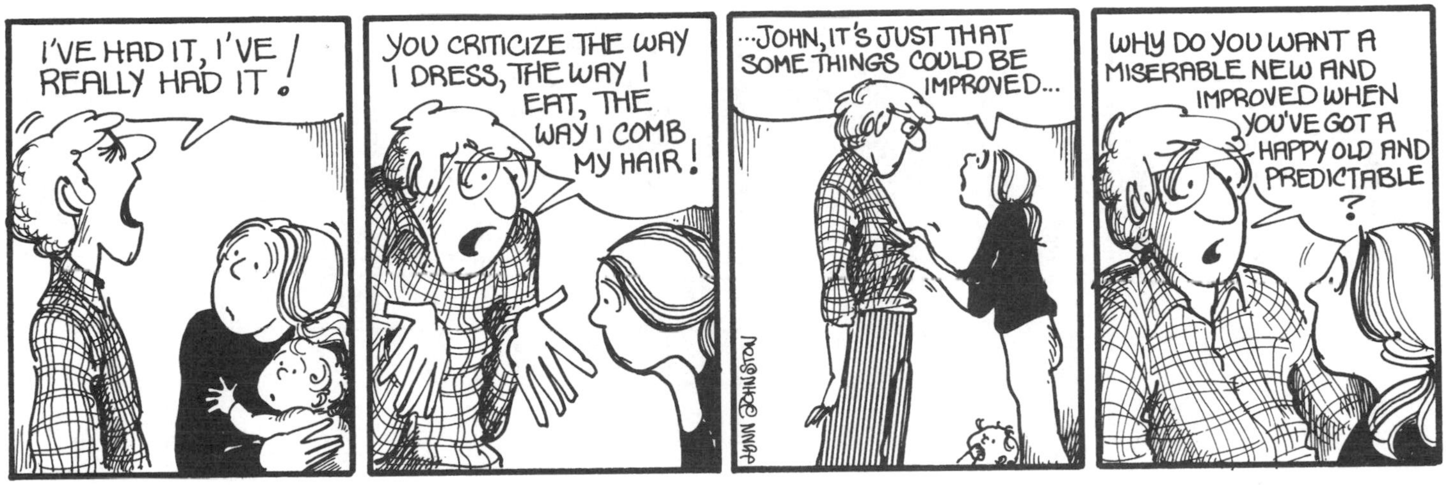
I'VE HAD IT, I'VE REALLY HAD IT!
YOU CRITICIZE THE WAY I DRESS, THE WAY I EAT, THE WAY I COMB MY HAIR!
LYNN JOHNSTON
...JOHN, IT'S JUST THAT SOME THINGS COULD BE IMPROVED...
WHY DO YOU WANT A MISERABLE NEW AND IMPROVED WHEN YOU'VE GOT A HAPPY OLD AND PREDICTABLE?

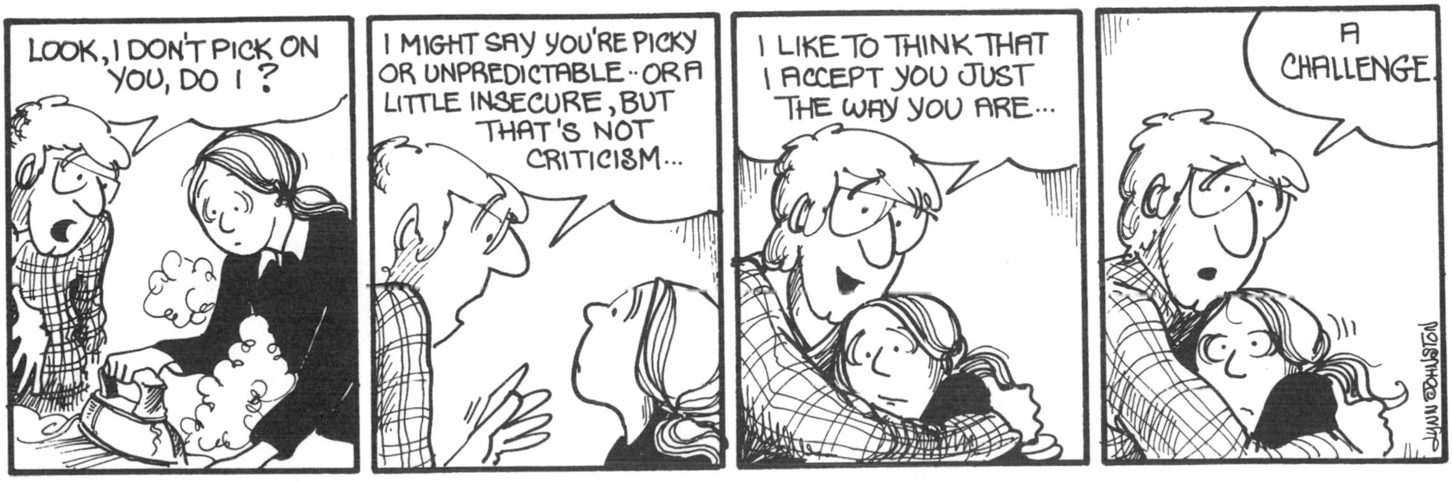
LOOK, I DON'T PICK ON YOU, DO I?
I MIGHT SAY YOU'RE PICKY OR UNPREDICTABLE.. OR A LITTLE INSECURE, BUT THAT'S NOT CRITICISM...
I LIKE TO THINK THAT I ACCEPT YOU JUST THE WAY YOU ARE...
A CHALLENGE.
LYNN JOHNSTON

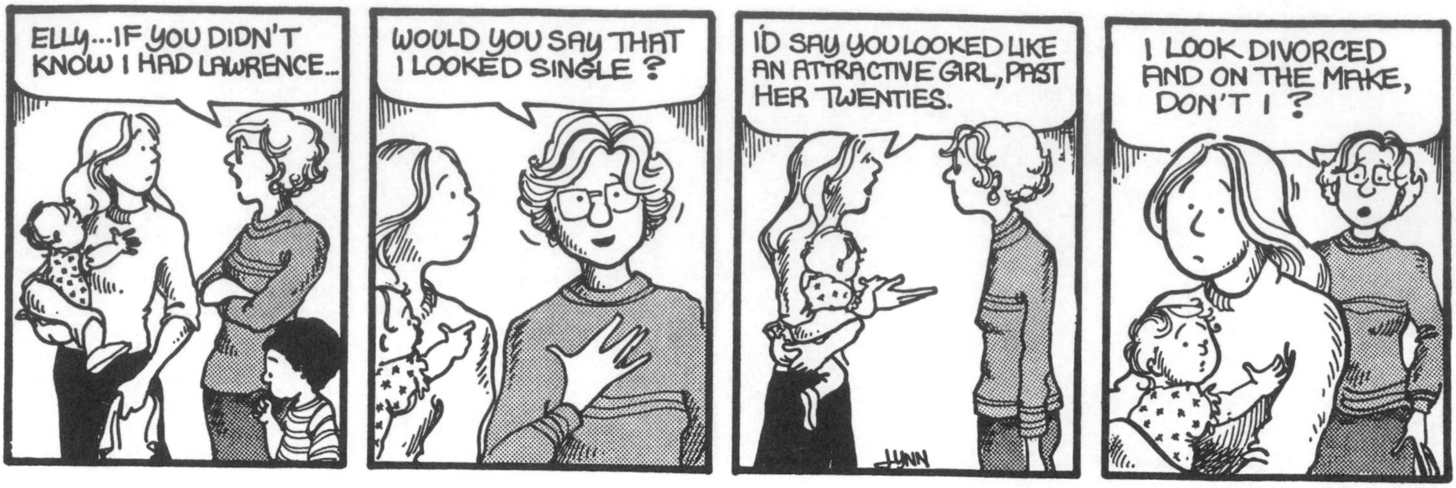
ELLY...IF YOU DIDN'T KNOW I HAD LAWRENCE...
WOULD YOU SAY THAT I LOOKED SINGLE?
I'D SAY YOU LOOKED LIKE AN ATTRACTIVE GIRL, PAST HER TWENTIES.
LYNN
I LOOK DIVORCED AND ON THE MAKE, DON'T I?

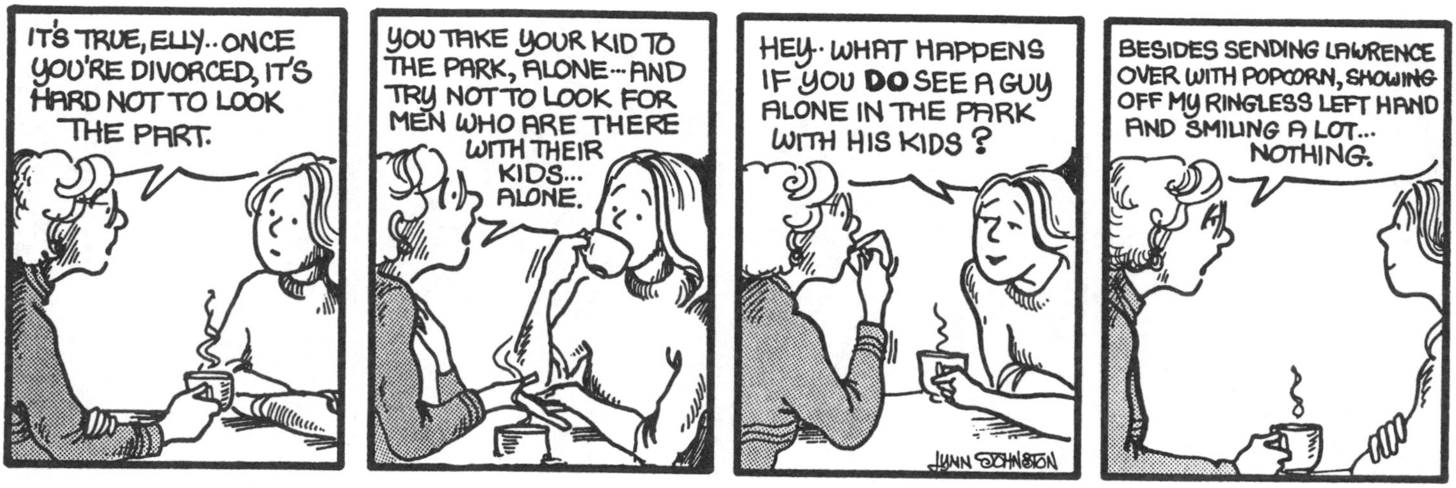
IT'S TRUE, ELLY.. ONCE YOU'RE DIVORCED, IT'S HARD NOT TO LOOK THE PART.
YOU TAKE YOUR KID TO THE PARK, ALONE...AND TRY NOT TO LOOK FOR MEN WHO ARE THERE WITH THEIR KIDS... ALONE.
HEY.. WHAT HAPPENS IF YOU **DO** SEE A GUY ALONE IN THE PARK WITH HIS KIDS?
LYNN JOHNSTON
BESIDES SENDING LAWRENCE OVER WITH POPCORN, SHOWING OFF MY RINGLESS LEFT HAND AND SMILING A LOT... NOTHING.

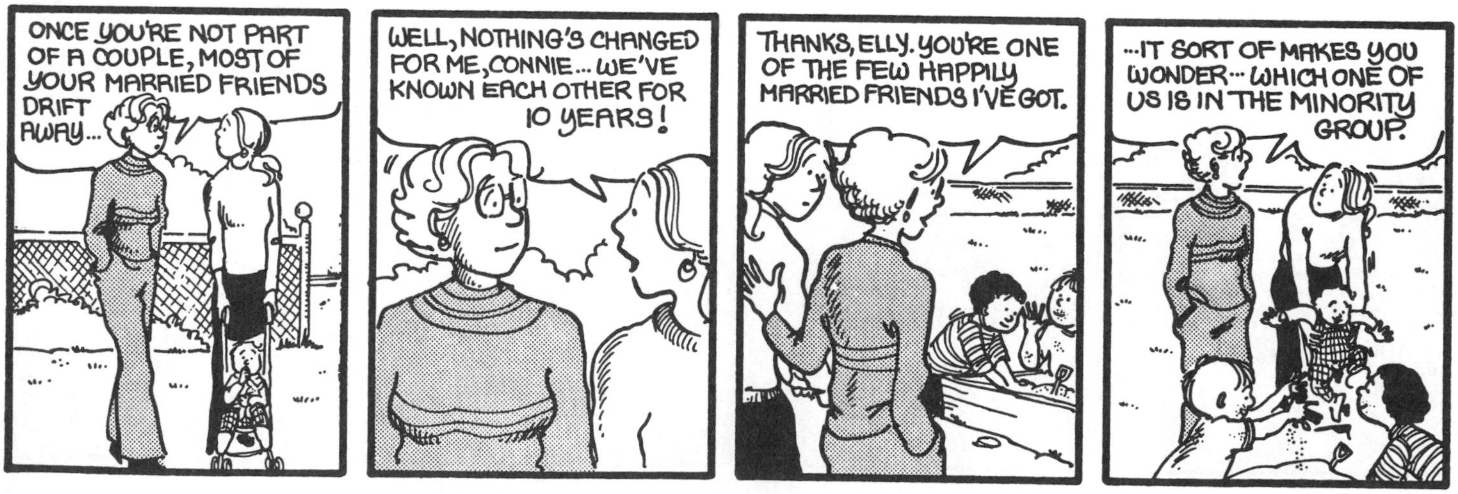
ONCE YOU'RE NOT PART OF A COUPLE, MOST OF YOUR MARRIED FRIENDS DRIFT AWAY...
WELL, NOTHING'S CHANGED FOR ME, CONNIE... WE'VE KNOWN EACH OTHER FOR 10 YEARS!
THANKS, ELLY. YOU'RE ONE OF THE FEW HAPPILY MARRIED FRIENDS I'VE GOT.
...IT SORT OF MAKES YOU WONDER... WHICH ONE OF US IS IN THE MINORITY GROUP.

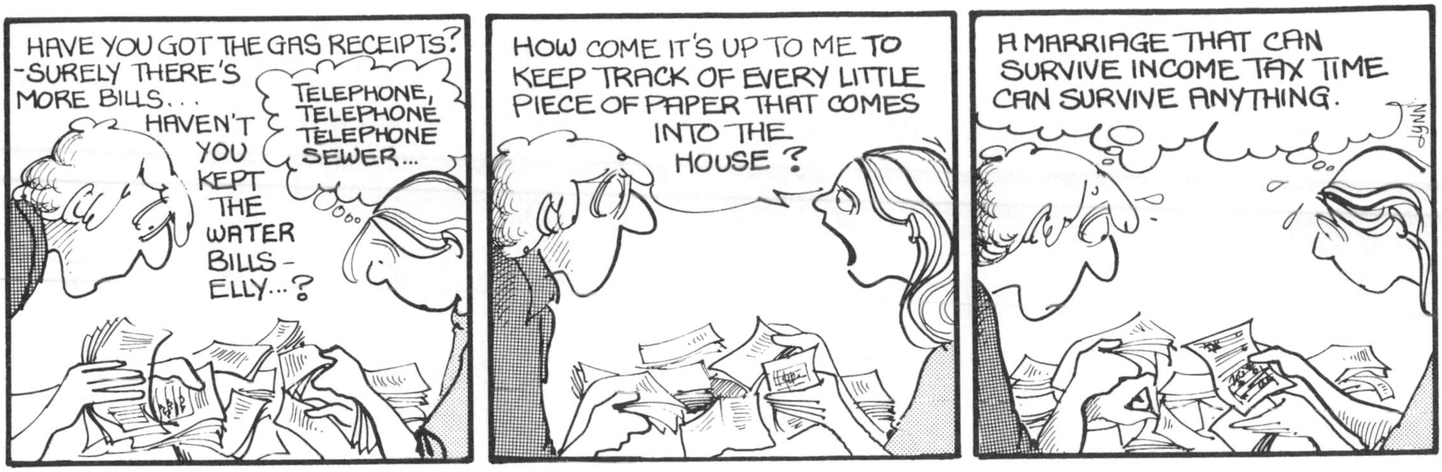
HAVE YOU GOT THE GAS RECEIPTS? -SURELY THERE'S MORE BILLS . . . HAVEN'T YOU KEPT THE WATER BILLS - ELLY...?
TELEPHONE, TELEPHONE TELEPHONE SEWER...
HOW COME IT'S UP TO ME TO KEEP TRACK OF EVERY LITTLE PIECE OF PAPER THAT COMES INTO THE HOUSE?
A MARRIAGE THAT CAN SURVIVE INCOME TAX TIME CAN SURVIVE ANYTHING.
LYNN

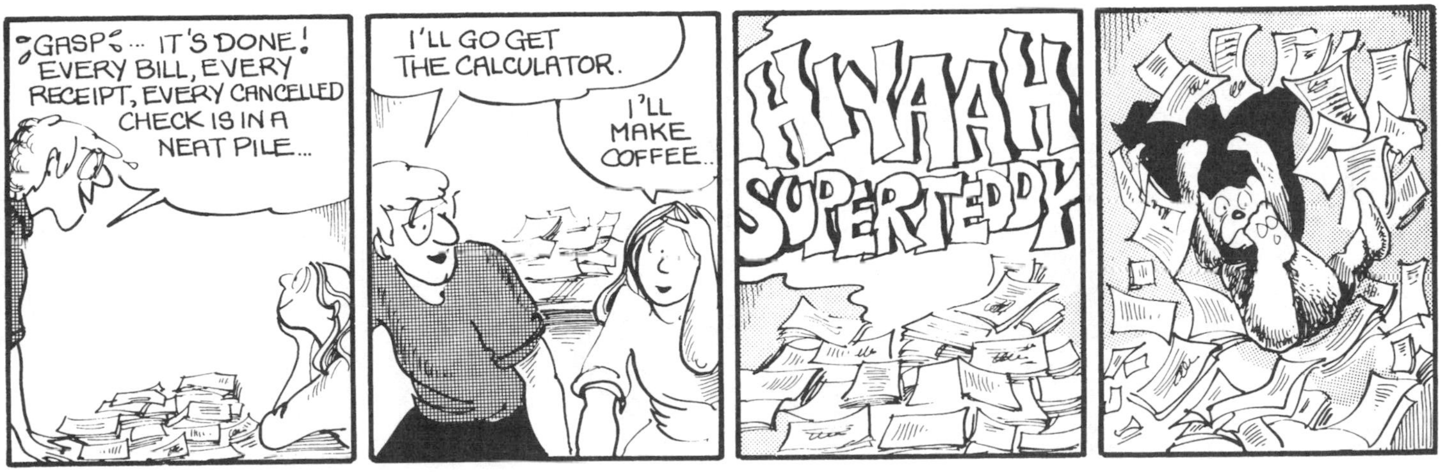
:GASP:... IT'S DONE! EVERY BILL, EVERY RECEIPT, EVERY CANCELLED CHECK IS IN A NEAT PILE...
I'LL GO GET THE CALCULATOR.
I'LL MAKE COFFEE...
HIYAAH SUPERTEDDY

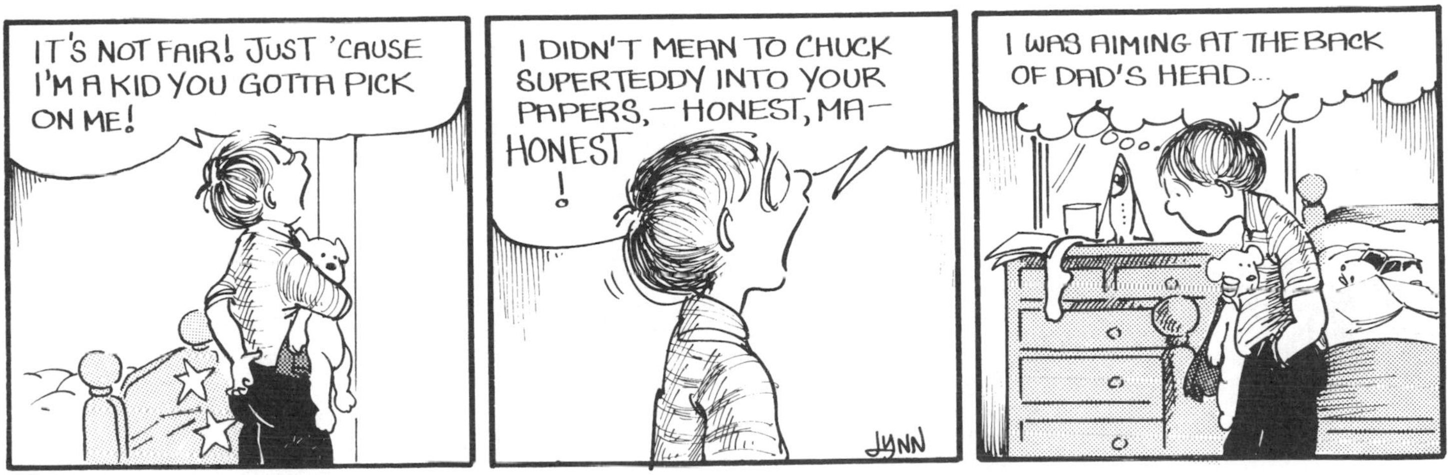
IT'S NOT FAIR! JUST 'CAUSE I'M A KID YOU GOTTA PICK ON ME!
I DIDN'T MEAN TO CHUCK SUPERTEDDY INTO YOUR PAPERS, — HONEST, MA — HONEST!
LYNN
I WAS AIMING AT THE BACK OF DAD'S HEAD...

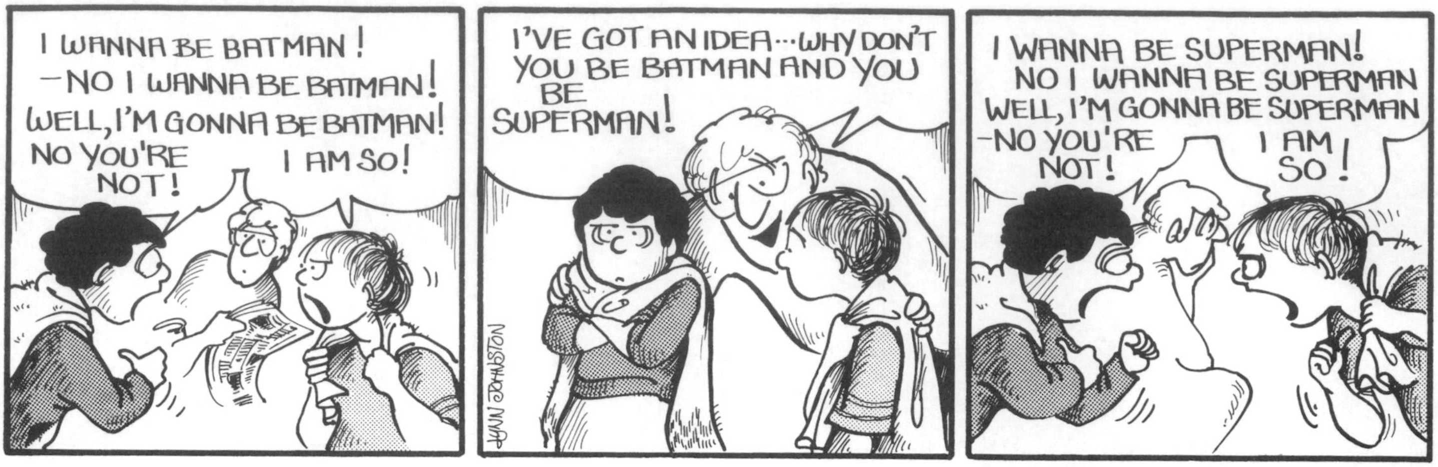
I WANNA BE BATMAN!
-NO I WANNA BE BATMAN!
WELL, I'M GONNA BE BATMAN!
NO YOU'RE NOT!
I AM SO!
I'VE GOT AN IDEA...WHY DON'T YOU BE BATMAN AND YOU BE SUPERMAN!
LYNN JOHNSTON
I WANNA BE SUPERMAN!
NO I WANNA BE SUPERMAN
WELL, I'M GONNA BE SUPERMAN
-NO YOU'RE NOT!
I AM SO!

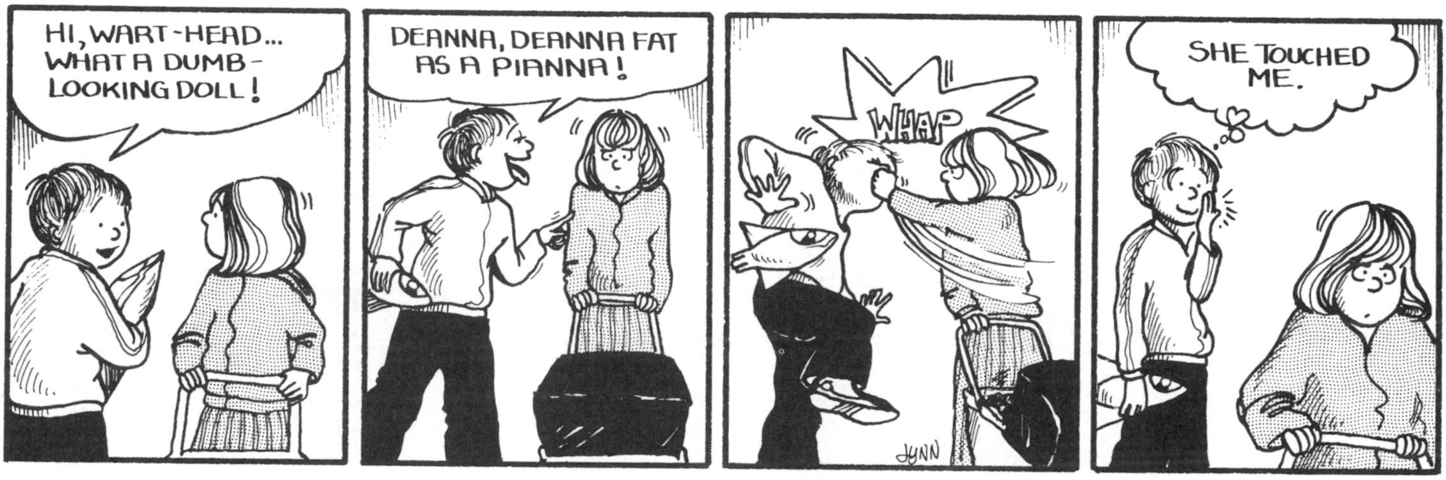
HI, WART-HEAD... WHAT A DUMB-LOOKING DOLL!
DEANNA, DEANNA FAT AS A PIANNA!
WHAP
LYNN
SHE TOUCHED ME.

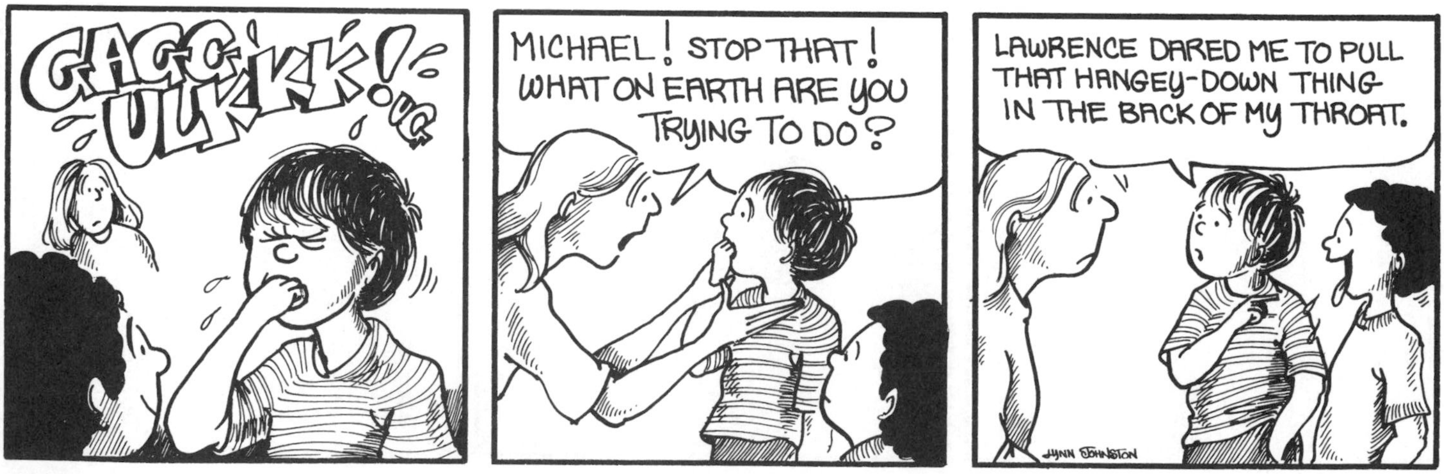
GAGG ULKKK! OUG
MICHAEL! STOP THAT! WHAT ON EARTH ARE YOU TRYING TO DO?
LAWRENCE DARED ME TO PULL THAT HANGEY-DOWN THING IN THE BACK OF MY THROAT.
LYNN JOHNSTON

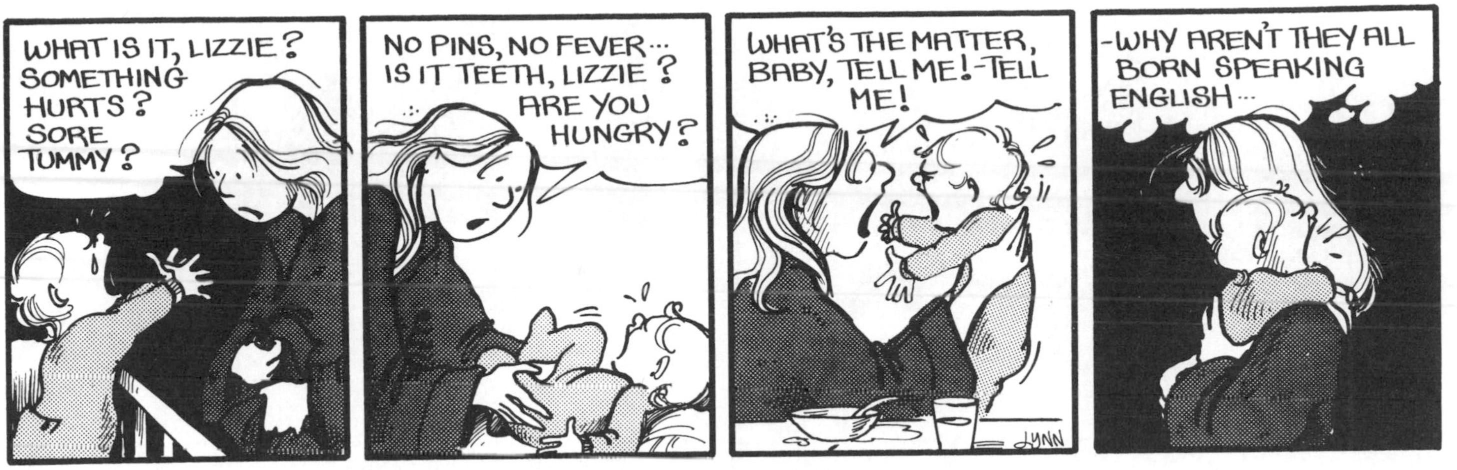
WHAT IS IT, LIZZIE? SOMETHING HURTS? SORE TUMMY?
NO PINS, NO FEVER... IS IT TEETH, LIZZIE? ARE YOU HUNGRY?
WHAT'S THE MATTER, BABY, TELL ME! -TELL ME!
LYNN
-WHY AREN'T THEY ALL BORN SPEAKING ENGLISH...

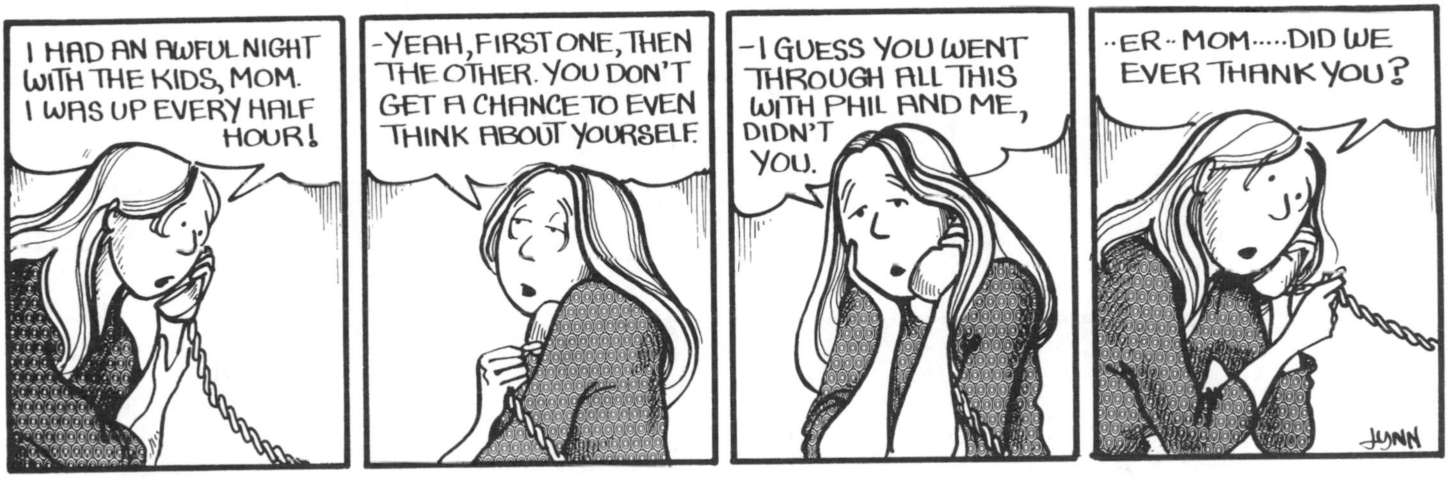
I HAD AN AWFUL NIGHT WITH THE KIDS, MOM. I WAS UP EVERY HALF HOUR!
-YEAH, FIRST ONE, THEN THE OTHER. YOU DON'T GET A CHANCE TO EVEN THINK ABOUT YOURSELF.
-I GUESS YOU WENT THROUGH ALL THIS WITH PHIL AND ME, DIDN'T YOU.
..ER..MOM.....DID WE EVER THANK YOU?
LYNN

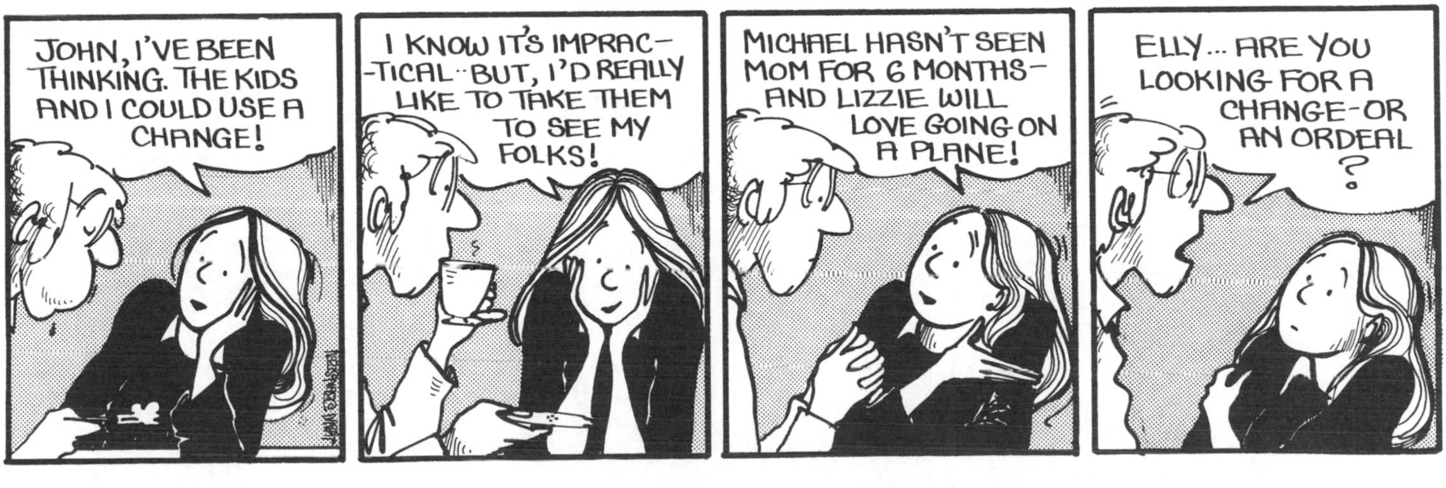
JOHN, I'VE BEEN THINKING. THE KIDS AND I COULD USE A CHANGE!
I KNOW IT'S IMPRAC- -TICAL..BUT, I'D REALLY LIKE TO TAKE THEM TO SEE MY FOLKS!
MICHAEL HASN'T SEEN MOM FOR 6 MONTHS- AND LIZZIE WILL LOVE GOING ON A PLANE!
ELLY... ARE YOU LOOKING FOR A CHANGE-OR AN ORDEAL ?

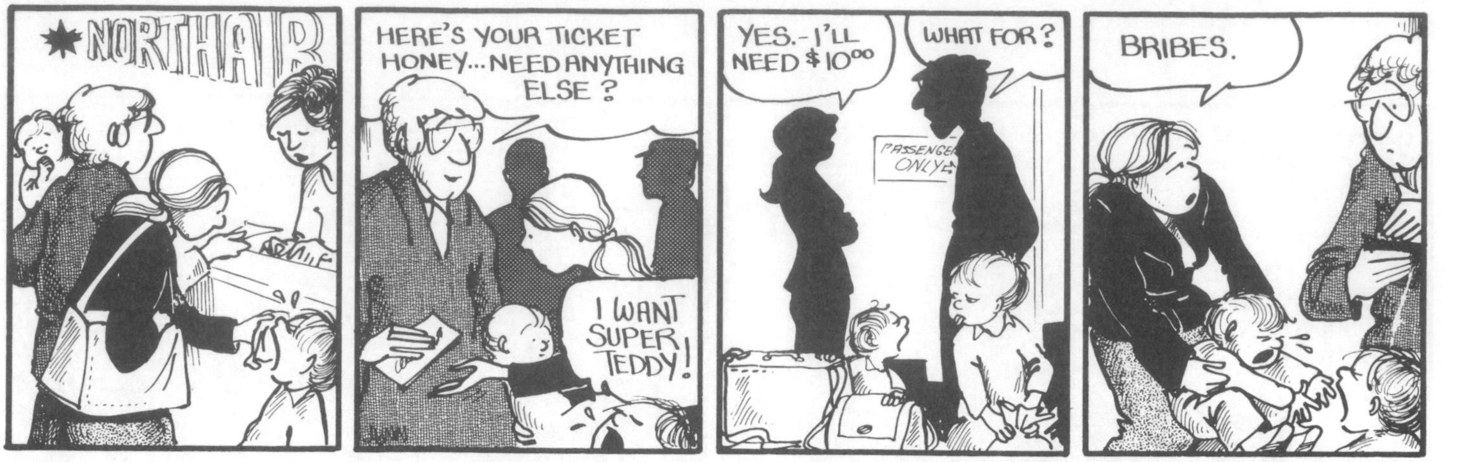
NORTHAIR
HERE'S YOUR TICKET HONEY... NEED ANYTHING ELSE ?
I WANT SUPER TEDDY!
YES.- I'LL NEED $10.00
WHAT FOR ?
PASSENGERS ONLY
BRIBES.

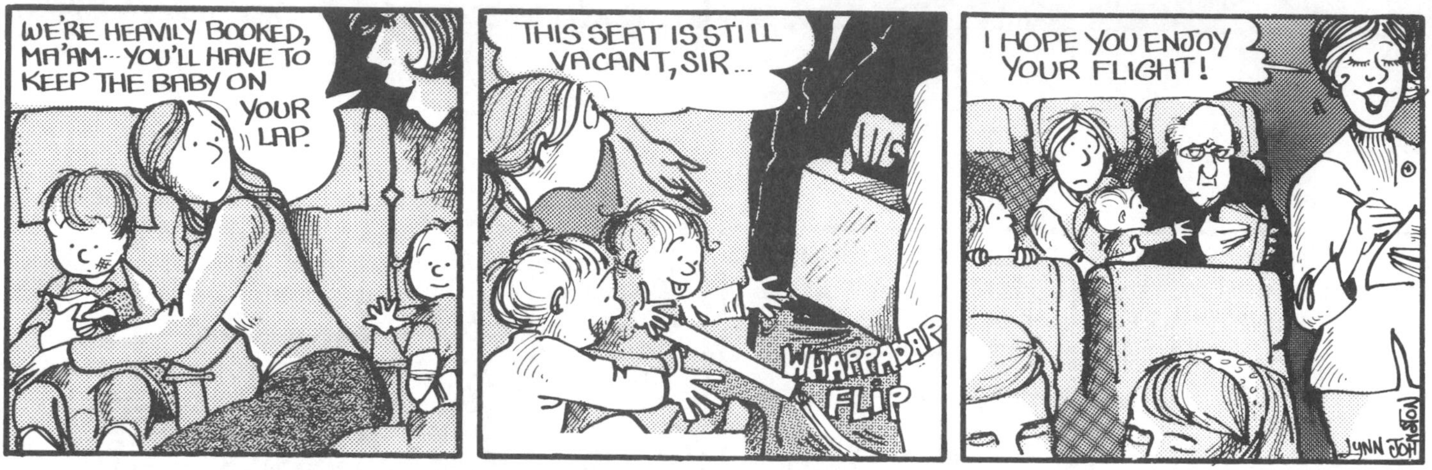
WE'RE HEAVILY BOOKED, MA'AM... YOU'LL HAVE TO KEEP THE BABY ON YOUR LAP.
THIS SEAT IS STILL VACANT, SIR...
WHAPPADAP
FLIP
I HOPE YOU ENJOY YOUR FLIGHT!

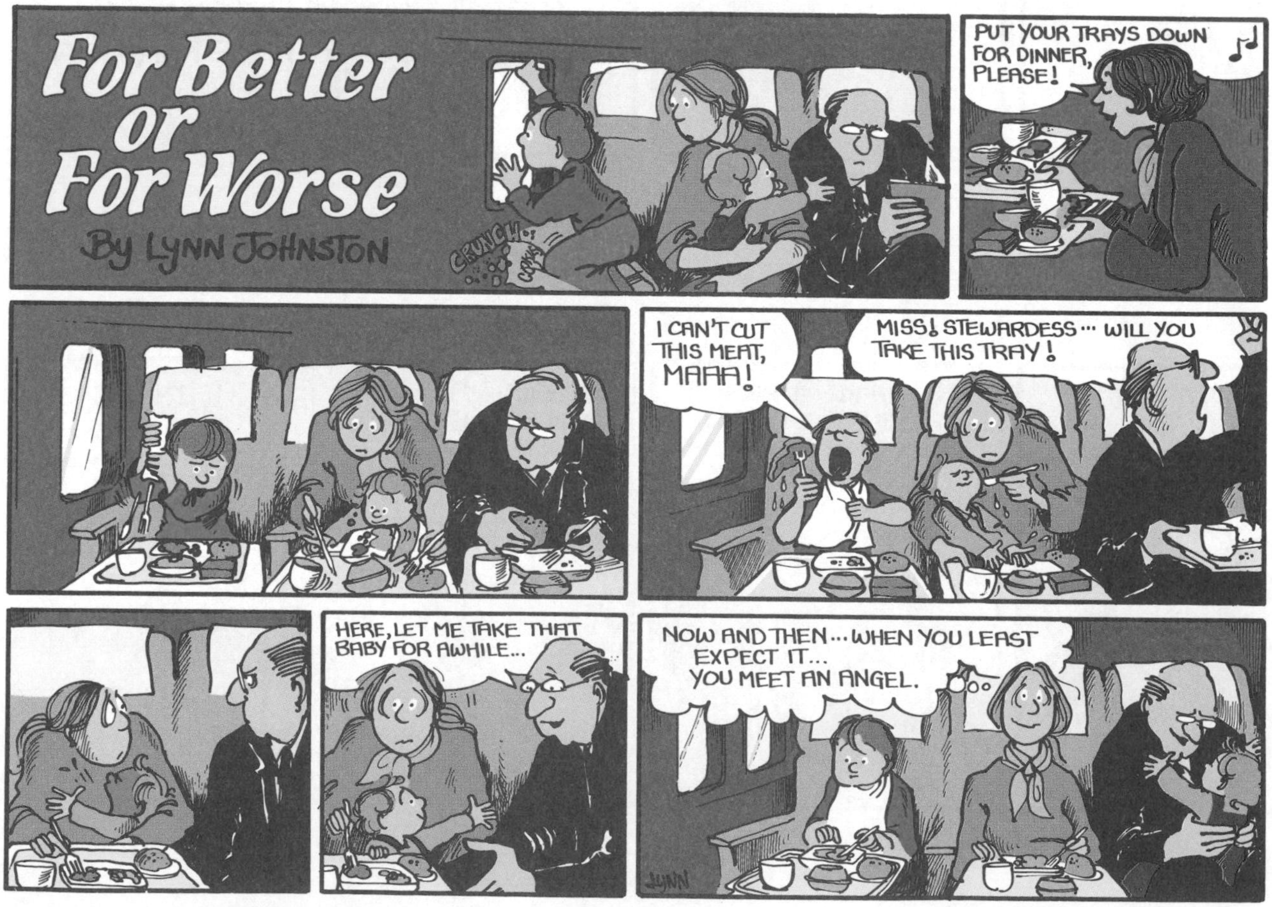
For Better or For Worse
By LYNN JOHNSTON
CRUNCH
PUT YOUR TRAYS DOWN FOR DINNER, PLEASE!
I CAN'T CUT THIS MEAT, MAAA!
MISS! STEWARDESS... WILL YOU TAKE THIS TRAY!
HERE, LET ME TAKE THAT BABY FOR AWHILE...
NOW AND THEN... WHEN YOU LEAST EXPECT IT... YOU MEET AN ANGEL.

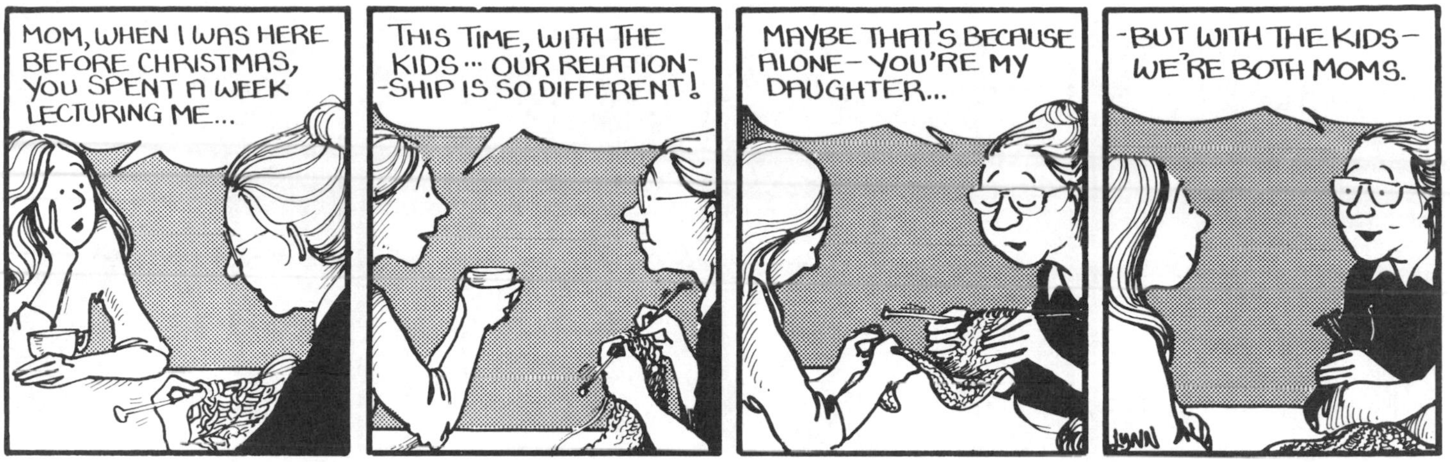
MOM, WHEN I WAS HERE BEFORE CHRISTMAS, YOU SPENT A WEEK LECTURING ME...
THIS TIME, WITH THE KIDS... OUR RELATION-SHIP IS SO DIFFERENT!
MAYBE THAT'S BECAUSE ALONE– YOU'RE MY DAUGHTER...
–BUT WITH THE KIDS– WE'RE BOTH MOMS.
LYNN

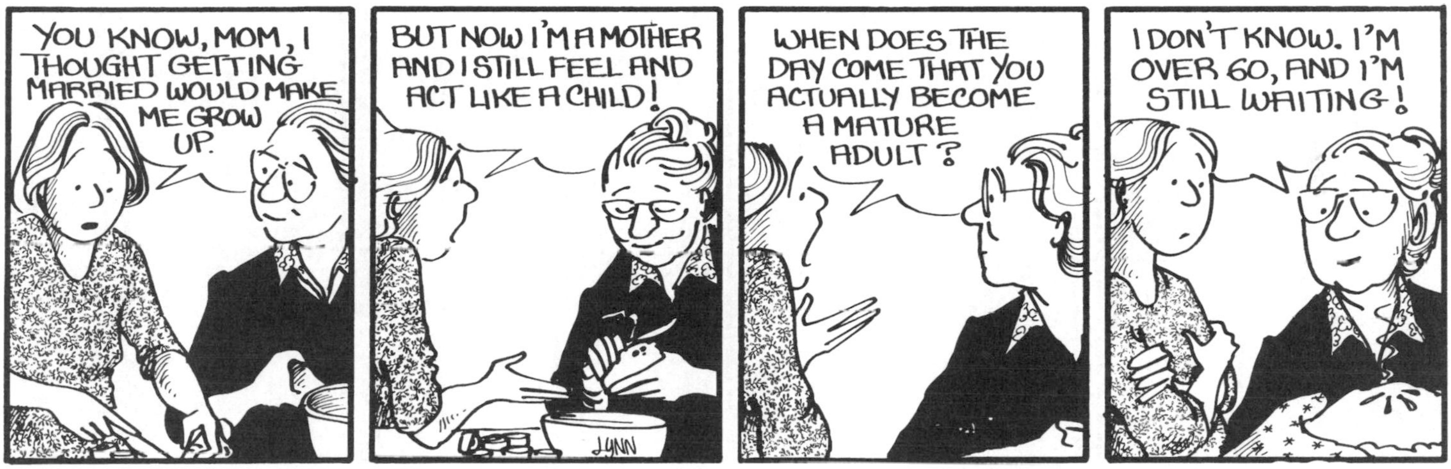
YOU KNOW, MOM, I THOUGHT GETTING MARRIED WOULD MAKE ME GROW UP.
BUT NOW I'M A MOTHER AND I STILL FEEL AND ACT LIKE A CHILD!
LYNN
WHEN DOES THE DAY COME THAT YOU ACTUALLY BECOME A MATURE ADULT?
I DON'T KNOW. I'M OVER 60, AND I'M STILL WAITING!

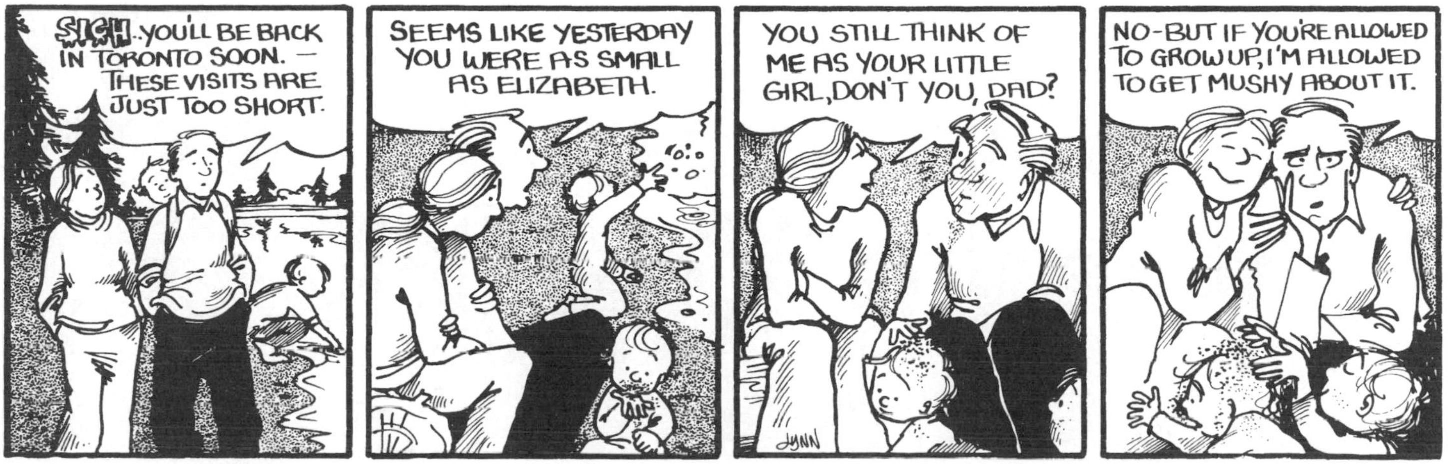
SIGH..YOU'LL BE BACK IN TORONTO SOON. – THESE VISITS ARE JUST TOO SHORT.
SEEMS LIKE YESTERDAY YOU WERE AS SMALL AS ELIZABETH.
YOU STILL THINK OF ME AS YOUR LITTLE GIRL, DON'T YOU, DAD?
LYNN
NO–BUT IF YOU'RE ALLOWED TO GROW UP, I'M ALLOWED TO GET MUSHY ABOUT IT.

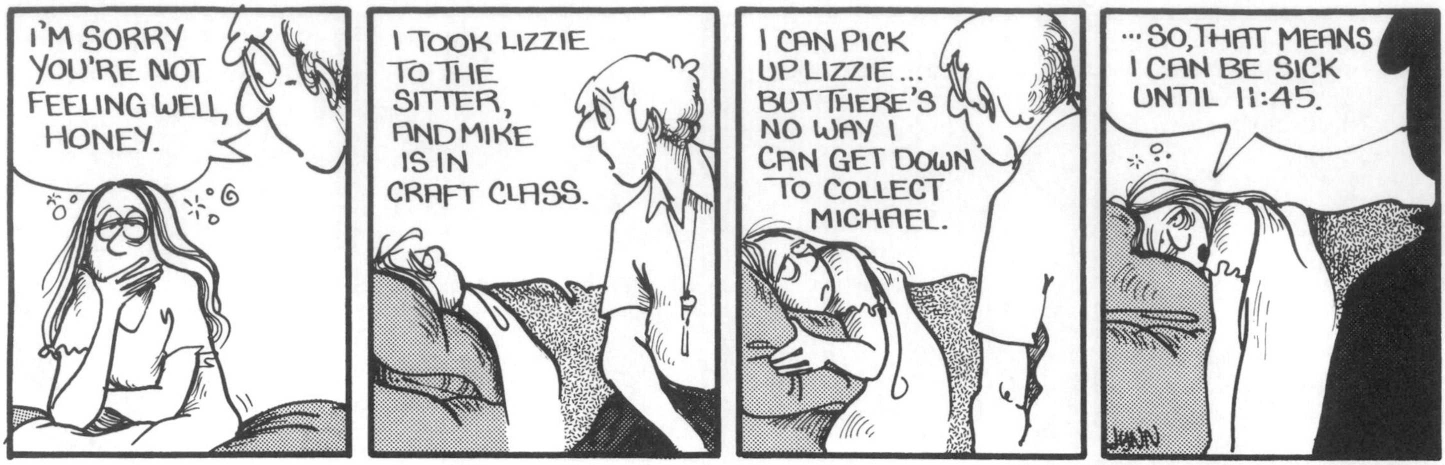
I'M SORRY YOU'RE NOT FEELING WELL, HONEY.
I TOOK LIZZIE TO THE SITTER, AND MIKE IS IN CRAFT CLASS.
I CAN PICK UP LIZZIE... BUT THERE'S NO WAY I CAN GET DOWN TO COLLECT MICHAEL.
...SO, THAT MEANS I CAN BE SICK UNTIL 11:45.
LYNN

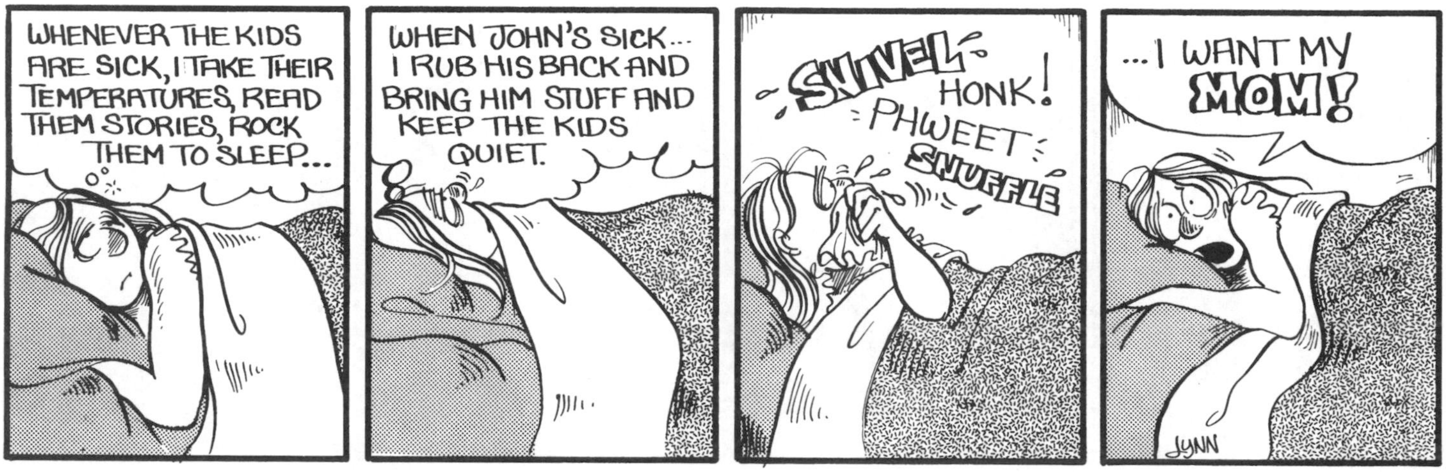
WHENEVER THE KIDS ARE SICK, I TAKE THEIR TEMPERATURES, READ THEM STORIES, ROCK THEM TO SLEEP...
WHEN JOHN'S SICK... I RUB HIS BACK AND BRING HIM STUFF AND KEEP THE KIDS QUIET.
SNIVEL
HONK!
PHWEET
SNUFFLE
...I WANT MY MOM!
LYNN

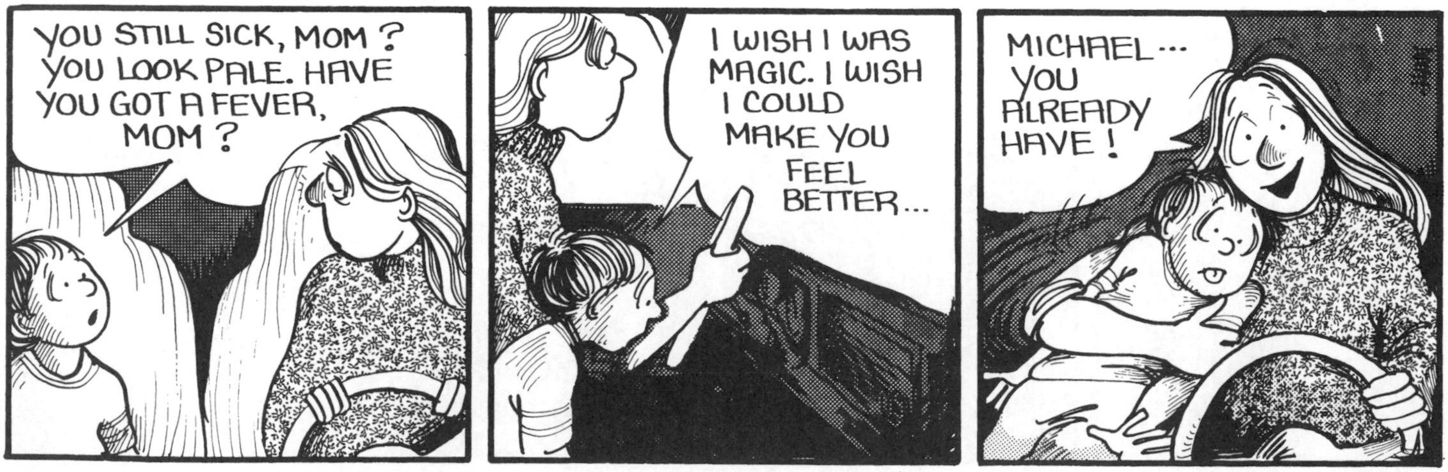
YOU STILL SICK, MOM? YOU LOOK PALE. HAVE YOU GOT A FEVER, MOM?
I WISH I WAS MAGIC. I WISH I COULD MAKE YOU FEEL BETTER...
MICHAEL... YOU ALREADY HAVE!

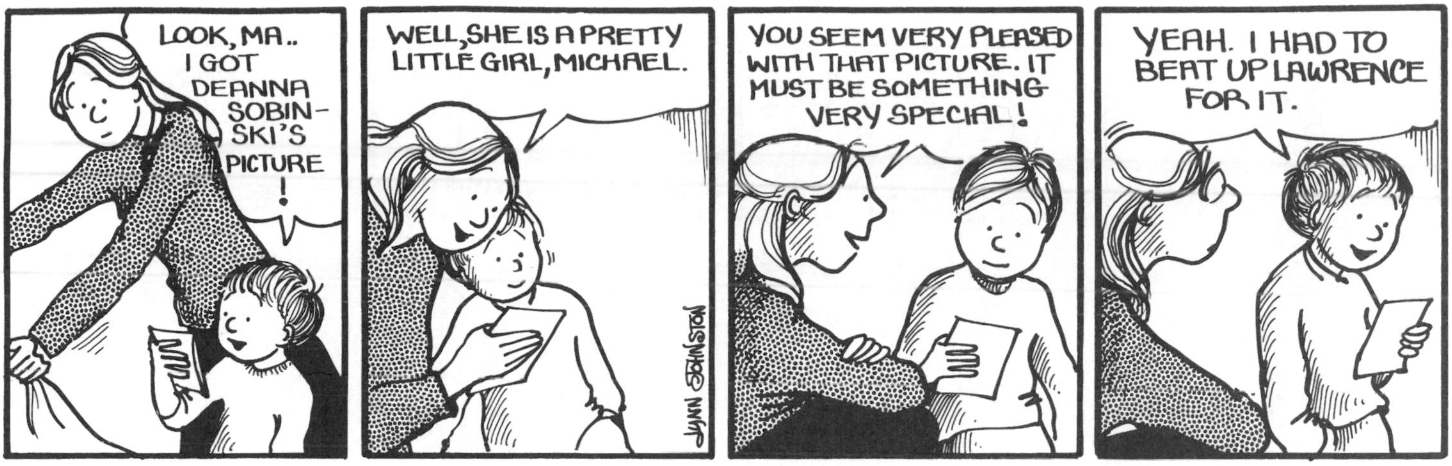

LOOK, MA.. I GOT DEANNA SOBIN-SKI'S PICTURE !
WELL, SHE IS A PRETTY LITTLE GIRL, MICHAEL.
LYNN JOHNSTON
YOU SEEM VERY PLEASED WITH THAT PICTURE. IT MUST BE SOMETHING VERY SPECIAL !
YEAH. I HAD TO BEAT UP LAWRENCE FOR IT.

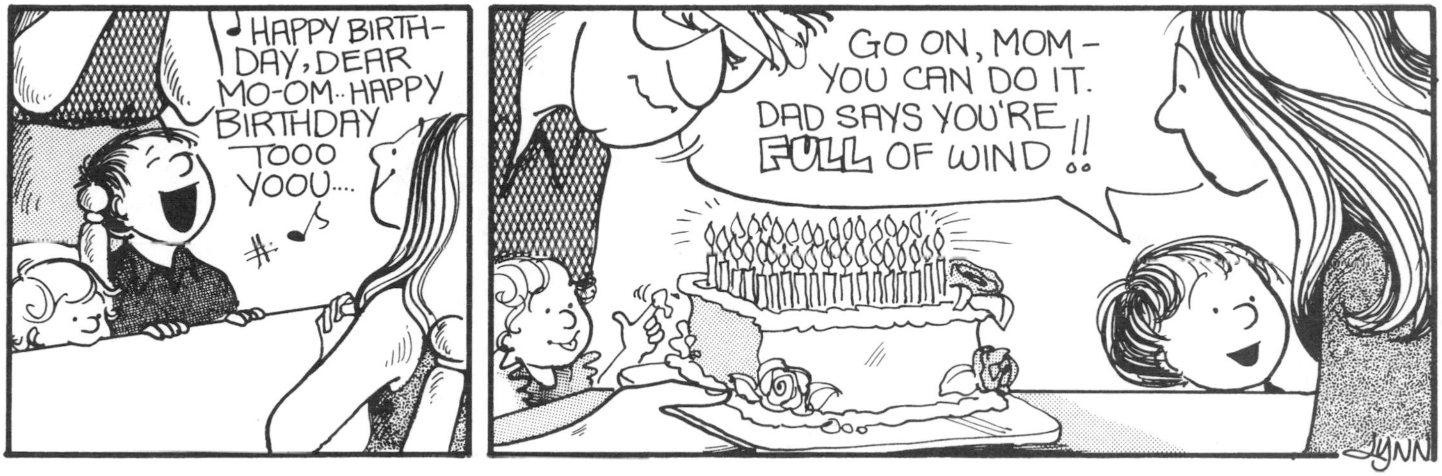

HAPPY BIRTH-DAY, DEAR MO-OM.. HAPPY BIRTHDAY TOOO YOOU....
GO ON, MOM - YOU CAN DO IT. DAD SAYS YOU'RE FULL OF WIND !!
LYNN

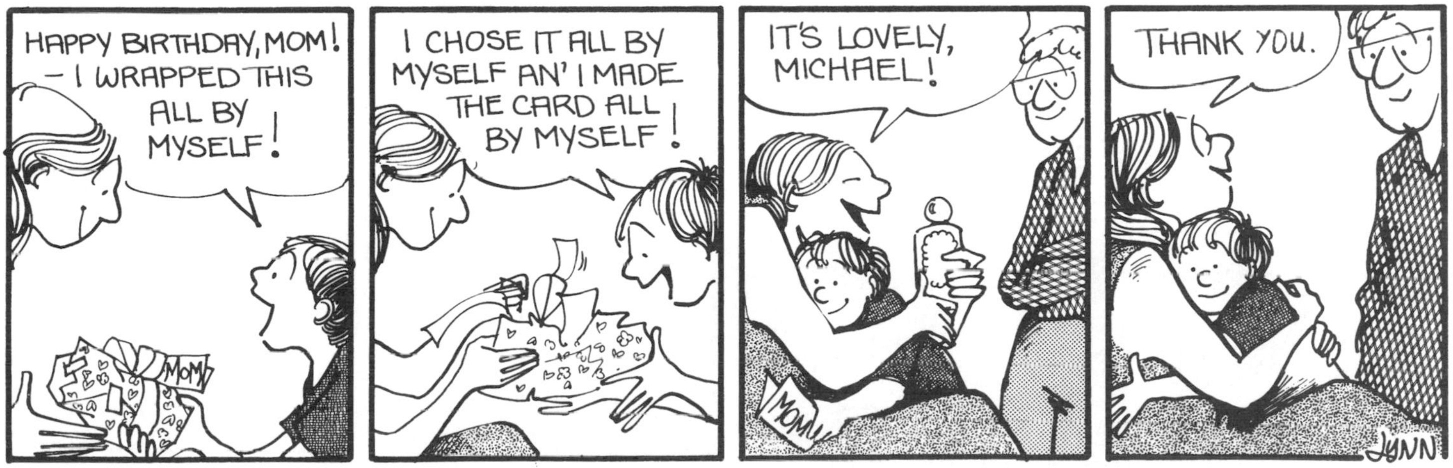

HAPPY BIRTHDAY, MOM! - I WRAPPED THIS ALL BY MYSELF !
MOM
I CHOSE IT ALL BY MYSELF AN' I MADE THE CARD ALL BY MYSELF !
IT'S LOVELY, MICHAEL!
MOM
THANK YOU.
LYNN

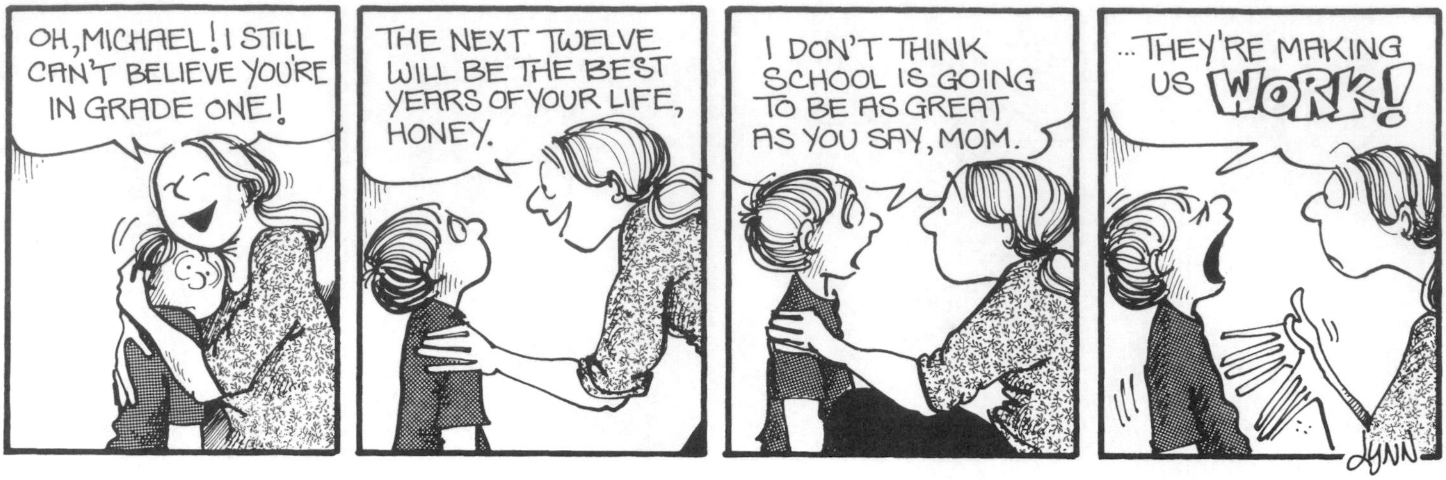

OH, MICHAEL! I STILL CAN'T BELIEVE YOU'RE IN GRADE ONE!
THE NEXT TWELVE WILL BE THE BEST YEARS OF YOUR LIFE, HONEY.
I DON'T THINK SCHOOL IS GOING TO BE AS GREAT AS YOU SAY, MOM.
...THEY'RE MAKING US WORK!
LYNN

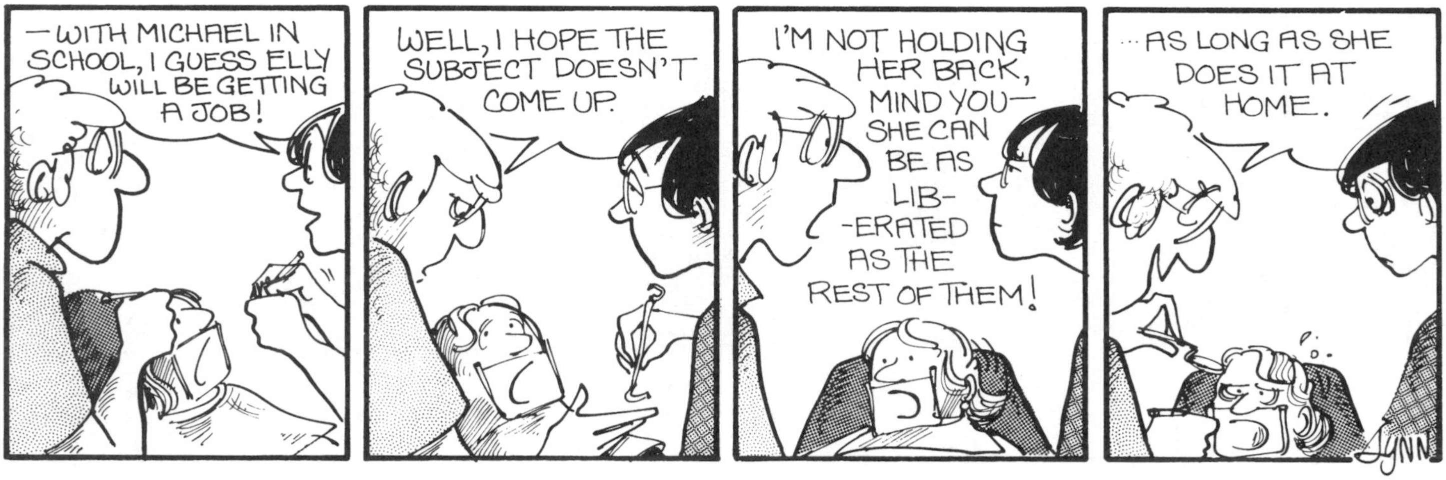

—WITH MICHAEL IN SCHOOL, I GUESS ELLY WILL BE GETTING A JOB!
WELL, I HOPE THE SUBJECT DOESN'T COME UP.
I'M NOT HOLDING HER BACK, MIND YOU— SHE CAN BE AS LIB- -ERATED AS THE REST OF THEM!
...AS LONG AS SHE DOES IT AT HOME.
LYNN

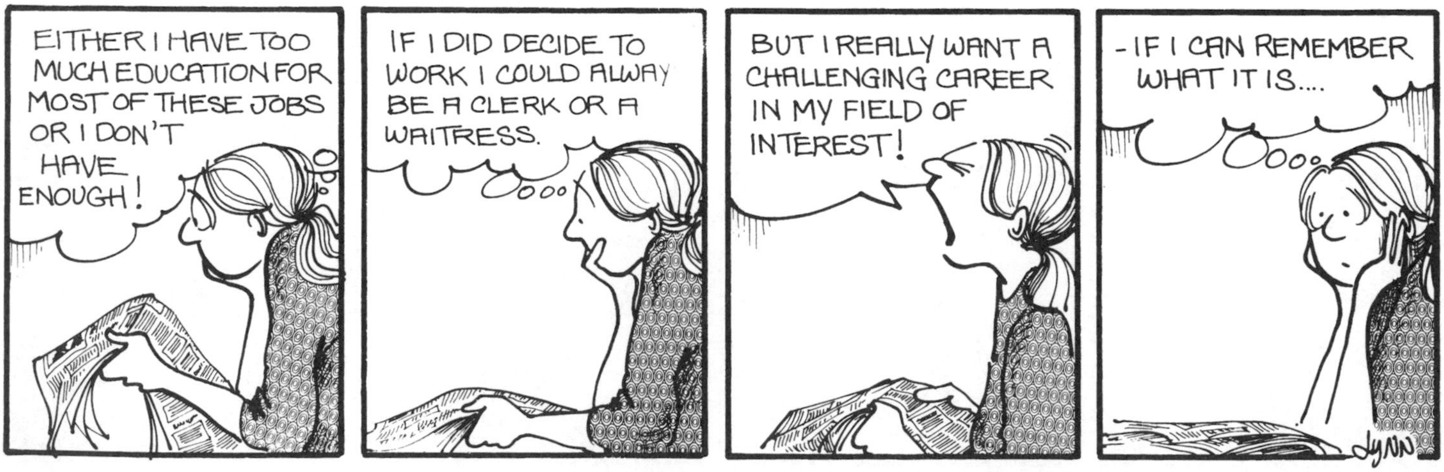

EITHER I HAVE TOO MUCH EDUCATION FOR MOST OF THESE JOBS OR I DON'T HAVE ENOUGH!
IF I DID DECIDE TO WORK I COULD ALWAY BE A CLERK OR A WAITRESS.
BUT I REALLY WANT A CHALLENGING CAREER IN MY FIELD OF INTEREST!
-IF I CAN REMEMBER WHAT IT IS....
LYNN

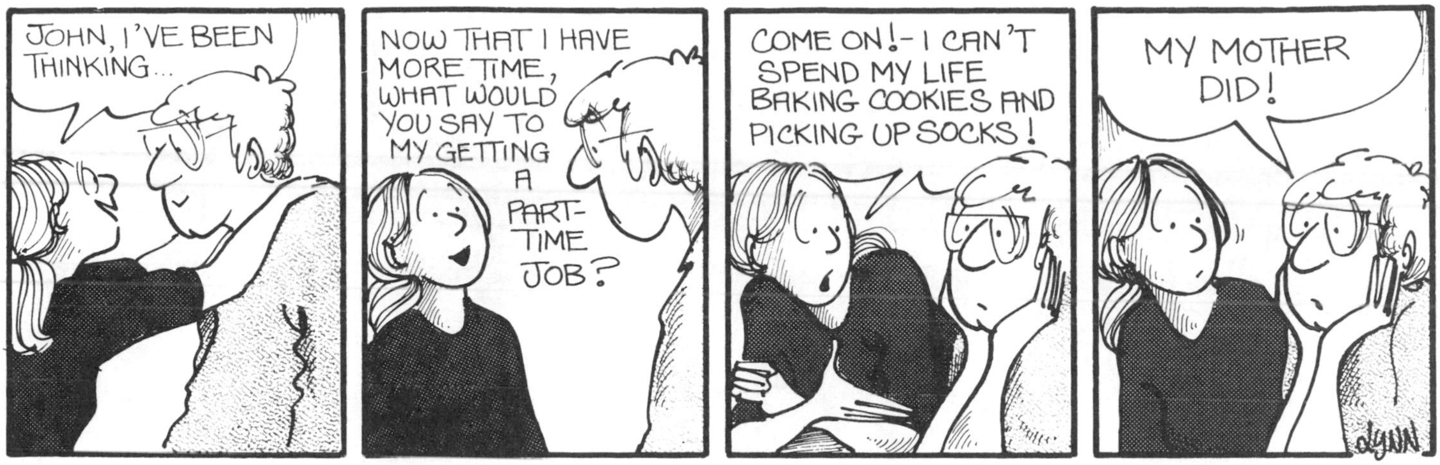
JOHN, I'VE BEEN THINKING...
NOW THAT I HAVE MORE TIME, WHAT WOULD YOU SAY TO MY GETTING A PART-TIME JOB?
COME ON!- I CAN'T SPEND MY LIFE BAKING COOKIES AND PICKING UP SOCKS!
MY MOTHER DID!
LYNN

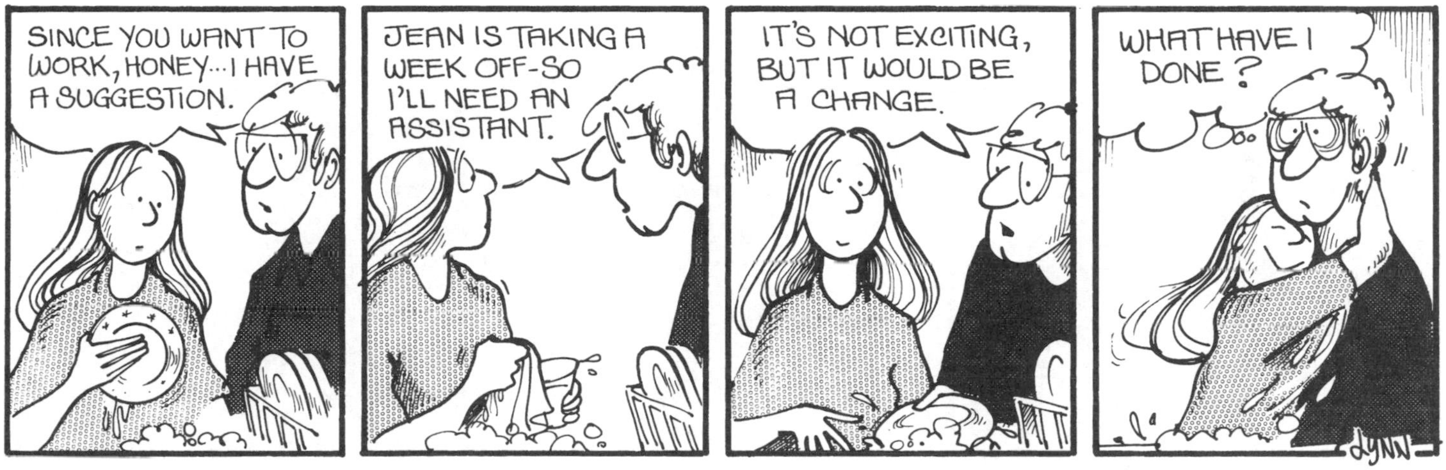
SINCE YOU WANT TO WORK, HONEY...I HAVE A SUGGESTION.
JEAN IS TAKING A WEEK OFF-SO I'LL NEED AN ASSISTANT.
IT'S NOT EXCITING, BUT IT WOULD BE A CHANGE.
WHAT HAVE I DONE?
LYNN

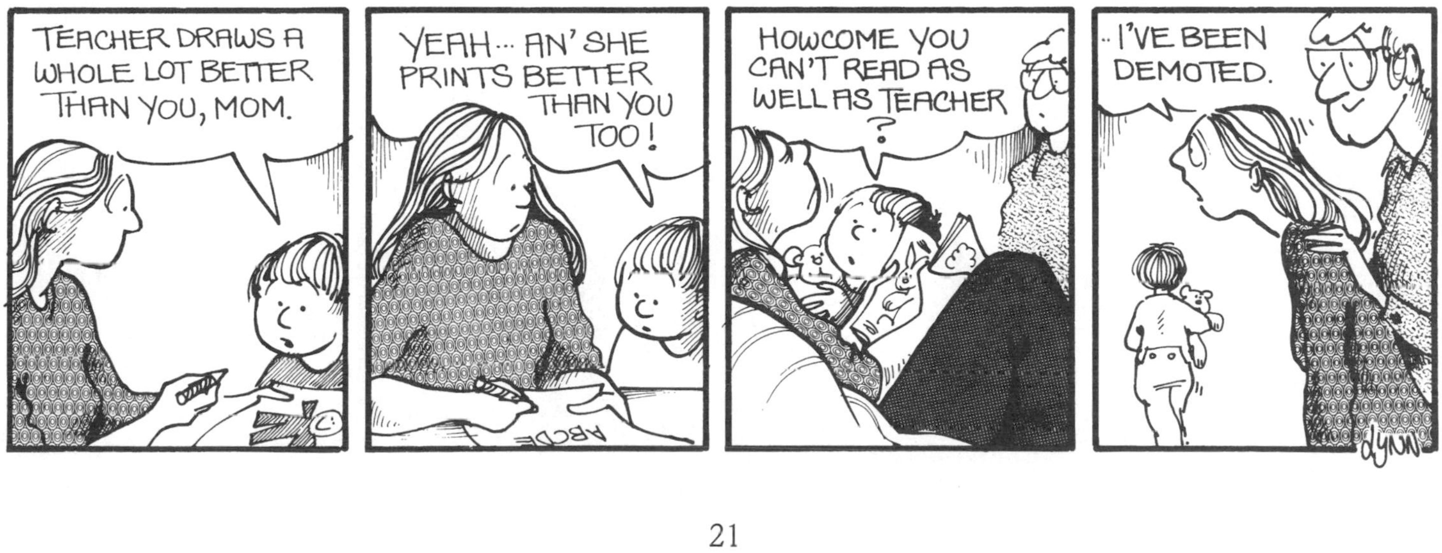
TEACHER DRAWS A WHOLE LOT BETTER THAN YOU, MOM.
YEAH... AN' SHE PRINTS BETTER THAN YOU TOO!
ABCDE
HOWCOME YOU CAN'T READ AS WELL AS TEACHER?
..I'VE BEEN DEMOTED.
LYNN

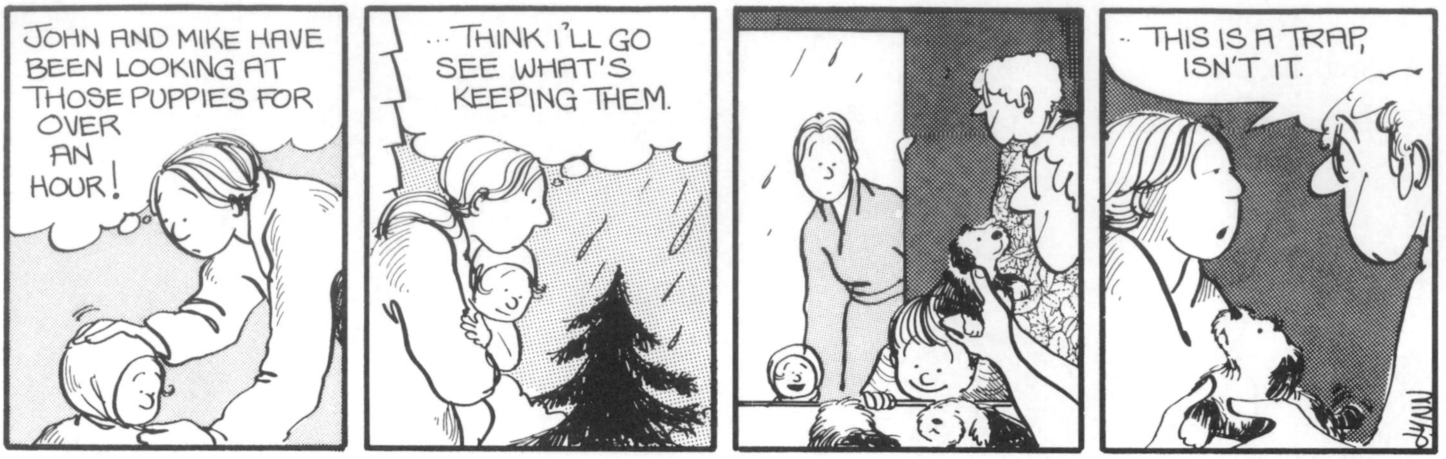
JOHN AND MIKE HAVE BEEN LOOKING AT THOSE PUPPIES FOR OVER AN HOUR!
...THINK I'LL GO SEE WHAT'S KEEPING THEM.
.. THIS IS A TRAP, ISN'T IT.

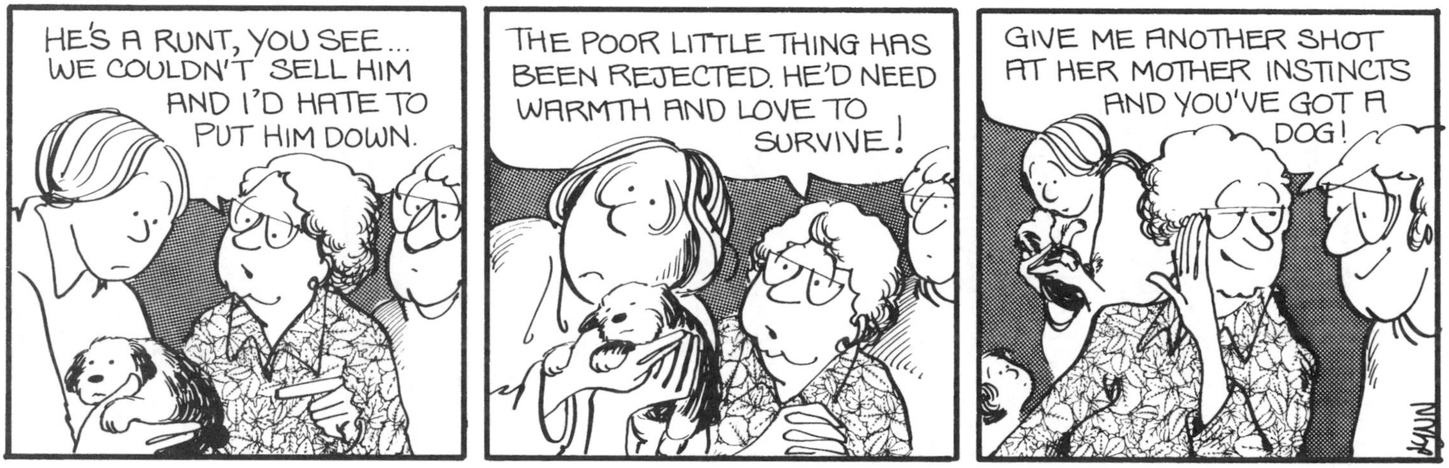
HE'S A RUNT, YOU SEE... WE COULDN'T SELL HIM AND I'D HATE TO PUT HIM DOWN.
THE POOR LITTLE THING HAS BEEN REJECTED. HE'D NEED WARMTH AND LOVE TO SURVIVE!
GIVE ME ANOTHER SHOT AT HER MOTHER INSTINCTS AND YOU'VE GOT A DOG!

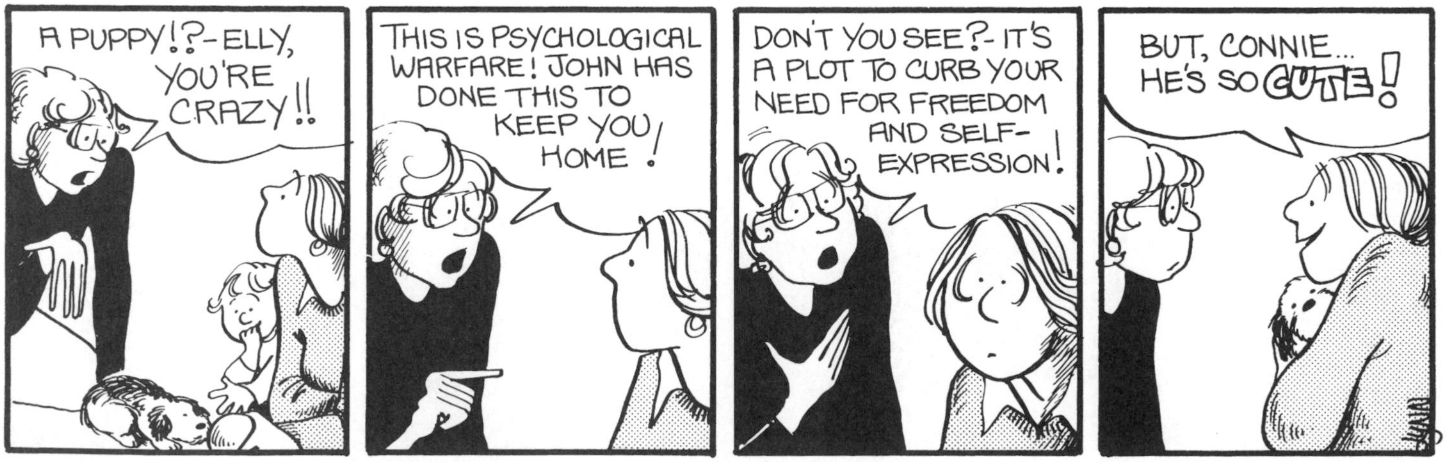
A PUPPY!?- ELLY, YOU'RE CRAZY!!
THIS IS PSYCHOLOGICAL WARFARE! JOHN HAS DONE THIS TO KEEP YOU HOME!
DON'T YOU SEE?- IT'S A PLOT TO CURB YOUR NEED FOR FREEDOM AND SELF-EXPRESSION!
BUT, CONNIE... HE'S SO CUTE!

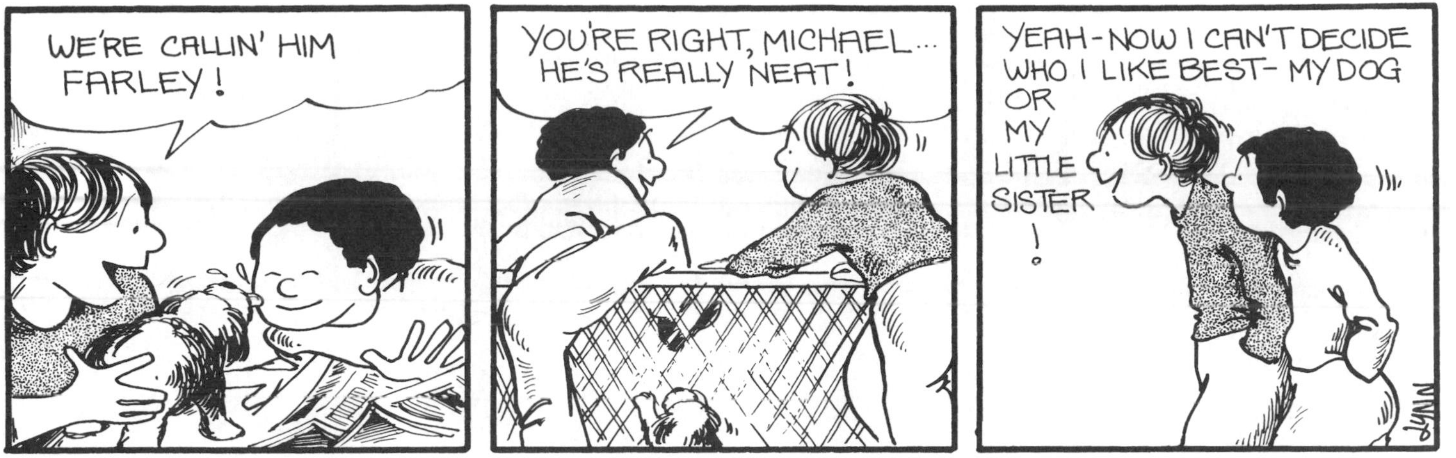
WE'RE CALLIN' HIM FARLEY!
YOU'RE RIGHT, MICHAEL... HE'S REALLY NEAT!
YEAH - NOW I CAN'T DECIDE WHO I LIKE BEST- MY DOG OR MY LITTLE SISTER!
LYNN

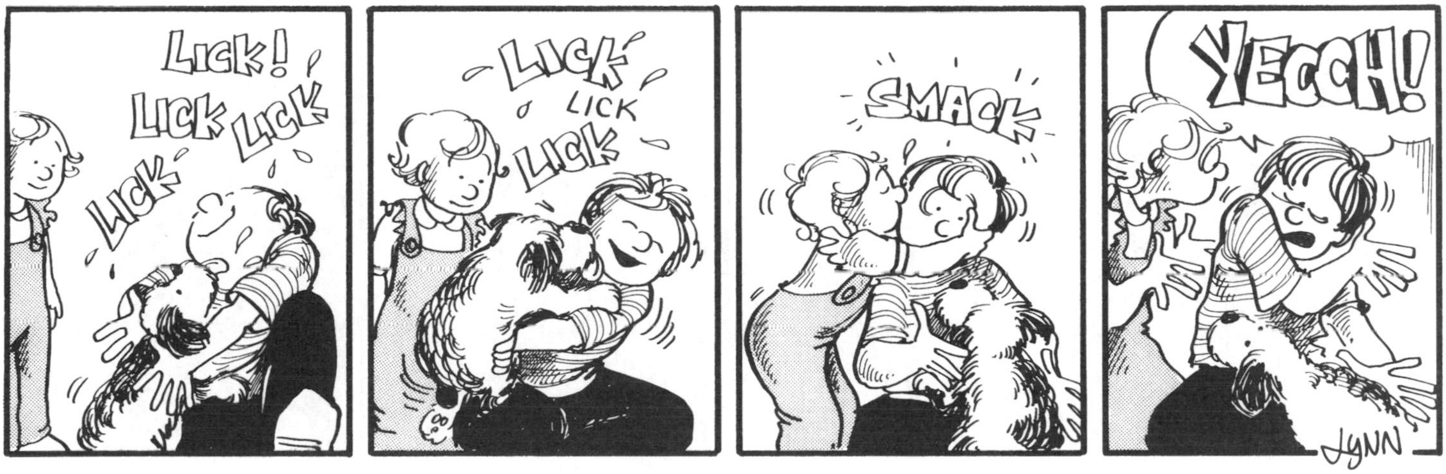
LICK! LICK LICK LICK
LICK LICK LICK
SMACK
YECCH!
LYNN

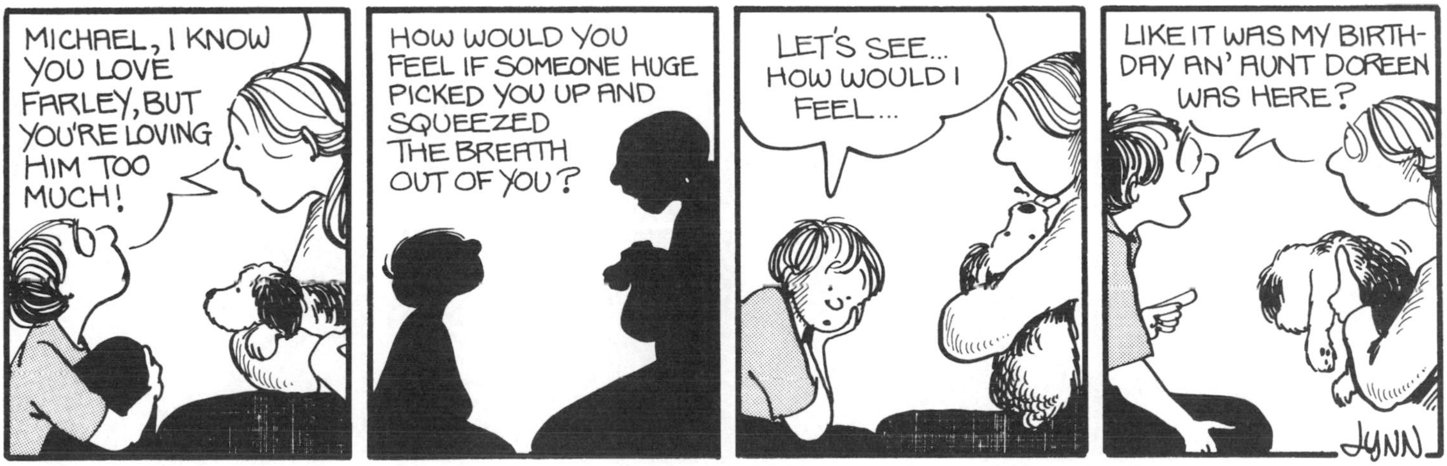
MICHAEL, I KNOW YOU LOVE FARLEY, BUT YOU'RE LOVING HIM TOO MUCH!
HOW WOULD YOU FEEL IF SOMEONE HUGE PICKED YOU UP AND SQUEEZED THE BREATH OUT OF YOU?
LET'S SEE... HOW WOULD I FEEL...
LIKE IT WAS MY BIRTHDAY AN' AUNT DOREEN WAS HERE?
LYNN

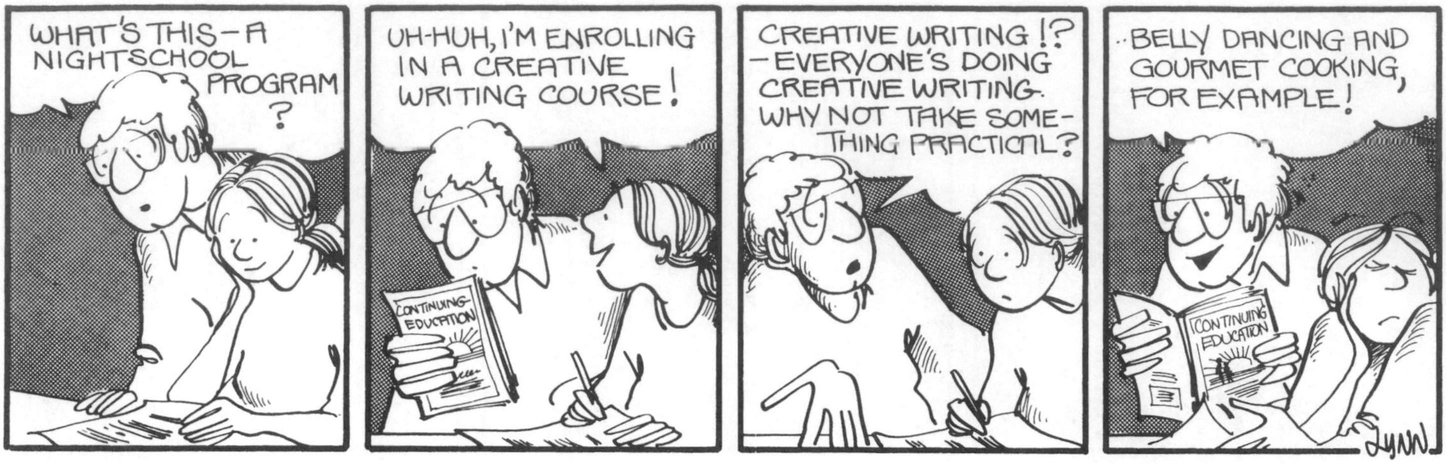
WHAT'S THIS—A NIGHTSCHOOL PROGRAM?
UH-HUH, I'M ENROLLING IN A CREATIVE WRITING COURSE!
CONTINUING EDUCATION
CREATIVE WRITING!? —EVERYONE'S DOING CREATIVE WRITING. WHY NOT TAKE SOMETHING PRACTICAL?
..BELLY DANCING AND GOURMET COOKING, FOR EXAMPLE!
CONTINUING EDUCATION
LYNN

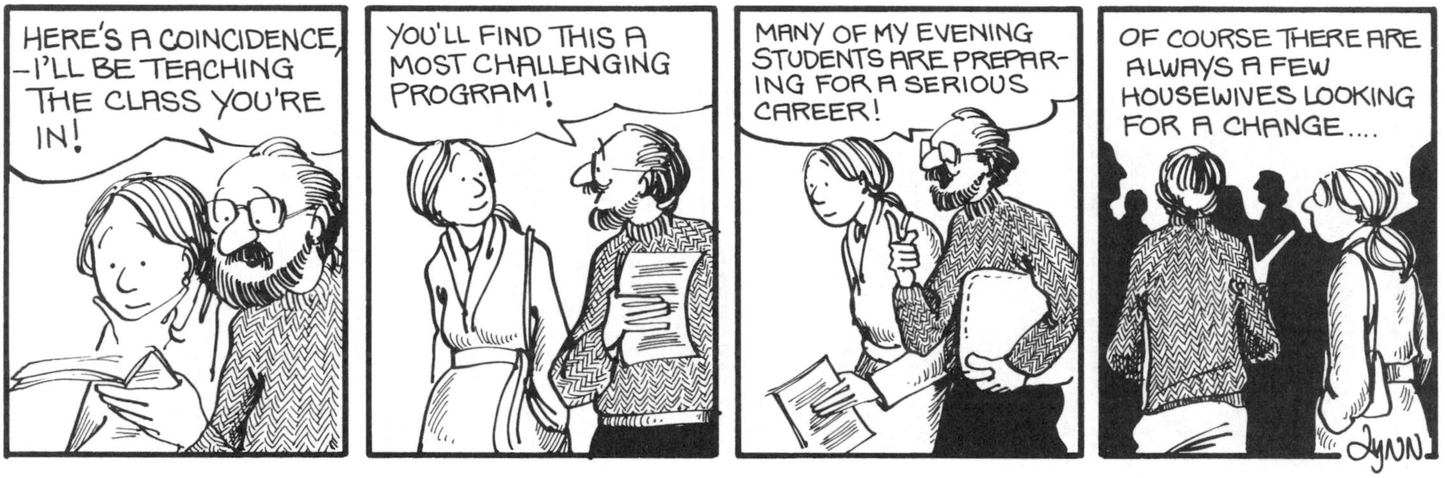
HERE'S A COINCIDENCE, —I'LL BE TEACHING THE CLASS YOU'RE IN!
YOU'LL FIND THIS A MOST CHALLENGING PROGRAM!
MANY OF MY EVENING STUDENTS ARE PREPARING FOR A SERIOUS CAREER!
OF COURSE THERE ARE ALWAYS A FEW HOUSEWIVES LOOKING FOR A CHANGE....
LYNN

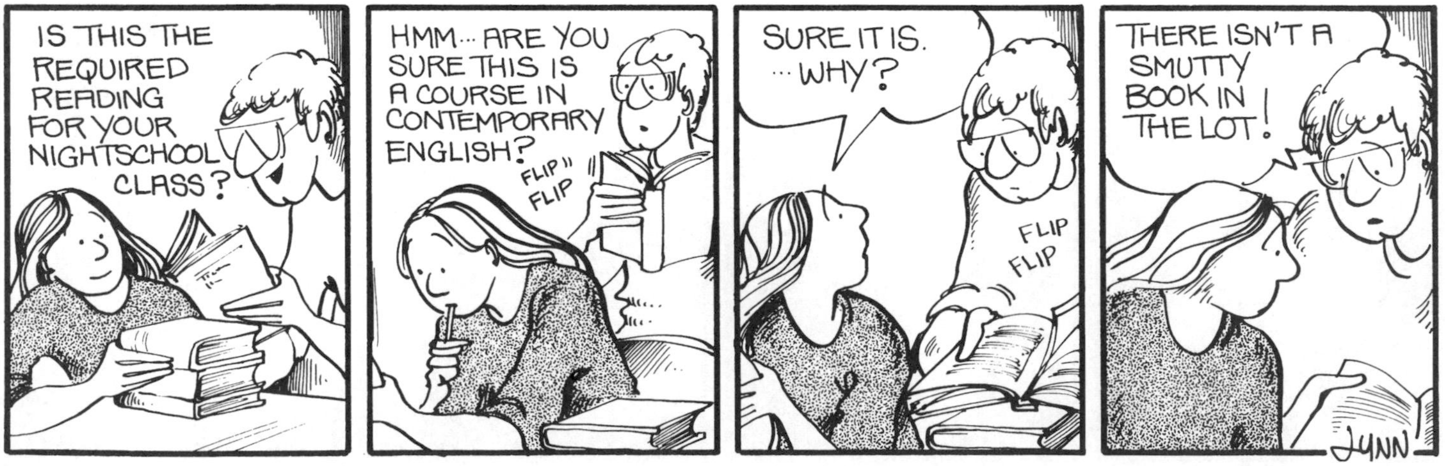
IS THIS THE REQUIRED READING FOR YOUR NIGHTSCHOOL CLASS?
HMM... ARE YOU SURE THIS IS A COURSE IN CONTEMPORARY ENGLISH?
FLIP FLIP
SURE IT IS. ...WHY?
FLIP FLIP
THERE ISN'T A SMUTTY BOOK IN THE LOT!
LYNN

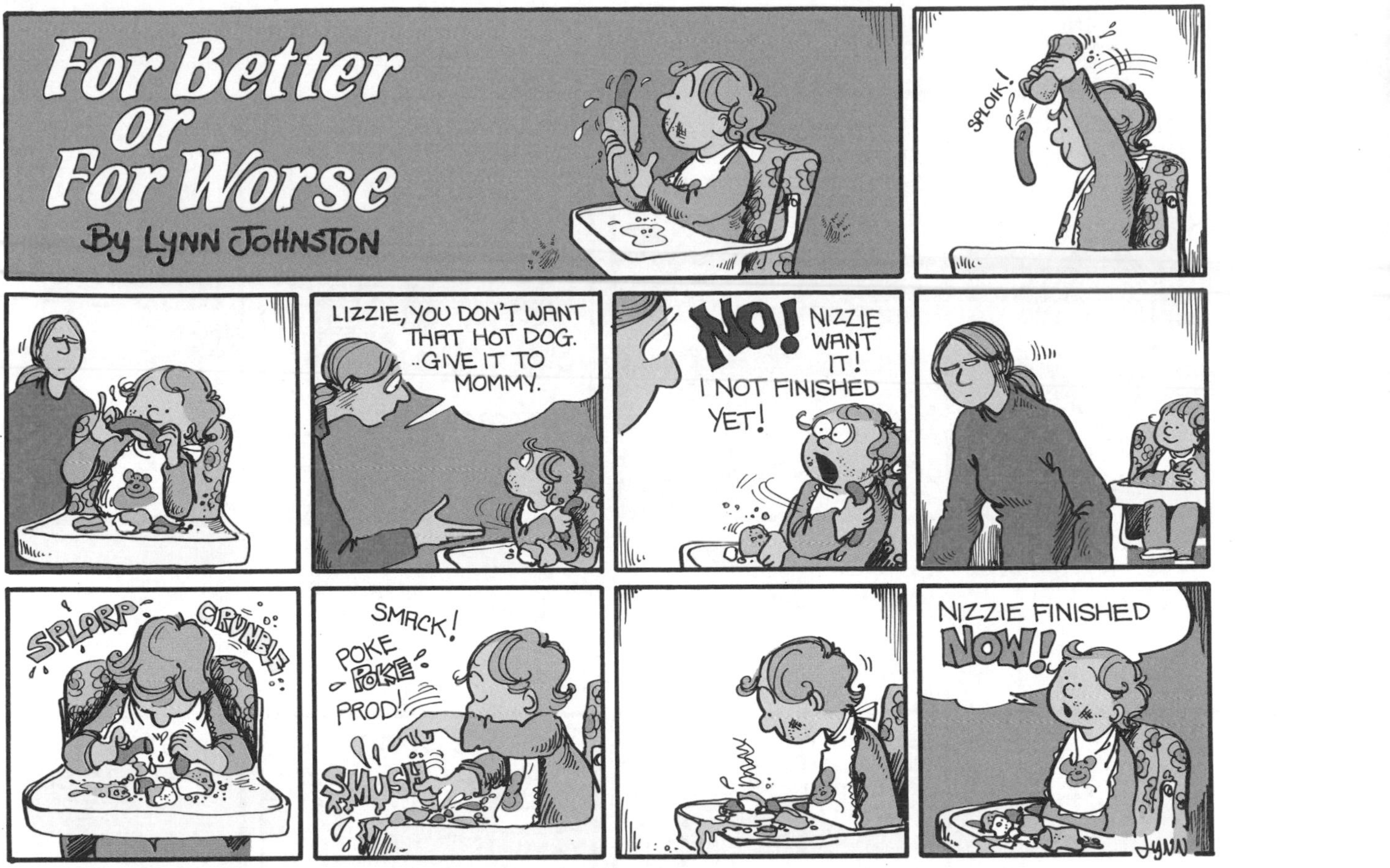
For Better or For Worse
By Lynn Johnston
SPLOIK!
LIZZIE, YOU DON'T WANT THAT HOT DOG. ..GIVE IT TO MOMMY.
NO! NIZZIE WANT IT! I NOT FINISHED YET!
SPLORP
CRUNBL
SMACK!
POKE
POKE
PROD!
SMUSH
NIZZIE FINISHED NOW!
LYNN

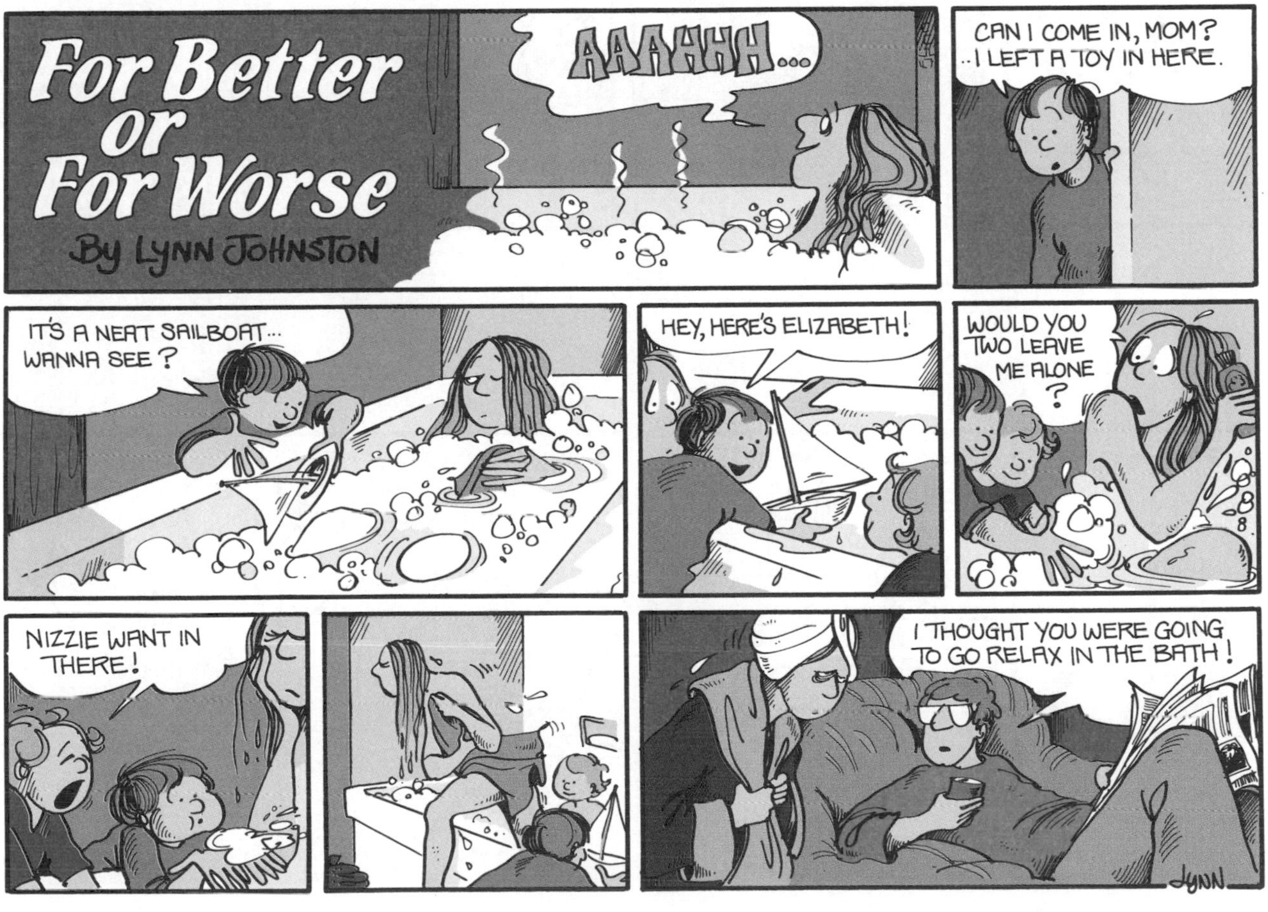
For Better or For Worse
By Lynn Johnston
AAAHHH...
CAN I COME IN, MOM? ..I LEFT A TOY IN HERE.
IT'S A NEAT SAILBOAT... WANNA SEE?
HEY, HERE'S ELIZABETH!
WOULD YOU TWO LEAVE ME ALONE?
NIZZIE WANT IN THERE!
I THOUGHT YOU WERE GOING TO GO RELAX IN THE BATH!
LYNN

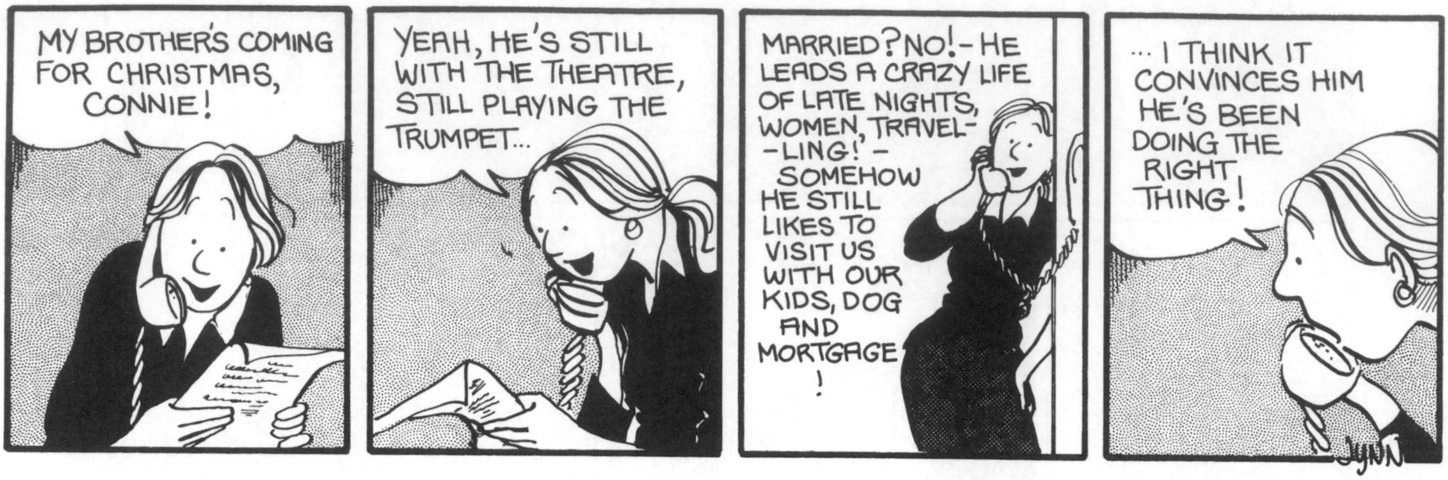
MY BROTHER'S COMING FOR CHRISTMAS, CONNIE!
YEAH, HE'S STILL WITH THE THEATRE, STILL PLAYING THE TRUMPET...
MARRIED? NO! - HE LEADS A CRAZY LIFE OF LATE NIGHTS, WOMEN, TRAVEL-LING! - SOMEHOW HE STILL LIKES TO VISIT US WITH OUR KIDS, DOG AND MORTGAGE!
... I THINK IT CONVINCES HIM HE'S BEEN DOING THE RIGHT THING!
LYNN

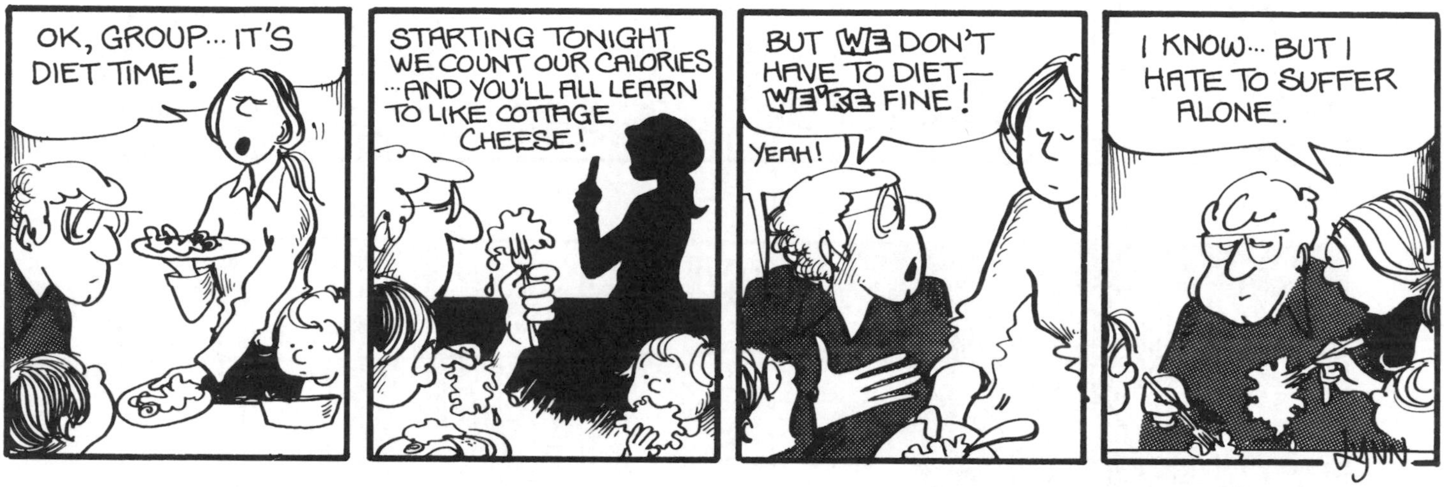
OK, GROUP... IT'S DIET TIME!
STARTING TONIGHT WE COUNT OUR CALORIES ...AND YOU'LL ALL LEARN TO LIKE COTTAGE CHEESE!
BUT WE DON'T HAVE TO DIET— WE'RE FINE!
YEAH!
I KNOW... BUT I HATE TO SUFFER ALONE.
LYNN

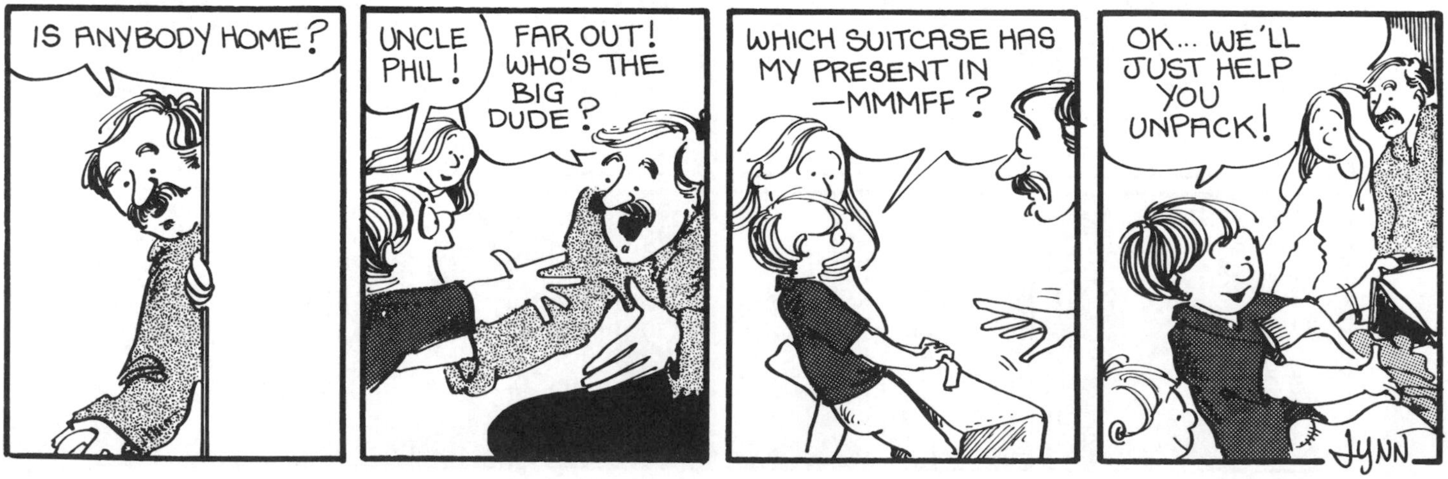
IS ANYBODY HOME?
UNCLE PHIL!
FAR OUT! WHO'S THE BIG DUDE?
WHICH SUITCASE HAS MY PRESENT IN —MMMFF?
OK... WE'LL JUST HELP YOU UNPACK!
LYNN

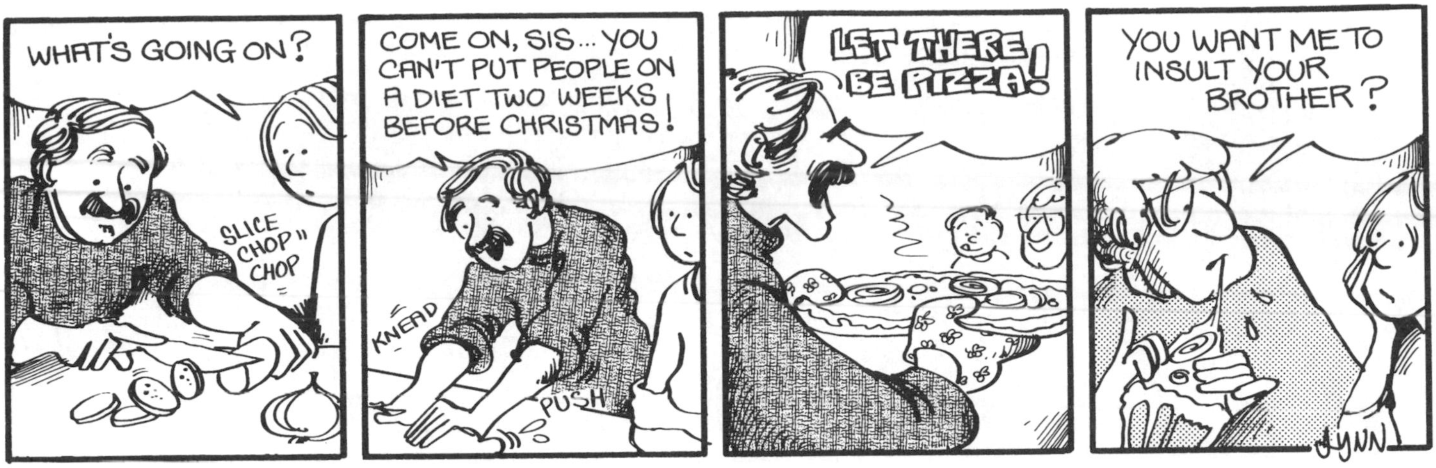
WHAT'S GOING ON?
SLICE CHOP" CHOP
COME ON, SIS... YOU CAN'T PUT PEOPLE ON A DIET TWO WEEKS BEFORE CHRISTMAS!
KNEAD
PUSH
LET THERE BE PIZZA!
YOU WANT ME TO INSULT YOUR BROTHER?
LYNN

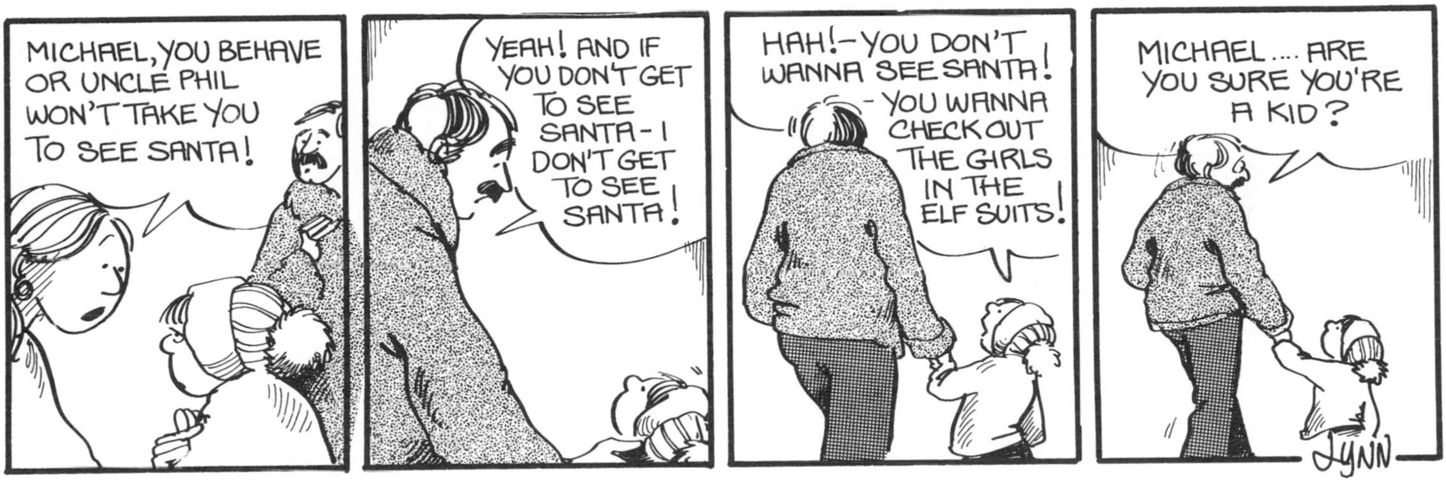
MICHAEL, YOU BEHAVE OR UNCLE PHIL WON'T TAKE YOU TO SEE SANTA!
YEAH! AND IF YOU DON'T GET TO SEE SANTA - I DON'T GET TO SEE SANTA!
HAH! - YOU DON'T WANNA SEE SANTA! - YOU WANNA CHECK OUT THE GIRLS IN THE ELF SUITS!
MICHAEL.... ARE YOU SURE YOU'RE A KID?
LYNN

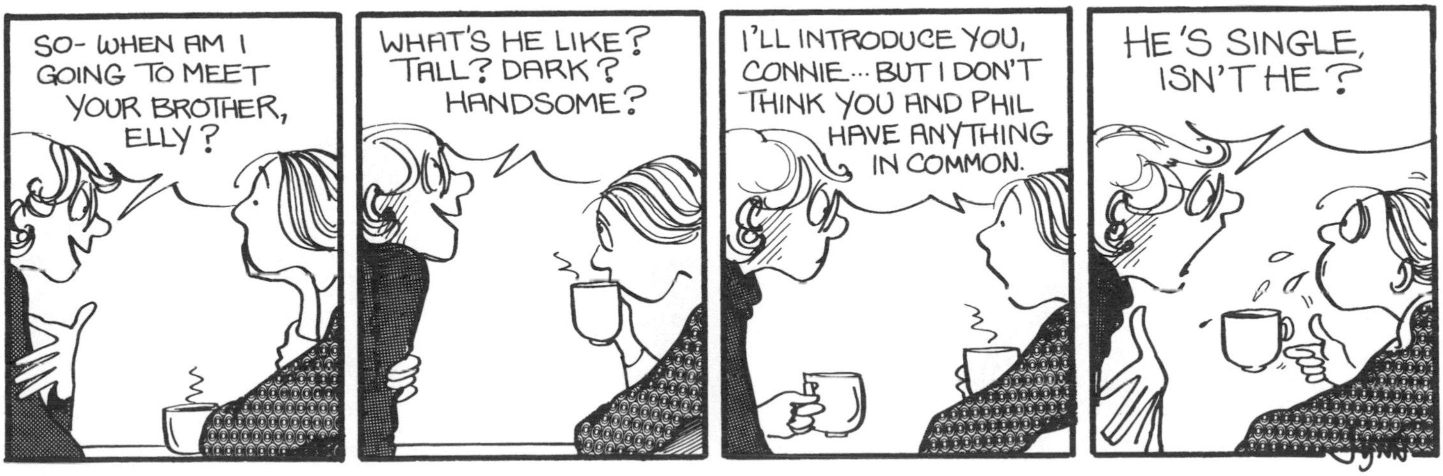
SO- WHEN AM I GOING TO MEET YOUR BROTHER, ELLY?
WHAT'S HE LIKE? TALL? DARK? HANDSOME?
I'LL INTRODUCE YOU, CONNIE... BUT I DON'T THINK YOU AND PHIL HAVE ANYTHING IN COMMON.
HE'S SINGLE, ISN'T HE?

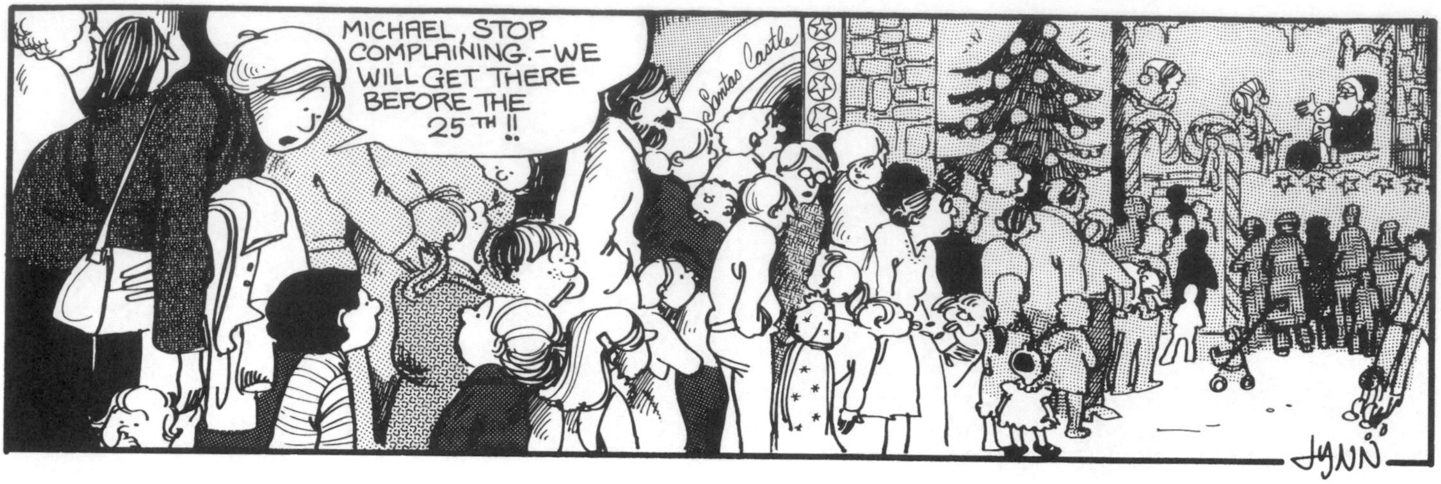
MICHAEL, STOP COMPLAINING.-WE WILL GET THERE BEFORE THE 25TH!!
Santas Castle
LYNN

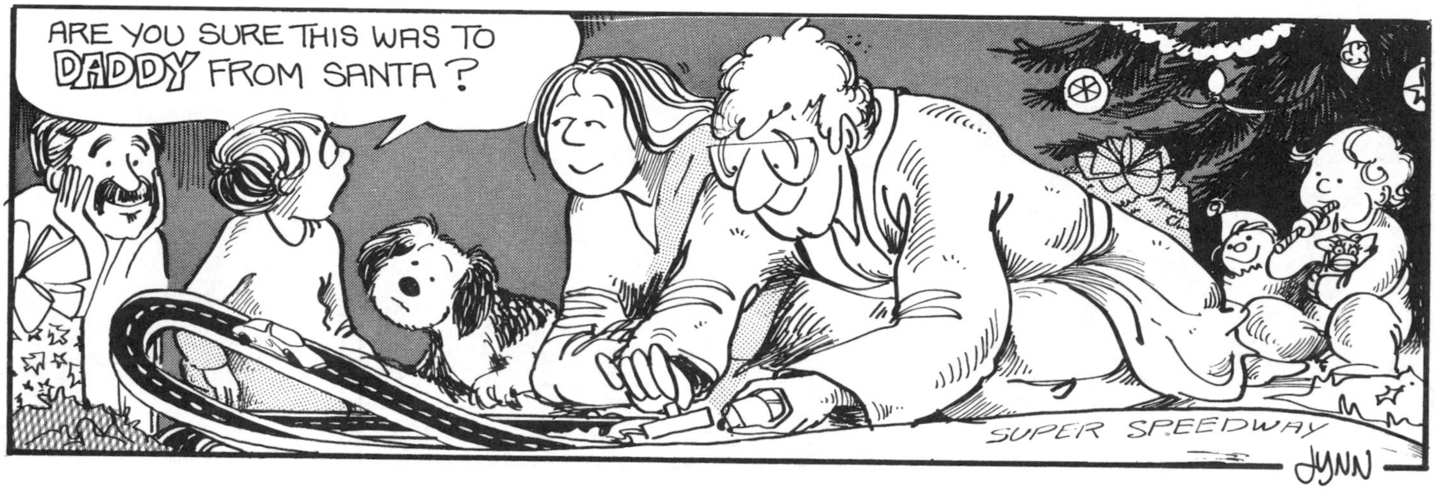
ARE YOU SURE THIS WAS TO DADDY FROM SANTA?
SUPER SPEEDWAY
LYNN

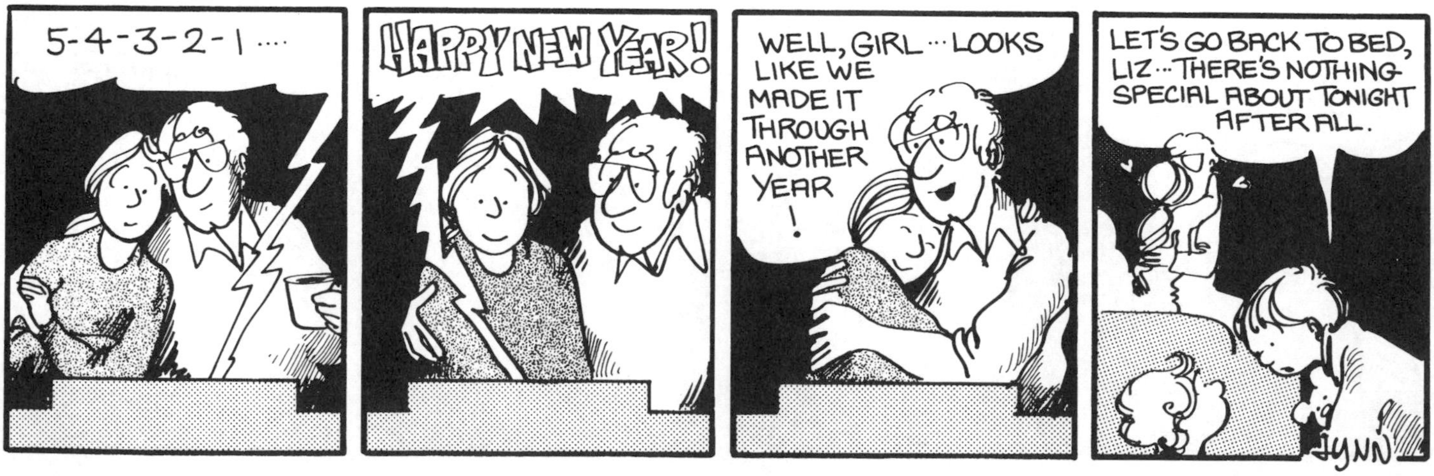
5-4-3-2-1....
HAPPY NEW YEAR!
WELL, GIRL... LOOKS LIKE WE MADE IT THROUGH ANOTHER YEAR!
LET'S GO BACK TO BED, LIZ... THERE'S NOTHING SPECIAL ABOUT TONIGHT AFTER ALL.
LYNN

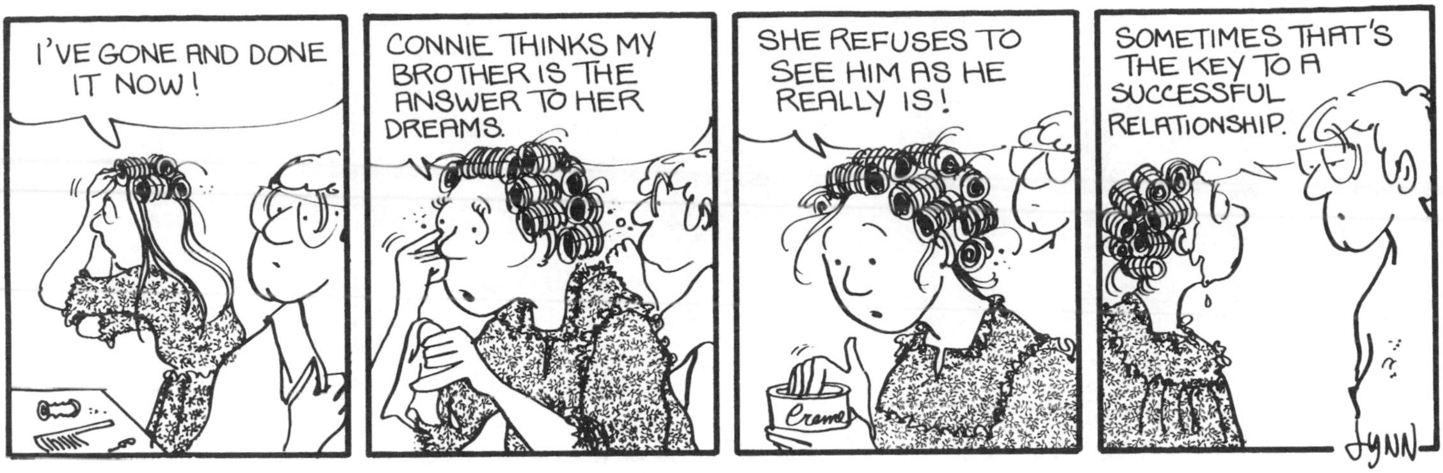
I'VE GONE AND DONE IT NOW!
CONNIE THINKS MY BROTHER IS THE ANSWER TO HER DREAMS.
SHE REFUSES TO SEE HIM AS HE REALLY IS!
Creme
SOMETIMES THAT'S THE KEY TO A SUCCESSFUL RELATIONSHIP.
Lynn

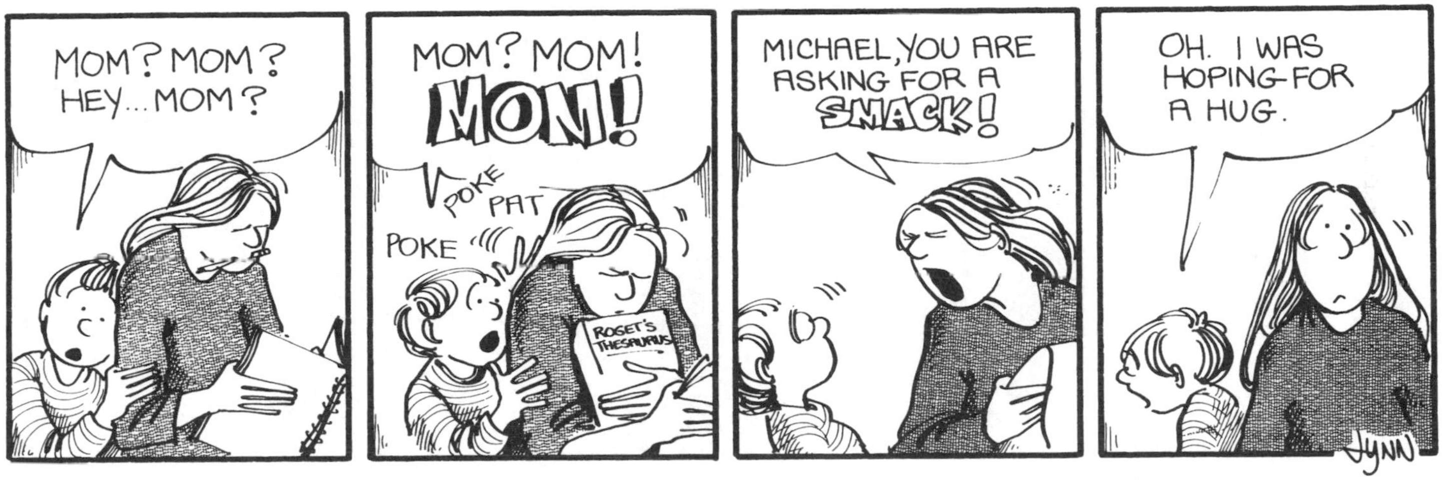
MOM? MOM? HEY... MOM?
MOM? MOM! MOM!
POKE
PAT
POKE
ROGET'S THESAURUS
MICHAEL, YOU ARE ASKING FOR A SMACK!
OH. I WAS HOPING FOR A HUG.
Lynn

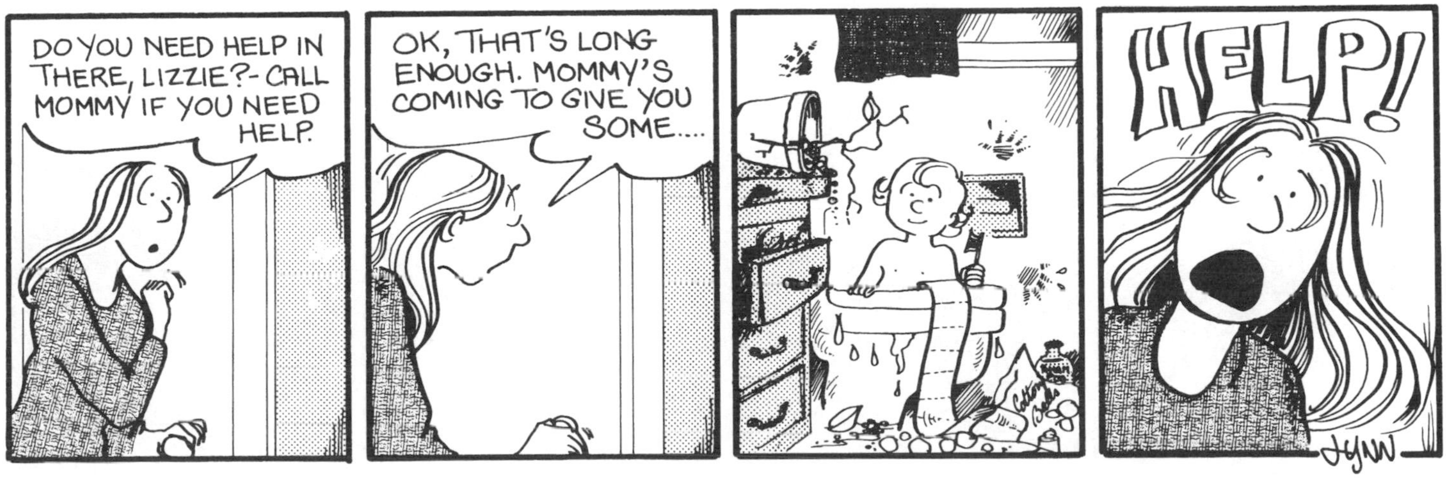
DO YOU NEED HELP IN THERE, LIZZIE?- CALL MOMMY IF YOU NEED HELP.
OK, THAT'S LONG ENOUGH. MOMMY'S COMING TO GIVE YOU SOME....
HELP!
Lynn

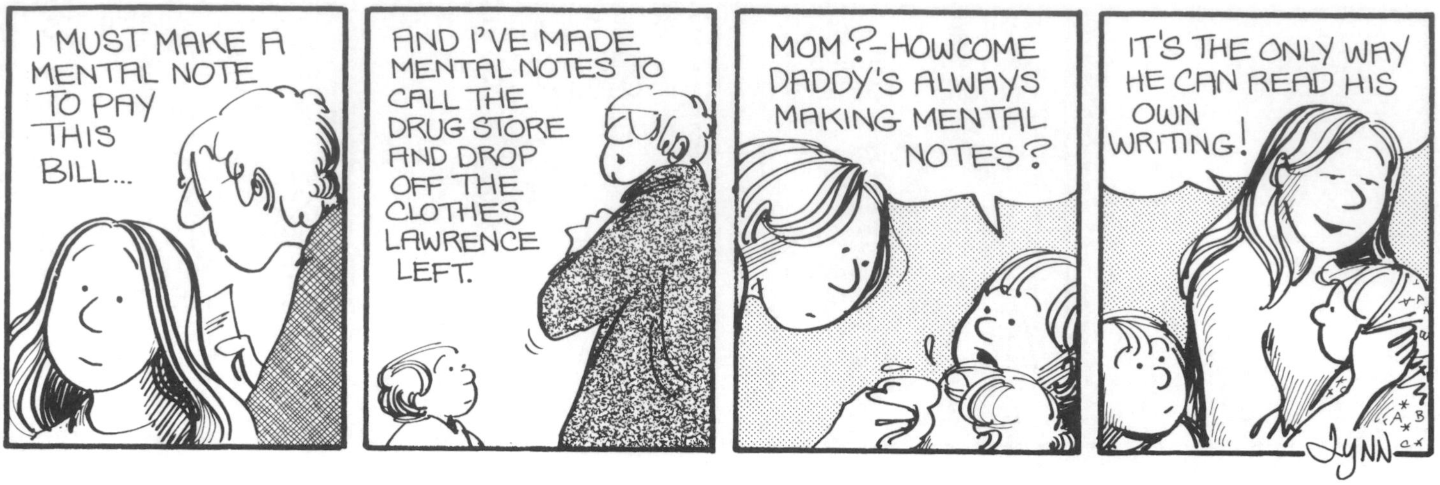
I MUST MAKE A MENTAL NOTE TO PAY THIS BILL...
AND I'VE MADE MENTAL NOTES TO CALL THE DRUG STORE AND DROP OFF THE CLOTHES LAWRENCE LEFT.
MOM?- HOWCOME DADDY'S ALWAYS MAKING MENTAL NOTES?
IT'S THE ONLY WAY HE CAN READ HIS OWN WRITING!
LYNN

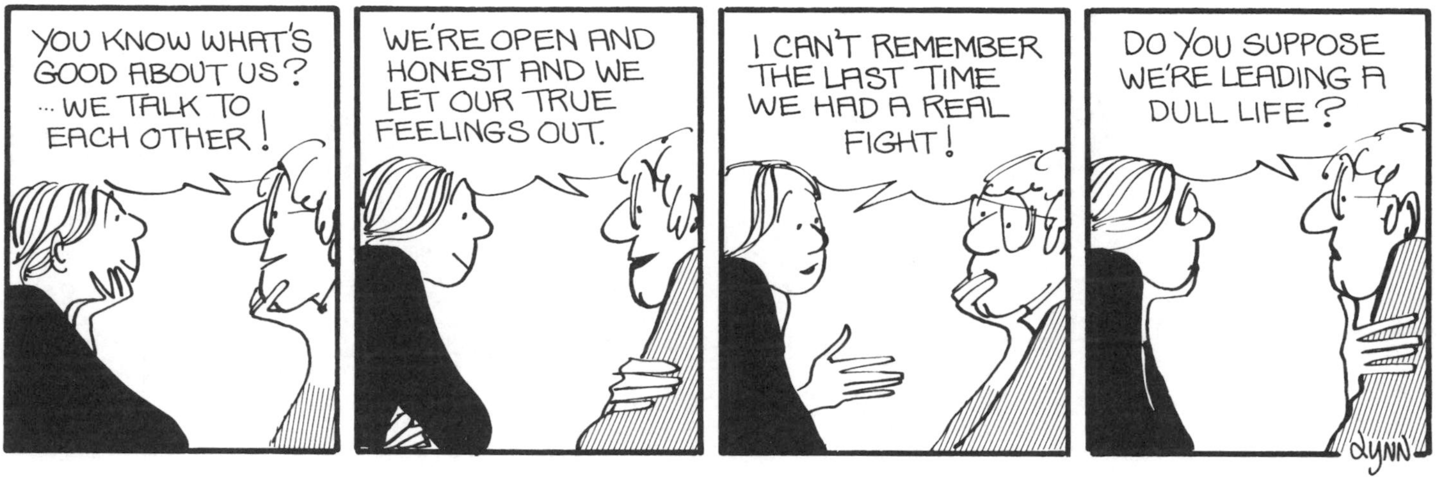
YOU KNOW WHAT'S GOOD ABOUT US? ... WE TALK TO EACH OTHER!
WE'RE OPEN AND HONEST AND WE LET OUR TRUE FEELINGS OUT.
I CAN'T REMEMBER THE LAST TIME WE HAD A REAL FIGHT!
DO YOU SUPPOSE WE'RE LEADING A DULL LIFE?
LYNN

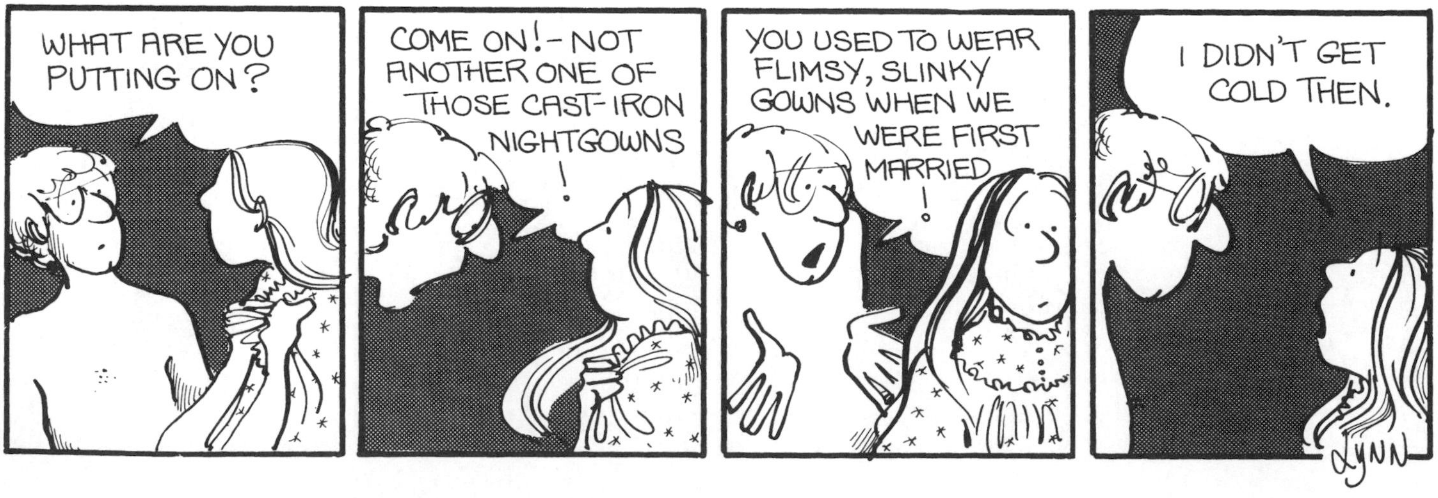
WHAT ARE YOU PUTTING ON?
COME ON!- NOT ANOTHER ONE OF THOSE CAST-IRON NIGHTGOWNS!
YOU USED TO WEAR FLIMSY, SLINKY GOWNS WHEN WE WERE FIRST MARRIED!
I DIDN'T GET COLD THEN.
LYNN

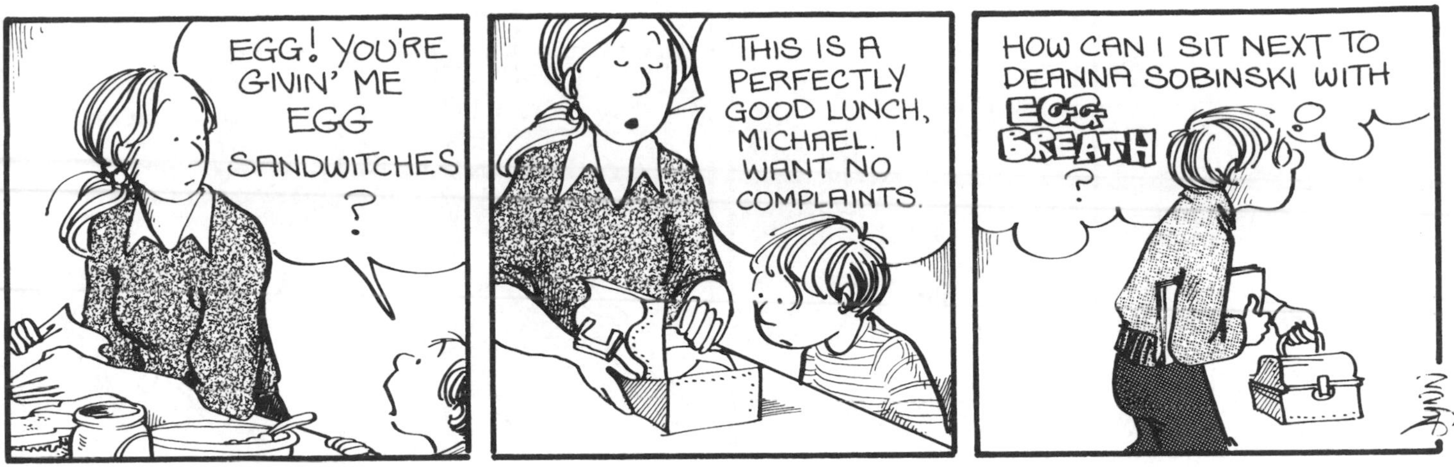
EGG! YOU'RE GIVIN' ME EGG SANDWITCHES?
THIS IS A PERFECTLY GOOD LUNCH, MICHAEL. I WANT NO COMPLAINTS.
HOW CAN I SIT NEXT TO DEANNA SOBINSKI WITH EGG BREATH?
LYNN

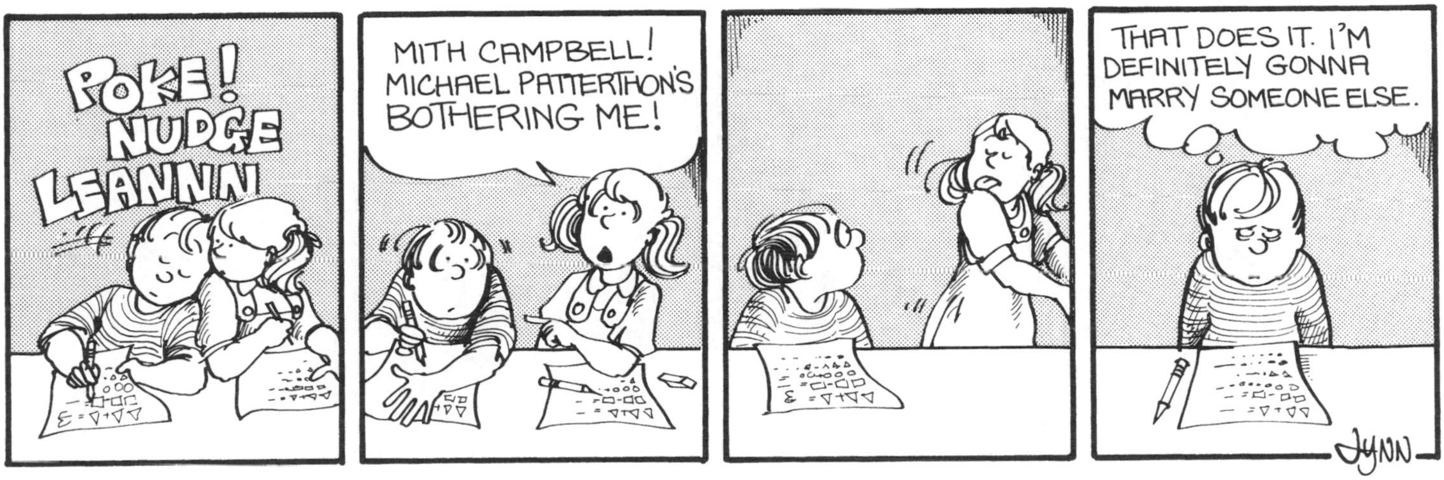
POKE! NUDGE LEANNN
MITH CAMPBELL! MICHAEL PATTERTHON'S BOTHERING ME!
THAT DOES IT. I'M DEFINITELY GONNA MARRY SOMEONE ELSE.
LYNN

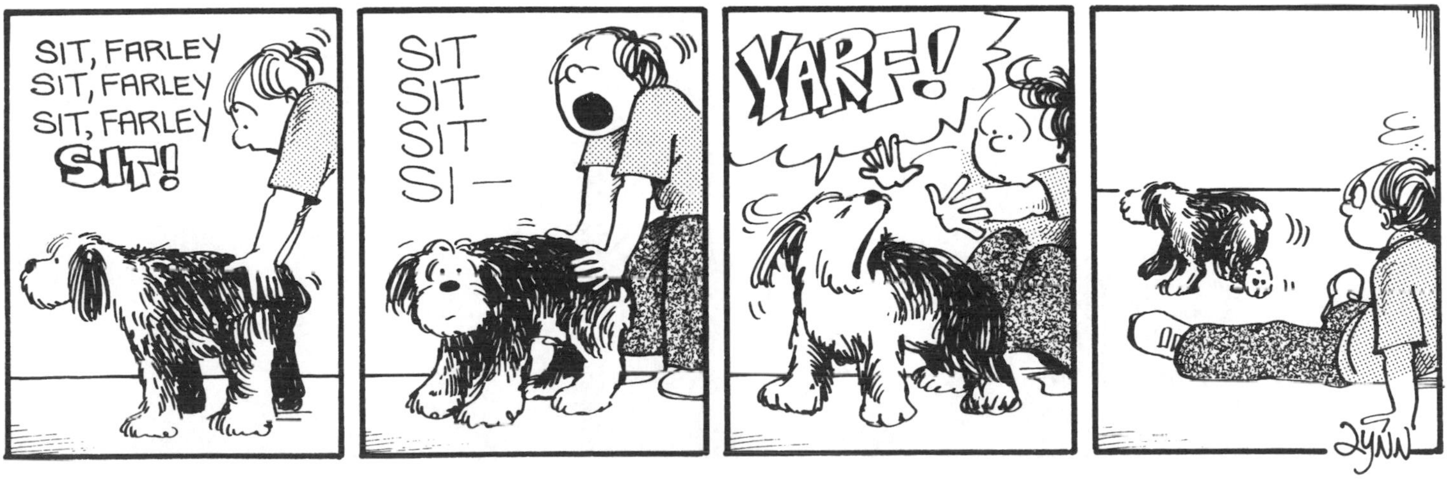
SIT, FARLEY SIT, FARLEY SIT, FARLEY SIT!
SIT SIT SIT SI—
YARF!
LYNN

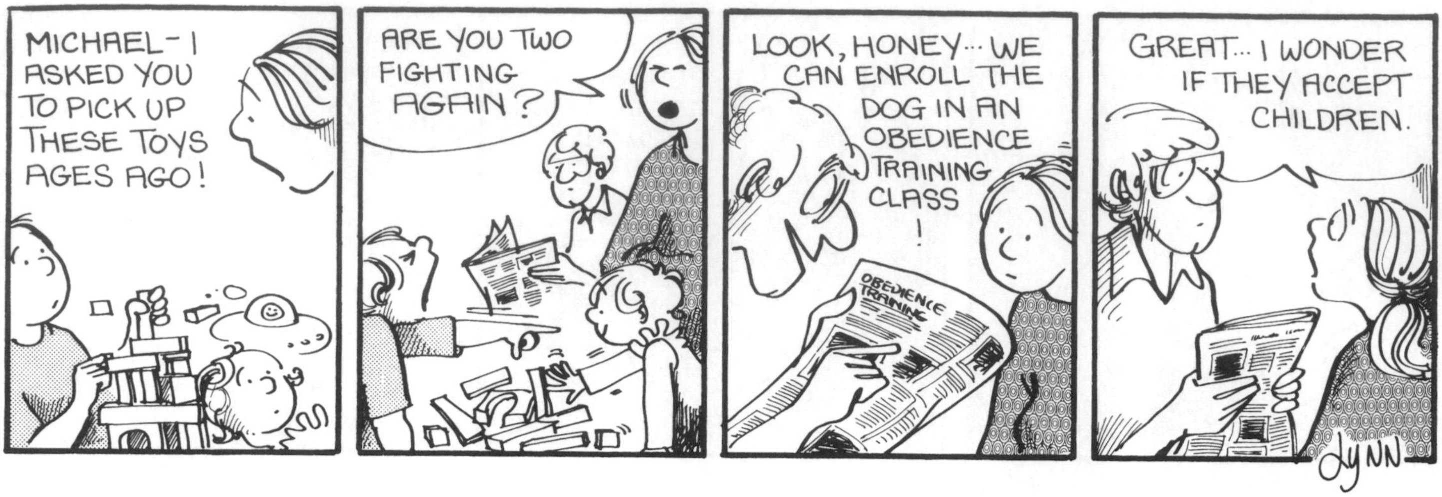
MICHAEL- I ASKED YOU TO PICK UP THESE TOYS AGES AGO!
ARE YOU TWO FIGHTING AGAIN?
LOOK, HONEY... WE CAN ENROLL THE DOG IN AN OBEDIENCE TRAINING CLASS!
OBEDIENCE TRAINING
GREAT... I WONDER IF THEY ACCEPT CHILDREN.
LYNN

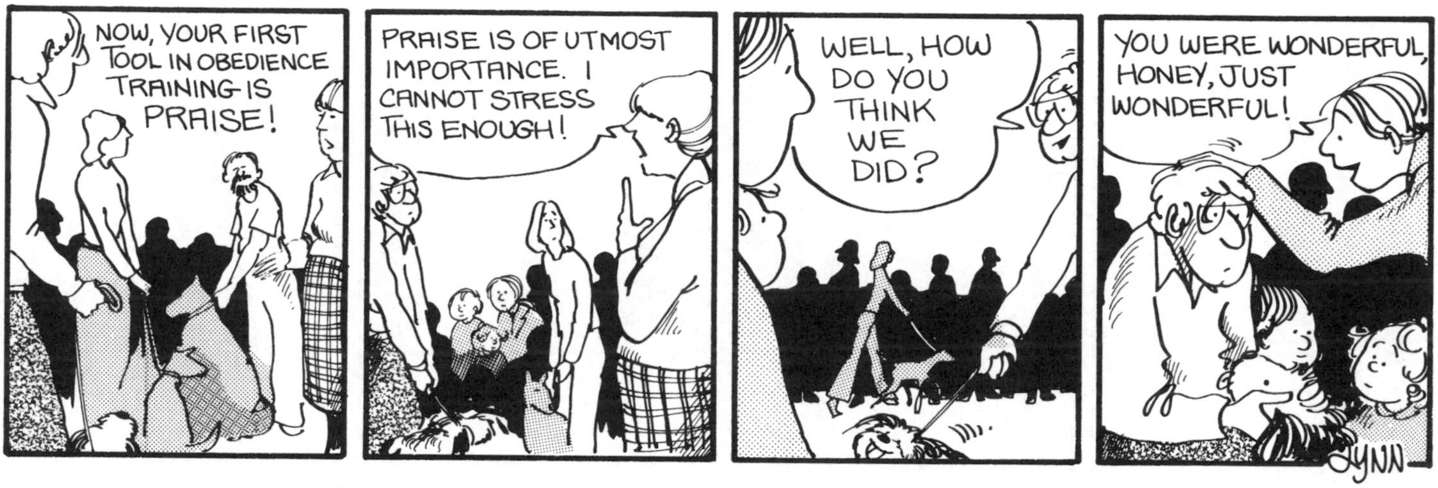
NOW, YOUR FIRST TOOL IN OBEDIENCE TRAINING IS PRAISE!
PRAISE IS OF UTMOST IMPORTANCE. I CANNOT STRESS THIS ENOUGH!
WELL, HOW DO YOU THINK WE DID?
YOU WERE WONDERFUL, HONEY, JUST WONDERFUL!
LYNN

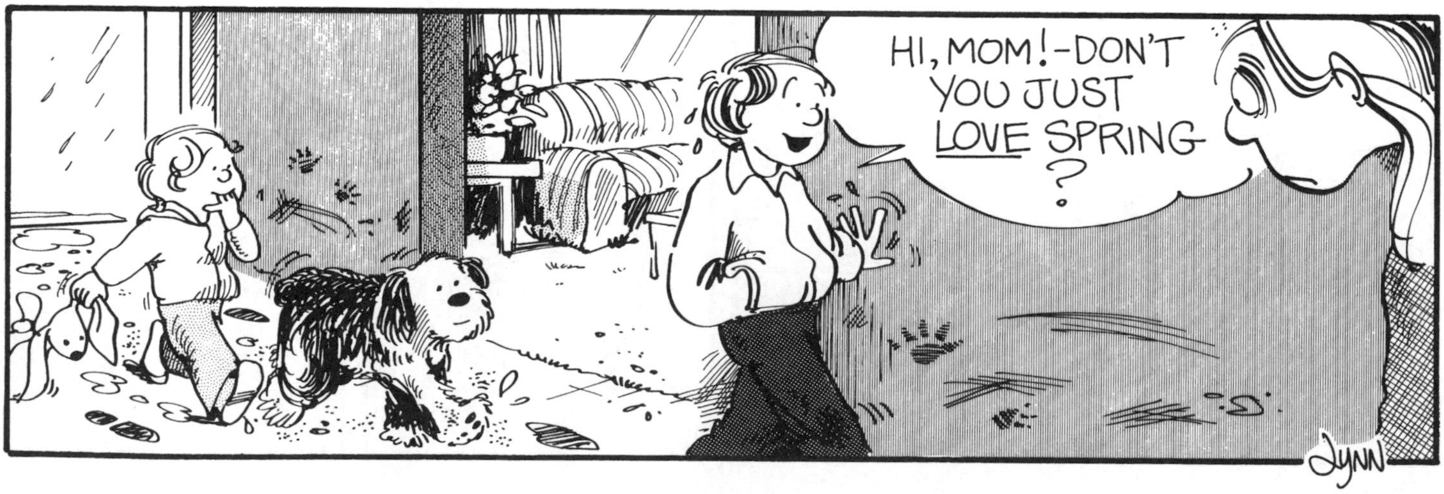
HI, MOM! - DON'T YOU JUST LOVE SPRING?
LYNN

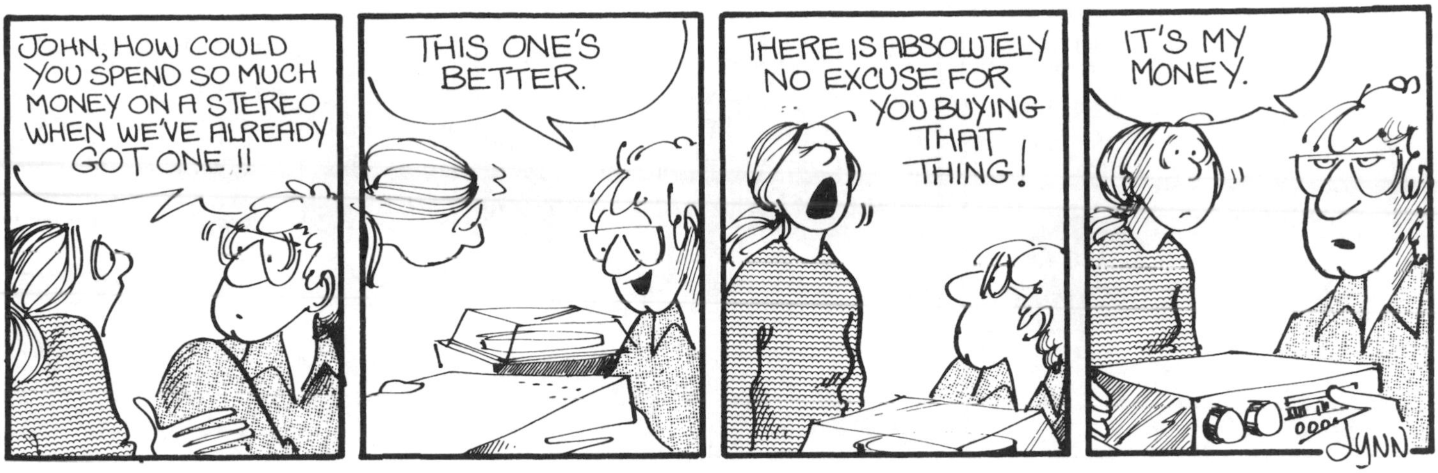
JOHN, HOW COULD YOU SPEND SO MUCH MONEY ON A STEREO WHEN WE'VE ALREADY GOT ONE !!
THIS ONE'S BETTER.
THERE IS ABSOLUTELY NO EXCUSE FOR YOU BUYING THAT THING!
IT'S MY MONEY.
LYNN

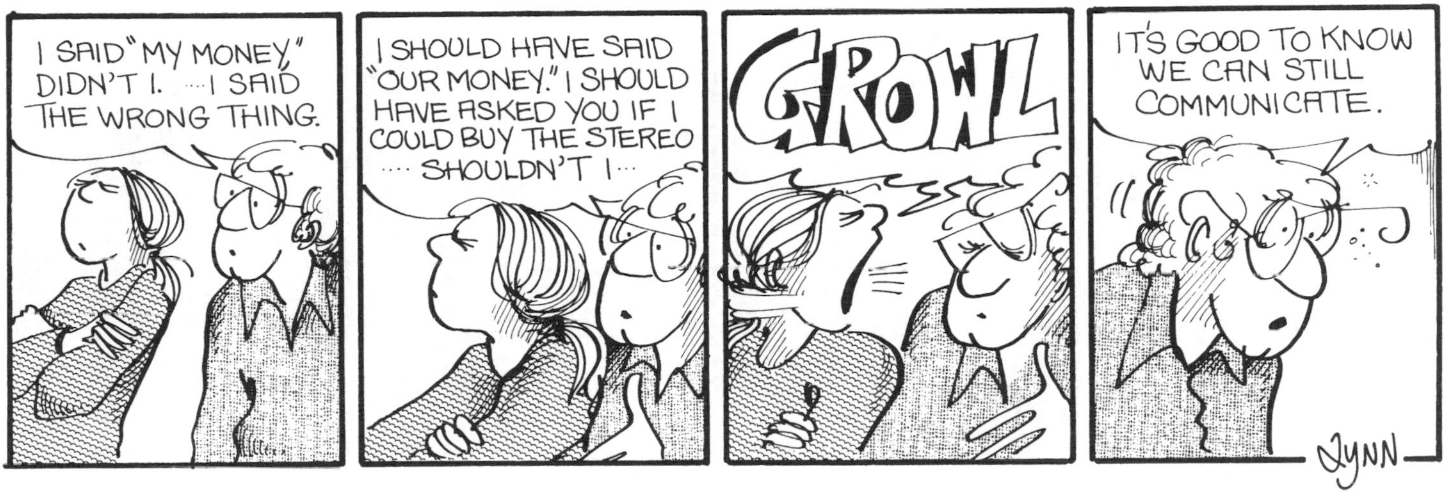
I SAID "MY MONEY," DIDN'T I. ....I SAID THE WRONG THING.
I SHOULD HAVE SAID "OUR MONEY." I SHOULD HAVE ASKED YOU IF I COULD BUY THE STEREO .... SHOULDN'T I...
GROWL
IT'S GOOD TO KNOW WE CAN STILL COMMUNICATE.
LYNN

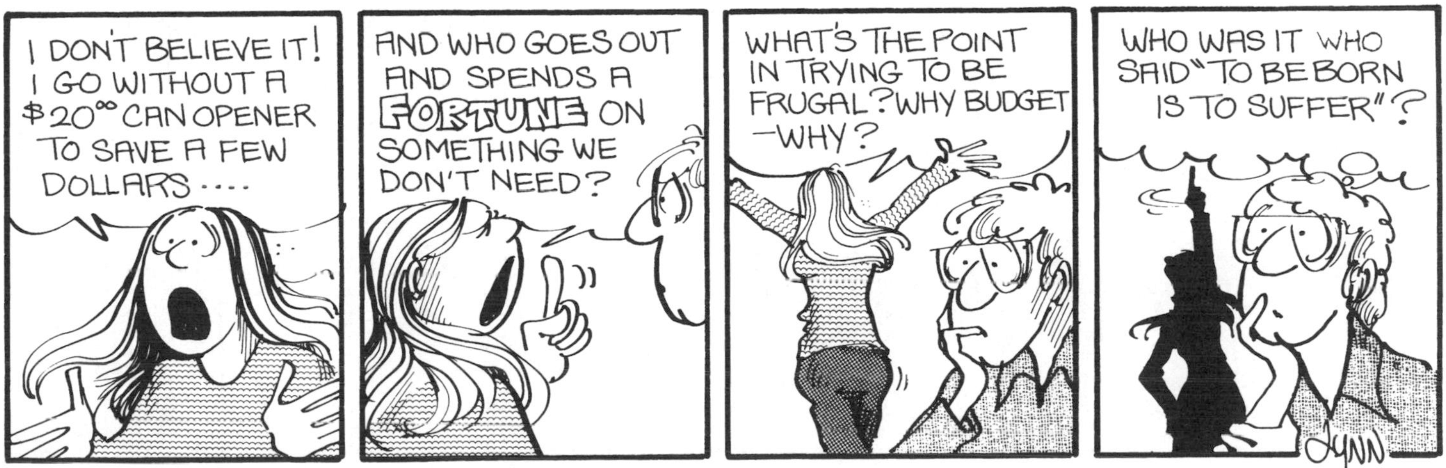
I DON'T BELIEVE IT! I GO WITHOUT A $20⁰⁰ CAN OPENER TO SAVE A FEW DOLLARS ....
AND WHO GOES OUT AND SPENDS A FORTUNE ON SOMETHING WE DON'T NEED?
WHAT'S THE POINT IN TRYING TO BE FRUGAL? WHY BUDGET —WHY?
WHO WAS IT WHO SAID "TO BE BORN IS TO SUFFER"?
LYNN

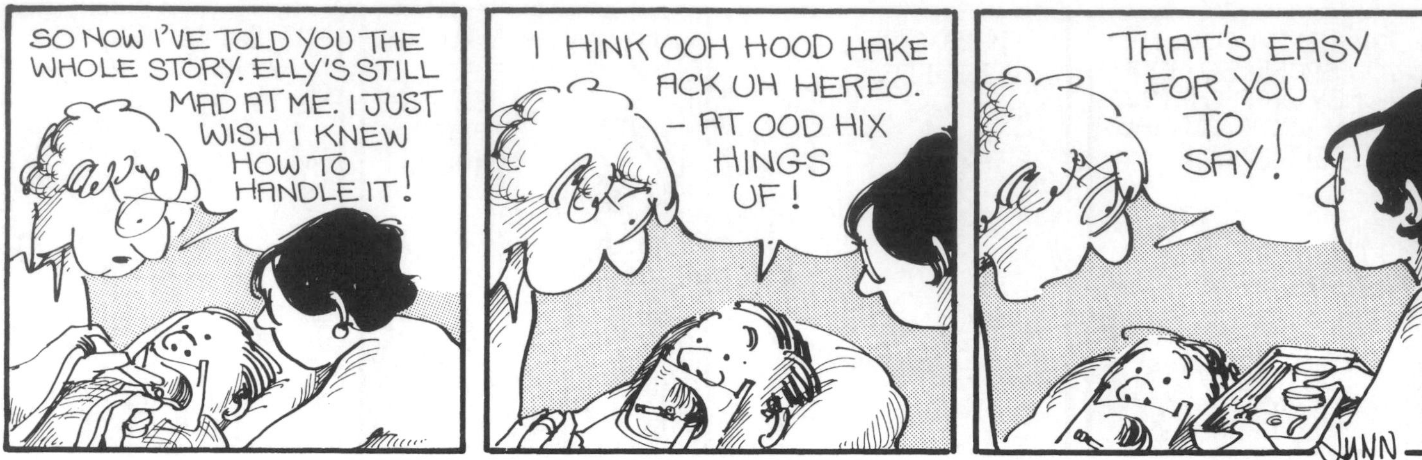
SO NOW I'VE TOLD YOU THE WHOLE STORY. ELLY'S STILL MAD AT ME. I JUST WISH I KNEW HOW TO HANDLE IT!
I HINK OOH HOOD HAKE ACK UH HEREO. - AT OOD HIX HINGS UF!
THAT'S EASY FOR YOU TO SAY!
LYNN

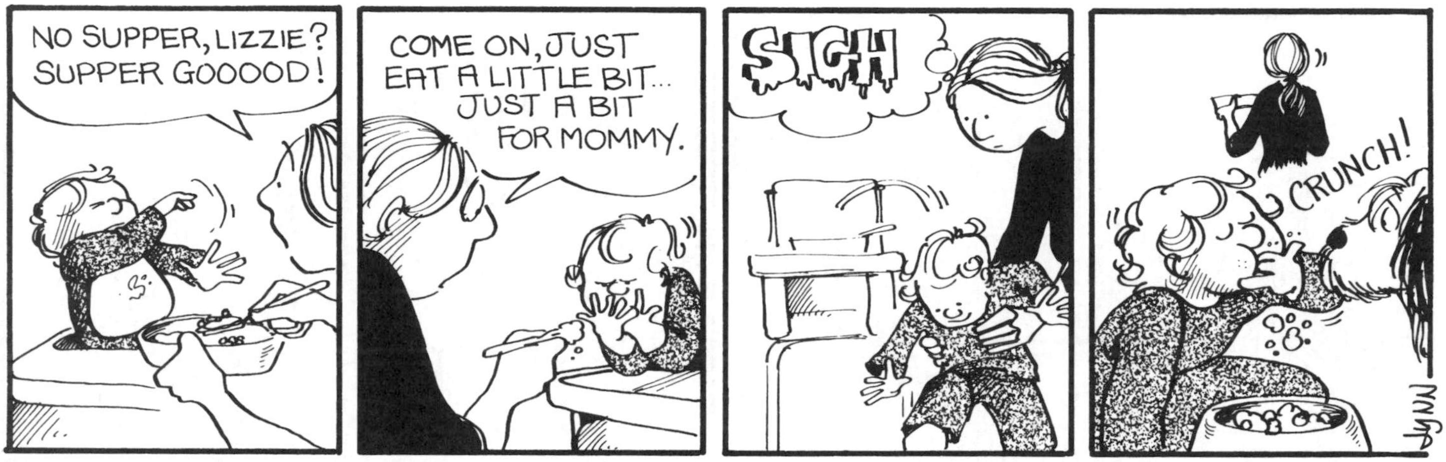
NO SUPPER, LIZZIE? SUPPER GOOOOD!
COME ON, JUST EAT A LITTLE BIT... JUST A BIT FOR MOMMY.
SIGH
CRUNCH!
LYNN

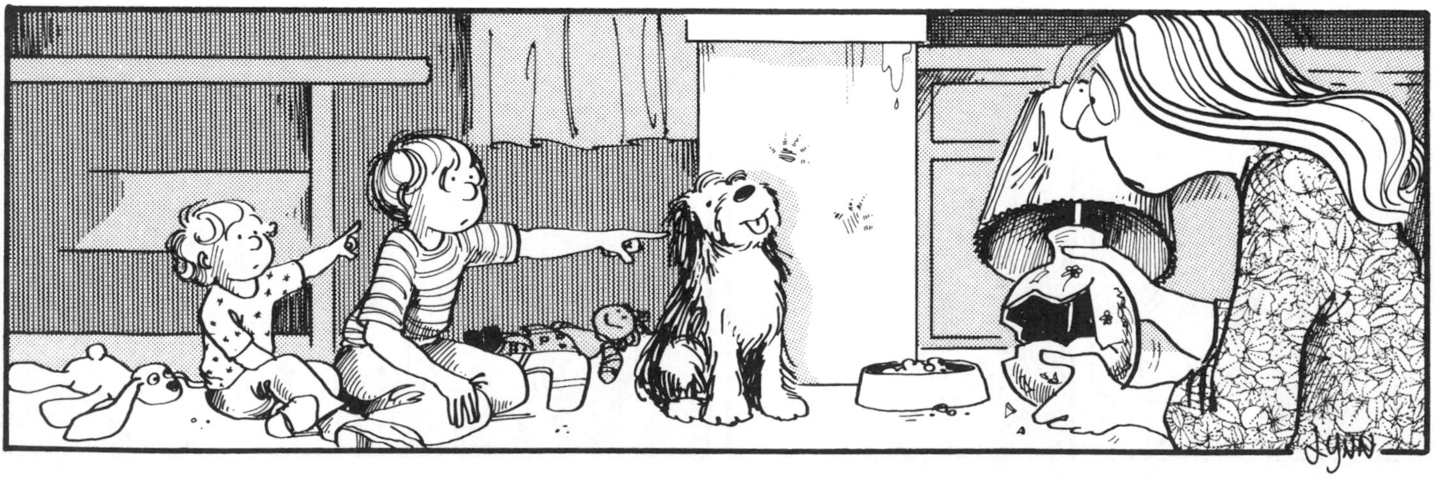
LYNN

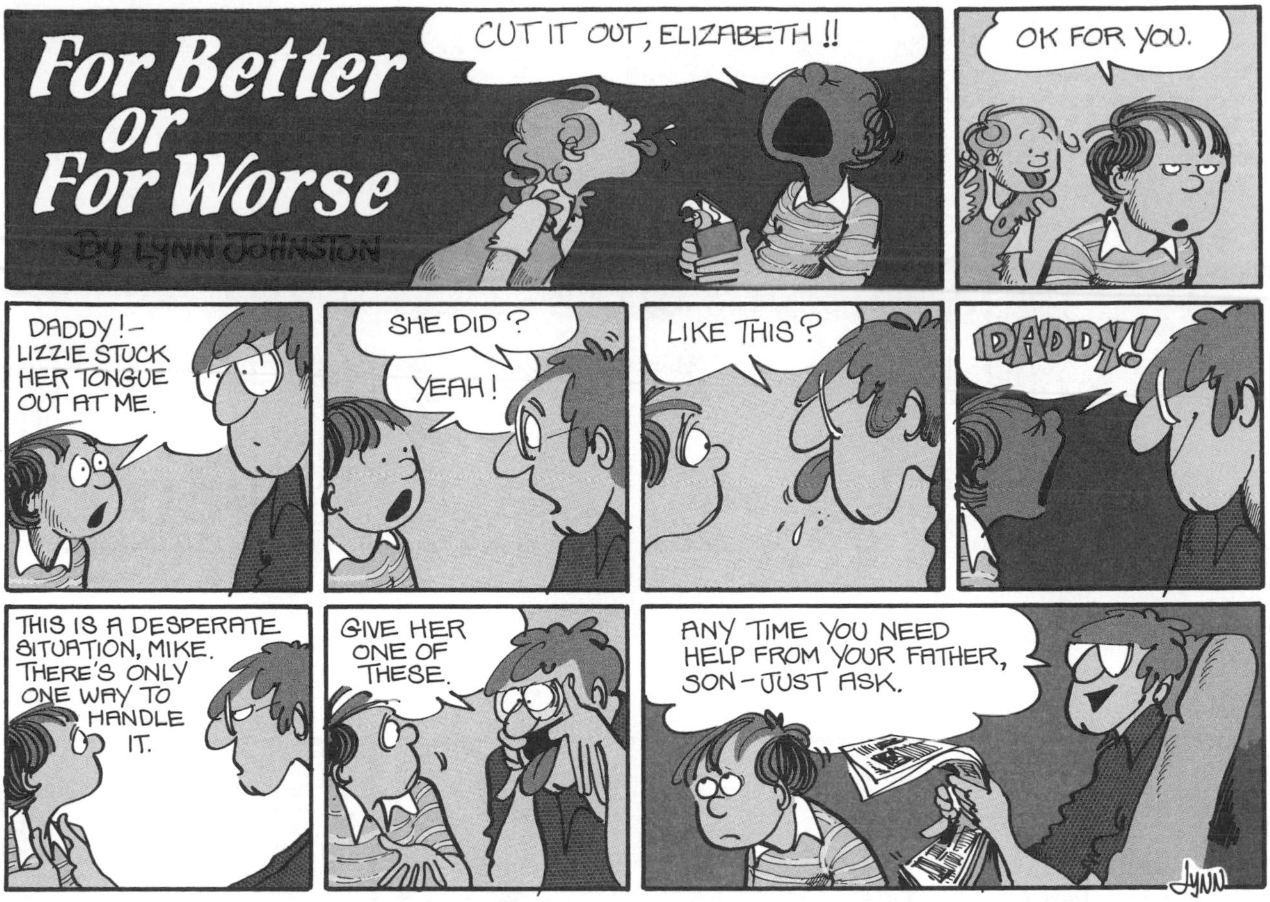
For Better or For Worse
By Lynn Johnston
CUT IT OUT, ELIZABETH !!
OK FOR YOU.
DADDY! - LIZZIE STUCK HER TONGUE OUT AT ME.
SHE DID ?
YEAH !
LIKE THIS ?
DADDY!
THIS IS A DESPERATE SITUATION, MIKE. THERE'S ONLY ONE WAY TO HANDLE IT.
GIVE HER ONE OF THESE.
ANY TIME YOU NEED HELP FROM YOUR FATHER, SON - JUST ASK.
LYNN

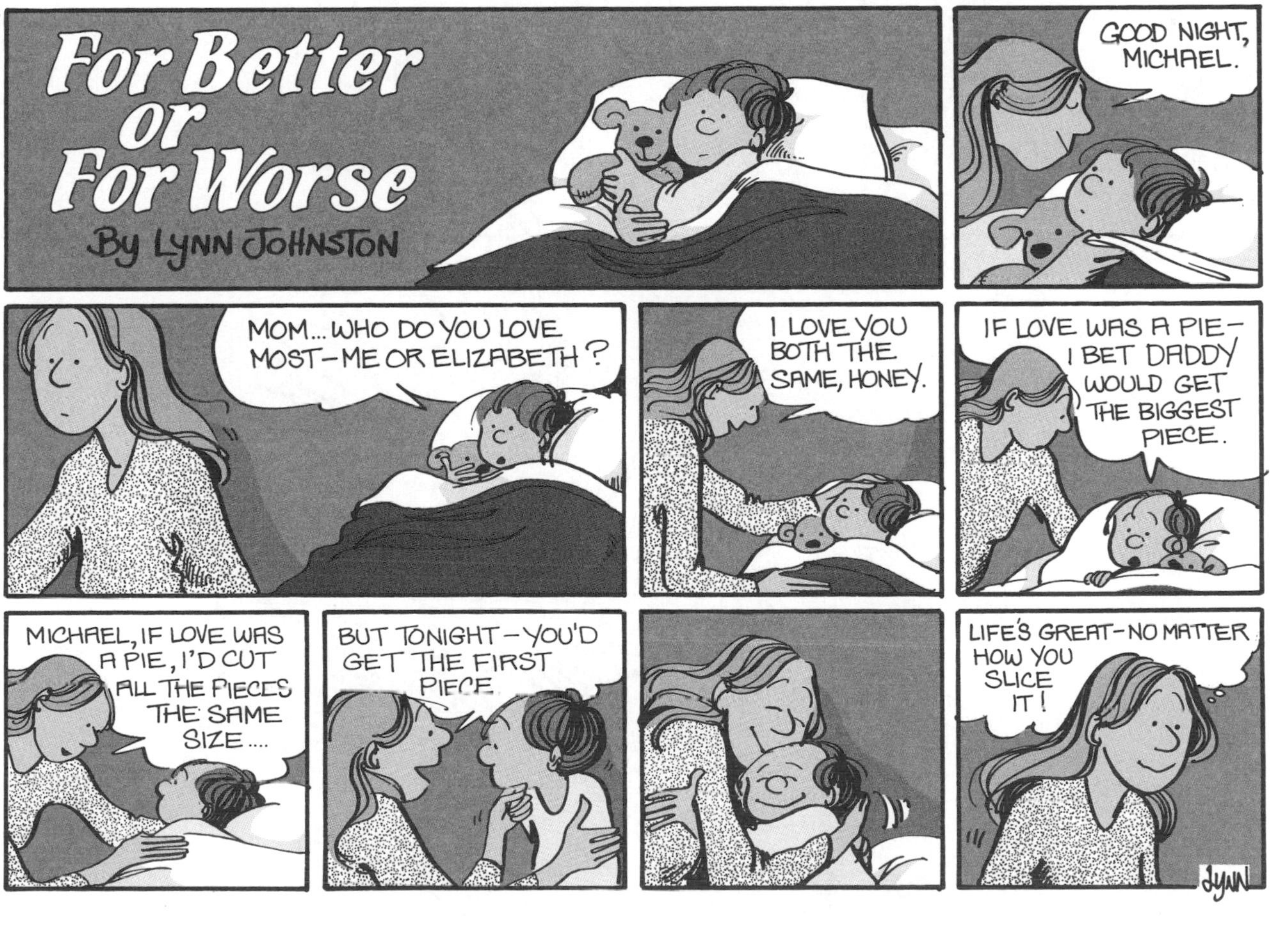
For Better or For Worse
By Lynn Johnston
GOOD NIGHT, MICHAEL.
MOM... WHO DO YOU LOVE MOST - ME OR ELIZABETH ?
I LOVE YOU BOTH THE SAME, HONEY.
IF LOVE WAS A PIE - I BET DADDY WOULD GET THE BIGGEST PIECE.
MICHAEL, IF LOVE WAS A PIE, I'D CUT ALL THE PIECES THE SAME SIZE....
BUT TONIGHT - YOU'D GET THE FIRST PIECE.
LIFE'S GREAT - NO MATTER HOW YOU SLICE IT !
LYNN

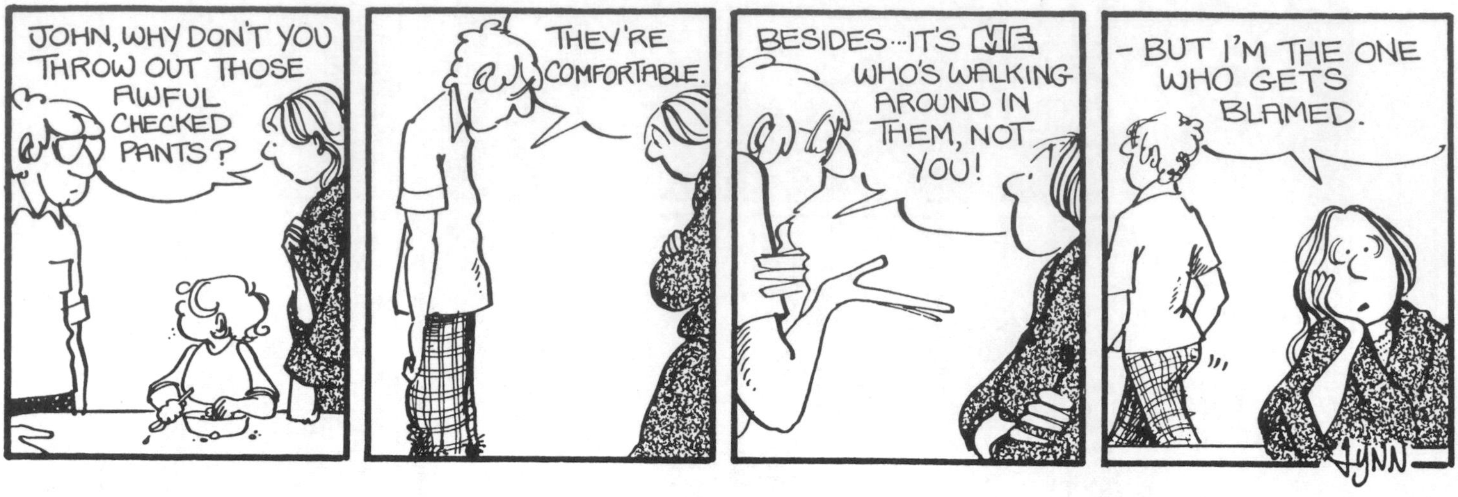
JOHN, WHY DON'T YOU THROW OUT THOSE AWFUL CHECKED PANTS?
THEY'RE COMFORTABLE.
BESIDES...IT'S ME WHO'S WALKING AROUND IN THEM, NOT YOU!
- BUT I'M THE ONE WHO GETS BLAMED.
LYNN

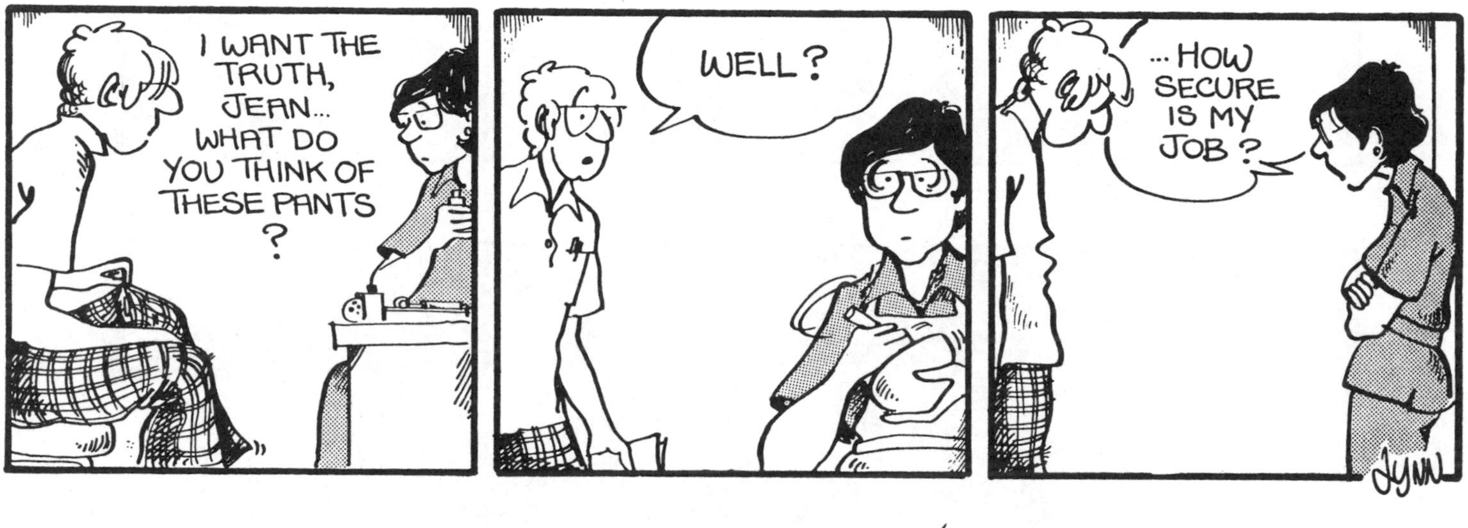
I WANT THE TRUTH, JEAN... WHAT DO YOU THINK OF THESE PANTS?
WELL?
...HOW SECURE IS MY JOB?
LYNN

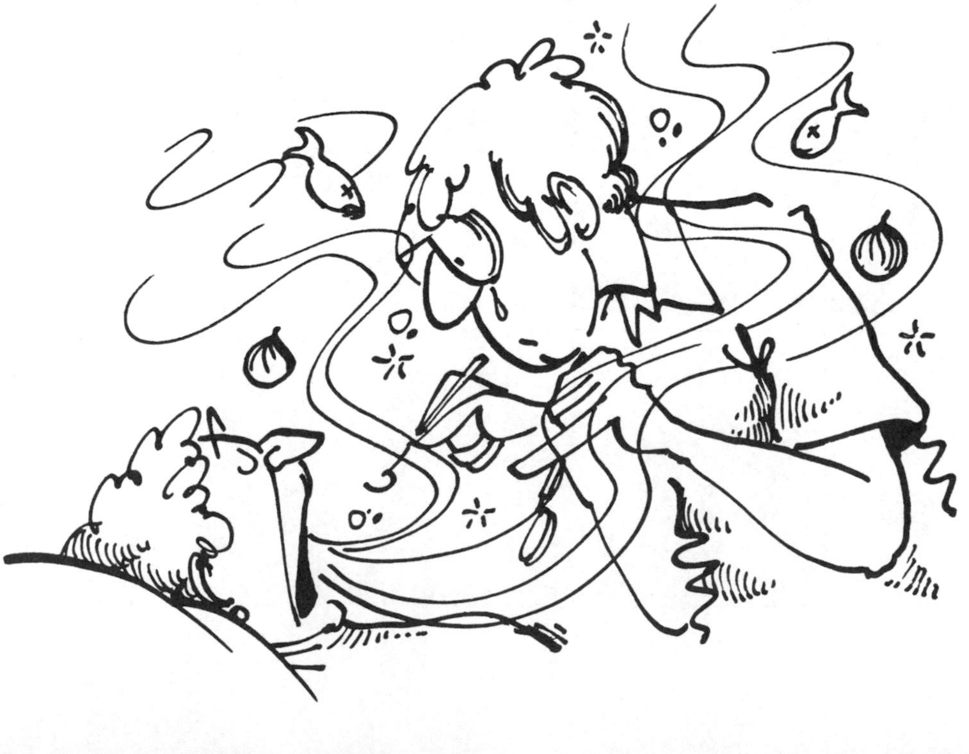

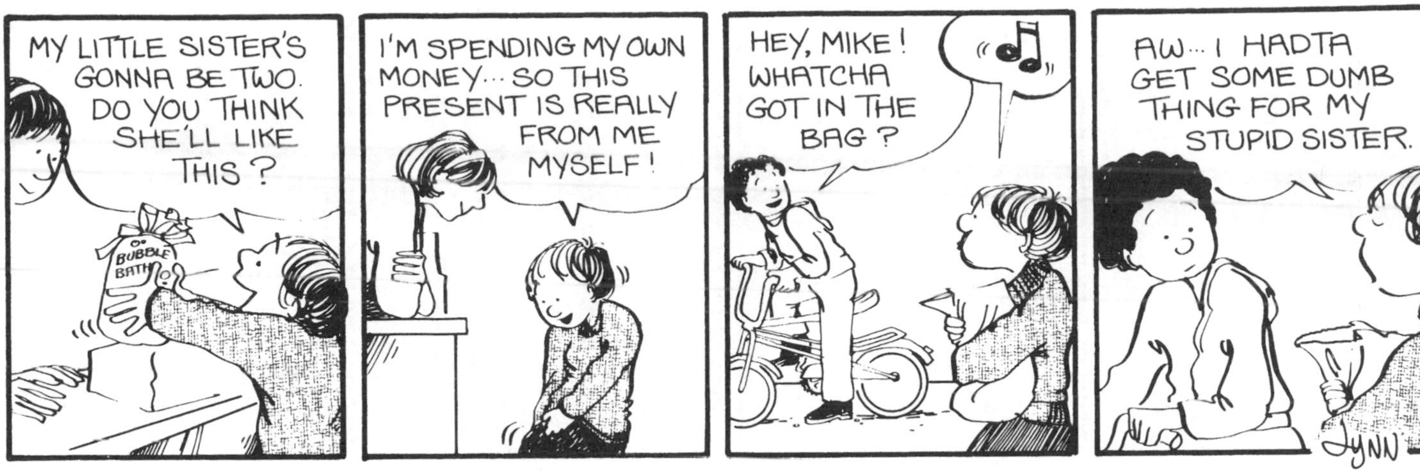
MY LITTLE SISTER'S GONNA BE TWO. DO YOU THINK SHE'LL LIKE THIS?
BUBBLE BATH
I'M SPENDING MY OWN MONEY... SO THIS PRESENT IS REALLY FROM ME MYSELF!
HEY, MIKE! WHATCHA GOT IN THE BAG?
AW... I HADTA GET SOME DUMB THING FOR MY STUPID SISTER.
LYNN

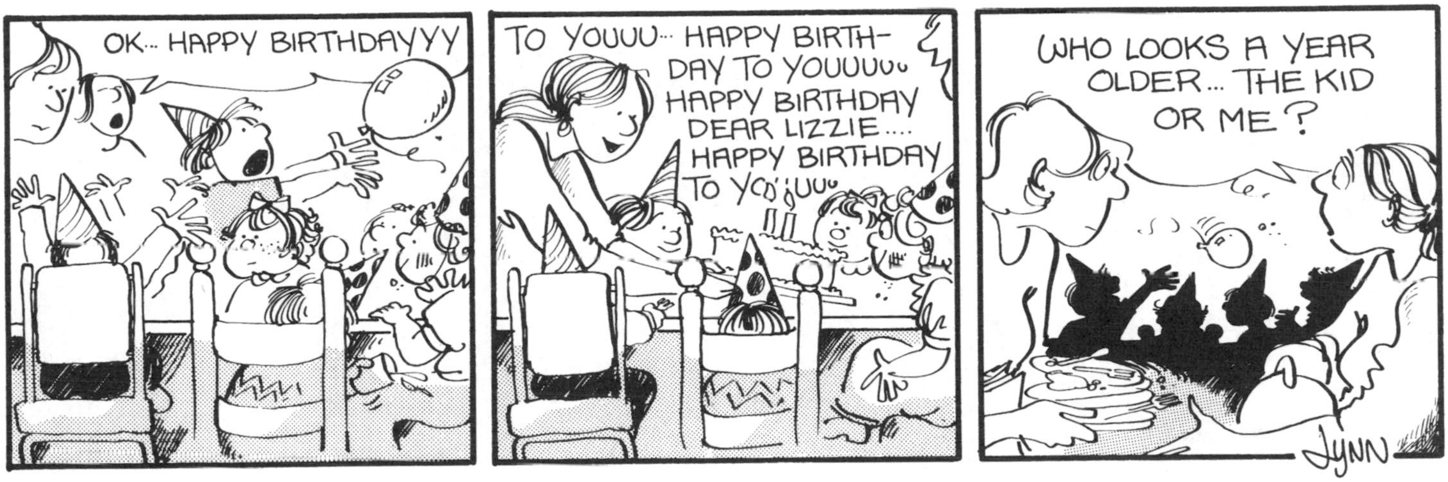
OK... HAPPY BIRTHDAYYY
TO YOUUU... HAPPY BIRTH-DAY TO YOUUUUU HAPPY BIRTHDAY DEAR LIZZIE.... HAPPY BIRTHDAY TO YOU
WHO LOOKS A YEAR OLDER... THE KID OR ME?
LYNN

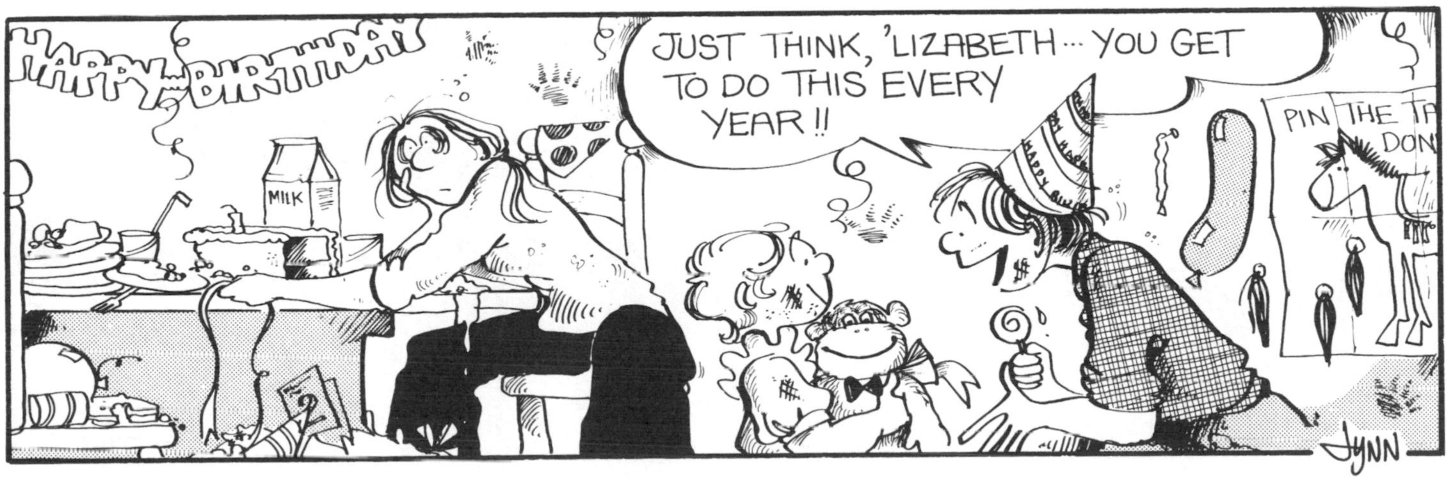
HAPPY BIRTHDAY
MILK
JUST THINK, 'LIZABETH... YOU GET TO DO THIS EVERY YEAR!!
LYNN

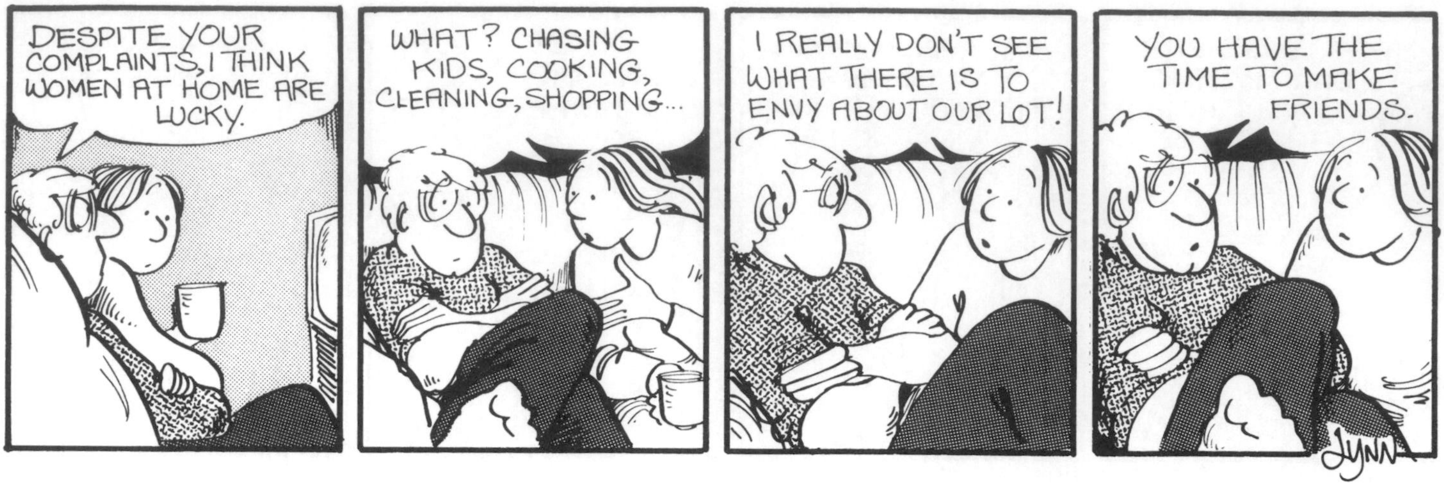
DESPITE YOUR COMPLAINTS, I THINK WOMEN AT HOME ARE LUCKY.
WHAT? CHASING KIDS, COOKING, CLEANING, SHOPPING...
I REALLY DON'T SEE WHAT THERE IS TO ENVY ABOUT OUR LOT!
YOU HAVE THE TIME TO MAKE FRIENDS.
LYNN

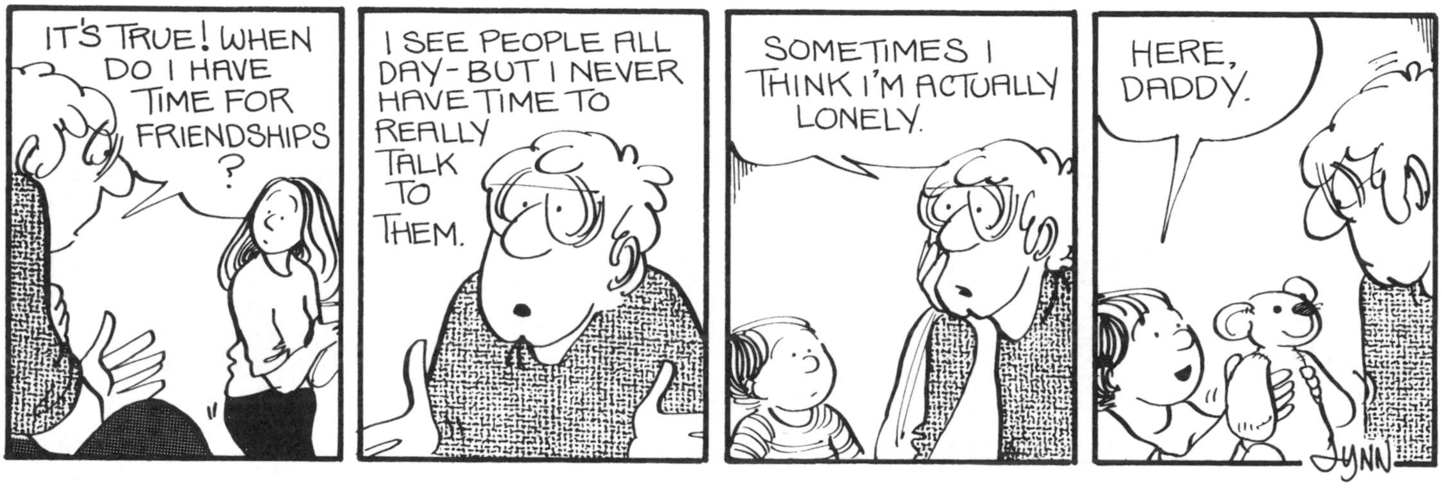
IT'S TRUE! WHEN DO I HAVE TIME FOR FRIENDSHIPS?
I SEE PEOPLE ALL DAY - BUT I NEVER HAVE TIME TO REALLY TALK TO THEM.
SOMETIMES I THINK I'M ACTUALLY LONELY.
HERE, DADDY.
LYNN

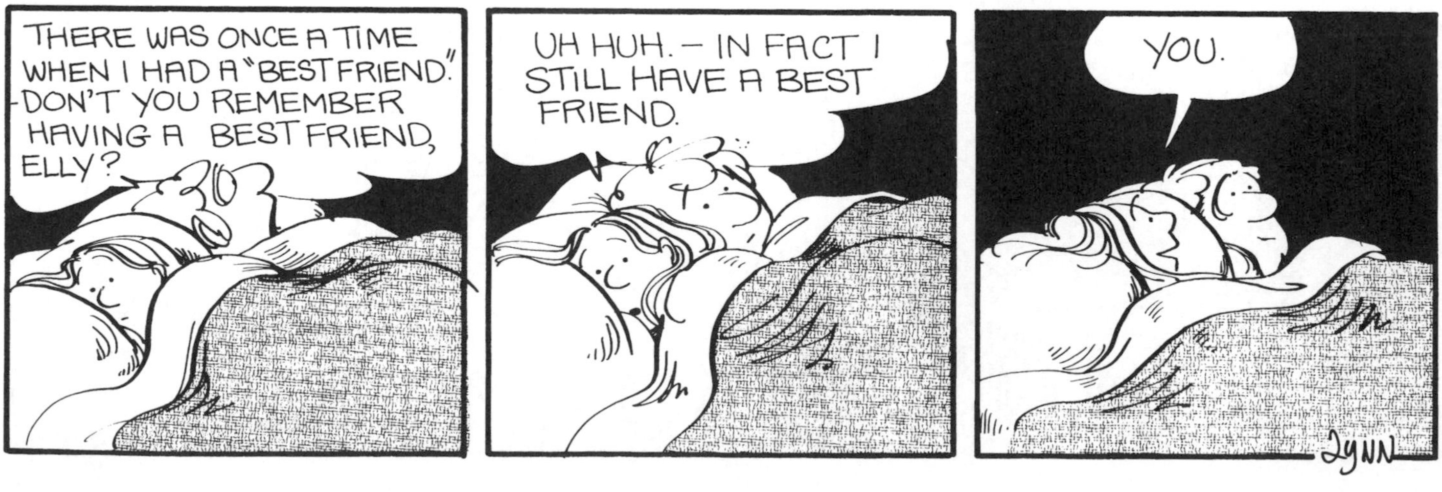
THERE WAS ONCE A TIME WHEN I HAD A "BEST FRIEND." DON'T YOU REMEMBER HAVING A BEST FRIEND, ELLY?
UH HUH. - IN FACT I STILL HAVE A BEST FRIEND.
YOU.
LYNN

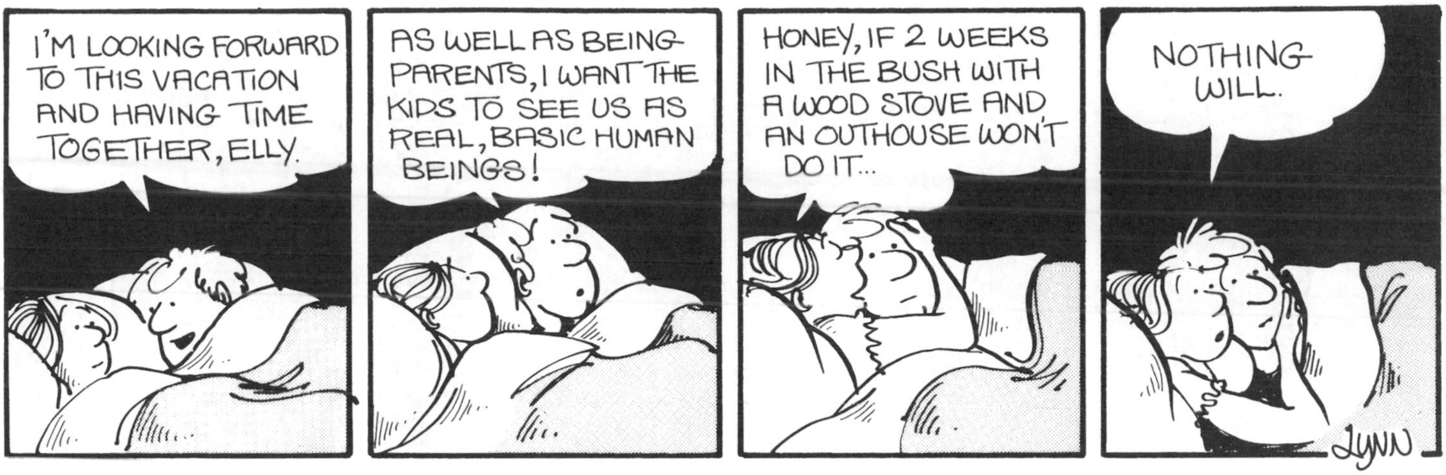
I'M LOOKING FORWARD TO THIS VACATION AND HAVING TIME TOGETHER, ELLY.
AS WELL AS BEING PARENTS, I WANT THE KIDS TO SEE US AS REAL, BASIC HUMAN BEINGS!
HONEY, IF 2 WEEKS IN THE BUSH WITH A WOOD STOVE AND AN OUTHOUSE WON'T DO IT...
NOTHING WILL.
LYNN

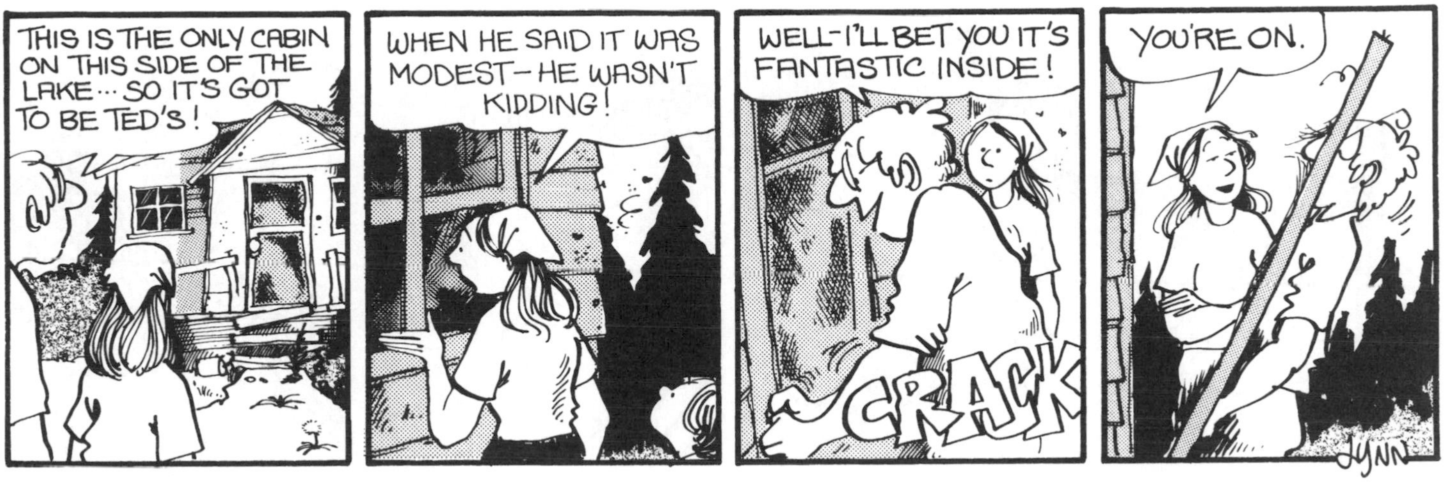
THIS IS THE ONLY CABIN ON THIS SIDE OF THE LAKE... SO IT'S GOT TO BE TED'S!
WHEN HE SAID IT WAS MODEST - HE WASN'T KIDDING!
WELL - I'LL BET YOU IT'S FANTASTIC INSIDE!
CRACK
YOU'RE ON.
LYNN

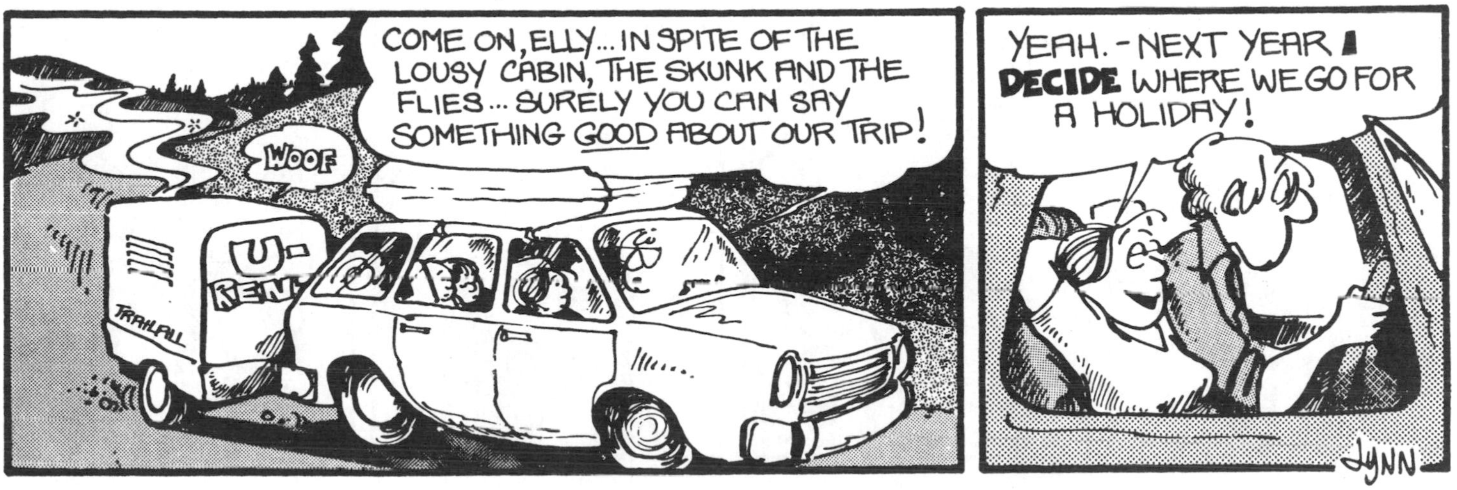
COME ON, ELLY... IN SPITE OF THE LOUSY CABIN, THE SKUNK AND THE FLIES... SURELY YOU CAN SAY SOMETHING GOOD ABOUT OUR TRIP!
WOOF
U-RENT
YEAH. - NEXT YEAR I DECIDE WHERE WE GO FOR A HOLIDAY!
LYNN

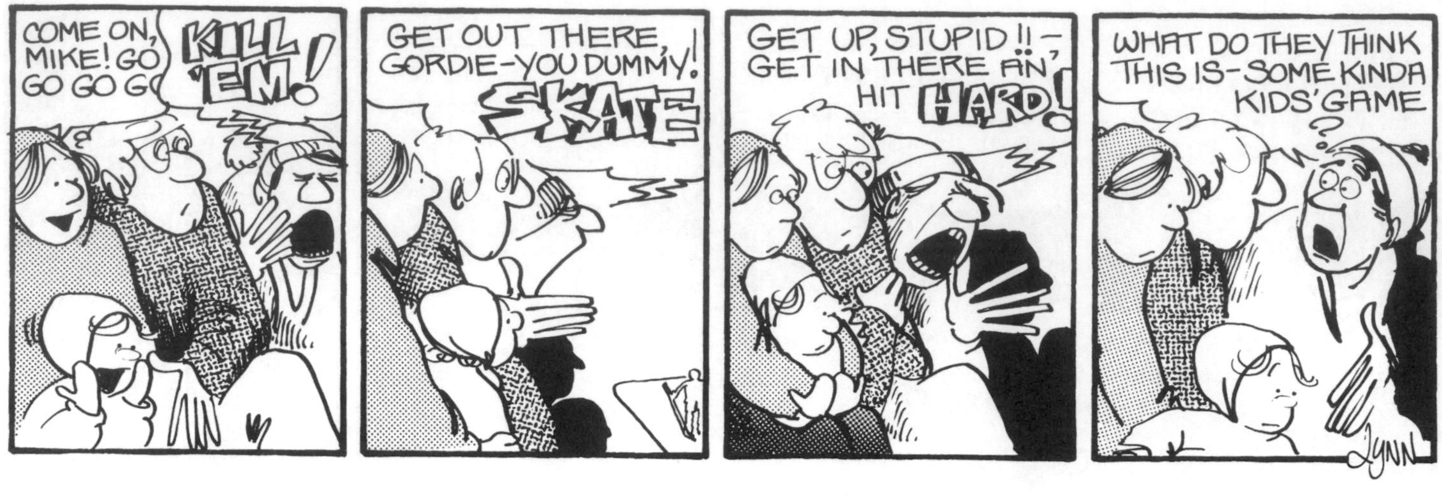

COME ON, MIKE! GO GO GO G
KILL 'EM!
GET OUT THERE, GORDIE-YOU DUMMY!
SKATE
GET UP, STUPID!! — GET IN THERE AN' HIT HARD!
WHAT DO THEY THINK THIS IS-SOME KINDA KIDS' GAME
?
LYNN

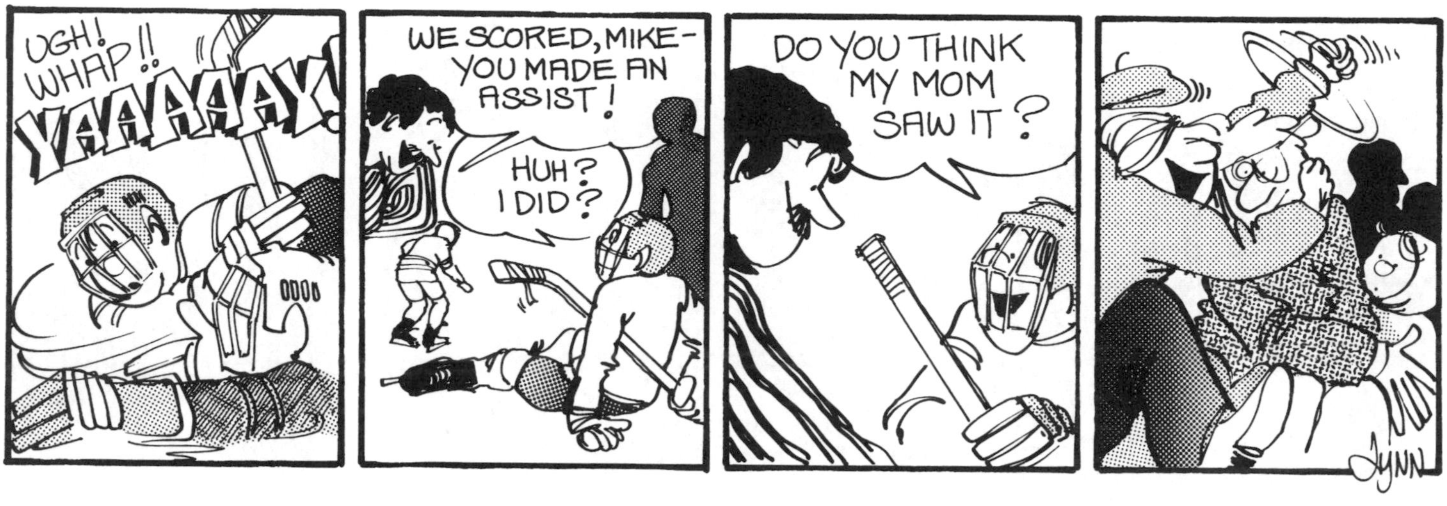

UGH!
WHAP!!
YAAAAAY!
WE SCORED, MIKE-YOU MADE AN ASSIST!
HUH? I DID?
DO YOU THINK MY MOM SAW IT?
LYNN

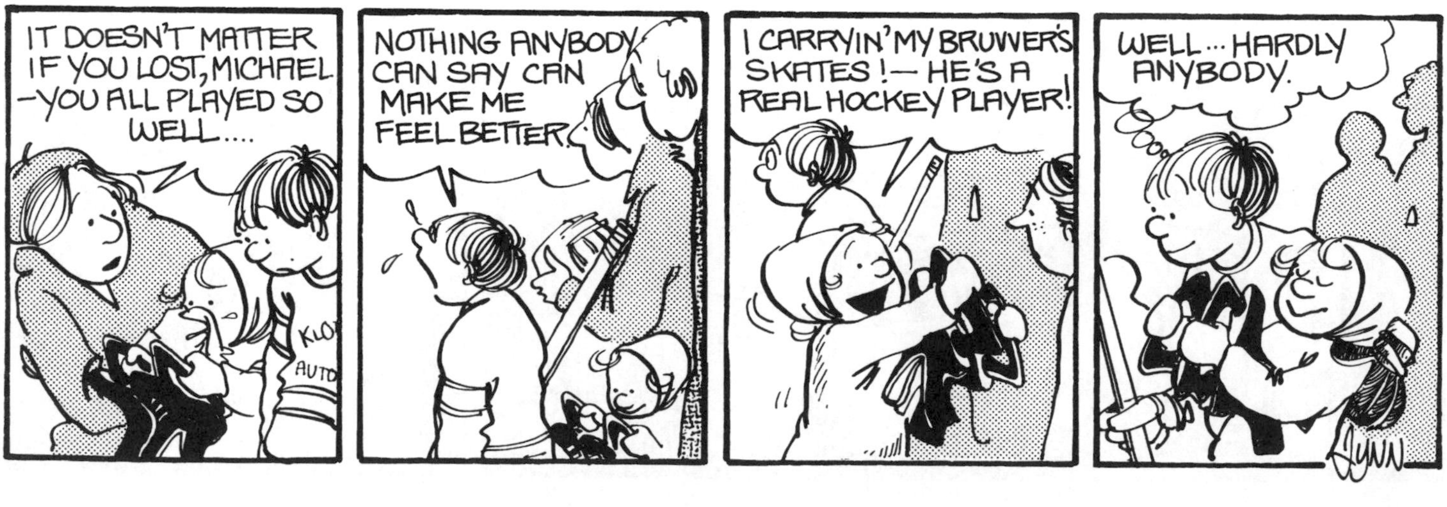

IT DOESN'T MATTER IF YOU LOST, MICHAEL -YOU ALL PLAYED SO WELL....
NOTHING ANYBODY CAN SAY CAN MAKE ME FEEL BETTER.
I CARRYIN' MY BRUVVER'S SKATES! — HE'S A REAL HOCKEY PLAYER!
WELL... HARDLY ANYBODY.
LYNN

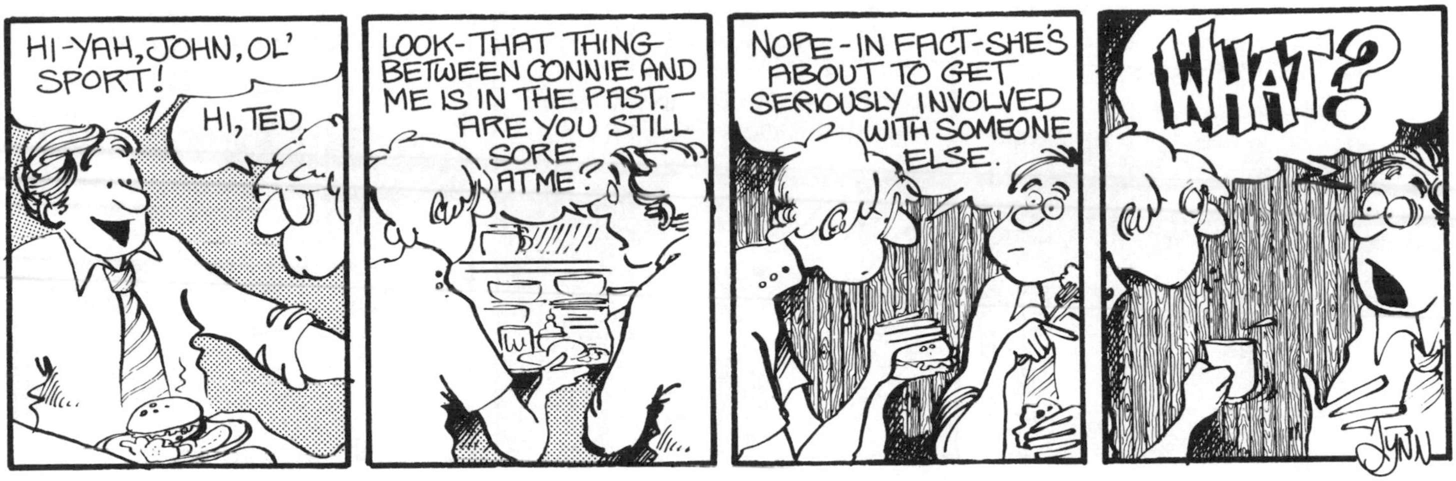
HI-YAH, JOHN, OL' SPORT!
HI, TED
LOOK-THAT THING BETWEEN CONNIE AND ME IS IN THE PAST.-ARE YOU STILL SORE AT ME?
NOPE-IN FACT-SHE'S ABOUT TO GET SERIOUSLY INVOLVED WITH SOMEONE ELSE.
WHAT?
LYNN

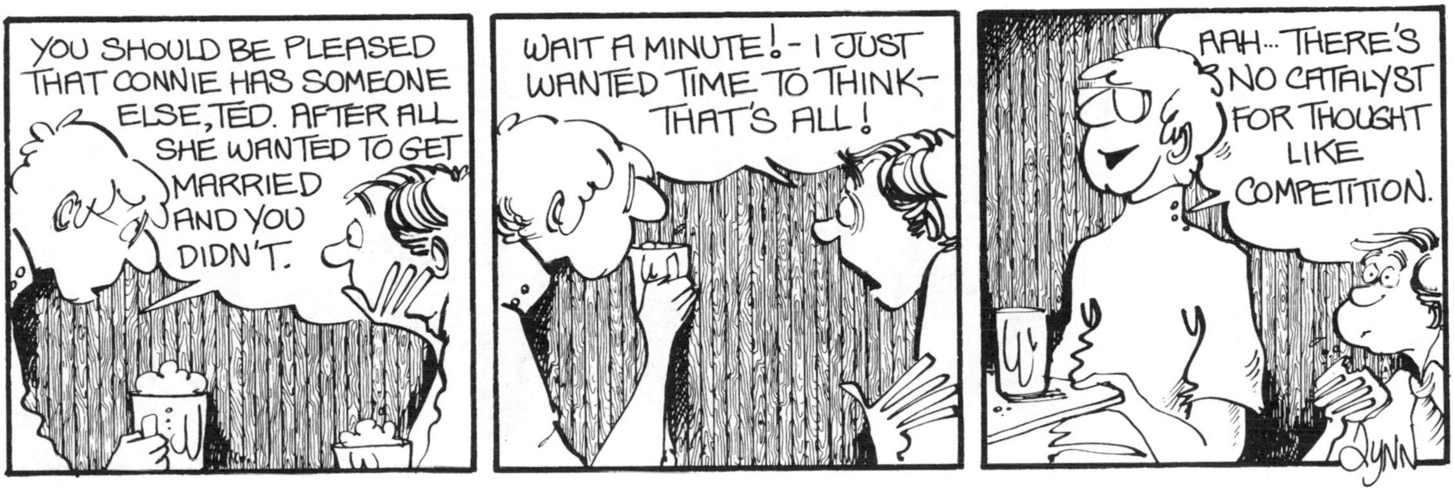
YOU SHOULD BE PLEASED THAT CONNIE HAS SOMEONE ELSE, TED. AFTER ALL SHE WANTED TO GET MARRIED AND YOU DIDN'T.
WAIT A MINUTE!-I JUST WANTED TIME TO THINK-THAT'S ALL!
AAH... THERE'S NO CATALYST FOR THOUGHT LIKE COMPETITION.
LYNN

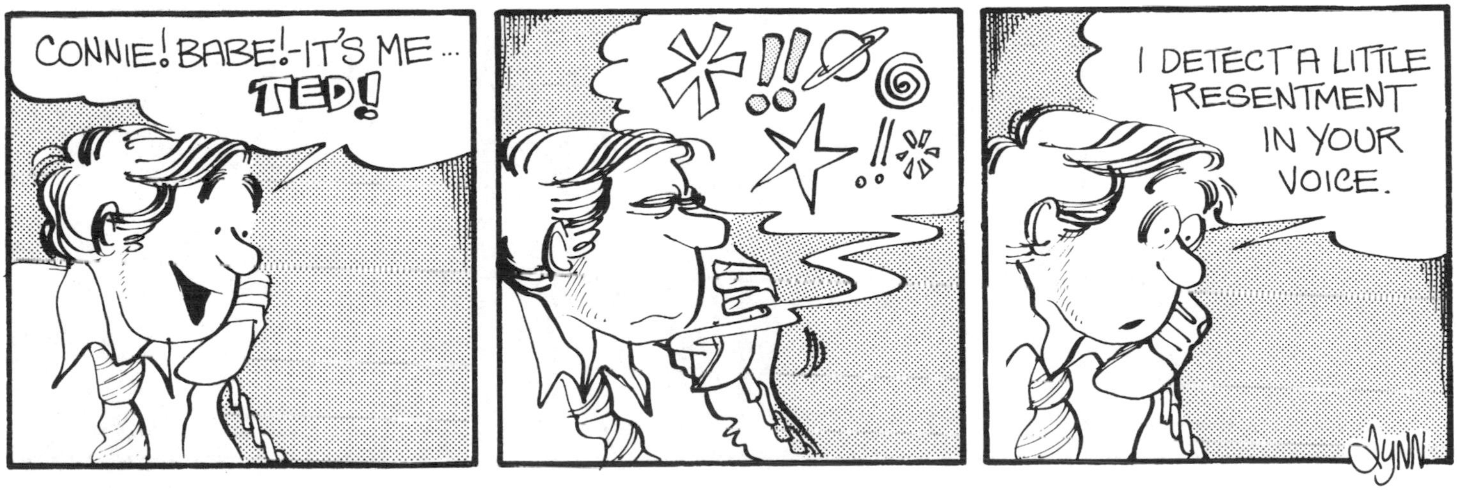
CONNIE! BABE!-IT'S ME... TED!
I DETECT A LITTLE RESENTMENT IN YOUR VOICE.
LYNN

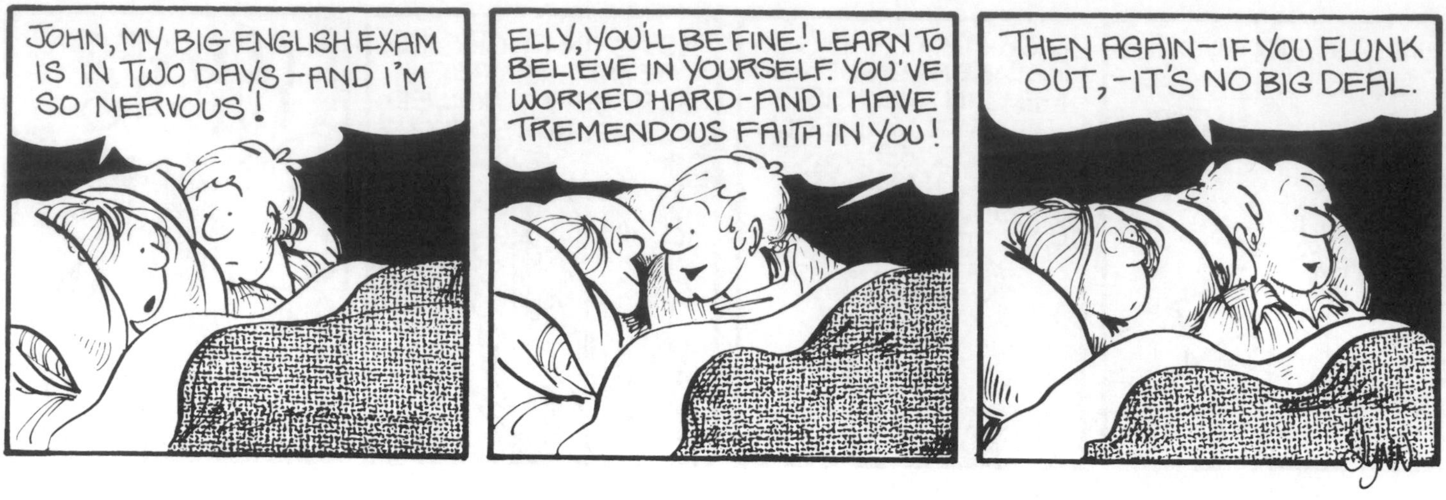
JOHN, MY BIG ENGLISH EXAM IS IN TWO DAYS—AND I'M SO NERVOUS!
ELLY, YOU'LL BE FINE! LEARN TO BELIEVE IN YOURSELF. YOU'VE WORKED HARD—AND I HAVE TREMENDOUS FAITH IN YOU!
THEN AGAIN—IF YOU FLUNK OUT,—IT'S NO BIG DEAL.
LYNN

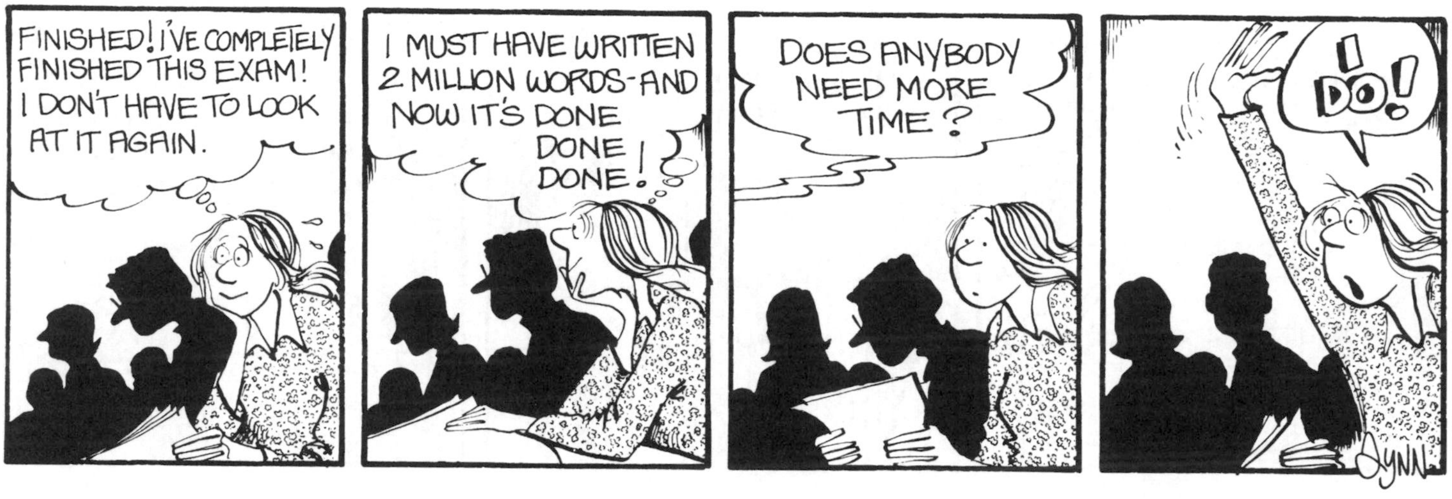
FINISHED! I'VE COMPLETELY FINISHED THIS EXAM! I DON'T HAVE TO LOOK AT IT AGAIN.
I MUST HAVE WRITTEN 2 MILLION WORDS-AND NOW IT'S DONE DONE! DONE!
DOES ANYBODY NEED MORE TIME?
I DO!
LYNN

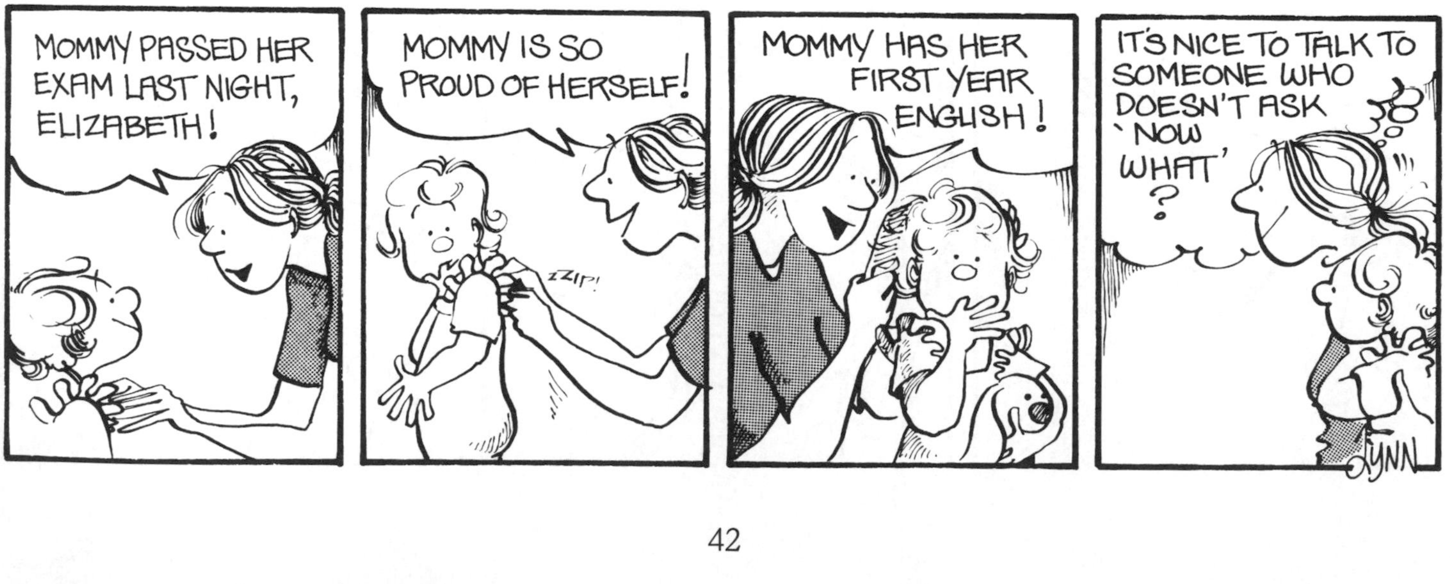
MOMMY PASSED HER EXAM LAST NIGHT, ELIZABETH!
MOMMY IS SO PROUD OF HERSELF!
ZZIP!
MOMMY HAS HER FIRST YEAR ENGLISH!
IT'S NICE TO TALK TO SOMEONE WHO DOESN'T ASK `NOW WHAT'?
LYNN

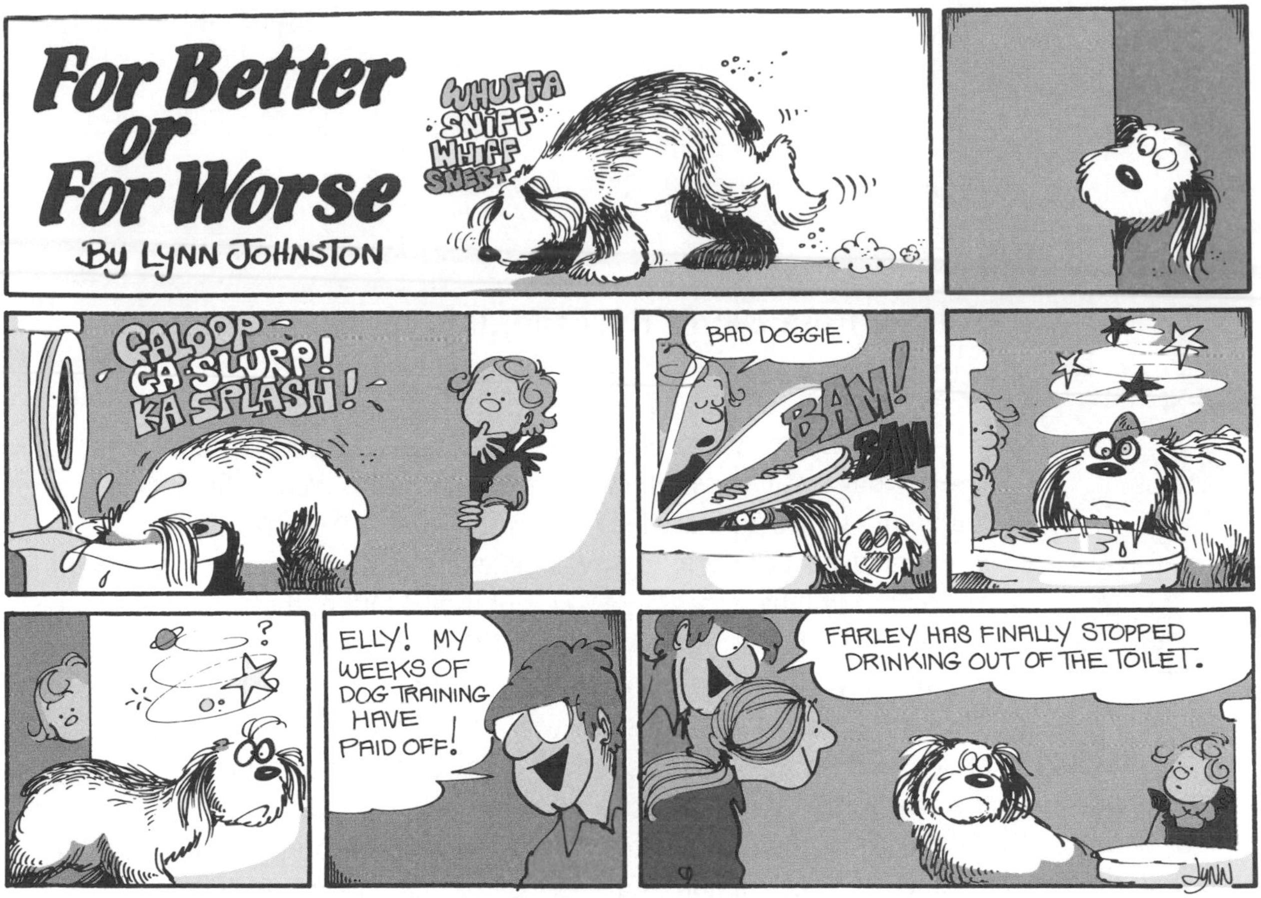
For Better or For Worse
By Lynn Johnston
WHUFFA SNIFF WHIFF SNERT
GALOOP-GA-SLURP! KA SPLASH!
BAD DOGGIE.
BAM!
BAM
?
ELLY! MY WEEKS OF DOG TRAINING HAVE PAID OFF!
FARLEY HAS FINALLY STOPPED DRINKING OUT OF THE TOILET.
LYNN

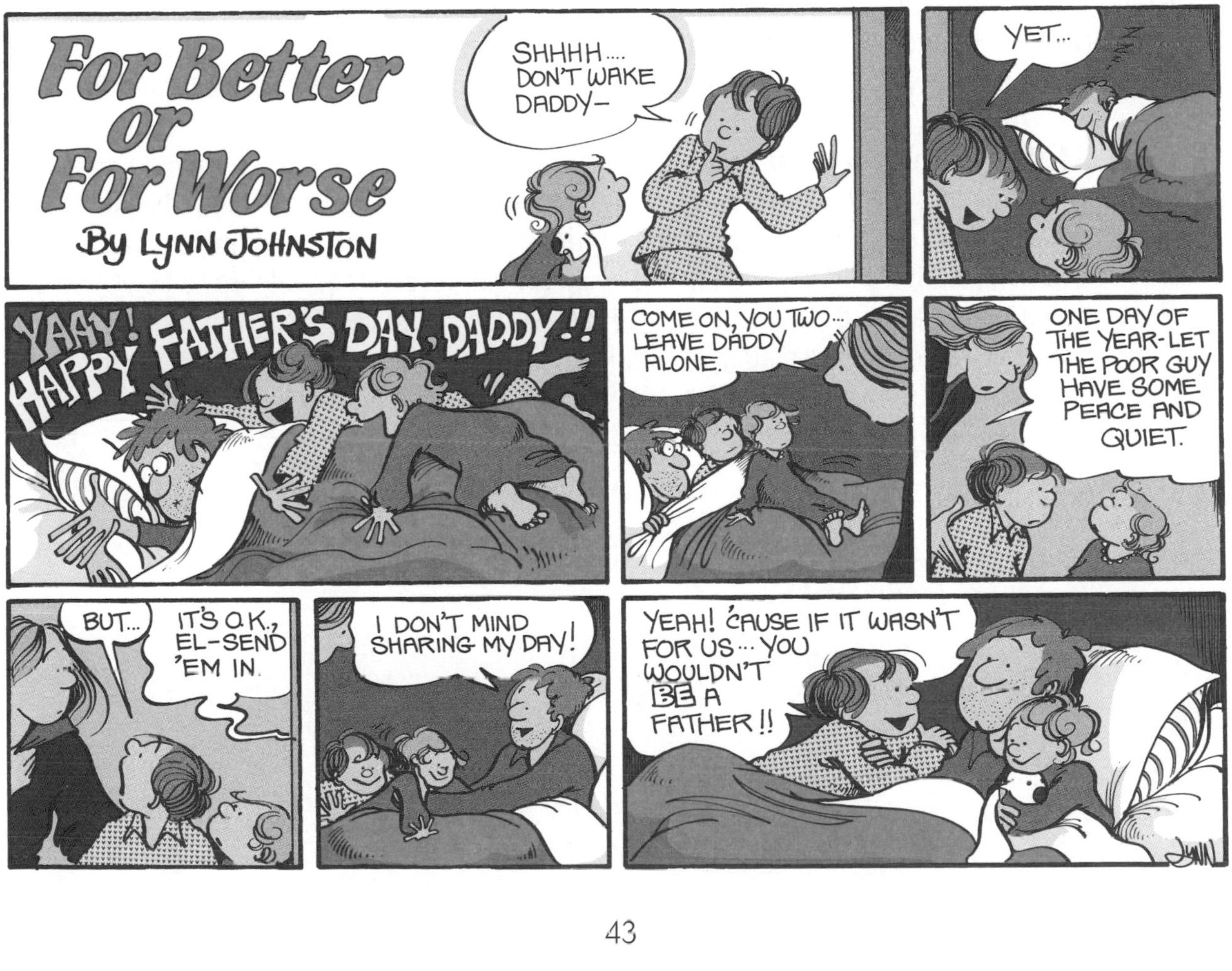
For Better or For Worse
By Lynn Johnston
SHHHH.... DON'T WAKE DADDY—
YET...
YAAY! HAPPY FATHER'S DAY, DADDY!!
COME ON, YOU TWO... LEAVE DADDY ALONE.
ONE DAY OF THE YEAR-LET THE POOR GUY HAVE SOME PEACE AND QUIET.
BUT...
IT'S O.K., EL-SEND 'EM IN.
I DON'T MIND SHARING MY DAY!
YEAH! 'CAUSE IF IT WASN'T FOR US... YOU WOULDN'T BE A FATHER!!
LYNN

A Note from Lynn's Husband, Rod Johnston

One good thing about having a comic strip modeled after you is this: Whenever you meet someone who reads the strip for the first time, your first impression has already been made. People immediately greet you with a smile. All that's left to do is ruin that first impression!

Some folks believe John is real and expect that somehow, when I turn to face them I will be only the thickness of paper! Often, they'll tell me of an incident from the strip that was identical to one they had, and they can't believe Lynn didn't see it happen in their house. They usually tell me how wonderful she is, that they have been affected in some way by the stories, and are comforted knowing that they are not experiencing life on their own. Discovering the fact that the same thing is happening to someone else brings him or her great comfort.

For Better or For Worse has been very good to us. It has allowed us to meet many amazing and wonderful people. Some have been famous, but most are ordinary people we've met, just because of the strip—people we would never have gotten to know otherwise. It has also allowed us as a family to travel to some unique places and see things we could never have imagined. We have lived a lifestyle that I certainly could never have imagined as a teenager. I couldn't have imagined even KNOWING people who get to do the things we do. Because of the way Lynn writes, almost all the feedback has been positive, which is very rare in this world.

Of course, many things that happen to us become fodder for the strip. Often I would come home from the clinic and say to Lynn, "A funny thing happened. It might be a good idea for you!" Of course, she wouldn't use it. However, if I did something dumb or said something embarrassing, guess what . . . it would become a great daily! If I said something she took offense to and blasted me for . . . it would end up in the strip! Luckily, I have a thick skin, and it is always fun to read the strips when they're done. As a matter of fact, I can often judge Lynn's mood by the strips she has just completed. With my usual man's intuition, I need all the help I can get!

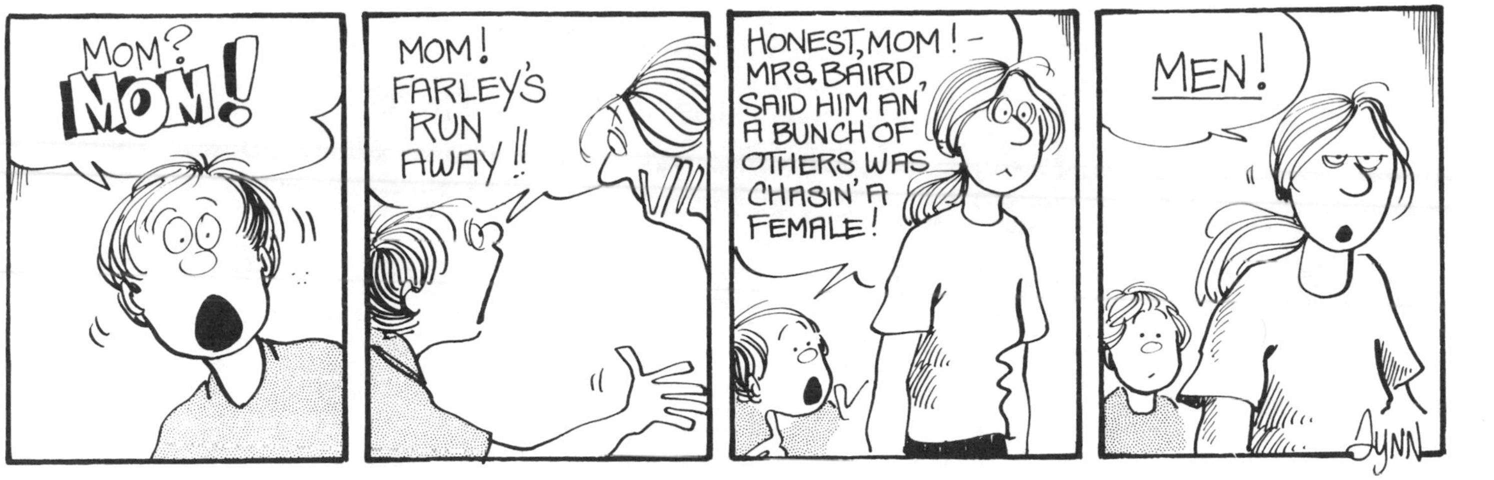
MOM? MOM!
MOM! FARLEY'S RUN AWAY!!
HONEST, MOM!– MRS. BAIRD, SAID HIM AN' A BUNCH OF OTHERS WAS CHASIN' A FEMALE!
MEN!
Lynn

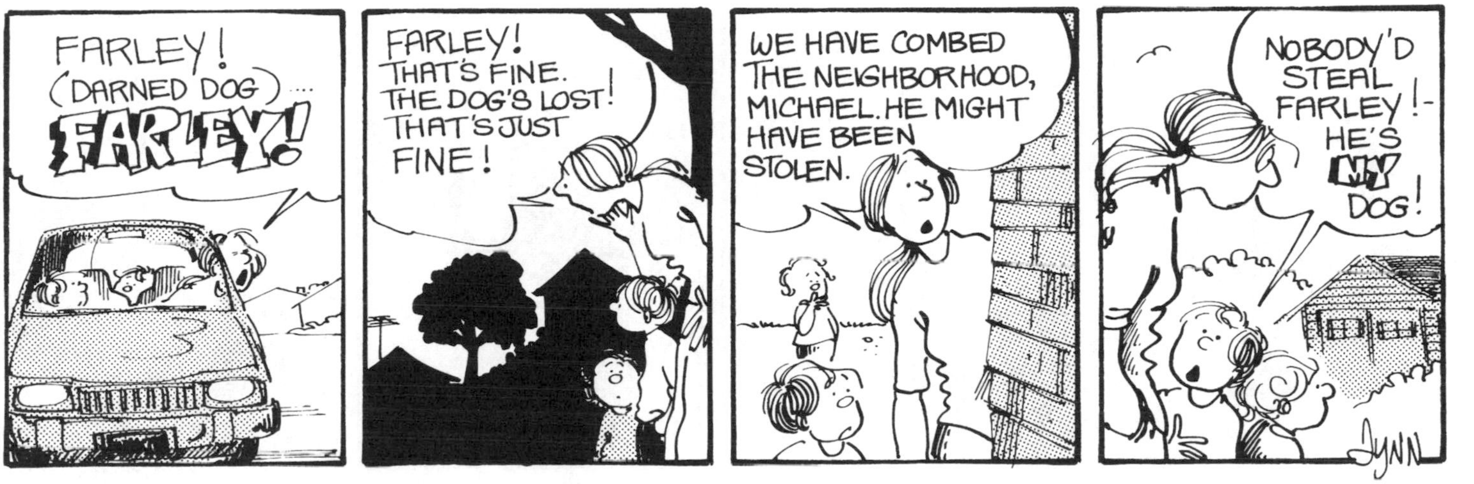
FARLEY! (DARNED DOG)... FARLEY!
FARLEY! THAT'S FINE. THE DOG'S LOST! THAT'S JUST FINE!
WE HAVE COMBED THE NEIGHBORHOOD, MICHAEL. HE MIGHT HAVE BEEN STOLEN.
NOBODY'D STEAL FARLEY!– HE'S MY DOG!
Lynn

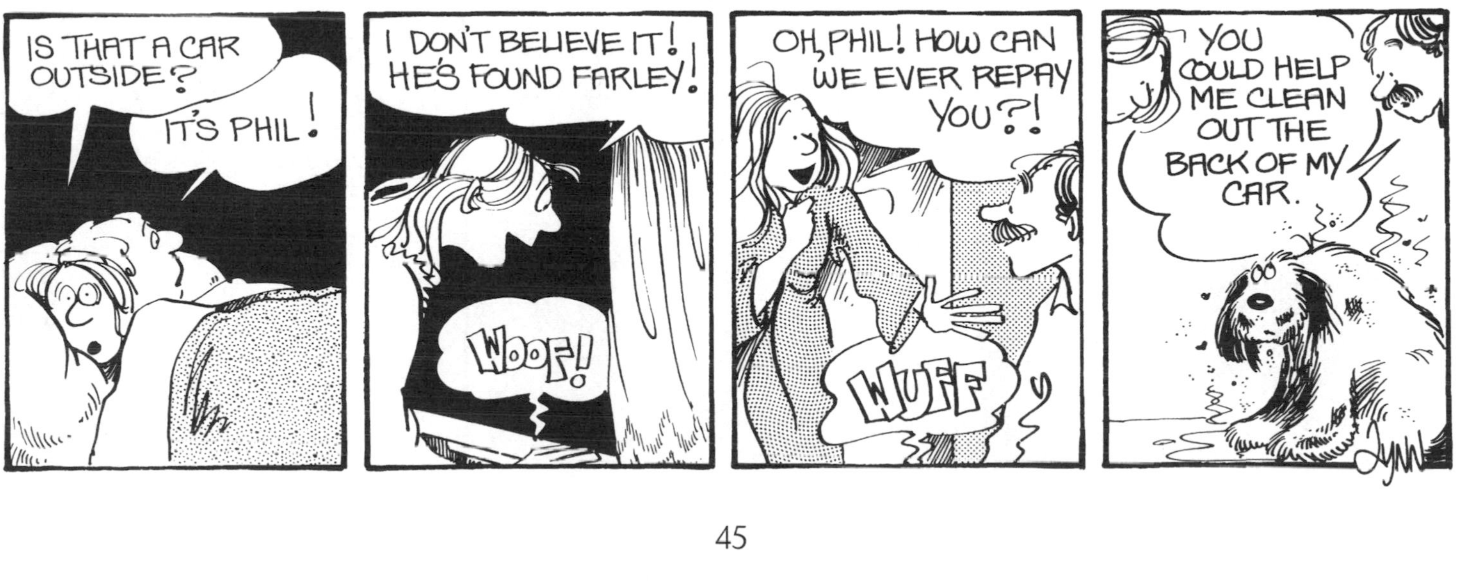
IS THAT A CAR OUTSIDE?
IT'S PHIL!
I DON'T BELIEVE IT! HE'S FOUND FARLEY!
WOOF!
OH, PHIL! HOW CAN WE EVER REPAY YOU?!
WUFF
YOU COULD HELP ME CLEAN OUT THE BACK OF MY CAR.
Lynn

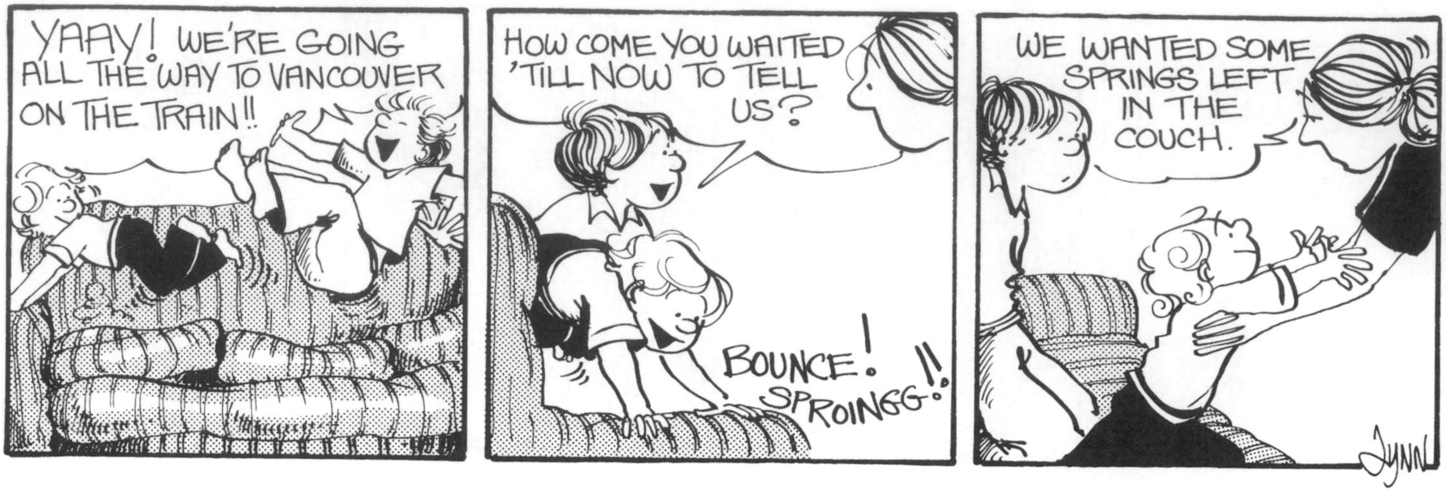
YAAY! WE'RE GOING ALL THE WAY TO VANCOUVER ON THE TRAIN!!
HOW COME YOU WAITED 'TILL NOW TO TELL US?
BOUNCE! SPROINGG!!
WE WANTED SOME SPRINGS LEFT IN THE COUCH.
Lynn

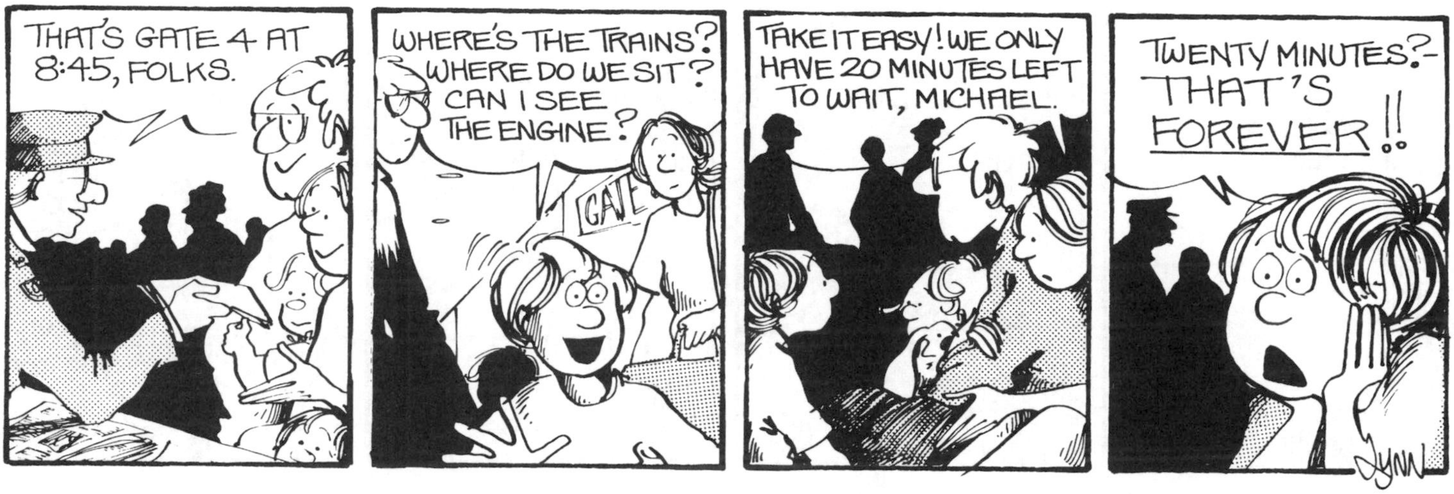
THAT'S GATE 4 AT 8:45, FOLKS.
WHERE'S THE TRAINS? WHERE DO WE SIT? CAN I SEE THE ENGINE?
GATE
TAKE IT EASY! WE ONLY HAVE 20 MINUTES LEFT TO WAIT, MICHAEL.
TWENTY MINUTES?- THAT'S FOREVER!!
Lynn

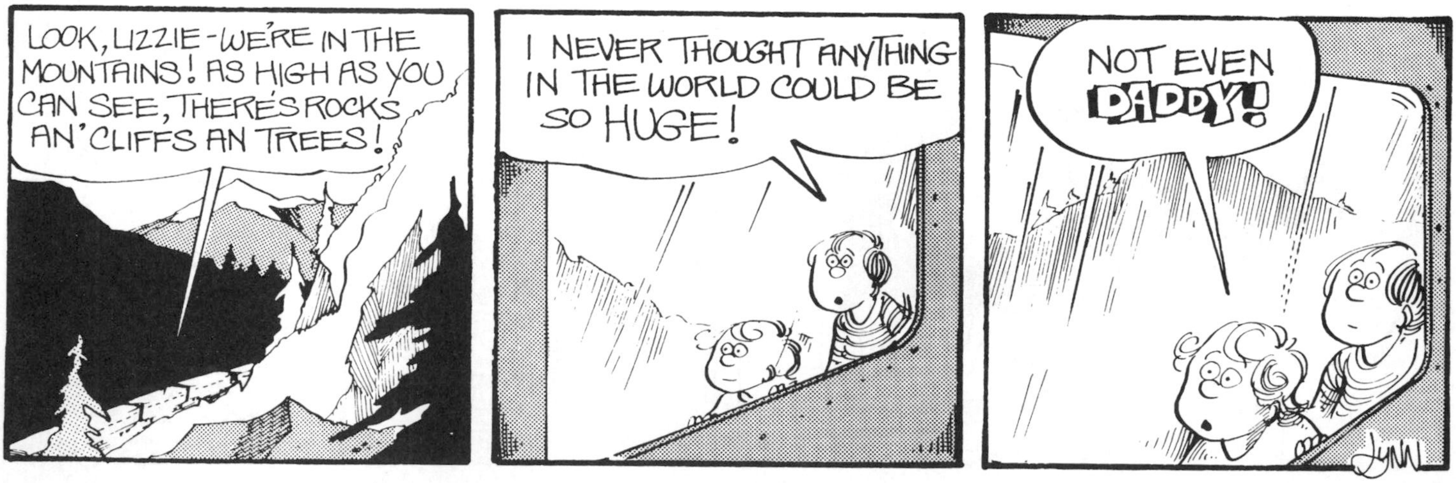
LOOK, LIZZIE-WE'RE IN THE MOUNTAINS! AS HIGH AS YOU CAN SEE, THERE'S ROCKS AN' CLIFFS AN TREES!
I NEVER THOUGHT ANYTHING IN THE WORLD COULD BE SO HUGE!
NOT EVEN DADDY!
Lynn

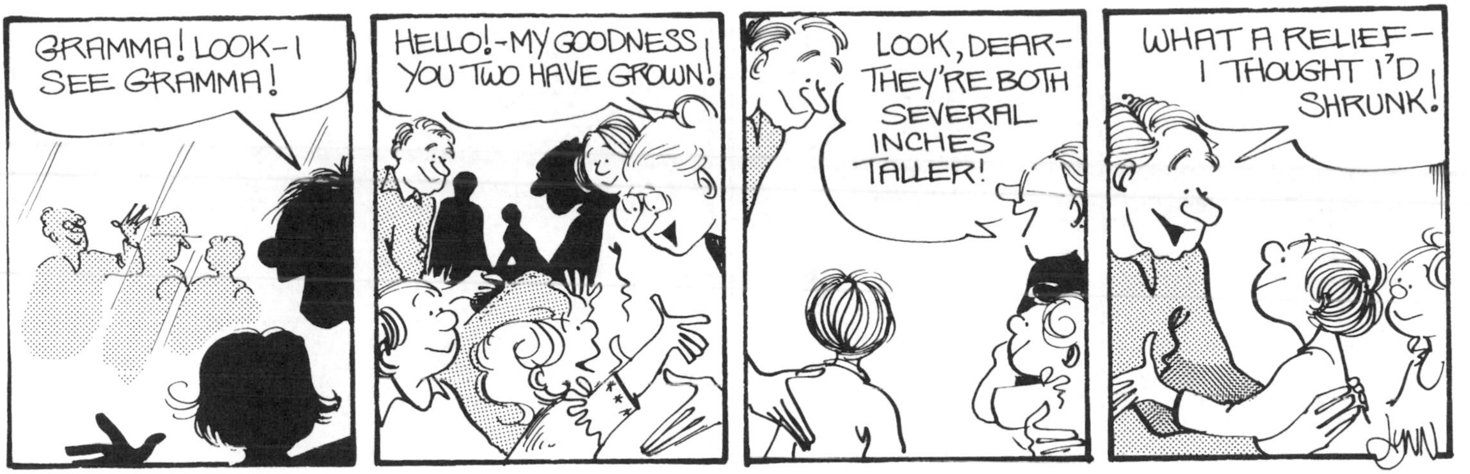
GRAMMA! LOOK-I SEE GRAMMA!
HELLO!-MY GOODNESS YOU TWO HAVE GROWN!
LOOK, DEAR-THEY'RE BOTH SEVERAL INCHES TALLER!
WHAT A RELIEF-I THOUGHT I'D SHRUNK!
LYNN

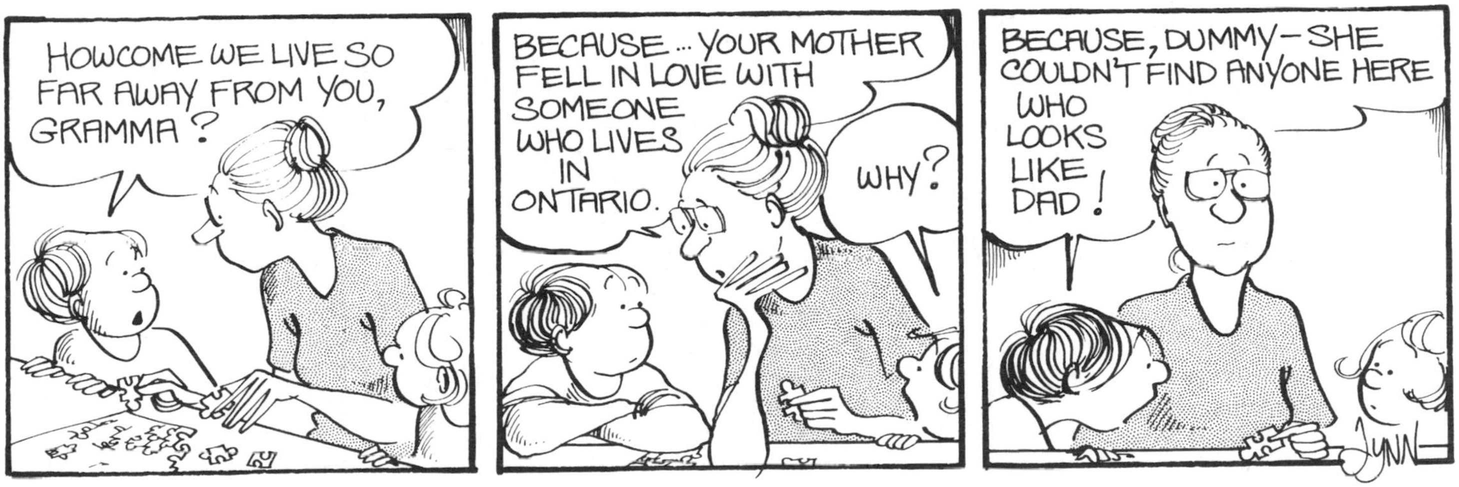
HOWCOME WE LIVE SO FAR AWAY FROM YOU, GRAMMA?
BECAUSE ... YOUR MOTHER FELL IN LOVE WITH SOMEONE WHO LIVES IN ONTARIO.
WHY?
BECAUSE, DUMMY-SHE COULDN'T FIND ANYONE HERE WHO LOOKS LIKE DAD!
LYNN

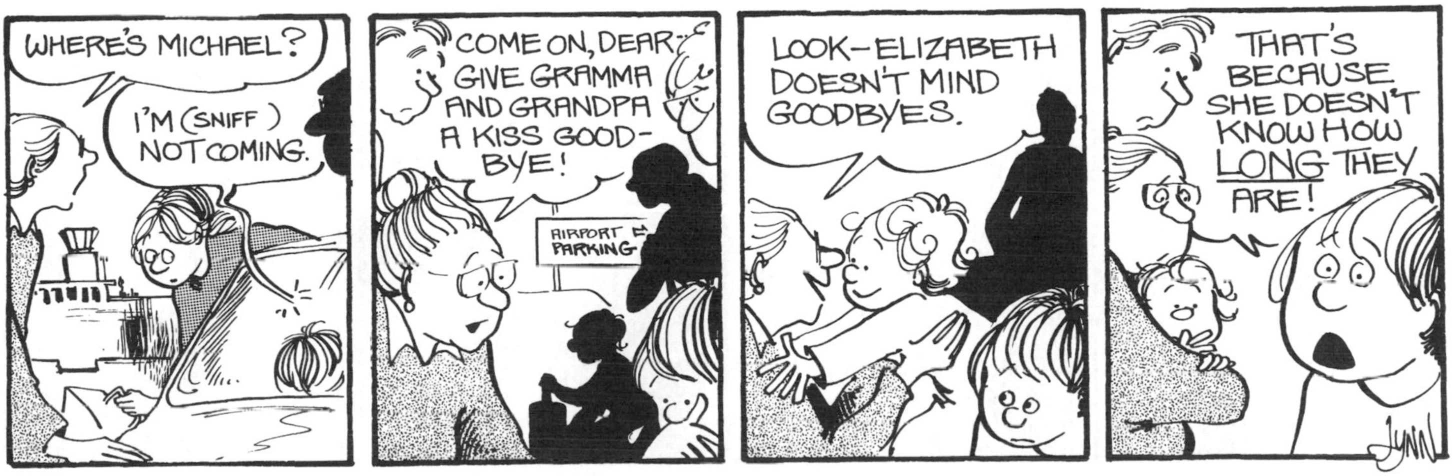
WHERE'S MICHAEL?
I'M (SNIFF) NOT COMING.
COME ON, DEAR-GIVE GRAMMA AND GRANDPA A KISS GOOD-BYE!
AIRPORT PARKING
LOOK-ELIZABETH DOESN'T MIND GOODBYES.
THAT'S BECAUSE SHE DOESN'T KNOW HOW LONG THEY ARE!
LYNN

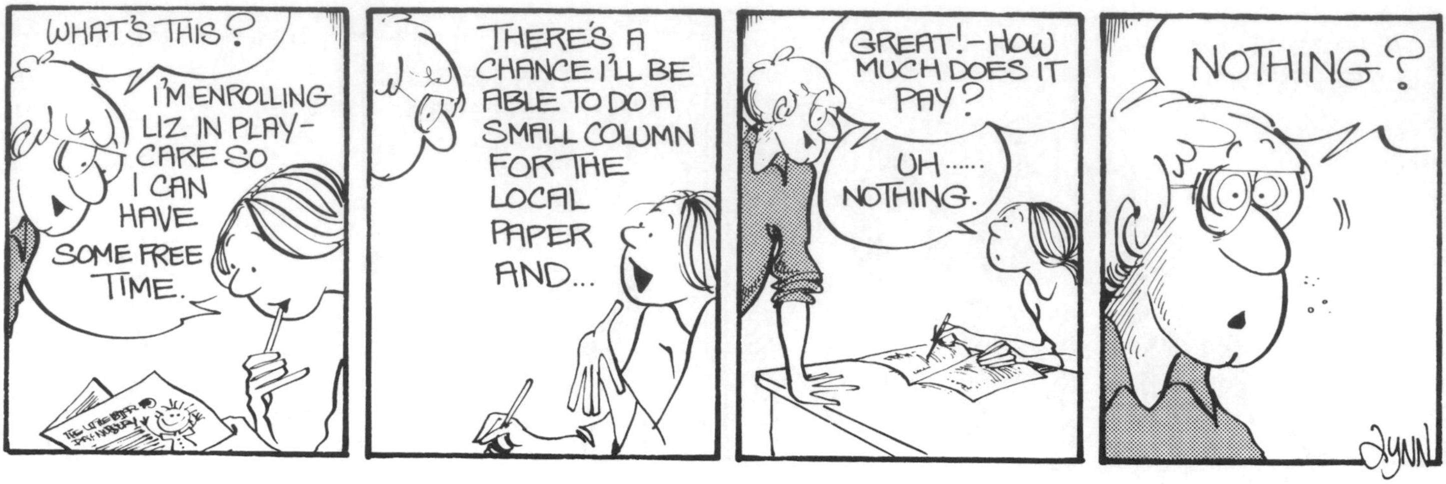
WHAT'S THIS?
I'M ENROLLING LIZ IN PLAY-CARE SO I CAN HAVE SOME FREE TIME.
THERE'S A CHANCE I'LL BE ABLE TO DO A SMALL COLUMN FOR THE LOCAL PAPER AND...
GREAT! - HOW MUCH DOES IT PAY?
UH...... NOTHING.
NOTHING?
LYNN

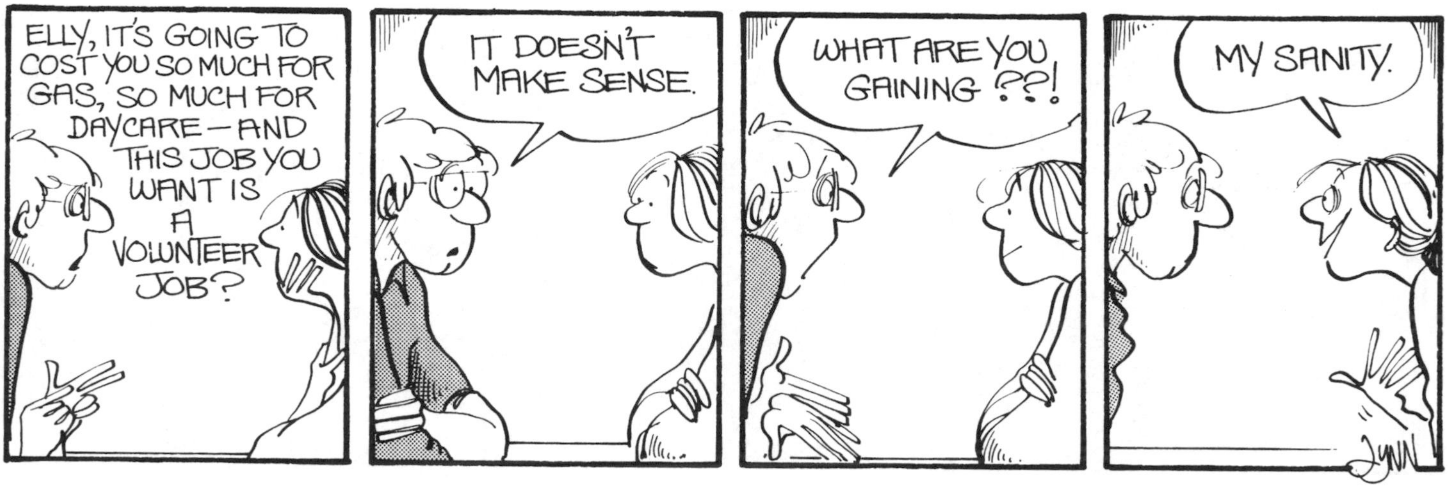
ELLY, IT'S GOING TO COST YOU SO MUCH FOR GAS, SO MUCH FOR DAYCARE - AND THIS JOB YOU WANT IS A VOLUNTEER JOB?
IT DOESN'T MAKE SENSE.
WHAT ARE YOU GAINING ??!
MY SANITY.
LYNN

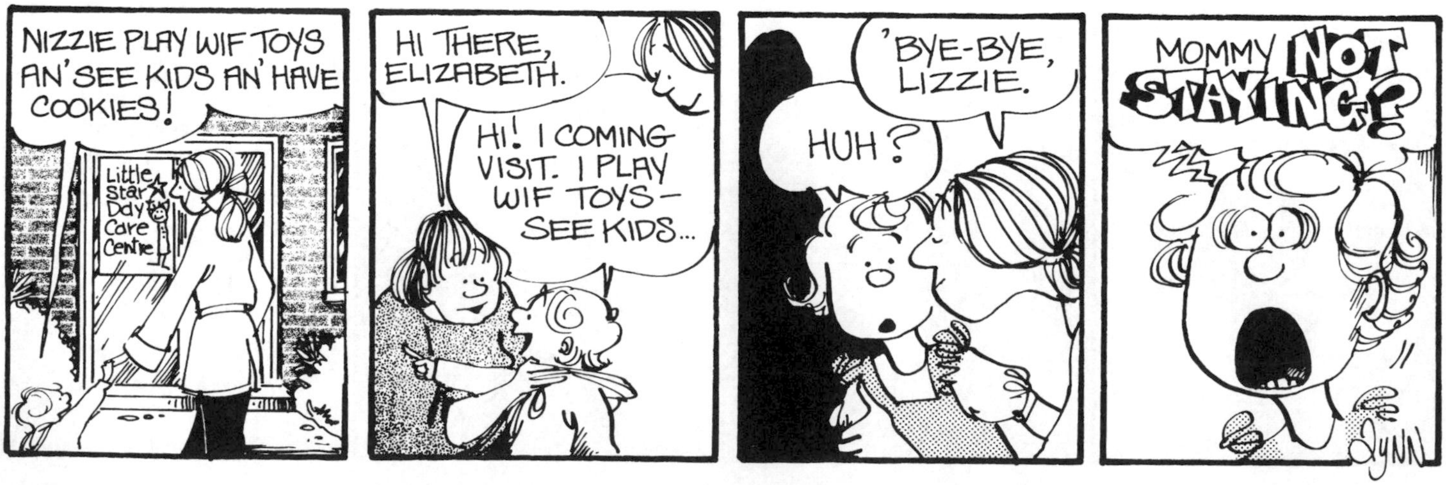
NIZZIE PLAY WIF TOYS AN' SEE KIDS AN' HAVE COOKIES!
Little Star Day Care Centre
HI THERE, ELIZABETH.
HI! I COMING VISIT. I PLAY WIF TOYS - SEE KIDS...
'BYE-BYE, LIZZIE.
HUH?
MOMMY NOT STAYING?
LYNN

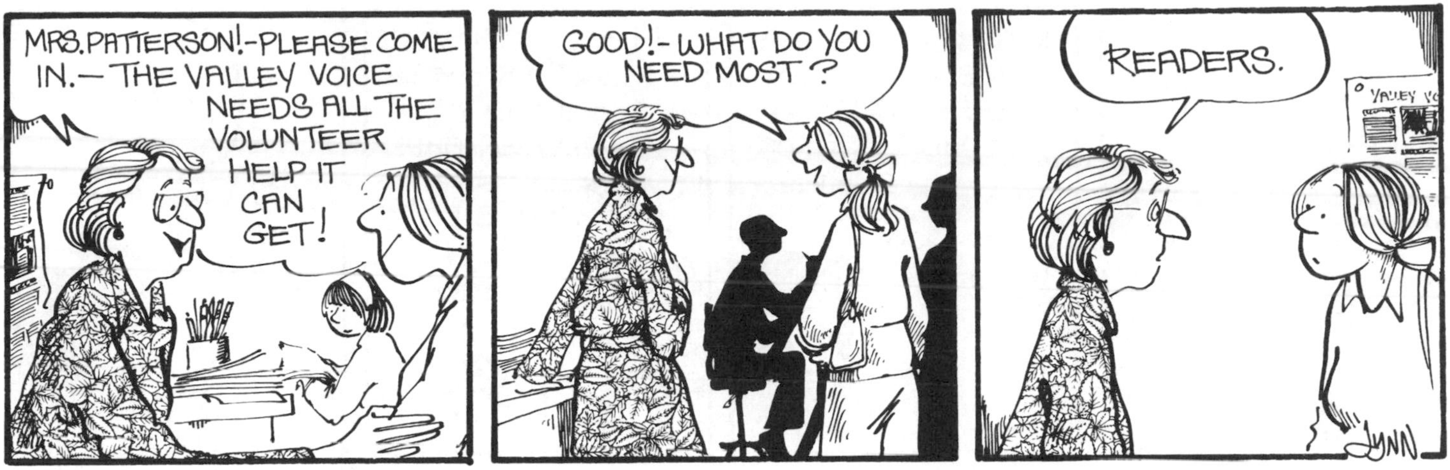
MRS. PATTERSON! - PLEASE COME IN. — THE VALLEY VOICE NEEDS ALL THE VOLUNTEER HELP IT CAN GET!
GOOD! - WHAT DO YOU NEED MOST?
READERS.
VALLEY VO
LYNN

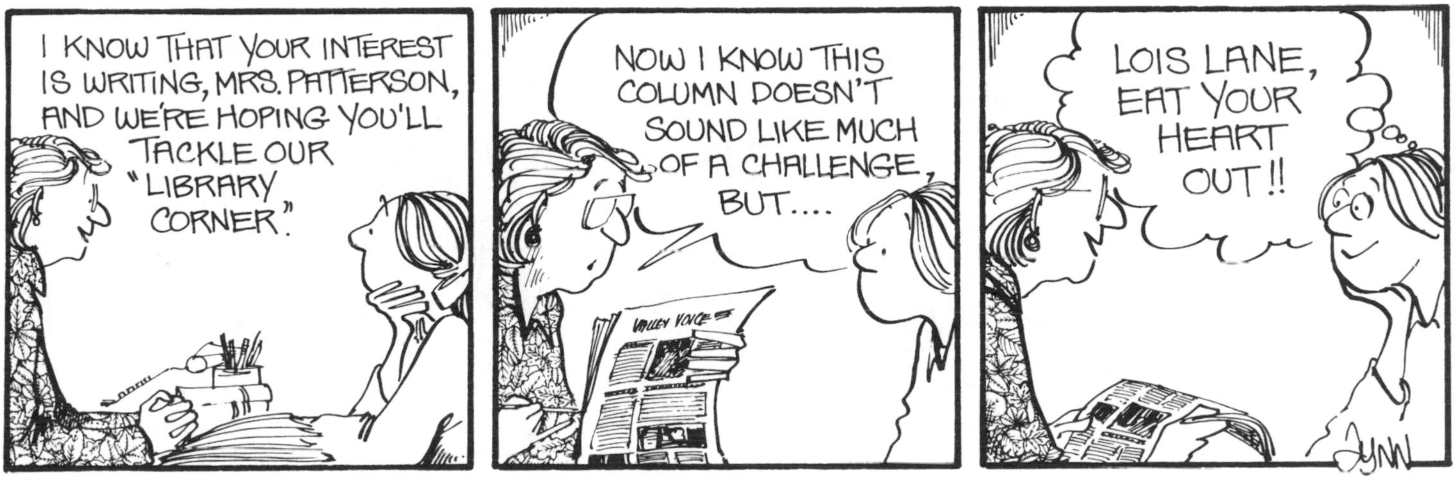
I KNOW THAT YOUR INTEREST IS WRITING, MRS. PATTERSON, AND WE'RE HOPING YOU'LL TACKLE OUR "LIBRARY CORNER".
NOW I KNOW THIS COLUMN DOESN'T SOUND LIKE MUCH OF A CHALLENGE, BUT....
VALLEY VOICE
LOIS LANE, EAT YOUR HEART OUT!!
LYNN

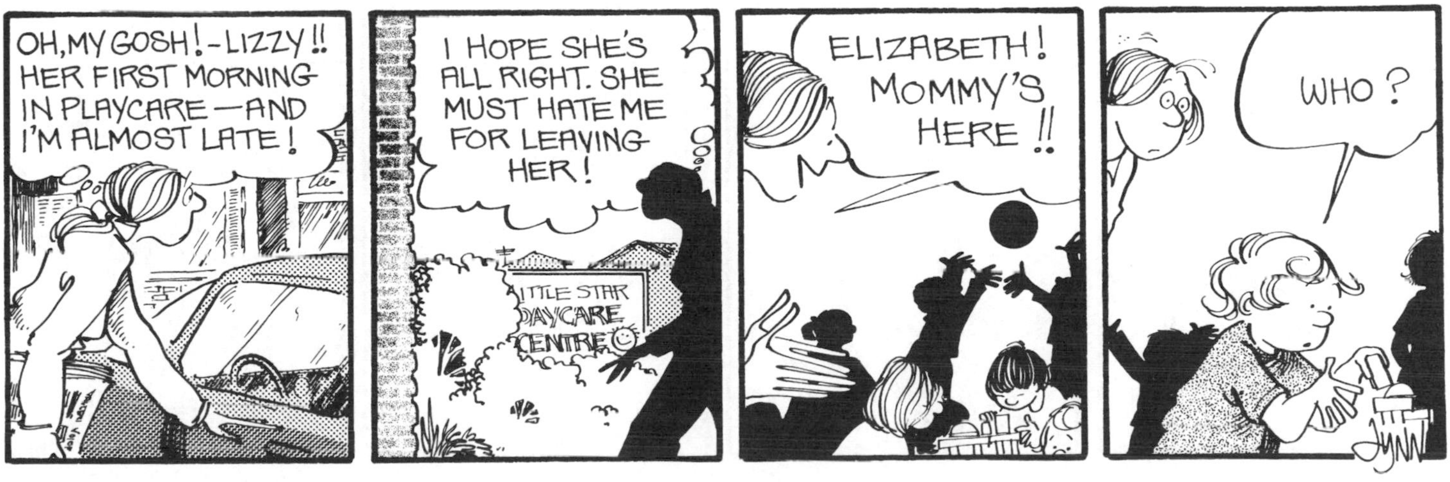
OH, MY GOSH! - LIZZY!! HER FIRST MORNING IN PLAYCARE — AND I'M ALMOST LATE!
I HOPE SHE'S ALL RIGHT. SHE MUST HATE ME FOR LEAVING HER!
ITTLE STAR
DAYCARE
CENTRE
ELIZABETH! MOMMY'S HERE!!
WHO?
LYNN

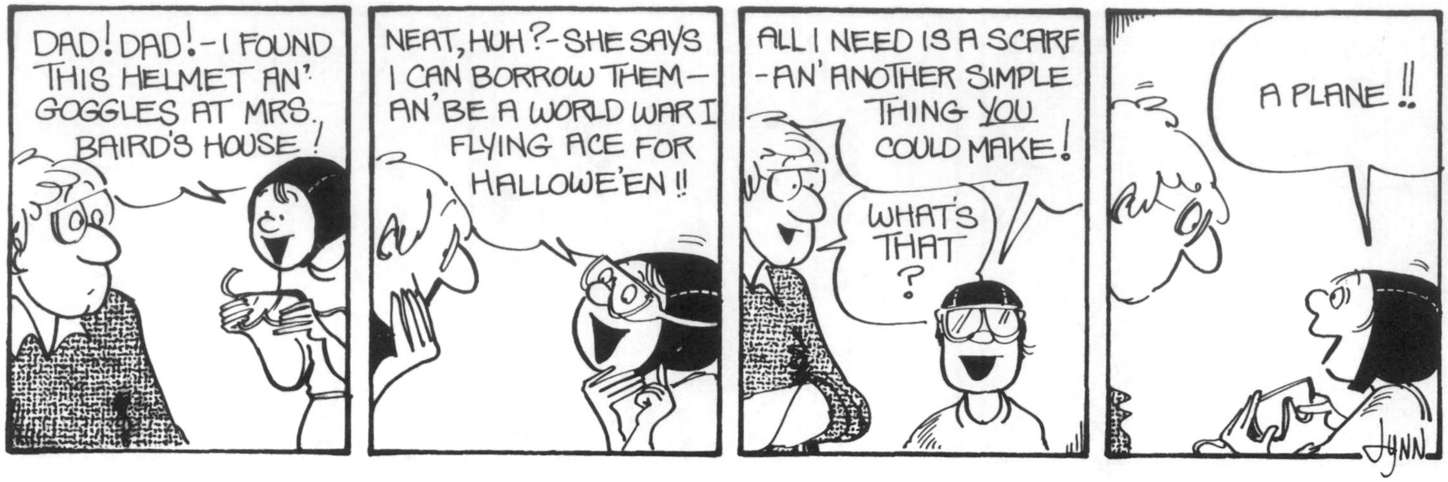
DAD! DAD! - I FOUND THIS HELMET AN' GOGGLES AT MRS. BAIRD'S HOUSE!
NEAT, HUH? - SHE SAYS I CAN BORROW THEM - AN' BE A WORLD WAR I FLYING ACE FOR HALLOWE'EN!!
ALL I NEED IS A SCARF - AN' ANOTHER SIMPLE THING YOU COULD MAKE!
WHAT'S THAT?
A PLANE!!
LYNN

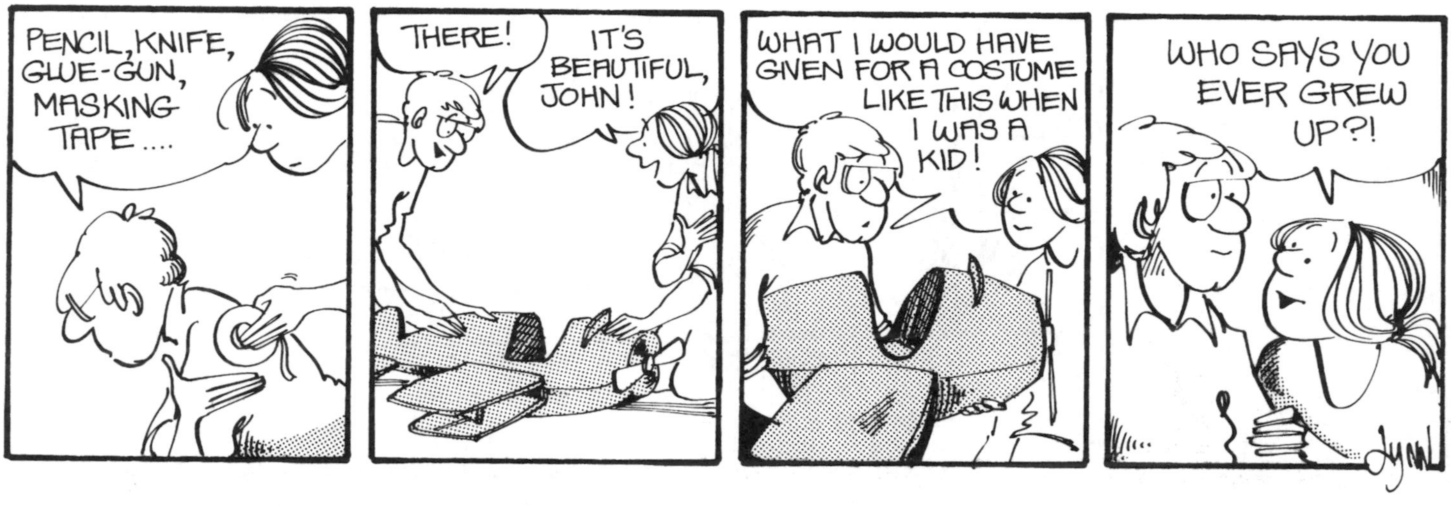
PENCIL, KNIFE, GLUE-GUN, MASKING TAPE....
THERE!
IT'S BEAUTIFUL, JOHN!
WHAT I WOULD HAVE GIVEN FOR A COSTUME LIKE THIS WHEN I WAS A KID!
WHO SAYS YOU EVER GREW UP?!
LYNN

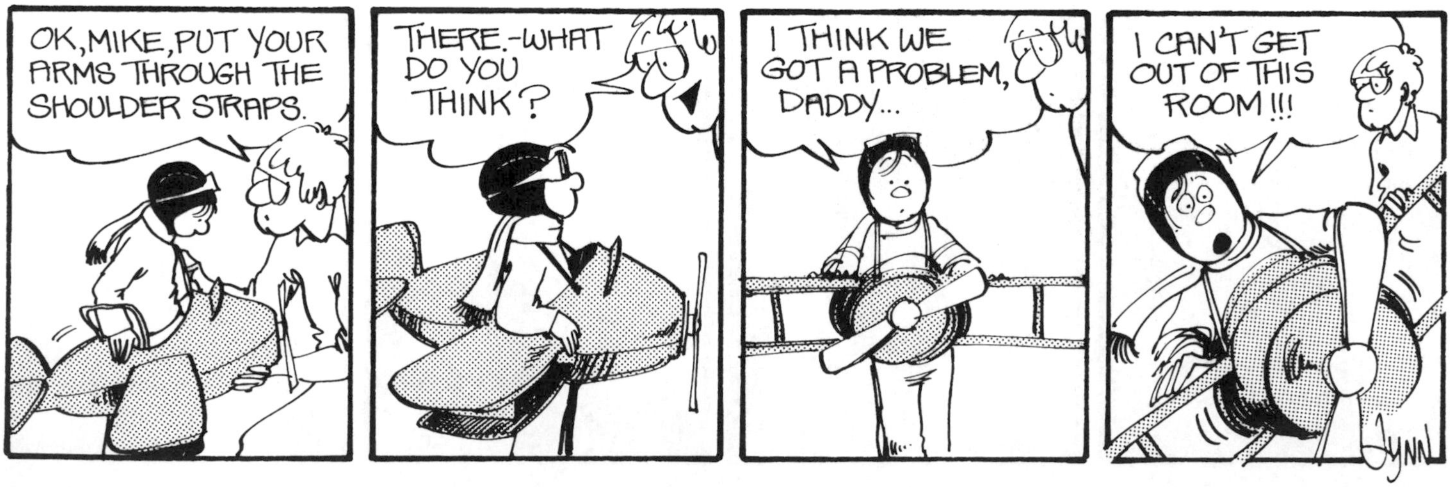
OK, MIKE, PUT YOUR ARMS THROUGH THE SHOULDER STRAPS.
THERE. - WHAT DO YOU THINK?
I THINK WE GOT A PROBLEM, DADDY...
I CAN'T GET OUT OF THIS ROOM!!!
LYNN

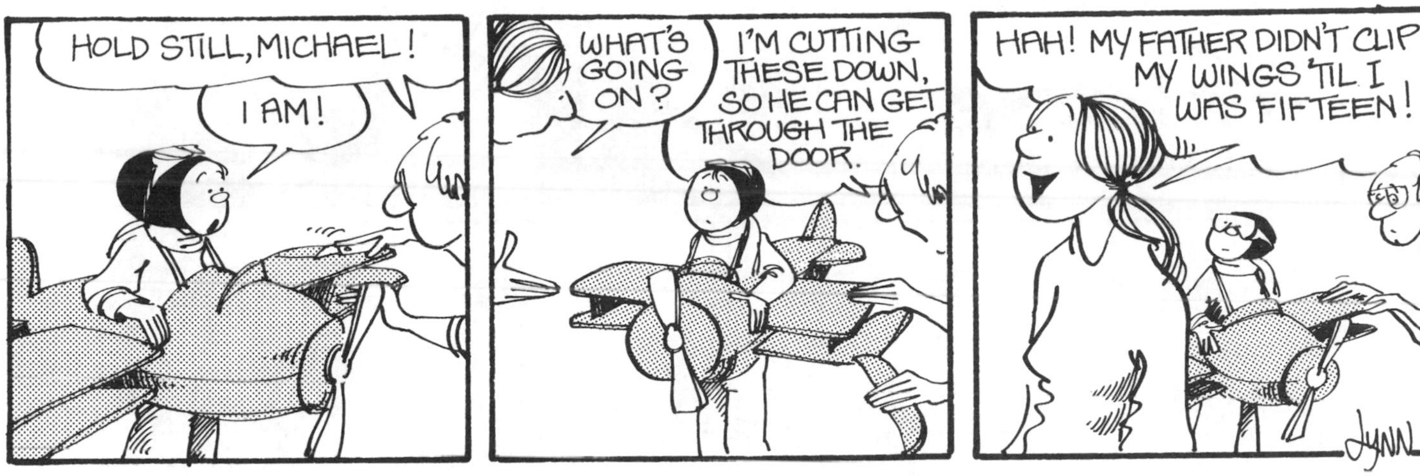
HOLD STILL, MICHAEL!
I AM!
WHAT'S GOING ON?
I'M CUTTING THESE DOWN, SO HE CAN GET THROUGH THE DOOR.
HAH! MY FATHER DIDN'T CLIP MY WINGS 'TIL I WAS FIFTEEN!
LYNN

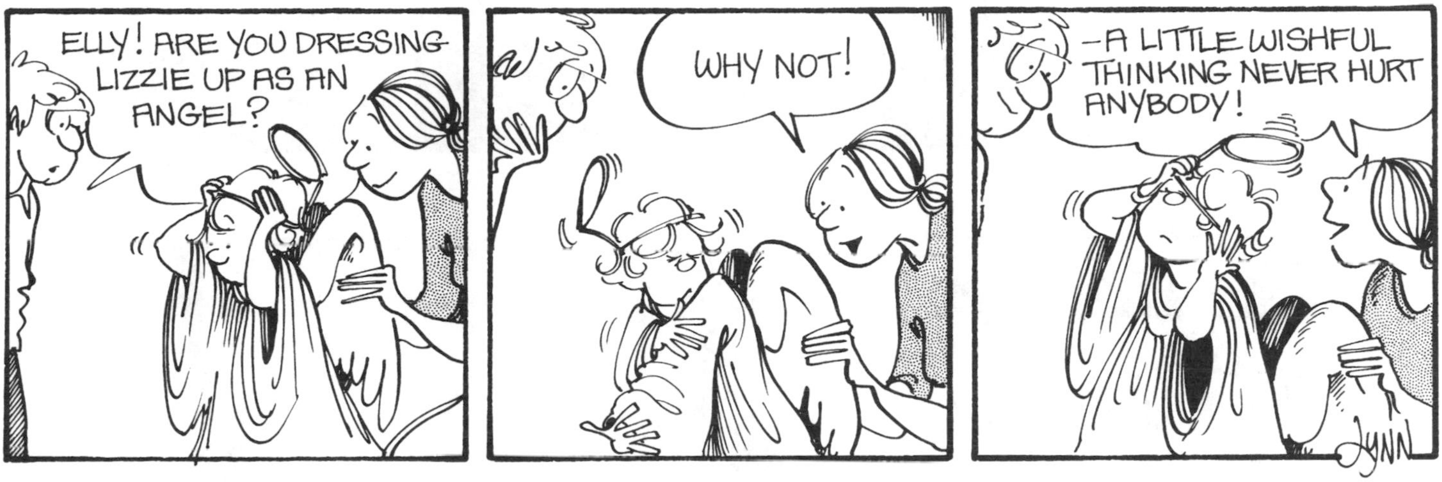
ELLY! ARE YOU DRESSING LIZZIE UP AS AN ANGEL?
WHY NOT!
-A LITTLE WISHFUL THINKING NEVER HURT ANYBODY!
LYNN

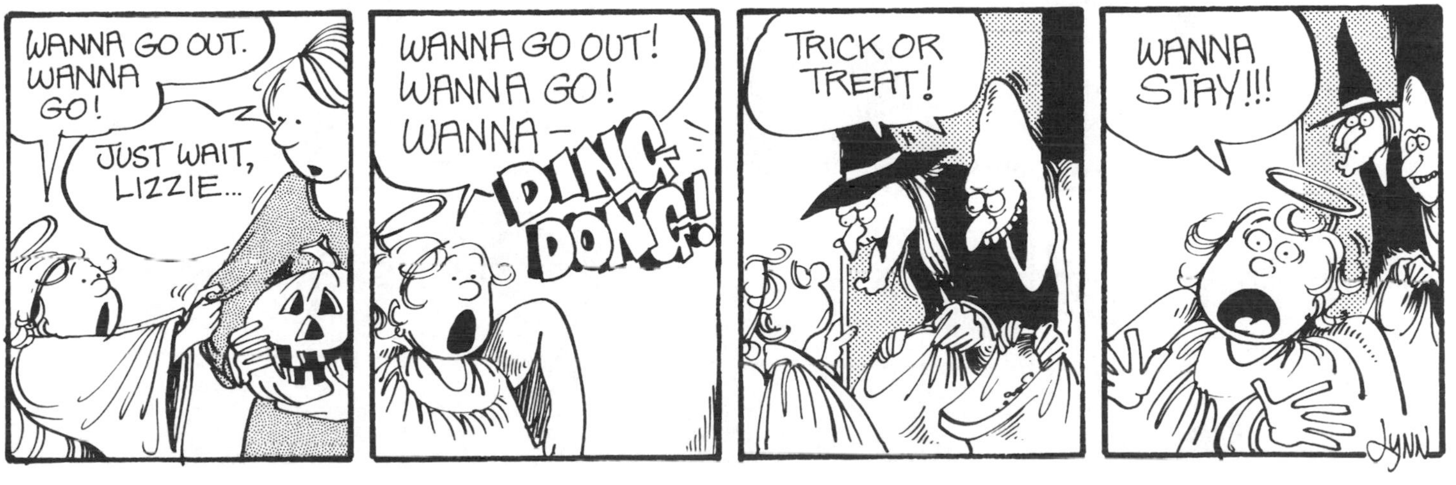
WANNA GO OUT. WANNA GO!
JUST WAIT, LIZZIE...
WANNA GO OUT! WANNA GO! WANNA -
DING DONG!
TRICK OR TREAT!
WANNA STAY!!!
LYNN

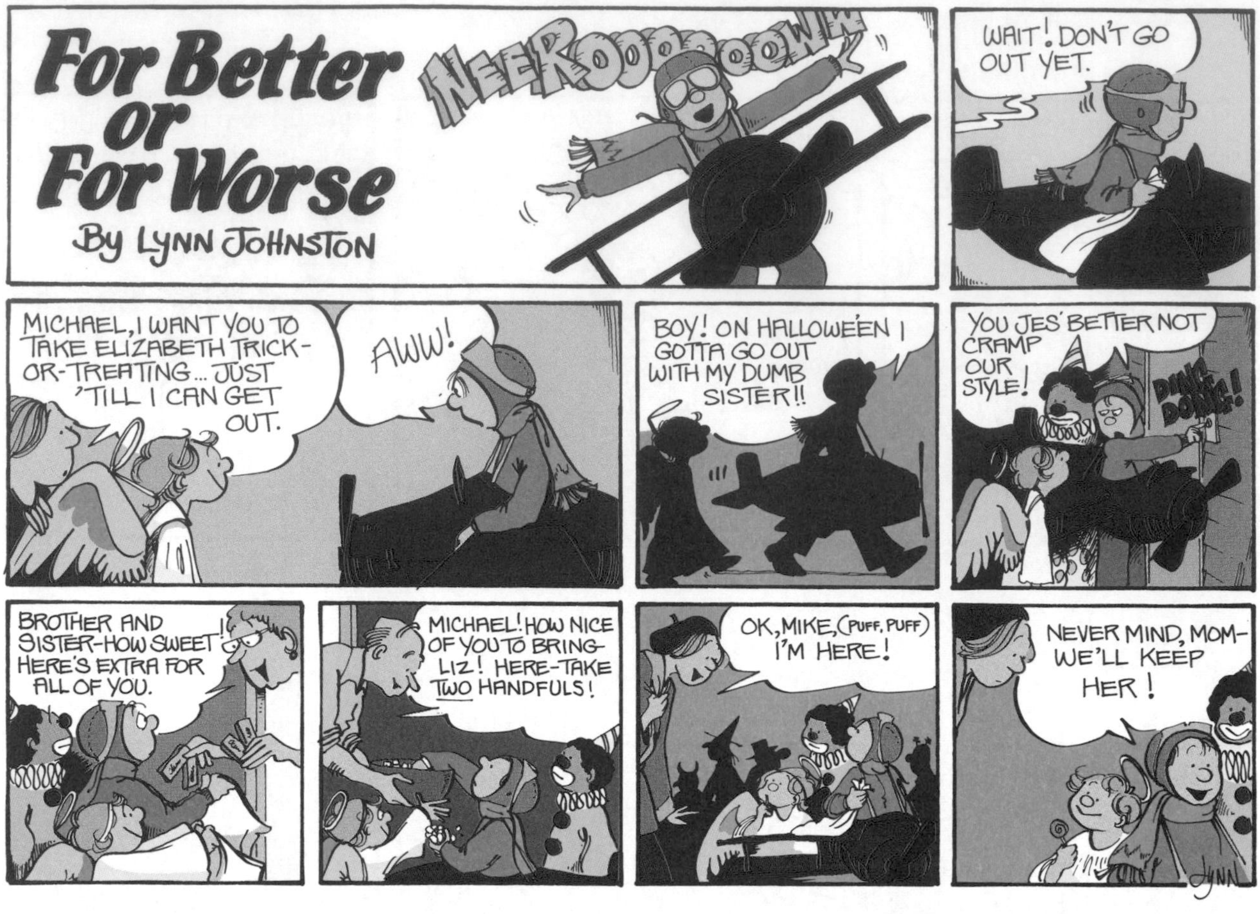
For Better or For Worse
By Lynn Johnston
NEEROOOOOOOWW
WAIT! DON'T GO OUT YET.
MICHAEL, I WANT YOU TO TAKE ELIZABETH TRICK-OR-TREATING... JUST 'TILL I CAN GET OUT.
AWW!
BOY! ON HALLOWE'EN I GOTTA GO OUT WITH MY DUMB SISTER!!
YOU JES' BETTER NOT CRAMP OUR STYLE!
DING DONG!
BROTHER AND SISTER-HOW SWEET! HERE'S EXTRA FOR ALL OF YOU.
MICHAEL! HOW NICE OF YOU TO BRING LIZ! HERE-TAKE TWO HANDFULS!
OK, MIKE, (PUFF, PUFF) I'M HERE!
NEVER MIND, MOM-WE'LL KEEP HER!
LYNN

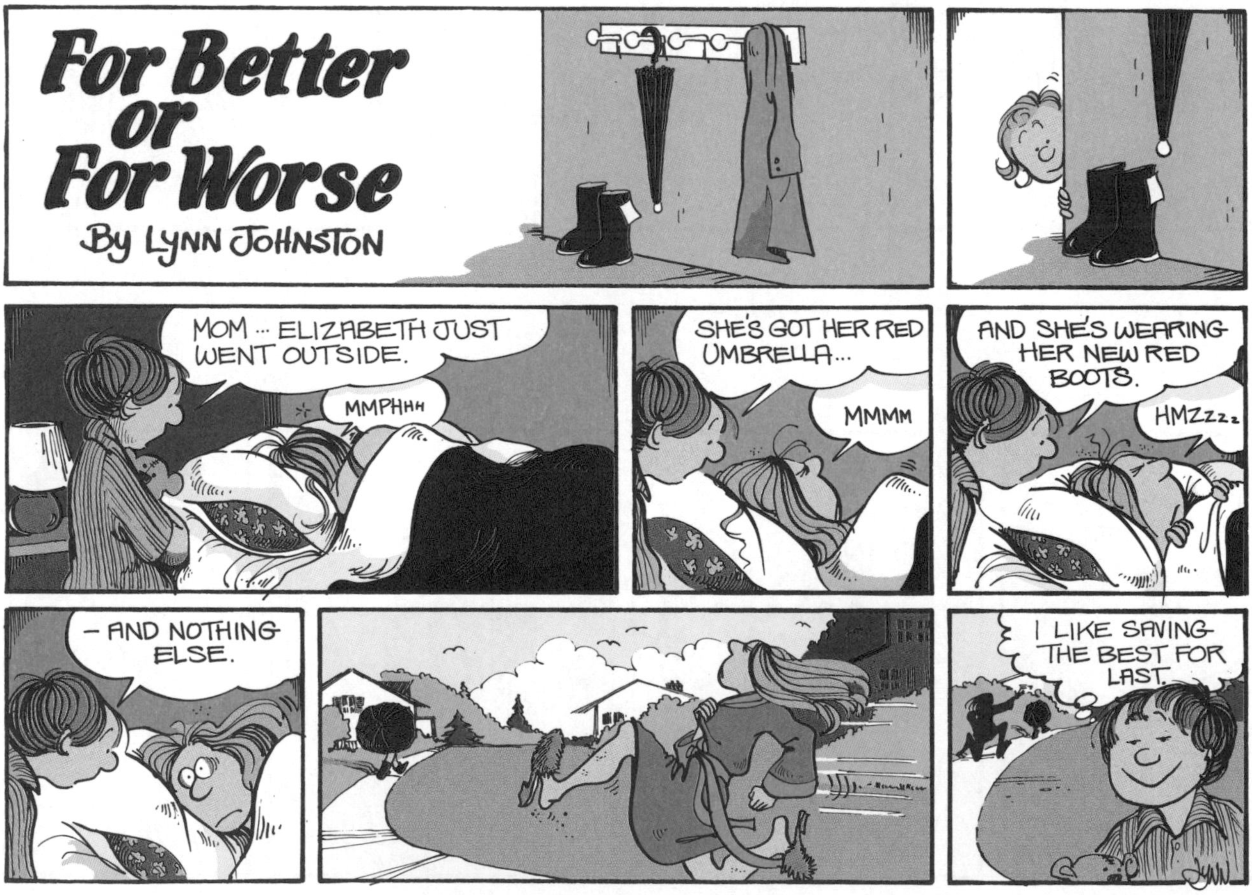
For Better or For Worse
By Lynn Johnston
MOM ... ELIZABETH JUST WENT OUTSIDE.
MMPHHH
SHE'S GOT HER RED UMBRELLA...
MMMM
AND SHE'S WEARING HER NEW RED BOOTS.
HMZzzz
– AND NOTHING ELSE.
I LIKE SAVING THE BEST FOR LAST.
LYNN

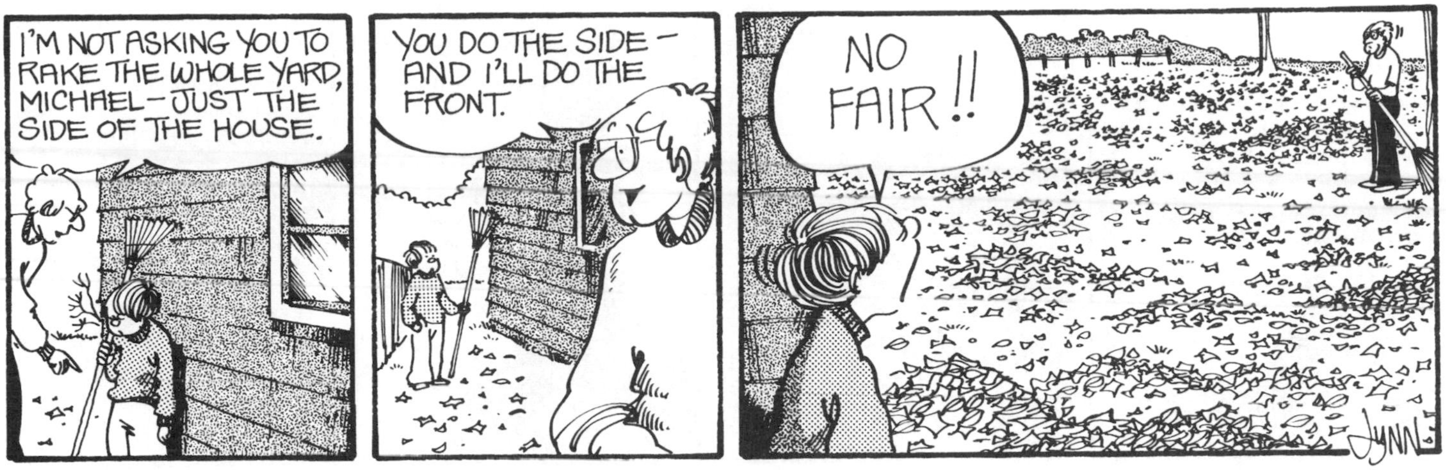
I'M NOT ASKING YOU TO RAKE THE WHOLE YARD, MICHAEL — JUST THE SIDE OF THE HOUSE.
YOU DO THE SIDE — AND I'LL DO THE FRONT.
NO FAIR!!
LYNN

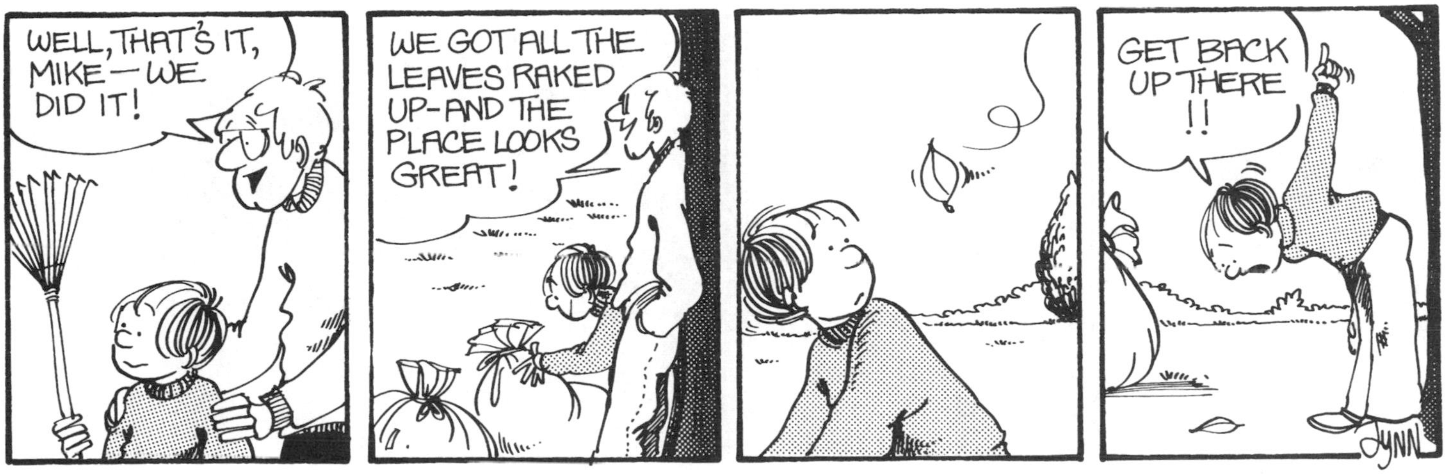
WELL, THAT'S IT, MIKE — WE DID IT!
WE GOT ALL THE LEAVES RAKED UP — AND THE PLACE LOOKS GREAT!
GET BACK UP THERE!!
LYNN

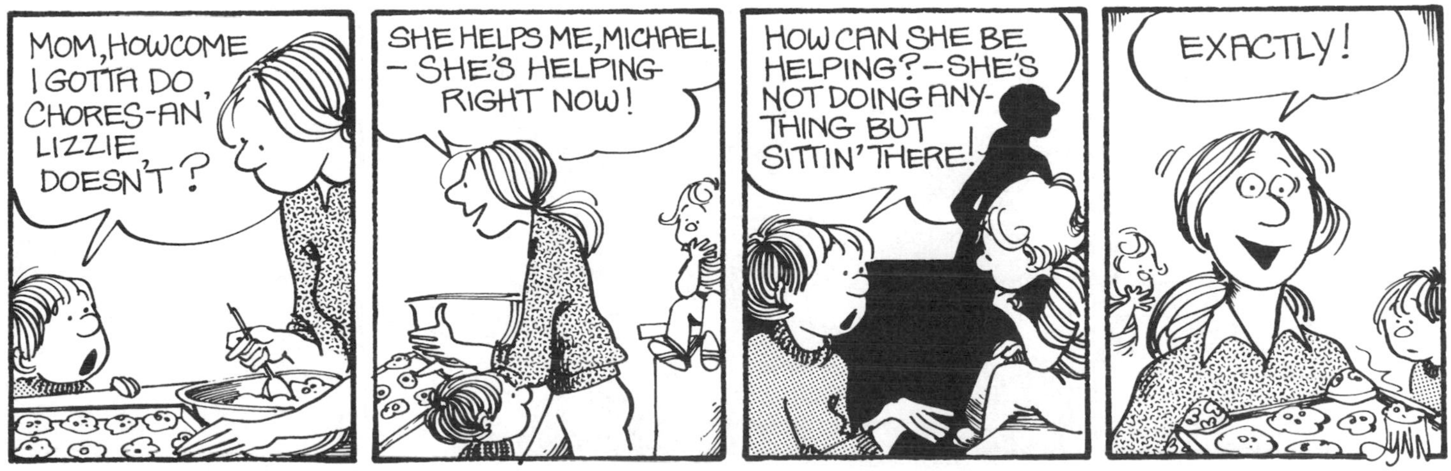
MOM, HOWCOME I GOTTA DO CHORES — AN' LIZZIE DOESN'T?
SHE HELPS ME, MICHAEL — SHE'S HELPING RIGHT NOW!
HOW CAN SHE BE HELPING? — SHE'S NOT DOING ANYTHING BUT SITTIN' THERE!
EXACTLY!
LYNN

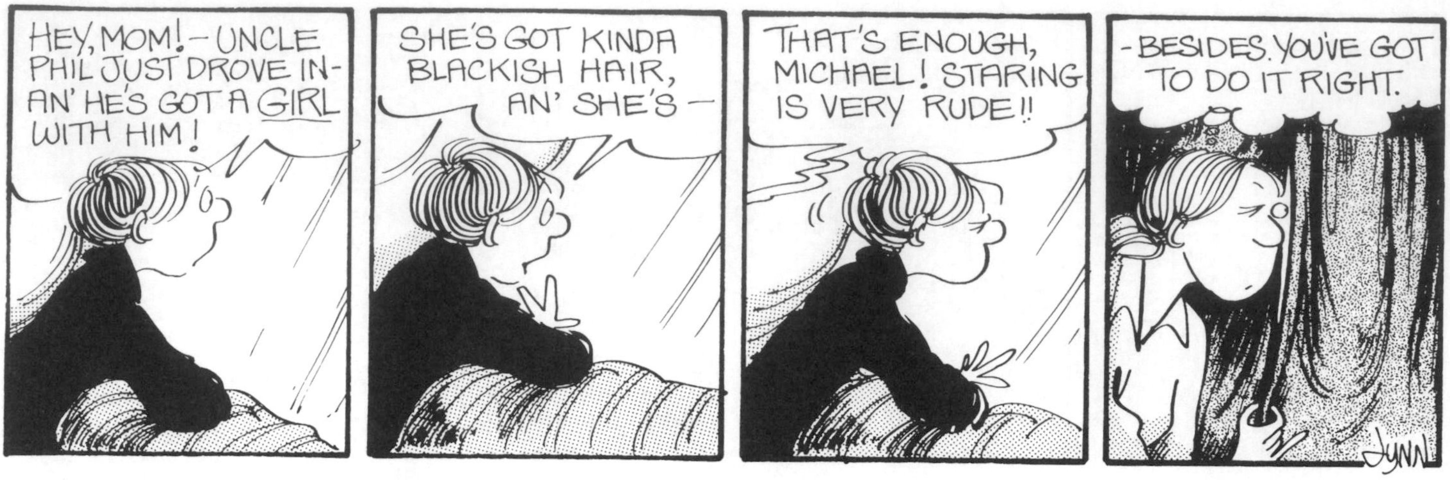
HEY, MOM! - UNCLE PHIL JUST DROVE IN - AN' HE'S GOT A GIRL WITH HIM!
SHE'S GOT KINDA BLACKISH HAIR, AN' SHE'S -
THAT'S ENOUGH, MICHAEL! STARING IS VERY RUDE!!
- BESIDES. YOU'VE GOT TO DO IT RIGHT.
LYNN

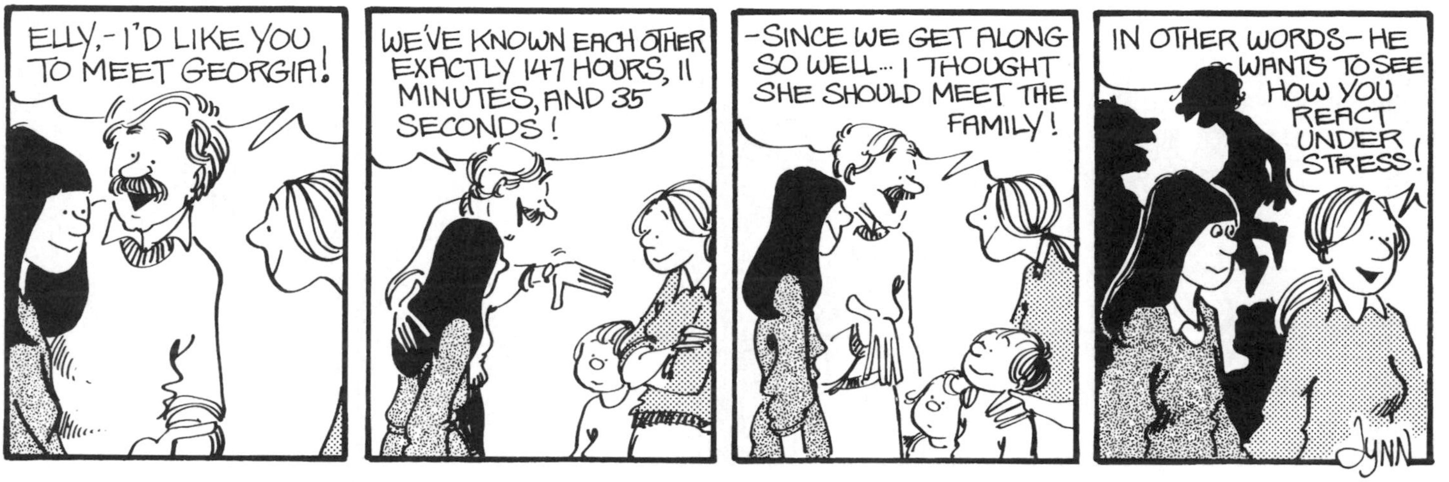
ELLY, - I'D LIKE YOU TO MEET GEORGIA!
WE'VE KNOWN EACH OTHER EXACTLY 147 HOURS, 11 MINUTES, AND 35 SECONDS!
- SINCE WE GET ALONG SO WELL... I THOUGHT SHE SHOULD MEET THE FAMILY!
IN OTHER WORDS - HE WANTS TO SEE HOW YOU REACT UNDER STRESS!
LYNN

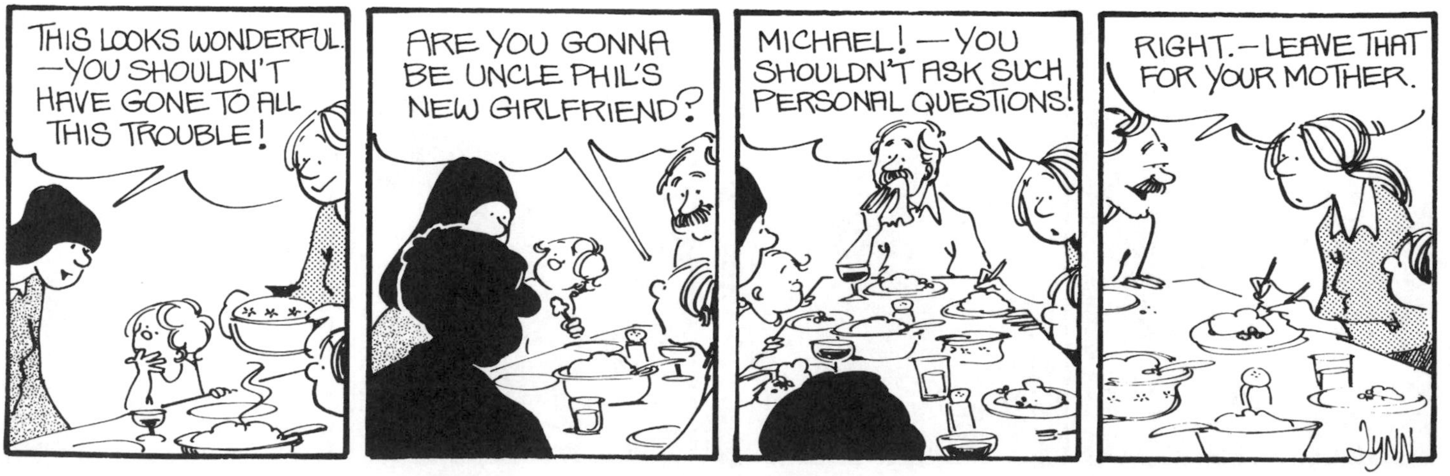
THIS LOOKS WONDERFUL. - YOU SHOULDN'T HAVE GONE TO ALL THIS TROUBLE!
ARE YOU GONNA BE UNCLE PHIL'S NEW GIRLFRIEND?
MICHAEL! — YOU SHOULDN'T ASK SUCH PERSONAL QUESTIONS!
RIGHT. - LEAVE THAT FOR YOUR MOTHER.
LYNN

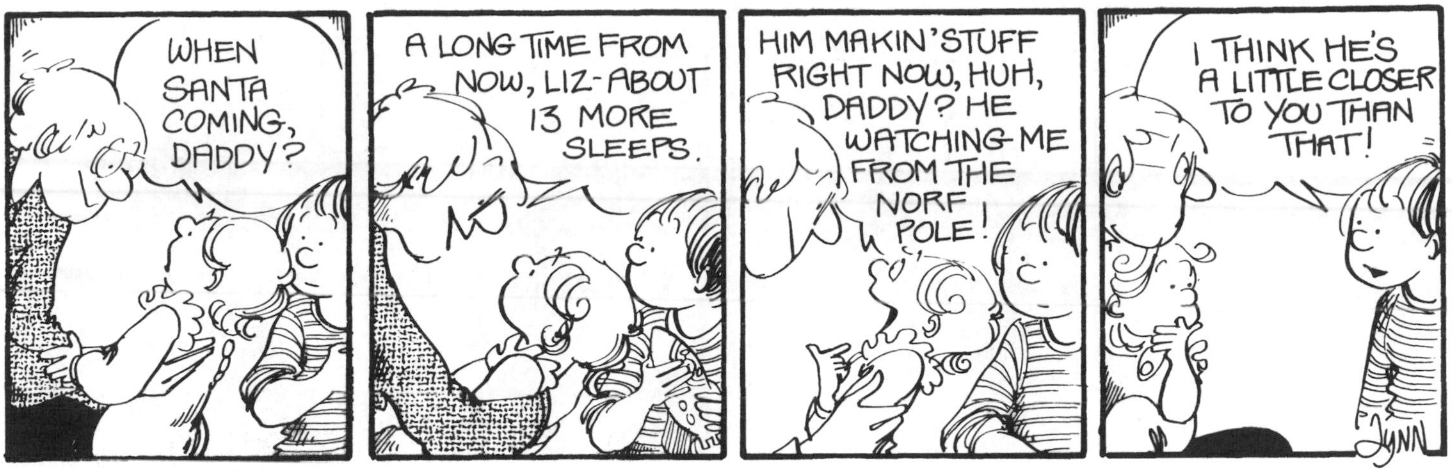
WHEN SANTA COMING, DADDY?
A LONG TIME FROM NOW, LIZ- ABOUT 13 MORE SLEEPS.
HIM MAKIN' STUFF RIGHT NOW, HUH, DADDY? HE WATCHING ME FROM THE NORF POLE!
I THINK HE'S A LITTLE CLOSER TO YOU THAN THAT!
LYNN

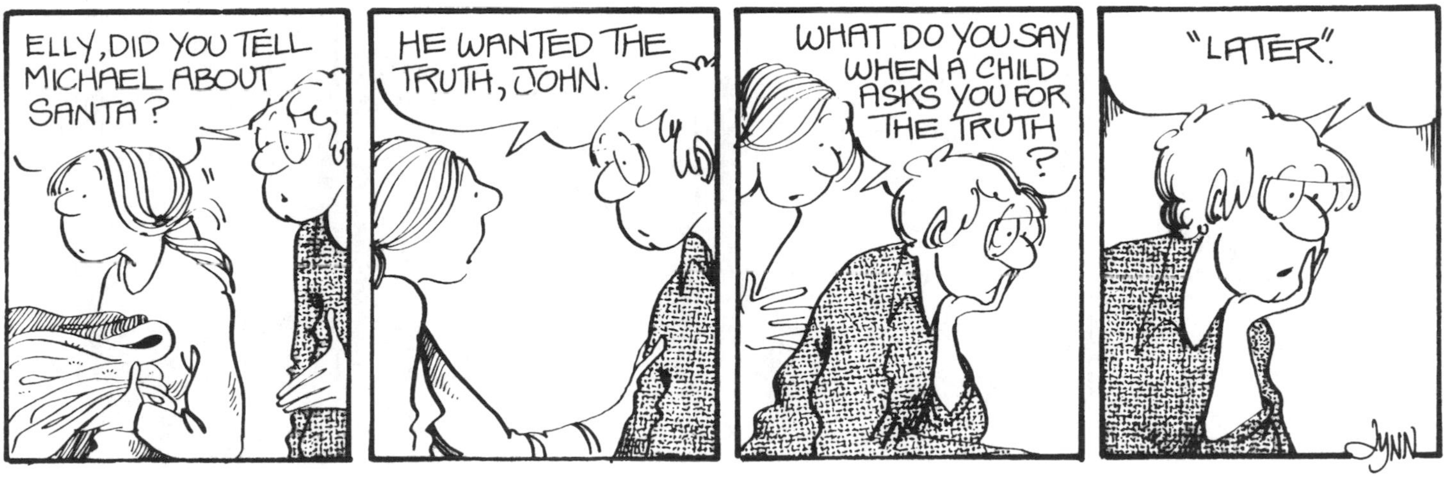
ELLY, DID YOU TELL MICHAEL ABOUT SANTA?
HE WANTED THE TRUTH, JOHN.
WHAT DO YOU SAY WHEN A CHILD ASKS YOU FOR THE TRUTH?
"LATER".
LYNN

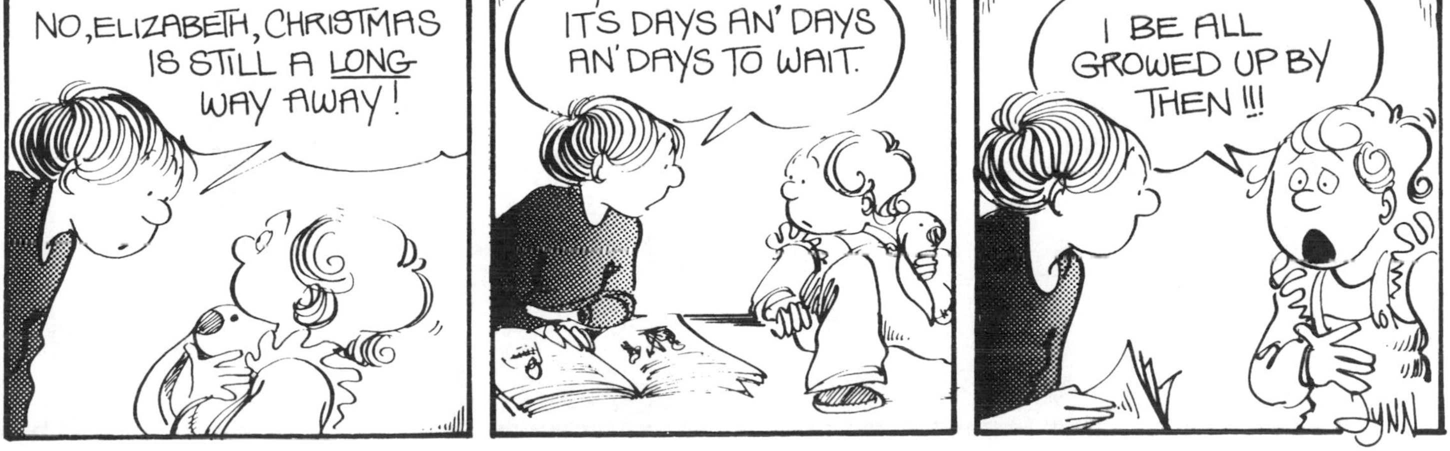
NO, ELIZABETH, CHRISTMAS IS STILL A LONG WAY AWAY!
IT'S DAYS AN' DAYS AN' DAYS TO WAIT.
I BE ALL GROWED UP BY THEN !!!
LYNN

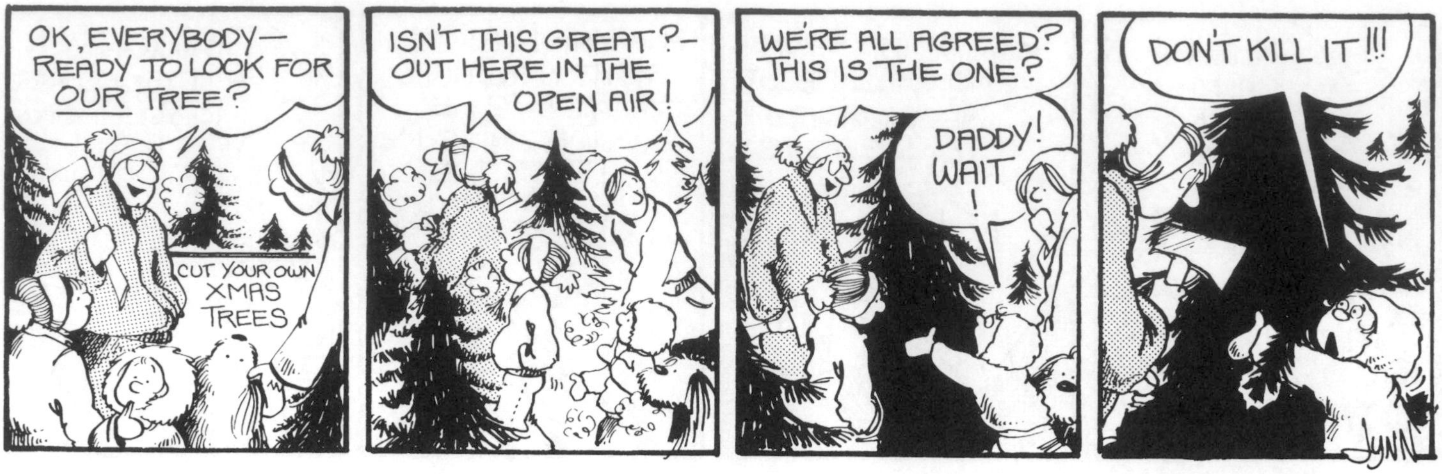
OK, EVERYBODY— READY TO LOOK FOR OUR TREE?
CUT YOUR OWN XMAS TREES
ISN'T THIS GREAT?- OUT HERE IN THE OPEN AIR!
WE'RE ALL AGREED? THIS IS THE ONE?
DADDY! WAIT!
DON'T KILL IT!!!
LYNN

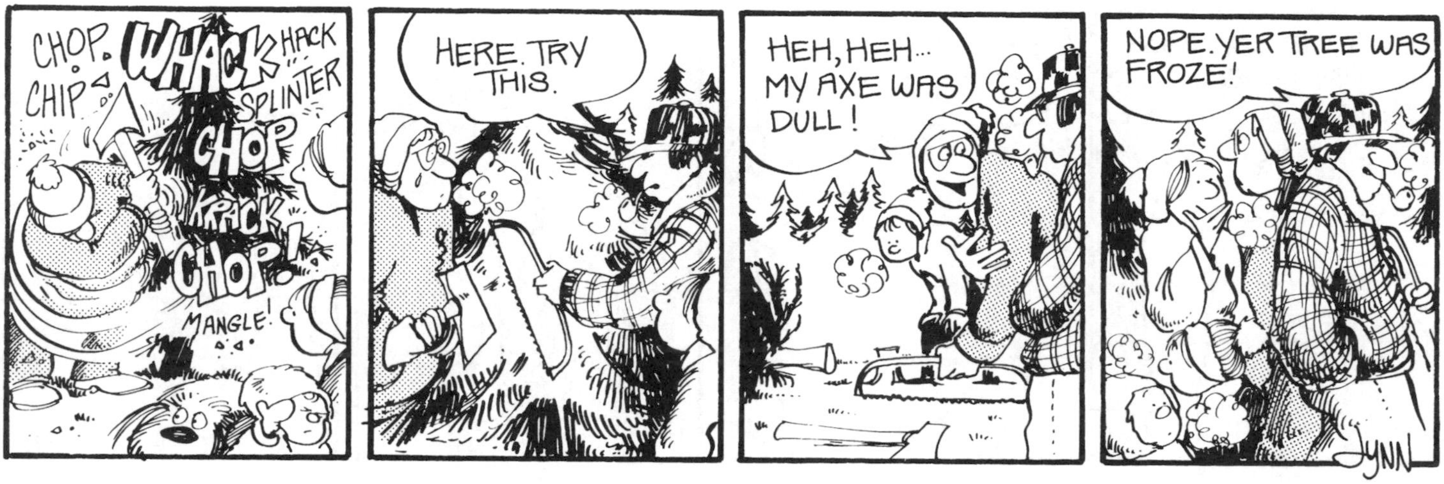
CHOP. CHIP WHACK HACK SPLINTER CHOP KRACK CHOP! MANGLE!
HERE. TRY THIS.
HEH, HEH... MY AXE WAS DULL!
NOPE. YER TREE WAS FROZE!
LYNN

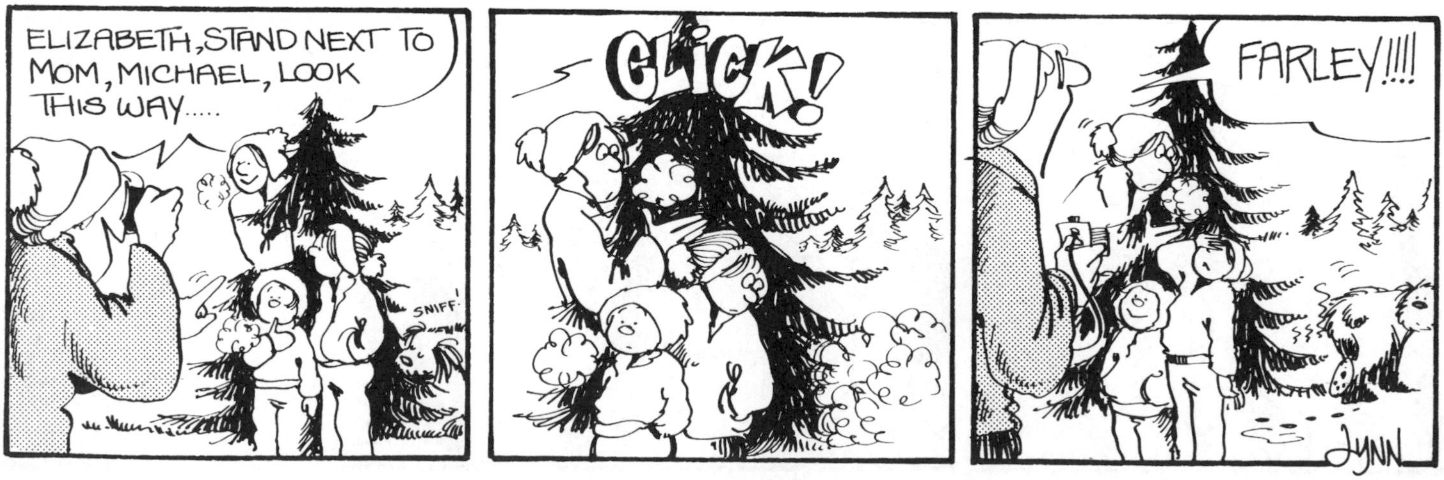
ELIZABETH, STAND NEXT TO MOM, MICHAEL, LOOK THIS WAY.....
SNIFF!
CLICK!
FARLEY!!!!
LYNN

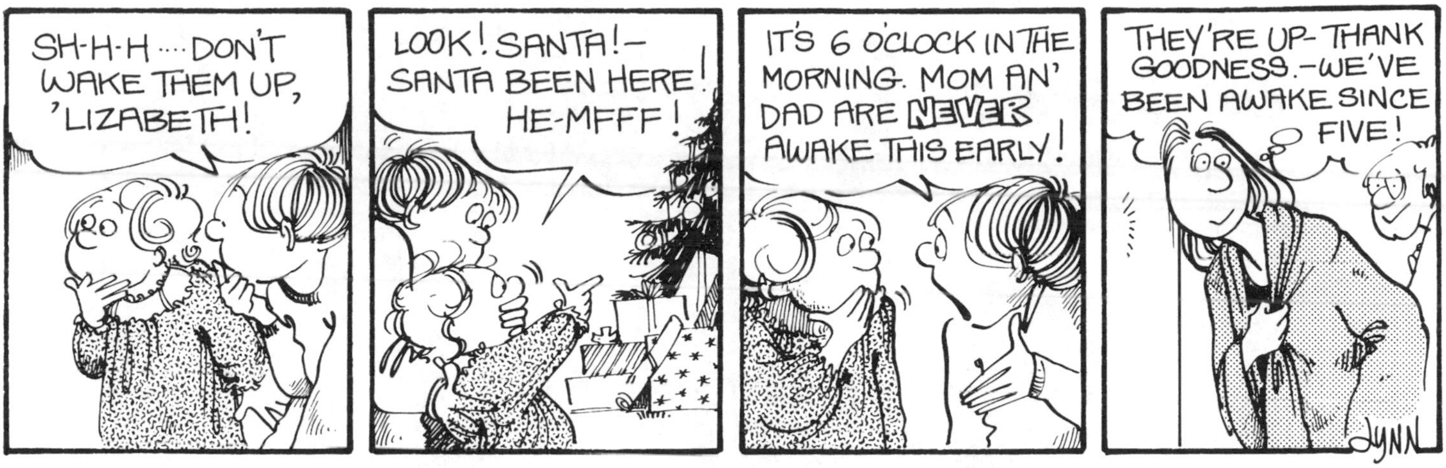
SH-H-H .... DON'T WAKE THEM UP, 'LIZABETH!
LOOK! SANTA! — SANTA BEEN HERE! HE-MFFF!
IT'S 6 O'CLOCK IN THE MORNING. MOM AN' DAD ARE NEVER AWAKE THIS EARLY!
THEY'RE UP- THANK GOODNESS.- WE'VE BEEN AWAKE SINCE FIVE!
LYNN

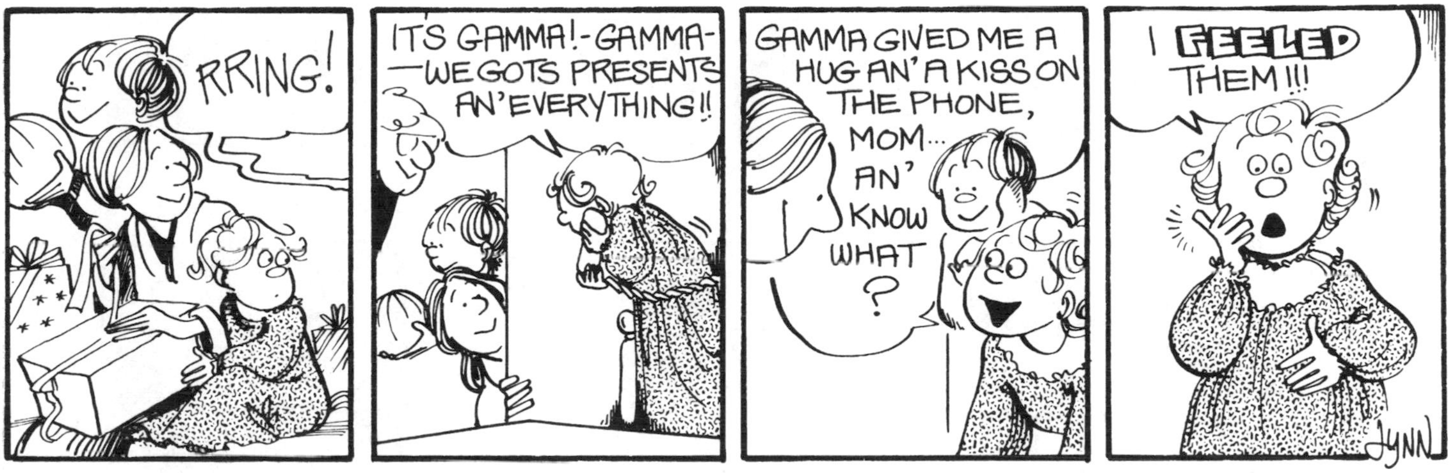
RRING!
IT'S GAMMA! - GAMMA- — WE GOTS PRESENTS AN' EVERYTHING!!
GAMMA GIVED ME A HUG AN' A KISS ON THE PHONE, MOM... AN' KNOW WHAT ?
I FEELED THEM!!!
LYNN

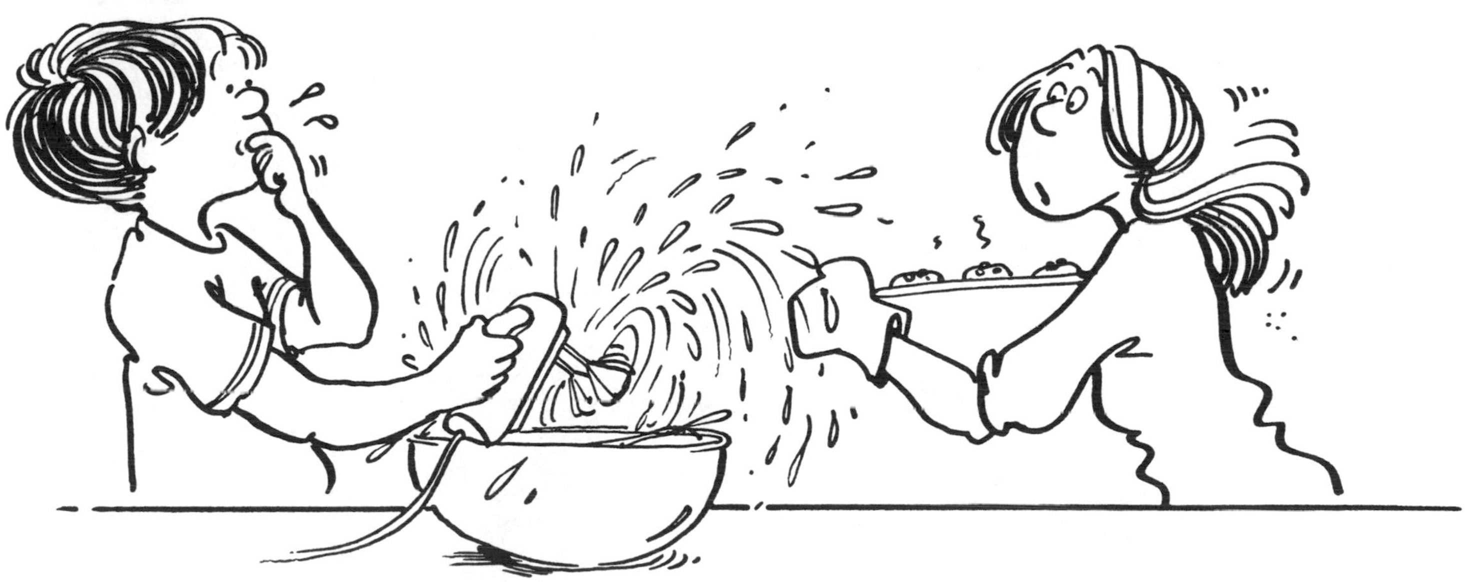

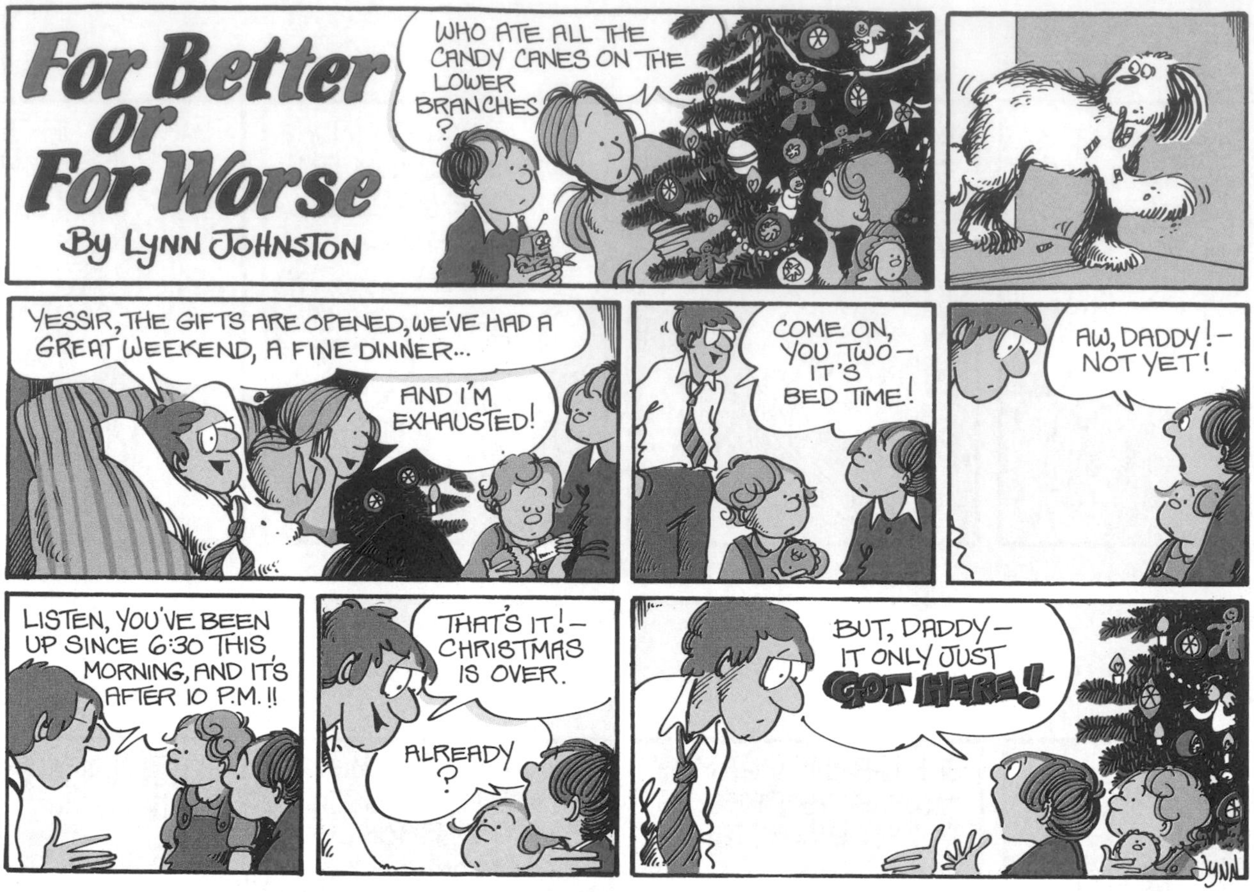
For Better or For Worse
By Lynn Johnston
WHO ATE ALL THE CANDY CANES ON THE LOWER BRANCHES ?
YESSIR, THE GIFTS ARE OPENED, WE'VE HAD A GREAT WEEKEND, A FINE DINNER...
AND I'M EXHAUSTED!
COME ON, YOU TWO— IT'S BED TIME!
AW, DADDY!— NOT YET!
LISTEN, YOU'VE BEEN UP SINCE 6:30 THIS MORNING, AND IT'S AFTER 10 P.M. !!
THAT'S IT!— CHRISTMAS IS OVER.
ALREADY ?
BUT, DADDY— IT ONLY JUST GOT HERE!!
LYNN

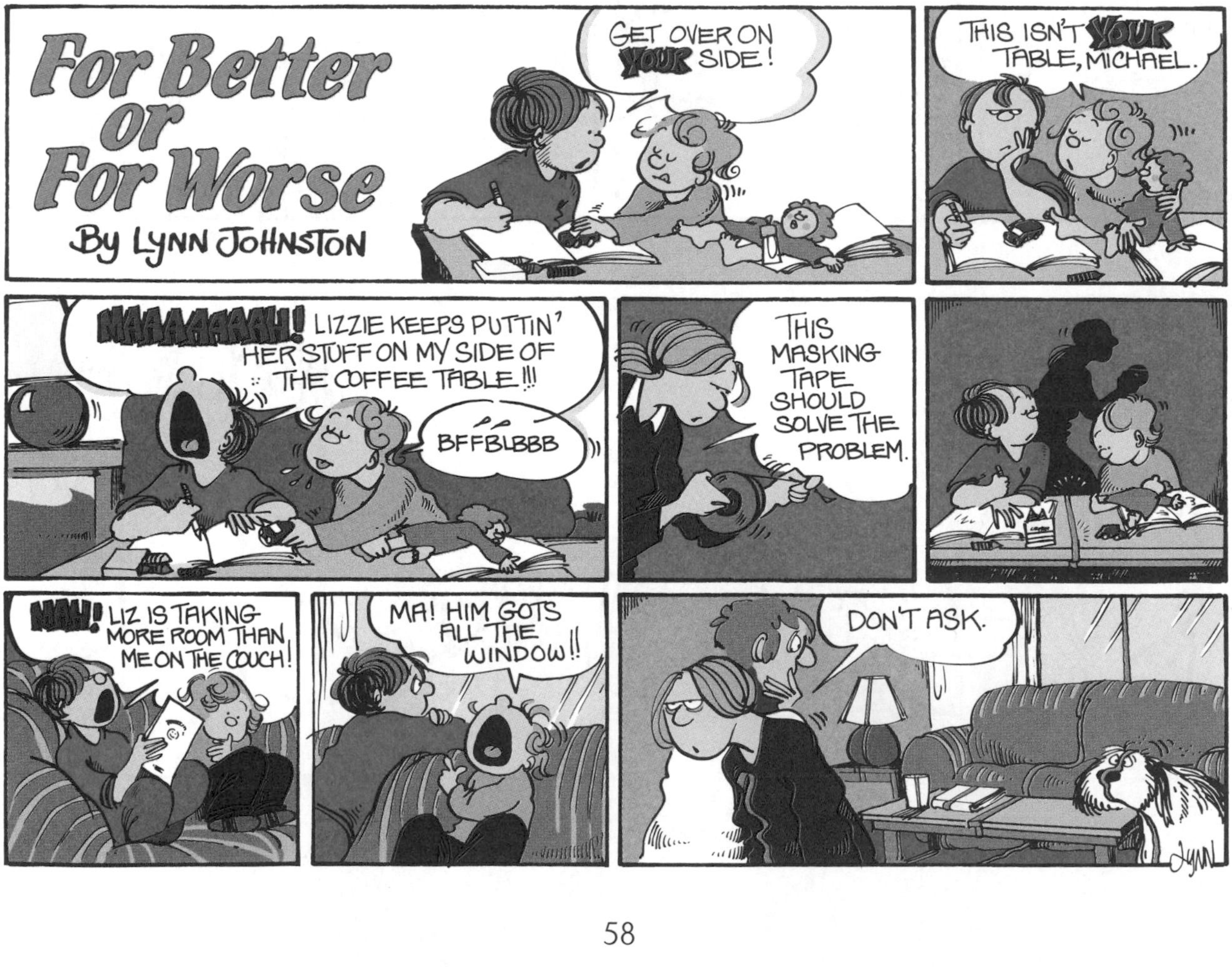
For Better or For Worse
By Lynn Johnston
GET OVER ON YOUR SIDE!
THIS ISN'T YOUR TABLE, MICHAEL.
WAAAAAAAH! LIZZIE KEEPS PUTTIN' HER STUFF ON MY SIDE OF THE COFFEE TABLE!!!
BFFBLBBB
THIS MASKING TAPE SHOULD SOLVE THE PROBLEM.
WAH! LIZ IS TAKING MORE ROOM THAN ME ON THE COUCH!
MA! HIM GOTS ALL THE WINDOW!!
DON'T ASK.
LYNN

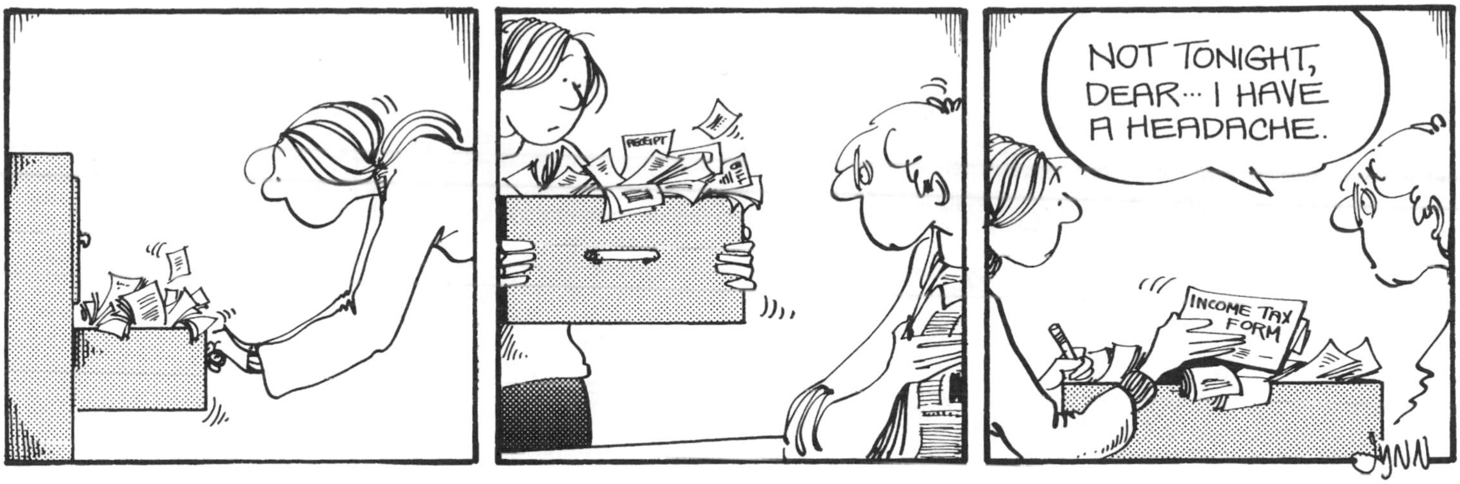
RECEIPT
INCOME TAX FORM
NOT TONIGHT, DEAR... I HAVE A HEADACHE.

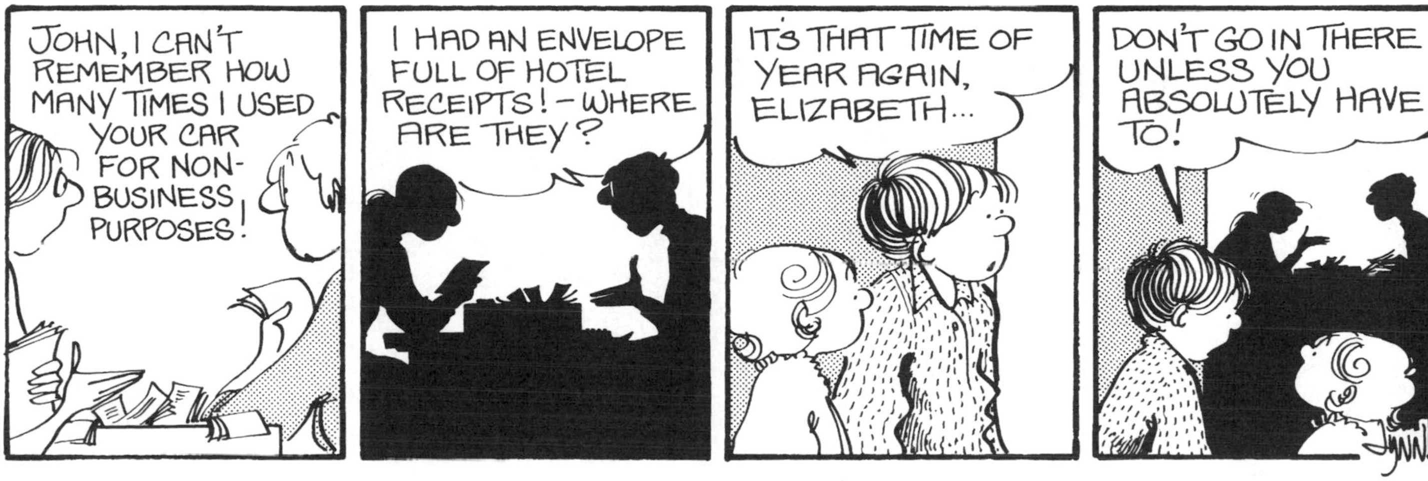
JOHN, I CAN'T REMEMBER HOW MANY TIMES I USED YOUR CAR FOR NON-BUSINESS PURPOSES!
I HAD AN ENVELOPE FULL OF HOTEL RECEIPTS! – WHERE ARE THEY?
IT'S THAT TIME OF YEAR AGAIN, ELIZABETH...
DON'T GO IN THERE UNLESS YOU ABSOLUTELY HAVE TO!

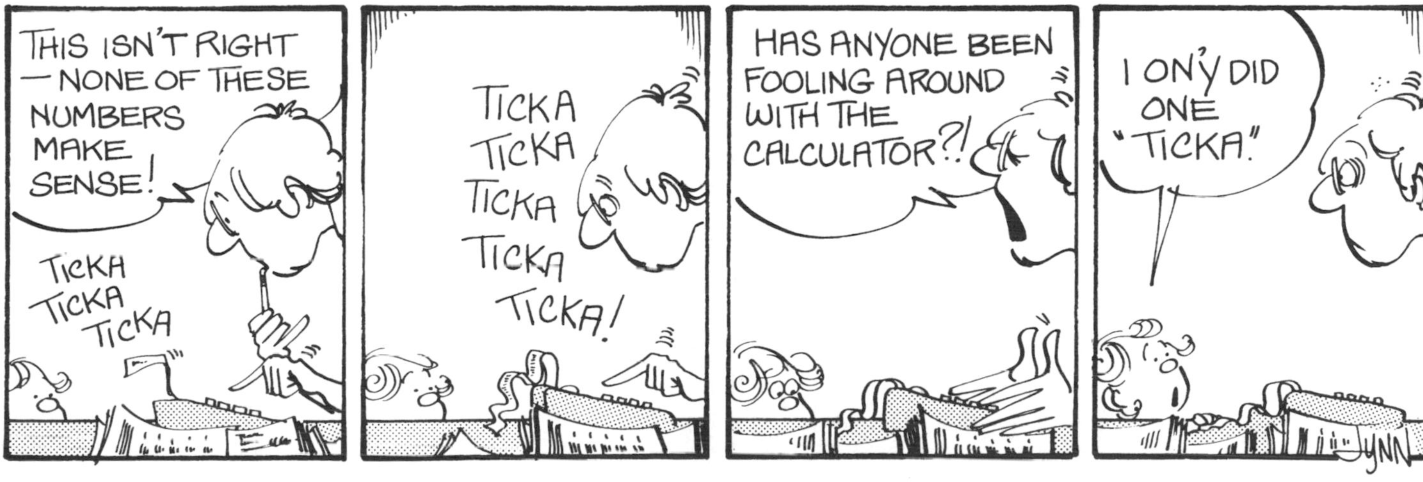
THIS ISN'T RIGHT – NONE OF THESE NUMBERS MAKE SENSE!
TICKA TICKA TICKA
TICKA TICKA TICKA TICKA TICKA!
HAS ANYONE BEEN FOOLING AROUND WITH THE CALCULATOR?!
I ON'Y DID ONE "TICKA."

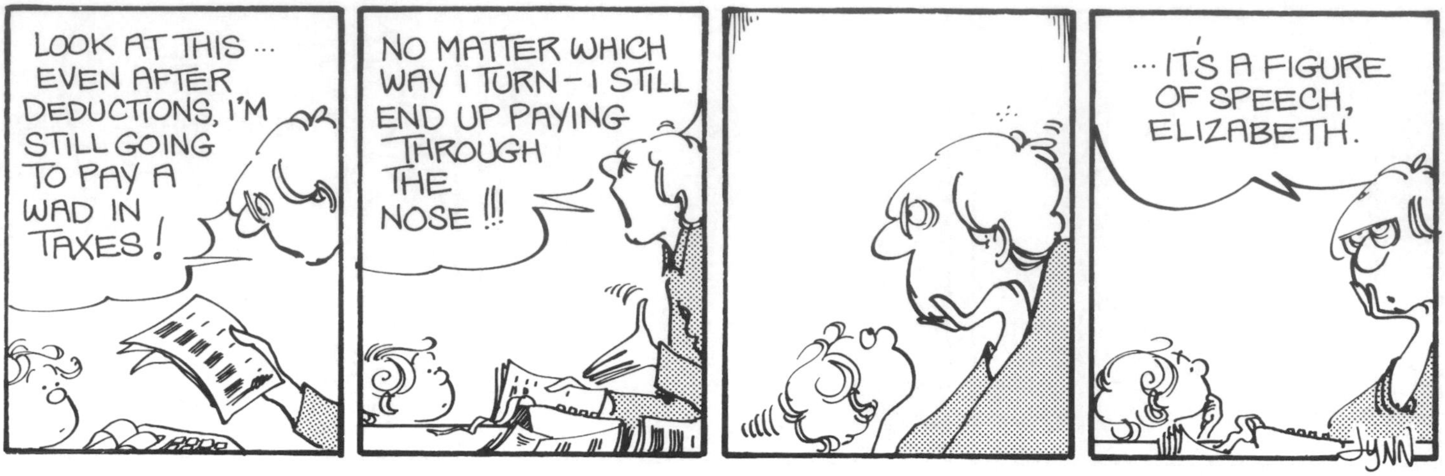
LOOK AT THIS ... EVEN AFTER DEDUCTIONS, I'M STILL GOING TO PAY A WAD IN TAXES!
NO MATTER WHICH WAY I TURN - I STILL END UP PAYING THROUGH THE NOSE!!!
... IT'S A FIGURE OF SPEECH, ELIZABETH.
LYNN

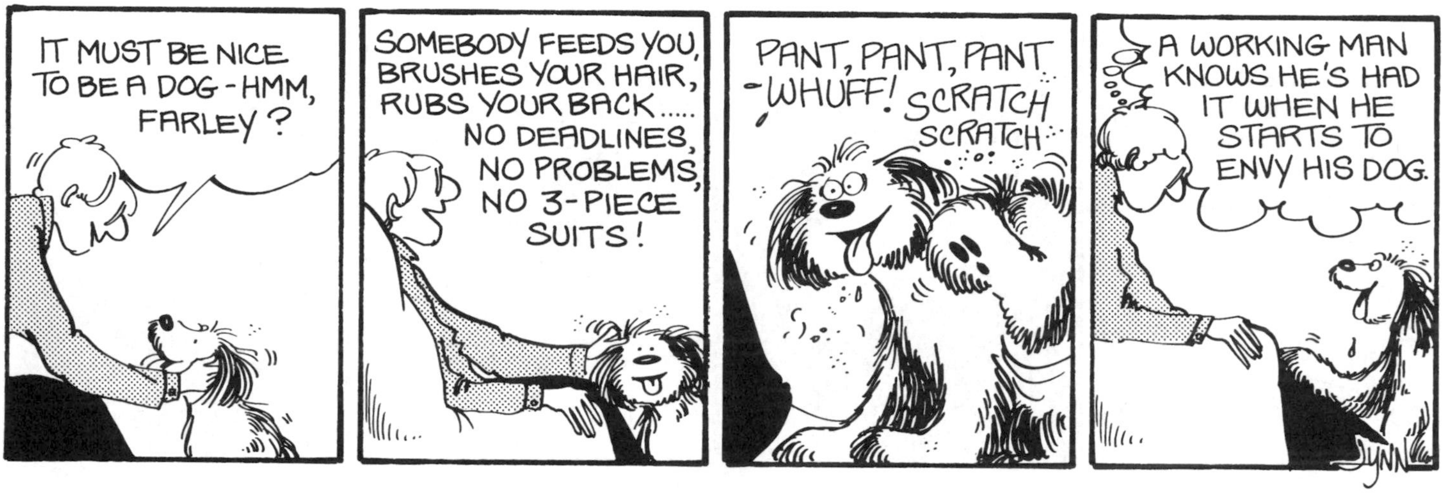
IT MUST BE NICE TO BE A DOG - HMM, FARLEY?
SOMEBODY FEEDS YOU, BRUSHES YOUR HAIR, RUBS YOUR BACK..... NO DEADLINES, NO PROBLEMS, NO 3-PIECE SUITS!
PANT, PANT, PANT
WHUFF!
SCRATCH SCRATCH
A WORKING MAN KNOWS HE'S HAD IT WHEN HE STARTS TO ENVY HIS DOG.
LYNN

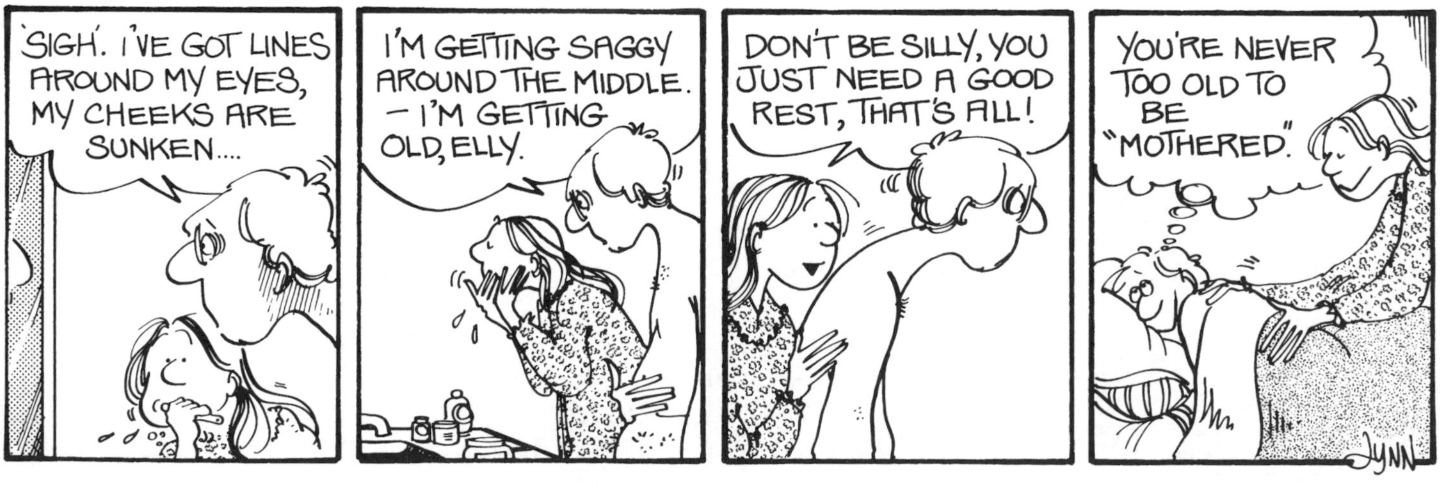
'SIGH'. I'VE GOT LINES AROUND MY EYES, MY CHEEKS ARE SUNKEN....
I'M GETTING SAGGY AROUND THE MIDDLE. - I'M GETTING OLD, ELLY.
DON'T BE SILLY, YOU JUST NEED A GOOD REST, THAT'S ALL!
YOU'RE NEVER TOO OLD TO BE "MOTHERED."
LYNN

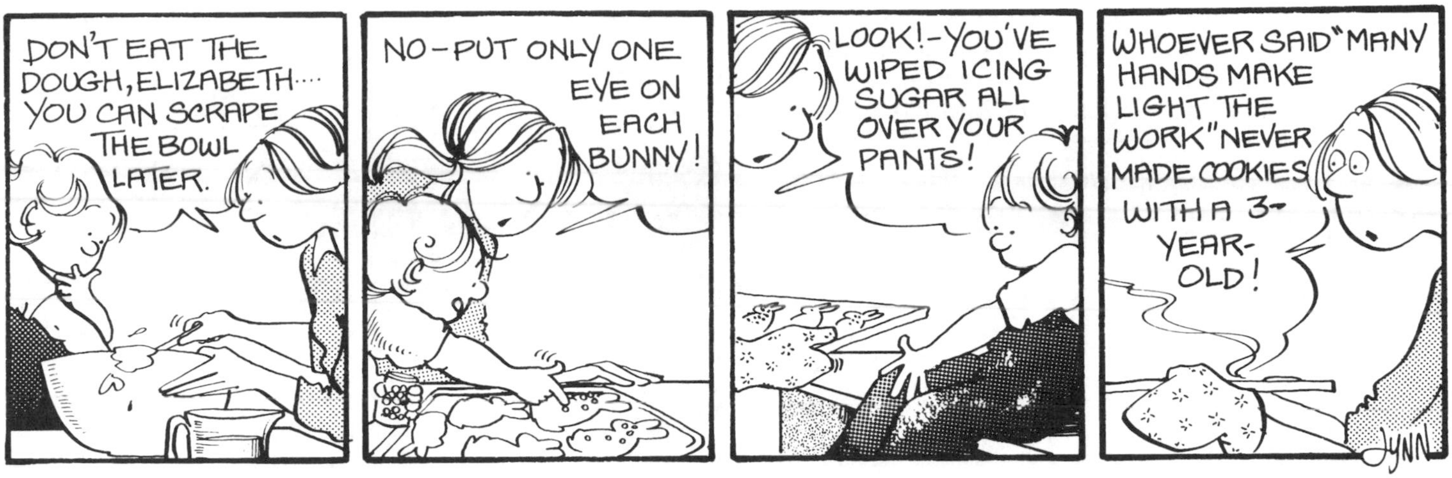
DON'T EAT THE DOUGH, ELIZABETH... YOU CAN SCRAPE THE BOWL LATER.
NO - PUT ONLY ONE EYE ON EACH BUNNY!
LOOK! - YOU'VE WIPED ICING SUGAR ALL OVER YOUR PANTS!
WHOEVER SAID "MANY HANDS MAKE LIGHT THE WORK" NEVER MADE COOKIES WITH A 3-YEAR-OLD!
LYNN

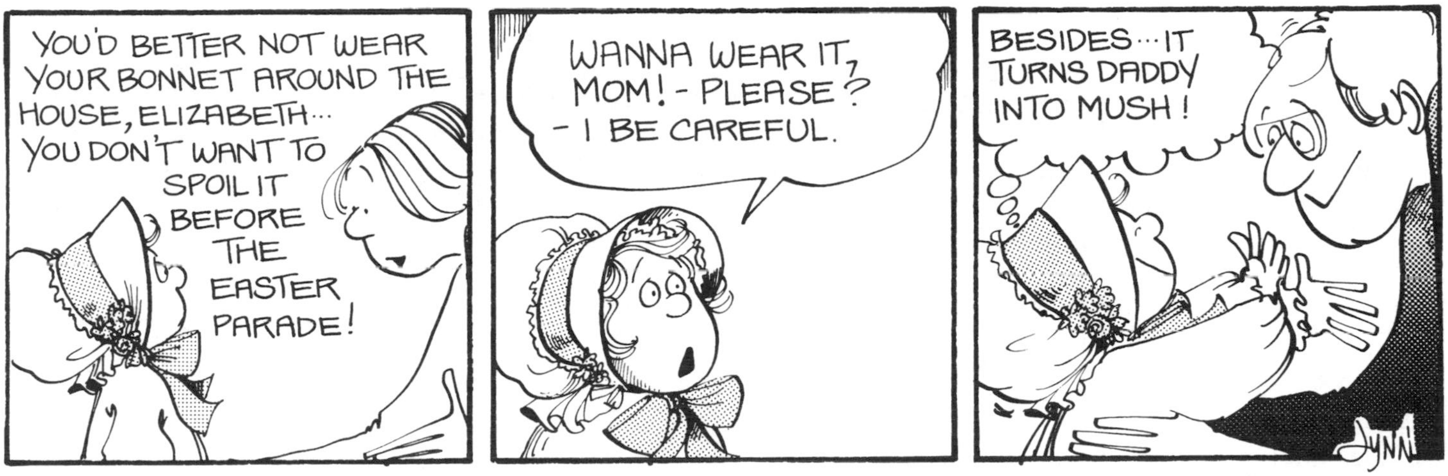
YOU'D BETTER NOT WEAR YOUR BONNET AROUND THE HOUSE, ELIZABETH... YOU DON'T WANT TO SPOIL IT BEFORE THE EASTER PARADE!
WANNA WEAR IT, MOM! - PLEASE? - I BE CAREFUL.
BESIDES... IT TURNS DADDY INTO MUSH!
LYNN

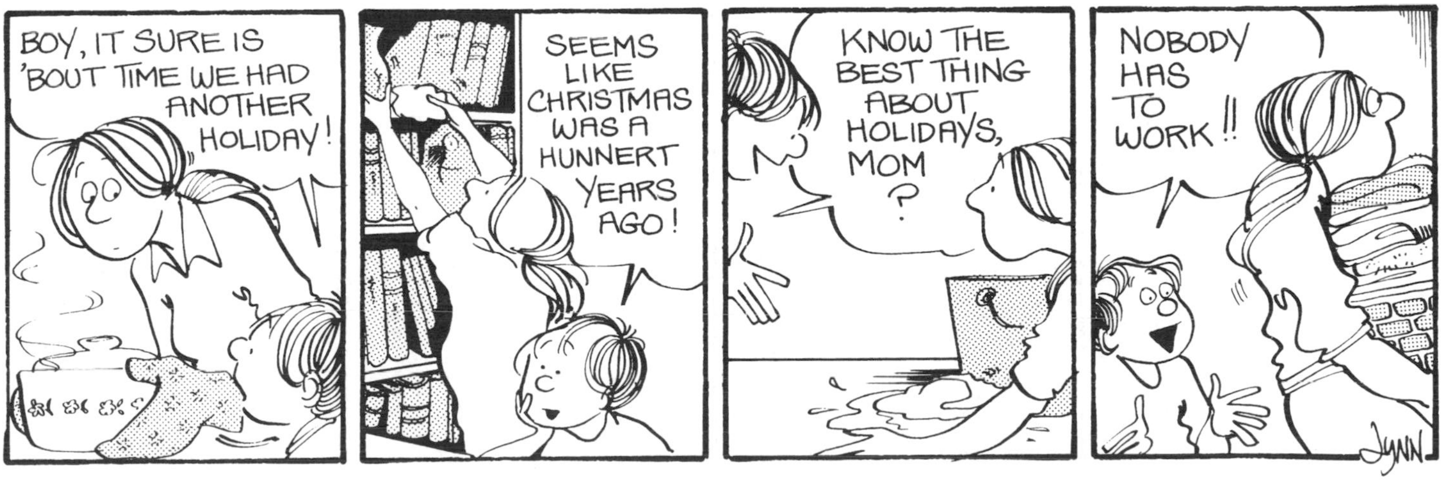
BOY, IT SURE IS 'BOUT TIME WE HAD ANOTHER HOLIDAY!
SEEMS LIKE CHRISTMAS WAS A HUNNERT YEARS AGO!
KNOW THE BEST THING ABOUT HOLIDAYS, MOM?
NOBODY HAS TO WORK!!
LYNN

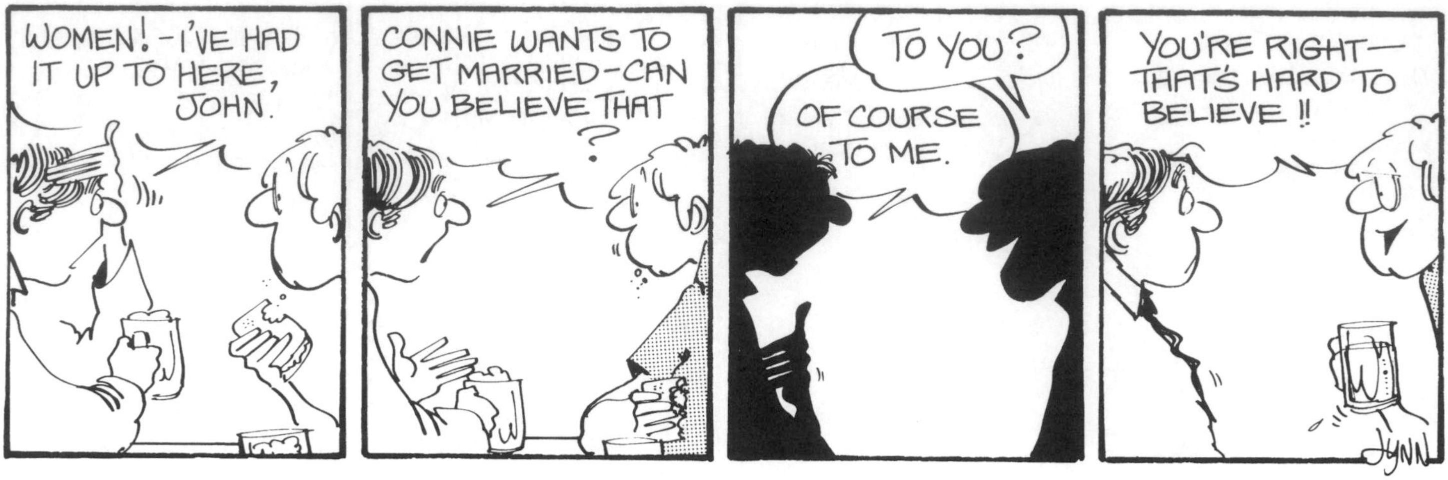
WOMEN! - I'VE HAD IT UP TO HERE, JOHN!
CONNIE WANTS TO GET MARRIED - CAN YOU BELIEVE THAT?
TO YOU?
OF COURSE TO ME.
YOU'RE RIGHT— THAT'S HARD TO BELIEVE !!
LYNN

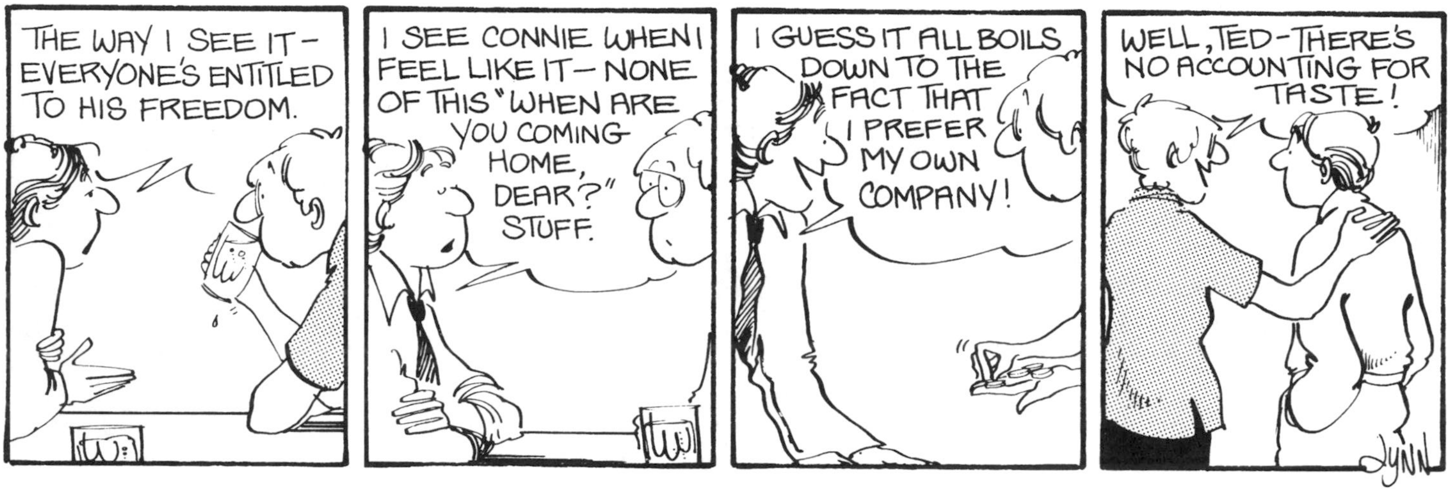
THE WAY I SEE IT - EVERYONE'S ENTITLED TO HIS FREEDOM.
I SEE CONNIE WHEN I FEEL LIKE IT— NONE OF THIS "WHEN ARE YOU COMING HOME, DEAR?" STUFF.
I GUESS IT ALL BOILS DOWN TO THE FACT THAT I PREFER MY OWN COMPANY!
WELL, TED - THERE'S NO ACCOUNTING FOR TASTE!
LYNN

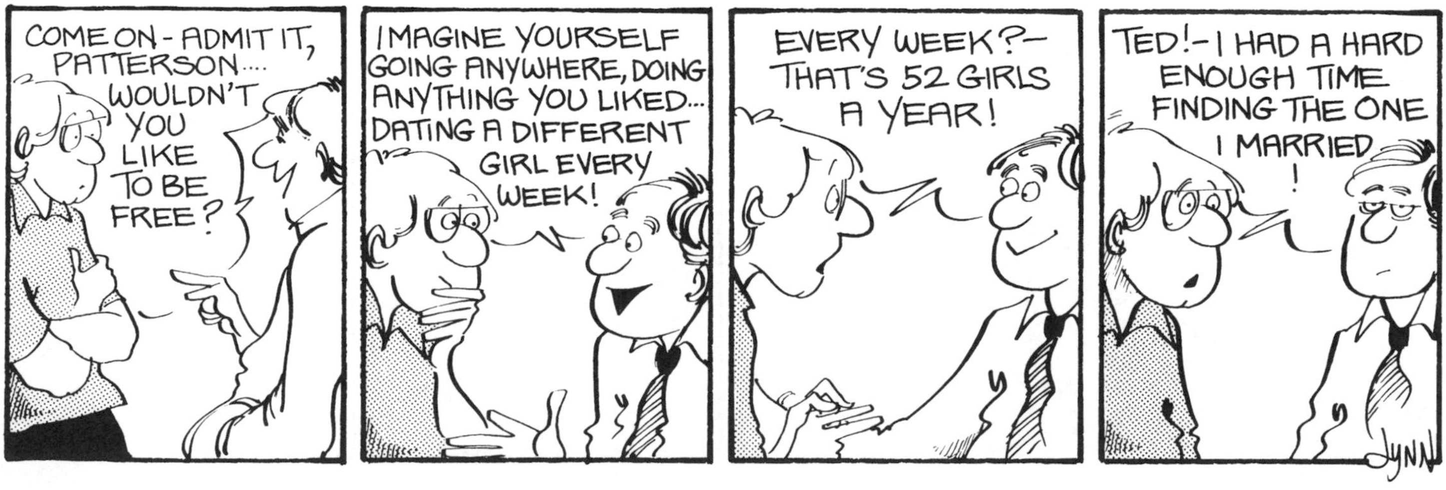
COME ON - ADMIT IT, PATTERSON.... WOULDN'T YOU LIKE TO BE FREE?
IMAGINE YOURSELF GOING ANYWHERE, DOING ANYTHING YOU LIKED... DATING A DIFFERENT GIRL EVERY WEEK!
EVERY WEEK?— THAT'S 52 GIRLS A YEAR!
TED! - I HAD A HARD ENOUGH TIME FINDING THE ONE I MARRIED!
LYNN

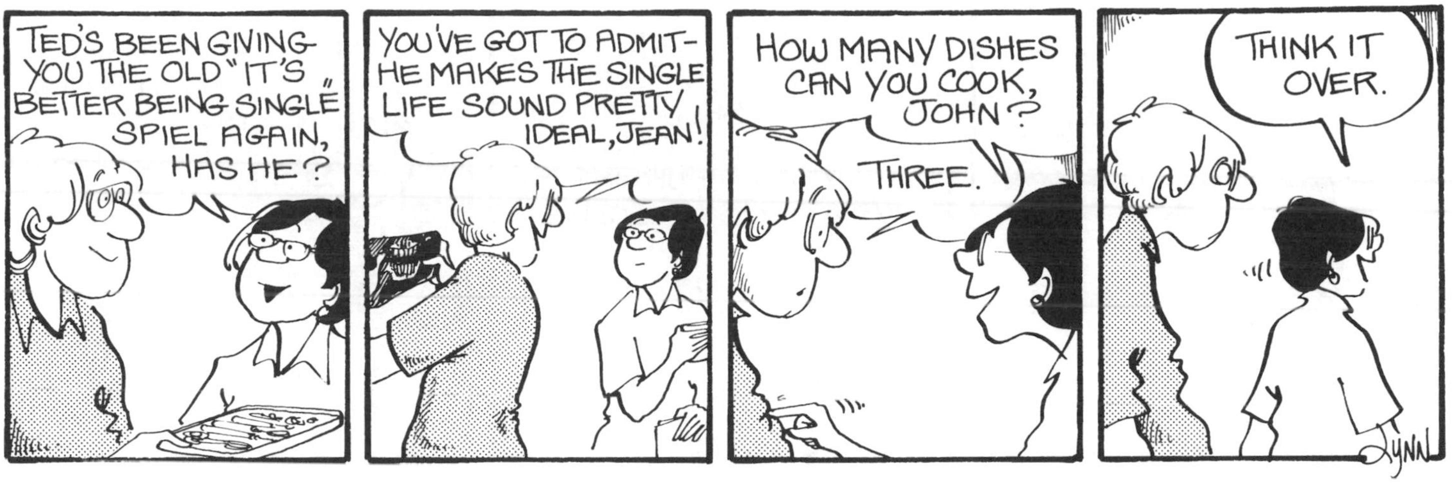
TED'S BEEN GIVING YOU THE OLD "IT'S BETTER BEING SINGLE" SPIEL AGAIN, HAS HE?
YOU'VE GOT TO ADMIT- HE MAKES THE SINGLE LIFE SOUND PRETTY IDEAL, JEAN!
HOW MANY DISHES CAN YOU COOK, JOHN?
THREE.
THINK IT OVER.
LYNN

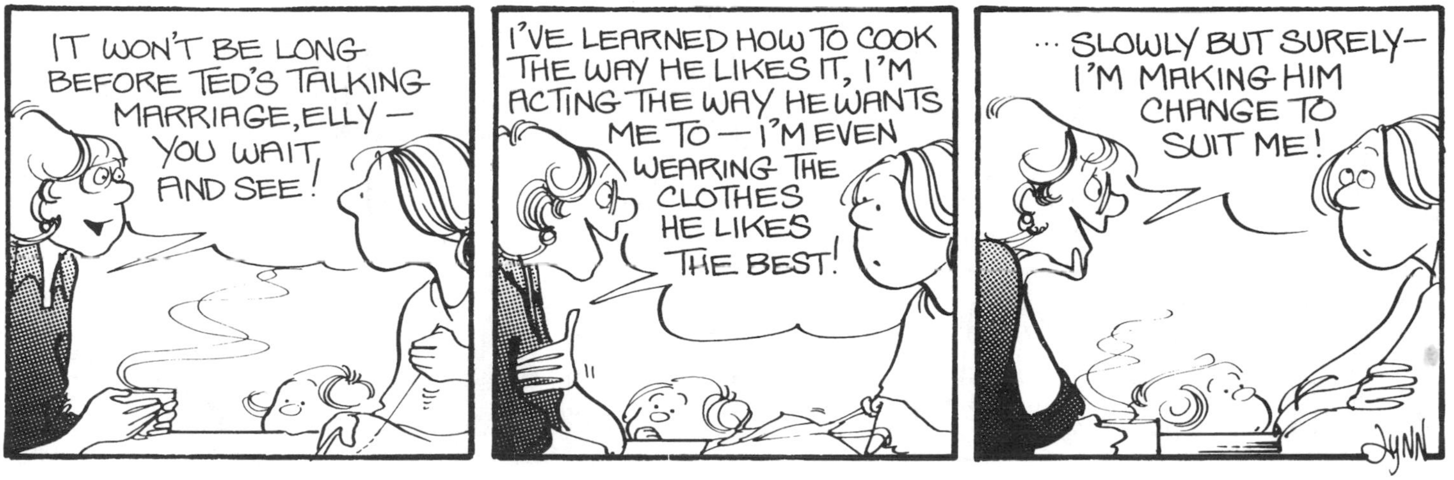
IT WON'T BE LONG BEFORE TED'S TALKING MARRIAGE, ELLY — YOU WAIT, AND SEE!
I'VE LEARNED HOW TO COOK THE WAY HE LIKES IT, I'M ACTING THE WAY HE WANTS ME TO — I'M EVEN WEARING THE CLOTHES HE LIKES THE BEST!
... SLOWLY BUT SURELY- I'M MAKING HIM CHANGE TO SUIT ME!
LYNN

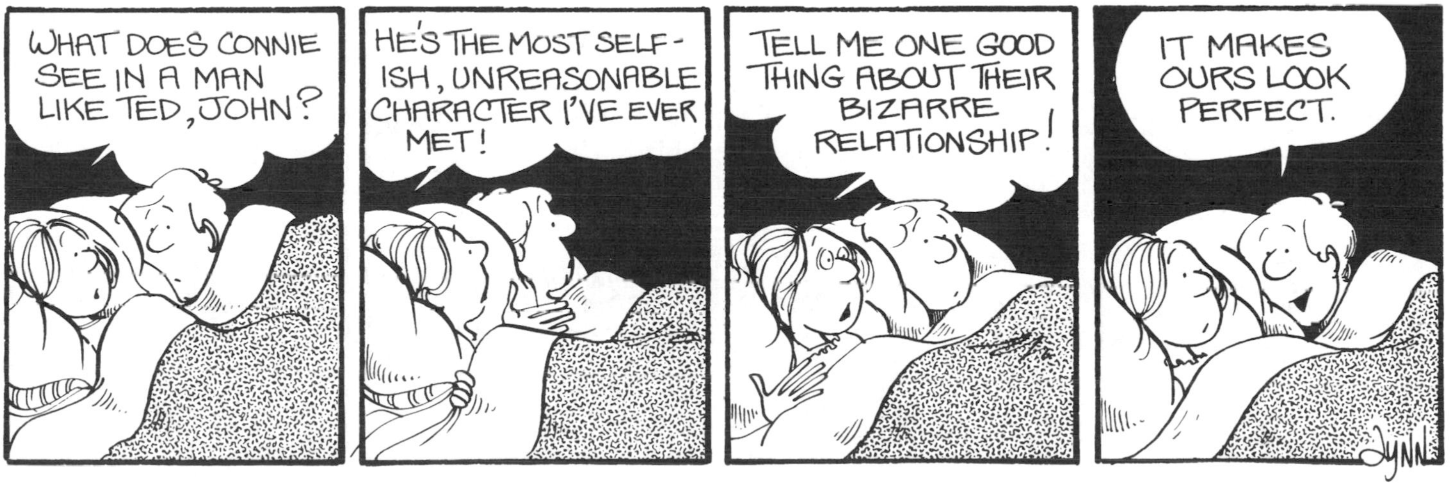
WHAT DOES CONNIE SEE IN A MAN LIKE TED, JOHN?
HE'S THE MOST SELF-ISH, UNREASONABLE CHARACTER I'VE EVER MET!
TELL ME ONE GOOD THING ABOUT THEIR BIZARRE RELATIONSHIP!
IT MAKES OURS LOOK PERFECT.
LYNN

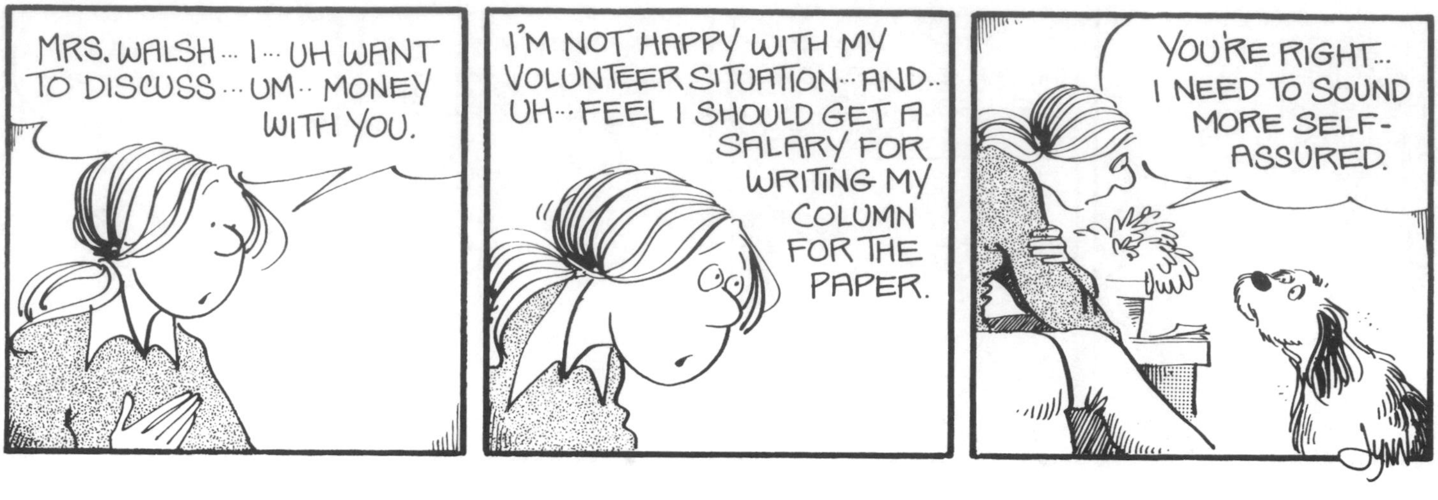
MRS. WALSH... I... UH WANT TO DISCUSS... UM.. MONEY WITH YOU.
I'M NOT HAPPY WITH MY VOLUNTEER SITUATION... AND.. UH... FEEL I SHOULD GET A SALARY FOR WRITING MY COLUMN FOR THE PAPER.
YOU'RE RIGHT... I NEED TO SOUND MORE SELF-ASSURED.
LYNN

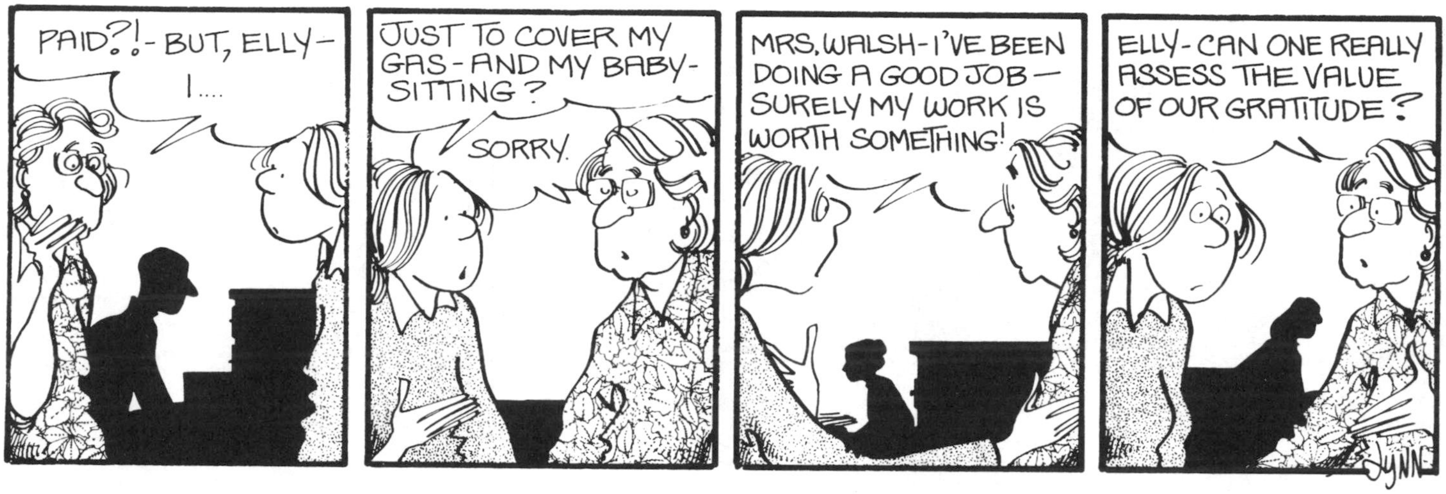
PAID?!- BUT, ELLY- I....
JUST TO COVER MY GAS- AND MY BABY-SITTING?
SORRY.
MRS. WALSH- I'VE BEEN DOING A GOOD JOB— SURELY MY WORK IS WORTH SOMETHING!
ELLY- CAN ONE REALLY ASSESS THE VALUE OF OUR GRATITUDE?
LYNN

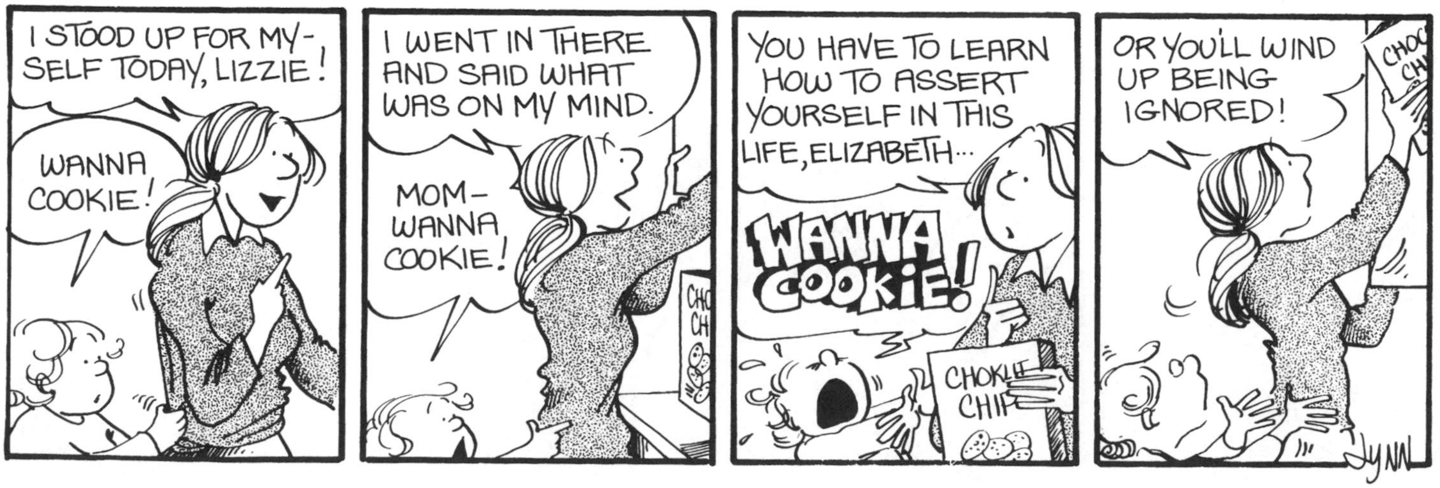
I STOOD UP FOR MY-SELF TODAY, LIZZIE!
WANNA COOKIE!
I WENT IN THERE AND SAID WHAT WAS ON MY MIND.
MOM- WANNA COOKIE!
YOU HAVE TO LEARN HOW TO ASSERT YOURSELF IN THIS LIFE, ELIZABETH...
WANNA COOKIE!
CHOKLE CHIP
OR YOU'LL WIND UP BEING IGNORED!
LYNN

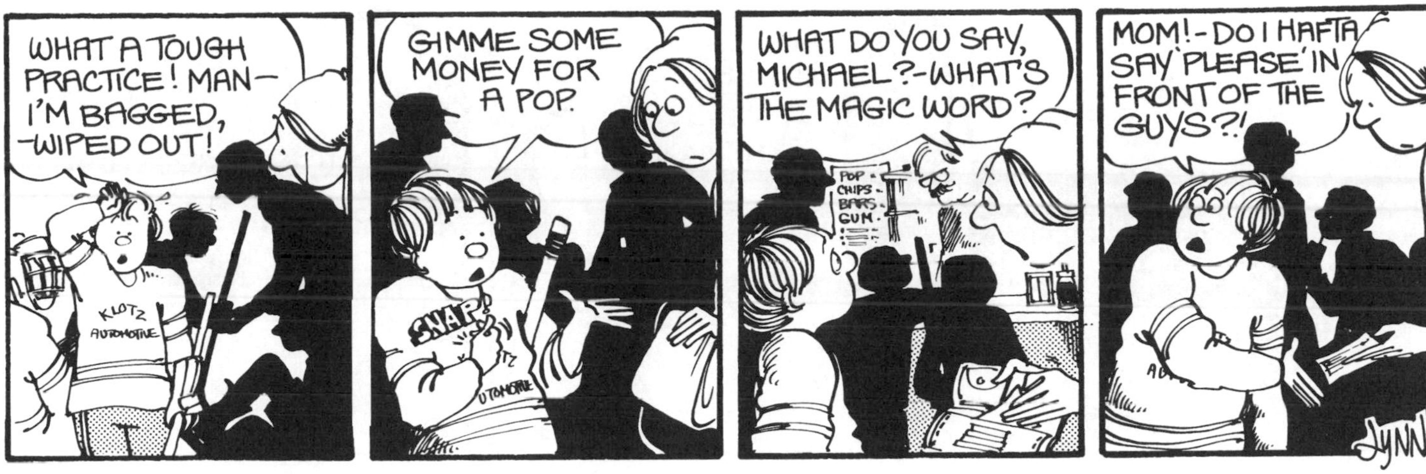

WHAT A TOUGH PRACTICE! MAN— I'M BAGGED, —WIPED OUT!
KLOTZ AUTOMOTIVE
GIMME SOME MONEY FOR A POP.
SNAP
WHAT DO YOU SAY, MICHAEL?-WHAT'S THE MAGIC WORD?
POP CHIPS BARS GUM
MOM!-DO I HAFTA SAY 'PLEASE' IN FRONT OF THE GUYS?!
LYNN

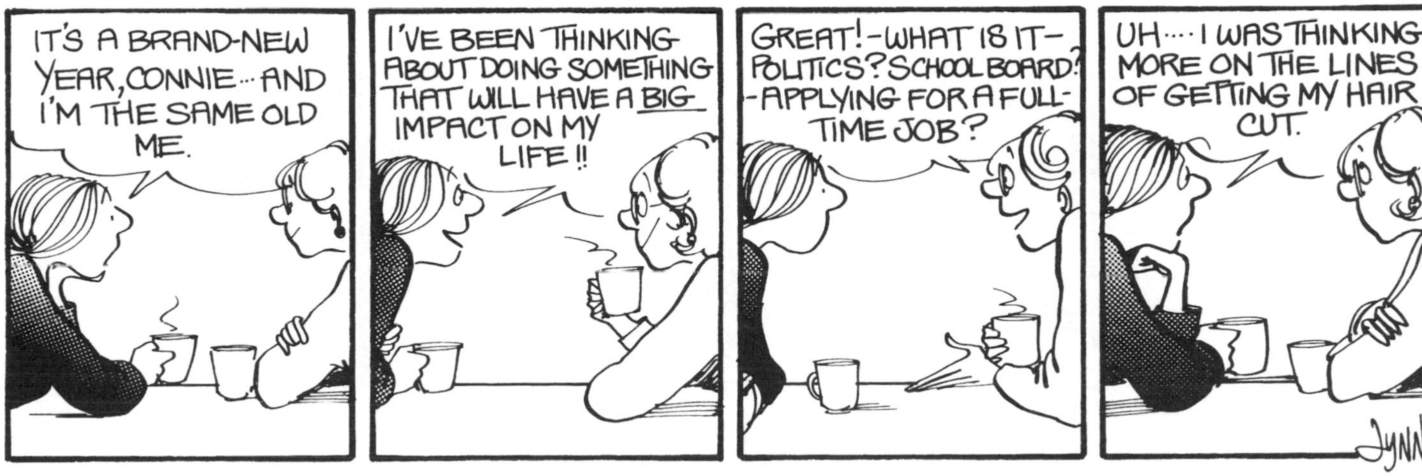

IT'S A BRAND-NEW YEAR, CONNIE... AND I'M THE SAME OLD ME.
I'VE BEEN THINKING ABOUT DOING SOMETHING THAT WILL HAVE A BIG IMPACT ON MY LIFE!!
GREAT!-WHAT IS IT-POLITICS? SCHOOL BOARD? -APPLYING FOR A FULL-TIME JOB?
UH.... I WAS THINKING MORE ON THE LINES OF GETTING MY HAIR CUT.
LYNN

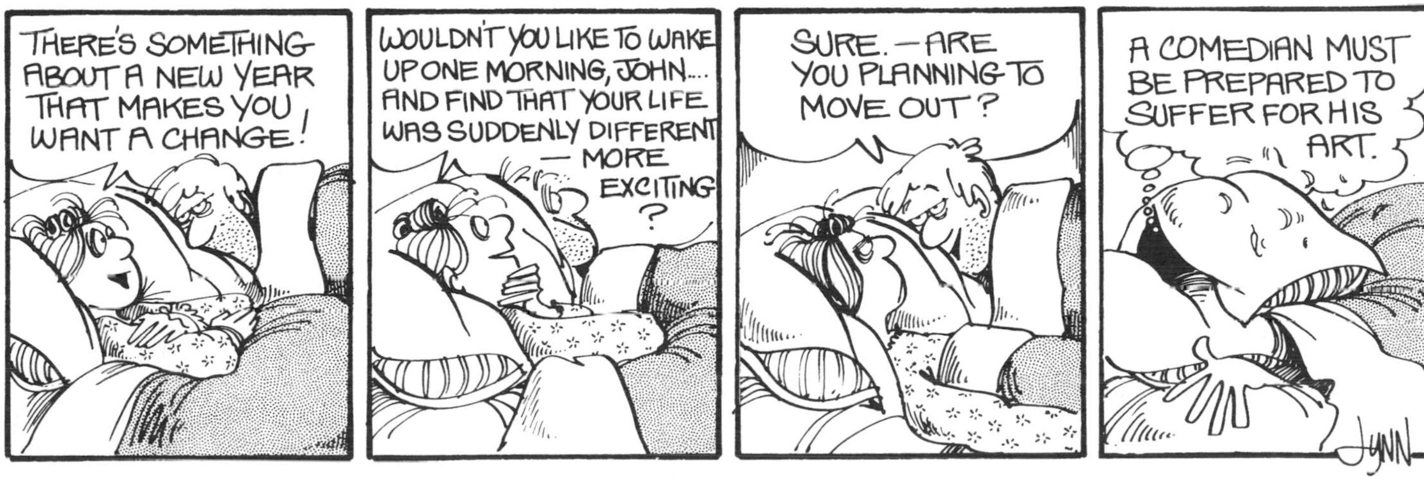

THERE'S SOMETHING ABOUT A NEW YEAR THAT MAKES YOU WANT A CHANGE!
WOULDN'T YOU LIKE TO WAKE UP ONE MORNING, JOHN.... AND FIND THAT YOUR LIFE WAS SUDDENLY DIFFERENT — MORE EXCITING?
SURE. —ARE YOU PLANNING TO MOVE OUT?
A COMEDIAN MUST BE PREPARED TO SUFFER FOR HIS ART.
LYNN

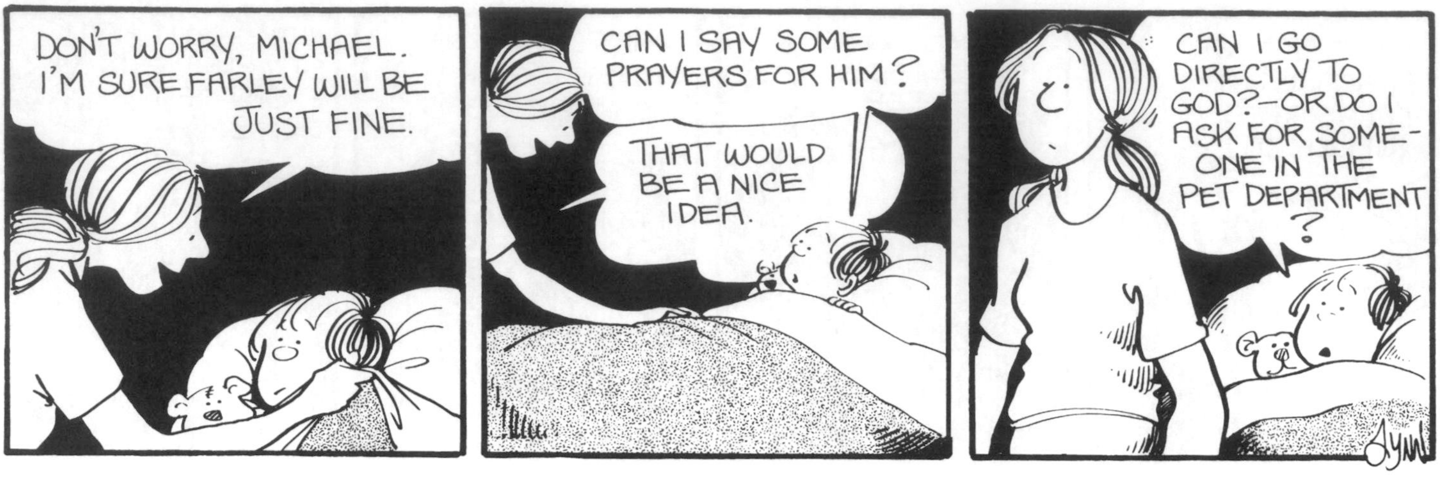
DON'T WORRY, MICHAEL. I'M SURE FARLEY WILL BE JUST FINE.
CAN I SAY SOME PRAYERS FOR HIM?
THAT WOULD BE A NICE IDEA.
CAN I GO DIRECTLY TO GOD?–OR DO I ASK FOR SOMEONE IN THE PET DEPARTMENT?
LYNN

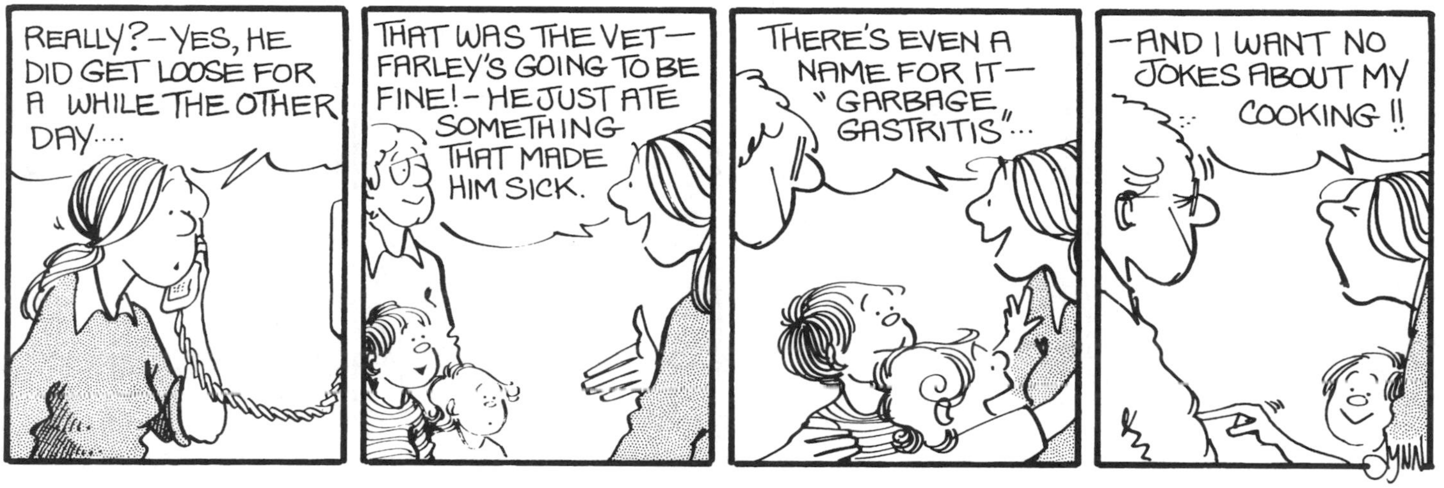
REALLY?–YES, HE DID GET LOOSE FOR A WHILE THE OTHER DAY....
THAT WAS THE VET–FARLEY'S GOING TO BE FINE!–HE JUST ATE SOMETHING THAT MADE HIM SICK.
THERE'S EVEN A NAME FOR IT–"GARBAGE GASTRITIS"...
–AND I WANT NO JOKES ABOUT MY COOKING!!
LYNN

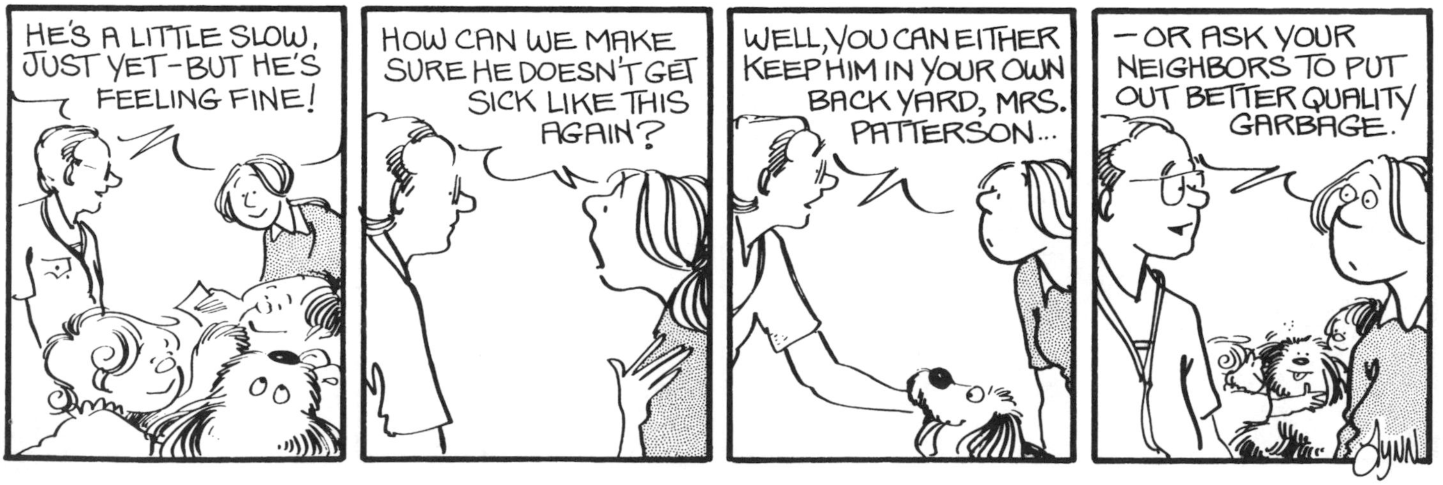
HE'S A LITTLE SLOW, JUST YET–BUT HE'S FEELING FINE!
HOW CAN WE MAKE SURE HE DOESN'T GET SICK LIKE THIS AGAIN?
WELL, YOU CAN EITHER KEEP HIM IN YOUR OWN BACK YARD, MRS. PATTERSON...
–OR ASK YOUR NEIGHBORS TO PUT OUT BETTER QUALITY GARBAGE.
LYNN

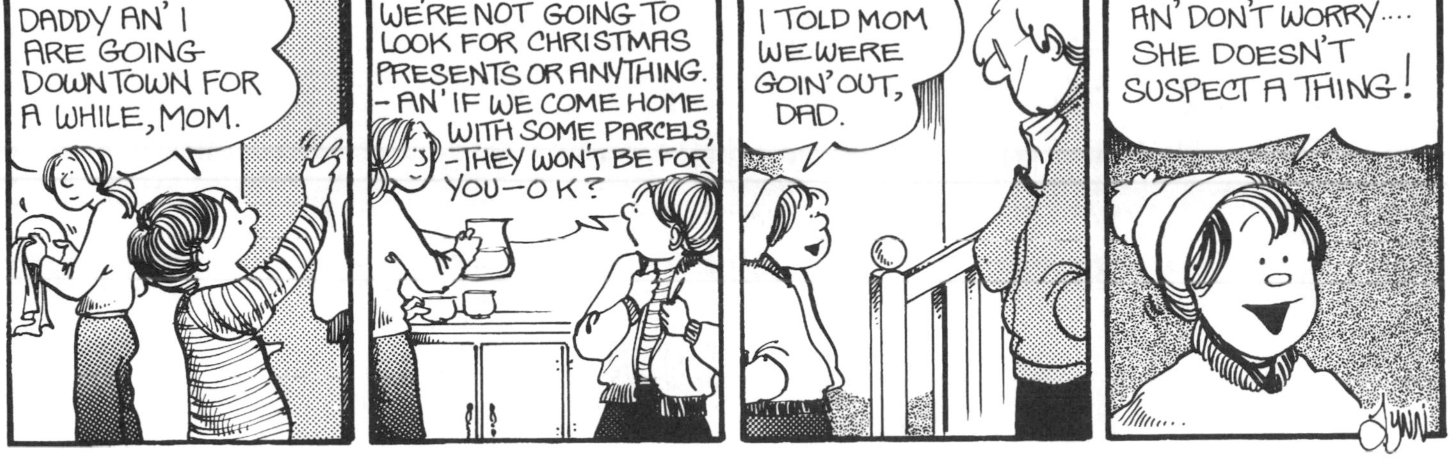
DADDY AN' I ARE GOING DOWNTOWN FOR A WHILE, MOM.
WE'RE NOT GOING TO LOOK FOR CHRISTMAS PRESENTS OR ANYTHING. – AN' IF WE COME HOME WITH SOME PARCELS, – THEY WON'T BE FOR YOU – O K?
I TOLD MOM WE WERE GOIN' OUT, DAD.
AN' DON'T WORRY.... SHE DOESN'T SUSPECT A THING!
LYNN

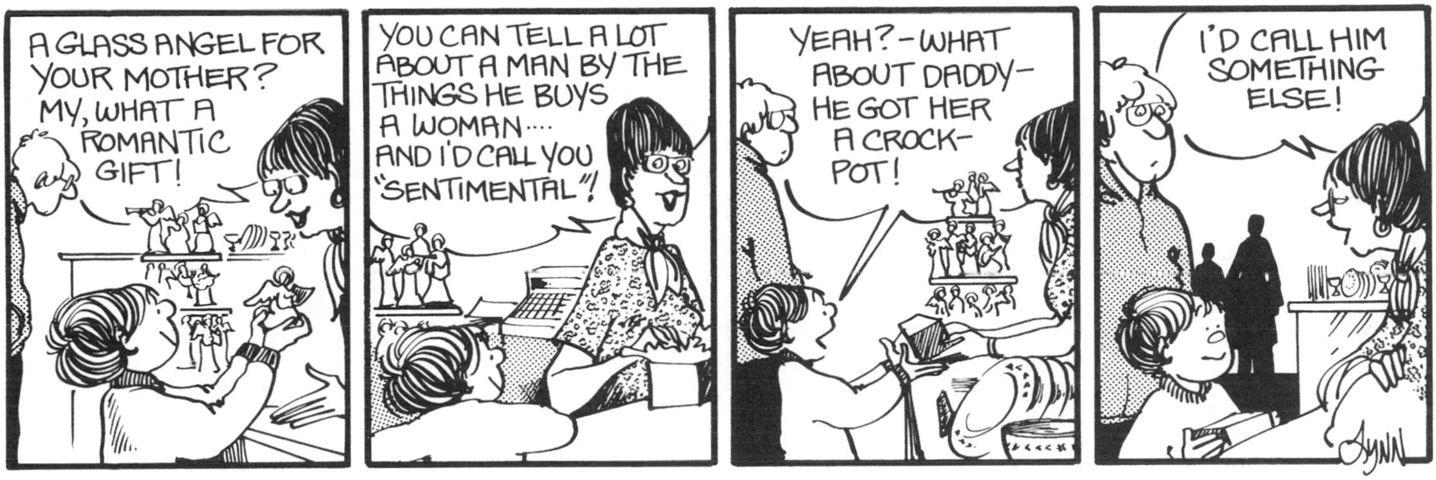
A GLASS ANGEL FOR YOUR MOTHER? MY, WHAT A ROMANTIC GIFT!
YOU CAN TELL A LOT ABOUT A MAN BY THE THINGS HE BUYS A WOMAN.... AND I'D CALL YOU "SENTIMENTAL"!
YEAH? – WHAT ABOUT DADDY – HE GOT HER A CROCK-POT!
I'D CALL HIM SOMETHING ELSE!
LYNN

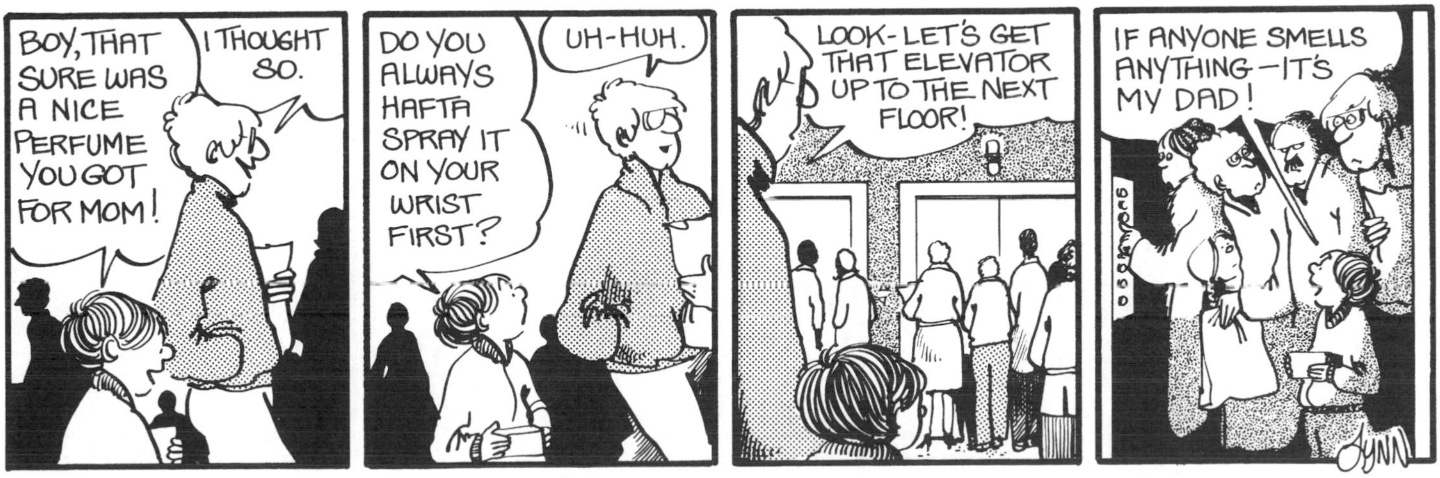
BOY, THAT SURE WAS A NICE PERFUME YOU GOT FOR MOM!
I THOUGHT SO.
DO YOU ALWAYS HAFTA SPRAY IT ON YOUR WRIST FIRST?
UH-HUH.
LOOK – LET'S GET THAT ELEVATOR UP TO THE NEXT FLOOR!
IF ANYONE SMELLS ANYTHING – IT'S MY DAD!
LYNN

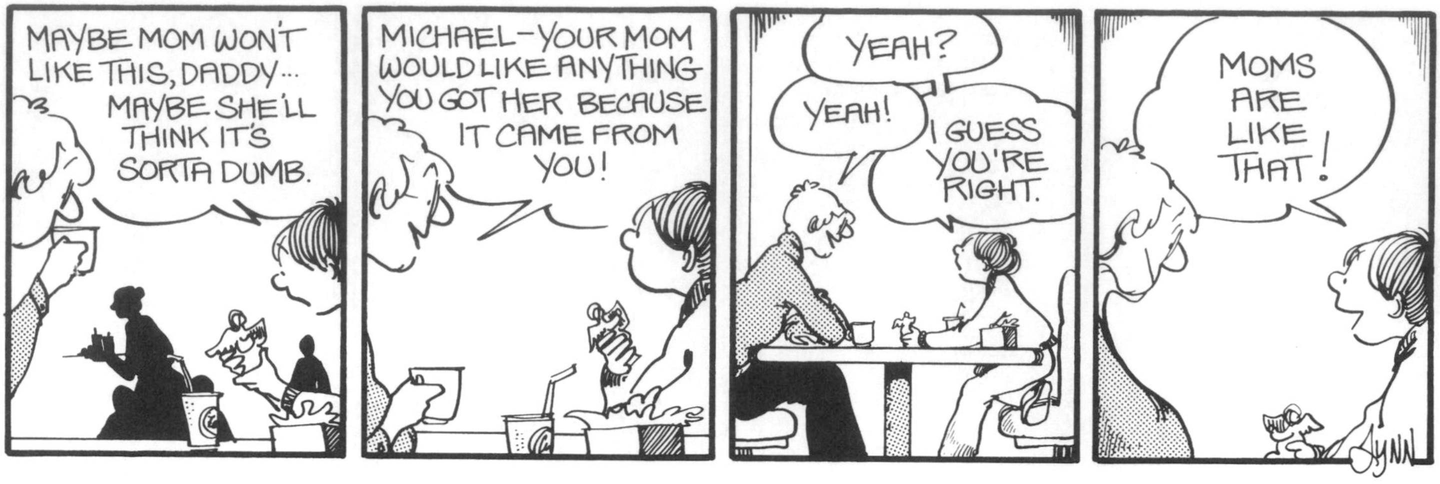
MAYBE MOM WON'T LIKE THIS, DADDY... MAYBE SHE'LL THINK IT'S SORTA DUMB.
MICHAEL–YOUR MOM WOULD LIKE ANYTHING YOU GOT HER BECAUSE IT CAME FROM YOU!
YEAH?
YEAH!
I GUESS YOU'RE RIGHT.
MOMS ARE LIKE THAT!

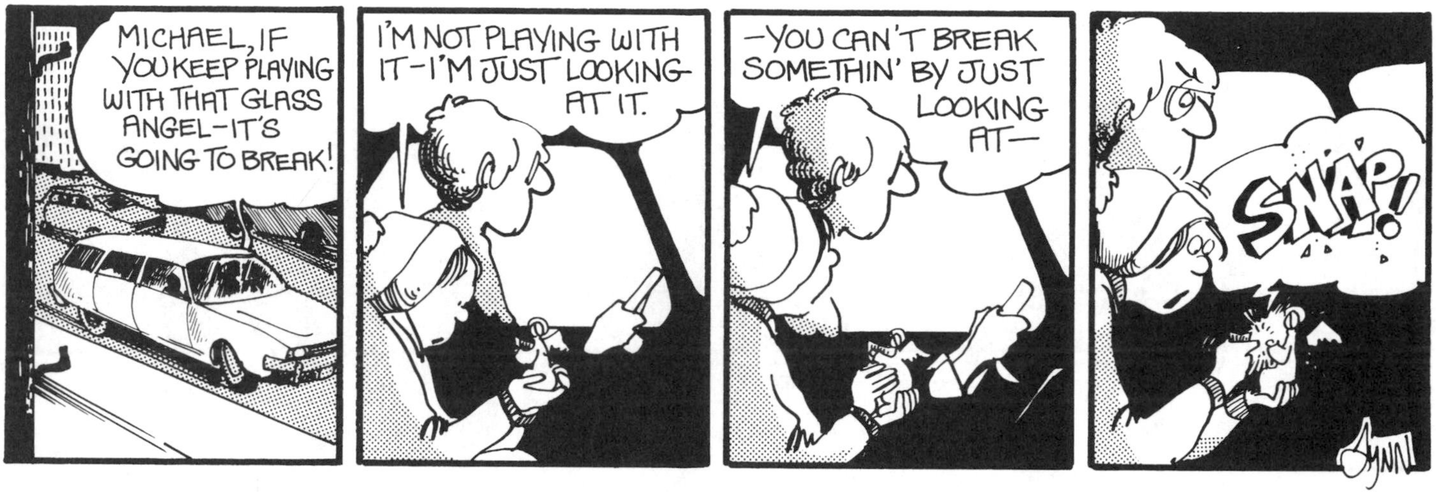
MICHAEL, IF YOU KEEP PLAYING WITH THAT GLASS ANGEL–IT'S GOING TO BREAK!
I'M NOT PLAYING WITH IT–I'M JUST LOOKING AT IT.
–YOU CAN'T BREAK SOMETHIN' BY JUST LOOKING AT—
SNAP!!

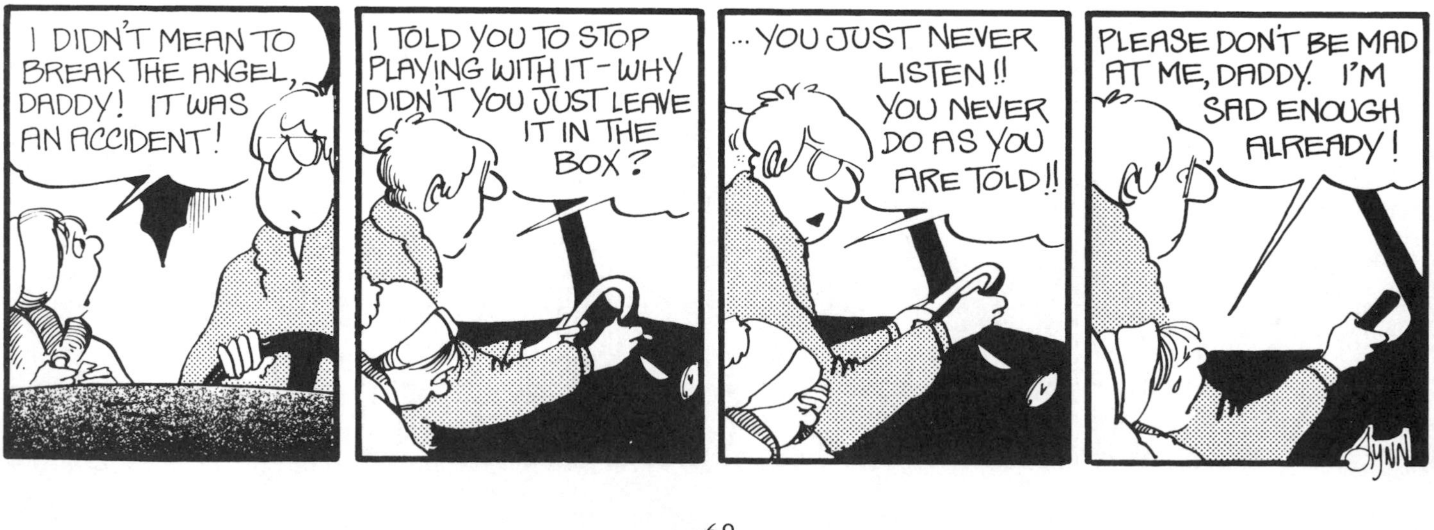
I DIDN'T MEAN TO BREAK THE ANGEL, DADDY! IT WAS AN ACCIDENT!
I TOLD YOU TO STOP PLAYING WITH IT–WHY DIDN'T YOU JUST LEAVE IT IN THE BOX?
...YOU JUST NEVER LISTEN!! YOU NEVER DO AS YOU ARE TOLD!!
PLEASE DON'T BE MAD AT ME, DADDY. I'M SAD ENOUGH ALREADY!

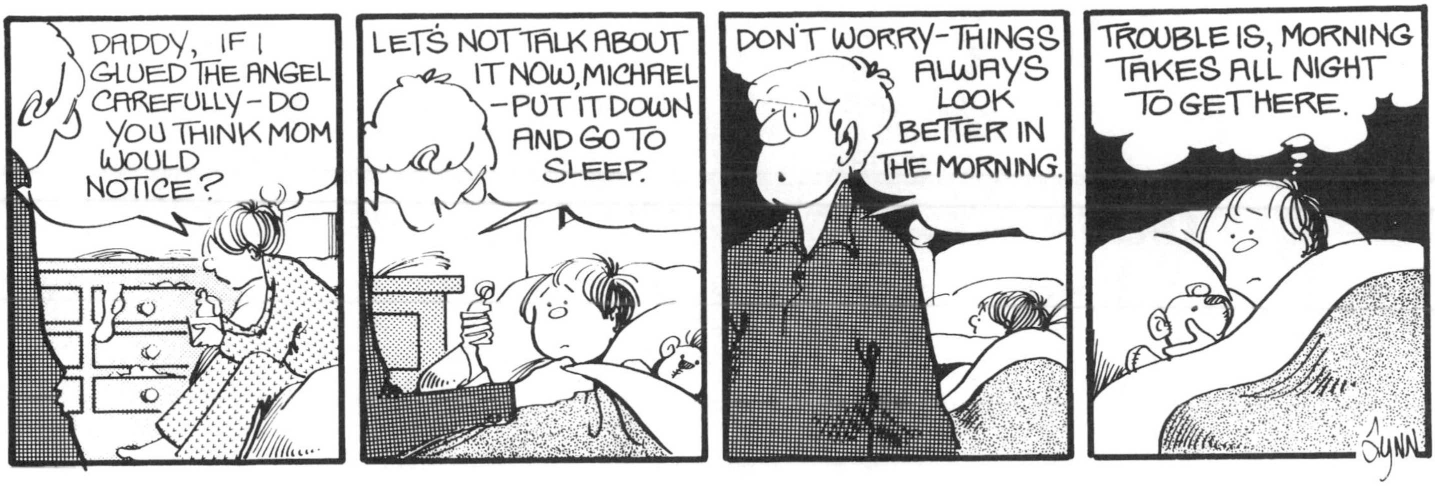
DADDY, IF I GLUED THE ANGEL CAREFULLY - DO YOU THINK MOM WOULD NOTICE?
LET'S NOT TALK ABOUT IT NOW, MICHAEL - PUT IT DOWN AND GO TO SLEEP.
DON'T WORRY - THINGS ALWAYS LOOK BETTER IN THE MORNING.
TROUBLE IS, MORNING TAKES ALL NIGHT TO GET HERE.
Lynn

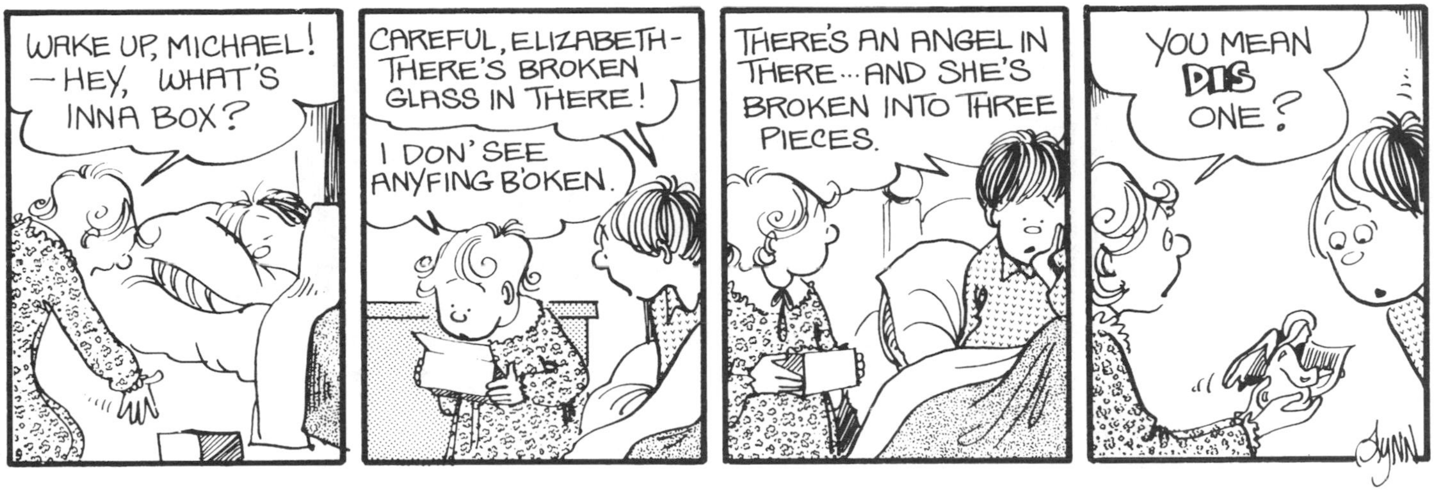
WAKE UP, MICHAEL! - HEY, WHAT'S INNA BOX?
CAREFUL, ELIZABETH - THERE'S BROKEN GLASS IN THERE!
I DON' SEE ANYFING B'OKEN.
THERE'S AN ANGEL IN THERE... AND SHE'S BROKEN INTO THREE PIECES.
YOU MEAN DIS ONE?
Lynn

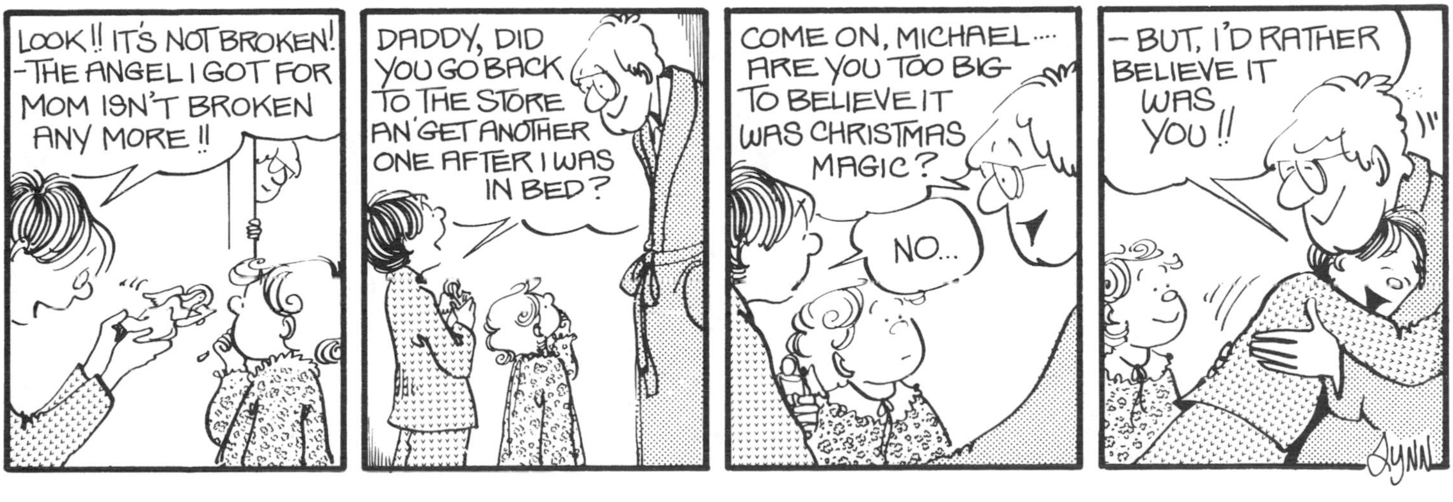
LOOK!! IT'S NOT BROKEN! - THE ANGEL I GOT FOR MOM ISN'T BROKEN ANY MORE!!
DADDY, DID YOU GO BACK TO THE STORE AN' GET ANOTHER ONE AFTER I WAS IN BED?
COME ON, MICHAEL.... ARE YOU TOO BIG TO BELIEVE IT WAS CHRISTMAS MAGIC?
NO...
- BUT, I'D RATHER BELIEVE IT WAS YOU!!
Lynn

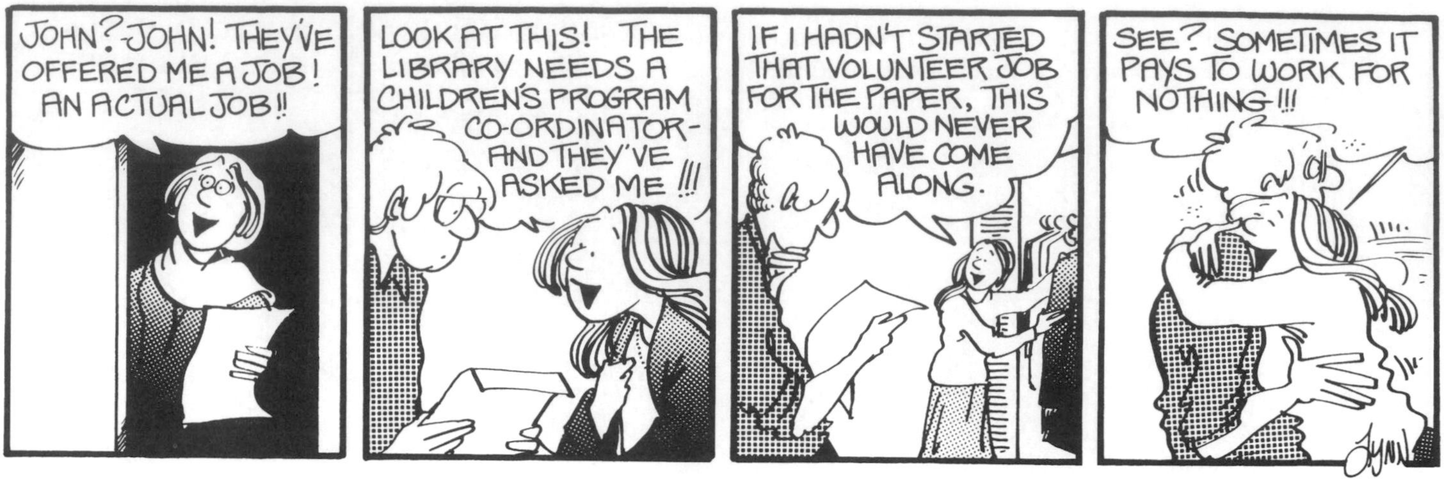
JOHN? JOHN! THEY'VE OFFERED ME A JOB! AN ACTUAL JOB!!
LOOK AT THIS! THE LIBRARY NEEDS A CHILDREN'S PROGRAM CO-ORDINATOR- AND THEY'VE ASKED ME!!!
IF I HADN'T STARTED THAT VOLUNTEER JOB FOR THE PAPER, THIS WOULD NEVER HAVE COME ALONG.
SEE? SOMETIMES IT PAYS TO WORK FOR NOTHING!!!
Lynn

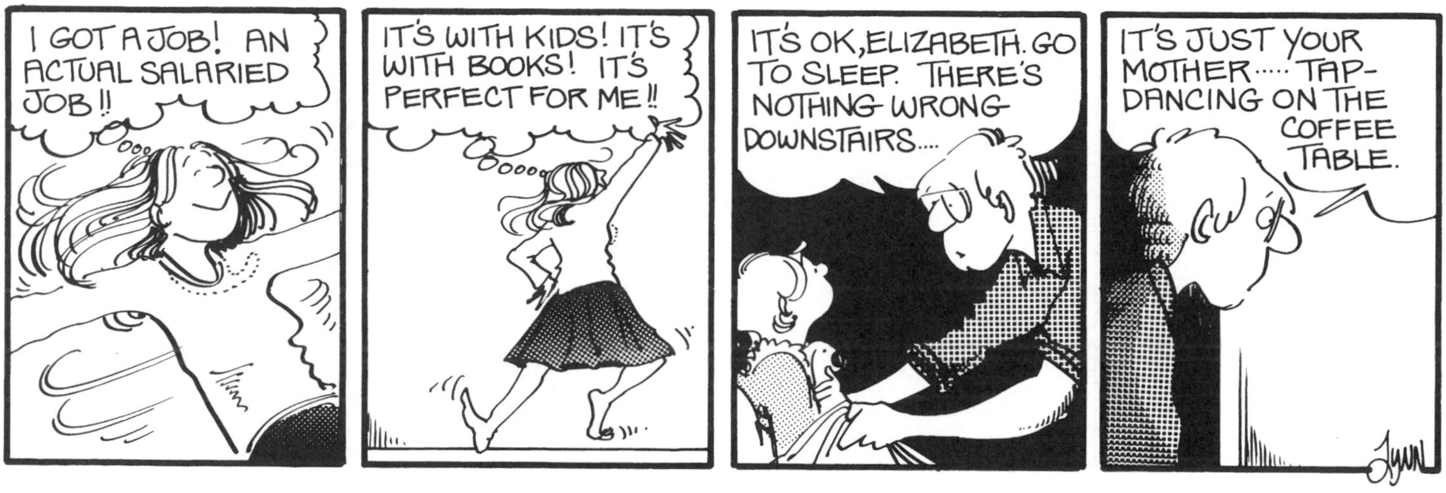
I GOT A JOB! AN ACTUAL SALARIED JOB!!
IT'S WITH KIDS! IT'S WITH BOOKS! IT'S PERFECT FOR ME!!
IT'S OK, ELIZABETH. GO TO SLEEP. THERE'S NOTHING WRONG DOWNSTAIRS....
IT'S JUST YOUR MOTHER..... TAP-DANCING ON THE COFFEE TABLE.
Lynn

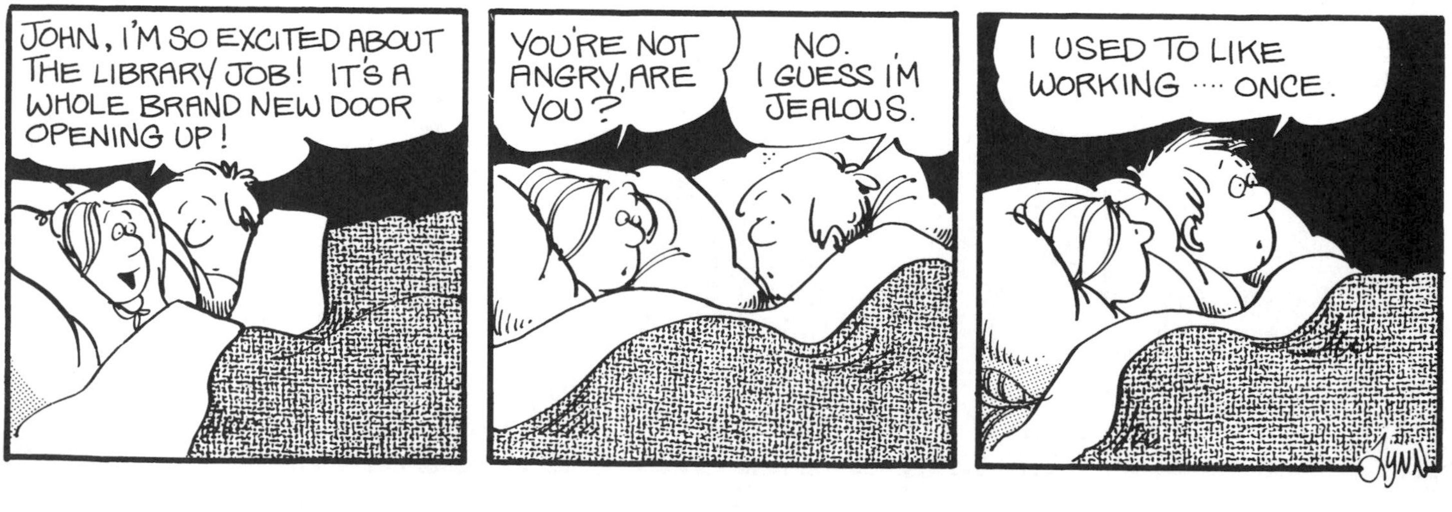
JOHN, I'M SO EXCITED ABOUT THE LIBRARY JOB! IT'S A WHOLE BRAND NEW DOOR OPENING UP!
YOU'RE NOT ANGRY, ARE YOU?
NO. I GUESS I'M JEALOUS.
I USED TO LIKE WORKING .... ONCE.
Lynn

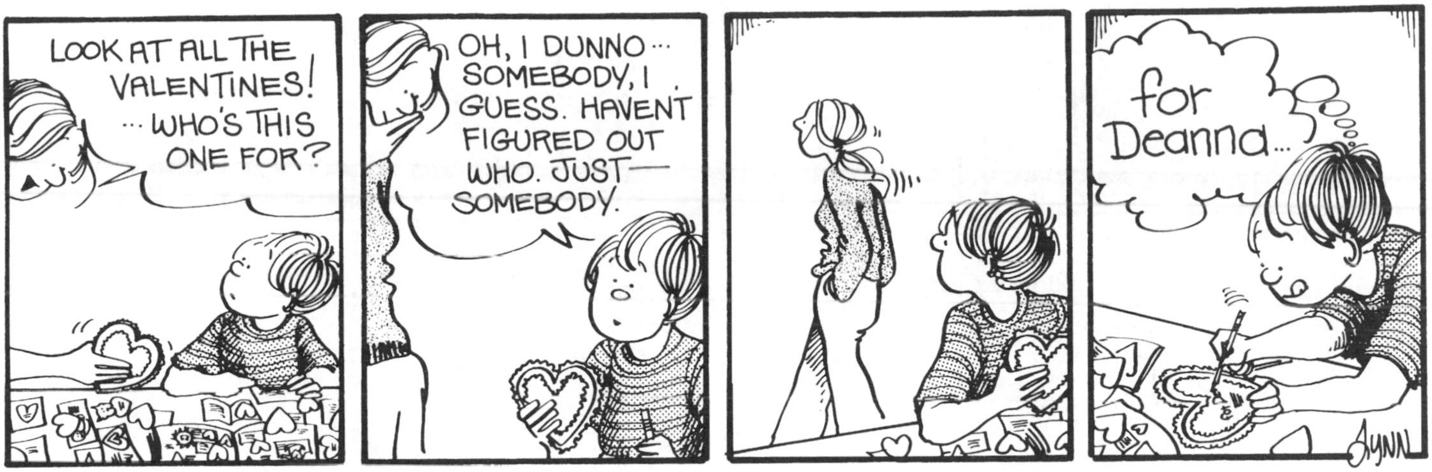
LOOK AT ALL THE VALENTINES! ...WHO'S THIS ONE FOR?
OH, I DUNNO... SOMEBODY, I GUESS. HAVEN'T FIGURED OUT WHO. JUST— SOMEBODY.
for Deanna...

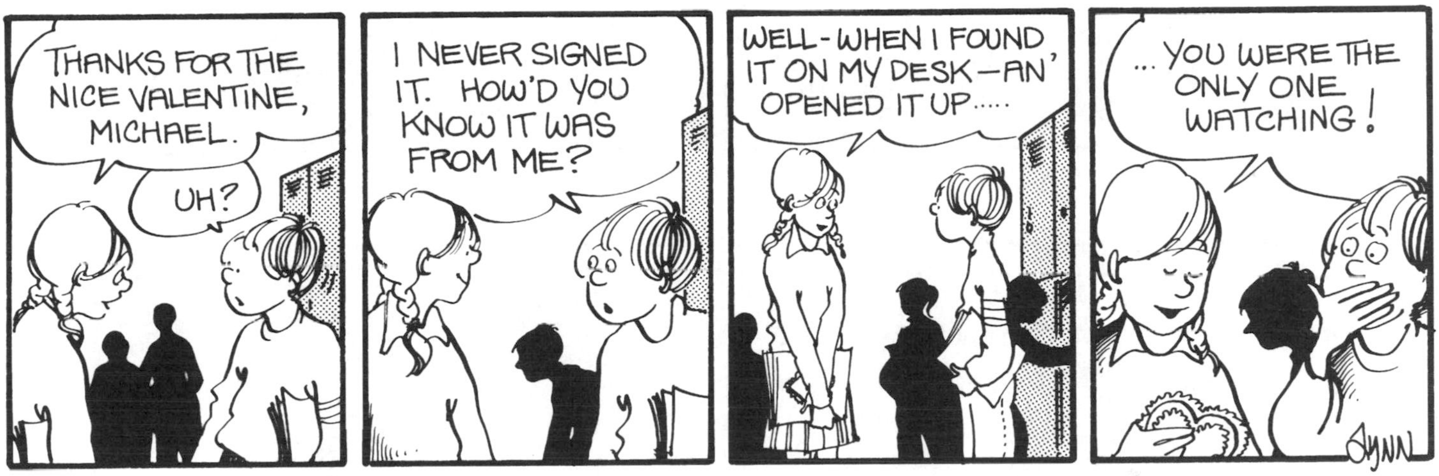
THANKS FOR THE NICE VALENTINE, MICHAEL.
UH?
I NEVER SIGNED IT. HOW'D YOU KNOW IT WAS FROM ME?
WELL- WHEN I FOUND IT ON MY DESK—AN' OPENED IT UP.....
...YOU WERE THE ONLY ONE WATCHING!

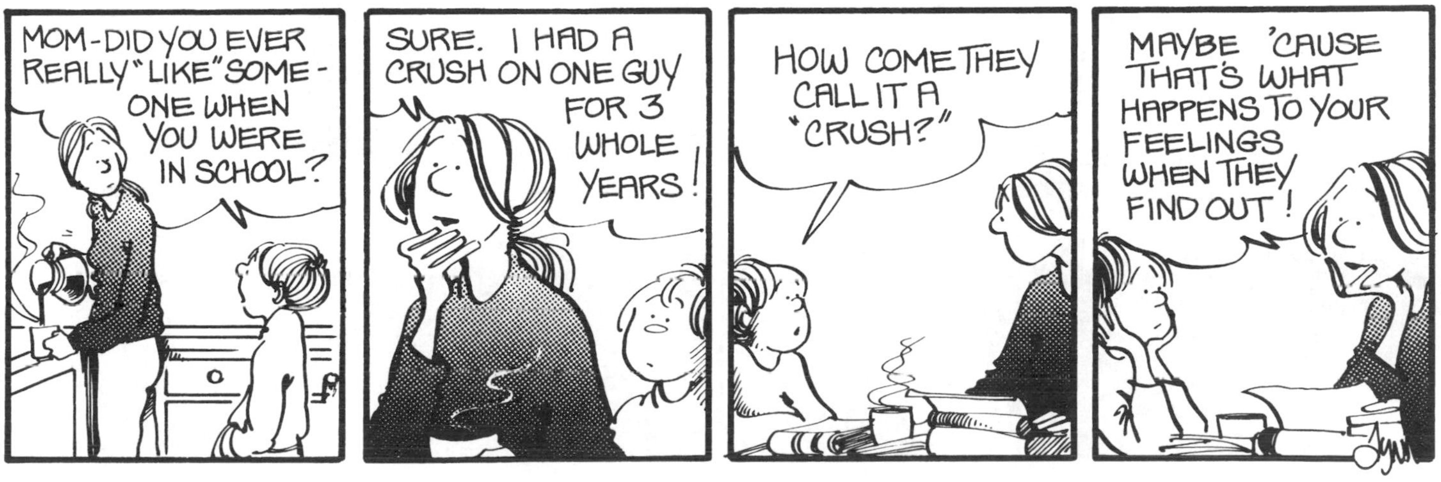
MOM-DID YOU EVER REALLY "LIKE" SOME-ONE WHEN YOU WERE IN SCHOOL?
SURE. I HAD A CRUSH ON ONE GUY FOR 3 WHOLE YEARS!
HOW COME THEY CALL IT A "CRUSH?"
MAYBE 'CAUSE THAT'S WHAT HAPPENS TO YOUR FEELINGS WHEN THEY FIND OUT!

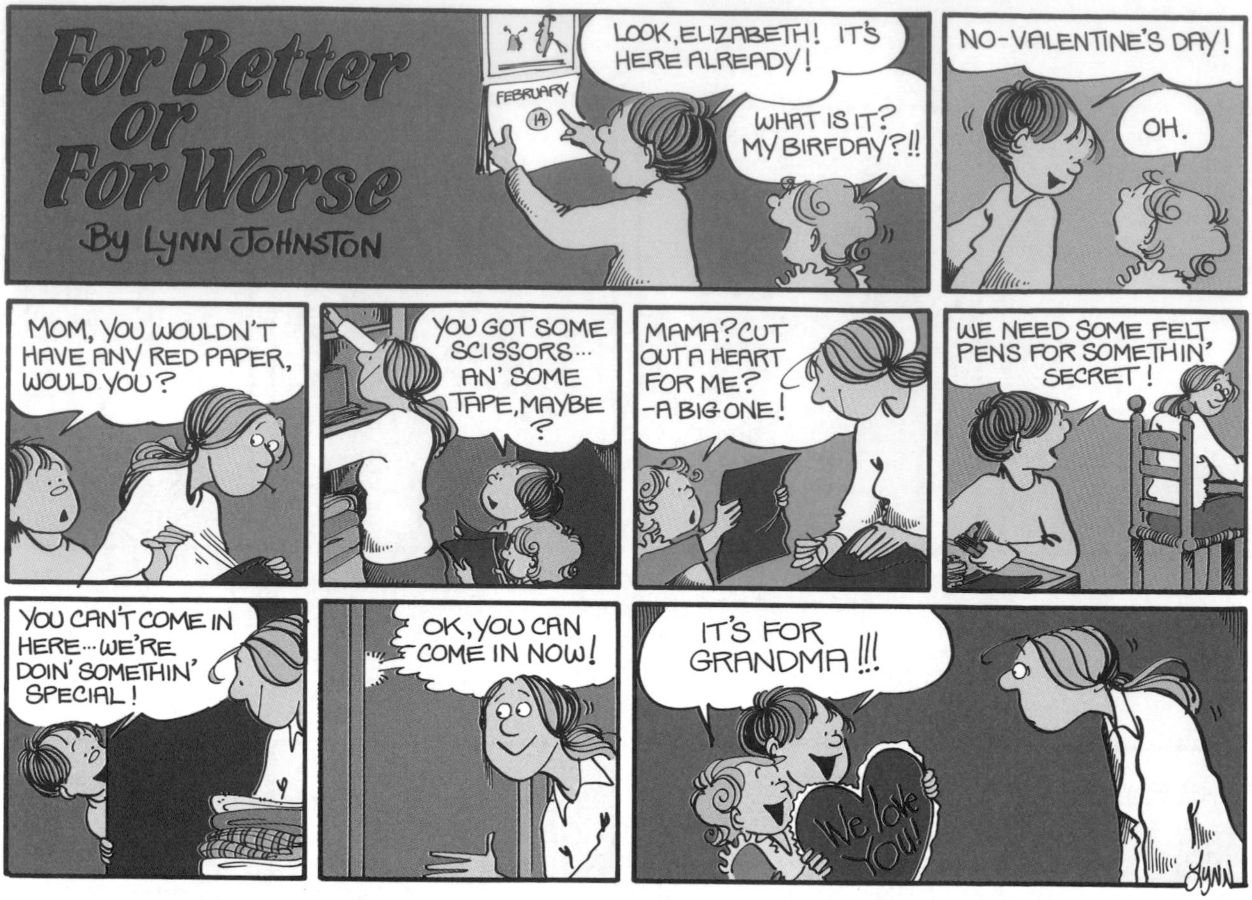
For Better or For Worse
By Lynn Johnston
FEBRUARY 14
LOOK, ELIZABETH! IT'S HERE ALREADY!
WHAT IS IT? MY BIRFDAY?!!
NO-VALENTINE'S DAY!
OH.
MOM, YOU WOULDN'T HAVE ANY RED PAPER, WOULD YOU?
YOU GOT SOME SCISSORS... AN' SOME TAPE, MAYBE?
MAMA? CUT OUT A HEART FOR ME? -A BIG ONE!
WE NEED SOME FELT PENS FOR SOMETHIN' SECRET!
YOU CAN'T COME IN HERE... WE'RE DOIN' SOMETHIN' SPECIAL!
OK, YOU CAN COME IN NOW!
IT'S FOR GRANDMA!!!
We love You!
LYNN

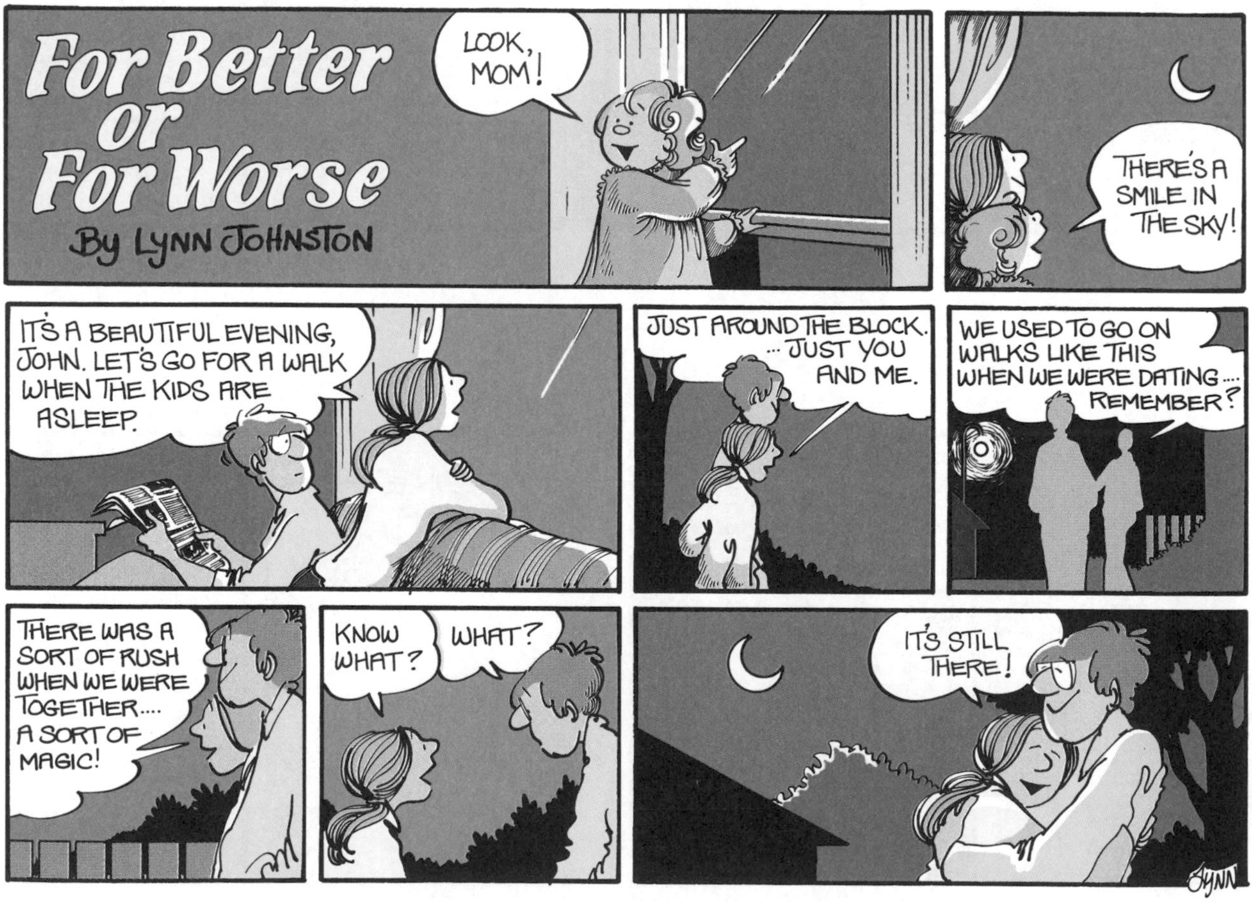
For Better or For Worse
By Lynn Johnston
LOOK, MOM!
THERE'S A SMILE IN THE SKY!
IT'S A BEAUTIFUL EVENING, JOHN. LET'S GO FOR A WALK WHEN THE KIDS ARE ASLEEP.
JUST AROUND THE BLOCK. ... JUST YOU AND ME.
WE USED TO GO ON WALKS LIKE THIS WHEN WE WERE DATING.... REMEMBER?
THERE WAS A SORT OF RUSH WHEN WE WERE TOGETHER.... A SORT OF MAGIC!
KNOW WHAT?
WHAT?
IT'S STILL THERE!
LYNN

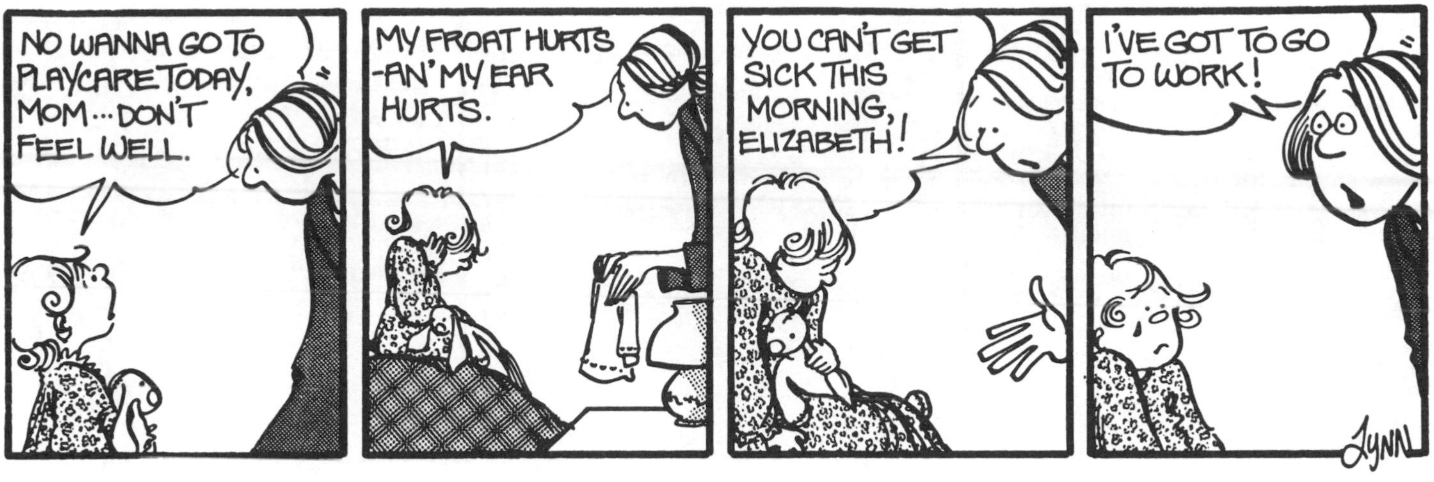
NO WANNA GO TO PLAYCARE TODAY, MOM... DON'T FEEL WELL.
MY FROAT HURTS -AN' MY EAR HURTS.
YOU CAN'T GET SICK THIS MORNING, ELIZABETH!
I'VE GOT TO GO TO WORK!
LYNN

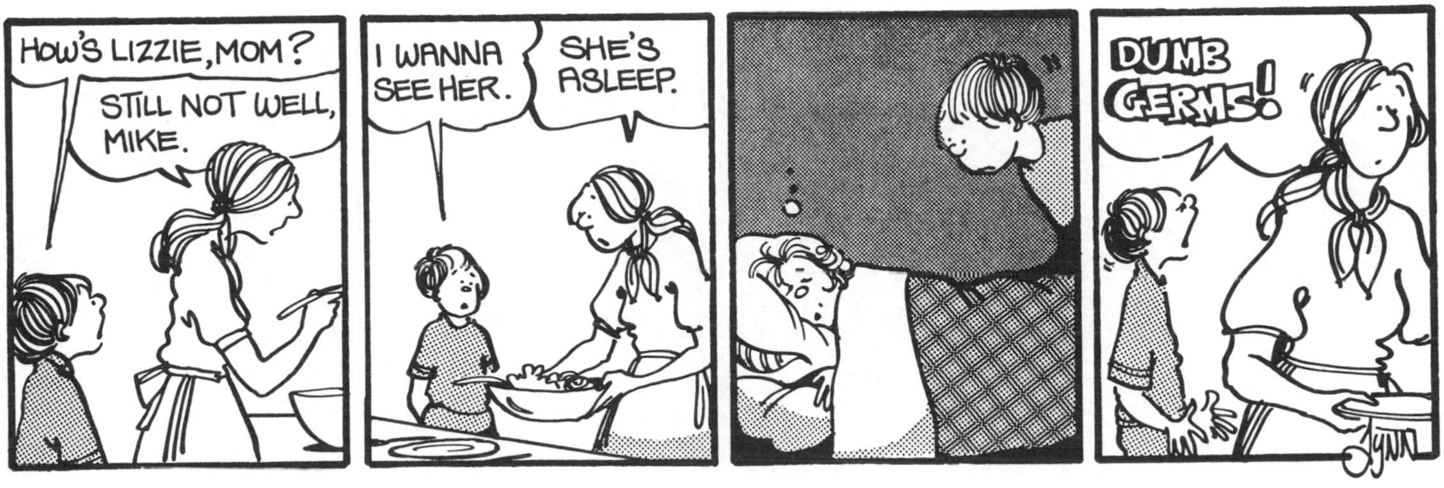
HOW'S LIZZIE, MOM?
STILL NOT WELL, MIKE.
I WANNA SEE HER.
SHE'S ASLEEP.
DUMB GERMS!
LYNN

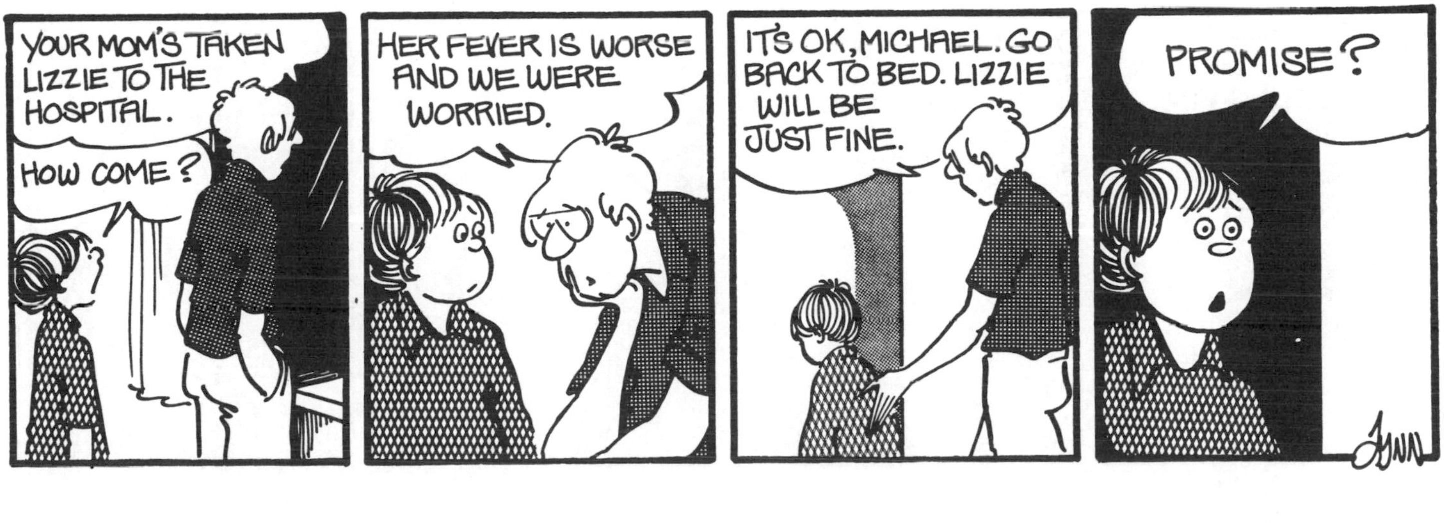
YOUR MOM'S TAKEN LIZZIE TO THE HOSPITAL.
HOW COME?
HER FEVER IS WORSE AND WE WERE WORRIED.
IT'S OK, MICHAEL. GO BACK TO BED. LIZZIE WILL BE JUST FINE.
PROMISE?
LYNN

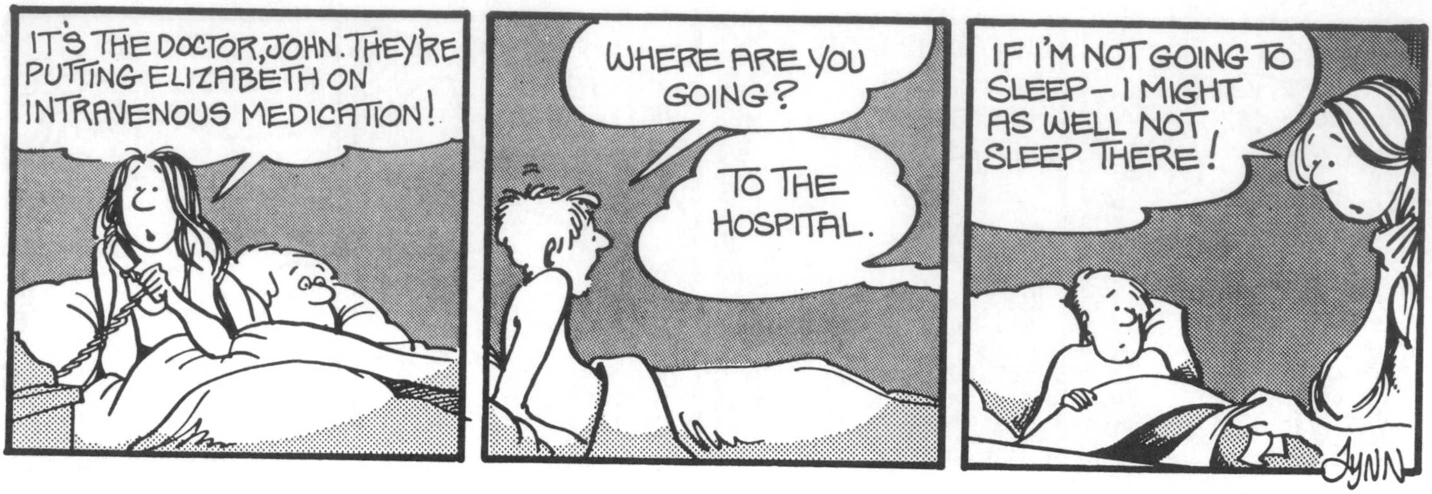
IT'S THE DOCTOR, JOHN. THEY'RE PUTTING ELIZABETH ON INTRAVENOUS MEDICATION!
WHERE ARE YOU GOING?
TO THE HOSPITAL.
IF I'M NOT GOING TO SLEEP– I MIGHT AS WELL NOT SLEEP THERE!
LYNN

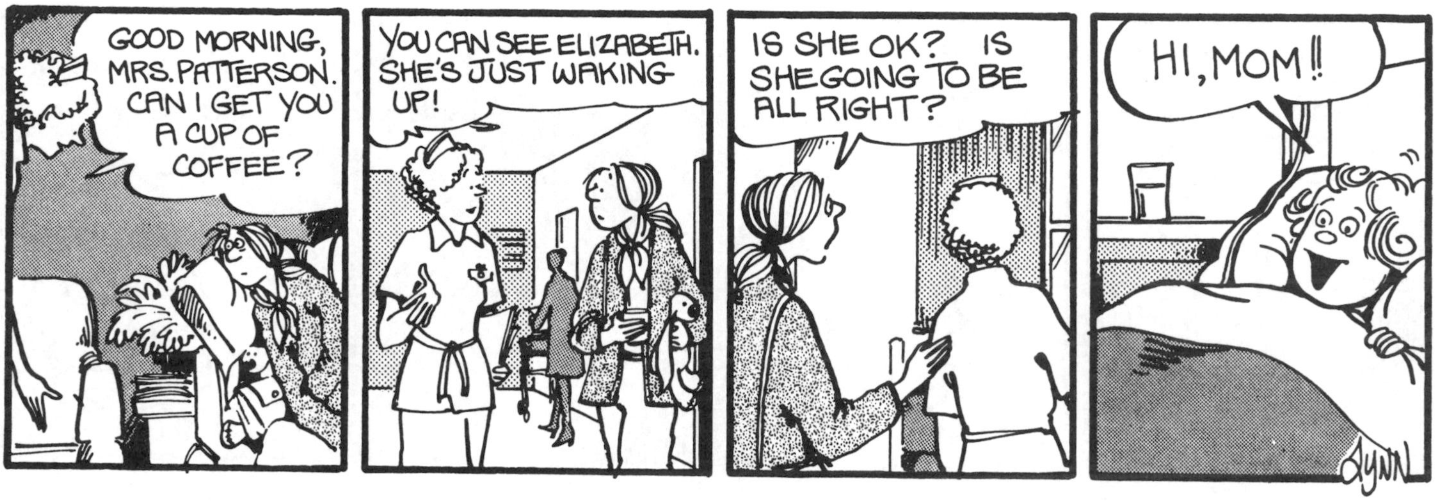
GOOD MORNING, MRS. PATTERSON. CAN I GET YOU A CUP OF COFFEE?
YOU CAN SEE ELIZABETH. SHE'S JUST WAKING UP!
IS SHE OK? IS SHE GOING TO BE ALL RIGHT?
HI, MOM!!
LYNN

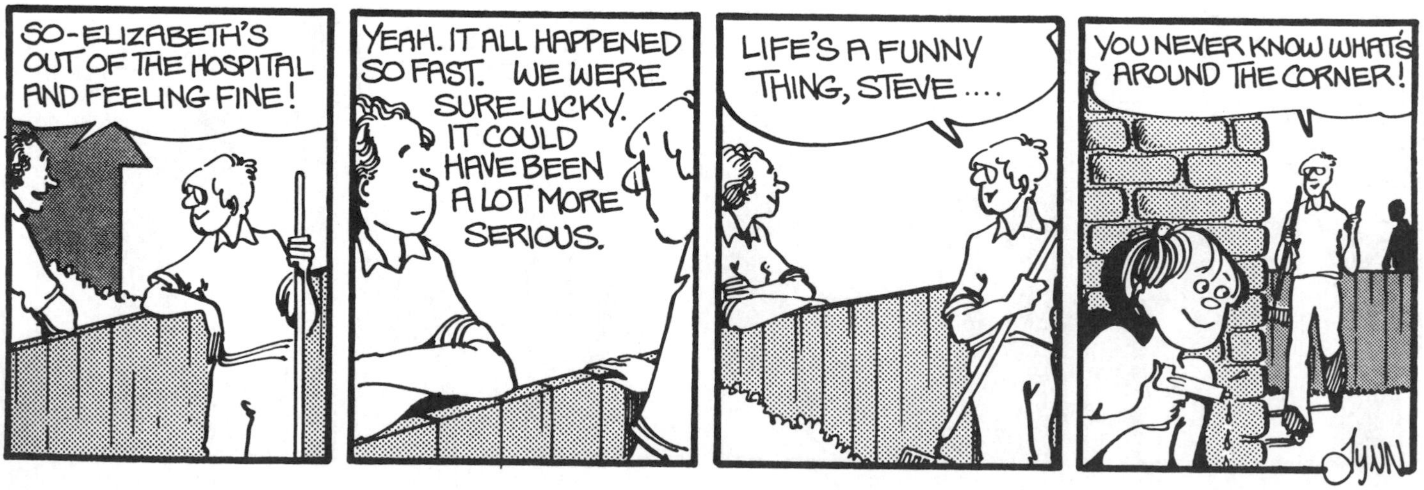
SO- ELIZABETH'S OUT OF THE HOSPITAL AND FEELING FINE!
YEAH. IT ALL HAPPENED SO FAST. WE WERE SURE LUCKY. IT COULD HAVE BEEN A LOT MORE SERIOUS.
LIFE'S A FUNNY THING, STEVE....
YOU NEVER KNOW WHAT'S AROUND THE CORNER!
LYNN

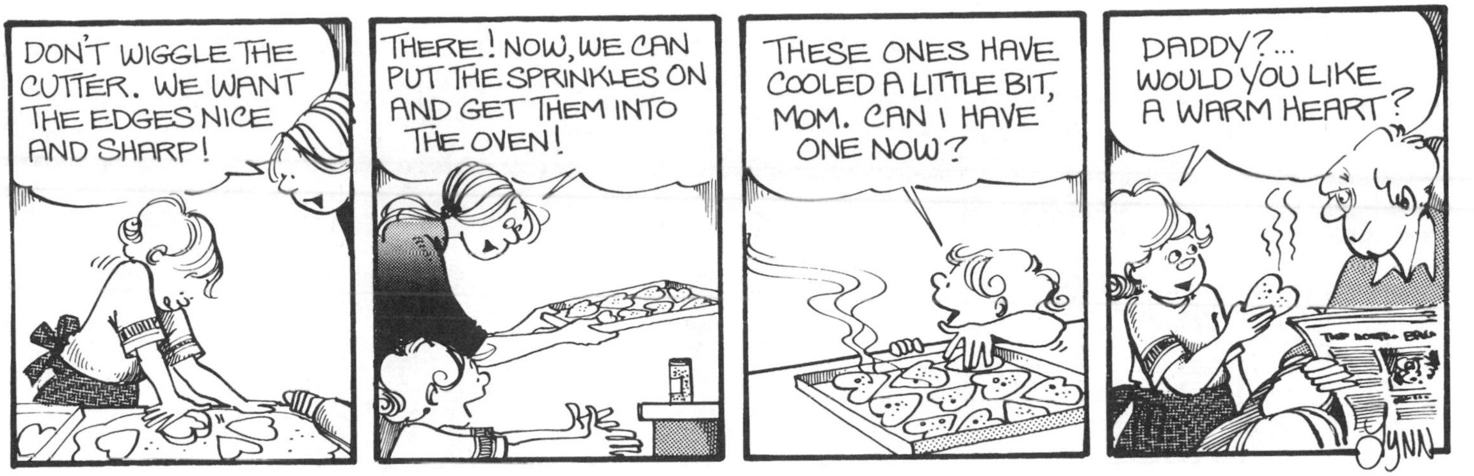
DON'T WIGGLE THE CUTTER. WE WANT THE EDGES NICE AND SHARP!
THERE! NOW, WE CAN PUT THE SPRINKLES ON AND GET THEM INTO THE OVEN!
THESE ONES HAVE COOLED A LITTLE BIT, MOM. CAN I HAVE ONE NOW?
DADDY?... WOULD YOU LIKE A WARM HEART?
LYNN

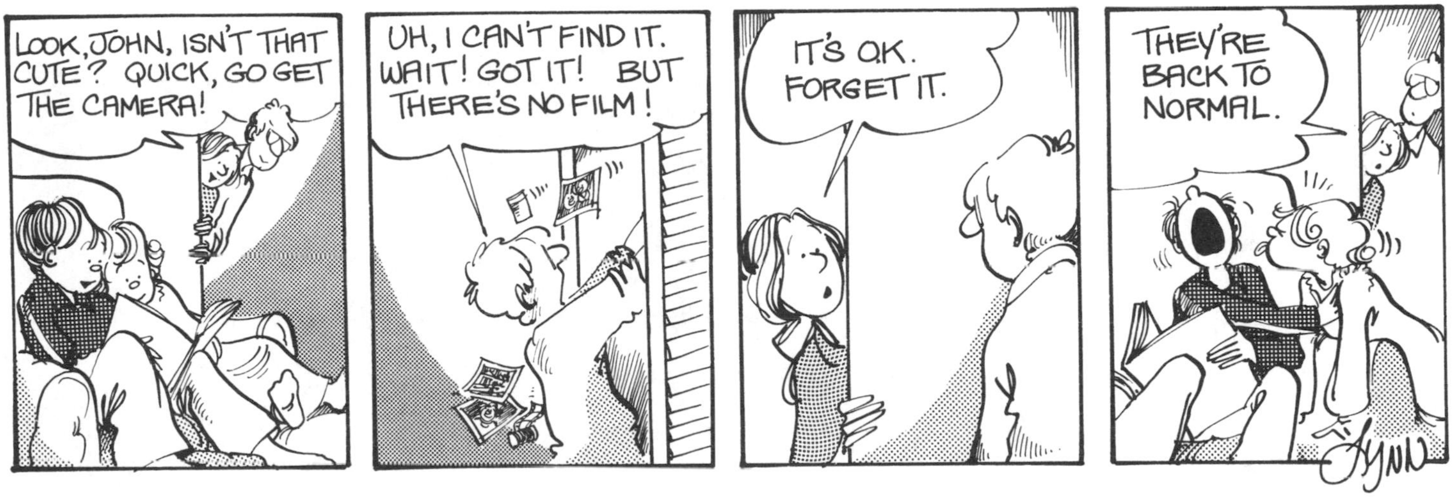
LOOK, JOHN, ISN'T THAT CUTE? QUICK, GO GET THE CAMERA!
UH, I CAN'T FIND IT. WAIT! GOT IT! BUT THERE'S NO FILM!
IT'S OK. FORGET IT.
THEY'RE BACK TO NORMAL.
LYNN

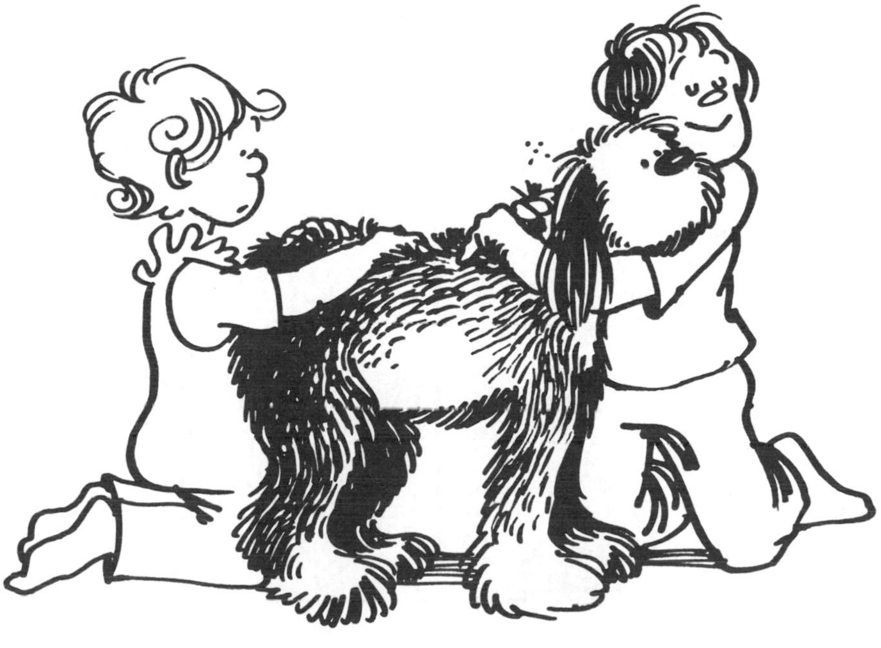

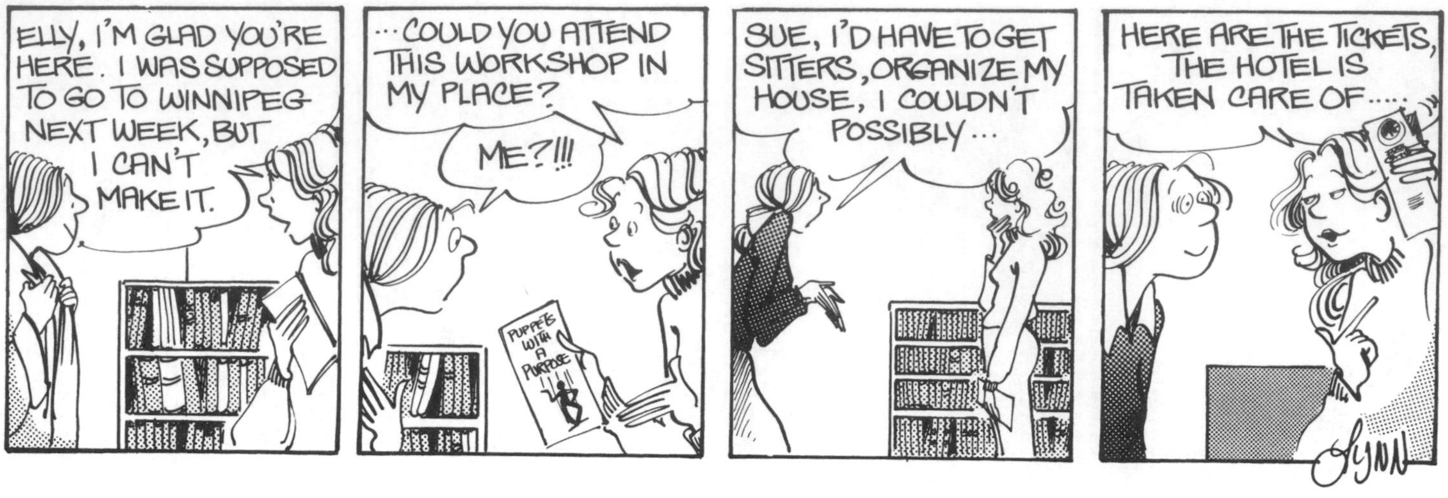
ELLY, I'M GLAD YOU'RE HERE. I WAS SUPPOSED TO GO TO WINNIPEG NEXT WEEK, BUT I CAN'T MAKE IT.
...COULD YOU ATTEND THIS WORKSHOP IN MY PLACE?
ME?!!!
PUPPETS WITH A PURPOSE
SUE, I'D HAVE TO GET SITTERS, ORGANIZE MY HOUSE, I COULDN'T POSSIBLY...
HERE ARE THE TICKETS, THE HOTEL IS TAKEN CARE OF.....
LYNN

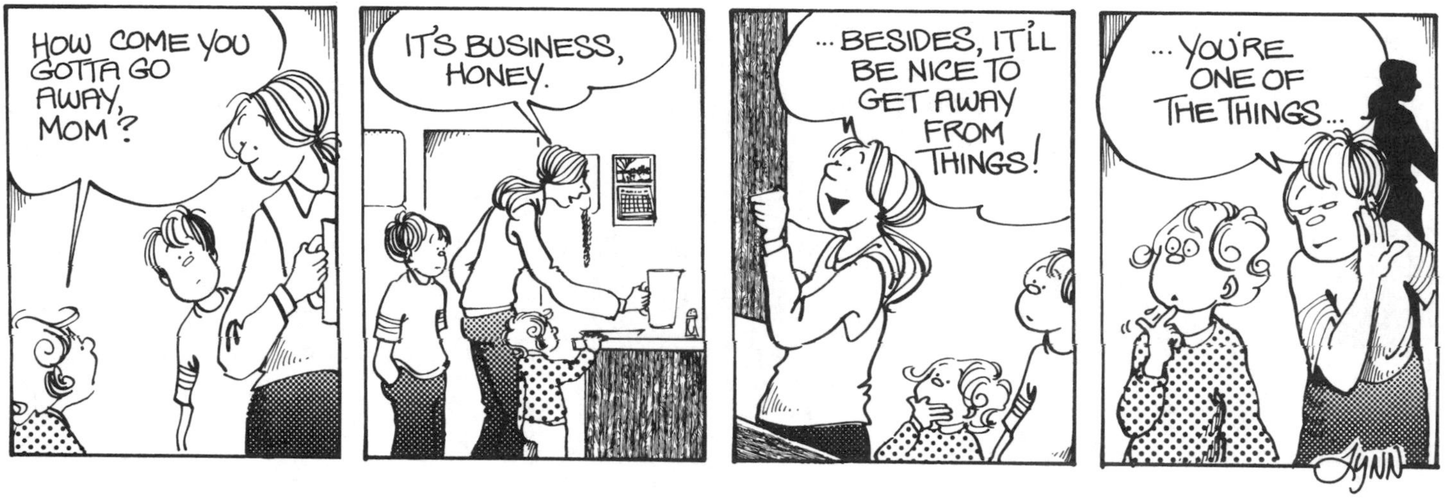
HOW COME YOU GOTTA GO AWAY, MOM?
IT'S BUSINESS, HONEY.
...BESIDES, IT'LL BE NICE TO GET AWAY FROM THINGS!
...YOU'RE ONE OF THE THINGS...
LYNN

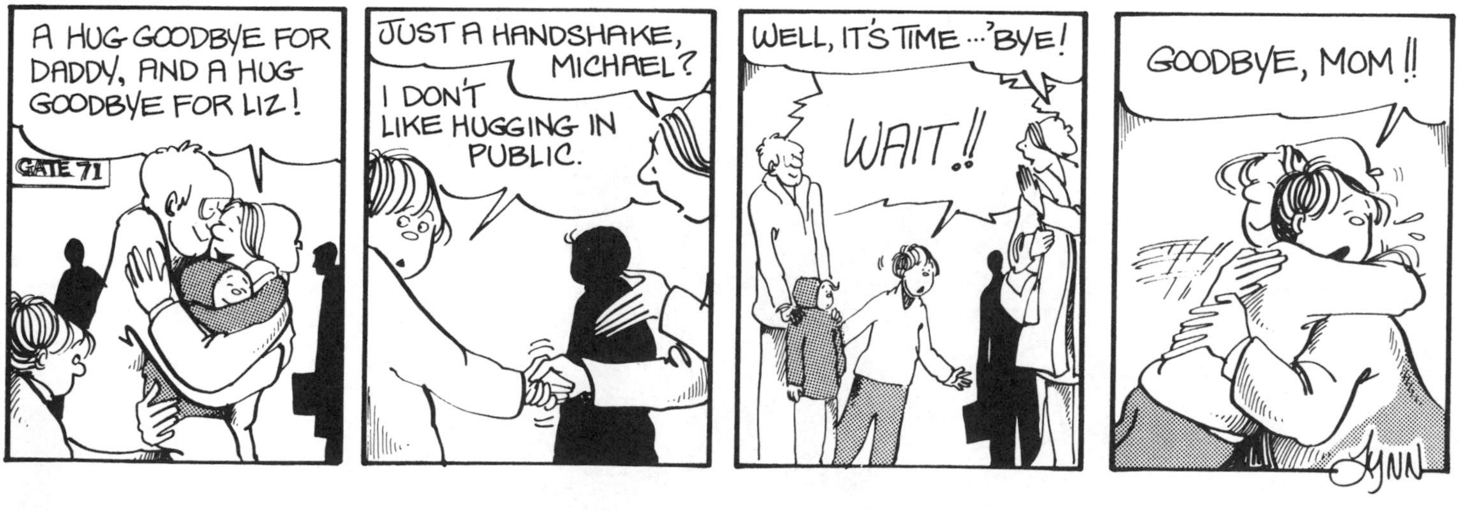
A HUG GOODBYE FOR DADDY, AND A HUG GOODBYE FOR LIZ!
GATE 71
JUST A HANDSHAKE, MICHAEL?
I DON'T LIKE HUGGING IN PUBLIC.
WELL, IT'S TIME...'BYE!
WAIT!!
GOODBYE, MOM!!
LYNN

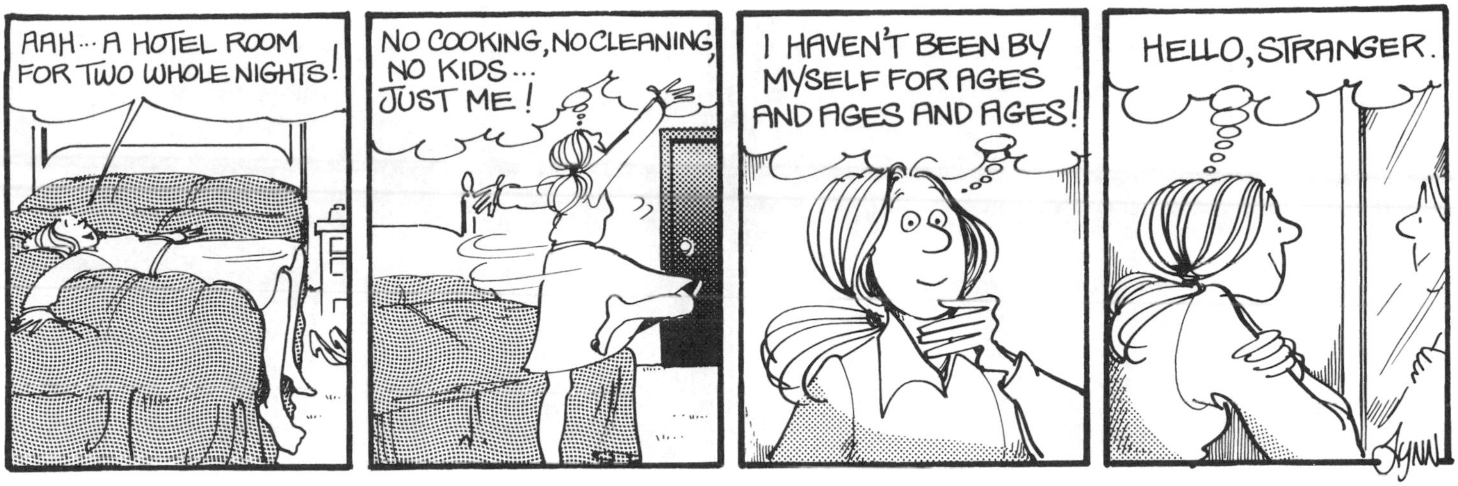
AAH... A HOTEL ROOM FOR TWO WHOLE NIGHTS!
NO COOKING, NO CLEANING, NO KIDS... JUST ME!
I HAVEN'T BEEN BY MYSELF FOR AGES AND AGES AND AGES!
HELLO, STRANGER.
LYNN

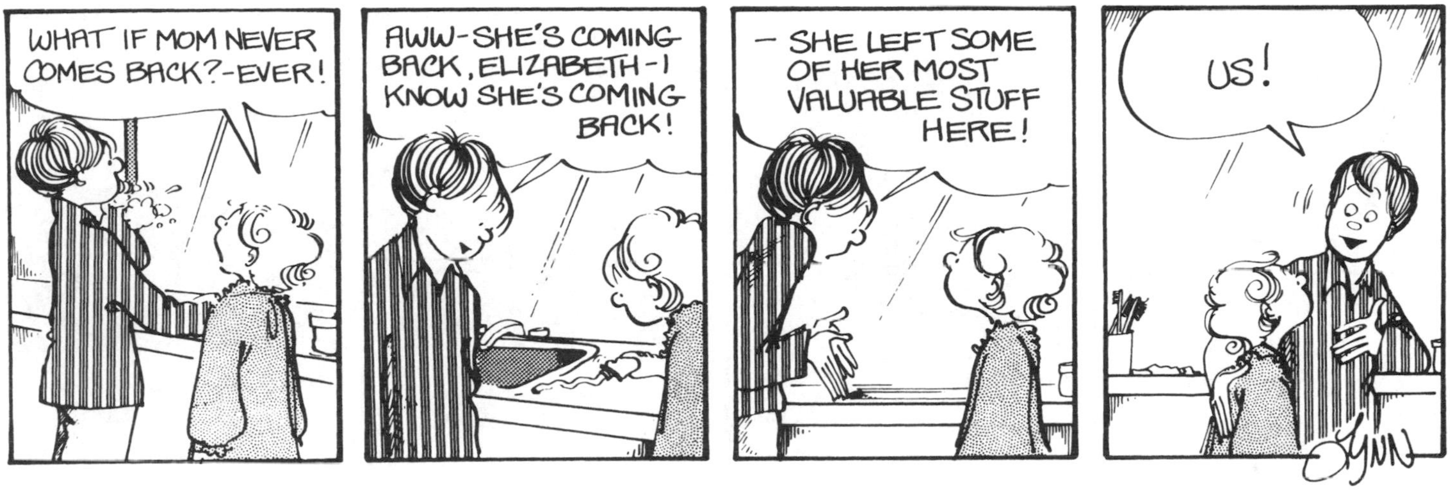
WHAT IF MOM NEVER COMES BACK?-EVER!
AWW-SHE'S COMING BACK, ELIZABETH-I KNOW SHE'S COMING BACK!
-SHE LEFT SOME OF HER MOST VALUABLE STUFF HERE!
US!
LYNN

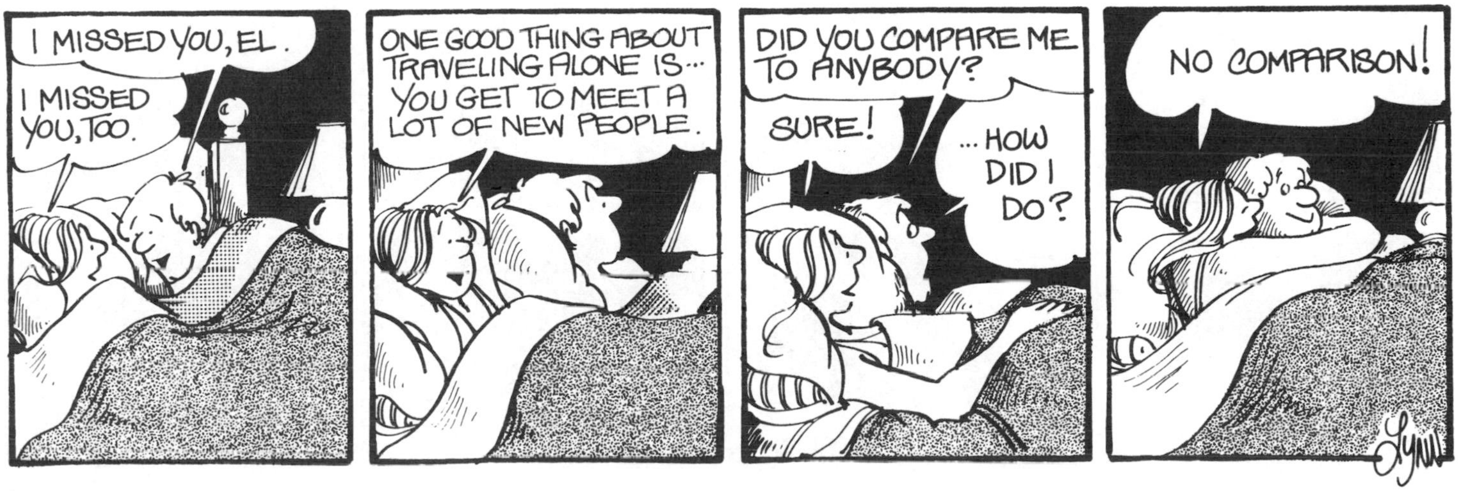
I MISSED YOU, EL.
I MISSED YOU, TOO.
ONE GOOD THING ABOUT TRAVELING ALONE IS... YOU GET TO MEET A LOT OF NEW PEOPLE.
DID YOU COMPARE ME TO ANYBODY?
SURE!
...HOW DID I DO?
NO COMPARISON!
LYNN

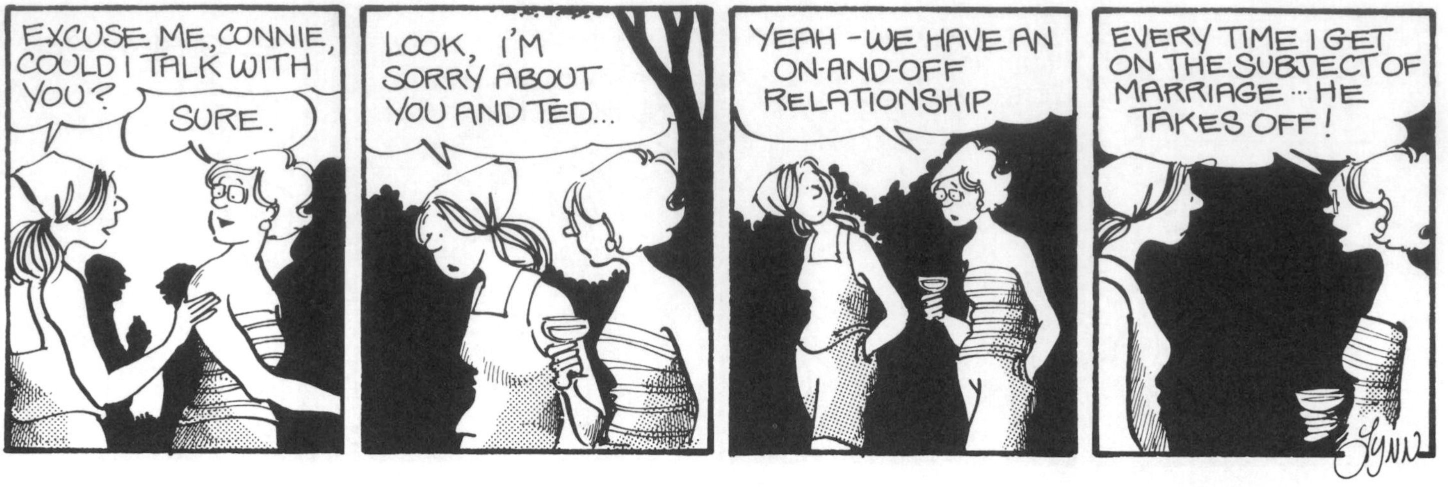
EXCUSE ME, CONNIE, COULD I TALK WITH YOU?
SURE.
LOOK, I'M SORRY ABOUT YOU AND TED...
YEAH - WE HAVE AN ON-AND-OFF RELATIONSHIP.
EVERY TIME I GET ON THE SUBJECT OF MARRIAGE ··· HE TAKES OFF!
Lynn

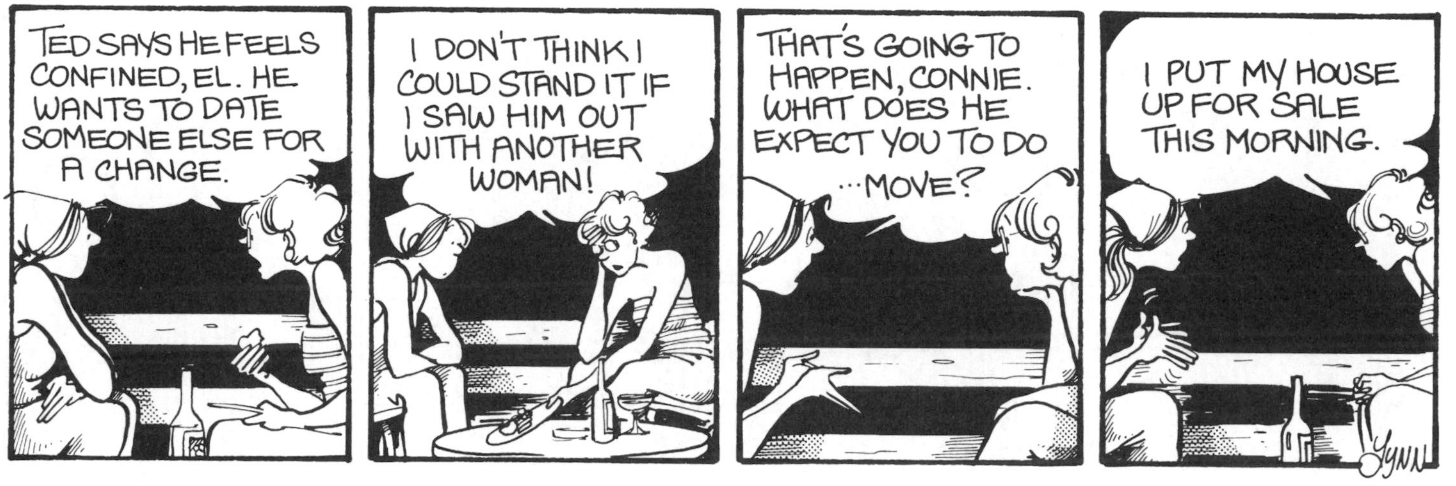
TED SAYS HE FEELS CONFINED, EL. HE WANTS TO DATE SOMEONE ELSE FOR A CHANGE.
I DON'T THINK I COULD STAND IT IF I SAW HIM OUT WITH ANOTHER WOMAN!
THAT'S GOING TO HAPPEN, CONNIE. WHAT DOES HE EXPECT YOU TO DO ...MOVE?
I PUT MY HOUSE UP FOR SALE THIS MORNING.
Lynn

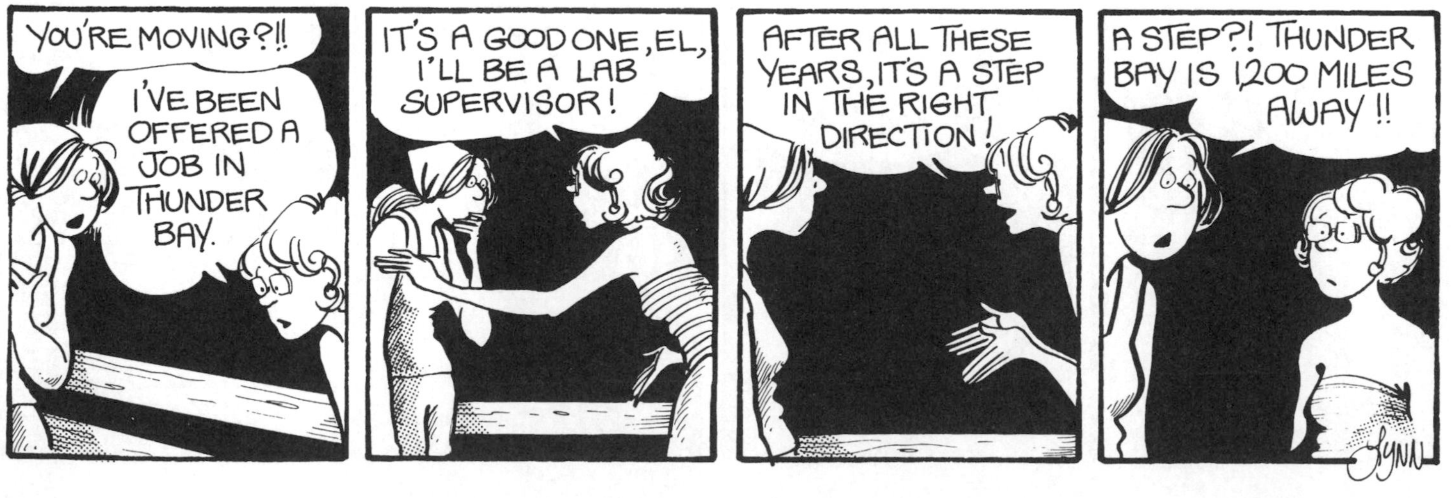
YOU'RE MOVING?!!
I'VE BEEN OFFERED A JOB IN THUNDER BAY.
IT'S A GOOD ONE, EL, I'LL BE A LAB SUPERVISOR!
AFTER ALL THESE YEARS, IT'S A STEP IN THE RIGHT DIRECTION!
A STEP?! THUNDER BAY IS 1,200 MILES AWAY!!
Lynn

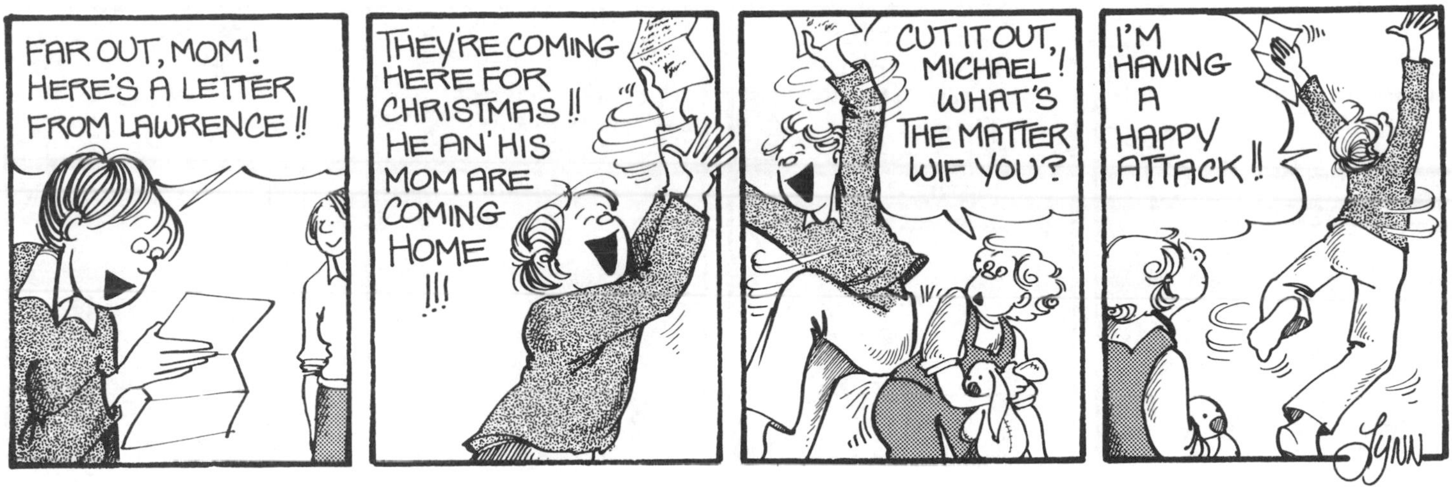
FAR OUT, MOM! HERE'S A LETTER FROM LAWRENCE!!
THEY'RE COMING HERE FOR CHRISTMAS!! HE AN' HIS MOM ARE COMING HOME!!!
CUT IT OUT, MICHAEL! WHAT'S THE MATTER WIF YOU?
I'M HAVING A HAPPY ATTACK!!
LYNN

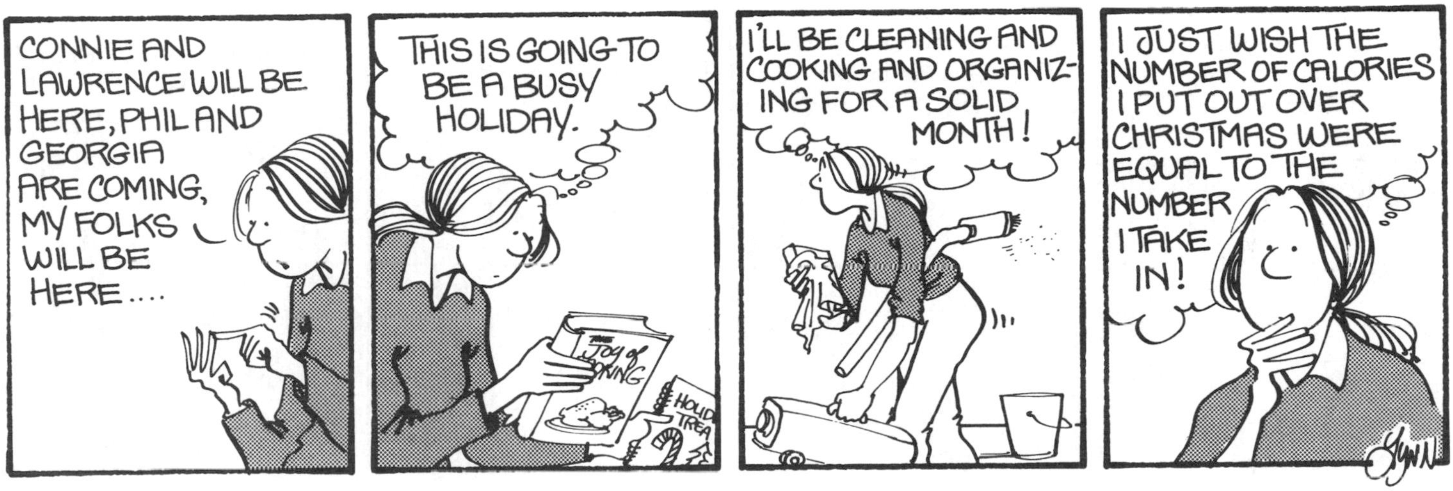
CONNIE AND LAWRENCE WILL BE HERE, PHIL AND GEORGIA ARE COMING, MY FOLKS WILL BE HERE....
THIS IS GOING TO BE A BUSY HOLIDAY.
I'LL BE CLEANING AND COOKING AND ORGANIZ-ING FOR A SOLID MONTH!
I JUST WISH THE NUMBER OF CALORIES I PUT OUT OVER CHRISTMAS WERE EQUAL TO THE NUMBER I TAKE IN!
LYNN

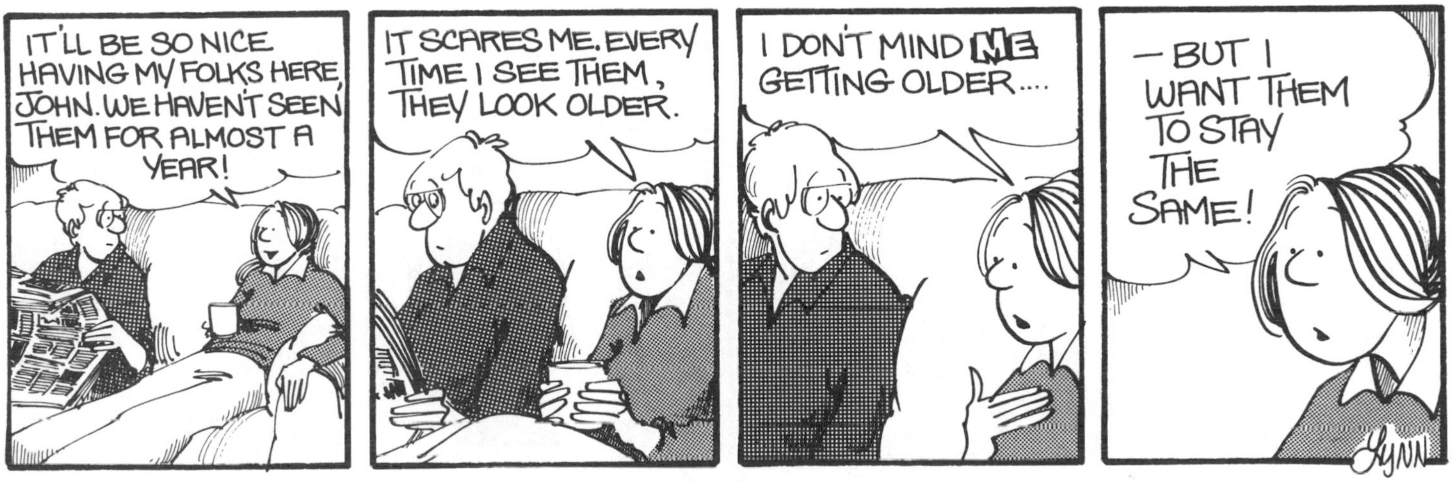
IT'LL BE SO NICE HAVING MY FOLKS HERE, JOHN. WE HAVEN'T SEEN THEM FOR ALMOST A YEAR!
IT SCARES ME. EVERY TIME I SEE THEM, THEY LOOK OLDER.
I DON'T MIND ME GETTING OLDER....
—BUT I WANT THEM TO STAY THE SAME!
LYNN

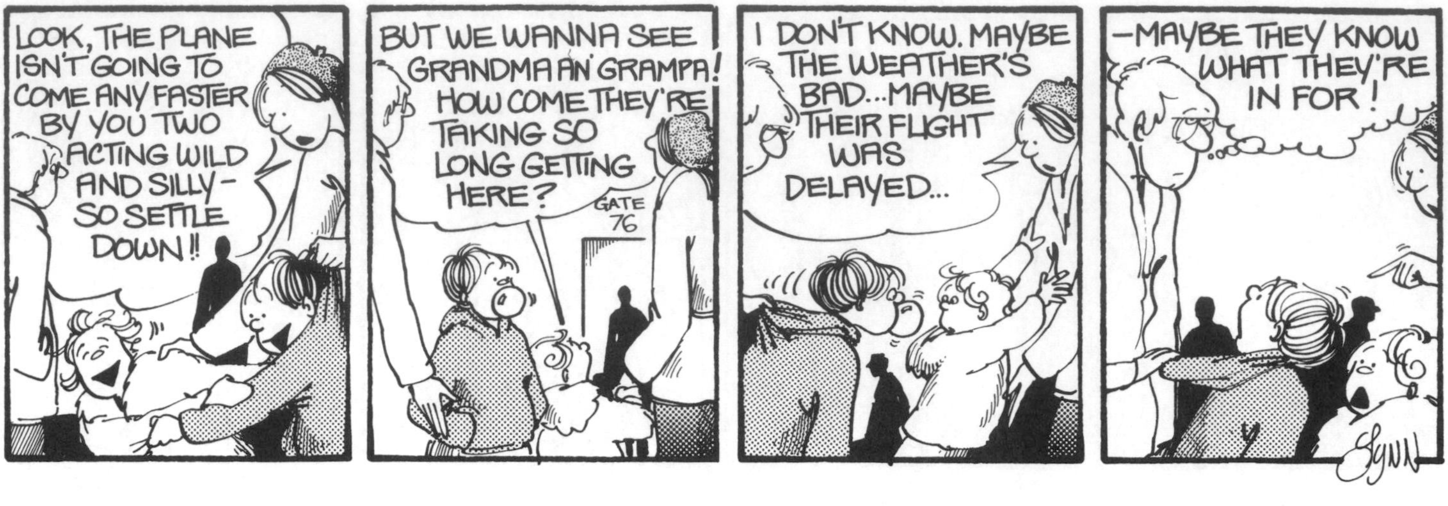
LOOK, THE PLANE ISN'T GOING TO COME ANY FASTER BY YOU TWO ACTING WILD AND SILLY - SO SETTLE DOWN!!
BUT WE WANNA SEE GRANDMA AN' GRAMPA! HOW COME THEY'RE TAKING SO LONG GETTING HERE?
GATE 76
I DON'T KNOW. MAYBE THE WEATHER'S BAD... MAYBE THEIR FLIGHT WAS DELAYED...
-MAYBE THEY KNOW WHAT THEY'RE IN FOR!
Lynn

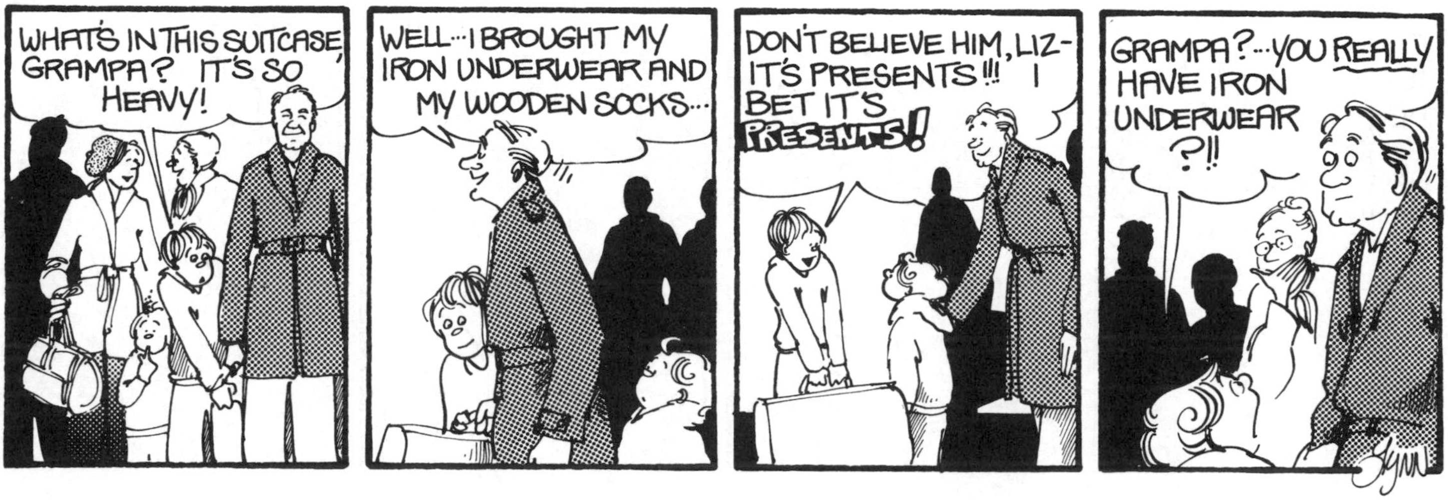
WHAT'S IN THIS SUITCASE, GRAMPA? IT'S SO HEAVY!
WELL... I BROUGHT MY IRON UNDERWEAR AND MY WOODEN SOCKS...
DON'T BELIEVE HIM, LIZ- IT'S PRESENTS!!! I BET IT'S PRESENTS!
GRAMPA?...YOU REALLY HAVE IRON UNDERWEAR ?!!
Lynn

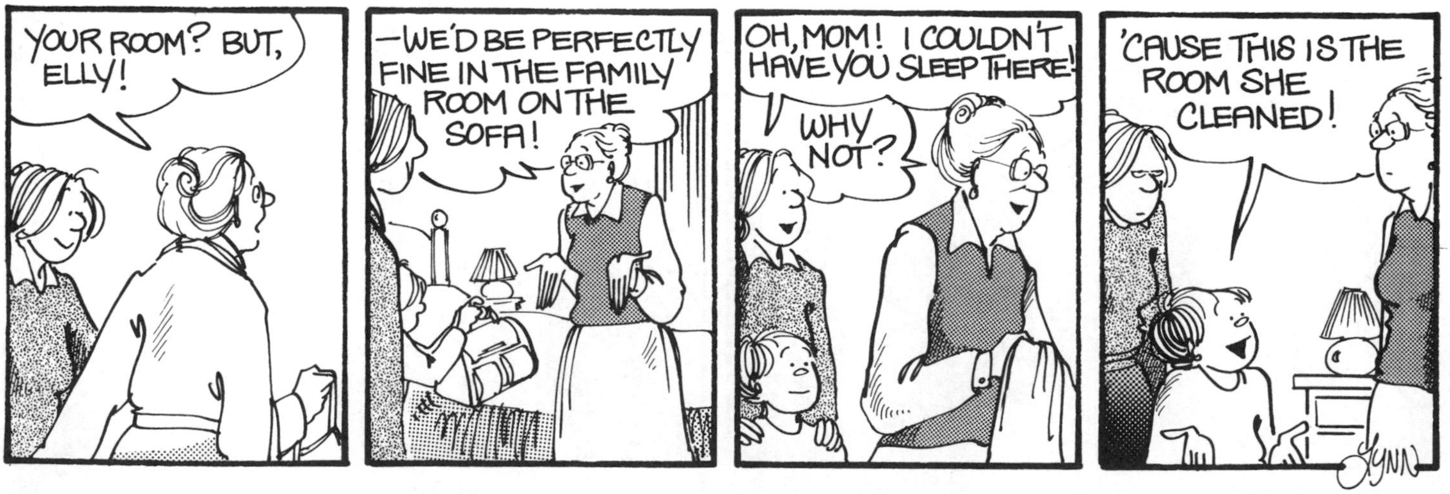
YOUR ROOM? BUT, ELLY!
-WE'D BE PERFECTLY FINE IN THE FAMILY ROOM ON THE SOFA!
OH, MOM! I COULDN'T HAVE YOU SLEEP THERE!
WHY NOT?
'CAUSE THIS IS THE ROOM SHE CLEANED!
Lynn

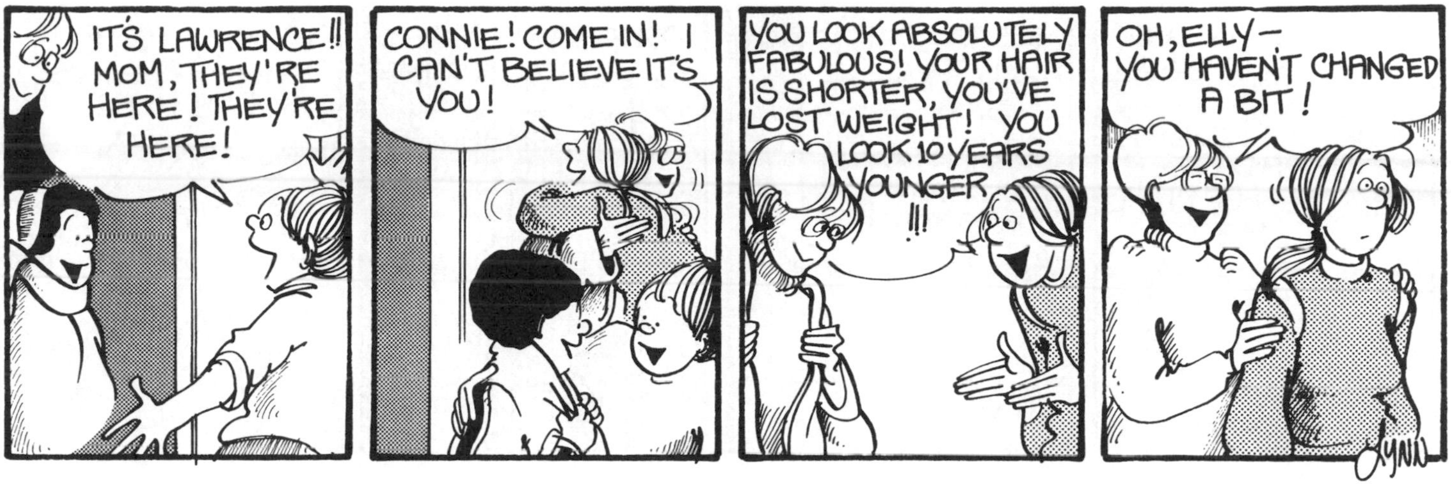
IT'S LAWRENCE!! MOM, THEY'RE HERE! THEY'RE HERE!
CONNIE! COME IN! I CAN'T BELIEVE IT'S YOU!
YOU LOOK ABSOLUTELY FABULOUS! YOUR HAIR IS SHORTER, YOU'VE LOST WEIGHT! YOU LOOK 10 YEARS YOUNGER!!!
OH, ELLY - YOU HAVEN'T CHANGED A BIT!
Lynn

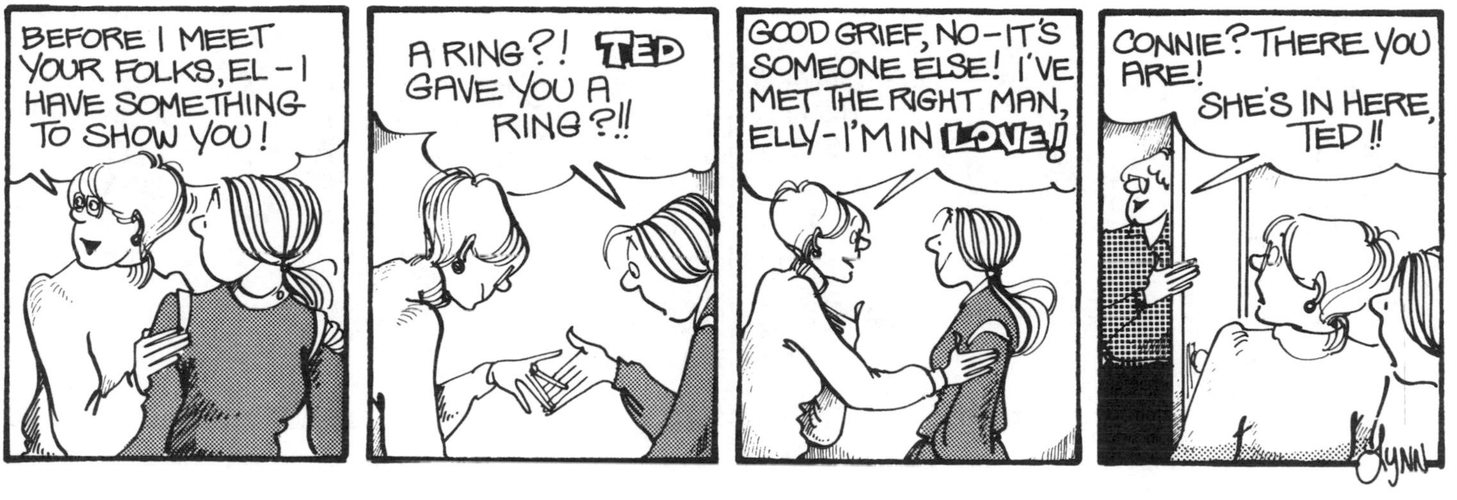
BEFORE I MEET YOUR FOLKS, EL - I HAVE SOMETHING TO SHOW YOU!
A RING?! TED GAVE YOU A RING?!!
GOOD GRIEF, NO - IT'S SOMEONE ELSE! I'VE MET THE RIGHT MAN, ELLY - I'M IN LOVE!
CONNIE? THERE YOU ARE!
SHE'S IN HERE, TED!!
Lynn

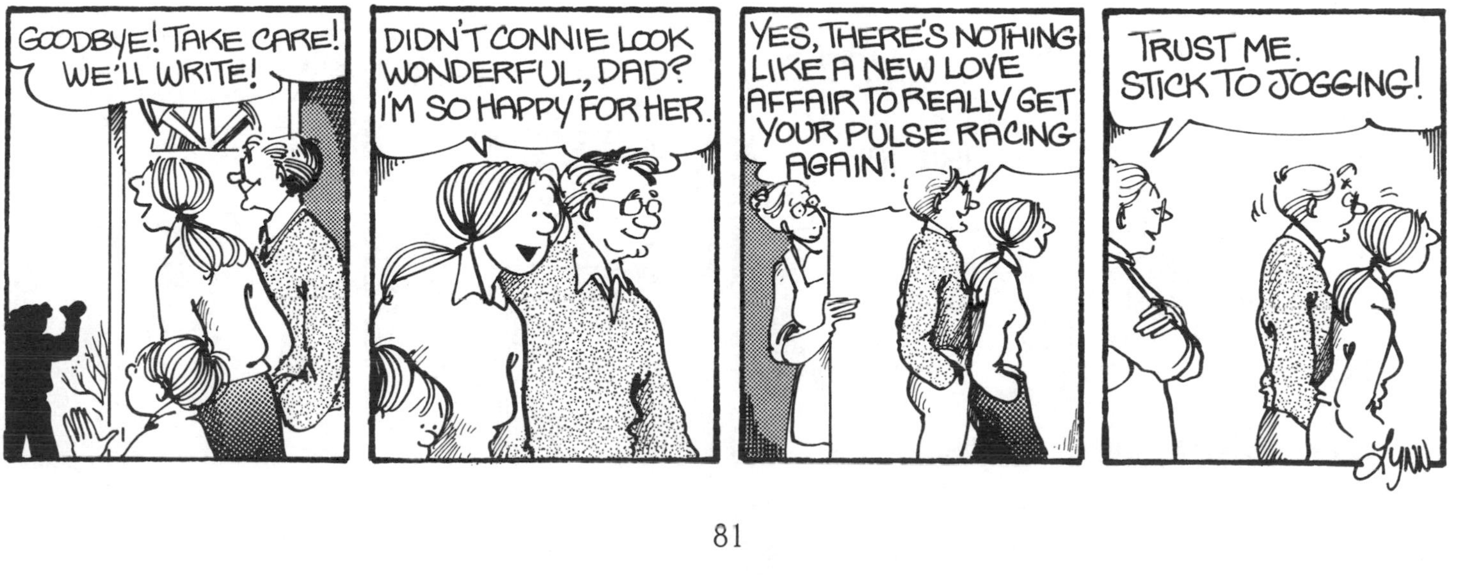
GOODBYE! TAKE CARE! WE'LL WRITE!
DIDN'T CONNIE LOOK WONDERFUL, DAD? I'M SO HAPPY FOR HER.
YES, THERE'S NOTHING LIKE A NEW LOVE AFFAIR TO REALLY GET YOUR PULSE RACING AGAIN!
TRUST ME. STICK TO JOGGING!
Lynn

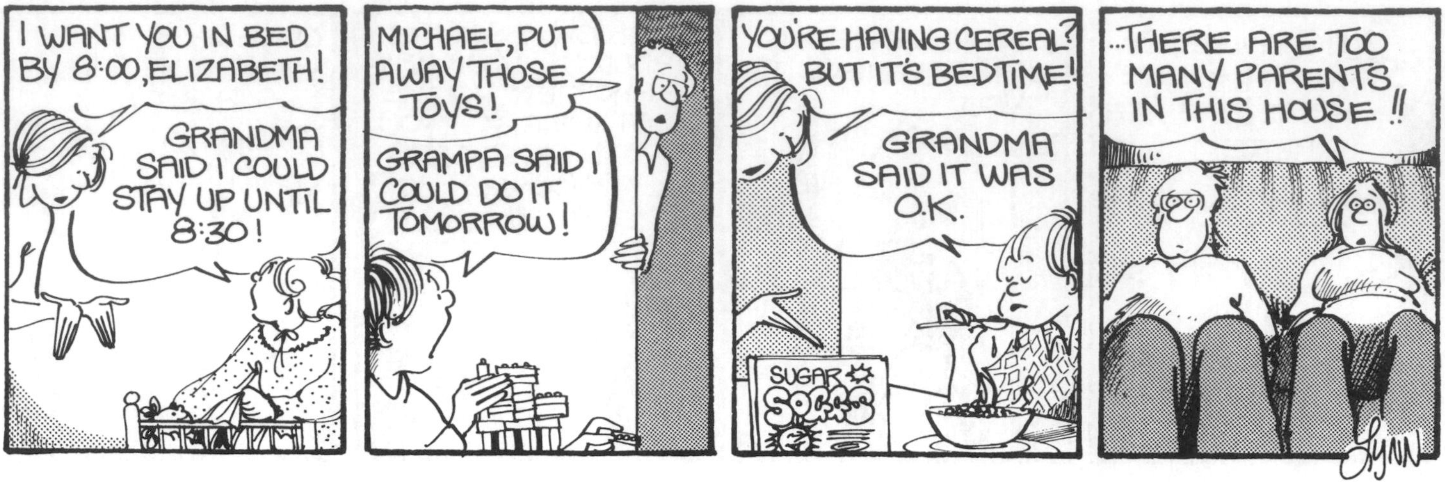
I WANT YOU IN BED BY 8:00, ELIZABETH!
GRANDMA SAID I COULD STAY UP UNTIL 8:30!
MICHAEL, PUT AWAY THOSE TOYS!
GRAMPA SAID I COULD DO IT TOMORROW!
YOU'RE HAVING CEREAL? BUT IT'S BEDTIME!
GRANDMA SAID IT WAS O.K.
SUGAR
...THERE ARE TOO MANY PARENTS IN THIS HOUSE!!
Lynn

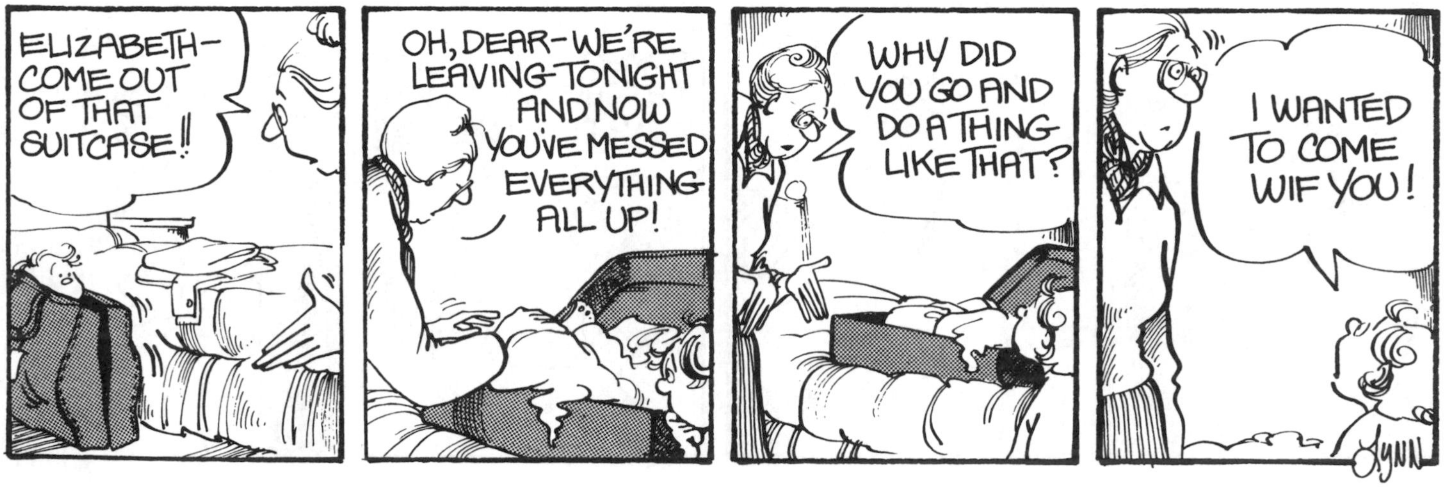
ELIZABETH- COME OUT OF THAT SUITCASE!!
OH, DEAR- WE'RE LEAVING TONIGHT AND NOW YOU'VE MESSED EVERYTHING ALL UP!
WHY DID YOU GO AND DO A THING LIKE THAT?
I WANTED TO COME WIF YOU!
Lynn

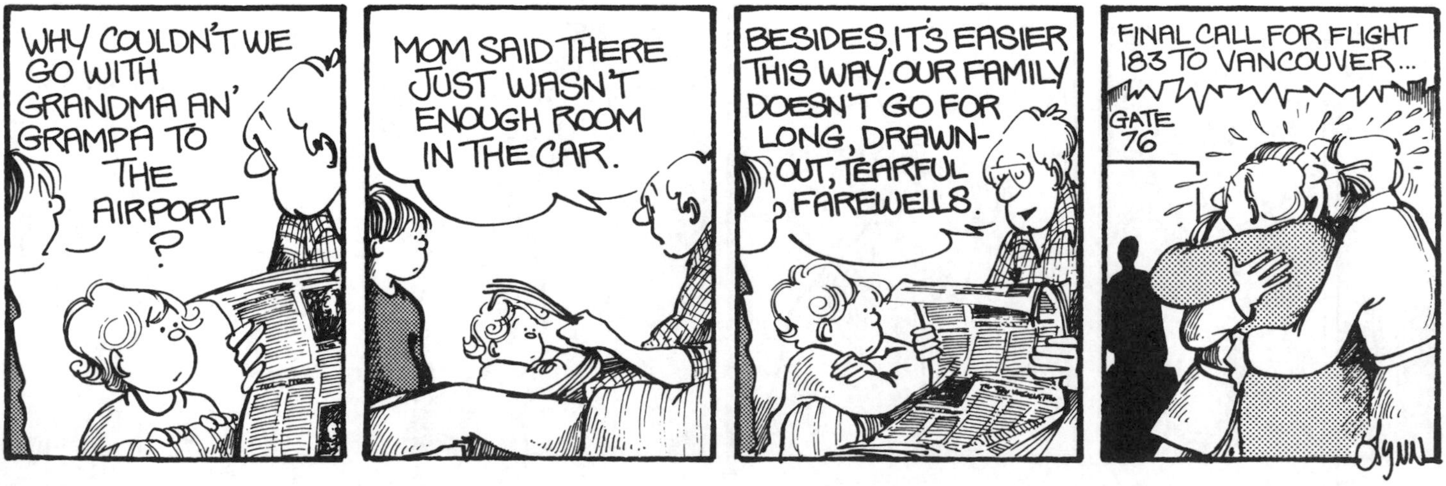
WHY COULDN'T WE GO WITH GRANDMA AN' GRAMPA TO THE AIRPORT?
MOM SAID THERE JUST WASN'T ENOUGH ROOM IN THE CAR.
BESIDES, IT'S EASIER THIS WAY. OUR FAMILY DOESN'T GO FOR LONG, DRAWN-OUT, TEARFUL FAREWELLS.
FINAL CALL FOR FLIGHT 183 TO VANCOUVER...
GATE 76
Lynn

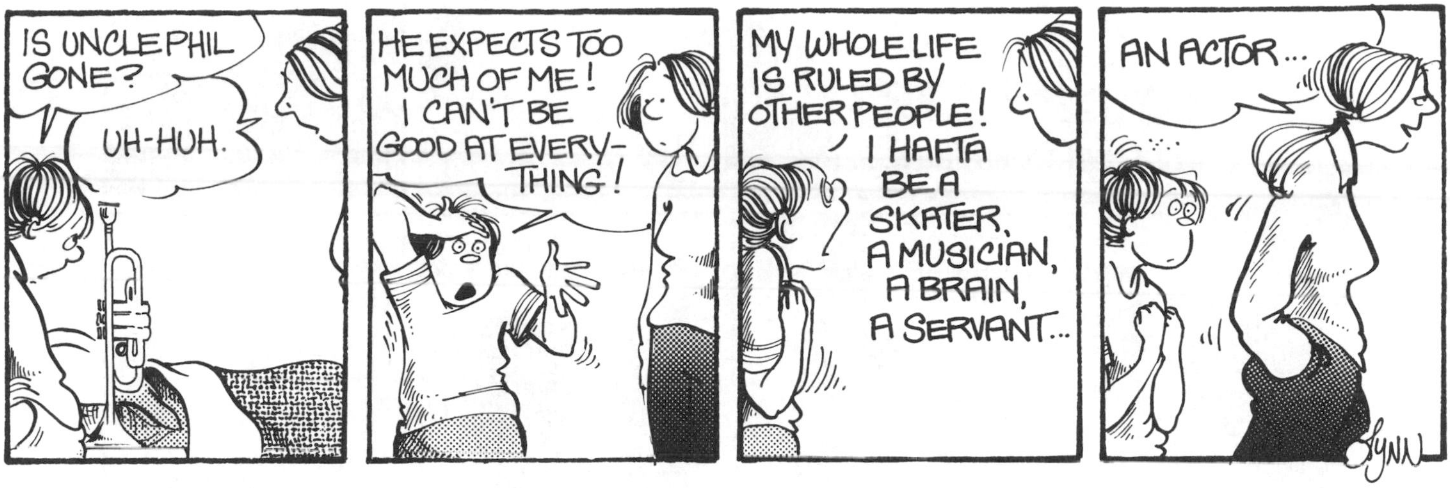
IS UNCLE PHIL GONE?
UH-HUH.
HE EXPECTS TOO MUCH OF ME! I CAN'T BE GOOD AT EVERYTHING!
MY WHOLE LIFE IS RULED BY OTHER PEOPLE!
I HAFTA BE A SKATER, A MUSICIAN, A BRAIN, A SERVANT...
AN ACTOR...
Lynn

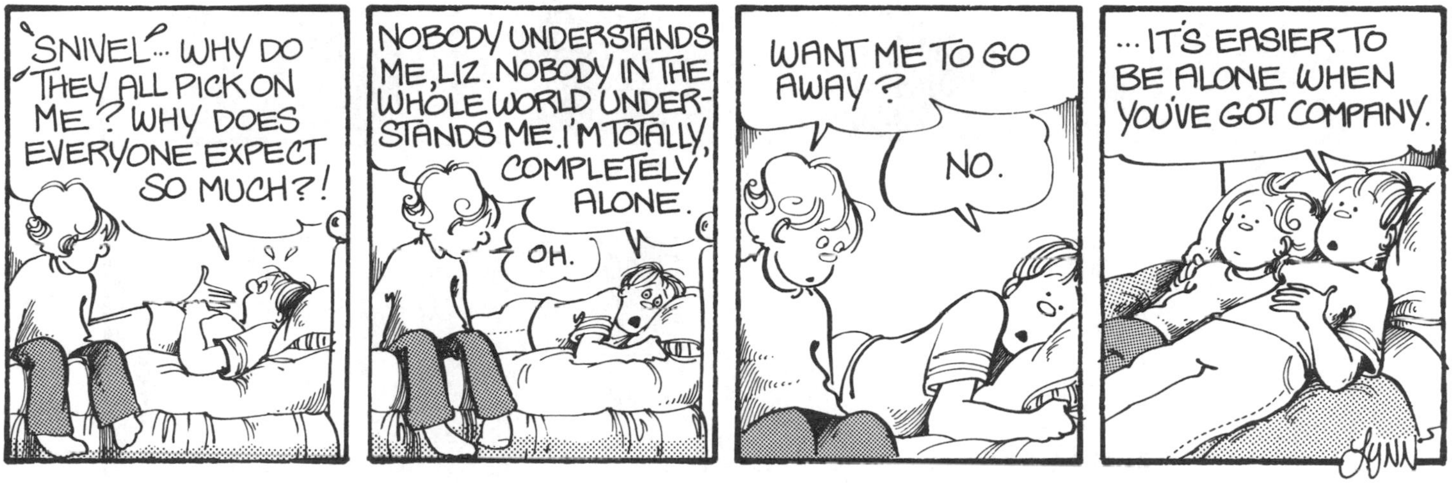
SNIVEL... WHY DO THEY ALL PICK ON ME? WHY DOES EVERYONE EXPECT SO MUCH?!
NOBODY UNDERSTANDS ME, LIZ. NOBODY IN THE WHOLE WORLD UNDERSTANDS ME. I'M TOTALLY, COMPLETELY ALONE.
OH.
WANT ME TO GO AWAY?
NO.
...IT'S EASIER TO BE ALONE WHEN YOU'VE GOT COMPANY.
Lynn

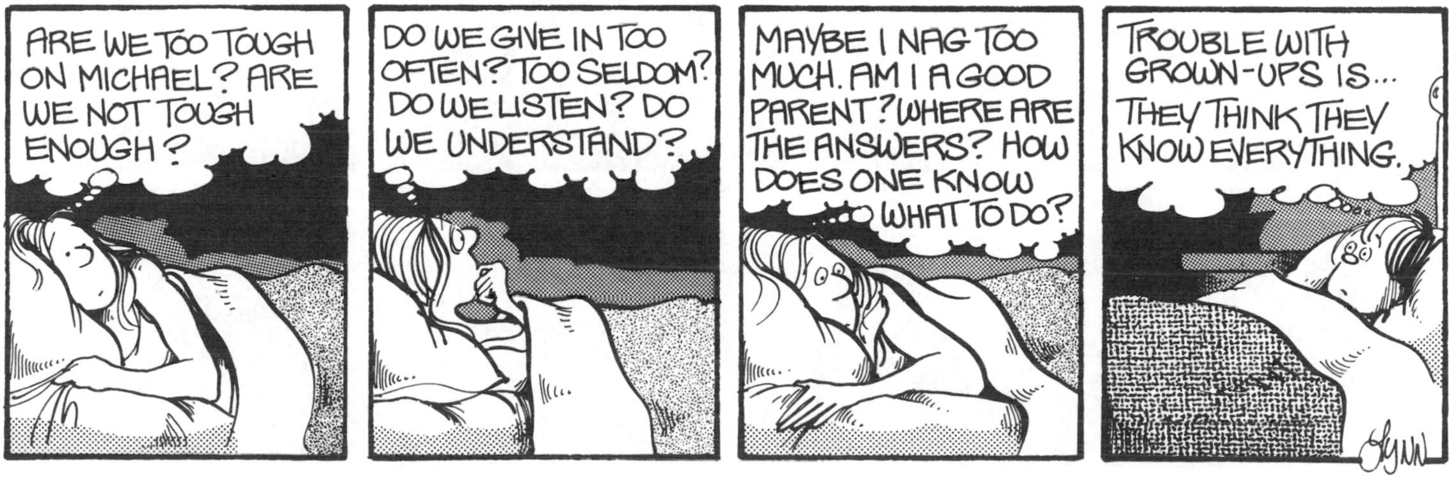
ARE WE TOO TOUGH ON MICHAEL? ARE WE NOT TOUGH ENOUGH?
DO WE GIVE IN TOO OFTEN? TOO SELDOM? DO WE LISTEN? DO WE UNDERSTAND?
MAYBE I NAG TOO MUCH. AM I A GOOD PARENT? WHERE ARE THE ANSWERS? HOW DOES ONE KNOW WHAT TO DO?
TROUBLE WITH GROWN-UPS IS... THEY THINK THEY KNOW EVERYTHING.
Lynn

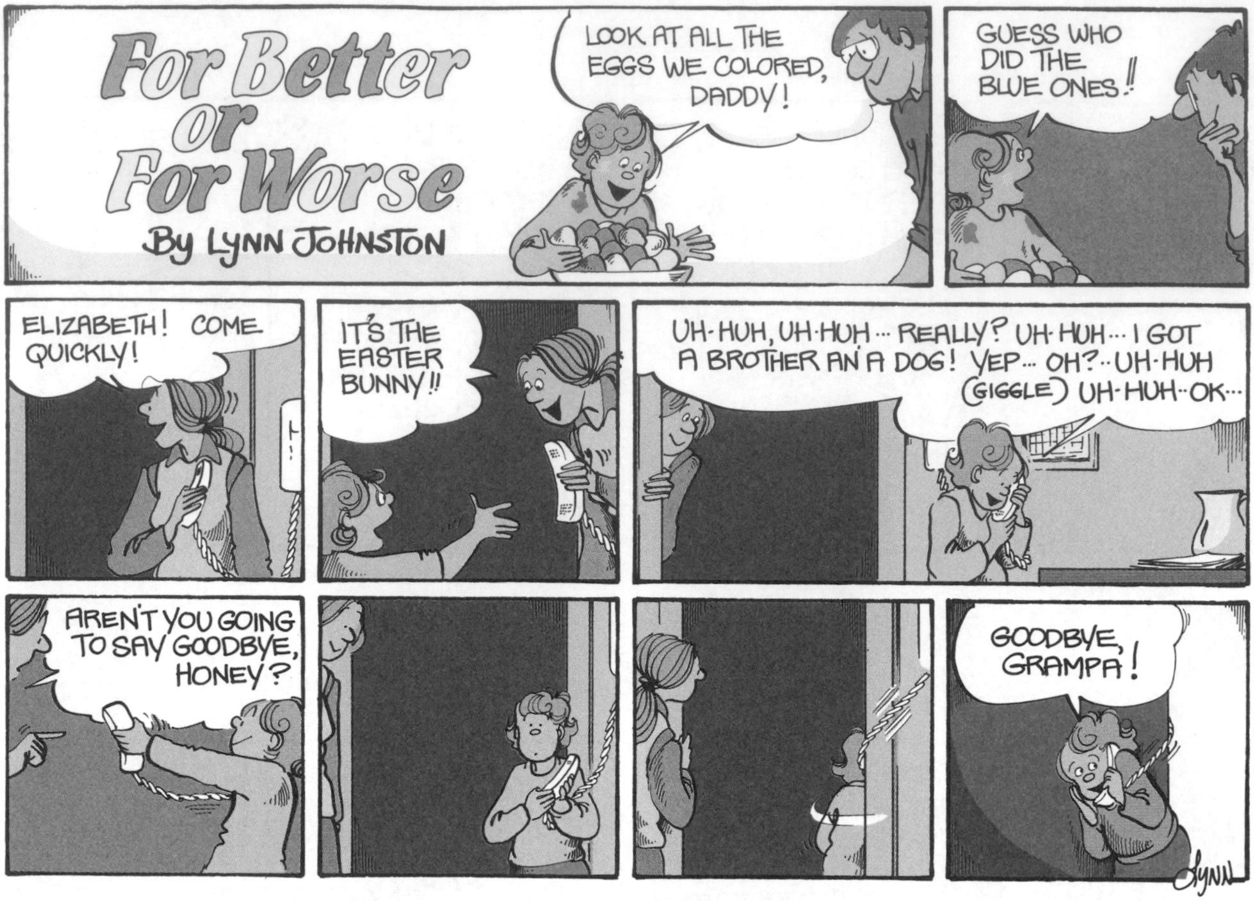
For Better or For Worse
By Lynn Johnston
LOOK AT ALL THE EGGS WE COLORED, DADDY!
GUESS WHO DID THE BLUE ONES!!
ELIZABETH! COME QUICKLY!
IT'S THE EASTER BUNNY!!
UH-HUH, UH-HUH... REALLY? UH-HUH... I GOT A BROTHER AN' A DOG! YEP... OH?.. UH-HUH (GIGGLE) UH-HUH..OK...
AREN'T YOU GOING TO SAY GOODBYE, HONEY?
GOODBYE, GRAMPA!
LYNN

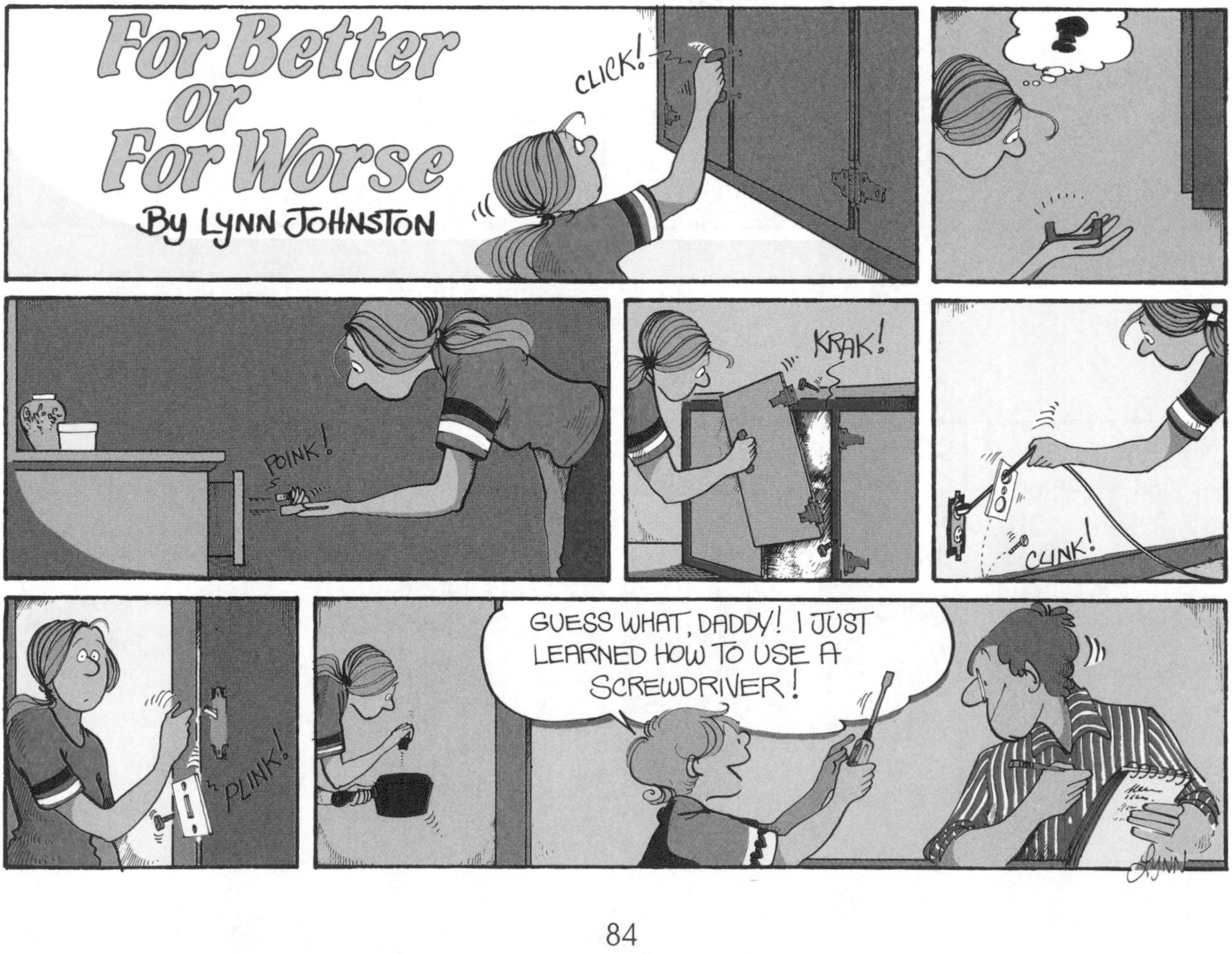
For Better or For Worse
By Lynn Johnston
CLICK!
?
POINK!
KRAK!
CLINK!
PLINK!
GUESS WHAT, DADDY! I JUST LEARNED HOW TO USE A SCREWDRIVER!
LYNN

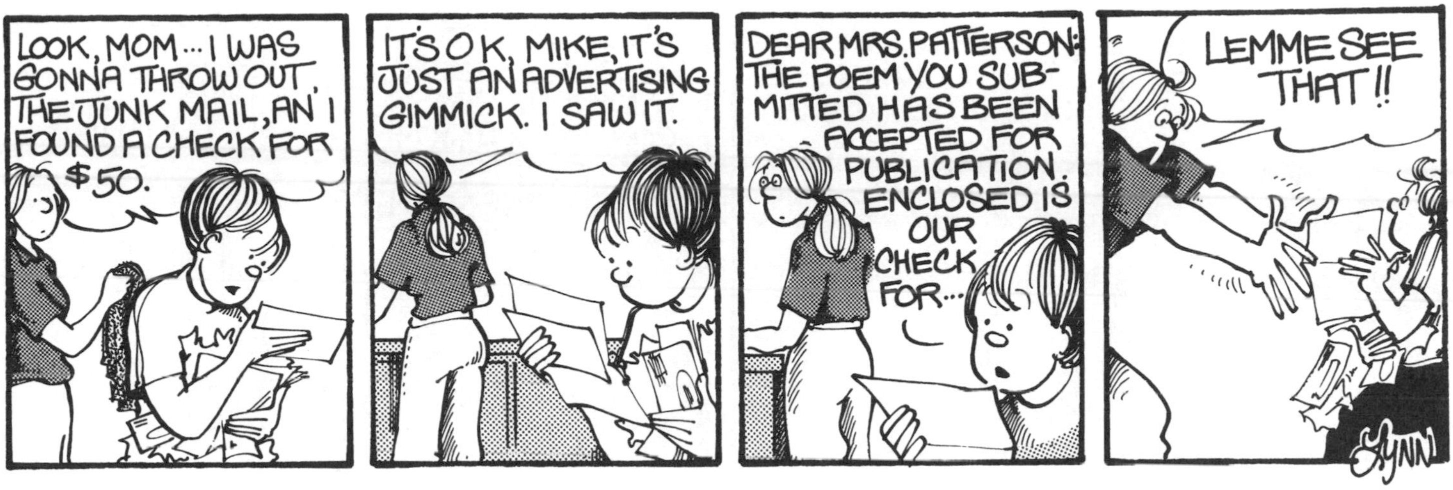
LOOK, MOM... I WAS GONNA THROW OUT THE JUNK MAIL, AN' I FOUND A CHECK FOR $50.
IT'S O K, MIKE, IT'S JUST AN ADVERTISING GIMMICK. I SAW IT.
DEAR MRS. PATTERSON: THE POEM YOU SUBMITTED HAS BEEN ACCEPTED FOR PUBLICATION. ENCLOSED IS OUR CHECK FOR...
LEMME SEE THAT!!
LYNN

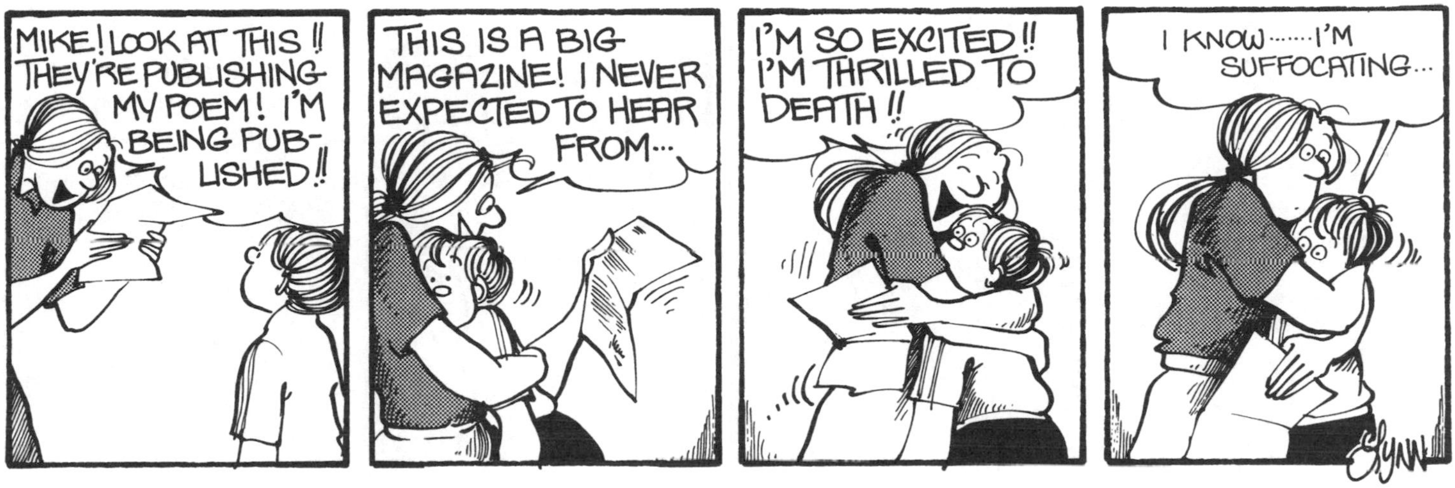
MIKE! LOOK AT THIS!! THEY'RE PUBLISHING MY POEM! I'M BEING PUBLISHED!!
THIS IS A BIG MAGAZINE! I NEVER EXPECTED TO HEAR FROM...
I'M SO EXCITED!! I'M THRILLED TO DEATH!!
I KNOW......I'M SUFFOCATING...
LYNN

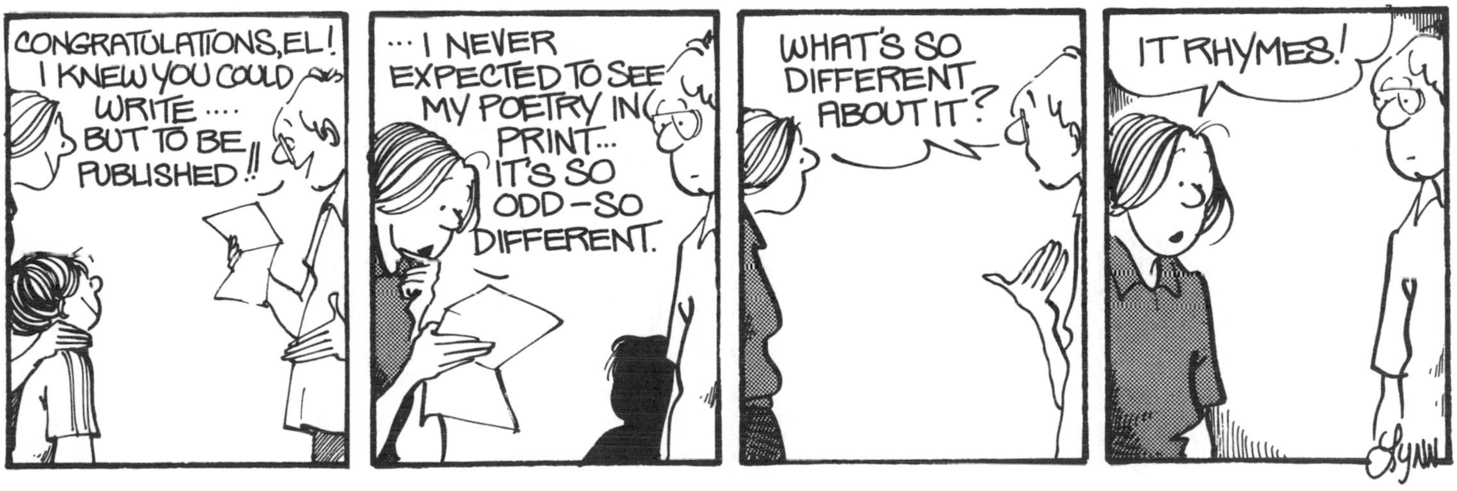
CONGRATULATIONS, EL! I KNEW YOU COULD WRITE.... BUT TO BE PUBLISHED!!
...I NEVER EXPECTED TO SEE MY POETRY IN PRINT... IT'S SO ODD - SO DIFFERENT.
WHAT'S SO DIFFERENT ABOUT IT?
IT RHYMES!
LYNN

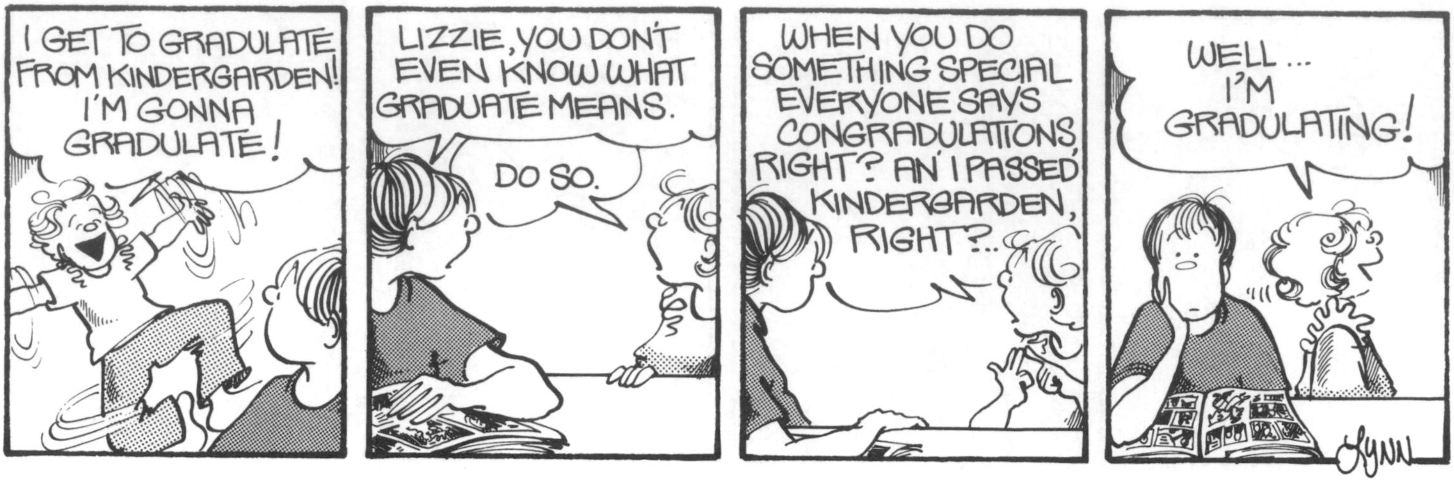
I GET TO GRADULATE FROM KINDERGARDEN! I'M GONNA GRADULATE!
LIZZIE, YOU DON'T EVEN KNOW WHAT GRADUATE MEANS.
DO SO.
WHEN YOU DO SOMETHING SPECIAL EVERYONE SAYS CONGRADULATIONS, RIGHT? AN' I PASSED KINDERGARDEN, RIGHT?...
WELL ... I'M GRADULATING!
LYNN

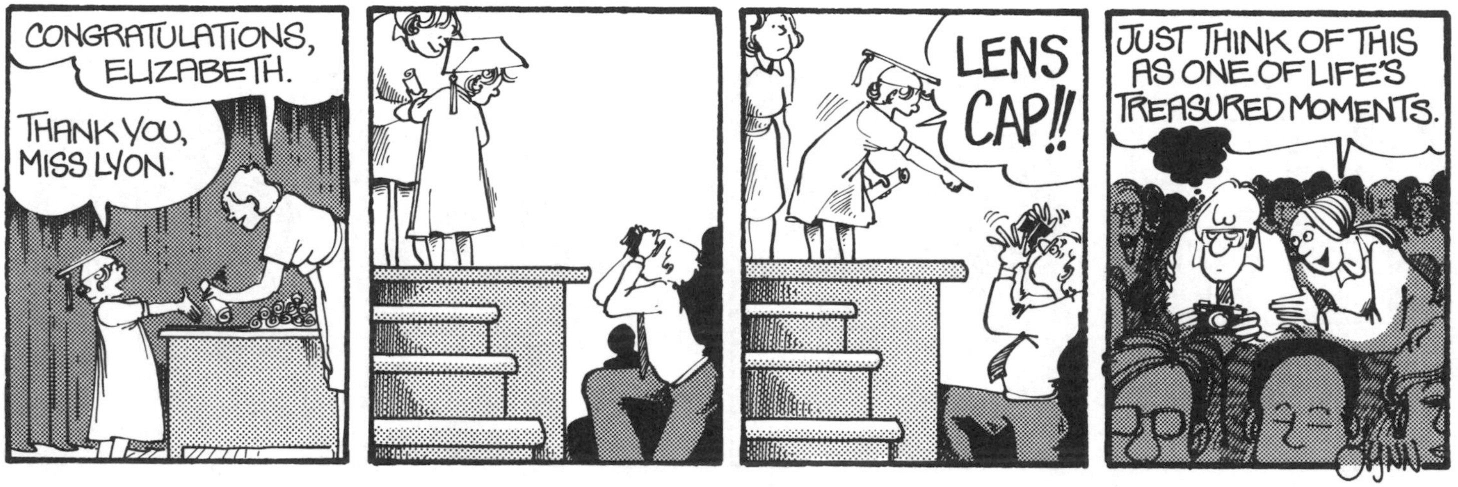
CONGRATULATIONS, ELIZABETH.
THANK YOU, MISS LYON.
LENS CAP!!
JUST THINK OF THIS AS ONE OF LIFE'S TREASURED MOMENTS.
LYNN

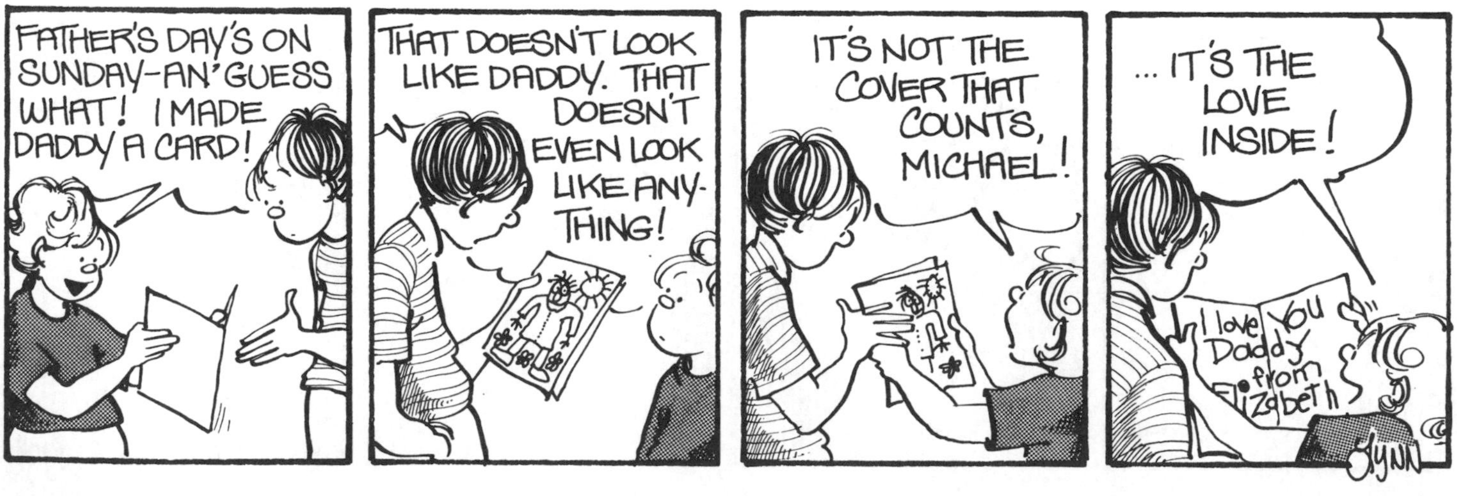
FATHER'S DAY'S ON SUNDAY-AN' GUESS WHAT! I MADE DADDY A CARD!
THAT DOESN'T LOOK LIKE DADDY. THAT DOESN'T EVEN LOOK LIKE ANY-THING!
IT'S NOT THE COVER THAT COUNTS, MICHAEL!
... IT'S THE LOVE INSIDE!
I love You Daddy from Elizabeth
LYNN

The Middle Years

From the beginning, FBorFW was received by readers with an enthusiasm that was both startling and enormously gratifying. Within five years, it was being consistently rated as one of the top three comics in both Canada and the United States. Considering the incredible quality of the competition, this was heady stuff.

I joined the National Cartoonists Society and took off with Rod to New York for the Reuben Awards, then held at the wonderful old Plaza Hotel, the backdrop for so many movies we'd seen. There I met some amazing people whose work I had admired, and even copied, for years: Will Eisner (*The Spirit*), Mort Drucker, Al Jaffee, Sergio Aragones from *Mad* magazine, and Gahan Wilson from *Playboy*, whose dark, demonic satire was admired by my art-school contemporaries to the point where we were all trying to outdo him. That's the way to learn cartooning. Find someone you admire and study what they do and how they do it! I told Mr. Wilson how much I loved his work. He responded dourly "Thank you . . . my mother says if I wasn't a cartoonist, I would have been a psychopath."

Jim Davis (*Garfield*) was there along with Mike Peters (*Mother Goose* and *Grimm*). We were the new kids on the block. And we hung together, in awe of the other guests. Dik Browne (*Hagar*), Mort Walker (*Beetle Bailey*), Milton Caniff (*Terry and the Pirates*)—so many of our heroes were in the same room with us, welcoming, accepting, glad to introduce us around. Rod and I sat with Bill and Bunny Hoest (*The Lockhorns*) and a lifelong friendship began with a room full of talented people—all vying for the same small pieces of newspaper real estate, yet supportive, complimentary, and so much fun to be with. I hadn't expected to be so readily accepted into the inner circle of famous comic artists. The NCS membership gave me even more reasons to leave home, as I attended board meetings and helped with the newsletter.

The arrogant twit I was trying to suppress was resurfacing and, oblivious to the frustration of my family, I bounced along, convinced I was good at everything, thank you, and peel me a grape! Success is something everyone dreams of, but in reality, it's a bit like a unicorn—the subject of great fantasies, but a troublesome beast to actually have around the house. Praise is seductive stuff. It's appallingly easy to make the mistake of believing one's own publicity!

I continued to work hard at the strip, however. I was never happy with what I did and would often throw out perfectly good stuff and do it again—because it wasn't good enough. I wanted to be the best. I wasn't in competition with other cartoonists—the competition was with myself. I couldn't wait for the paper (a day late) to see how the strip looked. The *Winnipeg Free Press* was one of our first clients, and they gave me a half page on Saturday, which is the day the colored comics run in Canada. This was great, since it allowed me to see my work in a large color format, pushing me to improve the coloring as best I could with the methods available at the time.

I began to put more and more detail into the backgrounds. I went to Buffalo, New York, to meet the folks who produced the color plates and sent the colored funnies to all the papers in North America. Tim Rosenthal, the guy in charge, was keen to see a cartoonist take an interest in the mechanics behind the scenes, and toured me through the labyrinth of cutting rooms. Color was done with a very time-consuming process using ruby lith—an acetate that had to be specially cut for every color the artist indicated, on what were like "paint by number" diagrams, sent with every strip. This system is too complicated to describe, but it worked. Tim introduced me to the photographers and the artists in the composition rooms; he showed me the huge presses and all the different methods editors chose to receive the comics. I was so impressed! Tim became someone I talked to often, and I called other cartoonists to tell them we had an ally in the system if we wanted to push for better and more variety in our color.

Computerized coloring was just starting to come onto the scene, and soon there were far more options to choose from. I hired another young artist and mom to do the color indication charts for me and discovered the joy of working with an assistant. Frances, like me, was a perfectionist. With her onboard, the Sunday page (as the color comics are called in the United States) took on a more polished look. She could devote more time to the color than I could, and she was so talented.

I also got help with the fan mail, which was arriving in larger and larger envelopes. It sometimes took a whole weekend to answer. My thinking was: If someone took the time and trouble to write, I should have the courtesy to answer. I know how nice it is to receive a response, so I wrote back to everyone, until I couldn't do it anymore. My family didn't get enough of my attention as it was! I worked together with Debbie, another Lynn Lake mom, who had beautiful handwriting and answered the letters with my voice. I would sign them and another great system was in place.

Despite the warm friendships, humorous goings-on, and great material, Lynn Lake irritated me enormously. Professionally, I was lonely. Cartooning is a solitary business and I yearned to have more contact with people who understood the lifestyle, shared the "in" jokes, and knew the challenges of the job.

We owned a magic carpet. At least, this is how I saw our airplane. Rod was a careful and well-prepared pilot who never took chances. I saw this wonderful machine as a way out. We often went to Winnipeg with the kids to go shopping, or visit friends, and sometimes we flew as far as Kansas City where we would meet with the people at the syndicate and talk about the next book, the next project. Rod enjoyed the flying and involvement with the wonderful people I knew and worked with, but he had a busy practice in town and sometimes felt like a glorified chauffeur.

There were times when I had to make a meeting or had an event to attend, and often the weather wouldn't be the best for small aircraft at lower altitudes. Still, I would insist, and Rod would fly me down to Winnipeg or wherever I had to be, dodging thunderstorms and possible freezing rain just to make an appointment. It's to his great credit as a pilot and the grace of God that we were not killed on some of the riskier trips.

My job involved all of us. My husband was now living with a different person than the one he married, and he amicably resigned himself to being "Mr. Lynn Johnston." Aaron and Kate accepted my work as kids do, but they never really knew how to react to the questions and the teasing. All too often, even when I was home and sitting in front of them, I was completely absent, mentally. Aaron was quick to learn my glazed "Patterson Mode" expression and take full advantage of it. "Can I have a raise in my allowance?" Because my answer to everything was "yes," both kids got in on the game. "Can we eat a bag of chips before dinner?" Katie would ask, "Can I cut up the front room curtains?!" They were (mostly!) joking, but it was an example of how deeply you can immerse yourself in a fantasy world and let the real one fend for itself. Kate once stood in front my drafting table eating a piece of cake.

"Can I have some of the cake on the counter?" she asked. "No," I said, "it's for company."

"Oh," she said and put it back. I didn't notice dessert had been mutilated until I was ready to serve it.

My mother-in-law was a rock and a realist. It was Ruth who shook me out of my periodic melancholy, and gave me both counsel and criticism. And it was Rod who kept our marriage together.

It says a great deal for his patience, understanding, and ability to tune me out entirely that we made it through this stage of our lives intact as a couple and a family. In fact, we sometimes debated whether we would have done so had it not been for a terrifying incident which occurred in the summer of 1984.

Our aircraft at the time was a Cessna 185, which was on Edo floats—the kind with retractable wheels for landing on both land and water. This was his transportation to the remote First Nations villages he traveled to every month to provide much needed dental care. It was also his pride and joy. Rod loved to fly, and almost any excuse was good enough to get him out to the airport, checklist in hand. When three canoeist friends from Hamilton asked if he would pick them up in the plane at the end of an arctic trip, he was happy to oblige. They were taking a strenuous trek down the Yathyked River which would end at a remote lake with the same name. On the appointed day, Rod flew into a bright blue sky. And vanished.

For three long, harrowing days, we waited for news from the Hercules aircraft and the search-and-rescue team onboard who scanned the sullen, empty landscape for signs of life—or death. Not one to pray for personal things, I asked all the powers that be to watch out for Rod and his friends and bring them home. Together with his family, I also prepared for the worst.

On the evening of the third day, the men were finally spotted huddled on the rocky shoreline near the overturned aircraft. The wind had caused it to roll over on takeoff. All that could be seen from the air were the floats. After being so long without food or shelter, Rod and his friends were starving, exhausted, hypothermic, and near their limit of endurance. Finding the men alive was a cause for celebration for the rescue team who were bracing themselves for a sad discovery. Had the team not found them, they would not have survived much longer.

For Rod it was a lesson in piloting and in humility. He said he used to wish he had a Mercedes-Benz, a huge workshop, and many other things, but when you are out in the barrens with no food or shelter, all that's important is warmth, a full stomach, and the love of your family.

For me, it was another chance. I had experienced the possibility of becoming a widow, and I was so very lucky to have my husband back. All our priorities were realigned. All of the quarrels and friction which seemed so important before suddenly became just as petty as they were.

Since our lives were by then inextricably entangled with those of the Pattersons, the incident eventually made its way onto the comics page. This marked a turning point for the strip as well as for us, personally. From 1987 on, the Pattersons no longer lived within a tight, self-absorbed circle. The story lines had focused almost exclusively on parenting, household chaos, and relationships within the family's close circle of friends. John and "Uncle Phil's" brush with death after a canoeing accident marked the first time the strip dealt with a genuine life-and-death situation. From then on, the harsh realities of the world intruded more often, the family's perspective widened, and the length, depth, and complexity of the story lines increased.

Soon, our lives would again be in transition as the mine in Lynn Lake gave notice of impending closure and everyone who could find work elsewhere sold what they could and moved away. We had purchased property near North Bay, Ontario, in preparation for the inevitable shutdown and moved to a log house in the countryside. The area was far enough into the north to suit the Johnstons. Rod's mom, dad, and brother, Ralph, all moved with us and we became neighbors again. It was still a five-minute walk to Ruth and Tom's house, which made everything seem as though it was all supposed to happen. Someone was writing us into a story line just as surely as I choreographed the lives of the Pattersons.

It was a timely transition. Aaron was entering grade six, Kate was starting grade one. The Patterson kids had also entered the school system. Both the real and the imaginary children were expanding their interests and awareness beyond their homes and families. They were developing a growing, if not always welcome, insight into the tougher issues of life. For parents, the day their youngest child goes off to school often marks a time when adult pursuits and career goals come back into focus.

My artwork changed again during this period. I was offered the opportunity to do six animated specials with an Ottawa studio, which meant that all the characters had to be drawn in three dimensions, sizes had to be right according to age, clothing styles were established, and expressions had to be drawn so the animators could follow my style and try to reproduce as many nuances of their personalities as possible. The family car had to be an actual car, and Farley the dog had to move and act like a real dog, with some leverage in the expression department. A lot of as-yet-unknown details had to be drawn. The most difficult job was to design the Pattersons' house, which on the outside looked like our house in Dundas but had the floor plan of the house in Lynn Lake. This implausible combination was an architect's nightmare and took the background designer and myself a full day to fabricate. Eventually, we had what looked like a set of contractor's plans, which included the garage, workshop, and a diagram of how the property sloped down toward a lane and ravine.

It was the first time I had seen what the house really looked like inside and out. Until then, I could stretch a room or change the position of a hallway, but now the house was an entity. Each room was drawn to show what the furniture was like, where the closets were, and what color schemes the family had chosen. Details were as precise as a photograph. Even an aerial view of the community had to be invented so the bus stop on the corner and the park down the street appeared in correct positions from every angle when outside "shots" were needed. It was an exhausting exercise, but it made my nonexistent people and places even more believable, even more accessible to the imagination.

From 1987 to 1995, lighter moments in the lives of the characters were balanced by more serious things. The strip dealt with real-world issues including political activism, alcoholism and child abuse, physical handicaps, the ego-crushing experience of being laid off, ethics in the press and—most controversial—the coming out of a gay teenager. The children were becoming adults, expressing themselves differently. Their appearances changed as did Elly's hairstyle.

Elly had a surprise pregnancy, and baby April came into the picture on April 1, 1992. This gave me the luxury of working with a character that was completely fictitious, about whom I could write anything without causing repercussion in Aaron and Kate's lives. Everyone continued to age and Farley the dog sired a litter of pups—one of which was adopted by the Pattersons. April was a toddler when the last serious story line of this period was written.

April fell into a rain-swollen creek. Once again, a member of the family found themselves in mortal danger, once again, there was a rescue just in time. This ending, however, was not entirely a happy one, as Farley the dog died from the stress of his heroic struggle to save April. It was the first time that death appeared onstage in the strip, with all the grief, guilt, and heartache that comes with it. It would not be the last time.

Charles Schulz was now one of my closest friends and confidants in the business. When I told him I had to do away with Farley, he was genuinely furious. I explained that I had no choice. Since the strip developed in real time, the dog was much older than he should be, and to allow him to stay in the strip would be contrary to everything I was doing. When you're working in real time, you have to deal with life spans! He was angry nonetheless, admonishing my decision. He threatened to have Snoopy hit by a truck at the same time and taken to the hospital. "Then nobody will care about your stupid story," he said. He was serious, so when the time came to write the series, I didn't tell him. The episode came as a surprise—and he never forgave me. Rather, he never forgave April for falling into the river in the first place! Like some readers, there are cartoonists who take these characters far too seriously.

These longer, more controversial stories sparked plenty of reader feedback. My favorite letter was from a man in Michigan who wrote: "You made me sick when you wrote that story about the gay kid in *For Better or For Worse*. After that, I completely stopped reading your strip. . . . Now that you have seen fit to kill off Farley the dog, I am NEVER going to read your lousy strip again!"

Lawrence's story and the death of Farley brought in an overwhelming flood of letters, but the stories of Sharon Edwards's paraplegia and Gordon Mayes's physical abuse at the hands of his alcoholic father also resulted in deeply emotional responses. Some readers approved of the topics and the way they were handled, some emphatically did not, but it was clear that everyone had been deeply moved one way or another and that the characters in the strip were believably real.

Although I never intended to be a conduit to open discussion about controversial subjects, I'm pleased to know that many of the strips have been used in presentations, parenting articles, books, and teaching aids. All of us face difficult issues in our lives. Death touches us all, sooner or later. Everyone, whether they are willing to admit it or not, has someone in their immediate family or circle of friends who is gay. Most of us know individuals who are disabled and others who are or have been the victims of physical abuse.

Since it is so important for me not to bring a character into the strip unless I can really "live" inside them and see the world as they do, I research my stories carefully, making sure the situations are accurate, possible, and fair. I have had the privilege of letting others speak through my characters. If the world is a stage, theirs are the most compelling performances, and their stories deserve to be told!

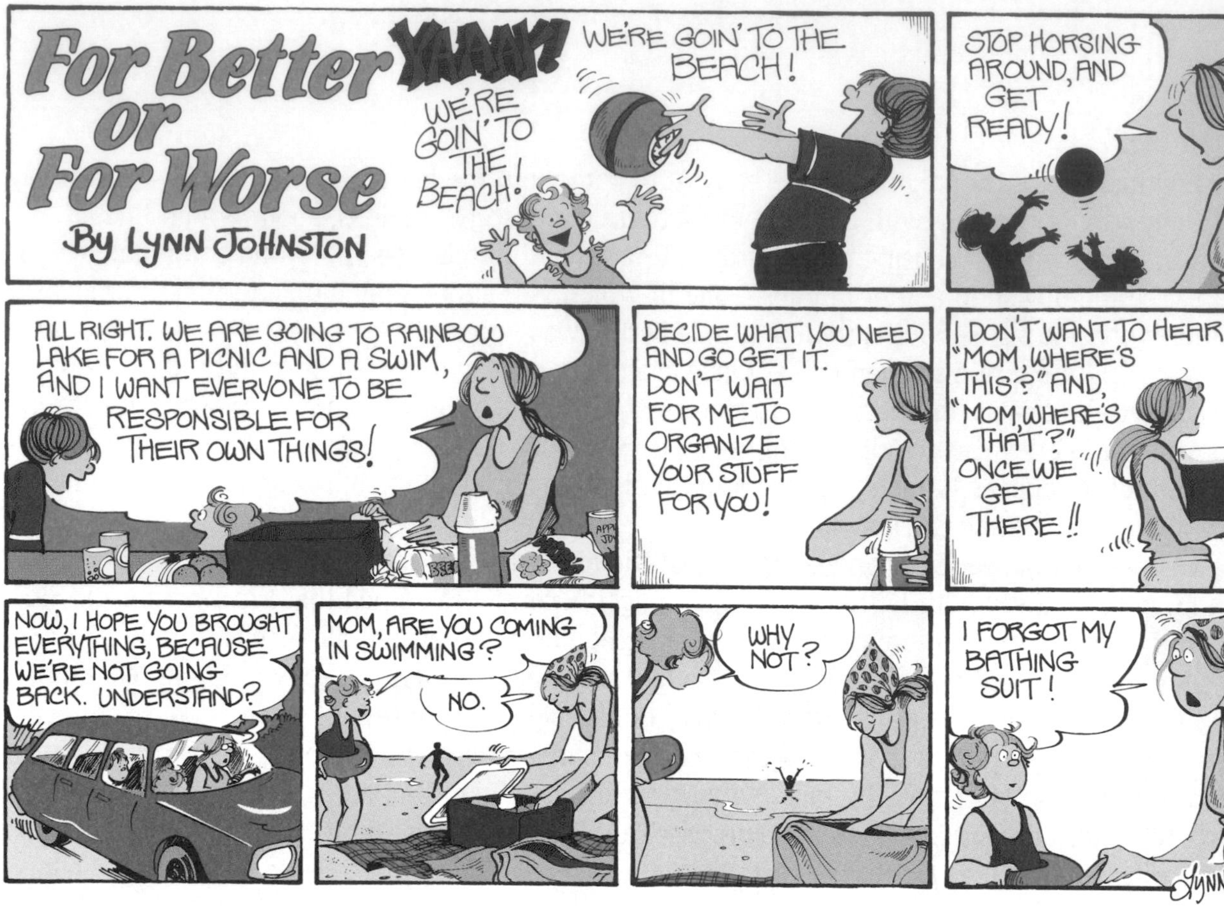
For Better or For Worse
By Lynn Johnston
YAAAAY!
WE'RE GOIN' TO THE BEACH!
WE'RE GOIN' TO THE BEACH!
STOP HORSING AROUND, AND GET READY!
ALL RIGHT. WE ARE GOING TO RAINBOW LAKE FOR A PICNIC AND A SWIM, AND I WANT EVERYONE TO BE RESPONSIBLE FOR THEIR OWN THINGS!
DECIDE WHAT YOU NEED AND GO GET IT. DON'T WAIT FOR ME TO ORGANIZE YOUR STUFF FOR YOU!
I DON'T WANT TO HEAR "MOM, WHERE'S THIS?" AND, "MOM, WHERE'S THAT?" ONCE WE GET THERE!!
NOW, I HOPE YOU BROUGHT EVERYTHING, BECAUSE WE'RE NOT GOING BACK. UNDERSTAND?
MOM, ARE YOU COMING IN SWIMMING?
NO.
WHY NOT?
I FORGOT MY BATHING SUIT!
LYNN

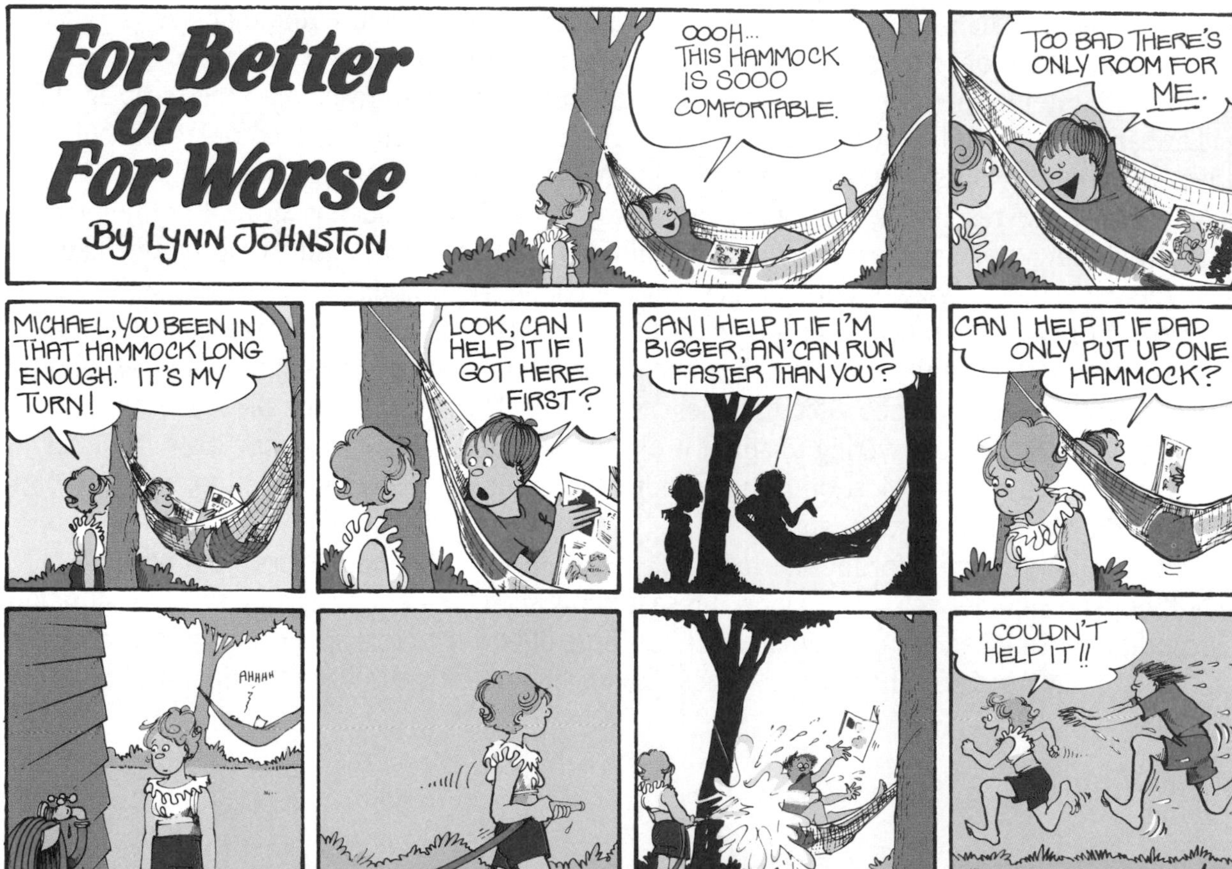
For Better or For Worse
By Lynn Johnston
OOOH... THIS HAMMOCK IS SOOO COMFORTABLE.
TOO BAD THERE'S ONLY ROOM FOR ME.
MICHAEL, YOU BEEN IN THAT HAMMOCK LONG ENOUGH. IT'S MY TURN!
LOOK, CAN I HELP IT IF I GOT HERE FIRST?
CAN I HELP IT IF I'M BIGGER, AN' CAN RUN FASTER THAN YOU?
CAN I HELP IT IF DAD ONLY PUT UP ONE HAMMOCK?
AHHHH
I COULDN'T HELP IT!!
LYNN

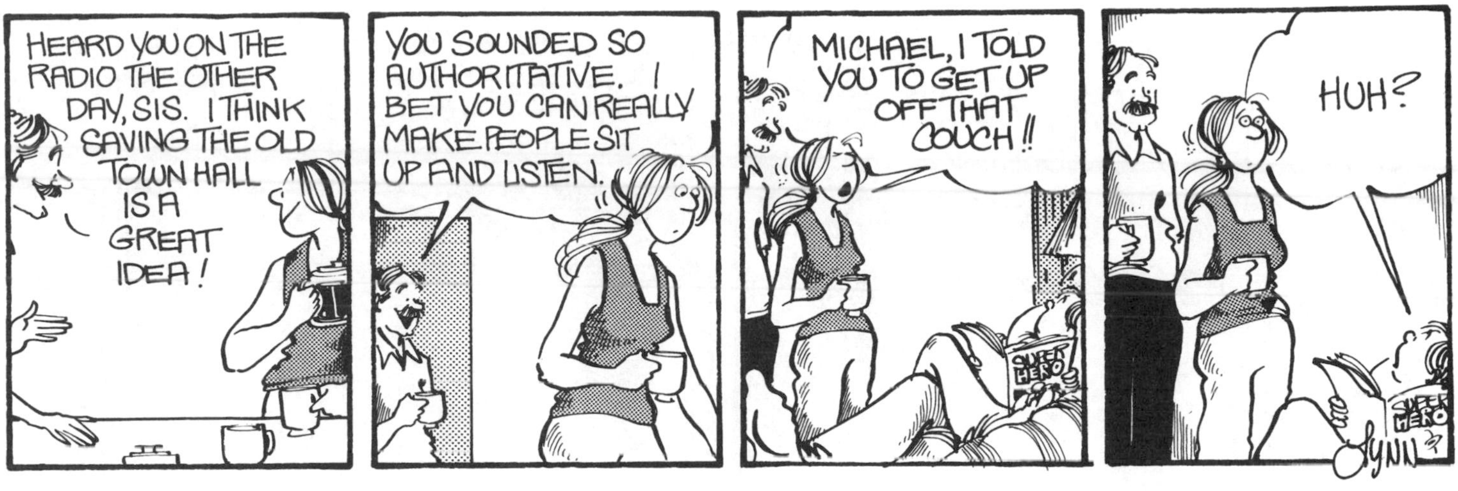
HEARD YOU ON THE RADIO THE OTHER DAY, SIS. I THINK SAVING THE OLD TOWN HALL IS A GREAT IDEA!
YOU SOUNDED SO AUTHORITATIVE. I BET YOU CAN REALLY MAKE PEOPLE SIT UP AND LISTEN.
MICHAEL, I TOLD YOU TO GET UP OFF THAT COUCH!!
SUPER HERO
HUH?
SUPER HERO
LYNN

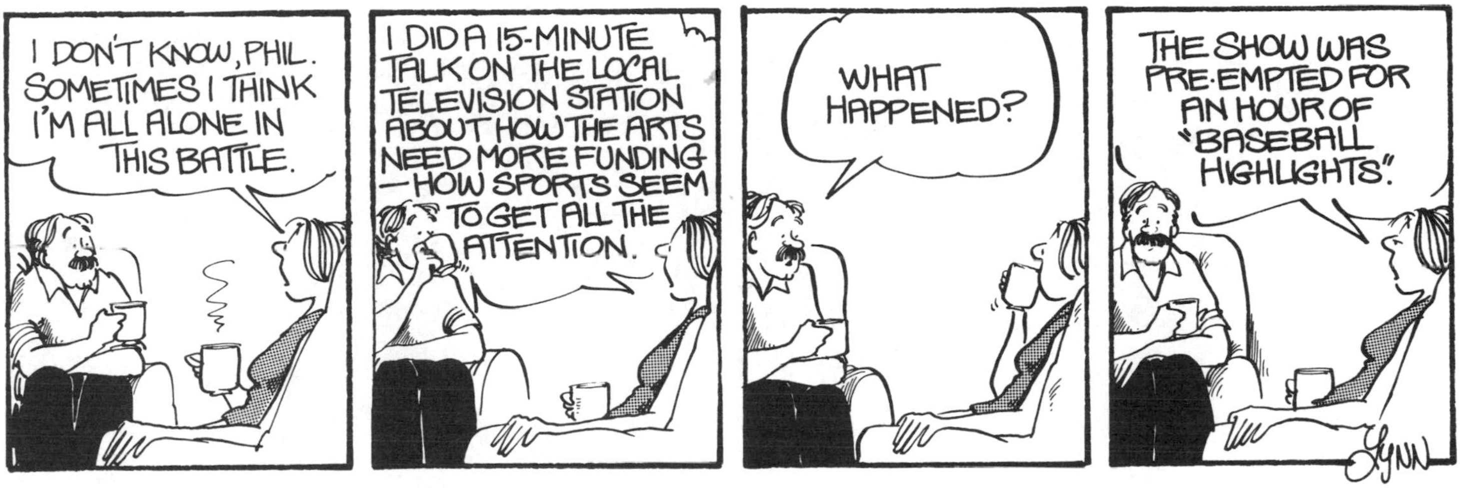
I DON'T KNOW, PHIL. SOMETIMES I THINK I'M ALL ALONE IN THIS BATTLE.
I DID A 15-MINUTE TALK ON THE LOCAL TELEVISION STATION ABOUT HOW THE ARTS NEED MORE FUNDING —HOW SPORTS SEEM TO GET ALL THE ATTENTION.
WHAT HAPPENED?
THE SHOW WAS PRE-EMPTED FOR AN HOUR OF "BASEBALL HIGHLIGHTS".
LYNN

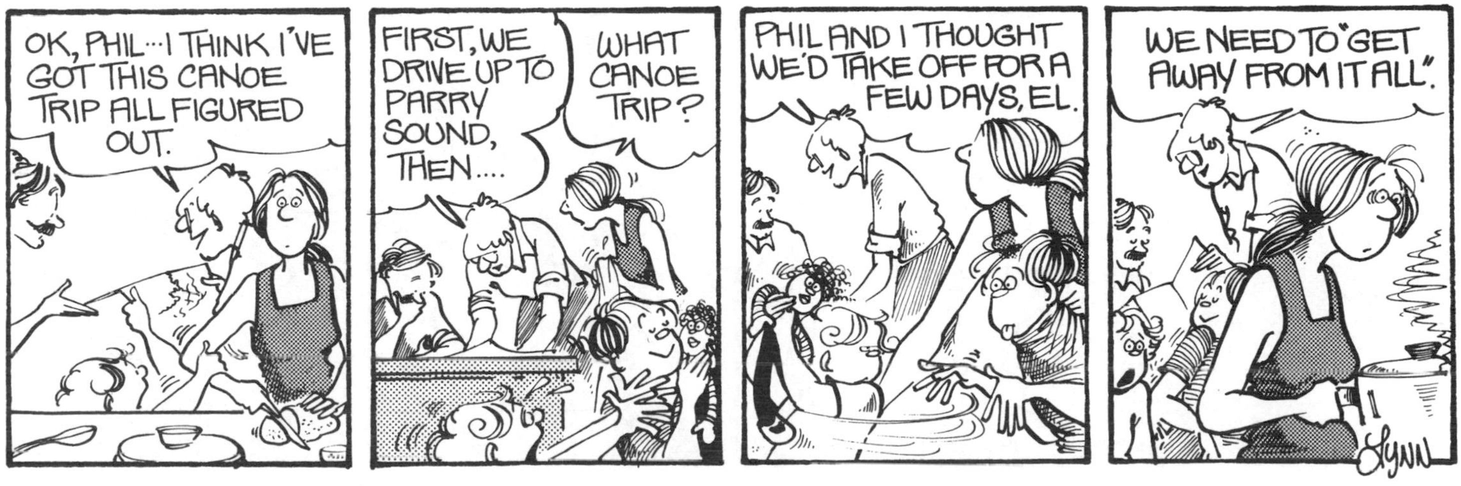
OK, PHIL···I THINK I'VE GOT THIS CANOE TRIP ALL FIGURED OUT.
FIRST, WE DRIVE UP TO PARRY SOUND, THEN....
WHAT CANOE TRIP?
PHIL AND I THOUGHT WE'D TAKE OFF FOR A FEW DAYS, EL.
WE NEED TO "GET AWAY FROM IT ALL".
LYNN

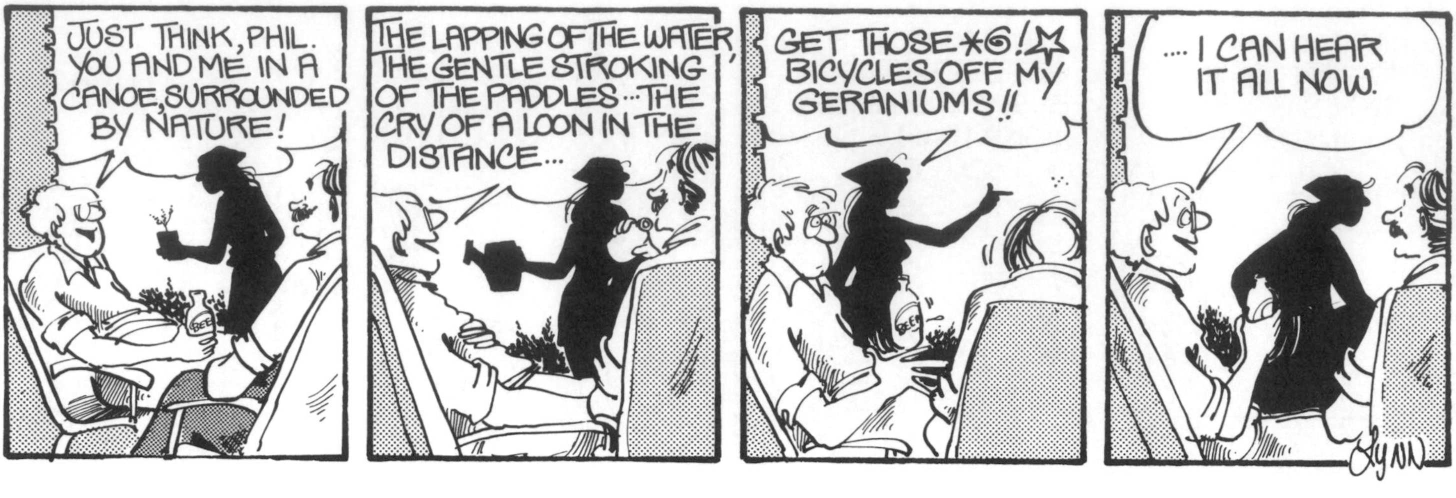
JUST THINK, PHIL. YOU AND ME IN A CANOE, SURROUNDED BY NATURE!
THE LAPPING OF THE WATER, THE GENTLE STROKING OF THE PADDLES... THE CRY OF A LOON IN THE DISTANCE...
GET THOSE *@! BICYCLES OFF MY GERANIUMS!!
.... I CAN HEAR IT ALL NOW.
LYNN

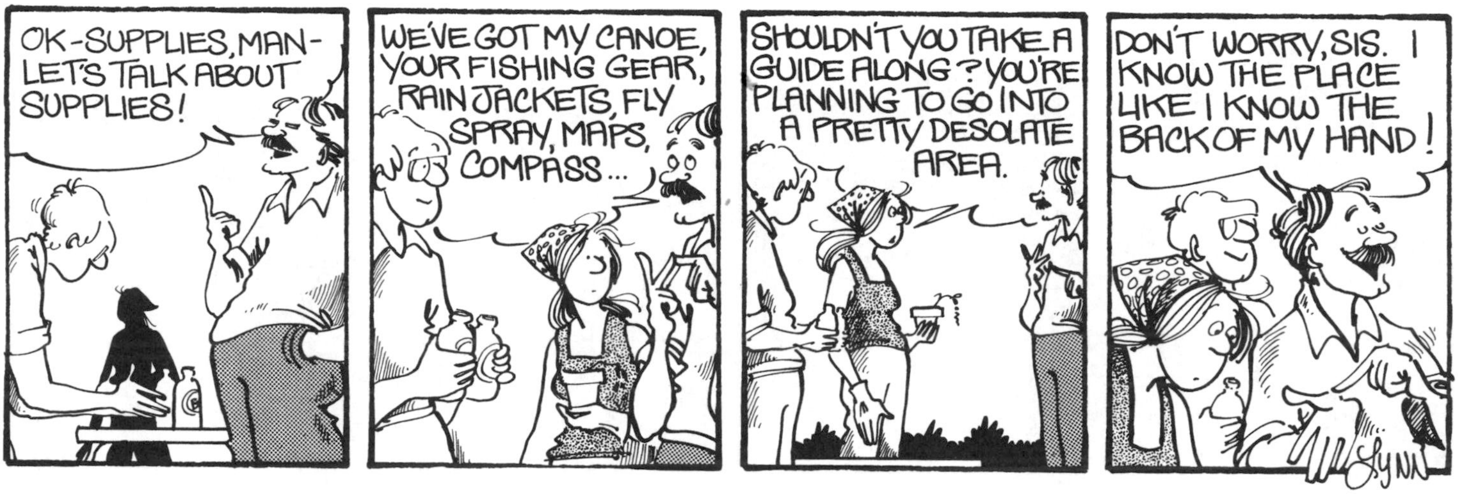
OK-SUPPLIES, MAN-LET'S TALK ABOUT SUPPLIES!
WE'VE GOT MY CANOE, YOUR FISHING GEAR, RAIN JACKETS, FLY SPRAY, MAPS, COMPASS...
SHOULDN'T YOU TAKE A GUIDE ALONG? YOU'RE PLANNING TO GO INTO A PRETTY DESOLATE AREA.
DON'T WORRY, SIS. I KNOW THE PLACE LIKE I KNOW THE BACK OF MY HAND!
LYNN

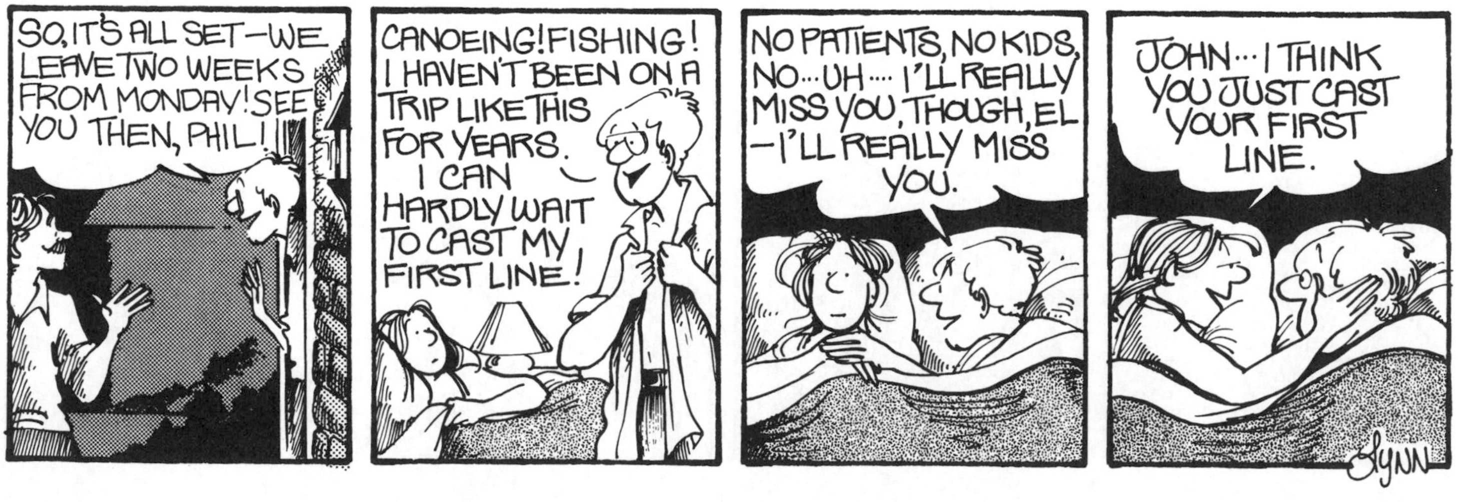
SO, IT'S ALL SET-WE LEAVE TWO WEEKS FROM MONDAY! SEE YOU THEN, PHIL!
CANOEING! FISHING! I HAVEN'T BEEN ON A TRIP LIKE THIS FOR YEARS.
I CAN HARDLY WAIT TO CAST MY FIRST LINE!
NO PATIENTS, NO KIDS, NO...UH.... I'LL REALLY MISS YOU, THOUGH, EL -I'LL REALLY MISS YOU.
JOHN... I THINK YOU JUST CAST YOUR FIRST LINE.
LYNN

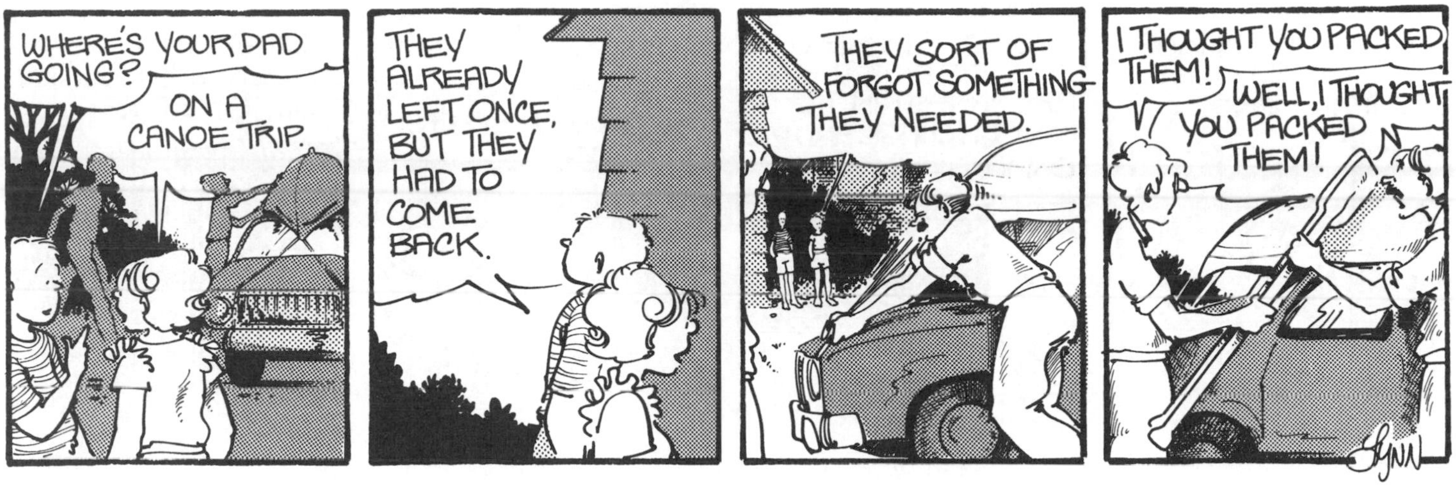
WHERE'S YOUR DAD GOING?
ON A CANOE TRIP.
THEY ALREADY LEFT ONCE, BUT THEY HAD TO COME BACK.
THEY SORT OF FORGOT SOMETHING THEY NEEDED.
I THOUGHT YOU PACKED THEM!
WELL, I THOUGHT YOU PACKED THEM!
LYNN

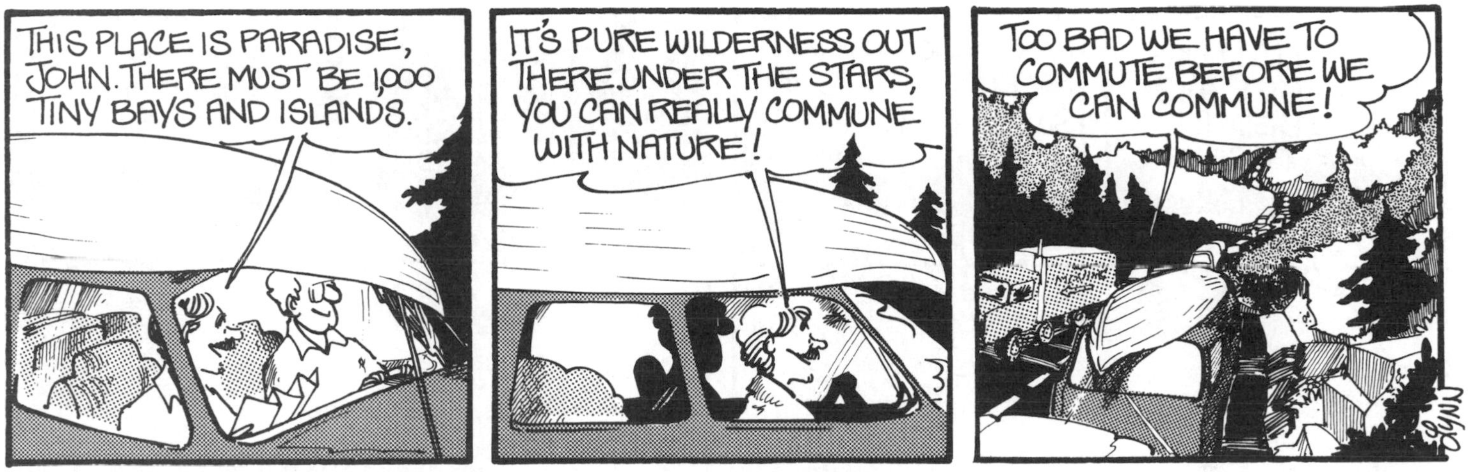
THIS PLACE IS PARADISE, JOHN. THERE MUST BE 1,000 TINY BAYS AND ISLANDS.
IT'S PURE WILDERNESS OUT THERE. UNDER THE STARS, YOU CAN REALLY COMMUNE WITH NATURE!
TOO BAD WE HAVE TO COMMUTE BEFORE WE CAN COMMUNE!
LYNN

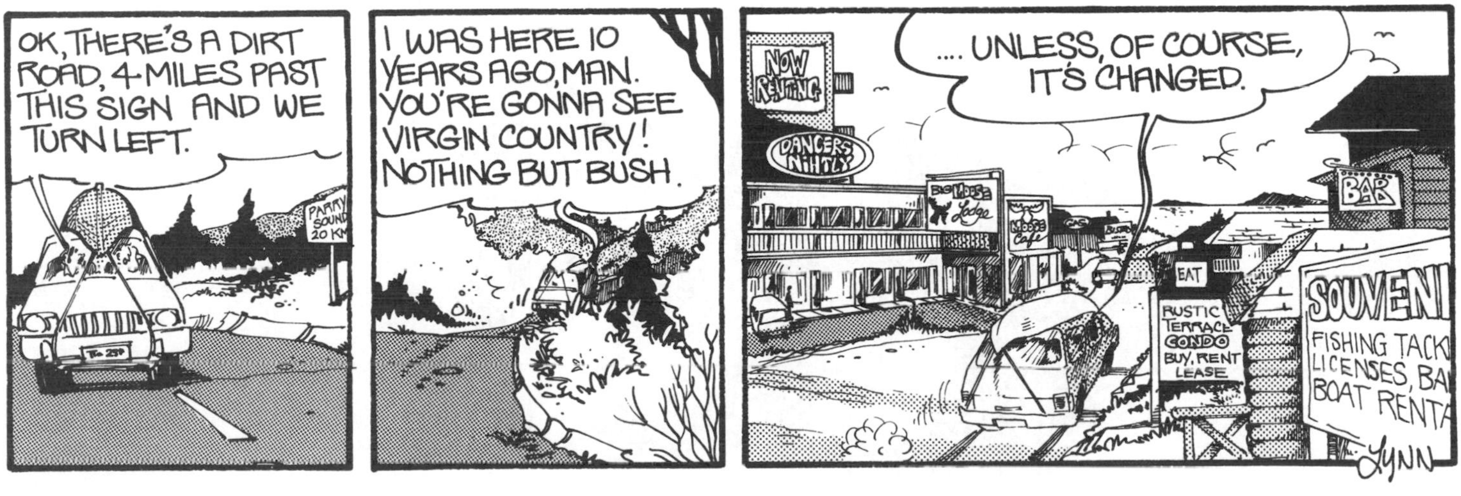
OK, THERE'S A DIRT ROAD, 4 MILES PAST THIS SIGN AND WE TURN LEFT.
PARRY SOUND 20 KM
I WAS HERE 10 YEARS AGO, MAN. YOU'RE GONNA SEE VIRGIN COUNTRY! NOTHING BUT BUSH.
.... UNLESS, OF COURSE, IT'S CHANGED.
NOW RENTING
DANCERS NIGHTLY
BIG MOOSE Lodge
BAR
EAT
RUSTIC TERRACE CONDO BUY, RENT LEASE
SOUVENI
FISHING TACK
LICENSES, BA
BOAT RENTA
LYNN

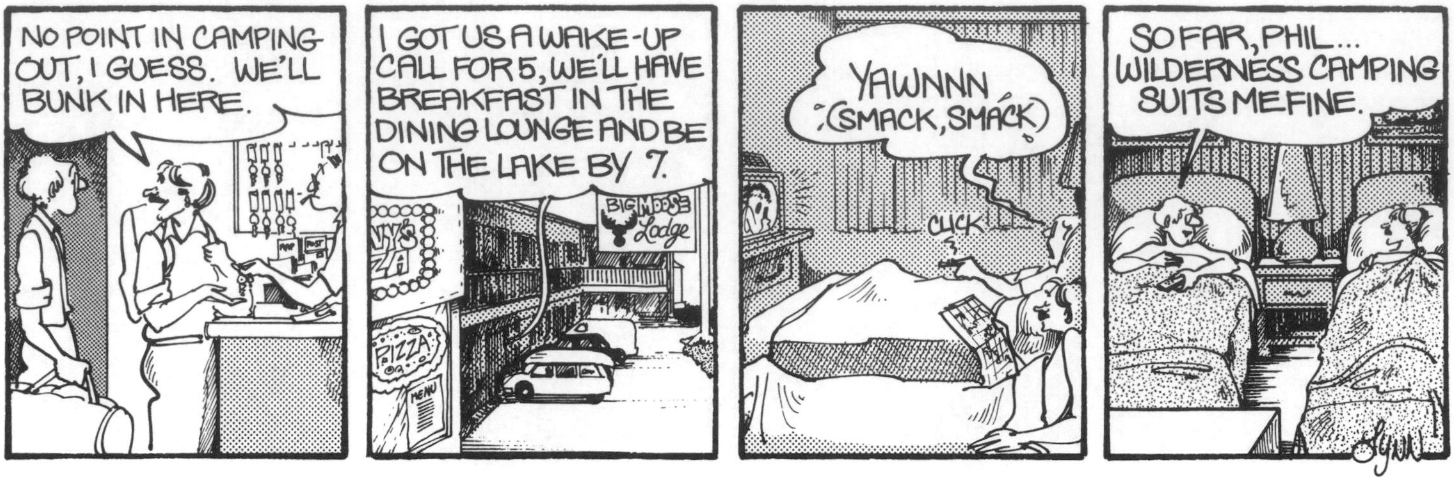
NO POINT IN CAMPING OUT, I GUESS. WE'LL BUNK IN HERE.
I GOT US A WAKE-UP CALL FOR 5, WE'LL HAVE BREAKFAST IN THE DINING LOUNGE AND BE ON THE LAKE BY 7.
BIG MOOSE Lodge
PIZZA
MENU
YAWNNN (SMACK, SMACK)
CLICK
SO FAR, PHIL... WILDERNESS CAMPING SUITS ME FINE.
Lynn

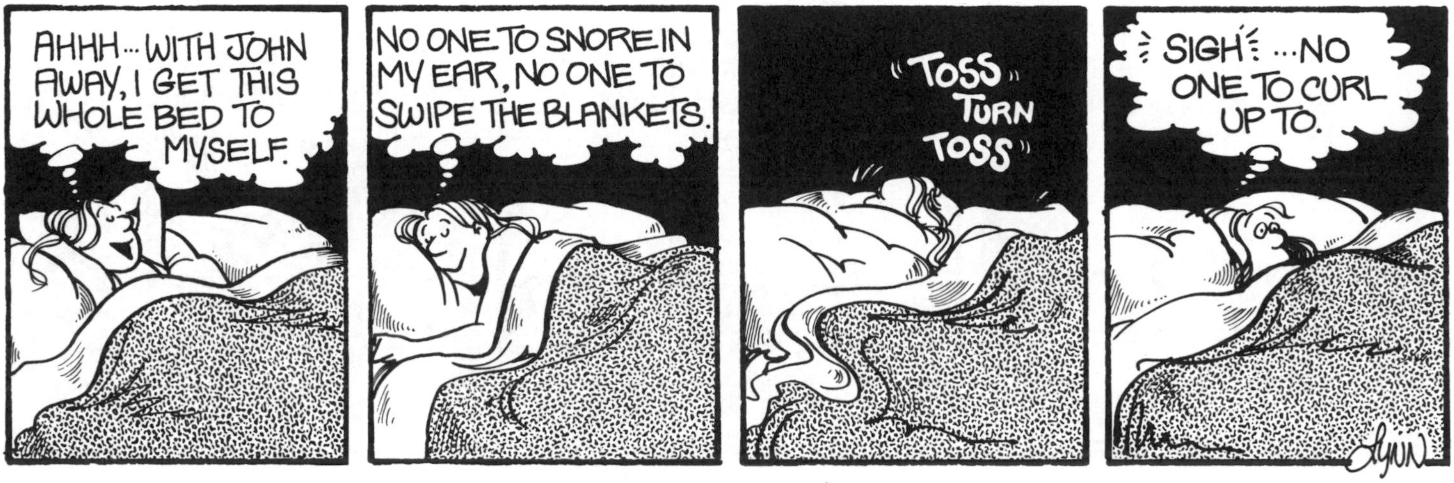
AHHH... WITH JOHN AWAY, I GET THIS WHOLE BED TO MYSELF.
NO ONE TO SNORE IN MY EAR, NO ONE TO SWIPE THE BLANKETS.
TOSS TURN TOSS
SIGH ...NO ONE TO CURL UP TO.
Lynn

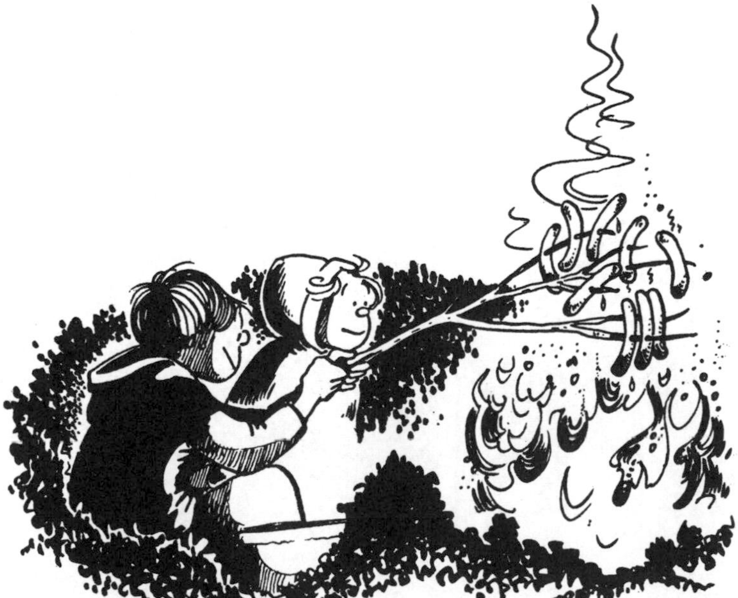

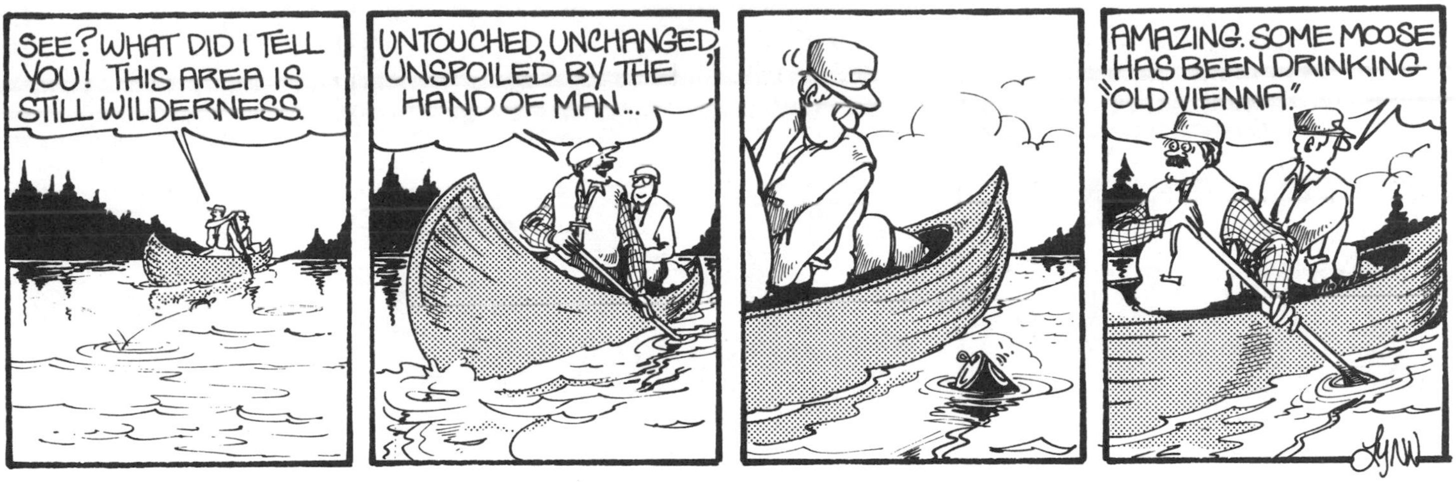
SEE? WHAT DID I TELL YOU! THIS AREA IS STILL WILDERNESS.
UNTOUCHED, UNCHANGED, UNSPOILED BY THE HAND OF MAN...
AMAZING. SOME MOOSE HAS BEEN DRINKING "OLD VIENNA."
LYNN

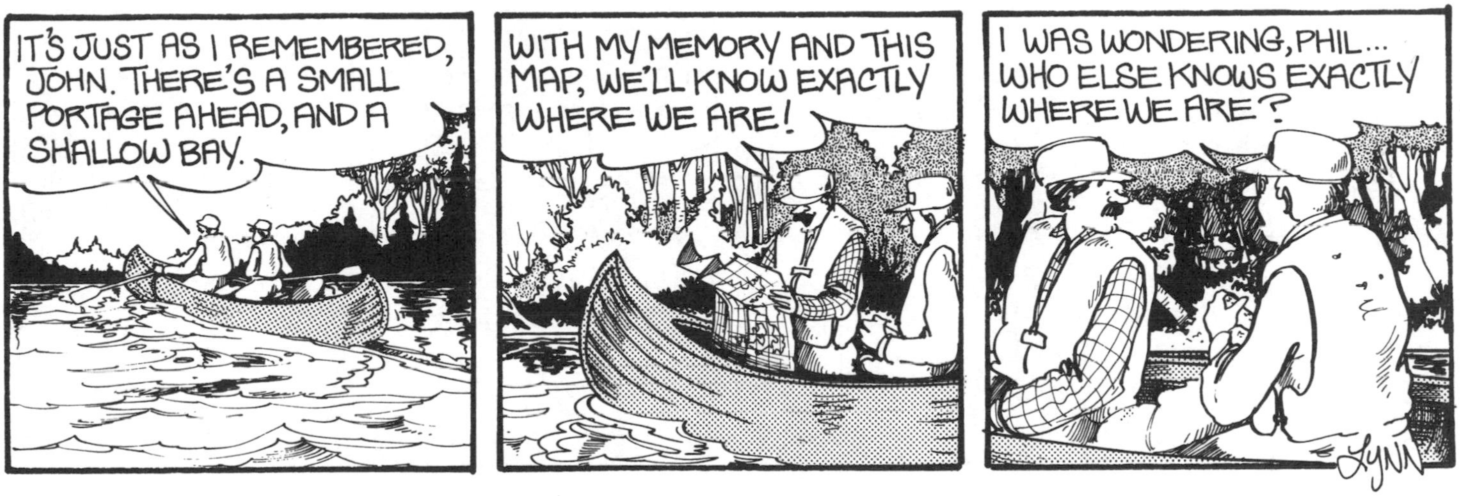
IT'S JUST AS I REMEMBERED, JOHN. THERE'S A SMALL PORTAGE AHEAD, AND A SHALLOW BAY.
WITH MY MEMORY AND THIS MAP, WE'LL KNOW EXACTLY WHERE WE ARE!
I WAS WONDERING, PHIL... WHO ELSE KNOWS EXACTLY WHERE WE ARE?
LYNN

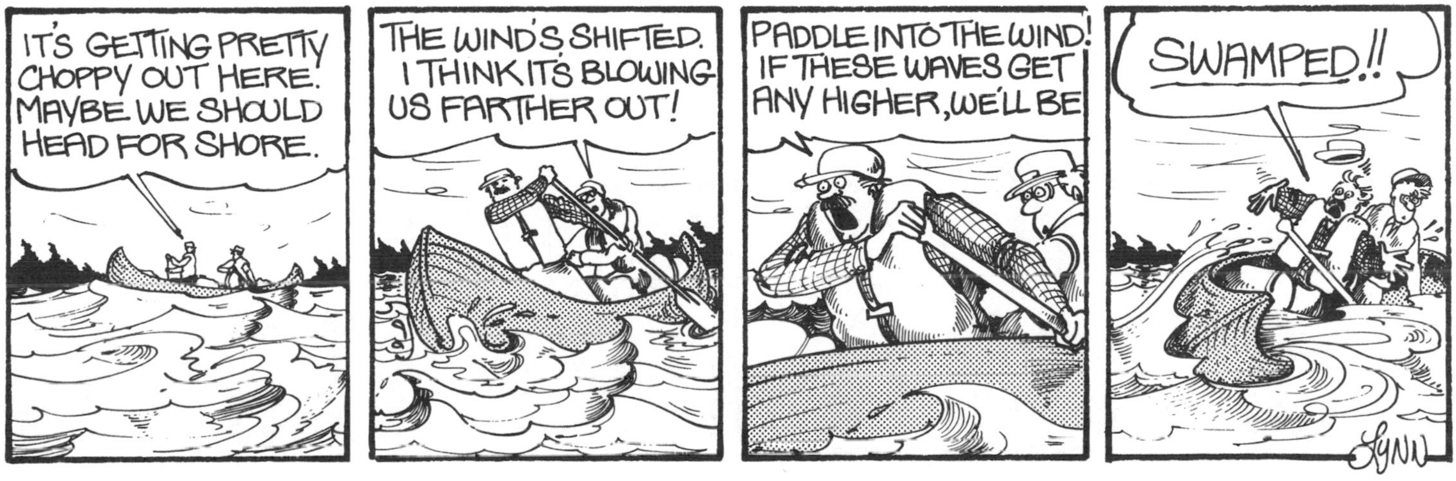
IT'S GETTING PRETTY CHOPPY OUT HERE. MAYBE WE SHOULD HEAD FOR SHORE.
THE WIND'S SHIFTED. I THINK IT'S BLOWING US FARTHER OUT!
PADDLE INTO THE WIND! IF THESE WAVES GET ANY HIGHER, WE'LL BE
SWAMPED!!
LYNN

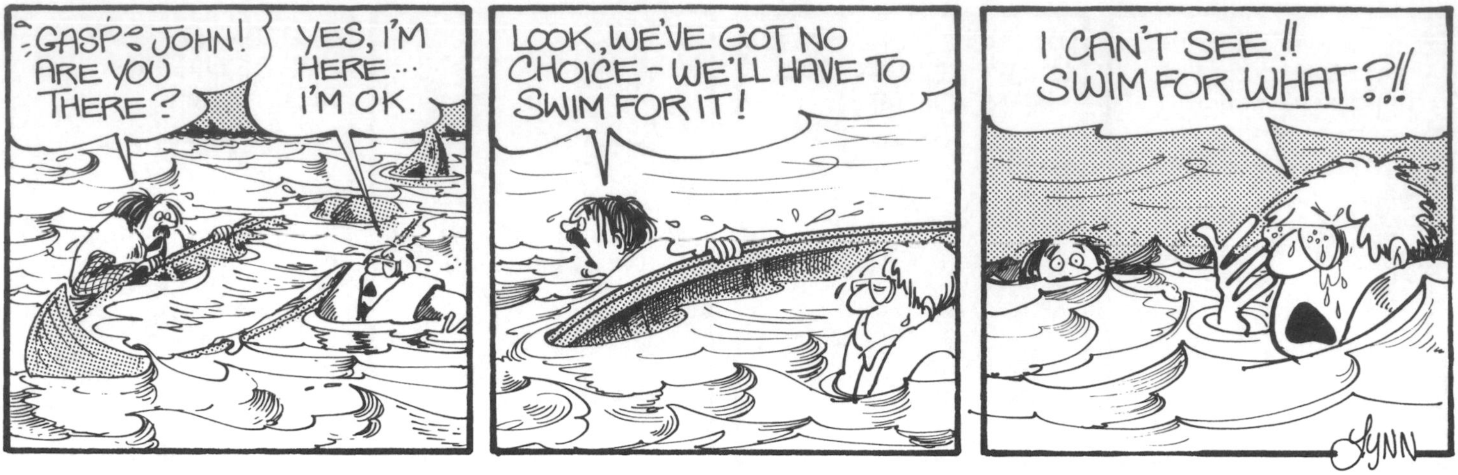
GASP JOHN! ARE YOU THERE?
YES, I'M HERE... I'M OK.
LOOK, WE'VE GOT NO CHOICE - WE'LL HAVE TO SWIM FOR IT!
I CAN'T SEE!! SWIM FOR WHAT?!!
LYNN

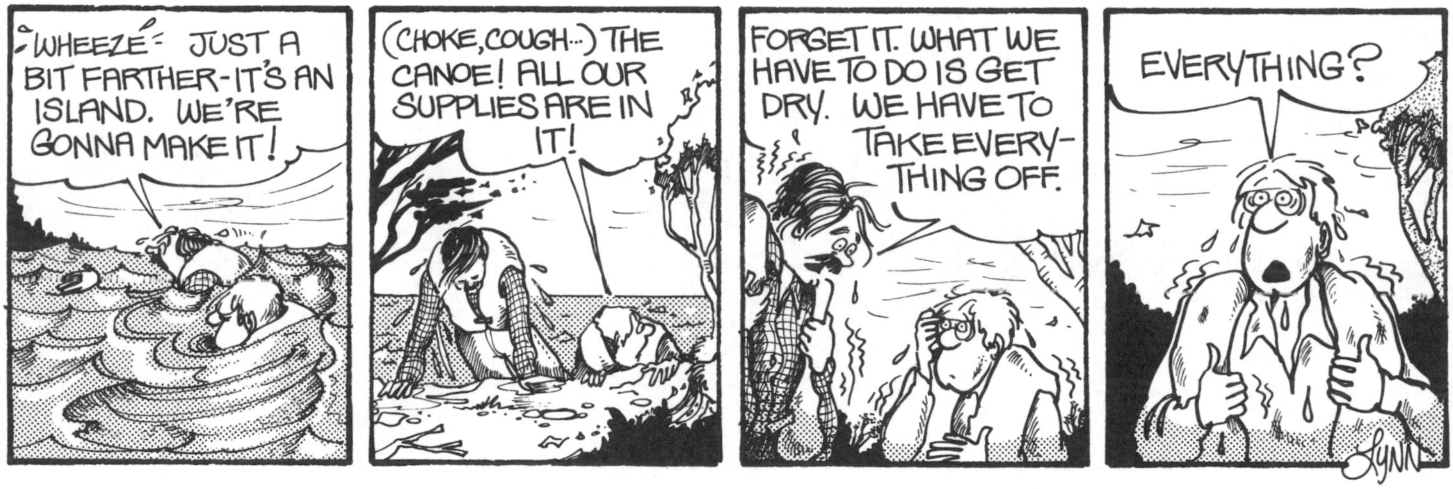
WHEEZE JUST A BIT FARTHER-IT'S AN ISLAND. WE'RE GONNA MAKE IT!
(CHOKE, COUGH...) THE CANOE! ALL OUR SUPPLIES ARE IN IT!
FORGET IT. WHAT WE HAVE TO DO IS GET DRY. WE HAVE TO TAKE EVERYTHING OFF.
EVERYTHING?
LYNN

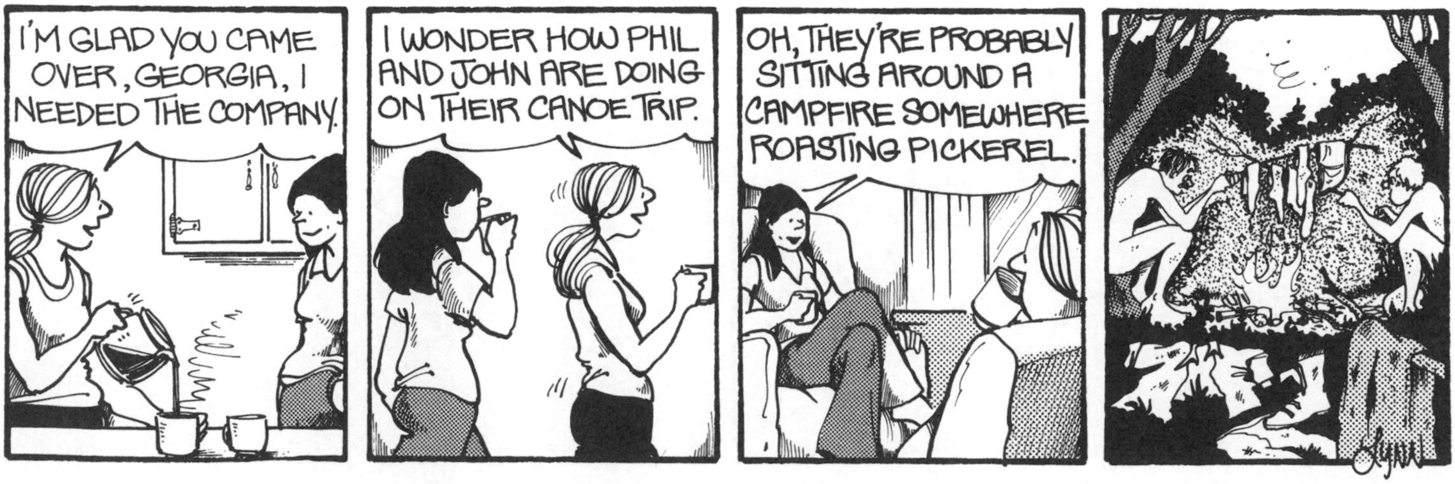
I'M GLAD YOU CAME OVER, GEORGIA, I NEEDED THE COMPANY.
I WONDER HOW PHIL AND JOHN ARE DOING ON THEIR CANOE TRIP.
OH, THEY'RE PROBABLY SITTING AROUND A CAMPFIRE SOMEWHERE ROASTING PICKEREL.
LYNN

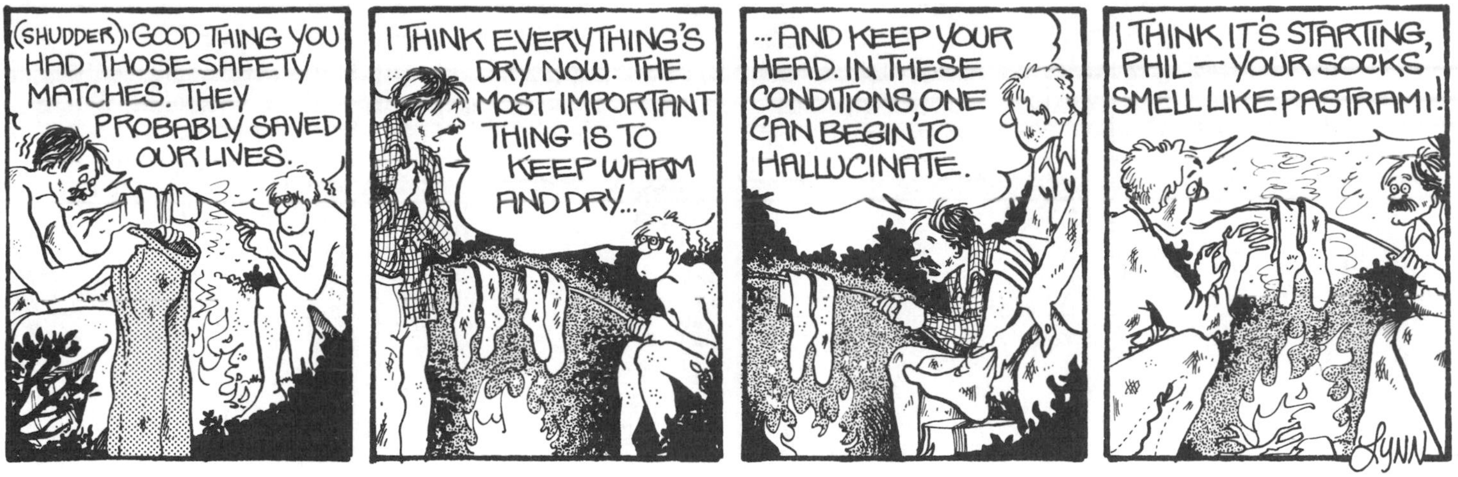
(SHUDDER) GOOD THING YOU HAD THOSE SAFETY MATCHES. THEY PROBABLY SAVED OUR LIVES.
I THINK EVERYTHING'S DRY NOW. THE MOST IMPORTANT THING IS TO KEEP WARM AND DRY...
...AND KEEP YOUR HEAD. IN THESE CONDITIONS, ONE CAN BEGIN TO HALLUCINATE.
I THINK IT'S STARTING, PHIL — YOUR SOCKS SMELL LIKE PASTRAMI!
LYNN

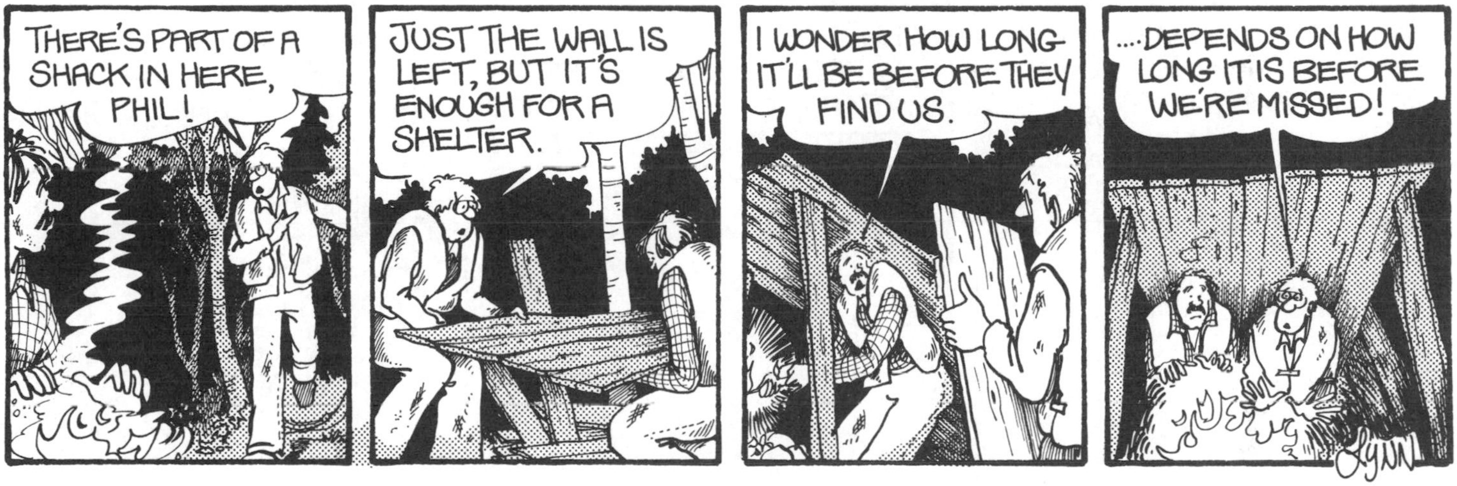
THERE'S PART OF A SHACK IN HERE, PHIL!
JUST THE WALL IS LEFT, BUT IT'S ENOUGH FOR A SHELTER.
I WONDER HOW LONG IT'LL BE BEFORE THEY FIND US.
....DEPENDS ON HOW LONG IT IS BEFORE WE'RE MISSED!
LYNN

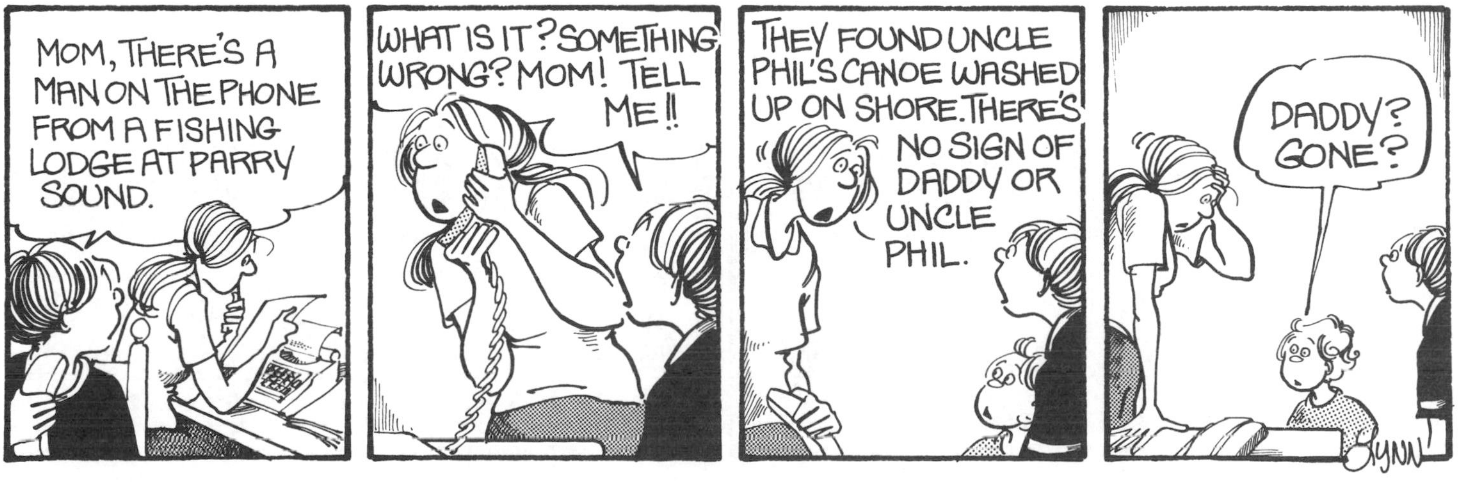
MOM, THERE'S A MAN ON THE PHONE FROM A FISHING LODGE AT PARRY SOUND.
WHAT IS IT? SOMETHING WRONG? MOM! TELL ME!!
THEY FOUND UNCLE PHIL'S CANOE WASHED UP ON SHORE. THERE'S NO SIGN OF DADDY OR UNCLE PHIL.
DADDY? GONE?
LYNN

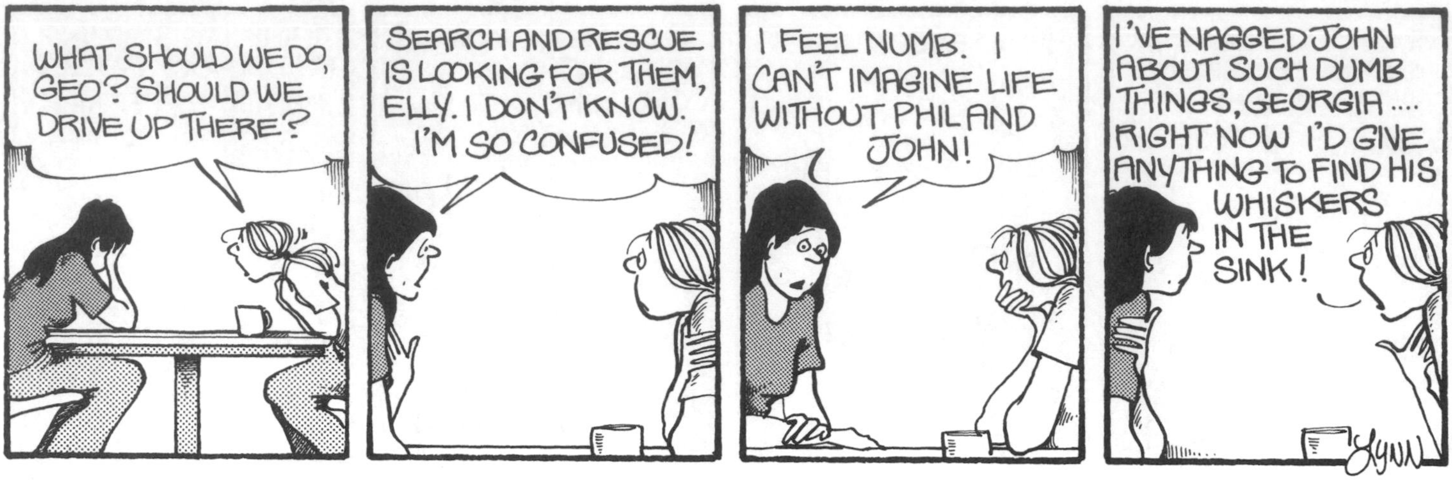
WHAT SHOULD WE DO, GEO? SHOULD WE DRIVE UP THERE?
SEARCH AND RESCUE IS LOOKING FOR THEM, ELLY. I DON'T KNOW. I'M SO CONFUSED!
I FEEL NUMB. I CAN'T IMAGINE LIFE WITHOUT PHIL AND JOHN!
I'VE NAGGED JOHN ABOUT SUCH DUMB THINGS, GEORGIA.... RIGHT NOW I'D GIVE ANYTHING TO FIND HIS WHISKERS IN THE SINK!
LYNN

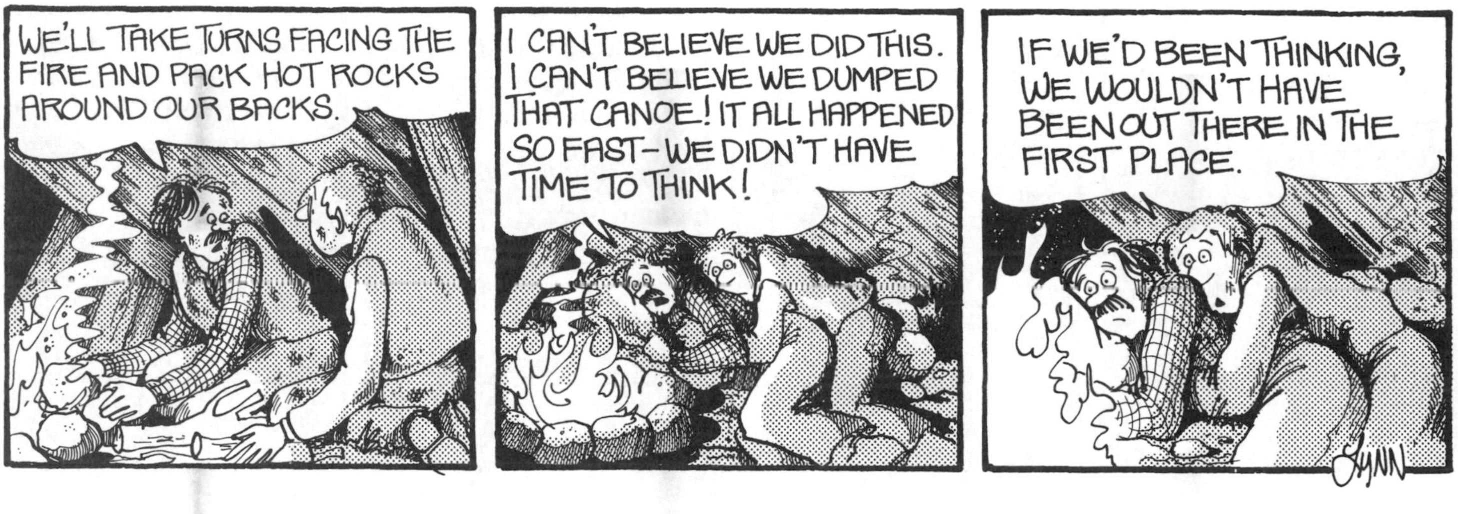
WE'LL TAKE TURNS FACING THE FIRE AND PACK HOT ROCKS AROUND OUR BACKS.
I CAN'T BELIEVE WE DID THIS. I CAN'T BELIEVE WE DUMPED THAT CANOE! IT ALL HAPPENED SO FAST- WE DIDN'T HAVE TIME TO THINK!
IF WE'D BEEN THINKING, WE WOULDN'T HAVE BEEN OUT THERE IN THE FIRST PLACE.
LYNN

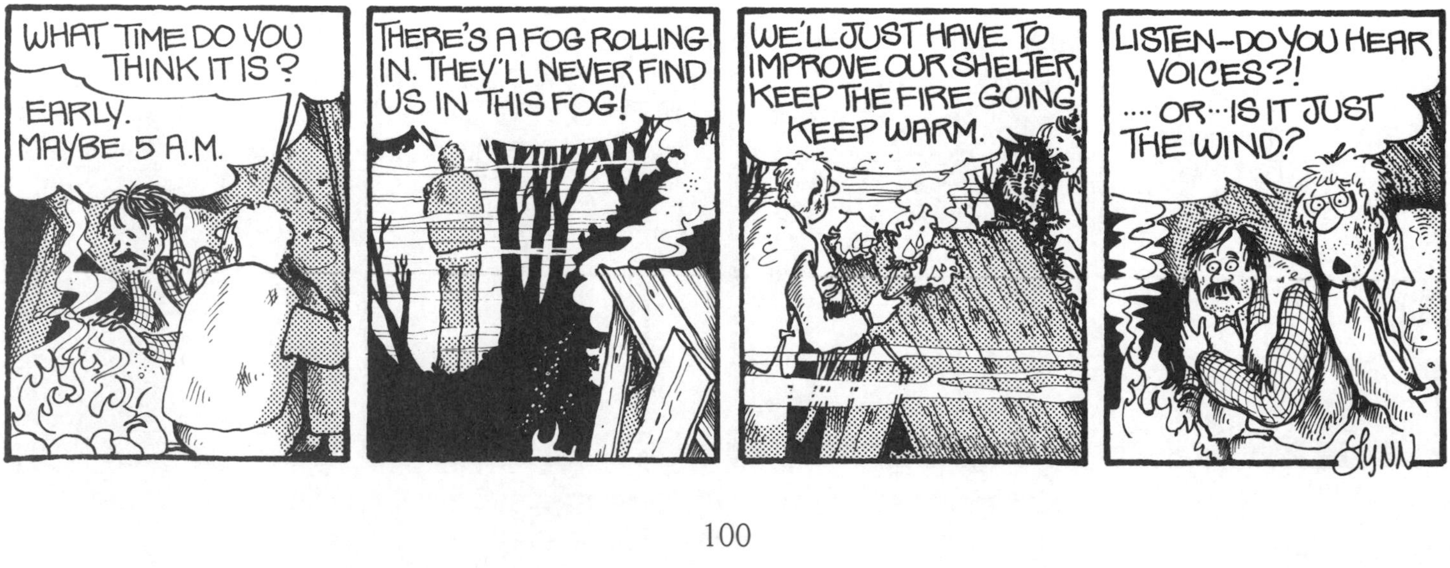
WHAT TIME DO YOU THINK IT IS?
EARLY. MAYBE 5 A.M.
THERE'S A FOG ROLLING IN. THEY'LL NEVER FIND US IN THIS FOG!
WE'LL JUST HAVE TO IMPROVE OUR SHELTER, KEEP THE FIRE GOING, KEEP WARM.
LISTEN--DO YOU HEAR VOICES?! ....OR...IS IT JUST THE WIND?
LYNN

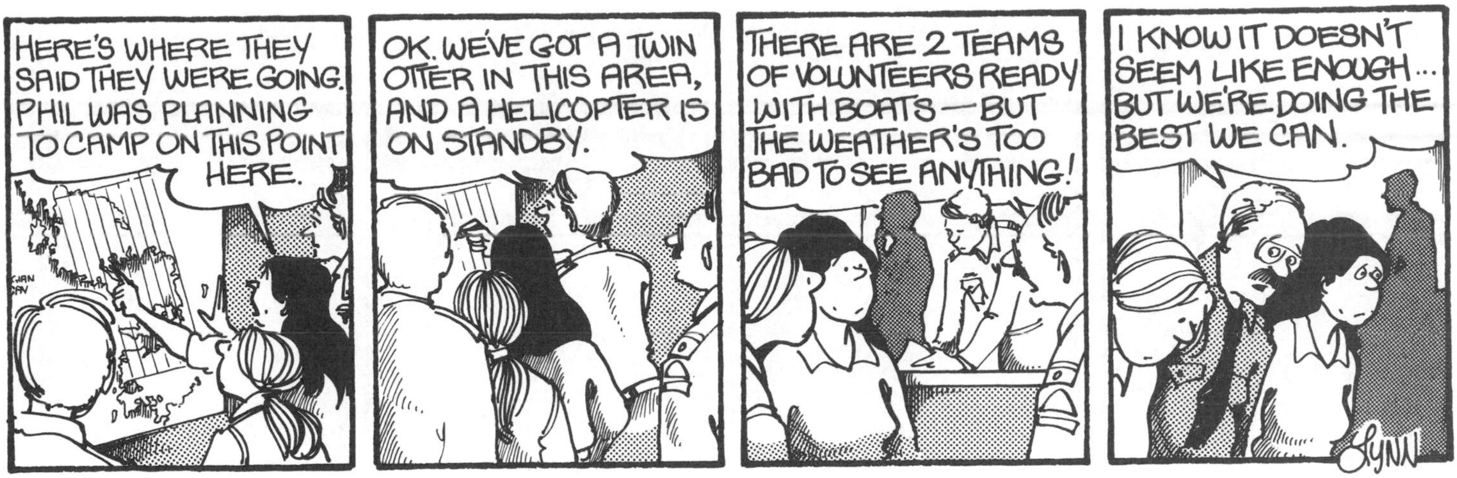
HERE'S WHERE THEY SAID THEY WERE GOING. PHIL WAS PLANNING TO CAMP ON THIS POINT HERE.
OK. WE'VE GOT A TWIN OTTER IN THIS AREA, AND A HELICOPTER IS ON STANDBY.
THERE ARE 2 TEAMS OF VOLUNTEERS READY WITH BOATS — BUT THE WEATHER'S TOO BAD TO SEE ANYTHING!
I KNOW IT DOESN'T SEEM LIKE ENOUGH... BUT WE'RE DOING THE BEST WE CAN.
LYNN

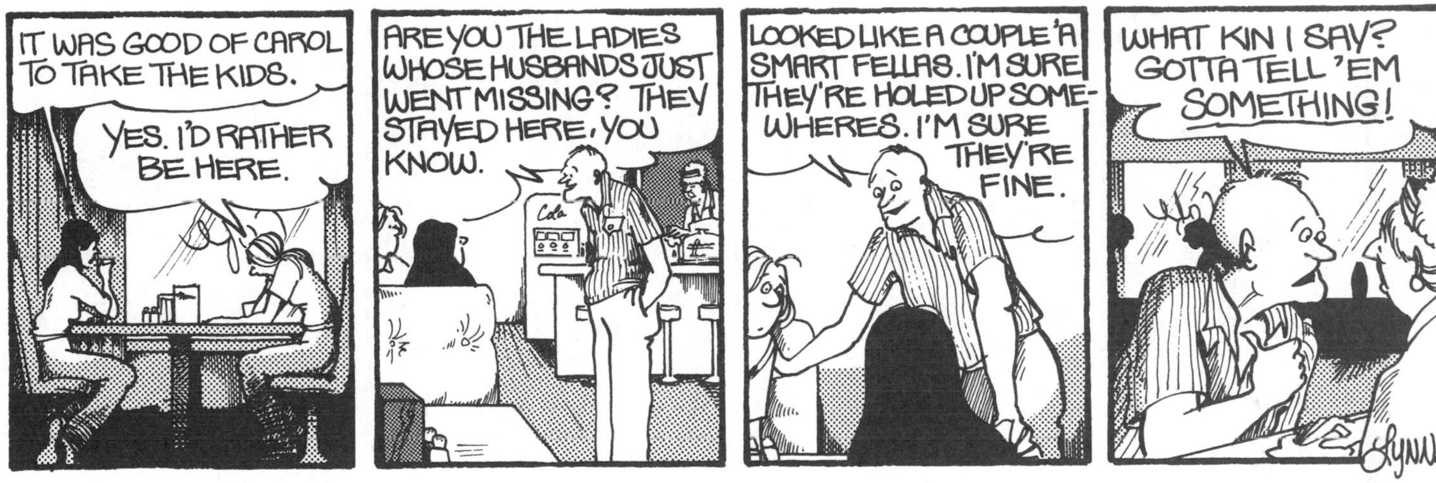
IT WAS GOOD OF CAROL TO TAKE THE KIDS.
YES. I'D RATHER BE HERE.
ARE YOU THE LADIES WHOSE HUSBANDS JUST WENT MISSING? THEY STAYED HERE, YOU KNOW.
LOOKED LIKE A COUPLE 'A SMART FELLAS. I'M SURE THEY'RE HOLED UP SOMEWHERES. I'M SURE THEY'RE FINE.
WHAT KIN I SAY? GOTTA TELL 'EM SOMETHING!
LYNN

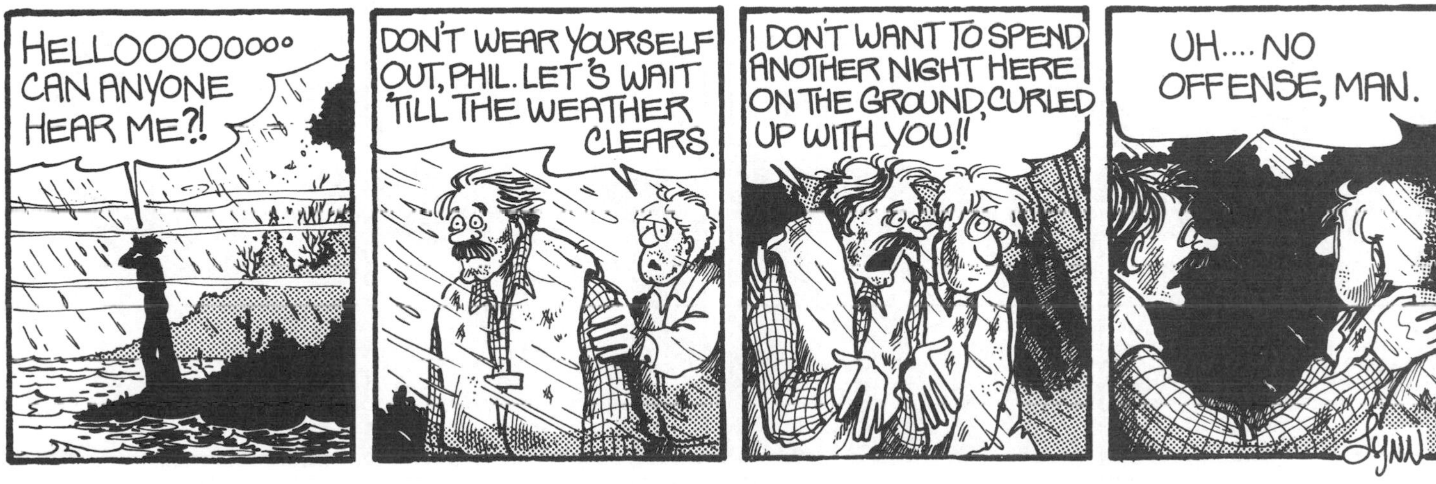
HELLOOOOOooo CAN ANYONE HEAR ME?!
DON'T WEAR YOURSELF OUT, PHIL. LET'S WAIT 'TILL THE WEATHER CLEARS.
I DON'T WANT TO SPEND ANOTHER NIGHT HERE ON THE GROUND, CURLED UP WITH YOU!!
UH.... NO OFFENSE, MAN.
LYNN

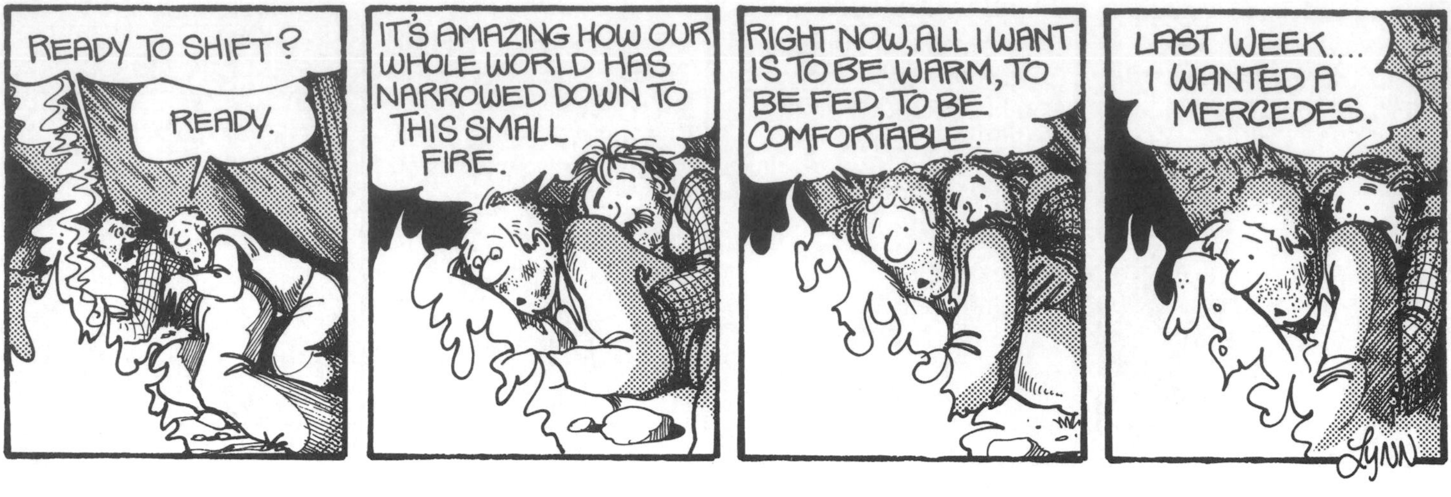
READY TO SHIFT?
READY.
IT'S AMAZING HOW OUR WHOLE WORLD HAS NARROWED DOWN TO THIS SMALL FIRE.
RIGHT NOW, ALL I WANT IS TO BE WARM, TO BE FED, TO BE COMFORTABLE.
LAST WEEK.... I WANTED A MERCEDES.

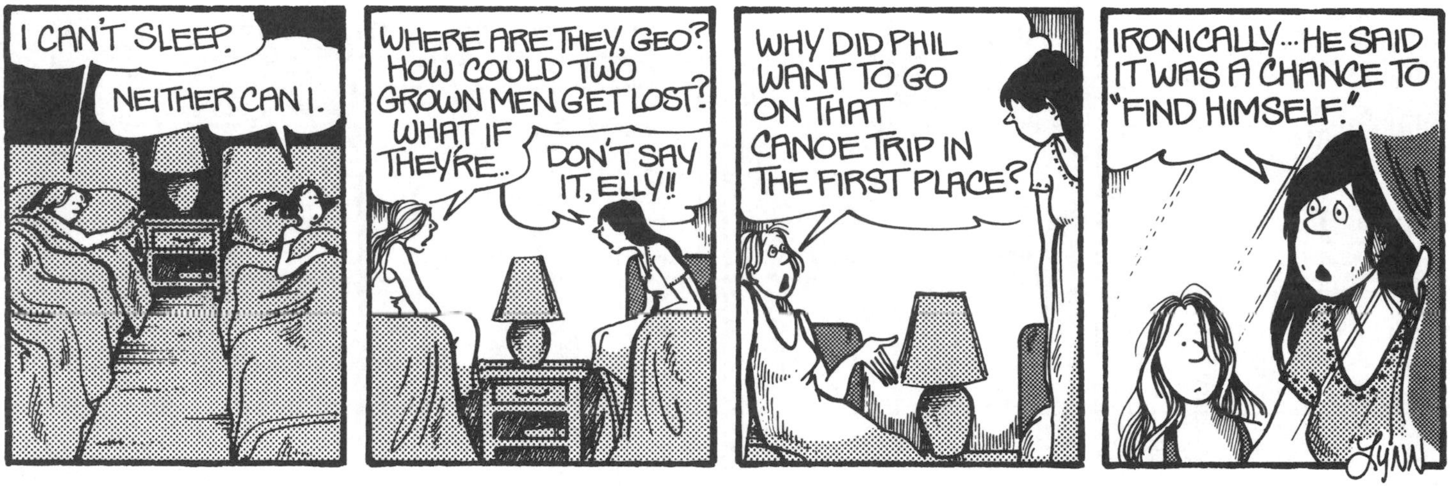
I CAN'T SLEEP.
NEITHER CAN I.
WHERE ARE THEY, GEO? HOW COULD TWO GROWN MEN GET LOST? WHAT IF THEY'RE..
DON'T SAY IT, ELLY!!
WHY DID PHIL WANT TO GO ON THAT CANOE TRIP IN THE FIRST PLACE?
IRONICALLY... HE SAID IT WAS A CHANCE TO "FIND HIMSELF."

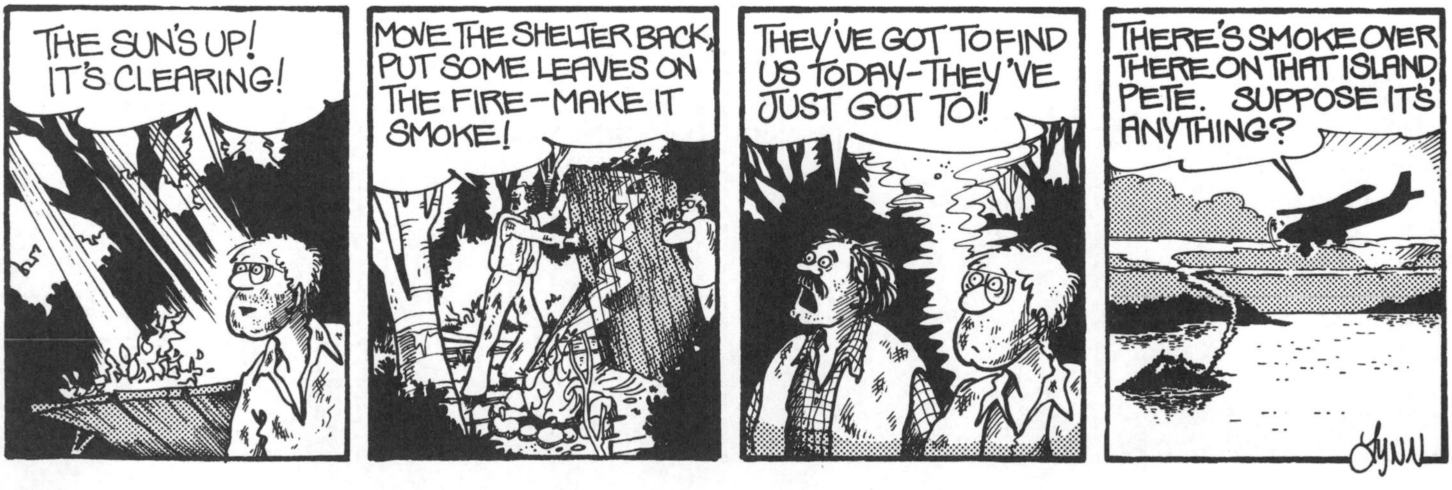
THE SUN'S UP! IT'S CLEARING!
MOVE THE SHELTER BACK, PUT SOME LEAVES ON THE FIRE - MAKE IT SMOKE!
THEY'VE GOT TO FIND US TODAY - THEY'VE JUST GOT TO!!
THERE'S SMOKE OVER THERE ON THAT ISLAND, PETE. SUPPOSE IT'S ANYTHING?

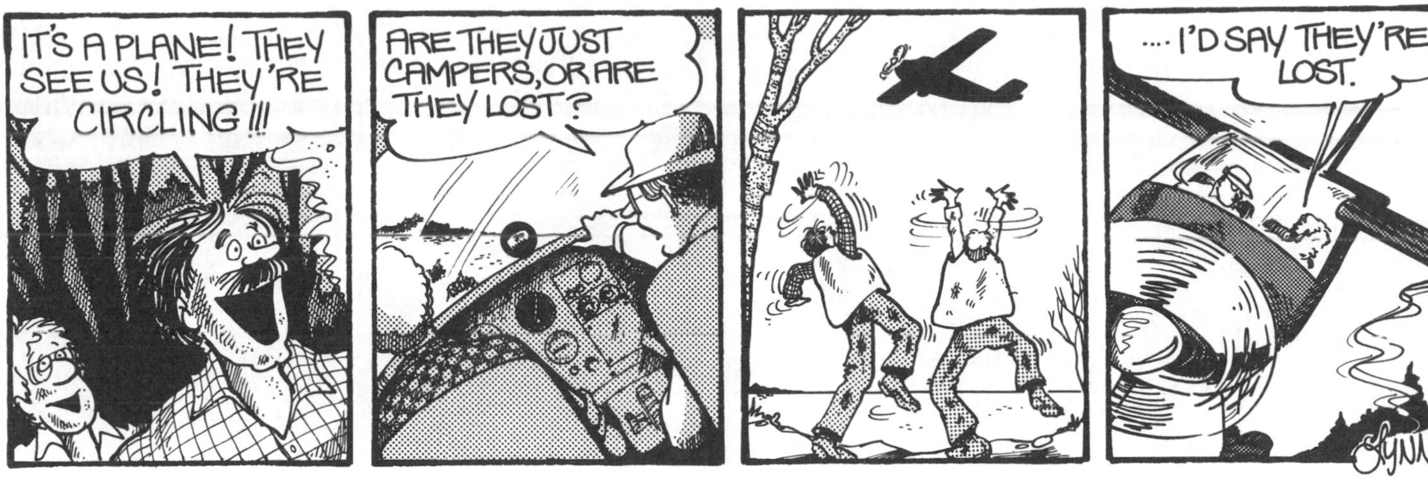
IT'S A PLANE! THEY SEE US! THEY'RE CIRCLING!!!
ARE THEY JUST CAMPERS, OR ARE THEY LOST?
....I'D SAY THEY'RE LOST.
LYNN

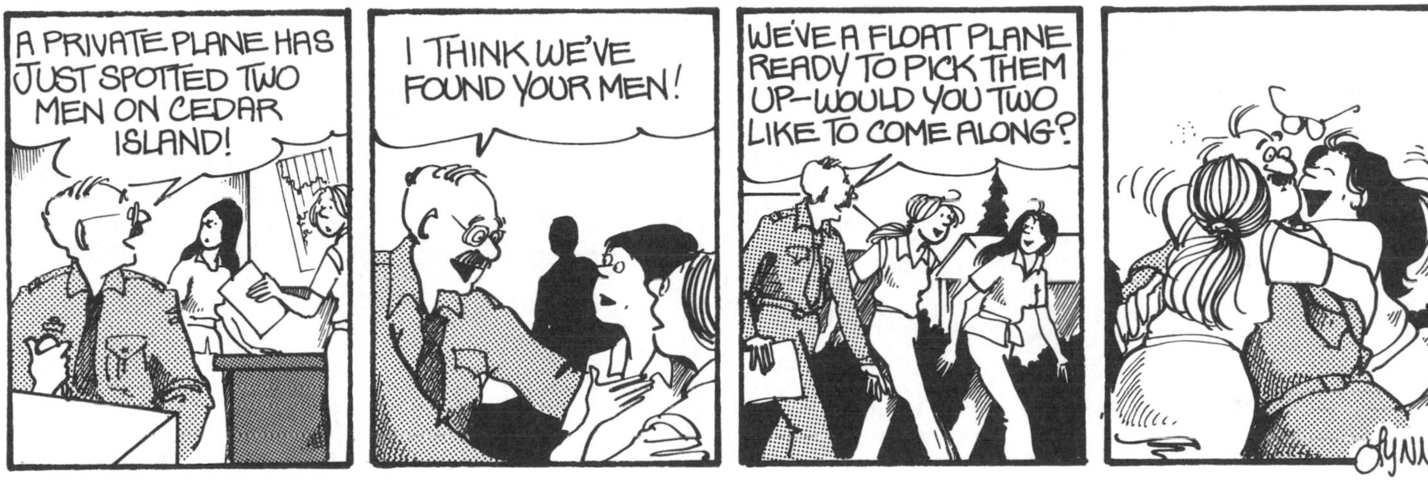
A PRIVATE PLANE HAS JUST SPOTTED TWO MEN ON CEDAR ISLAND!
I THINK WE'VE FOUND YOUR MEN!
WE'VE A FLOAT PLANE READY TO PICK THEM UP–WOULD YOU TWO LIKE TO COME ALONG?
LYNN

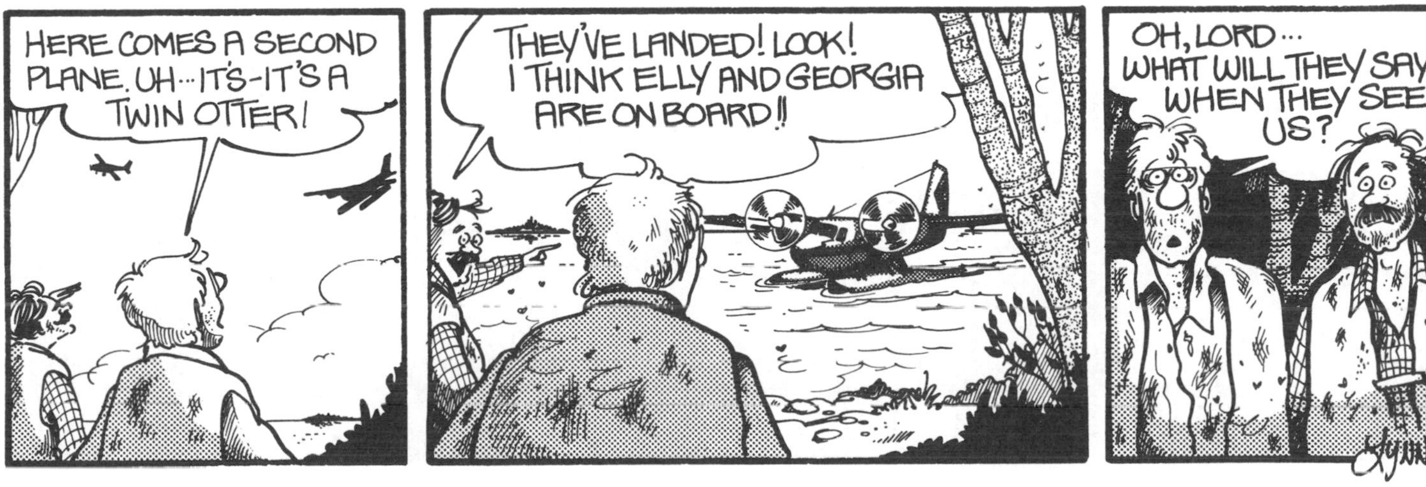
HERE COMES A SECOND PLANE. UH...IT'S-IT'S A TWIN OTTER!
THEY'VE LANDED! LOOK! I THINK ELLY AND GEORGIA ARE ON BOARD!!
OH, LORD... WHAT WILL THEY SAY WHEN THEY SEE US?
LYNN

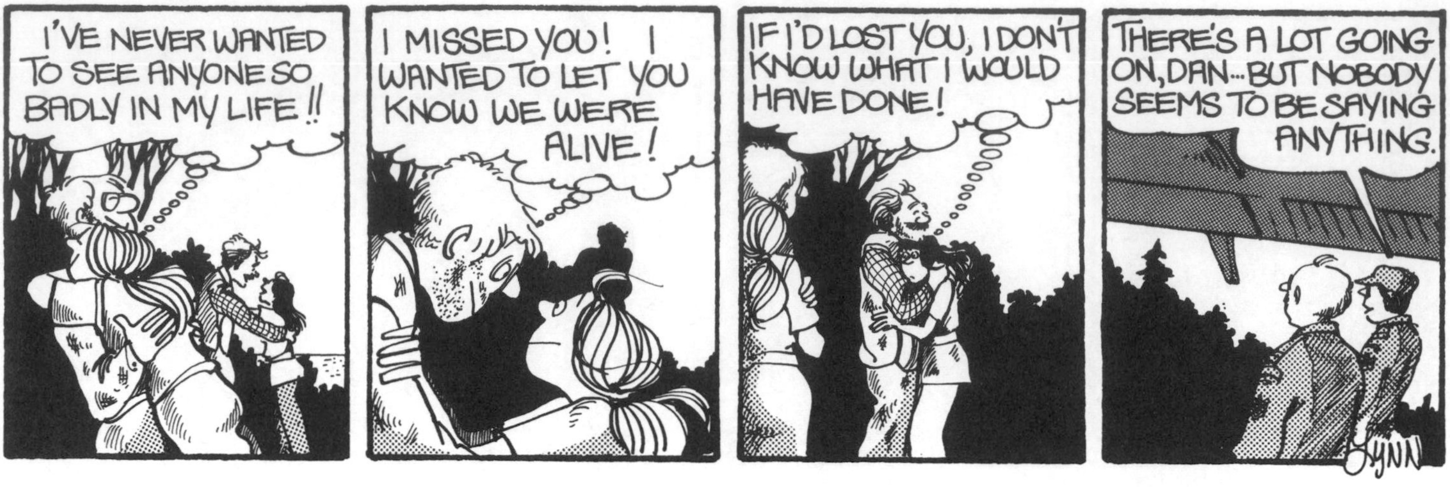
I'VE NEVER WANTED TO SEE ANYONE SO BADLY IN MY LIFE!!
I MISSED YOU! I WANTED TO LET YOU KNOW WE WERE ALIVE!
IF I'D LOST YOU, I DON'T KNOW WHAT I WOULD HAVE DONE!
THERE'S A LOT GOING ON, DAN... BUT NOBODY SEEMS TO BE SAYING ANYTHING.
LYNN

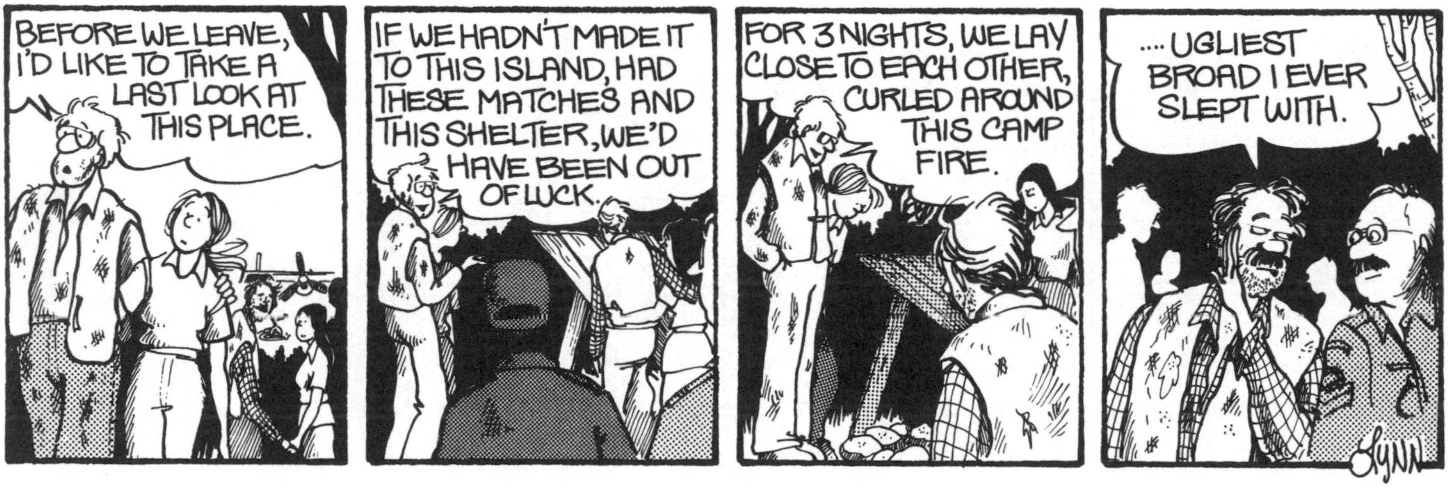
BEFORE WE LEAVE, I'D LIKE TO TAKE A LAST LOOK AT THIS PLACE.
IF WE HADN'T MADE IT TO THIS ISLAND, HAD THESE MATCHES AND THIS SHELTER, WE'D HAVE BEEN OUT OF LUCK.
FOR 3 NIGHTS, WE LAY CLOSE TO EACH OTHER, CURLED AROUND THIS CAMP FIRE.
....UGLIEST BROAD I EVER SLEPT WITH.
LYNN

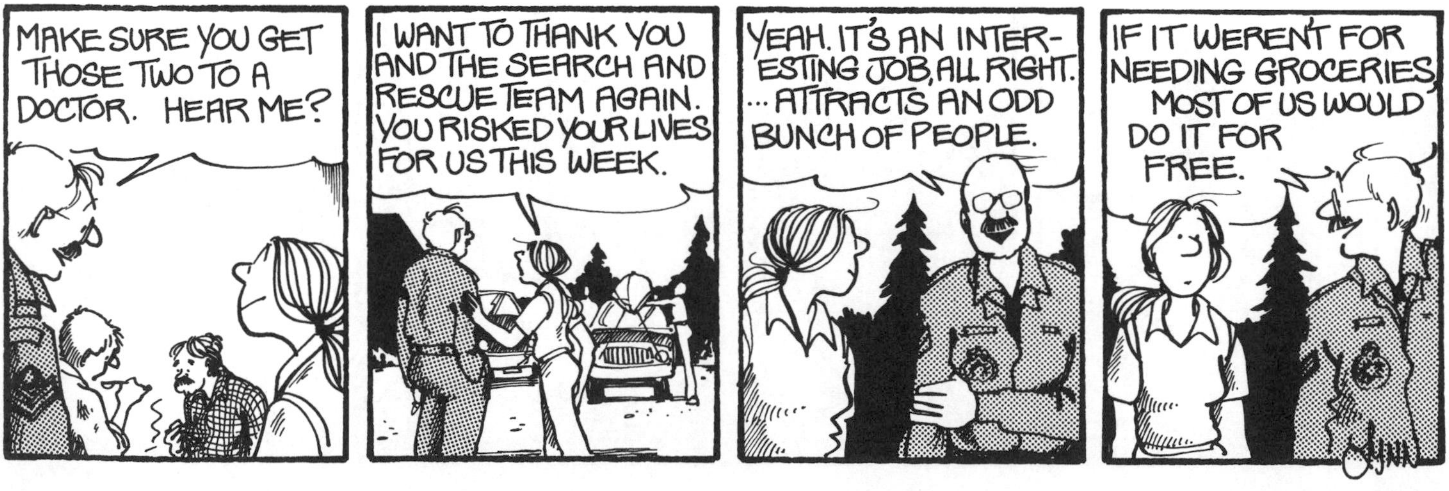
MAKE SURE YOU GET THOSE TWO TO A DOCTOR. HEAR ME?
I WANT TO THANK YOU AND THE SEARCH AND RESCUE TEAM AGAIN. YOU RISKED YOUR LIVES FOR US THIS WEEK.
YEAH. IT'S AN INTERESTING JOB, ALL RIGHT. ...ATTRACTS AN ODD BUNCH OF PEOPLE.
IF IT WEREN'T FOR NEEDING GROCERIES, MOST OF US WOULD DO IT FOR FREE.
LYNN

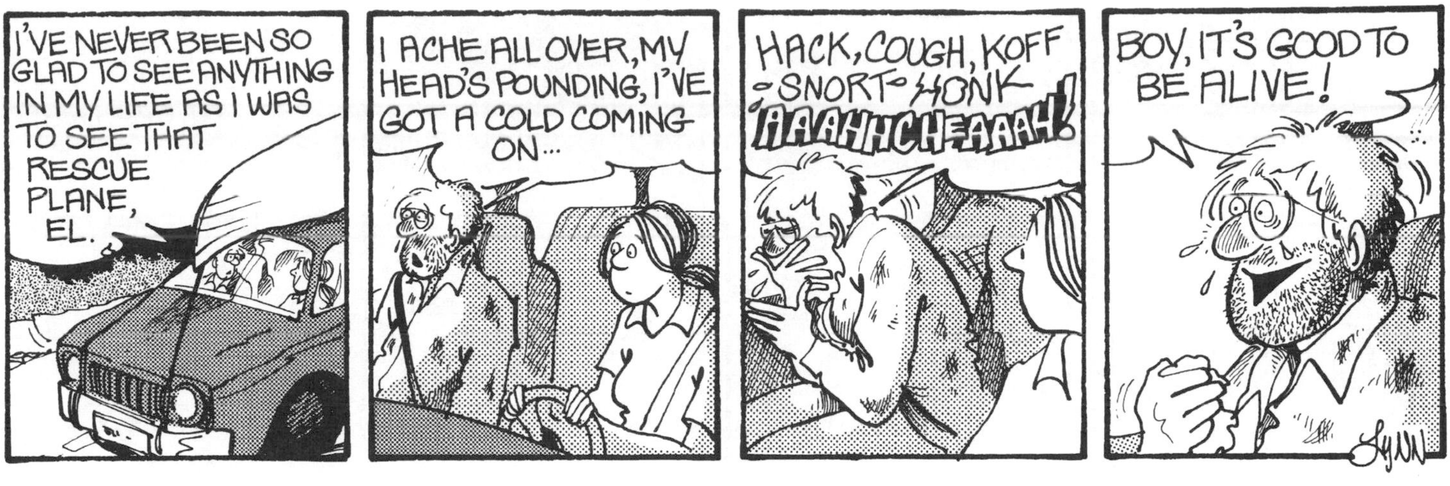
I'VE NEVER BEEN SO GLAD TO SEE ANYTHING IN MY LIFE AS I WAS TO SEE THAT RESCUE PLANE, EL.
I ACHE ALL OVER, MY HEAD'S POUNDING, I'VE GOT A COLD COMING ON...
HACK, COUGH, KOFF
SNORT
HONK
AAAHHCHEAAAH!
BOY, IT'S GOOD TO BE ALIVE!
LYNN

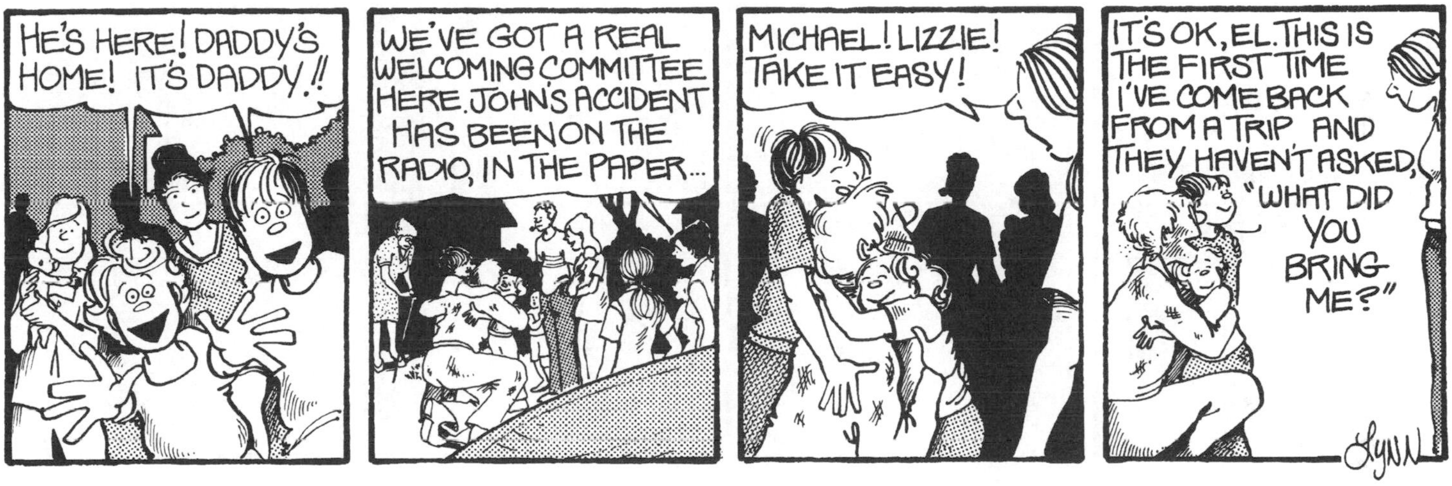
HE'S HERE! DADDY'S HOME! IT'S DADDY!!
WE'VE GOT A REAL WELCOMING COMMITTEE HERE. JOHN'S ACCIDENT HAS BEEN ON THE RADIO, IN THE PAPER...
MICHAEL! LIZZIE! TAKE IT EASY!
IT'S OK, EL. THIS IS THE FIRST TIME I'VE COME BACK FROM A TRIP AND THEY HAVEN'T ASKED, "WHAT DID YOU BRING ME?"
LYNN

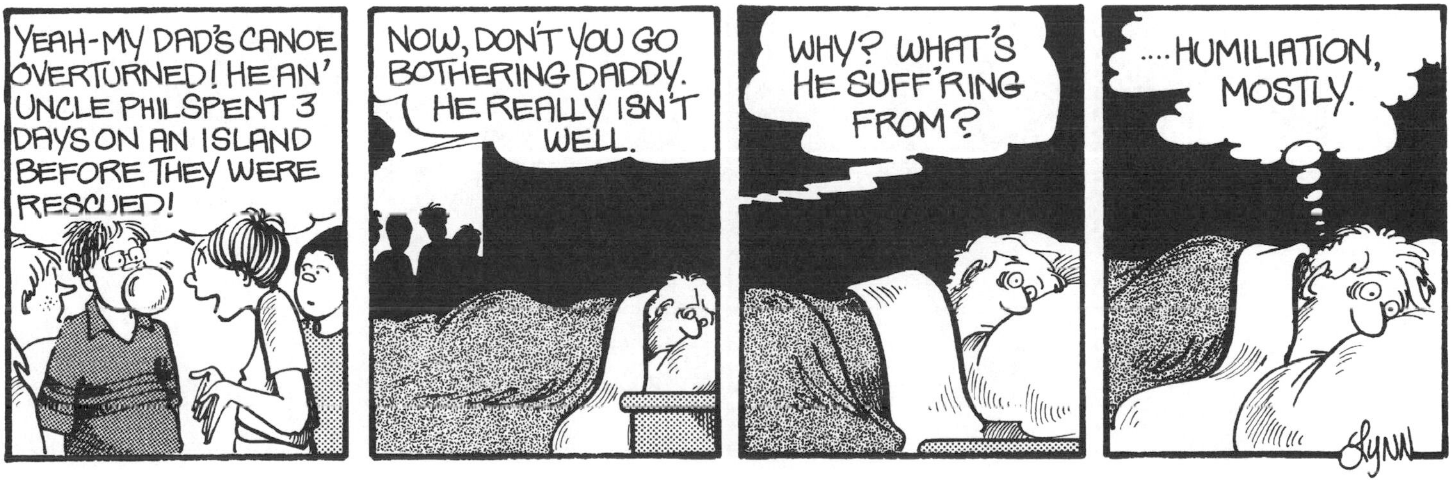
YEAH-MY DAD'S CANOE OVERTURNED! HE AN' UNCLE PHIL SPENT 3 DAYS ON AN ISLAND BEFORE THEY WERE RESCUED!
NOW, DON'T YOU GO BOTHERING DADDY. HE REALLY ISN'T WELL.
WHY? WHAT'S HE SUFF'RING FROM?
....HUMILIATION, MOSTLY.
LYNN

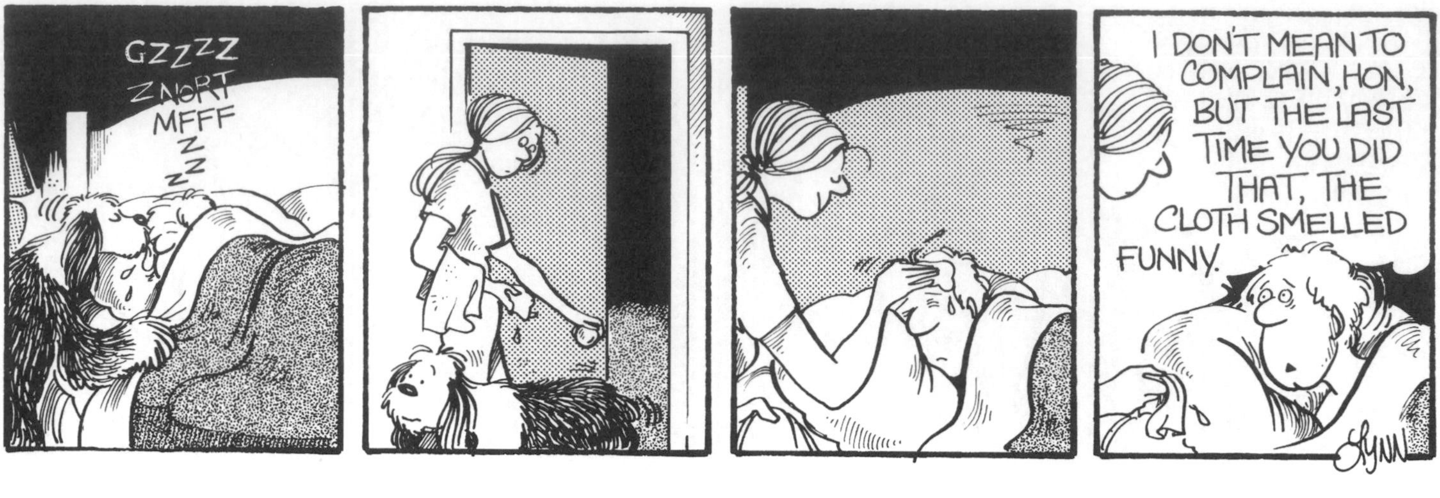
GZZZZ
ZNORT
MFFF
Z
Z
Z
I DON'T MEAN TO COMPLAIN, HON, BUT THE LAST TIME YOU DID THAT, THE CLOTH SMELLED FUNNY.
LYNN

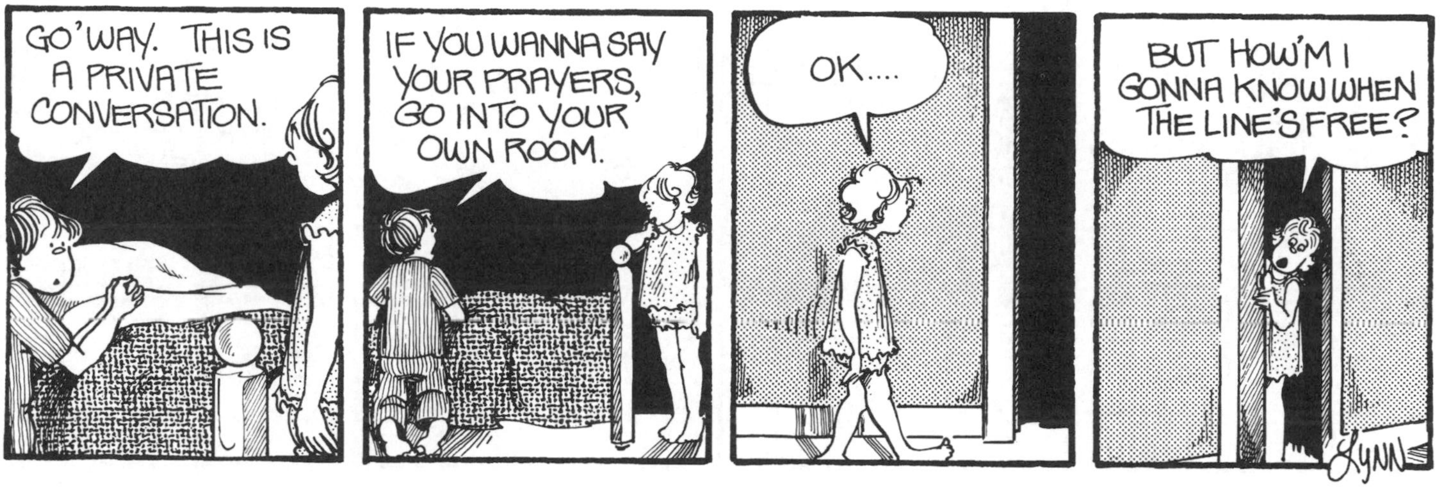
GO'WAY. THIS IS A PRIVATE CONVERSATION.
IF YOU WANNA SAY YOUR PRAYERS, GO INTO YOUR OWN ROOM.
OK....
BUT HOW'M I GONNA KNOW WHEN THE LINE'S FREE?
LYNN

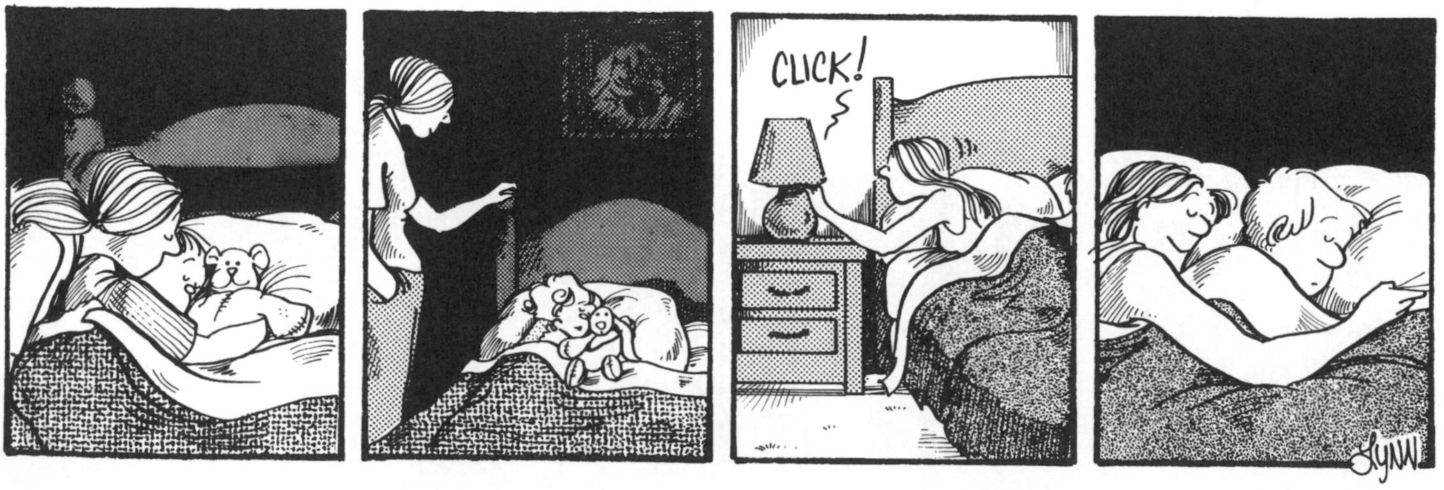
CLICK!
LYNN

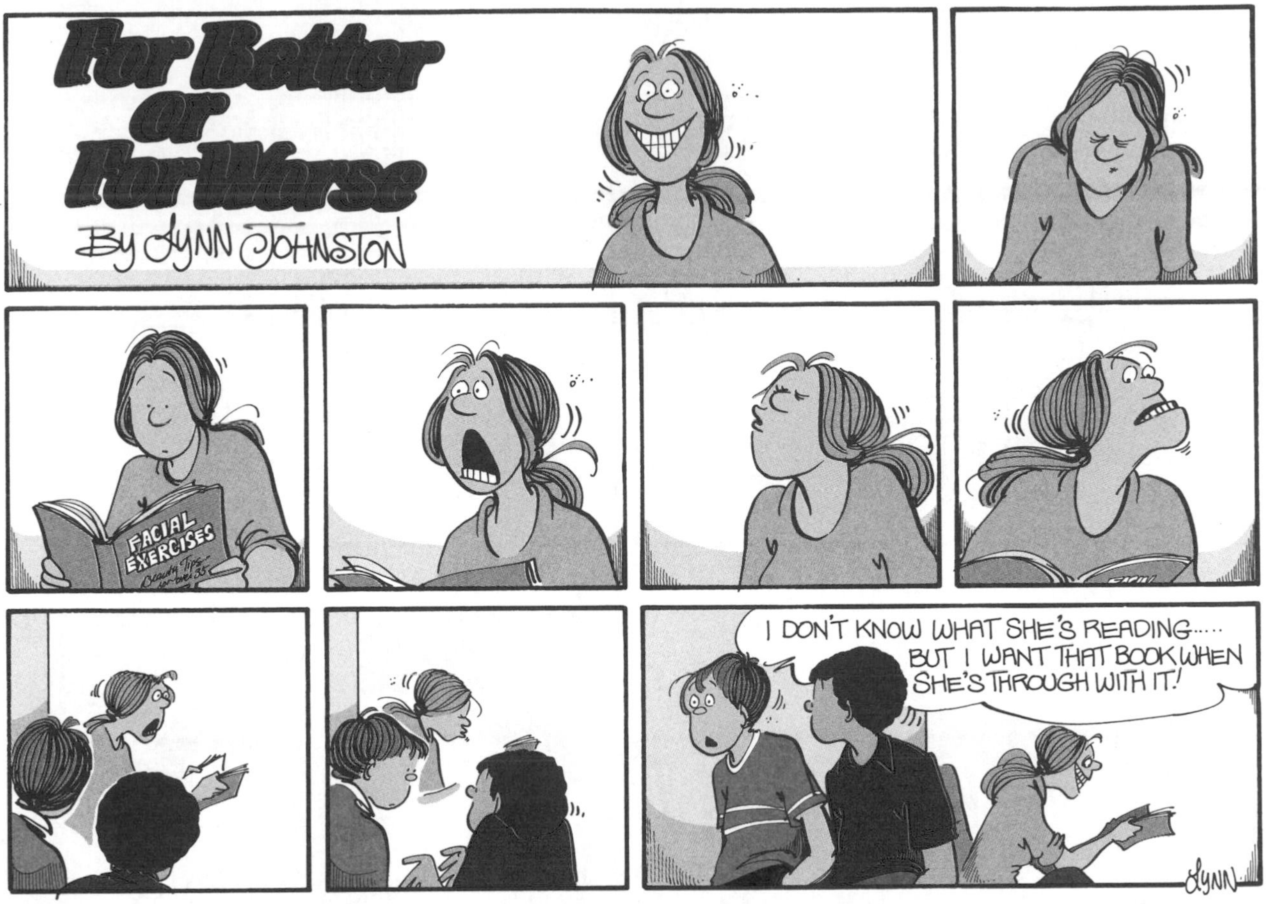
For Better or For Worse
By Lynn Johnston
FACIAL EXERCISES
I DON'T KNOW WHAT SHE'S READING..... BUT I WANT THAT BOOK WHEN SHE'S THROUGH WITH IT!
LYNN

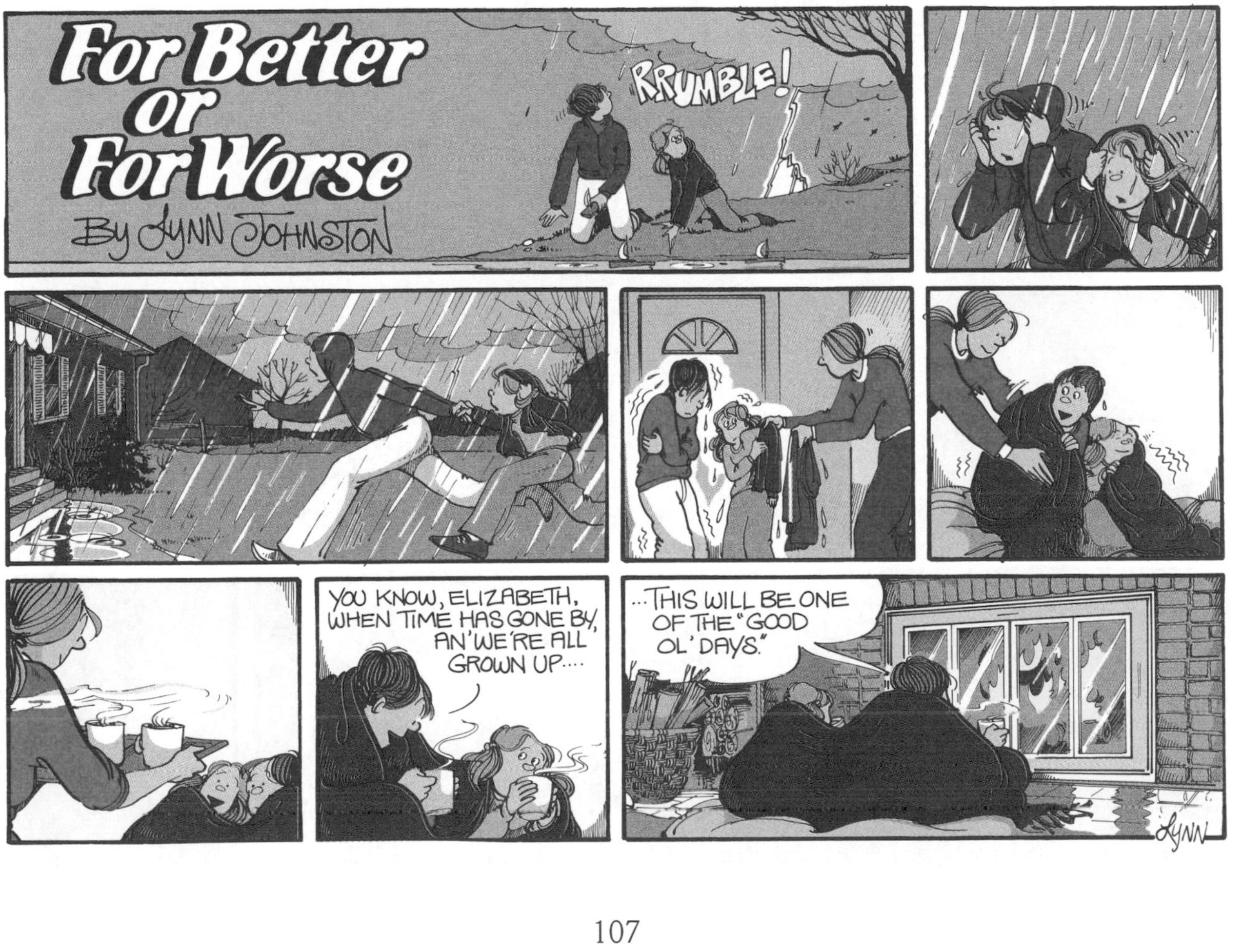
For Better or For Worse
By Lynn Johnston
RRUMBLE!
YOU KNOW, ELIZABETH, WHEN TIME HAS GONE BY, AN' WE'RE ALL GROWN UP....
...THIS WILL BE ONE OF THE "GOOD OL' DAYS."
LYNN

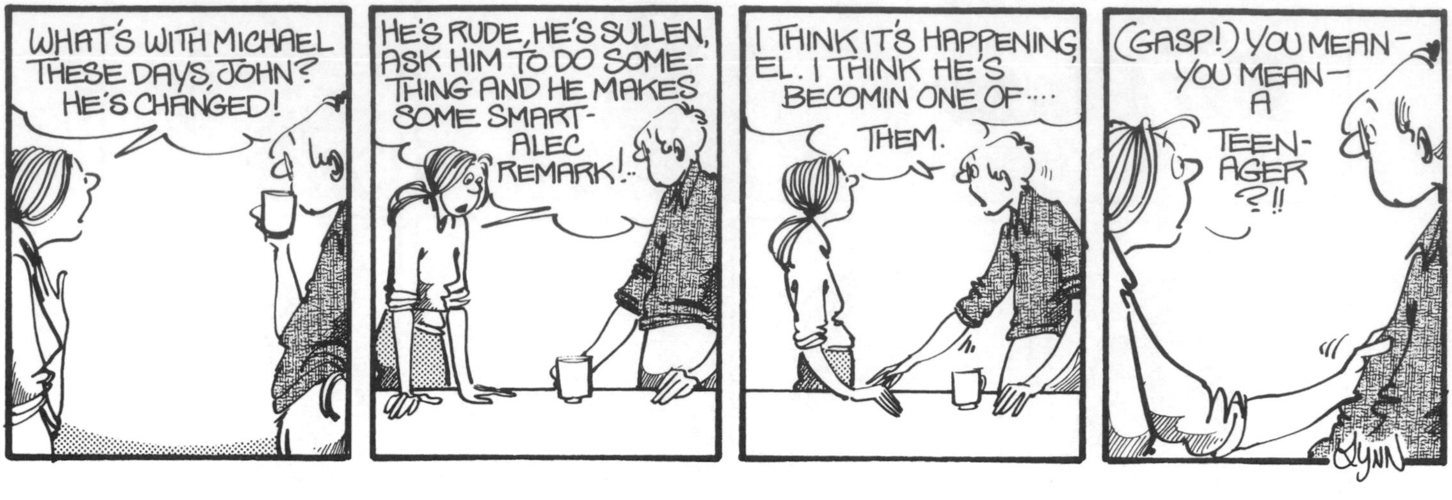
WHAT'S WITH MICHAEL THESE DAYS, JOHN? HE'S CHANGED!
HE'S RUDE, HE'S SULLEN, ASK HIM TO DO SOME-THING AND HE MAKES SOME SMART-ALEC REMARK!..
I THINK IT'S HAPPENING, EL. I THINK HE'S BECOMIN ONE OF....
THEM.
(GASP!) YOU MEAN- YOU MEAN- A TEEN-AGER ?!!
LYNN

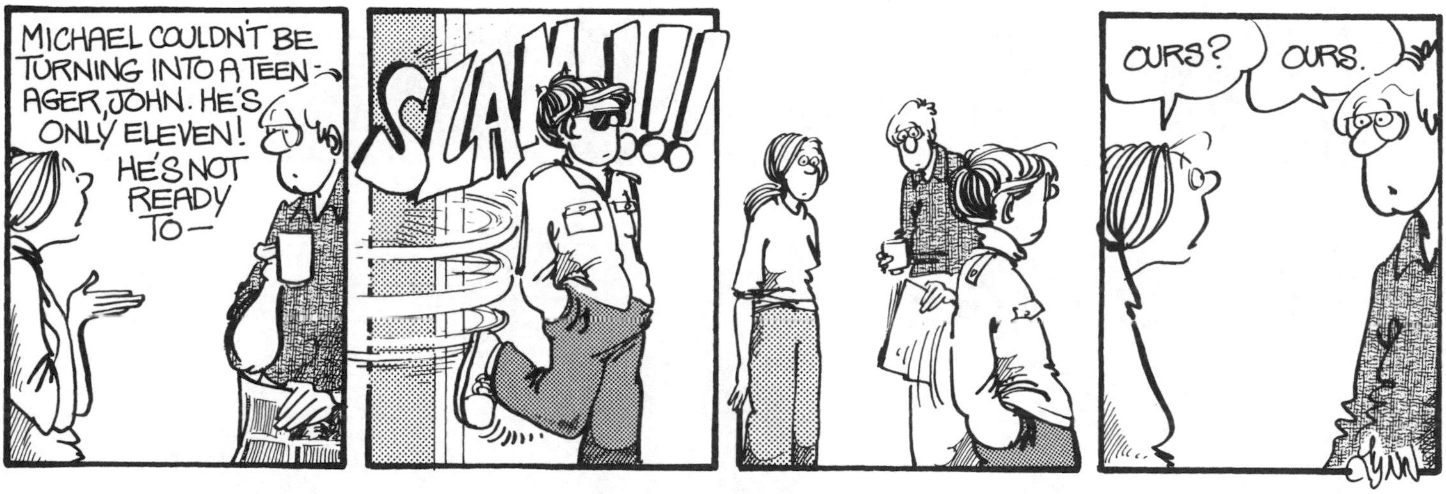
MICHAEL COULDN'T BE TURNING INTO A TEEN-AGER, JOHN. HE'S ONLY ELEVEN!
HE'S NOT READY TO—
SLAM!!!
OURS?
OURS.
LYNN

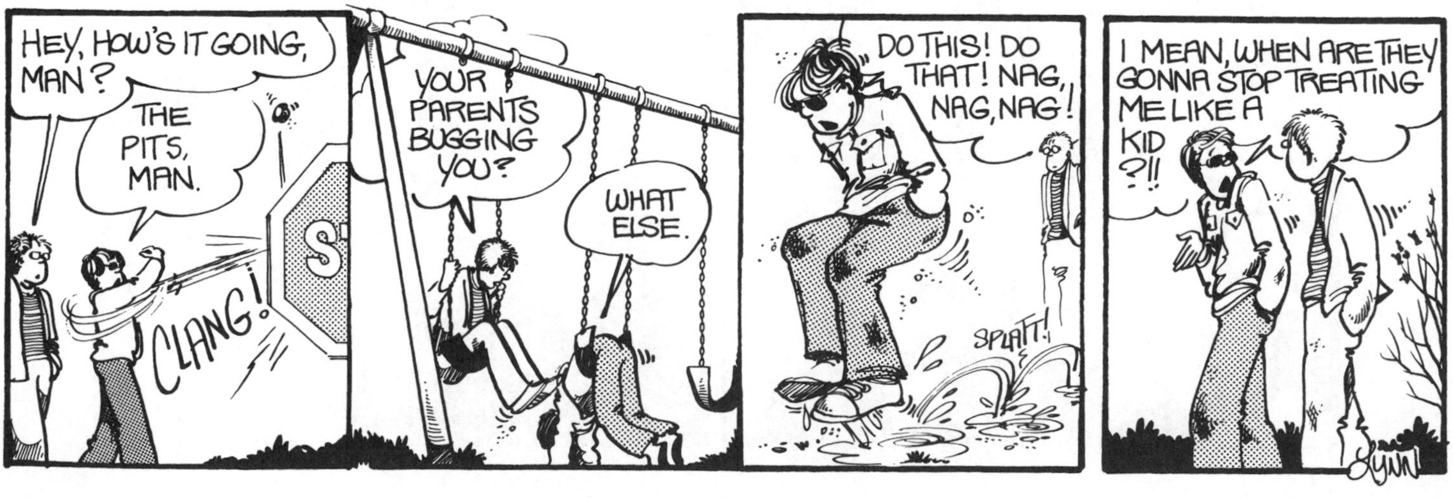
HEY, HOW'S IT GOING, MAN?
THE PITS, MAN.
CLANG!
YOUR PARENTS BUGGING YOU?
WHAT ELSE.
DO THIS! DO THAT! NAG, NAG, NAG!
SPLATT!
I MEAN, WHEN ARE THEY GONNA STOP TREATING ME LIKE A KID ?!!
LYNN

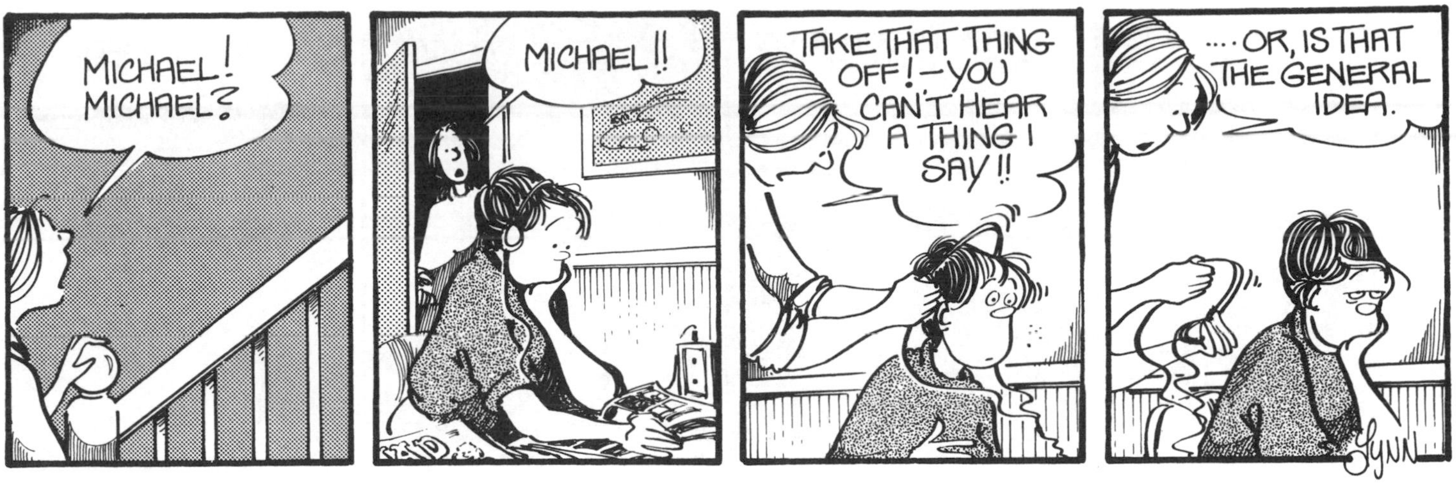
MICHAEL! MICHAEL?
MICHAEL!!
TAKE THAT THING OFF! —YOU CAN'T HEAR A THING I SAY!!
....OR, IS THAT THE GENERAL IDEA.
LYNN

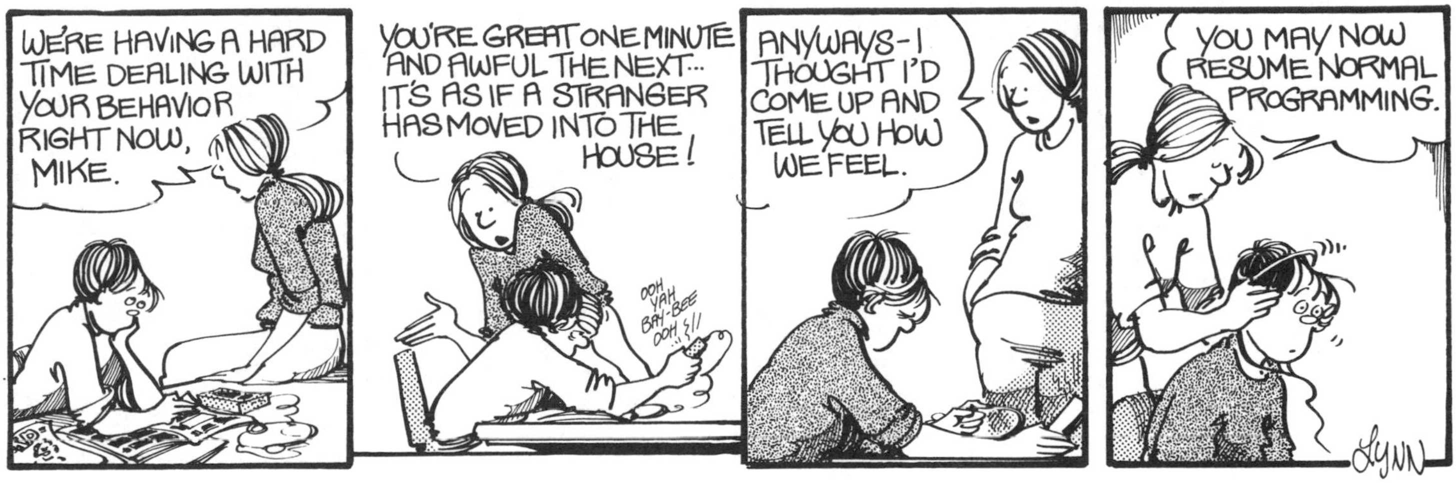
WE'RE HAVING A HARD TIME DEALING WITH YOUR BEHAVIOR RIGHT NOW, MIKE.
YOU'RE GREAT ONE MINUTE AND AWFUL THE NEXT... IT'S AS IF A STRANGER HAS MOVED INTO THE HOUSE!
OOH YAH BAY-BEE OOH!!
ANYWAYS- I THOUGHT I'D COME UP AND TELL YOU HOW WE FEEL.
YOU MAY NOW RESUME NORMAL PROGRAMMING.
LYNN

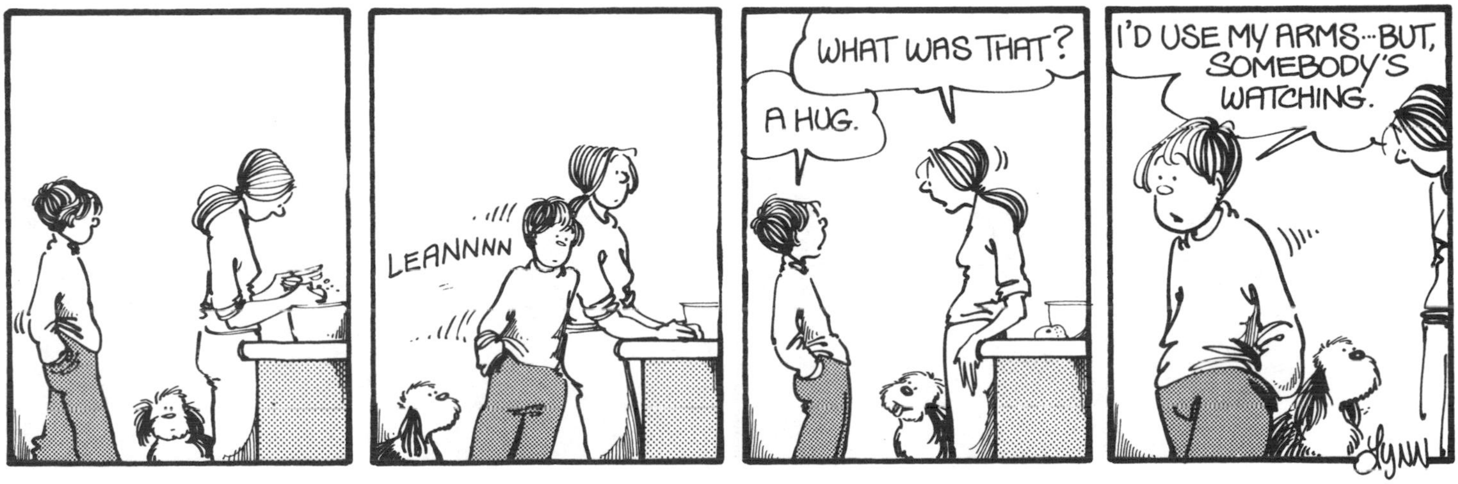
LEANNNN
WHAT WAS THAT?
A HUG.
I'D USE MY ARMS...BUT, SOMEBODY'S WATCHING.
LYNN

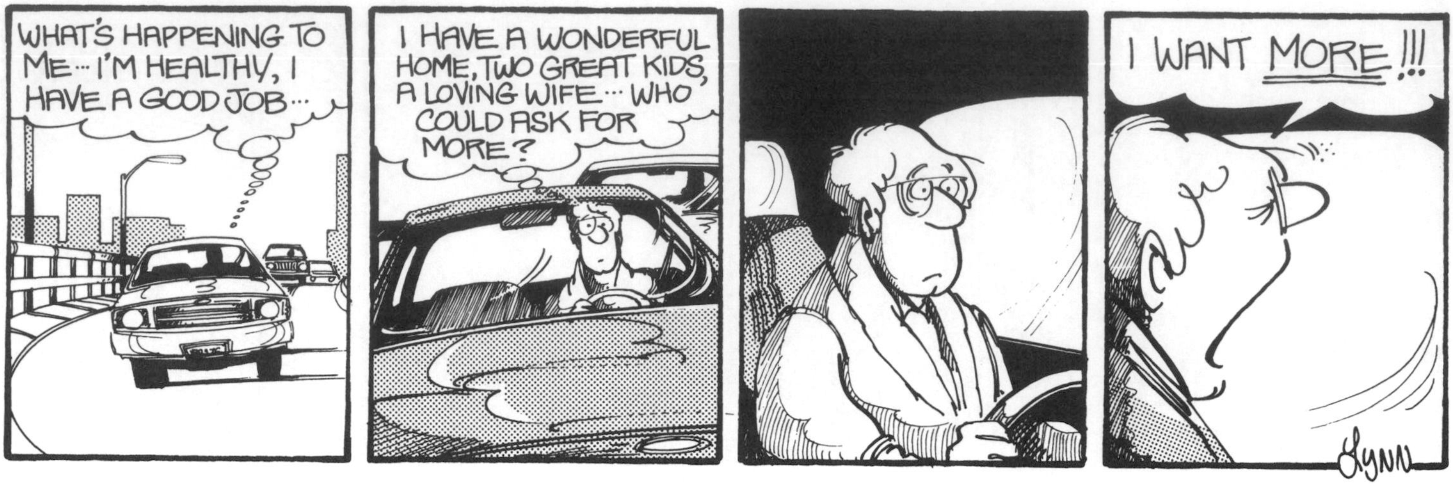
WHAT'S HAPPENING TO ME... I'M HEALTHY, I HAVE A GOOD JOB...
I HAVE A WONDERFUL HOME, TWO GREAT KIDS, A LOVING WIFE... WHO COULD ASK FOR MORE?
I WANT MORE!!!
LYNN

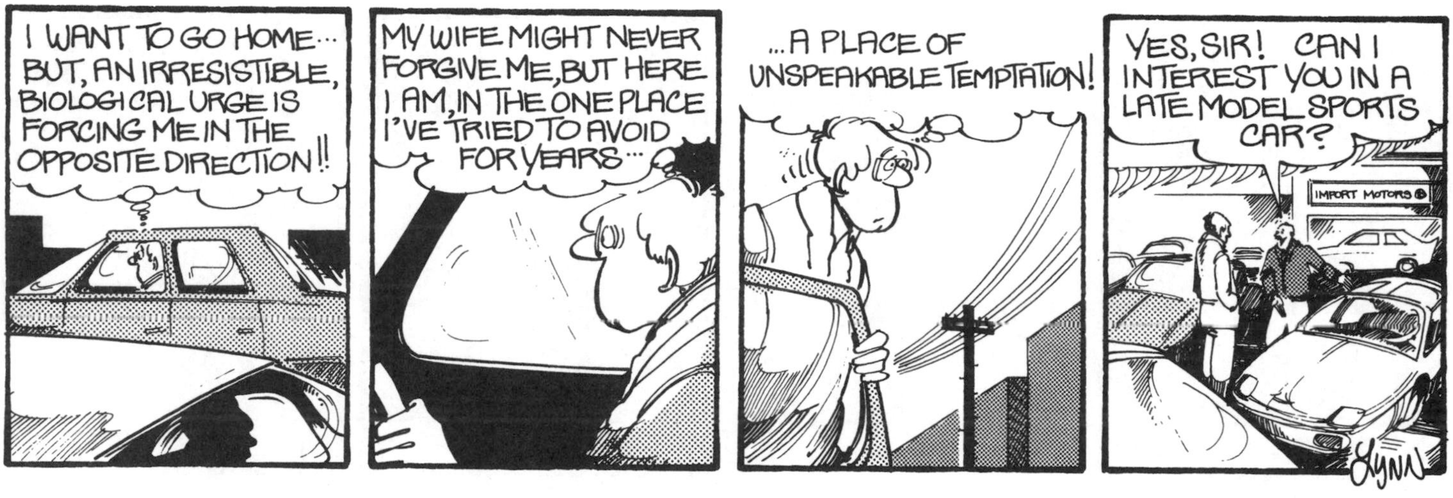
I WANT TO GO HOME... BUT, AN IRRESISTIBLE, BIOLOGICAL URGE IS FORCING ME IN THE OPPOSITE DIRECTION!!
MY WIFE MIGHT NEVER FORGIVE ME, BUT HERE I AM, IN THE ONE PLACE I'VE TRIED TO AVOID FOR YEARS...
...A PLACE OF UNSPEAKABLE TEMPTATION!
YES, SIR! CAN I INTEREST YOU IN A LATE MODEL SPORTS CAR?
IMPORT MOTORS
LYNN

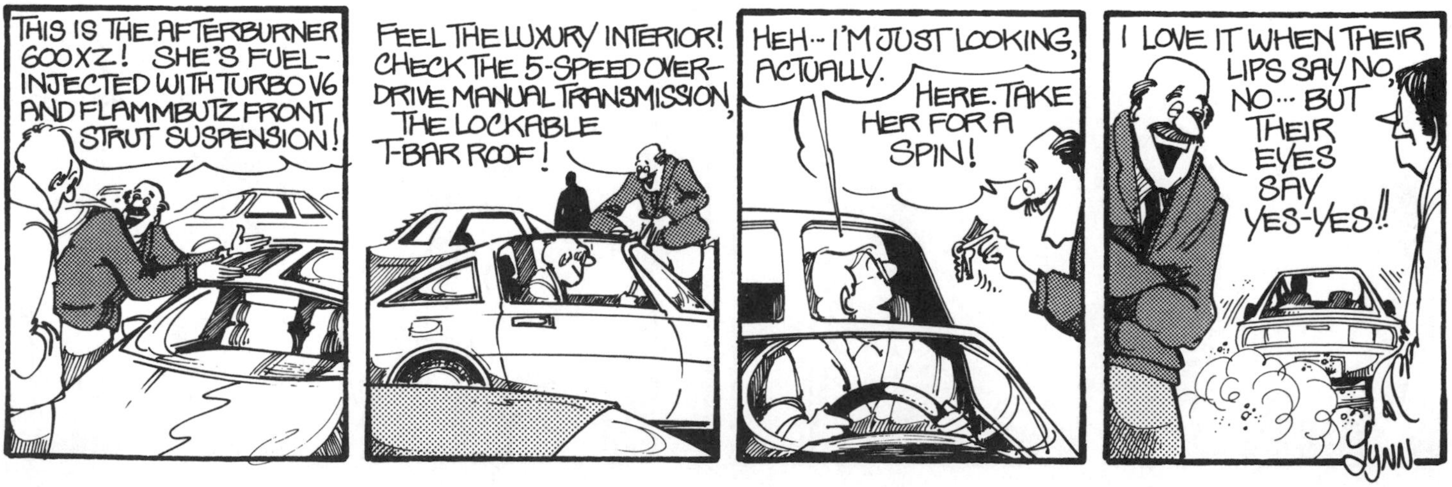
THIS IS THE AFTERBURNER 600XZ! SHE'S FUEL-INJECTED WITH TURBO V6 AND FLAMMBUTZ FRONT STRUT SUSPENSION!
FEEL THE LUXURY INTERIOR! CHECK THE 5-SPEED OVER-DRIVE MANUAL TRANSMISSION, THE LOCKABLE T-BAR ROOF!
HEH... I'M JUST LOOKING, ACTUALLY.
HERE. TAKE HER FOR A SPIN!
I LOVE IT WHEN THEIR LIPS SAY NO, NO... BUT THEIR EYES SAY YES-YES!!
LYNN

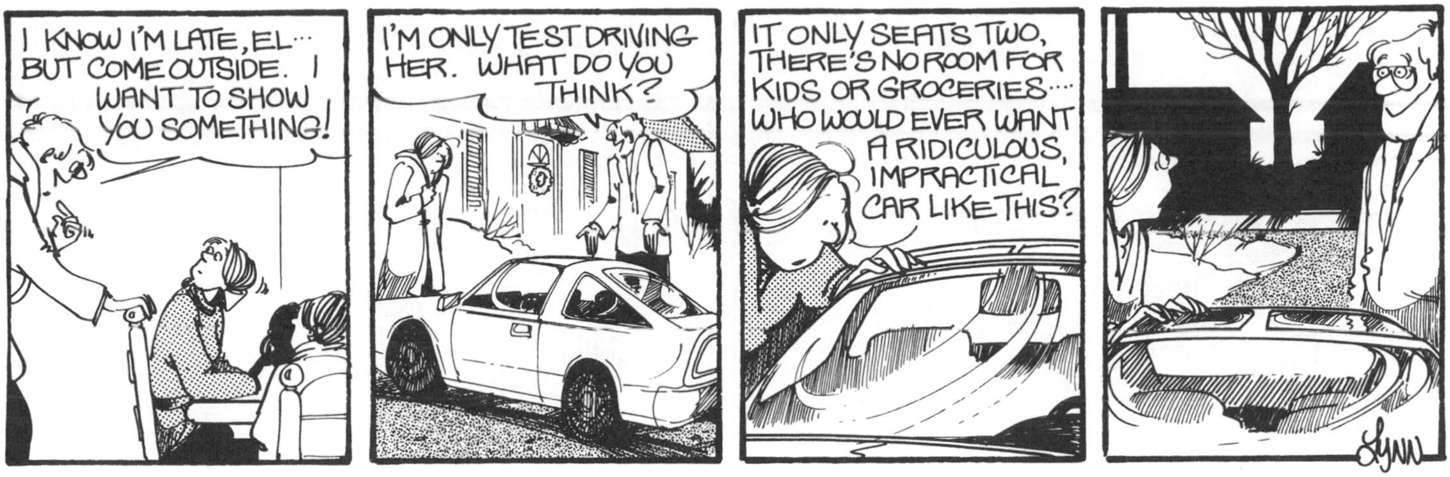
I KNOW I'M LATE, EL... BUT COME OUTSIDE. I WANT TO SHOW YOU SOMETHING!
I'M ONLY TEST DRIVING HER. WHAT DO YOU THINK?
IT ONLY SEATS TWO, THERE'S NO ROOM FOR KIDS OR GROCERIES.... WHO WOULD EVER WANT A RIDICULOUS, IMPRACTICAL CAR LIKE THIS?
Lynn

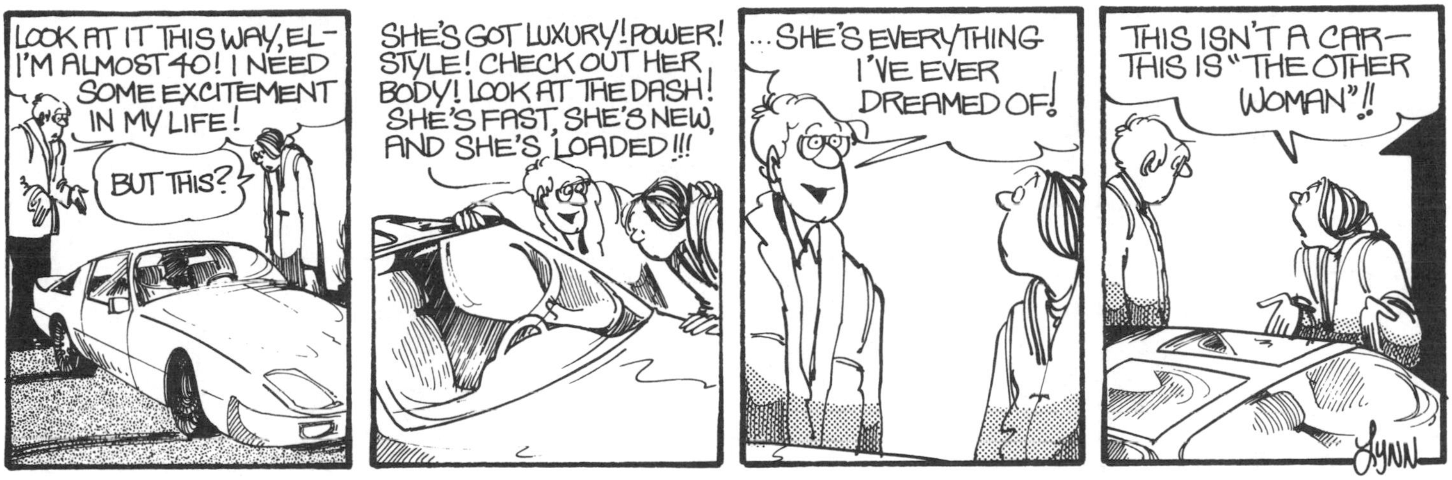
LOOK AT IT THIS WAY, EL- I'M ALMOST 40! I NEED SOME EXCITEMENT IN MY LIFE!
BUT THIS?
SHE'S GOT LUXURY! POWER! STYLE! CHECK OUT HER BODY! LOOK AT THE DASH! SHE'S FAST, SHE'S NEW, AND SHE'S LOADED!!!
...SHE'S EVERYTHING I'VE EVER DREAMED OF!
THIS ISN'T A CAR- THIS IS "THE OTHER WOMAN"!!
Lynn

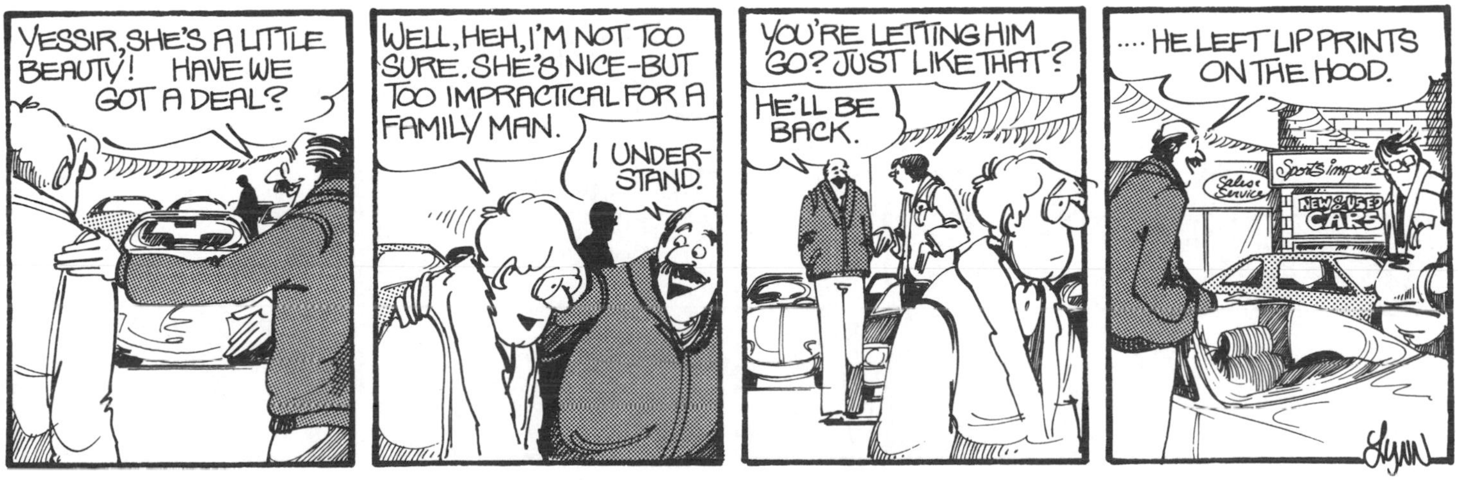
YESSIR, SHE'S A LITTLE BEAUTY! HAVE WE GOT A DEAL?
WELL, HEH, I'M NOT TOO SURE. SHE'S NICE-BUT TOO IMPRACTICAL FOR A FAMILY MAN.
I UNDERSTAND.
YOU'RE LETTING HIM GO? JUST LIKE THAT?
HE'LL BE BACK.
Sales & Service
Sports imports
NEW & USED CARS
.... HE LEFT LIP PRINTS ON THE HOOD.
Lynn

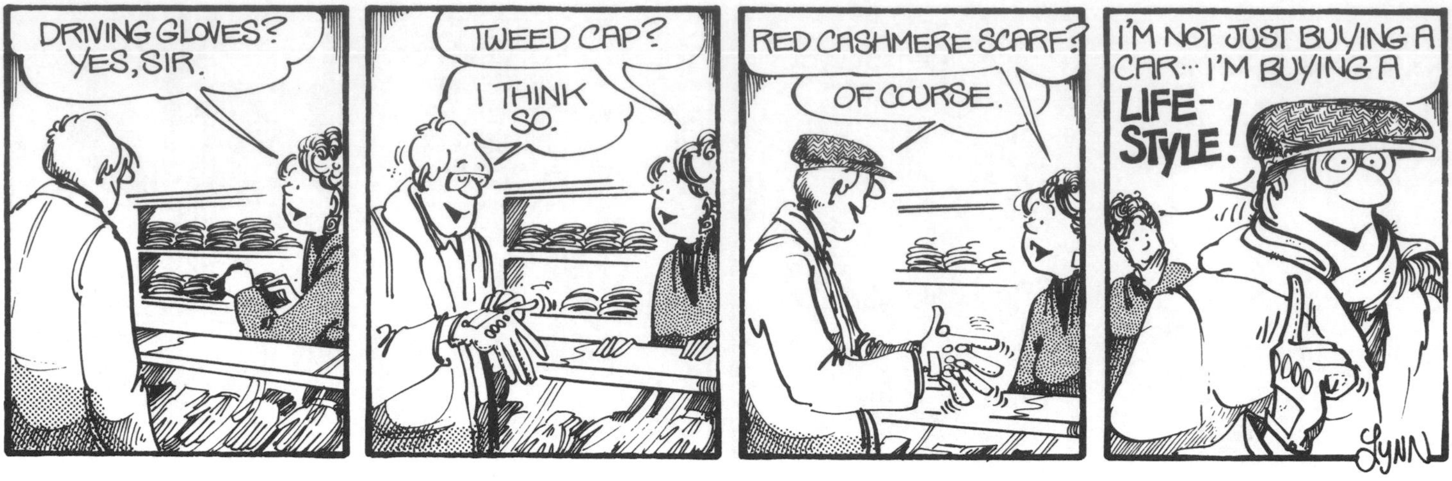
DRIVING GLOVES? YES, SIR.
TWEED CAP?
I THINK SO.
RED CASHMERE SCARF?
OF COURSE.
I'M NOT JUST BUYING A CAR··· I'M BUYING A LIFE-STYLE!

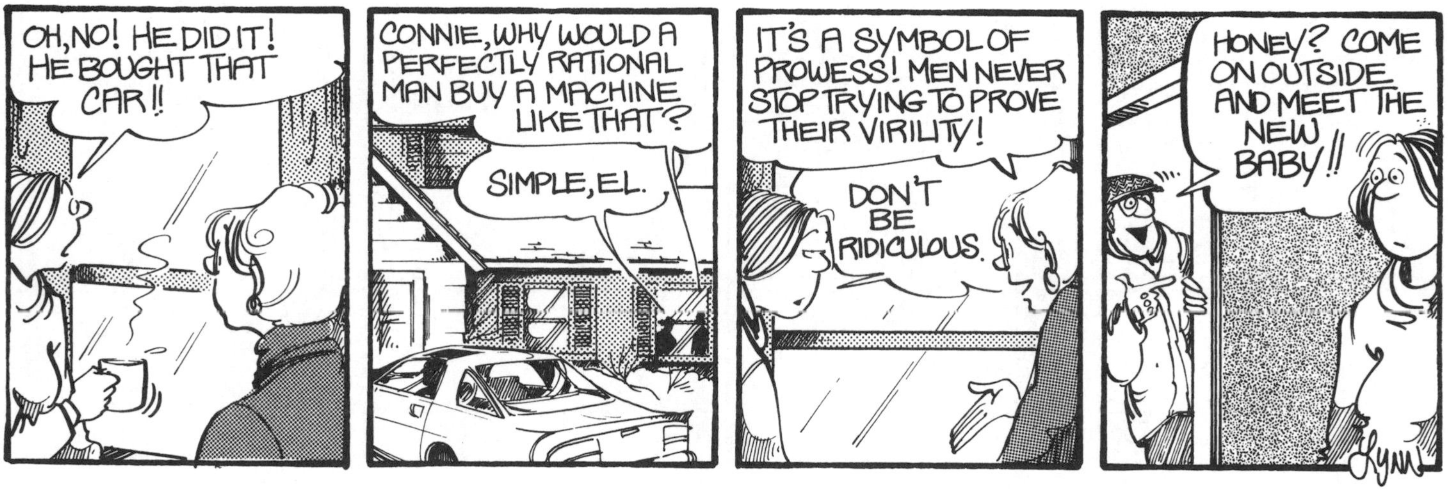
OH, NO! HE DID IT! HE BOUGHT THAT CAR!!
CONNIE, WHY WOULD A PERFECTLY RATIONAL MAN BUY A MACHINE LIKE THAT?
SIMPLE, EL.
IT'S A SYMBOL OF PROWESS! MEN NEVER STOP TRYING TO PROVE THEIR VIRILITY!
DON'T BE RIDICULOUS.
HONEY? COME ON OUTSIDE AND MEET THE NEW BABY!!

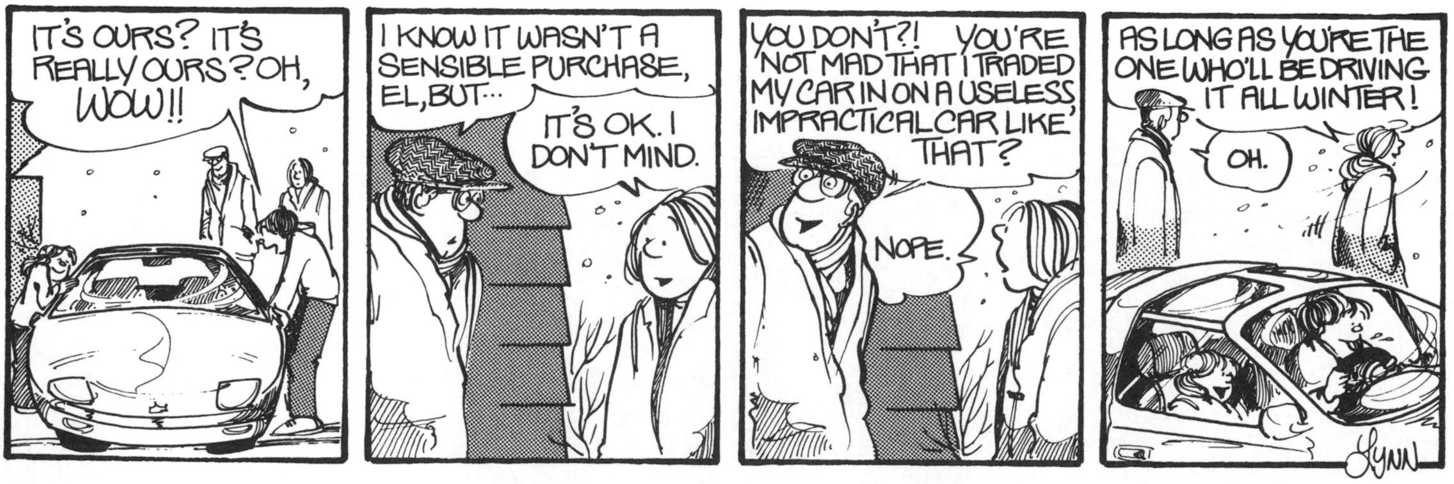
IT'S OURS? IT'S REALLY OURS? OH, WOW!!
I KNOW IT WASN'T A SENSIBLE PURCHASE, EL, BUT···
IT'S OK. I DON'T MIND.
YOU DON'T?! YOU'RE NOT MAD THAT I TRADED MY CAR IN ON A USELESS, IMPRACTICAL CAR LIKE THAT?
NOPE.
AS LONG AS YOU'RE THE ONE WHO'LL BE DRIVING IT ALL WINTER!
OH.

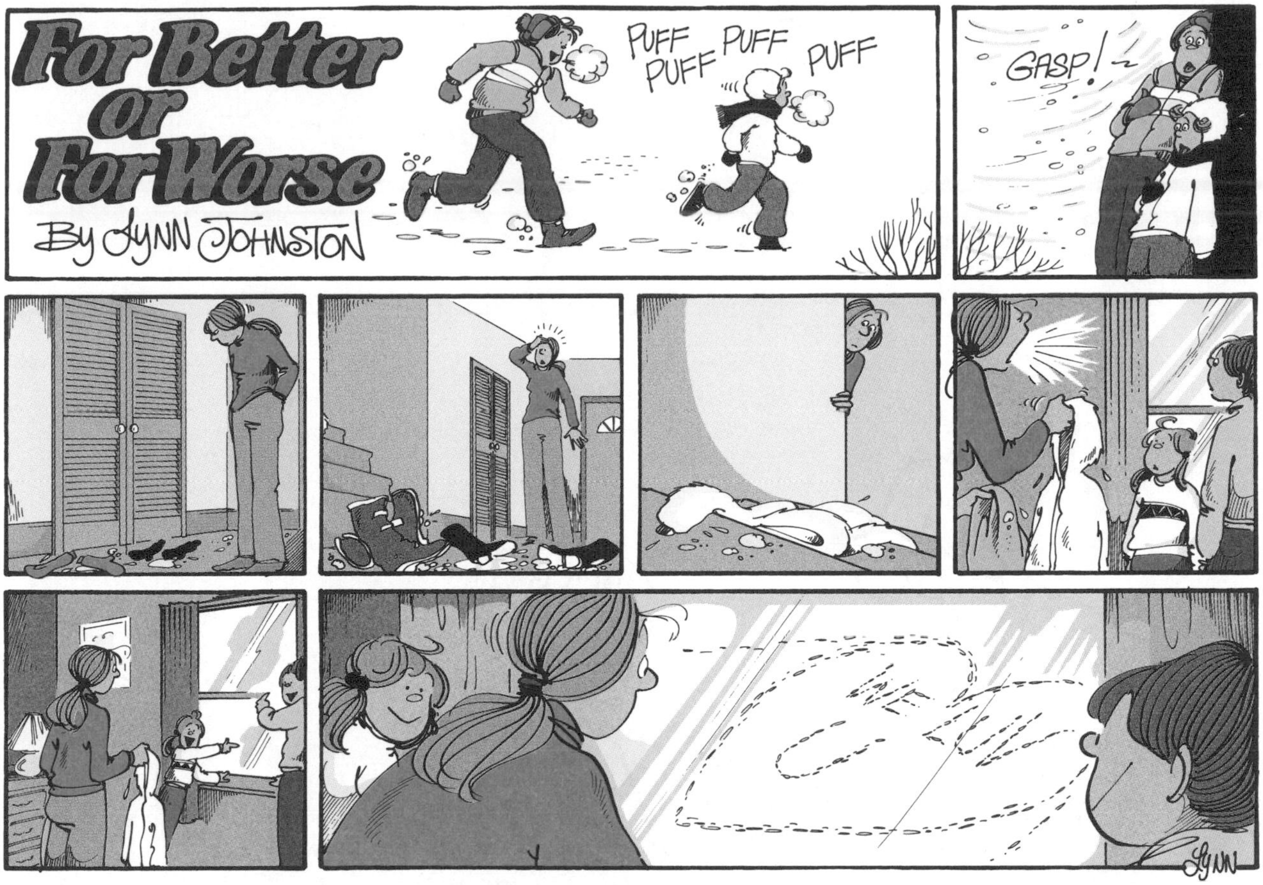
For Better or For Worse
By Lynn Johnston
PUFF PUFF PUFF PUFF
GASP!
LYNN

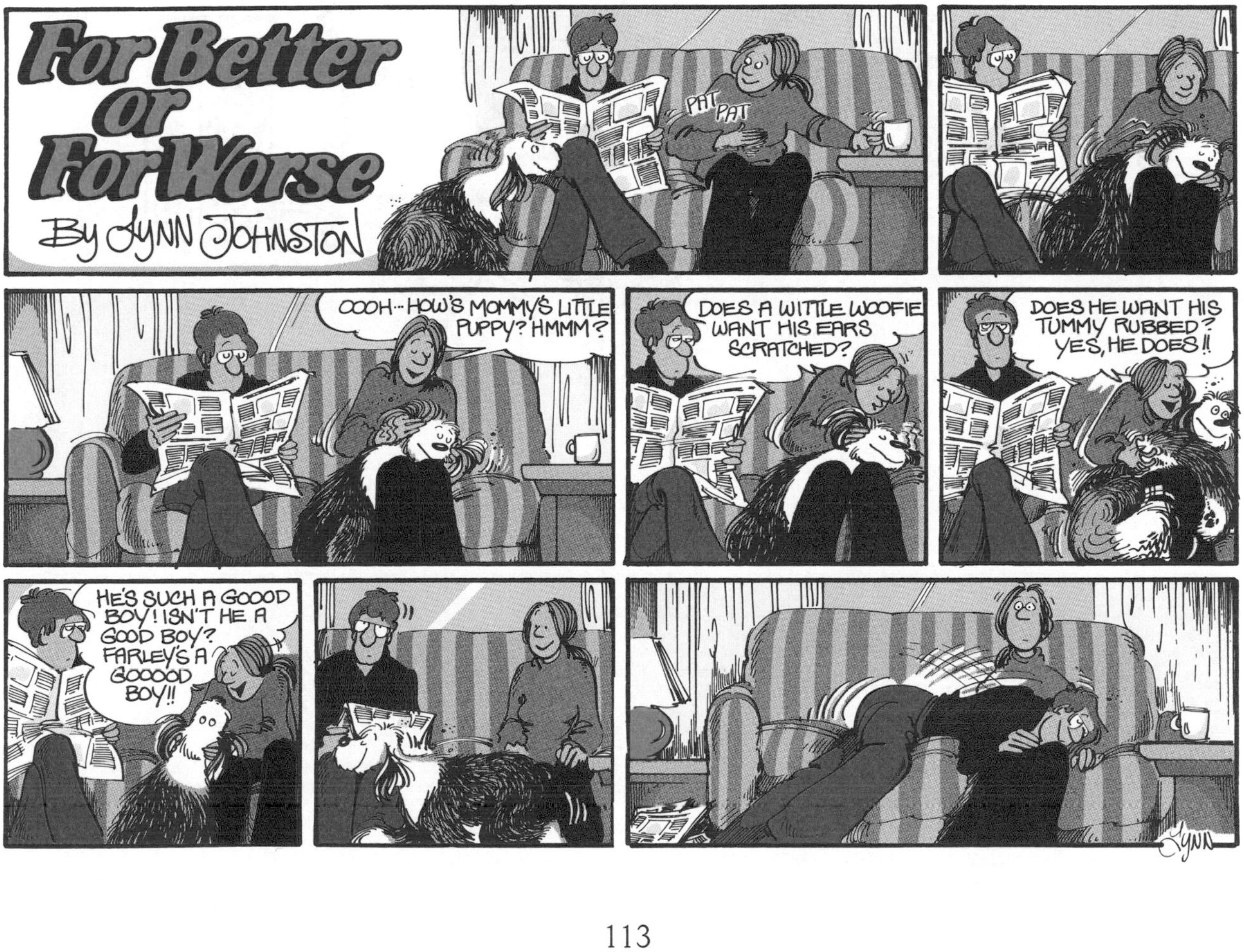
For Better or For Worse
By Lynn Johnston
PAT PAT
OOOH... HOW'S MOMMY'S LITTLE PUPPY? HMMM?
DOES A WITTLE WOOFIE WANT HIS EARS SCRATCHED?
DOES HE WANT HIS TUMMY RUBBED? YES, HE DOES!!
HE'S SUCH A GOOOD BOY! ISN'T HE A GOOD BOY? FARLEY'S A GOOOOD BOY!!
LYNN

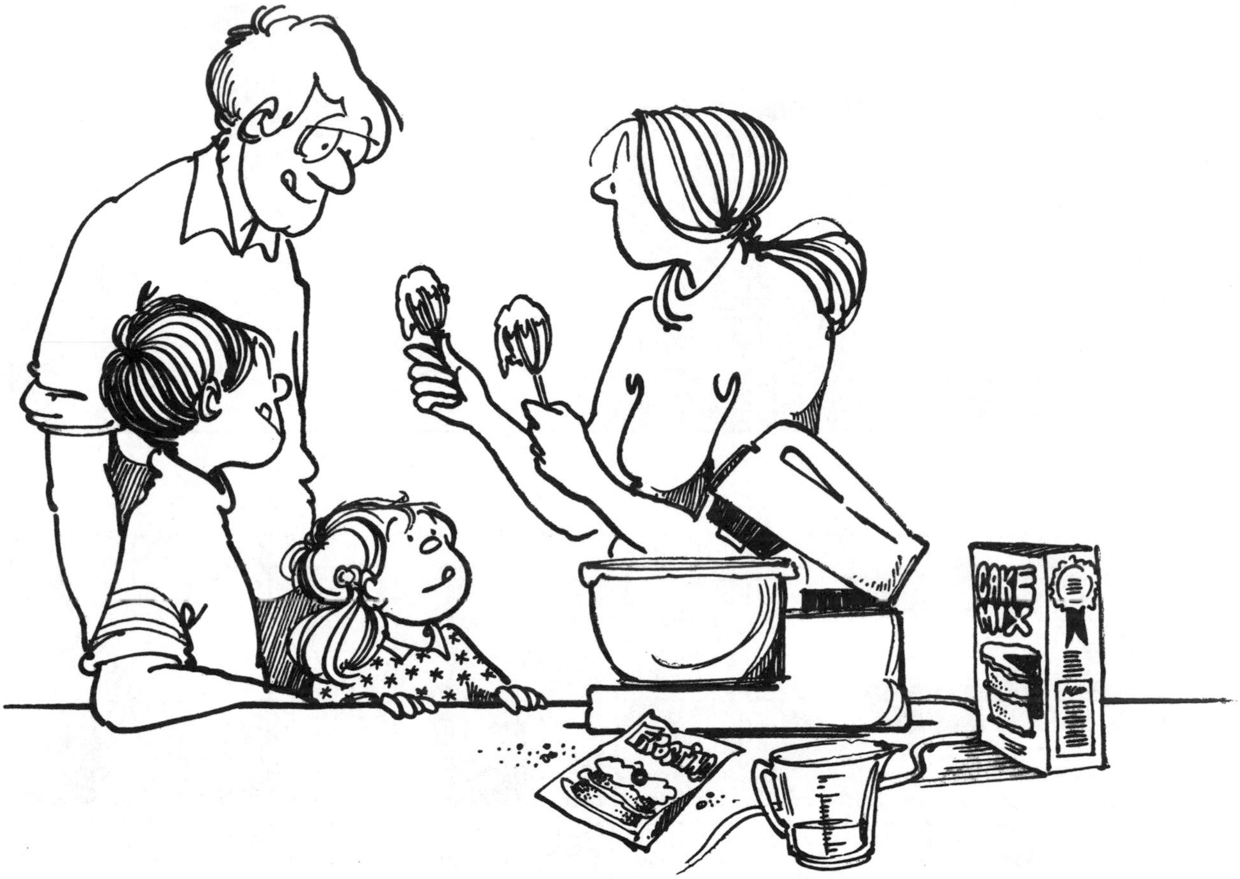
CAKE MIX

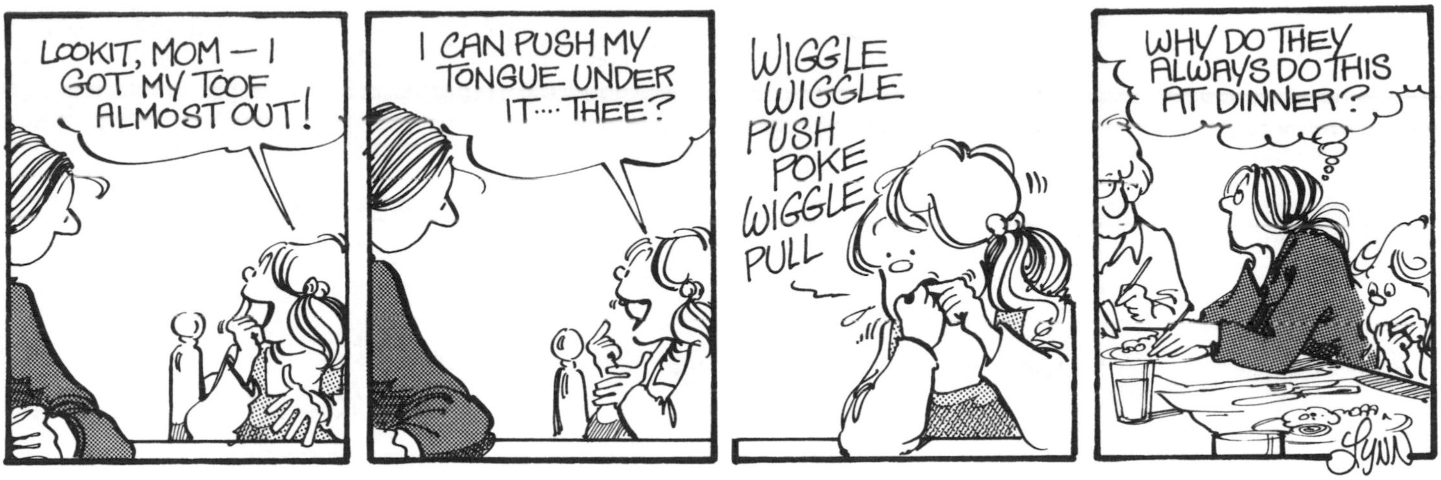
LOOKIT, MOM — I GOT MY TOOF ALMOST OUT!
I CAN PUSH MY TONGUE UNDER IT.... THEE?
WIGGLE WIGGLE PUSH POKE WIGGLE PULL
WHY DO THEY ALWAYS DO THIS AT DINNER?
LYNN

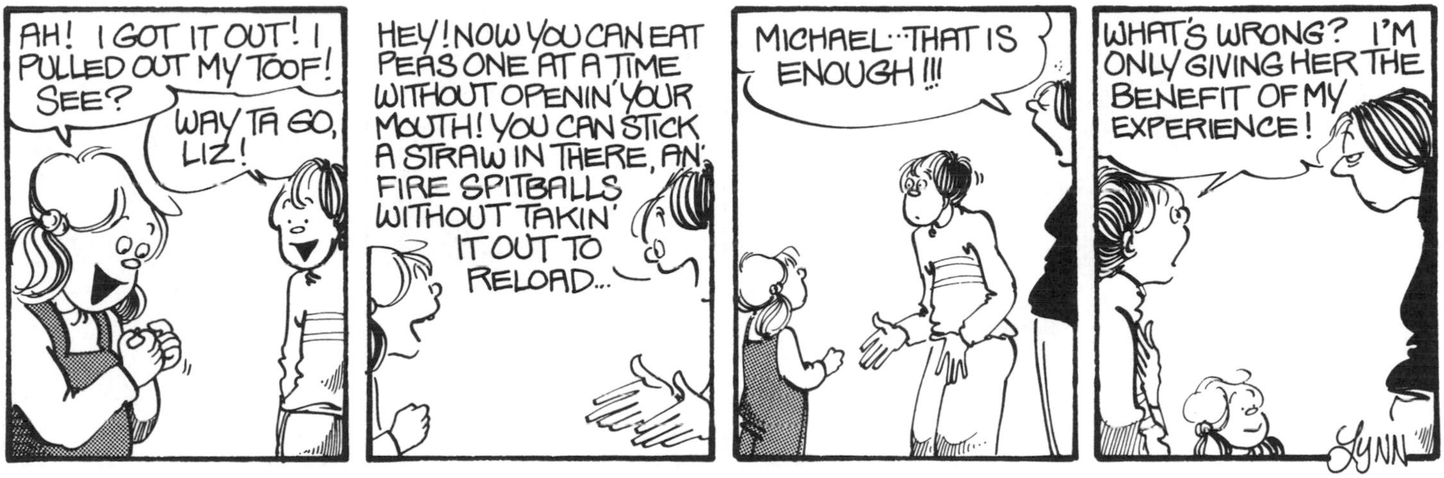
AH! I GOT IT OUT! I PULLED OUT MY TOOF! SEE?
WAY TA GO, LIZ!
HEY! NOW YOU CAN EAT PEAS ONE AT A TIME WITHOUT OPENIN' YOUR MOUTH! YOU CAN STICK A STRAW IN THERE, AN' FIRE SPITBALLS WITHOUT TAKIN' IT OUT TO RELOAD...
MICHAEL··· THAT IS ENOUGH!!!
WHAT'S WRONG? I'M ONLY GIVING HER THE BENEFIT OF MY EXPERIENCE!
LYNN

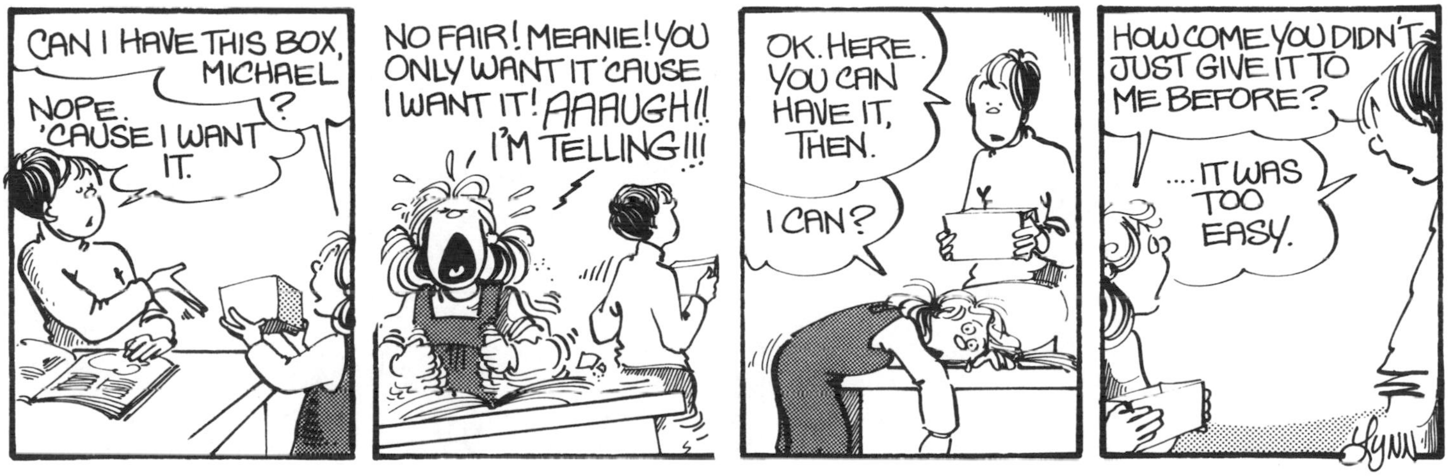
CAN I HAVE THIS BOX, MICHAEL?
NOPE. 'CAUSE I WANT IT.
NO FAIR! MEANIE! YOU ONLY WANT IT 'CAUSE I WANT IT! AAAUGH!! I'M TELLING!!!
OK. HERE. YOU CAN HAVE IT, THEN.
I CAN?
HOW COME YOU DIDN'T JUST GIVE IT TO ME BEFORE?
....IT WAS TOO EASY.
LYNN

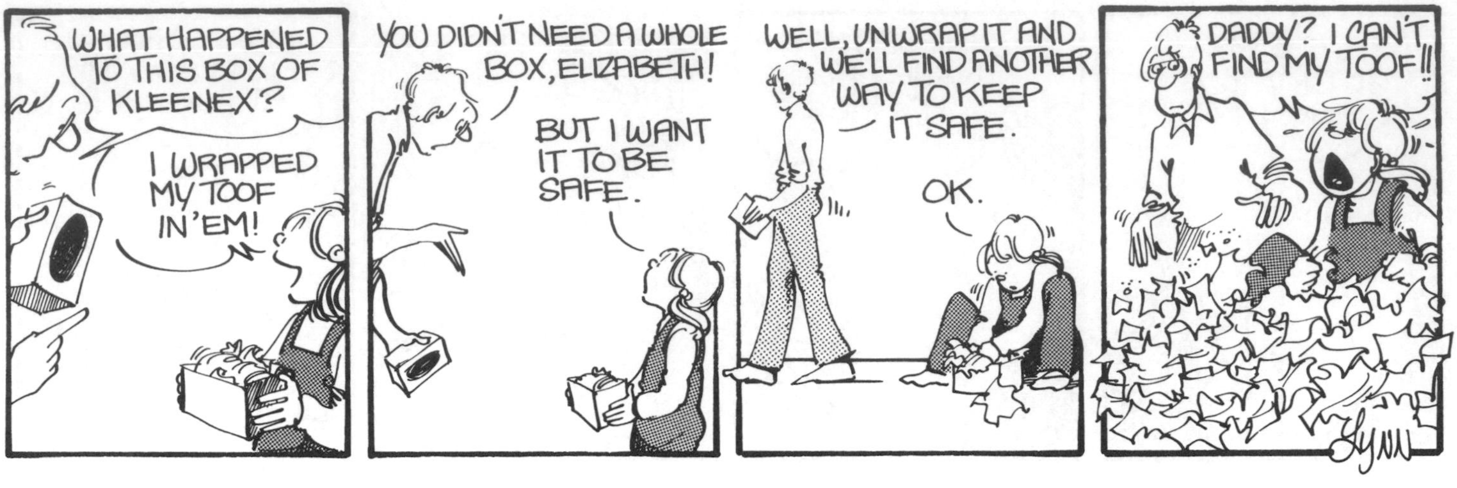
WHAT HAPPENED TO THIS BOX OF KLEENEX?
I WRAPPED MY TOOF IN'EM!
YOU DIDN'T NEED A WHOLE BOX, ELIZABETH!
BUT I WANT IT TO BE SAFE.
WELL, UNWRAP IT AND WE'LL FIND ANOTHER WAY TO KEEP IT SAFE.
OK.
DADDY? I CAN'T FIND MY TOOF!!
LYNN

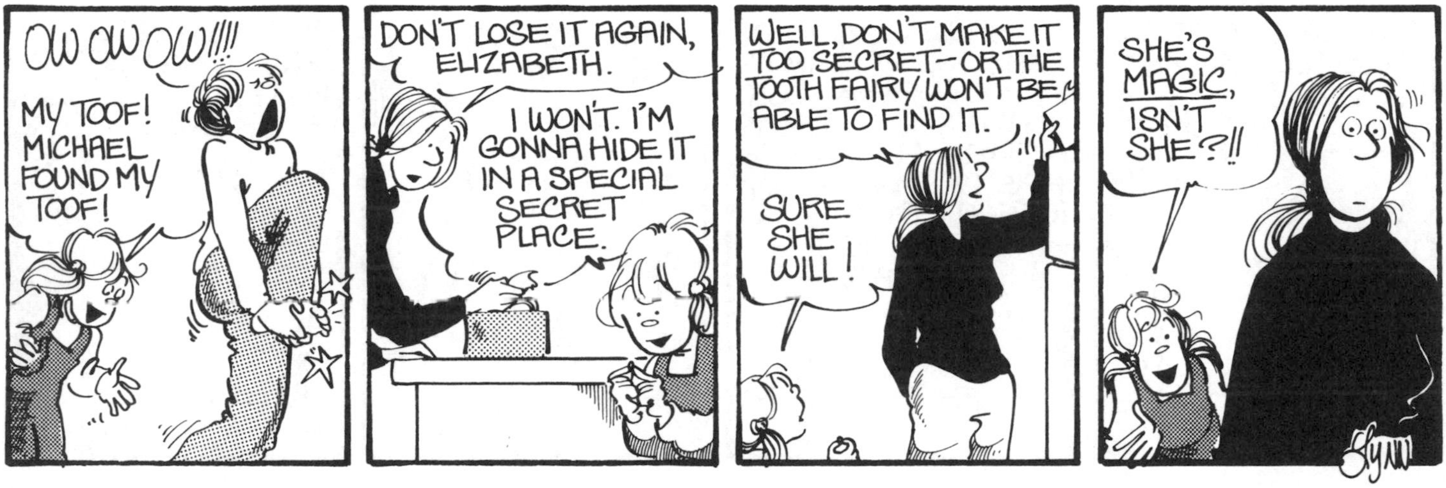
OW OW OW!!!!
MY TOOF! MICHAEL FOUND MY TOOF!
DON'T LOSE IT AGAIN, ELIZABETH.
I WON'T. I'M GONNA HIDE IT IN A SPECIAL SECRET PLACE.
WELL, DON'T MAKE IT TOO SECRET—OR THE TOOTH FAIRY WON'T BE ABLE TO FIND IT.
SURE SHE WILL!
SHE'S MAGIC, ISN'T SHE?!!
LYNN

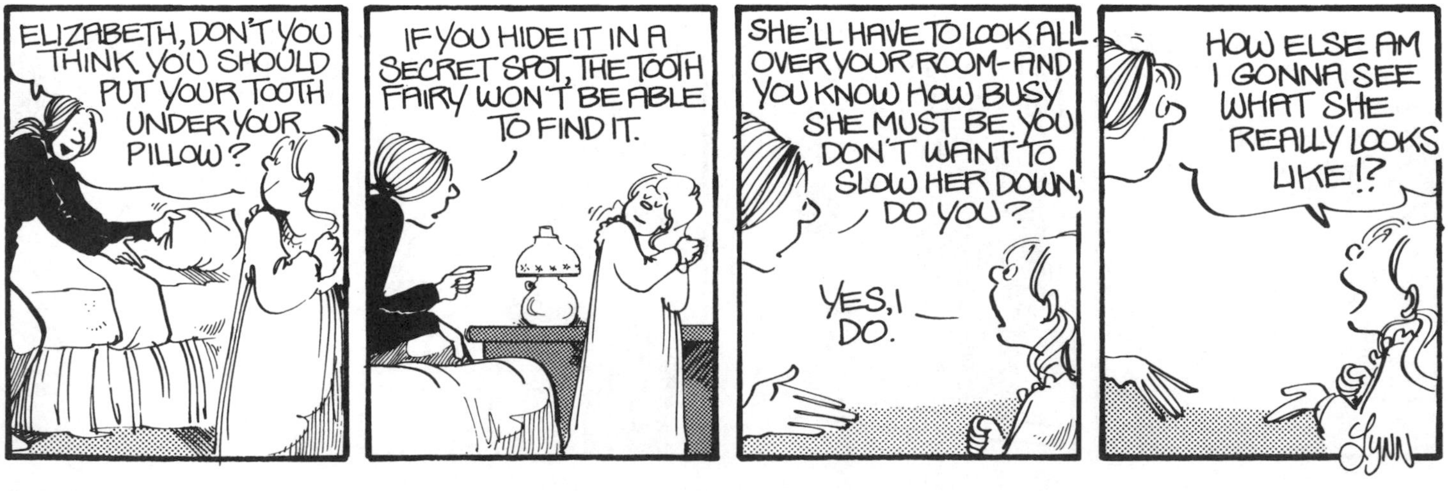
ELIZABETH, DON'T YOU THINK YOU SHOULD PUT YOUR TOOTH UNDER YOUR PILLOW?
IF YOU HIDE IT IN A SECRET SPOT, THE TOOTH FAIRY WON'T BE ABLE TO FIND IT.
SHE'LL HAVE TO LOOK ALL OVER YOUR ROOM—AND YOU KNOW HOW BUSY SHE MUST BE. YOU DON'T WANT TO SLOW HER DOWN, DO YOU?
YES, I DO.
HOW ELSE AM I GONNA SEE WHAT SHE REALLY LOOKS LIKE!?
LYNN

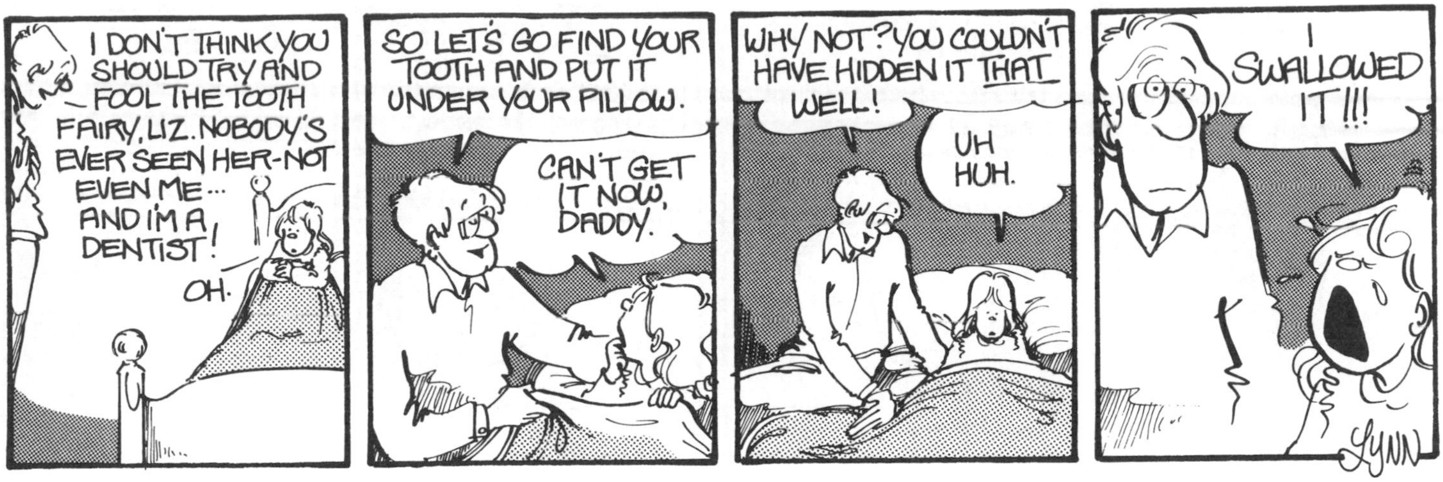
I DON'T THINK YOU SHOULD TRY AND FOOL THE TOOTH FAIRY, LIZ. NOBODY'S EVER SEEN HER-NOT EVEN ME... AND I'M A DENTIST!
OH.
SO LET'S GO FIND YOUR TOOTH AND PUT IT UNDER YOUR PILLOW.
CAN'T GET IT NOW, DADDY.
WHY NOT? YOU COULDN'T HAVE HIDDEN IT THAT WELL!
UH HUH.
I SWALLOWED IT!!!
LYNN

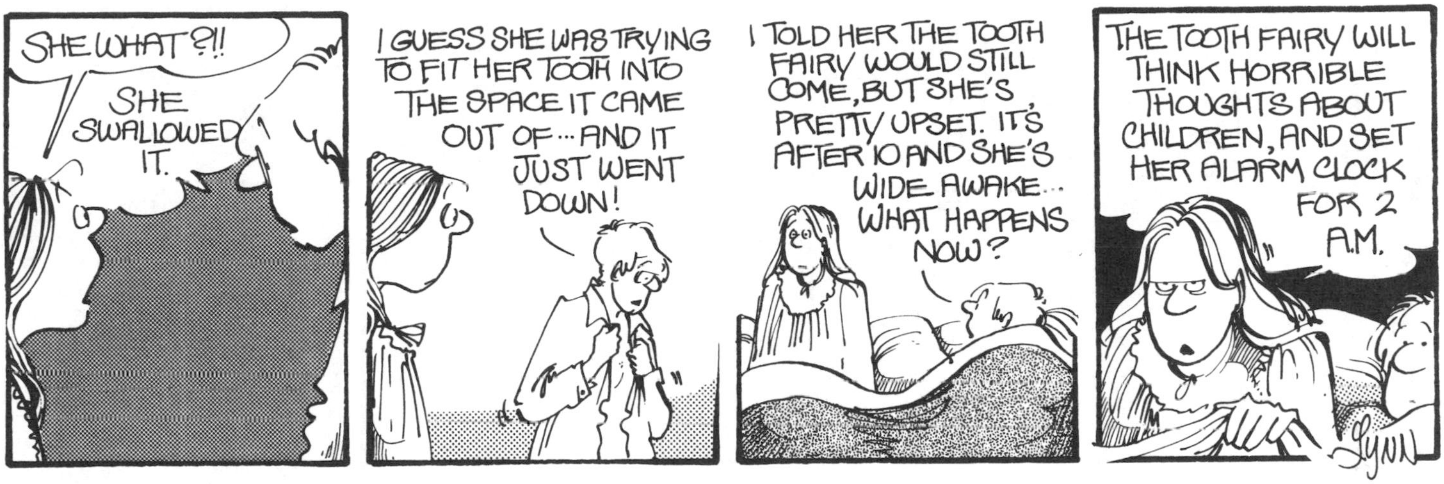
SHE WHAT?!!
SHE SWALLOWED IT.
I GUESS SHE WAS TRYING TO FIT HER TOOTH INTO THE SPACE IT CAME OUT OF... AND IT JUST WENT DOWN!
I TOLD HER THE TOOTH FAIRY WOULD STILL COME, BUT SHE'S PRETTY UPSET. IT'S AFTER 10 AND SHE'S WIDE AWAKE... WHAT HAPPENS NOW?
THE TOOTH FAIRY WILL THINK HORRIBLE THOUGHTS ABOUT CHILDREN, AND SET HER ALARM CLOCK FOR 2 A.M.
LYNN

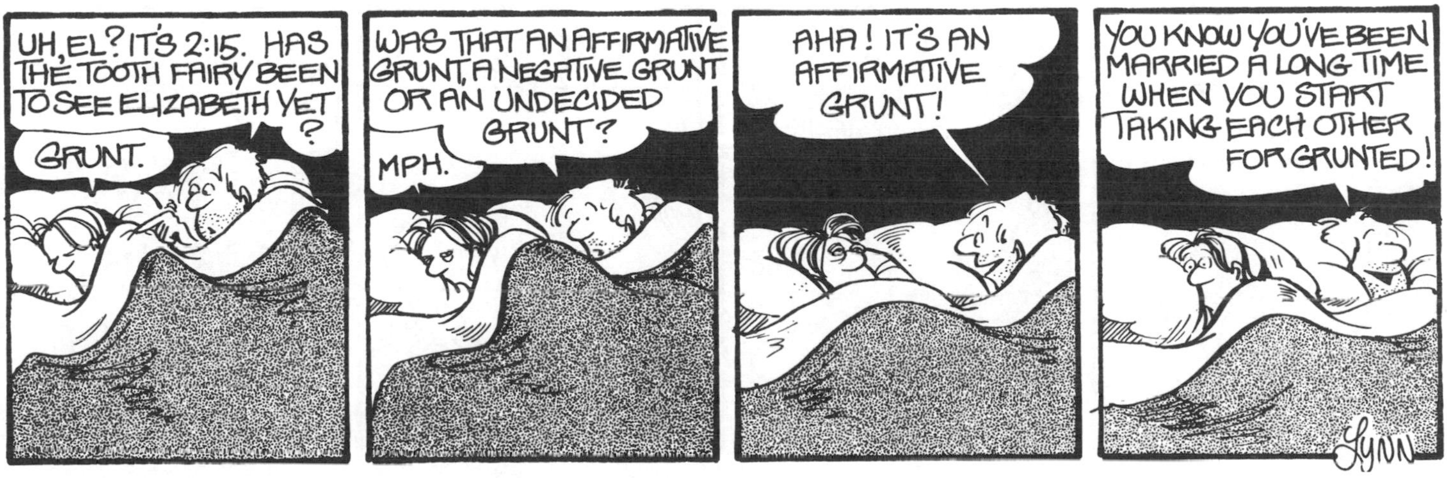
UH, EL? IT'S 2:15. HAS THE TOOTH FAIRY BEEN TO SEE ELIZABETH YET?
GRUNT.
WAS THAT AN AFFIRMATIVE GRUNT, A NEGATIVE GRUNT OR AN UNDECIDED GRUNT?
MPH.
AHA! IT'S AN AFFIRMATIVE GRUNT!
YOU KNOW YOU'VE BEEN MARRIED A LONG TIME WHEN YOU START TAKING EACH OTHER FOR GRUNTED!
LYNN

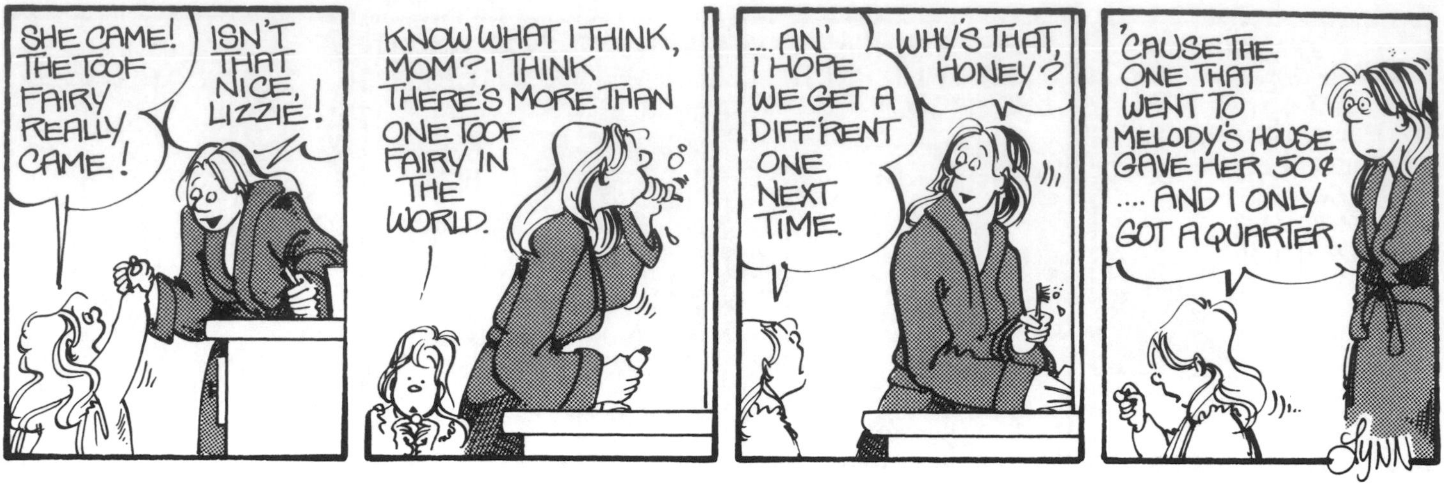
SHE CAME! THE TOOF FAIRY REALLY CAME!
ISN'T THAT NICE, LIZZIE!
KNOW WHAT I THINK, MOM? I THINK THERE'S MORE THAN ONE TOOF FAIRY IN THE WORLD.
.... AN' I HOPE WE GET A DIFF'RENT ONE NEXT TIME.
WHY'S THAT, HONEY?
'CAUSE THE ONE THAT WENT TO MELODY'S HOUSE GAVE HER 50¢ .... AND I ONLY GOT A QUARTER.
LYNN

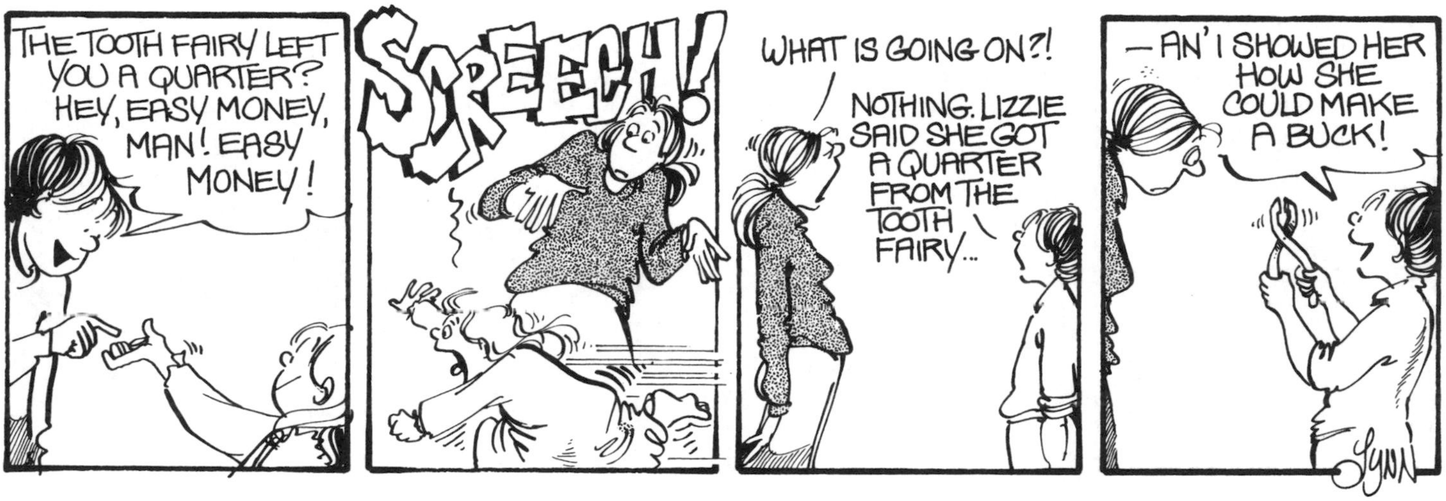
THE TOOTH FAIRY LEFT YOU A QUARTER? HEY, EASY MONEY, MAN! EASY MONEY!
SCREECH!
WHAT IS GOING ON?!
NOTHING. LIZZIE SAID SHE GOT A QUARTER FROM THE TOOTH FAIRY...
— AN' I SHOWED HER HOW SHE COULD MAKE A BUCK!
LYNN

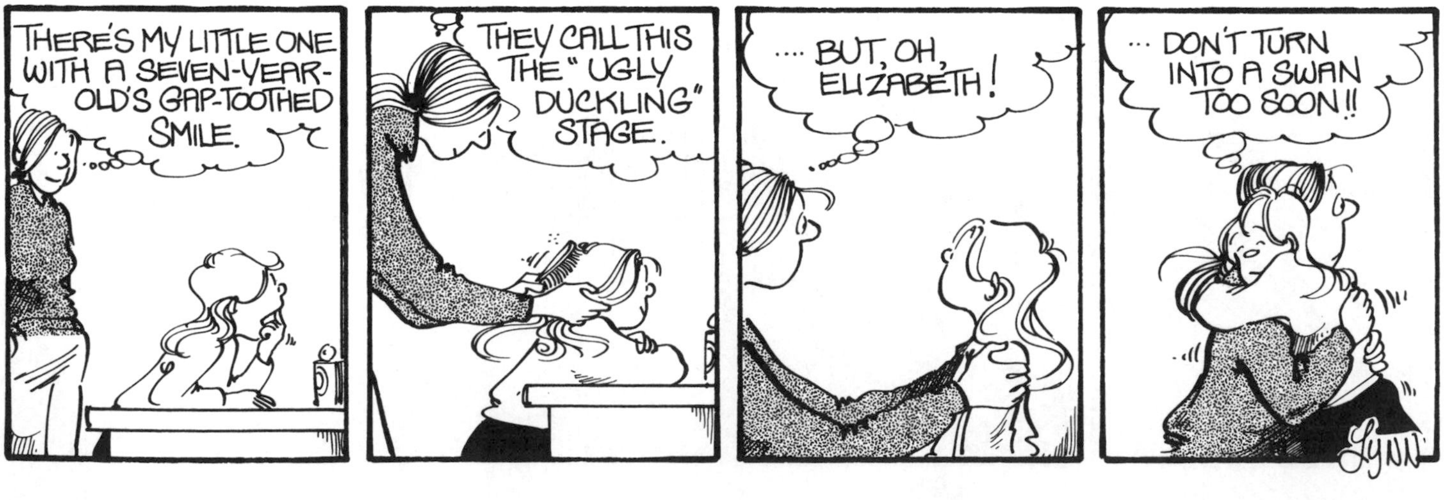
THERE'S MY LITTLE ONE WITH A SEVEN-YEAR-OLD'S GAP-TOOTHED SMILE.
THEY CALL THIS THE "UGLY DUCKLING" STAGE.
.... BUT, OH, ELIZABETH!
... DON'T TURN INTO A SWAN TOO SOON!!
LYNN

Growing Up with Ma — a Note from Lynn and Rod's Daughter, Kate Johnston

What was it like growing up in the Johnston household? Well it was pretty cool I must say. Mom worked out of the house, which meant she was always home when we needed her, but she worked all the time so Aaron and I spent quite a bit of time entertaining ourselves. She was always very interested in our lives and what our friends were up to. She was often able to use some of our stories in the strip. It is really cool to see one of my ideas or stories printed in a cartoon that is distributed worldwide.

Just as in the strip, she provided us with a warm, loving home that was full of fun and laughter. School, however, wasn't so great. Kids would tease us and pick on us because they just didn't understand, but we made some wonderful friends who will always be a part of our lives. As an adult (even though I am very proud of Mom), I don't generally let people in on that part of my life until they know me pretty well and I know this small fact won't change their opinion of me.

Since we lived in a small town, it didn't take long before Mom was a local celebrity. Sometimes people would point and whisper when they saw her around town, and some people would come over and chat her up. It was fun being at her side and feeling important, too.

Growing up in the Johnston household was great. Mom makes the best birthday cards ever! We always had great skating and Halloween costumes. How many kids get to sit in the audience of *The Joan Rivers Show* and see their mom up onstage? We had all kinds of opportunities that a lot of kids will never have. We have traveled all over the continent and have seen things that most kids will never see.

Both of my parents are creative, sarcastic, business-savvy, and successful. I have learned so much from both of them. Our parents have always encouraged us to use our talents (creativity runs deep in our genes), work hard, and do what makes us happy. Who knows where we will end up, but I sure am enjoying the adventure along the way.

Being the daughter of a popular, successful cartoonist is really cool. I have learned so much, and maybe she has learned from me as well. I can't wait to see what she does with her talents, outstanding staff, and all of her connections once the strip ends and she has time to concentrate on new exciting projects.

I adore my mother; she is my best friend in the world. She is an amazing person who has touched all of our lives. Not many people have accomplished what she has. You never cease to amaze me, Ma!

Love ya,
Kate

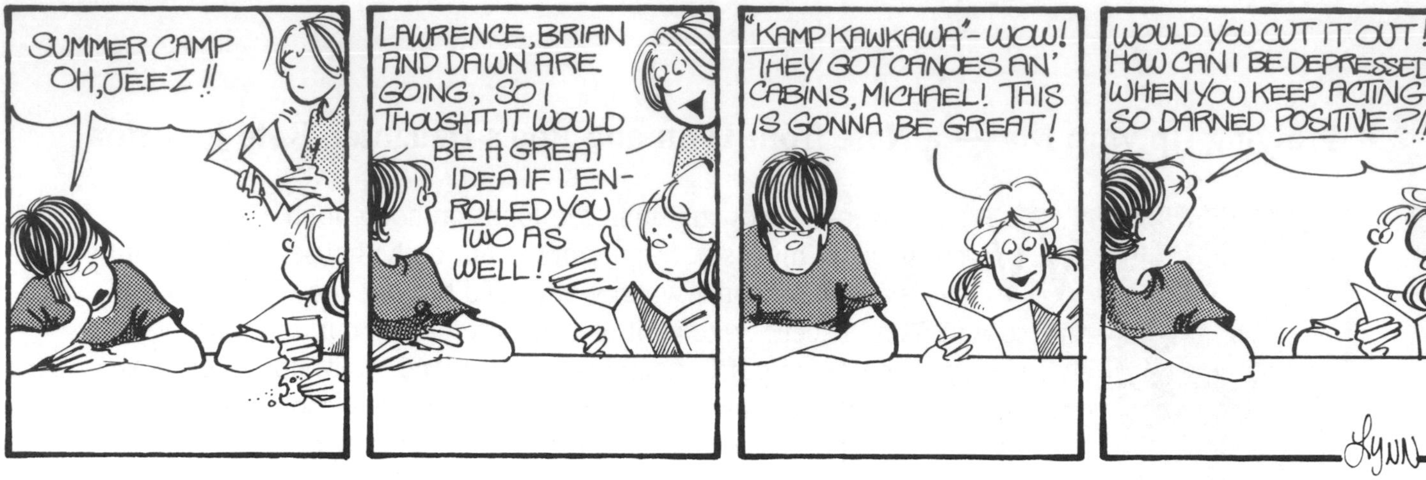
SUMMER CAMP OH, JEEZ!!
LAWRENCE, BRIAN AND DAWN ARE GOING, SO I THOUGHT IT WOULD BE A GREAT IDEA IF I ENROLLED YOU TWO AS WELL!
"KAMP KAWKAWA" - WOW! THEY GOT CANOES AN' CABINS, MICHAEL! THIS IS GONNA BE GREAT!
WOULD YOU CUT IT OUT! HOW CAN I BE DEPRESSED WHEN YOU KEEP ACTING SO DARNED POSITIVE?!!
Lynn

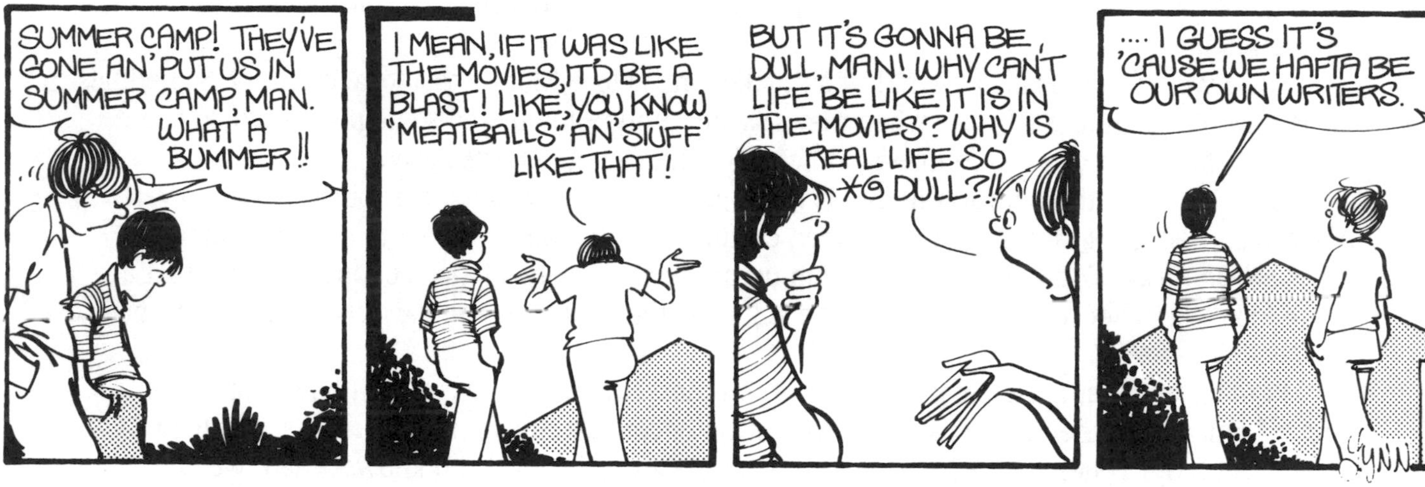
SUMMER CAMP! THEY'VE GONE AN' PUT US IN SUMMER CAMP, MAN. WHAT A BUMMER!!
I MEAN, IF IT WAS LIKE THE MOVIES, IT'D BE A BLAST! LIKE, YOU KNOW, "MEATBALLS" AN' STUFF LIKE THAT!
BUT IT'S GONNA BE DULL, MAN! WHY CAN'T LIFE BE LIKE IT IS IN THE MOVIES? WHY IS REAL LIFE SO *@ DULL?!!
.... I GUESS IT'S 'CAUSE WE HAFTA BE OUR OWN WRITERS.
Lynn

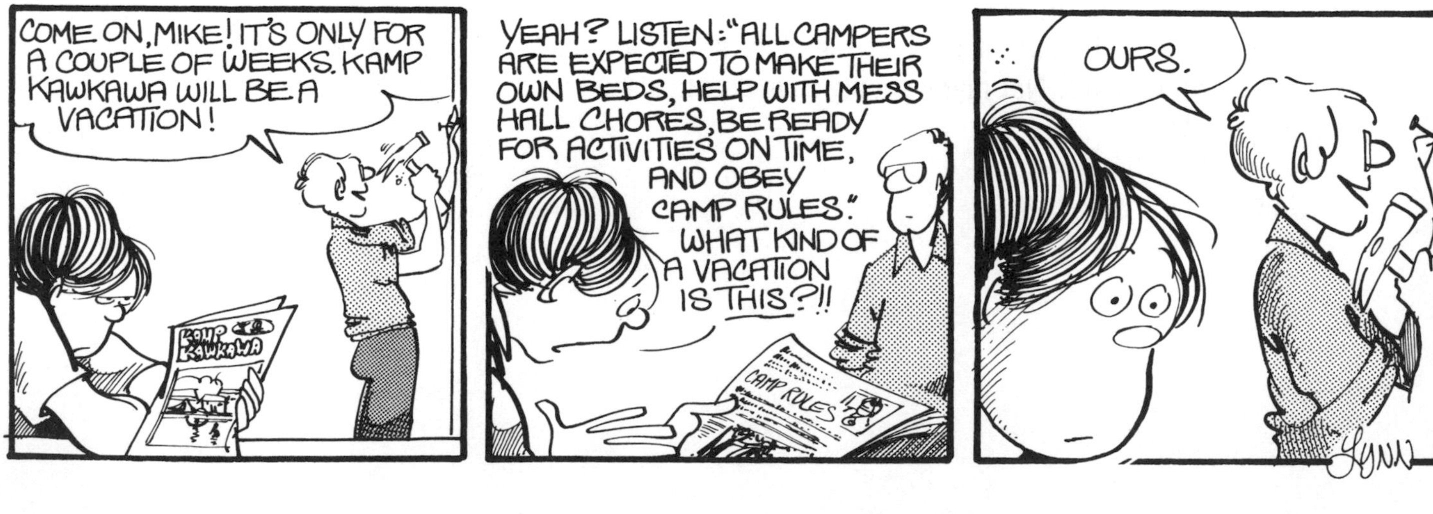
COME ON, MIKE! IT'S ONLY FOR A COUPLE OF WEEKS. KAMP KAWKAWA WILL BE A VACATION!
KAMP KAWKAWA
YEAH? LISTEN: "ALL CAMPERS ARE EXPECTED TO MAKE THEIR OWN BEDS, HELP WITH MESS HALL CHORES, BE READY FOR ACTIVITIES ON TIME, AND OBEY CAMP RULES." WHAT KIND OF A VACATION IS THIS?!!
CAMP RULES
OURS.
Lynn

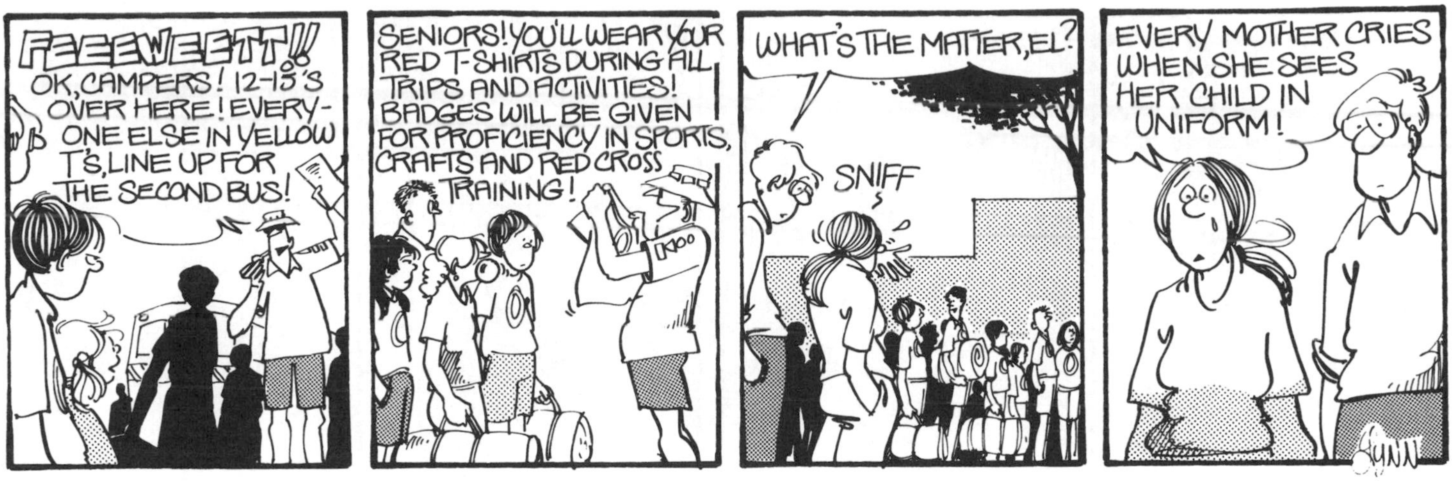
FEEEWEETT!!
OK, CAMPERS! 12-15'S OVER HERE! EVERY-ONE ELSE IN YELLOW T'S, LINE UP FOR THE SECOND BUS!
SENIORS! YOU'LL WEAR YOUR RED T-SHIRTS DURING ALL TRIPS AND ACTIVITIES! BADGES WILL BE GIVEN FOR PROFICIENCY IN SPORTS, CRAFTS AND RED CROSS TRAINING!
WHAT'S THE MATTER, EL?
SNIFF
EVERY MOTHER CRIES WHEN SHE SEES HER CHILD IN UNIFORM!
LYNN

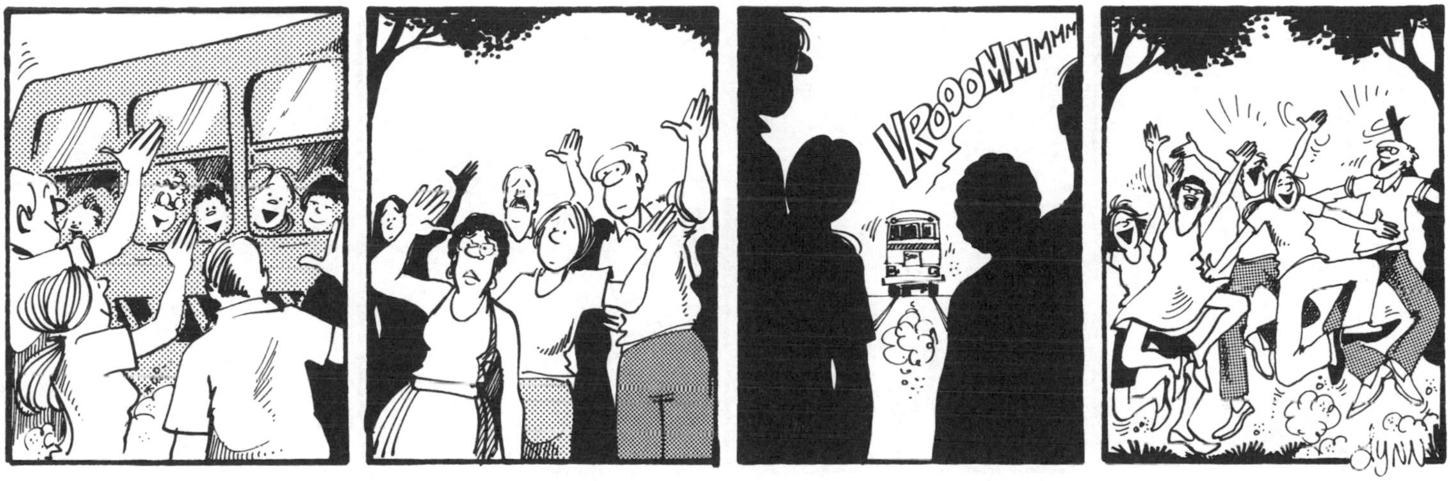
VROOOMMMMM
LYNN

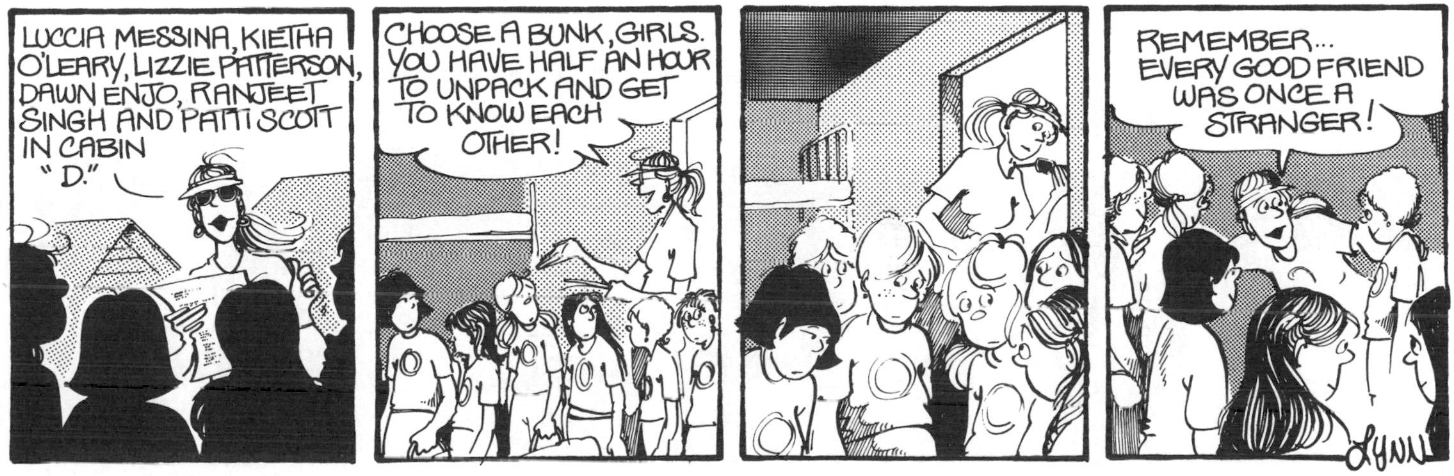
LUCCIA MESSINA, KIETHA O'LEARY, LIZZIE PATTERSON, DAWN ENJO, RANJEET SINGH AND PATTI SCOTT IN CABIN "D."
CHOOSE A BUNK, GIRLS. YOU HAVE HALF AN HOUR TO UNPACK AND GET TO KNOW EACH OTHER!
REMEMBER... EVERY GOOD FRIEND WAS ONCE A STRANGER!
LYNN

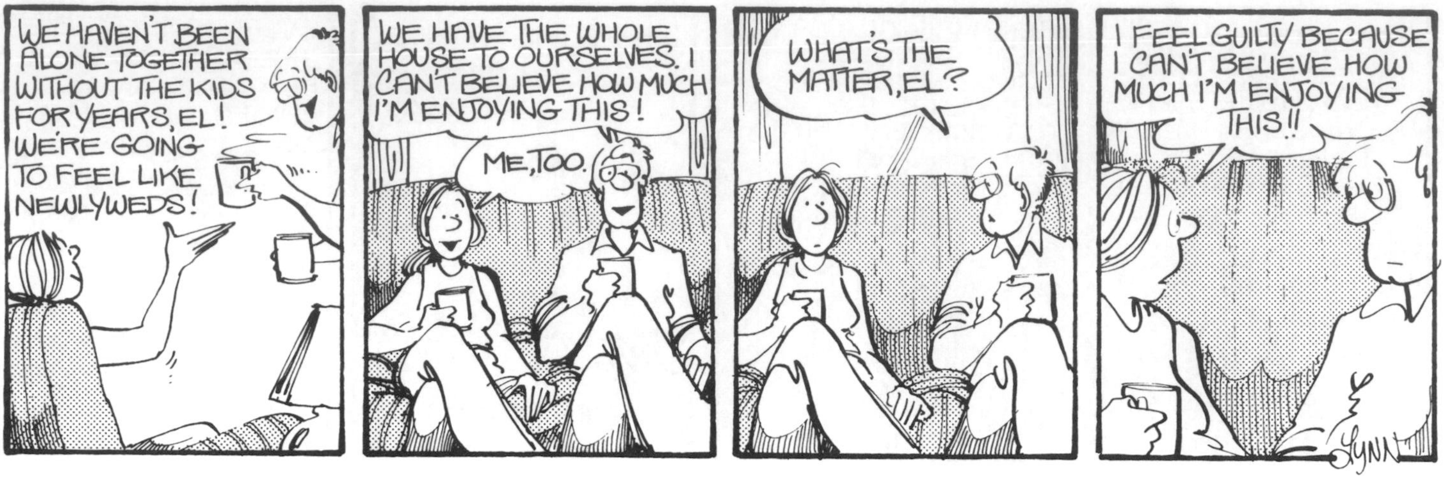
WE HAVEN'T BEEN ALONE TOGETHER WITHOUT THE KIDS FOR YEARS, EL! WE'RE GOING TO FEEL LIKE NEWLYWEDS!
WE HAVE THE WHOLE HOUSE TO OURSELVES. I CAN'T BELIEVE HOW MUCH I'M ENJOYING THIS!
ME, TOO.
WHAT'S THE MATTER, EL?
I FEEL GUILTY BECAUSE I CAN'T BELIEVE HOW MUCH I'M ENJOYING THIS!!
LYNN

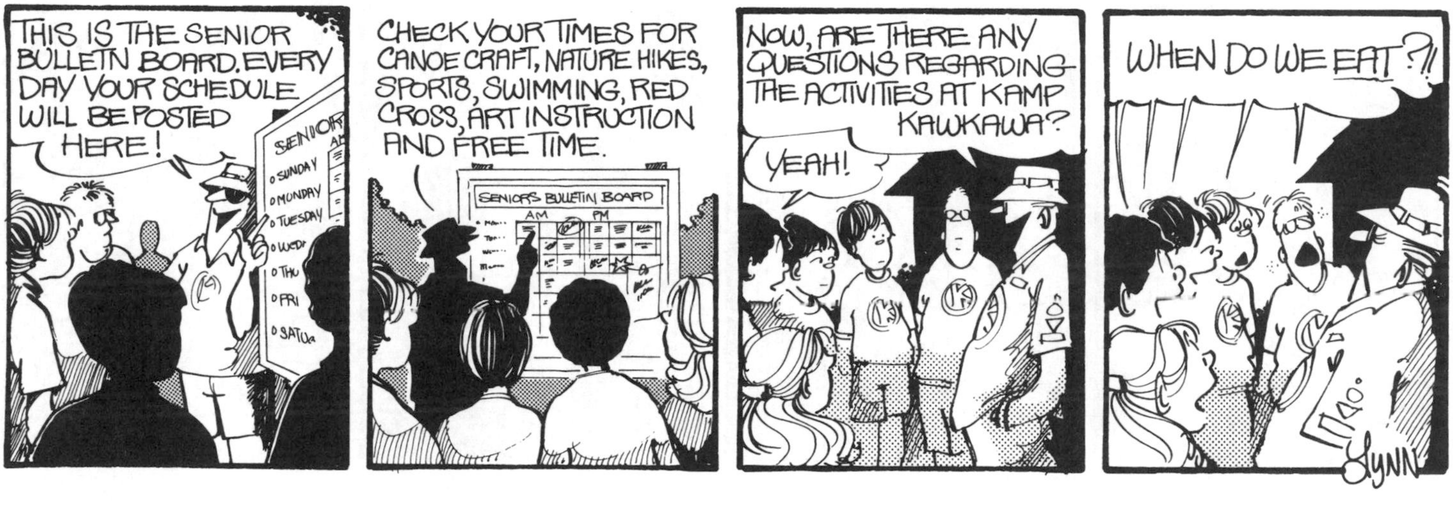
THIS IS THE SENIOR BULLETIN BOARD. EVERY DAY YOUR SCHEDULE WILL BE POSTED HERE!
SUNDAY
MONDAY
TUESDAY
CHECK YOUR TIMES FOR CANOE CRAFT, NATURE HIKES, SPORTS, SWIMMING, RED CROSS, ART INSTRUCTION AND FREE TIME.
SENIORS BULLETIN BOARD
AM
PM
NOW, ARE THERE ANY QUESTIONS REGARDING THE ACTIVITIES AT KAMP KAWKAWA?
YEAH!
WHEN DO WE EAT?!!
LYNN

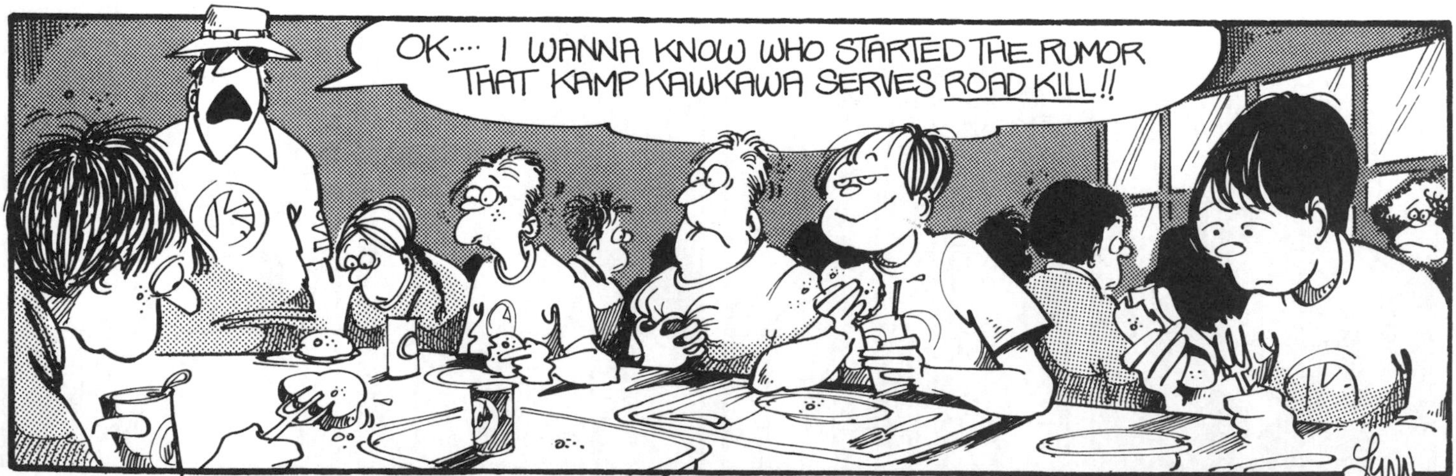
OK.... I WANNA KNOW WHO STARTED THE RUMOR THAT KAMP KAWKAWA SERVES ROAD KILL!!
LYNN

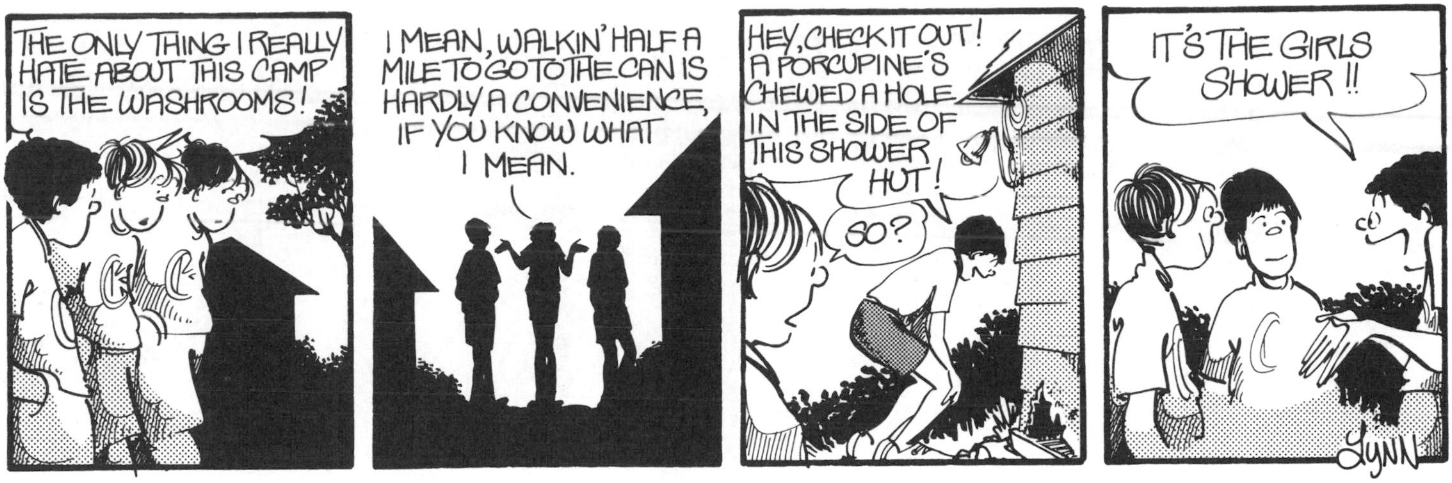
THE ONLY THING I REALLY HATE ABOUT THIS CAMP IS THE WASHROOMS!
I MEAN, WALKIN' HALF A MILE TO GO TO THE CAN IS HARDLY A CONVENIENCE, IF YOU KNOW WHAT I MEAN.
HEY, CHECK IT OUT! A PORCUPINE'S CHEWED A HOLE IN THE SIDE OF THIS SHOWER HUT!
SO?
IT'S THE GIRLS SHOWER!!
LYNN

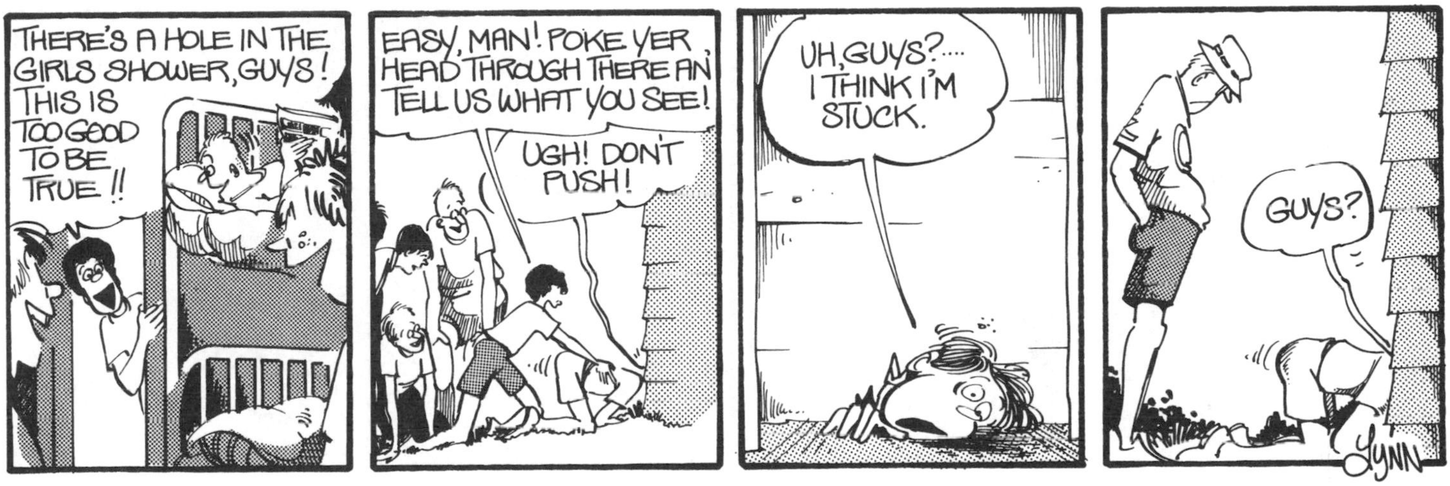
THERE'S A HOLE IN THE GIRLS SHOWER, GUYS! THIS IS TOO GOOD TO BE TRUE!!
EASY, MAN! POKE YER HEAD THROUGH THERE AN' TELL US WHAT YOU SEE!
UGH! DON'T PUSH!
UH, GUYS?.... I THINK I'M STUCK.
GUYS?
LYNN

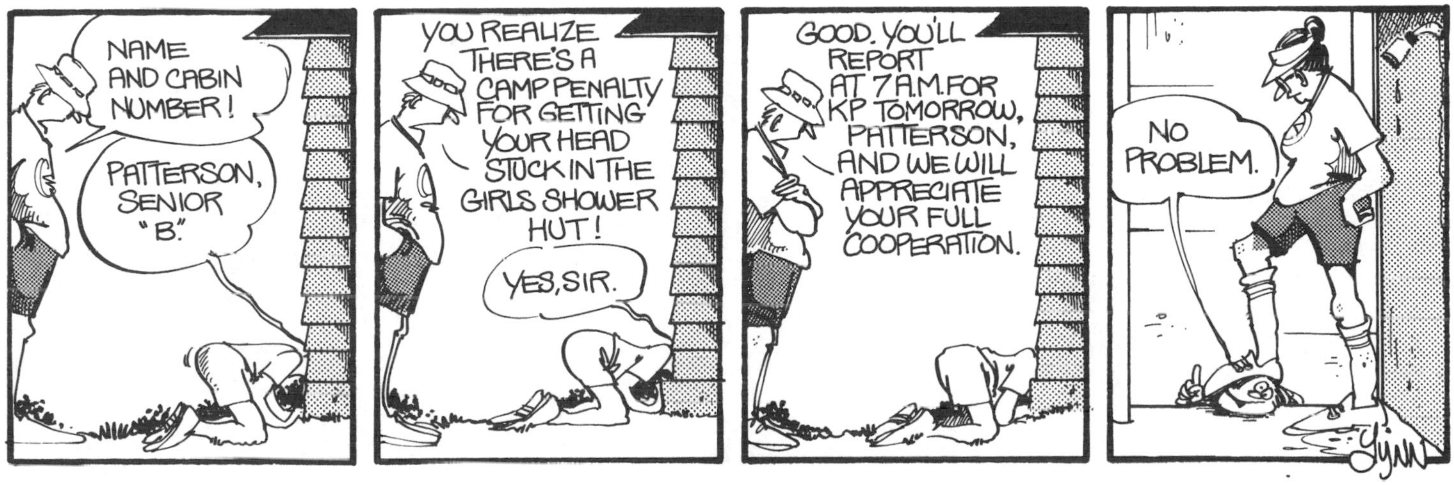
NAME AND CABIN NUMBER!
PATTERSON, SENIOR "B."
YOU REALIZE THERE'S A CAMP PENALTY FOR GETTING YOUR HEAD STUCK IN THE GIRLS SHOWER HUT!
YES, SIR.
GOOD. YOU'LL REPORT AT 7 A.M. FOR KP TOMORROW, PATTERSON, AND WE WILL APPRECIATE YOUR FULL COOPERATION.
NO PROBLEM.
LYNN

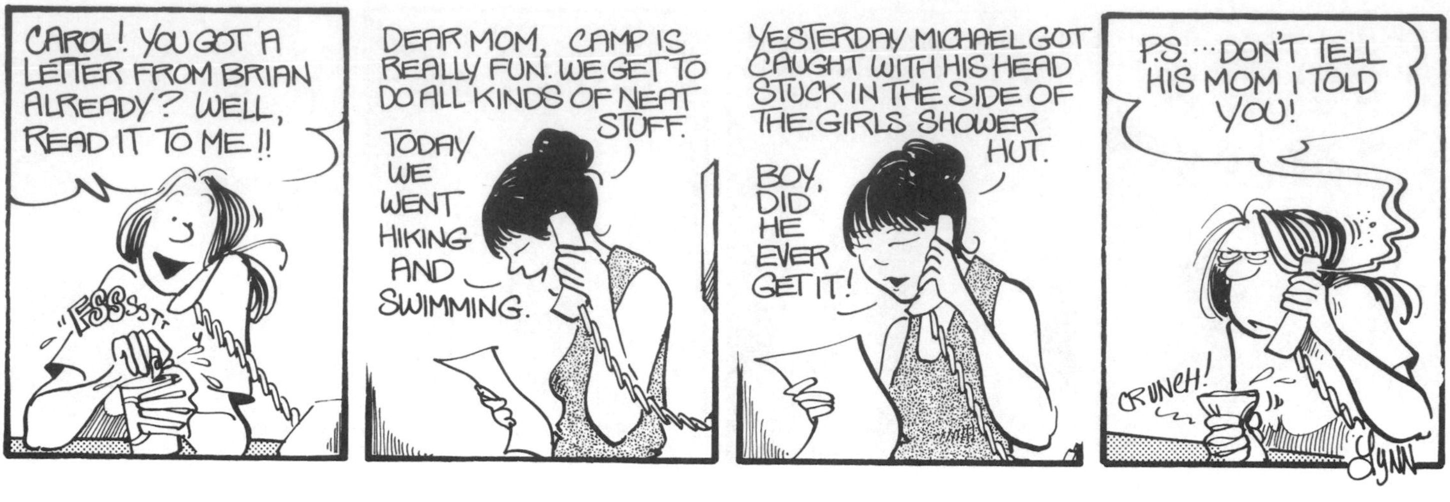
CAROL! YOU GOT A LETTER FROM BRIAN ALREADY? WELL, READ IT TO ME!!
FSSSSTT
DEAR MOM, CAMP IS REALLY FUN. WE GET TO DO ALL KINDS OF NEAT STUFF.
TODAY WE WENT HIKING AND SWIMMING.
YESTERDAY MICHAEL GOT CAUGHT WITH HIS HEAD STUCK IN THE SIDE OF THE GIRLS SHOWER HUT.
BOY, DID HE EVER GET IT!
P.S. ... DON'T TELL HIS MOM I TOLD YOU!
CRUNCH!
LYNN

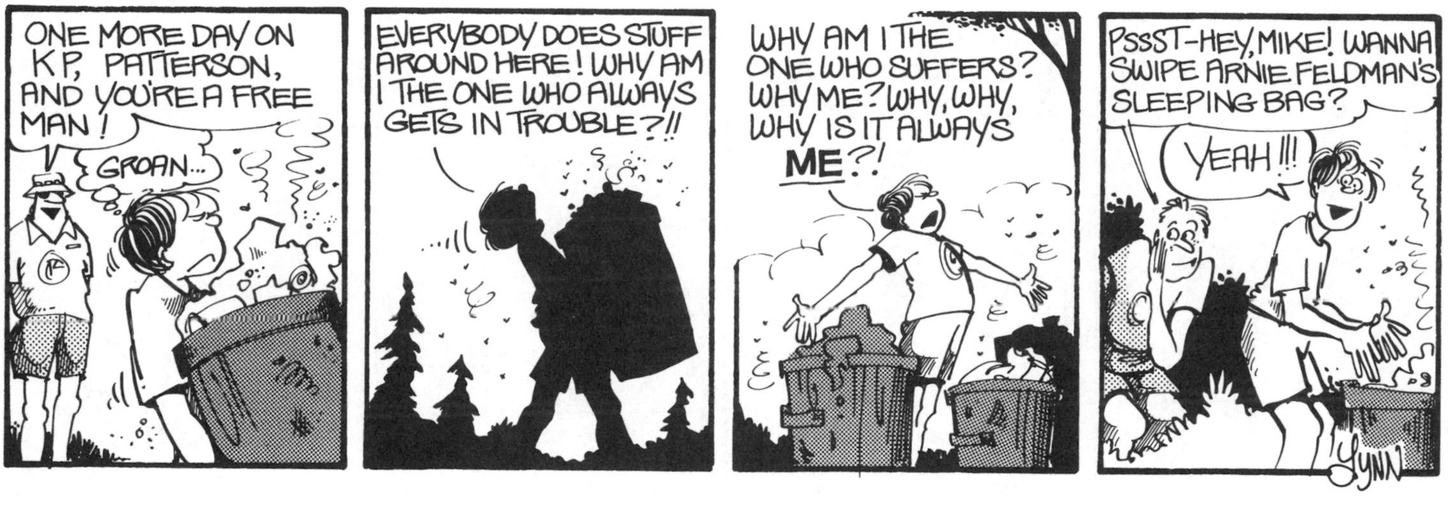
ONE MORE DAY ON K.P., PATTERSON, AND YOU'RE A FREE MAN!
GROAN...
EVERYBODY DOES STUFF AROUND HERE! WHY AM I THE ONE WHO ALWAYS GETS IN TROUBLE?!!
WHY AM I THE ONE WHO SUFFERS? WHY ME? WHY, WHY, WHY IS IT ALWAYS ME?!
PSSST-HEY, MIKE! WANNA SWIPE ARNIE FELDMAN'S SLEEPING BAG?
YEAH!!!
LYNN

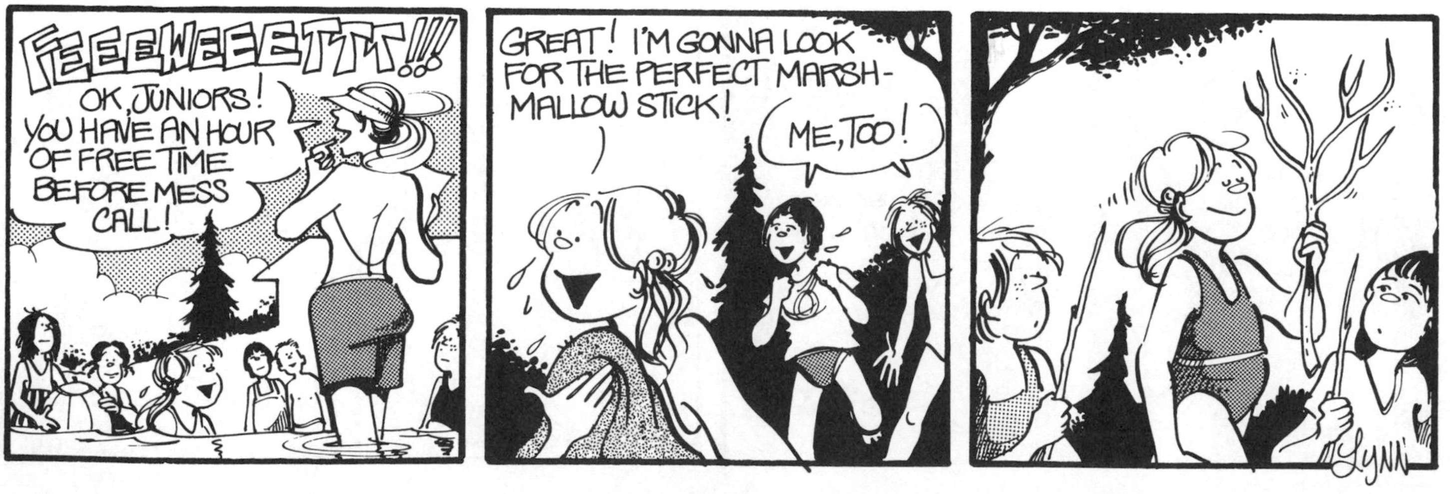
FEEEWEEETTT!!!
OK, JUNIORS! YOU HAVE AN HOUR OF FREE TIME BEFORE MESS CALL!
GREAT! I'M GONNA LOOK FOR THE PERFECT MARSH-MALLOW STICK!
ME, TOO!
LYNN

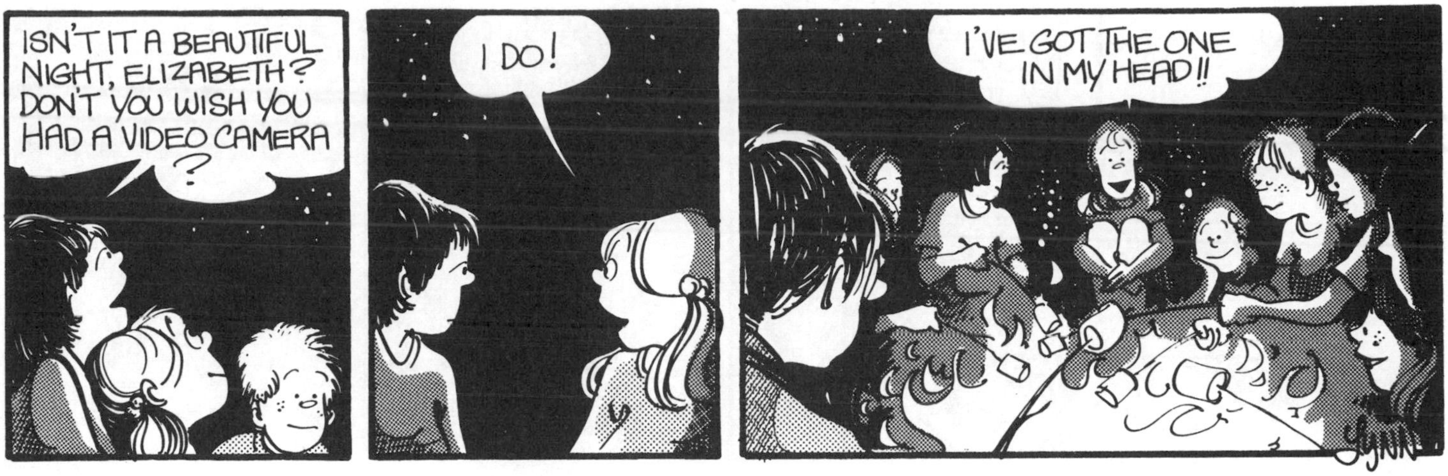
ISN'T IT A BEAUTIFUL NIGHT, ELIZABETH? DON'T YOU WISH YOU HAD A VIDEO CAMERA?
I DO!
I'VE GOT THE ONE IN MY HEAD!!
LYNN

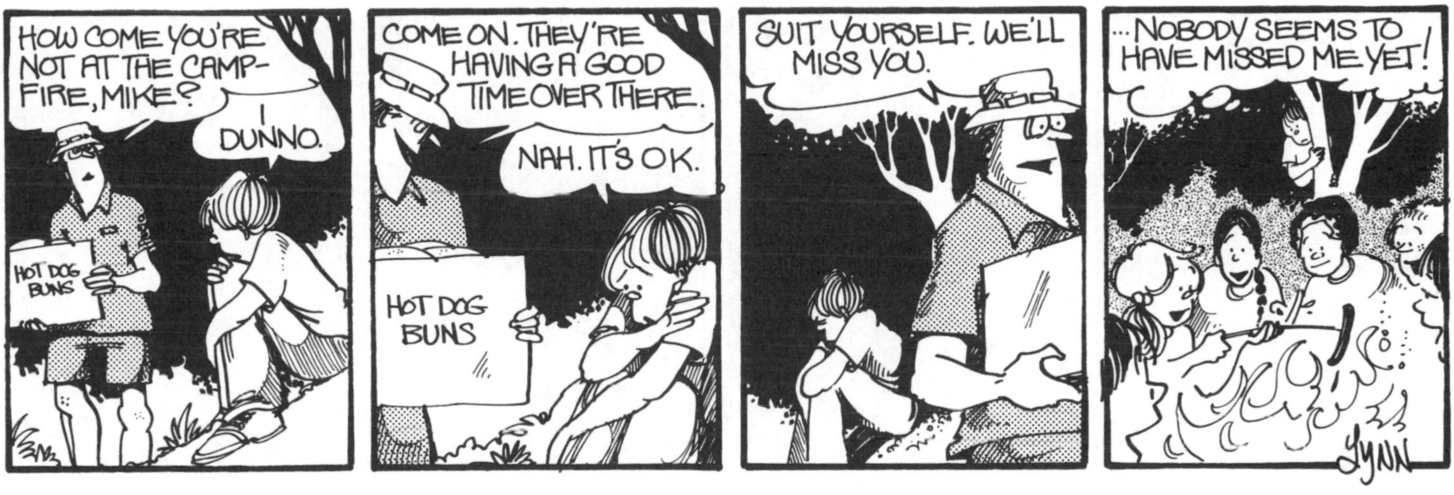
HOW COME YOU'RE NOT AT THE CAMP-FIRE, MIKE?
I DUNNO.
HOT DOG BUNS
COME ON. THEY'RE HAVING A GOOD TIME OVER THERE.
NAH. IT'S OK.
HOT DOG BUNS
SUIT YOURSELF. WE'LL MISS YOU.
...NOBODY SEEMS TO HAVE MISSED ME YET!
LYNN

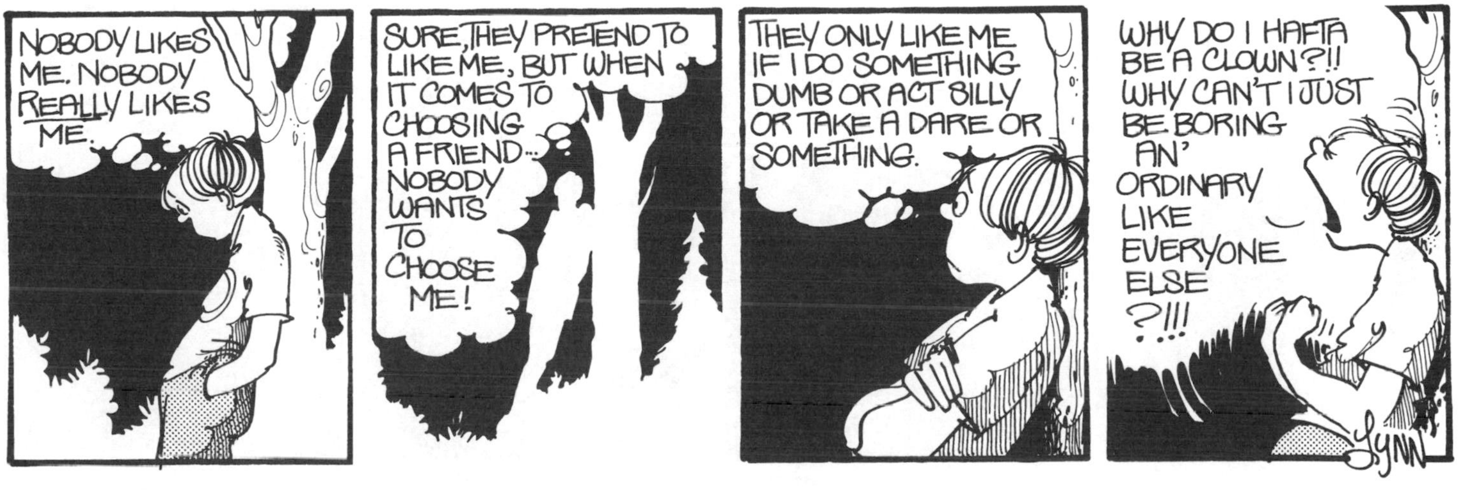
NOBODY LIKES ME. NOBODY REALLY LIKES ME.
SURE, THEY PRETEND TO LIKE ME, BUT WHEN IT COMES TO CHOOSING A FRIEND... NOBODY WANTS TO CHOOSE ME!
THEY ONLY LIKE ME IF I DO SOMETHING DUMB OR ACT SILLY OR TAKE A DARE OR SOMETHING.
WHY DO I HAFTA BE A CLOWN?!! WHY CAN'T I JUST BE BORING AN' ORDINARY LIKE EVERYONE ELSE?!!!
LYNN

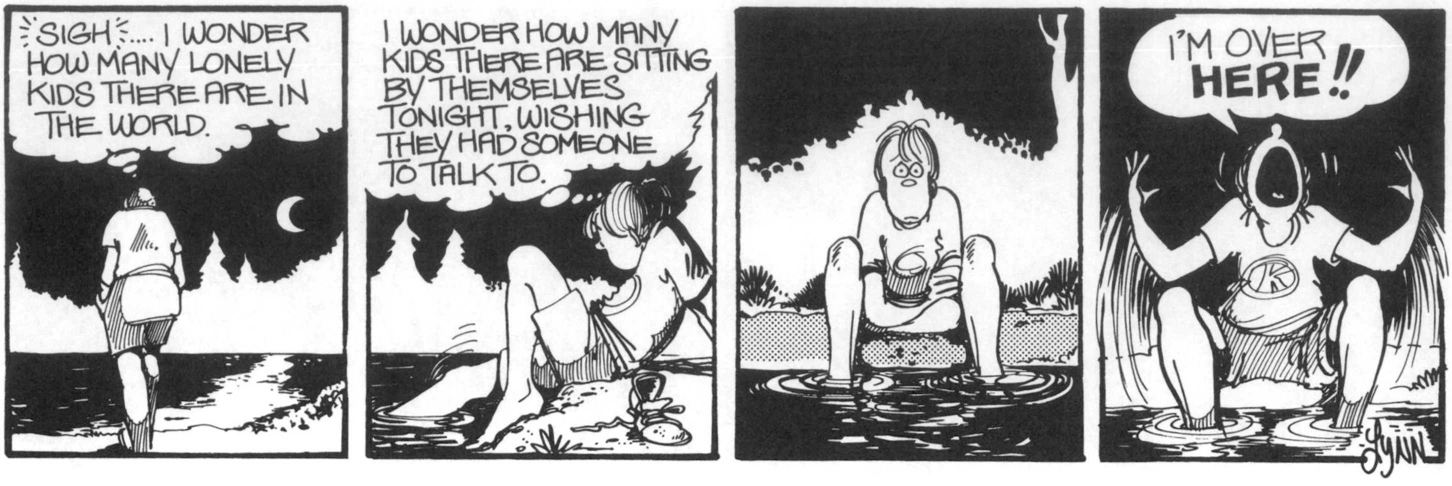

SIGH .... I WONDER HOW MANY LONELY KIDS THERE ARE IN THE WORLD.
I WONDER HOW MANY KIDS THERE ARE SITTING BY THEMSELVES TONIGHT, WISHING THEY HAD SOMEONE TO TALK TO.
I'M OVER HERE!!
LYNN

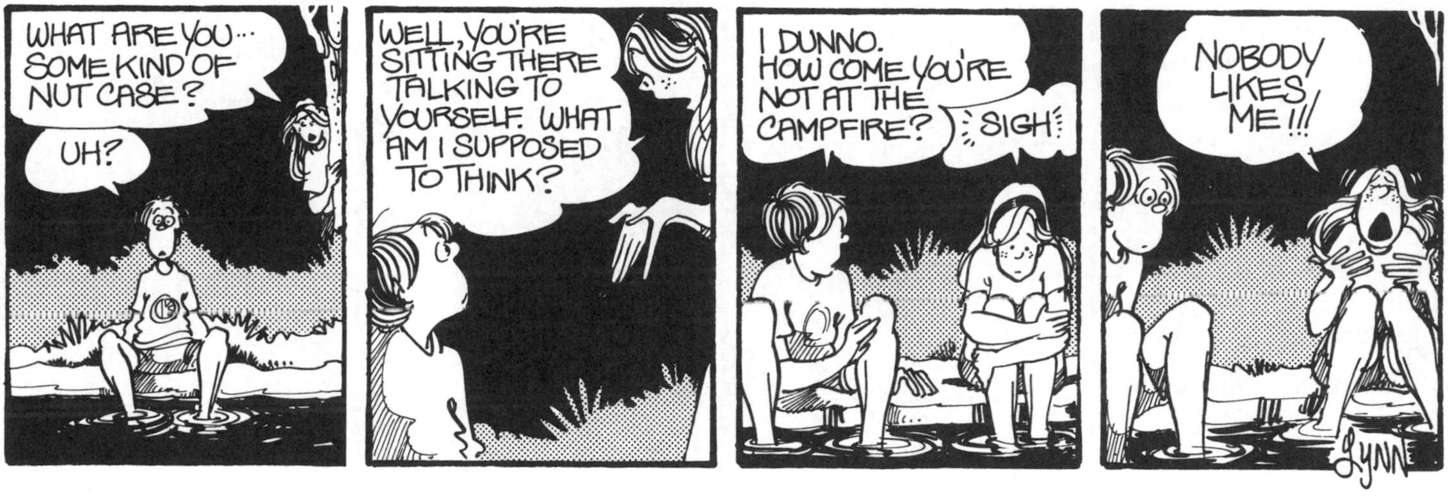

WHAT ARE YOU... SOME KIND OF NUT CASE?
UH?
WELL, YOU'RE SITTING THERE TALKING TO YOURSELF. WHAT AM I SUPPOSED TO THINK?
I DUNNO. HOW COME YOU'RE NOT AT THE CAMPFIRE?
SIGH
NOBODY LIKES ME!!!
LYNN

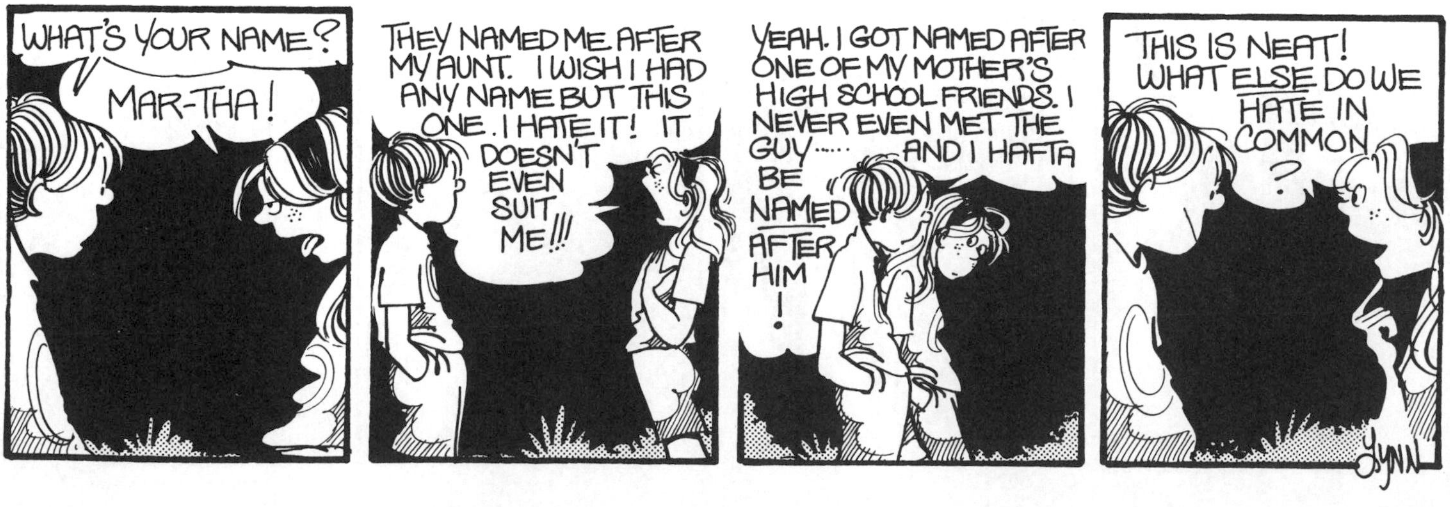

WHAT'S YOUR NAME?
MAR-THA!
THEY NAMED ME AFTER MY AUNT. I WISH I HAD ANY NAME BUT THIS ONE. I HATE IT! IT DOESN'T EVEN SUIT ME!!!
YEAH. I GOT NAMED AFTER ONE OF MY MOTHER'S HIGH SCHOOL FRIENDS. I NEVER EVEN MET THE GUY...... AND I HAFTA BE NAMED AFTER HIM!
THIS IS NEAT! WHAT ELSE DO WE HATE IN COMMON?
LYNN

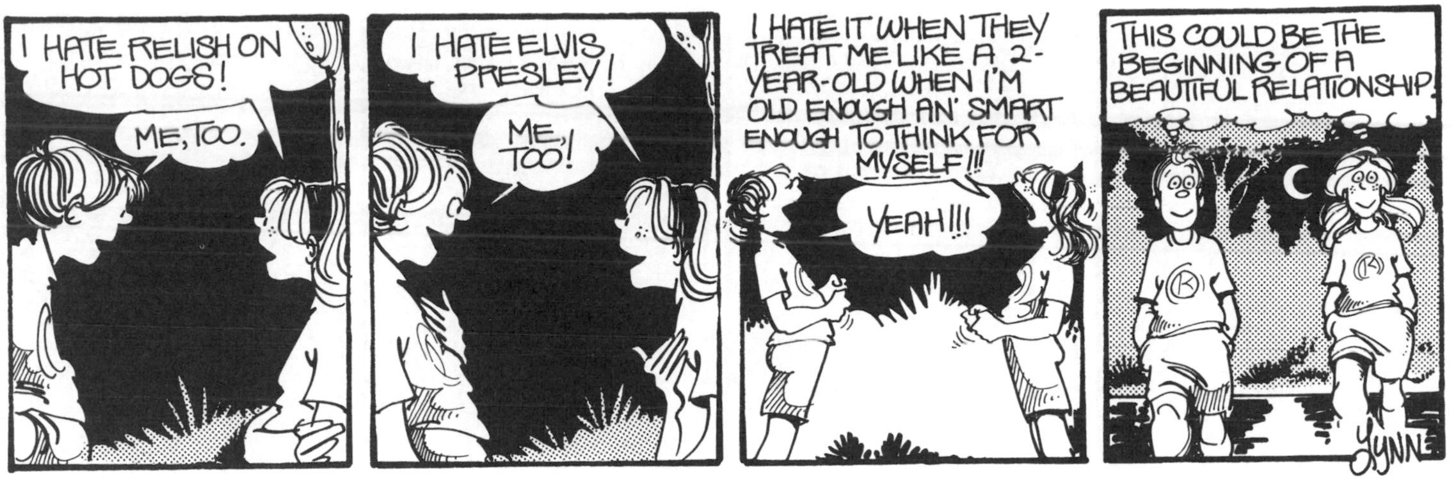
I HATE RELISH ON HOT DOGS!
ME, TOO.
I HATE ELVIS PRESLEY!
ME, TOO!
I HATE IT WHEN THEY TREAT ME LIKE A 2-YEAR-OLD WHEN I'M OLD ENOUGH AN' SMART ENOUGH TO THINK FOR MYSELF!!!
YEAH!!!
THIS COULD BE THE BEGINNING OF A BEAUTIFUL RELATIONSHIP.
LYNN

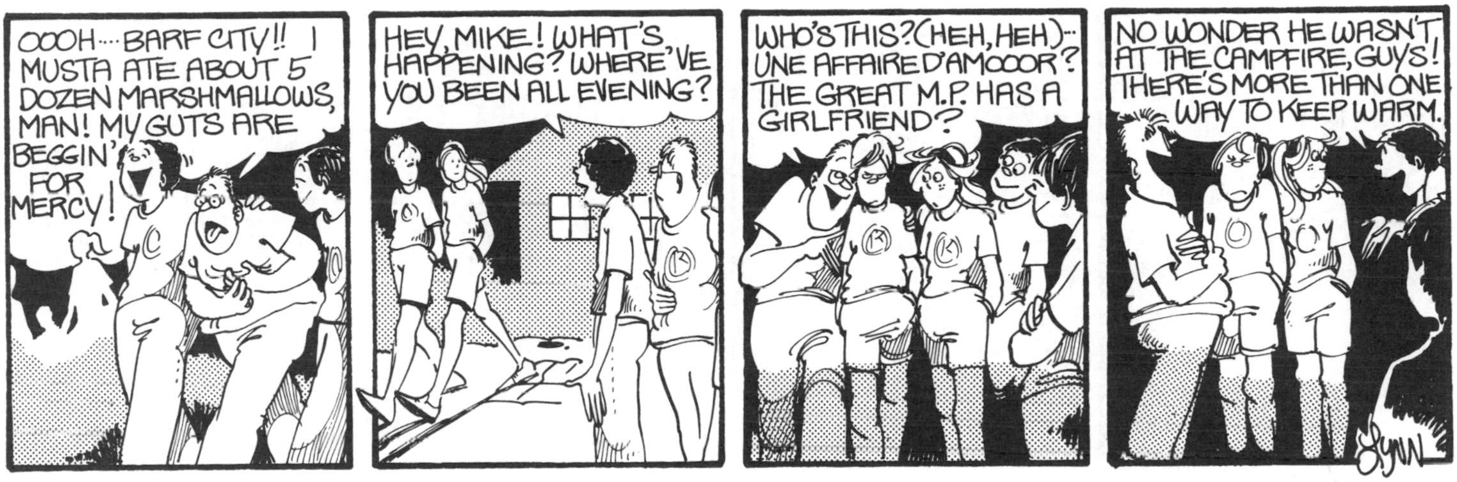
OOOH.... BARF CITY!! I MUSTA ATE ABOUT 5 DOZEN MARSHMALLOWS, MAN! MY GUTS ARE BEGGIN' FOR MERCY!
HEY, MIKE! WHAT'S HAPPENING? WHERE'VE YOU BEEN ALL EVENING?
WHO'S THIS? (HEH, HEH)... UNE AFFAIRE D'AMOOOR? THE GREAT M.P. HAS A GIRLFRIEND?
NO WONDER HE WASN'T AT THE CAMPFIRE, GUYS! THERE'S MORE THAN ONE WAY TO KEEP WARM.
LYNN

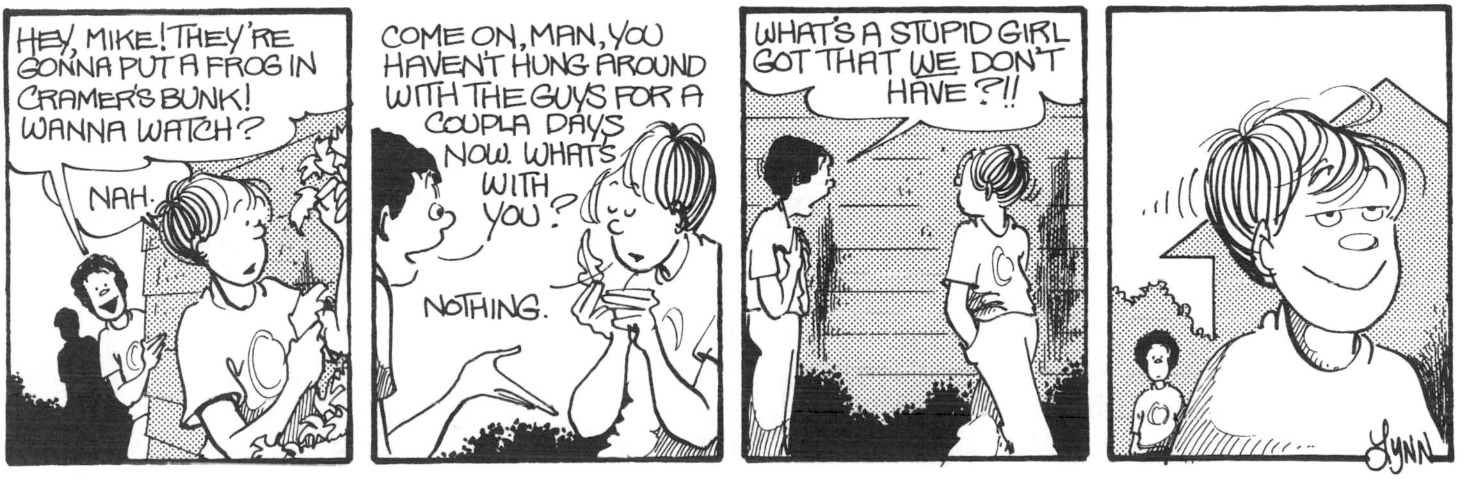
HEY, MIKE! THEY'RE GONNA PUT A FROG IN CRAMER'S BUNK! WANNA WATCH?
NAH.
COME ON, MAN, YOU HAVEN'T HUNG AROUND WITH THE GUYS FOR A COUPLA DAYS NOW. WHAT'S WITH YOU?
NOTHING.
WHAT'S A STUPID GIRL GOT THAT WE DON'T HAVE?!!
LYNN

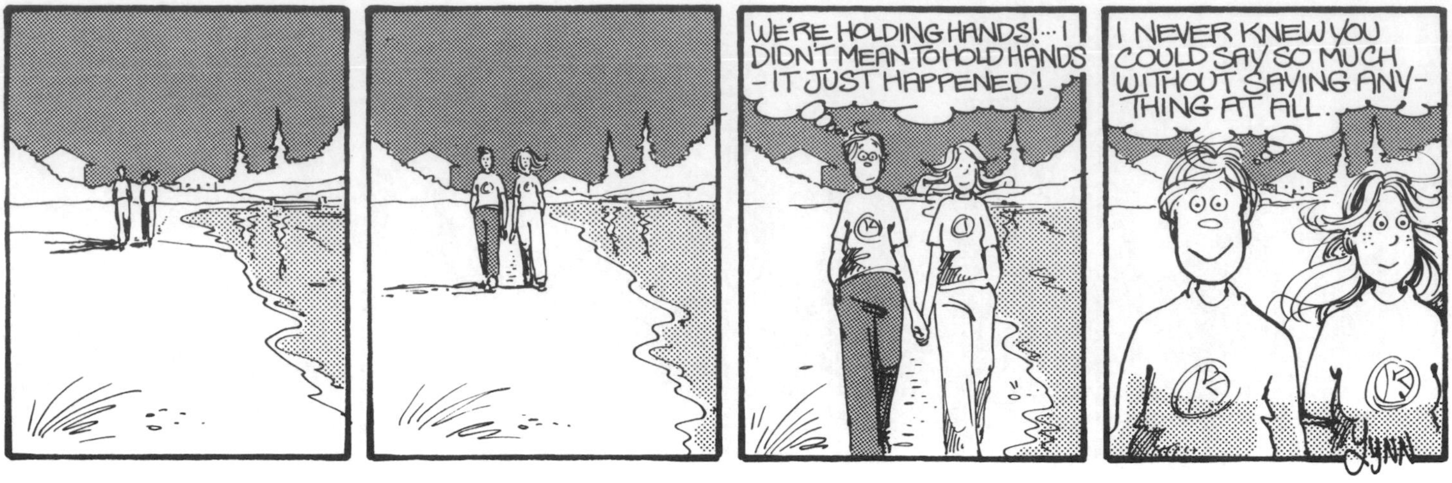
WE'RE HOLDING HANDS!... I DIDN'T MEAN TO HOLD HANDS - IT JUST HAPPENED!
I NEVER KNEW YOU COULD SAY SO MUCH WITHOUT SAYING ANY-THING AT ALL.
Lynn

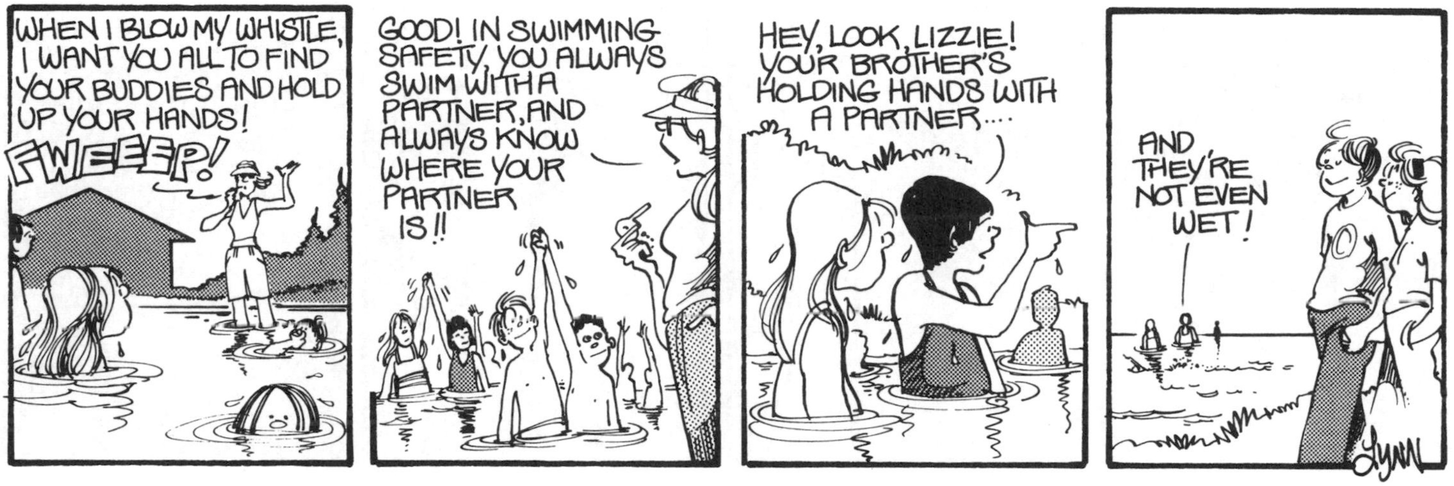
WHEN I BLOW MY WHISTLE, I WANT YOU ALL TO FIND YOUR BUDDIES AND HOLD UP YOUR HANDS!
FWEEEP!
GOOD! IN SWIMMING SAFETY, YOU ALWAYS SWIM WITH A PARTNER, AND ALWAYS KNOW WHERE YOUR PARTNER IS!!
HEY, LOOK, LIZZIE! YOUR BROTHER'S HOLDING HANDS WITH A PARTNER....
AND THEY'RE NOT EVEN WET!
Lynn

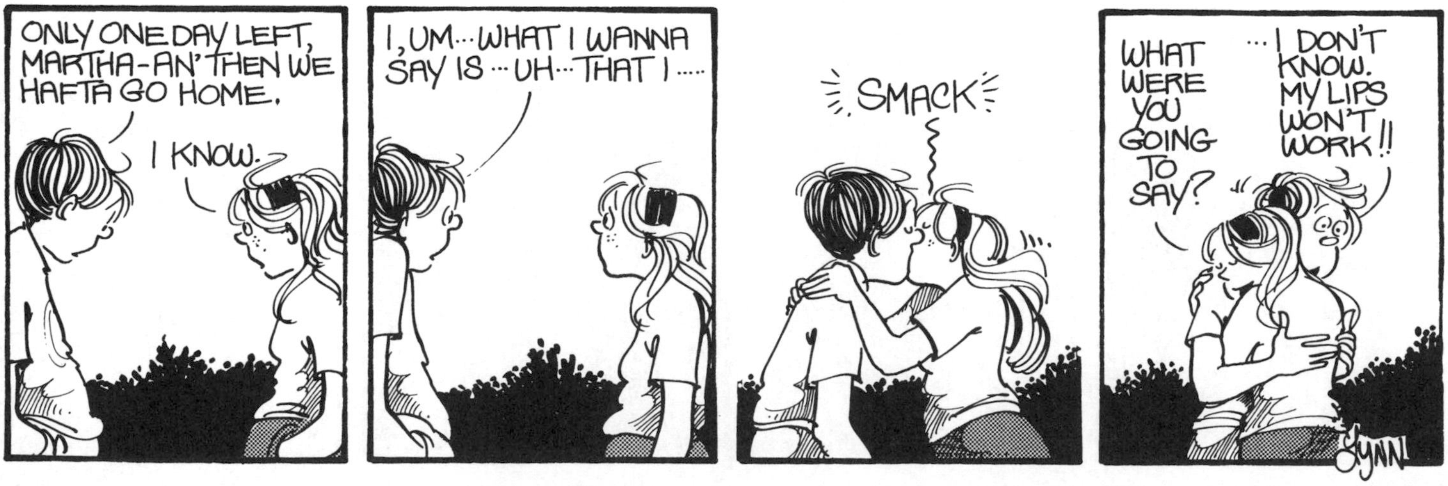
ONLY ONE DAY LEFT, MARTHA- AN' THEN WE HAFTA GO HOME.
I KNOW.
I, UM... WHAT I WANNA SAY IS... UH... THAT I....
SMACK
WHAT WERE YOU GOING TO SAY?
... I DON'T KNOW. MY LIPS WON'T WORK!!
Lynn

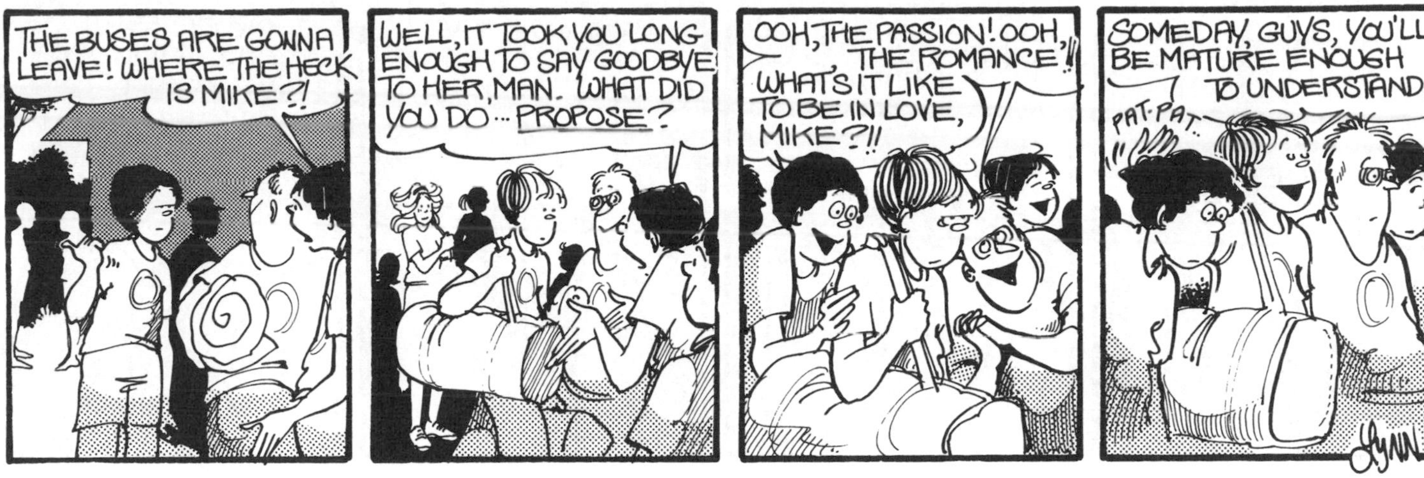
THE BUSES ARE GONNA LEAVE! WHERE THE HECK IS MIKE?!
WELL, IT TOOK YOU LONG ENOUGH TO SAY GOODBYE TO HER, MAN. WHAT DID YOU DO... PROPOSE?
OOH, THE PASSION! OOH, THE ROMANCE!!
WHAT'S IT LIKE TO BE IN LOVE, MIKE?!!
SOMEDAY, GUYS, YOU'LL BE MATURE ENOUGH TO UNDERSTAND.
PAT-PAT..
LYNN

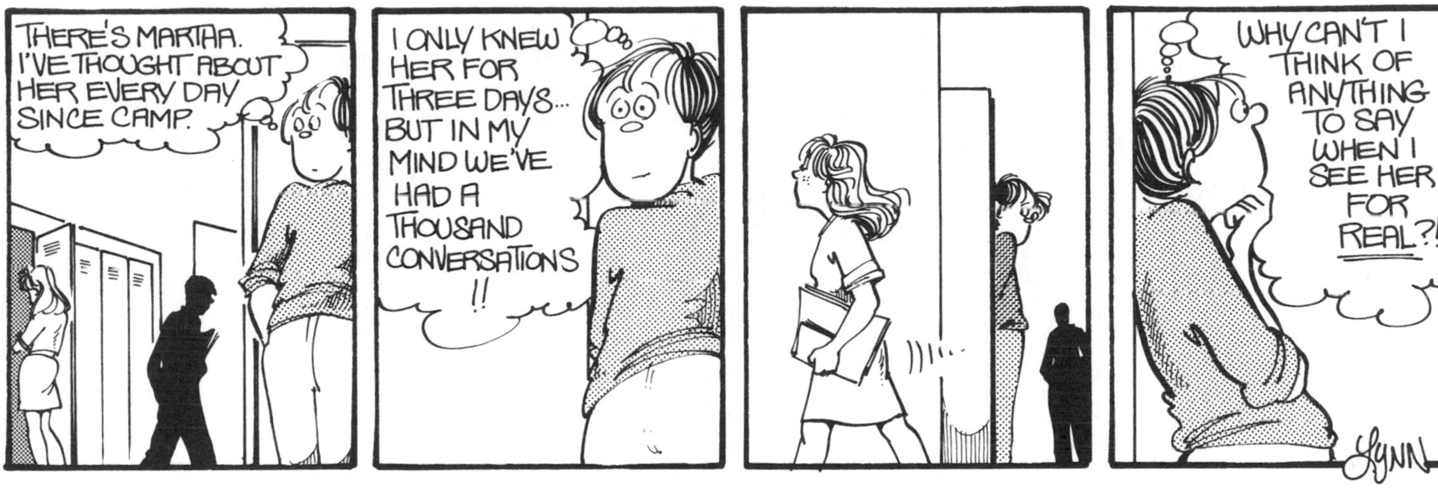
THERE'S MARTHA. I'VE THOUGHT ABOUT HER EVERY DAY SINCE CAMP.
I ONLY KNEW HER FOR THREE DAYS... BUT IN MY MIND WE'VE HAD A THOUSAND CONVERSATIONS!!
WHY CAN'T I THINK OF ANYTHING TO SAY WHEN I SEE HER FOR REAL?!!
LYNN

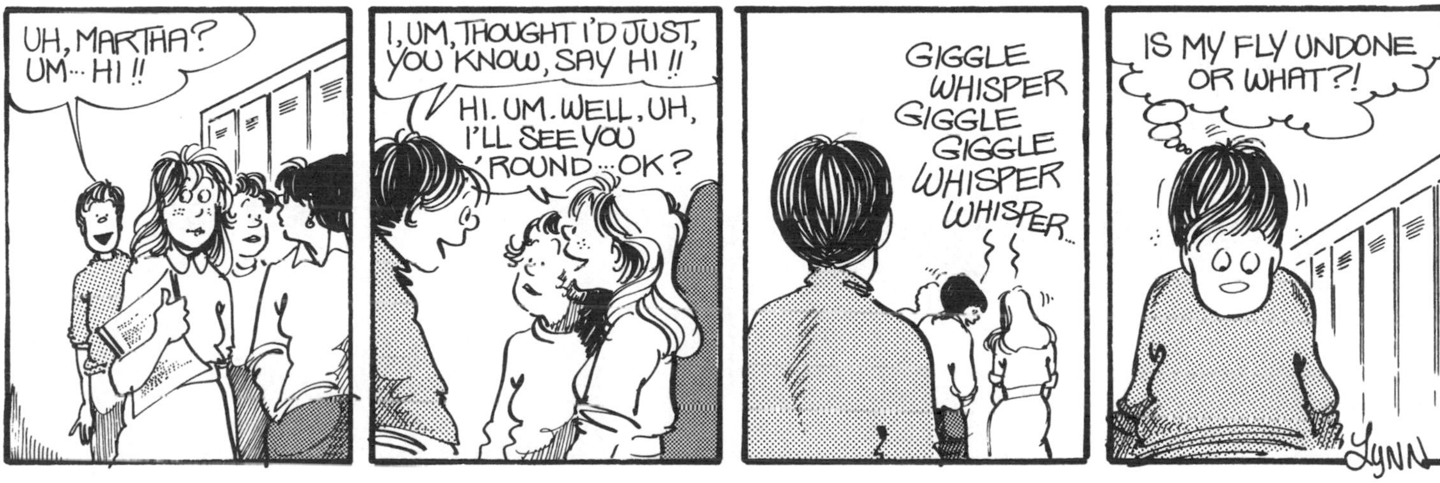
UH, MARTHA? UM... HI!!
I, UM, THOUGHT I'D JUST, YOU KNOW, SAY HI!!
HI. UM. WELL, UH, I'LL SEE YOU 'ROUND...OK?
GIGGLE WHISPER GIGGLE GIGGLE WHISPER WHISPER...
IS MY FLY UNDONE OR WHAT?!
LYNN

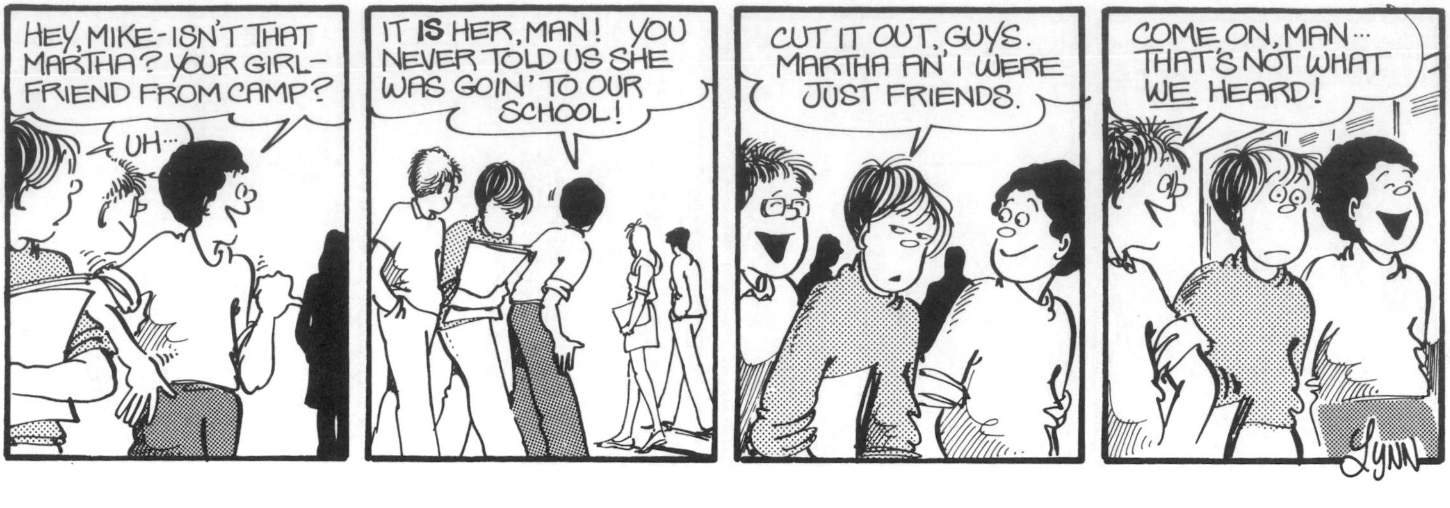
HEY, MIKE-ISN'T THAT MARTHA? YOUR GIRL-FRIEND FROM CAMP?
UH...
IT IS HER, MAN! YOU NEVER TOLD US SHE WAS GOIN' TO OUR SCHOOL!
CUT IT OUT, GUYS. MARTHA AN' I WERE JUST FRIENDS.
COME ON, MAN... THAT'S NOT WHAT WE HEARD!
LYNN

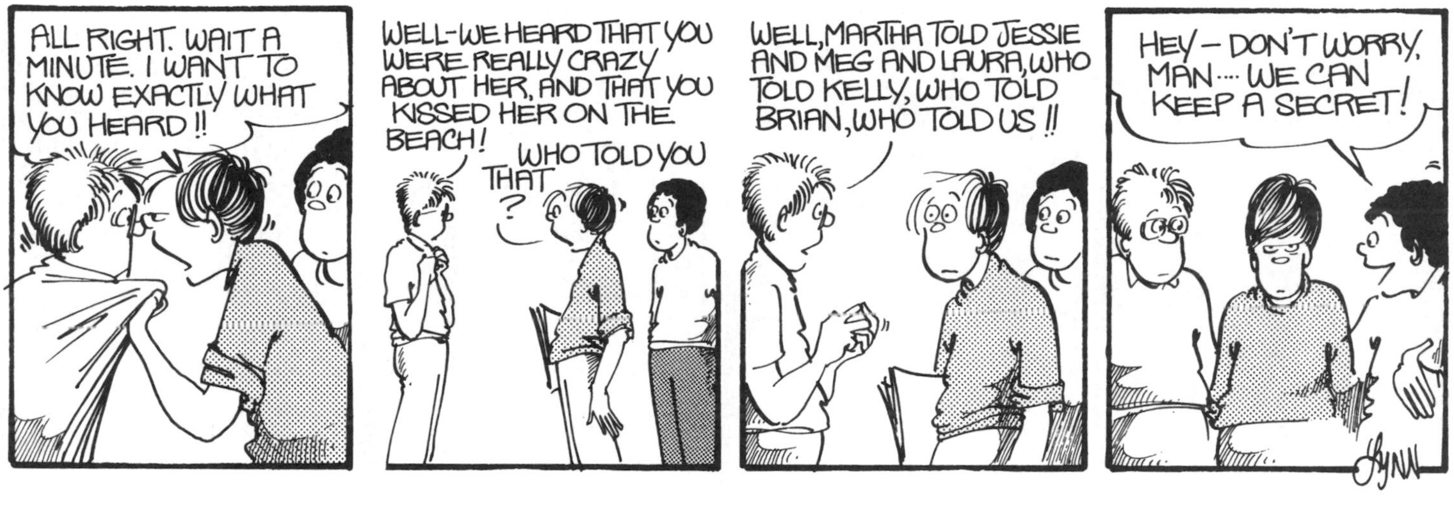
ALL RIGHT. WAIT A MINUTE. I WANT TO KNOW EXACTLY WHAT YOU HEARD!!
WELL-WE HEARD THAT YOU WERE REALLY CRAZY ABOUT HER, AND THAT YOU KISSED HER ON THE BEACH!
WHO TOLD YOU THAT?
WELL, MARTHA TOLD JESSIE AND MEG AND LAURA, WHO TOLD KELLY, WHO TOLD BRIAN, WHO TOLD US!!
HEY - DON'T WORRY, MAN.... WE CAN KEEP A SECRET!
LYNN

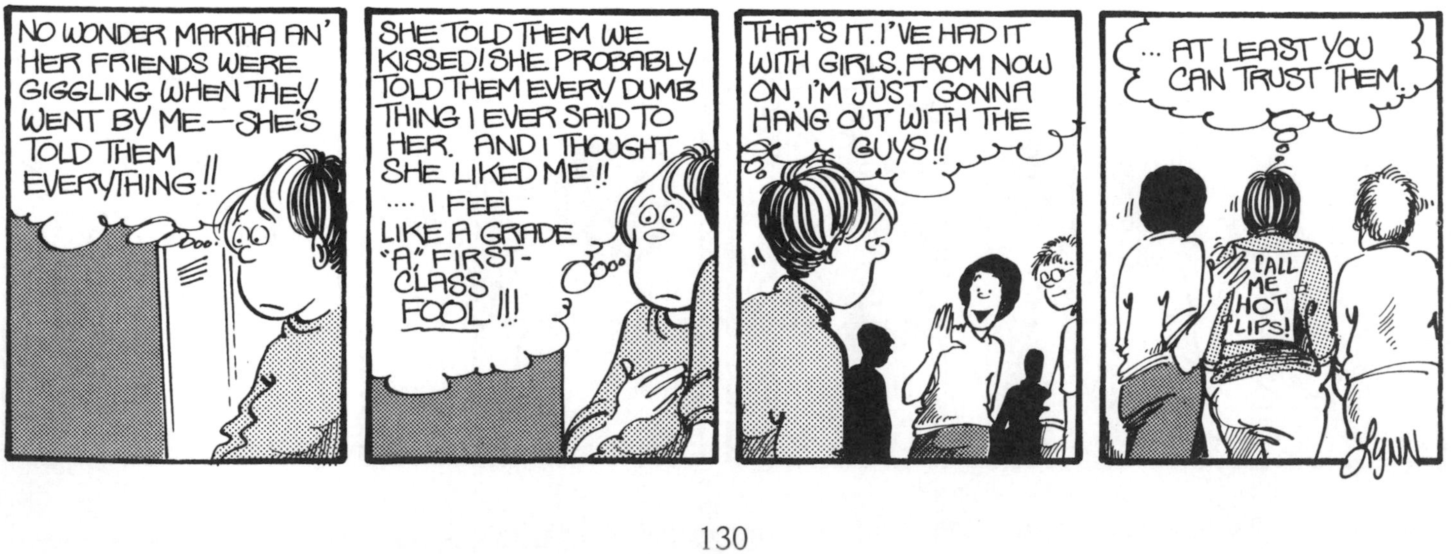
NO WONDER MARTHA AN' HER FRIENDS WERE GIGGLING WHEN THEY WENT BY ME—SHE'S TOLD THEM EVERYTHING!!
SHE TOLD THEM WE KISSED! SHE PROBABLY TOLD THEM EVERY DUMB THING I EVER SAID TO HER. AND I THOUGHT SHE LIKED ME!!
.... I FEEL LIKE A GRADE "A" FIRST-CLASS FOOL!!!
THAT'S IT. I'VE HAD IT WITH GIRLS. FROM NOW ON, I'M JUST GONNA HANG OUT WITH THE GUYS!!
... AT LEAST YOU CAN TRUST THEM.
CALL ME HOT LIPS!
LYNN

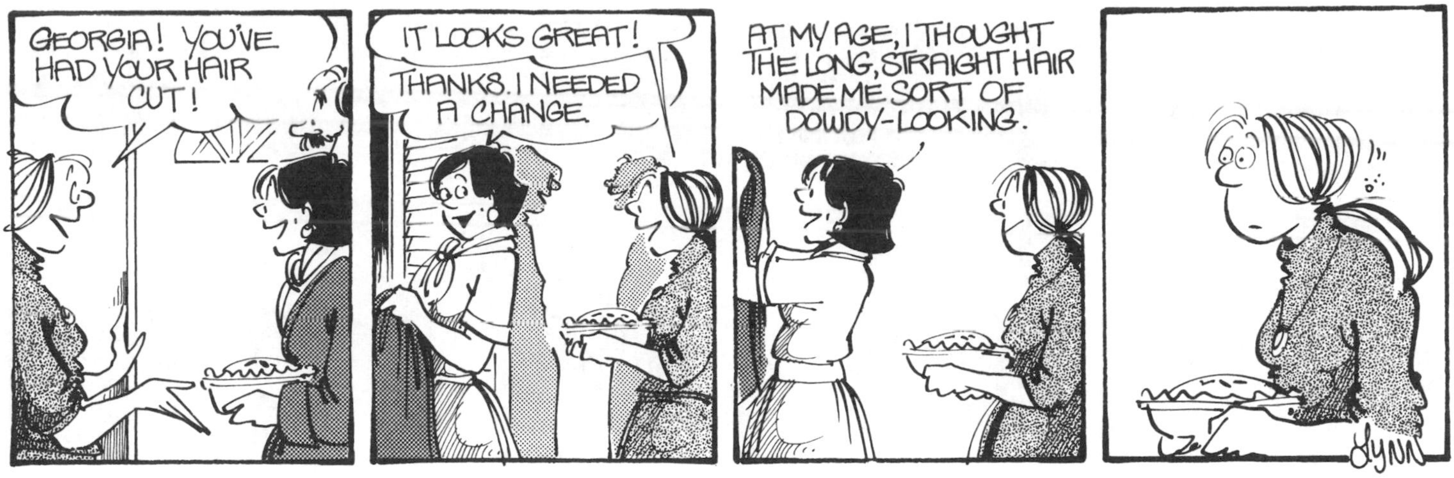
GEORGIA! YOU'VE HAD YOUR HAIR CUT!
IT LOOKS GREAT!
THANKS. I NEEDED A CHANGE.
AT MY AGE, I THOUGHT THE LONG, STRAIGHT HAIR MADE ME SORT OF DOWDY-LOOKING.
LYNN

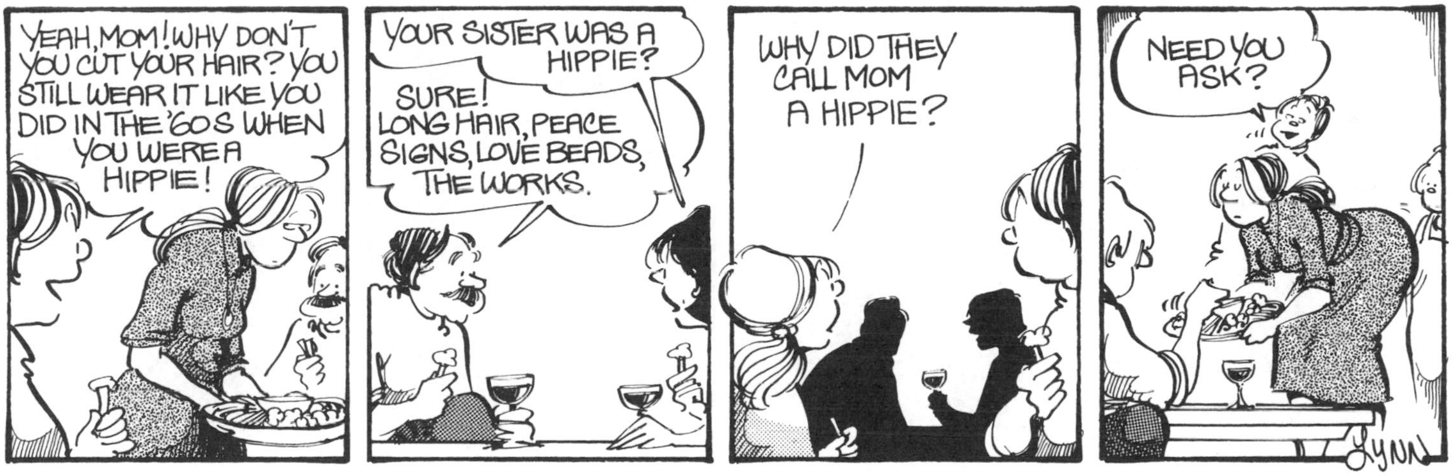
YEAH, MOM! WHY DON'T YOU CUT YOUR HAIR? YOU STILL WEAR IT LIKE YOU DID IN THE '60S WHEN YOU WERE A HIPPIE!
YOUR SISTER WAS A HIPPIE?
SURE! LONG HAIR, PEACE SIGNS, LOVE BEADS, THE WORKS.
WHY DID THEY CALL MOM A HIPPIE?
NEED YOU ASK?
LYNN

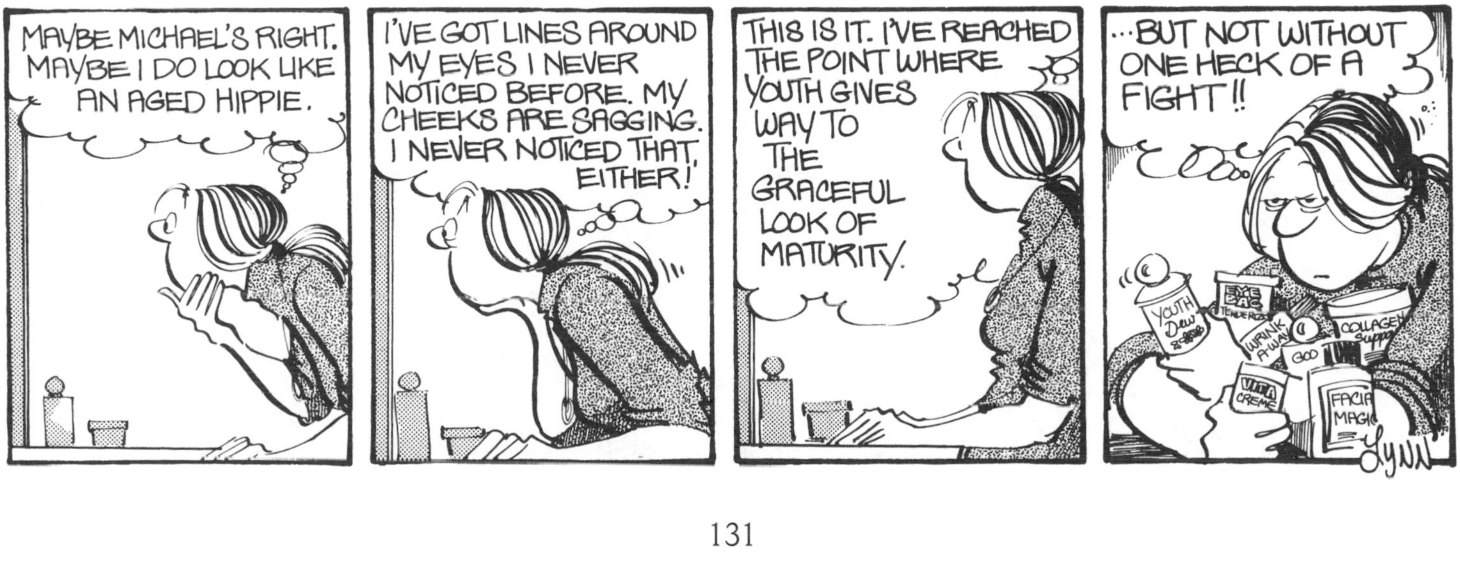
MAYBE MICHAEL'S RIGHT. MAYBE I DO LOOK LIKE AN AGED HIPPIE.
I'VE GOT LINES AROUND MY EYES I NEVER NOTICED BEFORE. MY CHEEKS ARE SAGGING. I NEVER NOTICED THAT, EITHER!
THIS IS IT. I'VE REACHED THE POINT WHERE YOUTH GIVES WAY TO THE GRACEFUL LOOK OF MATURITY.
...BUT NOT WITHOUT ONE HECK OF A FIGHT!!
YOUTH Dew
EYE BAG
WRINK A-WAY
GOO
VITA CREME
LYNN

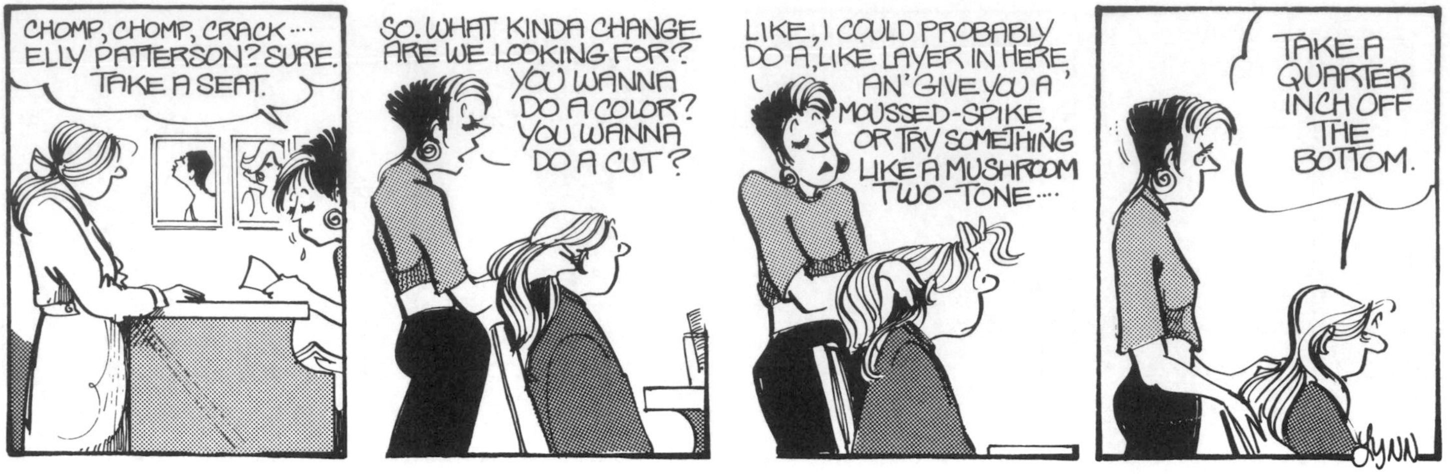
CHOMP, CHOMP, CRACK.... ELLY PATTERSON? SURE. TAKE A SEAT.
SO. WHAT KINDA CHANGE ARE WE LOOKING FOR? YOU WANNA DO A COLOR? YOU WANNA DO A CUT?
LIKE, I COULD PROBABLY DO A, LIKE LAYER IN HERE, AN' GIVE YOU A MOUSSED-SPIKE, OR TRY SOMETHING LIKE A MUSHROOM TWO-TONE....
TAKE A QUARTER INCH OFF THE BOTTOM.
LYNN

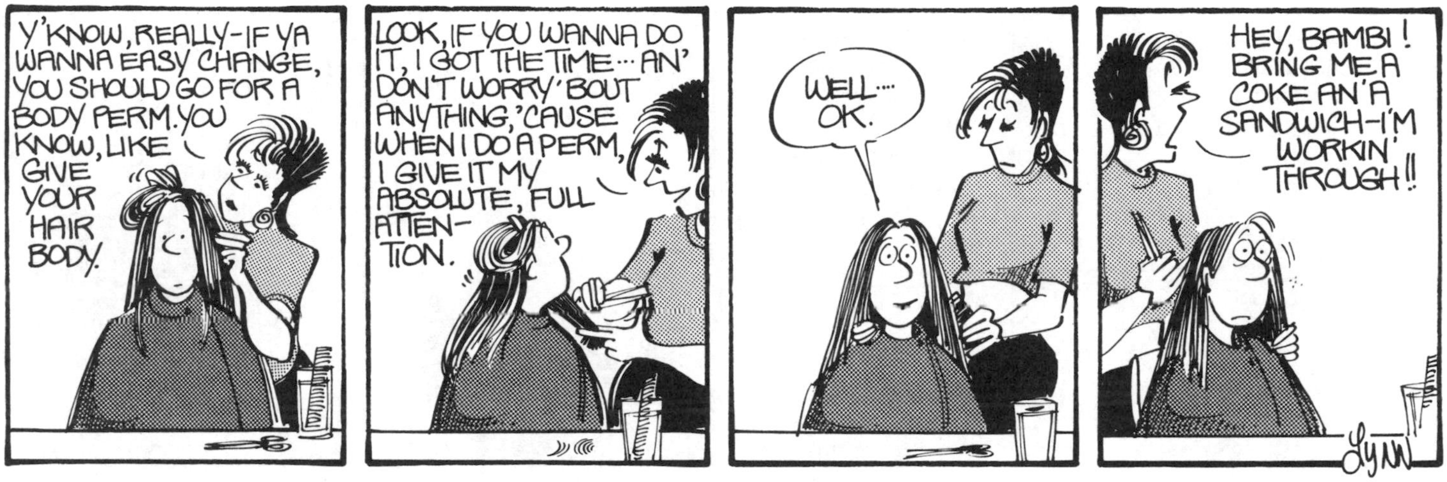
Y'KNOW, REALLY-IF YA WANNA EASY CHANGE, YOU SHOULD GO FOR A BODY PERM. YOU KNOW, LIKE GIVE YOUR HAIR BODY.
LOOK, IF YOU WANNA DO IT, I GOT THE TIME... AN' DON'T WORRY 'BOUT ANYTHING, 'CAUSE WHEN I DO A PERM, I GIVE IT MY ABSOLUTE, FULL ATTENTION.
WELL.... OK.
HEY, BAMBI! BRING ME A COKE AN' A SANDWICH-I'M WORKIN' THROUGH!!
LYNN

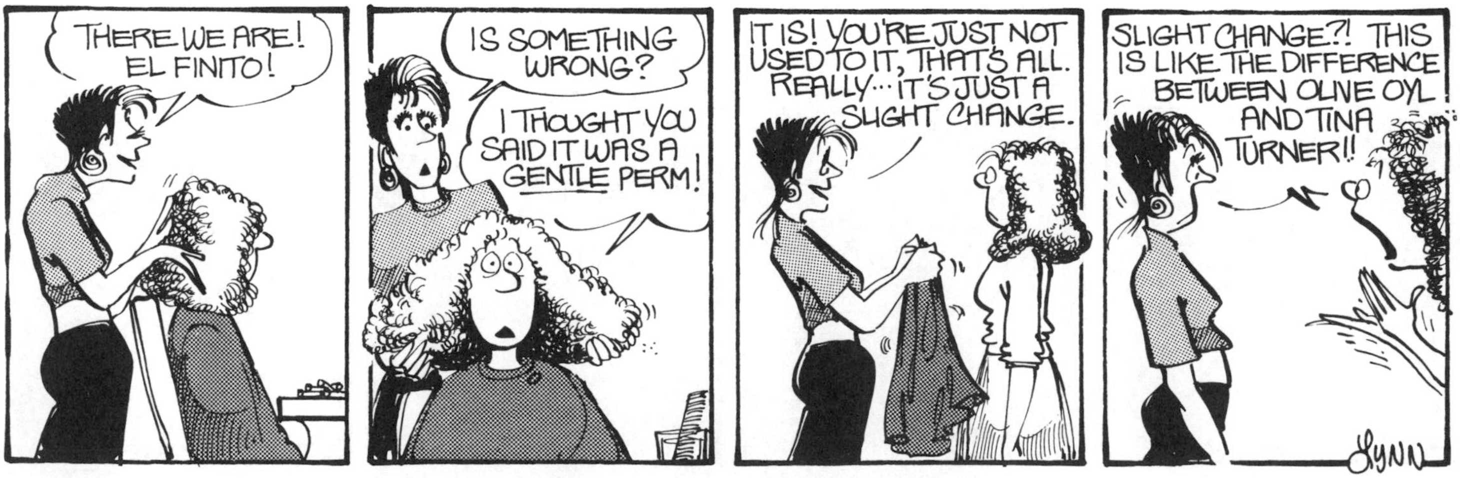
THERE WE ARE! EL FINITO!
IS SOMETHING WRONG?
I THOUGHT YOU SAID IT WAS A GENTLE PERM!
IT IS! YOU'RE JUST NOT USED TO IT, THAT'S ALL. REALLY... IT'S JUST A SLIGHT CHANGE.
SLIGHT CHANGE?! THIS IS LIKE THE DIFFERENCE BETWEEN OLIVE OYL AND TINA TURNER!!
LYNN

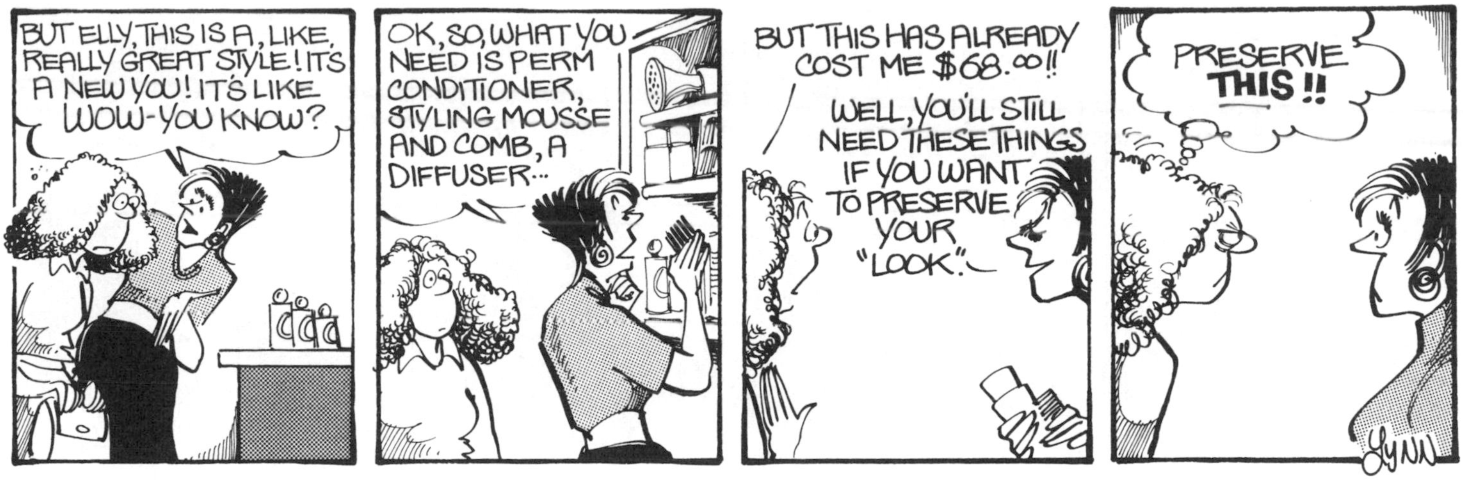
BUT ELLY, THIS IS A, LIKE, REALLY GREAT STYLE! IT'S A NEW YOU! IT'S LIKE WOW-YOU KNOW?
OK, SO, WHAT YOU NEED IS PERM CONDITIONER, STYLING MOUSSE AND COMB, A DIFFUSER...
BUT THIS HAS ALREADY COST ME $68.00!!
WELL, YOU'LL STILL NEED THESE THINGS IF YOU WANT TO PRESERVE YOUR "LOOK".
PRESERVE THIS!!

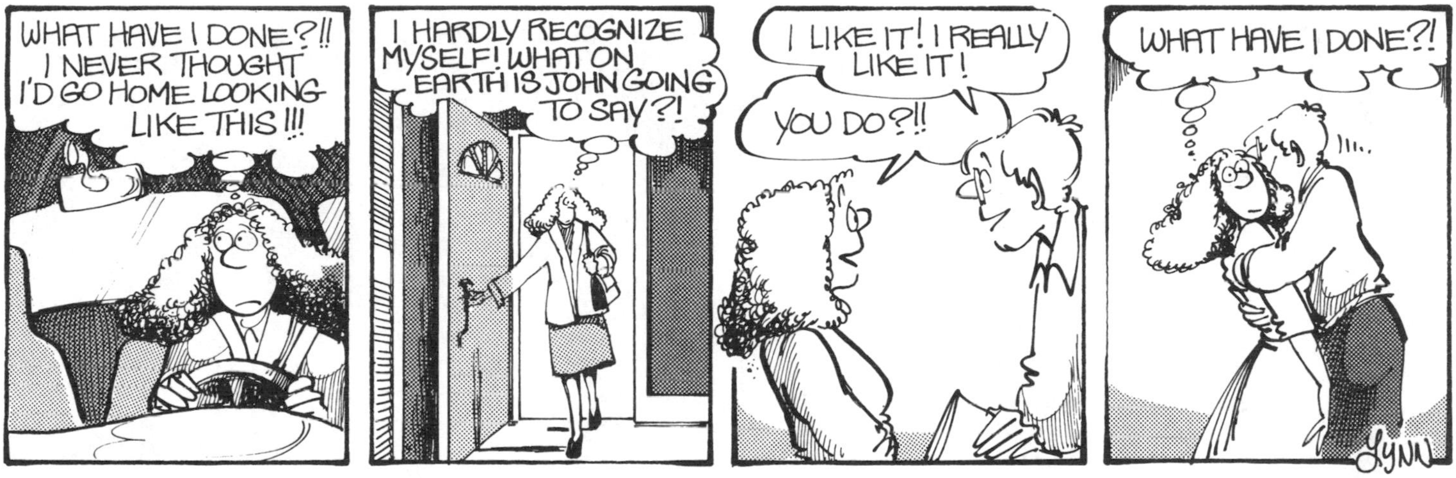
WHAT HAVE I DONE?!! I NEVER THOUGHT I'D GO HOME LOOKING LIKE THIS!!!
I HARDLY RECOGNIZE MYSELF! WHAT ON EARTH IS JOHN GOING TO SAY?!
I LIKE IT! I REALLY LIKE IT!
YOU DO?!!
WHAT HAVE I DONE?!

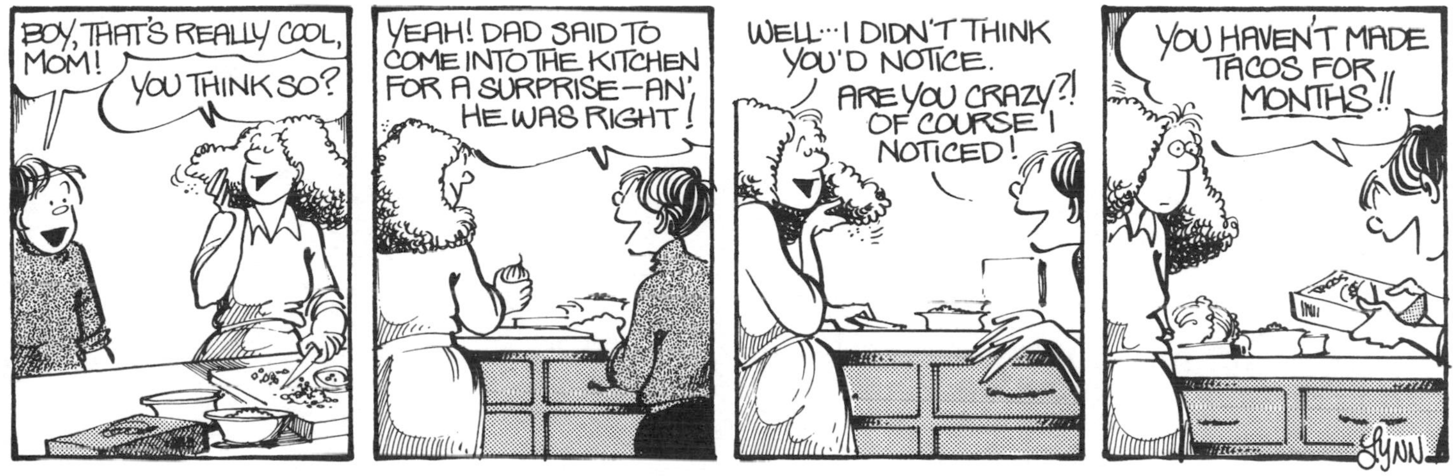
BOY, THAT'S REALLY COOL, MOM!
YOU THINK SO?
YEAH! DAD SAID TO COME INTO THE KITCHEN FOR A SURPRISE—AN' HE WAS RIGHT!
WELL... I DIDN'T THINK YOU'D NOTICE.
ARE YOU CRAZY?! OF COURSE I NOTICED!
YOU HAVEN'T MADE TACOS FOR MONTHS!!

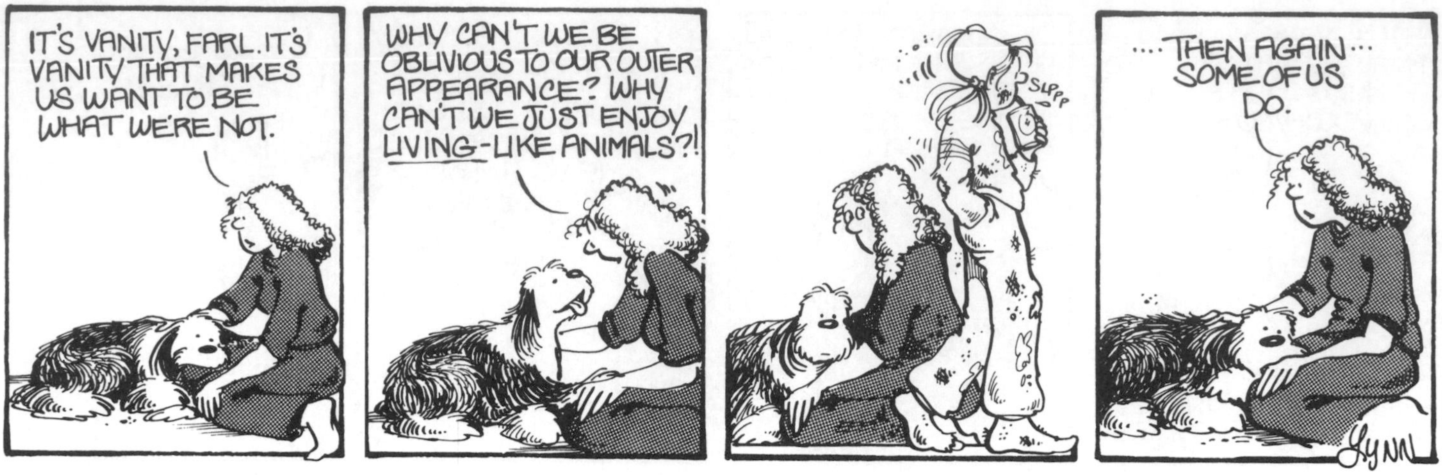
IT'S VANITY, FARL. IT'S VANITY THAT MAKES US WANT TO BE WHAT WE'RE NOT.
WHY CAN'T WE BE OBLIVIOUS TO OUR OUTER APPEARANCE? WHY CAN'T WE JUST ENJOY LIVING-LIKE ANIMALS?!
SLPPP
....THEN AGAIN.... SOME OF US DO.
LYNN

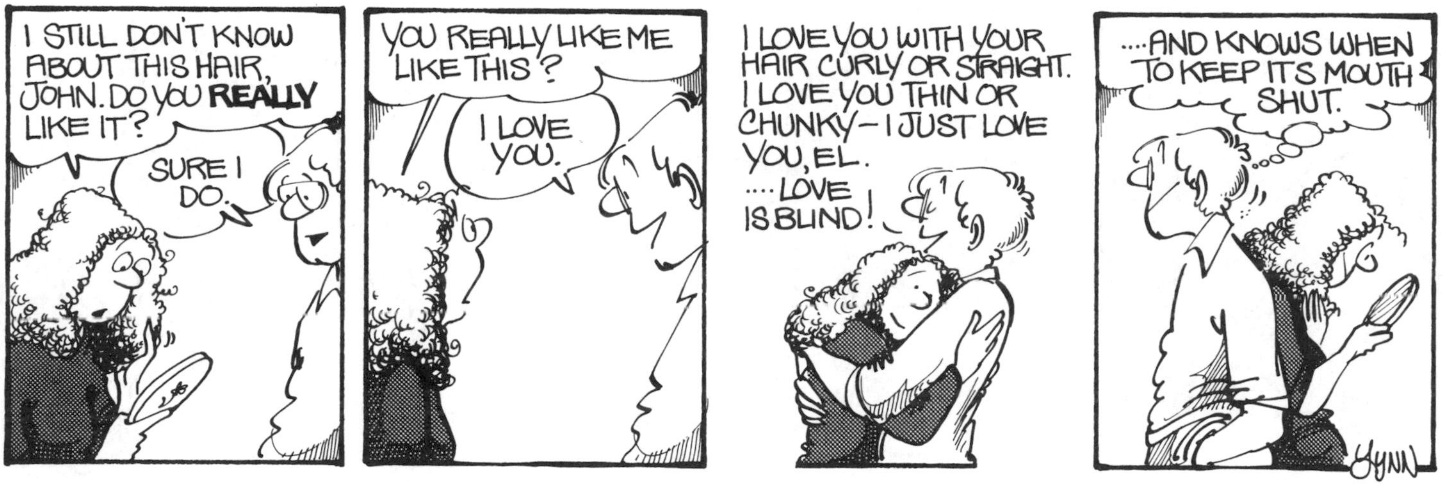
I STILL DON'T KNOW ABOUT THIS HAIR, JOHN. DO YOU **REALLY** LIKE IT?
SURE I DO.
YOU REALLY LIKE ME LIKE THIS?
I LOVE YOU.
I LOVE YOU WITH YOUR HAIR CURLY OR STRAIGHT. I LOVE YOU THIN OR CHUNKY—I JUST LOVE YOU, EL.
....LOVE IS BLIND!
....AND KNOWS WHEN TO KEEP ITS MOUTH SHUT.
LYNN

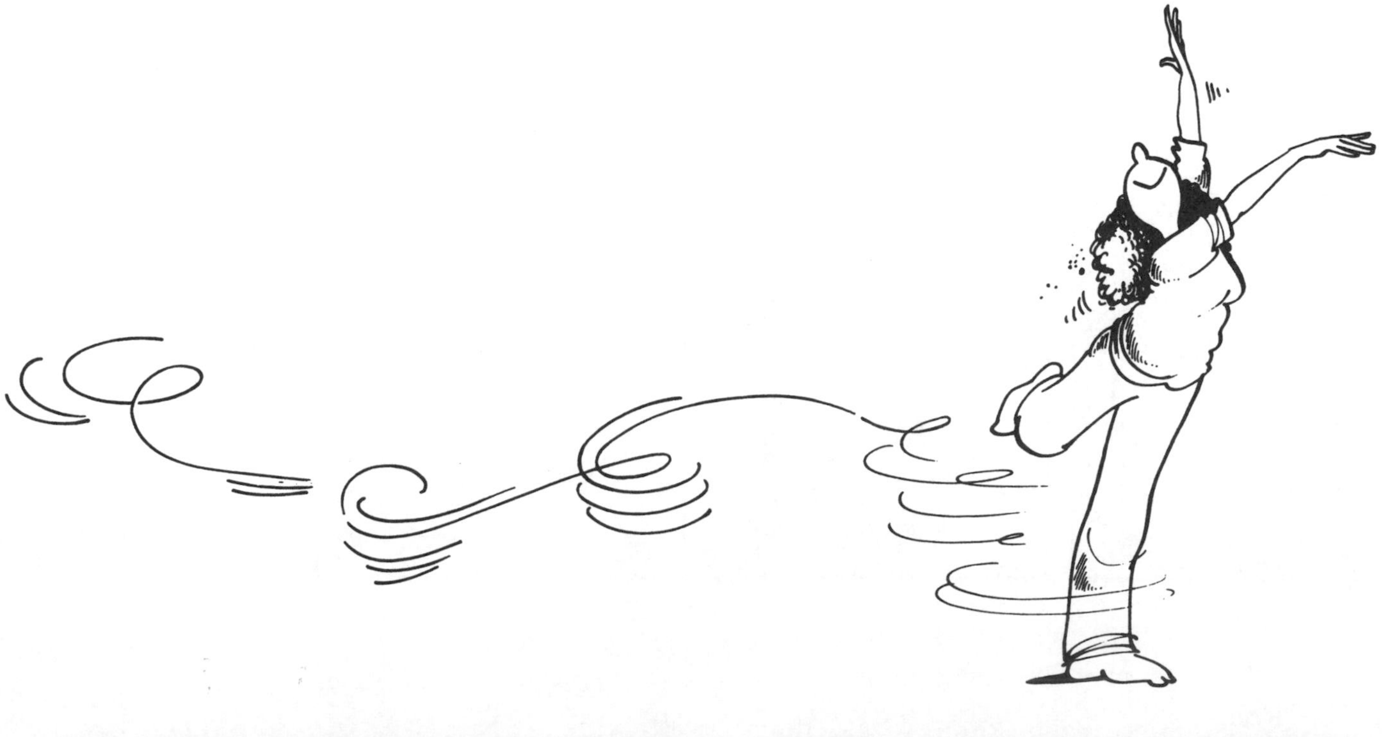

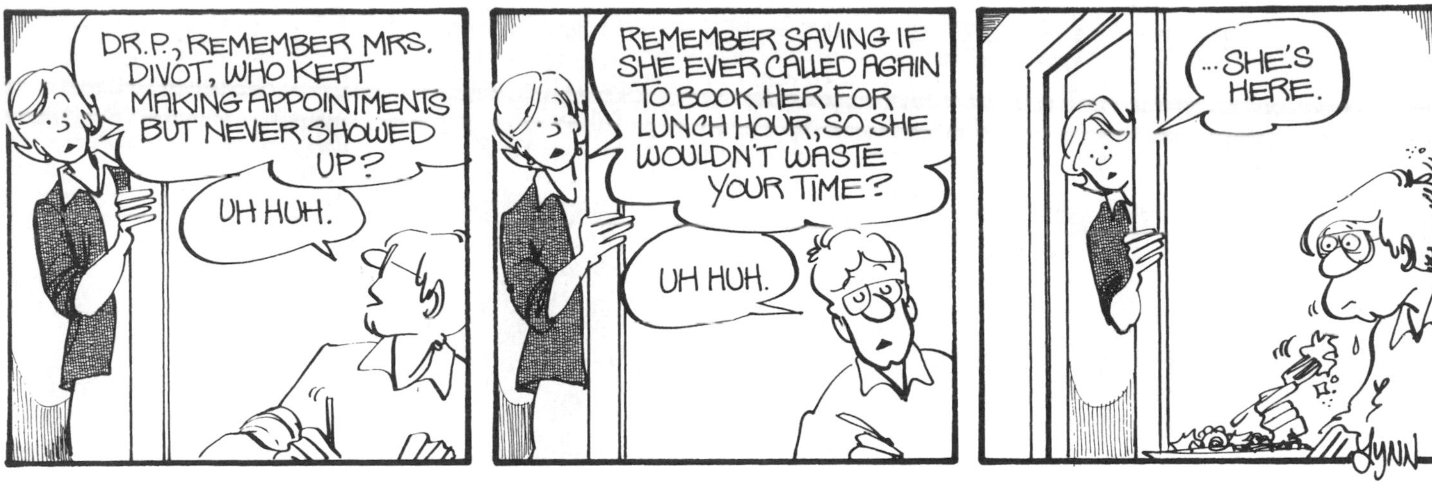
DR.P., REMEMBER MRS. DIVOT, WHO KEPT MAKING APPOINTMENTS BUT NEVER SHOWED UP?
UH HUH.
REMEMBER SAYING IF SHE EVER CALLED AGAIN TO BOOK HER FOR LUNCH HOUR, SO SHE WOULDN'T WASTE YOUR TIME?
UH HUH.
...SHE'S HERE.
LYNN

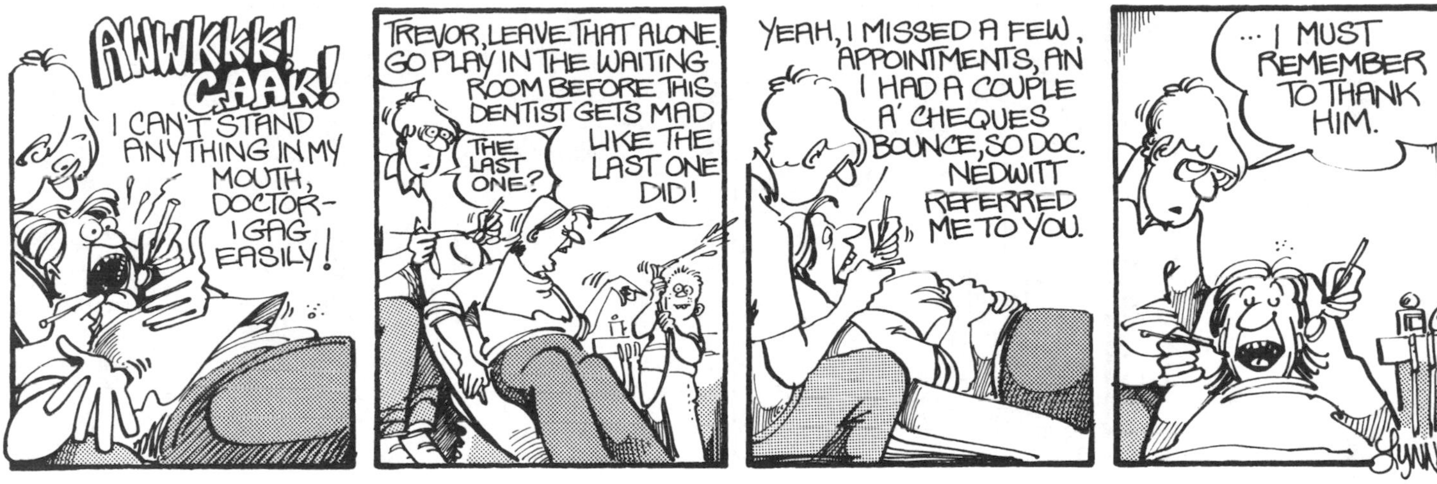
AWWKKK! GAAK!
I CAN'T STAND ANYTHING IN MY MOUTH, DOCTOR- I GAG EASILY!
TREVOR, LEAVE THAT ALONE. GO PLAY IN THE WAITING ROOM BEFORE THIS DENTIST GETS MAD LIKE THE LAST ONE DID!
THE LAST ONE?
YEAH, I MISSED A FEW, APPOINTMENTS, AN I HAD A COUPLE A' CHEQUES BOUNCE, SO DOC. NEDWITT REFERRED ME TO YOU.
... I MUST REMEMBER TO THANK HIM.
LYNN

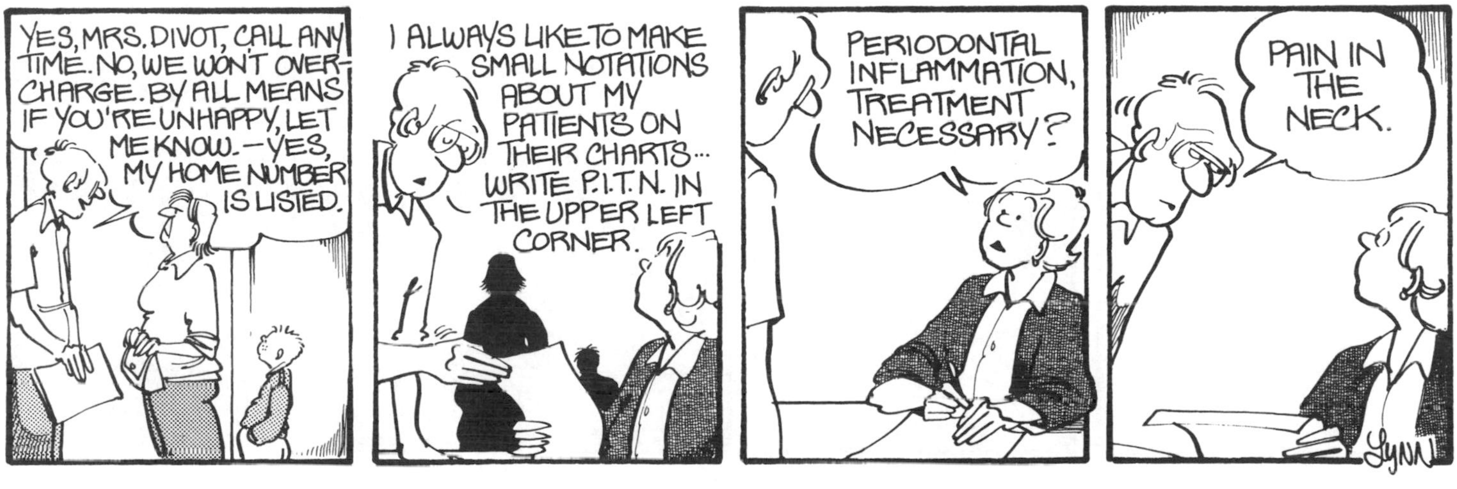
YES, MRS. DIVOT, CALL ANY TIME. NO, WE WON'T OVER-CHARGE. BY ALL MEANS IF YOU'RE UNHAPPY, LET ME KNOW.—YES, MY HOME NUMBER IS LISTED.
I ALWAYS LIKE TO MAKE SMALL NOTATIONS ABOUT MY PATIENTS ON THEIR CHARTS... WRITE P.I.T.N. IN THE UPPER LEFT CORNER.
PERIODONTAL INFLAMMATION, TREATMENT NECESSARY?
PAIN IN THE NECK.
LYNN

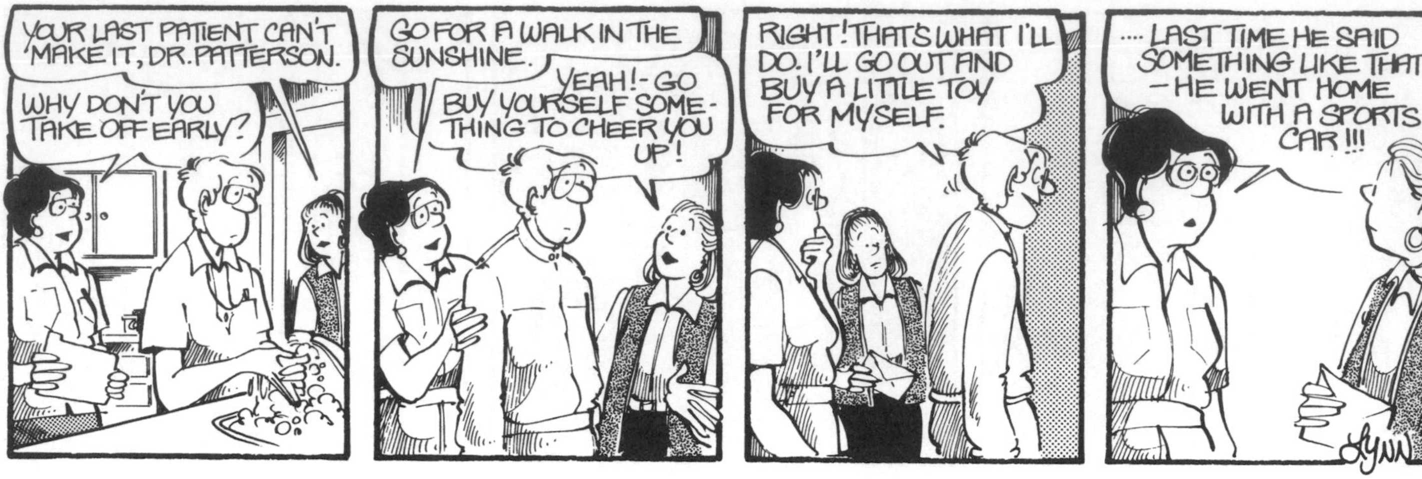
YOUR LAST PATIENT CAN'T MAKE IT, DR. PATTERSON.
WHY DON'T YOU TAKE OFF EARLY?
GO FOR A WALK IN THE SUNSHINE.
YEAH! - GO BUY YOURSELF SOMETHING TO CHEER YOU UP!
RIGHT! THAT'S WHAT I'LL DO. I'LL GO OUT AND BUY A LITTLE TOY FOR MYSELF.
.... LAST TIME HE SAID SOMETHING LIKE THAT - HE WENT HOME WITH A SPORTS CAR!!!
Lynn

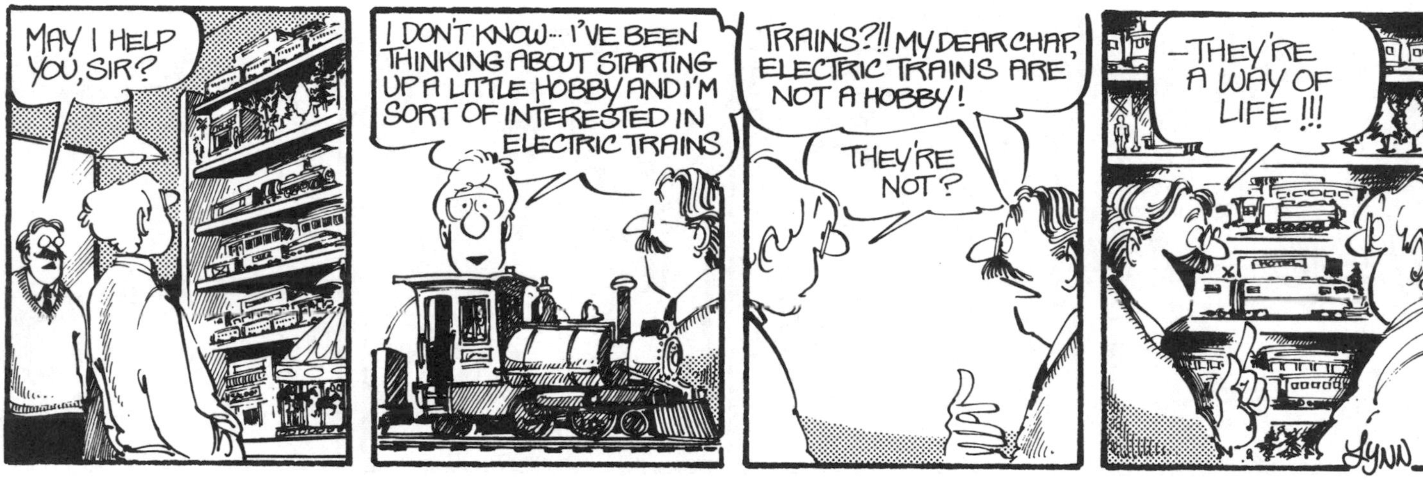
MAY I HELP YOU, SIR?
I DON'T KNOW... I'VE BEEN THINKING ABOUT STARTING UP A LITTLE HOBBY AND I'M SORT OF INTERESTED IN ELECTRIC TRAINS.
TRAINS?!! MY DEAR CHAP, ELECTRIC TRAINS ARE NOT A HOBBY!
THEY'RE NOT?
- THEY'RE A WAY OF LIFE!!!
Lynn

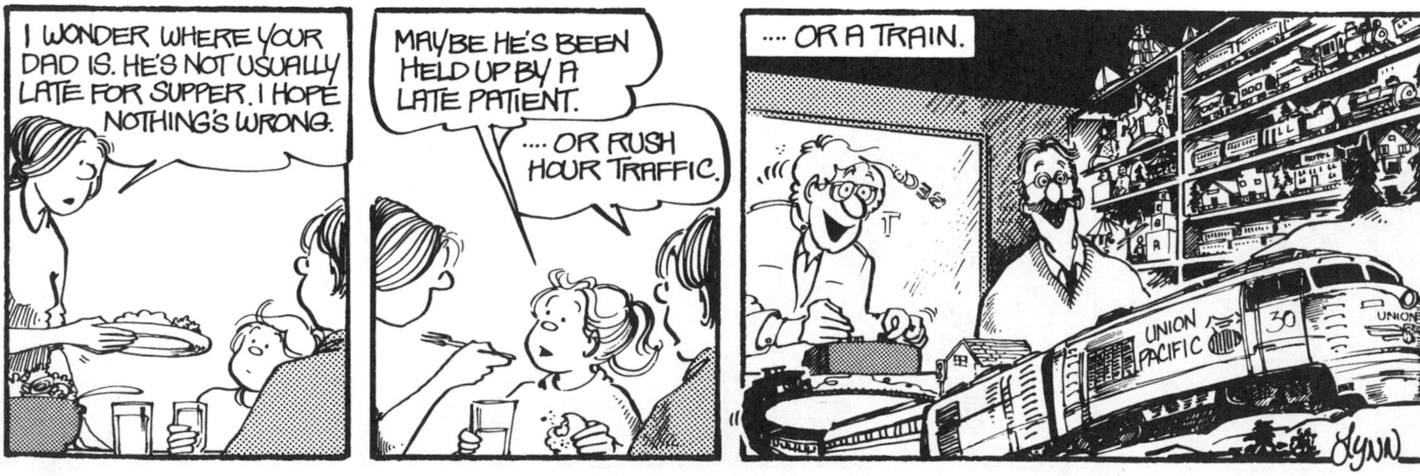
I WONDER WHERE YOUR DAD IS. HE'S NOT USUALLY LATE FOR SUPPER. I HOPE NOTHING'S WRONG.
MAYBE HE'S BEEN HELD UP BY A LATE PATIENT.
.... OR RUSH HOUR TRAFFIC.
.... OR A TRAIN.
UNION PACIFIC
30
Lynn

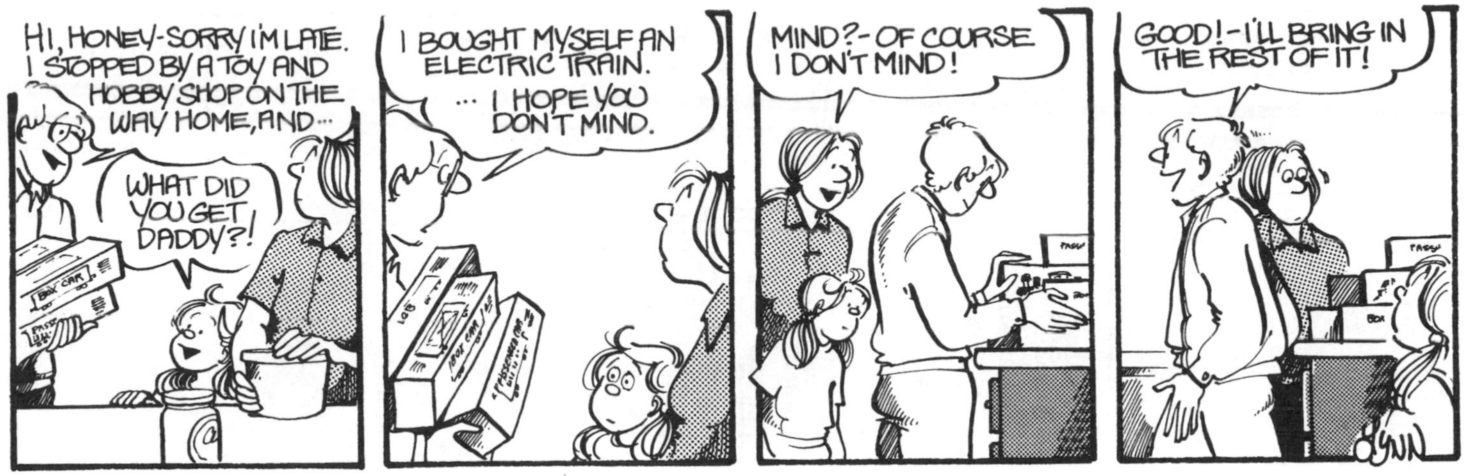
HI, HONEY-SORRY I'M LATE. I STOPPED BY A TOY AND HOBBY SHOP ON THE WAY HOME, AND...
WHAT DID YOU GET DADDY?!
I BOUGHT MYSELF AN ELECTRIC TRAIN.
... I HOPE YOU DON'T MIND.
MIND?- OF COURSE I DON'T MIND!
GOOD! - I'LL BRING IN THE REST OF IT!
LYNN

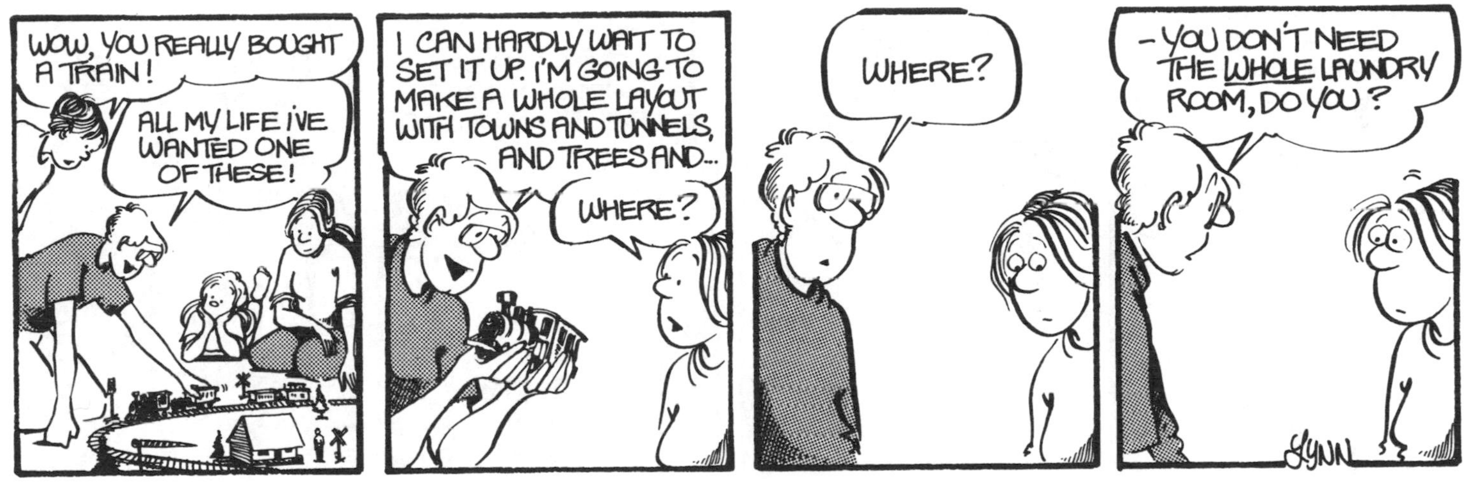
WOW, YOU REALLY BOUGHT A TRAIN!
ALL MY LIFE I'VE WANTED ONE OF THESE!
I CAN HARDLY WAIT TO SET IT UP. I'M GOING TO MAKE A WHOLE LAYOUT WITH TOWNS AND TUNNELS, AND TREES AND...
WHERE?
WHERE?
- YOU DON'T NEED THE WHOLE LAUNDRY ROOM, DO YOU?
LYNN

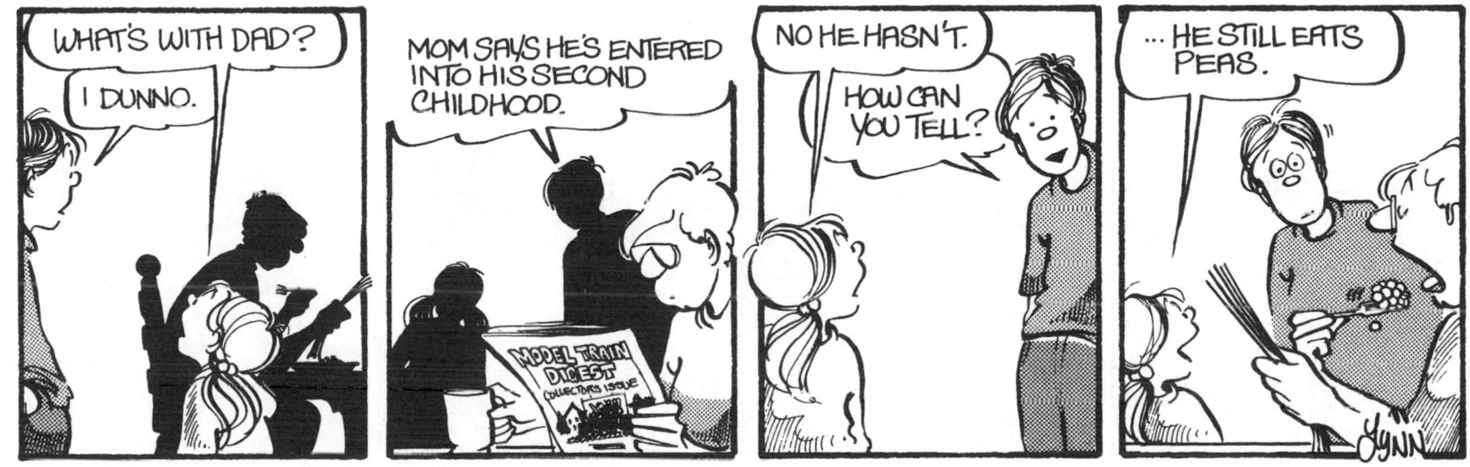
WHAT'S WITH DAD?
I DUNNO.
MOM SAYS HE'S ENTERED INTO HIS SECOND CHILDHOOD.
MODEL TRAIN DIGEST
COLLECTORS ISSUE
NO HE HASN'T.
HOW CAN YOU TELL?
... HE STILL EATS PEAS.
LYNN

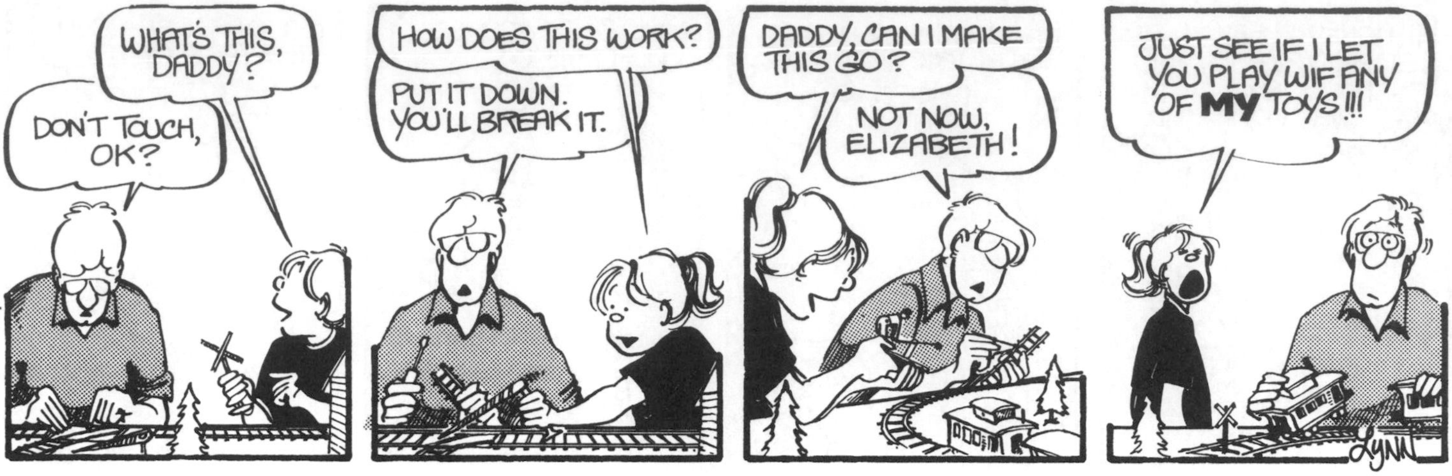
WHAT'S THIS, DADDY?
DON'T TOUCH, OK?
HOW DOES THIS WORK?
PUT IT DOWN. YOU'LL BREAK IT.
DADDY, CAN I MAKE THIS GO?
NOT NOW, ELIZABETH!
JUST SEE IF I LET YOU PLAY WIF ANY OF **MY** TOYS!!!
LYNN

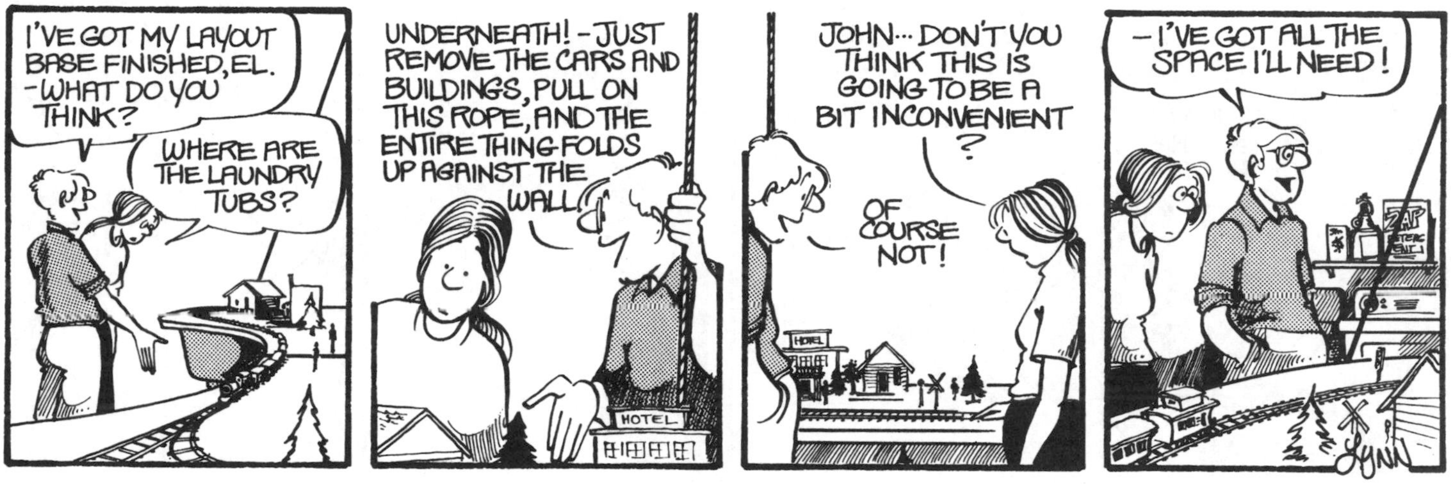
I'VE GOT MY LAYOUT BASE FINISHED, EL. -WHAT DO YOU THINK?
WHERE ARE THE LAUNDRY TUBS?
UNDERNEATH! -JUST REMOVE THE CARS AND BUILDINGS, PULL ON THIS ROPE, AND THE ENTIRE THING FOLDS UP AGAINST THE WALL
HOTEL
JOHN... DON'T YOU THINK THIS IS GOING TO BE A BIT INCONVENIENT?
OF COURSE NOT!
HOTEL
-I'VE GOT ALL THE SPACE I'LL NEED!
LYNN

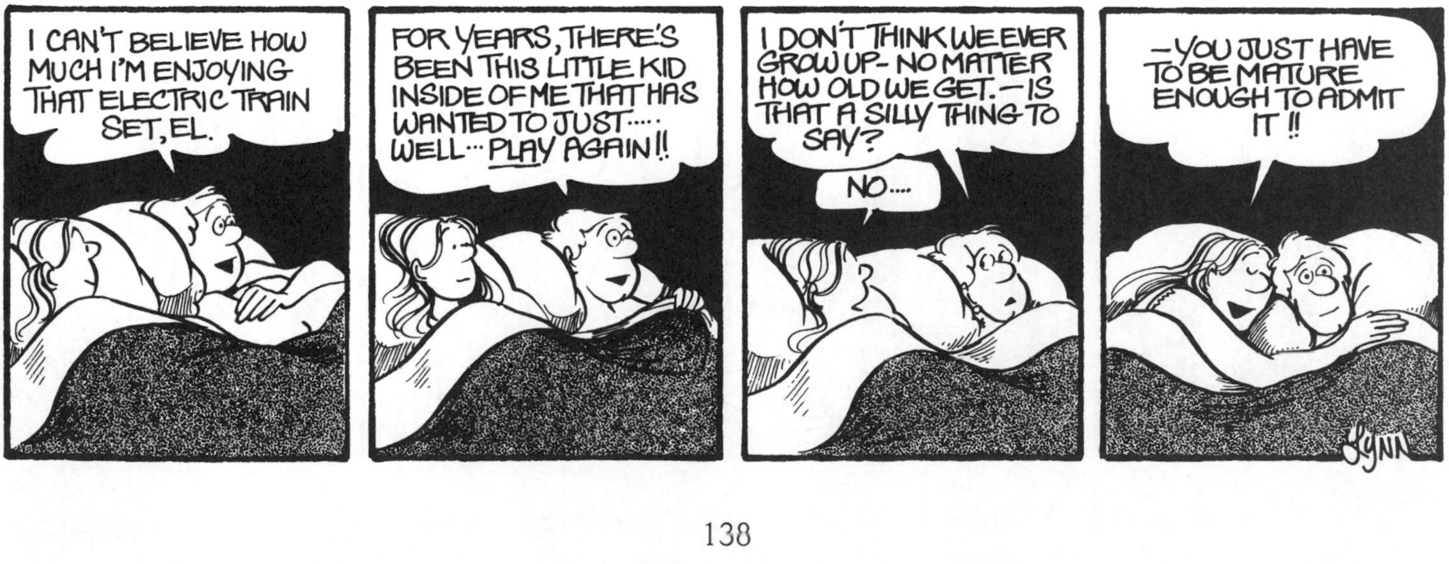
I CAN'T BELIEVE HOW MUCH I'M ENJOYING THAT ELECTRIC TRAIN SET, EL.
FOR YEARS, THERE'S BEEN THIS LITTLE KID INSIDE OF ME THAT HAS WANTED TO JUST..... WELL... PLAY AGAIN!!
I DON'T THINK WE EVER GROW UP- NO MATTER HOW OLD WE GET. -IS THAT A SILLY THING TO SAY?
NO....
-YOU JUST HAVE TO BE MATURE ENOUGH TO ADMIT IT!!
LYNN

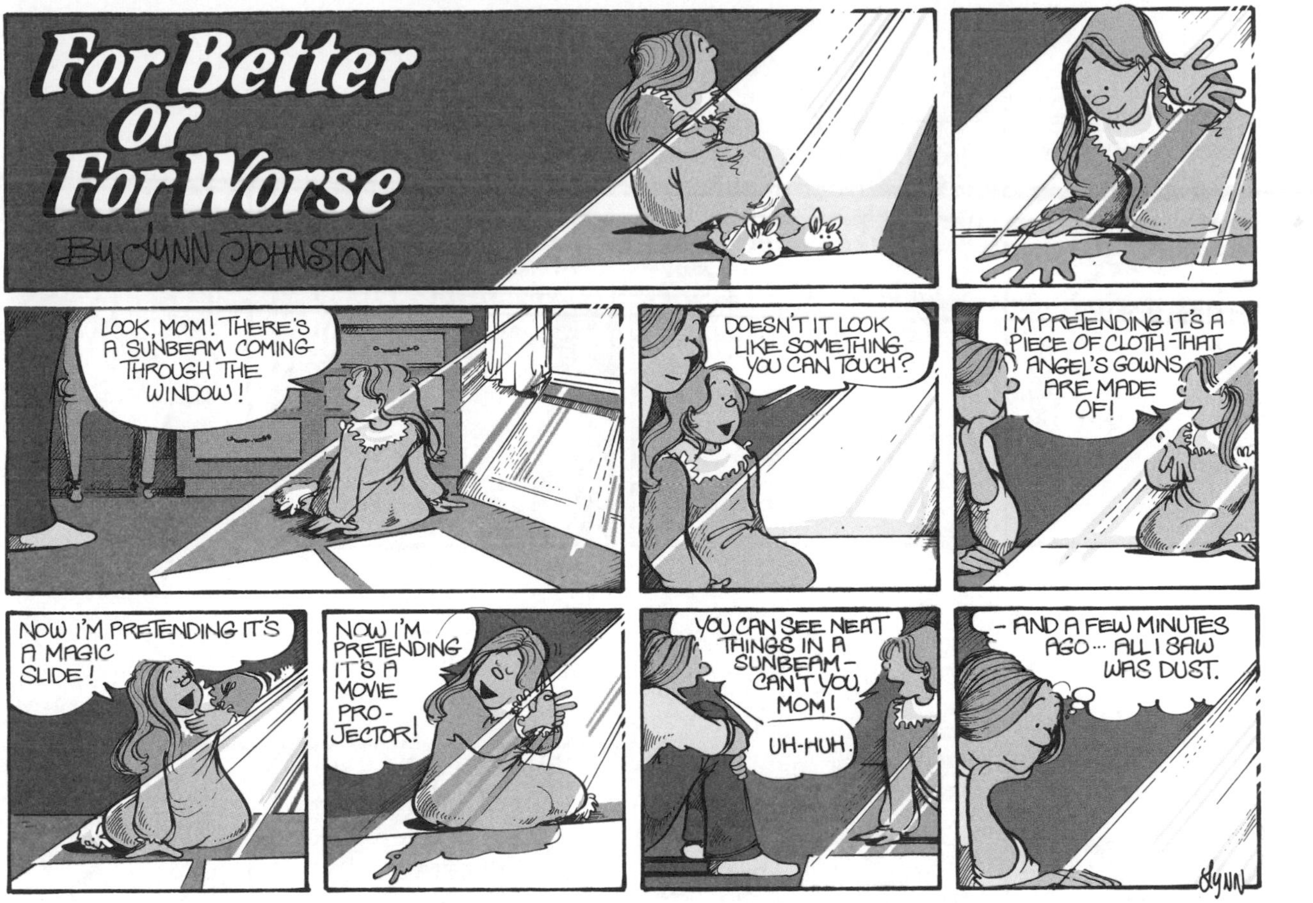
For Better or For Worse
By Lynn Johnston
LOOK, MOM! THERE'S A SUNBEAM COMING THROUGH THE WINDOW!
DOESN'T IT LOOK LIKE SOMETHING YOU CAN TOUCH?
I'M PRETENDING IT'S A PIECE OF CLOTH-THAT ANGEL'S GOWNS ARE MADE OF!
NOW I'M PRETENDING IT'S A MAGIC SLIDE!
NOW I'M PRETENDING IT'S A MOVIE PRO-JECTOR!
YOU CAN SEE NEAT THINGS IN A SUNBEAM- CAN'T YOU, MOM!
UH-HUH.
- AND A FEW MINUTES AGO... ALL I SAW WAS DUST.
Lynn

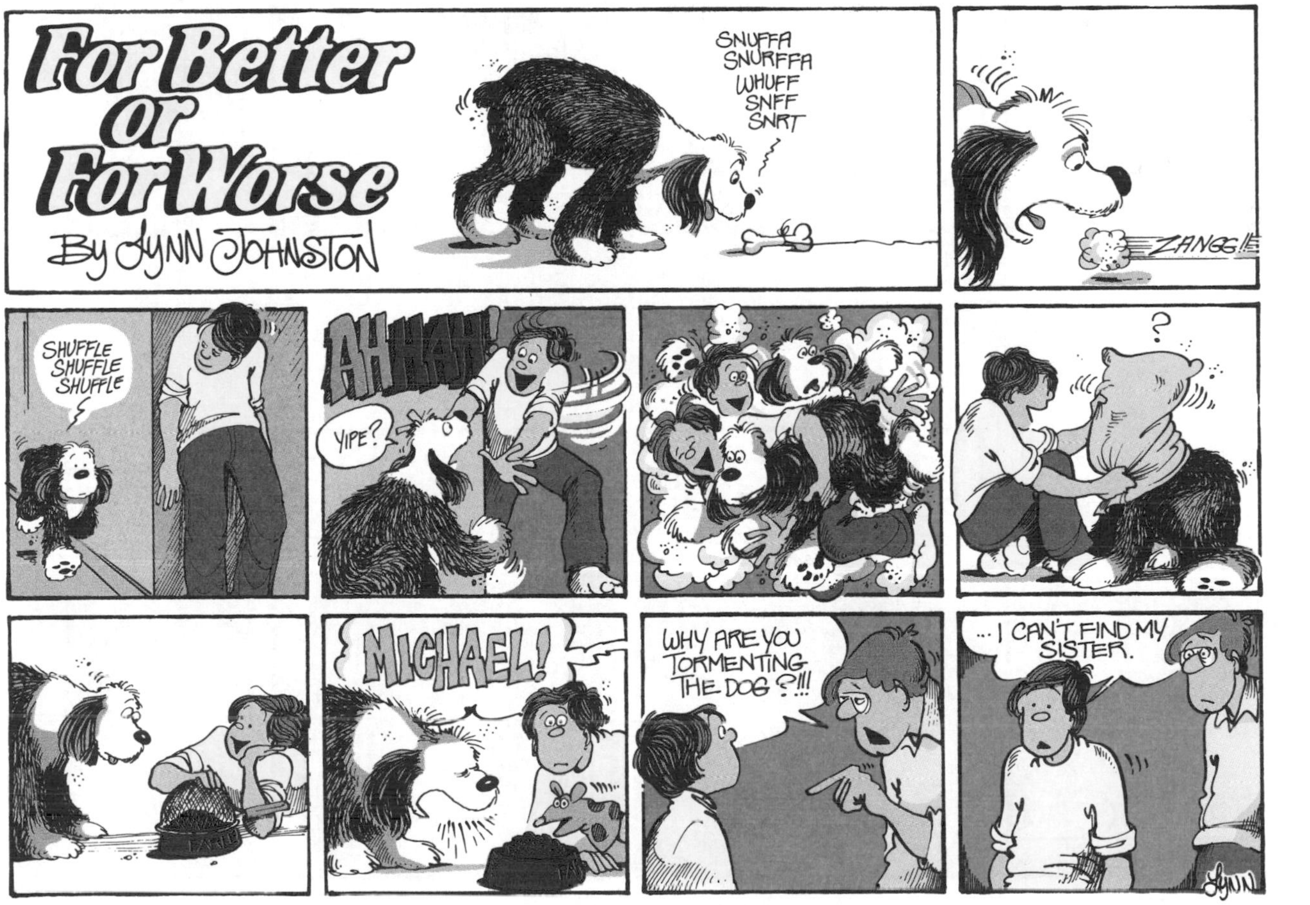
For Better or For Worse
By Lynn Johnston
SNUFFA SNURFFA WHUFF SNFF SNRT
ZANGG!
SHUFFLE SHUFFLE SHUFFLE
AH HAH!
YIPE?
?
MICHAEL!
WHY ARE YOU TORMENTING THE DOG?!!!
... I CAN'T FIND MY SISTER.
Lynn

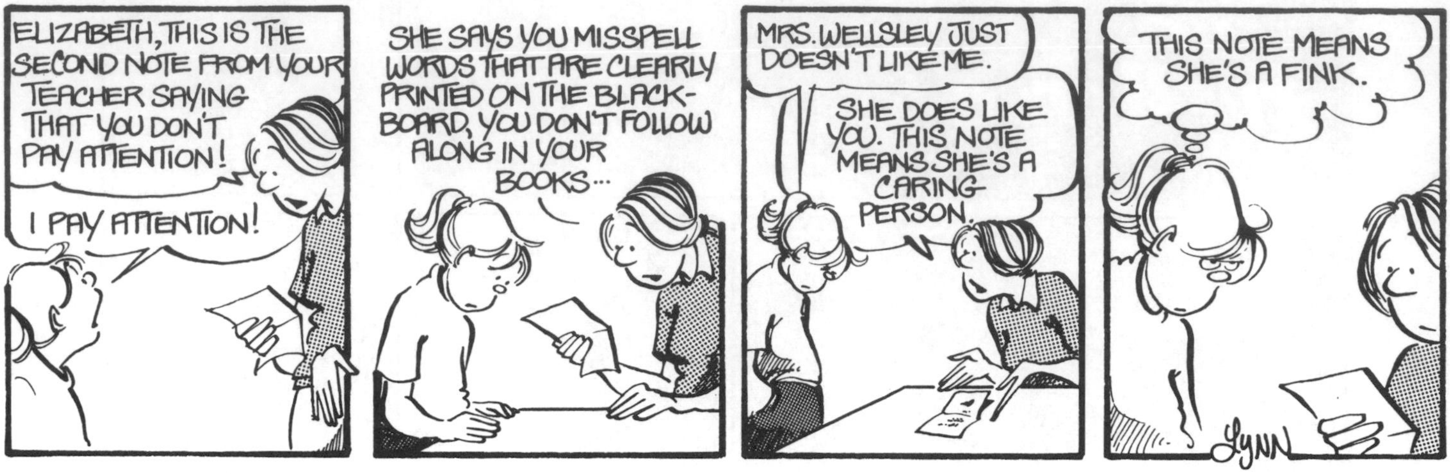
ELIZABETH, THIS IS THE SECOND NOTE FROM YOUR TEACHER SAYING THAT YOU DON'T PAY ATTENTION!
I PAY ATTENTION!
SHE SAYS YOU MISSPELL WORDS THAT ARE CLEARLY PRINTED ON THE BLACK-BOARD, YOU DON'T FOLLOW ALONG IN YOUR BOOKS...
MRS. WELLSLEY JUST DOESN'T LIKE ME.
SHE DOES LIKE YOU. THIS NOTE MEANS SHE'S A CARING PERSON.
THIS NOTE MEANS SHE'S A FINK.
LYNN

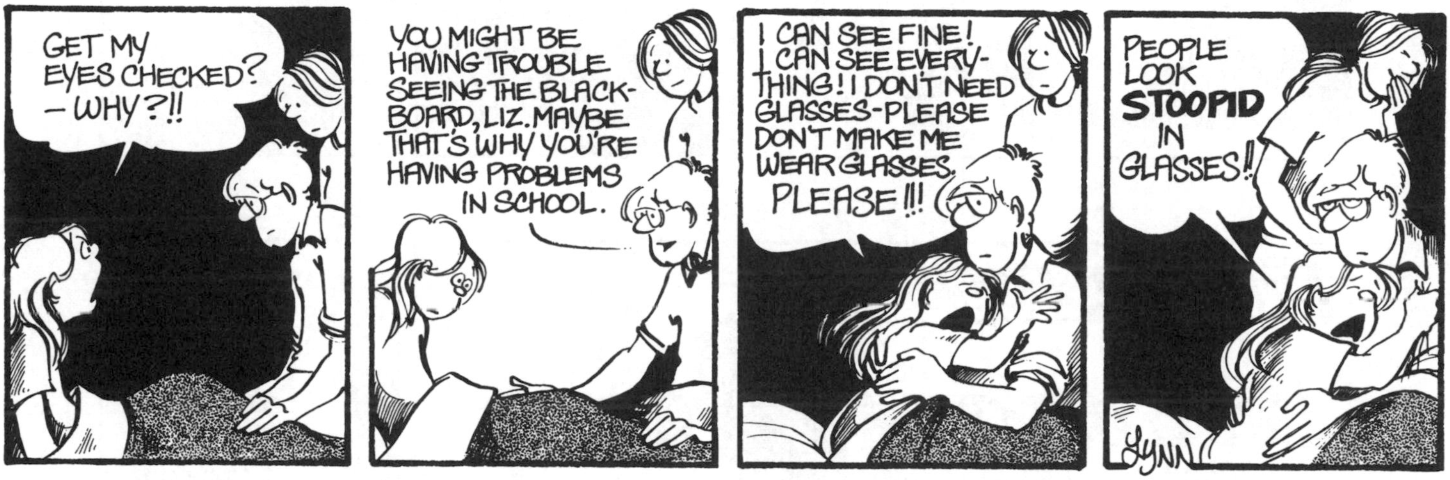
GET MY EYES CHECKED? - WHY?!!
YOU MIGHT BE HAVING TROUBLE SEEING THE BLACK-BOARD, LIZ. MAYBE THAT'S WHY YOU'RE HAVING PROBLEMS IN SCHOOL.
I CAN SEE FINE! I CAN SEE EVERY-THING! I DON'T NEED GLASSES - PLEASE DON'T MAKE ME WEAR GLASSES. PLEASE!!!
PEOPLE LOOK STOOPID IN GLASSES!!
LYNN

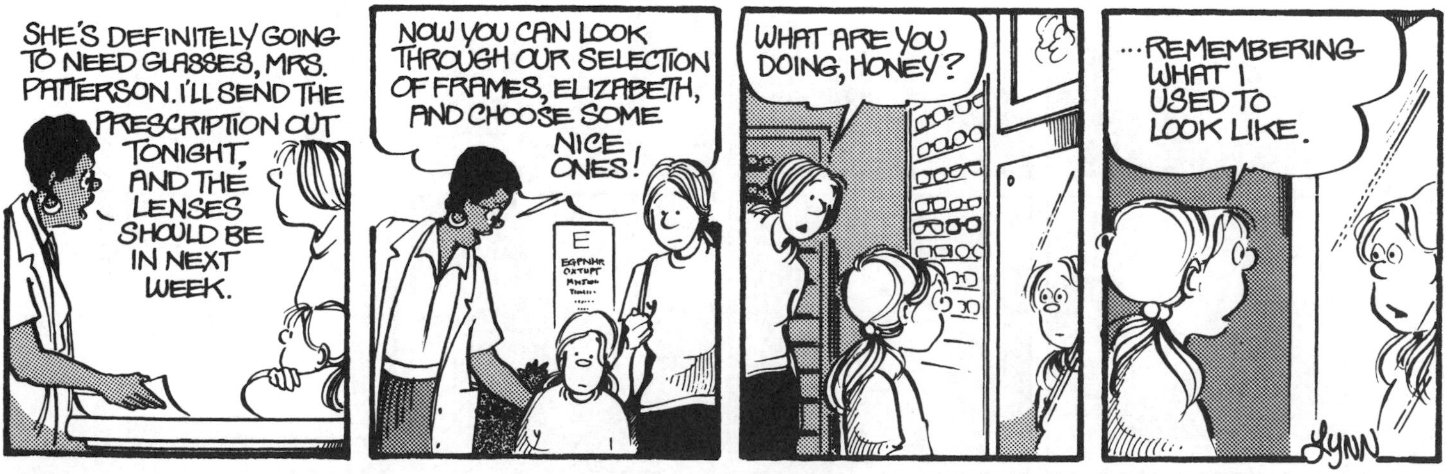
SHE'S DEFINITELY GOING TO NEED GLASSES, MRS. PATTERSON. I'LL SEND THE PRESCRIPTION OUT TONIGHT, AND THE LENSES SHOULD BE IN NEXT WEEK.
NOW YOU CAN LOOK THROUGH OUR SELECTION OF FRAMES, ELIZABETH, AND CHOOSE SOME NICE ONES!
E
WHAT ARE YOU DOING, HONEY?
...REMEMBERING WHAT I USED TO LOOK LIKE.
LYNN

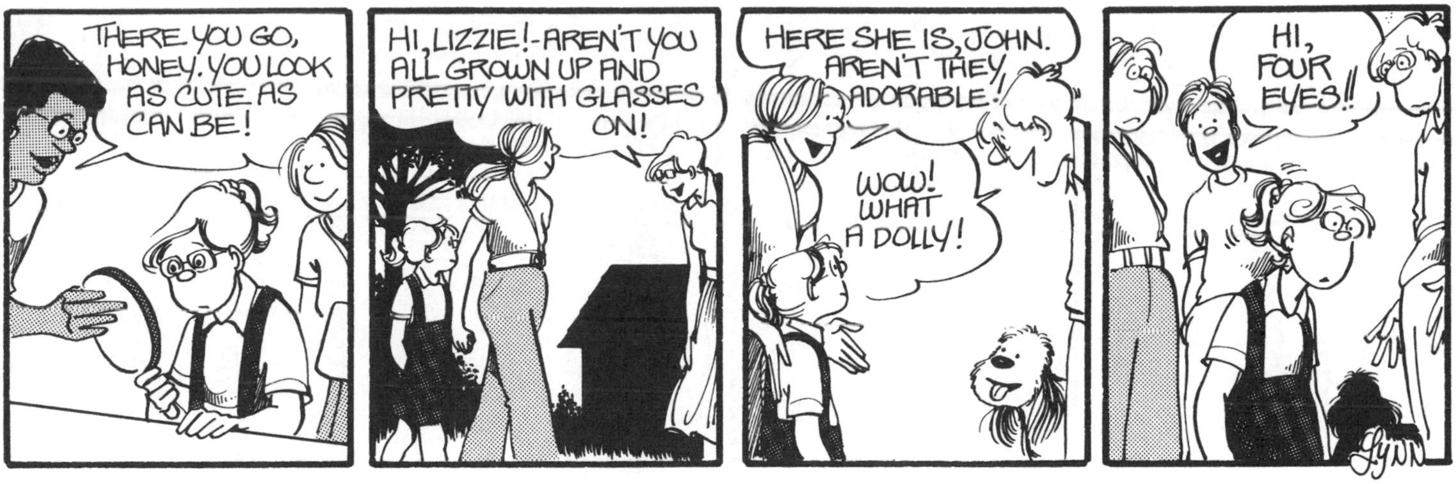
THERE YOU GO, HONEY. YOU LOOK AS CUTE AS CAN BE!
HI, LIZZIE!-AREN'T YOU ALL GROWN UP AND PRETTY WITH GLASSES ON!
HERE SHE IS, JOHN. AREN'T THEY ADORABLE!
WOW! WHAT A DOLLY!
HI, FOUR EYES!!
LYNN

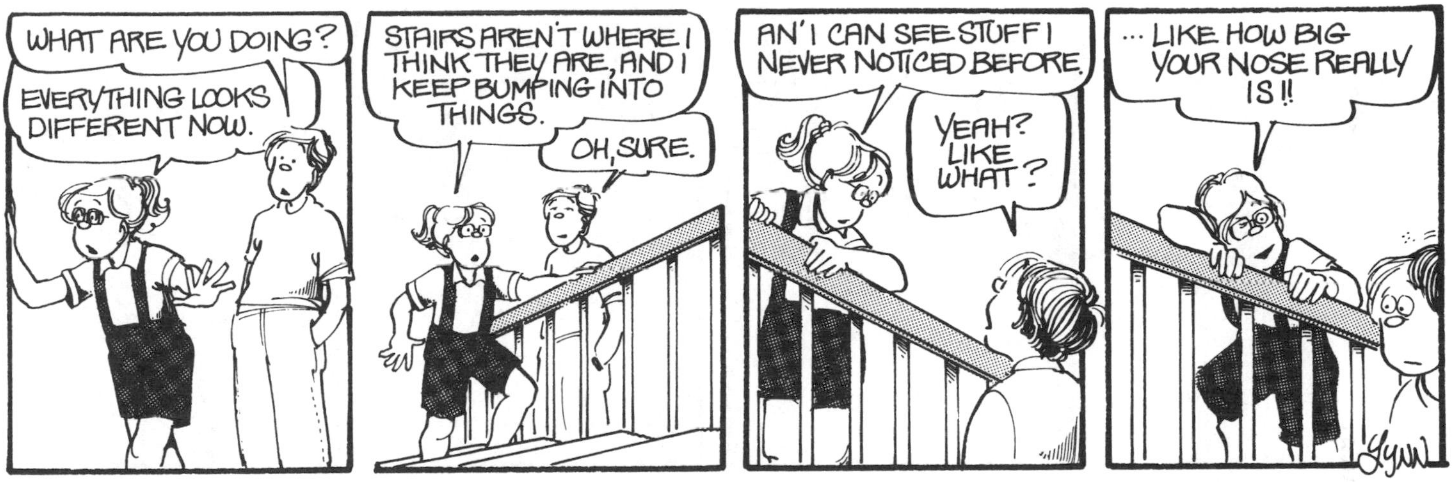
WHAT ARE YOU DOING?
EVERYTHING LOOKS DIFFERENT NOW.
STAIRS AREN'T WHERE I THINK THEY ARE, AND I KEEP BUMPING INTO THINGS.
OH, SURE.
AN' I CAN SEE STUFF I NEVER NOTICED BEFORE.
YEAH? LIKE WHAT?
... LIKE HOW BIG YOUR NOSE REALLY IS!!
LYNN

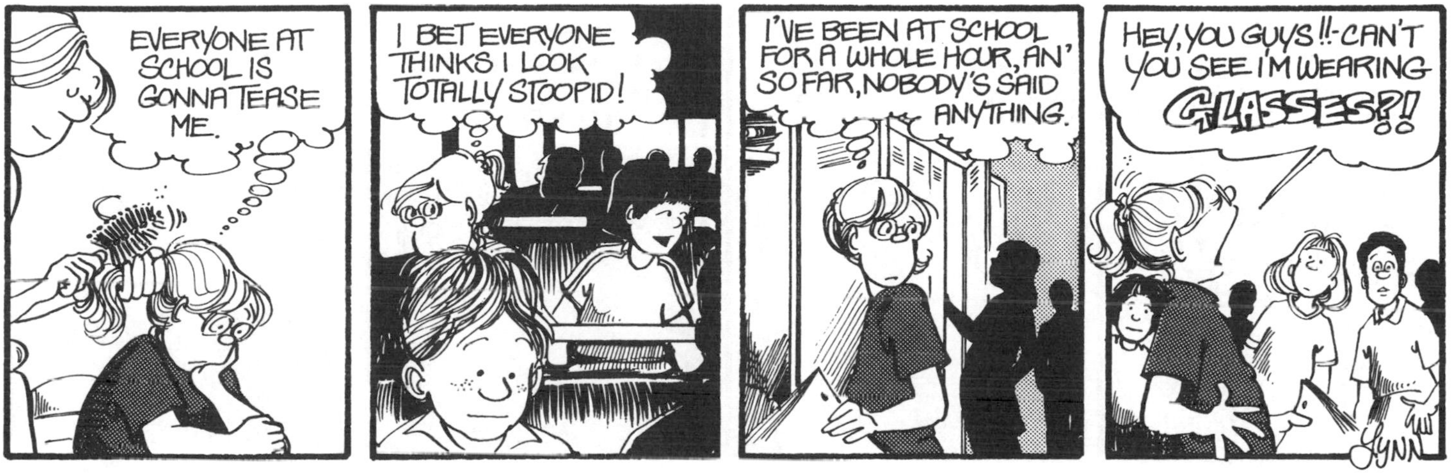
EVERYONE AT SCHOOL IS GONNA TEASE ME.
I BET EVERYONE THINKS I LOOK TOTALLY STOOPID!
I'VE BEEN AT SCHOOL FOR A WHOLE HOUR, AN' SO FAR, NOBODY'S SAID ANYTHING.
HEY, YOU GUYS!!-CAN'T YOU SEE I'M WEARING GLASSES?!
LYNN

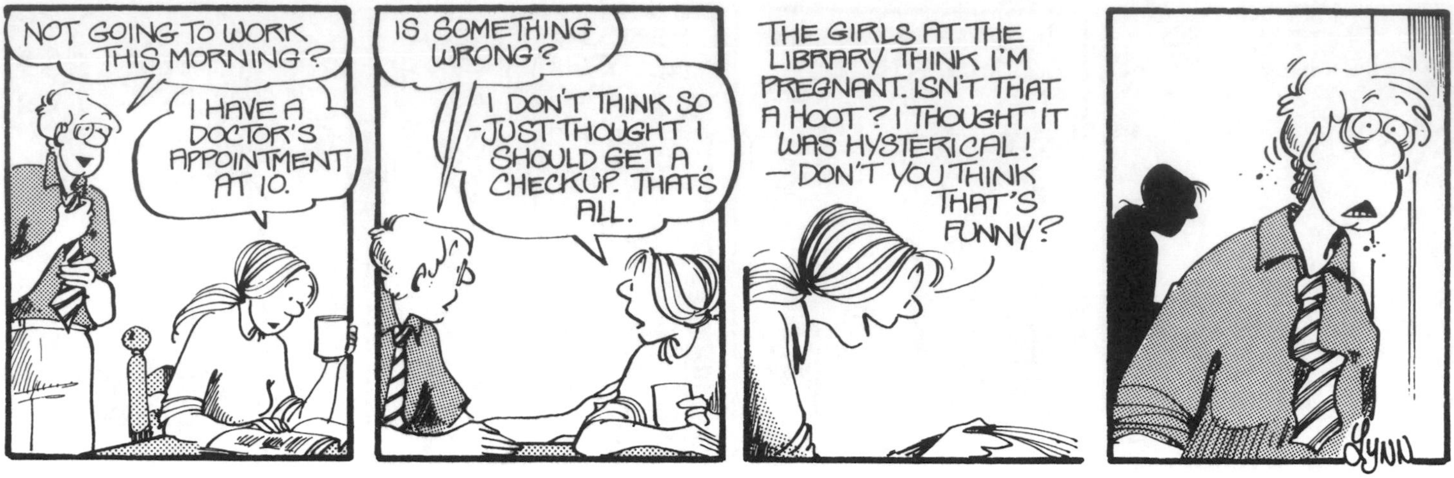
NOT GOING TO WORK THIS MORNING?
I HAVE A DOCTOR'S APPOINTMENT AT 10.
IS SOMETHING WRONG?
I DON'T THINK SO -JUST THOUGHT I SHOULD GET A CHECKUP. THAT'S ALL.
THE GIRLS AT THE LIBRARY THINK I'M PREGNANT. ISN'T THAT A HOOT? I THOUGHT IT WAS HYSTERICAL! — DON'T YOU THINK THAT'S FUNNY?
LYNN

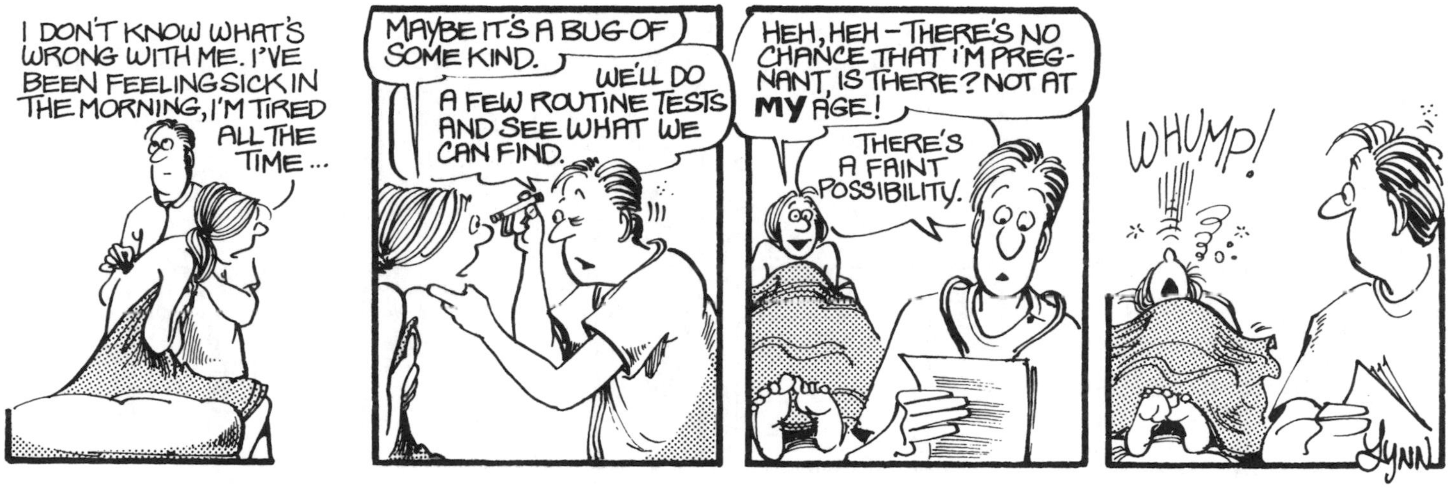
I DON'T KNOW WHAT'S WRONG WITH ME. I'VE BEEN FEELING SICK IN THE MORNING, I'M TIRED ALL THE TIME...
MAYBE IT'S A BUG OF SOME KIND.
WE'LL DO A FEW ROUTINE TESTS AND SEE WHAT WE CAN FIND.
HEH, HEH — THERE'S NO CHANCE THAT I'M PREGNANT, IS THERE? NOT AT MY AGE!
THERE'S A FAINT POSSIBILITY.
WHUMP!
LYNN

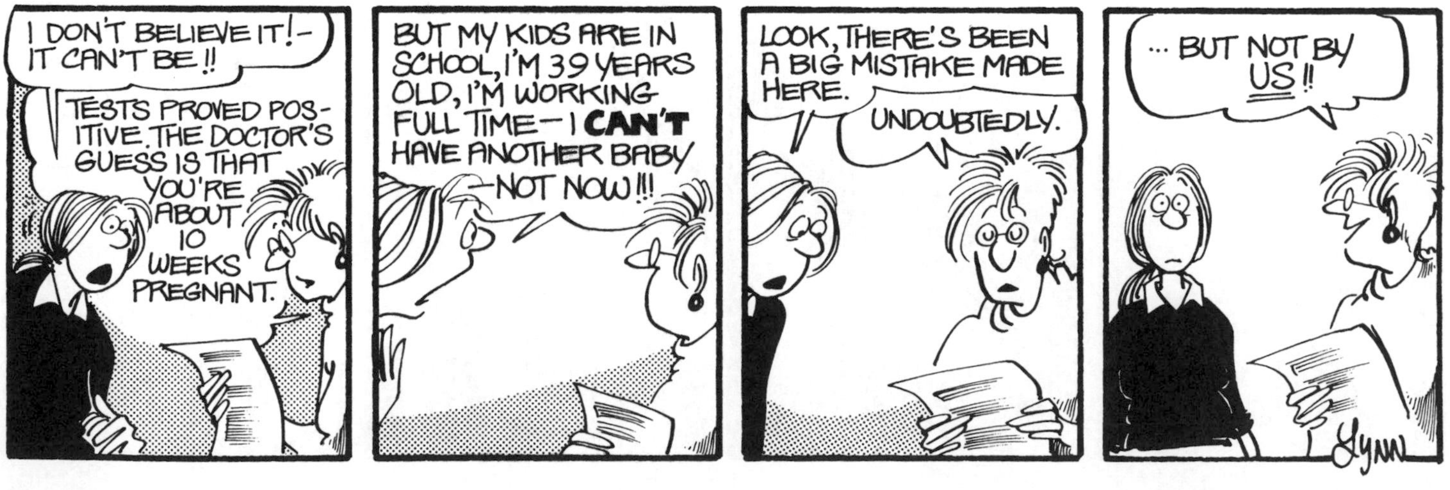
I DON'T BELIEVE IT! — IT CAN'T BE!!
TESTS PROVED POSITIVE. THE DOCTOR'S GUESS IS THAT YOU'RE ABOUT 10 WEEKS PREGNANT.
BUT MY KIDS ARE IN SCHOOL, I'M 39 YEARS OLD, I'M WORKING FULL TIME — I CAN'T HAVE ANOTHER BABY — NOT NOW!!!
LOOK, THERE'S BEEN A BIG MISTAKE MADE HERE.
UNDOUBTEDLY.
... BUT NOT BY US!!
LYNN

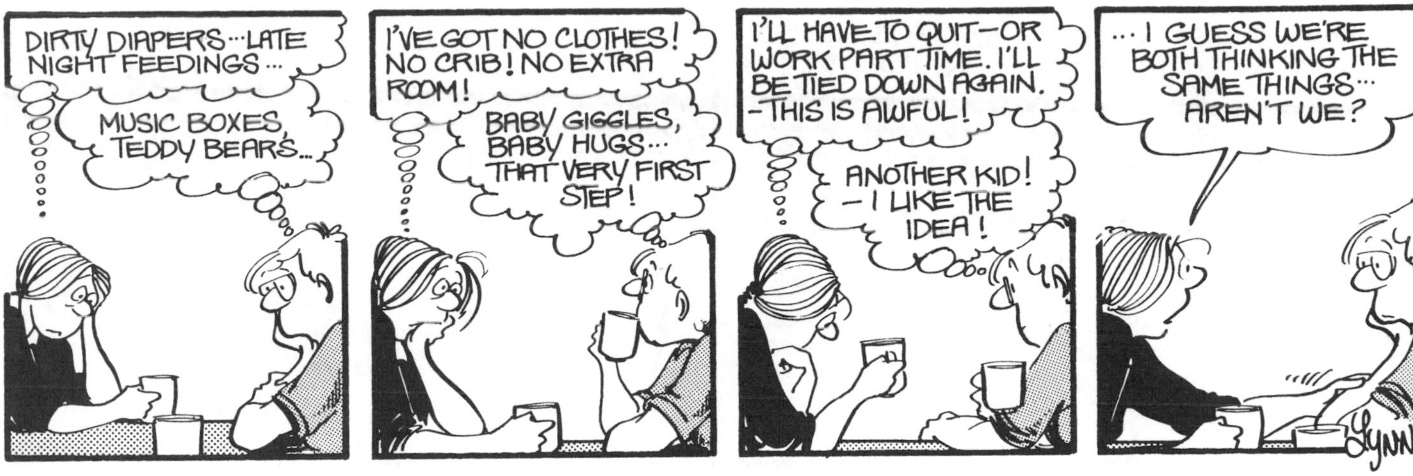
DIRTY DIAPERS...LATE NIGHT FEEDINGS...
MUSIC BOXES, TEDDY BEARS...
I'VE GOT NO CLOTHES! NO CRIB! NO EXTRA ROOM!
BABY GIGGLES, BABY HUGS... THAT VERY FIRST STEP!
I'LL HAVE TO QUIT—OR WORK PART TIME. I'LL BE TIED DOWN AGAIN. -THIS IS AWFUL!
ANOTHER KID! - I LIKE THE IDEA!
... I GUESS WE'RE BOTH THINKING THE SAME THINGS... AREN'T WE?
LYNN

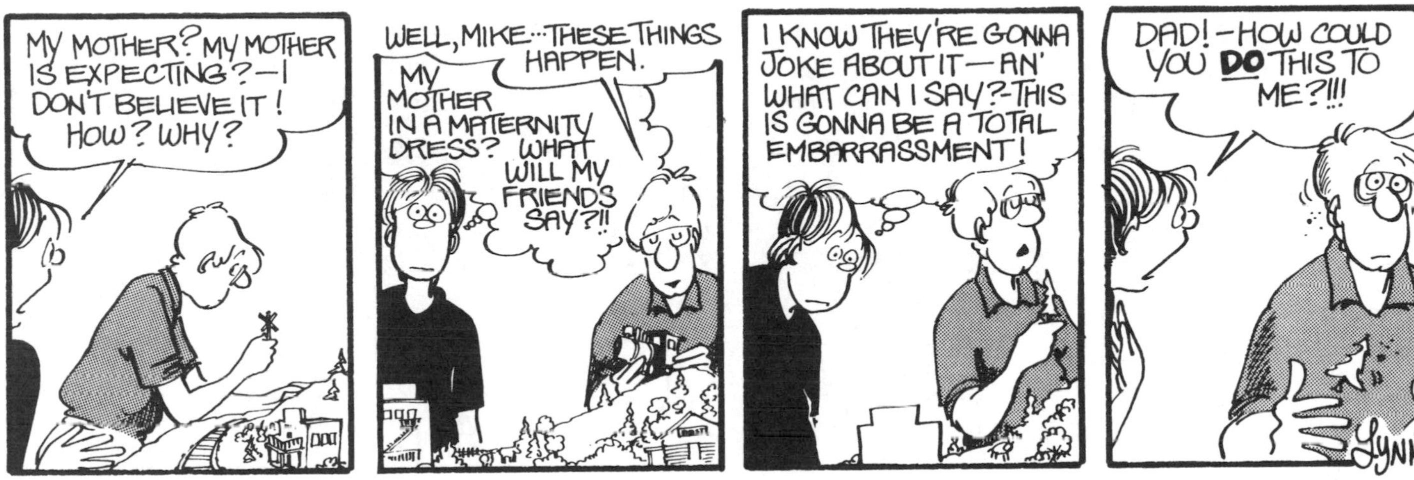
MY MOTHER? MY MOTHER IS EXPECTING?-I DON'T BELIEVE IT! HOW? WHY?
WELL, MIKE...THESE THINGS HAPPEN.
MY MOTHER IN A MATERNITY DRESS? WHAT WILL MY FRIENDS SAY?!!
I KNOW THEY'RE GONNA JOKE ABOUT IT—AN' WHAT CAN I SAY?-THIS IS GONNA BE A TOTAL EMBARRASSMENT!
DAD! -HOW COULD YOU **DO** THIS TO ME?!!!
LYNN

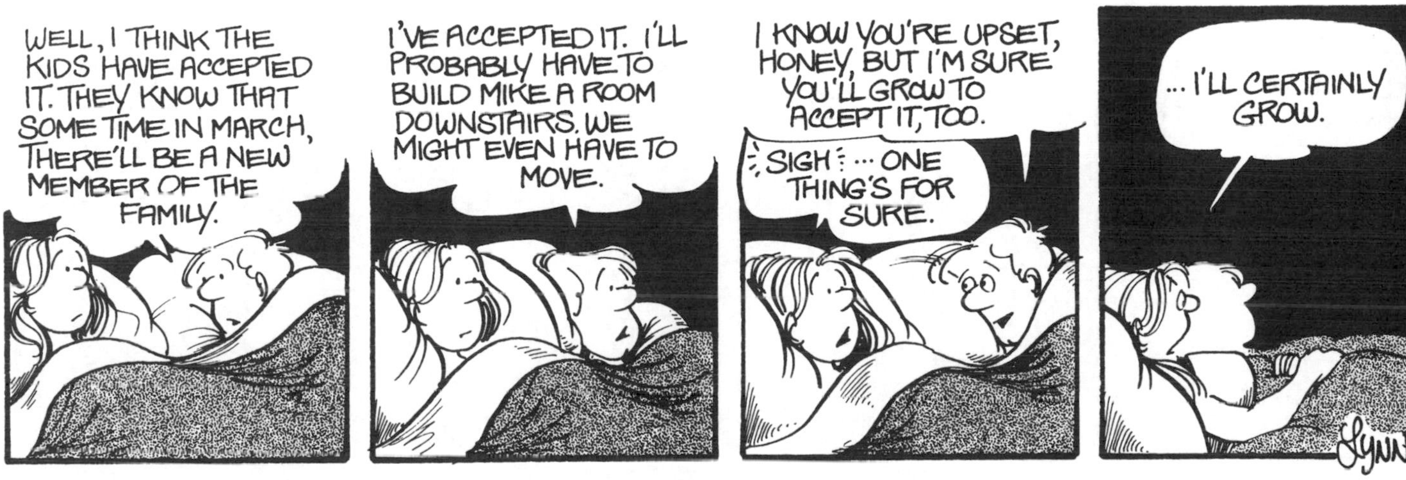
WELL, I THINK THE KIDS HAVE ACCEPTED IT. THEY KNOW THAT SOME TIME IN MARCH, THERE'LL BE A NEW MEMBER OF THE FAMILY.
I'VE ACCEPTED IT. I'LL PROBABLY HAVE TO BUILD MIKE A ROOM DOWNSTAIRS. WE MIGHT EVEN HAVE TO MOVE.
I KNOW YOU'RE UPSET, HONEY, BUT I'M SURE YOU'LL GROW TO ACCEPT IT, TOO.
SIGH ... ONE THING'S FOR SURE.
... I'LL CERTAINLY GROW.
LYNN

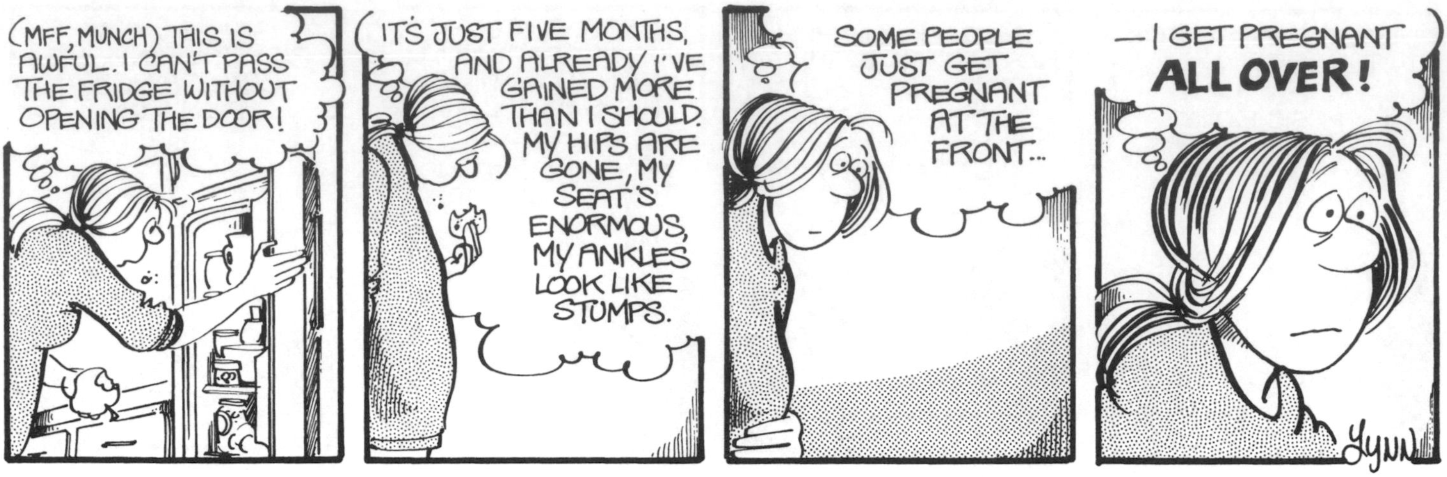
(MFF, MUNCH) THIS IS AWFUL. I CAN'T PASS THE FRIDGE WITHOUT OPENING THE DOOR!
IT'S JUST FIVE MONTHS, AND ALREADY I'VE GAINED MORE THAN I SHOULD. MY HIPS ARE GONE, MY SEAT'S ENORMOUS, MY ANKLES LOOK LIKE STUMPS.
SOME PEOPLE JUST GET PREGNANT AT THE FRONT...
— I GET PREGNANT
ALL OVER!
LYNN

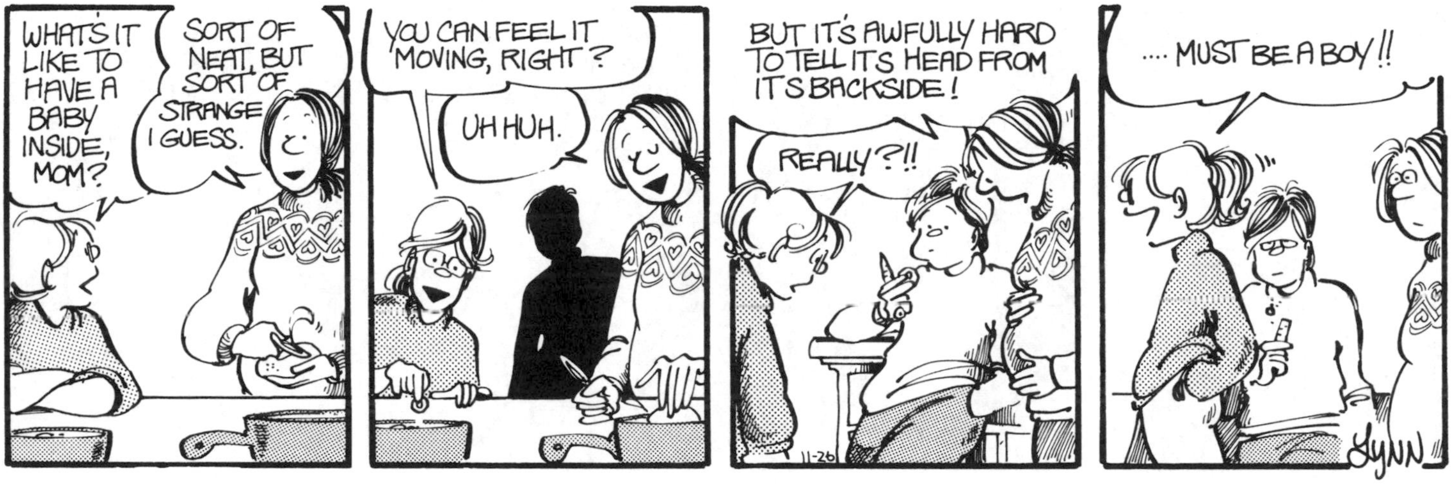
WHAT'S IT LIKE TO HAVE A BABY INSIDE, MOM?
SORT OF NEAT, BUT SORT OF STRANGE I GUESS.
YOU CAN FEEL IT MOVING, RIGHT?
UH HUH.
BUT IT'S AWFULLY HARD TO TELL ITS HEAD FROM ITS BACKSIDE!
REALLY?!!
11-26
.... MUST BE A BOY!!
LYNN

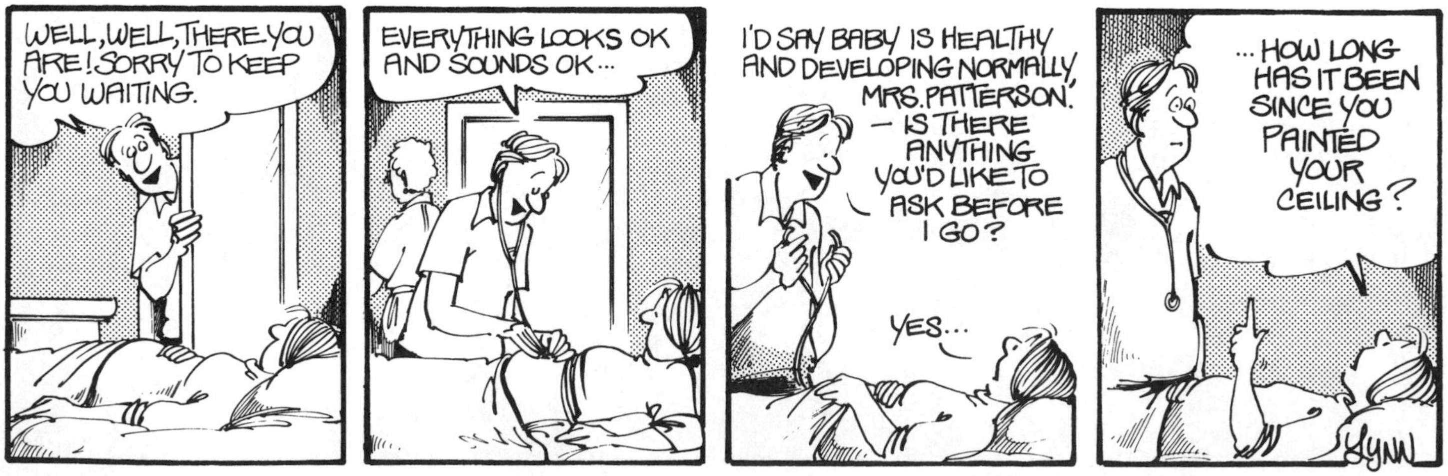
WELL, WELL, THERE YOU ARE! SORRY TO KEEP YOU WAITING.
EVERYTHING LOOKS OK AND SOUNDS OK...
I'D SAY BABY IS HEALTHY AND DEVELOPING NORMALLY, MRS. PATTERSON. — IS THERE ANYTHING YOU'D LIKE TO ASK BEFORE I GO?
YES...
... HOW LONG HAS IT BEEN SINCE YOU PAINTED YOUR CEILING?
LYNN

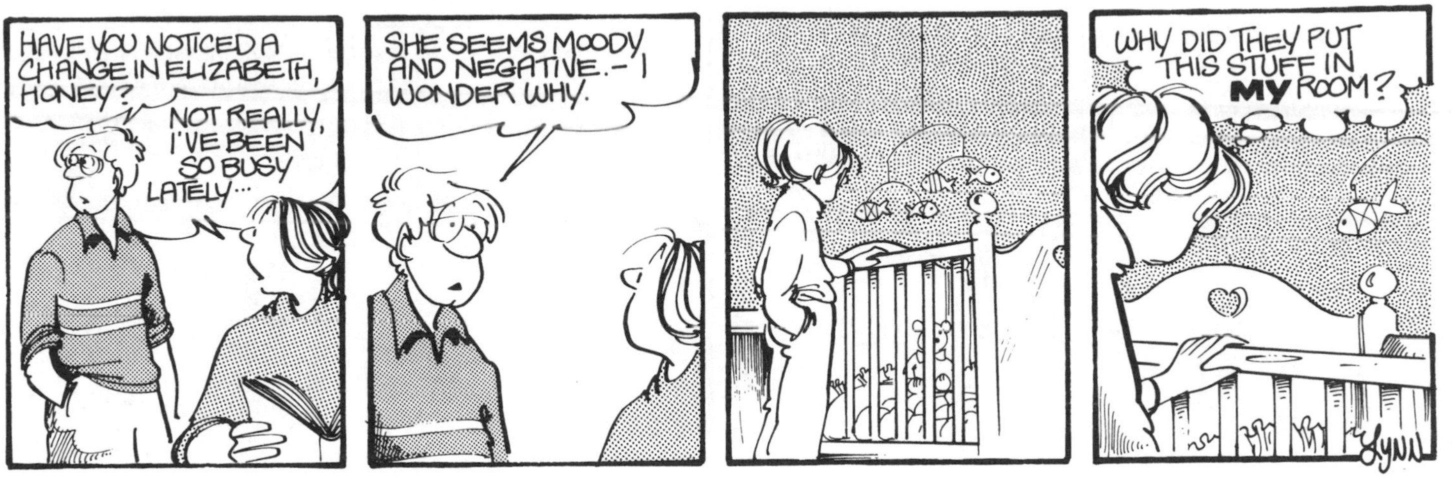
HAVE YOU NOTICED A CHANGE IN ELIZABETH, HONEY?
NOT REALLY, I'VE BEEN SO BUSY LATELY...
SHE SEEMS MOODY AND NEGATIVE. - I WONDER WHY.
WHY DID THEY PUT THIS STUFF IN MY ROOM?
LYNN

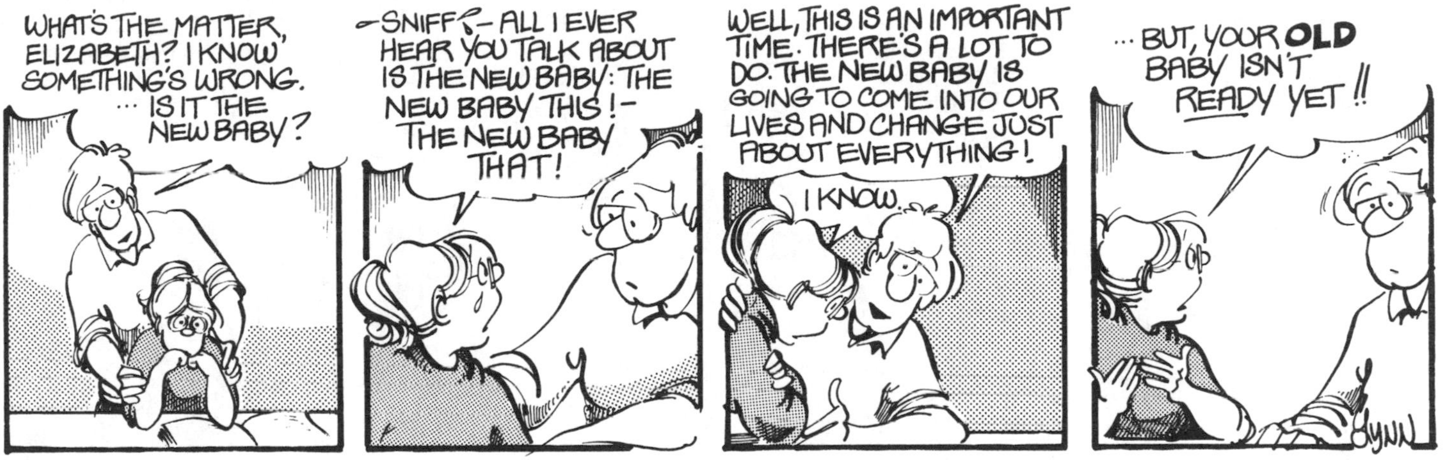
WHAT'S THE MATTER, ELIZABETH? I KNOW SOMETHING'S WRONG. ... IS IT THE NEW BABY?
-SNIFF- ALL I EVER HEAR YOU TALK ABOUT IS THE NEW BABY: THE NEW BABY THIS! - THE NEW BABY THAT!
WELL, THIS IS AN IMPORTANT TIME. THERE'S A LOT TO DO. THE NEW BABY IS GOING TO COME INTO OUR LIVES AND CHANGE JUST ABOUT EVERYTHING!
I KNOW.
... BUT, YOUR OLD BABY ISN'T READY YET!!
LYNN

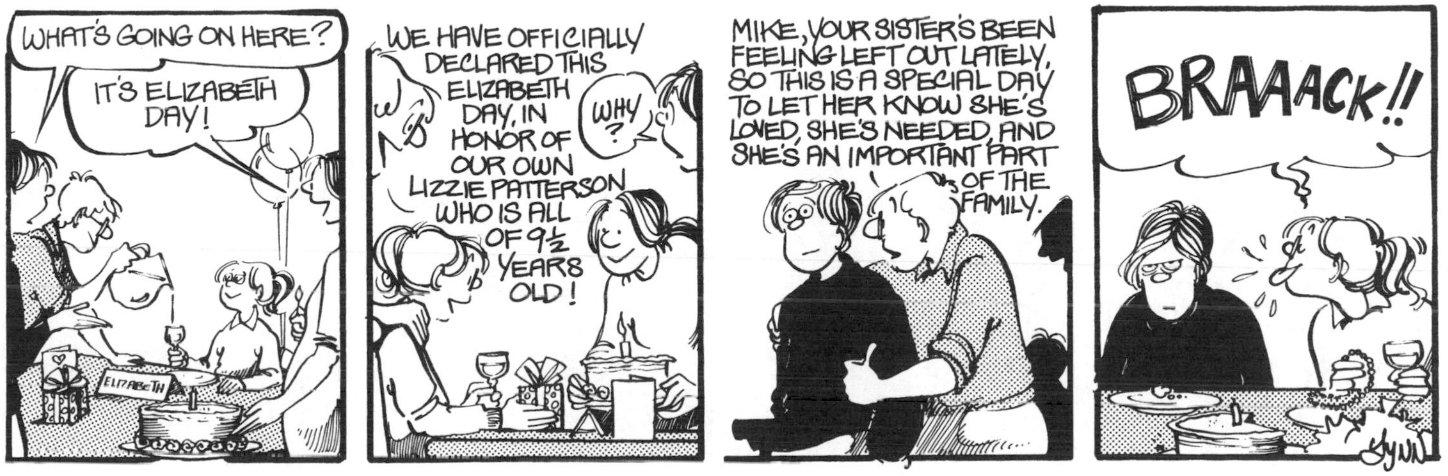
WHAT'S GOING ON HERE?
IT'S ELIZABETH DAY!
ELIZABETH
WE HAVE OFFICIALLY DECLARED THIS ELIZABETH DAY, IN HONOR OF OUR OWN LIZZIE PATTERSON WHO IS ALL OF 9½ YEARS OLD!
WHY?
MIKE, YOUR SISTER'S BEEN FEELING LEFT OUT LATELY, SO THIS IS A SPECIAL DAY TO LET HER KNOW SHE'S LOVED, SHE'S NEEDED, AND SHE'S AN IMPORTANT PART OF THE FAMILY.
BRAAACK!!
LYNN

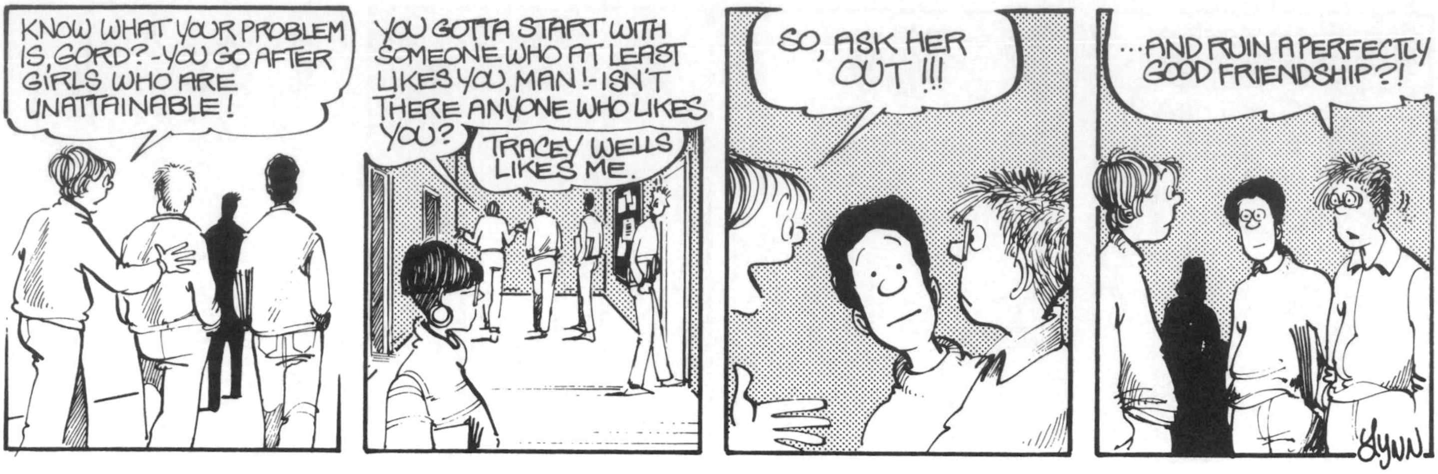
KNOW WHAT YOUR PROBLEM IS, GORD?-YOU GO AFTER GIRLS WHO ARE UNATTAINABLE!
YOU GOTTA START WITH SOMEONE WHO AT LEAST LIKES YOU, MAN!-ISN'T THERE ANYONE WHO LIKES YOU?
TRACEY WELLS LIKES ME.
SO, ASK HER OUT!!!
...AND RUIN A PERFECTLY GOOD FRIENDSHIP?!
LYNN

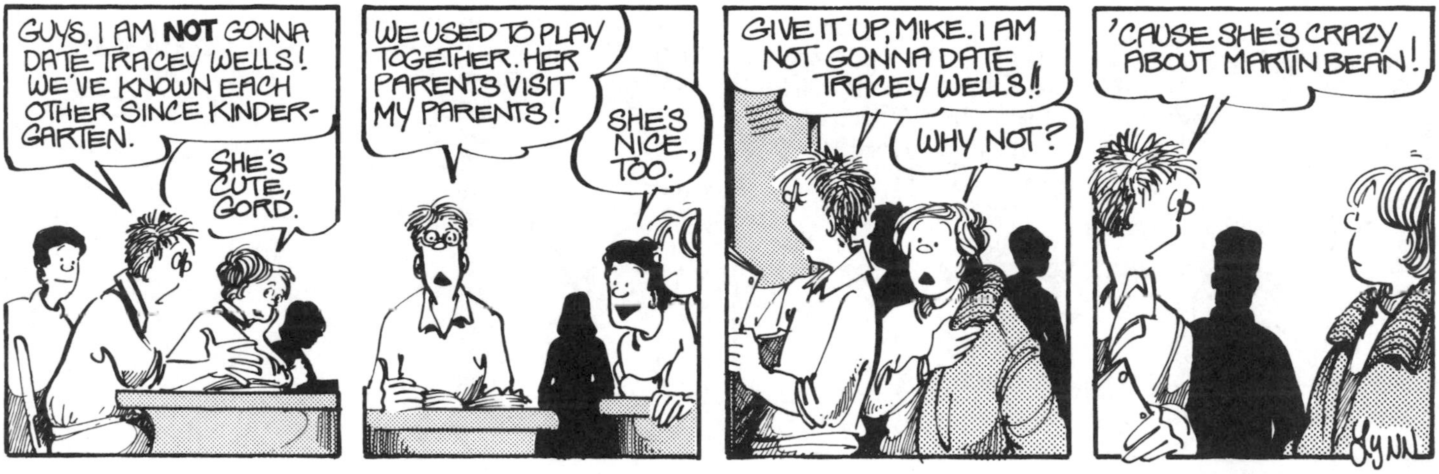
GUYS, I AM NOT GONNA DATE TRACEY WELLS! WE'VE KNOWN EACH OTHER SINCE KINDER-GARTEN.
SHE'S CUTE, GORD.
WE USED TO PLAY TOGETHER. HER PARENTS VISIT MY PARENTS!
SHE'S NICE, TOO.
GIVE IT UP, MIKE. I AM NOT GONNA DATE TRACEY WELLS!!
WHY NOT?
'CAUSE SHE'S CRAZY ABOUT MARTIN BEAN!
LYNN

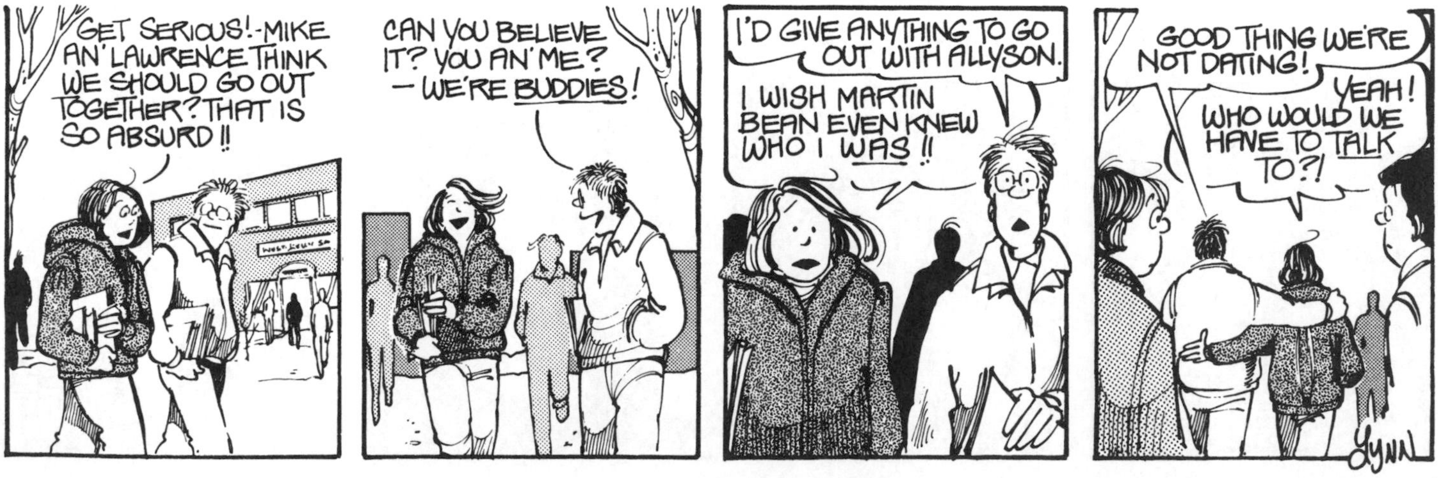
GET SERIOUS!-MIKE AN' LAWRENCE THINK WE SHOULD GO OUT TOGETHER? THAT IS SO ABSURD!!
CAN YOU BELIEVE IT? YOU AN' ME? — WE'RE BUDDIES!
I'D GIVE ANYTHING TO GO OUT WITH ALLYSON.
I WISH MARTIN BEAN EVEN KNEW WHO I WAS!!
GOOD THING WE'RE NOT DATING!
YEAH! WHO WOULD WE HAVE TO TALK TO?!
LYNN

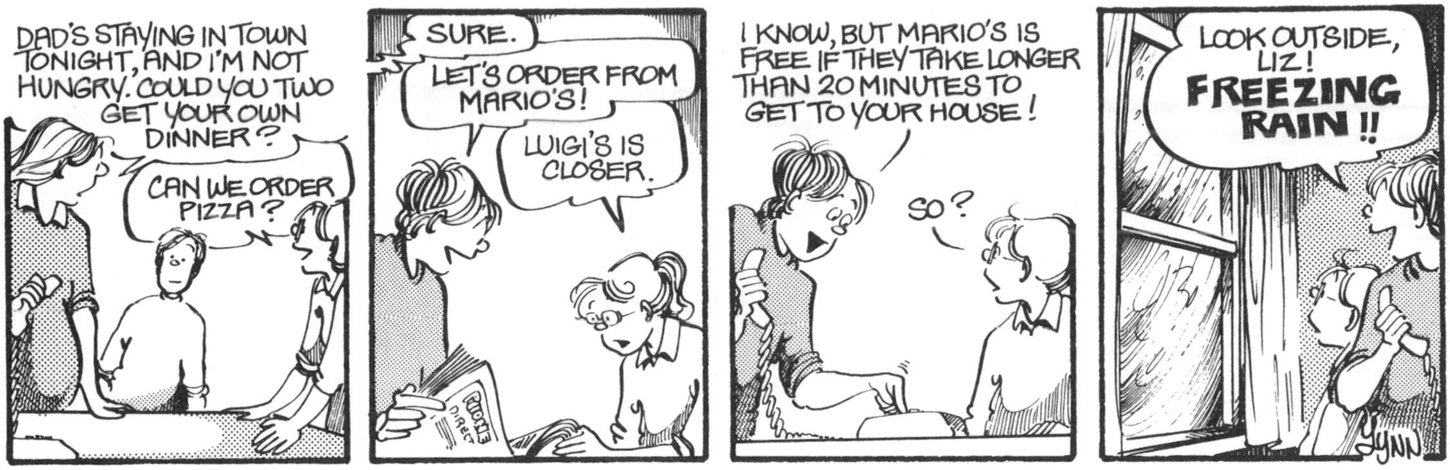
DAD'S STAYING IN TOWN TONIGHT, AND I'M NOT HUNGRY. COULD YOU TWO GET YOUR OWN DINNER?
CAN WE ORDER PIZZA?
SURE.
LET'S ORDER FROM MARIO'S!
LUIGI'S IS CLOSER.
I KNOW, BUT MARIO'S IS FREE IF THEY TAKE LONGER THAN 20 MINUTES TO GET TO YOUR HOUSE!
SO?
LOOK OUTSIDE, LIZ!
FREEZING RAIN!!
LYNN

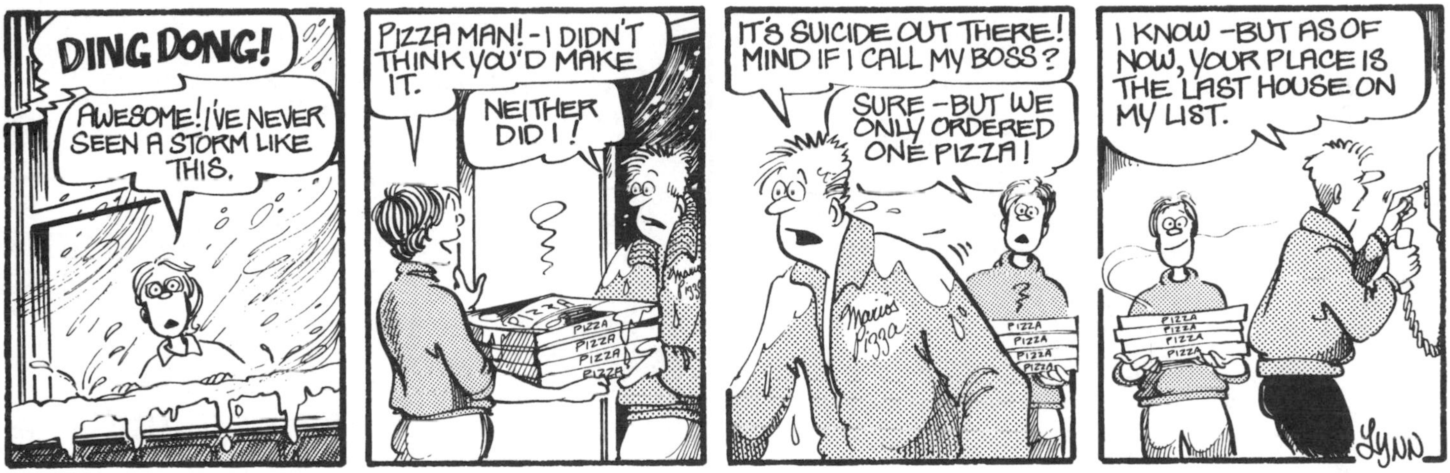
DING DONG!
AWESOME! I'VE NEVER SEEN A STORM LIKE THIS.
PIZZA MAN! - I DIDN'T THINK YOU'D MAKE IT.
NEITHER DID I!
IT'S SUICIDE OUT THERE! MIND IF I CALL MY BOSS?
SURE - BUT WE ONLY ORDERED ONE PIZZA!
I KNOW - BUT AS OF NOW, YOUR PLACE IS THE LAST HOUSE ON MY LIST.
LYNN

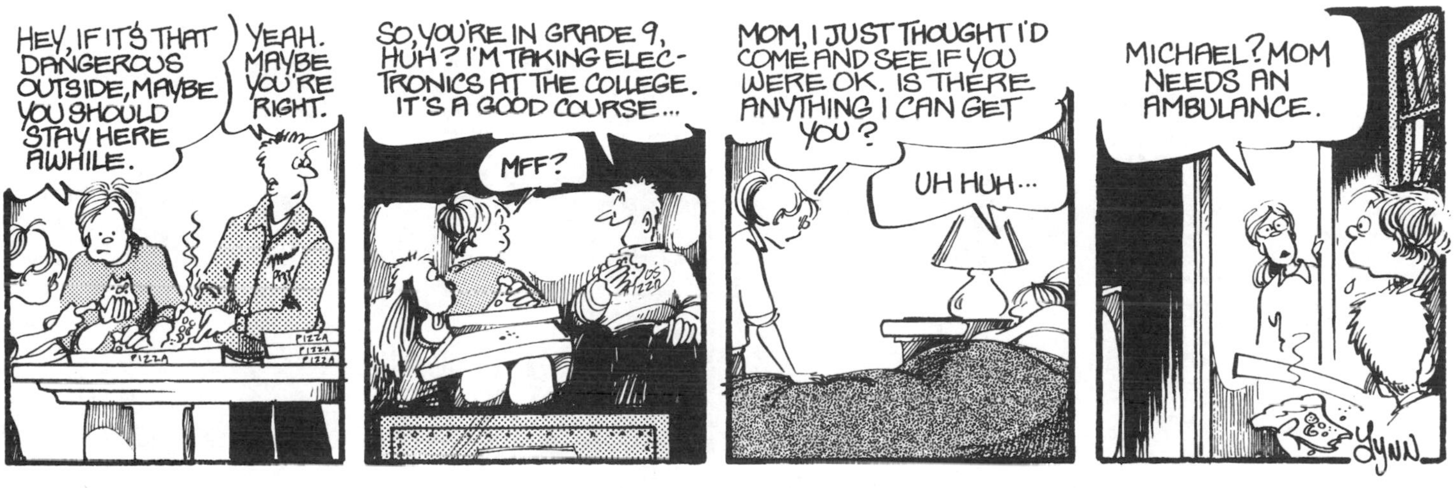
HEY, IF IT'S THAT DANGEROUS OUTSIDE, MAYBE YOU SHOULD STAY HERE AWHILE.
YEAH. MAYBE YOU'RE RIGHT.
SO, YOU'RE IN GRADE 9, HUH? I'M TAKING ELEC-TRONICS AT THE COLLEGE. IT'S A GOOD COURSE...
MFF?
MOM, I JUST THOUGHT I'D COME AND SEE IF YOU WERE OK. IS THERE ANYTHING I CAN GET YOU?
UH HUH...
MICHAEL? MOM NEEDS AN AMBULANCE.
LYNN

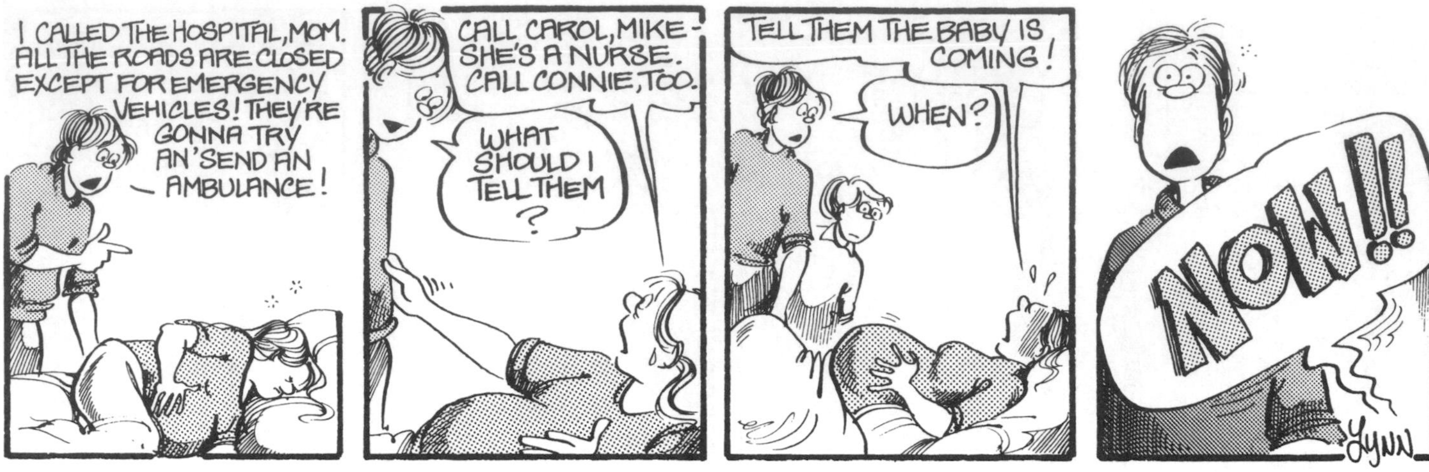
I CALLED THE HOSPITAL, MOM. ALL THE ROADS ARE CLOSED EXCEPT FOR EMERGENCY VEHICLES! THEY'RE GONNA TRY AN' SEND AN AMBULANCE!
CALL CAROL, MIKE- SHE'S A NURSE. CALL CONNIE, TOO.
WHAT SHOULD I TELL THEM?
TELL THEM THE BABY IS COMING!
WHEN?
NOW!!
LYNN

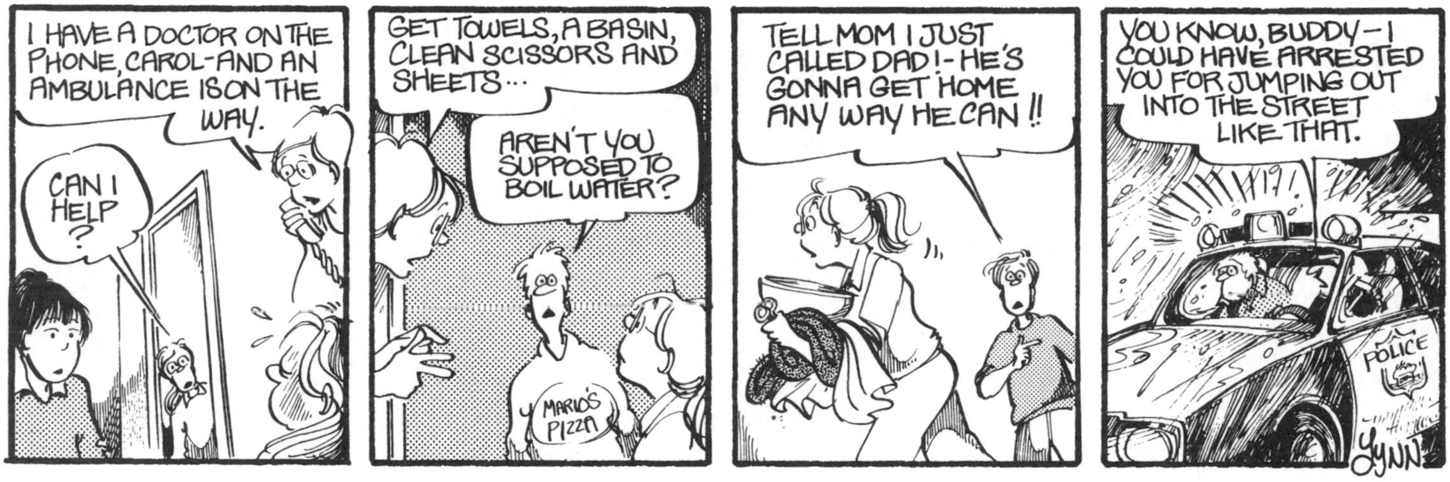
I HAVE A DOCTOR ON THE PHONE, CAROL-AND AN AMBULANCE IS ON THE WAY.
CAN I HELP?
GET TOWELS, A BASIN, CLEAN SCISSORS AND SHEETS...
AREN'T YOU SUPPOSED TO BOIL WATER?
MARIO'S PIZZA
TELL MOM I JUST CALLED DAD!- HE'S GONNA GET HOME ANY WAY HE CAN!!
YOU KNOW, BUDDY-I COULD HAVE ARRESTED YOU FOR JUMPING OUT INTO THE STREET LIKE THAT.
POLICE
LYNN

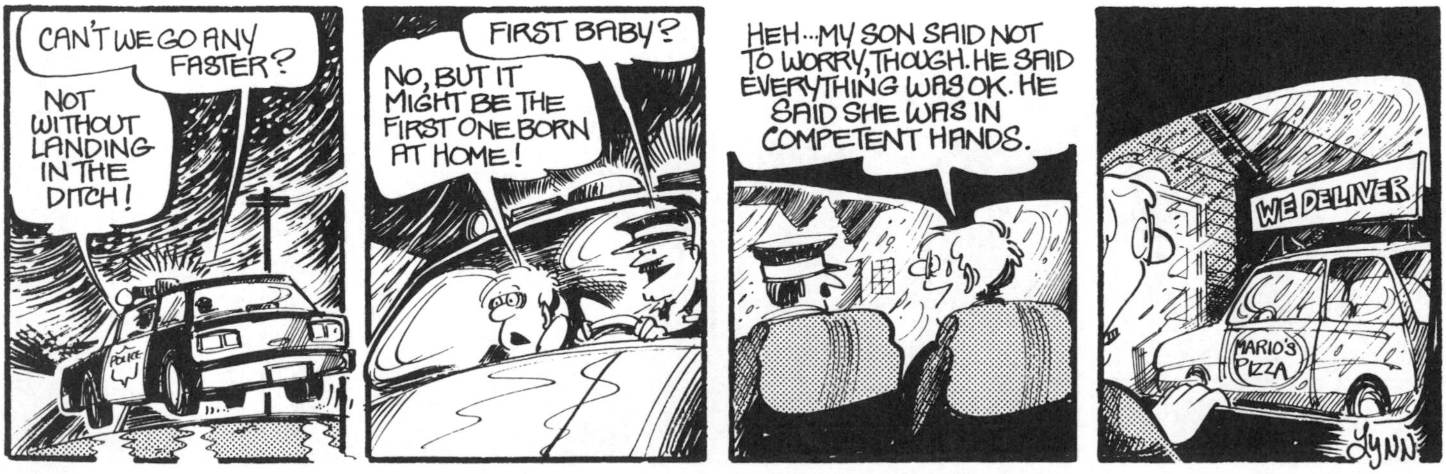
CAN'T WE GO ANY FASTER?
NOT WITHOUT LANDING IN THE DITCH!
FIRST BABY?
NO, BUT IT MIGHT BE THE FIRST ONE BORN AT HOME!
HEH...MY SON SAID NOT TO WORRY, THOUGH. HE SAID EVERYTHING WAS OK. HE SAID SHE WAS IN COMPETENT HANDS.
WE DELIVER
MARIO'S PIZZA
LYNN

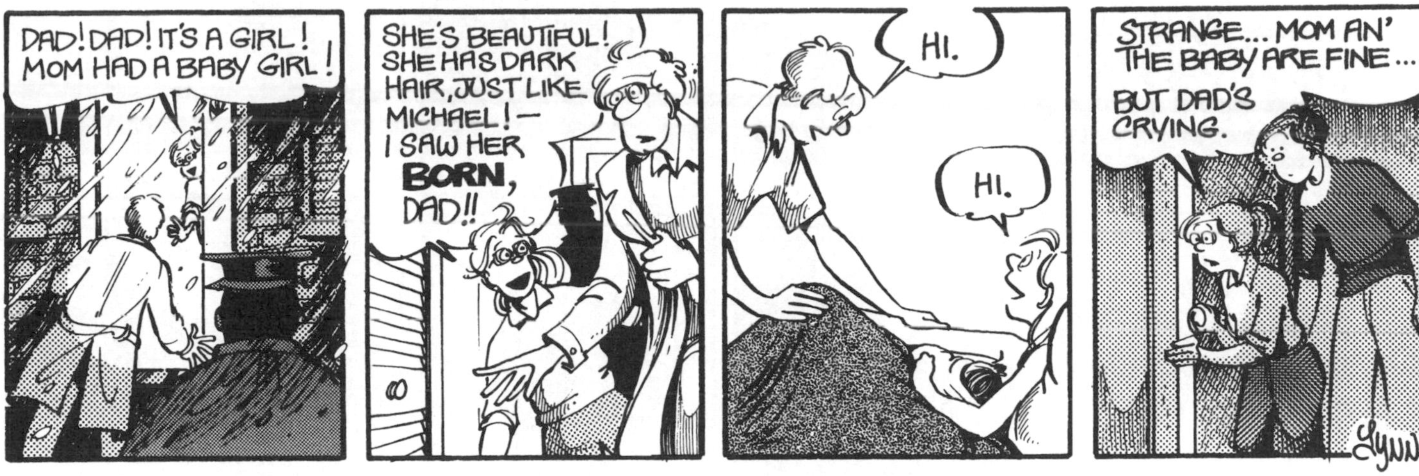
DAD! DAD! IT'S A GIRL! MOM HAD A BABY GIRL!
SHE'S BEAUTIFUL! SHE HAS DARK HAIR, JUST LIKE MICHAEL! — I SAW HER BORN, DAD!!
HI.
HI.
STRANGE... MOM AN' THE BABY ARE FINE... BUT DAD'S CRYING.
LYNN

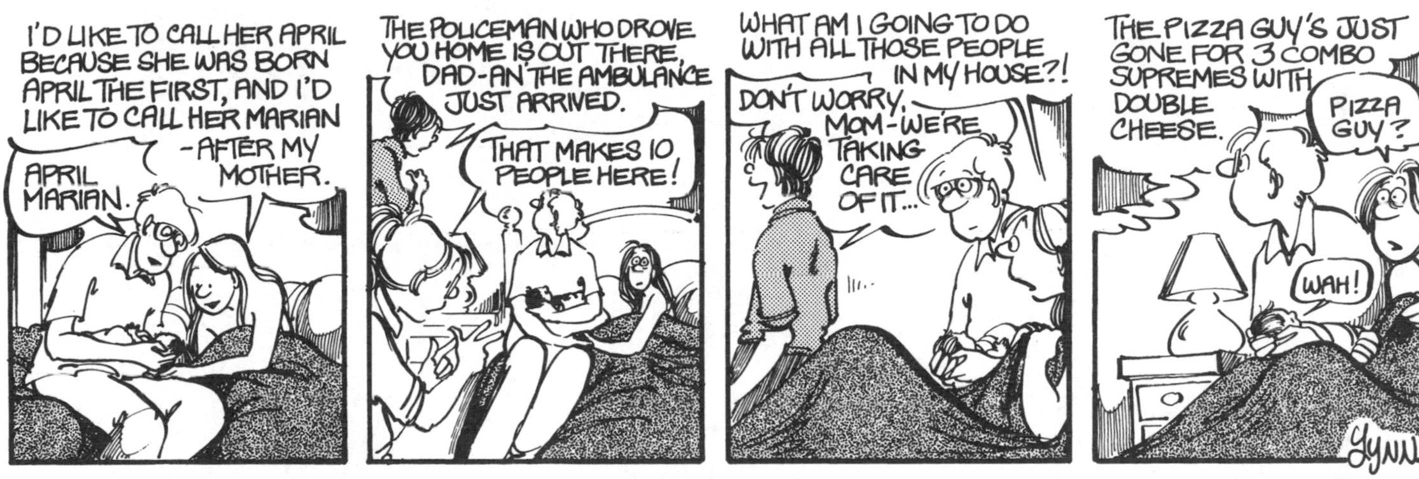
I'D LIKE TO CALL HER APRIL BECAUSE SHE WAS BORN APRIL THE FIRST, AND I'D LIKE TO CALL HER MARIAN - AFTER MY MOTHER.
APRIL MARIAN.
THE POLICEMAN WHO DROVE YOU HOME IS OUT THERE, DAD-AN' THE AMBULANCE JUST ARRIVED.
THAT MAKES 10 PEOPLE HERE!
WHAT AM I GOING TO DO WITH ALL THOSE PEOPLE IN MY HOUSE?!
DON'T WORRY, MOM - WE'RE TAKING CARE OF IT...
THE PIZZA GUY'S JUST GONE FOR 3 COMBO SUPREMES WITH DOUBLE CHEESE.
PIZZA GUY?
WAH!
LYNN

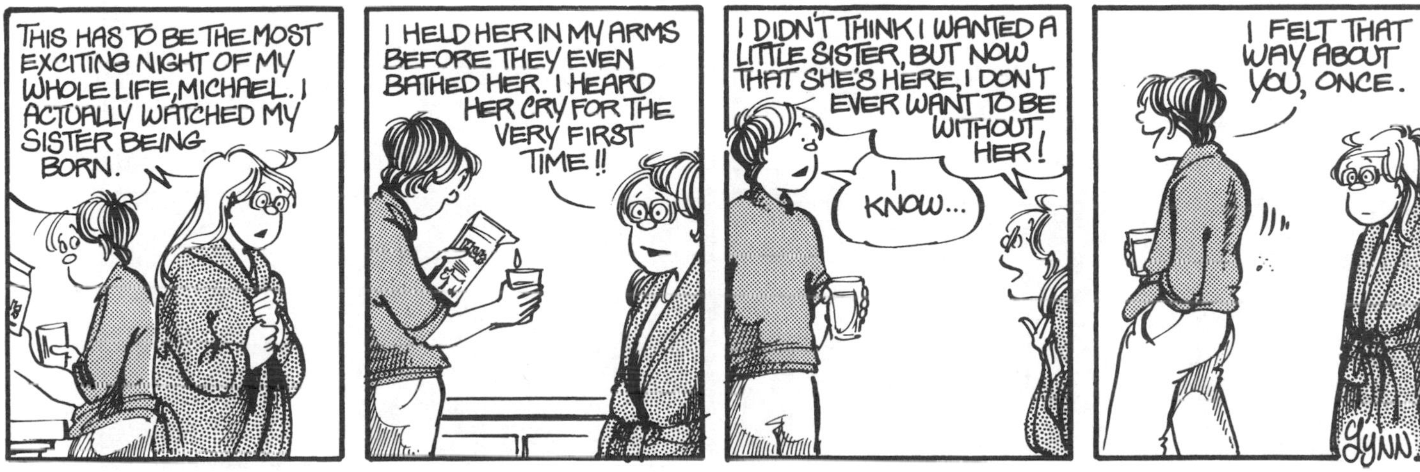
THIS HAS TO BE THE MOST EXCITING NIGHT OF MY WHOLE LIFE, MICHAEL. I ACTUALLY WATCHED MY SISTER BEING BORN.
I HELD HER IN MY ARMS BEFORE THEY EVEN BATHED HER. I HEARD HER CRY FOR THE VERY FIRST TIME!!
I DIDN'T THINK I WANTED A LITTLE SISTER, BUT NOW THAT SHE'S HERE, I DON'T EVER WANT TO BE WITHOUT HER!
I KNOW...
I FELT THAT WAY ABOUT YOU, ONCE.
LYNN

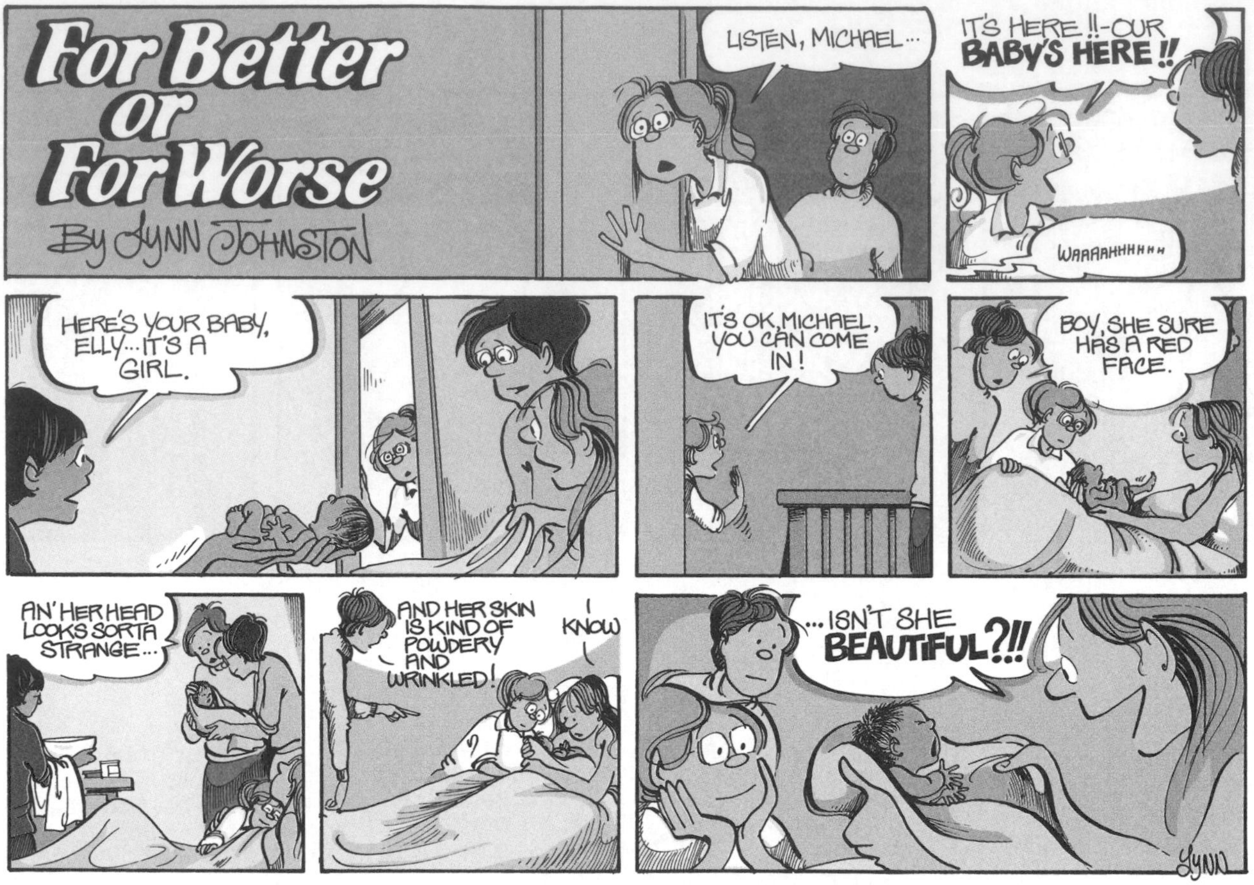
For Better or For Worse
By Lynn Johnston
LISTEN, MICHAEL...
IT'S HERE !!-OUR BABY'S HERE !!
WAAAAHHHHHH
HERE'S YOUR BABY, ELLY... IT'S A GIRL.
IT'S OK, MICHAEL, YOU CAN COME IN!
BOY, SHE SURE HAS A RED FACE.
AN' HER HEAD LOOKS SORTA STRANGE...
AND HER SKIN IS KIND OF POWDERY AND WRINKLED!
I KNOW
...ISN'T SHE BEAUTIFUL?!!
Lynn

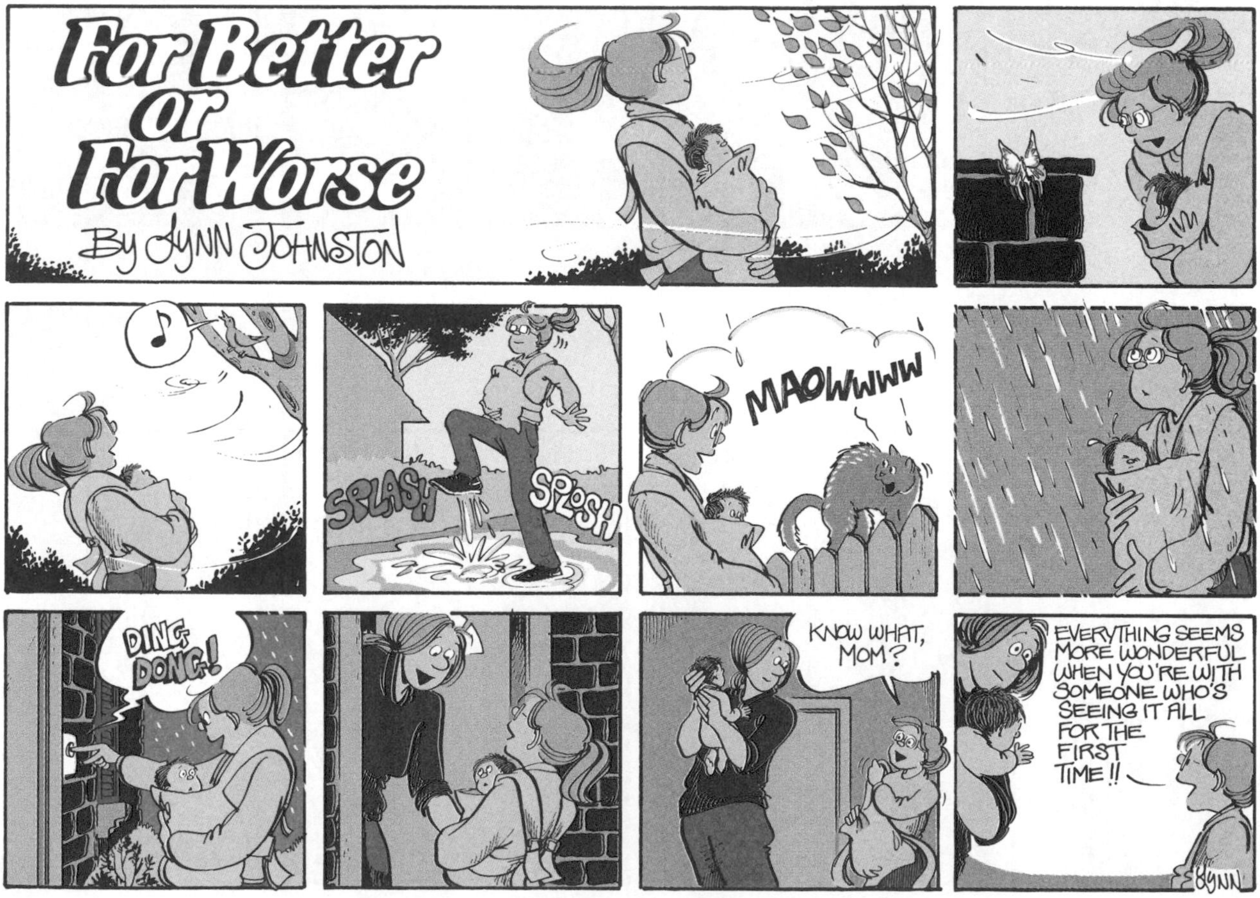
For Better or For Worse
By Lynn Johnston
SPLASH
SPLOSH
MAOWWWW
DING DONG!
KNOW WHAT, MOM?
EVERYTHING SEEMS MORE WONDERFUL WHEN YOU'RE WITH SOMEONE WHO'S SEEING IT ALL FOR THE FIRST TIME!!
Lynn

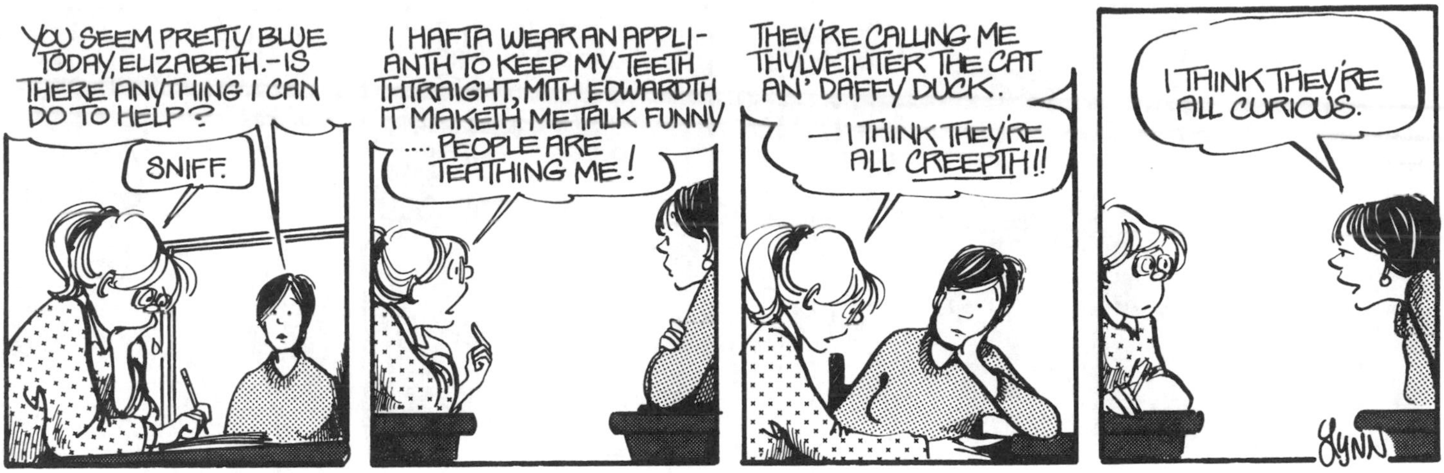
YOU SEEM PRETTY BLUE TODAY, ELIZABETH.–IS THERE ANYTHING I CAN DO TO HELP?
SNIFF.
I HAFTA WEAR AN APPLIANTH TO KEEP MY TEETH THTRAIGHT, MITH EDWARDTH. IT MAKETH ME TALK FUNNY .... PEOPLE ARE TEATHING ME!
THEY'RE CALLING ME THYLVETHTER THE CAT AN' DAFFY DUCK.
—I THINK THEY'RE ALL CREEPTH!!
I THINK THEY'RE ALL CURIOUS.
LYNN

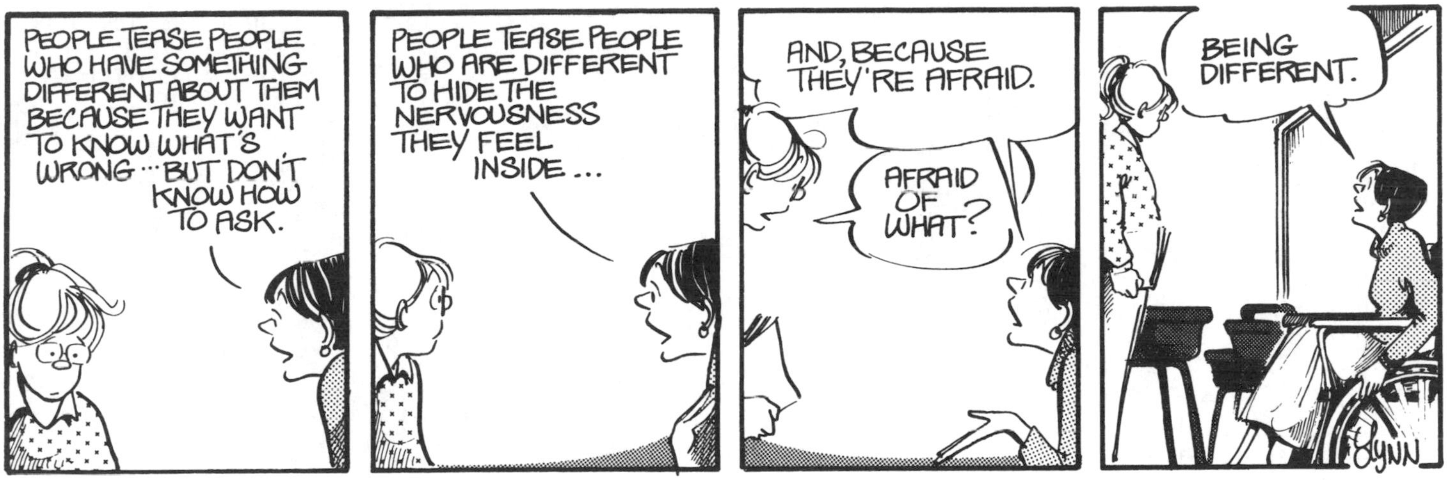
PEOPLE TEASE PEOPLE WHO HAVE SOMETHING DIFFERENT ABOUT THEM BECAUSE THEY WANT TO KNOW WHAT'S WRONG ··· BUT DON'T KNOW HOW TO ASK.
PEOPLE TEASE PEOPLE WHO ARE DIFFERENT TO HIDE THE NERVOUSNESS THEY FEEL INSIDE ...
AND, BECAUSE THEY'RE AFRAID.
AFRAID OF WHAT?
BEING DIFFERENT.
LYNN

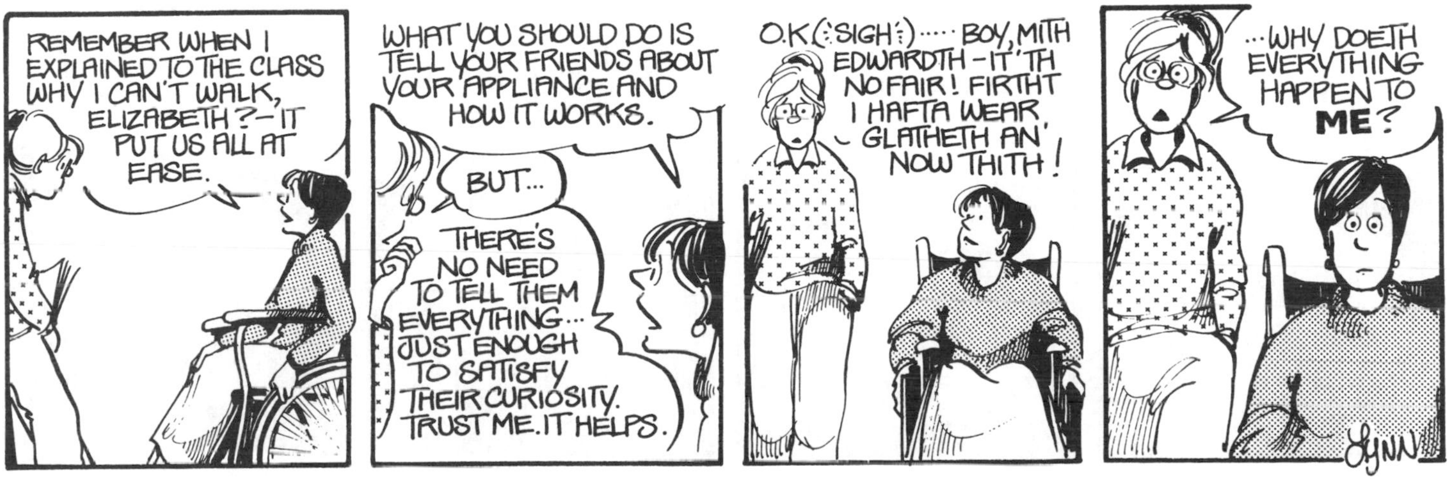
REMEMBER WHEN I EXPLAINED TO THE CLASS WHY I CAN'T WALK, ELIZABETH?–IT PUT US ALL AT EASE.
WHAT YOU SHOULD DO IS TELL YOUR FRIENDS ABOUT YOUR APPLIANCE AND HOW IT WORKS.
BUT...
THERE'S NO NEED TO TELL THEM EVERYTHING... JUST ENOUGH TO SATISFY THEIR CURIOSITY. TRUST ME. IT HELPS.
O.K (SIGH) ····· BOY, MITH EDWARDTH – IT'TH NO FAIR! FIRTHT I HAFTA WEAR GLATHETH AN' NOW THITH!
...WHY DOETH EVERYTHING HAPPEN TO ME?
LYNN

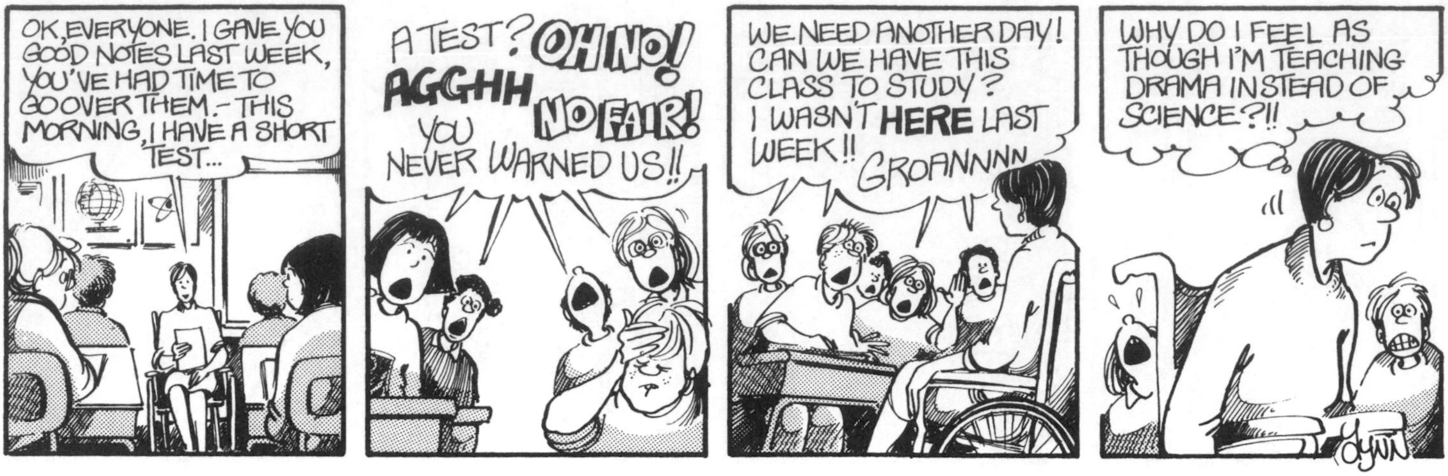
OK, EVERYONE. I GAVE YOU GOOD NOTES LAST WEEK, YOU'VE HAD TIME TO GO OVER THEM.- THIS MORNING, I HAVE A SHORT TEST...
A TEST?
OH NO!
AGGHH
NO FAIR!
YOU NEVER WARNED US!!
WE NEED ANOTHER DAY! CAN WE HAVE THIS CLASS TO STUDY? I WASN'T HERE LAST WEEK!!
GROANNNN
WHY DO I FEEL AS THOUGH I'M TEACHING DRAMA INSTEAD OF SCIENCE?!!
LYNN

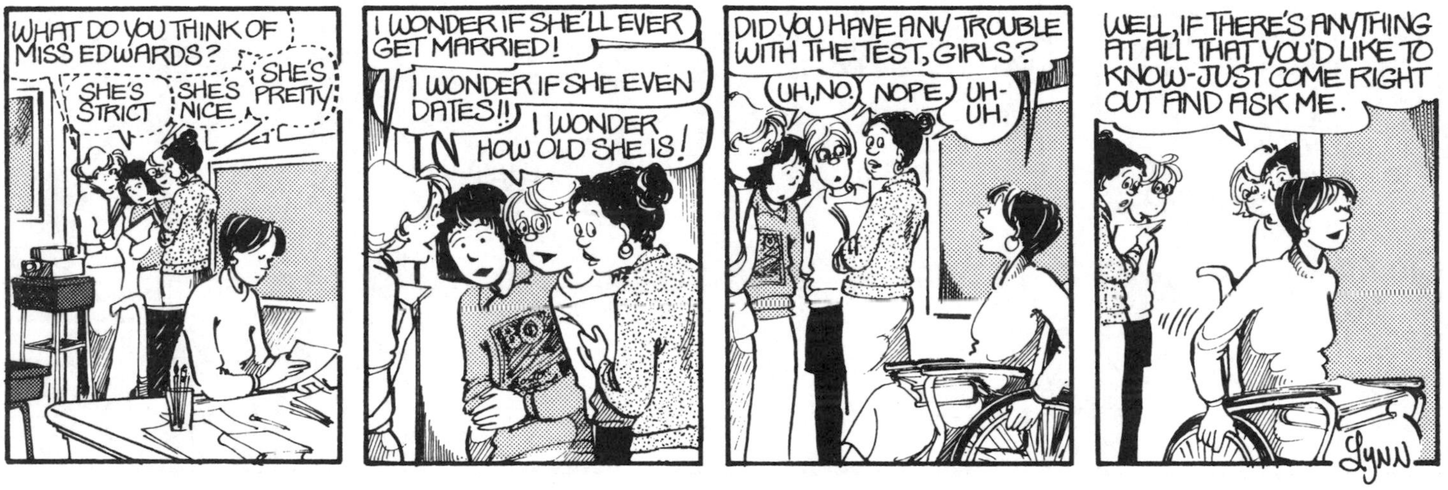
WHAT DO YOU THINK OF MISS EDWARDS?
SHE'S STRICT
SHE'S NICE
SHE'S PRETTY
I WONDER IF SHE'LL EVER GET MARRIED!
I WONDER IF SHE EVEN DATES!!
I WONDER HOW OLD SHE IS!
DID YOU HAVE ANY TROUBLE WITH THE TEST, GIRLS?
UH, NO.
NOPE.
UH-UH.
WELL, IF THERE'S ANYTHING AT ALL THAT YOU'D LIKE TO KNOW-JUST COME RIGHT OUT AND ASK ME.
LYNN

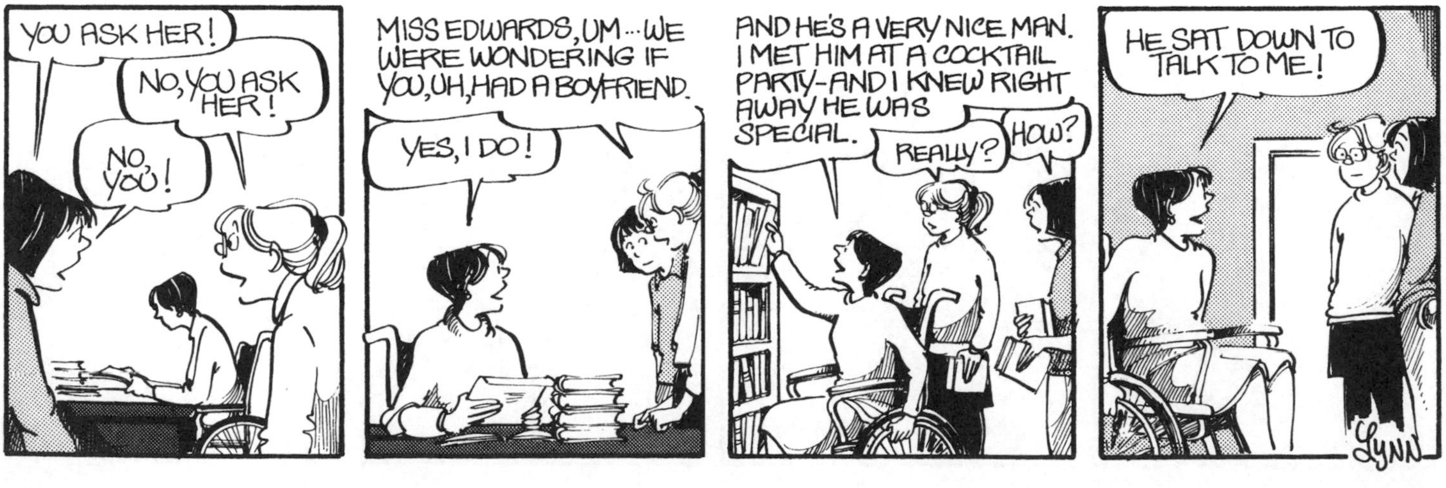
YOU ASK HER!
NO, YOU ASK HER!
NO, YOU!
MISS EDWARDS, UM...WE WERE WONDERING IF YOU, UH, HAD A BOYFRIEND.
YES, I DO!
AND HE'S A VERY NICE MAN. I MET HIM AT A COCKTAIL PARTY-AND I KNEW RIGHT AWAY HE WAS SPECIAL.
REALLY?
HOW?
HE SAT DOWN TO TALK TO ME!
LYNN

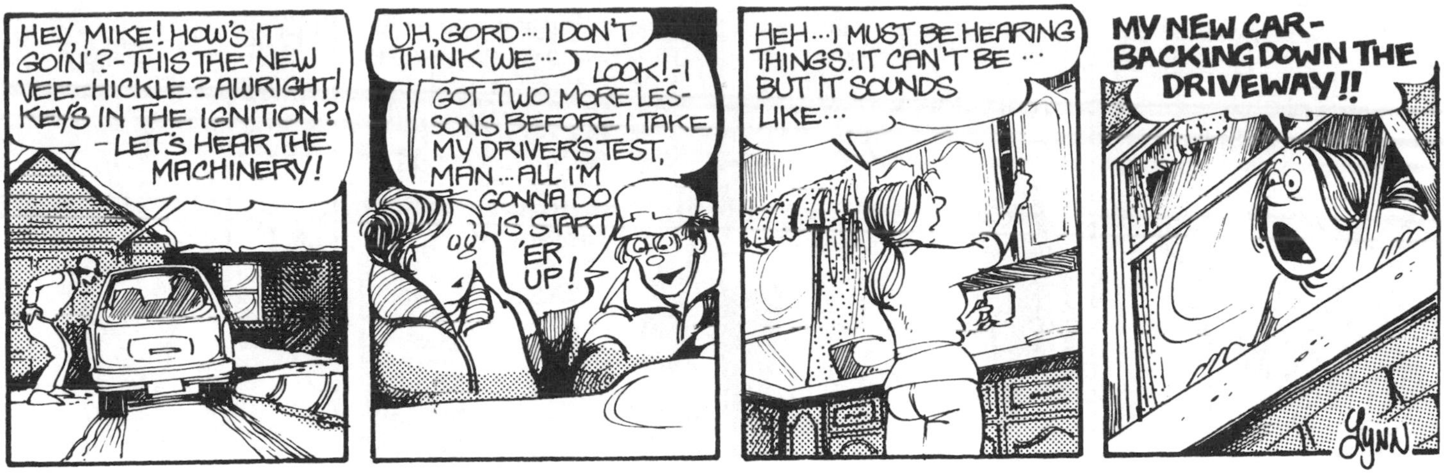
HEY, MIKE! HOW'S IT GOIN'?-THIS THE NEW VEE-HICKLE? AWRIGHT! KEY'S IN THE IGNITION? - LET'S HEAR THE MACHINERY!
UH, GORD... I DON'T THINK WE...
LOOK!-I GOT TWO MORE LESSONS BEFORE I TAKE MY DRIVER'S TEST, MAN... ALL I'M GONNA DO IS START 'ER UP!
HEH... I MUST BE HEARING THINGS. IT CAN'T BE ... BUT IT SOUNDS LIKE...
MY NEW CAR-BACKING DOWN THE DRIVEWAY!!
Lynn

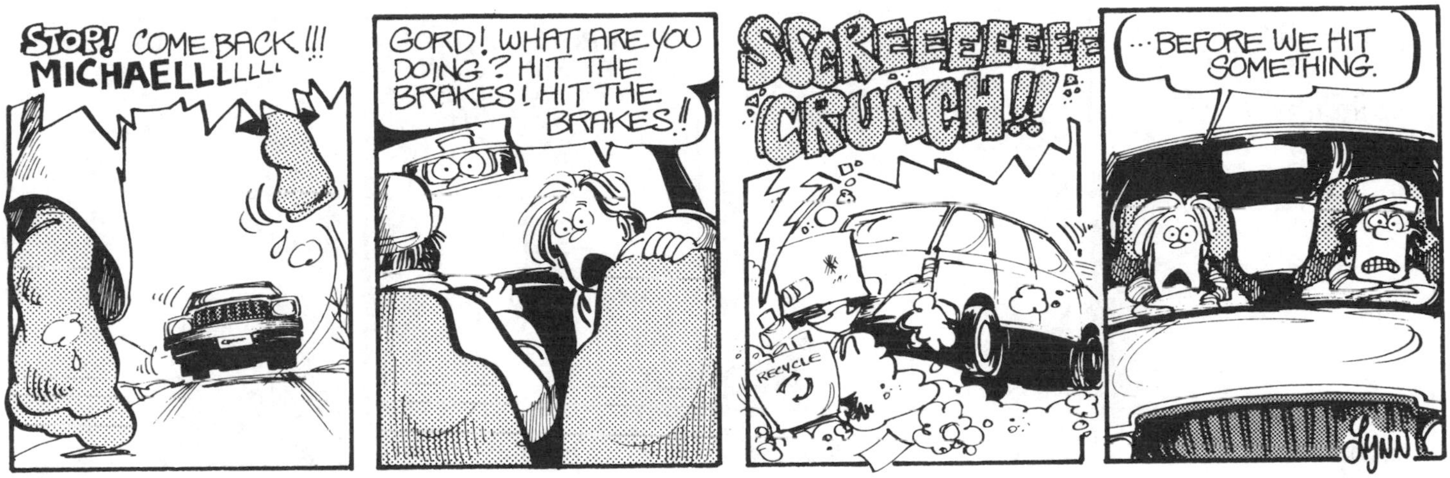
STOP! COME BACK!!! MICHAELLLLLLL
GORD! WHAT ARE YOU DOING? HIT THE BRAKES! HIT THE BRAKES!!
SSCREEEEEEEE
CRUNCH!!
RECYCLE
...BEFORE WE HIT SOMETHING.
Lynn

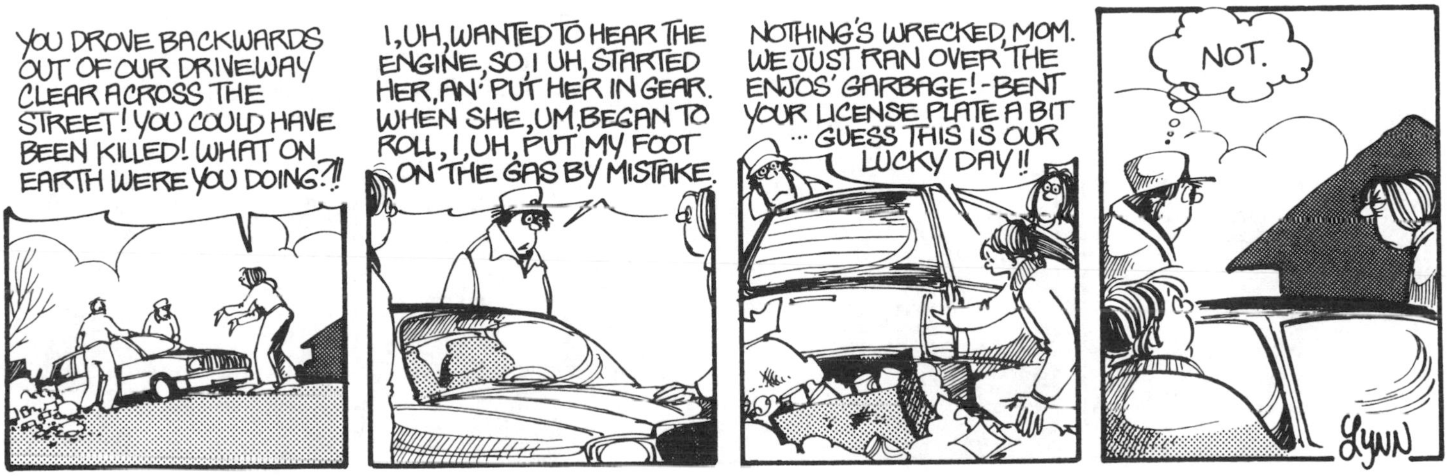
YOU DROVE BACKWARDS OUT OF OUR DRIVEWAY CLEAR ACROSS THE STREET! YOU COULD HAVE BEEN KILLED! WHAT ON EARTH WERE YOU DOING?!!
I, UH, WANTED TO HEAR THE ENGINE, SO, I UH, STARTED HER, AN' PUT HER IN GEAR. WHEN SHE, UM, BEGAN TO ROLL, I, UH, PUT MY FOOT ON THE GAS BY MISTAKE.
NOTHING'S WRECKED, MOM. WE JUST RAN OVER THE ENJOS' GARBAGE!-BENT YOUR LICENSE PLATE A BIT ... GUESS THIS IS OUR LUCKY DAY!!
NOT.
Lynn

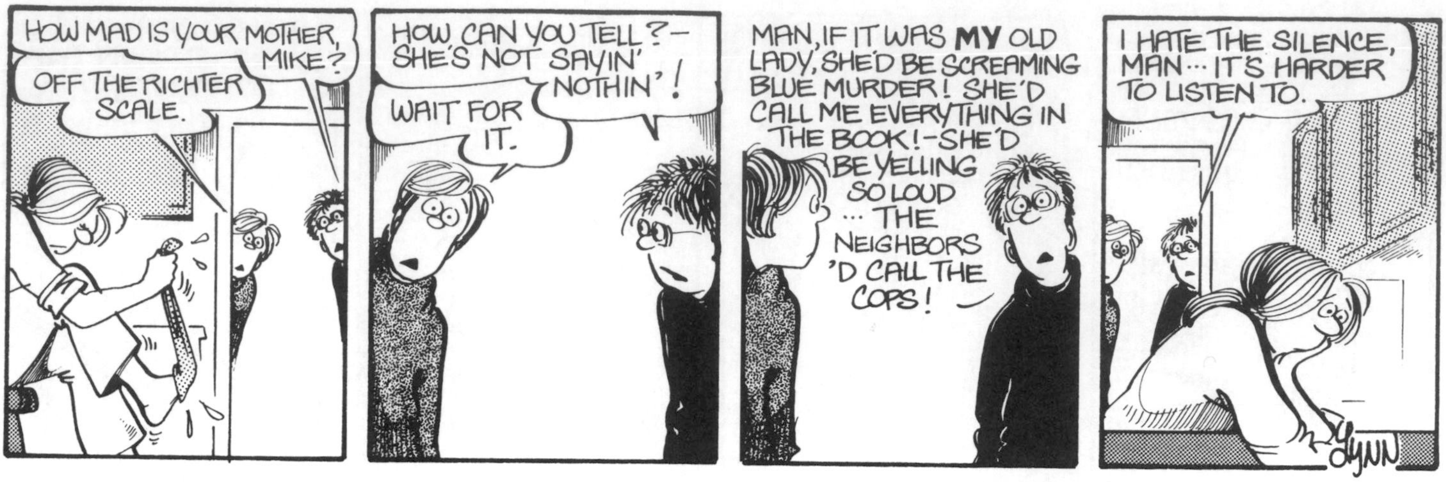
HOW MAD IS YOUR MOTHER, MIKE?
OFF THE RICHTER SCALE.
HOW CAN YOU TELL?—SHE'S NOT SAYIN' NOTHIN'!
WAIT FOR IT.
MAN, IF IT WAS MY OLD LADY, SHE'D BE SCREAMING BLUE MURDER! SHE'D CALL ME EVERYTHING IN THE BOOK!—SHE'D BE YELLING SO LOUD ... THE NEIGHBORS 'D CALL THE COPS!
I HATE THE SILENCE, MAN ... IT'S HARDER TO LISTEN TO.
LYNN

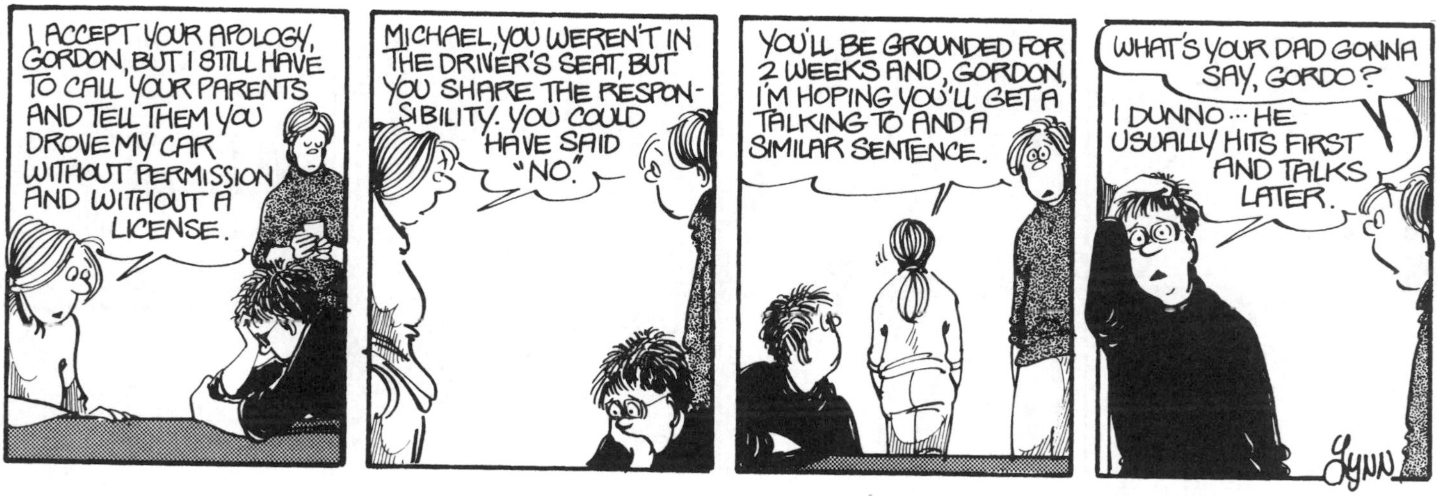
I ACCEPT YOUR APOLOGY, GORDON, BUT I STILL HAVE TO CALL YOUR PARENTS AND TELL THEM YOU DROVE MY CAR WITHOUT PERMISSION AND WITHOUT A LICENSE.
MICHAEL, YOU WEREN'T IN THE DRIVER'S SEAT, BUT YOU SHARE THE RESPONSIBILITY. YOU COULD HAVE SAID "NO."
YOU'LL BE GROUNDED FOR 2 WEEKS AND, GORDON, I'M HOPING YOU'LL GET A TALKING TO AND A SIMILAR SENTENCE.
WHAT'S YOUR DAD GONNA SAY, GORDO?
I DUNNO ... HE USUALLY HITS FIRST AND TALKS LATER.
LYNN

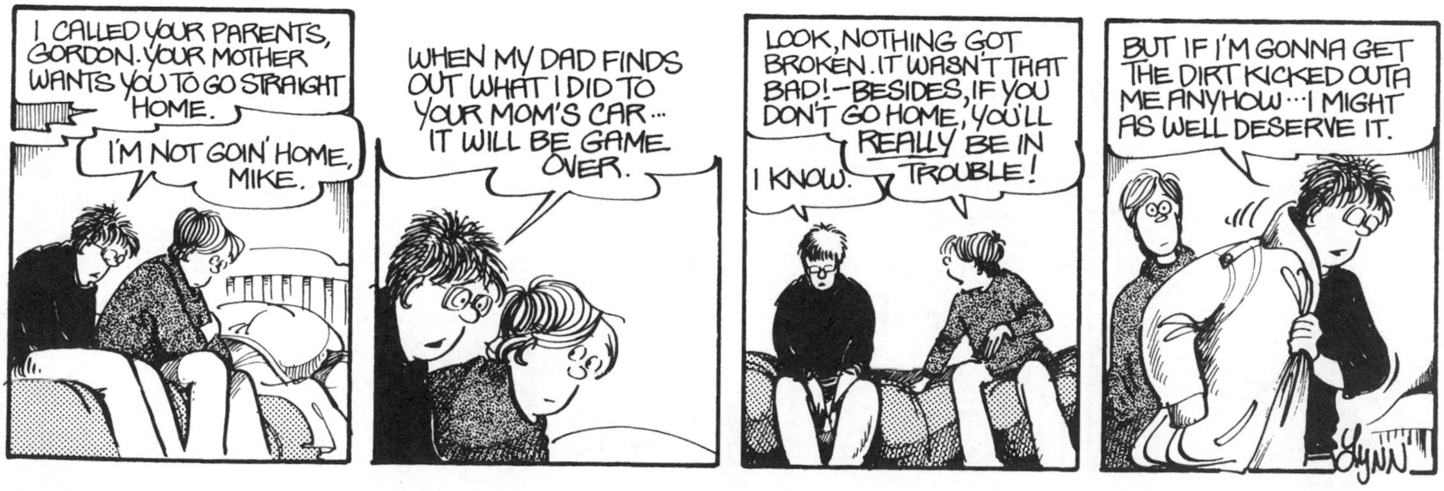
I CALLED YOUR PARENTS, GORDON. YOUR MOTHER WANTS YOU TO GO STRAIGHT HOME.
I'M NOT GOIN' HOME, MIKE.
WHEN MY DAD FINDS OUT WHAT I DID TO YOUR MOM'S CAR ... IT WILL BE GAME OVER.
LOOK, NOTHING GOT BROKEN. IT WASN'T THAT BAD!—BESIDES, IF YOU DON'T GO HOME, YOU'LL REALLY BE IN TROUBLE!
I KNOW.
BUT IF I'M GONNA GET THE DIRT KICKED OUTA ME ANYHOW ... I MIGHT AS WELL DESERVE IT.
LYNN

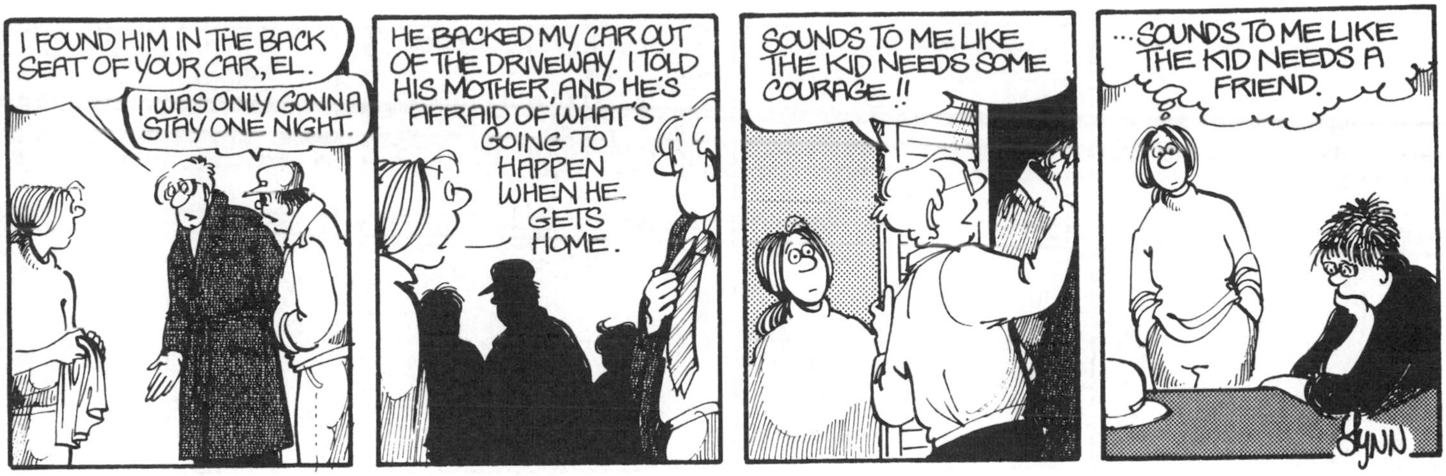
I FOUND HIM IN THE BACK SEAT OF YOUR CAR, EL.
I WAS ONLY GONNA STAY ONE NIGHT.
HE BACKED MY CAR OUT OF THE DRIVEWAY. I TOLD HIS MOTHER, AND HE'S AFRAID OF WHAT'S GOING TO HAPPEN WHEN HE GETS HOME.
SOUNDS TO ME LIKE THE KID NEEDS SOME COURAGE!!
...SOUNDS TO ME LIKE THE KID NEEDS A FRIEND.
LYNN

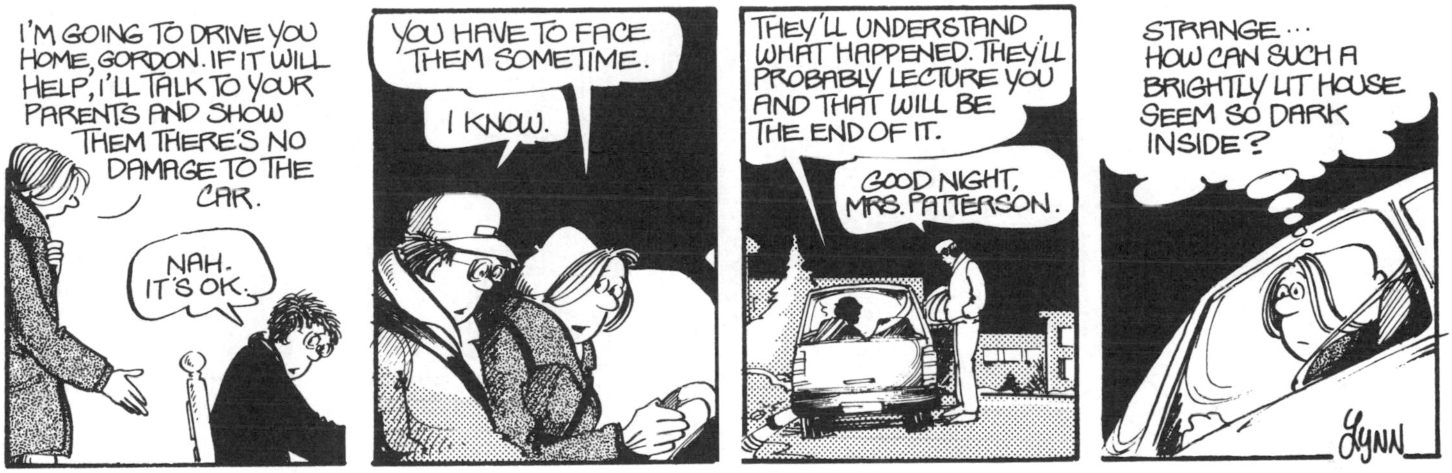
I'M GOING TO DRIVE YOU HOME, GORDON. IF IT WILL HELP, I'LL TALK TO YOUR PARENTS AND SHOW THEM THERE'S NO DAMAGE TO THE CAR.
NAH. IT'S OK.
YOU HAVE TO FACE THEM SOMETIME.
I KNOW.
THEY'LL UNDERSTAND WHAT HAPPENED. THEY'LL PROBABLY LECTURE YOU AND THAT WILL BE THE END OF IT.
GOOD NIGHT, MRS. PATTERSON.
STRANGE... HOW CAN SUCH A BRIGHTLY LIT HOUSE SEEM SO DARK INSIDE?
LYNN

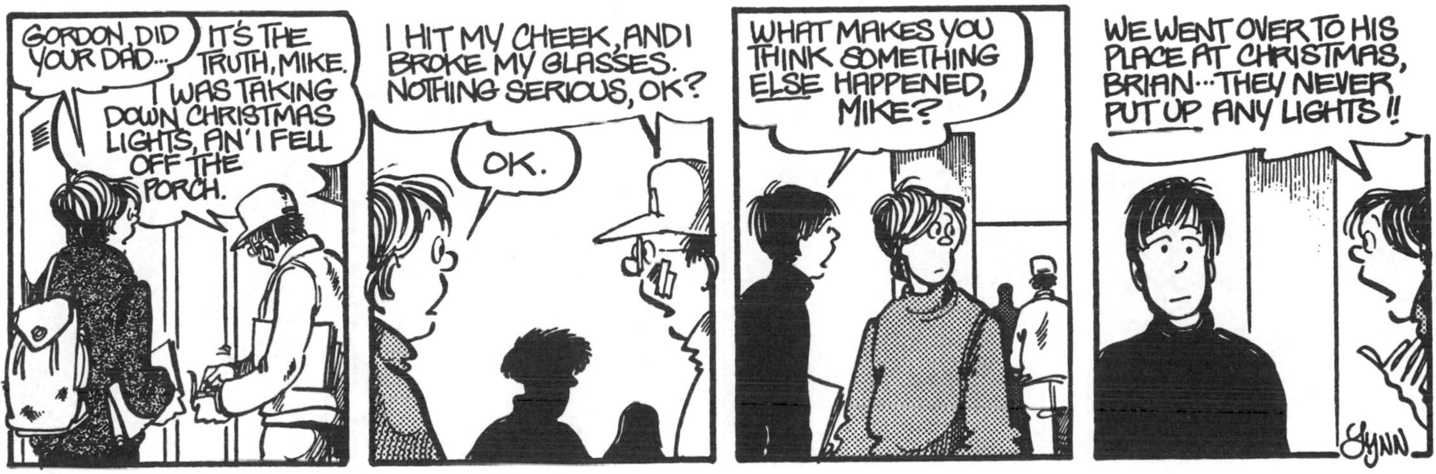
GORDON, DID YOUR DAD...
IT'S THE TRUTH, MIKE. I WAS TAKING DOWN CHRISTMAS LIGHTS, AN' I FELL OFF THE PORCH.
I HIT MY CHEEK, AND I BROKE MY GLASSES. NOTHING SERIOUS, OK?
OK.
WHAT MAKES YOU THINK SOMETHING ELSE HAPPENED, MIKE?
WE WENT OVER TO HIS PLACE AT CHRISTMAS, BRIAN... THEY NEVER PUT UP ANY LIGHTS!!
LYNN

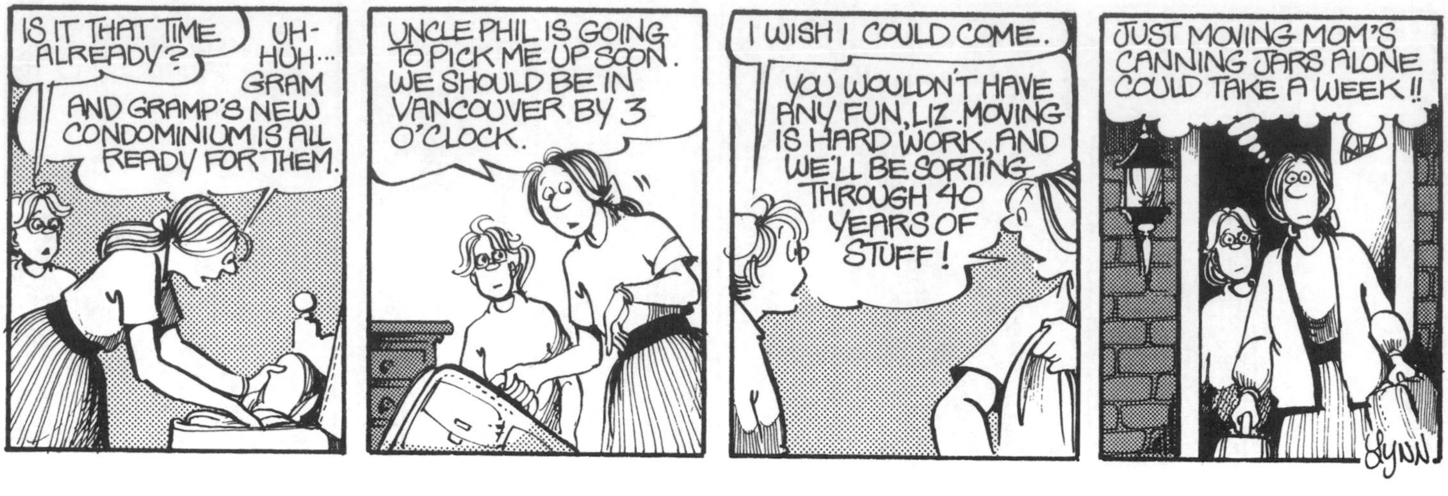
IS IT THAT TIME ALREADY?
UH-HUH... GRAM AND GRAMP'S NEW CONDOMINIUM IS ALL READY FOR THEM.
UNCLE PHIL IS GOING TO PICK ME UP SOON. WE SHOULD BE IN VANCOUVER BY 3 O'CLOCK.
I WISH I COULD COME.
YOU WOULDN'T HAVE ANY FUN, LIZ. MOVING IS HARD WORK, AND WE'LL BE SORTING THROUGH 40 YEARS OF STUFF!
JUST MOVING MOM'S CANNING JARS ALONE COULD TAKE A WEEK!!
LYNN

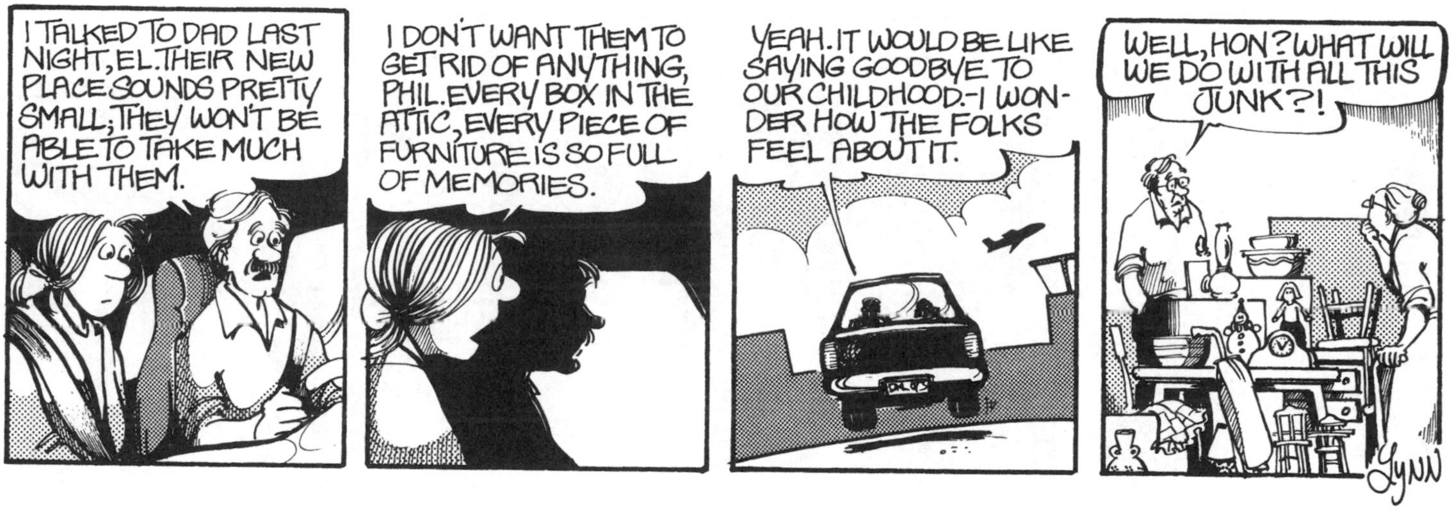
I TALKED TO DAD LAST NIGHT, EL. THEIR NEW PLACE SOUNDS PRETTY SMALL; THEY WON'T BE ABLE TO TAKE MUCH WITH THEM.
I DON'T WANT THEM TO GET RID OF ANYTHING, PHIL. EVERY BOX IN THE ATTIC, EVERY PIECE OF FURNITURE IS SO FULL OF MEMORIES.
YEAH. IT WOULD BE LIKE SAYING GOODBYE TO OUR CHILDHOOD.-I WONDER HOW THE FOLKS FEEL ABOUT IT.
WELL, HON? WHAT WILL WE DO WITH ALL THIS JUNK?!
LYNN

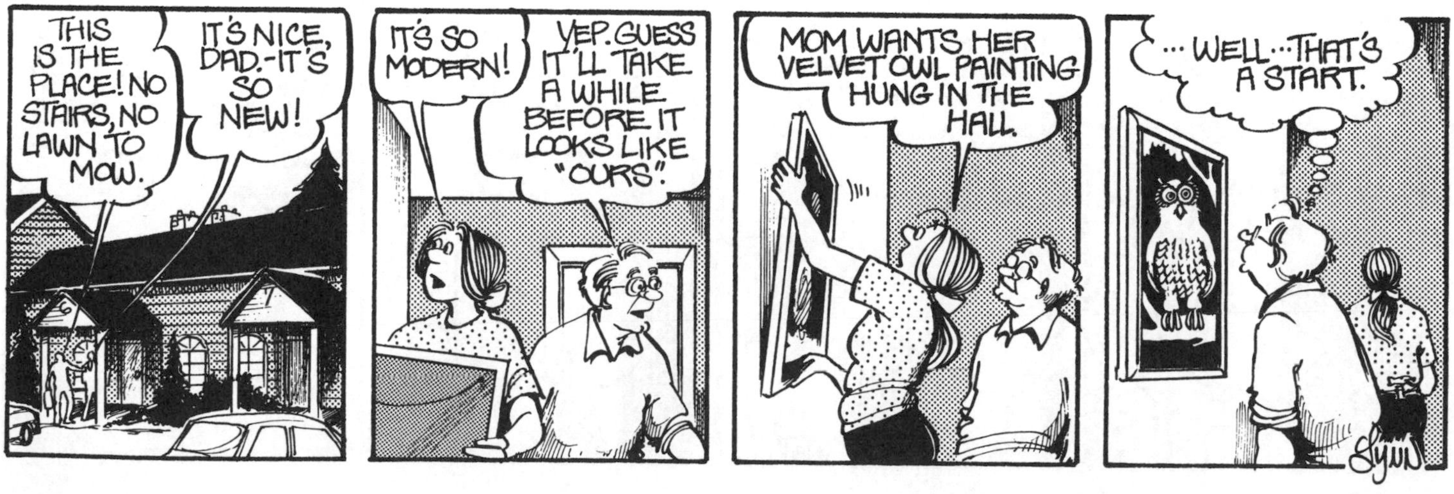
THIS IS THE PLACE! NO STAIRS, NO LAWN TO MOW.
IT'S NICE, DAD.-IT'S SO NEW!
IT'S SO MODERN!
YEP. GUESS IT'LL TAKE A WHILE BEFORE IT LOOKS LIKE "OURS".
MOM WANTS HER VELVET OWL PAINTING HUNG IN THE HALL.
...WELL...THAT'S A START.
LYNN

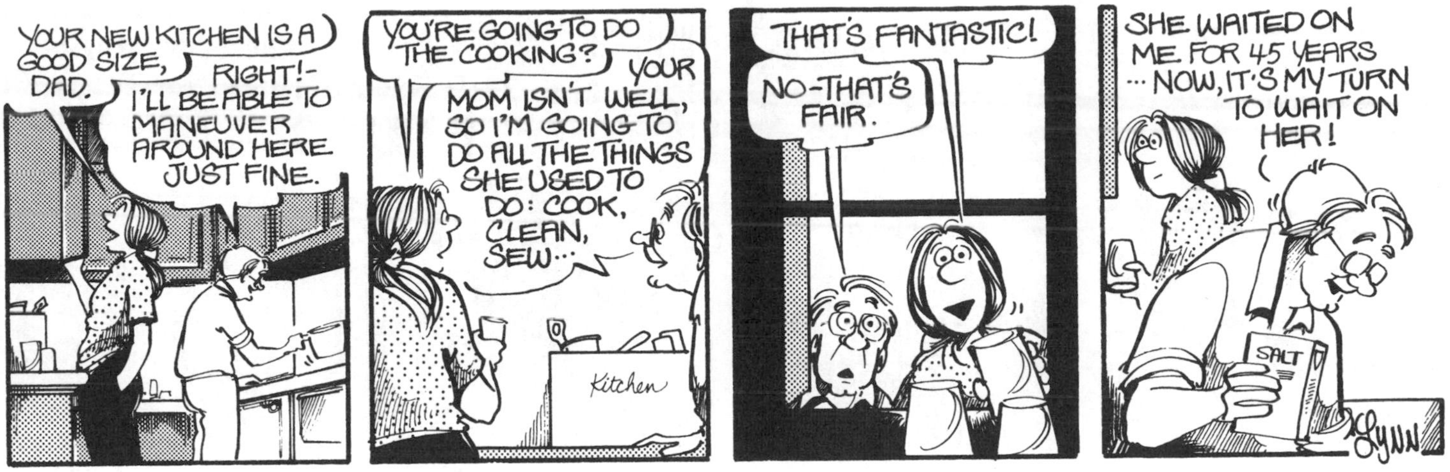
YOUR NEW KITCHEN IS A GOOD SIZE, DAD.
RIGHT!- I'LL BE ABLE TO MANEUVER AROUND HERE JUST FINE.
YOU'RE GOING TO DO THE COOKING?
YOUR MOM ISN'T WELL, SO I'M GOING TO DO ALL THE THINGS SHE USED TO DO: COOK, CLEAN, SEW...
Kitchen
THAT'S FANTASTIC!
NO-THAT'S FAIR.
SHE WAITED ON ME FOR 45 YEARS ... NOW, IT'S MY TURN TO WAIT ON HER!
SALT
Lynn

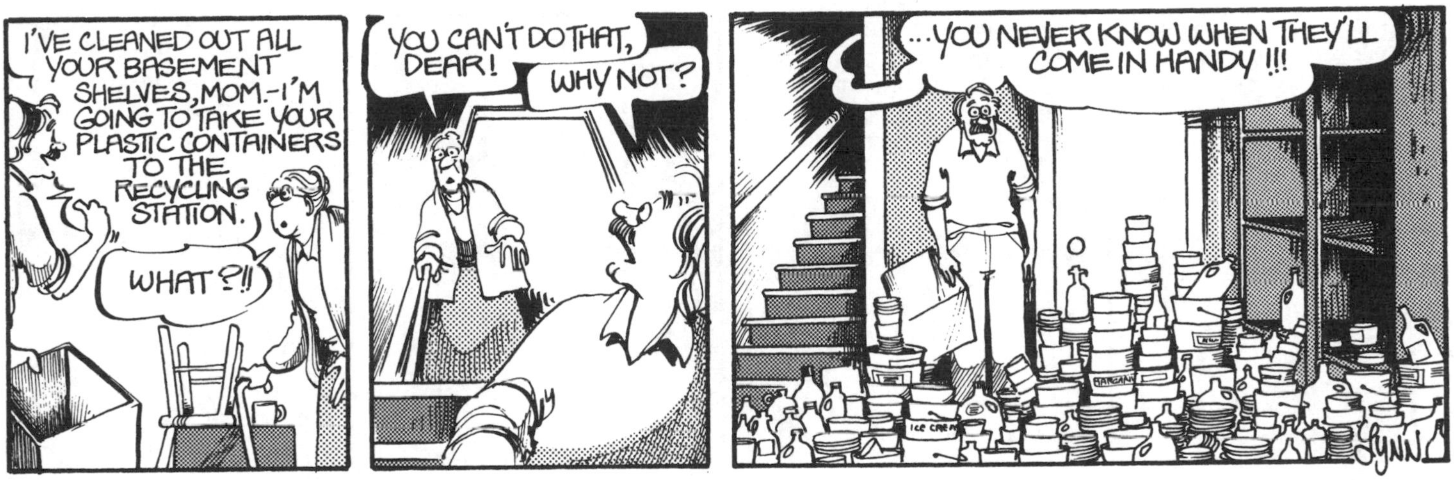
I'VE CLEANED OUT ALL YOUR BASEMENT SHELVES, MOM.- I'M GOING TO TAKE YOUR PLASTIC CONTAINERS TO THE RECYCLING STATION.
WHAT ?!!
YOU CAN'T DO THAT, DEAR!
WHY NOT?
...YOU NEVER KNOW WHEN THEY'LL COME IN HANDY !!!
Lynn

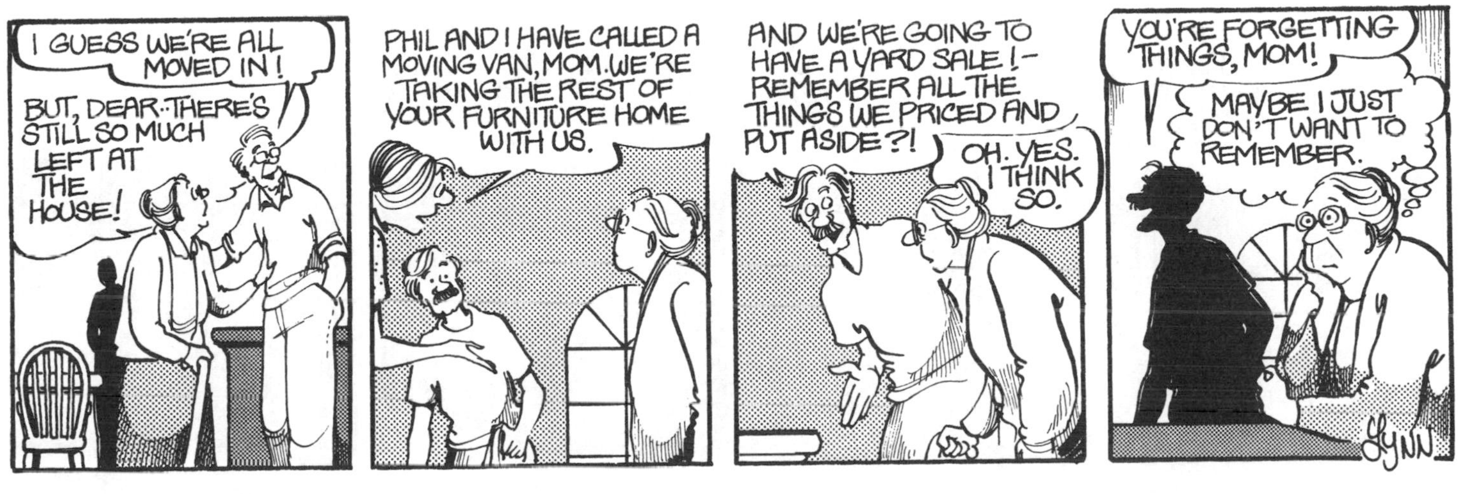
I GUESS WE'RE ALL MOVED IN!
BUT, DEAR: THERE'S STILL SO MUCH LEFT AT THE HOUSE!
PHIL AND I HAVE CALLED A MOVING VAN, MOM. WE'RE TAKING THE REST OF YOUR FURNITURE HOME WITH US.
AND WE'RE GOING TO HAVE A YARD SALE!- REMEMBER ALL THE THINGS WE PRICED AND PUT ASIDE?!
OH. YES. I THINK SO.
YOU'RE FORGETTING THINGS, MOM!
MAYBE I JUST DON'T WANT TO REMEMBER.
Lynn

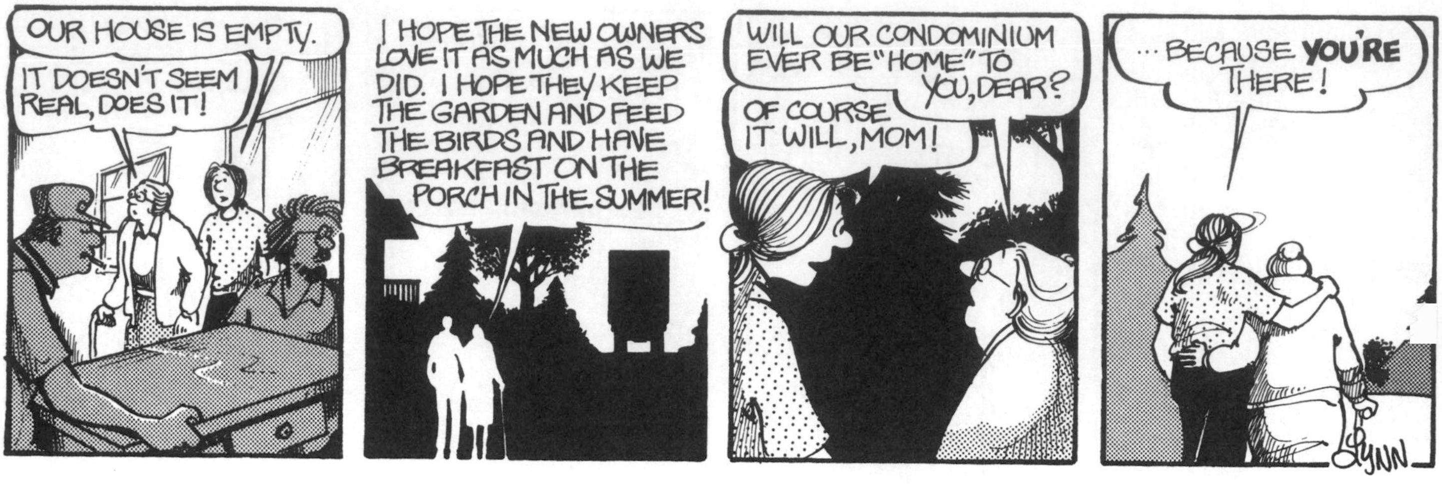
OUR HOUSE IS EMPTY.
IT DOESN'T SEEM REAL, DOES IT!
I HOPE THE NEW OWNERS LOVE IT AS MUCH AS WE DID. I HOPE THEY KEEP THE GARDEN AND FEED THE BIRDS AND HAVE BREAKFAST ON THE PORCH IN THE SUMMER!
WILL OUR CONDOMINIUM EVER BE "HOME" TO YOU, DEAR?
OF COURSE IT WILL, MOM!
... BECAUSE **YOU'RE** THERE!
LYNN

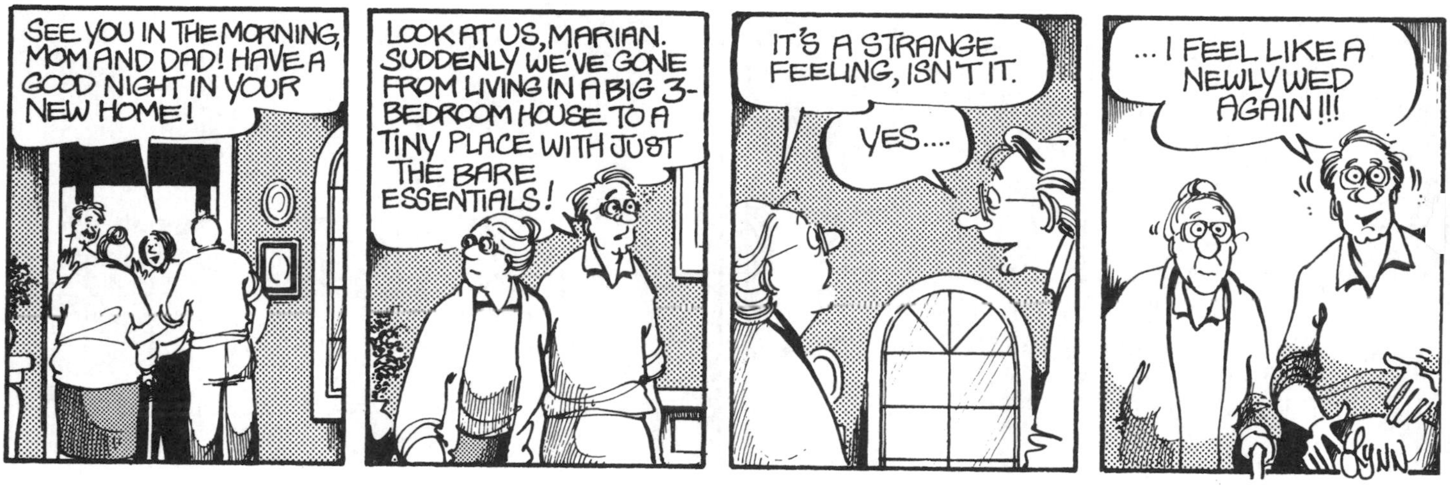
SEE YOU IN THE MORNING, MOM AND DAD! HAVE A GOOD NIGHT IN YOUR NEW HOME!
LOOK AT US, MARIAN. SUDDENLY WE'VE GONE FROM LIVING IN A BIG 3-BEDROOM HOUSE TO A TINY PLACE WITH JUST THE BARE ESSENTIALS!
IT'S A STRANGE FEELING, ISN'T IT.
YES....
... I FEEL LIKE A NEWLYWED AGAIN!!!
LYNN

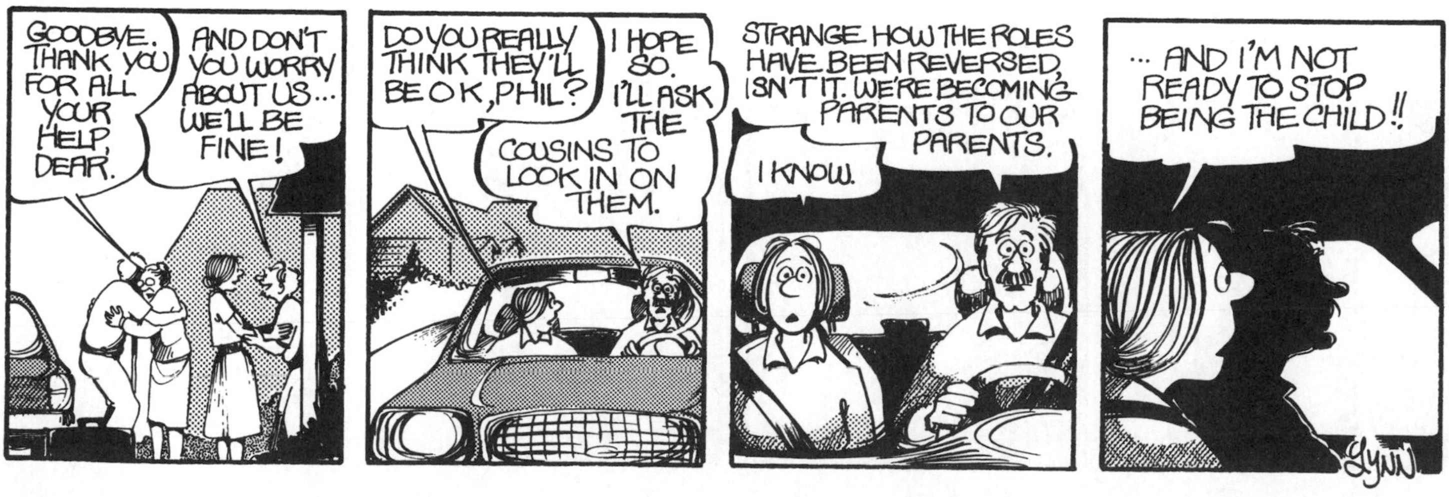
GOODBYE. THANK YOU FOR ALL YOUR HELP, DEAR.
AND DON'T YOU WORRY ABOUT US... WE'LL BE FINE!
DO YOU REALLY THINK THEY'LL BE OK, PHIL?
I HOPE SO. I'LL ASK THE COUSINS TO LOOK IN ON THEM.
STRANGE HOW THE ROLES HAVE BEEN REVERSED, ISN'T IT. WE'RE BECOMING PARENTS TO OUR PARENTS.
I KNOW.
... AND I'M NOT READY TO STOP BEING THE CHILD!!
LYNN

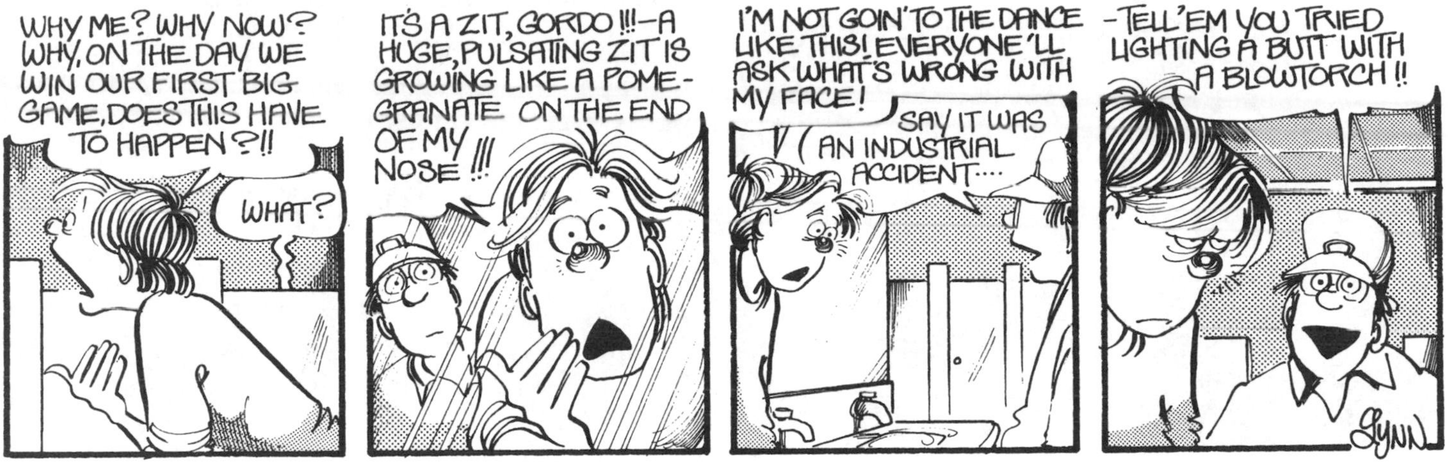
WHY ME? WHY NOW? WHY, ON THE DAY WE WIN OUR FIRST BIG GAME, DOES THIS HAVE TO HAPPEN?!!
WHAT?
IT'S A ZIT, GORDO!!! —A HUGE, PULSATING ZIT IS GROWING LIKE A POMEGRANATE ON THE END OF MY NOSE!!!
I'M NOT GOIN' TO THE DANCE LIKE THIS! EVERYONE'LL ASK WHAT'S WRONG WITH MY FACE!
SAY IT WAS AN INDUSTRIAL ACCIDENT....
—TELL 'EM YOU TRIED LIGHTING A BUTT WITH A BLOWTORCH!!
LYNN

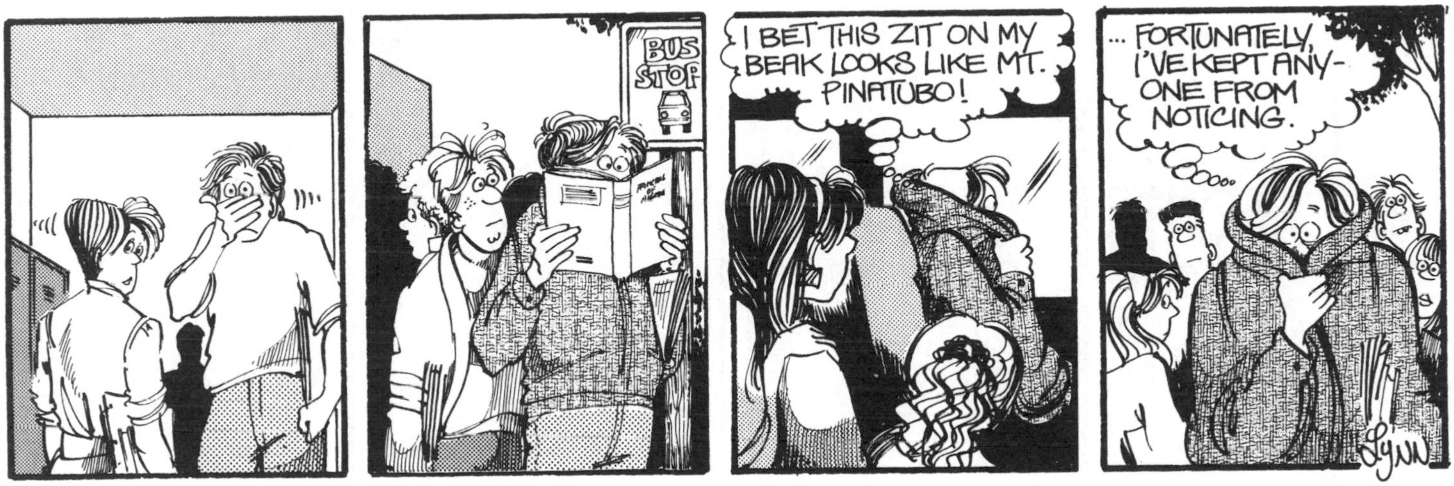
BUS STOP
I BET THIS ZIT ON MY BEAK LOOKS LIKE MT. PINATUBO!
... FORTUNATELY, I'VE KEPT ANYONE FROM NOTICING.
LYNN

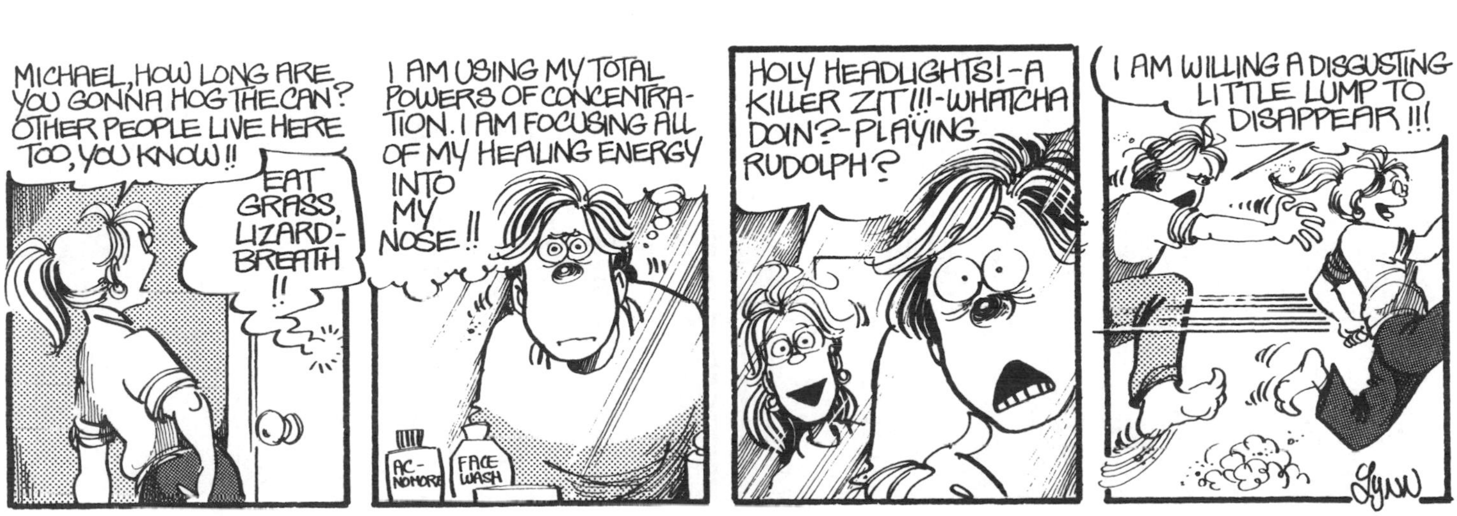
MICHAEL, HOW LONG ARE YOU GONNA HOG THE CAN? OTHER PEOPLE LIVE HERE TOO, YOU KNOW!!
EAT GRASS, LIZARD-BREATH!!
I AM USING MY TOTAL POWERS OF CONCENTRATION. I AM FOCUSING ALL OF MY HEALING ENERGY INTO MY NOSE!!
AC-NOMORE
FACE WASH
HOLY HEADLIGHTS! —A KILLER ZIT!!! —WHATCHA DOIN? —PLAYING RUDOLPH?
I AM WILLING A DISGUSTING LITTLE LUMP TO DISAPPEAR!!!
LYNN

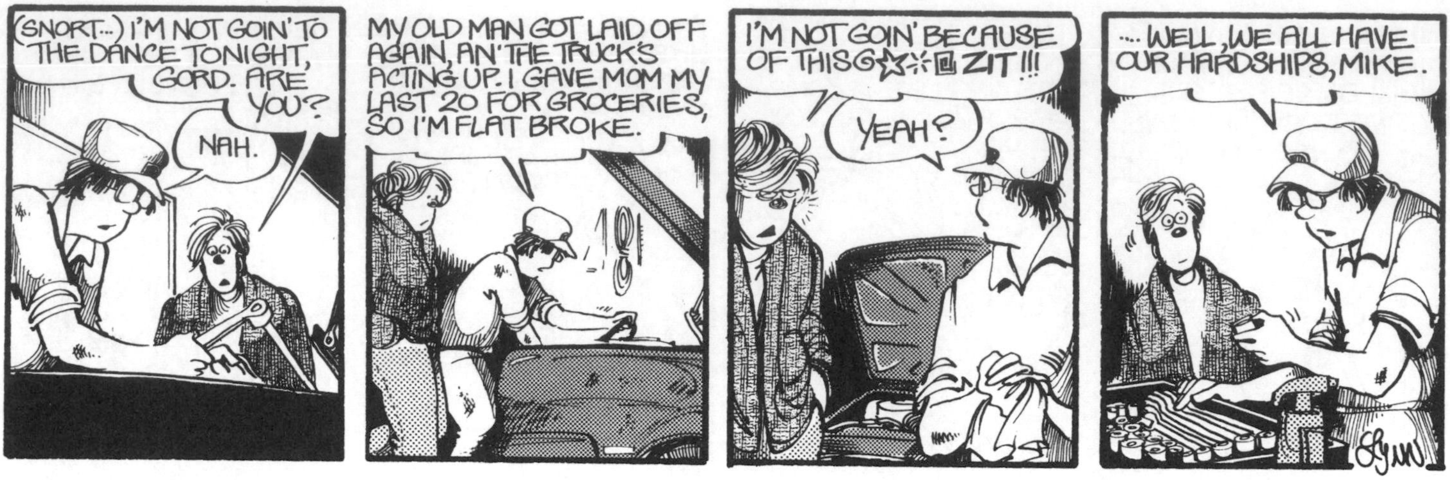
(SNORT...) I'M NOT GOIN' TO THE DANCE TONIGHT, GORD. ARE YOU?
NAH.
MY OLD MAN GOT LAID OFF AGAIN, AN' THE TRUCK'S ACTING UP. I GAVE MOM MY LAST 20 FOR GROCERIES, SO I'M FLAT BROKE.
I'M NOT GOIN' BECAUSE OF THIS G☆※@ ZIT!!!
YEAH?
... WELL, WE ALL HAVE OUR HARDSHIPS, MIKE.
LYNN

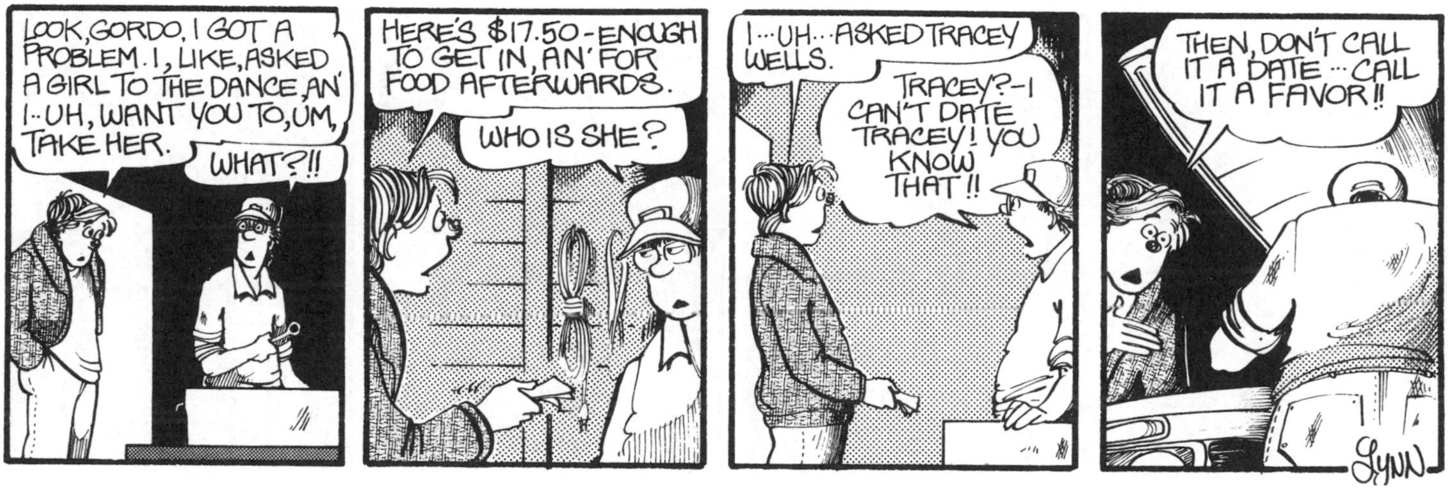
LOOK, GORDO, I GOT A PROBLEM. I, LIKE, ASKED A GIRL TO THE DANCE, AN' I..UH, WANT YOU TO, UM, TAKE HER.
WHAT?!!
HERE'S $17.50 - ENOUGH TO GET IN, AN' FOR FOOD AFTERWARDS.
WHO IS SHE?
I...UH...ASKED TRACEY WELLS.
TRACEY?-I CAN'T DATE TRACEY! YOU KNOW THAT!!
THEN, DON'T CALL IT A DATE...CALL IT A FAVOR!!
LYNN

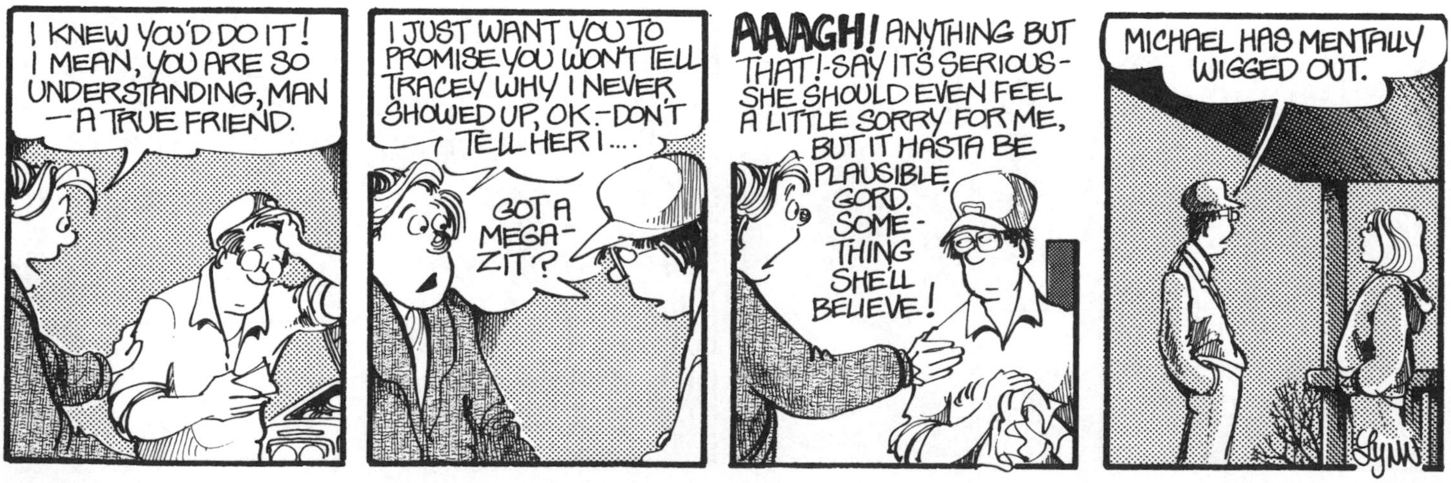
I KNEW YOU'D DO IT! I MEAN, YOU ARE SO UNDERSTANDING, MAN — A TRUE FRIEND.
I JUST WANT YOU TO PROMISE YOU WON'T TELL TRACEY WHY I NEVER SHOWED UP, OK.- DON'T TELL HER I....
GOT A MEGA-ZIT?
AAAGH! ANYTHING BUT THAT!-SAY IT'S SERIOUS- SHE SHOULD EVEN FEEL A LITTLE SORRY FOR ME, BUT IT HASTA BE PLAUSIBLE, GORD. SOMETHING SHE'LL BELIEVE!
MICHAEL HAS MENTALLY WIGGED OUT.
LYNN

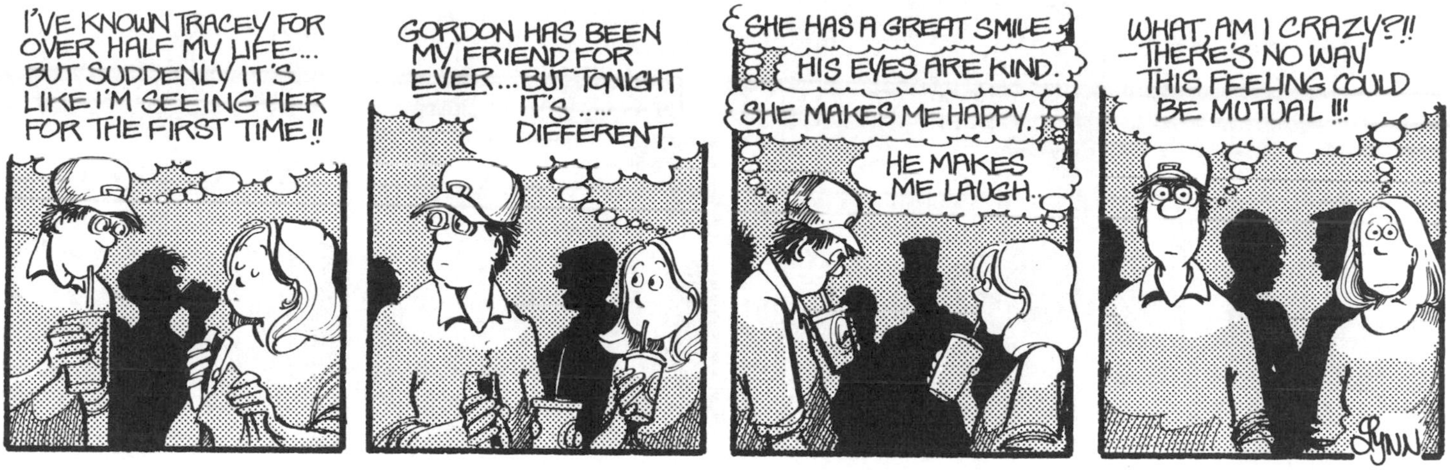
I'VE KNOWN TRACEY FOR OVER HALF MY LIFE... BUT SUDDENLY IT'S LIKE I'M SEEING HER FOR THE FIRST TIME!!
GORDON HAS BEEN MY FRIEND FOR EVER... BUT TONIGHT IT'S ..... DIFFERENT.
SHE HAS A GREAT SMILE.
HIS EYES ARE KIND.
SHE MAKES ME HAPPY.
HE MAKES ME LAUGH.
WHAT, AM I CRAZY?!! -THERE'S NO WAY THIS FEELING COULD BE MUTUAL!!!
LYNN

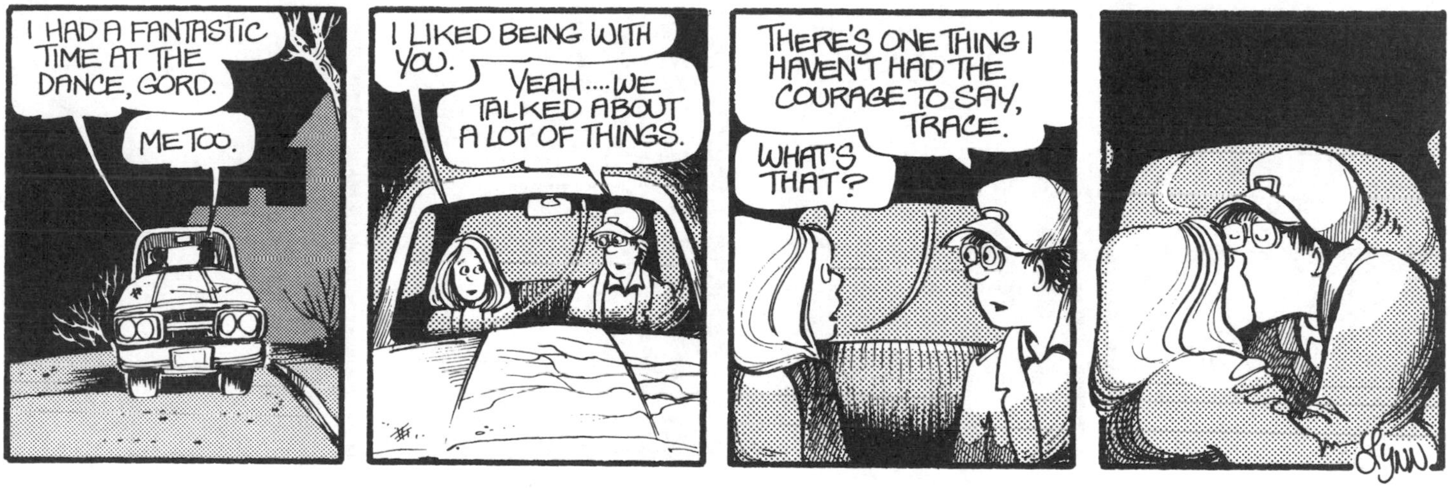
I HAD A FANTASTIC TIME AT THE DANCE, GORD.
ME TOO.
I LIKED BEING WITH YOU.
YEAH.... WE TALKED ABOUT A LOT OF THINGS.
THERE'S ONE THING I HAVEN'T HAD THE COURAGE TO SAY, TRACE.
WHAT'S THAT?
LYNN

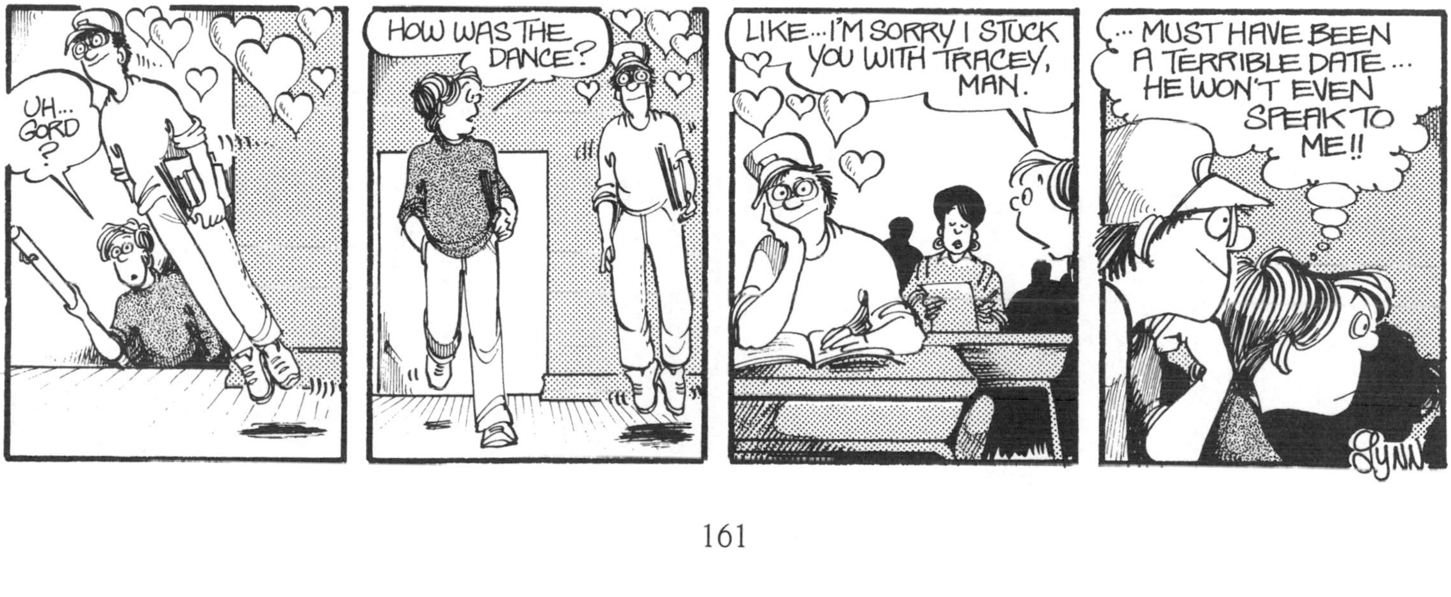
UH... GORD?
HOW WAS THE DANCE?
LIKE... I'M SORRY I STUCK YOU WITH TRACEY, MAN.
... MUST HAVE BEEN A TERRIBLE DATE... HE WON'T EVEN SPEAK TO ME!!
LYNN

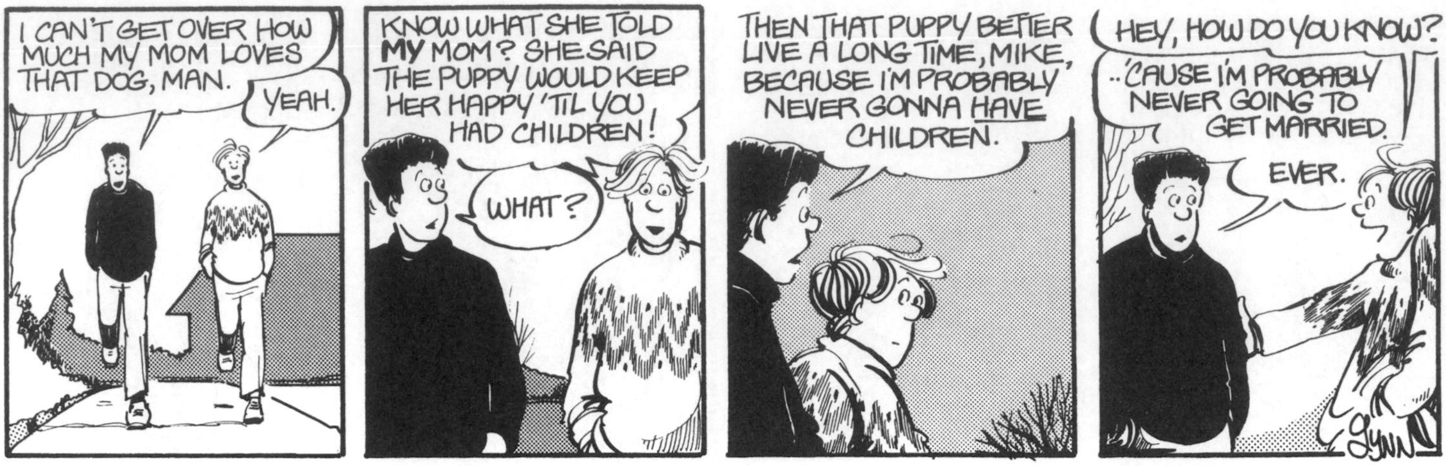
I CAN'T GET OVER HOW MUCH MY MOM LOVES THAT DOG, MAN.
YEAH.
KNOW WHAT SHE TOLD MY MOM? SHE SAID THE PUPPY WOULD KEEP HER HAPPY 'TIL YOU HAD CHILDREN!
WHAT?
THEN THAT PUPPY BETTER LIVE A LONG TIME, MIKE, BECAUSE I'M PROBABLY NEVER GONNA HAVE CHILDREN.
HEY, HOW DO YOU KNOW?
..'CAUSE I'M PROBABLY NEVER GOING TO GET MARRIED.
EVER.
LYNN

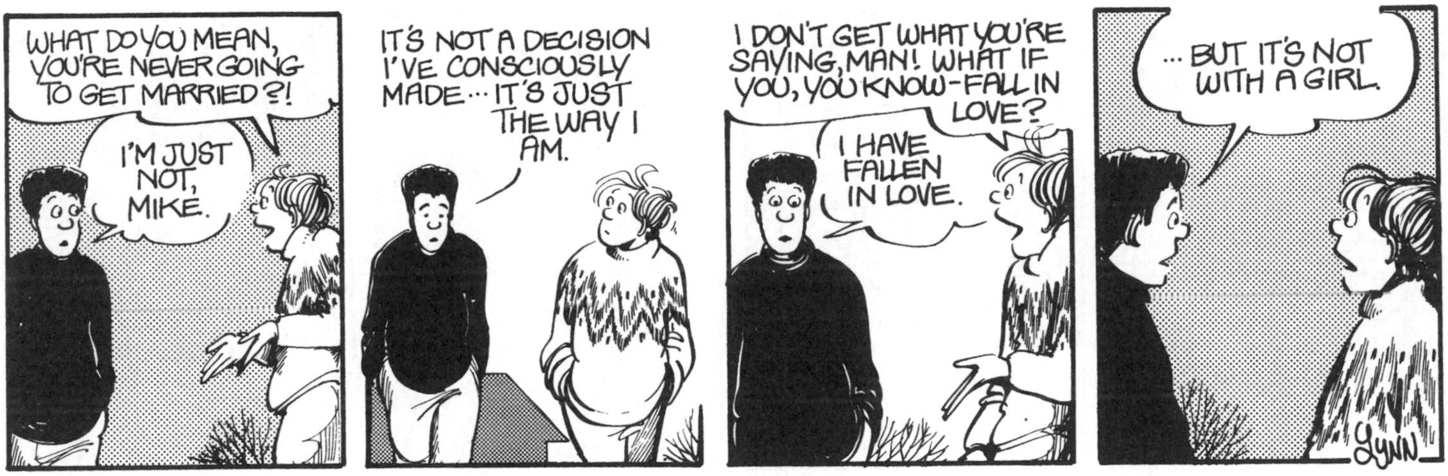
WHAT DO YOU MEAN, YOU'RE NEVER GOING TO GET MARRIED?!
I'M JUST NOT, MIKE.
IT'S NOT A DECISION I'VE CONSCIOUSLY MADE... IT'S JUST THE WAY I AM.
I DON'T GET WHAT YOU'RE SAYING, MAN! WHAT IF YOU, YOU KNOW-FALL IN LOVE?
I HAVE FALLEN IN LOVE.
... BUT IT'S NOT WITH A GIRL.
LYNN

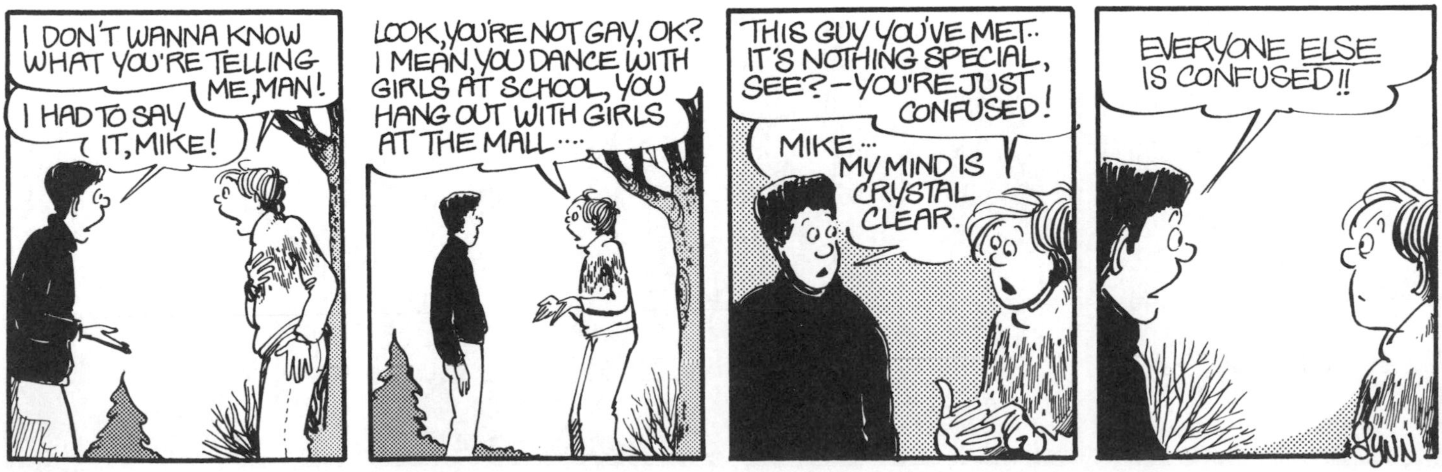
I DON'T WANNA KNOW WHAT YOU'RE TELLING ME, MAN!
I HAD TO SAY IT, MIKE!
LOOK, YOU'RE NOT GAY, OK? I MEAN, YOU DANCE WITH GIRLS AT SCHOOL, YOU HANG OUT WITH GIRLS AT THE MALL....
THIS GUY YOU'VE MET.. IT'S NOTHING SPECIAL, SEE?-YOU'RE JUST CONFUSED!
MIKE... MY MIND IS CRYSTAL CLEAR.
EVERYONE ELSE IS CONFUSED!!
LYNN

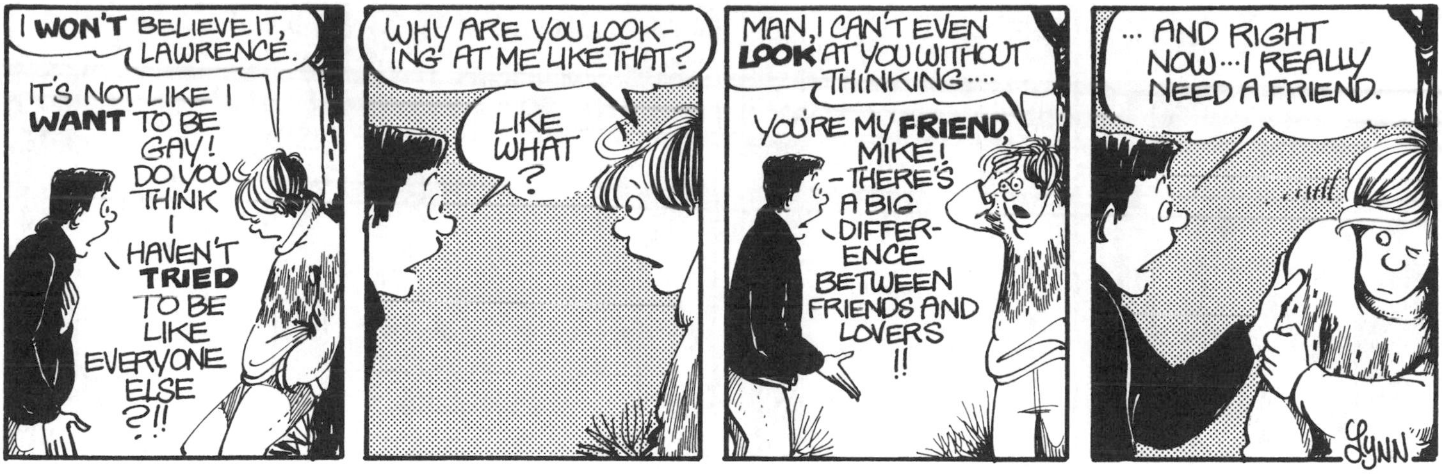
I WON'T BELIEVE IT, LAWRENCE.
IT'S NOT LIKE I WANT TO BE GAY! DO YOU THINK I HAVEN'T TRIED TO BE LIKE EVERYONE ELSE ?!!
WHY ARE YOU LOOKING AT ME LIKE THAT?
LIKE WHAT ?
MAN, I CAN'T EVEN LOOK AT YOU WITHOUT THINKING....
YOU'RE MY FRIEND, MIKE! - THERE'S A BIG DIFFERENCE BETWEEN FRIENDS AND LOVERS !!
... AND RIGHT NOW... I REALLY NEED A FRIEND.
LYNN

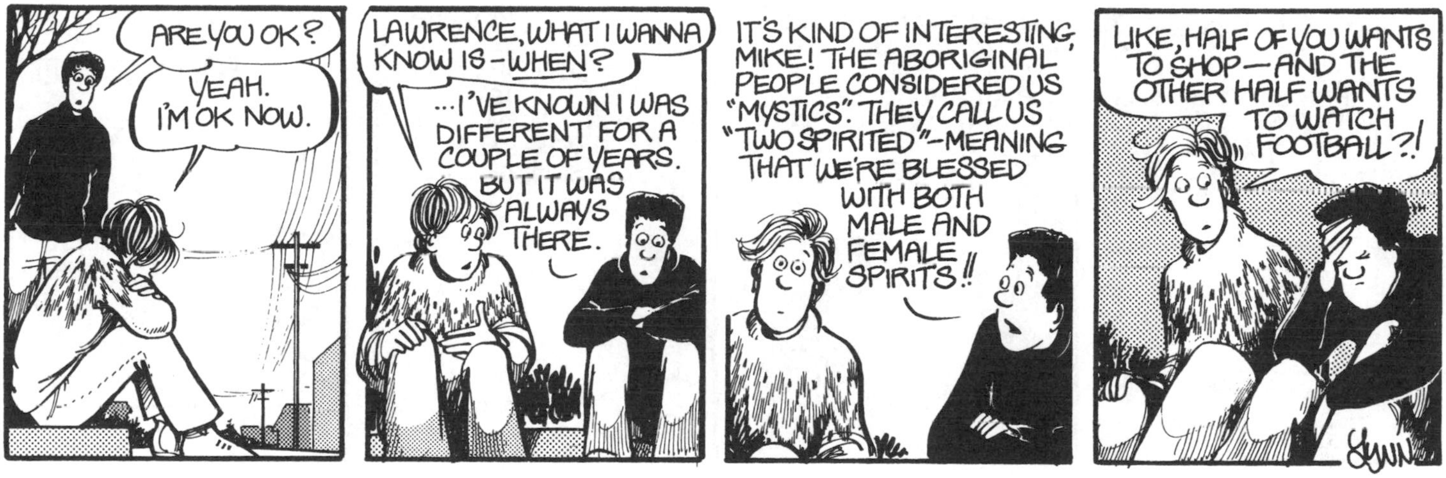
ARE YOU OK?
YEAH. I'M OK NOW.
LAWRENCE, WHAT I WANNA KNOW IS - WHEN?
...I'VE KNOWN I WAS DIFFERENT FOR A COUPLE OF YEARS. BUT IT WAS ALWAYS THERE.
IT'S KIND OF INTERESTING, MIKE! THE ABORIGINAL PEOPLE CONSIDERED US "MYSTICS". THEY CALL US "TWO SPIRITED" - MEANING THAT WE'RE BLESSED WITH BOTH MALE AND FEMALE SPIRITS!!
LIKE, HALF OF YOU WANTS TO SHOP — AND THE OTHER HALF WANTS TO WATCH FOOTBALL?!
LYNN

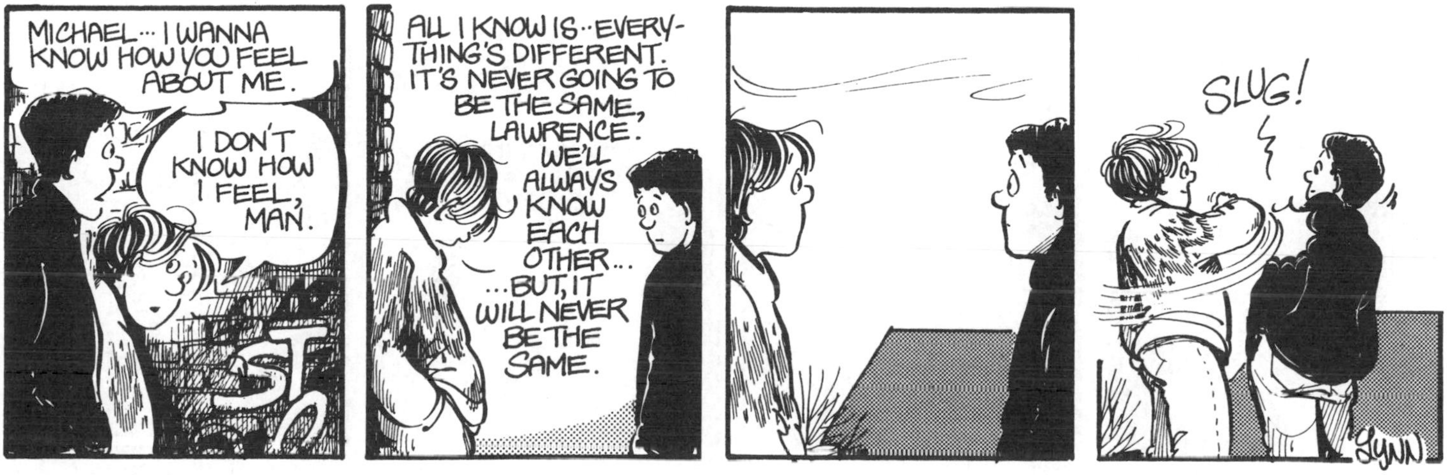
MICHAEL... I WANNA KNOW HOW YOU FEEL ABOUT ME.
I DON'T KNOW HOW I FEEL, MAN.
ALL I KNOW IS.. EVERYTHING'S DIFFERENT. IT'S NEVER GOING TO BE THE SAME, LAWRENCE.
WE'LL ALWAYS KNOW EACH OTHER...
...BUT, IT WILL NEVER BE THE SAME.
SLUG!
LYNN

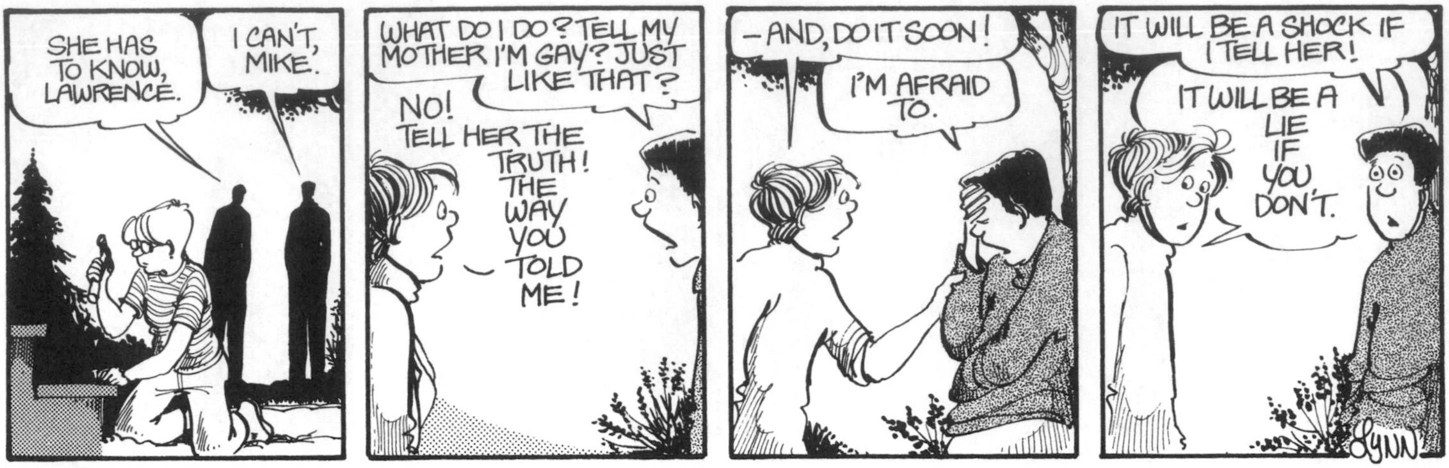
SHE HAS TO KNOW, LAWRENCE.
I CAN'T, MIKE.
WHAT DO I DO? TELL MY MOTHER I'M GAY? JUST LIKE THAT?
NO! TELL HER THE TRUTH! THE WAY YOU TOLD ME!
– AND, DO IT SOON!
I'M AFRAID TO.
IT WILL BE A SHOCK IF I TELL HER!
IT WILL BE A LIE IF YOU DON'T.
LYNN

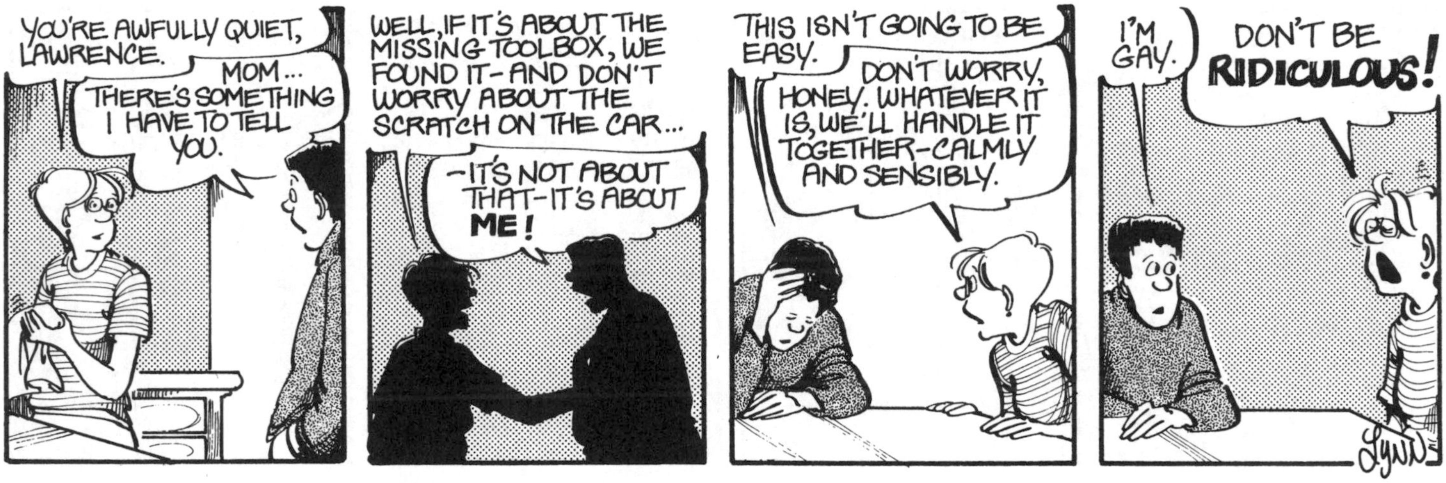
YOU'RE AWFULLY QUIET, LAWRENCE.
MOM... THERE'S SOMETHING I HAVE TO TELL YOU.
WELL, IF IT'S ABOUT THE MISSING TOOLBOX, WE FOUND IT – AND DON'T WORRY ABOUT THE SCRATCH ON THE CAR...
– IT'S NOT ABOUT THAT – IT'S ABOUT ME!
THIS ISN'T GOING TO BE EASY.
DON'T WORRY, HONEY. WHATEVER IT IS, WE'LL HANDLE IT TOGETHER – CALMLY AND SENSIBLY.
I'M GAY.
DON'T BE RIDICULOUS!
LYNN

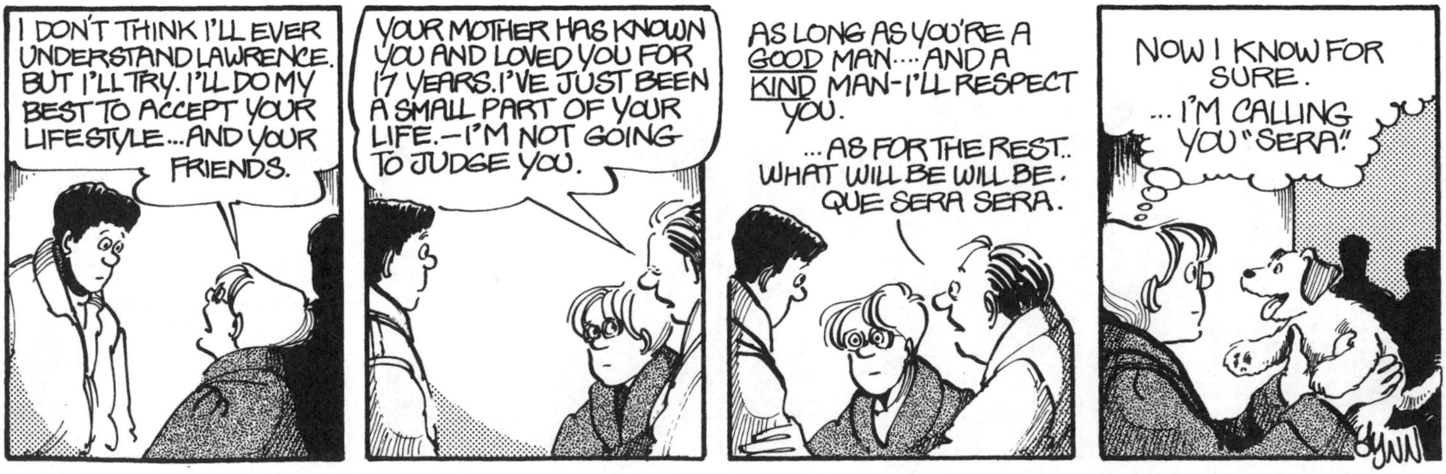
I DON'T THINK I'LL EVER UNDERSTAND LAWRENCE. BUT I'LL TRY. I'LL DO MY BEST TO ACCEPT YOUR LIFESTYLE... AND YOUR FRIENDS.
YOUR MOTHER HAS KNOWN YOU AND LOVED YOU FOR 17 YEARS. I'VE JUST BEEN A SMALL PART OF YOUR LIFE. – I'M NOT GOING TO JUDGE YOU.
AS LONG AS YOU'RE A GOOD MAN.... AND A KIND MAN – I'LL RESPECT YOU.
... AS FOR THE REST.. WHAT WILL BE WILL BE. QUE SERA SERA.
NOW I KNOW FOR SURE.
... I'M CALLING YOU "SERA."
LYNN

A Note from Lynn's Brother-in-Law, Ralph Johnston

The first time I "met" Lynn, I didn't actually meet her. I had finished high school in Lynn Lake, the small northern Manitoba mining town I had grown up in, and ventured across the Atlantic to study textile design at a college in Scotland. (Lynn Lake, coincidentally was named for the man who discovered the ore body. His last name was "Lynn.")

My brother Rod (then living in Hamilton) took advantage of having a brother so far away and came to visit me over the New Year's holidays. When he arrived, his big news was he had a new girlfriend, an artist, who had sent along a gift for me.

It was a cartoon painting by Lynn of me (with my face drawn from my high school photo) at an imaginary kilt-weaving competition. In the background was a model displaying my entry—a wild, gaudy, artsy kilt. Staring at my entry, taking notes with something akin to dismay, was one of the middle-aged judges. In another one of those odd quirks of coincidence, this judge was the spitting image of my design teacher at the time, Tom Stillie—a wry, experienced Scotsman who patiently put up with what we design students called "creative brilliance." Not only had she caught him perfectly (not knowing he even existed) but she drew him in his trademark dark blue checked suit! Not bad for someone who had never met either of us.

Over the next few years, Lynn, with young Aaron, and then baby Kate, became more and more part of our family. My own relationship with them was long distance, since we were usually a few thousand miles apart. They were in southern Ontario when I was still in Scotland, and when I moved to southern Ontario, they moved to Lynn Lake.

One distinct advantage of living away from Lynn was getting her newsletters. The move to northern Manitoba was a considerable cultural shock to the city girl she was then, and she responded by sending out sporadic newsletters, detailing the eye-rolling events of day-to-day life, liberally sprinkled with boisterous drawings. There was the porcupine roadkill she had picked up for a friend to get the quills (for native quill work) that got stuffed in a bag, put in the freezer, and forgotten until one painful day . . .

There was the morning Lynn was at the small Lynn Lake airport, waiting for the flight out. Also waiting at the airport was a stripper, flown up from Winnipeg the day before for a wild party, who now, tired and bedraggled, was waiting for the flight out. The airline agent leaned over to the stripper, pointed to Lynn, and said, "She does a strip too, you know." The woman eyed Lynn over, then snorted with disgust, "Why don't they hire local?"

Eventually, I too moved to Lynn Lake. It was lots of fun having Lynn in our family. She got along well with my parents, and living in the same town was good for both her and them. As well as the fun of having a creative, generous-hearted, adventurous sister-in-law around, we got to be in on some of the action when her three books, and then the cartoon strip, began to take off.

We got to dine with Adrienne Clarkson and her camera crew (before Adrienne became Governor General of Canada). We got to meet other cartoonists and artists who came by to visit, and we got to watch the media interview her.

Having an inside view of a strip like Lynn's was educational. Not only was there hoopla and attention, but a lot of trial and tribulation—not to mention steady hard work on her part. In fact, Lynn has incredible focus. When she was getting some work out for a deadline one time, I passed through her studio into a basement room, and found the floor flooded with a couple of inches of water.

"Lynn," I said, "there's some water on the floor in here."

"Um hmm," she muttered, focused intently on her work.

"Lynn, there's a lot of water on the floor in here!"

"Um hmm," she nodded. "Probably the sump pump flooded." She pointed at a panel to access the sump pump, and kept working.

I opened it and jiggled the sump pump to get it going.

"Do you have a shop vac?" I asked.

"Um . . . yes." She pointed in the general direction of the garage.

Seventeen shop vac loads of water later, she was still working intently. A deadline was due, and mere floods weren't going to distract her from what needed to be done.

Just as once she realized that Lawrence the neighbor boy in the strip was gay, nothing was going to distract her from having him come out in her family-based strip when the time was right. And she did.

Lawrence's coming out in 1993 was actually a few years in the planning. As her gay brother-in-law, I was the one consulted during the early planning stages, and then my partner, Chuck, and I got to watch events unfold. In the days just before the story ran, the media got wind of it, and a barrage of negative outrage began. It shook Lynn badly. Anything gay-positive receives a rough reception in some quarters, and we were expecting some reaction—but the force of the onslaught still came as a surprise. There were literally nonstop calls requesting interviews, and complaints and concerns from papers across the continent—and this before anything had appeared in print!

Then the episode began running, and the positive calls and letters started coming in to balance the negative. That month, Lynn got three thousand letters about Lawrence coming out! Some were negative, but polite, while others were incredibly vitriolic, like the one that started, "Dear Madam Pervert." Others were incredible, heartwarming personal stories of struggle and triumph and courage.

It was a tumultuous time for all of us, but I was proud of Lynn for pushing the boundaries, and glad to have been part of it. Eventually the furor died down, of course, and *For Better or For Worse* continued on its poignant, funny, family way, with new adventures and new episodes.

It's hard to believe it's been 25 years since Lynn first walked down to the Lynn Lake bus depot to ship her week's worth of strips off, then stopped in at the Hudson Bay Store for groceries on the way back home.

How time flies! But what a wonderful world you've created in all those years!

Many thanks, Lynn!

Ralph

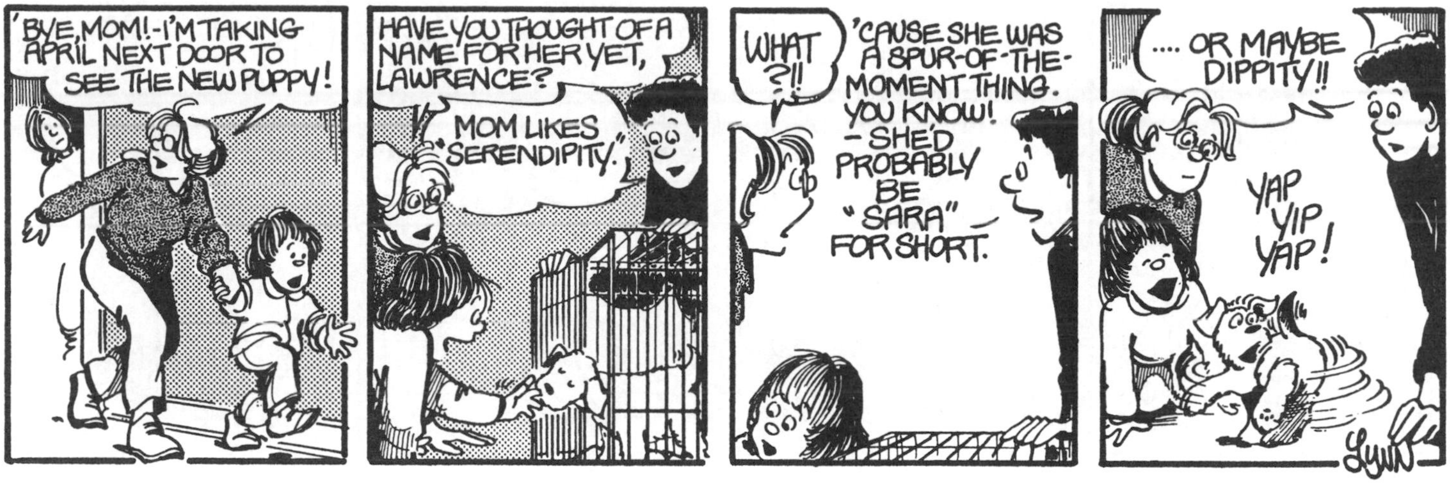

'BYE, MOM! - I'M TAKING APRIL NEXT DOOR TO SEE THE NEW PUPPY!
HAVE YOU THOUGHT OF A NAME FOR HER YET, LAWRENCE?
MOM LIKES "SERENDIPITY."
WHAT ?!!
'CAUSE SHE WAS A SPUR-OF-THE-MOMENT THING. YOU KNOW! - SHE'D PROBABLY BE "SARA" FOR SHORT.
.... OR MAYBE DIPPITY!!
YAP YIP YAP!
LYNN

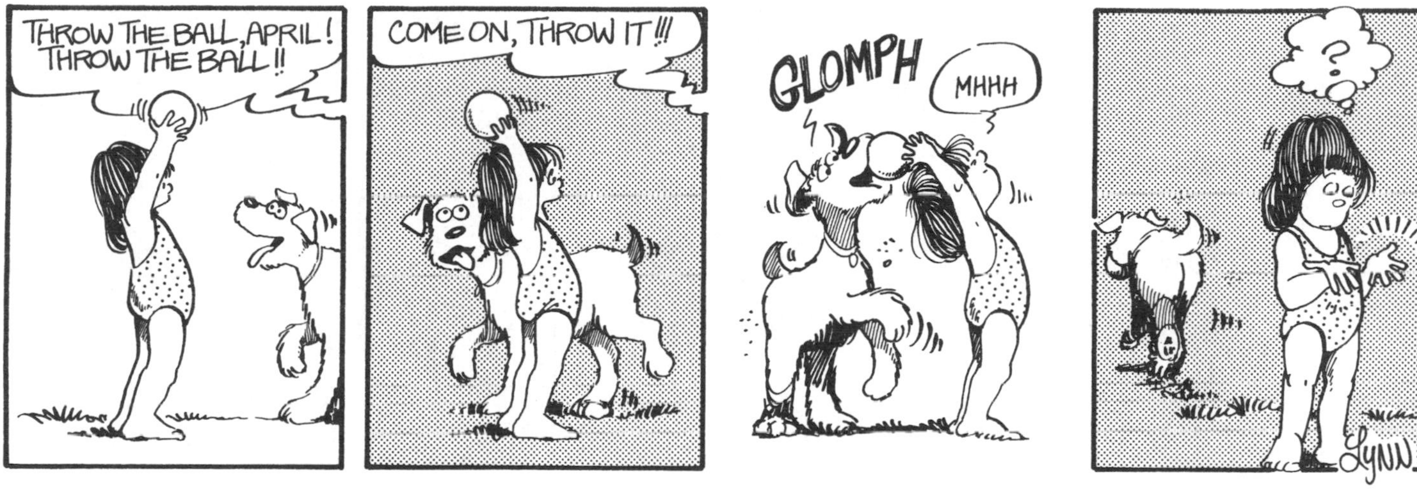

THROW THE BALL, APRIL! THROW THE BALL!!
COME ON, THROW IT!!!
GLOMPH
MHHH
?
LYNN

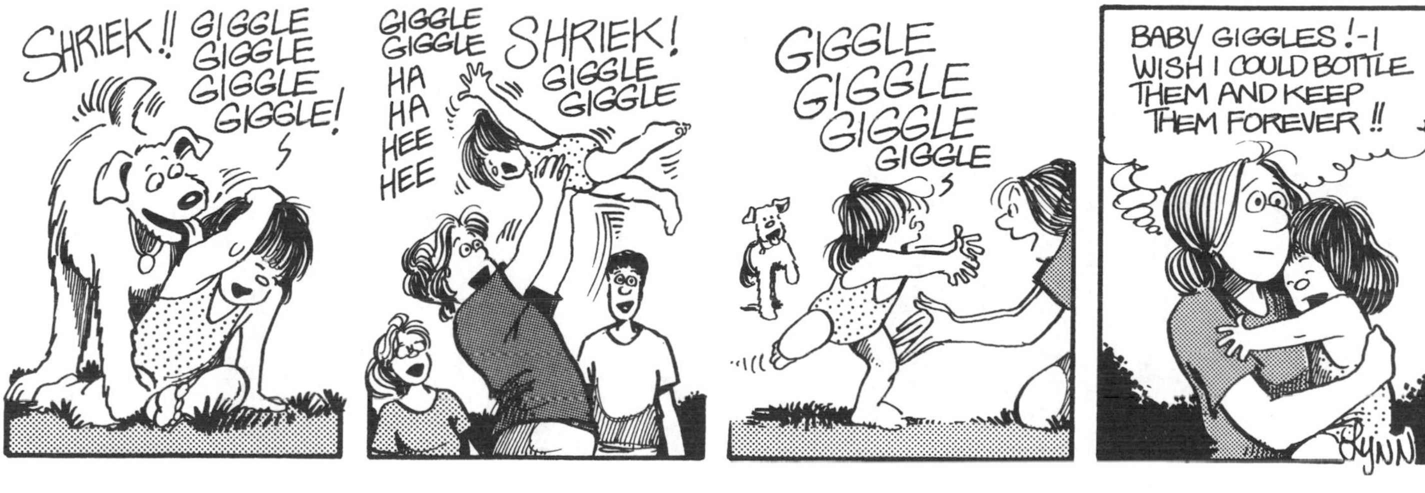

SHRIEK!! GIGGLE GIGGLE GIGGLE GIGGLE!
GIGGLE GIGGLE HA HA HEE HEE SHRIEK! GIGGLE GIGGLE
GIGGLE GIGGLE GIGGLE GIGGLE
BABY GIGGLES! - I WISH I COULD BOTTLE THEM AND KEEP THEM FOREVER!!
LYNN

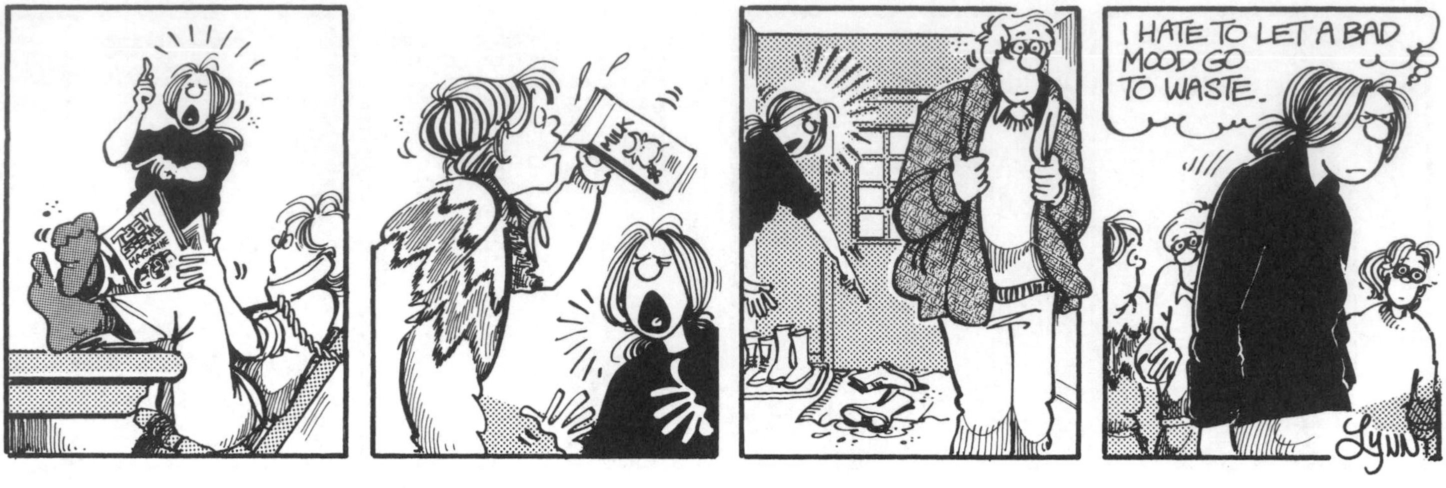

MILK
I HATE TO LET A BAD MOOD GO TO WASTE.
LYNN

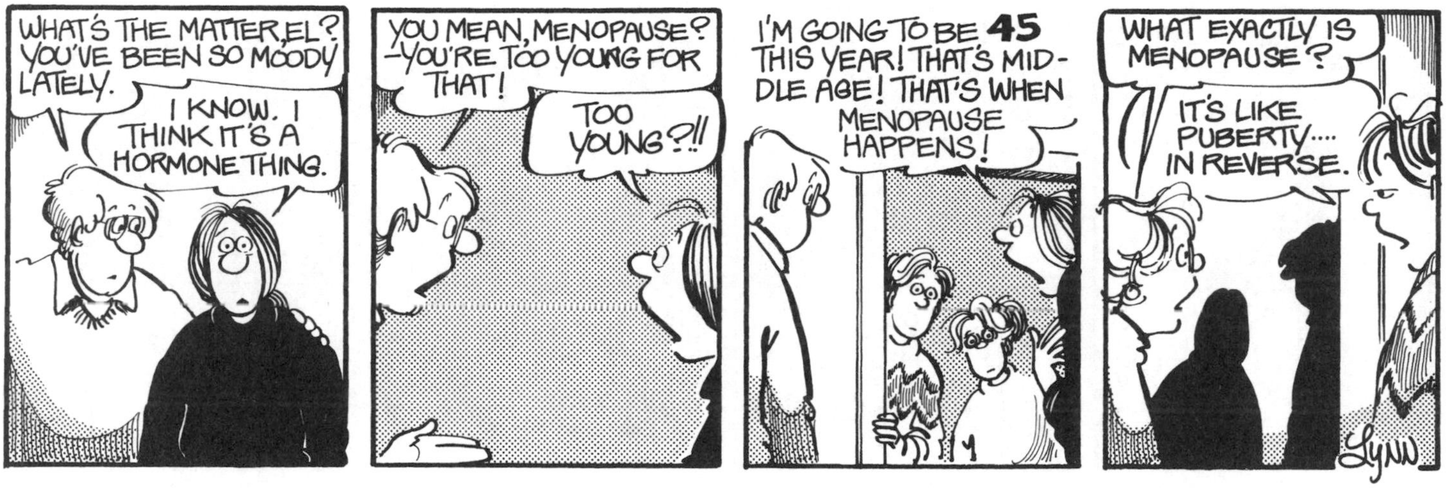

WHAT'S THE MATTER, EL? YOU'VE BEEN SO MOODY LATELY.
I KNOW. I THINK IT'S A HORMONE THING.
YOU MEAN, MENOPAUSE? -YOU'RE TOO YOUNG FOR THAT!
TOO YOUNG?!!
I'M GOING TO BE 45 THIS YEAR! THAT'S MIDDLE AGE! THAT'S WHEN MENOPAUSE HAPPENS!
WHAT EXACTLY IS MENOPAUSE?
IT'S LIKE PUBERTY.... IN REVERSE.
LYNN

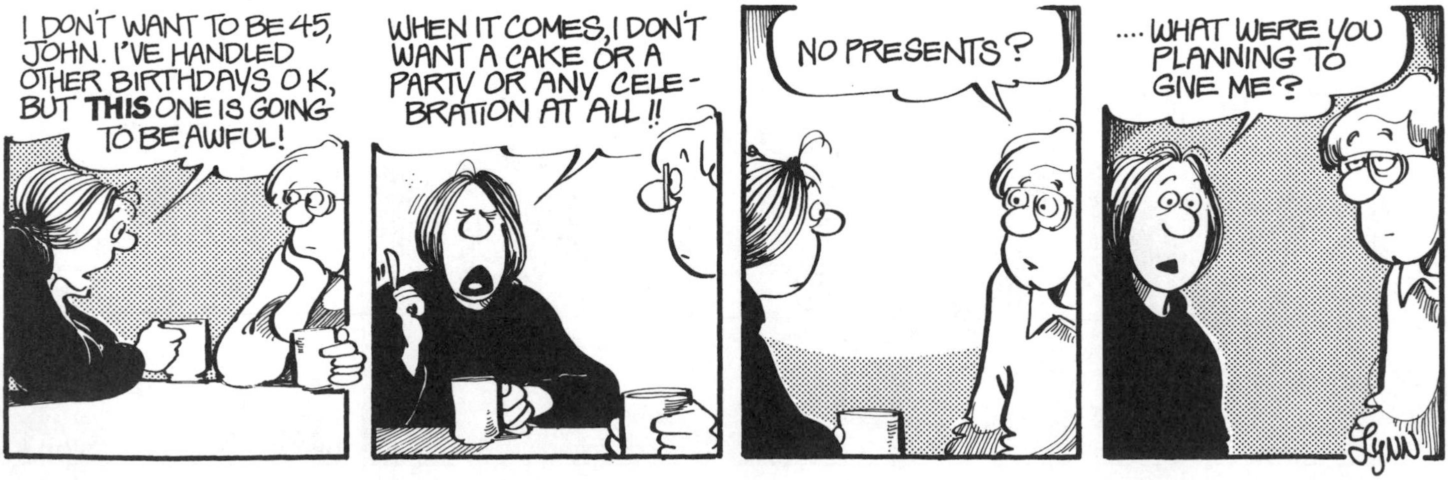

I DON'T WANT TO BE 45, JOHN. I'VE HANDLED OTHER BIRTHDAYS O K, BUT THIS ONE IS GOING TO BE AWFUL!
WHEN IT COMES, I DON'T WANT A CAKE OR A PARTY OR ANY CELEBRATION AT ALL!!
NO PRESENTS?
....WHAT WERE YOU PLANNING TO GIVE ME?
LYNN

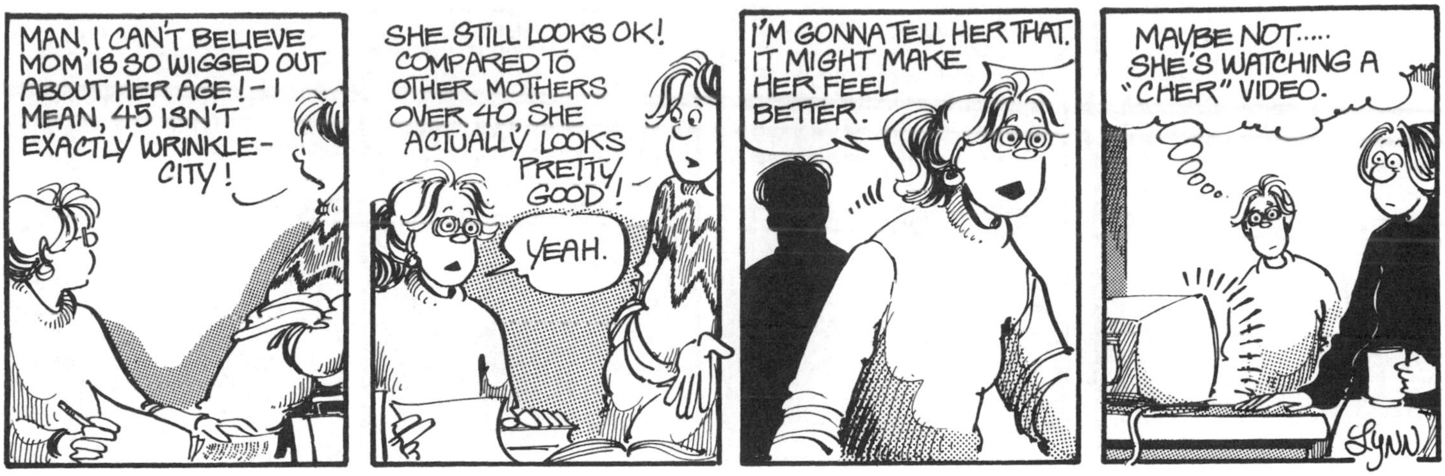
MAN, I CAN'T BELIEVE MOM IS SO WIGGED OUT ABOUT HER AGE! - I MEAN, 45 ISN'T EXACTLY WRINKLE-CITY!
SHE STILL LOOKS OK! COMPARED TO OTHER MOTHERS OVER 40, SHE ACTUALLY LOOKS PRETTY GOOD!
YEAH.
I'M GONNA TELL HER THAT. IT MIGHT MAKE HER FEEL BETTER.
MAYBE NOT..... SHE'S WATCHING A "CHER" VIDEO.
LYNN

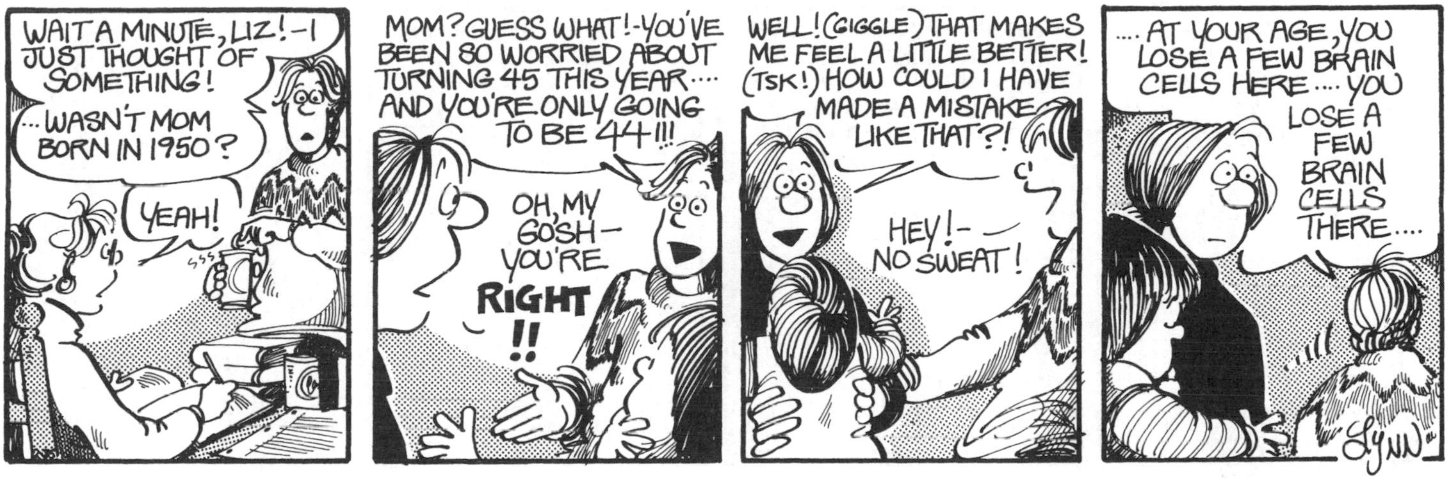
WAIT A MINUTE, LIZ! - I JUST THOUGHT OF SOMETHING!
...WASN'T MOM BORN IN 1950?
YEAH!
MOM? GUESS WHAT! - YOU'VE BEEN SO WORRIED ABOUT TURNING 45 THIS YEAR.... AND YOU'RE ONLY GOING TO BE 44!!!
OH, MY GOSH - YOU'RE RIGHT!!
WELL! (GIGGLE) THAT MAKES ME FEEL A LITTLE BETTER! (TSK!) HOW COULD I HAVE MADE A MISTAKE LIKE THAT?!
HEY! - NO SWEAT!
.... AT YOUR AGE, YOU LOSE A FEW BRAIN CELLS HERE .... YOU LOSE A FEW BRAIN CELLS THERE....
LYNN

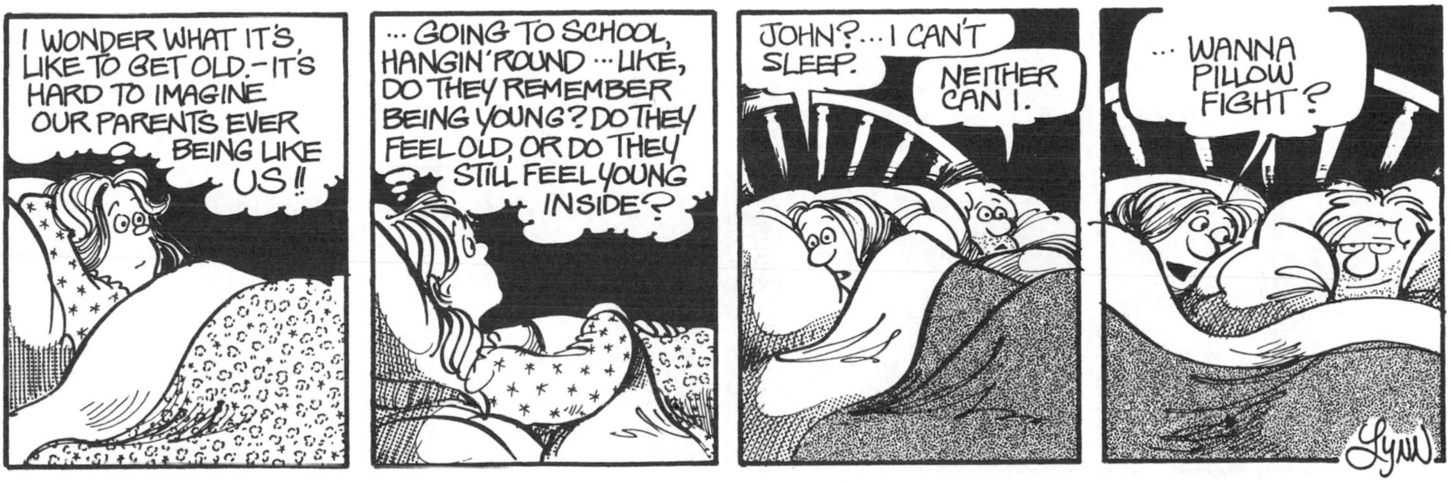
I WONDER WHAT IT'S LIKE TO GET OLD. - IT'S HARD TO IMAGINE OUR PARENTS EVER BEING LIKE US!!
... GOING TO SCHOOL, HANGIN' ROUND ... LIKE, DO THEY REMEMBER BEING YOUNG? DO THEY FEEL OLD, OR DO THEY STILL FEEL YOUNG INSIDE?
JOHN?... I CAN'T SLEEP.
NEITHER CAN I.
... WANNA PILLOW FIGHT?
LYNN

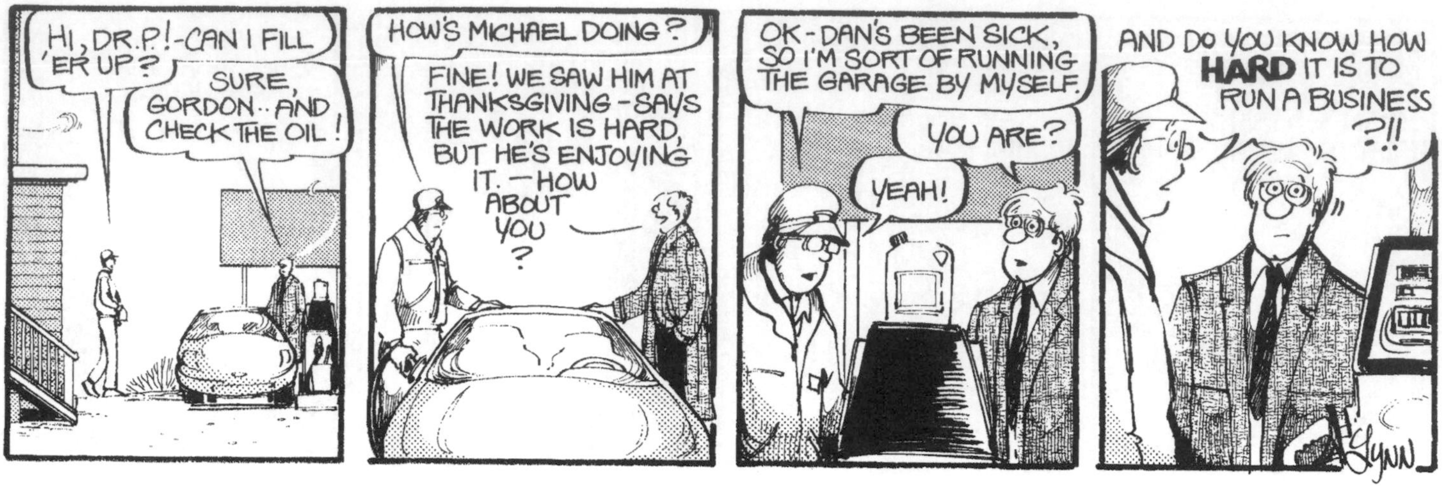
HI, DR. P! - CAN I FILL 'ER UP?
SURE, GORDON.. AND CHECK THE OIL!
HOW'S MICHAEL DOING?
FINE! WE SAW HIM AT THANKSGIVING - SAYS THE WORK IS HARD, BUT HE'S ENJOYING IT. - HOW ABOUT YOU?
OK - DAN'S BEEN SICK, SO I'M SORT OF RUNNING THE GARAGE BY MYSELF.
YOU ARE?
YEAH!
AND DO YOU KNOW HOW HARD IT IS TO RUN A BUSINESS?!!
LYNN

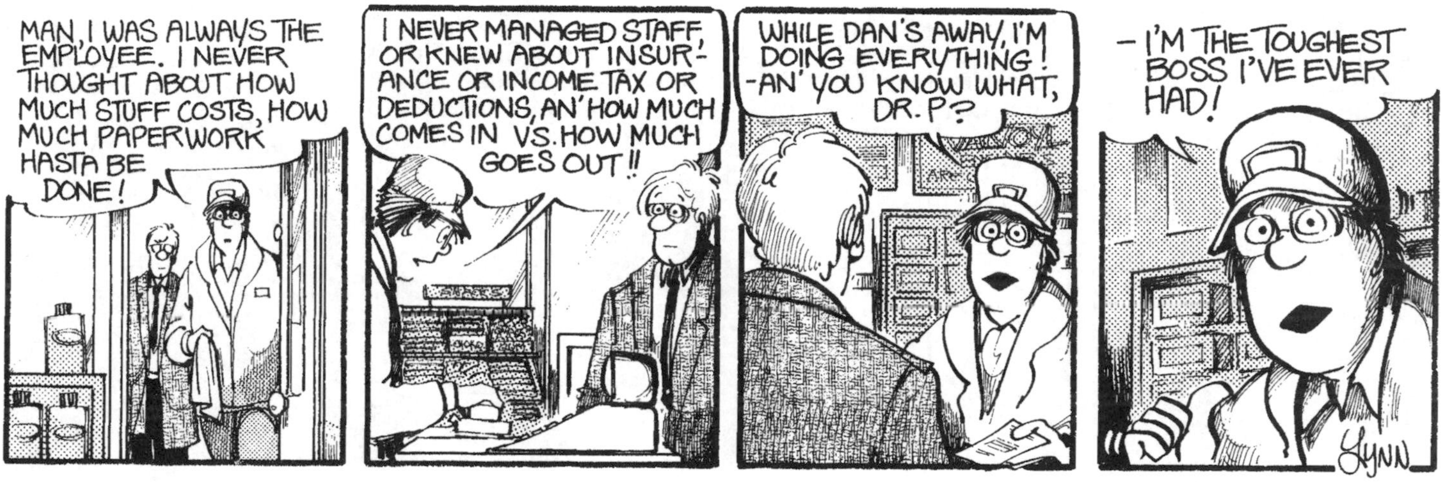
MAN, I WAS ALWAYS THE EMPLOYEE. I NEVER THOUGHT ABOUT HOW MUCH STUFF COSTS, HOW MUCH PAPERWORK HASTA BE DONE!
I NEVER MANAGED STAFF, OR KNEW ABOUT INSURANCE OR INCOME TAX OR DEDUCTIONS, AN' HOW MUCH COMES IN VS. HOW MUCH GOES OUT!!
WHILE DAN'S AWAY, I'M DOING EVERYTHING! - AN' YOU KNOW WHAT, DR. P?
- I'M THE TOUGHEST BOSS I'VE EVER HAD!
LYNN

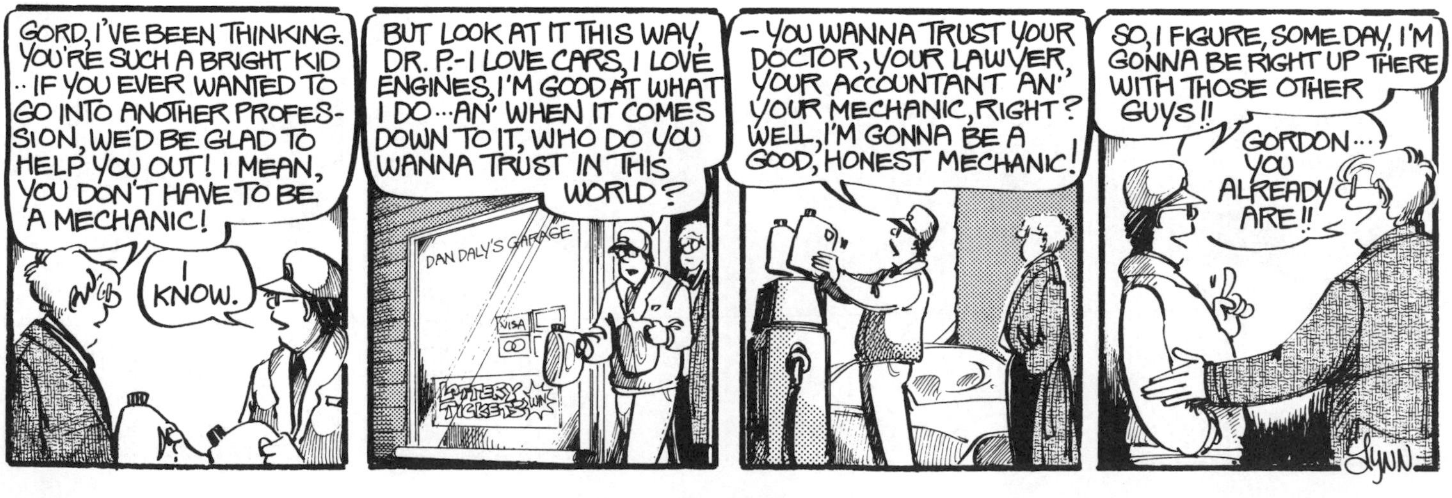
GORD, I'VE BEEN THINKING. YOU'RE SUCH A BRIGHT KID .. IF YOU EVER WANTED TO GO INTO ANOTHER PROFESSION, WE'D BE GLAD TO HELP YOU OUT! I MEAN, YOU DON'T HAVE TO BE A MECHANIC!
I KNOW.
BUT LOOK AT IT THIS WAY, DR. P. - I LOVE CARS, I LOVE ENGINES, I'M GOOD AT WHAT I DO... AN' WHEN IT COMES DOWN TO IT, WHO DO YOU WANNA TRUST IN THIS WORLD?
DAN DALY'S GARAGE
VISA
LOTTERY TICKETS
WIN
- YOU WANNA TRUST YOUR DOCTOR, YOUR LAWYER, YOUR ACCOUNTANT AN' YOUR MECHANIC, RIGHT? WELL, I'M GONNA BE A GOOD, HONEST MECHANIC!
SO, I FIGURE, SOME DAY, I'M GONNA BE RIGHT UP THERE WITH THOSE OTHER GUYS!!
GORDON... YOU ALREADY ARE!!
LYNN

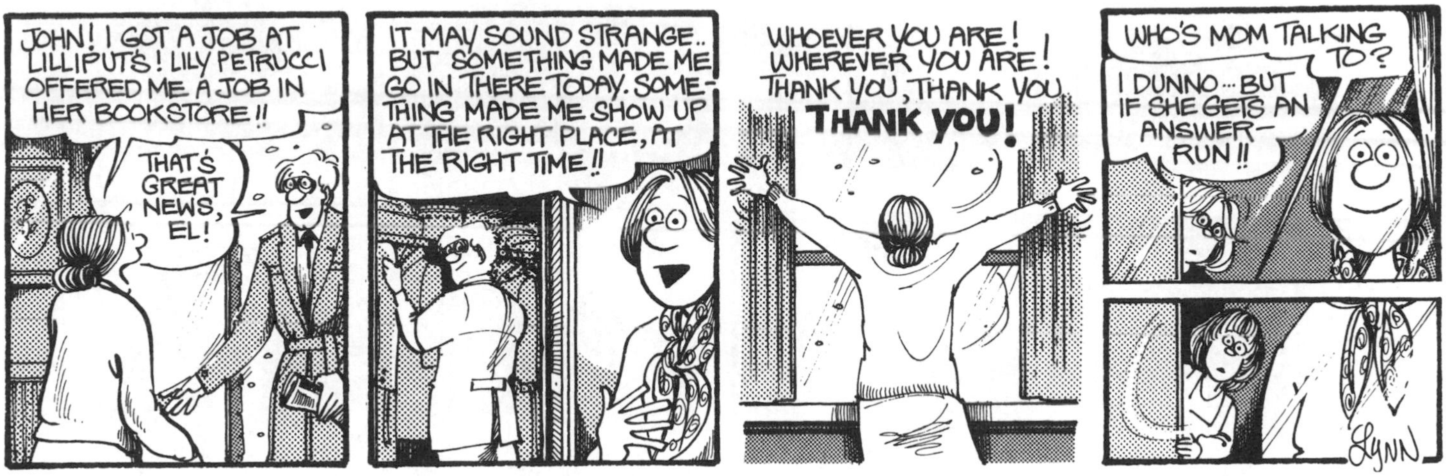
JOHN! I GOT A JOB AT LILLIPUTS! LILY PETRUCCI OFFERED ME A JOB IN HER BOOKSTORE!!
THAT'S GREAT NEWS, EL!
IT MAY SOUND STRANGE.. BUT SOMETHING MADE ME GO IN THERE TODAY. SOMETHING MADE ME SHOW UP AT THE RIGHT PLACE, AT THE RIGHT TIME!!
WHOEVER YOU ARE! WHEREVER YOU ARE! THANK YOU, THANK YOU THANK YOU!
WHO'S MOM TALKING TO?
I DUNNO... BUT IF SHE GETS AN ANSWER– RUN!!
LYNN

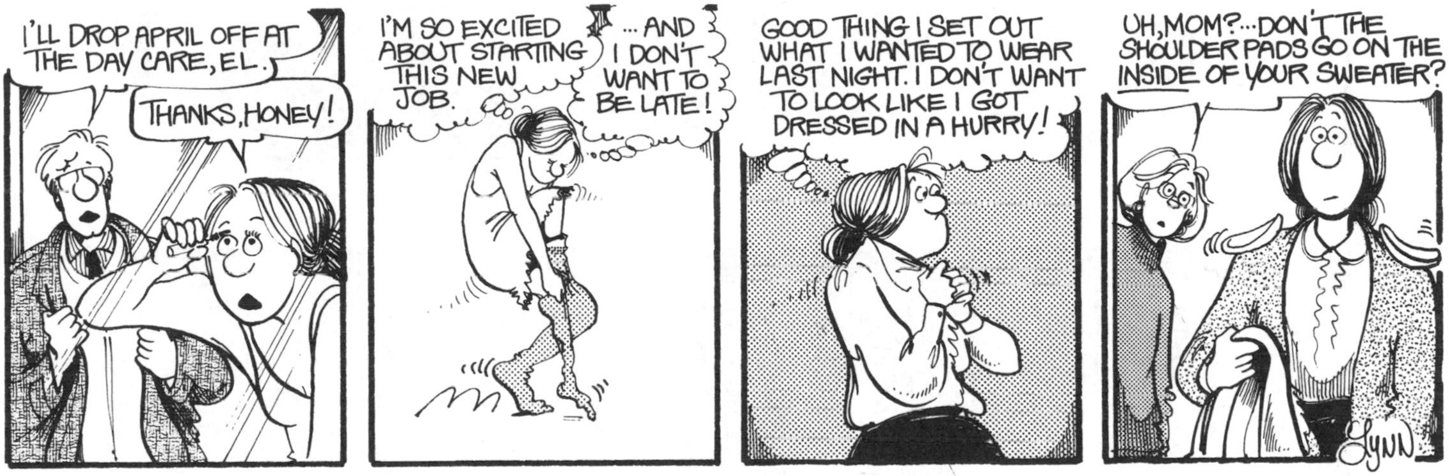
I'LL DROP APRIL OFF AT THE DAY CARE, EL.
THANKS, HONEY!
I'M SO EXCITED ABOUT STARTING THIS NEW JOB.
...AND I DON'T WANT TO BE LATE!
GOOD THING I SET OUT WHAT I WANTED TO WEAR LAST NIGHT. I DON'T WANT TO LOOK LIKE I GOT DRESSED IN A HURRY!
UH, MOM?... DON'T THE SHOULDER PADS GO ON THE INSIDE OF YOUR SWEATER?
LYNN

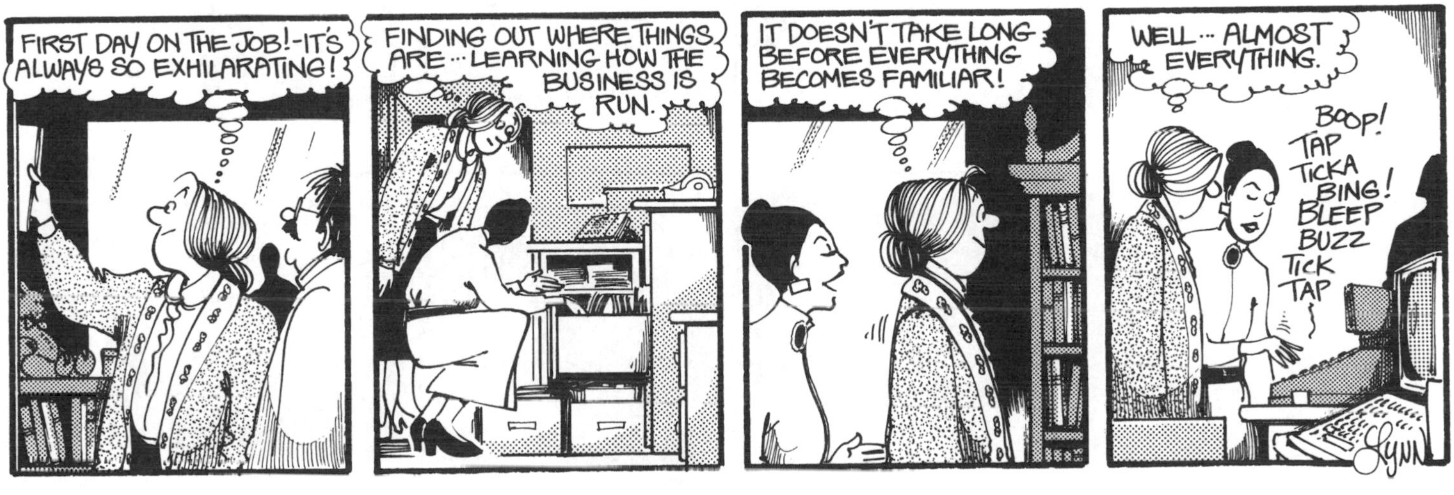
FIRST DAY ON THE JOB! - IT'S ALWAYS SO EXHILARATING!
FINDING OUT WHERE THINGS ARE... LEARNING HOW THE BUSINESS IS RUN.
IT DOESN'T TAKE LONG BEFORE EVERYTHING BECOMES FAMILIAR!
WELL... ALMOST EVERYTHING.
BOOP! TAP TICKA BING! BLEEP BUZZ TICK TAP
LYNN

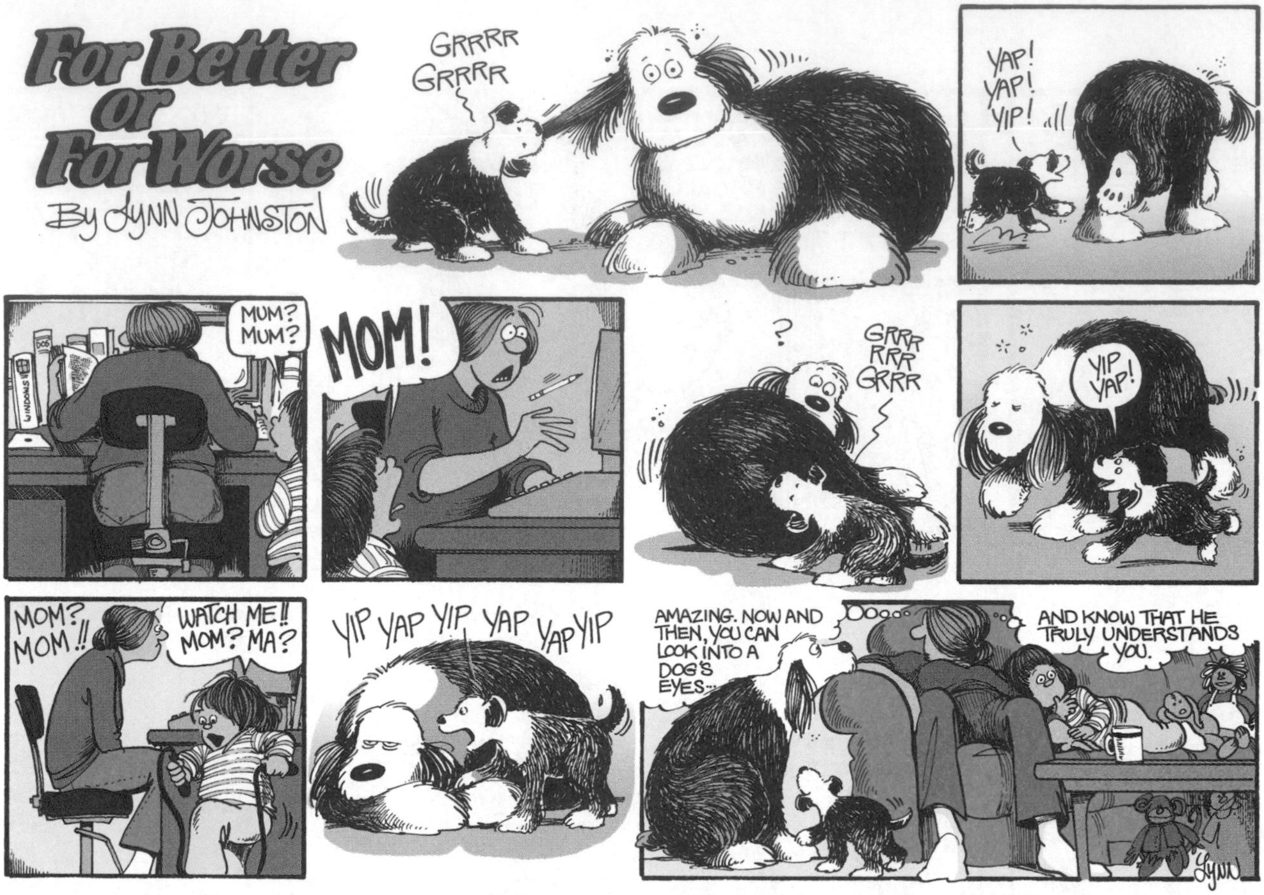
For Better or For Worse
By Lynn Johnston
GRRRR GRRRR
YAP! YAP! YIP!
MUM? MUM?
MOM!
?
GRRR RRR GRRR
YIP YAP!
MOM? MOM!!
WATCH ME!! MOM? MA?
YIP YAP YIP YAP YAP YIP
AMAZING. NOW AND THEN, YOU CAN LOOK INTO A DOG'S EYES...
AND KNOW THAT HE TRULY UNDERSTANDS YOU.
LYNN

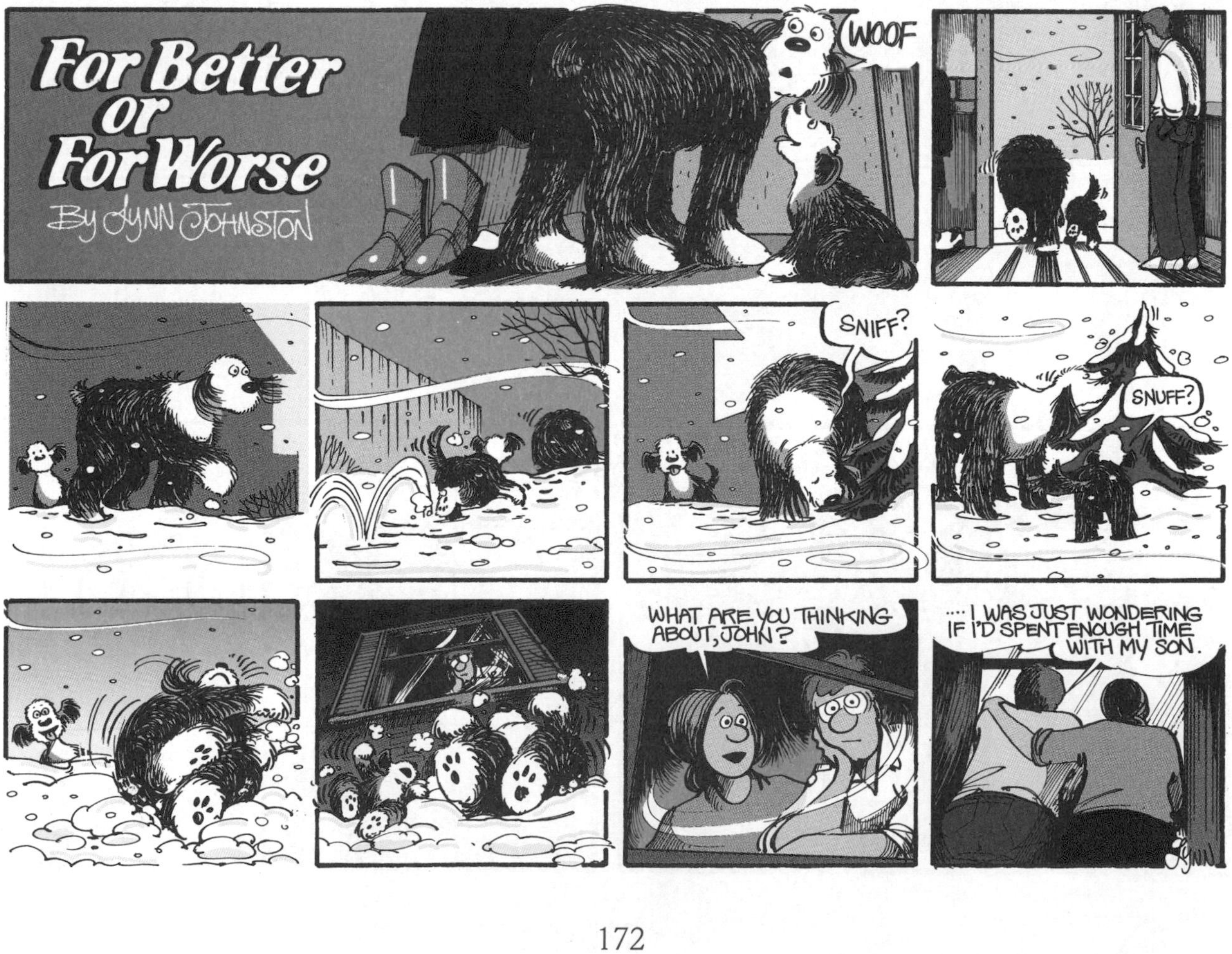
For Better or For Worse
By Lynn Johnston
WOOF
SNIFF?
SNUFF?
WHAT ARE YOU THINKING ABOUT, JOHN?
.... I WAS JUST WONDERING IF I'D SPENT ENOUGH TIME WITH MY SON.
LYNN

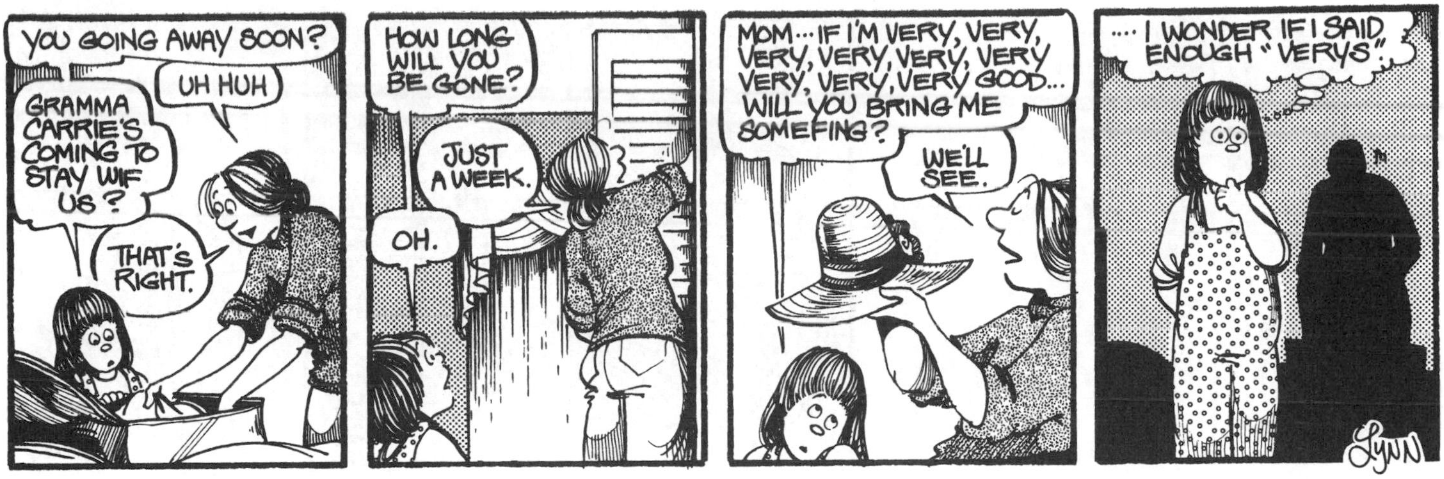
YOU GOING AWAY SOON?
UH HUH
GRAMMA CARRIE'S COMING TO STAY WIF US?
THAT'S RIGHT.
HOW LONG WILL YOU BE GONE?
JUST A WEEK.
OH.
MOM... IF I'M VERY, VERY, VERY, VERY, VERY, VERY VERY, VERY, VERY GOOD... WILL YOU BRING ME SOMEFING?
WE'LL SEE.
.... I WONDER IF I SAID ENOUGH "VERYS".
LYNN

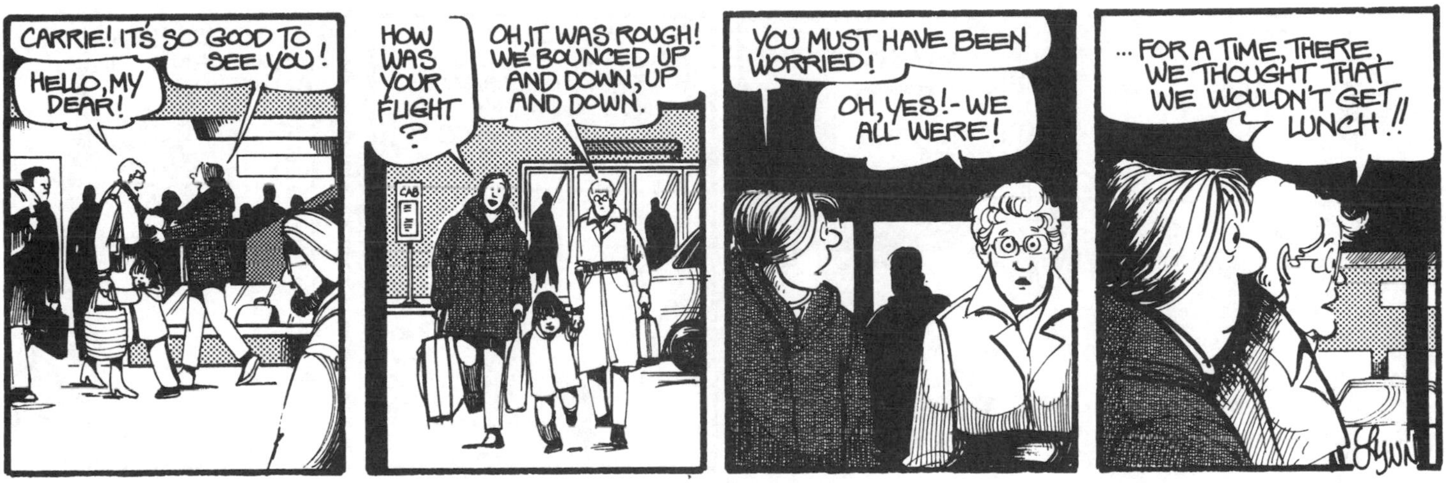
CARRIE! IT'S SO GOOD TO SEE YOU!
HELLO, MY DEAR!
HOW WAS YOUR FLIGHT?
OH, IT WAS ROUGH! WE BOUNCED UP AND DOWN, UP AND DOWN.
CAB
YOU MUST HAVE BEEN WORRIED!
OH, YES! - WE ALL WERE!
... FOR A TIME, THERE, WE THOUGHT THAT WE WOULDN'T GET LUNCH!!
LYNN

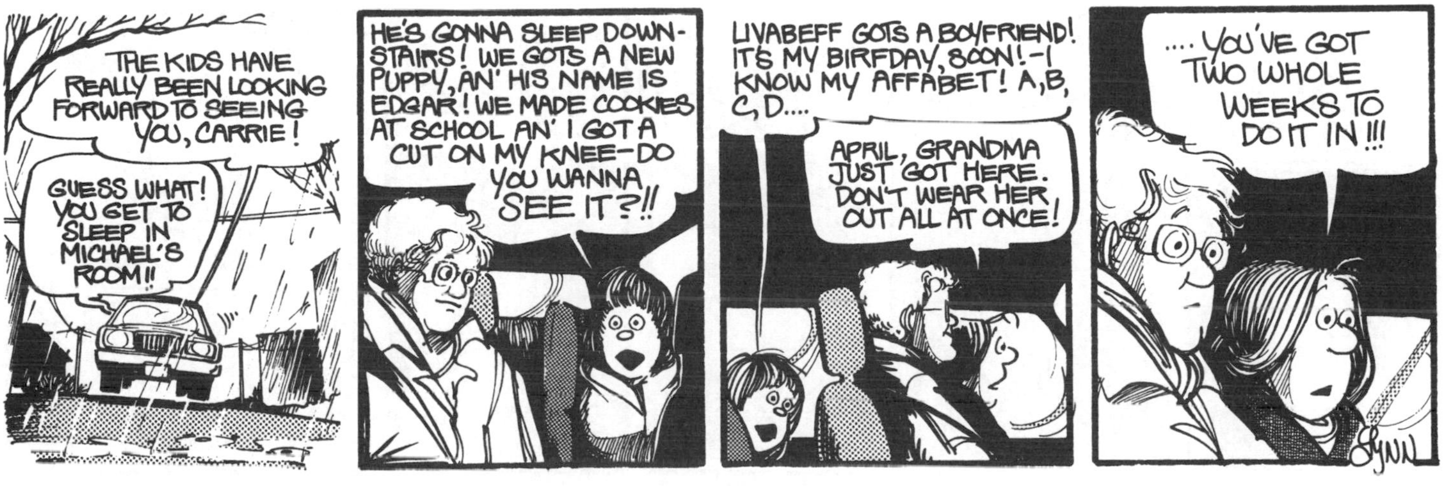
THE KIDS HAVE REALLY BEEN LOOKING FORWARD TO SEEING YOU, CARRIE!
GUESS WHAT! YOU GET TO SLEEP IN MICHAEL'S ROOM!!
HE'S GONNA SLEEP DOWN-STAIRS! WE GOTS A NEW PUPPY, AN' HIS NAME IS EDGAR! WE MADE COOKIES AT SCHOOL AN' I GOT A CUT ON MY KNEE-DO YOU WANNA SEE IT?!!
LIVABEFF GOTS A BOYFRIEND! IT'S MY BIRFDAY, SOON! - I KNOW MY AFFABET! A, B, C, D....
APRIL, GRANDMA JUST GOT HERE. DON'T WEAR HER OUT ALL AT ONCE!
.... YOU'VE GOT TWO WHOLE WEEKS TO DO IT IN!!!
LYNN

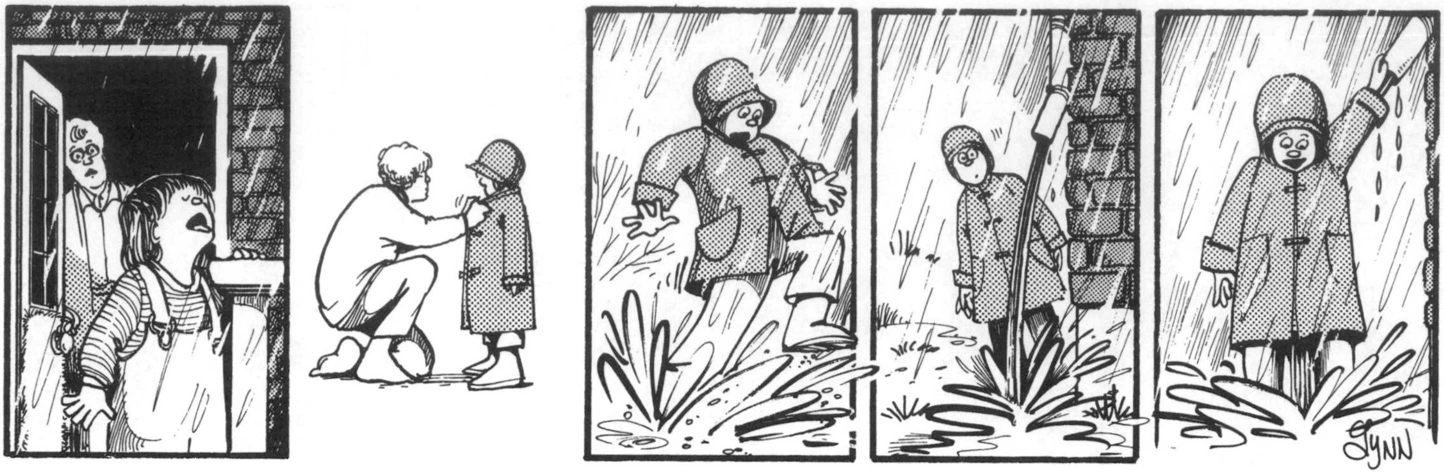

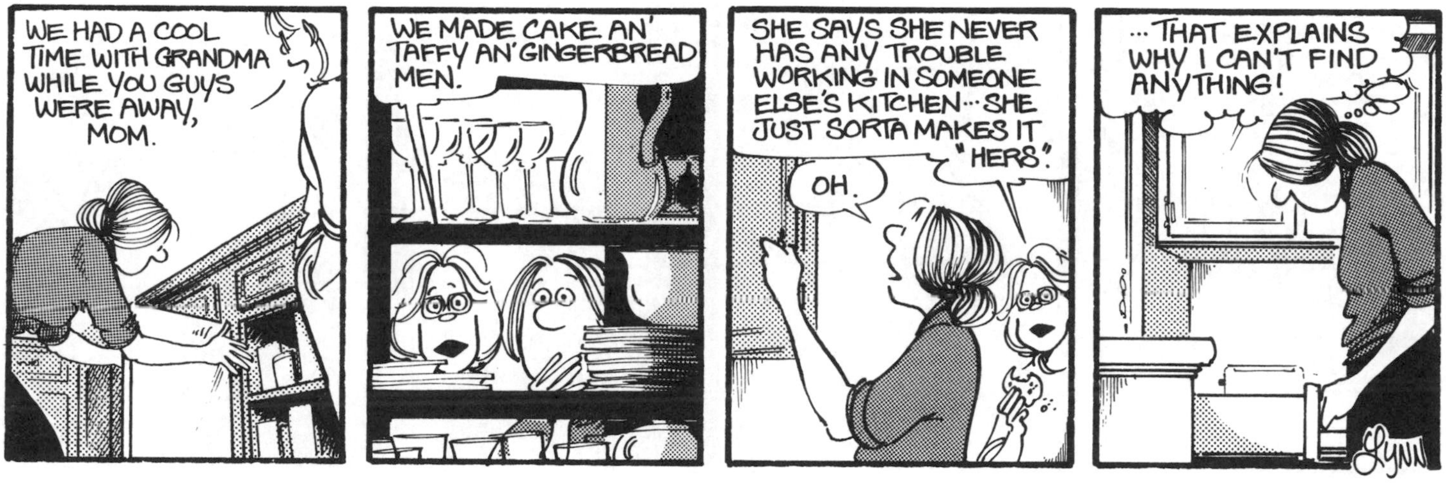
WE HAD A COOL TIME WITH GRANDMA WHILE YOU GUYS WERE AWAY, MOM.
WE MADE CAKE AN' TAFFY AN' GINGERBREAD MEN.
SHE SAYS SHE NEVER HAS ANY TROUBLE WORKING IN SOMEONE ELSE'S KITCHEN... SHE JUST SORTA MAKES IT "HERS."
OH.
...THAT EXPLAINS WHY I CAN'T FIND ANYTHING!

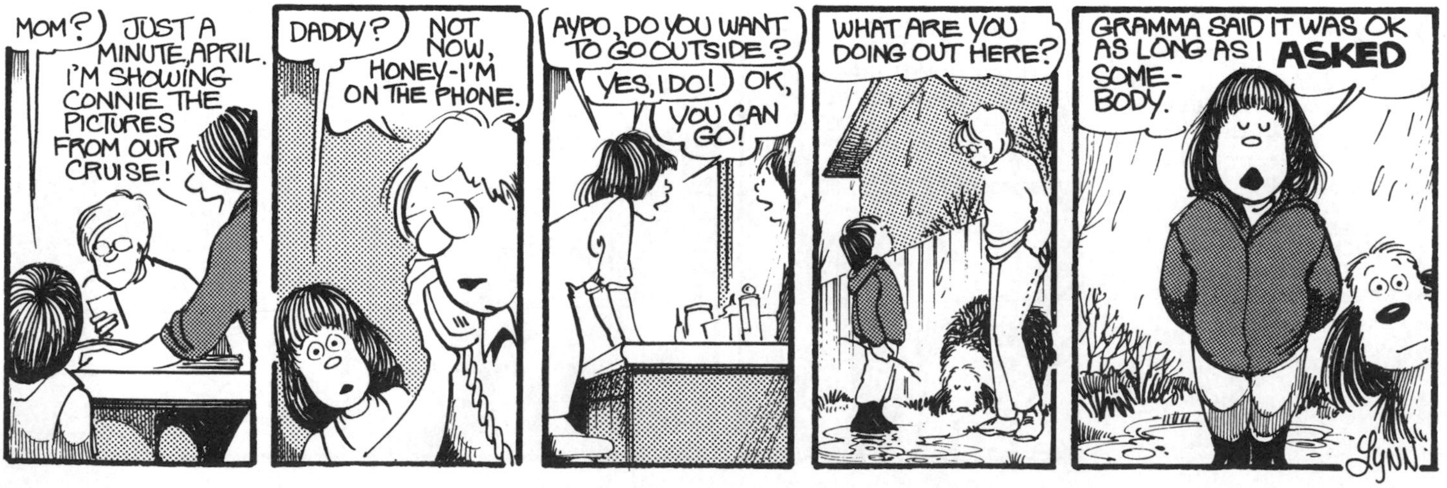
MOM?
JUST A MINUTE, APRIL. I'M SHOWING CONNIE THE PICTURES FROM OUR CRUISE!
DADDY?
NOT NOW, HONEY-I'M ON THE PHONE.
AYPO, DO YOU WANT TO GO OUTSIDE?
YES, I DO!
OK, YOU CAN GO!
WHAT ARE YOU DOING OUT HERE?
GRAMMA SAID IT WAS OK AS LONG AS I ASKED SOME-BODY.

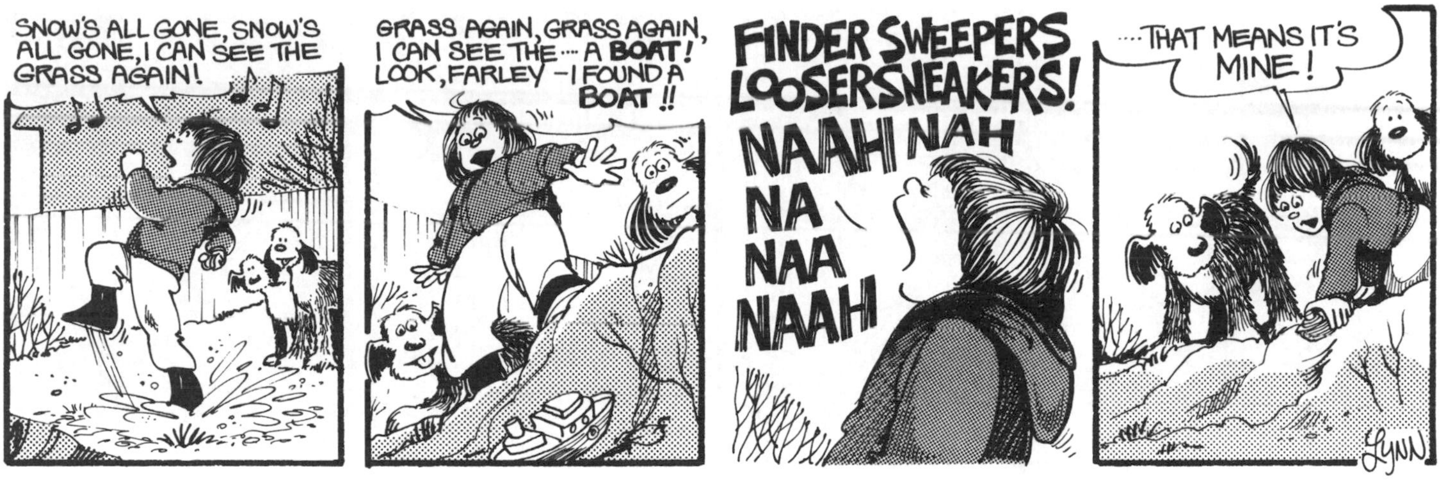
SNOW'S ALL GONE, SNOW'S ALL GONE, I CAN SEE THE GRASS AGAIN!
GRASS AGAIN, GRASS AGAIN, I CAN SEE THE ···· A BOAT! LOOK, FARLEY – I FOUND A BOAT !!
FINDER SWEEPERS LOOSERSNEAKERS!
NAAH NAH NA NAA NAAH
···· THAT MEANS IT'S MINE!
LYNN

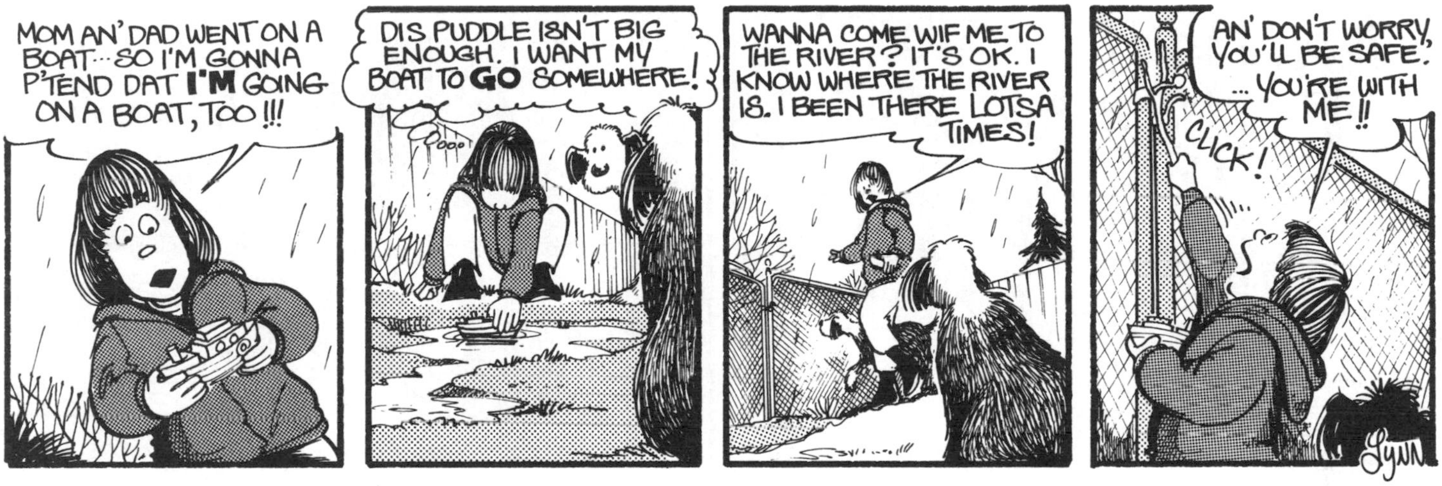
MOM AN' DAD WENT ON A BOAT ··· SO I'M GONNA P'TEND DAT I'M GOING ON A BOAT, TOO !!!
DIS PUDDLE ISN'T BIG ENOUGH. I WANT MY BOAT TO GO SOMEWHERE!
WANNA COME WIF ME TO THE RIVER? IT'S OK. I KNOW WHERE THE RIVER IS. I BEEN THERE LOTSA TIMES!
AN' DON'T WORRY, YOU'LL BE SAFE. ... YOU'RE WITH ME!!
CLICK!
LYNN

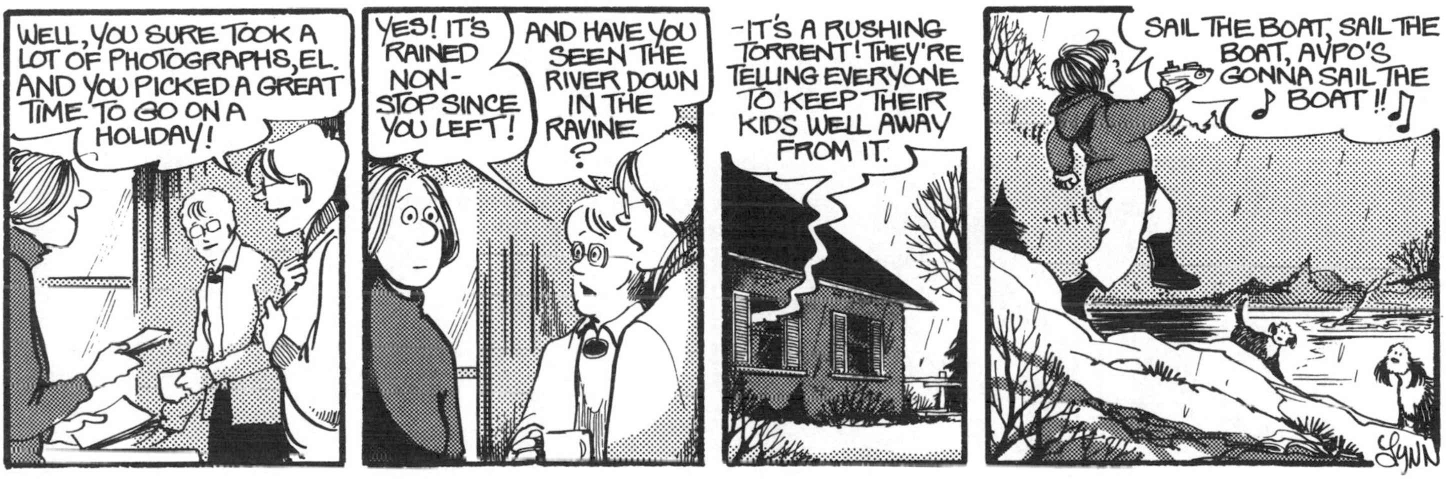
WELL, YOU SURE TOOK A LOT OF PHOTOGRAPHS, EL. AND YOU PICKED A GREAT TIME TO GO ON A HOLIDAY!
YES! IT'S RAINED NON-STOP SINCE YOU LEFT!
AND HAVE YOU SEEN THE RIVER DOWN IN THE RAVINE?
–IT'S A RUSHING TORRENT! THEY'RE TELLING EVERYONE TO KEEP THEIR KIDS WELL AWAY FROM IT.
SAIL THE BOAT, SAIL THE BOAT, AYPO'S GONNA SAIL THE BOAT!!
LYNN

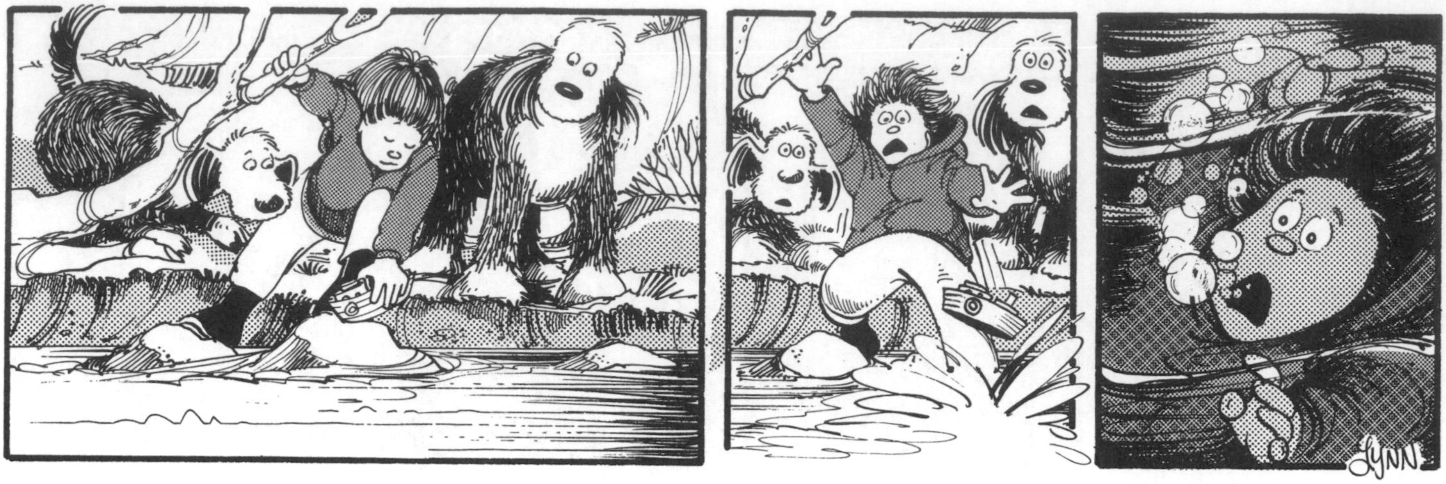
LYNN

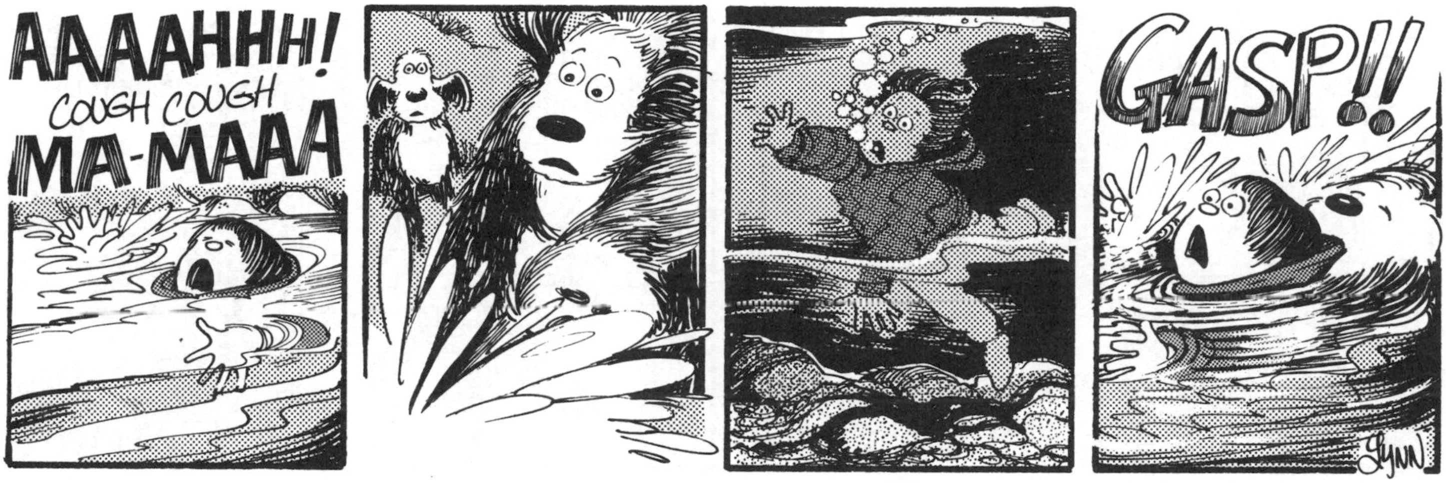
AAAAHHH!
COUGH COUGH
MA-MAAA
GASP!!
LYNN

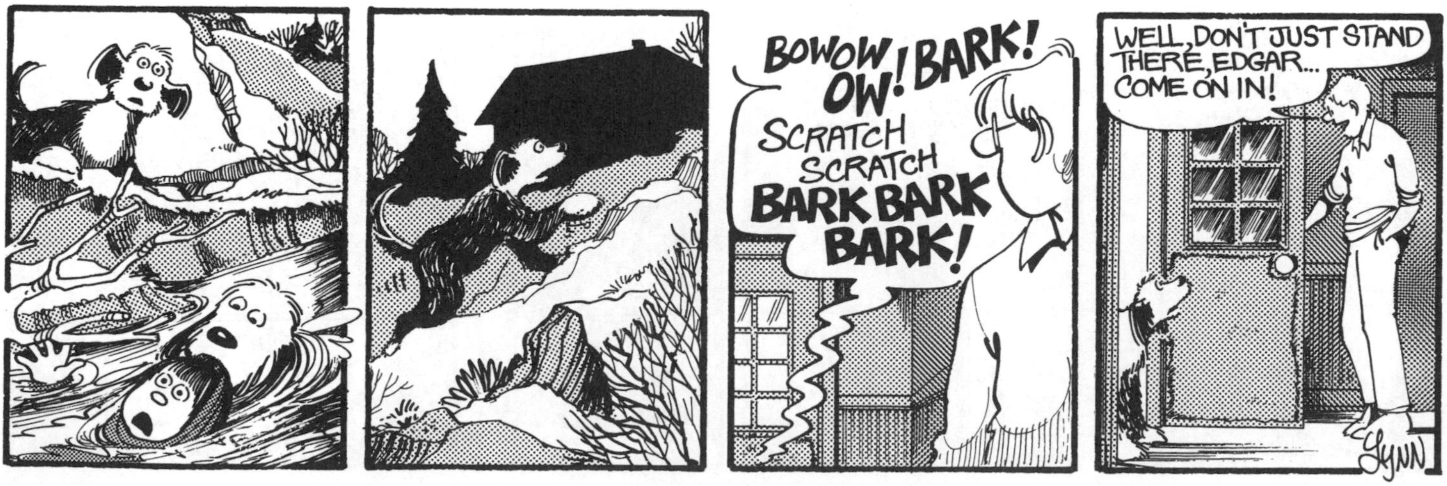
BOWOW OW! BARK!
SCRATCH SCRATCH
BARK BARK BARK!
WELL, DON'T JUST STAND THERE, EDGAR... COME ON IN!
LYNN

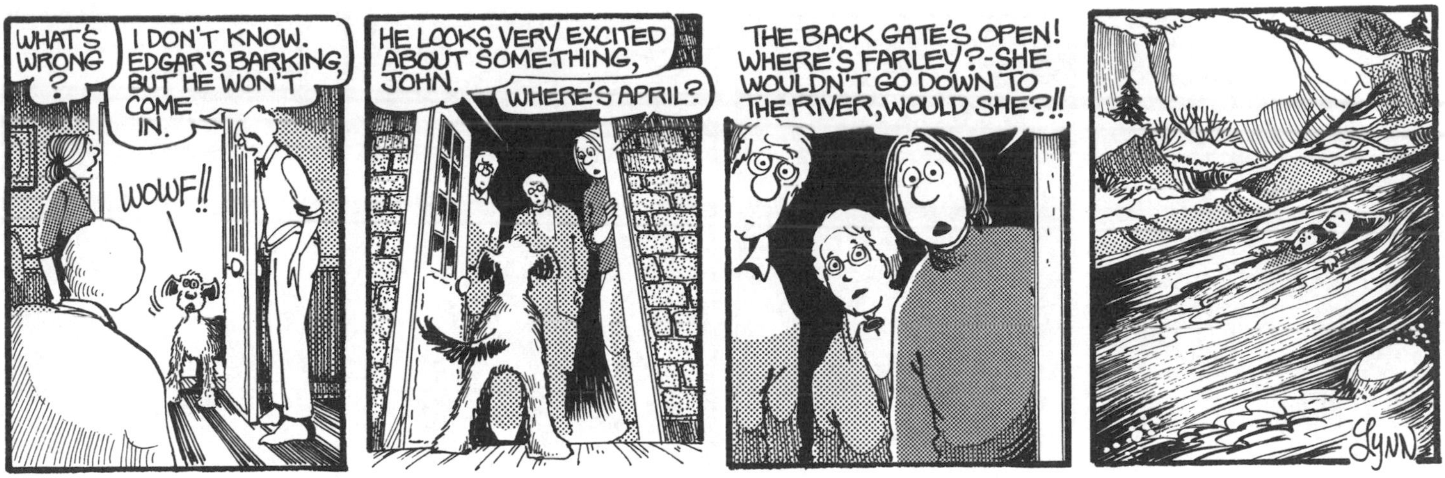
WHAT'S WRONG?
I DON'T KNOW. EDGAR'S BARKING, BUT HE WON'T COME IN.
WOWF!!
HE LOOKS VERY EXCITED ABOUT SOMETHING, JOHN.
WHERE'S APRIL?
THE BACK GATE'S OPEN! WHERE'S FARLEY?-SHE WOULDN'T GO DOWN TO THE RIVER, WOULD SHE?!!
LYNN

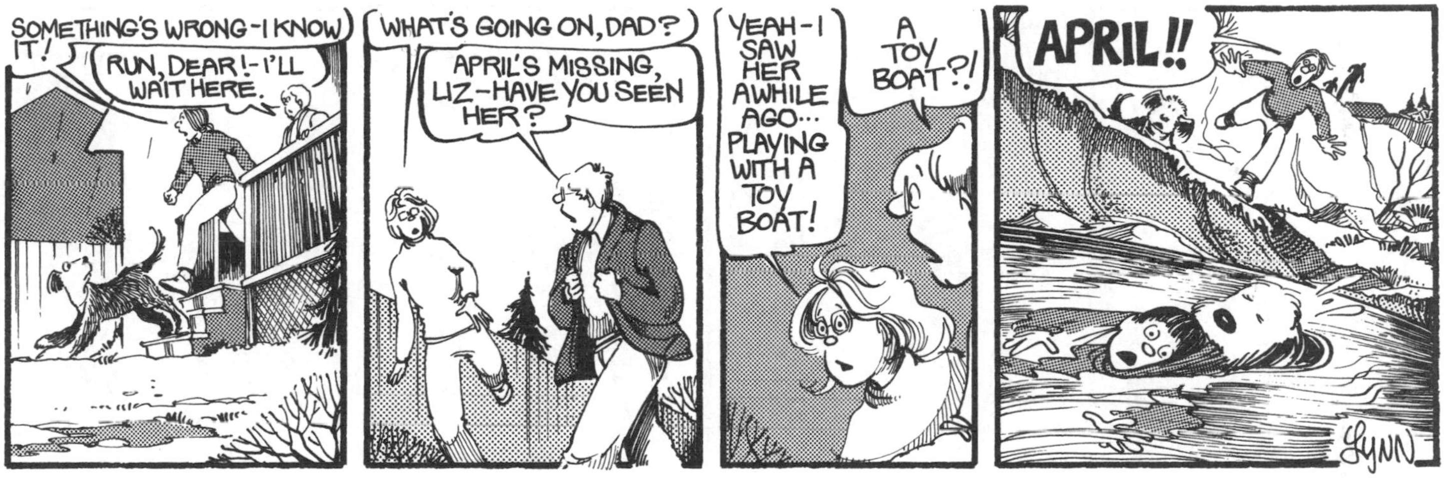
SOMETHING'S WRONG-I KNOW IT!
RUN, DEAR!-I'LL WAIT HERE.
WHAT'S GOING ON, DAD?
APRIL'S MISSING, LIZ-HAVE YOU SEEN HER?
YEAH-I SAW HER AWHILE AGO... PLAYING WITH A TOY BOAT!
A TOY BOAT?!
APRIL!!
LYNN

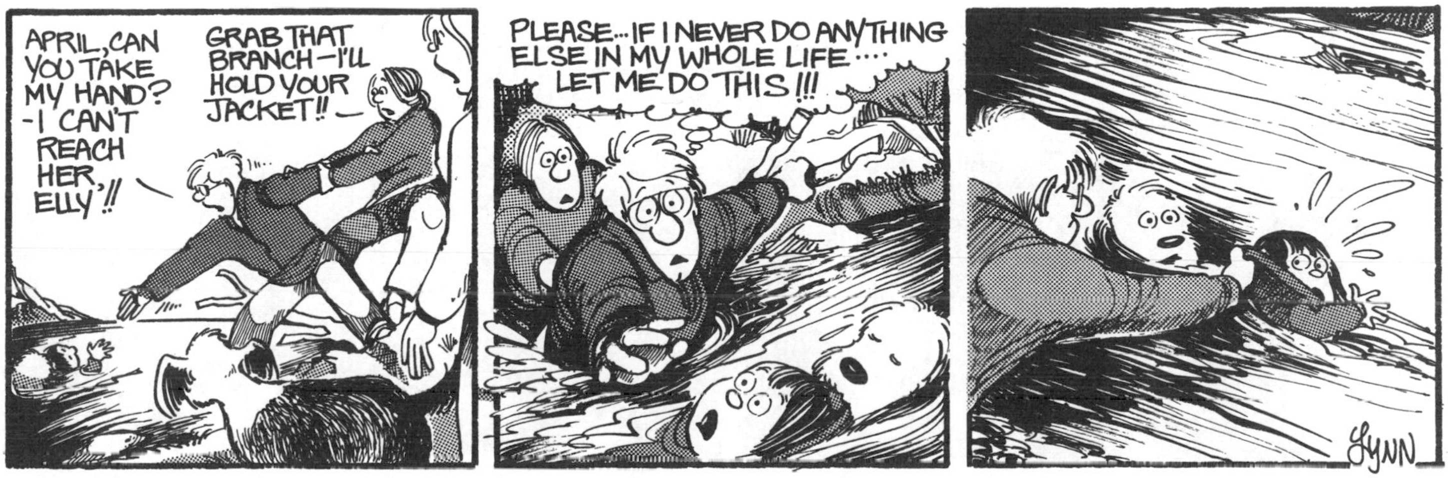
APRIL, CAN YOU TAKE MY HAND? -I CAN'T REACH HER, ELLY!!
GRAB THAT BRANCH-I'LL HOLD YOUR JACKET!!
PLEASE... IF I NEVER DO ANYTHING ELSE IN MY WHOLE LIFE.... LET ME DO THIS!!!
LYNN

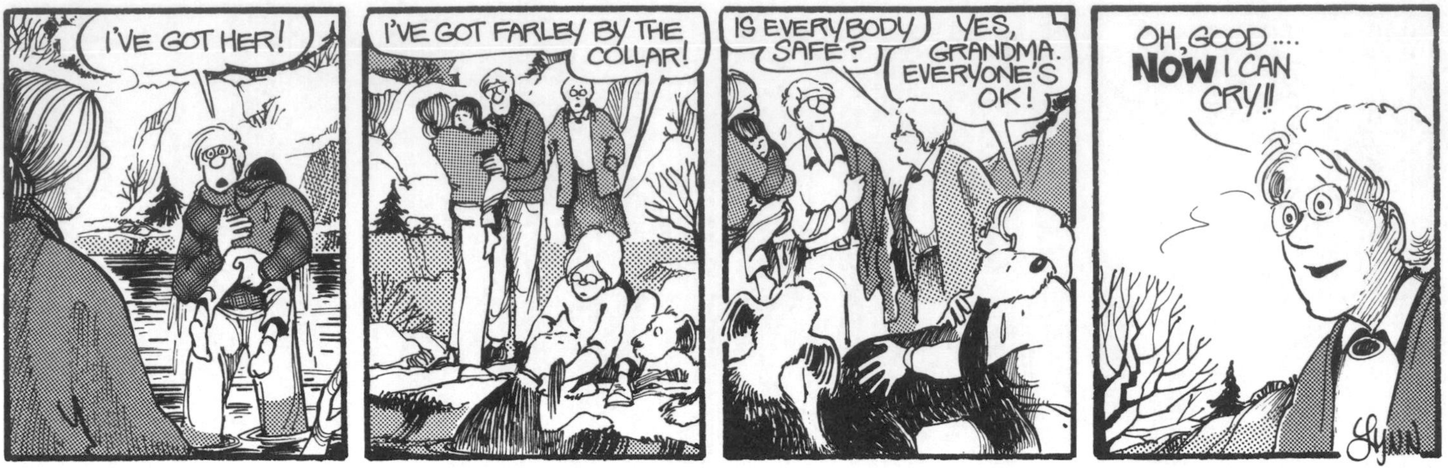
I'VE GOT HER!
I'VE GOT FARLEY BY THE COLLAR!
IS EVERYBODY SAFE?
YES, GRANDMA. EVERYONE'S OK!
OH, GOOD.... NOW I CAN CRY!!
LYNN

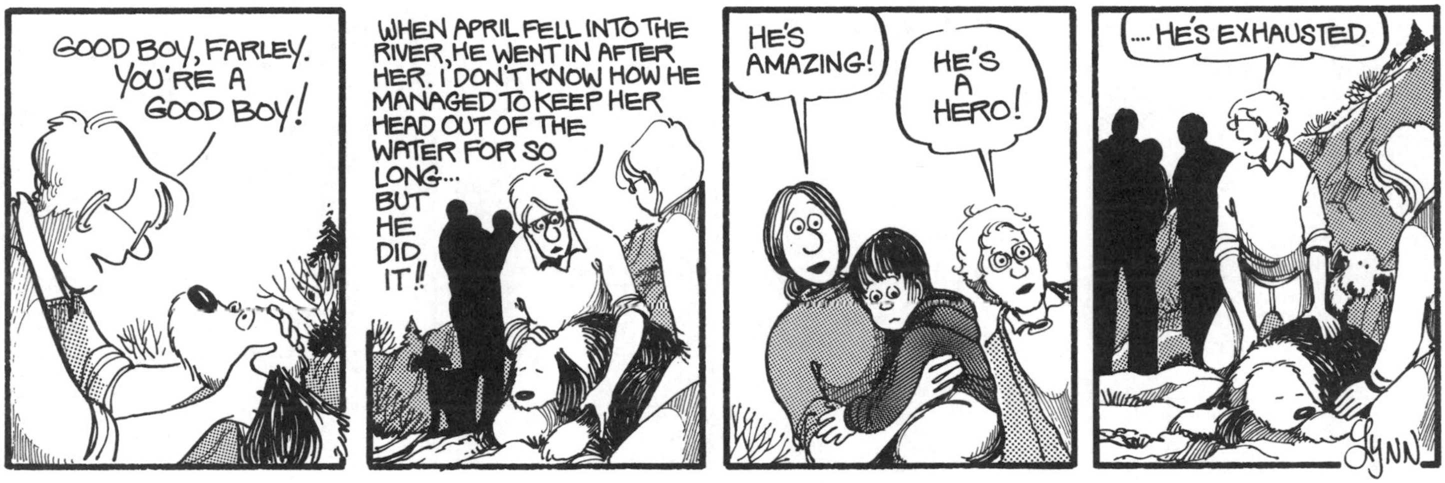
GOOD BOY, FARLEY. YOU'RE A GOOD BOY!
WHEN APRIL FELL INTO THE RIVER, HE WENT IN AFTER HER. I DON'T KNOW HOW HE MANAGED TO KEEP HER HEAD OUT OF THE WATER FOR SO LONG... BUT HE DID IT!!
HE'S AMAZING!
HE'S A HERO!
.... HE'S EXHAUSTED.
LYNN

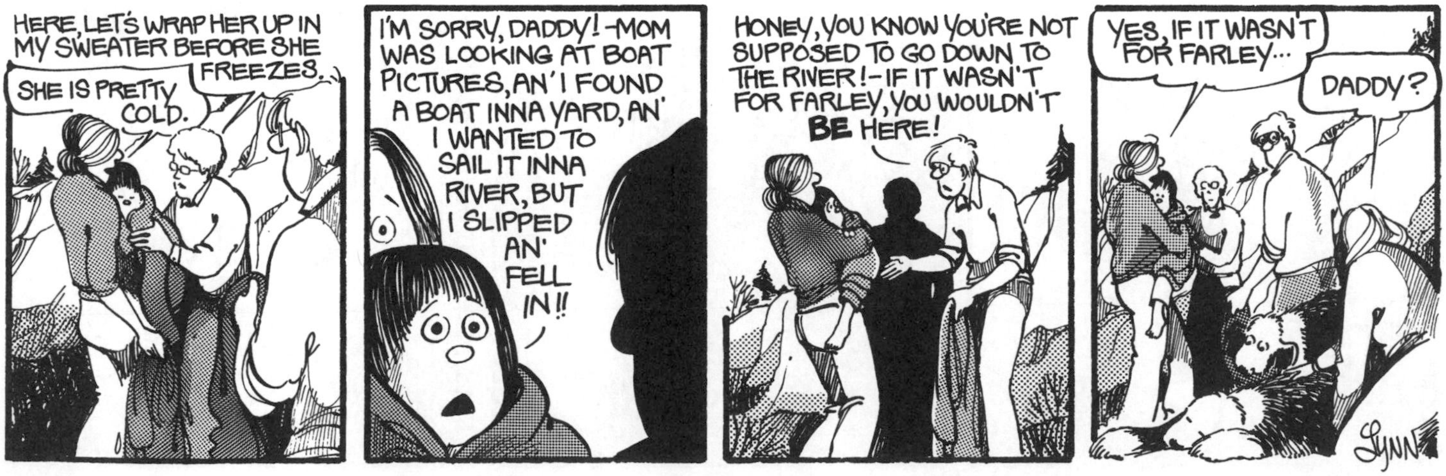
HERE, LET'S WRAP HER UP IN MY SWEATER BEFORE SHE FREEZES.
SHE IS PRETTY COLD.
I'M SORRY, DADDY! -MOM WAS LOOKING AT BOAT PICTURES, AN' I FOUND A BOAT INNA YARD, AN' I WANTED TO SAIL IT INNA RIVER, BUT I SLIPPED AN' FELL IN!!
HONEY, YOU KNOW YOU'RE NOT SUPPOSED TO GO DOWN TO THE RIVER! -IF IT WASN'T FOR FARLEY, YOU WOULDN'T BE HERE!
YES, IF IT WASN'T FOR FARLEY...
DADDY?
LYNN

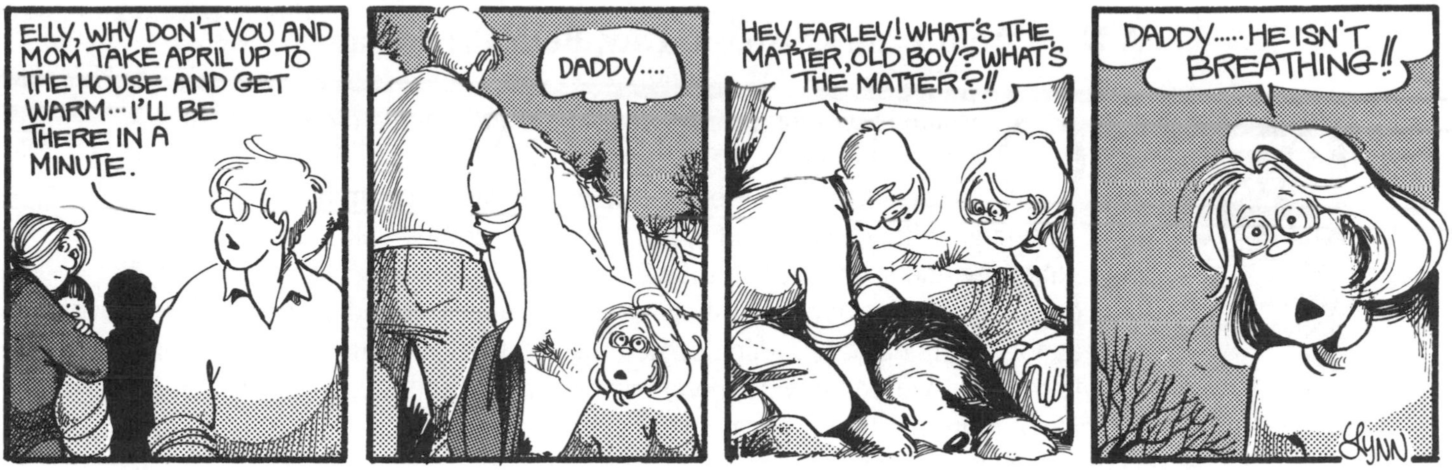
ELLY, WHY DON'T YOU AND MOM TAKE APRIL UP TO THE HOUSE AND GET WARM... I'LL BE THERE IN A MINUTE.
DADDY....
HEY, FARLEY! WHAT'S THE MATTER, OLD BOY? WHAT'S THE MATTER?!!
DADDY..... HE ISN'T BREATHING!!
LYNN

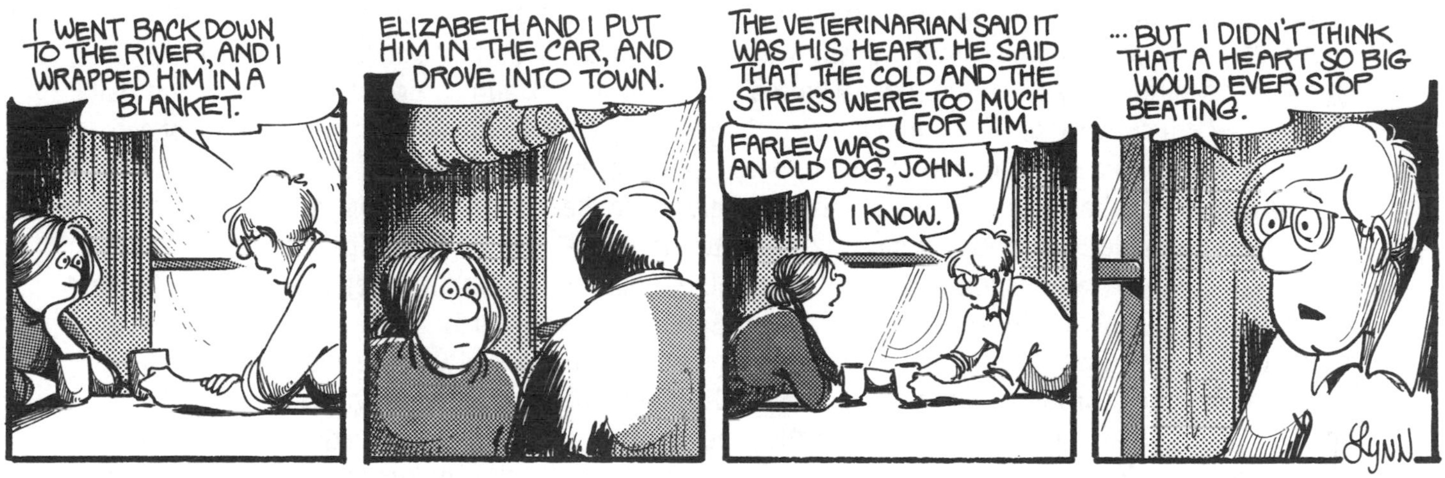
I WENT BACK DOWN TO THE RIVER, AND I WRAPPED HIM IN A BLANKET.
ELIZABETH AND I PUT HIM IN THE CAR, AND DROVE INTO TOWN.
THE VETERINARIAN SAID IT WAS HIS HEART. HE SAID THAT THE COLD AND THE STRESS WERE TOO MUCH FOR HIM.
FARLEY WAS AN OLD DOG, JOHN.
I KNOW.
... BUT I DIDN'T THINK THAT A HEART SO BIG WOULD EVER STOP BEATING.
LYNN

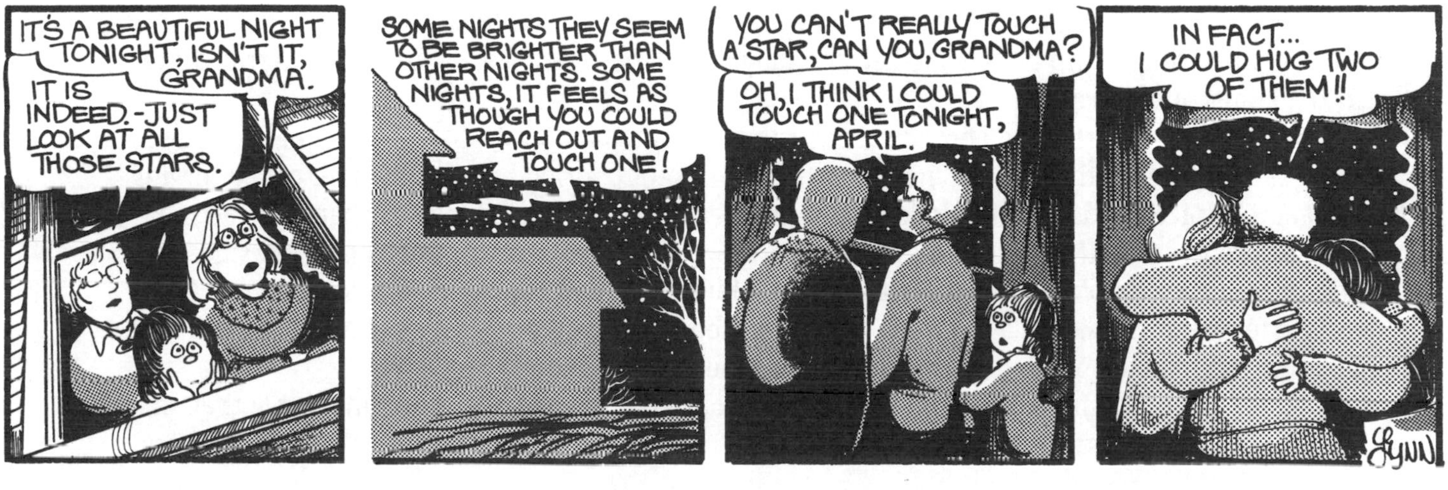
IT'S A BEAUTIFUL NIGHT TONIGHT, ISN'T IT, GRANDMA.
IT IS INDEED.-JUST LOOK AT ALL THOSE STARS.
SOME NIGHTS THEY SEEM TO BE BRIGHTER THAN OTHER NIGHTS. SOME NIGHTS, IT FEELS AS THOUGH YOU COULD REACH OUT AND TOUCH ONE!
YOU CAN'T REALLY TOUCH A STAR, CAN YOU, GRANDMA?
OH, I THINK I COULD TOUCH ONE TONIGHT, APRIL.
IN FACT... I COULD HUG TWO OF THEM!!
LYNN

A Note from Lynn's Sister-in-Law, Beth Cruikshank

Our family was long considered, in our little hometown of Lynn Lake, to be so heavily into arts and crafts as to be verging on weirdness. Half the basement of our bungalow home was taken up by my mother's weaving studio, chock-full of four-harness floor looms, spinning wheels, bobbin winders, and a small mountain of yarns. The other half housed Dad's carpentry and lapidary workshop, where his rock saw and tumbler roared almost nightly. Brother Ralph carried the creative weaving on where Mom left off and worked toward a professional career in music, while brother Rod indulged in erratic orgies of more traditionally male types of creativity, including model building, electronic kits, mechanics, disc-jockeying, and model railroading.

Still, when Lynn married Rod and joined the ranks, there was no doubt at all that the artistic level in the family had just kicked up by several orders of magnitude.

Lynn's talent for drawing really is astonishing. In her prime, she could draw faster and more fluently than she could talk, and she's never been any slouch at that, either. Time and again, we would watch amazed as she impatiently grabbed up an envelope or scrap of notepaper and whipped off a drawing of someone or something she was trying to describe. Her instinctive ability to depict any bodily position, any facial expression with a few rapid strokes and squiggles of the pen, and nail these note-perfect every time, invariably left us boggling. No one in the family was really surprised when her cartoon books, and later the strip, became as successful as they did.

Having a "real" artist in the family has definitely made life more interesting. All our homes are enlivened by wonderful bits of "Lynn art," the family anecdotes include a number of richly bizarre entanglements with famous folk, the media, and other offshoots of Lynn's fame, and we never quite know what will show up in the mail. Once, Lynn sent us a case of Spam—why, we never knew; another time, two dozen rubber chickens. One memorable Christmas, we received a hundred false noses/moustaches, Groucho Marx-style. Our holiday family photos that year were exceptionally interesting! And then, of course, there were the times when she had bouts of artistic temperament . . .

I remember, in the early days of the strip, sitting in my mother's tiny kitchen in Lynn Lake with a coffee cup in one hand and a cookie in the other, watching with interest while Lynn threw a truly excellent panic attack. It made her nuts whenever she had one of those days when everything she drew looked (to her) sickeningly second-rate. None of the rest of us could see these fatal flaws, mind you. The strips she was raging about as purest plug-ugly cow-droppings seemed pretty much her usual wonderfully drawn stuff. But to Lynn, if it isn't excellent, it isn't good enough, and in the early months of the strip before she became fully confident in her work, "bad days" terrified her into a lather of self-loathing.

It was both entertaining and educational to watch my mother deal with the situation. She let Lynn vent, made soothing noises now and then, and kept pouring her a little more coffee, urging yet another slice of succulent date loaf or plump peanut butter cookie into her hands. It wasn't long before the fear fit passed and Lynn settled down to happily indulge in calories and small-town gossip with the rest of us. Like Alice B. Toklas, Mom had found the recipe for dealing with an artistic temperament—just add a dash of comfort food to unlimited servings of affection, et voila!—an artist too replete and content to worry about much of anything.

All of us in the immediate family have found ourselves involved, at one time or another, in support or contribution to Lynn's strip. All the kids have provided excellent story ideas at times, just by being kids. Many of us have been morphed into secondary cartoon characters. And all of us have provided advice at times and whatever expertise we could offer on the story lines.

My particular role, since the beginning of FBorFW, has been the unique honor of serving as the main "family veterinarian" to the Pattersons' various mythical pets. This has led to some interesting, if slightly bizarre, discussions with Lynn. The one I remember best went something like this:

"You're going to kill off Farley? Lynn, you can't DO that!"

"I have no choice." The voice on the phone sounded unusually grim. "You know my strip runs in real time. And since you just told me sheepdogs don't usually live past twelve, and Farley is already thirteen—well . . ."

"Wow!" I contemplated the likely reader reaction with awe. "So how are you going to do it? How on earth do you bump off the family dog in three panels and a punch line, and hope to get away with it?"

"I don't know. Farley is getting older and more feeble these days, so the setup is there. But I can't see the end yet."

"Well, there's one thing I can tell you about the end!" I said, with sudden conviction. "After all the abuse that poor dog has taken from those kids over the years, and the way you've made him the butt and fool of the family, you HAVE to give him back his dignity when he goes. Farley has to die a hero!"

"A hero?" Lynn said, startled. "Farley? Oh, come on! He's old and tired, and besides, everyone knows he's basically pretty dumb. He can't do some brilliant Lassie thing, like smashing through the window of the burning building and turning the combination of the lock with his teeth to rescue little Timmy before the dynamite goes off in the mine!"

"He doesn't need to have brains, just a bit of sheepdog instinct!" I said, "It's deep-rooted in them to protect their flocks, you know. Like April, for instance. Farley and April are close—he's bound to be protective of her. Have him rescue April in some simple way."

"How?" The skepticism was now tinged with interest. "It has to be believable."

"Well, there's a ravine behind the Pattersons' house, with a creek in it, right? Nothing is more of a kid magnet than running water. I've sometimes wondered why the kids never go down there. So have April fall into the creek when it's high and Farley drag her out. Simple, believable, minimum brains required. But definitely strenuous enough to set off a fatal heart attack in the poor old mutt."

"Hmm!"

"It's perfect!" I continued, warming to my theme. "Farley gets to die relatively painlessly, a hero, with dignity. Elly and John are then spared having to make the awful decision to take him on that last gloomy trip to the vet. What could be better?"

There was a lengthy silence.

"I'll think about it," Lynn said finally.

The subject never arose again, and I soon forgot our conversation. Then I turned to the comics section of the paper one spring day and saw April headed down to the ravine with a toy boat in her hand and Farley and Edgar at her heels. I had proposed the idea frivolously, without much real thought. But as the story unfolded, I found myself wrenched with anxiety for April, and in tears by the conclusion. Lynn's ability to tell a story powerfully and well has never been better illustrated. And beyond a doubt, she gave Farley back his dignity in a most satisfying way in the end. Just as the doctor ordered!

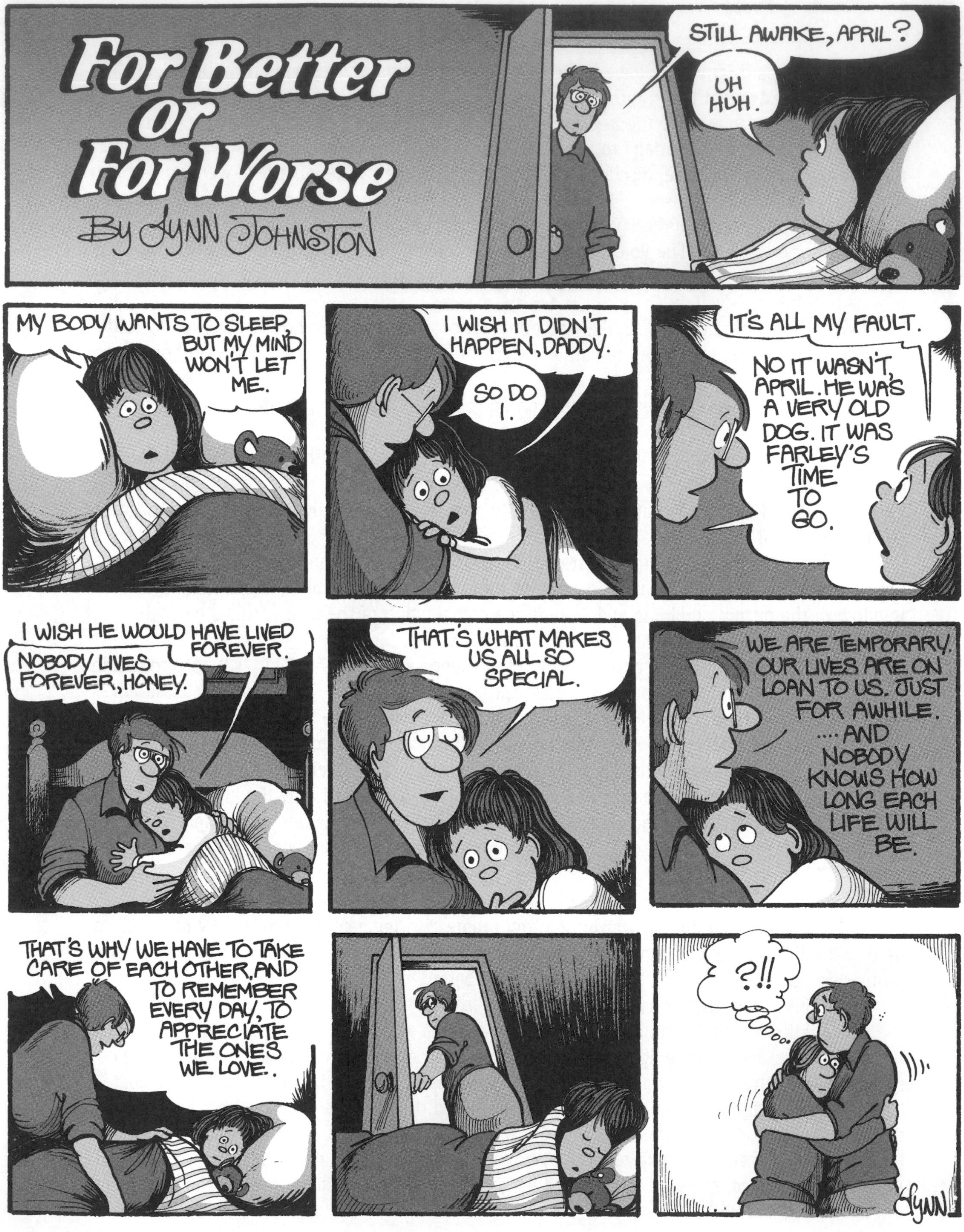
For Better or For Worse
By Lynn Johnston
STILL AWAKE, APRIL?
UH HUH.
MY BODY WANTS TO SLEEP, BUT MY MIND WON'T LET ME.
I WISH IT DIDN'T HAPPEN, DADDY.
SO DO I.
IT'S ALL MY FAULT.
NO IT WASN'T, APRIL. HE WAS A VERY OLD DOG. IT WAS FARLEY'S TIME TO GO.
I WISH HE WOULD HAVE LIVED FOREVER.
NOBODY LIVES FOREVER, HONEY.
THAT'S WHAT MAKES US ALL SO SPECIAL.
WE ARE TEMPORARY. OUR LIVES ARE ON LOAN TO US. JUST FOR AWHILE.
....AND NOBODY KNOWS HOW LONG EACH LIFE WILL BE.
THAT'S WHY WE HAVE TO TAKE CARE OF EACH OTHER, AND TO REMEMBER EVERY DAY, TO APPRECIATE THE ONES WE LOVE..
?!!
Lynn

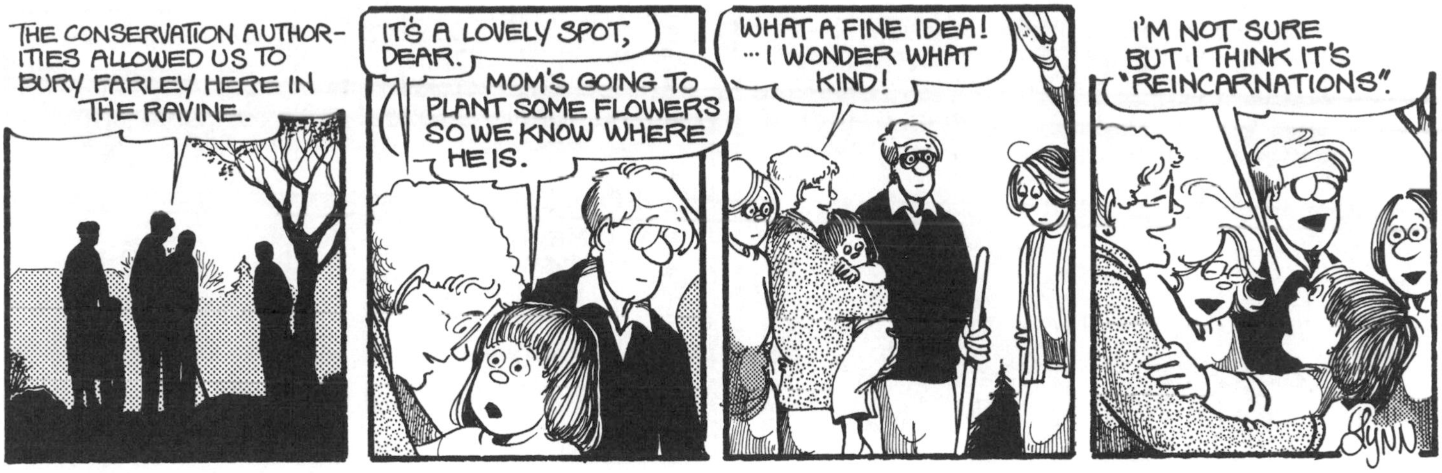
THE CONSERVATION AUTHORITIES ALLOWED US TO BURY FARLEY HERE IN THE RAVINE.
IT'S A LOVELY SPOT, DEAR.
MOM'S GOING TO PLANT SOME FLOWERS SO WE KNOW WHERE HE IS.
WHAT A FINE IDEA! ...I WONDER WHAT KIND!
I'M NOT SURE BUT I THINK IT'S "REINCARNATIONS".

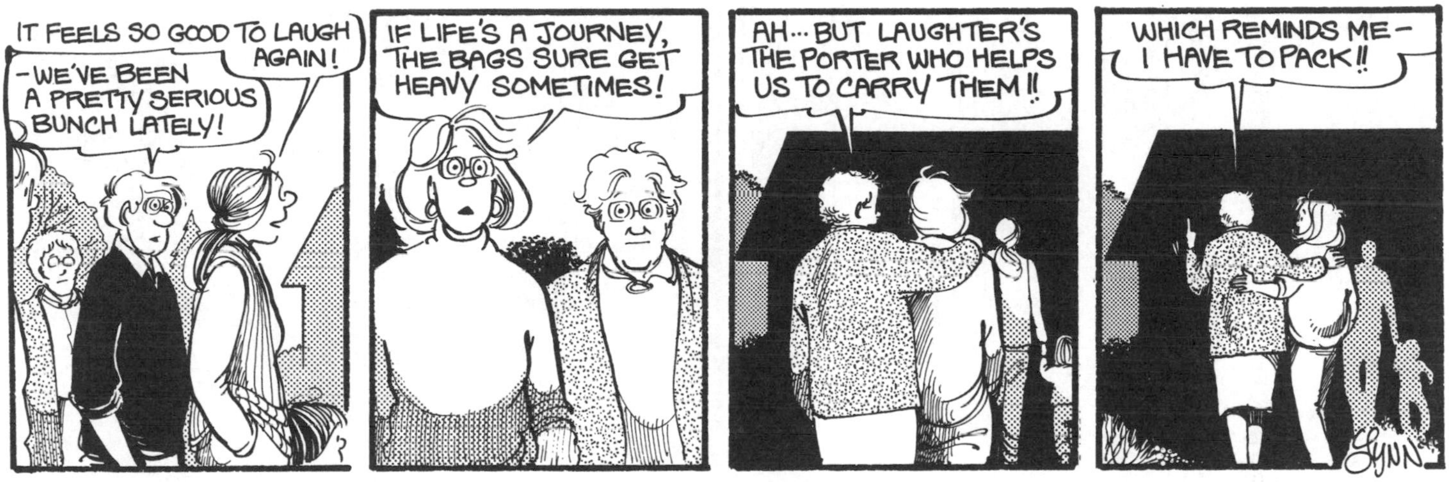
IT FEELS SO GOOD TO LAUGH AGAIN!
-WE'VE BEEN A PRETTY SERIOUS BUNCH LATELY!
IF LIFE'S A JOURNEY, THE BAGS SURE GET HEAVY SOMETIMES!
AH... BUT LAUGHTER'S THE PORTER WHO HELPS US TO CARRY THEM!!
WHICH REMINDS ME - I HAVE TO PACK!!

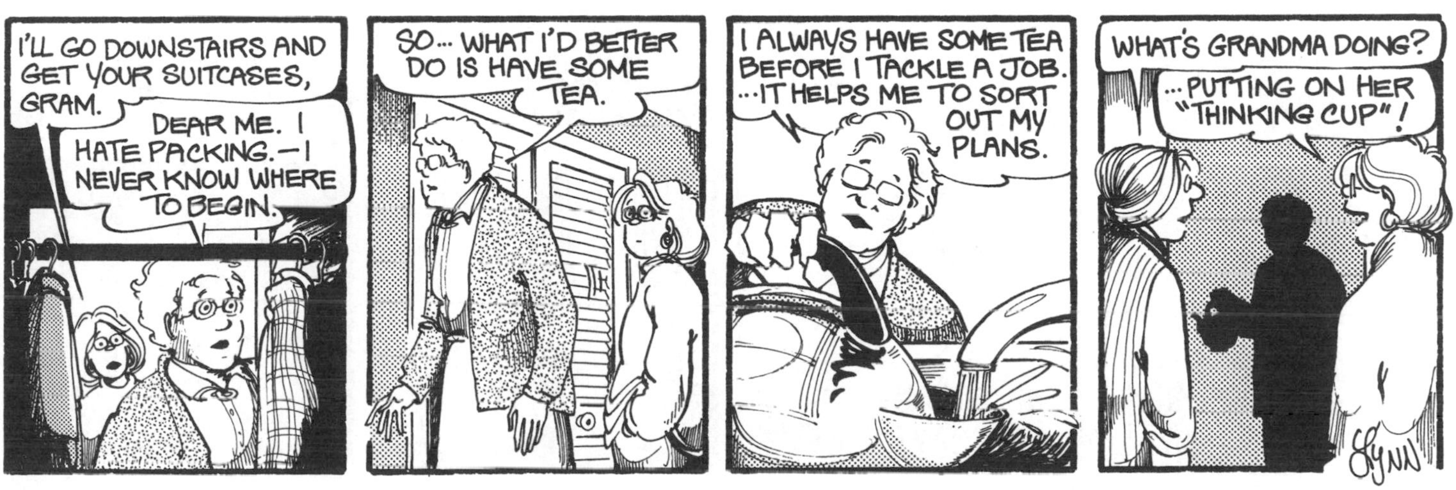
I'LL GO DOWNSTAIRS AND GET YOUR SUITCASES, GRAM.
DEAR ME. I HATE PACKING. - I NEVER KNOW WHERE TO BEGIN.
SO... WHAT I'D BETTER DO IS HAVE SOME TEA.
I ALWAYS HAVE SOME TEA BEFORE I TACKLE A JOB. ...IT HELPS ME TO SORT OUT MY PLANS.
WHAT'S GRANDMA DOING?
...PUTTING ON HER "THINKING CUP"!

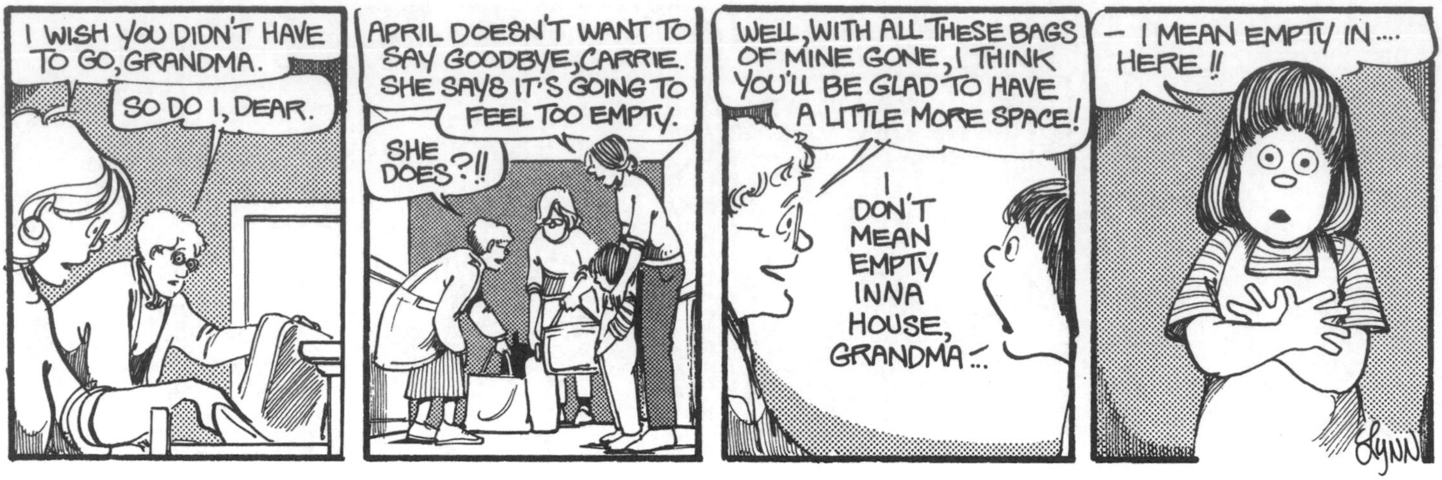
I WISH YOU DIDN'T HAVE TO GO, GRANDMA.
SO DO I, DEAR.
APRIL DOESN'T WANT TO SAY GOODBYE, CARRIE. SHE SAYS IT'S GOING TO FEEL TOO EMPTY.
SHE DOES?!!
WELL, WITH ALL THESE BAGS OF MINE GONE, I THINK YOU'LL BE GLAD TO HAVE A LITTLE MORE SPACE!
I DON'T MEAN EMPTY INNA HOUSE, GRANDMA...
– I MEAN EMPTY IN.... HERE!!

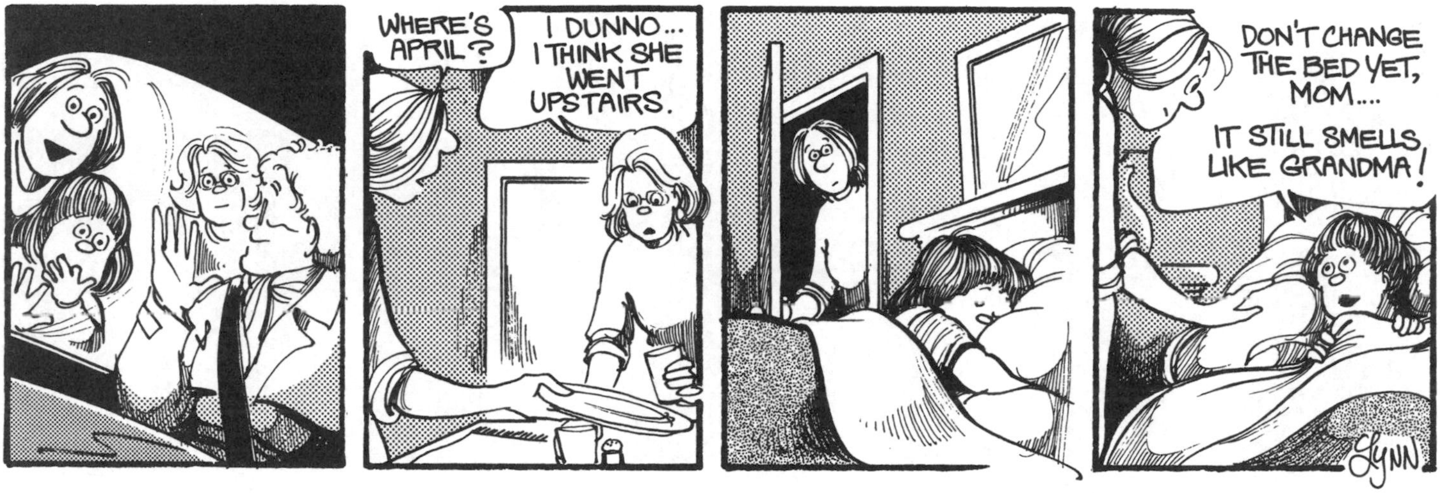
WHERE'S APRIL?
I DUNNO... I THINK SHE WENT UPSTAIRS.
DON'T CHANGE THE BED YET, MOM....
IT STILL SMELLS LIKE GRANDMA!

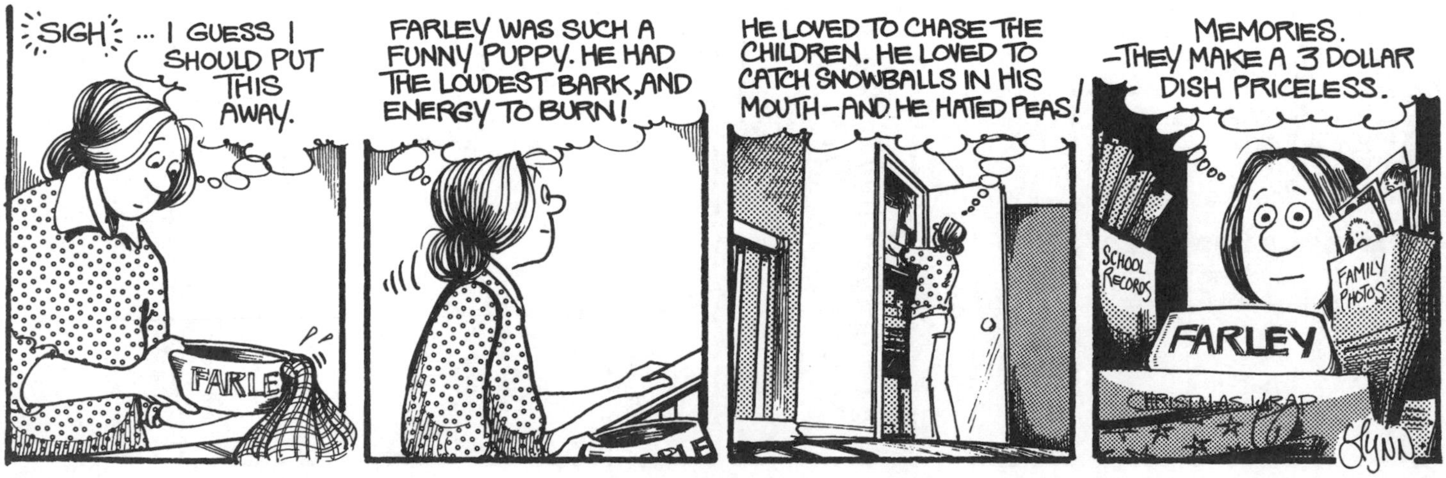
SIGH ... I GUESS I SHOULD PUT THIS AWAY.
FARLE
FARLEY WAS SUCH A FUNNY PUPPY. HE HAD THE LOUDEST BARK, AND ENERGY TO BURN!
HE LOVED TO CHASE THE CHILDREN. HE LOVED TO CATCH SNOWBALLS IN HIS MOUTH – AND HE HATED PEAS!
MEMORIES. – THEY MAKE A 3 DOLLAR DISH PRICELESS.
SCHOOL RECORDS
FAMILY PHOTOS
FARLEY
CHRISTMAS WRAP

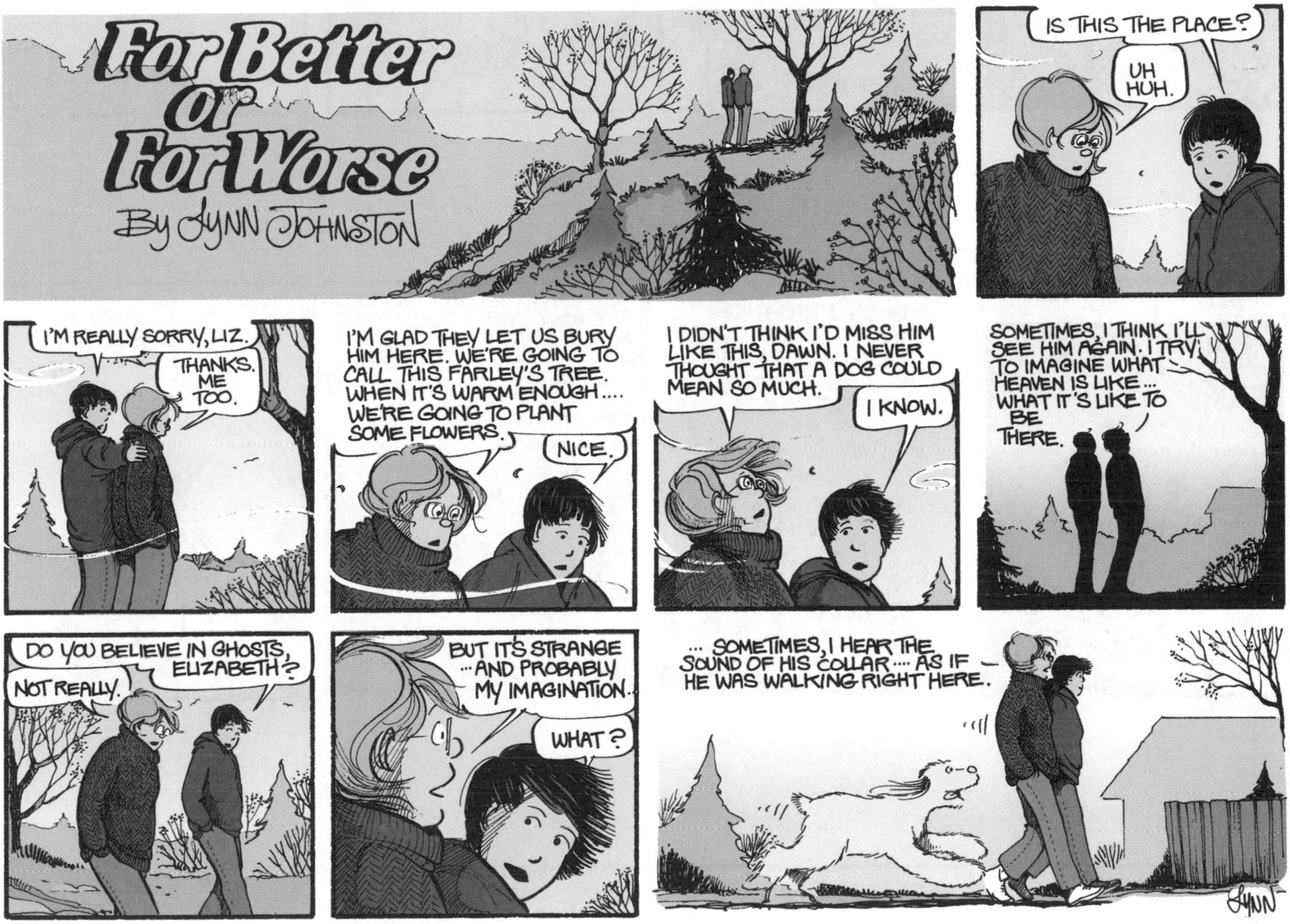
For Better or For Worse
By Lynn Johnston
IS THIS THE PLACE?
UH HUH.
I'M REALLY SORRY, LIZ.
THANKS. ME TOO.
I'M GLAD THEY LET US BURY HIM HERE. WE'RE GOING TO CALL THIS FARLEY'S TREE. WHEN IT'S WARM ENOUGH.... WE'RE GOING TO PLANT SOME FLOWERS.
NICE.
I DIDN'T THINK I'D MISS HIM LIKE THIS, DAWN. I NEVER THOUGHT THAT A DOG COULD MEAN SO MUCH.
I KNOW.
SOMETIMES, I THINK I'LL SEE HIM AGAIN. I TRY TO IMAGINE WHAT HEAVEN IS LIKE... WHAT IT'S LIKE TO BE THERE.
DO YOU BELIEVE IN GHOSTS, ELIZABETH?
NOT REALLY.
BUT IT'S STRANGE ...AND PROBABLY MY IMAGINATION..
WHAT?
... SOMETIMES, I HEAR THE SOUND OF HIS COLLAR.... AS IF HE WAS WALKING RIGHT HERE.
Lynn

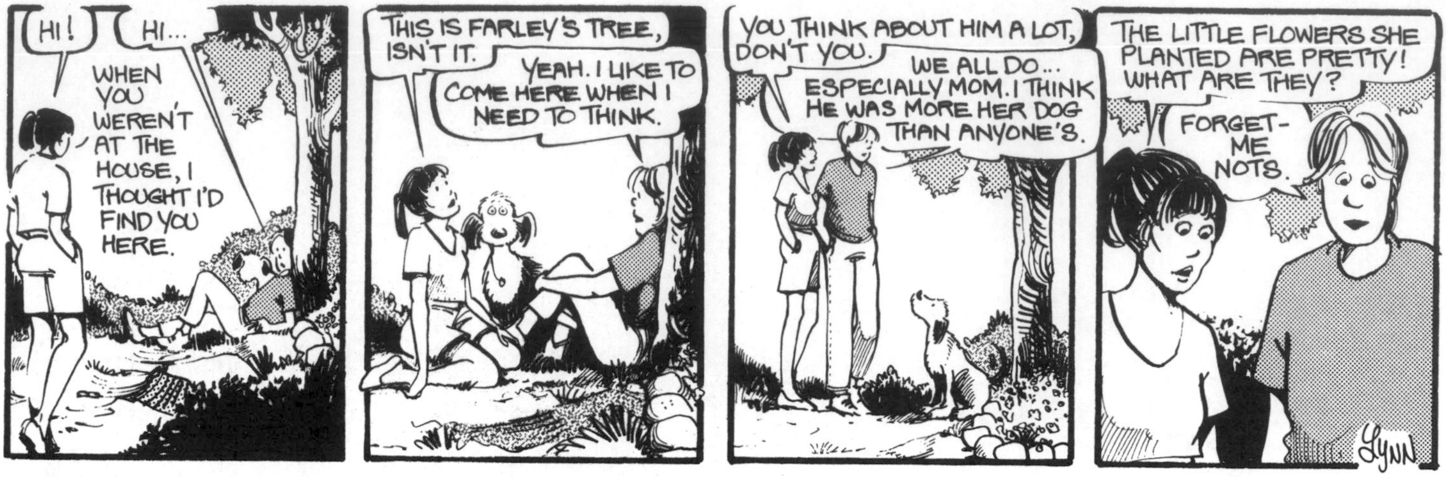
HI!
HI...
WHEN YOU WEREN'T AT THE HOUSE, I THOUGHT I'D FIND YOU HERE.
THIS IS FARLEY'S TREE, ISN'T IT.
YEAH. I LIKE TO COME HERE WHEN I NEED TO THINK.
YOU THINK ABOUT HIM A LOT, DON'T YOU.
WE ALL DO... ESPECIALLY MOM. I THINK HE WAS MORE HER DOG THAN ANYONE'S.
THE LITTLE FLOWERS SHE PLANTED ARE PRETTY! WHAT ARE THEY?
FORGET-ME NOTS.
Lynn

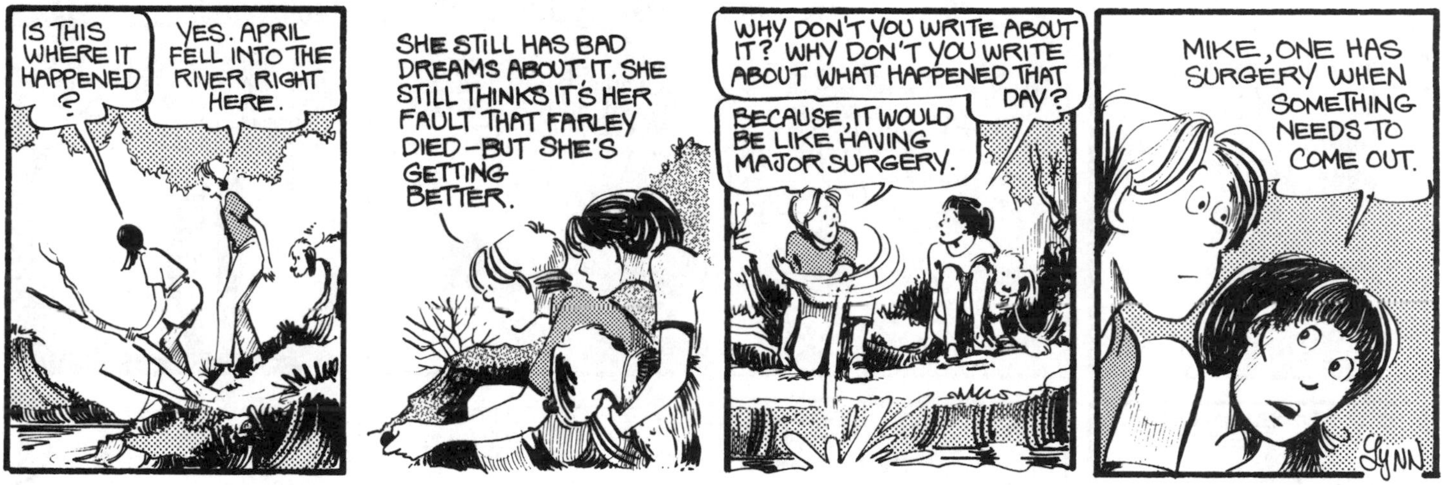
IS THIS WHERE IT HAPPENED?
YES. APRIL FELL INTO THE RIVER RIGHT HERE.
SHE STILL HAS BAD DREAMS ABOUT IT. SHE STILL THINKS IT'S HER FAULT THAT FARLEY DIED—BUT SHE'S GETTING BETTER.
WHY DON'T YOU WRITE ABOUT IT? WHY DON'T YOU WRITE ABOUT WHAT HAPPENED THAT DAY?
BECAUSE, IT WOULD BE LIKE HAVING MAJOR SURGERY.
MIKE, ONE HAS SURGERY WHEN SOMETHING NEEDS TO COME OUT.
Lynn

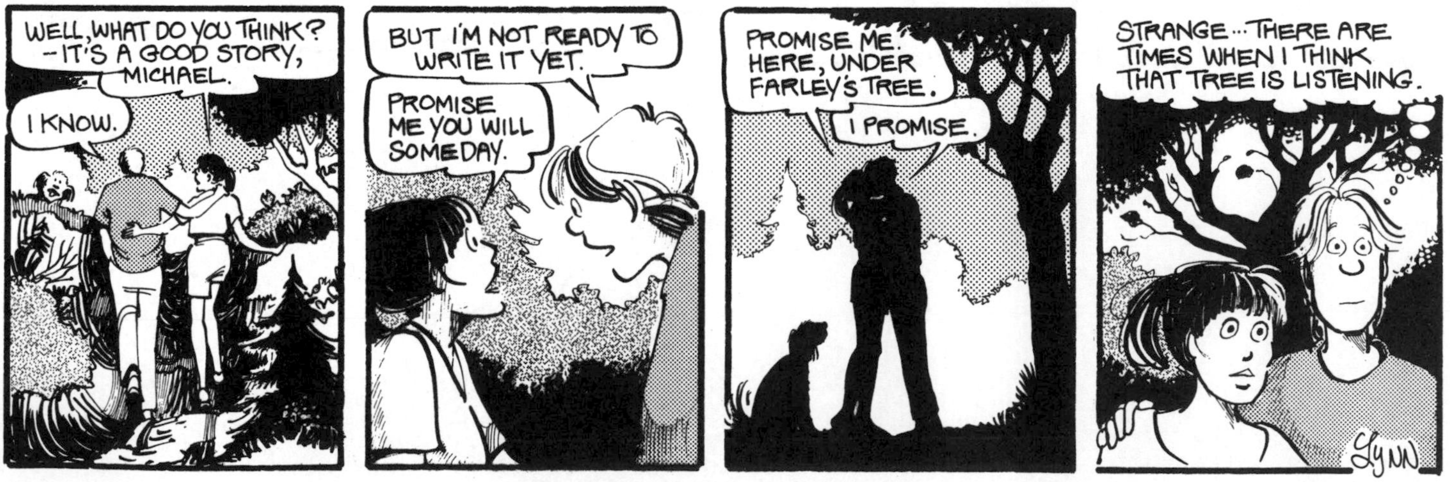
WELL, WHAT DO YOU THINK? —IT'S A GOOD STORY, MICHAEL.
I KNOW.
BUT I'M NOT READY TO WRITE IT YET.
PROMISE ME YOU WILL SOMEDAY.
PROMISE ME. HERE, UNDER FARLEY'S TREE.
I PROMISE.
STRANGE... THERE ARE TIMES WHEN I THINK THAT TREE IS LISTENING.
Lynn

I want to thank Beth Cruikshank for helping me write the text for this book.
Without her, I'd still be procrastinating!
—Lynn

The Later Years

In some ways April's misadventure and Farley's death marked another point of transition for FBorFW. In the strip, John and Elly had reached the stage of having to accept, as gracefully as possible, the turning of the generational wheel. They were no longer young adults, wrestling with the hassles of raising small children and trying to carve out satisfying careers while juggling mortgage payments. Their children and their children's friends were growing into that role. Despite having a young daughter still at home, they were now among the ranks of the middle aged, potential grandparents—almost retirees! Elly was discussing the miseries of menopause and John was ogling sports cars to make up for his lack of speed in other areas.

It was a time to draw back and focus once again on relationships, but this time with a more philosophical view about who we are. Where are we going? A gentler, wry tone emerged, which was different again from the bittersweet humor of the early years or the ups and downs of the middle years when I touched on some troublesome issues and gained so much attention.

It was never exactly calculated, but the lives of the Pattersons always seemed to intertwine with our own. My parents were gone, and in 1994 we lost Rod's mom, who had been both mom and mentor to me. His dad passed away two years later, and family gatherings would never be the same. During that time, health problems began to surface as a major concern for us, too.

Rod developed a heart condition called atrial fibrillation (isn't it great to have actual names for these things?) and I inherited a neurological disease called Dystonia. The form I have is called Spasmodic Torticollis, which means "twisting spasms" in medicalese. When I lie down, my head twists to the left—and hard! Weird, hum? Anyway, it's a permanent part of my physical works now, and other than depression and fatigue, it's OK to live with. Others have it worse!

My eyesight was also a problem. I could no longer put out the volume of work I once did. I made the difficult decision to hire another artist to work with me. It wasn't easy to find someone who could put up with my *gottadoitnow* and it's *gottabegood* way of working. I was also nervous about letting anyone else touch my strip!

I was lucky to eventually find the right person with the right set of skills and the ability to work under pressure. I continued to write and draw the strip, and ink the characters, and Laura Piché did the rest. With someone younger (and so talented!) to work with, I started to turn each panel into a *workofart*. I drew every shingle on the roof, every tile in the bathrooms. I wanted the audience to see the pattern on the couch, read the signs in the supermarkets, and feel as though they knew the environment as well as I did. Laura completed the lettering and coloring and any design work that had to be done, including book covers and calendar art.

I also hired an executive director to handle the licensing agreements. Nancy Vincent is the brains behind the business and Liuba Liamzina does all the bookkeeping. The correspondence, now about 90 percent e-mail, was answered with the help of another mom who worked at home. We outgrew the basement of our house and built a studio on a small private lake nearby. Another graphic designer/colorist was added to the team and a Web site was set up with the help of a friend of our son's. (I LOVE young people!)

I now felt like part of a team, and it gave me confidence to push the story lines again into real-life experiences. I had people with whom I could discuss ideas and who would read the pencil roughs with an eye for detail, check my spelling, and add stories of their own to the ones I had filed in my mental Rolodex. For years, Rod and his parents had been my editors (before the editors at the syndicate saw anything). But with the studio no longer at the house and Rod busy with his practice, a fledgling model railway business, and volunteer work, he had little opportunity to pass judgment on the comics.

With the staff's blessing and a call to my dad's sister, Bessie, I decided to write about the death of my mother, using images and conversations that actually took place. For my brother, Alan, who could not be there when she died, I changed history. Both Elly and "Uncle Phil" were at her side as she gently slipped away.

I rewrote history again by having Grandpa Jim, Elly and Phil's father, continue on with his life, eventually moving from Vancouver to Ontario to live with his daughter. In reality, our dad died a year after our mother, but the character has kept him alive. Jim Richards talks, dresses, tells tall tales, and loves a kitchen music jam, just like Dad did. If Dad were alive, he would have taught my daughter how to play the guitar, and he would have fallen in love again because Mom made him promise to do so. Dad (his name was Merv Ridgway, and mom's name was Ursula) always wanted a Sheltie dog, so it was almost like giving a gift to his spirit when Dixie was written into the saga! So, Grandpa Jim has not only survived several years in the strip, he has a Sheltie dog and has found the second love of his life in Iris, who married him, takes care of him, and loves him—warts and all! This is the life I would have wished for our dad, but writing about him like this has been wonderful therapy.

I have also kept Rod's parents alive. "Carrie and Will Patterson" reside in a small farming community just outside Winnipeg, near John's sister, Bev, and her husband, Dan. They appear too rarely in the strip, but exist nonetheless in good health and good spirits.

It has also been fun to shake off the creaks and groans of middle age and relive the joys and hassles of being young again through Michael, Deanna, Elizabeth, and their friends as they become adults.

Here, too, some whiffs of wish fulfillment have crept in. I've been accused, for example of being too kind to Mike's friend, Gordon. Unkempt, homely, and the victim of abuse, he was a loser in his childhood days. The complaint is that he has now been overly compensated with a loving, strife-free marriage to a wonderful, caring wife who has borne him two adorable children, and has a business that is far too successful to be true.

Well, what's wrong with that? Shouldn't hard work, good management, integrity, and the ability to save be rewarded? So what if his life has been turned around? Who would not want a happy ending for someone like Gordon, if we had the power to give it to them? There is great satisfaction in being able to play God—and besides, we've all known people like Gordon Mayes: gentle, courageous individuals who neither allow the survival of a harsh childhood to corrupt them nor use it as an excuse for failure. It's always gratifying to see how many like Gordon do succeed, far beyond everyone's expectations.

Partly because my work is being closely scrutinized by readers and partly in defiance of my dwindling eyesight, I have become frustratingly obsessive about detail. I draw with the use of models, and my collection of miniatures grows weekly. I have model cars, musical instruments, bicycles, a wheelchair—things like shoes and basketballs, baseball gloves and shopping carts I've scored at key chain and fridge magnet sections of kid's wear and gift shops. I use a Polaroid camera whenever a body position is too awkward to re-create from memory, and the assortment of really odd poses are worthy of a scrapbook someday.

In early drawings of Elly making a midnight visit to toddler Elizabeth's room to see if she was frightened by an electrical storm, the backgrounds were sketchy outlines of bed clothes, and window and door frames. In 2000, when she did the same for April, the final panel showed the pattern on the wallpaper and every book on the bookshelf.

The characters have become more realistic, too. Elly's face no longer splits in half when she hollers at kids or pets, and her eyes don't bug out of her head as much as they used to. The classic "rubber face" cartooning has morphed into a more realistic style—and I really can't explain why! Michael is a pretty good-looking young man, with an attractive wife and beautiful baby. What happened to the goofy expressions and exaggerated body language? I really don't know. I do know that the art has, let's say, matured. I'm a better artist than I used to be and I'm a much more careful writer. The writing is more of a challenge than the drawing because I must give each character center stage from time to time, without losing story lines that have been started.

I have more stories in my head than I could ever tell in the strip—because I have just one statement a day, just 30 seconds every 24 hours to reveal what's happening next! I want to tell you about Brian Enjo's rediscovery of his Japanese roots, the ups and downs of Uncle Phil's music career, the ongoing self-discovery of Weed and Candace, and about Annie's difficult marriage. I want to write about Connie, her husband, Greg, and his two daughters, now adults with children of their own. People want to know what's happening with Lawrence and his partner Nicholas, about Gordon's family, and whatever became of Mrs. Dingle, Aunt Fiona, Cousin Laura, and that idiot Ted!

All these stories would be so much fun to explore, but I have to make careful choices, work with the central characters, and write about things that matter most to me and hopefully to my readers as well.

When I write, I am each character. I am also an observer, hovering around them like a spirit, waiting for them to react or to speak again. I am always aware of where the Pattersons are, what their friends and neighbors are doing, what the weather is like, and how the pets are surviving without the constant attention they were used to before Elly became a store owner and Grandpa moved to his own digs. The hardest part of the job now is to see the world through the eyes of the young people, to dig into the past and recall our baby days. Without frustration, there is no "funny." Really good family humor comes from the subtle things that go on, the day-to-day irritations that drive parents of young children crazy. I don't have that miserably wonderful stimulation anymore, so I rely on my young moms at work to remind me. Then I can walk into Michael and Deanna's home, hear the bath-time bawling, and smell the leftovers.

My personal experiences now are the complications of growing older—finding hairs growing where no hair ever grew, losing the desire to party till you drop, finding yourself seriously admiring a hunky recording star and discovering he's the same age as your son!

I'm ready to be a grandparent, with all the passion one has for a child of your own. Rod and I discuss wills and cremation versus burial at sea. We are about to buy a plot near Rod's parents, Ruth and Tom—is this stuff fodder for the funny pages? Not really. And so I focus on fabricating stories. The interpersonal relationships and the challenges my imaginary people are facing are more realistic and more complex than before. The challenge for me now is to become a better artist, a better writer, and to keep producing stuff that's both fun and funny. Laughter fills my spirit and feeds my soul and it's something I love to share.

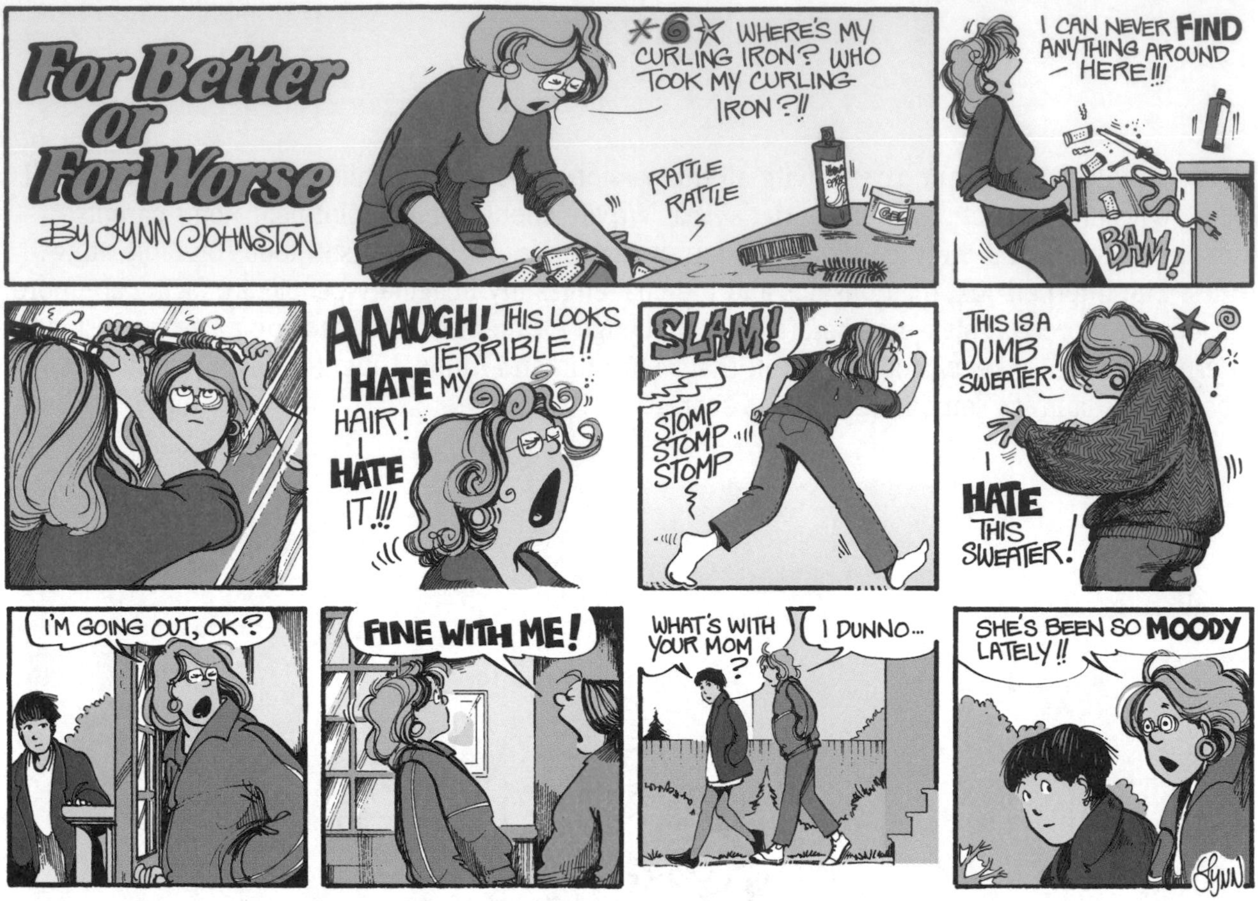
For Better or For Worse
By Lynn Johnston
*@☆ WHERE'S MY CURLING IRON? WHO TOOK MY CURLING IRON?!!
RATTLE RATTLE
I CAN NEVER FIND ANYTHING AROUND - HERE!!!
BAM!
AAAUGH! THIS LOOKS TERRIBLE!!
I HATE MY HAIR! I HATE IT!!!
SLAM!
STOMP STOMP STOMP
THIS IS A DUMB SWEATER!
I HATE THIS SWEATER!
I'M GOING OUT, OK?
FINE WITH ME!
WHAT'S WITH YOUR MOM?
I DUNNO...
SHE'S BEEN SO MOODY LATELY!!
LYNN

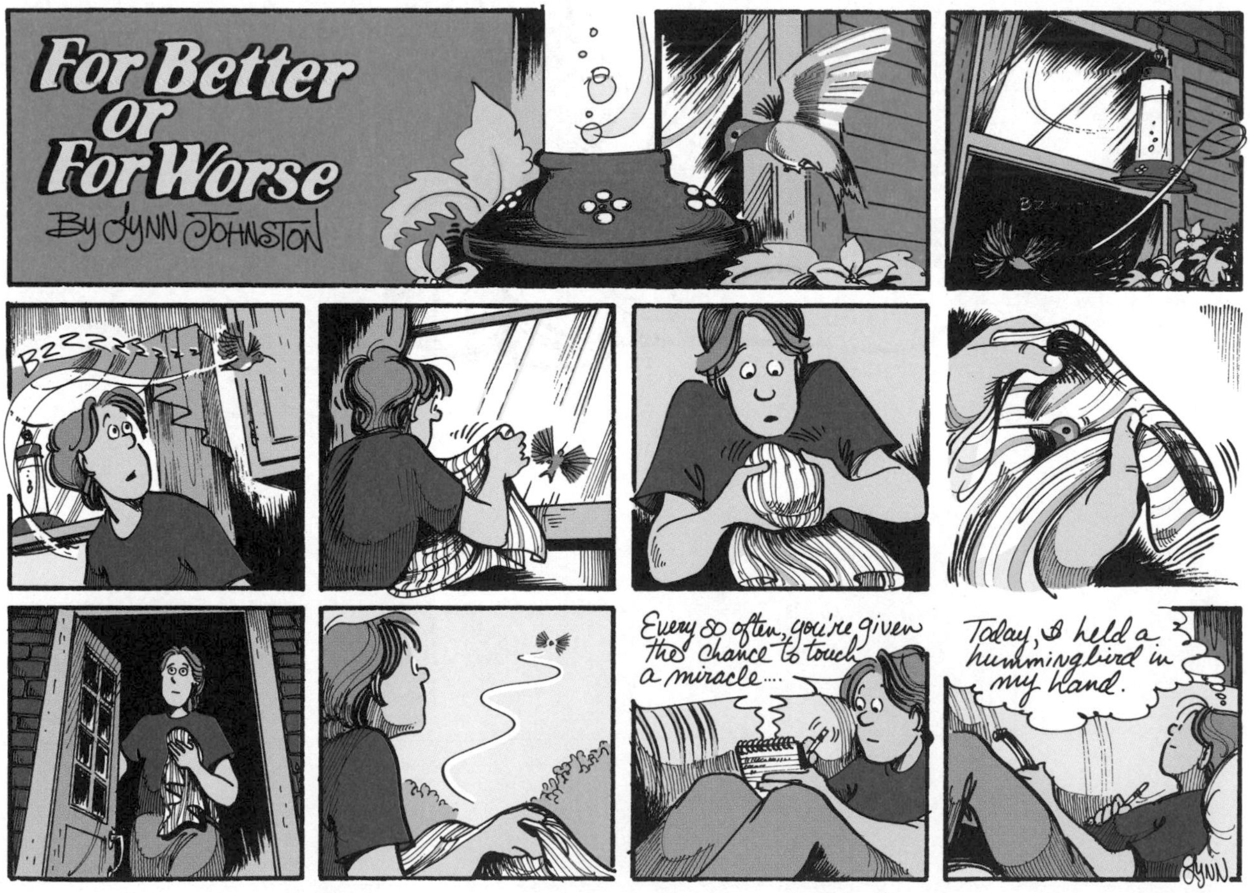
For Better or For Worse
By Lynn Johnston
BZZZZZZZZZ
Every so often, you're given the chance to touch a miracle....
Today, I held a hummingbird in my hand.
LYNN

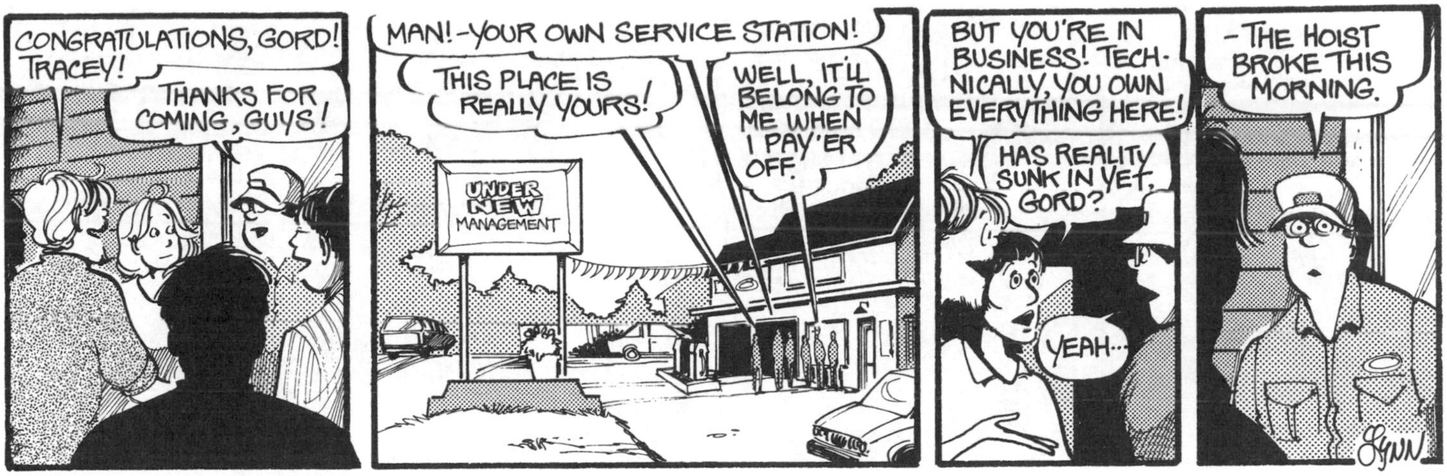
CONGRATULATIONS, GORD! TRACEY!
THANKS FOR COMING, GUYS!
MAN! -YOUR OWN SERVICE STATION!
THIS PLACE IS REALLY YOURS!
WELL, IT'LL BELONG TO ME WHEN I PAY 'ER OFF.
UNDER NEW MANAGEMENT
BUT YOU'RE IN BUSINESS! TECHNICALLY, YOU OWN EVERYTHING HERE!
HAS REALITY SUNK IN YET, GORD?
YEAH...
-THE HOIST BROKE THIS MORNING.
LYNN

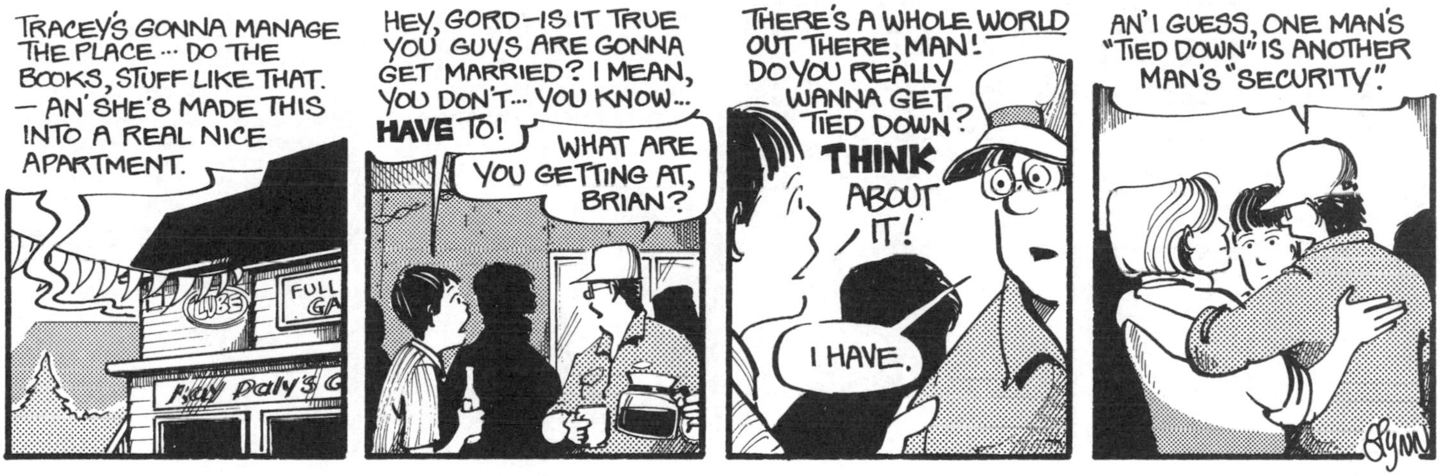
TRACEY'S GONNA MANAGE THE PLACE ... DO THE BOOKS, STUFF LIKE THAT. — AN' SHE'S MADE THIS INTO A REAL NICE APARTMENT.
LUBE
HEY, GORD—IS IT TRUE YOU GUYS ARE GONNA GET MARRIED? I MEAN, YOU DON'T... YOU KNOW... HAVE TO!
WHAT ARE YOU GETTING AT, BRIAN?
THERE'S A WHOLE WORLD OUT THERE, MAN! DO YOU REALLY WANNA GET TIED DOWN? THINK ABOUT IT!
I HAVE.
AN' I GUESS, ONE MAN'S "TIED DOWN" IS ANOTHER MAN'S "SECURITY".
LYNN

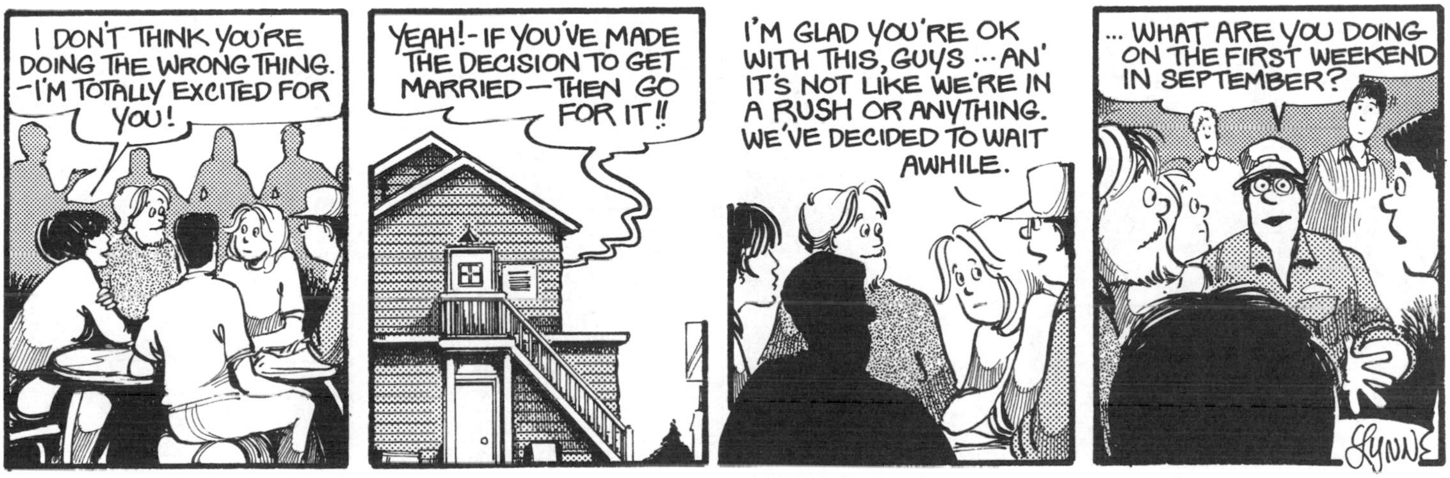
I DON'T THINK YOU'RE DOING THE WRONG THING. -I'M TOTALLY EXCITED FOR YOU!
YEAH! -IF YOU'VE MADE THE DECISION TO GET MARRIED—THEN GO FOR IT!!
I'M GLAD YOU'RE OK WITH THIS, GUYS ... AN' IT'S NOT LIKE WE'RE IN A RUSH OR ANYTHING. WE'VE DECIDED TO WAIT AWHILE.
... WHAT ARE YOU DOING ON THE FIRST WEEKEND IN SEPTEMBER?
LYNN

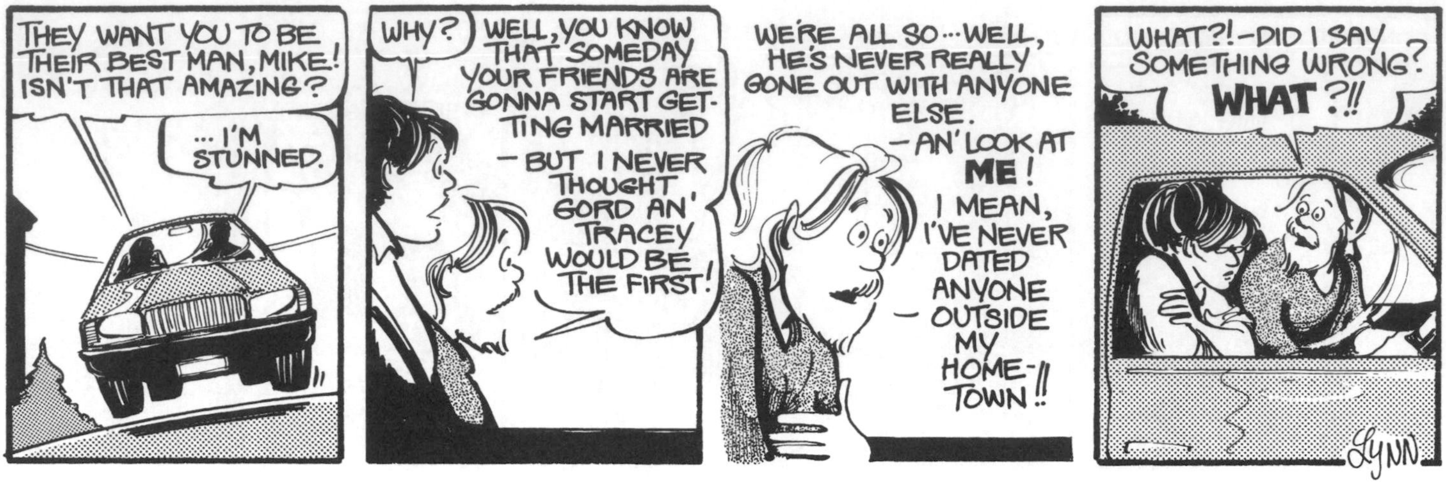
THEY WANT YOU TO BE THEIR BEST MAN, MIKE! ISN'T THAT AMAZING?
... I'M STUNNED.
WHY?
WELL, YOU KNOW THAT SOMEDAY YOUR FRIENDS ARE GONNA START GETTING MARRIED
— BUT I NEVER THOUGHT GORD AN' TRACEY WOULD BE THE FIRST!
WE'RE ALL SO... WELL, HE'S NEVER REALLY GONE OUT WITH ANYONE ELSE.
— AN' LOOK AT ME!
I MEAN, I'VE NEVER DATED ANYONE OUTSIDE MY HOME-TOWN!!
WHAT?!—DID I SAY SOMETHING WRONG? WHAT?!!
LYNN

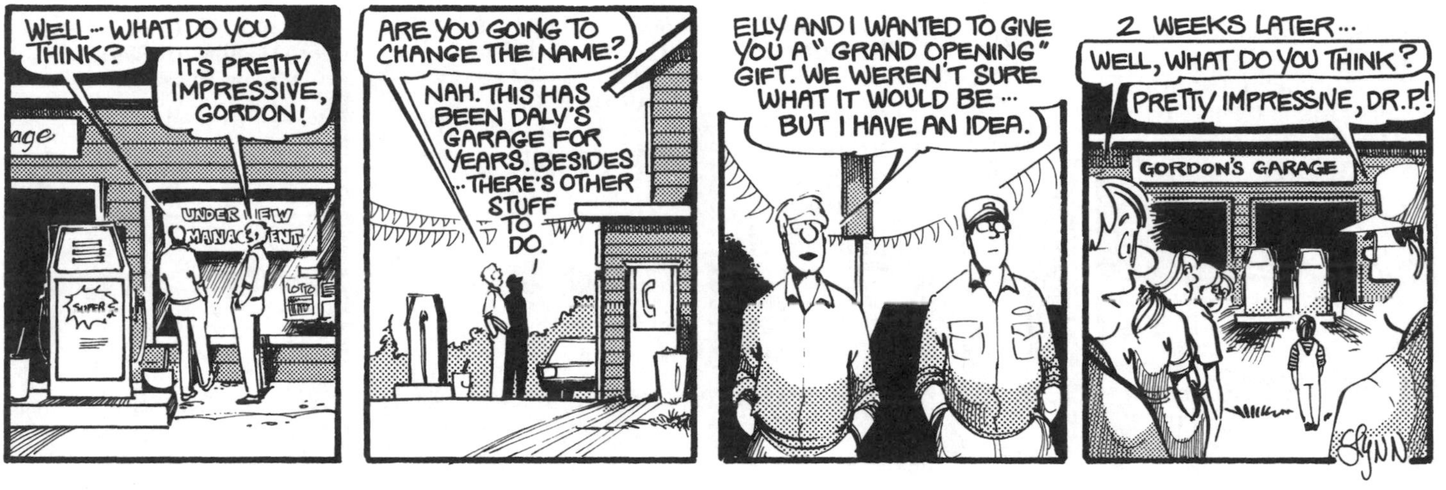
WELL... WHAT DO YOU THINK?
IT'S PRETTY IMPRESSIVE, GORDON!
ARE YOU GOING TO CHANGE THE NAME?
NAH. THIS HAS BEEN DALY'S GARAGE FOR YEARS. BESIDES ...THERE'S OTHER STUFF TO DO.
ELLY AND I WANTED TO GIVE YOU A "GRAND OPENING" GIFT. WE WEREN'T SURE WHAT IT WOULD BE ...
BUT I HAVE AN IDEA.
2 WEEKS LATER...
WELL, WHAT DO YOU THINK?
PRETTY IMPRESSIVE, DR. P.!
GORDON'S GARAGE
LYNN

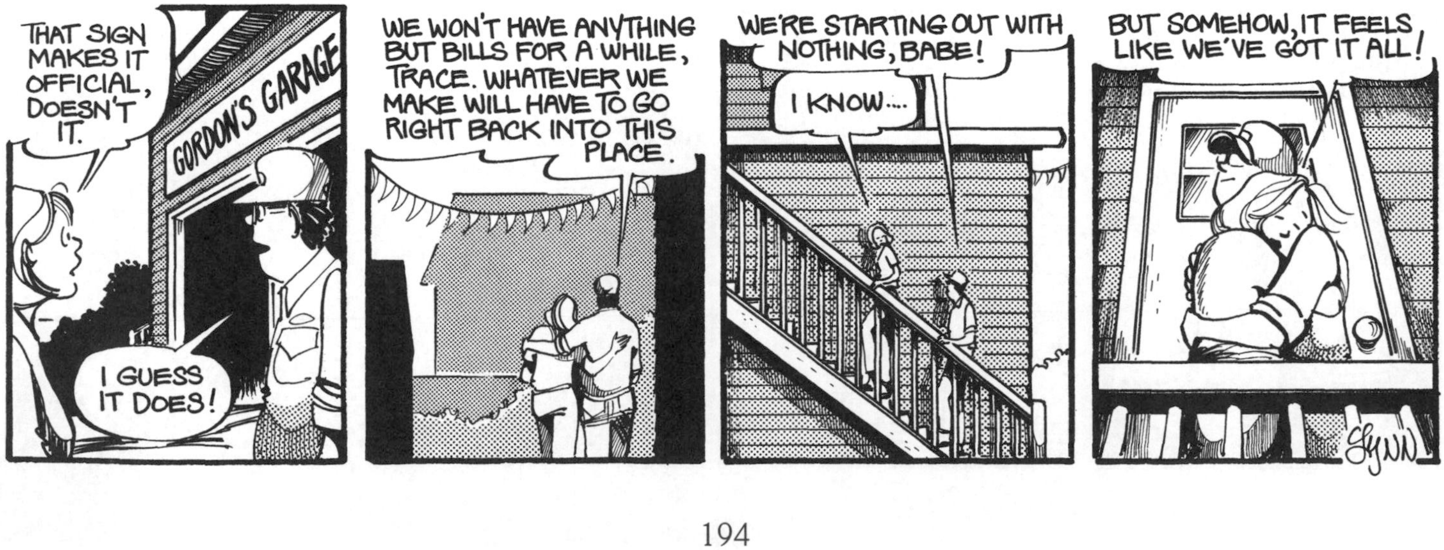
THAT SIGN MAKES IT OFFICIAL, DOESN'T IT.
GORDON'S GARAGE
I GUESS IT DOES!
WE WON'T HAVE ANYTHING BUT BILLS FOR A WHILE, TRACE. WHATEVER WE MAKE WILL HAVE TO GO RIGHT BACK INTO THIS PLACE.
WE'RE STARTING OUT WITH NOTHING, BABE!
I KNOW....
BUT SOMEHOW, IT FEELS LIKE WE'VE GOT IT ALL!
LYNN

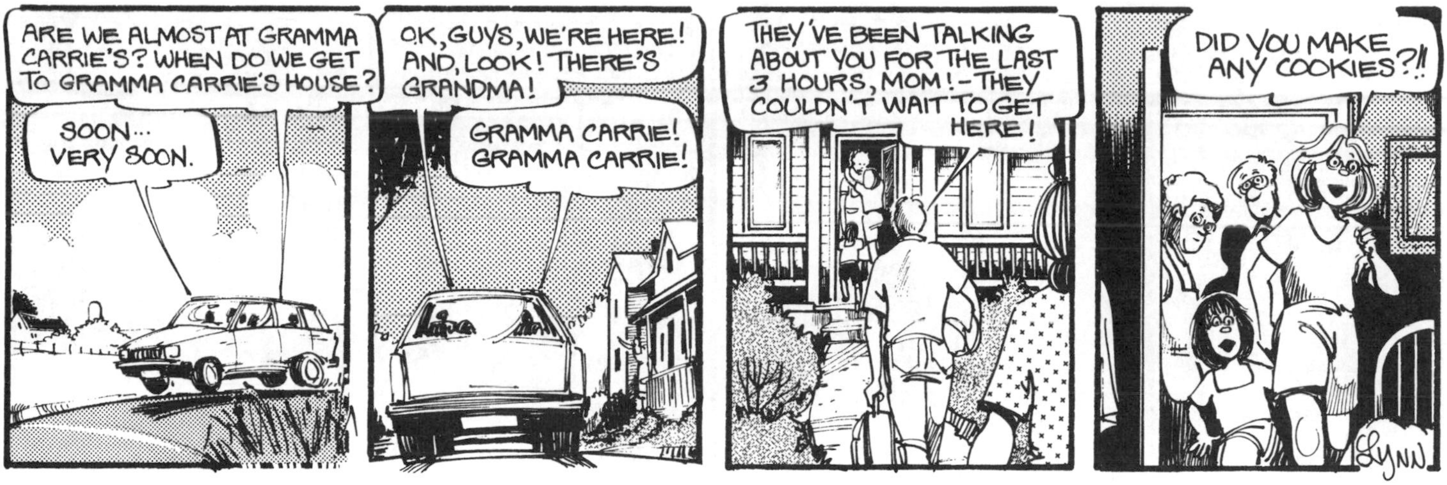
ARE WE ALMOST AT GRAMMA CARRIE'S? WHEN DO WE GET TO GRAMMA CARRIE'S HOUSE?
SOON... VERY SOON.
O.K, GUYS, WE'RE HERE! AND, LOOK! THERE'S GRANDMA!
GRAMMA CARRIE! GRAMMA CARRIE!
THEY'VE BEEN TALKING ABOUT YOU FOR THE LAST 3 HOURS, MOM! - THEY COULDN'T WAIT TO GET HERE!
DID YOU MAKE ANY COOKIES?!!
LYNN

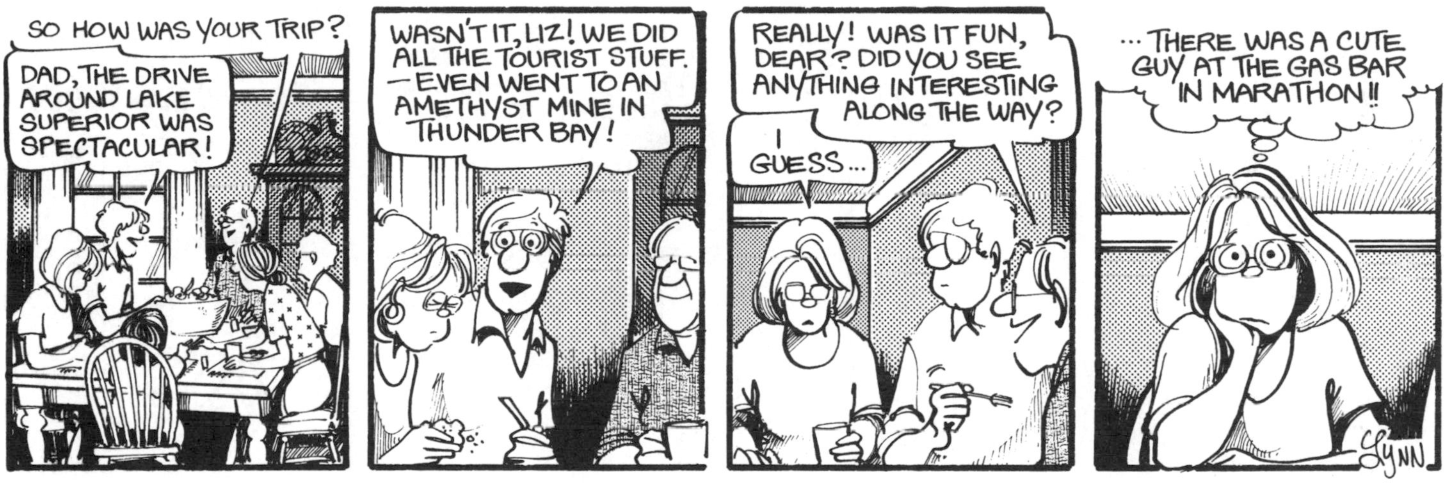
SO HOW WAS YOUR TRIP?
DAD, THE DRIVE AROUND LAKE SUPERIOR WAS SPECTACULAR!
WASN'T IT, LIZ! WE DID ALL THE TOURIST STUFF. - EVEN WENT TO AN AMETHYST MINE IN THUNDER BAY!
REALLY! WAS IT FUN, DEAR? DID YOU SEE ANYTHING INTERESTING ALONG THE WAY?
I GUESS...
... THERE WAS A CUTE GUY AT THE GAS BAR IN MARATHON!!
LYNN

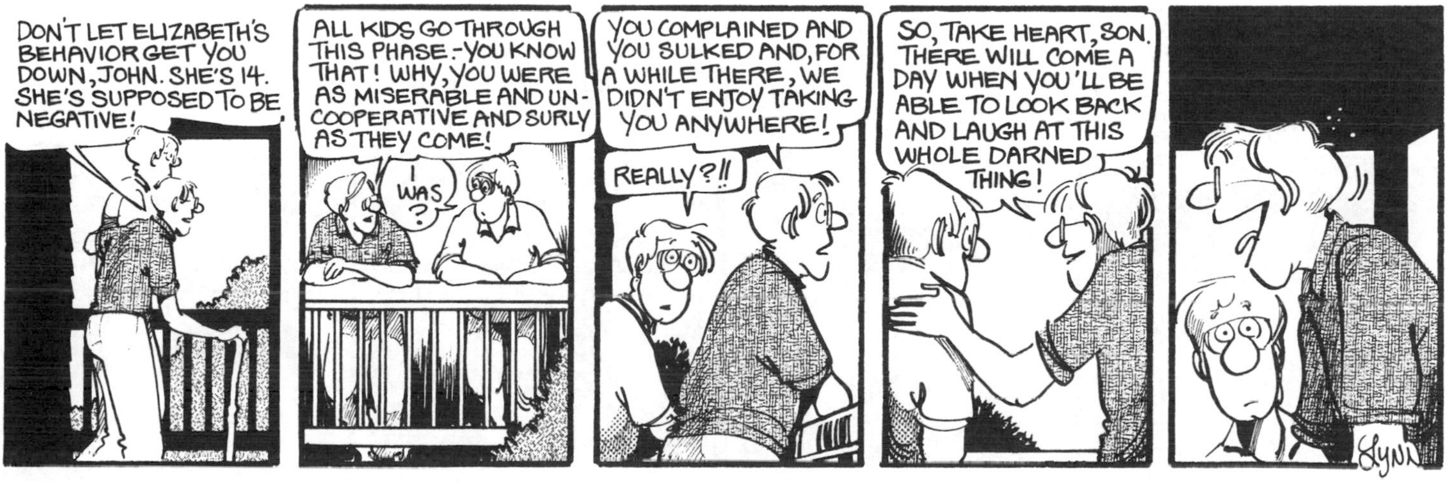
DON'T LET ELIZABETH'S BEHAVIOR GET YOU DOWN, JOHN. SHE'S 14. SHE'S SUPPOSED TO BE NEGATIVE!
ALL KIDS GO THROUGH THIS PHASE. - YOU KNOW THAT! WHY, YOU WERE AS MISERABLE AND UN-COOPERATIVE AND SURLY AS THEY COME!
I WAS?
YOU COMPLAINED AND YOU SULKED AND, FOR A WHILE THERE, WE DIDN'T ENJOY TAKING YOU ANYWHERE!
REALLY?!!
SO, TAKE HEART, SON. THERE WILL COME A DAY WHEN YOU'LL BE ABLE TO LOOK BACK AND LAUGH AT THIS WHOLE DARNED THING!
LYNN

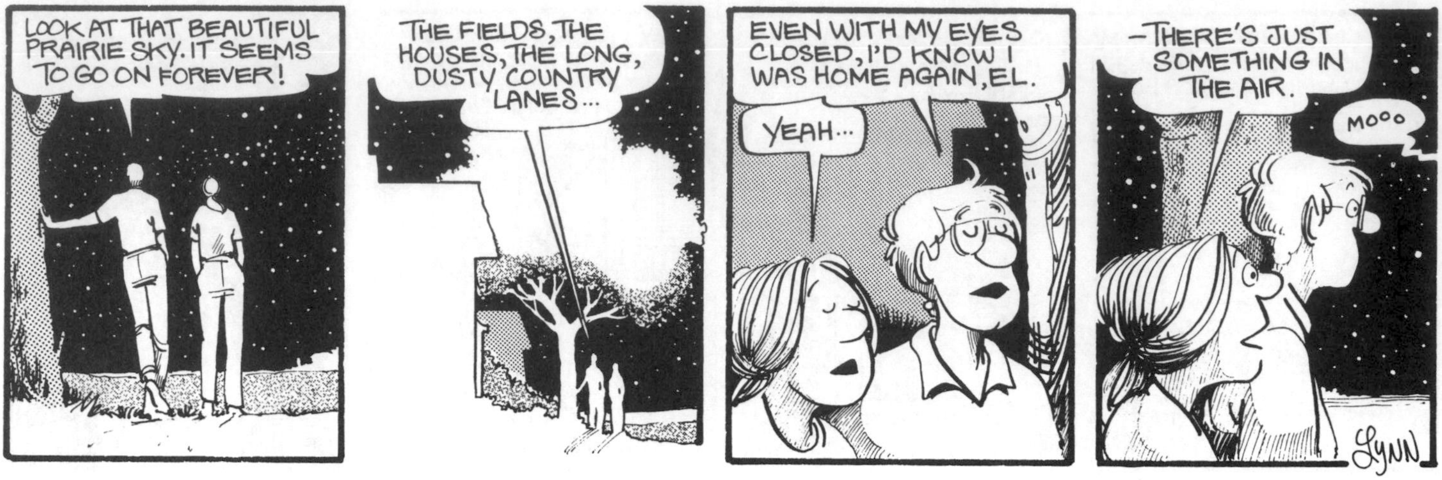
LOOK AT THAT BEAUTIFUL PRAIRIE SKY. IT SEEMS TO GO ON FOREVER!
THE FIELDS, THE HOUSES, THE LONG, DUSTY COUNTRY LANES...
EVEN WITH MY EYES CLOSED, I'D KNOW I WAS HOME AGAIN, EL.
YEAH...
-THERE'S JUST SOMETHING IN THE AIR.
MOOO
LYNN

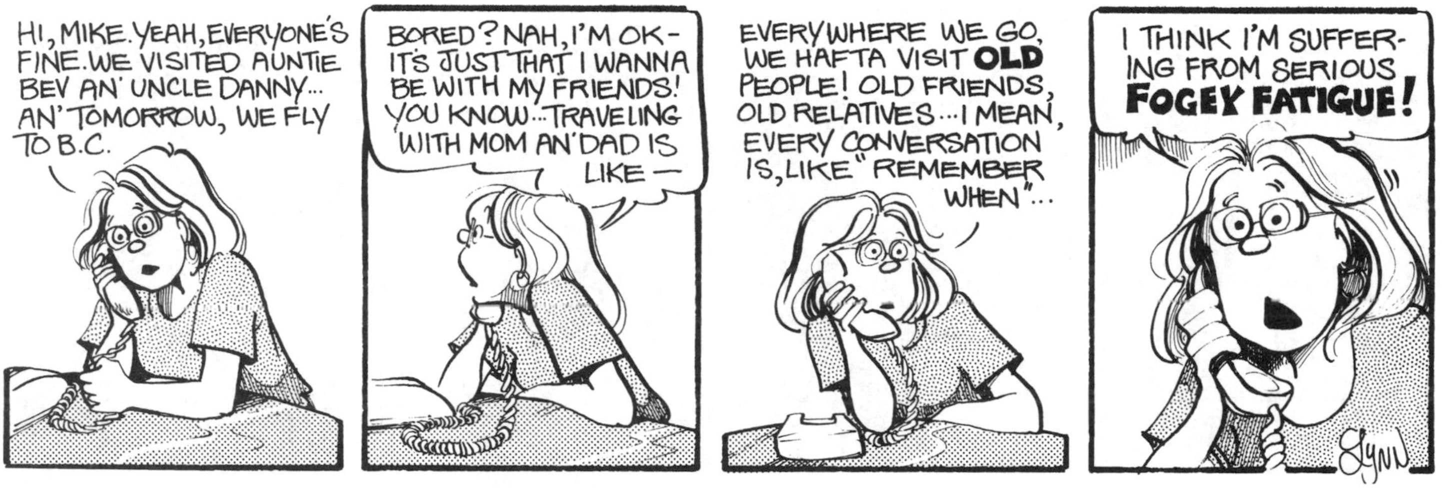
HI, MIKE. YEAH, EVERYONE'S FINE. WE VISITED AUNTIE BEV AN' UNCLE DANNY... AN' TOMORROW, WE FLY TO B.C.
BORED? NAH, I'M OK- IT'S JUST THAT I WANNA BE WITH MY FRIENDS! YOU KNOW... TRAVELING WITH MOM AN' DAD IS LIKE —
EVERYWHERE WE GO, WE HAFTA VISIT OLD PEOPLE! OLD FRIENDS, OLD RELATIVES... I MEAN, EVERY CONVERSATION IS, LIKE "REMEMBER WHEN"...
I THINK I'M SUFFERING FROM SERIOUS FOGEY FATIGUE!
LYNN

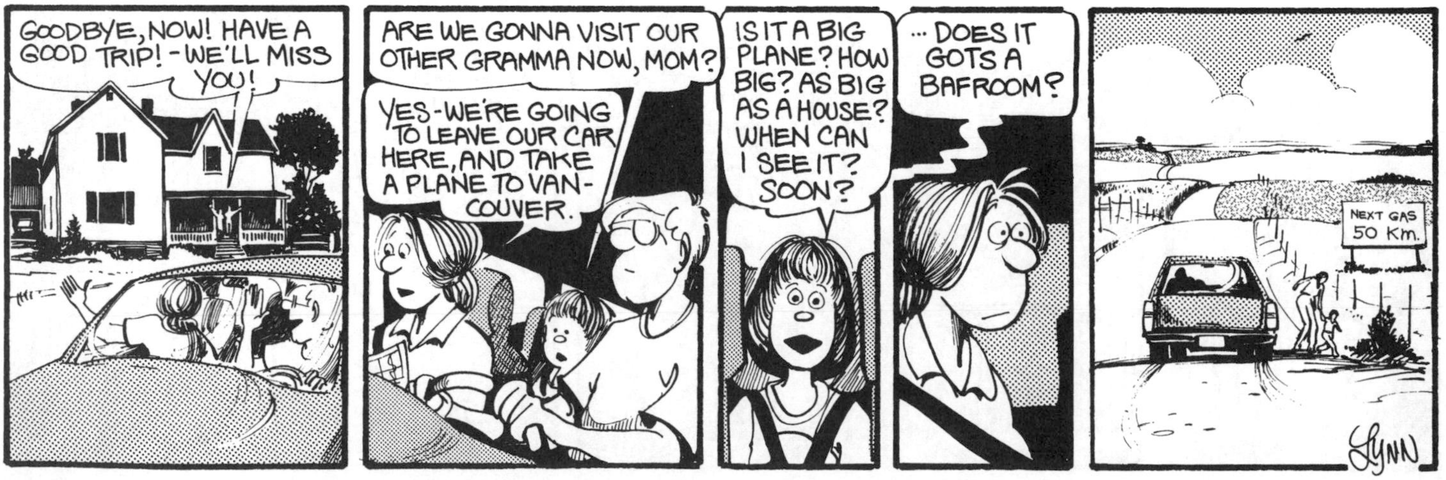
GOODBYE, NOW! HAVE A GOOD TRIP! - WE'LL MISS YOU!
ARE WE GONNA VISIT OUR OTHER GRAMMA NOW, MOM?
YES - WE'RE GOING TO LEAVE OUR CAR HERE, AND TAKE A PLANE TO VANCOUVER.
IS IT A BIG PLANE? HOW BIG? AS BIG AS A HOUSE? WHEN CAN I SEE IT? SOON?
... DOES IT GOTS A BAFROOM?
NEXT GAS 50 Km.
LYNN

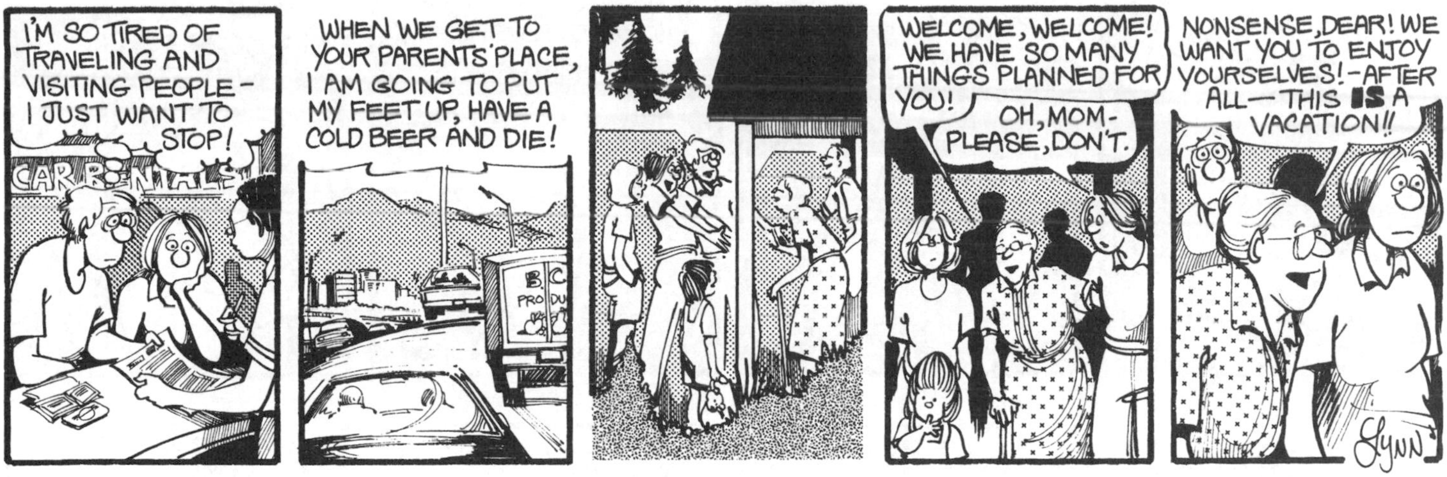
I'M SO TIRED OF TRAVELING AND VISITING PEOPLE - I JUST WANT TO STOP!
CAR RENTALS
WHEN WE GET TO YOUR PARENTS' PLACE, I AM GOING TO PUT MY FEET UP, HAVE A COLD BEER AND DIE!
WELCOME, WELCOME! WE HAVE SO MANY THINGS PLANNED FOR YOU!
OH, MOM- PLEASE, DON'T.
NONSENSE, DEAR! WE WANT YOU TO ENJOY YOURSELVES! - AFTER ALL — THIS **IS** A VACATION!!
LYNN

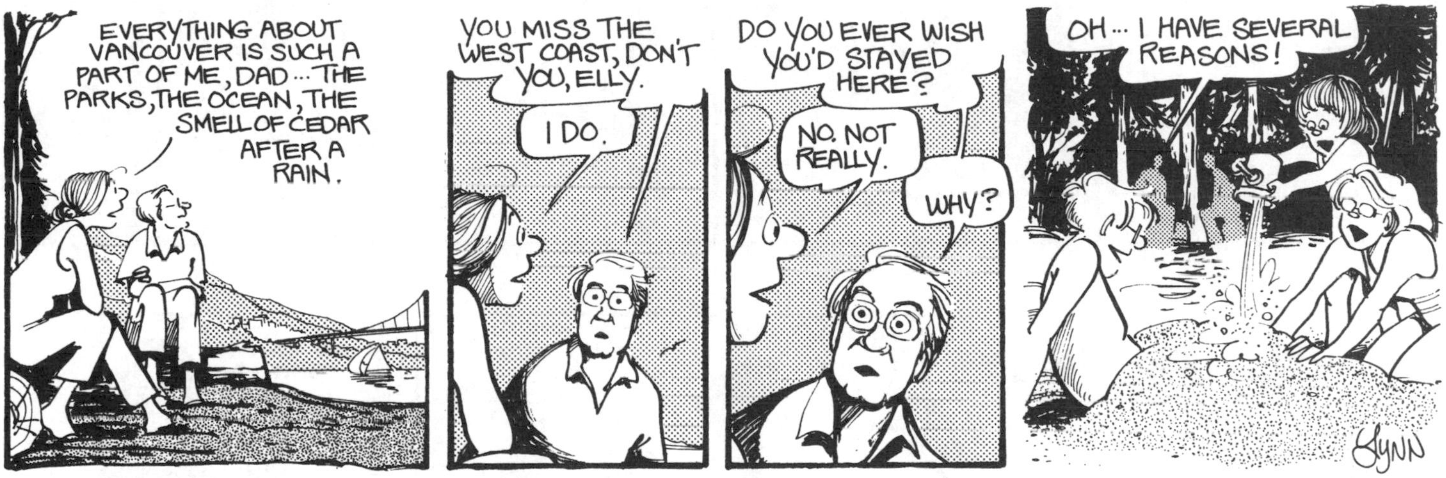
EVERYTHING ABOUT VANCOUVER IS SUCH A PART OF ME, DAD ... THE PARKS, THE OCEAN, THE SMELL OF CEDAR AFTER A RAIN.
YOU MISS THE WEST COAST, DON'T YOU, ELLY.
I DO.
DO YOU EVER WISH YOU'D STAYED HERE?
NO. NOT REALLY.
WHY?
OH ... I HAVE SEVERAL REASONS!
LYNN

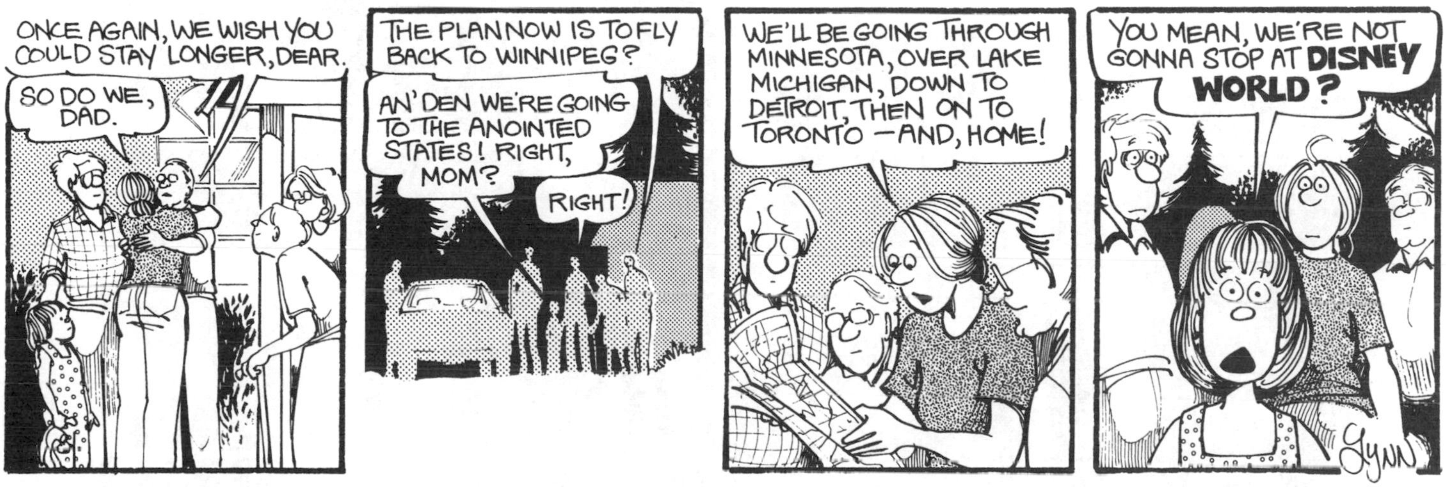
ONCE AGAIN, WE WISH YOU COULD STAY LONGER, DEAR.
SO DO WE, DAD.
THE PLAN NOW IS TO FLY BACK TO WINNIPEG?
AN' DEN WE'RE GOING TO THE ANOINTED STATES! RIGHT, MOM?
RIGHT!
WE'LL BE GOING THROUGH MINNESOTA, OVER LAKE MICHIGAN, DOWN TO DETROIT, THEN ON TO TORONTO — AND, HOME!
YOU MEAN, WE'RE NOT GONNA STOP AT **DISNEY WORLD?**
LYNN

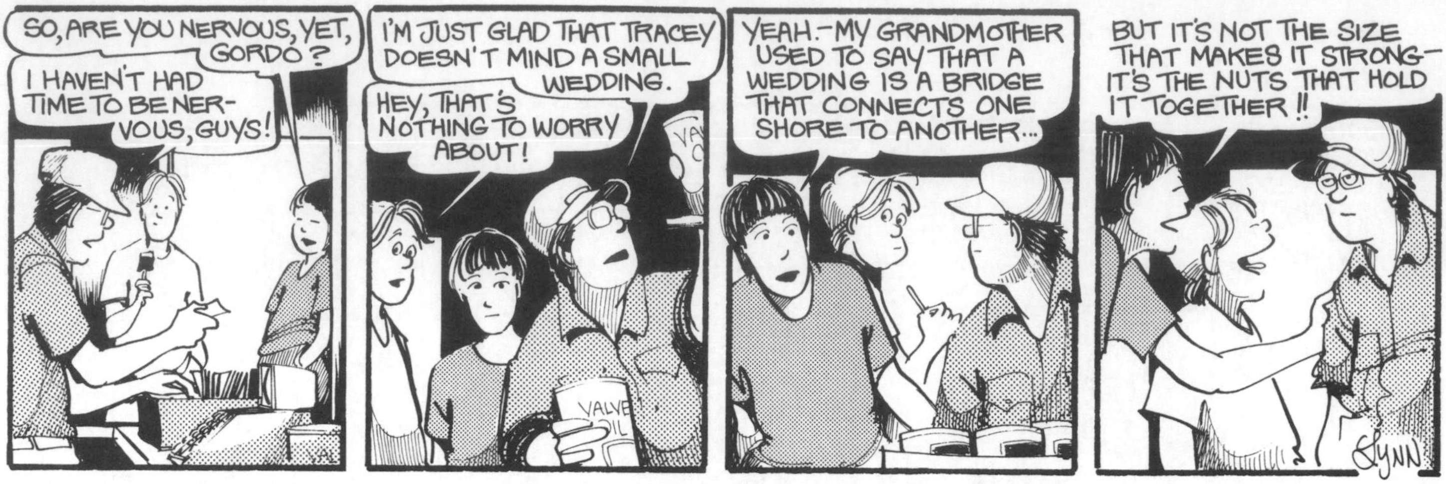
SO, ARE YOU NERVOUS, YET, GORDO?
I HAVEN'T HAD TIME TO BE NER-VOUS, GUYS!
I'M JUST GLAD THAT TRACEY DOESN'T MIND A SMALL WEDDING.
HEY, THAT'S NOTHING TO WORRY ABOUT!
VALVE OIL
YEAH.—MY GRANDMOTHER USED TO SAY THAT A WEDDING IS A BRIDGE THAT CONNECTS ONE SHORE TO ANOTHER...
BUT IT'S NOT THE SIZE THAT MAKES IT STRONG—IT'S THE NUTS THAT HOLD IT TOGETHER!!
LYNN

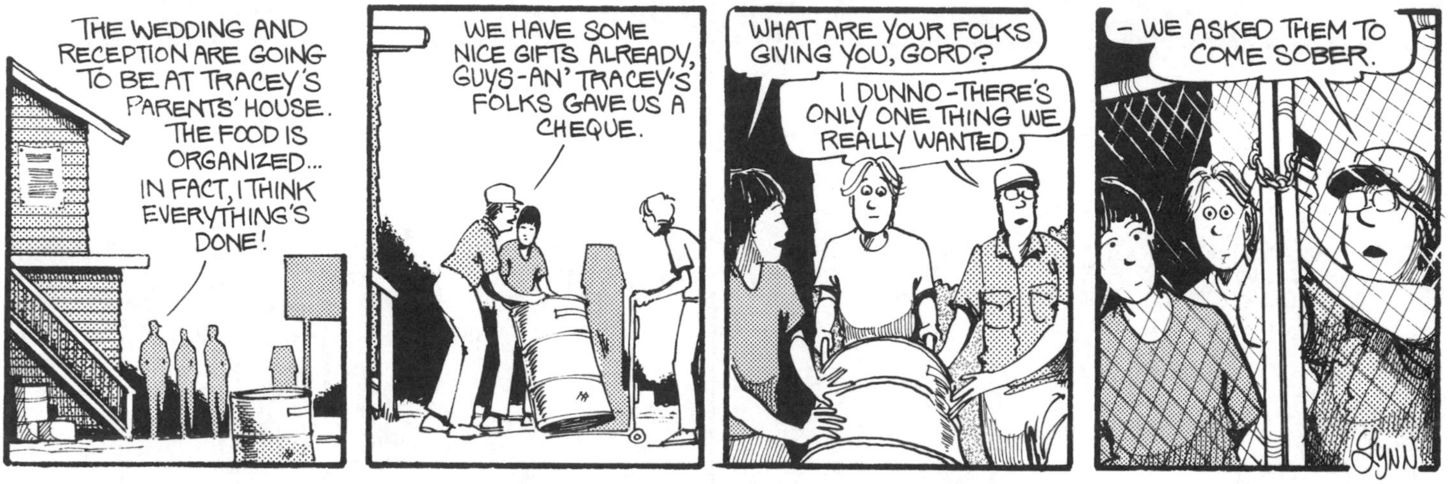
THE WEDDING AND RECEPTION ARE GOING TO BE AT TRACEY'S PARENTS' HOUSE. THE FOOD IS ORGANIZED... IN FACT, I THINK EVERYTHING'S DONE!
WE HAVE SOME NICE GIFTS ALREADY, GUYS—AN' TRACEY'S FOLKS GAVE US A CHEQUE.
WHAT ARE YOUR FOLKS GIVING YOU, GORD?
I DUNNO—THERE'S ONLY ONE THING WE REALLY WANTED.
—WE ASKED THEM TO COME SOBER.
LYNN

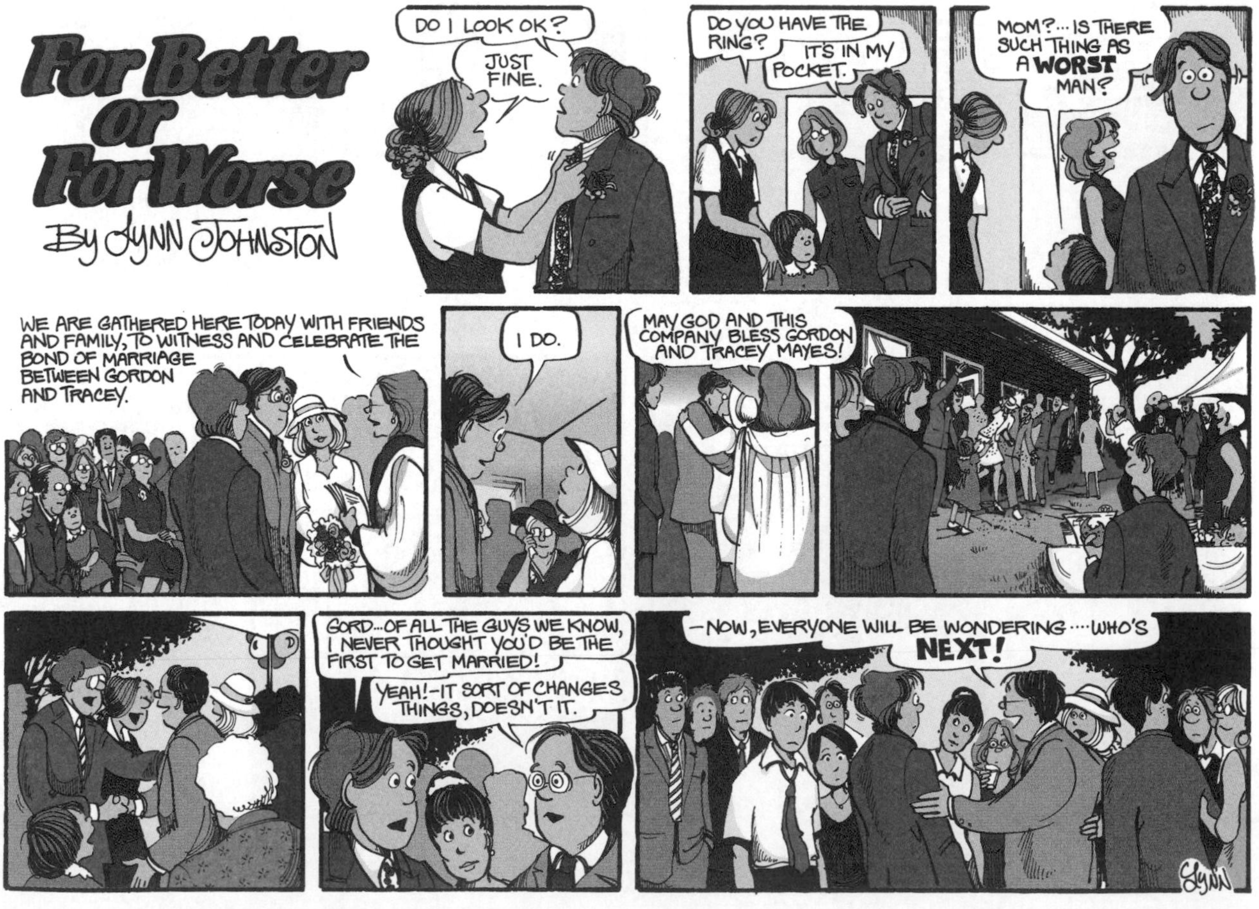
For Better or For Worse
By Lynn Johnston
DO I LOOK OK?
JUST FINE.
DO YOU HAVE THE RING?
IT'S IN MY POCKET.
MOM?... IS THERE SUCH THING AS A WORST MAN?
WE ARE GATHERED HERE TODAY WITH FRIENDS AND FAMILY, TO WITNESS AND CELEBRATE THE BOND OF MARRIAGE BETWEEN GORDON AND TRACEY.
I DO.
MAY GOD AND THIS COMPANY BLESS GORDON AND TRACEY MAYES!
GORD... OF ALL THE GUYS WE KNOW, I NEVER THOUGHT YOU'D BE THE FIRST TO GET MARRIED!
YEAH!—IT SORT OF CHANGES THINGS, DOESN'T IT.
—NOW, EVERYONE WILL BE WONDERING.... WHO'S NEXT!
LYNN

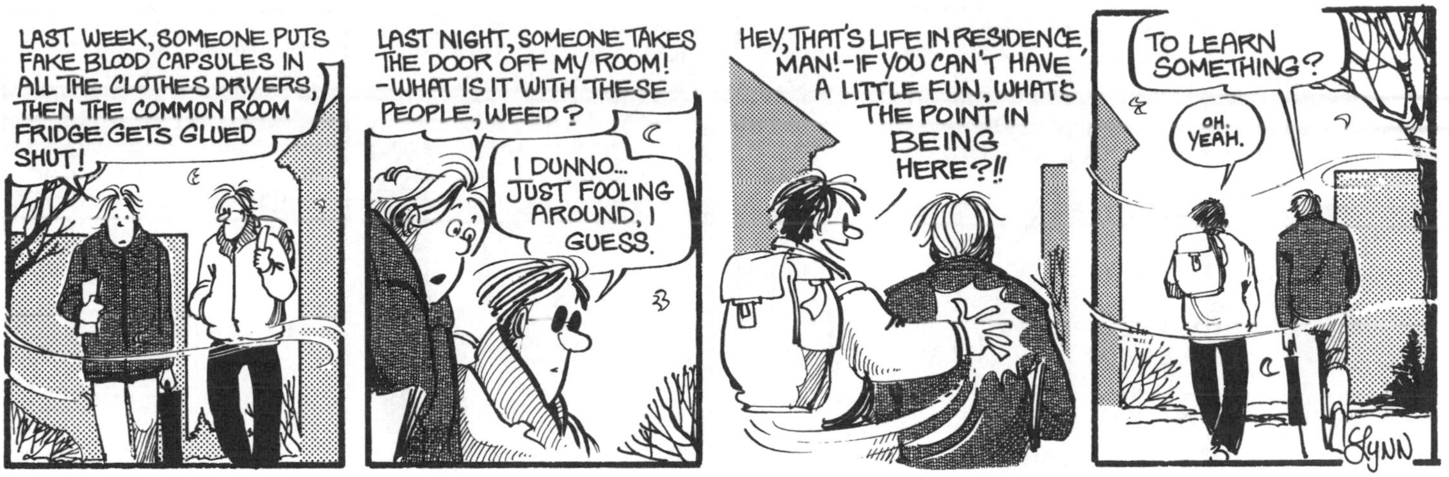
LAST WEEK, SOMEONE PUTS FAKE BLOOD CAPSULES IN ALL THE CLOTHES DRYERS, THEN THE COMMON ROOM FRIDGE GETS GLUED SHUT!
LAST NIGHT, SOMEONE TAKES THE DOOR OFF MY ROOM! -WHAT IS IT WITH THESE PEOPLE, WEED?
I DUNNO... JUST FOOLING AROUND, I GUESS.
HEY, THAT'S LIFE IN RESIDENCE, MAN! -IF YOU CAN'T HAVE A LITTLE FUN, WHAT'S THE POINT IN BEING HERE?!!
TO LEARN SOMETHING?
OH. YEAH.
LYNN

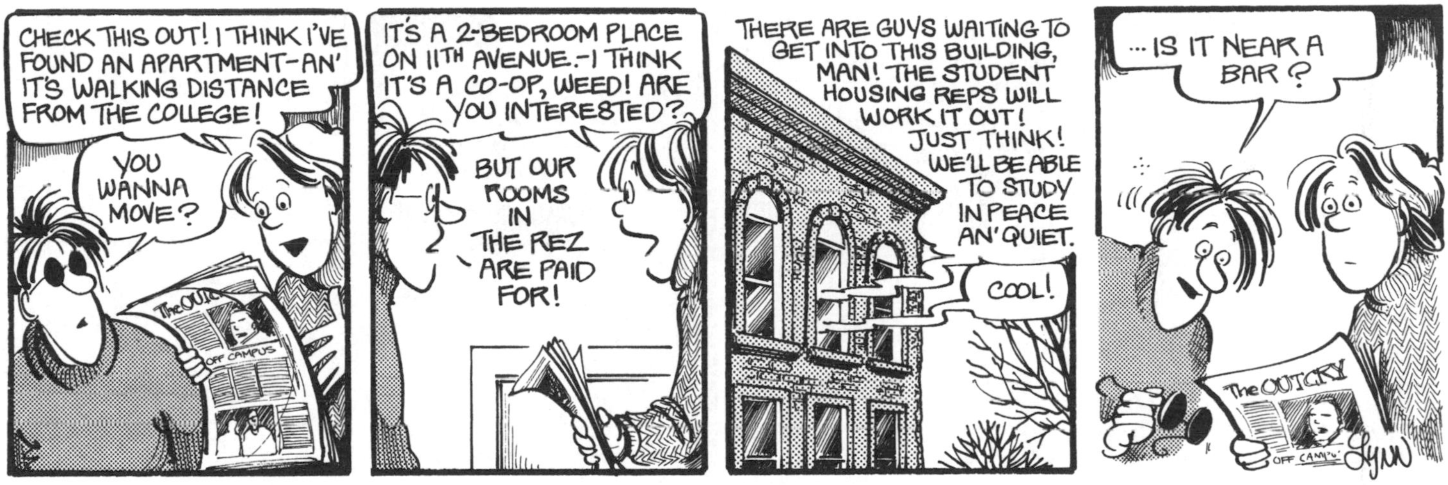
CHECK THIS OUT! I THINK I'VE FOUND AN APARTMENT-AN' IT'S WALKING DISTANCE FROM THE COLLEGE!
YOU WANNA MOVE?
OFF CAMPUS
IT'S A 2-BEDROOM PLACE ON 11TH AVENUE.-I THINK IT'S A CO-OP, WEED! ARE YOU INTERESTED?
BUT OUR ROOMS IN THE REZ ARE PAID FOR!
THERE ARE GUYS WAITING TO GET INTO THIS BUILDING, MAN! THE STUDENT HOUSING REPS WILL WORK IT OUT! JUST THINK! WE'LL BE ABLE TO STUDY IN PEACE AN' QUIET.
COOL!
...IS IT NEAR A BAR?
The OUTCRY
OFF CAMPUS
LYNN

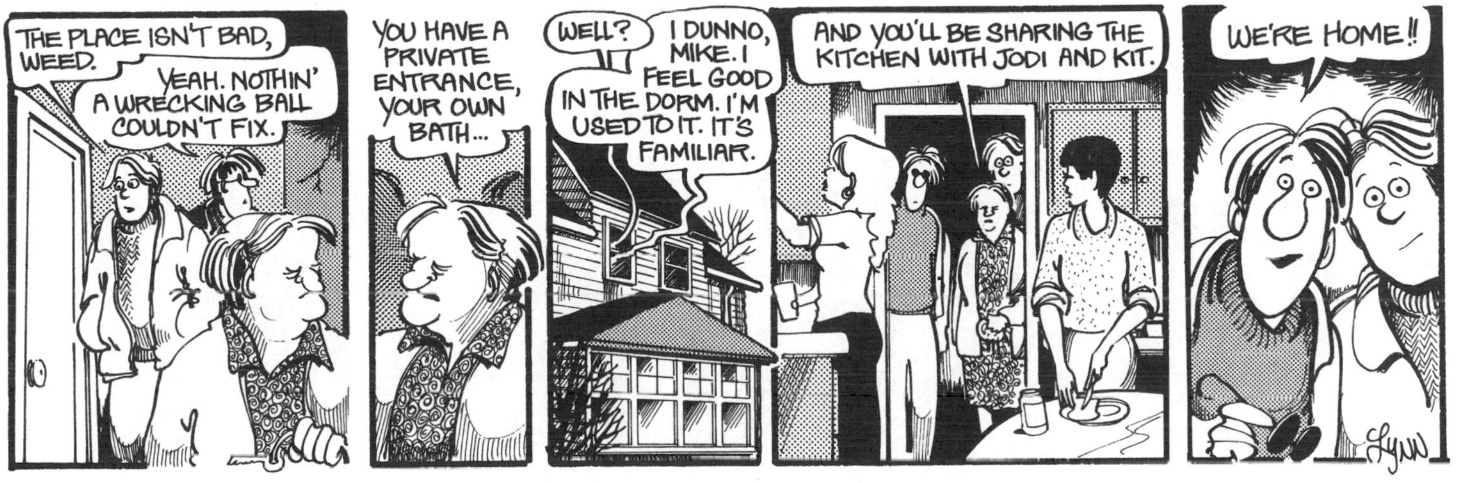
THE PLACE ISN'T BAD, WEED.
YEAH. NOTHIN' A WRECKING BALL COULDN'T FIX.
YOU HAVE A PRIVATE ENTRANCE, YOUR OWN BATH...
WELL?
I DUNNO, MIKE. I FEEL GOOD IN THE DORM. I'M USED TO IT. IT'S FAMILIAR.
AND YOU'LL BE SHARING THE KITCHEN WITH JODI AND KIT.
WE'RE HOME!!
LYNN

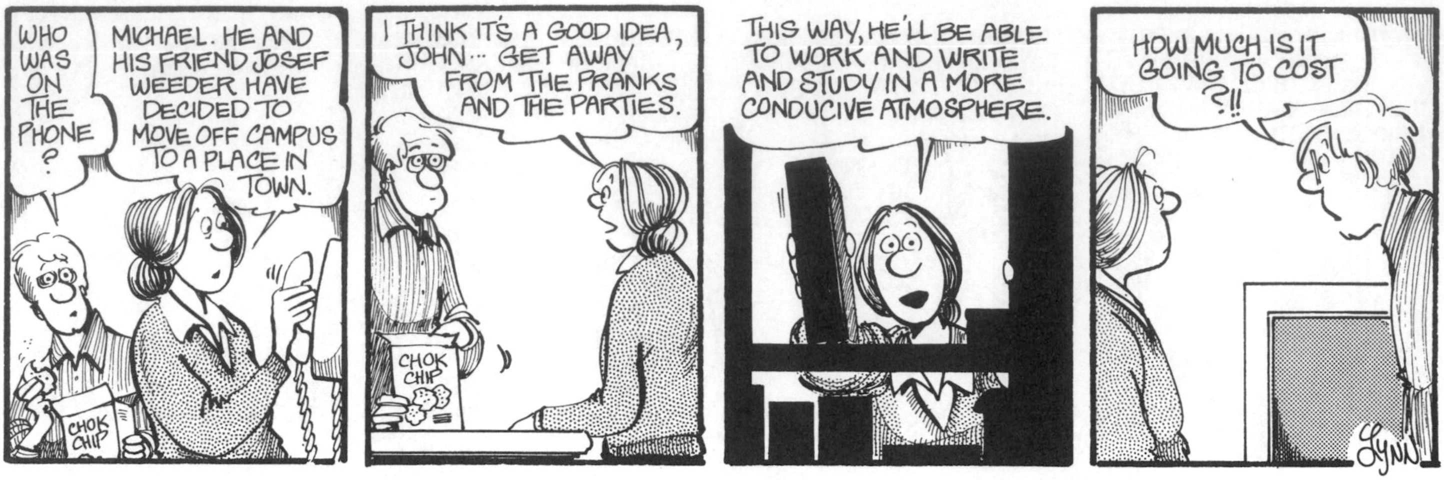
WHO WAS ON THE PHONE ?
MICHAEL. HE AND HIS FRIEND JOSEF WEEDER HAVE DECIDED TO MOVE OFF CAMPUS TO A PLACE IN TOWN.
CHOK CHIP
I THINK IT'S A GOOD IDEA, JOHN... GET AWAY FROM THE PRANKS AND THE PARTIES.
THIS WAY, HE'LL BE ABLE TO WORK AND WRITE AND STUDY IN A MORE CONDUCIVE ATMOSPHERE.
HOW MUCH IS IT GOING TO COST ?!!
LYNN

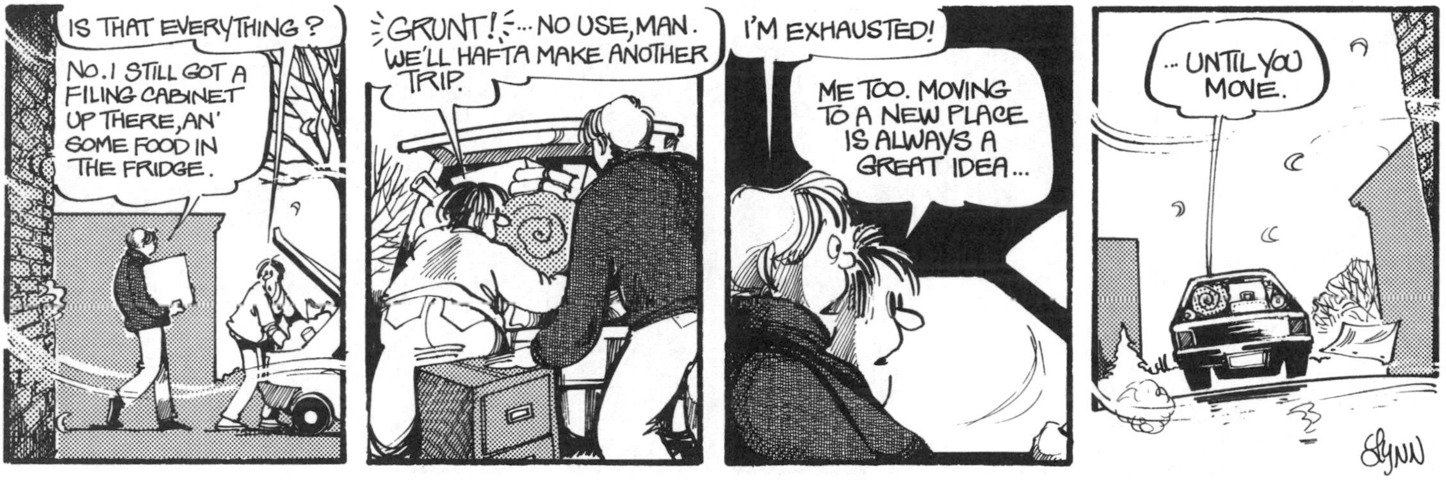
IS THAT EVERYTHING ?
NO. I STILL GOT A FILING CABINET UP THERE, AN' SOME FOOD IN THE FRIDGE.
GRUNT! ... NO USE, MAN. WE'LL HAFTA MAKE ANOTHER TRIP.
I'M EXHAUSTED!
ME TOO. MOVING TO A NEW PLACE IS ALWAYS A GREAT IDEA...
... UNTIL YOU MOVE.
LYNN

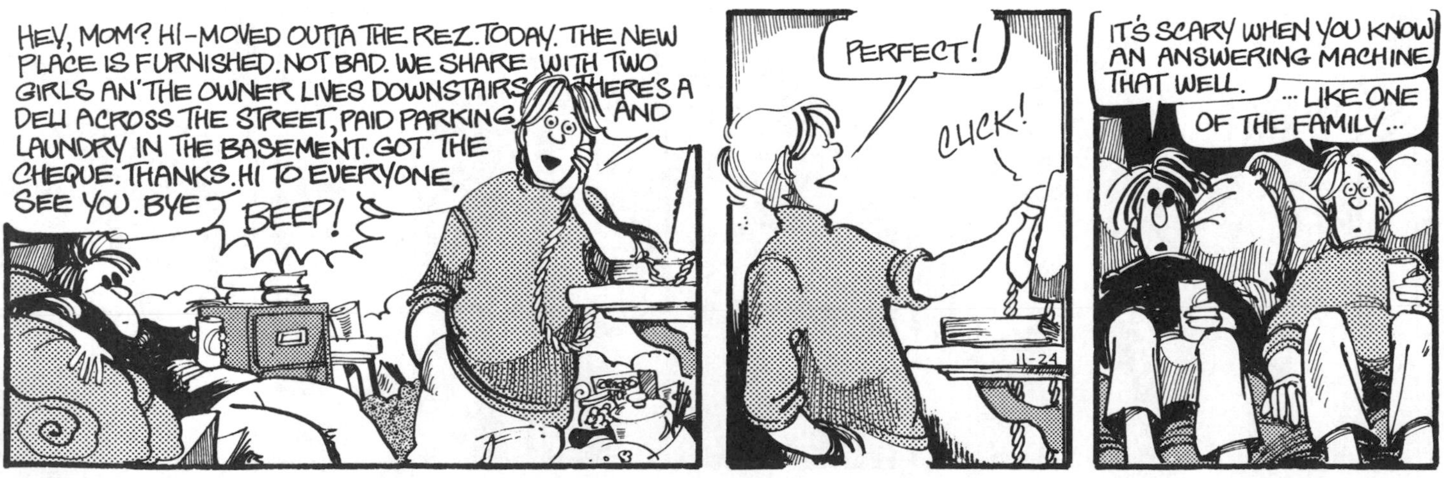
HEY, MOM? HI-MOVED OUTTA THE REZ. TODAY. THE NEW PLACE IS FURNISHED. NOT BAD. WE SHARE WITH TWO GIRLS AN' THE OWNER LIVES DOWNSTAIRS. THERE'S A DELI ACROSS THE STREET, PAID PARKING AND LAUNDRY IN THE BASEMENT. GOT THE CHEQUE. THANKS. HI TO EVERYONE. SEE YOU. BYE
BEEP!
PERFECT!
CLICK!
11-24
IT'S SCARY WHEN YOU KNOW AN ANSWERING MACHINE THAT WELL.
... LIKE ONE OF THE FAMILY...

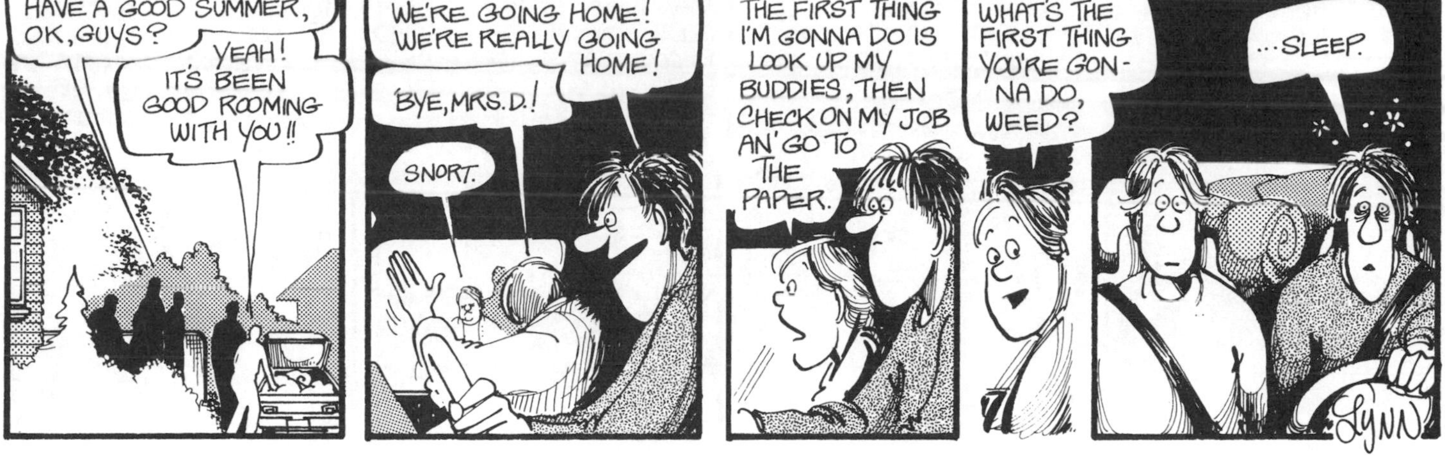
HAVE A GOOD SUMMER, OK, GUYS?
YEAH! IT'S BEEN GOOD ROOMING WITH YOU!!
WE'RE GOING HOME! WE'RE REALLY GOING HOME!
'BYE, MRS. D.!
SNORT.
THE FIRST THING I'M GONNA DO IS LOOK UP MY BUDDIES, THEN CHECK ON MY JOB AN' GO TO THE PAPER.
WHAT'S THE FIRST THING YOU'RE GON-NA DO, WEED?
...SLEEP.
LYNN

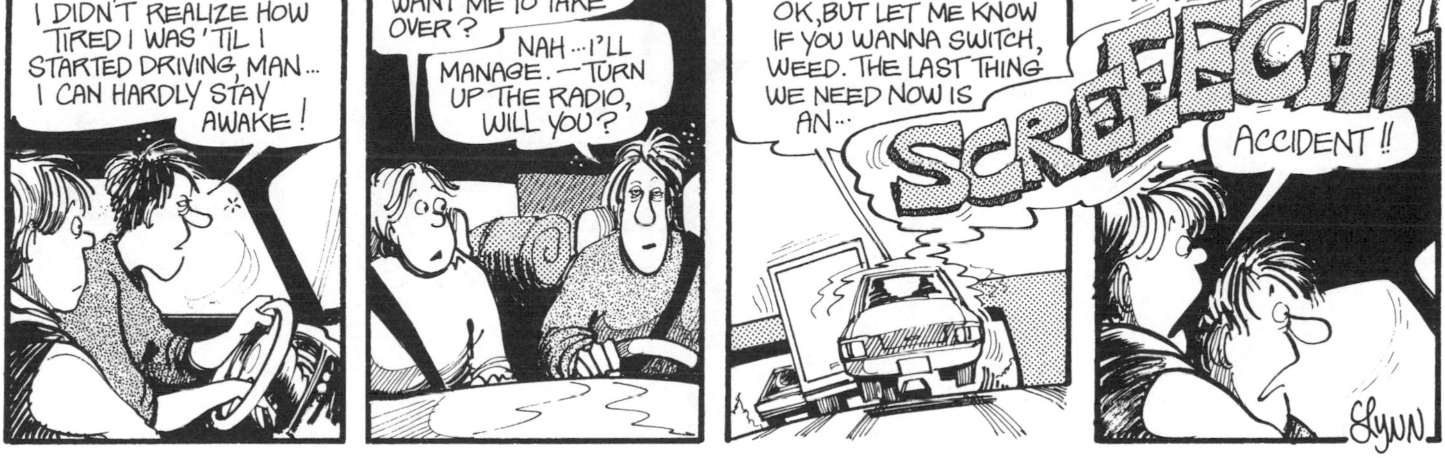
I DIDN'T REALIZE HOW TIRED I WAS 'TIL I STARTED DRIVING, MAN... I CAN HARDLY STAY AWAKE!
WANT ME TO TAKE OVER?
NAH...I'LL MANAGE. —TURN UP THE RADIO, WILL YOU?
OK, BUT LET ME KNOW IF YOU WANNA SWITCH, WEED. THE LAST THING WE NEED NOW IS AN...
SCREEECH!!
ACCIDENT!!
LYNN

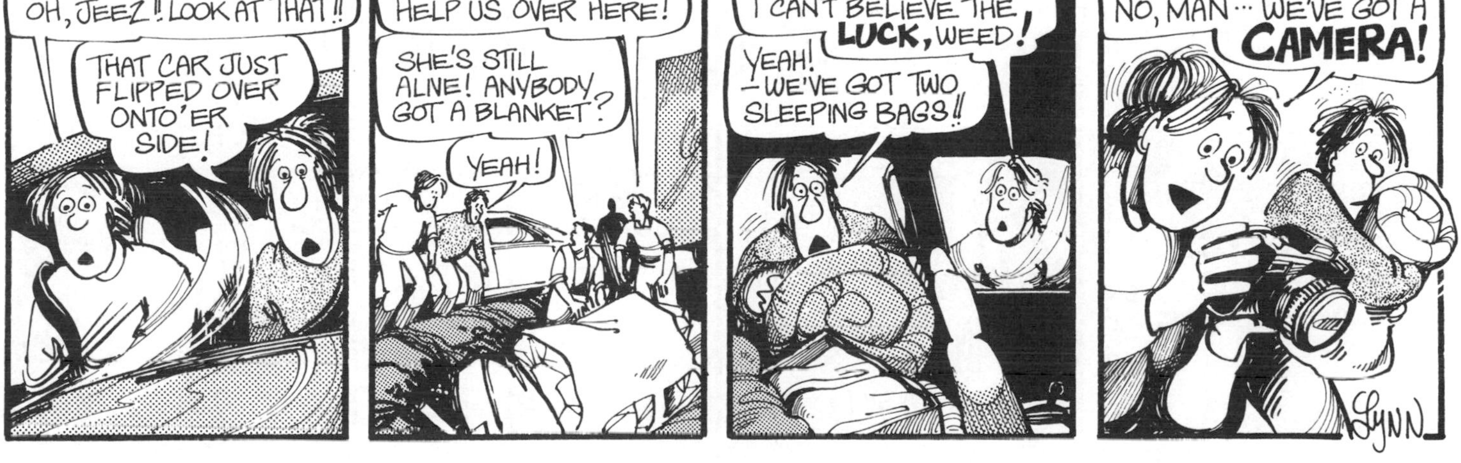
OH, JEEZ!! LOOK AT THAT!!
THAT CAR JUST FLIPPED OVER ONTO 'ER SIDE!
HELP US OVER HERE!
SHE'S STILL ALIVE! ANYBODY GOT A BLANKET?
YEAH!
I CAN'T BELIEVE THE LUCK, WEED!
YEAH! —WE'VE GOT TWO SLEEPING BAGS!!
NO, MAN... WE'VE GOT A CAMERA!
LYNN

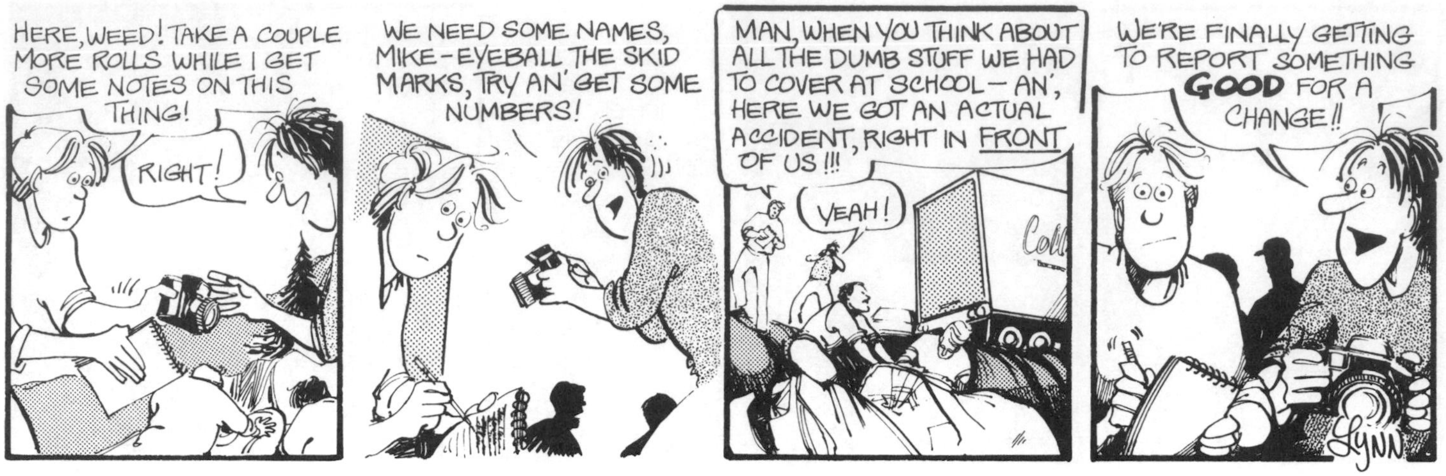
HERE, WEED! TAKE A COUPLE MORE ROLLS WHILE I GET SOME NOTES ON THIS THING!
RIGHT!
WE NEED SOME NAMES, MIKE - EYEBALL THE SKID MARKS, TRY AN' GET SOME NUMBERS!
MAN, WHEN YOU THINK ABOUT ALL THE DUMB STUFF WE HAD TO COVER AT SCHOOL — AN', HERE WE GOT AN ACTUAL ACCIDENT, RIGHT IN FRONT OF US !!!
YEAH!
WE'RE FINALLY GETTING TO REPORT SOMETHING GOOD FOR A CHANGE!!
LYNN

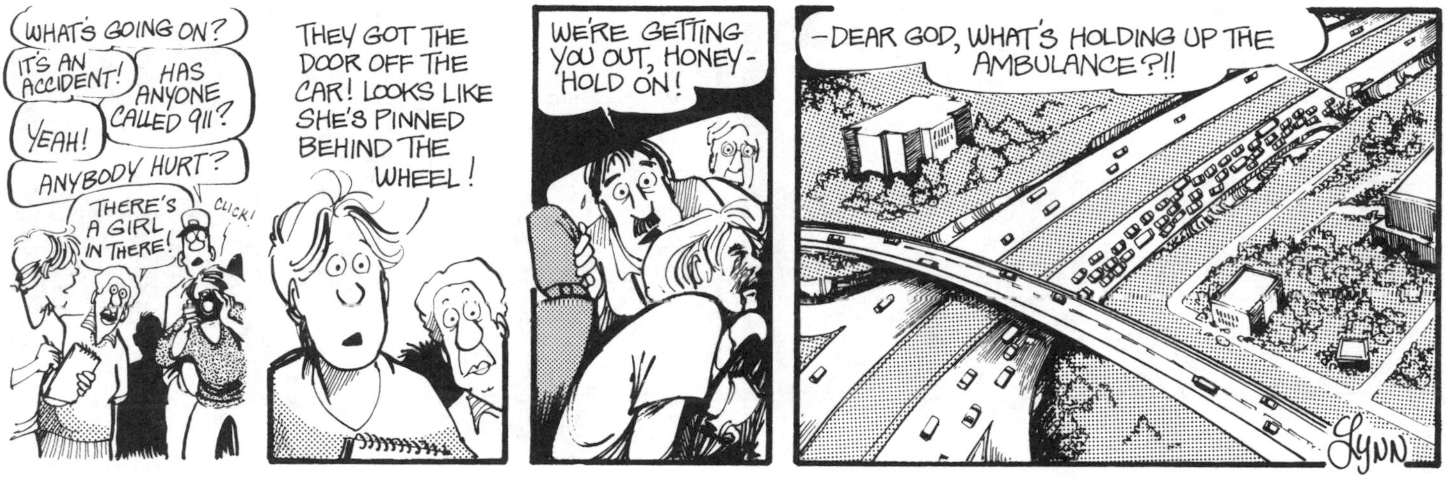
WHAT'S GOING ON?
IT'S AN ACCIDENT!
HAS ANYONE CALLED 911?
YEAH!
ANYBODY HURT?
THERE'S A GIRL IN THERE!
CLICK!
THEY GOT THE DOOR OFF THE CAR! LOOKS LIKE SHE'S PINNED BEHIND THE WHEEL!
WE'RE GETTING YOU OUT, HONEY - HOLD ON!
— DEAR GOD, WHAT'S HOLDING UP THE AMBULANCE?!!
LYNN

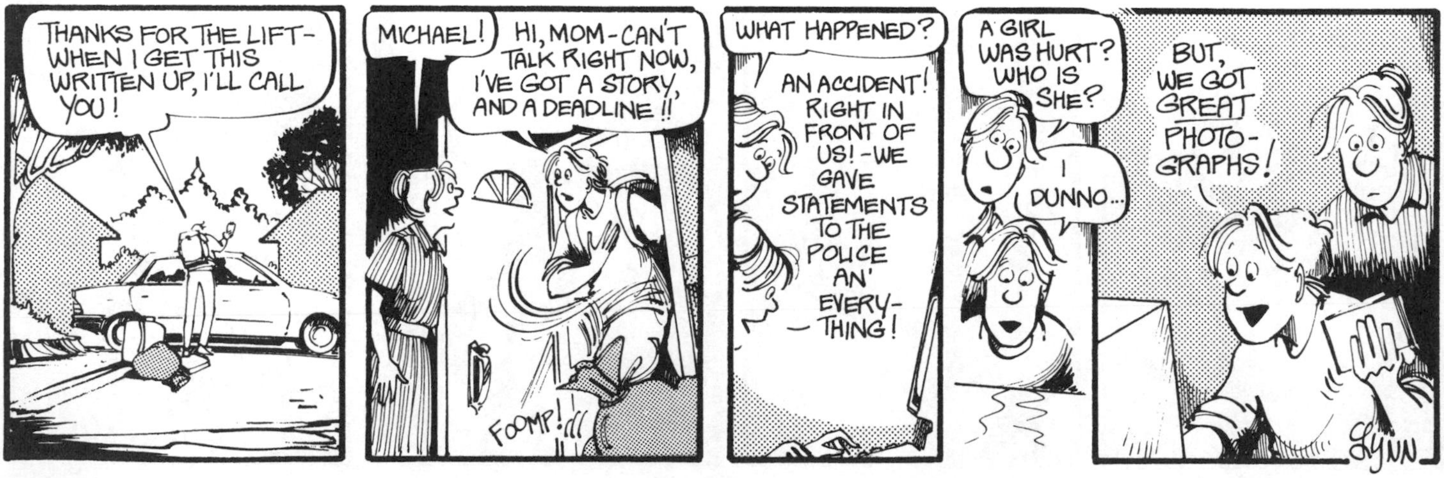
THANKS FOR THE LIFT - WHEN I GET THIS WRITTEN UP, I'LL CALL YOU!
MICHAEL!
HI, MOM - CAN'T TALK RIGHT NOW, I'VE GOT A STORY, AND A DEADLINE!!
FOOMP!
WHAT HAPPENED?
AN ACCIDENT! RIGHT IN FRONT OF US! - WE GAVE STATEMENTS TO THE POLICE AN' EVERY- THING!
A GIRL WAS HURT? WHO IS SHE?
I DUNNO...
BUT, WE GOT GREAT PHOTO- GRAPHS!
LYNN

Panel 1: IT'S HERE! YESS! WE DID IT! - WE GOT ONTO THE FRONT PAGE !!!

Panel 2: LET'S SEE .... NEAR FATAL ACCIDENT ..... YAH, TA, TA ... WAIT A SECOND! — WAIT A SECOND! .... SOME BUTT-BRAIN HAS EDITED MY STUFF !!

Panel 3: I WROTE A GREAT STORY, AN' THEY PRINTED **HALF** OF IT !!!

DO THEY SAY WHO THE VICTIM WAS?

I DUNNO. I DON'T CARE ABOUT THAT RIGHT NOW.

Panel 4: WELL, YOU SHOULD .....

YOU KNOW HER.

Panel 5: 20-YEAR-OLD DEANNA SOBINSKI SUFFERED MULTIPLE INJURIES WHEN SHE LOST CONTROL OF HER CAR YESTERDAY.

IT WAS DEANNA?

Panel 6: ACCORDING TO WITNESSES, THE CAR BROKE THROUGH A BARRICADE AND ROLLED ONCE, CRUSHING THE DRIVER'S SIDE OF THE VEHICLE.

DEANNA!

Panel 7: MISS SOBINSKI WAS FREED BY TWO QUICK-THINKING TRUCK DRIVERS WHO ARE CREDITED WITH SAVING HER LIFE.

I THOUGHT SHE WAS, YOU KNOW, JUST ANOTHER PERSON !!!

Panel 8: NOBODY IS "JUST ANOTHER PERSON", MICHAEL!

Panel 9: WHO'S DEANNA SOBINSKI?

WE WENT TO ELEMENTARY SCHOOL TOGETHER. I HAD A CRUSH ON HER! SHE WAS A CUTE LITTLE KID ... BUT THEY MOVED AND WE LOST TOUCH.

Panel 10: SHE ALMOST DIED YESTERDAY ... AND WE TOOK **PICTURES!** - ALL WE COULD THINK ABOUT WAS GETTING A STORY ONTO THE FRONT PAGE OF THE PAPER!

Panel 11: HOW COULD I HAVE BEEN SO INSENSITIVE?

YEAH ... THAT WAS AMAZINGLY INSENSITIVE!

Panel 12: LIZ ... MICHAEL DOESN'T NEED YOU TO CRITICIZE HIM RIGHT NOW!

HE'S DOING WELL ENOUGH ON HIS OWN.

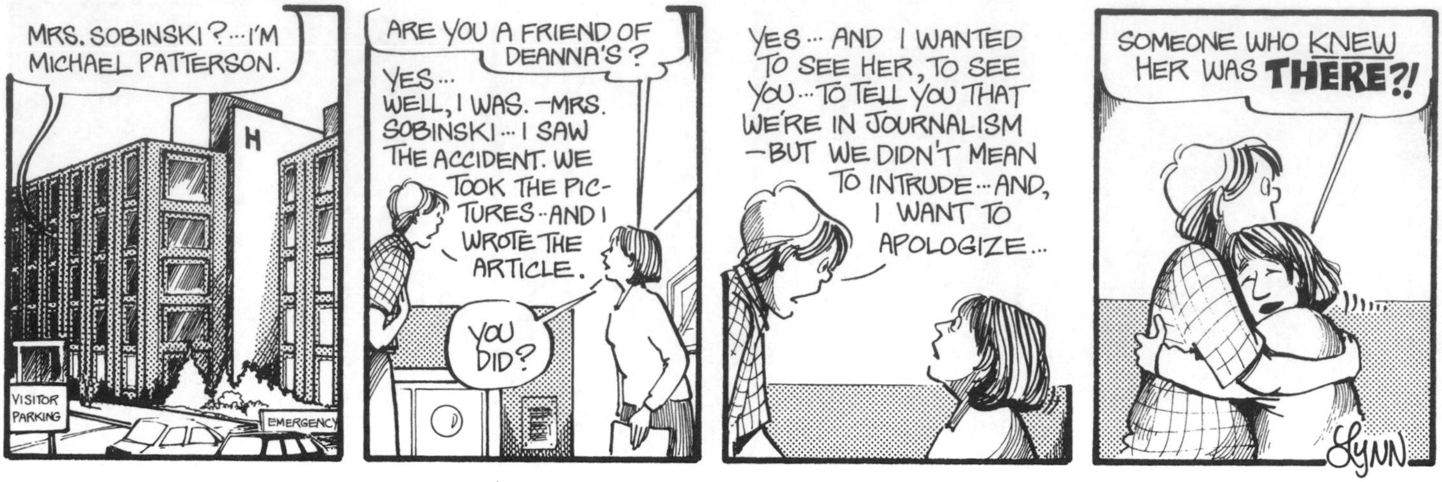
MRS. SOBINSKI? ... I'M MICHAEL PATTERSON.
VISITOR PARKING
EMERGENCY
H
ARE YOU A FRIEND OF DEANNA'S?
YES ... WELL, I WAS. –MRS. SOBINSKI ... I SAW THE ACCIDENT. WE TOOK THE PICTURES .. AND I WROTE THE ARTICLE.
YOU DID?
YES ... AND I WANTED TO SEE HER, TO SEE YOU ... TO TELL YOU THAT WE'RE IN JOURNALISM –BUT WE DIDN'T MEAN TO INTRUDE ... AND, I WANT TO APOLOGIZE ...
SOMEONE WHO KNEW HER WAS **THERE**?!
LYNN

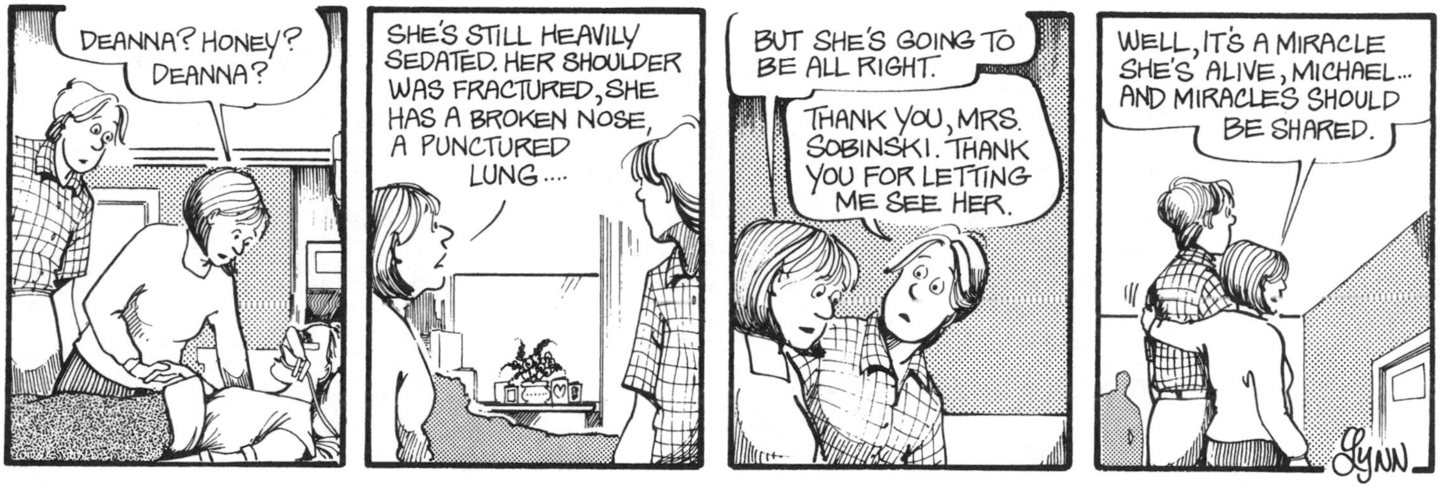
DEANNA? HONEY? DEANNA?
SHE'S STILL HEAVILY SEDATED. HER SHOULDER WAS FRACTURED, SHE HAS A BROKEN NOSE, A PUNCTURED LUNG ....
BUT SHE'S GOING TO BE ALL RIGHT.
THANK YOU, MRS. SOBINSKI. THANK YOU FOR LETTING ME SEE HER.
WELL, IT'S A MIRACLE SHE'S ALIVE, MICHAEL ... AND MIRACLES SHOULD BE SHARED.
LYNN

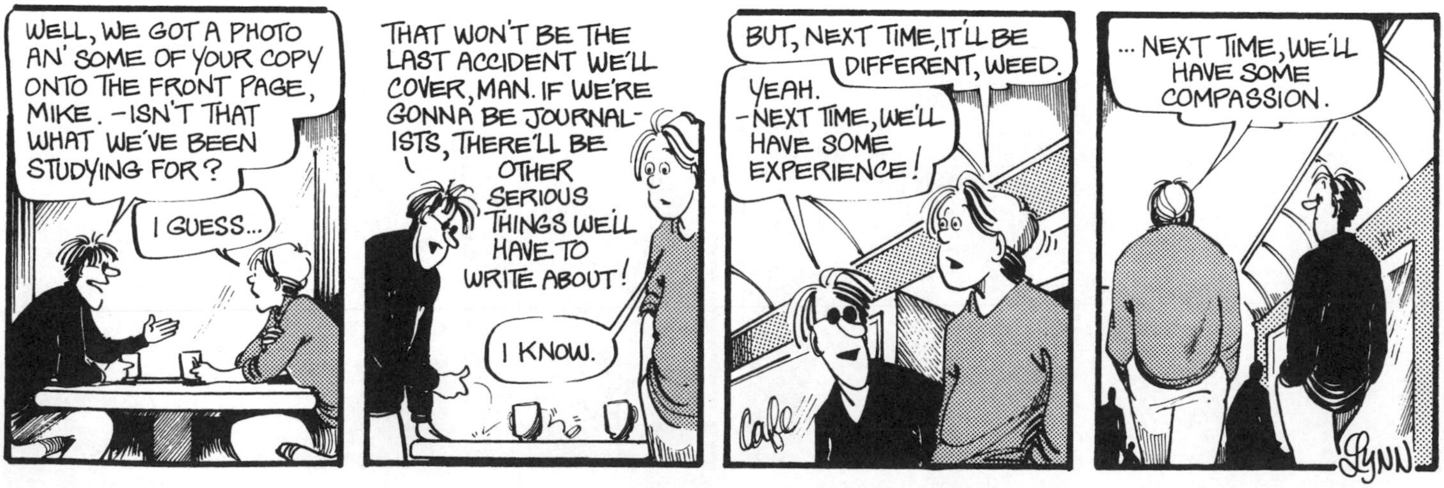
WELL, WE GOT A PHOTO AN' SOME OF YOUR COPY ONTO THE FRONT PAGE, MIKE. –ISN'T THAT WHAT WE'VE BEEN STUDYING FOR?
I GUESS ...
THAT WON'T BE THE LAST ACCIDENT WE'LL COVER, MAN. IF WE'RE GONNA BE JOURNALISTS, THERE'LL BE OTHER SERIOUS THINGS WE'LL HAVE TO WRITE ABOUT!
I KNOW.
BUT, NEXT TIME, IT'LL BE DIFFERENT, WEED.
YEAH. –NEXT TIME, WE'LL HAVE SOME EXPERIENCE!
Cafe
... NEXT TIME, WE'LL HAVE SOME COMPASSION.
LYNN

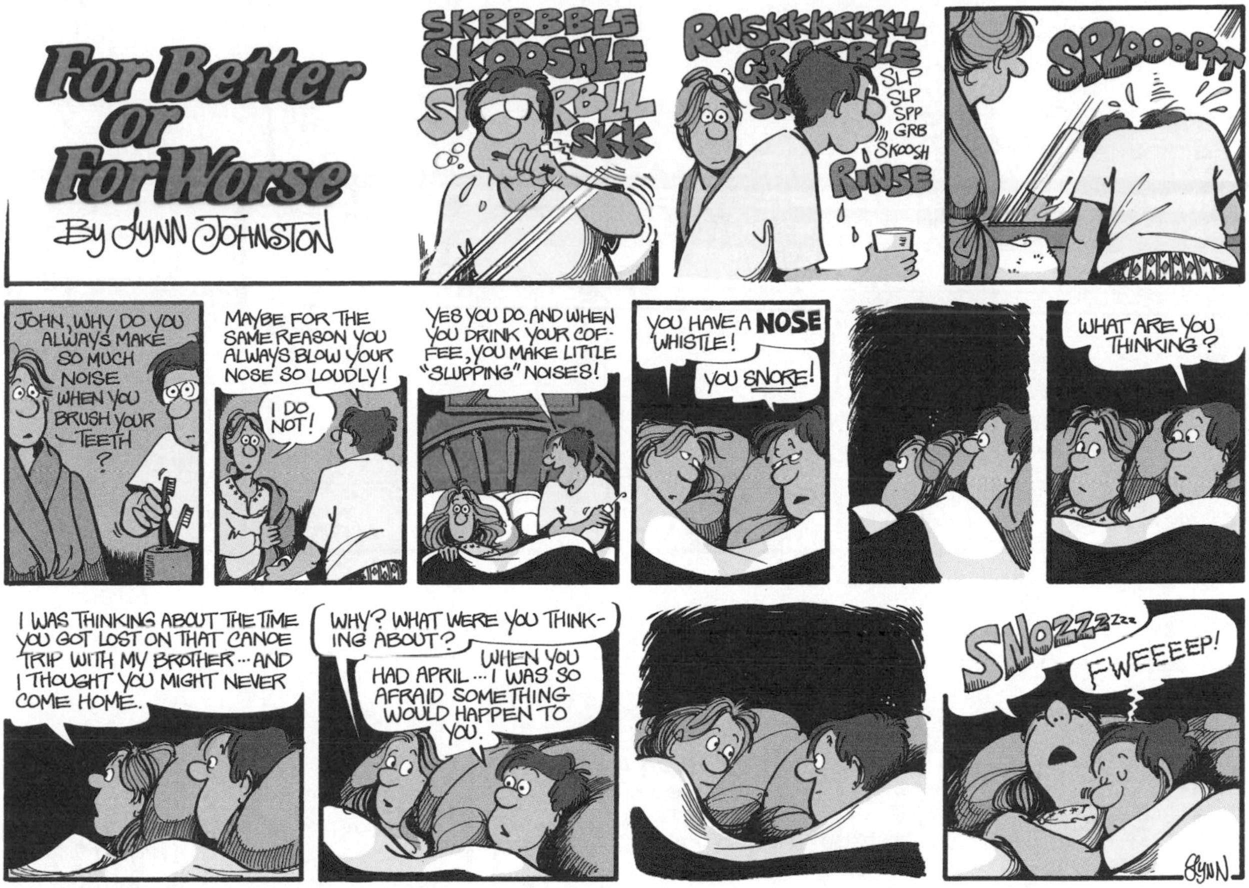
For Better or For Worse
By Lynn Johnston
SKRRBBLE SKOOSHLE SKRBLL SKK
RINSKKKRKKLL GRRBBLE SK
SLP SLP SPP GRB SKOOSH
RINSE
SPLOOOPTT
JOHN, WHY DO YOU ALWAYS MAKE SO MUCH NOISE WHEN YOU BRUSH YOUR TEETH?
MAYBE FOR THE SAME REASON YOU ALWAYS BLOW YOUR NOSE SO LOUDLY!
I DO NOT!
YES YOU DO. AND WHEN YOU DRINK YOUR COFFEE, YOU MAKE LITTLE "SLUPPING" NOISES!
YOU HAVE A NOSE WHISTLE!
YOU SNORE!
WHAT ARE YOU THINKING?
I WAS THINKING ABOUT THE TIME YOU GOT LOST ON THAT CANOE TRIP WITH MY BROTHER... AND I THOUGHT YOU MIGHT NEVER COME HOME.
WHY? WHAT WERE YOU THINKING ABOUT?
WHEN YOU HAD APRIL... I WAS SO AFRAID SOMETHING WOULD HAPPEN TO YOU.
SNOZZZzzz
FWEEEEP!
Lynn

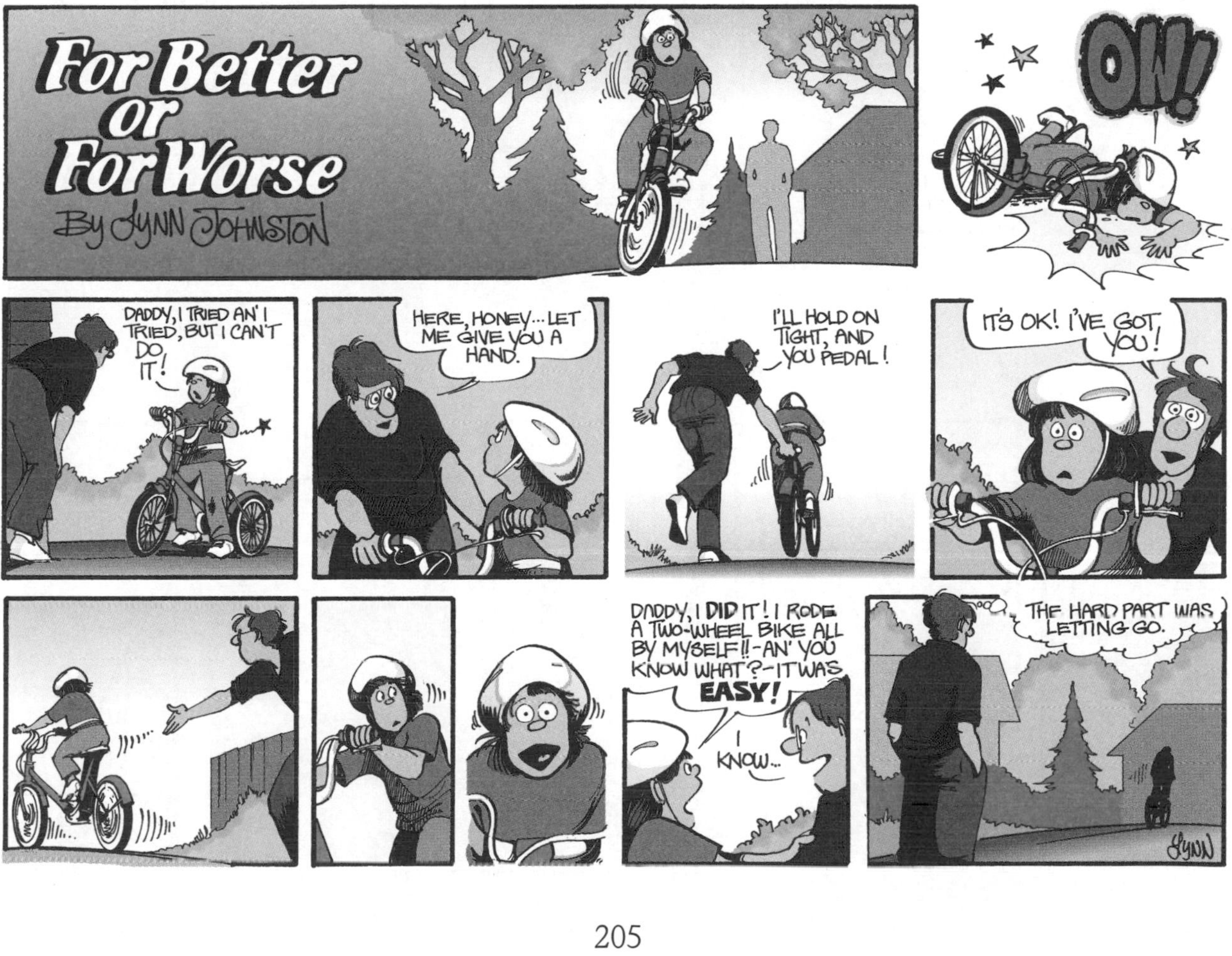
For Better or For Worse
By Lynn Johnston
OW!
DADDY, I TRIED AN' I TRIED, BUT I CAN'T DO IT!
HERE, HONEY... LET ME GIVE YOU A HAND.
I'LL HOLD ON TIGHT, AND YOU PEDAL!
IT'S OK! I'VE GOT YOU!
DADDY, I DID IT! I RODE A TWO-WHEEL BIKE ALL BY MYSELF!! -AN' YOU KNOW WHAT?- IT WAS EASY!
I KNOW...
THE HARD PART WAS LETTING GO.
Lynn

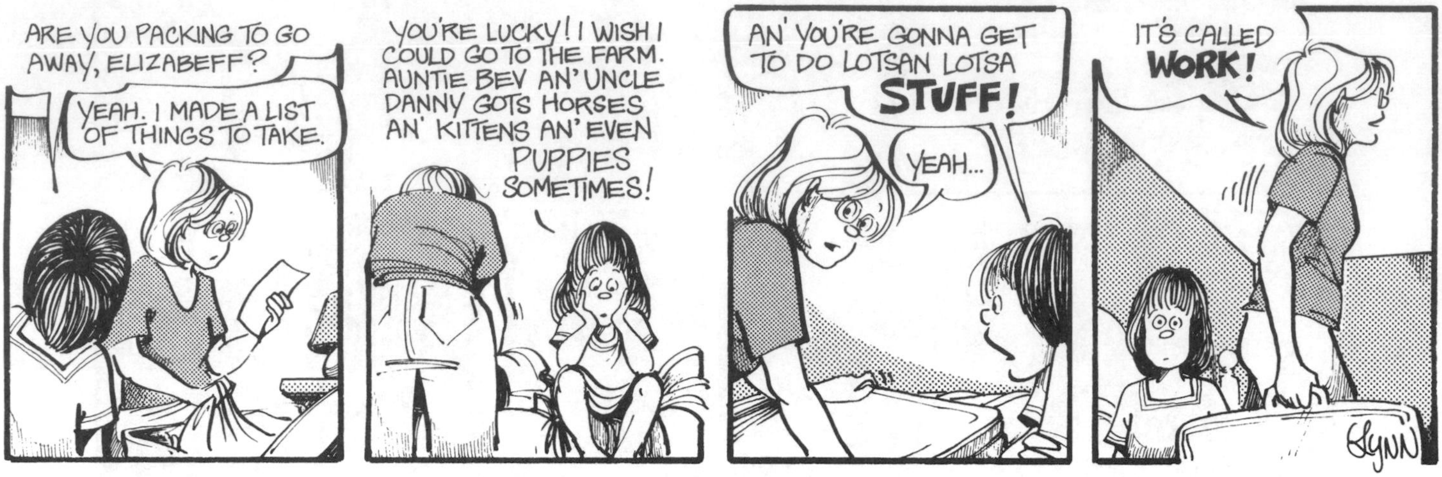
ARE YOU PACKING TO GO AWAY, ELIZABEFF?
YEAH. I MADE A LIST OF THINGS TO TAKE.
YOU'RE LUCKY! I WISH I COULD GO TO THE FARM. AUNTIE BEV AN' UNCLE DANNY GOTS HORSES AN' KITTENS AN' EVEN PUPPIES SOMETIMES!
AN' YOU'RE GONNA GET TO DO LOTSAN LOTSA STUFF!
YEAH...
IT'S CALLED WORK!
LYNN

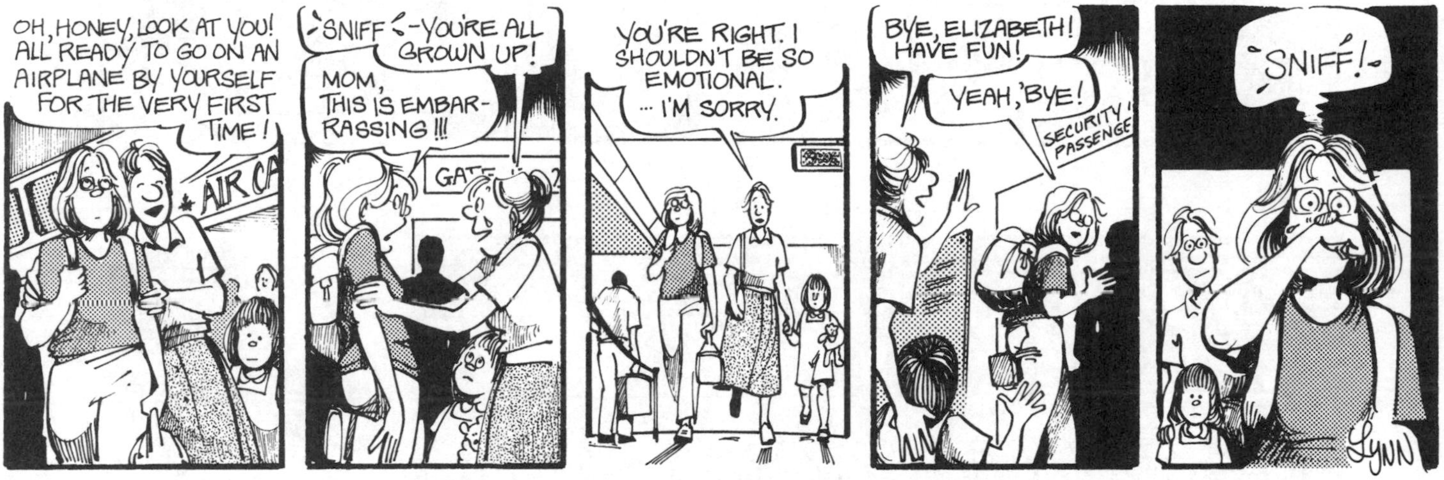
OH, HONEY, LOOK AT YOU! ALL READY TO GO ON AN AIRPLANE BY YOURSELF FOR THE VERY FIRST TIME!
SNIFF -YOU'RE ALL GROWN UP!
MOM, THIS IS EMBARRASSING!!!
YOU'RE RIGHT. I SHOULDN'T BE SO EMOTIONAL. ... I'M SORRY.
BYE, ELIZABETH! HAVE FUN!
YEAH, 'BYE!
SECURITY PASSENGE
SNIFF!
LYNN

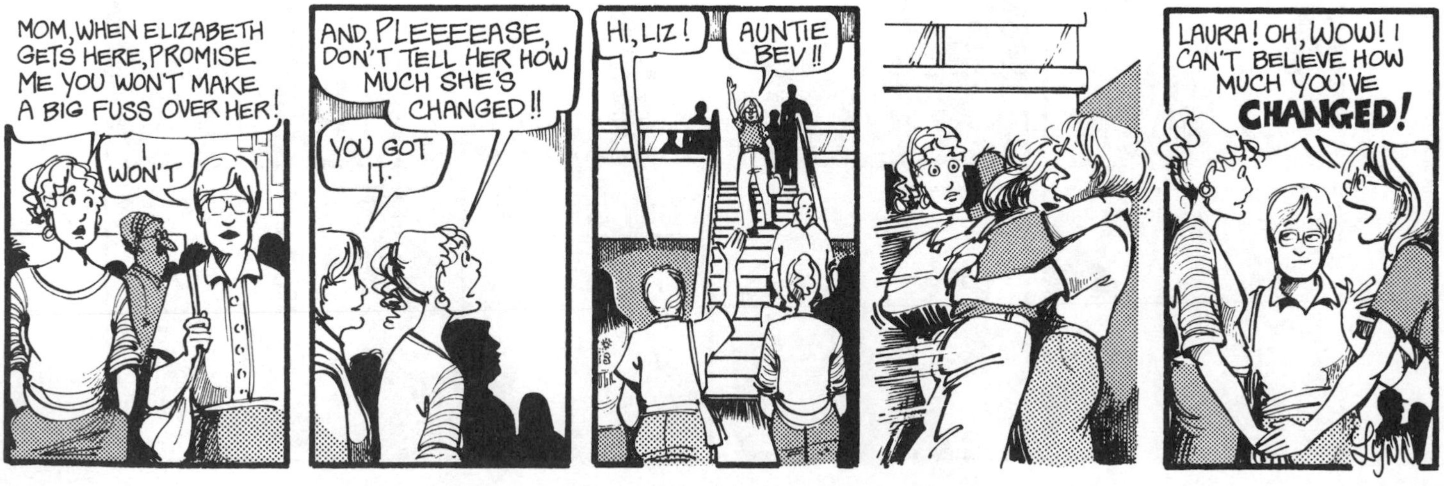
MOM, WHEN ELIZABETH GETS HERE, PROMISE ME YOU WON'T MAKE A BIG FUSS OVER HER!
I WON'T
AND, PLEEEEASE, DON'T TELL HER HOW MUCH SHE'S CHANGED!!
YOU GOT IT.
HI, LIZ!
AUNTIE BEV!!
LAURA! OH, WOW! I CAN'T BELIEVE HOW MUCH YOU'VE CHANGED!
LYNN

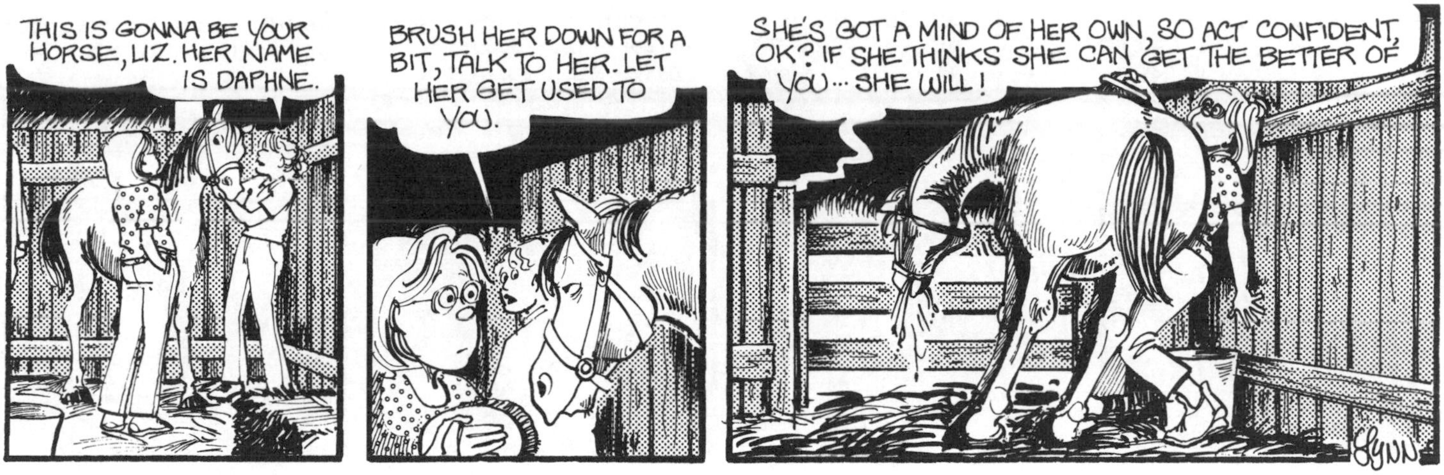
THIS IS GONNA BE YOUR HORSE, LIZ. HER NAME IS DAPHNE.
BRUSH HER DOWN FOR A BIT, TALK TO HER. LET HER GET USED TO YOU.
SHE'S GOT A MIND OF HER OWN, SO ACT CONFIDENT, OK? IF SHE THINKS SHE CAN GET THE BETTER OF YOU... SHE WILL!
LYNN

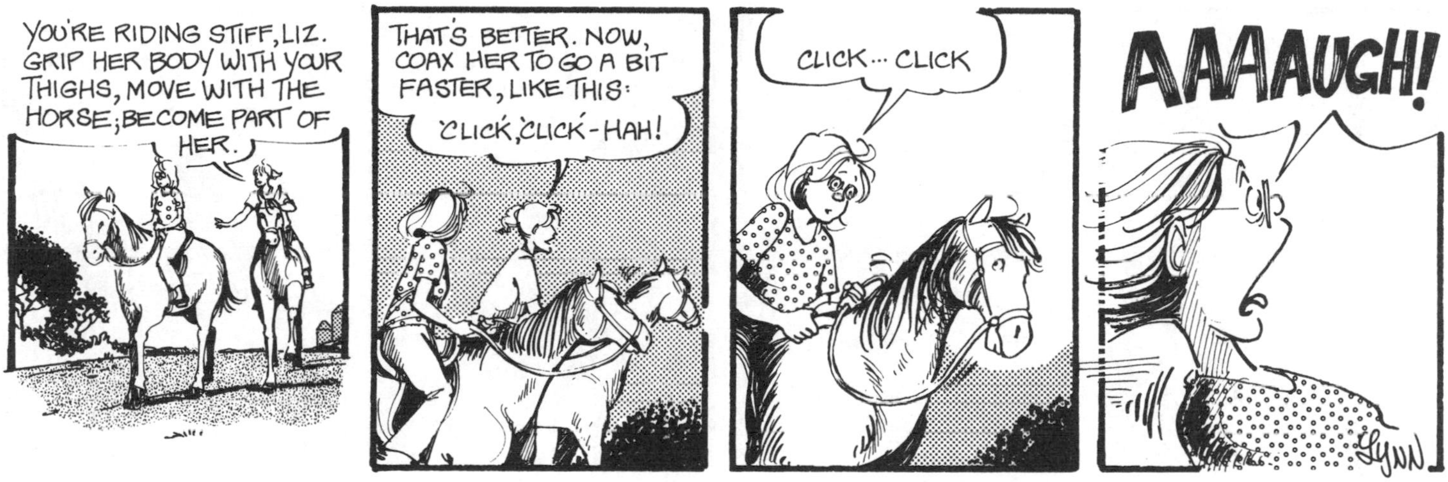
YOU'RE RIDING STIFF, LIZ. GRIP HER BODY WITH YOUR THIGHS, MOVE WITH THE HORSE; BECOME PART OF HER.
THAT'S BETTER. NOW, COAX HER TO GO A BIT FASTER, LIKE THIS:
'CLICK, 'CLICK-HAH!
CLICK... CLICK
AAAAUGH!
LYNN

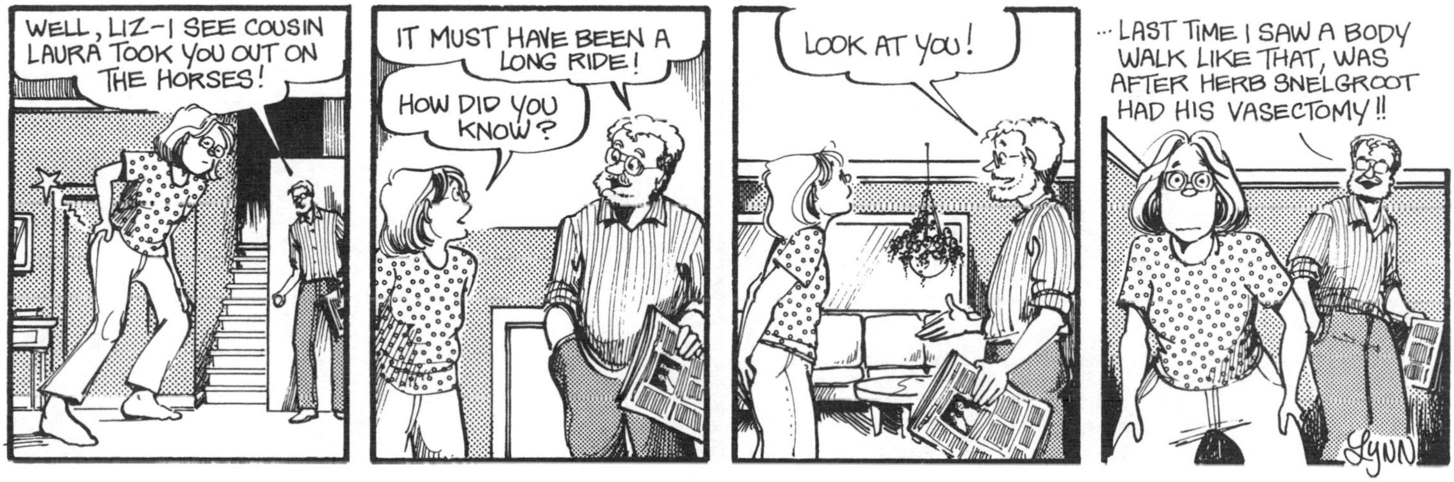
WELL, LIZ-I SEE COUSIN LAURA TOOK YOU OUT ON THE HORSES!
IT MUST HAVE BEEN A LONG RIDE!
HOW DID YOU KNOW?
LOOK AT YOU!
...LAST TIME I SAW A BODY WALK LIKE THAT, WAS AFTER HERB SNELGROOT HAD HIS VASECTOMY!!
LYNN

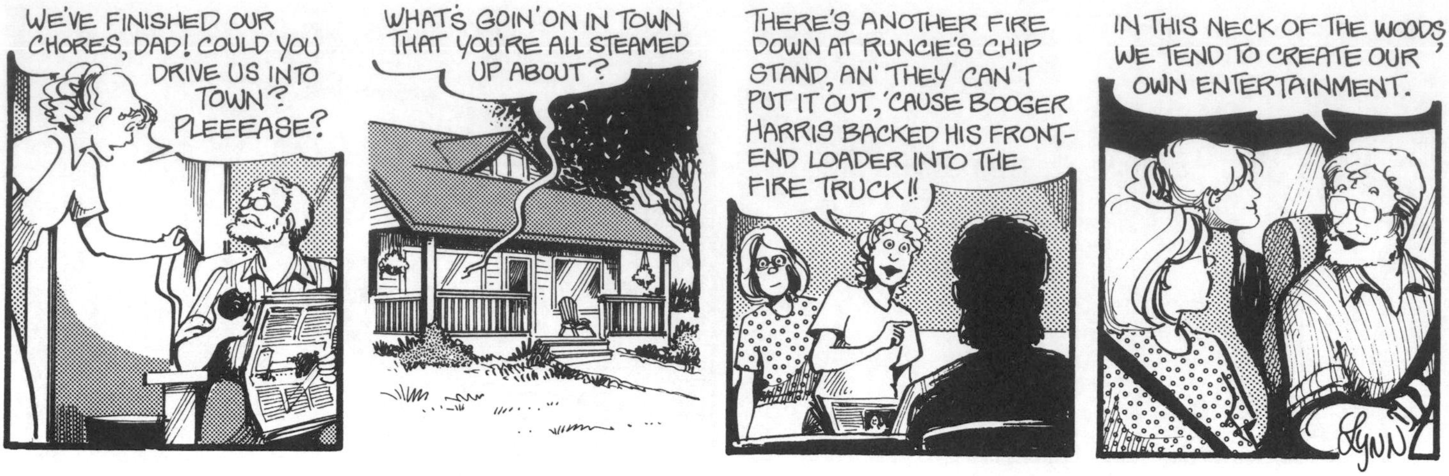
WE'VE FINISHED OUR CHORES, DAD! COULD YOU DRIVE US INTO TOWN? PLEEEASE?
WHAT'S GOIN' ON IN TOWN THAT YOU'RE ALL STEAMED UP ABOUT?
THERE'S ANOTHER FIRE DOWN AT RUNCIE'S CHIP STAND, AN' THEY CAN'T PUT IT OUT, 'CAUSE BOOGER HARRIS BACKED HIS FRONT-END LOADER INTO THE FIRE TRUCK!!
IN THIS NECK OF THE WOODS, WE TEND TO CREATE OUR OWN ENTERTAINMENT.
LYNN

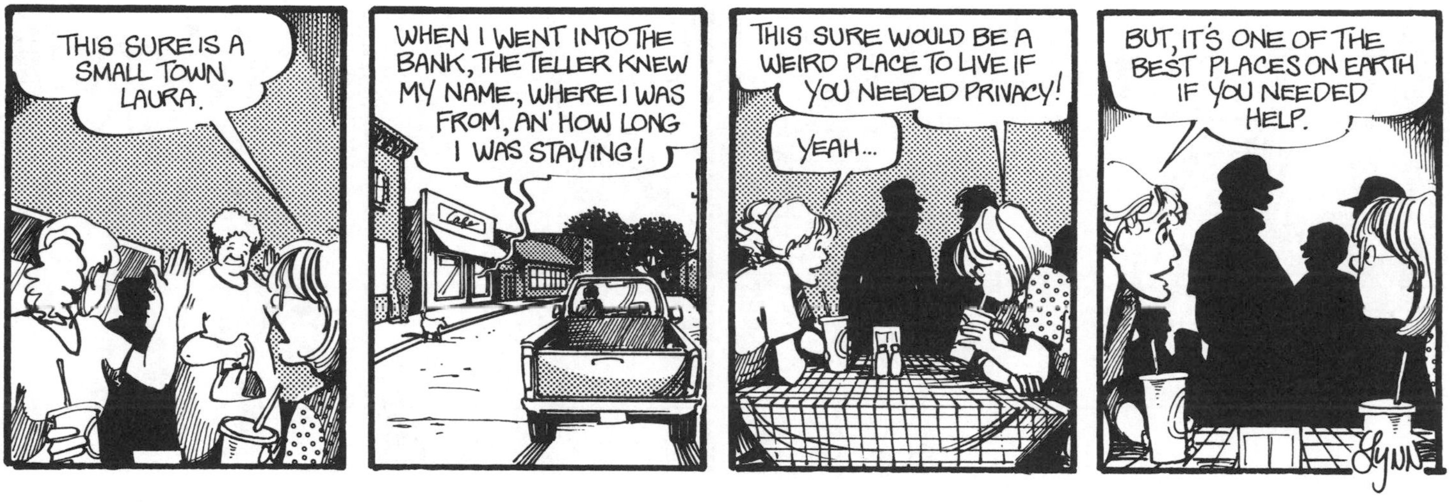
THIS SURE IS A SMALL TOWN, LAURA.
WHEN I WENT INTO THE BANK, THE TELLER KNEW MY NAME, WHERE I WAS FROM, AN' HOW LONG I WAS STAYING!
THIS SURE WOULD BE A WEIRD PLACE TO LIVE IF YOU NEEDED PRIVACY!
YEAH...
BUT, IT'S ONE OF THE BEST PLACES ON EARTH IF YOU NEEDED HELP.
LYNN

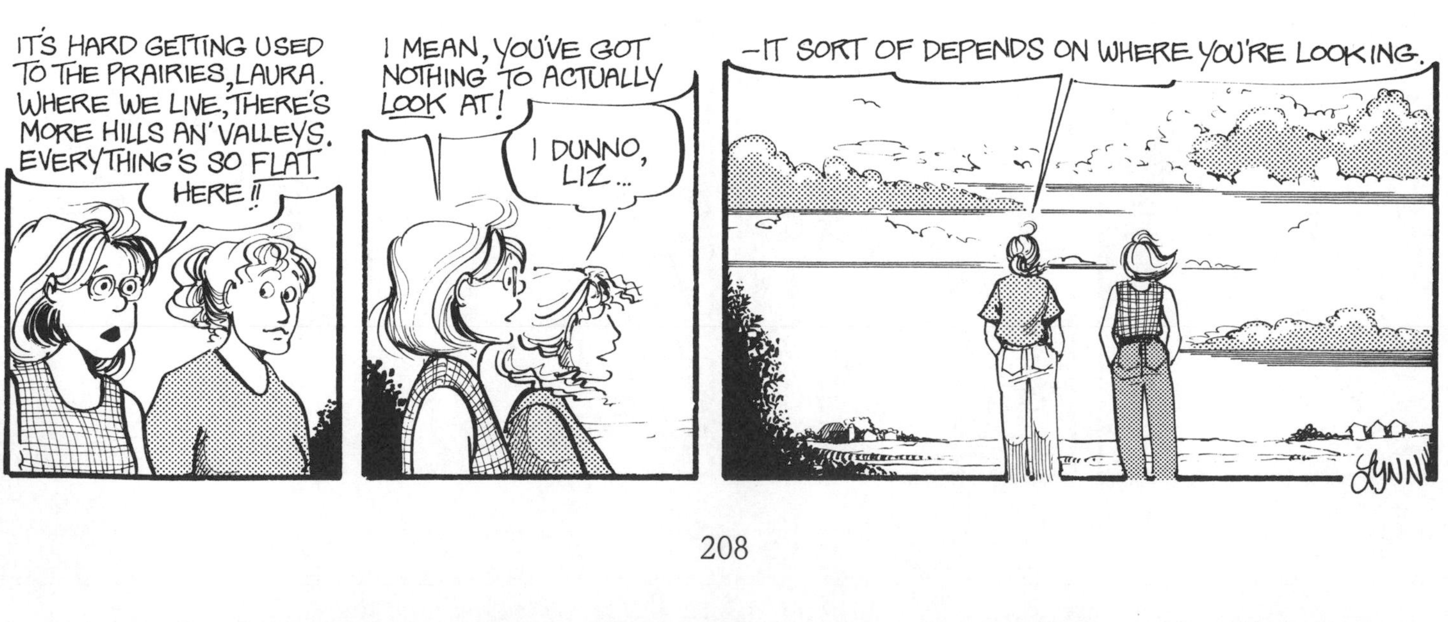
IT'S HARD GETTING USED TO THE PRAIRIES, LAURA. WHERE WE LIVE, THERE'S MORE HILLS AN' VALLEYS. EVERYTHING'S SO FLAT HERE!!
I MEAN, YOU'VE GOT NOTHING TO ACTUALLY LOOK AT!
I DUNNO, LIZ...
—IT SORT OF DEPENDS ON WHERE YOU'RE LOOKING.
LYNN

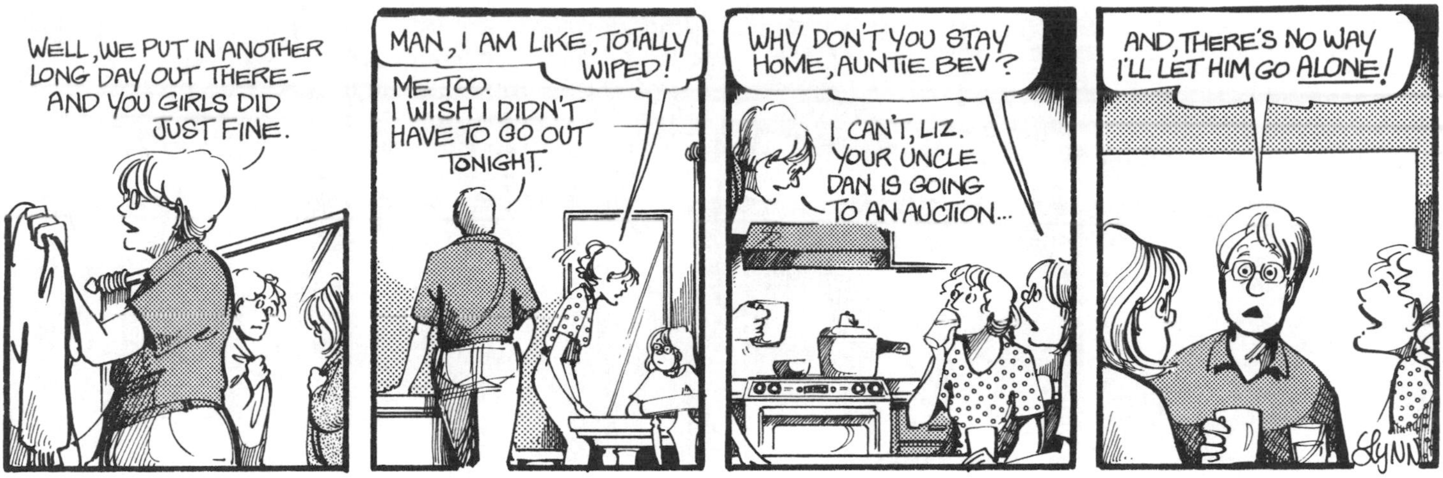
WELL, WE PUT IN ANOTHER LONG DAY OUT THERE— AND YOU GIRLS DID JUST FINE.
MAN, I AM LIKE, TOTALLY WIPED!
ME TOO. I WISH I DIDN'T HAVE TO GO OUT TONIGHT.
WHY DON'T YOU STAY HOME, AUNTIE BEV?
I CAN'T, LIZ. YOUR UNCLE DAN IS GOING TO AN AUCTION...
AND, THERE'S NO WAY I'LL LET HIM GO ALONE!
LYNN

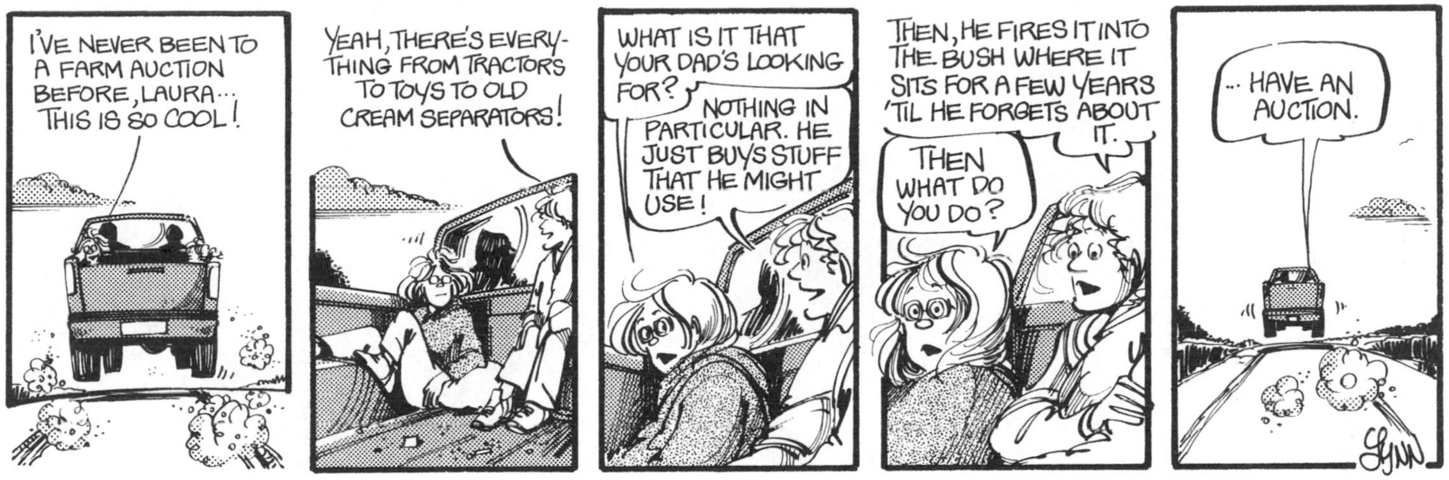
I'VE NEVER BEEN TO A FARM AUCTION BEFORE, LAURA... THIS IS SO COOL!
YEAH, THERE'S EVERYTHING FROM TRACTORS TO TOYS TO OLD CREAM SEPARATORS!
WHAT IS IT THAT YOUR DAD'S LOOKING FOR?
NOTHING IN PARTICULAR. HE JUST BUYS STUFF THAT HE MIGHT USE!
THEN, HE FIRES IT INTO THE BUSH WHERE IT SITS FOR A FEW YEARS 'TIL HE FORGETS ABOUT IT.
THEN WHAT DO YOU DO?
... HAVE AN AUCTION.
LYNN

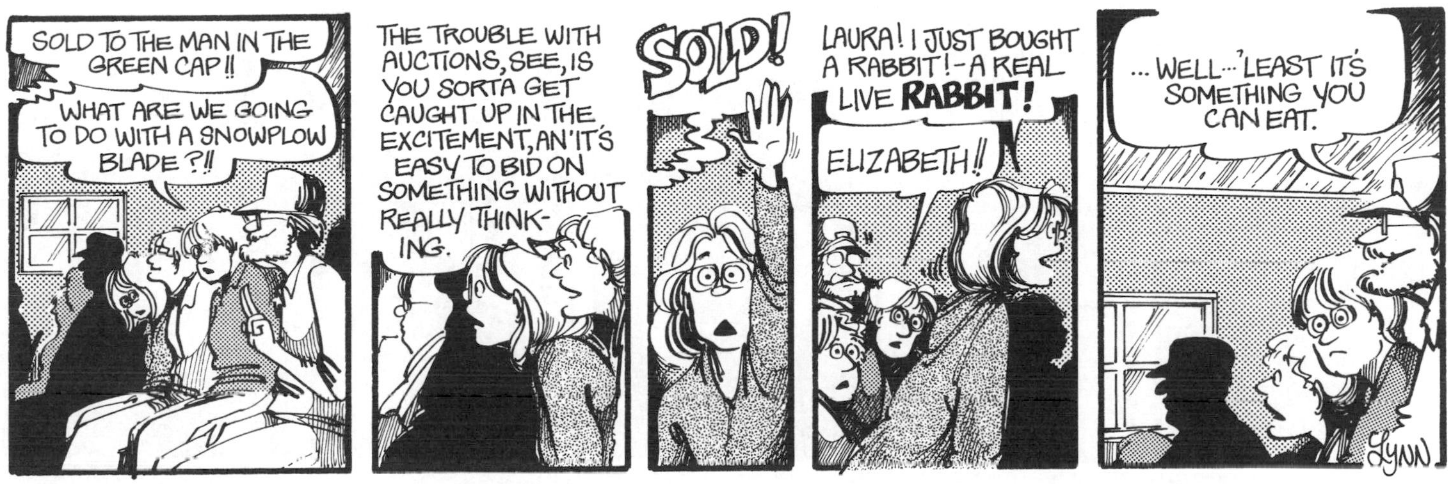
SOLD TO THE MAN IN THE GREEN CAP!!
WHAT ARE WE GOING TO DO WITH A SNOWPLOW BLADE?!!
THE TROUBLE WITH AUCTIONS, SEE, IS YOU SORTA GET CAUGHT UP IN THE EXCITEMENT, AN'IT'S EASY TO BID ON SOMETHING WITHOUT REALLY THINKING.
SOLD!
LAURA! I JUST BOUGHT A RABBIT! -A REAL LIVE RABBIT!
ELIZABETH!!
... WELL... 'LEAST IT'S SOMETHING YOU CAN EAT.
LYNN

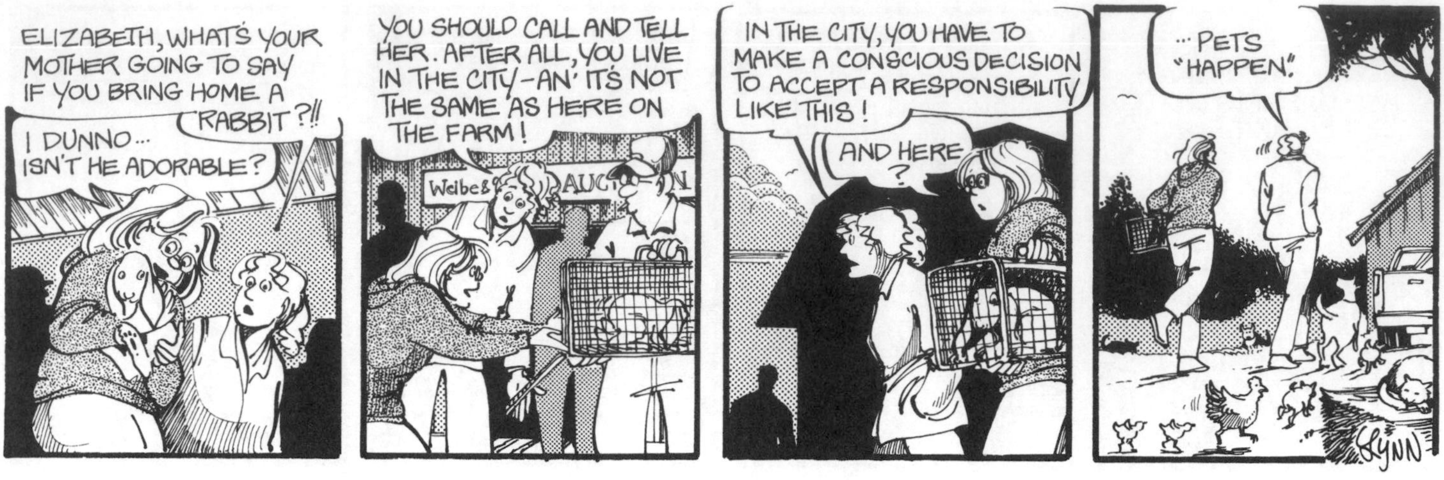
ELIZABETH, WHAT'S YOUR MOTHER GOING TO SAY IF YOU BRING HOME A RABBIT?!!
I DUNNO... ISN'T HE ADORABLE?
YOU SHOULD CALL AND TELL HER. AFTER ALL, YOU LIVE IN THE CITY-AN' IT'S NOT THE SAME AS HERE ON THE FARM!
AUCTION
IN THE CITY, YOU HAVE TO MAKE A CONSCIOUS DECISION TO ACCEPT A RESPONSIBILITY LIKE THIS!
AND HERE?
...PETS "HAPPEN."
LYNN

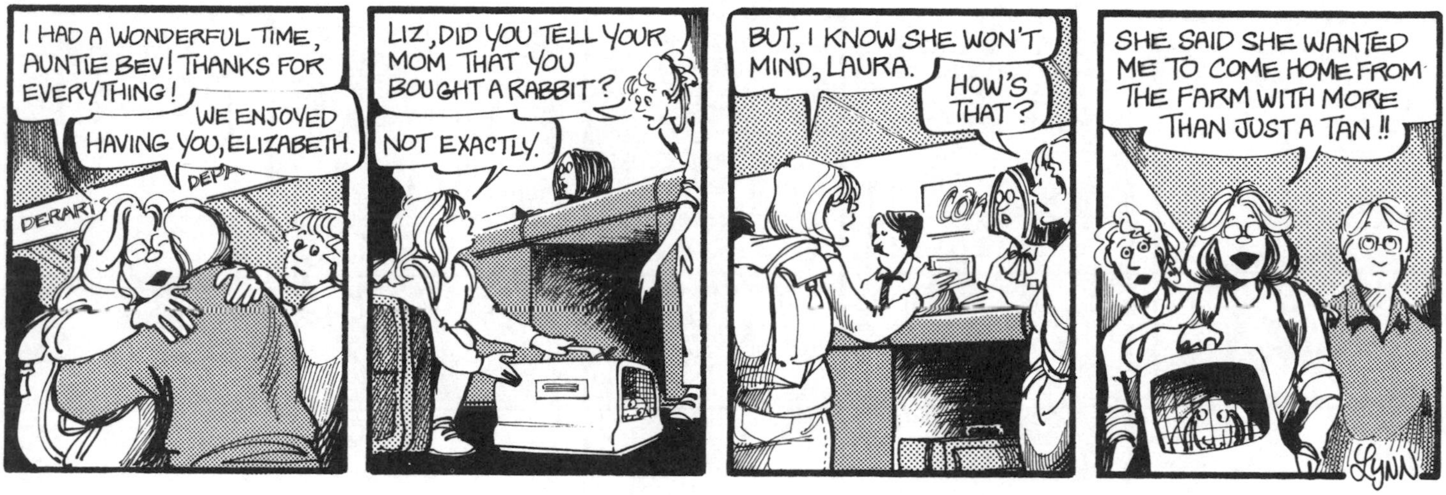
I HAD A WONDERFUL TIME, AUNTIE BEV! THANKS FOR EVERYTHING!
WE ENJOYED HAVING YOU, ELIZABETH.
LIZ, DID YOU TELL YOUR MOM THAT YOU BOUGHT A RABBIT?
NOT EXACTLY.
BUT, I KNOW SHE WON'T MIND, LAURA.
HOW'S THAT?
SHE SAID SHE WANTED ME TO COME HOME FROM THE FARM WITH MORE THAN JUST A TAN!!
LYNN

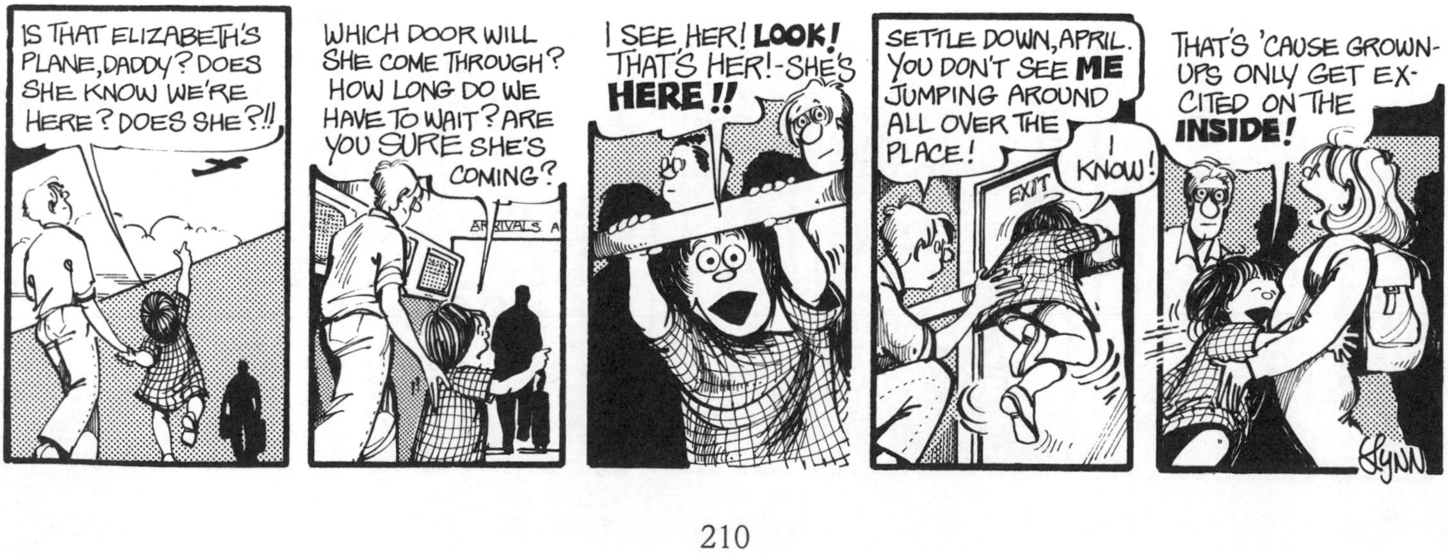
IS THAT ELIZABETH'S PLANE, DADDY? DOES SHE KNOW WE'RE HERE? DOES SHE?!!
WHICH DOOR WILL SHE COME THROUGH? HOW LONG DO WE HAVE TO WAIT? ARE YOU SURE SHE'S COMING?
ARRIVALS A
I SEE HER! **LOOK!** THAT'S HER!-SHE'S **HERE!!**
SETTLE DOWN, APRIL. YOU DON'T SEE **ME** JUMPING AROUND ALL OVER THE PLACE!
EXIT
I KNOW!
THAT'S 'CAUSE GROWN-UPS ONLY GET EXCITED ON THE **INSIDE!**
LYNN

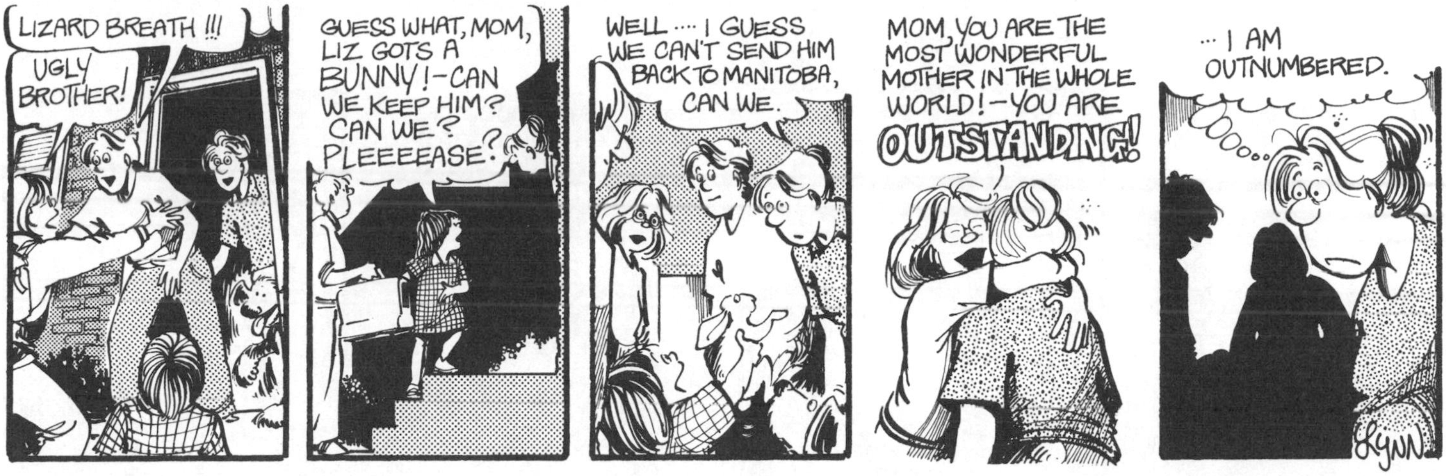
LIZARD BREATH !!!
UGLY BROTHER!
GUESS WHAT, MOM, LIZ GOTS A BUNNY! - CAN WE KEEP HIM? CAN WE? PLEEEEEASE?
WELL .... I GUESS WE CAN'T SEND HIM BACK TO MANITOBA, CAN WE.
MOM, YOU ARE THE MOST WONDERFUL MOTHER IN THE WHOLE WORLD! - YOU ARE
OUTSTANDING!
... I AM OUTNUMBERED.
LYNN

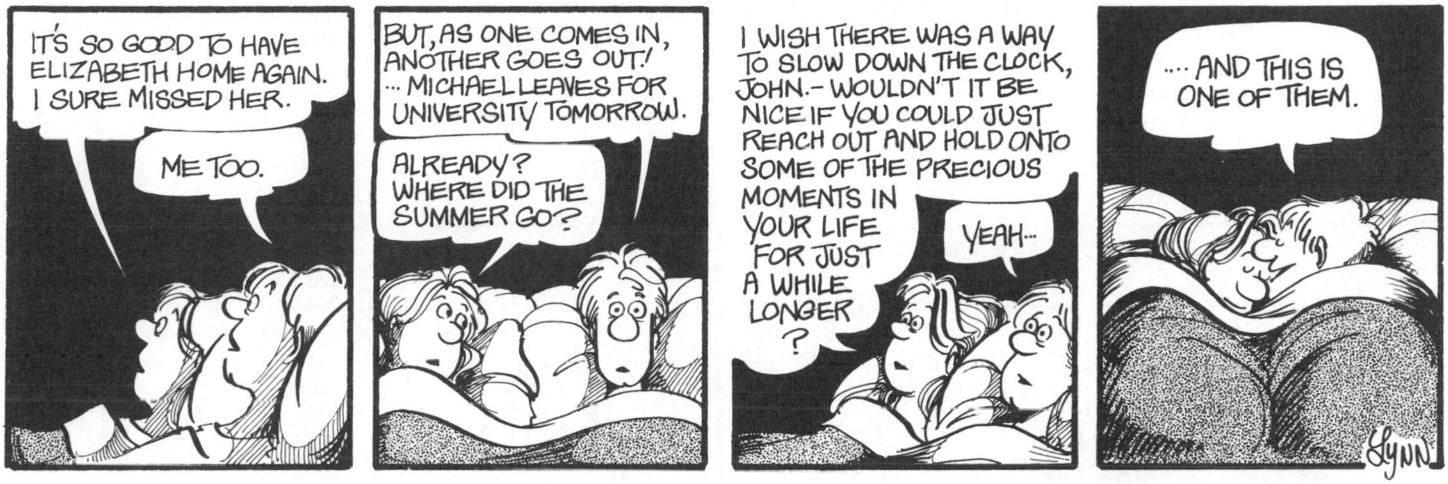
IT'S SO GOOD TO HAVE ELIZABETH HOME AGAIN. I SURE MISSED HER.
ME TOO.
BUT, AS ONE COMES IN, ANOTHER GOES OUT! ... MICHAEL LEAVES FOR UNIVERSITY TOMORROW.
ALREADY? WHERE DID THE SUMMER GO?
I WISH THERE WAS A WAY TO SLOW DOWN THE CLOCK, JOHN. - WOULDN'T IT BE NICE IF YOU COULD JUST REACH OUT AND HOLD ONTO SOME OF THE PRECIOUS MOMENTS IN YOUR LIFE FOR JUST A WHILE LONGER?
YEAH...
.... AND THIS IS ONE OF THEM.
LYNN

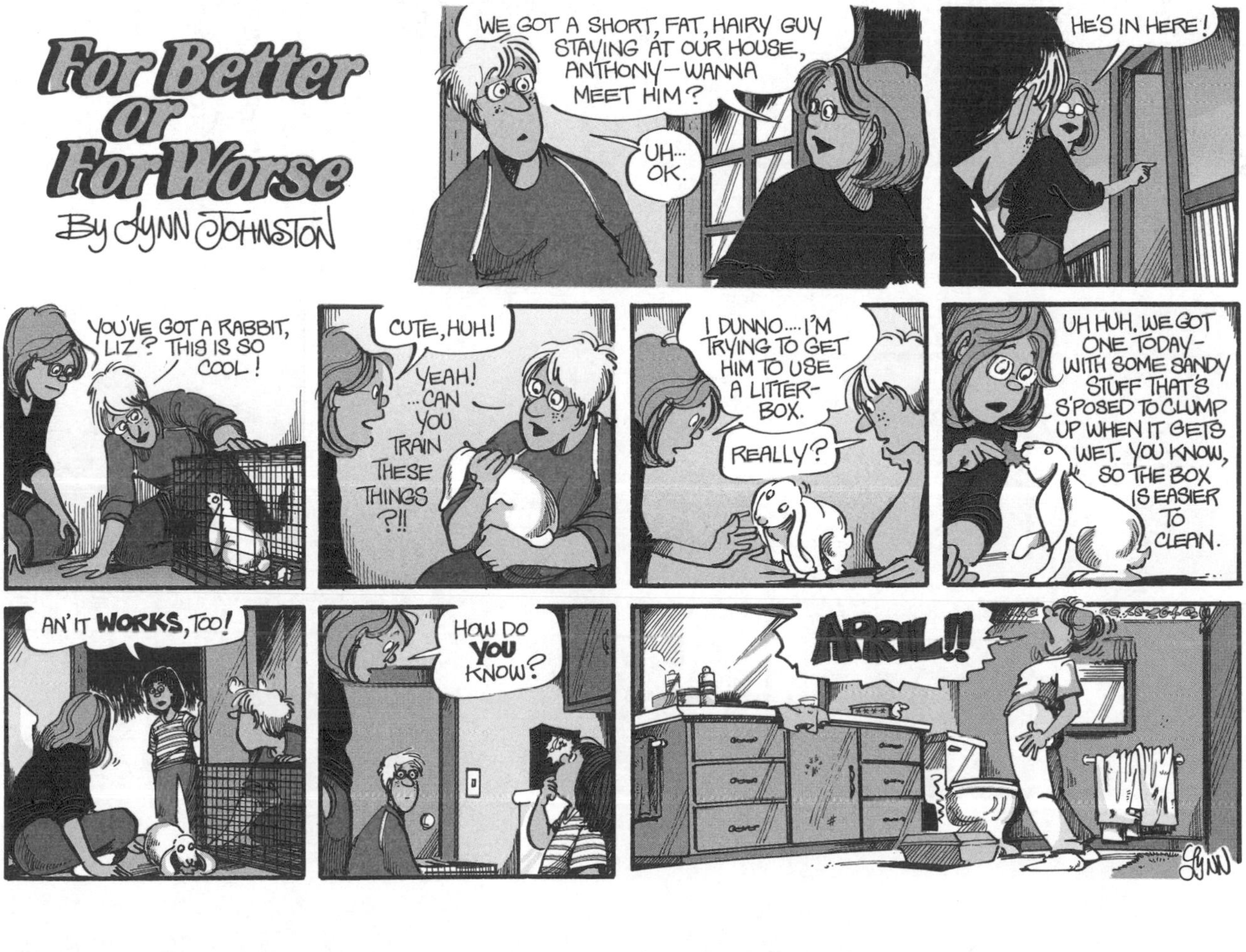
For Better or For Worse
By LYNN JOHNSTON
WE GOT A SHORT, FAT, HAIRY GUY STAYING AT OUR HOUSE, ANTHONY - WANNA MEET HIM?
UH... OK.
HE'S IN HERE!
YOU'VE GOT A RABBIT, LIZ? THIS IS SO COOL!
CUTE, HUH!
YEAH! ...CAN YOU TRAIN THESE THINGS?!!
I DUNNO.... I'M TRYING TO GET HIM TO USE A LITTER-BOX.
REALLY?
UH HUH. WE GOT ONE TODAY - WITH SOME SANDY STUFF THAT'S S'POSED TO CLUMP UP WHEN IT GETS WET. YOU KNOW, SO THE BOX IS EASIER TO CLEAN.
AN' IT WORKS, TOO!
HOW DO YOU KNOW?
APRIL!!
LYNN

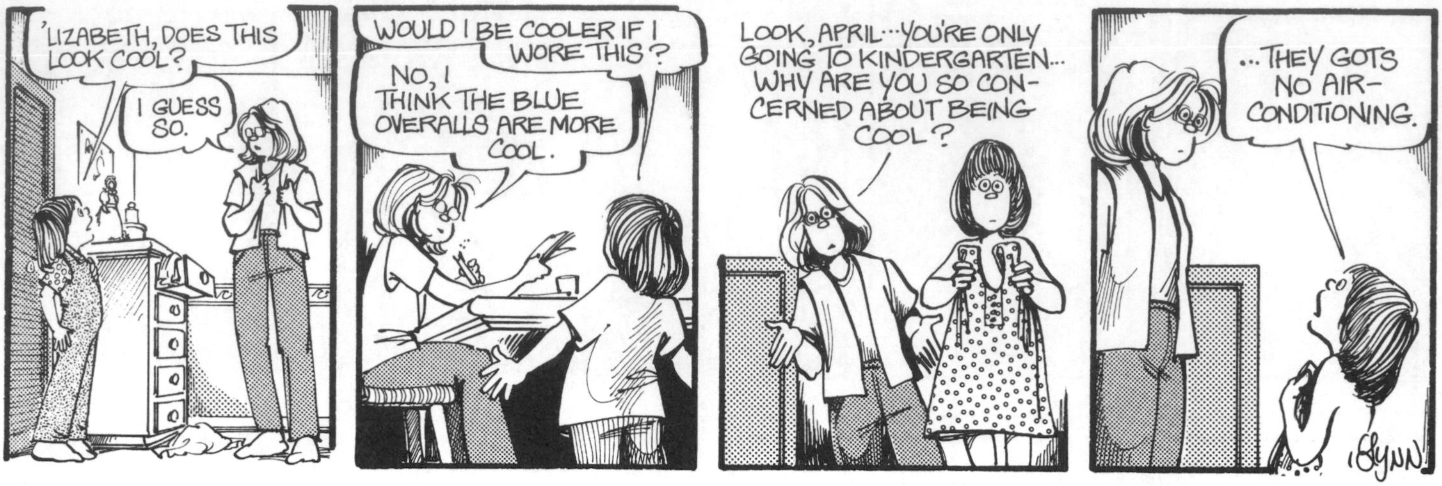
'LIZABETH, DOES THIS LOOK COOL?
I GUESS SO.
WOULD I BE COOLER IF I WORE THIS?
NO, I THINK THE BLUE OVERALLS ARE MORE COOL.
LOOK, APRIL... YOU'RE ONLY GOING TO KINDERGARTEN... WHY ARE YOU SO CONCERNED ABOUT BEING COOL?
...THEY GOTS NO AIR-CONDITIONING.
LYNN

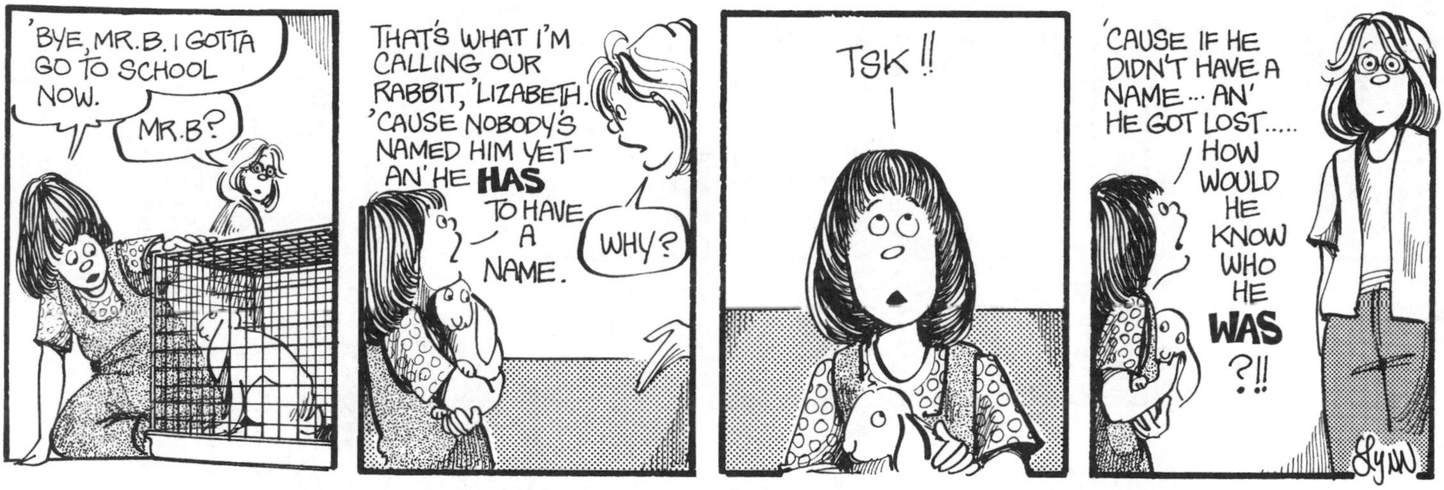
'BYE, MR. B. I GOTTA GO TO SCHOOL NOW.
MR. B?
THAT'S WHAT I'M CALLING OUR RABBIT, 'LIZABETH. 'CAUSE NOBODY'S NAMED HIM YET— AN' HE HAS TO HAVE A NAME.
WHY?
TSK!!
'CAUSE IF HE DIDN'T HAVE A NAME... AN' HE GOT LOST.....
HOW WOULD HE KNOW WHO HE WAS ?!!
LYNN

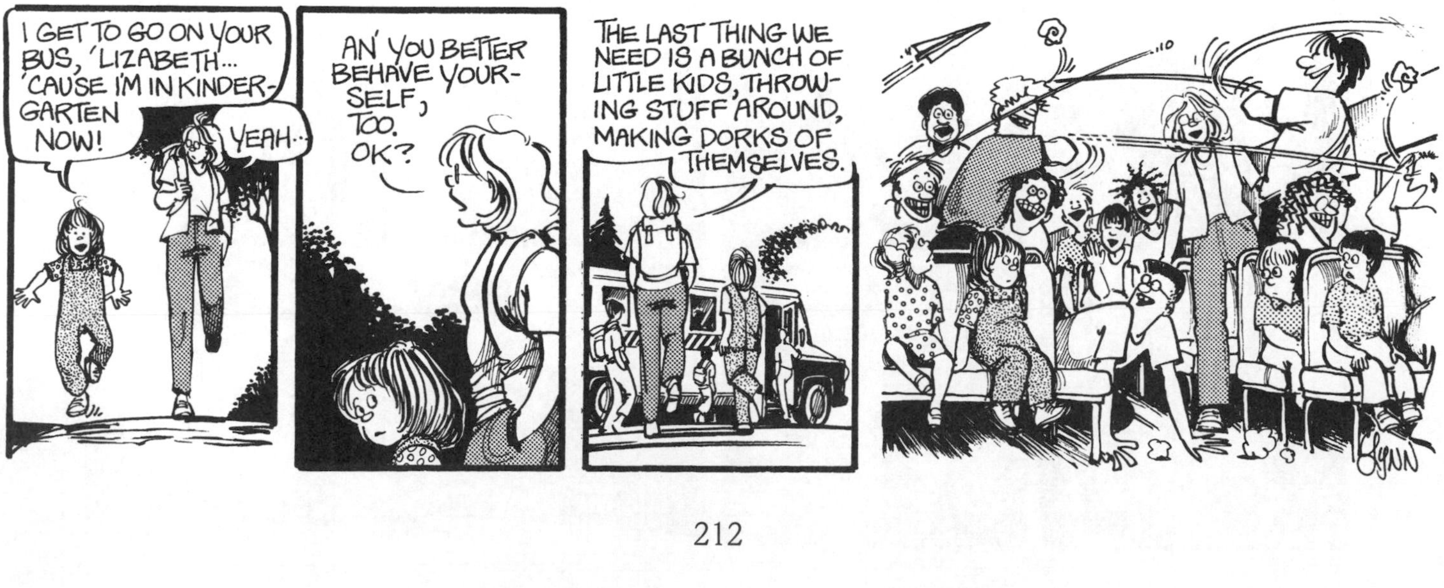
I GET TO GO ON YOUR BUS, 'LIZABETH... 'CAUSE I'M IN KINDERGARTEN NOW!
YEAH...
AN' YOU BETTER BEHAVE YOURSELF, TOO. OK?
THE LAST THING WE NEED IS A BUNCH OF LITTLE KIDS, THROWING STUFF AROUND, MAKING DORKS OF THEMSELVES.
LYNN

Panel 1: KINDERGARTEN'S GONNA BE COOL, APRIL! LOOKIT ALL THE STUFF WE GET TO USE! — YAH!

(labels: PAPER GLOSS, BLUE, GLUE, POWDER PAINT, RED, BALSA STICKS)

Panel 2: WHATSA MATTER? — I DON'T KNOW ANYBODY BESIDES YOU AN' DUNCAN, BECKY.

Panel 3: SO? — SO? — LOOK AROUND, GUYS!

Panel 4: ... EVERYBODY'S STRANGE EXCEPT **US!**

Panel 5: EVERYBODY'S STANDING UP AN' SAYING THEIR NAMES IN FRONT OF THE CLASS.

Panel 6: IT'S ALMOST MY TURN ... ALMOST ... ALMOST .... I'M **NEXT!**

Panel 7: ERK! — **MY NAME IS APRIL PATTERSON !!**

Panel 8: SOMETIMES YOU GOTTA GET WORDS OUT FAST ... OR THEY WON'T COME OUT AT ALL !

Panel 9: SO, HOW WAS YOUR FIRST WEEK IN KINDERGARTEN, APRIL? — AWESOME!

Panel 10: WE'RE ALL IN COLOR GROUPS AN' WE DO GAMES, AN' WE DO STUFF ON THE COMPUTERS AN' WE HAVE SONGS AN' PUZZLES AN' STORIES.

Panel 11: WELL, IT SOUNDS LIKE FUN TO ME !! — YEAH, BUT YOU KNOW WHAT, DAD?

Panel 12: ... I THINK THEY'RE TRYING TO FOOL US INTO LEARNING SOMETHING !

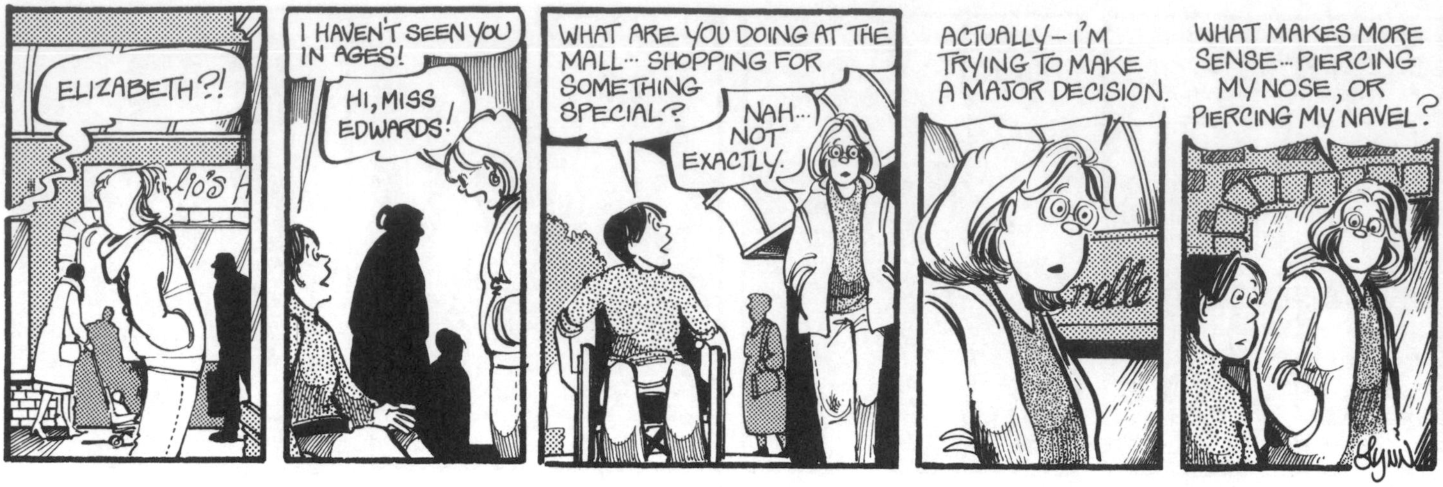
ELIZABETH?!
Lo's
I HAVEN'T SEEN YOU IN AGES!
HI, MISS EDWARDS!
WHAT ARE YOU DOING AT THE MALL... SHOPPING FOR SOMETHING SPECIAL?
NAH... NOT EXACTLY.
ACTUALLY - I'M TRYING TO MAKE A MAJOR DECISION.
WHAT MAKES MORE SENSE... PIERCING MY NOSE, OR PIERCING MY NAVEL?
Lynn

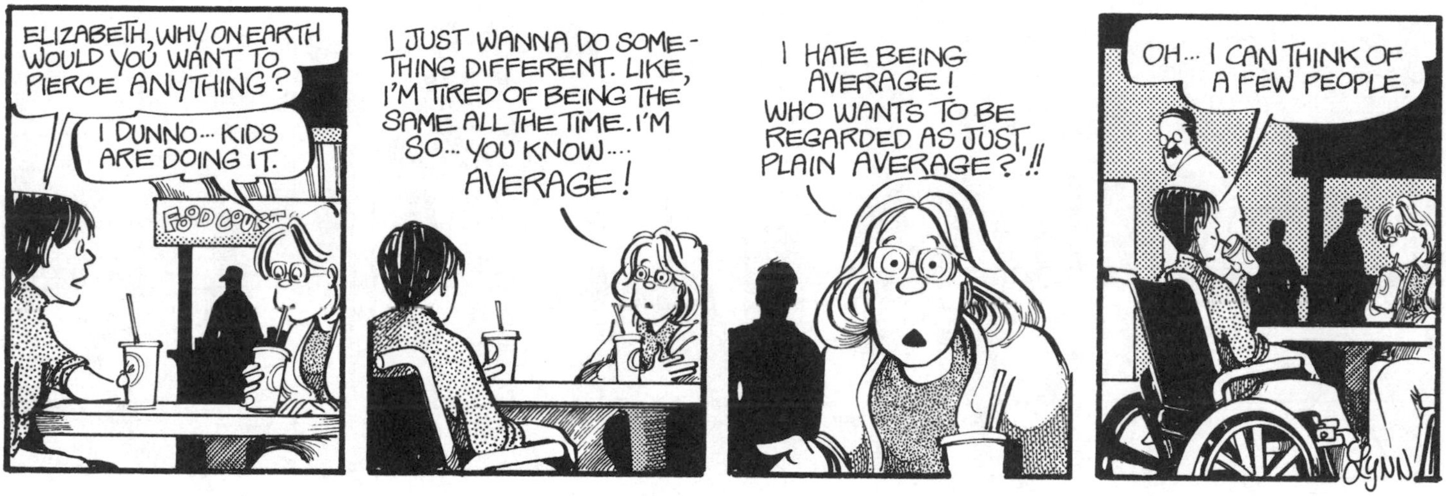
ELIZABETH, WHY ON EARTH WOULD YOU WANT TO PIERCE ANYTHING?
I DUNNO... KIDS ARE DOING IT.
FOOD COURT
I JUST WANNA DO SOMETHING DIFFERENT. LIKE, I'M TIRED OF BEING THE SAME ALL THE TIME. I'M SO... YOU KNOW.... AVERAGE!
I HATE BEING AVERAGE! WHO WANTS TO BE REGARDED AS JUST, PLAIN AVERAGE?!!
OH... I CAN THINK OF A FEW PEOPLE.
Lynn

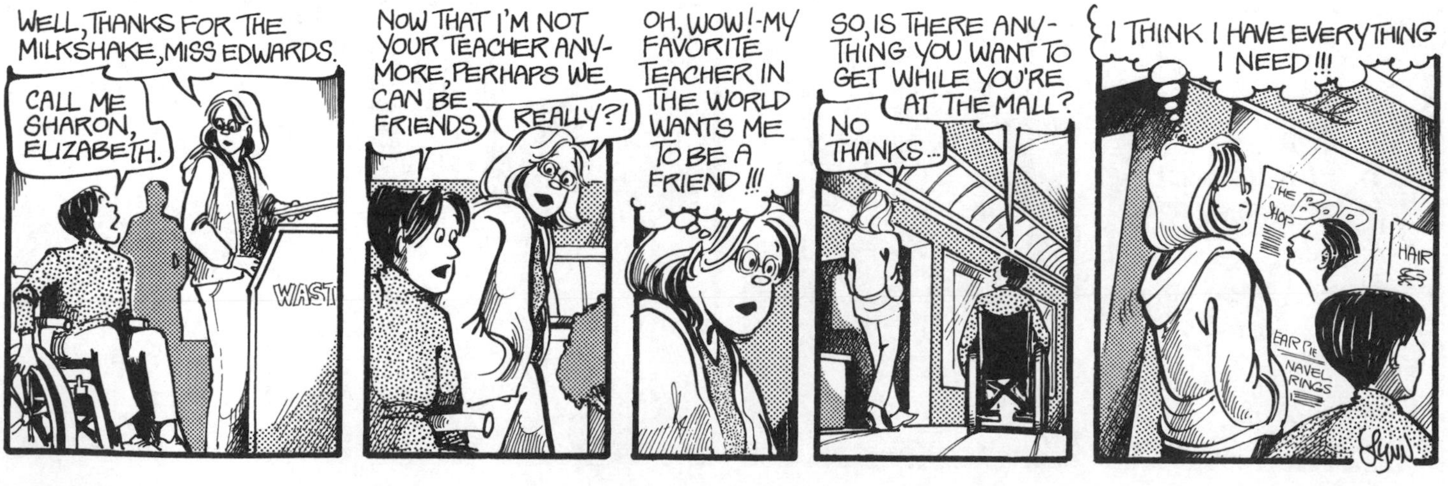
WELL, THANKS FOR THE MILKSHAKE, MISS EDWARDS.
CALL ME SHARON, ELIZABETH.
WAST
NOW THAT I'M NOT YOUR TEACHER ANYMORE, PERHAPS WE CAN BE FRIENDS.
REALLY?!
OH, WOW! - MY FAVORITE TEACHER IN THE WORLD WANTS ME TO BE A FRIEND!!!
SO, IS THERE ANYTHING YOU WANT TO GET WHILE YOU'RE AT THE MALL?
NO THANKS...
I THINK I HAVE EVERYTHING I NEED!!!
THE BOD SHOP
HAIR
EAR PIE
NAVEL RINGS
Lynn

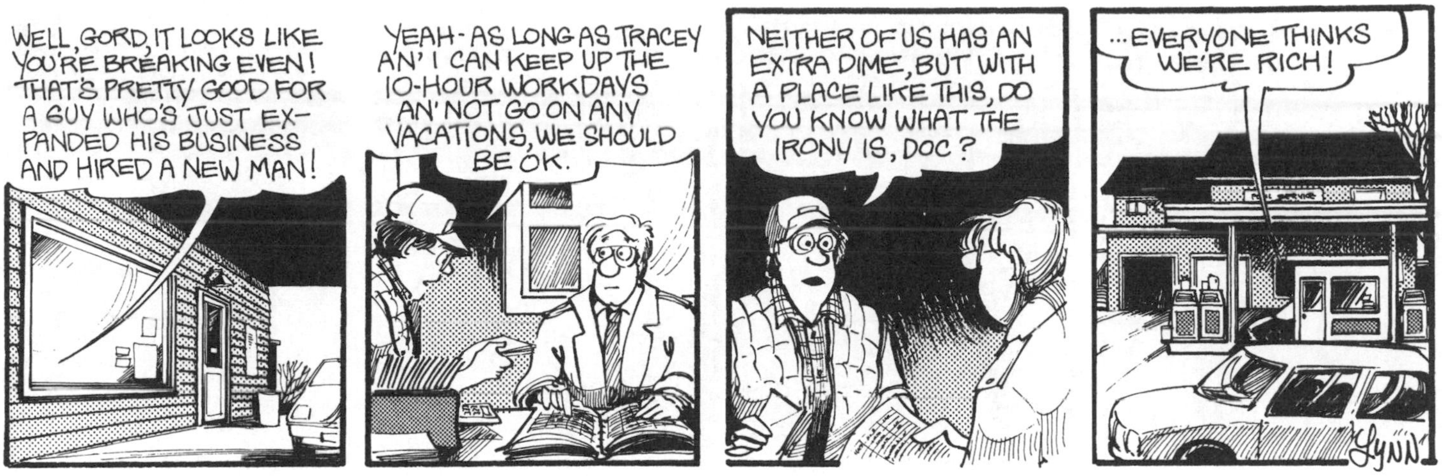
WELL, GORD, IT LOOKS LIKE YOU'RE BREAKING EVEN! THAT'S PRETTY GOOD FOR A GUY WHO'S JUST EXPANDED HIS BUSINESS AND HIRED A NEW MAN!
YEAH - AS LONG AS TRACEY AN' I CAN KEEP UP THE 10-HOUR WORKDAYS AN' NOT GO ON ANY VACATIONS, WE SHOULD BE OK.
NEITHER OF US HAS AN EXTRA DIME, BUT WITH A PLACE LIKE THIS, DO YOU KNOW WHAT THE IRONY IS, DOC?
...EVERYONE THINKS WE'RE RICH!
LYNN

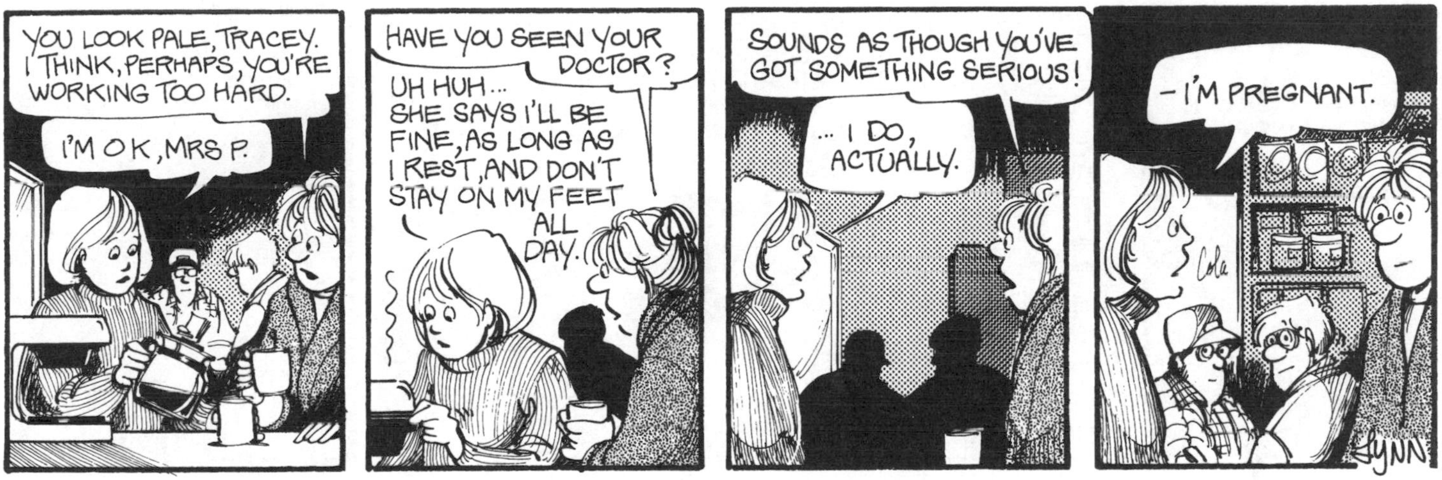
YOU LOOK PALE, TRACEY. I THINK, PERHAPS, YOU'RE WORKING TOO HARD.
I'M OK, MRS P.
HAVE YOU SEEN YOUR DOCTOR?
UH HUH... SHE SAYS I'LL BE FINE, AS LONG AS I REST, AND DON'T STAY ON MY FEET ALL DAY.
SOUNDS AS THOUGH YOU'VE GOT SOMETHING SERIOUS!
... I DO, ACTUALLY.
- I'M PREGNANT.
Cola
LYNN

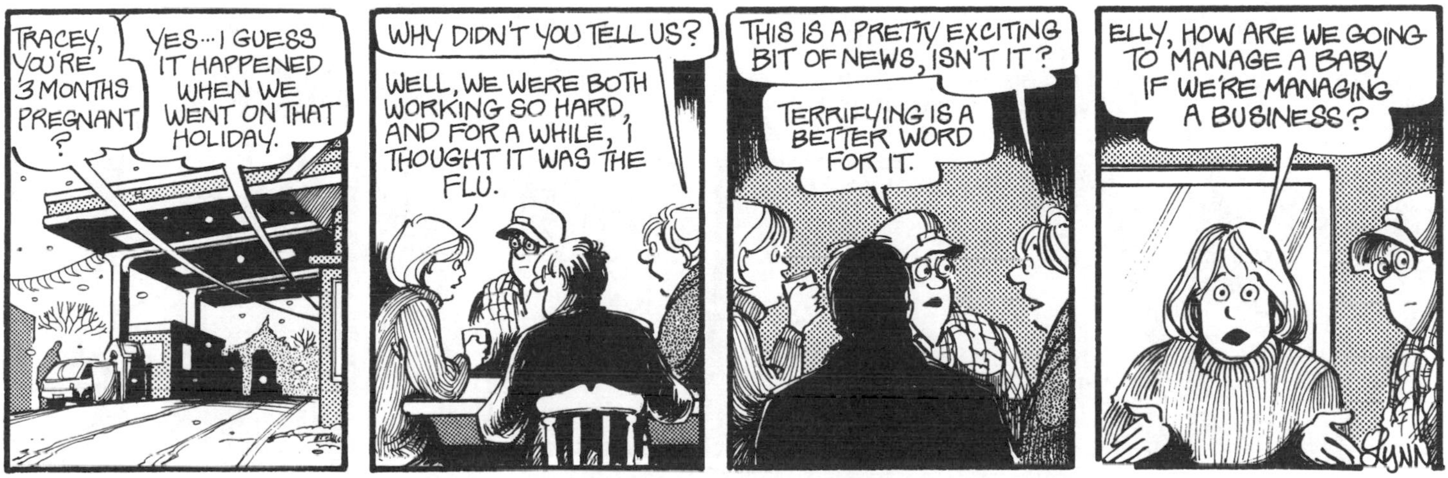
TRACEY, YOU'RE 3 MONTHS PREGNANT?
YES... I GUESS IT HAPPENED WHEN WE WENT ON THAT HOLIDAY.
WHY DIDN'T YOU TELL US?
WELL, WE WERE BOTH WORKING SO HARD, AND FOR A WHILE, I THOUGHT IT WAS THE FLU.
THIS IS A PRETTY EXCITING BIT OF NEWS, ISN'T IT?
TERRIFYING IS A BETTER WORD FOR IT.
ELLY, HOW ARE WE GOING TO MANAGE A BABY IF WE'RE MANAGING A BUSINESS?
LYNN

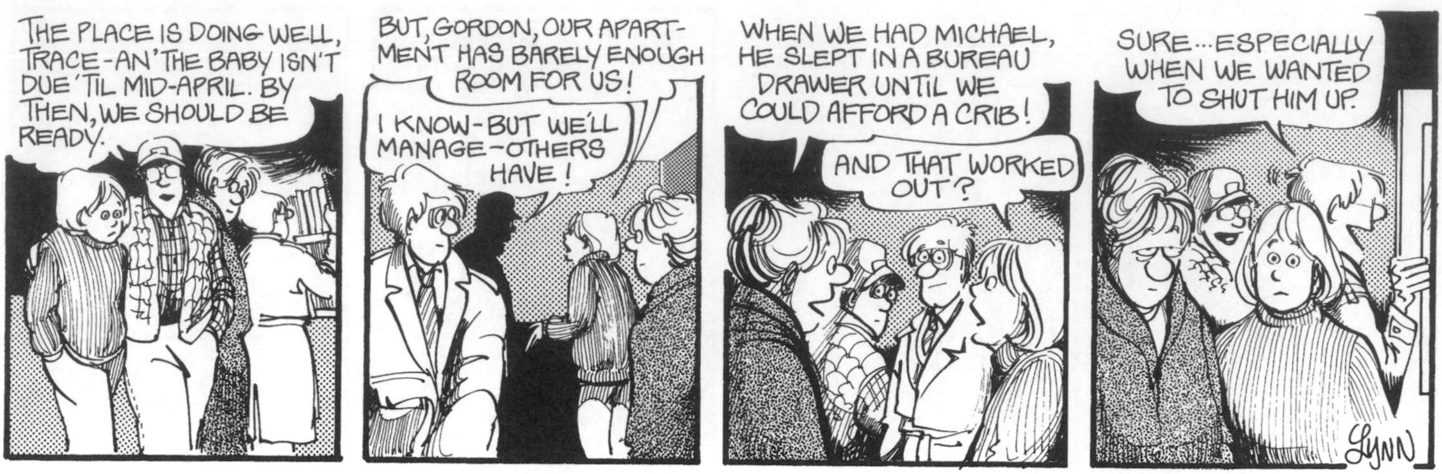
THE PLACE IS DOING WELL, TRACE - AN' THE BABY ISN'T DUE 'TIL MID-APRIL. BY THEN, WE SHOULD BE READY.
BUT, GORDON, OUR APARTMENT HAS BARELY ENOUGH ROOM FOR US!
I KNOW - BUT WE'LL MANAGE - OTHERS HAVE!
WHEN WE HAD MICHAEL, HE SLEPT IN A BUREAU DRAWER UNTIL WE COULD AFFORD A CRIB!
AND THAT WORKED OUT?
SURE... ESPECIALLY WHEN WE WANTED TO SHUT HIM UP.
Lynn

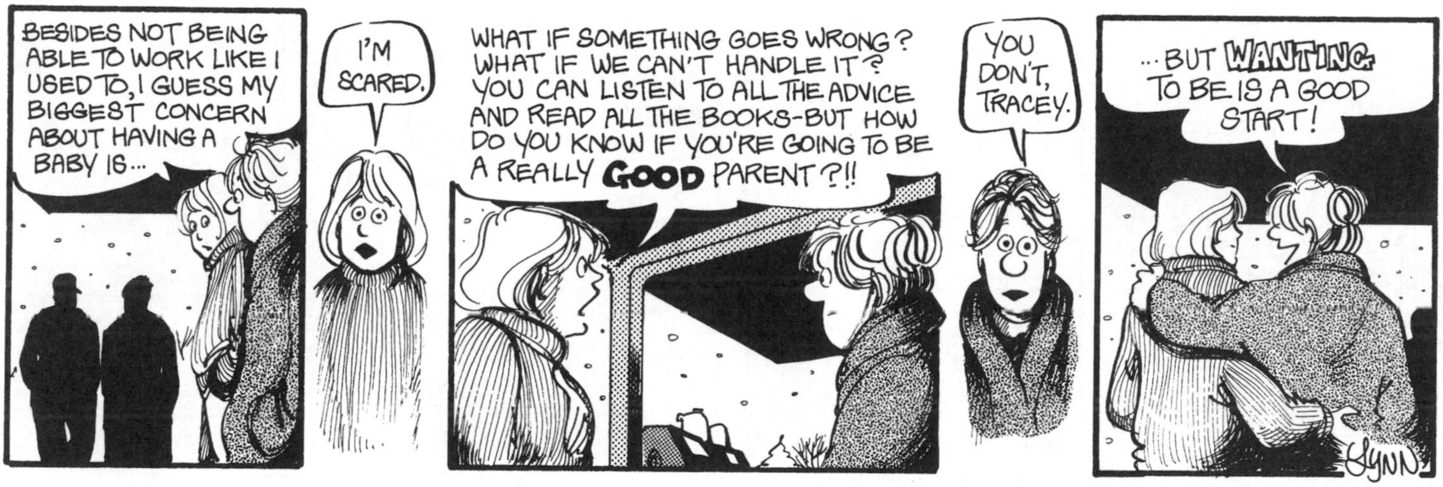
BESIDES NOT BEING ABLE TO WORK LIKE I USED TO, I GUESS MY BIGGEST CONCERN ABOUT HAVING A BABY IS...
I'M SCARED.
WHAT IF SOMETHING GOES WRONG? WHAT IF WE CAN'T HANDLE IT? YOU CAN LISTEN TO ALL THE ADVICE AND READ ALL THE BOOKS - BUT HOW DO YOU KNOW IF YOU'RE GOING TO BE A REALLY GOOD PARENT?!!
YOU DON'T, TRACEY.
... BUT WANTING TO BE IS A GOOD START!
Lynn

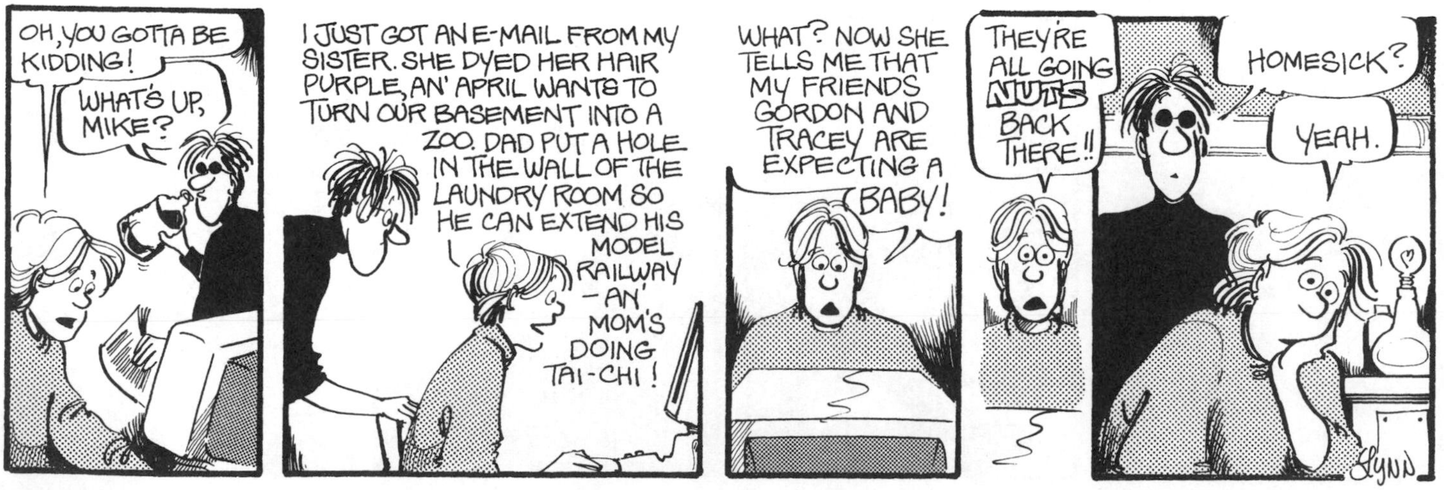
OH, YOU GOTTA BE KIDDING!
WHAT'S UP, MIKE?
I JUST GOT AN E-MAIL FROM MY SISTER. SHE DYED HER HAIR PURPLE, AN' APRIL WANTS TO TURN OUR BASEMENT INTO A ZOO. DAD PUT A HOLE IN THE WALL OF THE LAUNDRY ROOM SO HE CAN EXTEND HIS MODEL RAILWAY - AN' MOM'S DOING TAI-CHI!
WHAT? NOW SHE TELLS ME THAT MY FRIENDS GORDON AND TRACEY ARE EXPECTING A BABY!
THEY'RE ALL GOING NUTS BACK THERE!!
HOMESICK?
YEAH.
Lynn

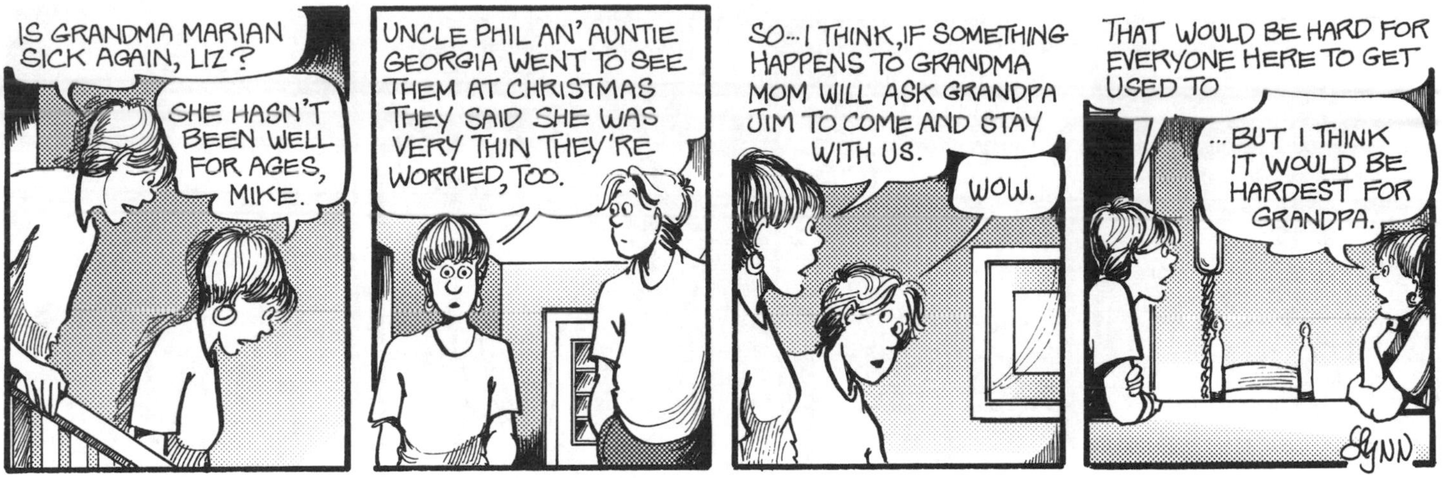
IS GRANDMA MARIAN SICK AGAIN, LIZ?
SHE HASN'T BEEN WELL FOR AGES, MIKE.
UNCLE PHIL AN' AUNTIE GEORGIA WENT TO SEE THEM AT CHRISTMAS THEY SAID SHE WAS VERY THIN THEY'RE WORRIED, TOO.
SO...I THINK, IF SOMETHING HAPPENS TO GRANDMA MOM WILL ASK GRANDPA JIM TO COME AND STAY WITH US.
WOW.
THAT WOULD BE HARD FOR EVERYONE HERE TO GET USED TO
...BUT I THINK IT WOULD BE HARDEST FOR GRANDPA.
LYNN

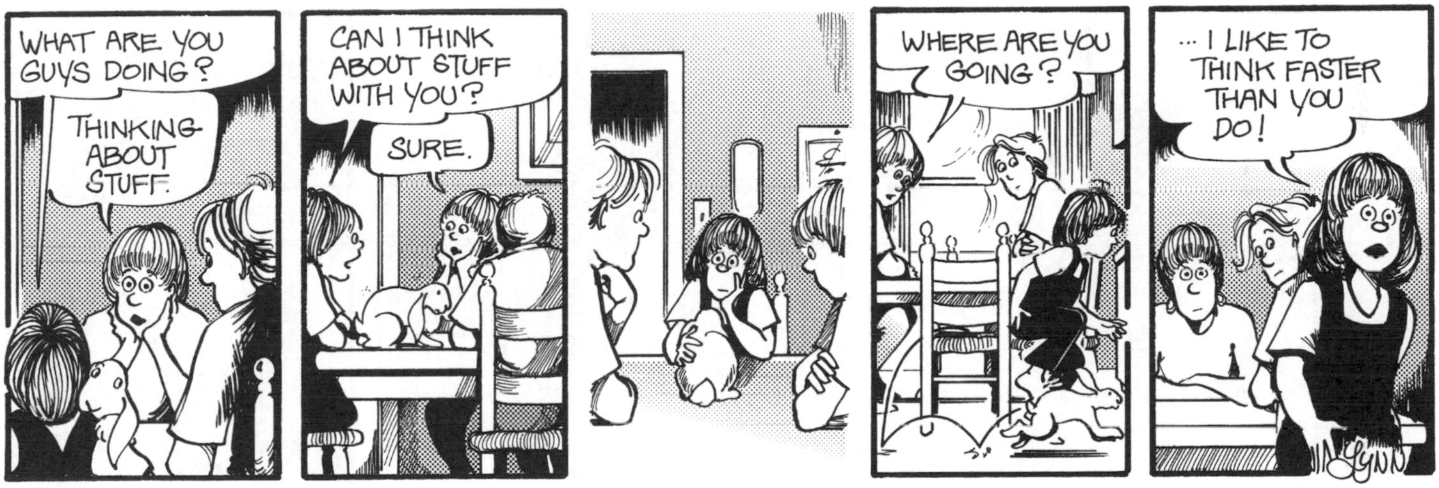
WHAT ARE YOU GUYS DOING?
THINKING ABOUT STUFF
CAN I THINK ABOUT STUFF WITH YOU?
SURE.
WHERE ARE YOU GOING?
...I LIKE TO THINK FASTER THAN YOU DO!
LYNN

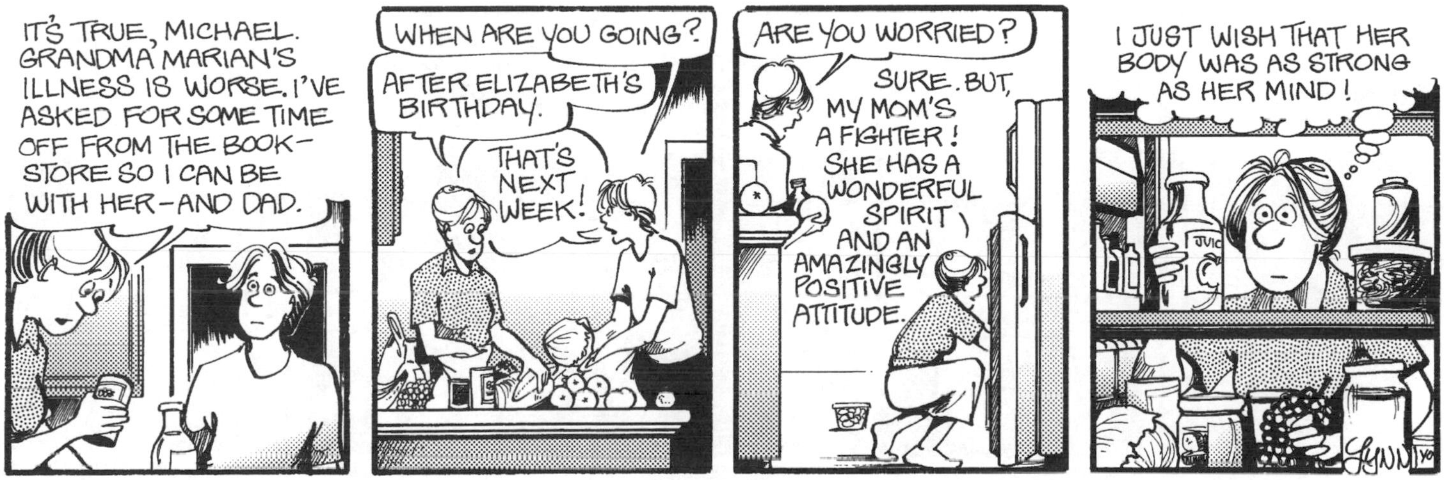
IT'S TRUE, MICHAEL. GRANDMA MARIAN'S ILLNESS IS WORSE. I'VE ASKED FOR SOME TIME OFF FROM THE BOOK-STORE SO I CAN BE WITH HER-AND DAD.
WHEN ARE YOU GOING?
AFTER ELIZABETH'S BIRTHDAY.
THAT'S NEXT WEEK!
ARE YOU WORRIED?
SURE. BUT, MY MOM'S A FIGHTER! SHE HAS A WONDERFUL SPIRIT, AND AN AMAZINGLY POSITIVE ATTITUDE.
I JUST WISH THAT HER BODY WAS AS STRONG AS HER MIND!
LYNN

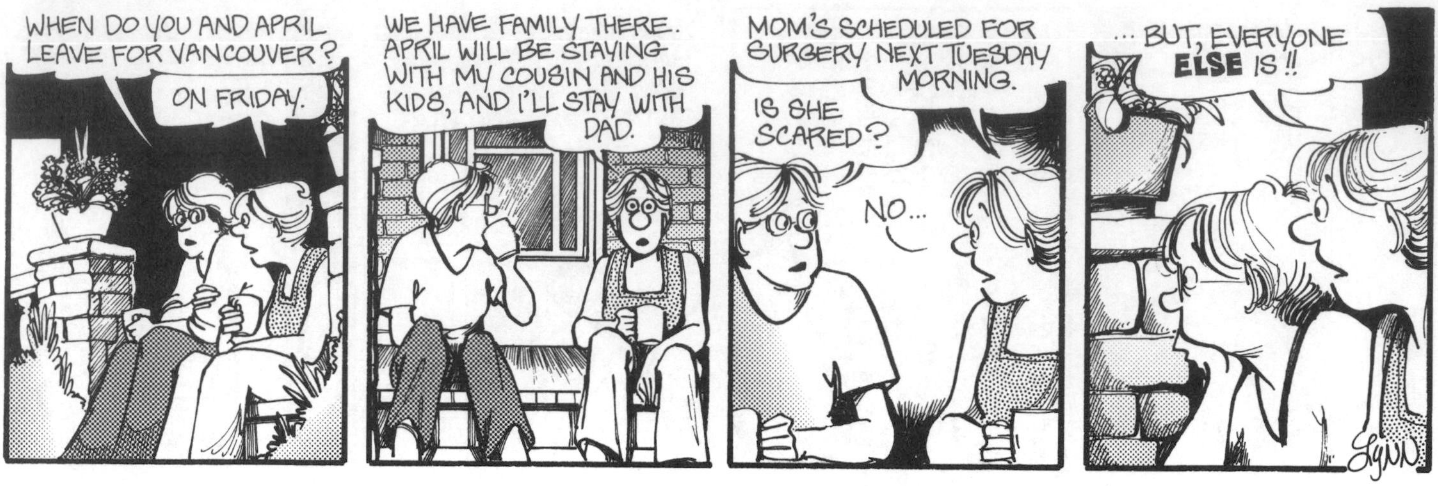
WHEN DO YOU AND APRIL LEAVE FOR VANCOUVER?
ON FRIDAY.
WE HAVE FAMILY THERE. APRIL WILL BE STAYING WITH MY COUSIN AND HIS KIDS, AND I'LL STAY WITH DAD.
MOM'S SCHEDULED FOR SURGERY NEXT TUESDAY MORNING.
IS SHE SCARED?
NO...
... BUT, EVERYONE ELSE IS!!
LYNN

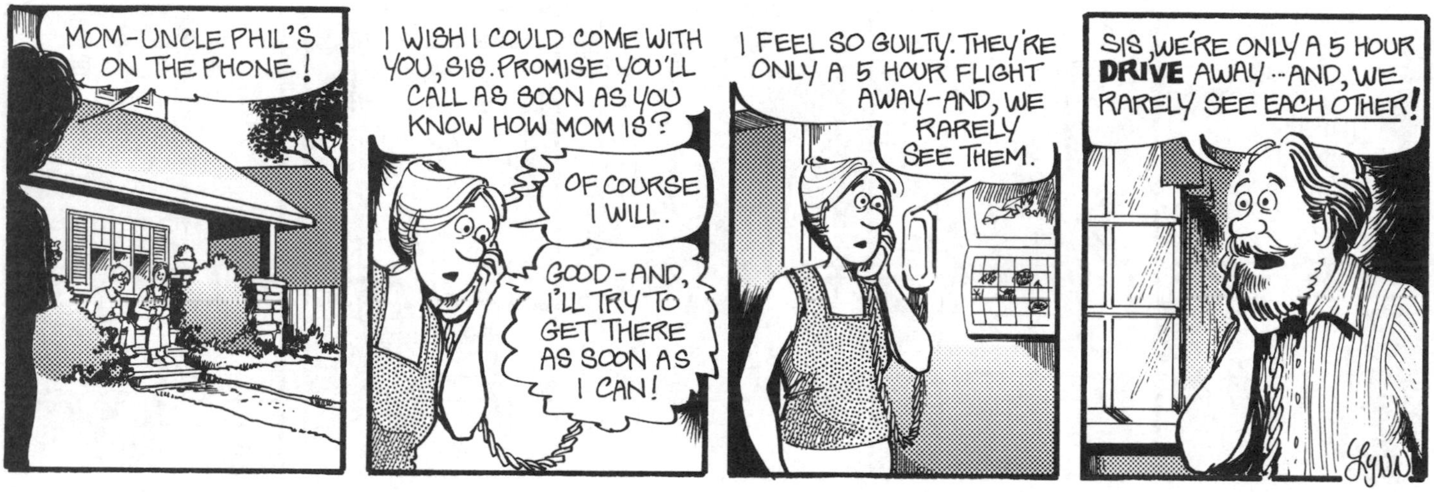
MOM-UNCLE PHIL'S ON THE PHONE!
I WISH I COULD COME WITH YOU, SIS. PROMISE YOU'LL CALL AS SOON AS YOU KNOW HOW MOM IS?
OF COURSE I WILL.
GOOD-AND, I'LL TRY TO GET THERE AS SOON AS I CAN!
I FEEL SO GUILTY. THEY'RE ONLY A 5 HOUR FLIGHT AWAY-AND, WE RARELY SEE THEM.
SIS, WE'RE ONLY A 5 HOUR DRIVE AWAY -- AND, WE RARELY SEE EACH OTHER!
LYNN

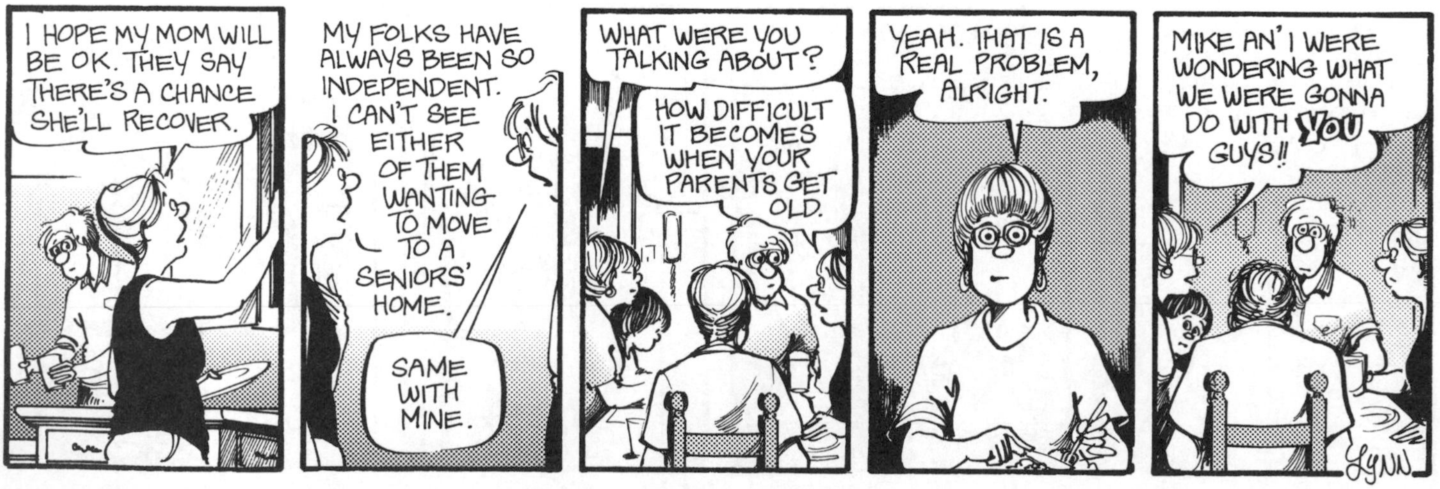
I HOPE MY MOM WILL BE OK. THEY SAY THERE'S A CHANCE SHE'LL RECOVER.
MY FOLKS HAVE ALWAYS BEEN SO INDEPENDENT. I CAN'T SEE EITHER OF THEM WANTING TO MOVE TO A SENIORS' HOME.
SAME WITH MINE.
WHAT WERE YOU TALKING ABOUT?
HOW DIFFICULT IT BECOMES WHEN YOUR PARENTS GET OLD.
YEAH. THAT IS A REAL PROBLEM, ALRIGHT.
MIKE AN' I WERE WONDERING WHAT WE WERE GONNA DO WITH YOU GUYS!!
LYNN

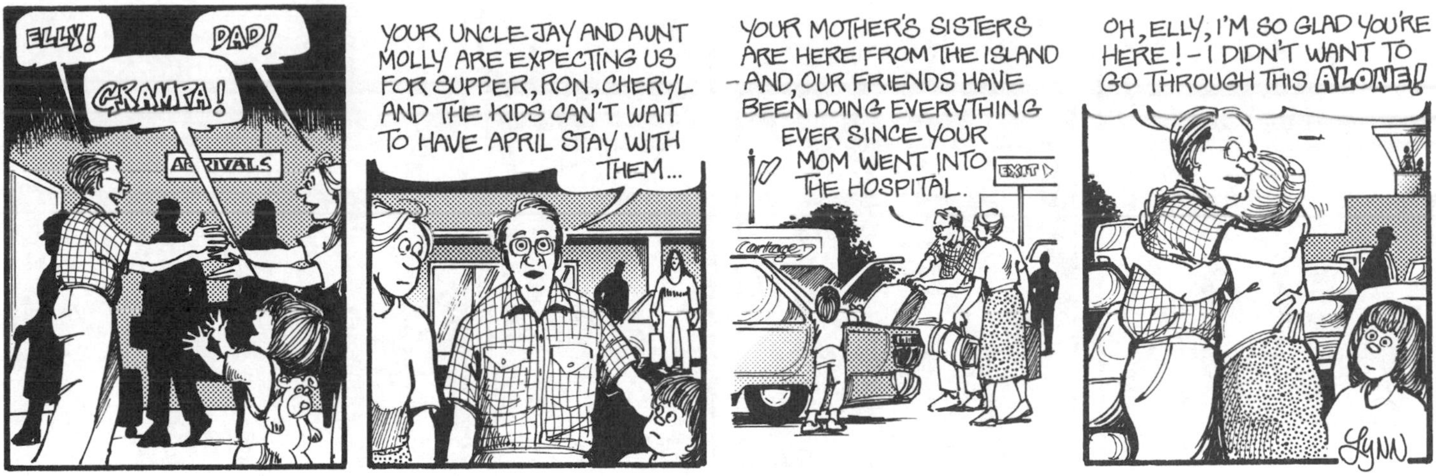
ELLY!
DAD!
GRAMPA!
ARRIVALS
YOUR UNCLE JAY AND AUNT MOLLY ARE EXPECTING US FOR SUPPER, RON, CHERYL AND THE KIDS CAN'T WAIT TO HAVE APRIL STAY WITH THEM...
YOUR MOTHER'S SISTERS ARE HERE FROM THE ISLAND - AND, OUR FRIENDS HAVE BEEN DOING EVERYTHING EVER SINCE YOUR MOM WENT INTO THE HOSPITAL.
EXIT
OH, ELLY, I'M SO GLAD YOU'RE HERE! - I DIDN'T WANT TO GO THROUGH THIS ALONE!
LYNN

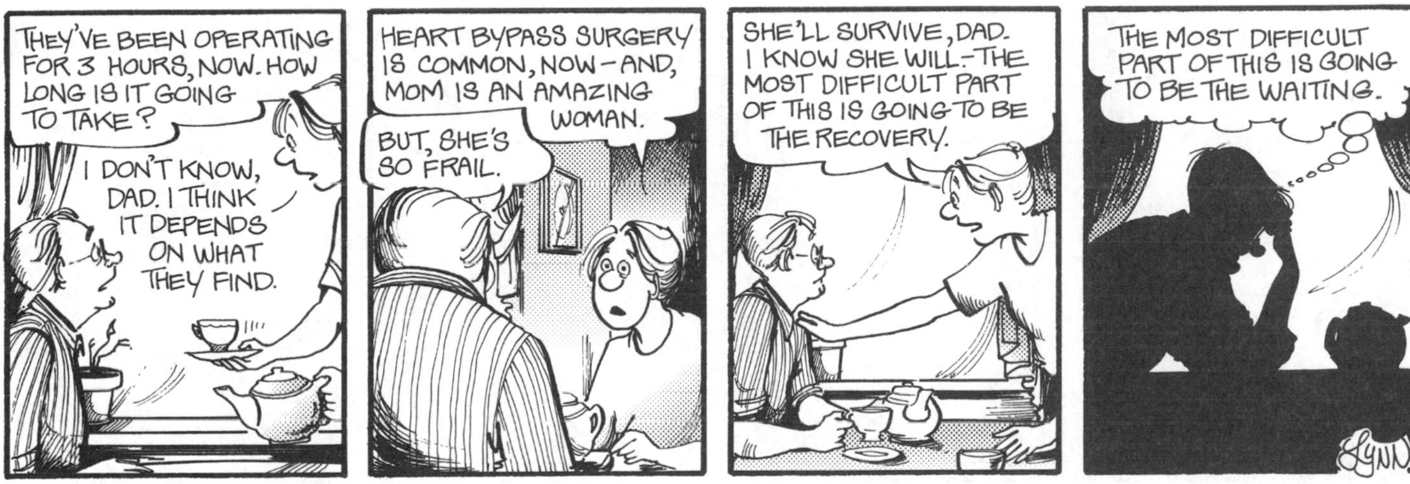
THEY'VE BEEN OPERATING FOR 3 HOURS, NOW. HOW LONG IS IT GOING TO TAKE?
I DON'T KNOW, DAD. I THINK IT DEPENDS ON WHAT THEY FIND.
HEART BYPASS SURGERY IS COMMON, NOW - AND, MOM IS AN AMAZING WOMAN.
BUT, SHE'S SO FRAIL.
SHE'LL SURVIVE, DAD. I KNOW SHE WILL. - THE MOST DIFFICULT PART OF THIS IS GOING TO BE THE RECOVERY.
THE MOST DIFFICULT PART OF THIS IS GOING TO BE THE WAITING.
LYNN

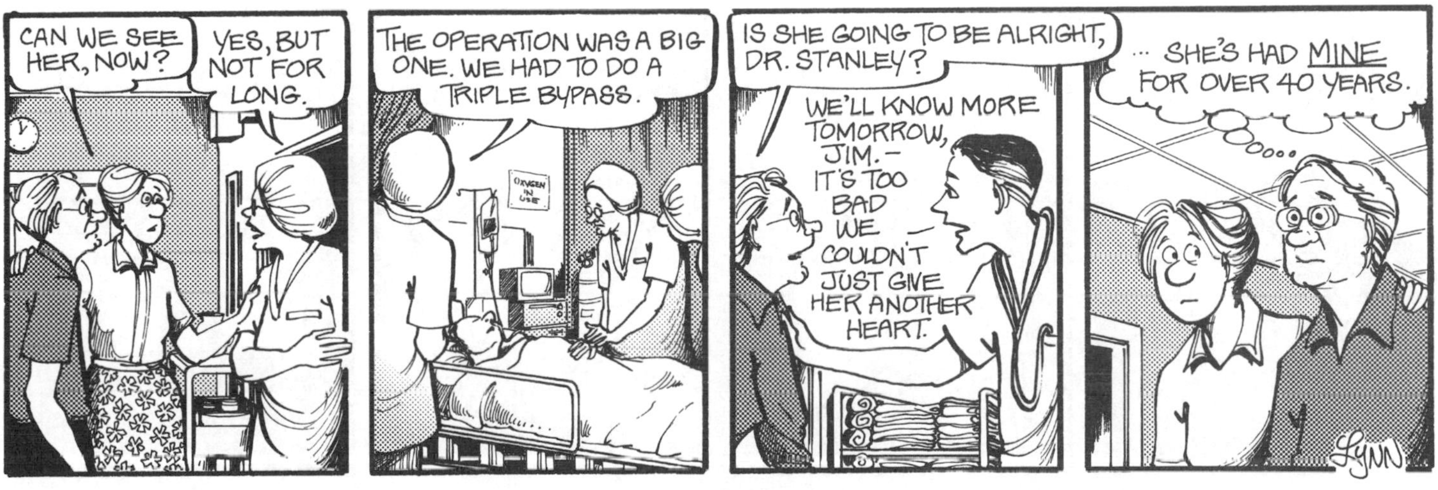
CAN WE SEE HER, NOW?
YES, BUT NOT FOR LONG.
THE OPERATION WAS A BIG ONE. WE HAD TO DO A TRIPLE BYPASS.
OXYGEN IN USE
IS SHE GOING TO BE ALRIGHT, DR. STANLEY?
WE'LL KNOW MORE TOMORROW, JIM. - IT'S TOO BAD WE COULDN'T JUST GIVE HER ANOTHER HEART.
... SHE'S HAD MINE FOR OVER 40 YEARS.
LYNN

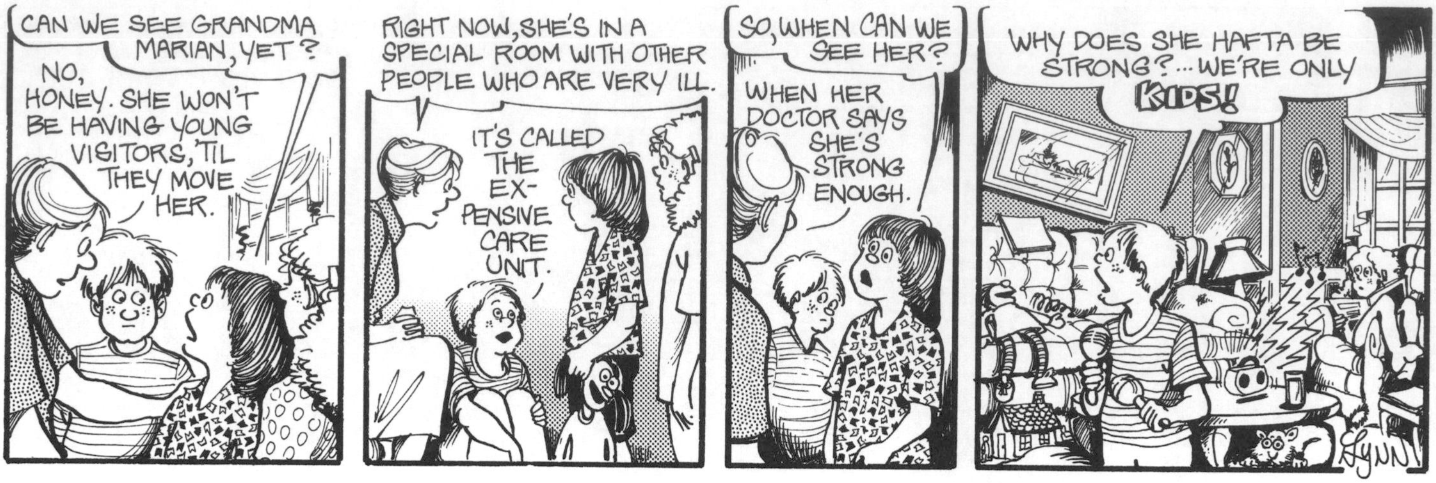
CAN WE SEE GRANDMA MARIAN, YET?
NO, HONEY. SHE WON'T BE HAVING YOUNG VISITORS, 'TIL THEY MOVE HER.
RIGHT NOW, SHE'S IN A SPECIAL ROOM WITH OTHER PEOPLE WHO ARE VERY ILL.
IT'S CALLED THE EX-PENSIVE CARE UNIT.
SO, WHEN CAN WE SEE HER?
WHEN HER DOCTOR SAYS SHE'S STRONG ENOUGH.
WHY DOES SHE HAFTA BE STRONG?... WE'RE ONLY KIDS!
LYNN

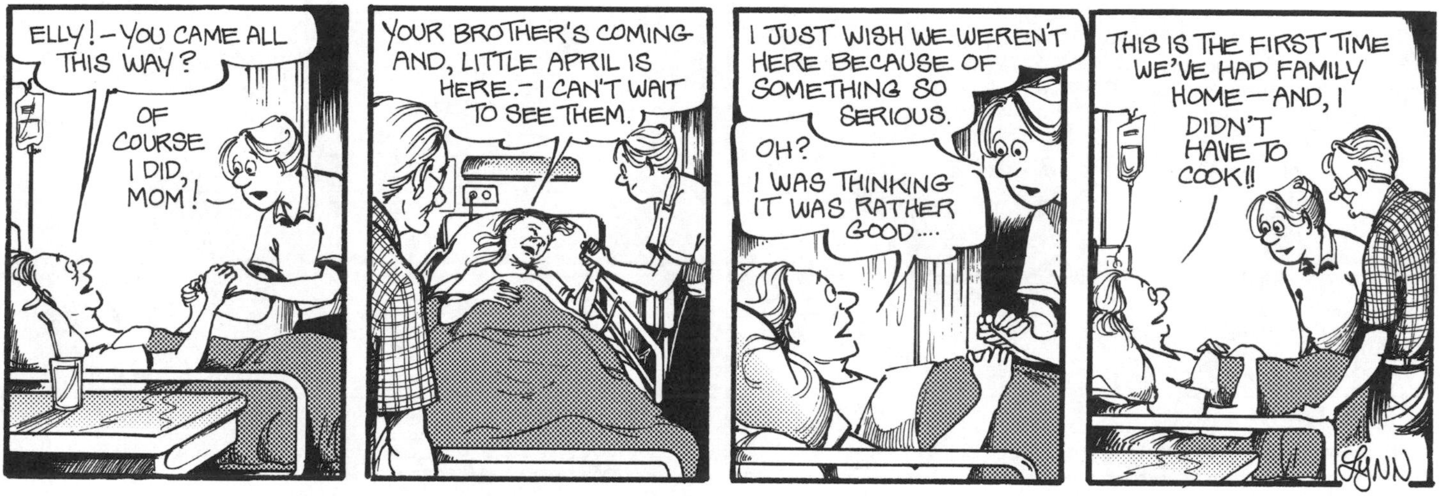
ELLY! – YOU CAME ALL THIS WAY?
OF COURSE I DID, MOM!
YOUR BROTHER'S COMING AND, LITTLE APRIL IS HERE. – I CAN'T WAIT TO SEE THEM.
I JUST WISH WE WEREN'T HERE BECAUSE OF SOMETHING SO SERIOUS.
OH? I WAS THINKING IT WAS RATHER GOOD....
THIS IS THE FIRST TIME WE'VE HAD FAMILY HOME – AND, I DIDN'T HAVE TO COOK!!
LYNN

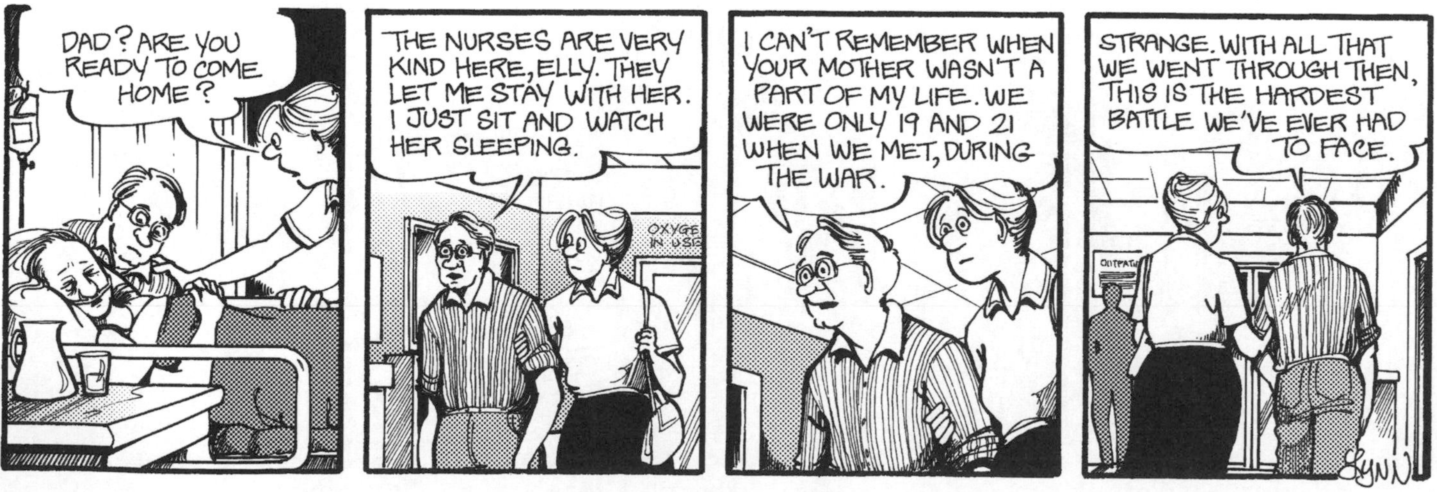
DAD? ARE YOU READY TO COME HOME?
THE NURSES ARE VERY KIND HERE, ELLY. THEY LET ME STAY WITH HER. I JUST SIT AND WATCH HER SLEEPING.
OXYGEN IN USE
I CAN'T REMEMBER WHEN YOUR MOTHER WASN'T A PART OF MY LIFE. WE WERE ONLY 19 AND 21 WHEN WE MET, DURING THE WAR.
STRANGE. WITH ALL THAT WE WENT THROUGH THEN, THIS IS THE HARDEST BATTLE WE'VE EVER HAD TO FACE.
LYNN

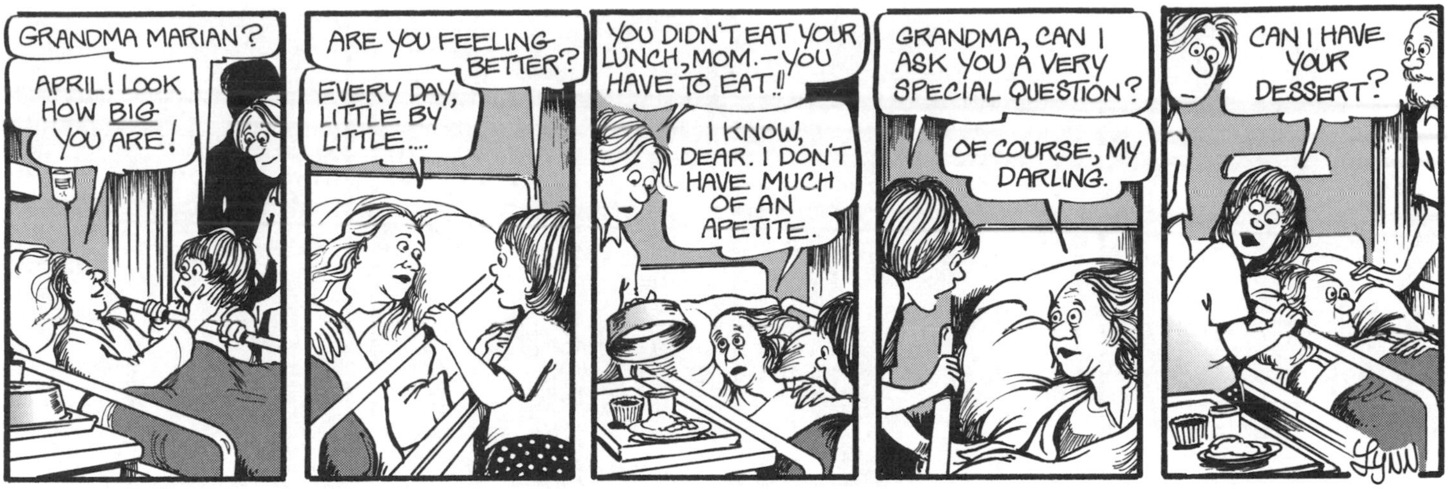
GRANDMA MARIAN?
APRIL! LOOK HOW BIG YOU ARE!
ARE YOU FEELING BETTER?
EVERY DAY, LITTLE BY LITTLE....
YOU DIDN'T EAT YOUR LUNCH, MOM.—YOU HAVE TO EAT!!
I KNOW, DEAR. I DON'T HAVE MUCH OF AN APETITE.
GRANDMA, CAN I ASK YOU A VERY SPECIAL QUESTION?
OF COURSE, MY DARLING.
CAN I HAVE YOUR DESSERT?
Lynn

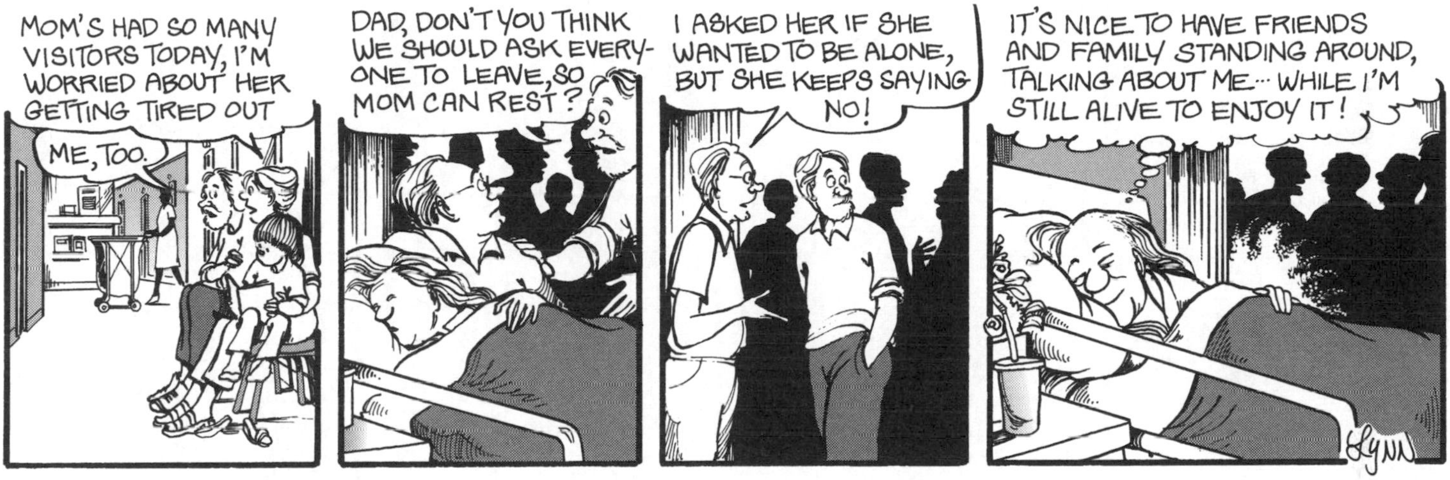
MOM'S HAD SO MANY VISITORS TODAY, I'M WORRIED ABOUT HER GETTING TIRED OUT
ME, TOO.
DAD, DON'T YOU THINK WE SHOULD ASK EVERY-ONE TO LEAVE, SO MOM CAN REST?
I ASKED HER IF SHE WANTED TO BE ALONE, BUT SHE KEEPS SAYING NO!
IT'S NICE TO HAVE FRIENDS AND FAMILY STANDING AROUND, TALKING ABOUT ME... WHILE I'M STILL ALIVE TO ENJOY IT!
Lynn

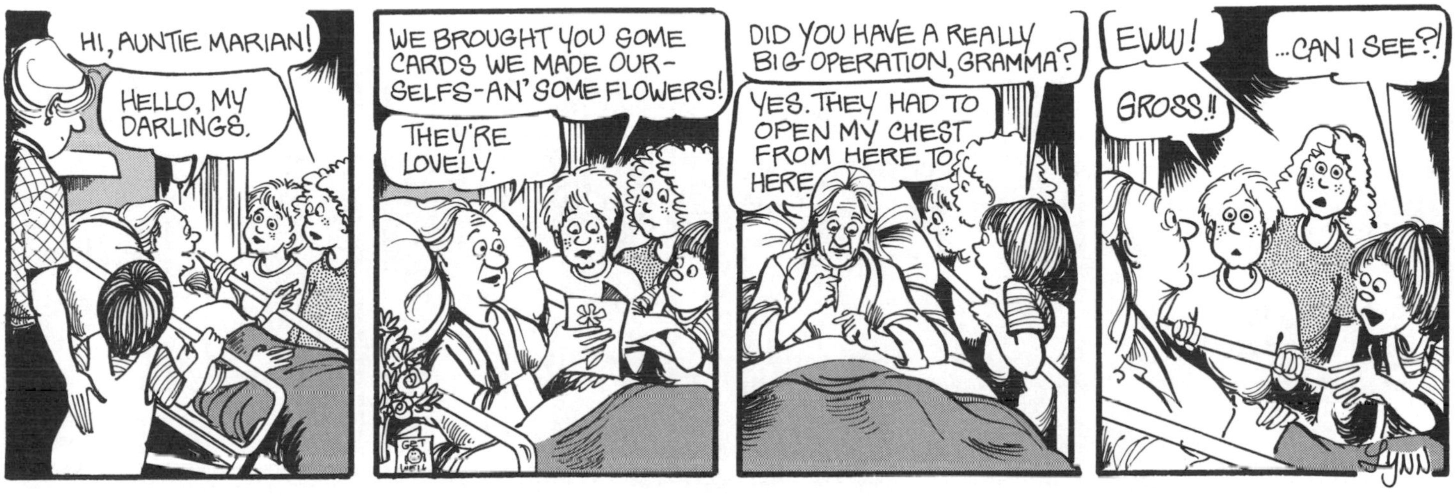
HI, AUNTIE MARIAN!
HELLO, MY DARLINGS.
WE BROUGHT YOU SOME CARDS WE MADE OUR-SELFS-AN' SOME FLOWERS!
THEY'RE LOVELY.
DID YOU HAVE A REALLY BIG OPERATION, GRAMMA?
YES. THEY HAD TO OPEN MY CHEST FROM HERE TO HERE.
EWW!
GROSS!!
...CAN I SEE?!
Lynn

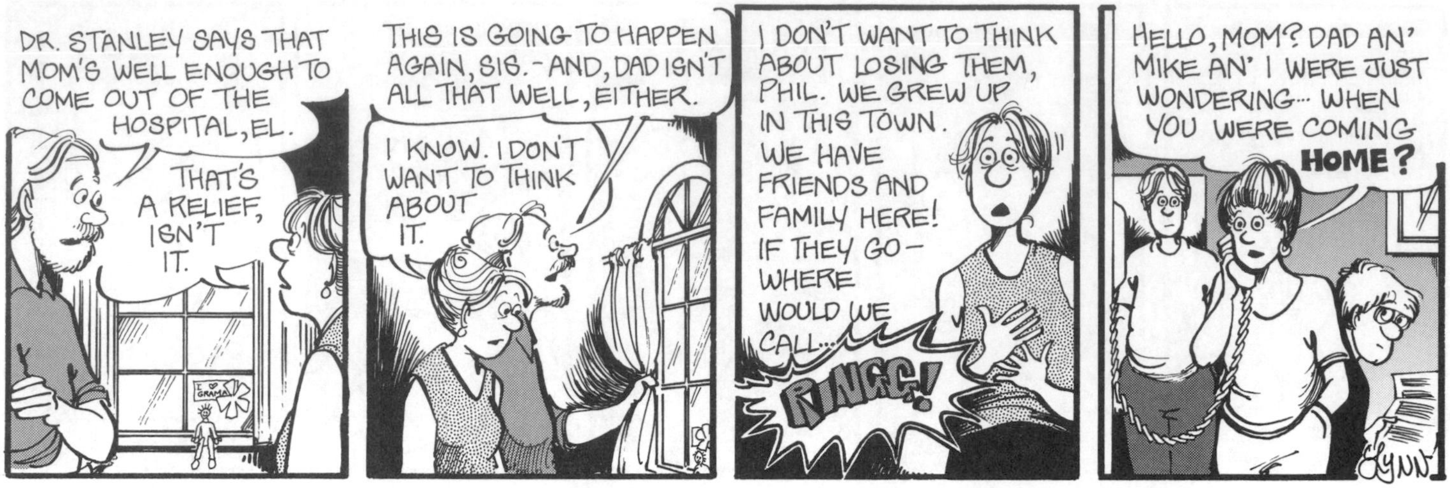
DR. STANLEY SAYS THAT MOM'S WELL ENOUGH TO COME OUT OF THE HOSPITAL, EL.
THAT'S A RELIEF, ISN'T IT.
THIS IS GOING TO HAPPEN AGAIN, SIS. - AND, DAD ISN'T ALL THAT WELL, EITHER.
I KNOW. I DON'T WANT TO THINK ABOUT IT.
I DON'T WANT TO THINK ABOUT LOSING THEM, PHIL. WE GREW UP IN THIS TOWN. WE HAVE FRIENDS AND FAMILY HERE! IF THEY GO— WHERE WOULD WE CALL...
RINGG!
HELLO, MOM? DAD AN' MIKE AN' I WERE JUST WONDERING... WHEN YOU WERE COMING HOME?
LYNN

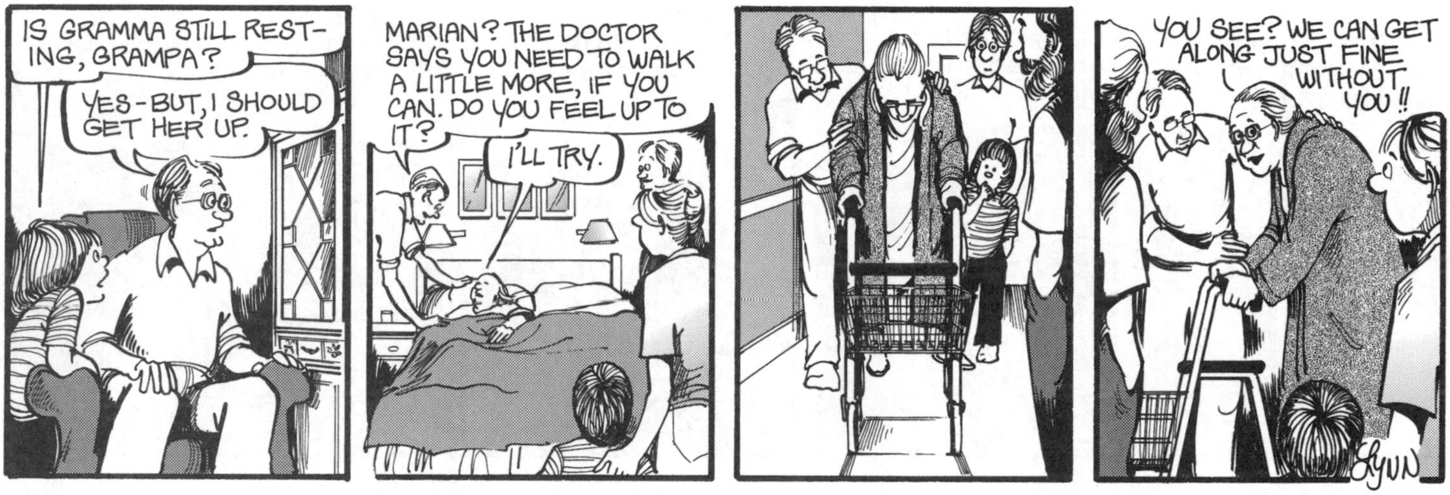
IS GRAMMA STILL RESTING, GRAMPA?
YES - BUT, I SHOULD GET HER UP.
MARIAN? THE DOCTOR SAYS YOU NEED TO WALK A LITTLE MORE, IF YOU CAN. DO YOU FEEL UP TO IT?
I'LL TRY.
YOU SEE? WE CAN GET ALONG JUST FINE WITHOUT YOU!!
LYNN

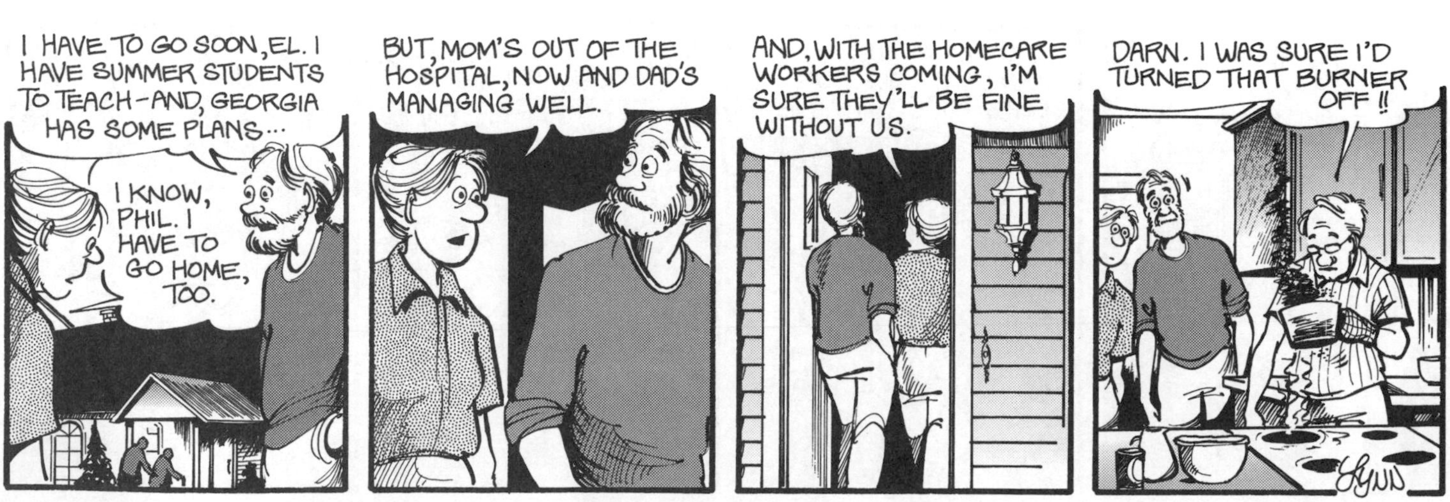
I HAVE TO GO SOON, EL. I HAVE SUMMER STUDENTS TO TEACH - AND, GEORGIA HAS SOME PLANS...
I KNOW, PHIL. I HAVE TO GO HOME, TOO.
BUT, MOM'S OUT OF THE HOSPITAL, NOW AND DAD'S MANAGING WELL.
AND, WITH THE HOMECARE WORKERS COMING, I'M SURE THEY'LL BE FINE WITHOUT US.
DARN. I WAS SURE I'D TURNED THAT BURNER OFF!!
LYNN

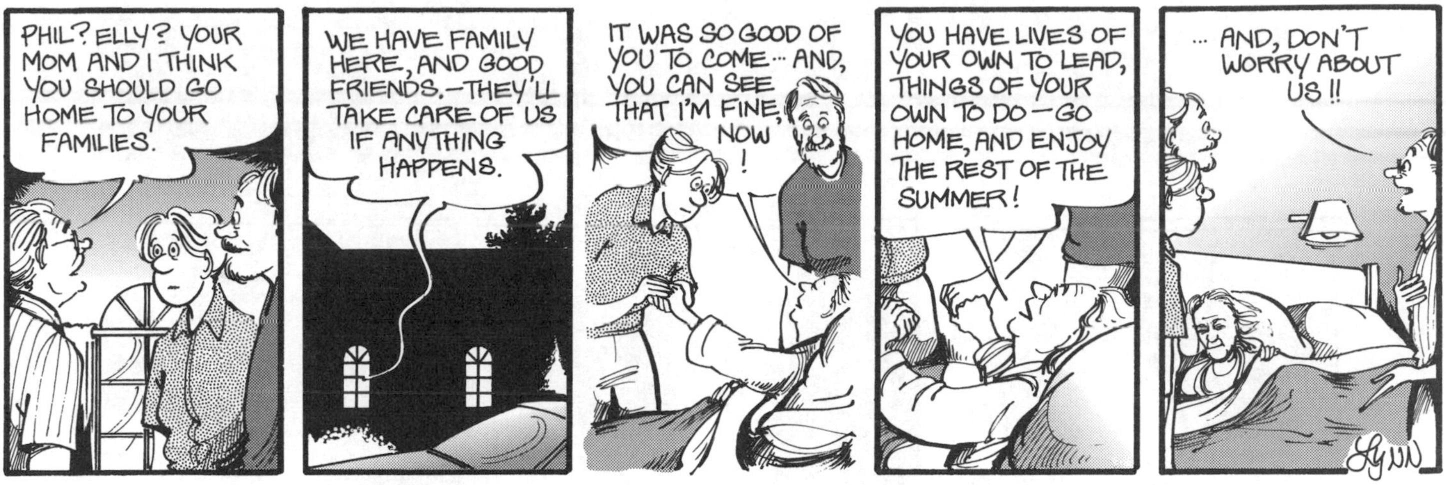
PHIL? ELLY? YOUR MOM AND I THINK YOU SHOULD GO HOME TO YOUR FAMILIES.
WE HAVE FAMILY HERE, AND GOOD FRIENDS.–THEY'LL TAKE CARE OF US IF ANYTHING HAPPENS.
IT WAS SO GOOD OF YOU TO COME... AND, YOU CAN SEE THAT I'M FINE, NOW!
YOU HAVE LIVES OF YOUR OWN TO LEAD, THINGS OF YOUR OWN TO DO–GO HOME, AND ENJOY THE REST OF THE SUMMER!
... AND, DON'T WORRY ABOUT US !!
LYNN

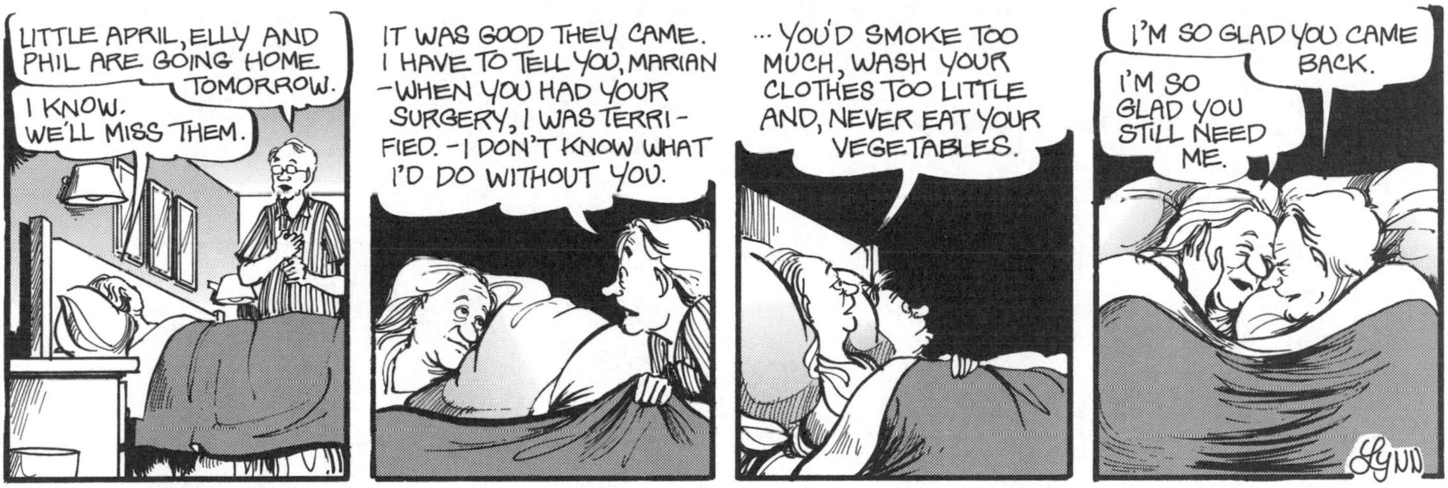
LITTLE APRIL, ELLY AND PHIL ARE GOING HOME TOMORROW.
I KNOW. WE'LL MISS THEM.
IT WAS GOOD THEY CAME. I HAVE TO TELL YOU, MARIAN –WHEN YOU HAD YOUR SURGERY, I WAS TERRI-FIED. –I DON'T KNOW WHAT I'D DO WITHOUT YOU.
... YOU'D SMOKE TOO MUCH, WASH YOUR CLOTHES TOO LITTLE AND, NEVER EAT YOUR VEGETABLES.
I'M SO GLAD YOU CAME BACK.
I'M SO GLAD YOU STILL NEED ME.
LYNN

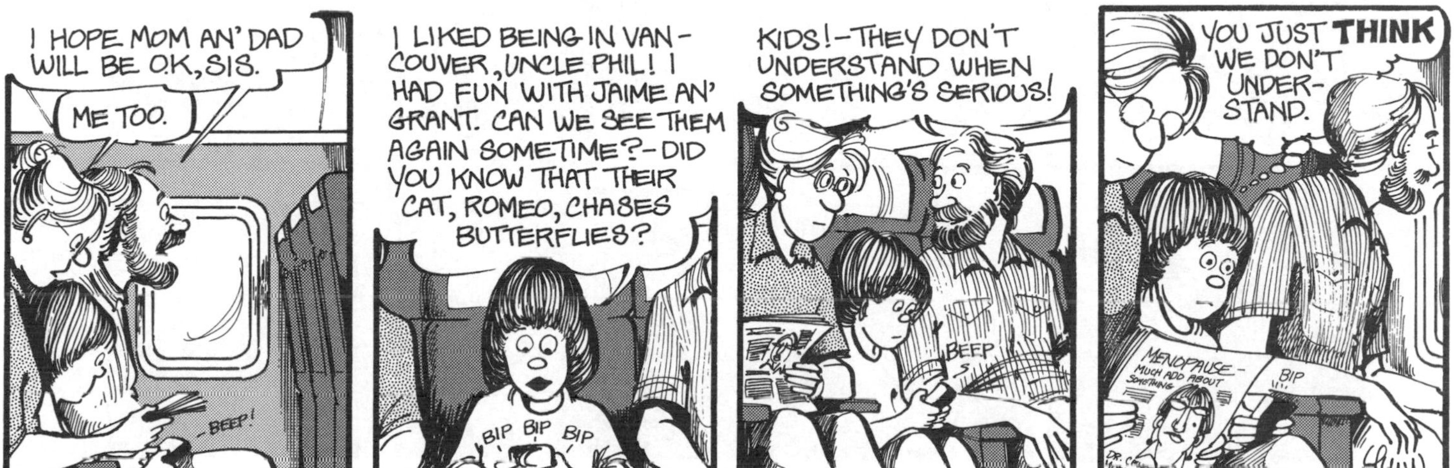
I HOPE MOM AN' DAD WILL BE O.K, SIS.
ME TOO.
-BEEP!
I LIKED BEING IN VAN-COUVER, UNCLE PHIL! I HAD FUN WITH JAIME AN' GRANT. CAN WE SEE THEM AGAIN SOMETIME?–DID YOU KNOW THAT THEIR CAT, ROMEO, CHASES BUTTERFLIES?
BIP BIP BIP
KIDS!–THEY DON'T UNDERSTAND WHEN SOMETHING'S SERIOUS!
BEEP
YOU JUST **THINK** WE DON'T UNDER-STAND.
MENOPAUSE– MUCH ADO ABOUT SOMETHING
BIP
LYNN

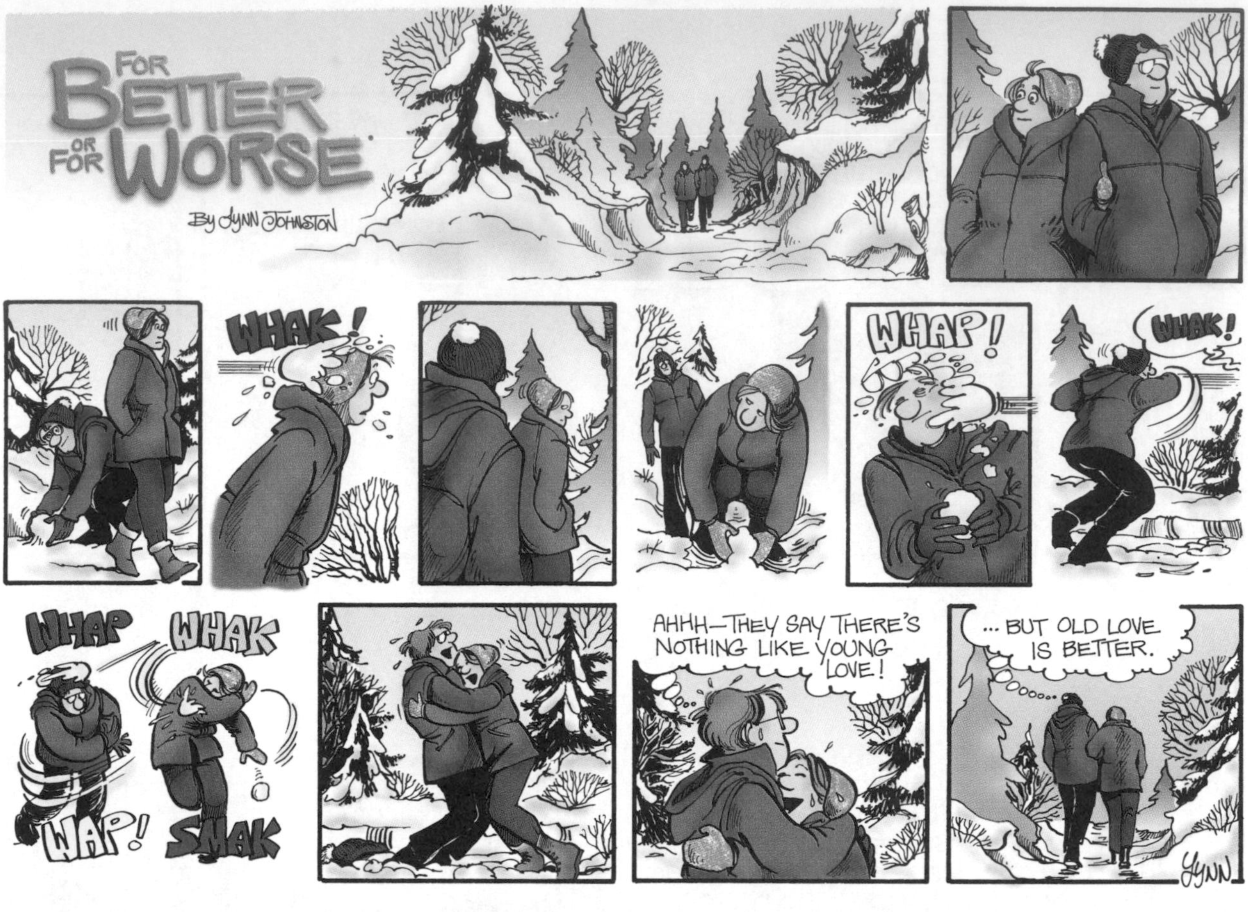
FOR BETTER OR FOR WORSE
By Lynn Johnston
WHAK!
WHAP!
WHAK!
WHAP
WHAK
WAP!
SMAK
AHHH—THEY SAY THERE'S NOTHING LIKE YOUNG LOVE!
... BUT OLD LOVE IS BETTER.
Lynn

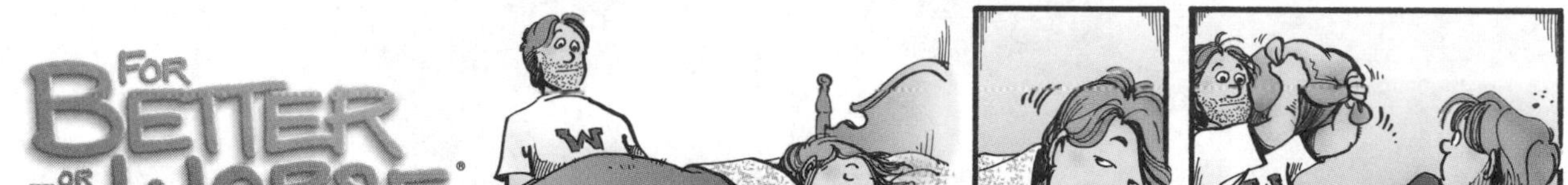
FOR BETTER OR FOR WORSE
By Lynn Johnston
WHUMP!
POW
WHAP
WHAK
WHAP WHACK!
HAH!
WHAP!
WHAP!
POW!
SHHHHHH
RIGHT. ANOTHER CARDINAL FAMILY RULE:
IF I DIDN'T SEE IT... IT DIDN'T HAPPEN.
Lynn

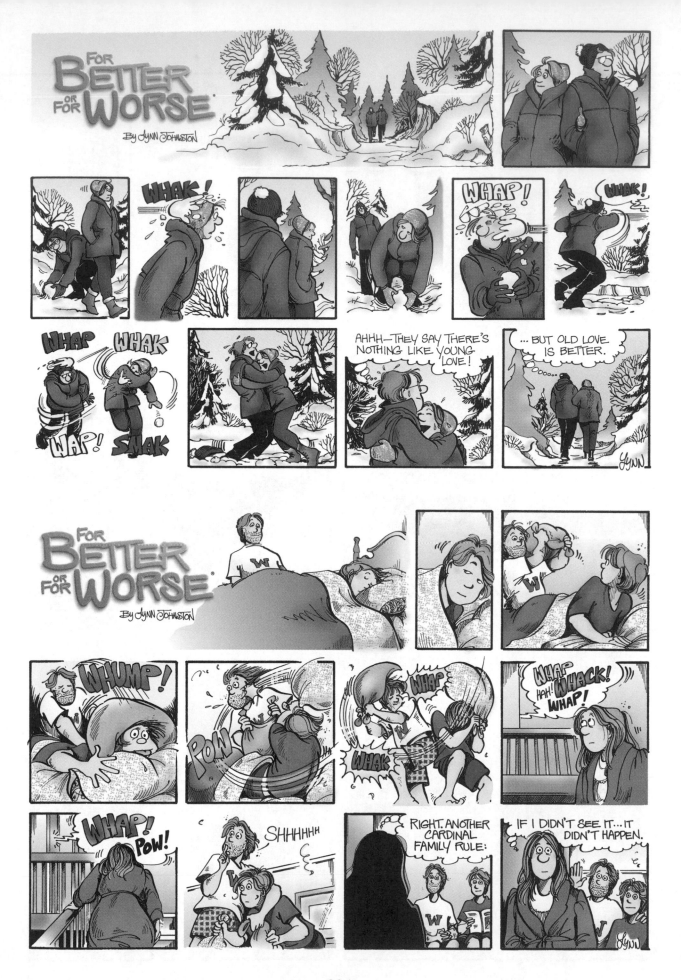

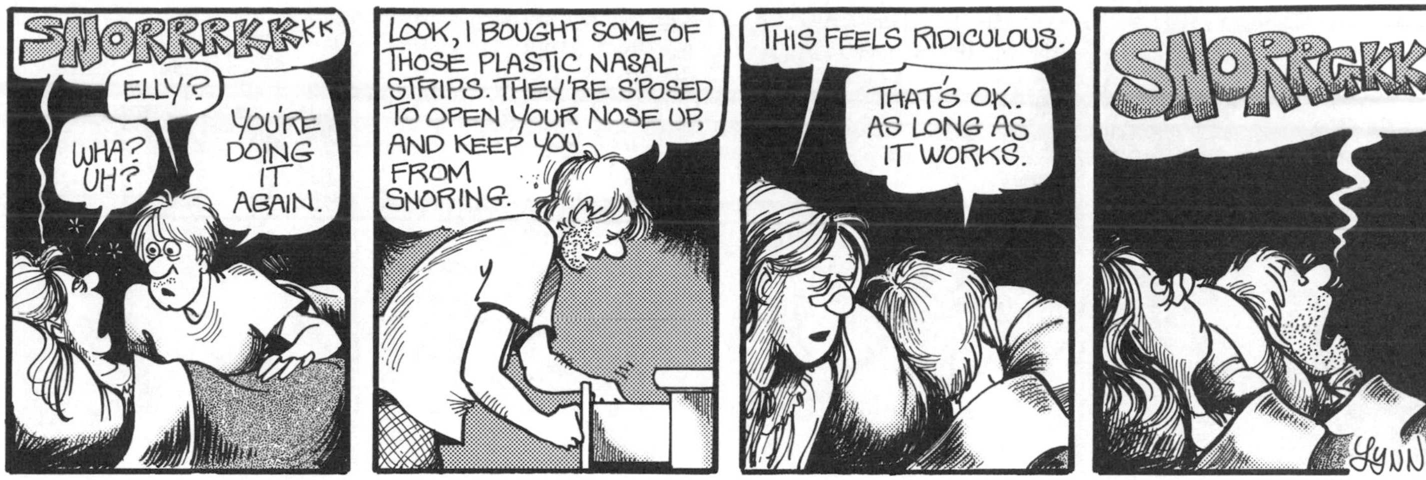
SNORRRKKKKK
ELLY?
WHA? UH?
YOU'RE DOING IT AGAIN.
LOOK, I BOUGHT SOME OF THOSE PLASTIC NASAL STRIPS. THEY'RE S'POSED TO OPEN YOUR NOSE UP, AND KEEP YOU FROM SNORING.
THIS FEELS RIDICULOUS.
THAT'S OK. AS LONG AS IT WORKS.
SNORRGKK..
LYNN

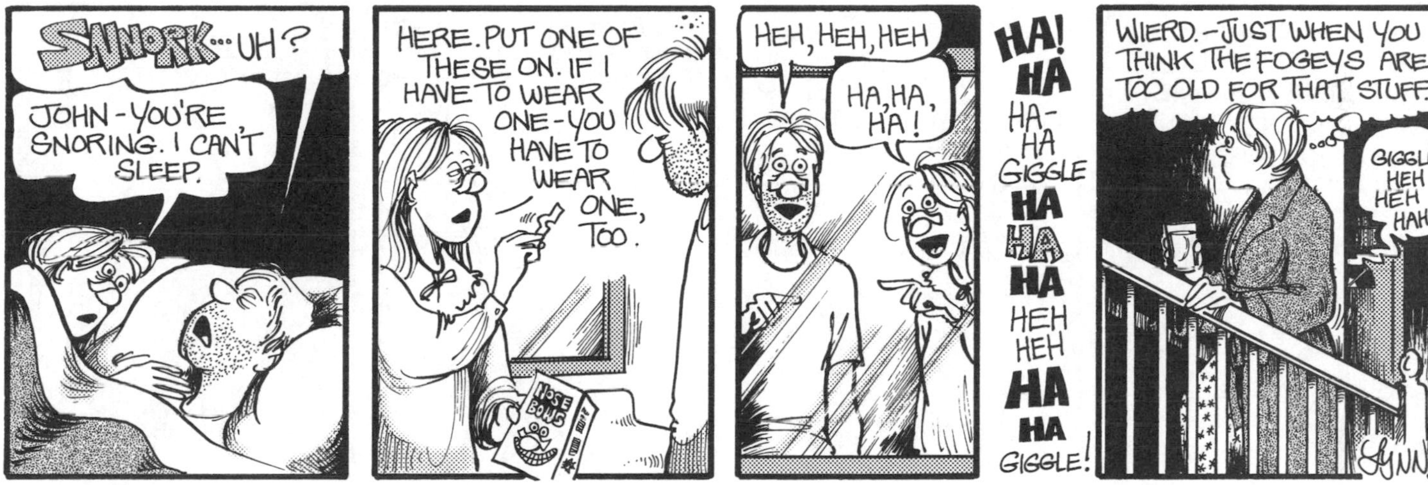
SNNORK... UH?
JOHN - YOU'RE SNORING. I CAN'T SLEEP.
HERE. PUT ONE OF THESE ON. IF I HAVE TO WEAR ONE - YOU HAVE TO WEAR ONE, TOO.
NOSE BOND
HEH, HEH, HEH
HA, HA, HA!
HA! HA HA- HA GIGGLE HA HA HA HEH HEH HA HA GIGGLE!
WIERD. - JUST WHEN YOU THINK THE FOGEYS ARE TOO OLD FOR THAT STUFF.
GIGGLE HEH HEH HAH!
LYNN

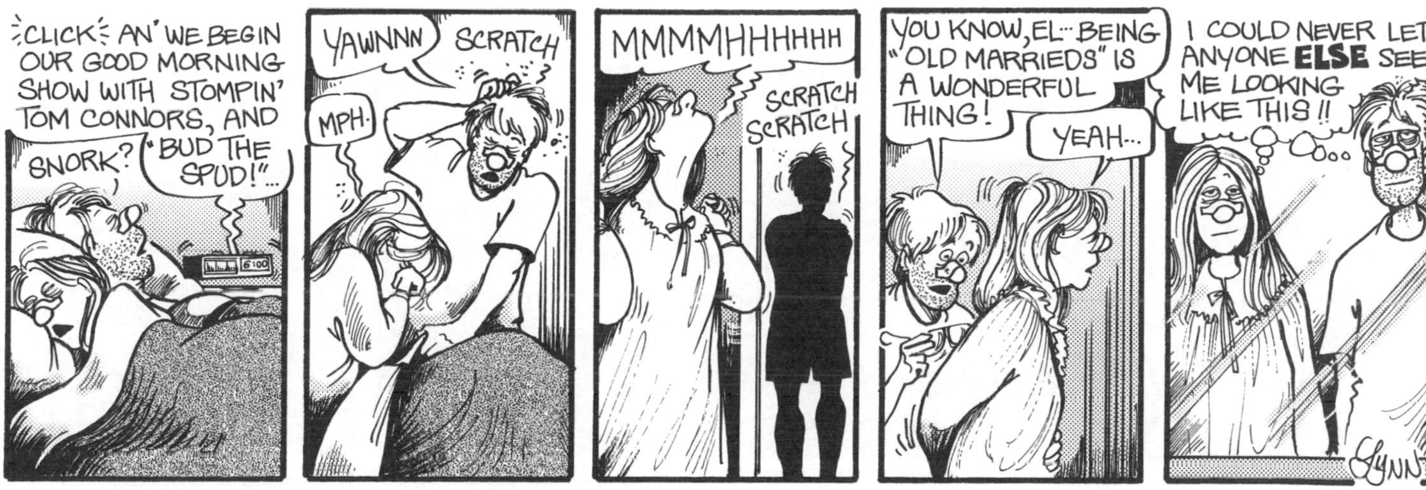
CLICK AN' WE BEGIN OUR GOOD MORNING SHOW WITH STOMPIN' TOM CONNORS, AND "BUD THE SPUD!"...
SNORK?
6:00
YAWNNN
SCRATCH
MPH.
MMMMHHHHHH
SCRATCH SCRATCH
YOU KNOW, EL... BEING "OLD MARRIEDS" IS A WONDERFUL THING!
YEAH...
I COULD NEVER LET ANYONE **ELSE** SEE ME LOOKING LIKE THIS!!
LYNN

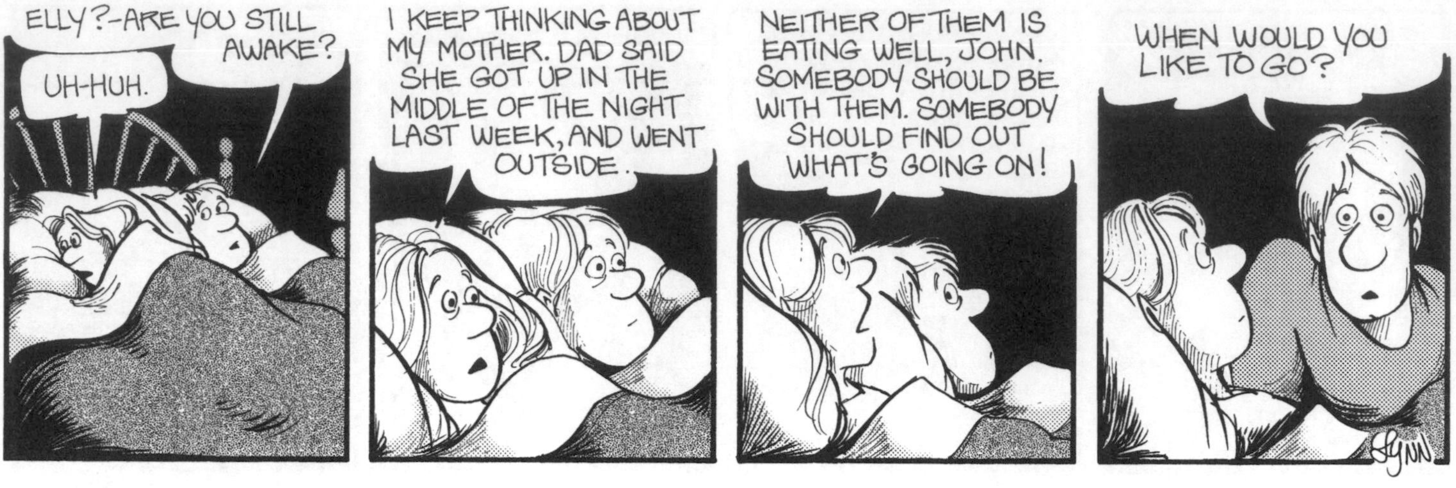
ELLY?-ARE YOU STILL AWAKE?
UH-HUH.
I KEEP THINKING ABOUT MY MOTHER. DAD SAID SHE GOT UP IN THE MIDDLE OF THE NIGHT LAST WEEK, AND WENT OUTSIDE.
NEITHER OF THEM IS EATING WELL, JOHN. SOMEBODY SHOULD BE WITH THEM. SOMEBODY SHOULD FIND OUT WHAT'S GOING ON!
WHEN WOULD YOU LIKE TO GO?
LYNN

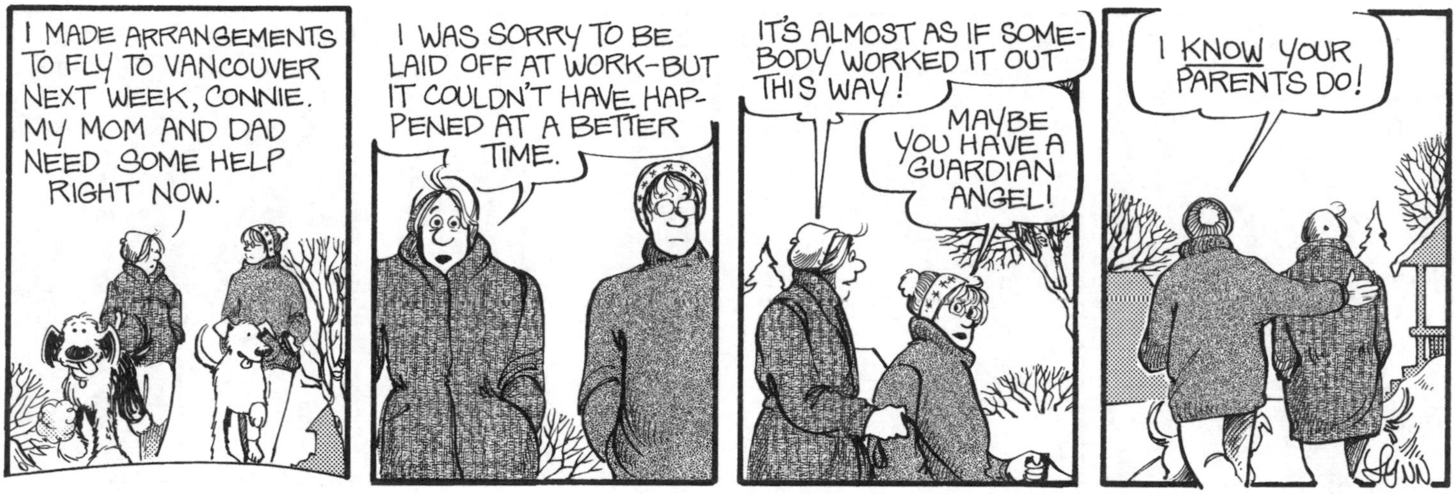
I MADE ARRANGEMENTS TO FLY TO VANCOUVER NEXT WEEK, CONNIE. MY MOM AND DAD NEED SOME HELP RIGHT NOW.
I WAS SORRY TO BE LAID OFF AT WORK-BUT IT COULDN'T HAVE HAPPENED AT A BETTER TIME.
IT'S ALMOST AS IF SOMEBODY WORKED IT OUT THIS WAY!
MAYBE YOU HAVE A GUARDIAN ANGEL!
I KNOW YOUR PARENTS DO!
LYNN

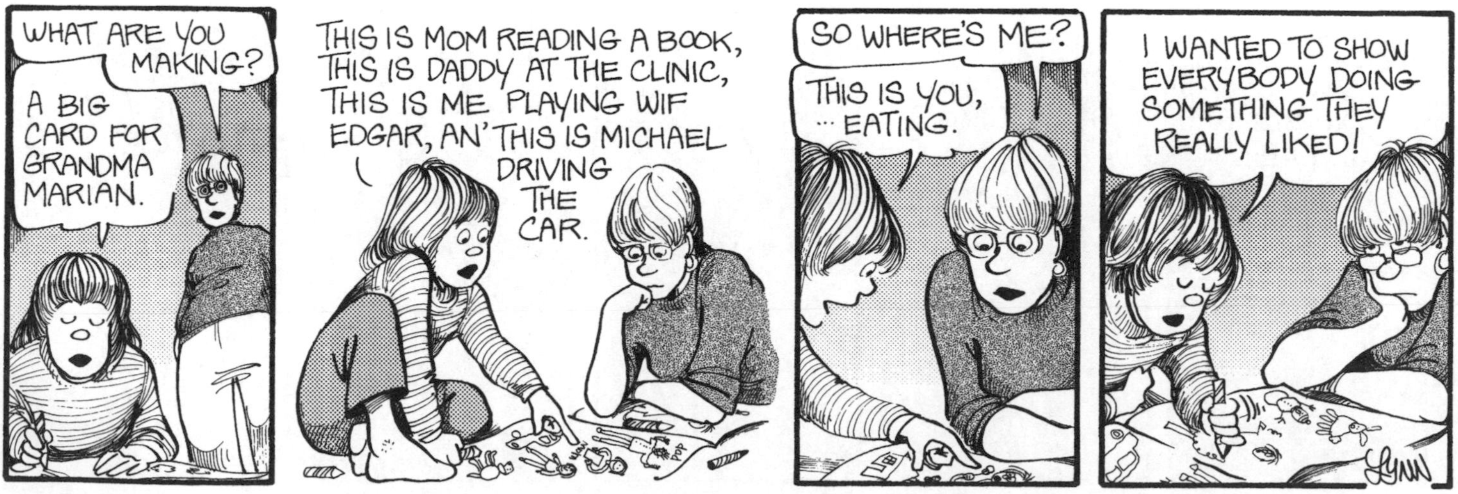
WHAT ARE YOU MAKING?
A BIG CARD FOR GRANDMA MARIAN.
THIS IS MOM READING A BOOK, THIS IS DADDY AT THE CLINIC, THIS IS ME PLAYING WIF EDGAR, AN' THIS IS MICHAEL DRIVING THE CAR.
SO WHERE'S ME?
THIS IS YOU, ... EATING.
I WANTED TO SHOW EVERYBODY DOING SOMETHING THEY REALLY LIKED!
LYNN

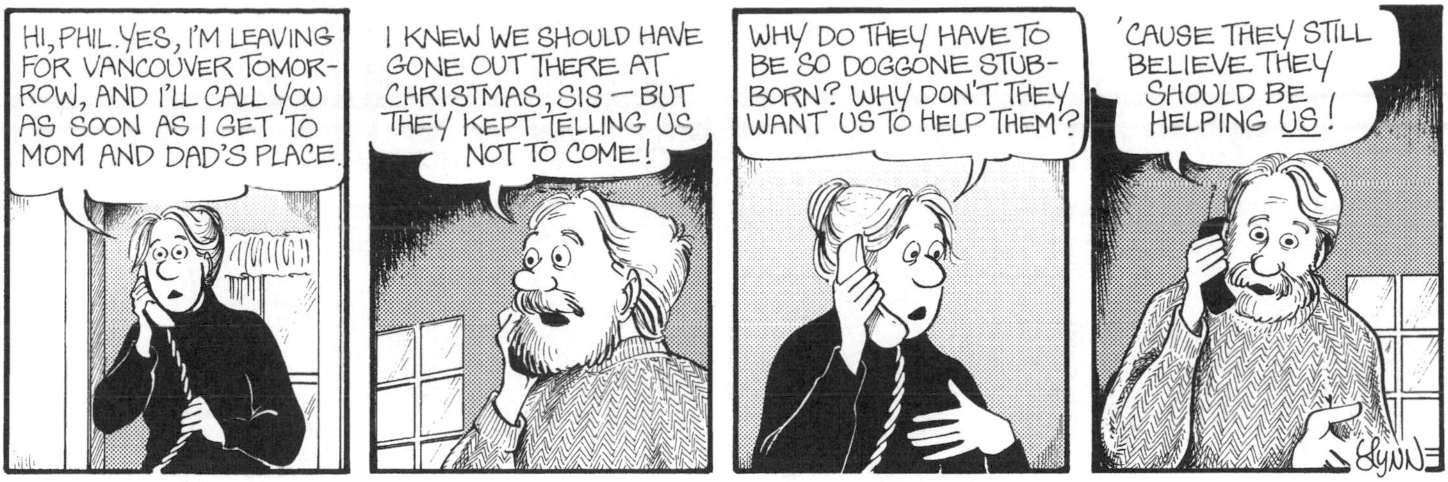
HI, PHIL. YES, I'M LEAVING FOR VANCOUVER TOMORROW, AND I'LL CALL YOU AS SOON AS I GET TO MOM AND DAD'S PLACE.
I KNEW WE SHOULD HAVE GONE OUT THERE AT CHRISTMAS, SIS — BUT THEY KEPT TELLING US NOT TO COME!
WHY DO THEY HAVE TO BE SO DOGGONE STUBBORN? WHY DON'T THEY WANT US TO HELP THEM?
'CAUSE THEY STILL BELIEVE THEY SHOULD BE HELPING US!
LYNN

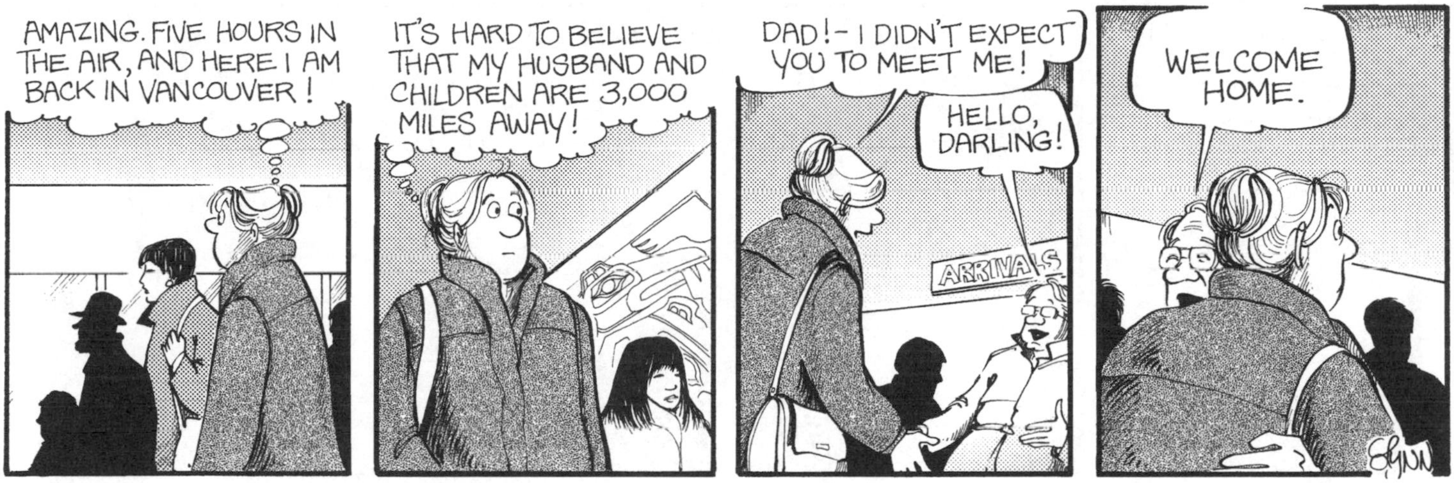
AMAZING. FIVE HOURS IN THE AIR, AND HERE I AM BACK IN VANCOUVER!
IT'S HARD TO BELIEVE THAT MY HUSBAND AND CHILDREN ARE 3,000 MILES AWAY!
DAD! - I DIDN'T EXPECT YOU TO MEET ME!
HELLO, DARLING!
ARRIVALS
WELCOME HOME.
LYNN

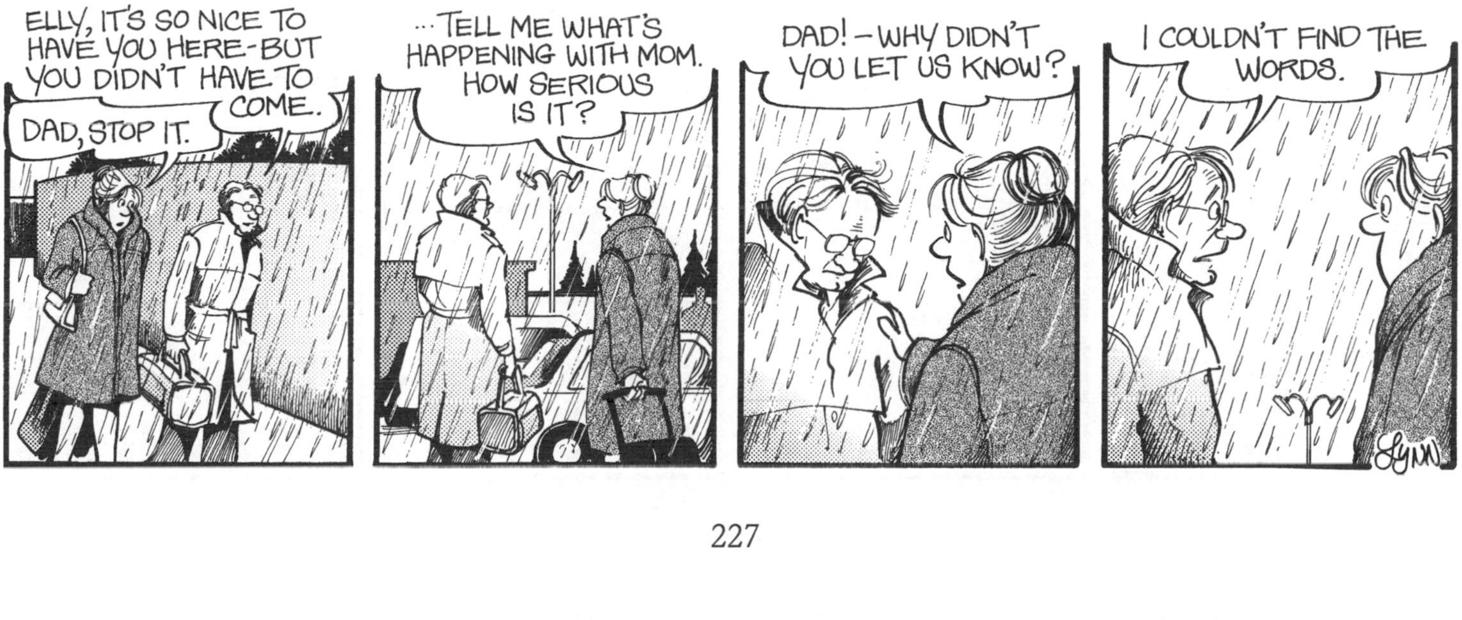
ELLY, IT'S SO NICE TO HAVE YOU HERE - BUT YOU DIDN'T HAVE TO COME.
DAD, STOP IT.
...TELL ME WHAT'S HAPPENING WITH MOM. HOW SERIOUS IS IT?
DAD! — WHY DIDN'T YOU LET US KNOW?
I COULDN'T FIND THE WORDS.
LYNN

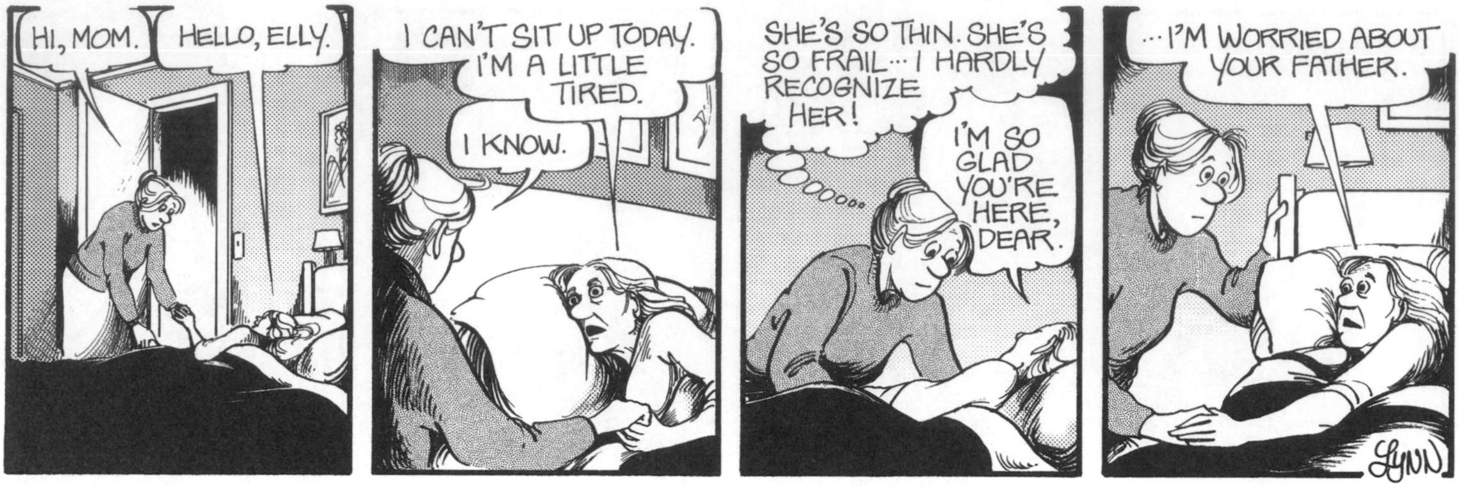
HI, MOM.
HELLO, ELLY.
I CAN'T SIT UP TODAY. I'M A LITTLE TIRED.
I KNOW.
SHE'S SO THIN. SHE'S SO FRAIL... I HARDLY RECOGNIZE HER!
I'M SO GLAD YOU'RE HERE, DEAR.
...I'M WORRIED ABOUT YOUR FATHER.
LYNN

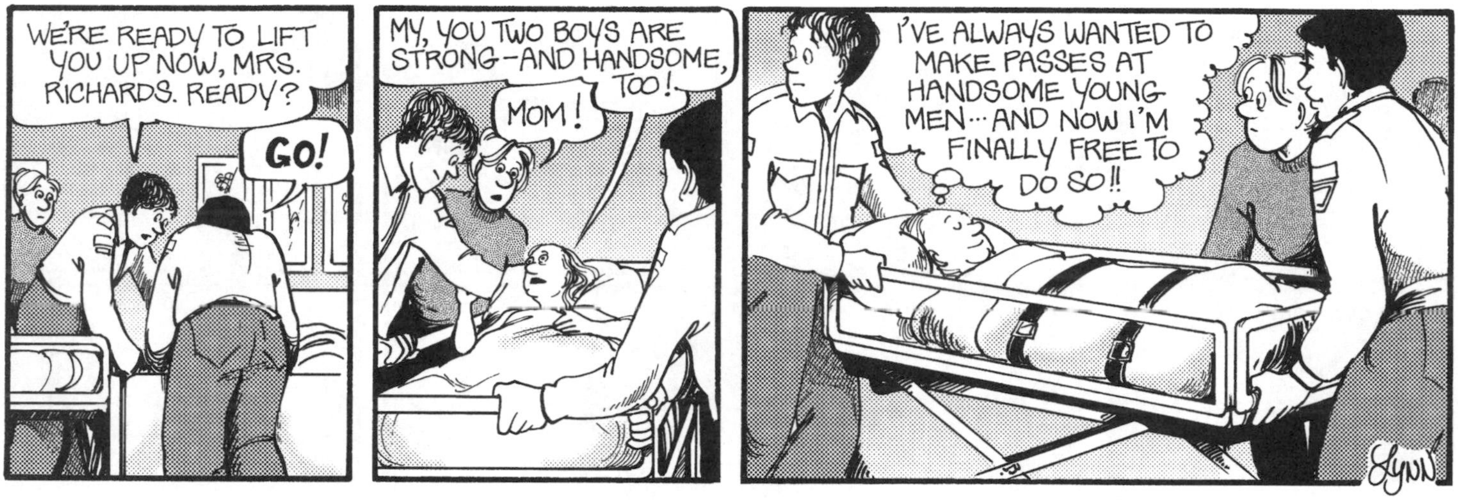
WE'RE READY TO LIFT YOU UP NOW, MRS. RICHARDS. READY?
GO!
MY, YOU TWO BOYS ARE STRONG—AND HANDSOME, TOO!
MOM!
I'VE ALWAYS WANTED TO MAKE PASSES AT HANDSOME YOUNG MEN... AND NOW I'M FINALLY FREE TO DO SO!!
LYNN

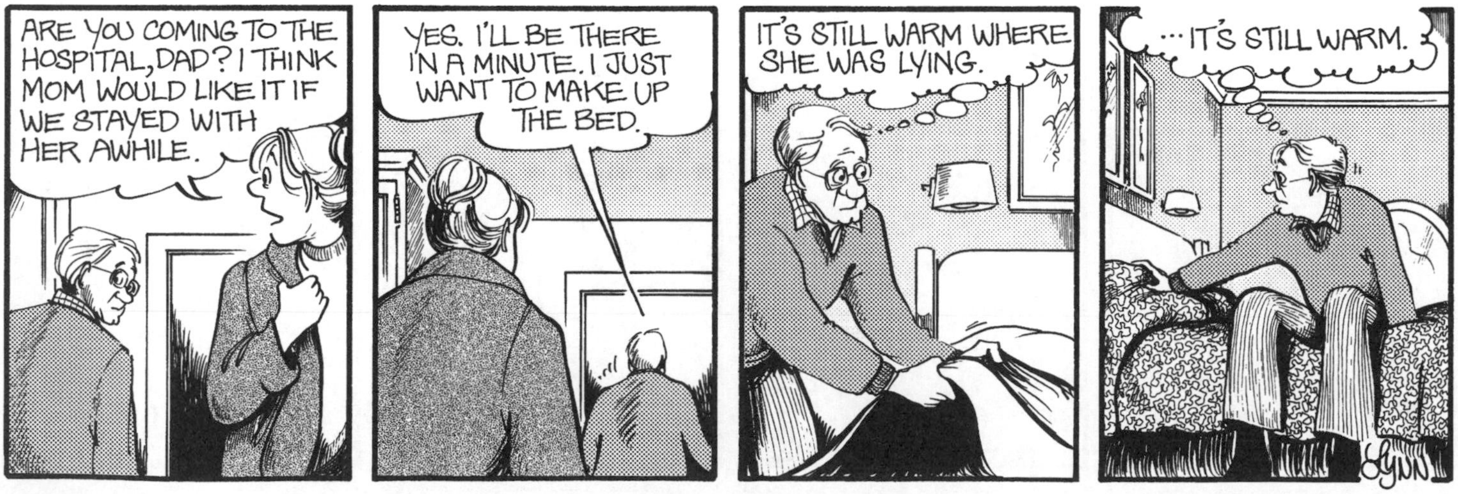
ARE YOU COMING TO THE HOSPITAL, DAD? I THINK MOM WOULD LIKE IT IF WE STAYED WITH HER AWHILE.
YES. I'LL BE THERE IN A MINUTE. I JUST WANT TO MAKE UP THE BED.
IT'S STILL WARM WHERE SHE WAS LYING.
...IT'S STILL WARM.
LYNN

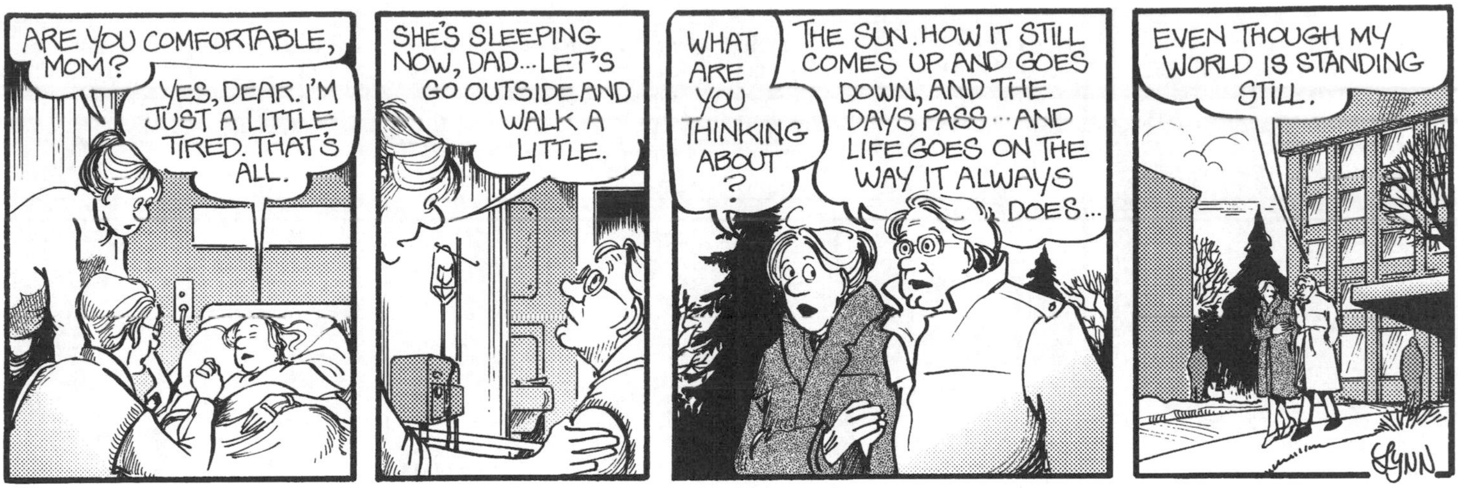
ARE YOU COMFORTABLE, MOM?
YES, DEAR. I'M JUST A LITTLE TIRED. THAT'S ALL.
SHE'S SLEEPING NOW, DAD... LET'S GO OUTSIDE AND WALK A LITTLE.
WHAT ARE YOU THINKING ABOUT?
THE SUN. HOW IT STILL COMES UP AND GOES DOWN, AND THE DAYS PASS... AND LIFE GOES ON THE WAY IT ALWAYS DOES...
EVEN THOUGH MY WORLD IS STANDING STILL.
LYNN

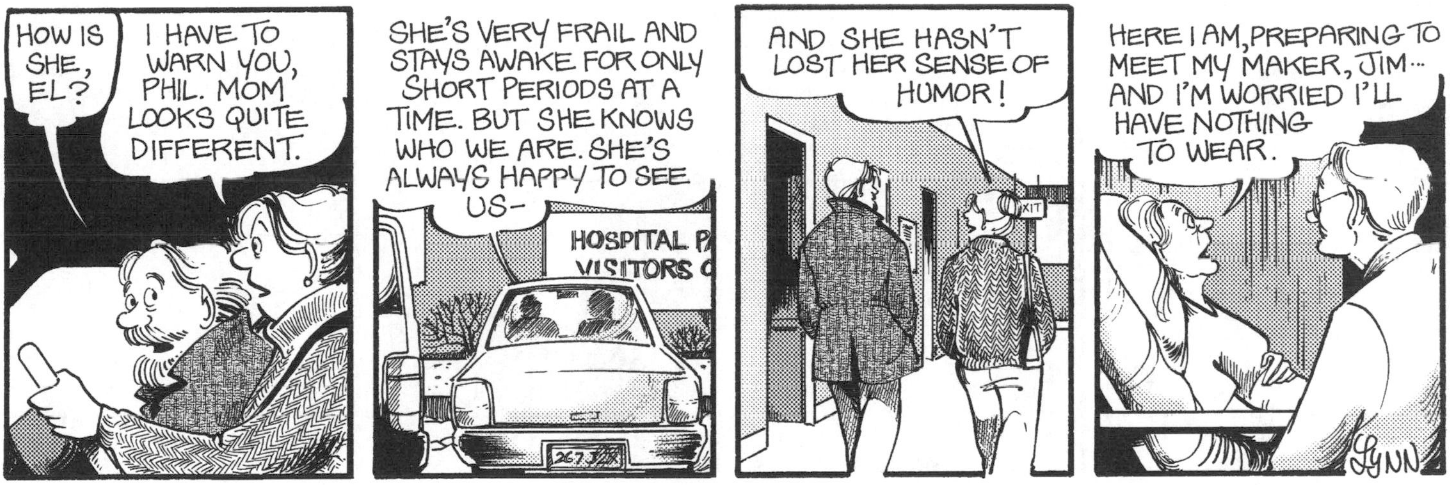
HOW IS SHE, EL?
I HAVE TO WARN YOU, PHIL. MOM LOOKS QUITE DIFFERENT.
SHE'S VERY FRAIL AND STAYS AWAKE FOR ONLY SHORT PERIODS AT A TIME. BUT SHE KNOWS WHO WE ARE. SHE'S ALWAYS HAPPY TO SEE US-
AND SHE HASN'T LOST HER SENSE OF HUMOR!
HERE I AM, PREPARING TO MEET MY MAKER, JIM... AND I'M WORRIED I'LL HAVE NOTHING TO WEAR.
LYNN

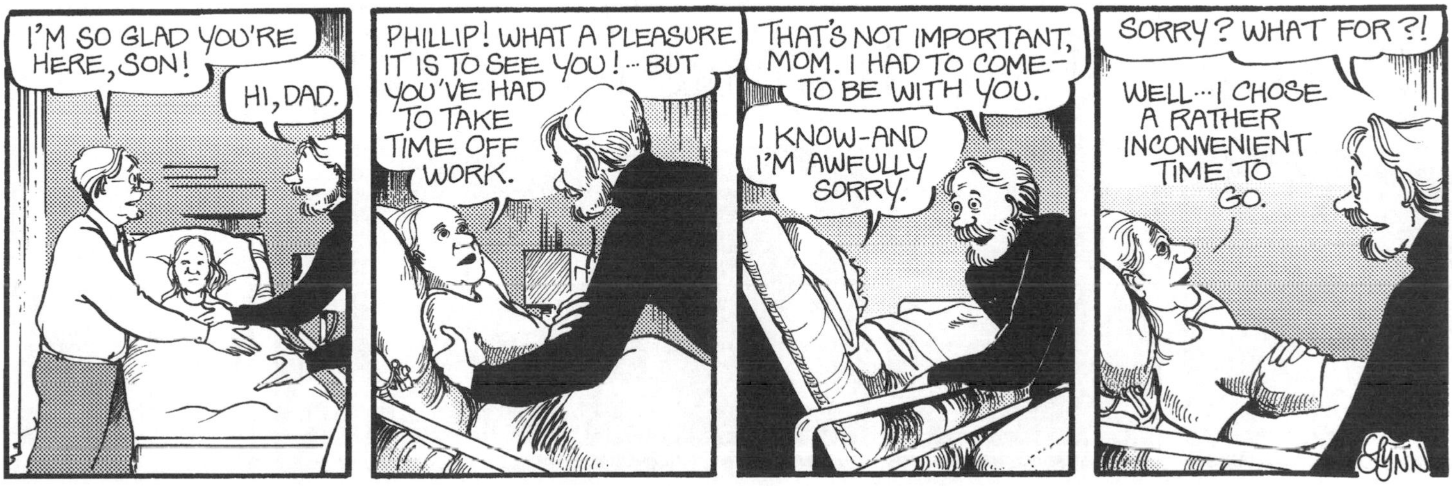
I'M SO GLAD YOU'RE HERE, SON!
HI, DAD.
PHILLIP! WHAT A PLEASURE IT IS TO SEE YOU! ... BUT YOU'VE HAD TO TAKE TIME OFF WORK.
THAT'S NOT IMPORTANT, MOM. I HAD TO COME- TO BE WITH YOU.
I KNOW-AND I'M AWFULLY SORRY.
SORRY? WHAT FOR?!
WELL... I CHOSE A RATHER INCONVENIENT TIME TO GO.
LYNN

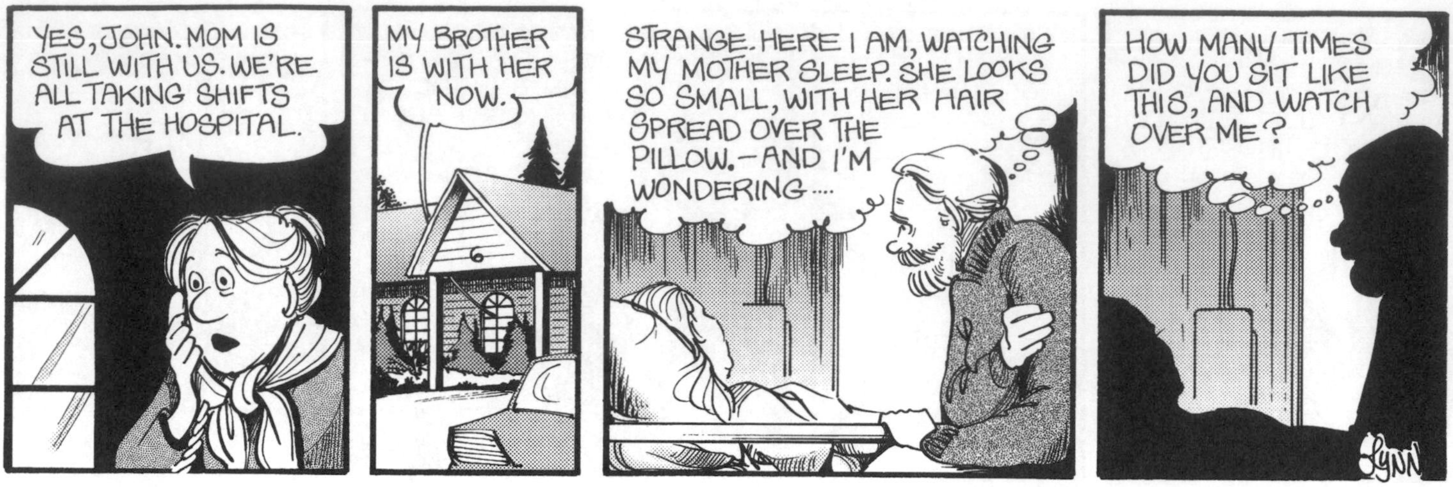
YES, JOHN. MOM IS STILL WITH US. WE'RE ALL TAKING SHIFTS AT THE HOSPITAL.
MY BROTHER IS WITH HER NOW.
STRANGE. HERE I AM, WATCHING MY MOTHER SLEEP. SHE LOOKS SO SMALL, WITH HER HAIR SPREAD OVER THE PILLOW.—AND I'M WONDERING....
HOW MANY TIMES DID YOU SIT LIKE THIS, AND WATCH OVER ME?
LYNN

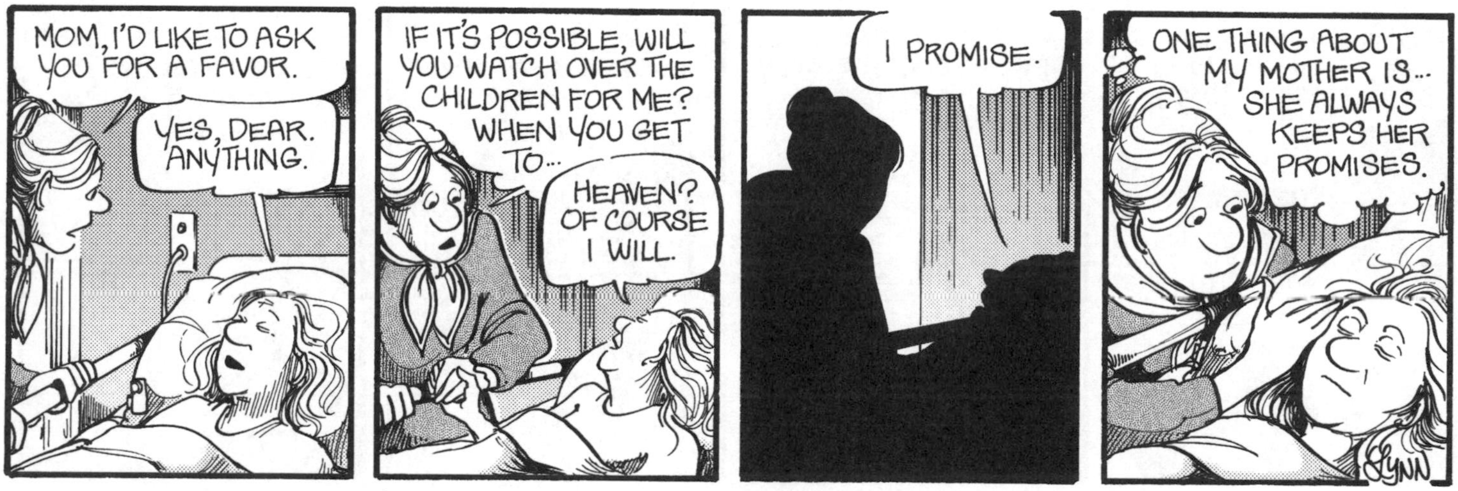
MOM, I'D LIKE TO ASK YOU FOR A FAVOR.
YES, DEAR. ANYTHING.
IF IT'S POSSIBLE, WILL YOU WATCH OVER THE CHILDREN FOR ME? WHEN YOU GET TO...
HEAVEN? OF COURSE I WILL.
I PROMISE.
ONE THING ABOUT MY MOTHER IS... SHE ALWAYS KEEPS HER PROMISES.
LYNN

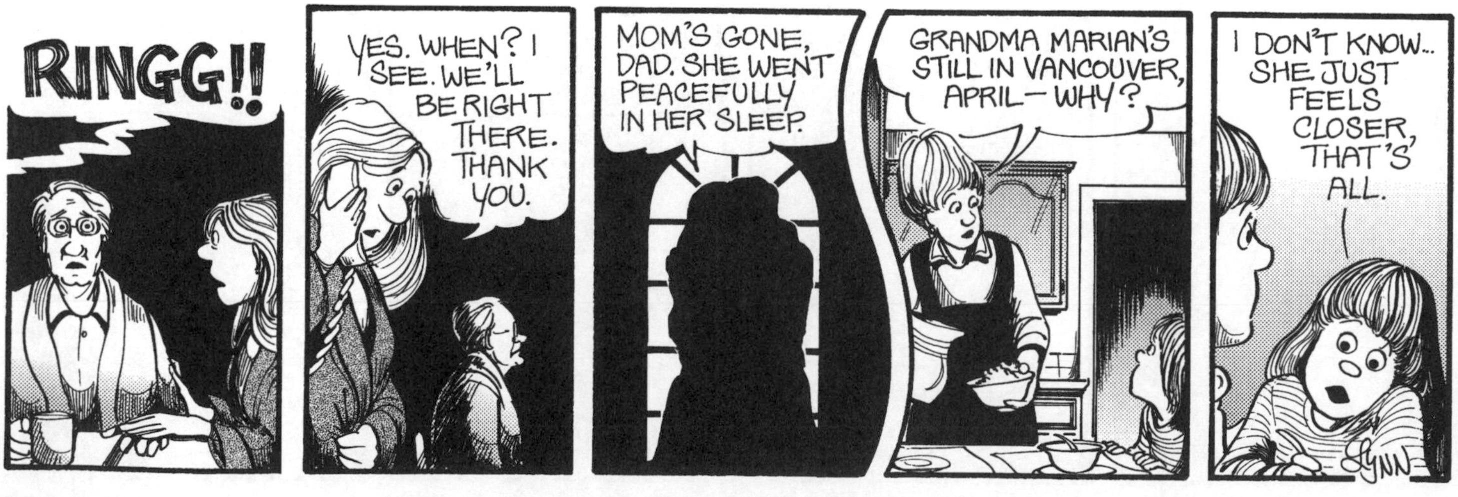
RINGG!!
YES. WHEN? I SEE. WE'LL BE RIGHT THERE. THANK YOU.
MOM'S GONE, DAD. SHE WENT PEACEFULLY IN HER SLEEP.
GRANDMA MARIAN'S STILL IN VANCOUVER, APRIL— WHY?
I DON'T KNOW... SHE JUST FEELS CLOSER, THAT'S ALL.
LYNN

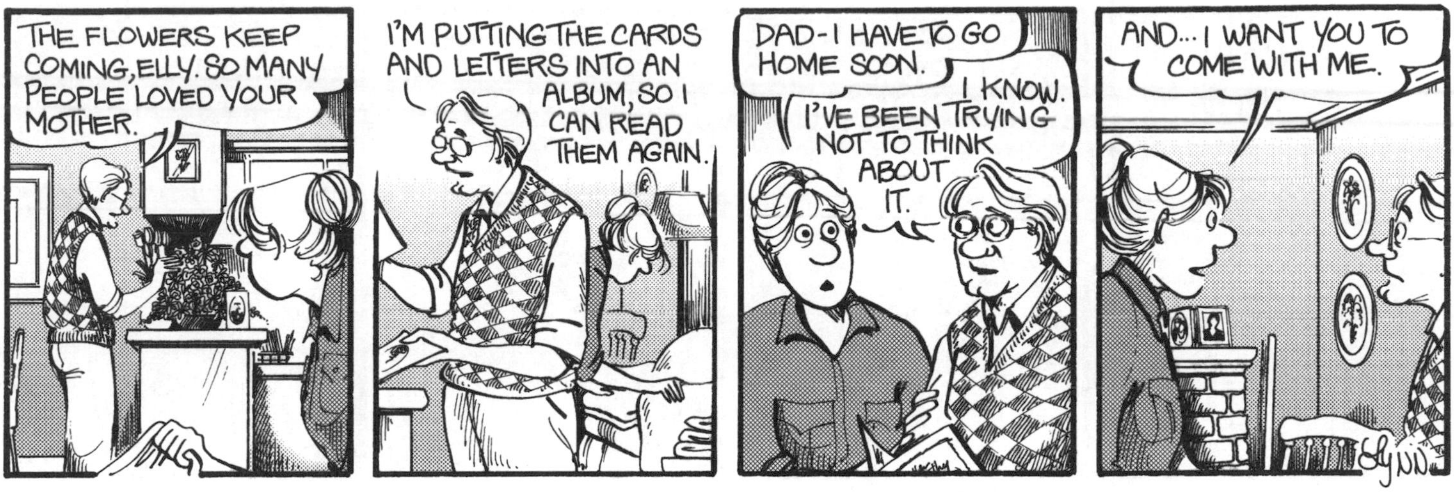
THE FLOWERS KEEP COMING, ELLY. SO MANY PEOPLE LOVED YOUR MOTHER.
I'M PUTTING THE CARDS AND LETTERS INTO AN ALBUM, SO I CAN READ THEM AGAIN.
DAD- I HAVE TO GO HOME SOON.
I KNOW. I'VE BEEN TRYING NOT TO THINK ABOUT IT.
AND... I WANT YOU TO COME WITH ME.
LYNN

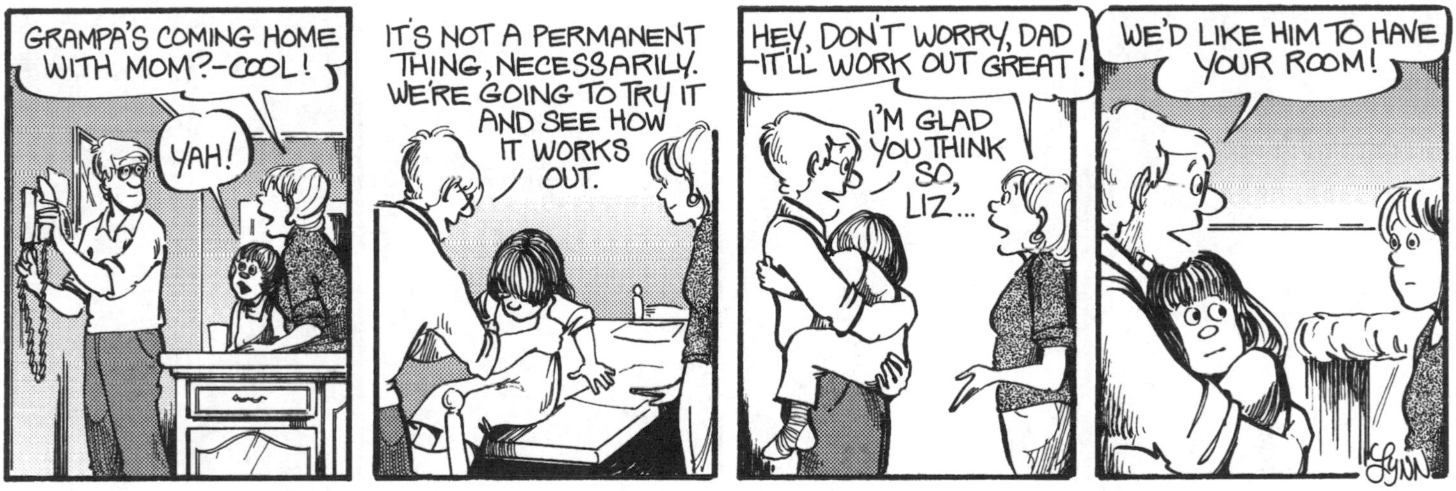
GRAMPA'S COMING HOME WITH MOM?-COOL!
YAH!
IT'S NOT A PERMANENT THING, NECESSARILY. WE'RE GOING TO TRY IT AND SEE HOW IT WORKS OUT.
HEY, DON'T WORRY, DAD -IT'LL WORK OUT GREAT!
I'M GLAD YOU THINK SO, LIZ...
WE'D LIKE HIM TO HAVE YOUR ROOM!
LYNN

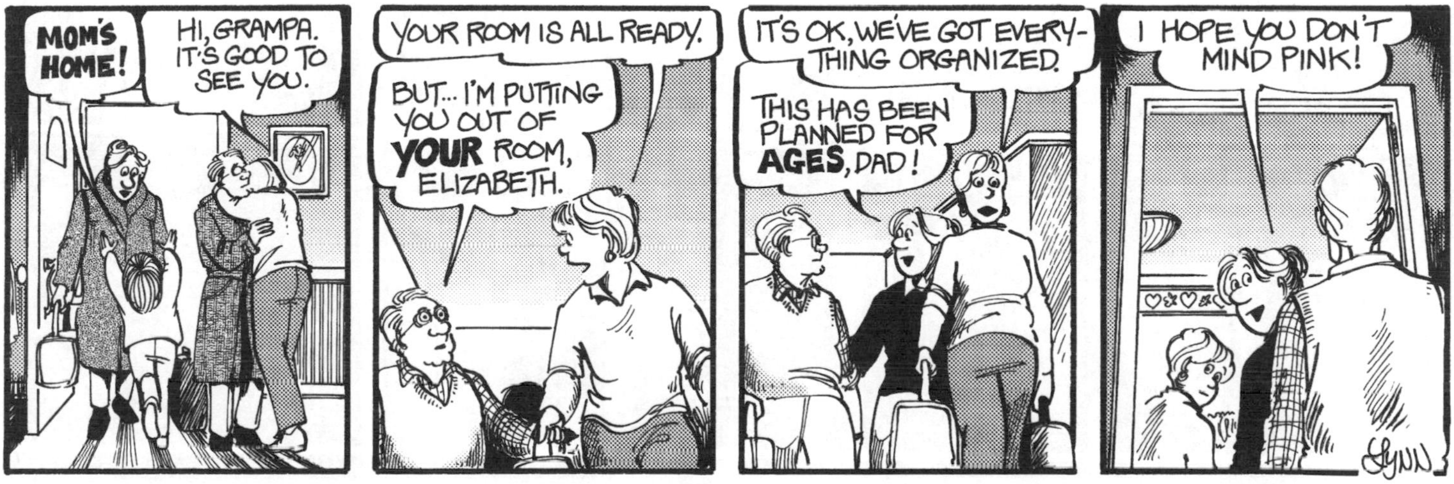
MOM'S HOME!
HI, GRAMPA. IT'S GOOD TO SEE YOU.
YOUR ROOM IS ALL READY.
BUT... I'M PUTTING YOU OUT OF YOUR ROOM, ELIZABETH.
IT'S OK, WE'VE GOT EVERYTHING ORGANIZED.
THIS HAS BEEN PLANNED FOR AGES, DAD!
I HOPE YOU DON'T MIND PINK!
LYNN

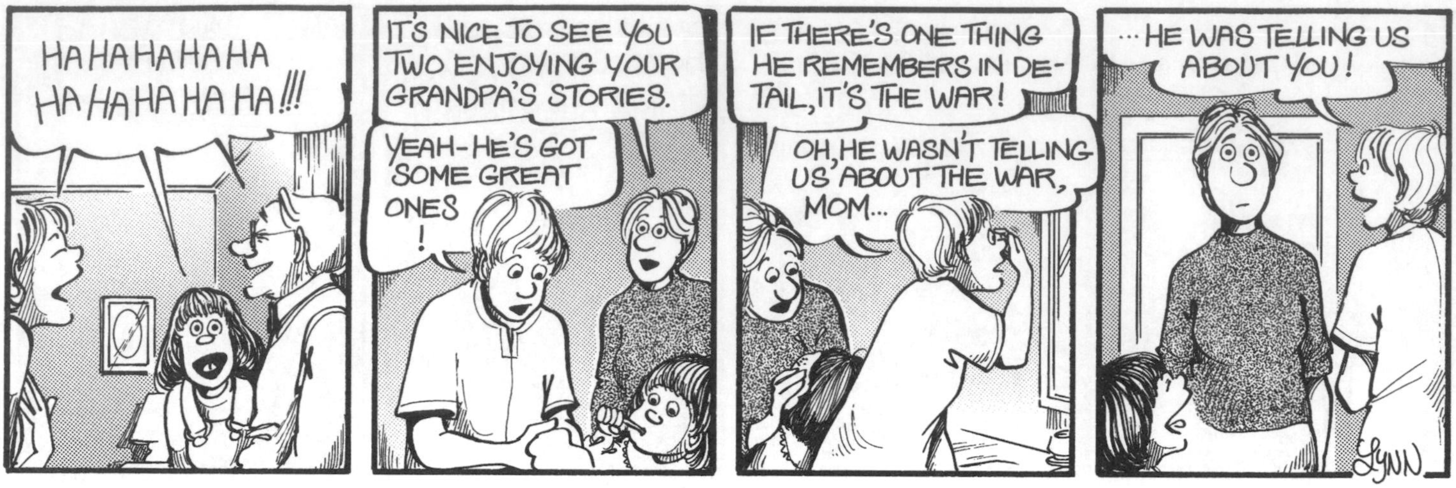
HA HA HA HA HA HA HA HA HA HA HA HA HA!!!
IT'S NICE TO SEE YOU TWO ENJOYING YOUR GRANDPA'S STORIES.
YEAH - HE'S GOT SOME GREAT ONES!
IF THERE'S ONE THING HE REMEMBERS IN DETAIL, IT'S THE WAR!
OH, HE WASN'T TELLING US ABOUT THE WAR, MOM...
...HE WAS TELLING US ABOUT YOU!
LYNN

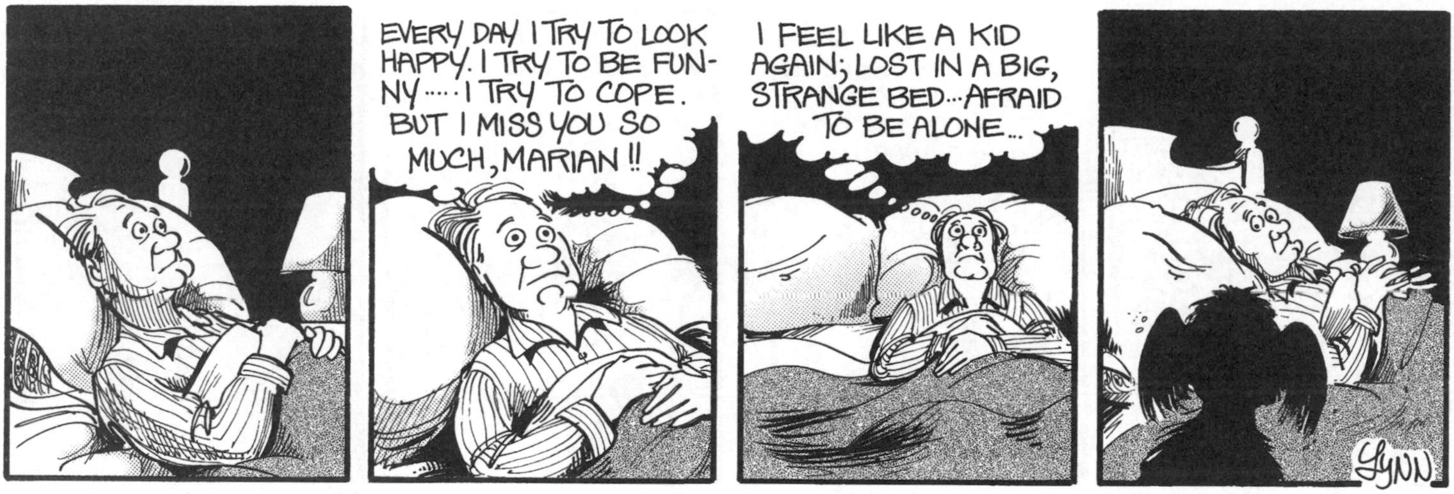
EVERY DAY I TRY TO LOOK HAPPY. I TRY TO BE FUNNY..... I TRY TO COPE. BUT I MISS YOU SO MUCH, MARIAN!!
I FEEL LIKE A KID AGAIN; LOST IN A BIG, STRANGE BED... AFRAID TO BE ALONE...
LYNN

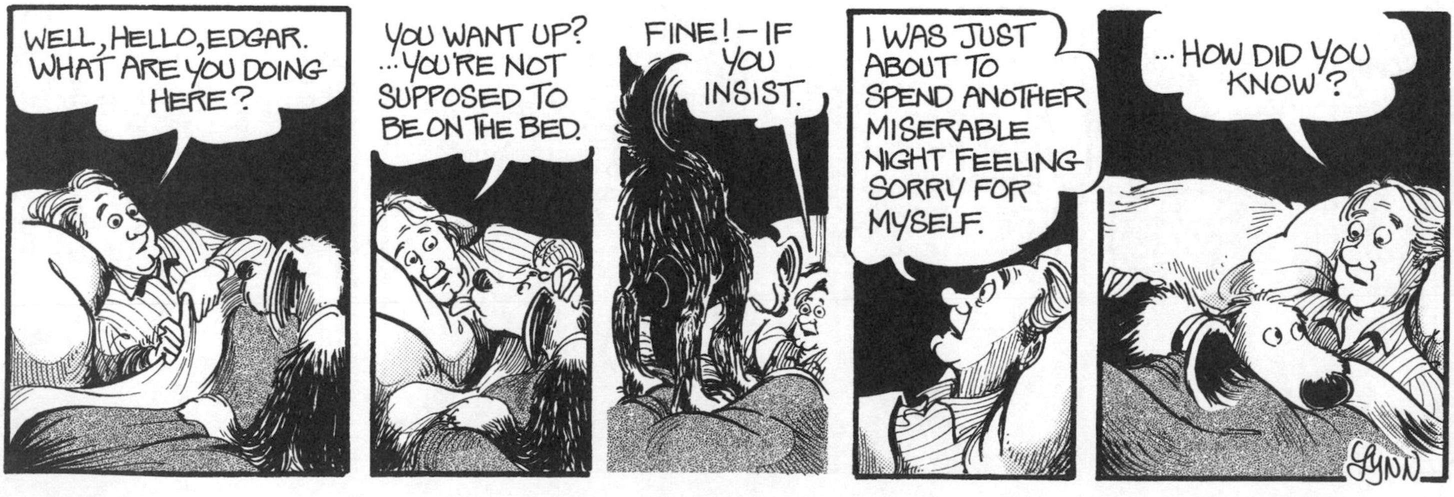
WELL, HELLO, EDGAR. WHAT ARE YOU DOING HERE?
YOU WANT UP? ...YOU'RE NOT SUPPOSED TO BE ON THE BED.
FINE! - IF YOU INSIST.
I WAS JUST ABOUT TO SPEND ANOTHER MISERABLE NIGHT FEELING SORRY FOR MYSELF.
...HOW DID YOU KNOW?
LYNN

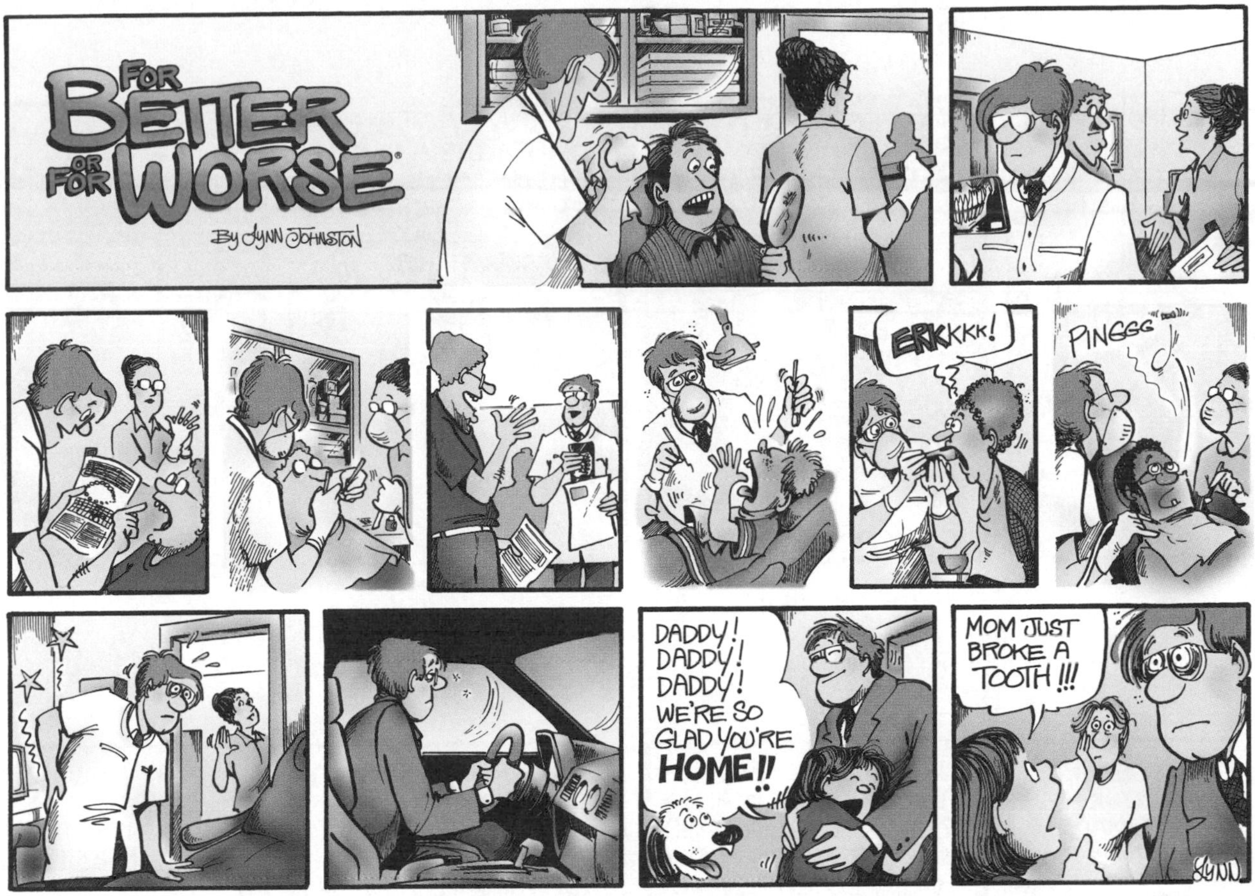
FOR BETTER OR FOR WORSE
By Lynn Johnston
ERKKKK!
PINGGG
DADDY! DADDY! DADDY! WE'RE SO GLAD YOU'RE HOME!!
MOM JUST BROKE A TOOTH!!!
LYNN

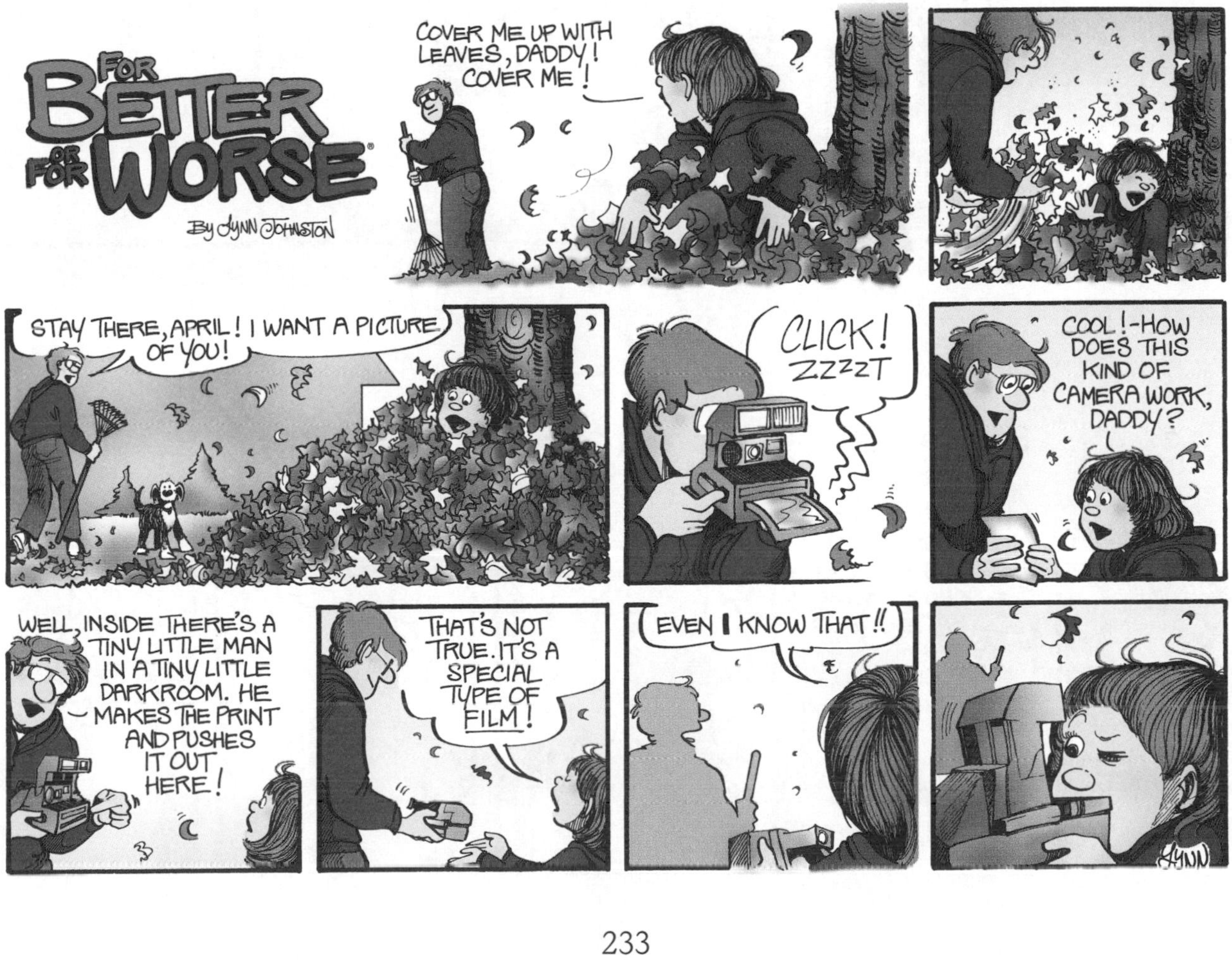
FOR BETTER OR FOR WORSE
By Lynn Johnston
COVER ME UP WITH LEAVES, DADDY! COVER ME!
STAY THERE, APRIL! I WANT A PICTURE OF YOU!
CLICK! ZZZZT
COOL!-HOW DOES THIS KIND OF CAMERA WORK, DADDY?
WELL, INSIDE THERE'S A TINY LITTLE MAN IN A TINY LITTLE DARKROOM. HE MAKES THE PRINT AND PUSHES IT OUT HERE!
THAT'S NOT TRUE. IT'S A SPECIAL TYPE OF FILM!
EVEN I KNOW THAT!!
LYNN

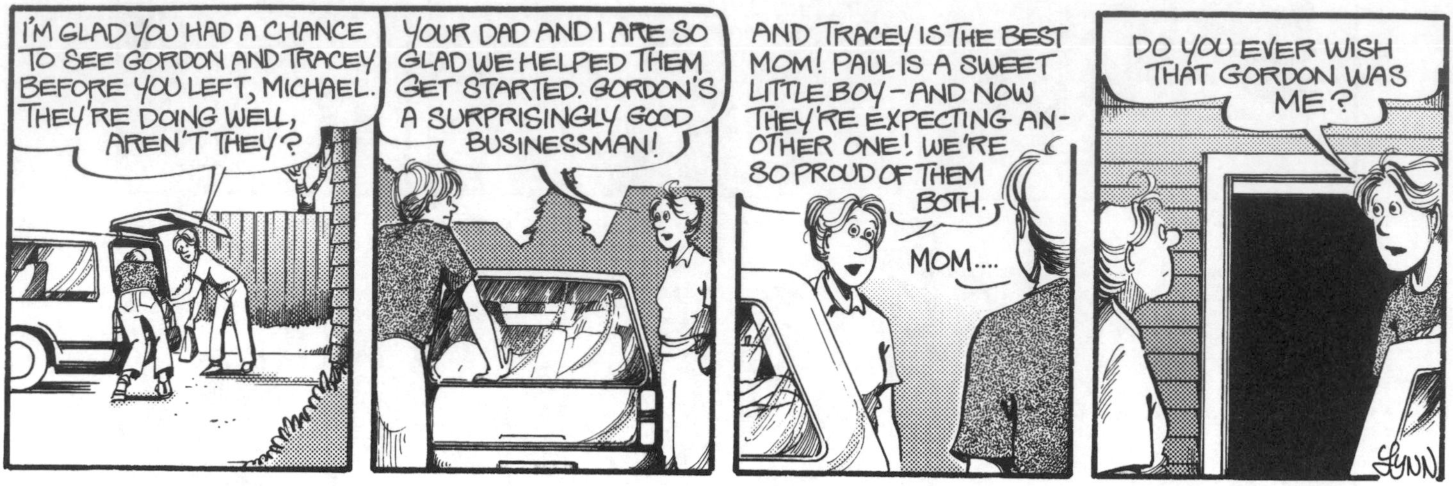
I'M GLAD YOU HAD A CHANCE TO SEE GORDON AND TRACEY BEFORE YOU LEFT, MICHAEL. THEY'RE DOING WELL, AREN'T THEY?
YOUR DAD AND I ARE SO GLAD WE HELPED THEM GET STARTED. GORDON'S A SURPRISINGLY GOOD BUSINESSMAN!
AND TRACEY IS THE BEST MOM! PAUL IS A SWEET LITTLE BOY - AND NOW THEY'RE EXPECTING ANOTHER ONE! WE'RE SO PROUD OF THEM BOTH.
MOM....
DO YOU EVER WISH THAT GORDON WAS ME?
LYNN

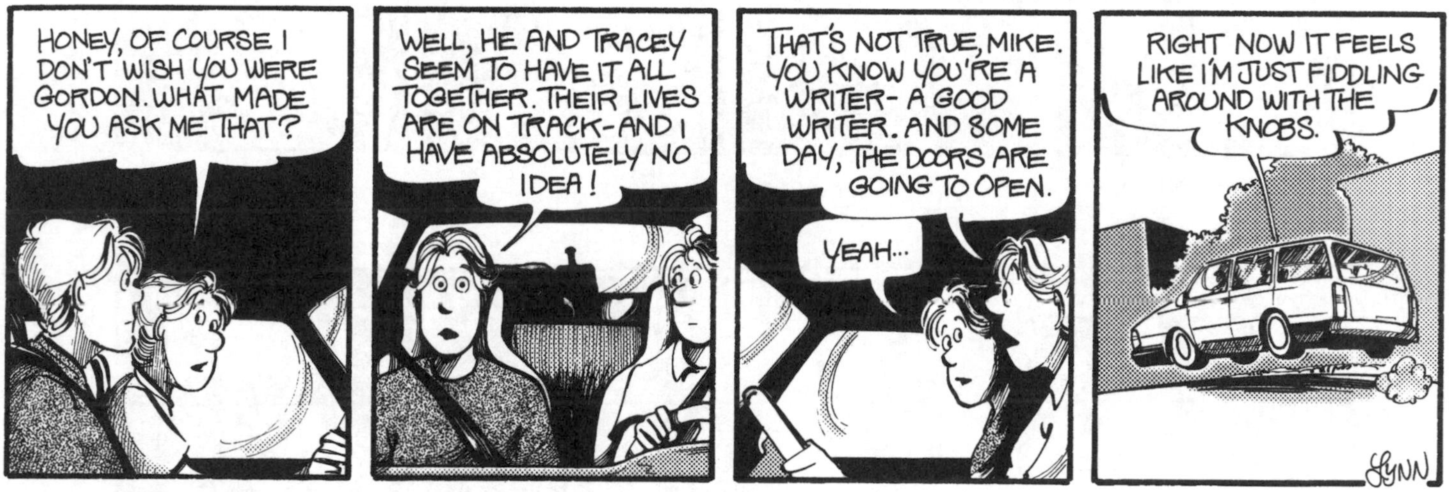
HONEY, OF COURSE I DON'T WISH YOU WERE GORDON. WHAT MADE YOU ASK ME THAT?
WELL, HE AND TRACEY SEEM TO HAVE IT ALL TOGETHER. THEIR LIVES ARE ON TRACK - AND I HAVE ABSOLUTELY NO IDEA!
THAT'S NOT TRUE, MIKE. YOU KNOW YOU'RE A WRITER - A GOOD WRITER. AND SOME DAY, THE DOORS ARE GOING TO OPEN.
YEAH...
RIGHT NOW IT FEELS LIKE I'M JUST FIDDLING AROUND WITH THE KNOBS.
LYNN

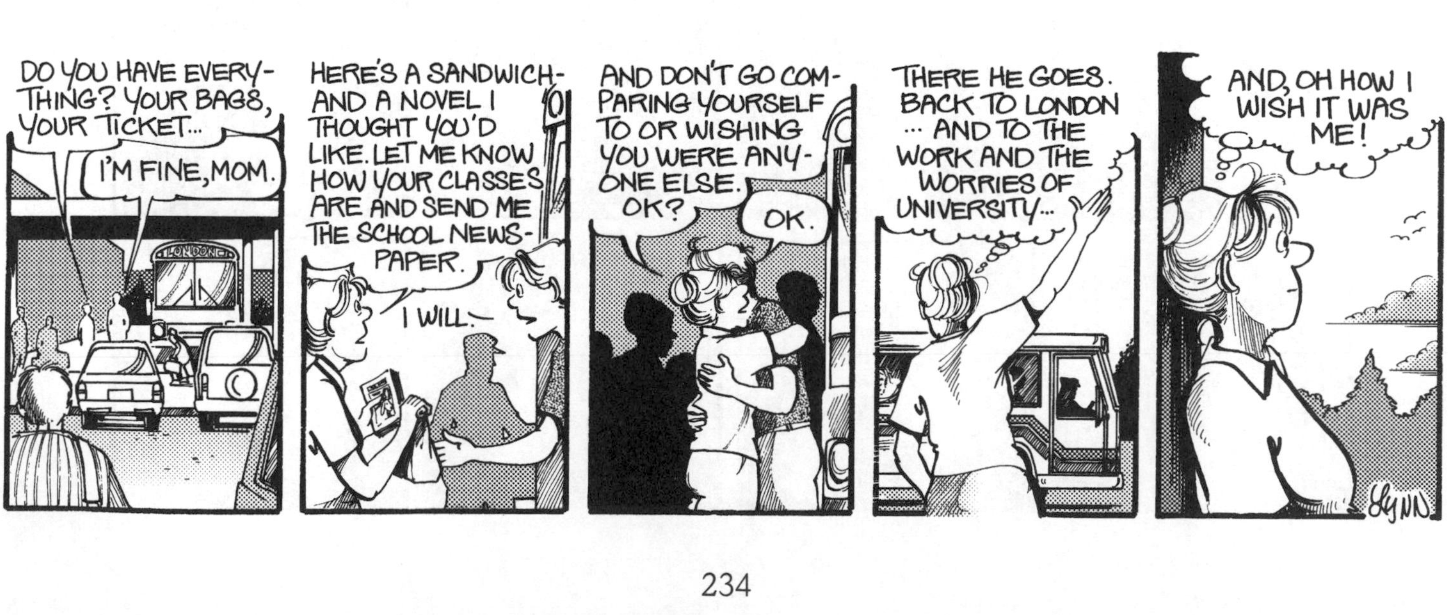
DO YOU HAVE EVERYTHING? YOUR BAGS, YOUR TICKET...
I'M FINE, MOM.
LONDON
HERE'S A SANDWICH - AND A NOVEL I THOUGHT YOU'D LIKE. LET ME KNOW HOW YOUR CLASSES ARE AND SEND ME THE SCHOOL NEWSPAPER.
I WILL.
AND DON'T GO COMPARING YOURSELF TO OR WISHING YOU WERE ANYONE ELSE. OK?
OK.
THERE HE GOES. BACK TO LONDON ... AND TO THE WORK AND THE WORRIES OF UNIVERSITY...
AND, OH HOW I WISH IT WAS ME!
LYNN

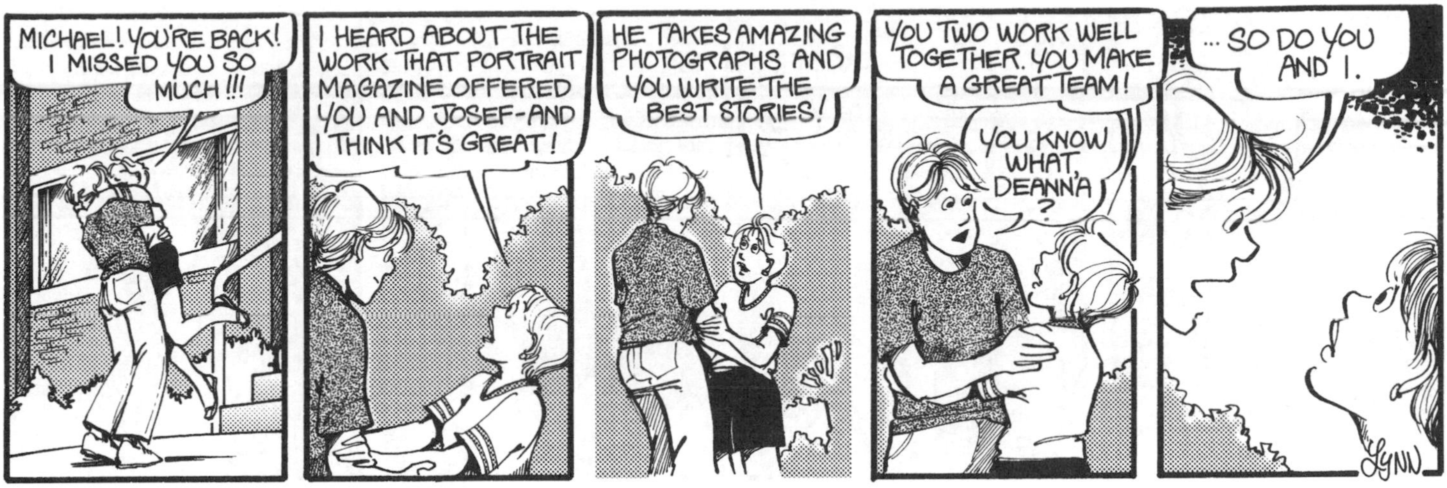
MICHAEL! YOU'RE BACK! I MISSED YOU SO MUCH!!!
I HEARD ABOUT THE WORK THAT PORTRAIT MAGAZINE OFFERED YOU AND JOSEF-AND I THINK IT'S GREAT!
HE TAKES AMAZING PHOTOGRAPHS AND YOU WRITE THE BEST STORIES!
YOU TWO WORK WELL TOGETHER. YOU MAKE A GREAT TEAM!
YOU KNOW WHAT, DEANNA?
... SO DO YOU AND I.
LYNN

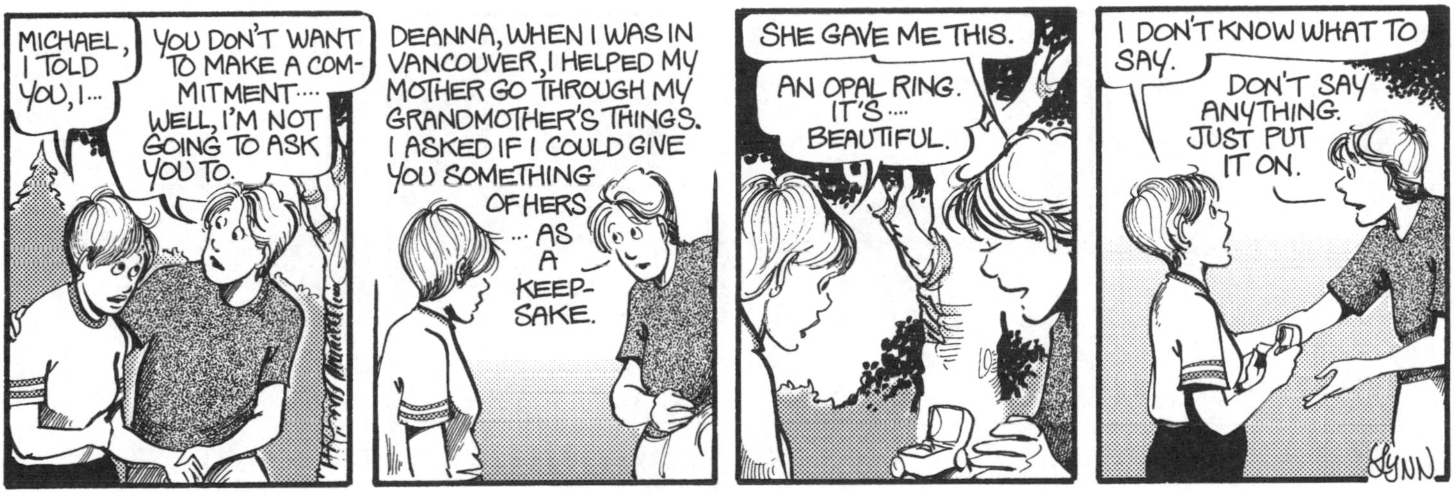
MICHAEL, I TOLD YOU, I...
YOU DON'T WANT TO MAKE A COMMITMENT.... WELL, I'M NOT GOING TO ASK YOU TO.
DEANNA, WHEN I WAS IN VANCOUVER, I HELPED MY MOTHER GO THROUGH MY GRANDMOTHER'S THINGS. I ASKED IF I COULD GIVE YOU SOMETHING OF HERS ... AS A KEEPSAKE.
SHE GAVE ME THIS.
AN OPAL RING. IT'S .... BEAUTIFUL.
I DON'T KNOW WHAT TO SAY.
DON'T SAY ANYTHING. JUST PUT IT ON.
LYNN

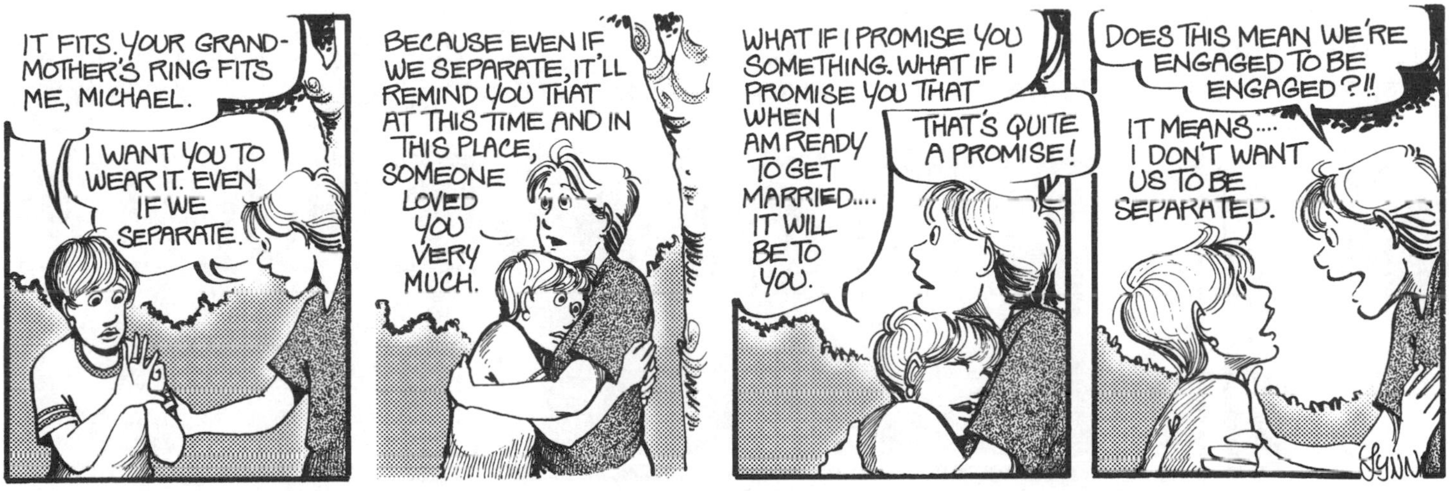
IT FITS. YOUR GRANDMOTHER'S RING FITS ME, MICHAEL.
I WANT YOU TO WEAR IT. EVEN IF WE SEPARATE.
BECAUSE EVEN IF WE SEPARATE, IT'LL REMIND YOU THAT AT THIS TIME AND IN THIS PLACE, SOMEONE LOVED YOU VERY MUCH.
WHAT IF I PROMISE YOU SOMETHING. WHAT IF I PROMISE YOU THAT WHEN I AM READY TO GET MARRIED.... IT WILL BE TO YOU.
THAT'S QUITE A PROMISE!
DOES THIS MEAN WE'RE ENGAGED TO BE ENGAGED?!!
IT MEANS.... I DON'T WANT US TO BE SEPARATED.
LYNN

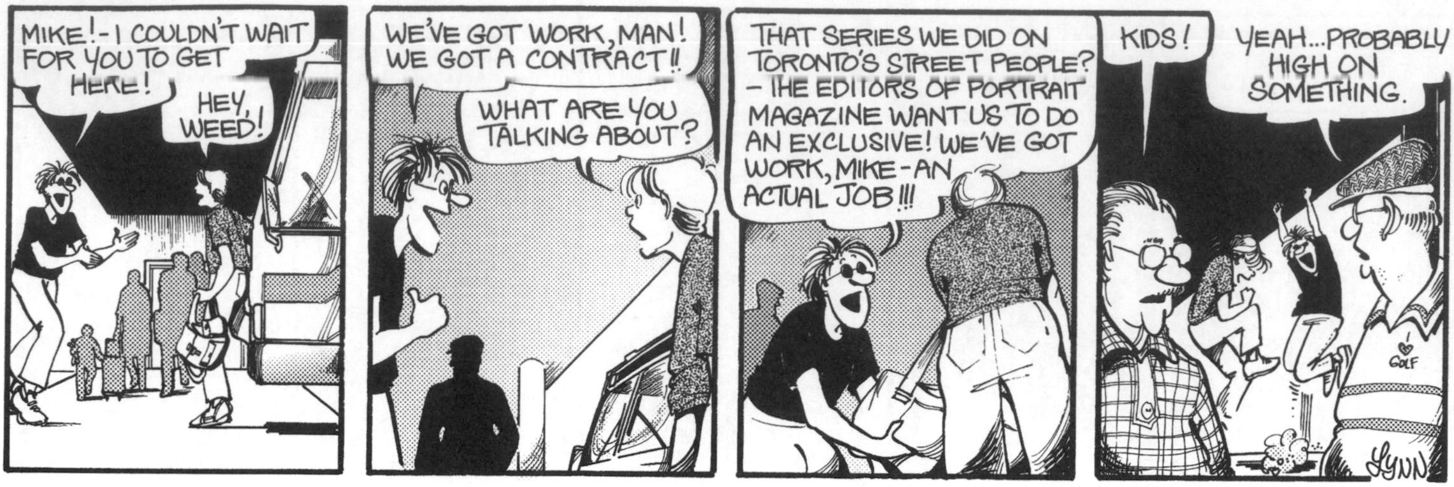
MIKE! - I COULDN'T WAIT FOR YOU TO GET HERE!
HEY, WEED!
WE'VE GOT WORK, MAN! WE GOT A CONTRACT!!
WHAT ARE YOU TALKING ABOUT?
THAT SERIES WE DID ON TORONTO'S STREET PEOPLE? - THE EDITORS OF PORTRAIT MAGAZINE WANT US TO DO AN EXCLUSIVE! WE'VE GOT WORK, MIKE - AN ACTUAL JOB!!!
KIDS!
YEAH...PROBABLY HIGH ON SOMETHING.
LYNN

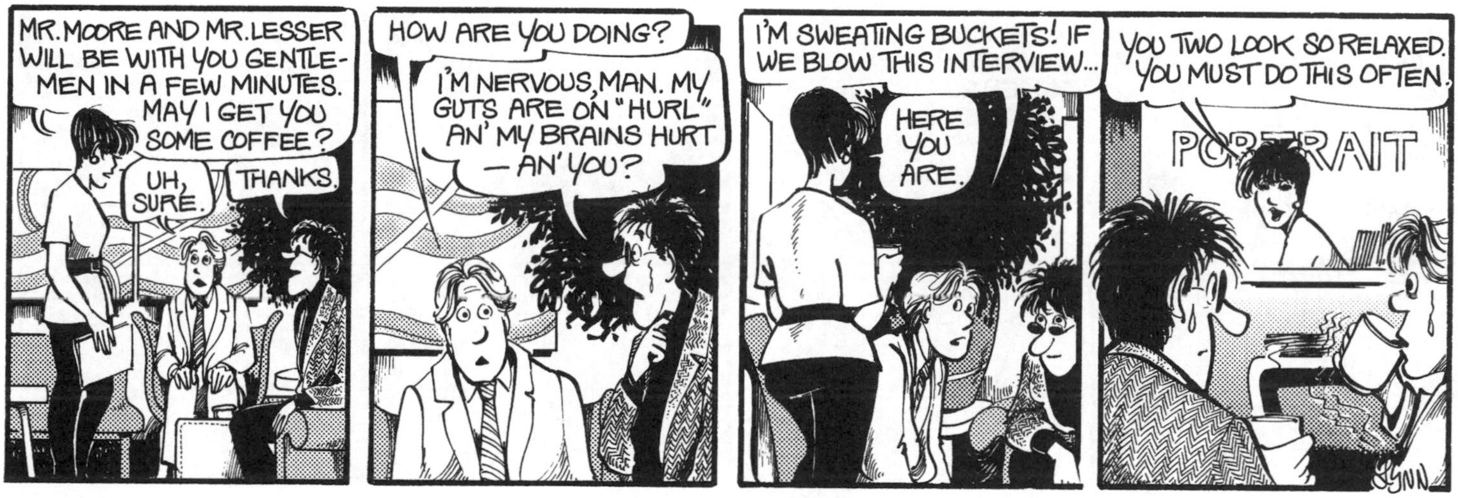
MR. MOORE AND MR. LESSER WILL BE WITH YOU GENTLEMEN IN A FEW MINUTES. MAY I GET YOU SOME COFFEE?
UH, SURE.
THANKS.
HOW ARE YOU DOING?
I'M NERVOUS, MAN. MY GUTS ARE ON "HURL" AN' MY BRAINS HURT — AN' YOU?
I'M SWEATING BUCKETS! IF WE BLOW THIS INTERVIEW...
HERE YOU ARE.
YOU TWO LOOK SO RELAXED. YOU MUST DO THIS OFTEN.
LYNN

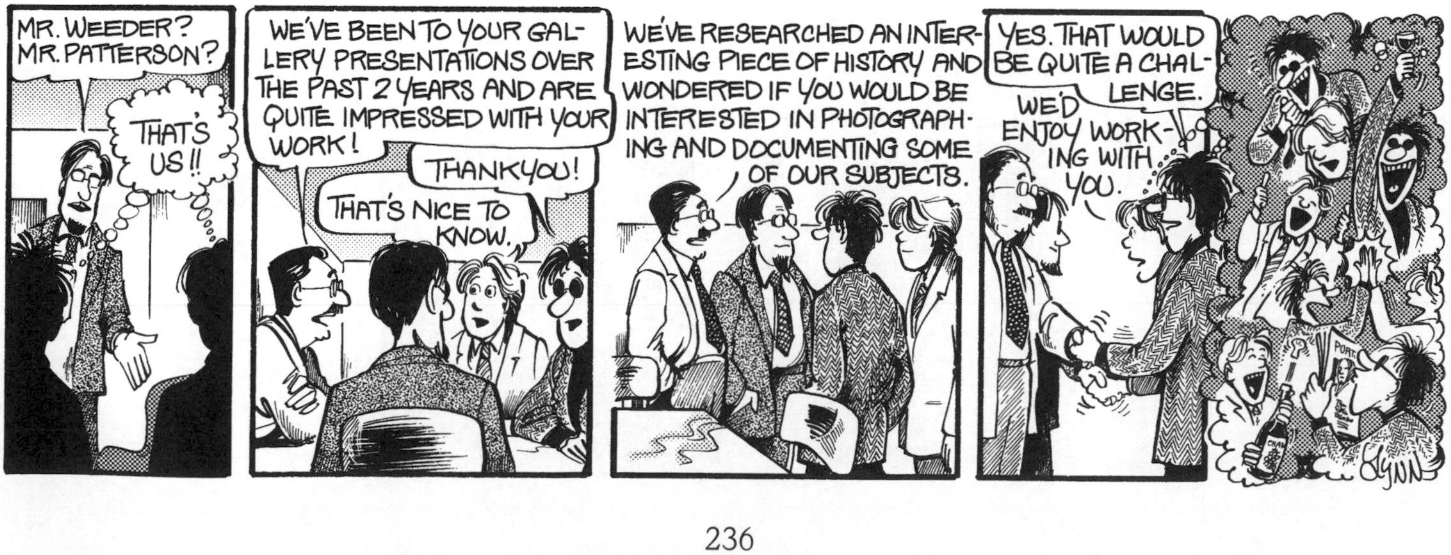
MR. WEEDER? MR. PATTERSON?
THAT'S US!!
WE'VE BEEN TO YOUR GALLERY PRESENTATIONS OVER THE PAST 2 YEARS AND ARE QUITE IMPRESSED WITH YOUR WORK!
THANKYOU!
THAT'S NICE TO KNOW.
WE'VE RESEARCHED AN INTERESTING PIECE OF HISTORY AND WONDERED IF YOU WOULD BE INTERESTED IN PHOTOGRAPHING AND DOCUMENTING SOME OF OUR SUBJECTS.
YES. THAT WOULD BE QUITE A CHALLENGE.
WE'D ENJOY WORKING WITH YOU.
LYNN

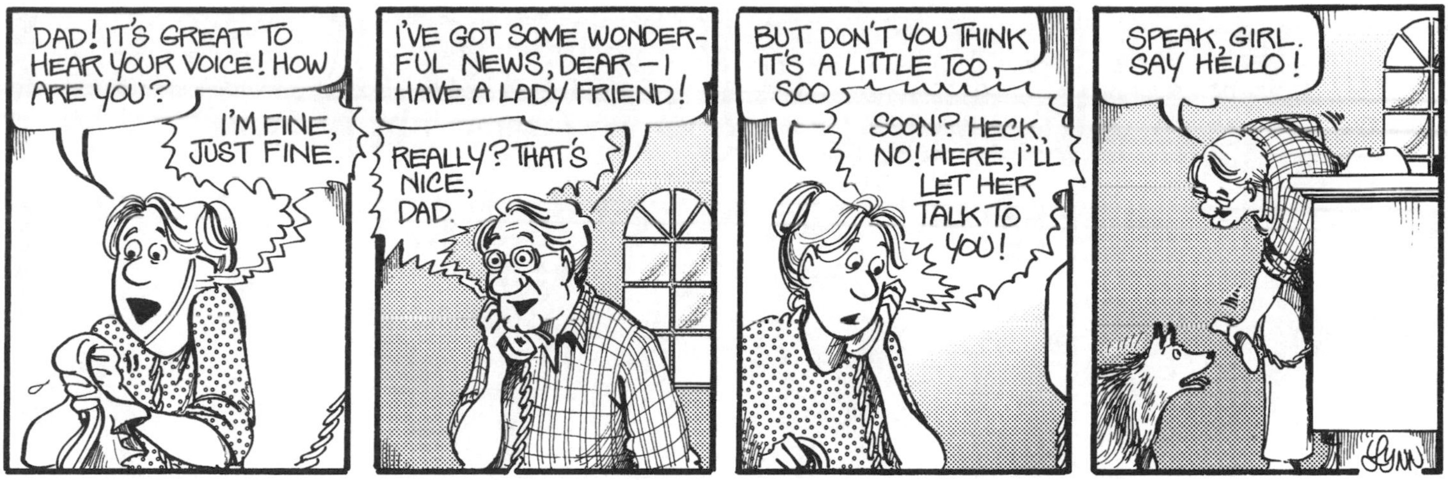
DAD! IT'S GREAT TO HEAR YOUR VOICE! HOW ARE YOU?
I'M FINE, JUST FINE.
I'VE GOT SOME WONDERFUL NEWS, DEAR — I HAVE A LADY FRIEND!
REALLY? THAT'S NICE, DAD.
BUT DON'T YOU THINK IT'S A LITTLE TOO, SOO
SOON? HECK NO! HERE, I'LL LET HER TALK TO YOU!
SPEAK, GIRL. SAY HELLO!
LYNN

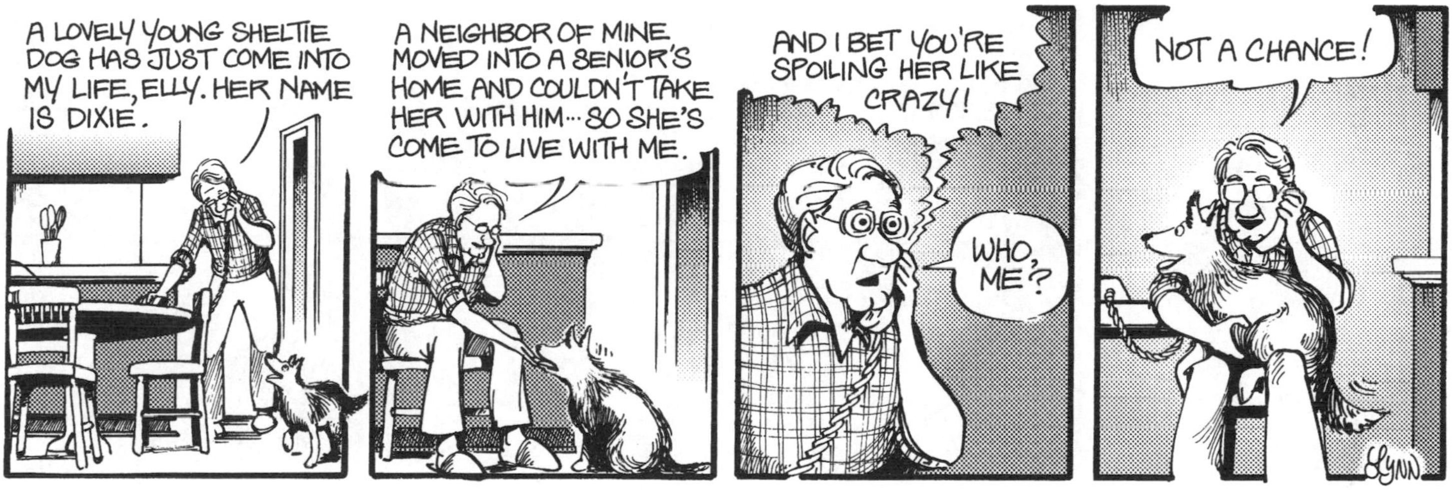
A LOVELY YOUNG SHELTIE DOG HAS JUST COME INTO MY LIFE, ELLY. HER NAME IS DIXIE.
A NEIGHBOR OF MINE MOVED INTO A SENIOR'S HOME AND COULDN'T TAKE HER WITH HIM... SO SHE'S COME TO LIVE WITH ME.
AND I BET YOU'RE SPOILING HER LIKE CRAZY!
WHO, ME?
NOT A CHANCE!
LYNN

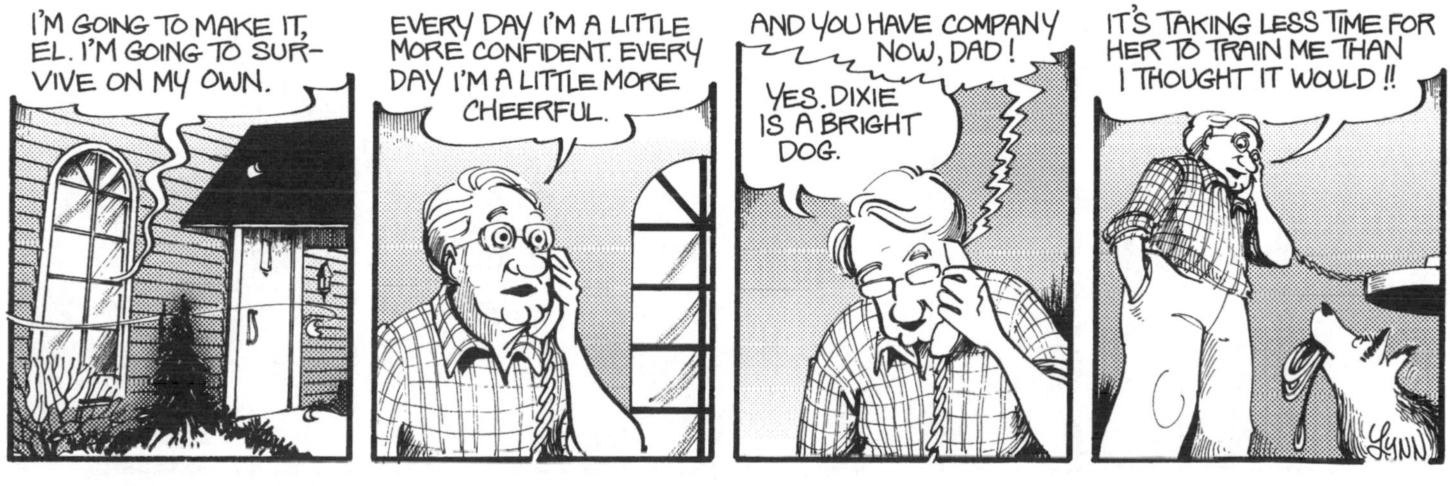
I'M GOING TO MAKE IT, EL. I'M GOING TO SURVIVE ON MY OWN.
EVERY DAY I'M A LITTLE MORE CONFIDENT. EVERY DAY I'M A LITTLE MORE CHEERFUL.
AND YOU HAVE COMPANY NOW, DAD!
YES. DIXIE IS A BRIGHT DOG.
IT'S TAKING LESS TIME FOR HER TO TRAIN ME THAN I THOUGHT IT WOULD!!
LYNN

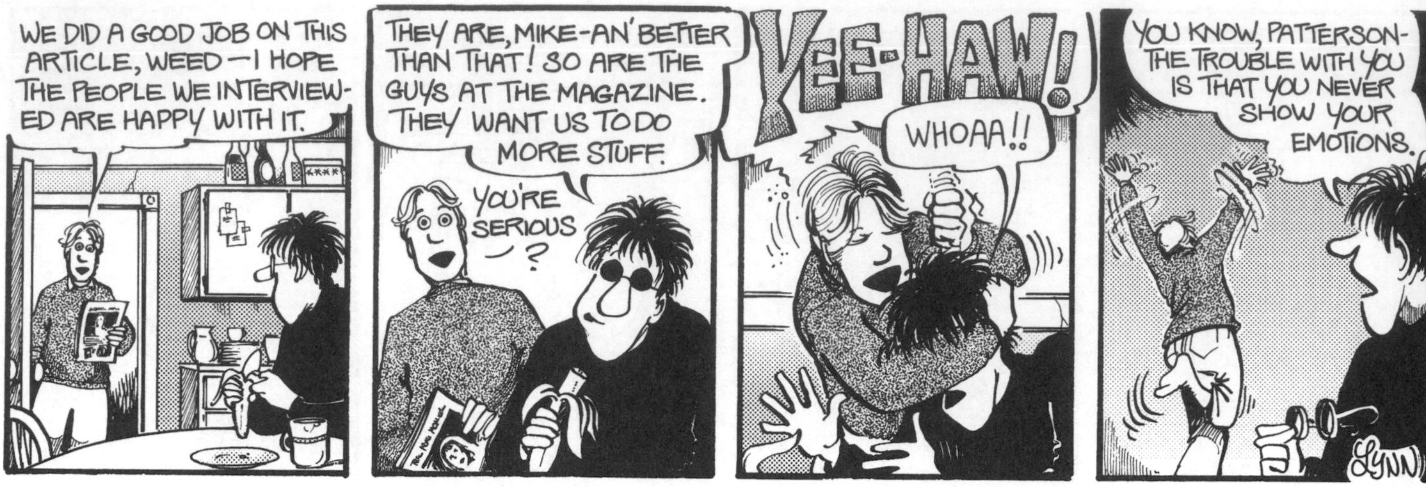

WE DID A GOOD JOB ON THIS ARTICLE, WEED—I HOPE THE PEOPLE WE INTERVIEWED ARE HAPPY WITH IT.
THEY ARE, MIKE-AN' BETTER THAN THAT! SO ARE THE GUYS AT THE MAGAZINE. THEY WANT US TO DO MORE STUFF.
YOU'RE SERIOUS?
YEE-HAW!
WHOAA!!
YOU KNOW, PATTERSON-THE TROUBLE WITH YOU IS THAT YOU NEVER SHOW YOUR EMOTIONS.
LYNN

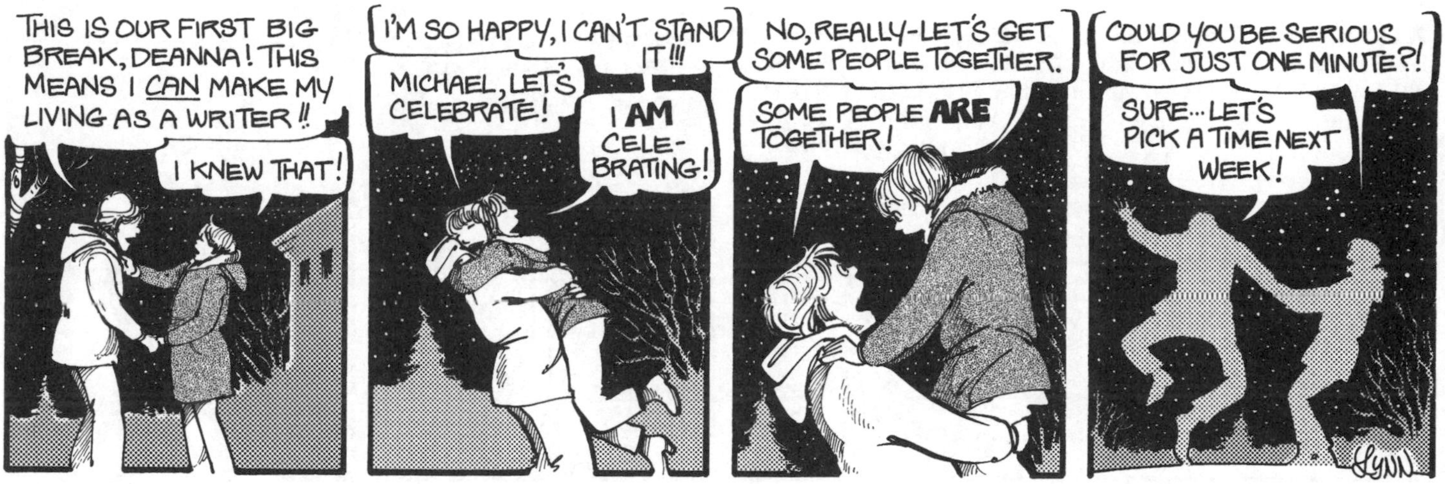

THIS IS OUR FIRST BIG BREAK, DEANNA! THIS MEANS I CAN MAKE MY LIVING AS A WRITER!!
I KNEW THAT!
I'M SO HAPPY, I CAN'T STAND IT!!!
MICHAEL, LET'S CELEBRATE!
I AM CELEBRATING!
NO, REALLY-LET'S GET SOME PEOPLE TOGETHER.
SOME PEOPLE ARE TOGETHER!
COULD YOU BE SERIOUS FOR JUST ONE MINUTE?!
SURE... LET'S PICK A TIME NEXT WEEK!
LYNN

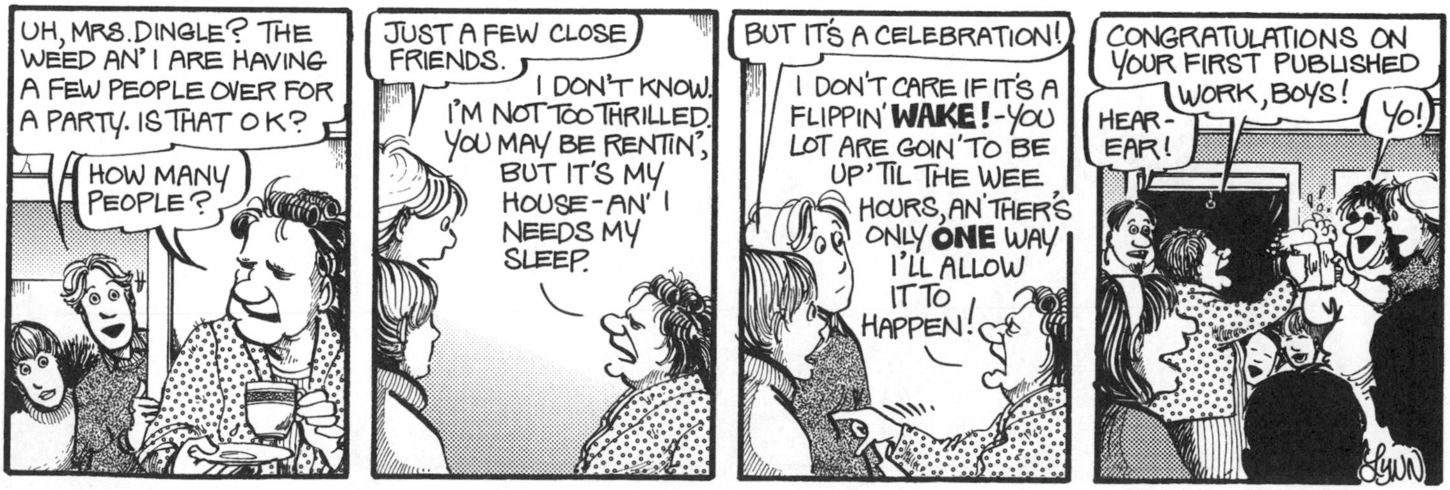

UH, MRS. DINGLE? THE WEED AN' I ARE HAVING A FEW PEOPLE OVER FOR A PARTY. IS THAT OK?
HOW MANY PEOPLE?
JUST A FEW CLOSE FRIENDS.
I DON'T KNOW. I'M NOT TOO THRILLED. YOU MAY BE RENTIN', BUT IT'S MY HOUSE-AN' I NEEDS MY SLEEP.
BUT IT'S A CELEBRATION!
I DON'T CARE IF IT'S A FLIPPIN' WAKE!-YOU LOT ARE GOIN' TO BE UP 'TIL THE WEE HOURS, AN' THER'S ONLY ONE WAY I'LL ALLOW IT TO HAPPEN!
CONGRATULATIONS ON YOUR FIRST PUBLISHED WORK, BOYS!
HEAR-EAR!
YO!
LYNN

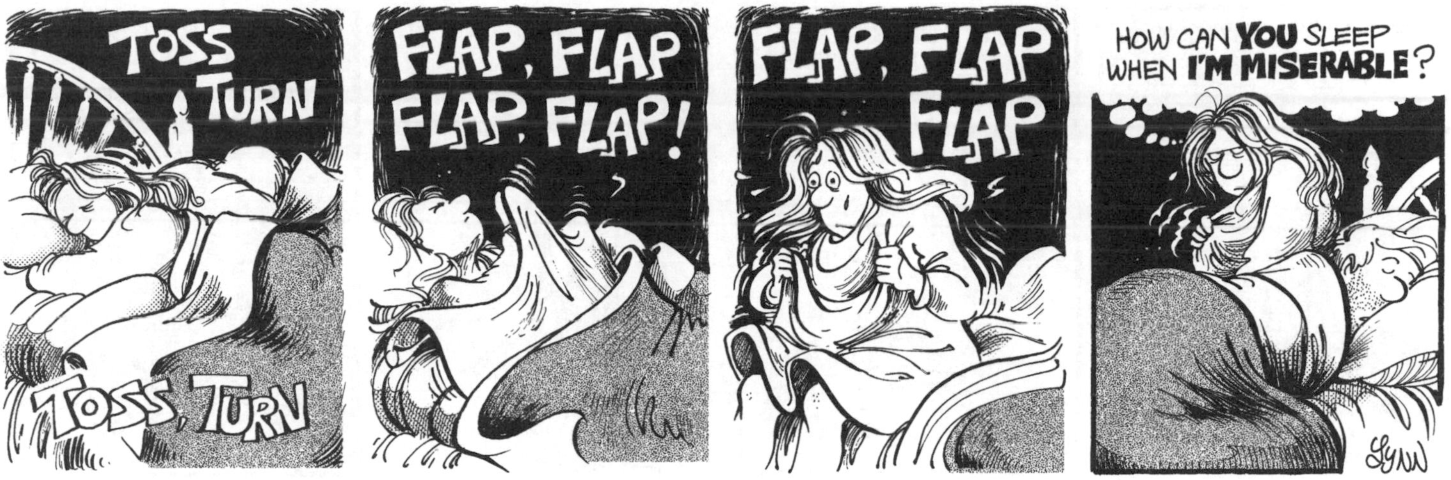
TOSS TURN
TOSS, TURN
FLAP, FLAP FLAP, FLAP!
FLAP, FLAP FLAP
HOW CAN YOU SLEEP WHEN I'M MISERABLE?
LYNN

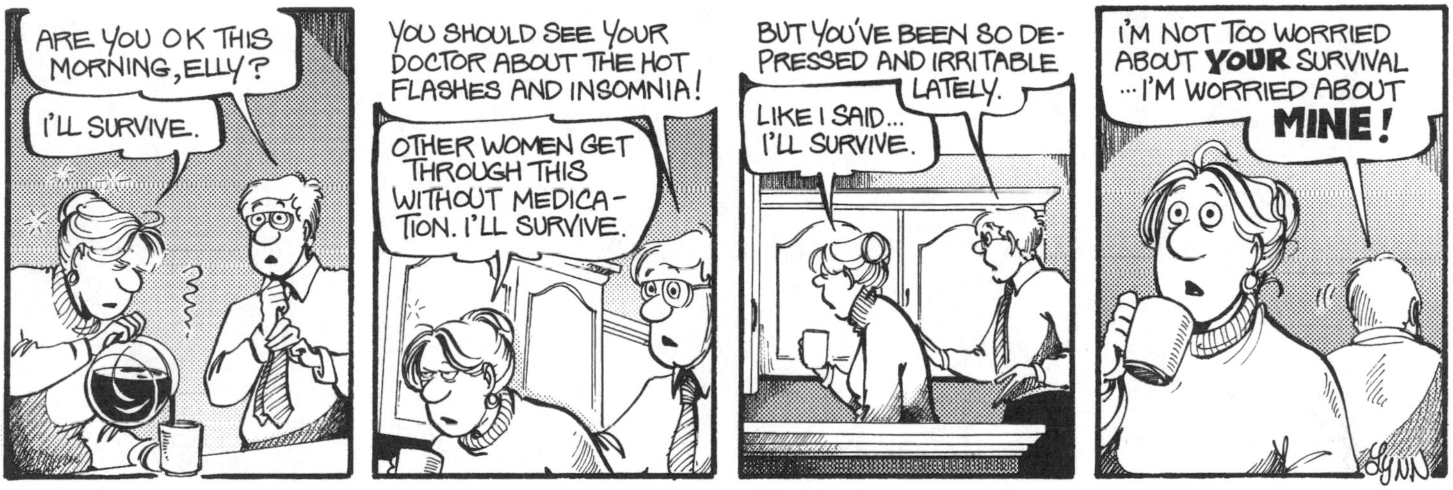
ARE YOU OK THIS MORNING, ELLY?
I'LL SURVIVE.
YOU SHOULD SEE YOUR DOCTOR ABOUT THE HOT FLASHES AND INSOMNIA!
OTHER WOMEN GET THROUGH THIS WITHOUT MEDICA-TION. I'LL SURVIVE.
BUT YOU'VE BEEN SO DE-PRESSED AND IRRITABLE LATELY.
LIKE I SAID... I'LL SURVIVE.
I'M NOT TOO WORRIED ABOUT YOUR SURVIVAL ...I'M WORRIED ABOUT MINE!
LYNN

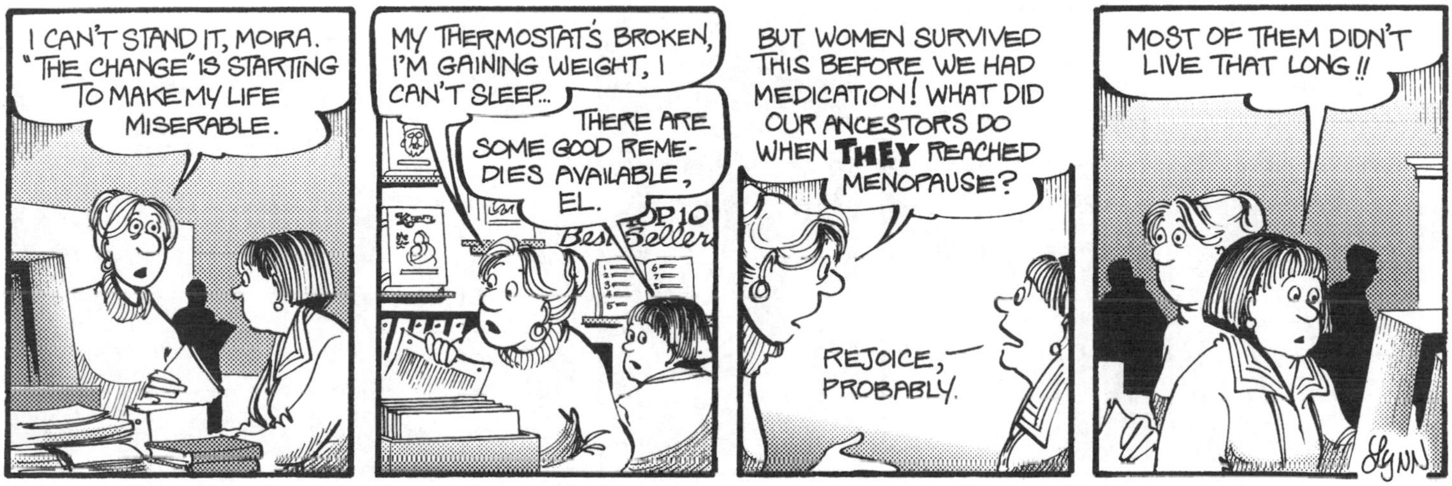
I CAN'T STAND IT, MOIRA. "THE CHANGE" IS STARTING TO MAKE MY LIFE MISERABLE.
MY THERMOSTAT'S BROKEN, I'M GAINING WEIGHT, I CAN'T SLEEP...
THERE ARE SOME GOOD REME-DIES AVAILABLE, EL.
TOP 10 Best Sellers
BUT WOMEN SURVIVED THIS BEFORE WE HAD MEDICATION! WHAT DID OUR ANCESTORS DO WHEN THEY REACHED MENOPAUSE?
REJOICE, PROBABLY.
MOST OF THEM DIDN'T LIVE THAT LONG!!
LYNN

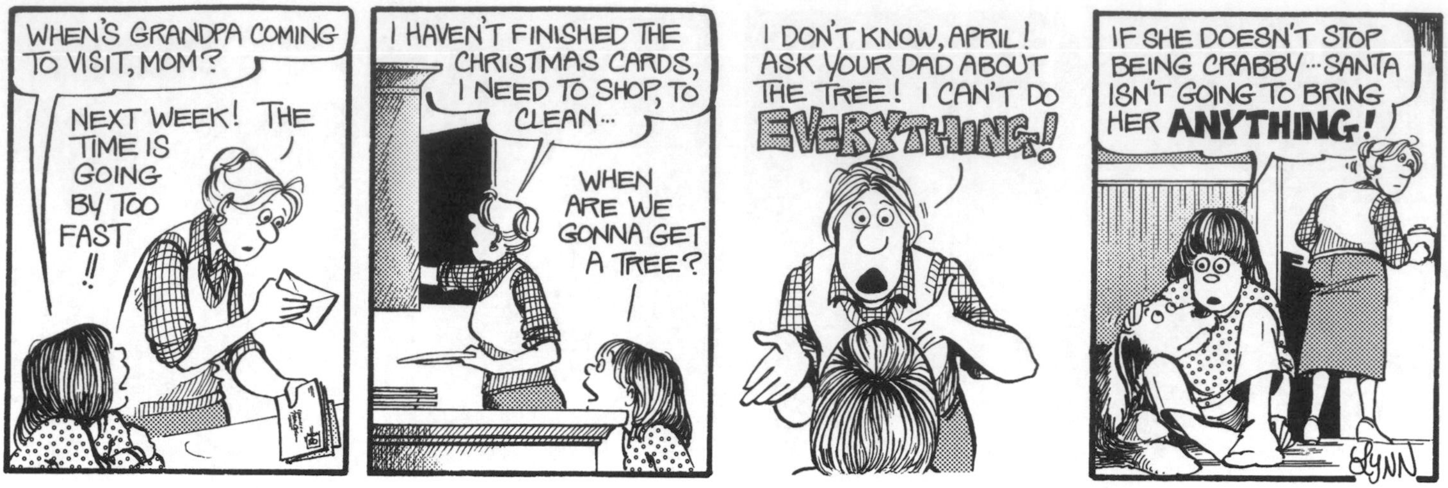
WHEN'S GRANDPA COMING TO VISIT, MOM?
NEXT WEEK! THE TIME IS GOING BY TOO FAST!!
I HAVEN'T FINISHED THE CHRISTMAS CARDS, I NEED TO SHOP, TO CLEAN...
WHEN ARE WE GONNA GET A TREE?
I DON'T KNOW, APRIL! ASK YOUR DAD ABOUT THE TREE! I CAN'T DO EVERYTHING!
IF SHE DOESN'T STOP BEING CRABBY...SANTA ISN'T GOING TO BRING HER ANYTHING!
LYNN

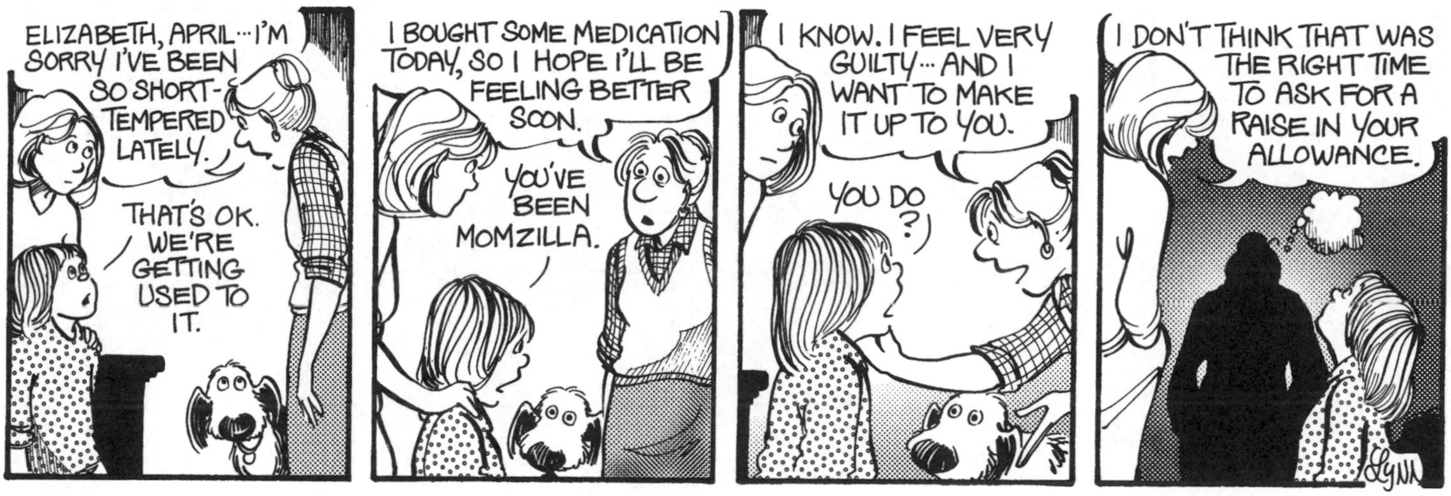
ELIZABETH, APRIL...I'M SORRY I'VE BEEN SO SHORT-TEMPERED LATELY.
THAT'S OK. WE'RE GETTING USED TO IT.
I BOUGHT SOME MEDICATION TODAY, SO I HOPE I'LL BE FEELING BETTER SOON.
YOU'VE BEEN MOMZILLA.
I KNOW. I FEEL VERY GUILTY...AND I WANT TO MAKE IT UP TO YOU.
YOU DO?
I DON'T THINK THAT WAS THE RIGHT TIME TO ASK FOR A RAISE IN YOUR ALLOWANCE.
LYNN

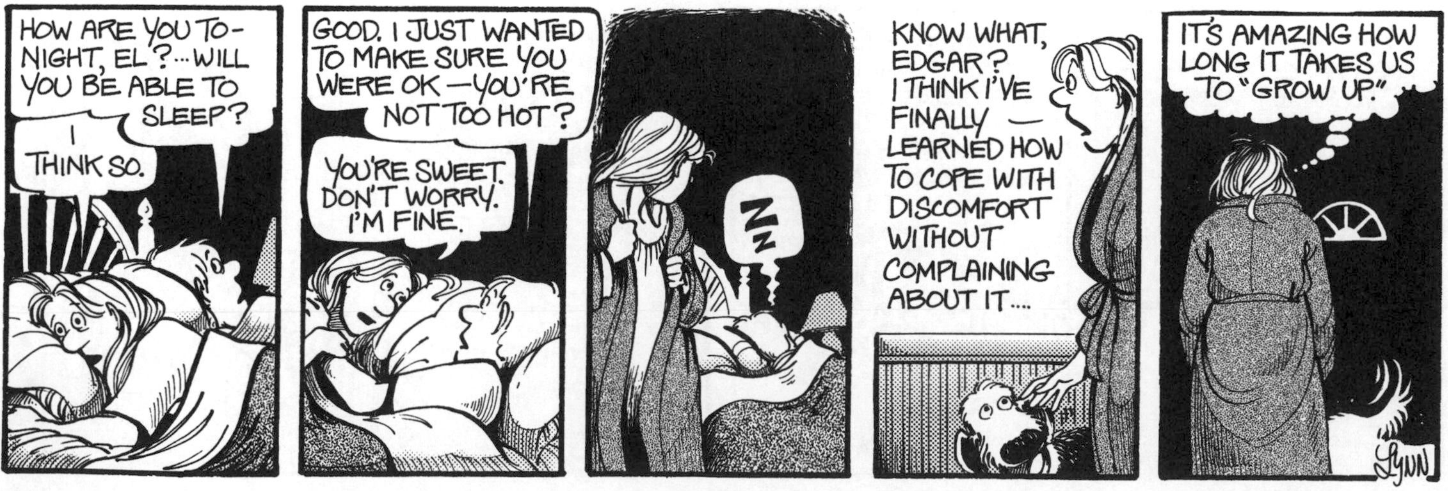
HOW ARE YOU TO-NIGHT, EL?...WILL YOU BE ABLE TO SLEEP?
I THINK SO.
GOOD. I JUST WANTED TO MAKE SURE YOU WERE OK—YOU'RE NOT TOO HOT?
YOU'RE SWEET. DON'T WORRY. I'M FINE.
ZZ
KNOW WHAT, EDGAR? I THINK I'VE FINALLY—LEARNED HOW TO COPE WITH DISCOMFORT WITHOUT COMPLAINING ABOUT IT....
IT'S AMAZING HOW LONG IT TAKES US TO "GROW UP."
LYNN

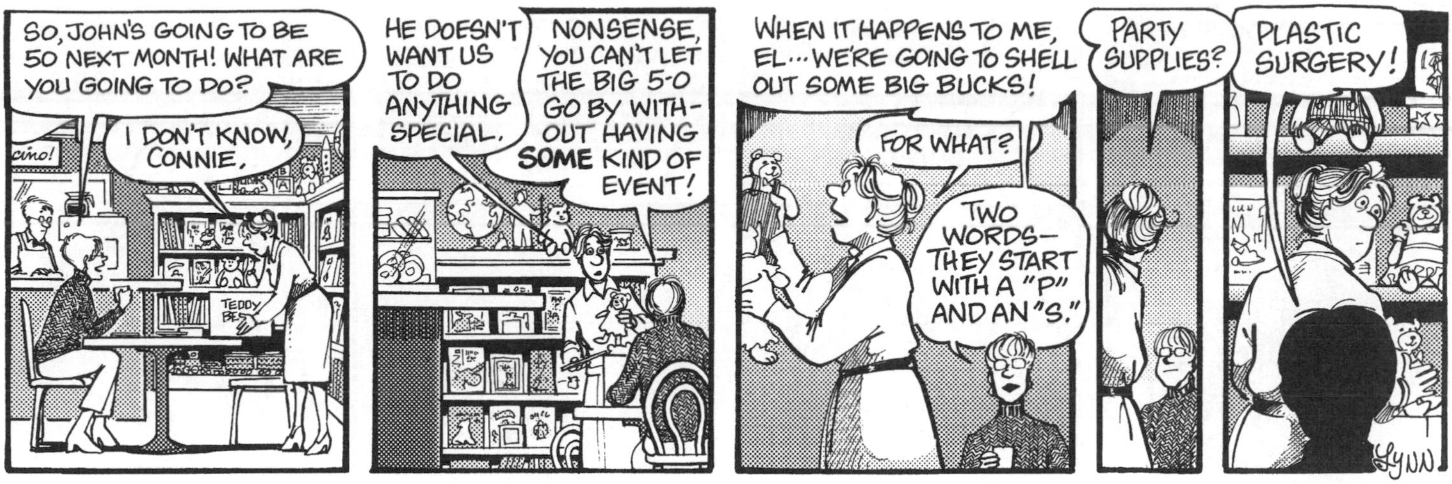
SO, JOHN'S GOING TO BE 50 NEXT MONTH! WHAT ARE YOU GOING TO DO?
I DON'T KNOW, CONNIE.
HE DOESN'T WANT US TO DO ANYTHING SPECIAL.
NONSENSE, YOU CAN'T LET THE BIG 5-0 GO BY WITHOUT HAVING SOME KIND OF EVENT!
WHEN IT HAPPENS TO ME, EL... WE'RE GOING TO SHELL OUT SOME BIG BUCKS!
FOR WHAT?
TWO WORDS– THEY START WITH A "P" AND AN "S."
PARTY SUPPLIES?
PLASTIC SURGERY!

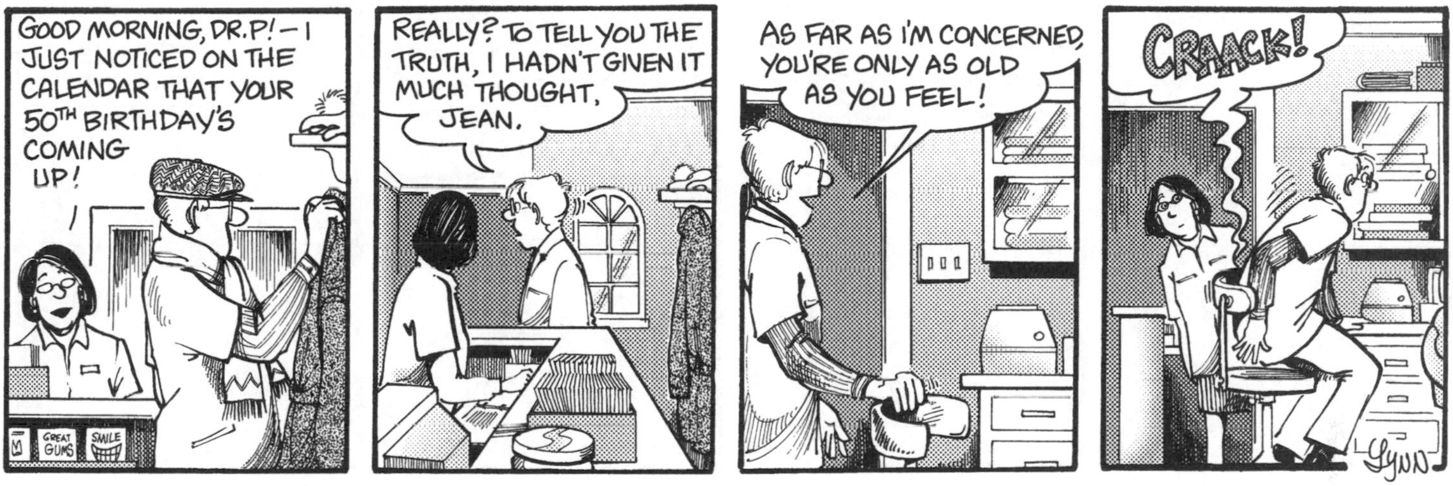
GOOD MORNING, DR. P! – I JUST NOTICED ON THE CALENDAR THAT YOUR 50TH BIRTHDAY'S COMING UP!
REALLY? TO TELL YOU THE TRUTH, I HADN'T GIVEN IT MUCH THOUGHT, JEAN.
AS FAR AS I'M CONCERNED, YOU'RE ONLY AS OLD AS YOU FEEL!
CRAACK!

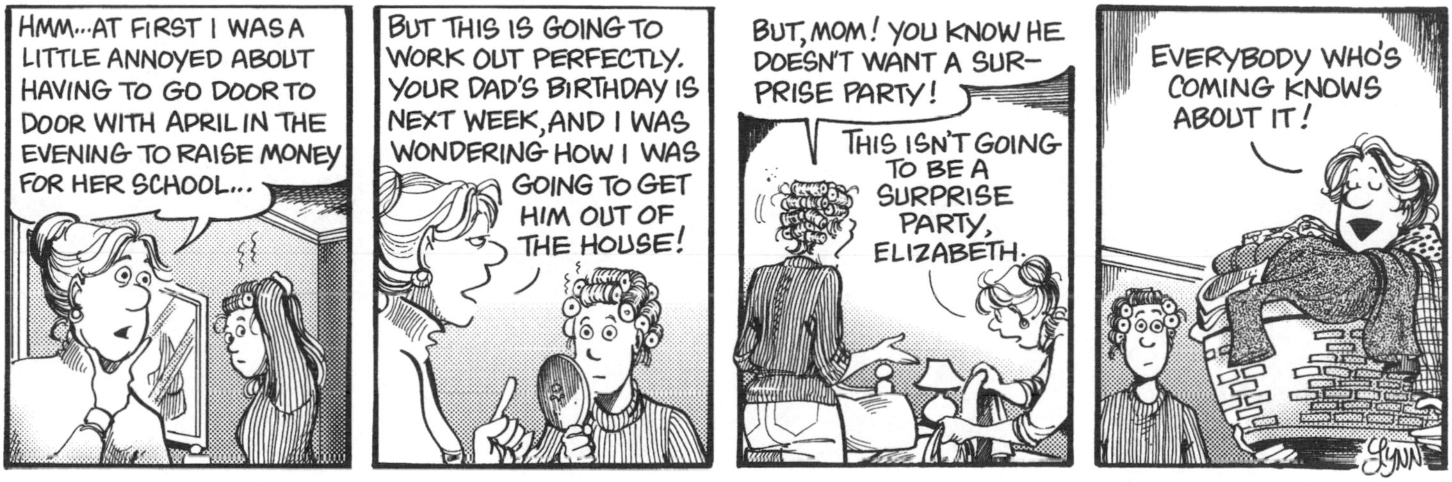
HMM... AT FIRST I WAS A LITTLE ANNOYED ABOUT HAVING TO GO DOOR TO DOOR WITH APRIL IN THE EVENING TO RAISE MONEY FOR HER SCHOOL...
BUT THIS IS GOING TO WORK OUT PERFECTLY. YOUR DAD'S BIRTHDAY IS NEXT WEEK, AND I WAS WONDERING HOW I WAS GOING TO GET HIM OUT OF THE HOUSE!
BUT, MOM! YOU KNOW HE DOESN'T WANT A SURPRISE PARTY!
THIS ISN'T GOING TO BE A SURPRISE PARTY, ELIZABETH.
EVERYBODY WHO'S COMING KNOWS ABOUT IT!

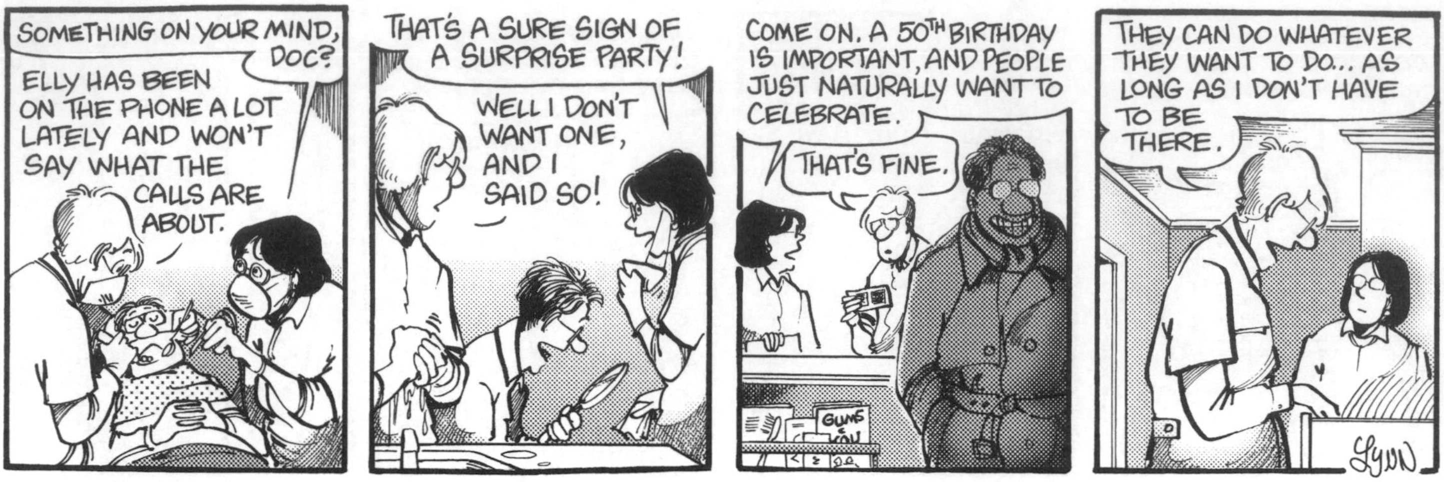
SOMETHING ON YOUR MIND, DOC?
ELLY HAS BEEN ON THE PHONE A LOT LATELY AND WON'T SAY WHAT THE CALLS ARE ABOUT.
THAT'S A SURE SIGN OF A SURPRISE PARTY!
WELL I DON'T WANT ONE, AND I SAID SO!
COME ON. A 50TH BIRTHDAY IS IMPORTANT, AND PEOPLE JUST NATURALLY WANT TO CELEBRATE.
THAT'S FINE.
THEY CAN DO WHATEVER THEY WANT TO DO... AS LONG AS I DON'T HAVE TO BE THERE.
LYNN

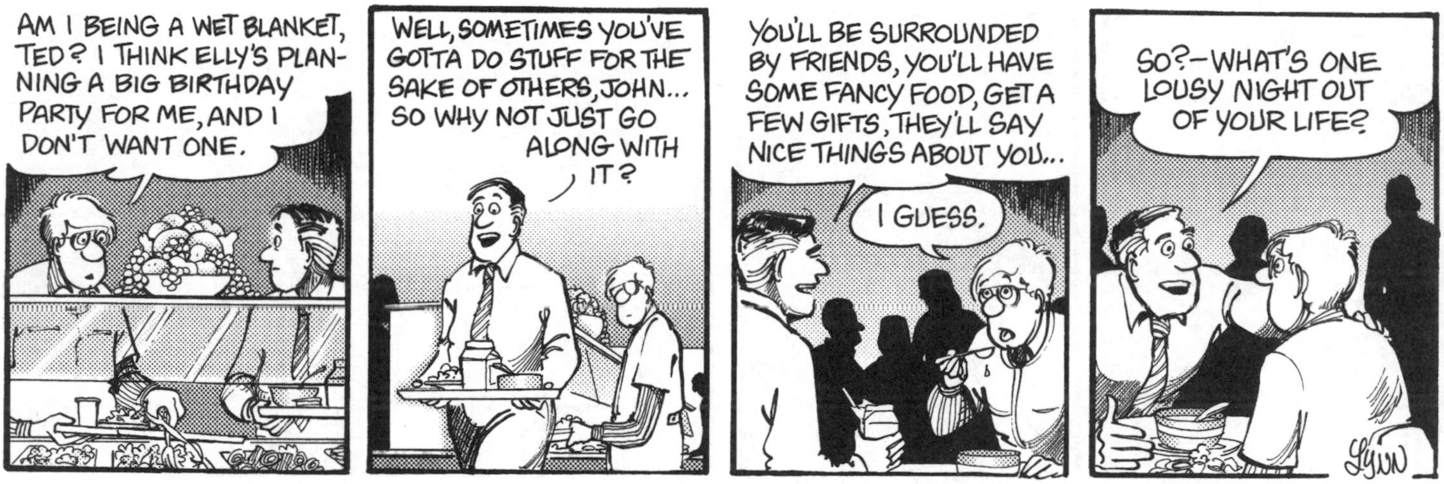
AM I BEING A WET BLANKET, TED? I THINK ELLY'S PLANNING A BIG BIRTHDAY PARTY FOR ME, AND I DON'T WANT ONE.
WELL, SOMETIMES YOU'VE GOTTA DO STUFF FOR THE SAKE OF OTHERS, JOHN... SO WHY NOT JUST GO ALONG WITH IT?
YOU'LL BE SURROUNDED BY FRIENDS, YOU'LL HAVE SOME FANCY FOOD, GET A FEW GIFTS, THEY'LL SAY NICE THINGS ABOUT YOU...
I GUESS.
SO?–WHAT'S ONE LOUSY NIGHT OUT OF YOUR LIFE?
LYNN

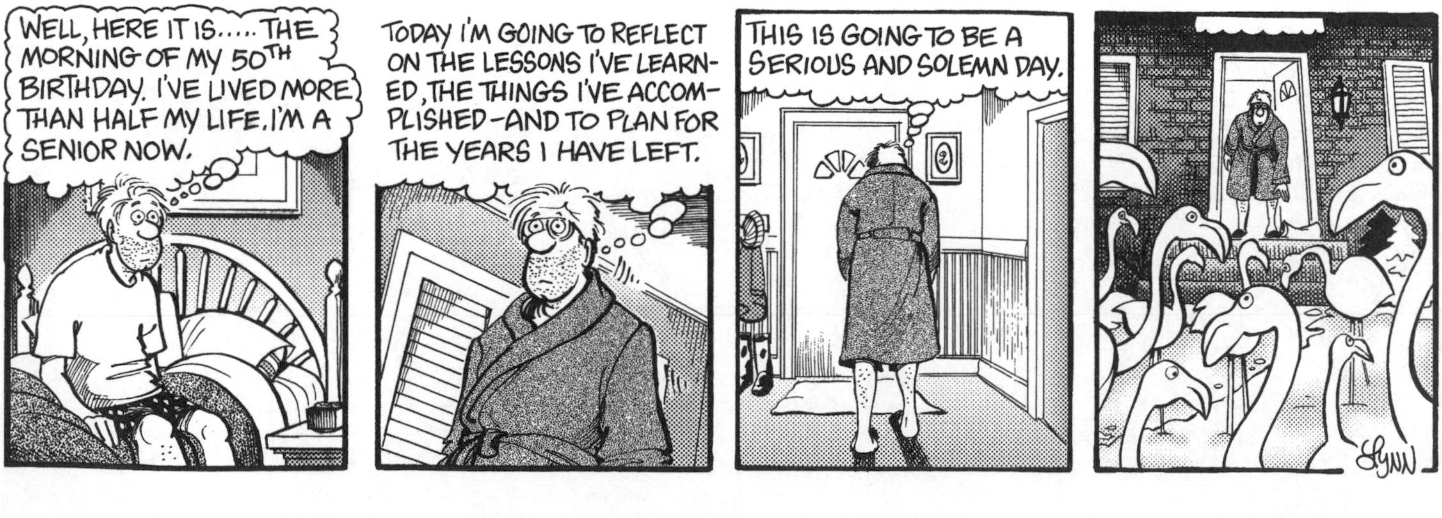
WELL, HERE IT IS..... THE MORNING OF MY 50TH BIRTHDAY. I'VE LIVED MORE THAN HALF MY LIFE. I'M A SENIOR NOW.
TODAY I'M GOING TO REFLECT ON THE LESSONS I'VE LEARNED, THE THINGS I'VE ACCOMPLISHED–AND TO PLAN FOR THE YEARS I HAVE LEFT.
THIS IS GOING TO BE A SERIOUS AND SOLEMN DAY.
LYNN

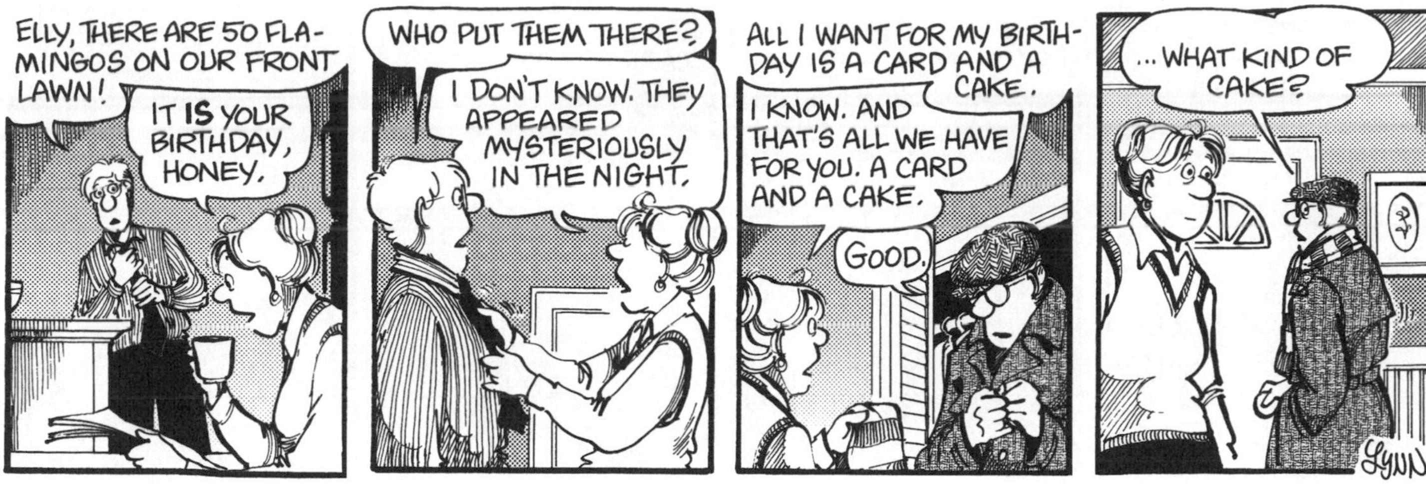
ELLY, THERE ARE 50 FLAMINGOS ON OUR FRONT LAWN!
IT IS YOUR BIRTHDAY, HONEY.
WHO PUT THEM THERE?
I DON'T KNOW. THEY APPEARED MYSTERIOUSLY IN THE NIGHT.
ALL I WANT FOR MY BIRTHDAY IS A CARD AND A CAKE.
I KNOW. AND THAT'S ALL WE HAVE FOR YOU. A CARD AND A CAKE.
GOOD.
... WHAT KIND OF CAKE?
LYNN

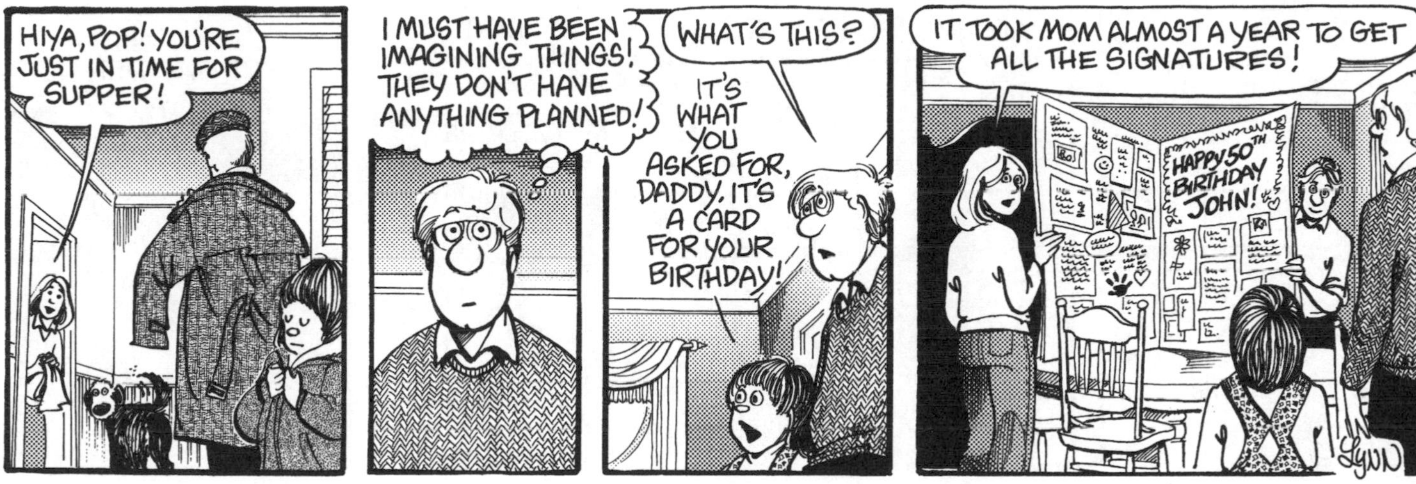
HIYA, POP! YOU'RE JUST IN TIME FOR SUPPER!
I MUST HAVE BEEN IMAGINING THINGS! THEY DON'T HAVE ANYTHING PLANNED!
WHAT'S THIS?
IT'S WHAT YOU ASKED FOR, DADDY. IT'S A CARD FOR YOUR BIRTHDAY!
IT TOOK MOM ALMOST A YEAR TO GET ALL THE SIGNATURES!
HAPPY 50TH BIRTHDAY JOHN!
LYNN

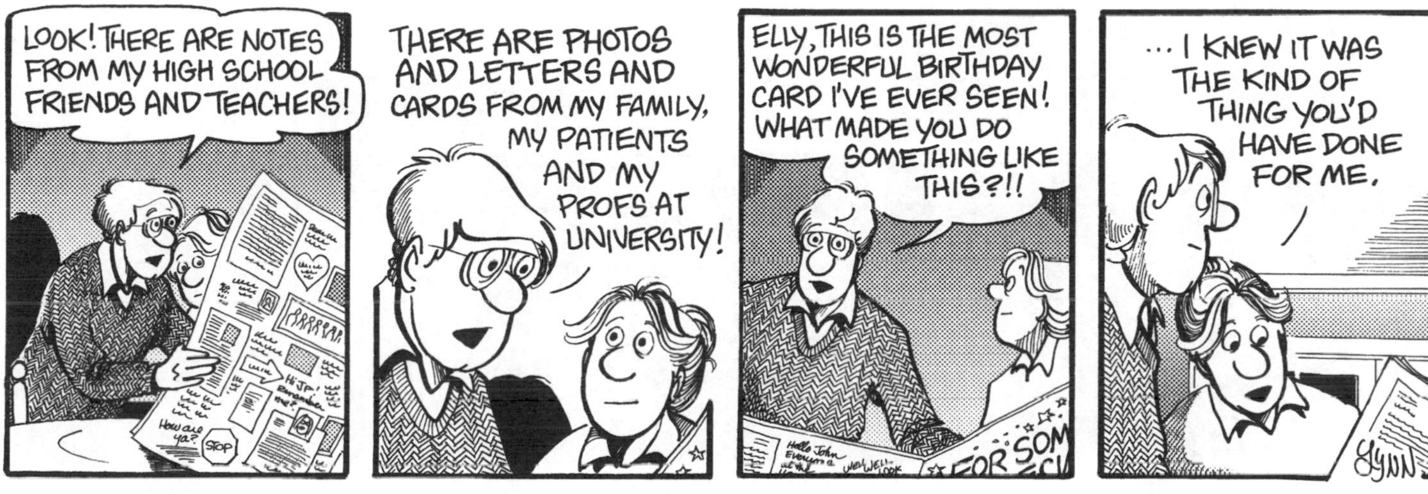
LOOK! THERE ARE NOTES FROM MY HIGH SCHOOL FRIENDS AND TEACHERS!
How are ya?
STOP
THERE ARE PHOTOS AND LETTERS AND CARDS FROM MY FAMILY, MY PATIENTS AND MY PROFS AT UNIVERSITY!
ELLY, THIS IS THE MOST WONDERFUL BIRTHDAY CARD I'VE EVER SEEN! WHAT MADE YOU DO SOMETHING LIKE THIS?!!
... I KNEW IT WAS THE KIND OF THING YOU'D HAVE DONE FOR ME.
LYNN

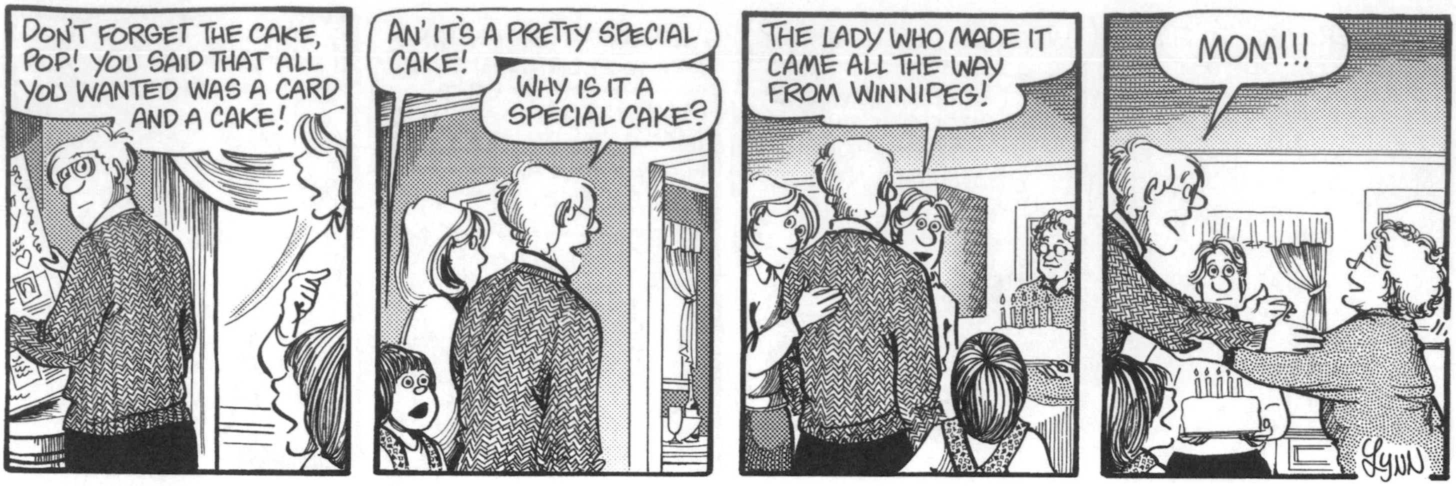
DON'T FORGET THE CAKE, POP! YOU SAID THAT ALL YOU WANTED WAS A CARD AND A CAKE!
AN' IT'S A PRETTY SPECIAL CAKE!
WHY IS IT A SPECIAL CAKE?
THE LADY WHO MADE IT CAME ALL THE WAY FROM WINNIPEG!
MOM!!!
LYNN

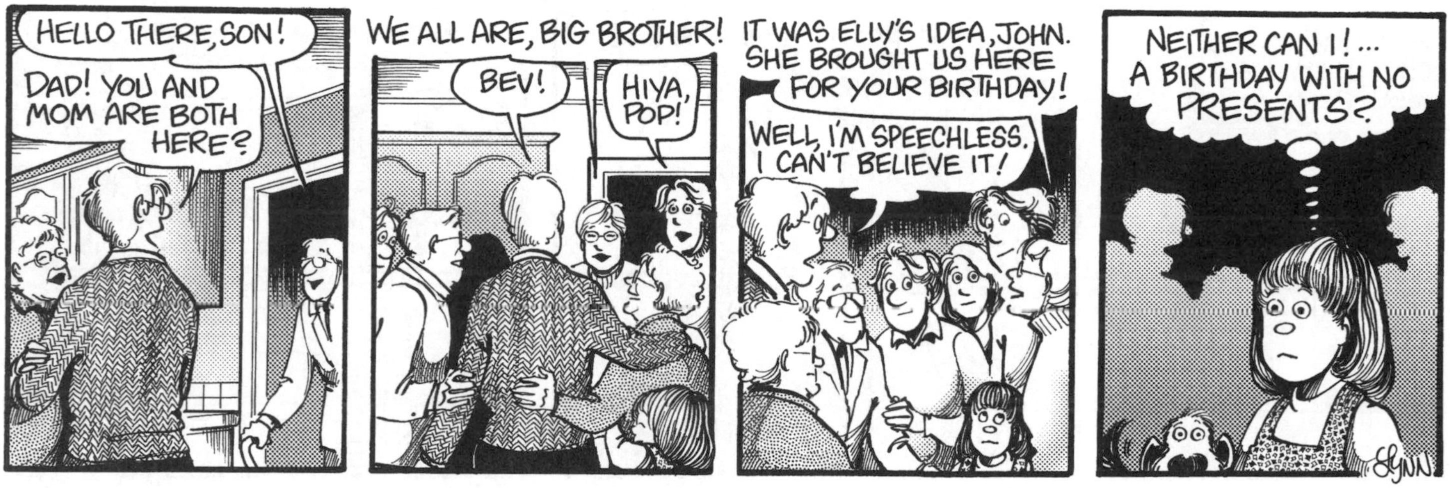
HELLO THERE, SON!
DAD! YOU AND MOM ARE BOTH HERE?
WE ALL ARE, BIG BROTHER!
BEV!
HIYA, POP!
IT WAS ELLY'S IDEA, JOHN. SHE BROUGHT US HERE FOR YOUR BIRTHDAY!
WELL, I'M SPEECHLESS. I CAN'T BELIEVE IT!
NEITHER CAN I!... A BIRTHDAY WITH NO PRESENTS?
LYNN

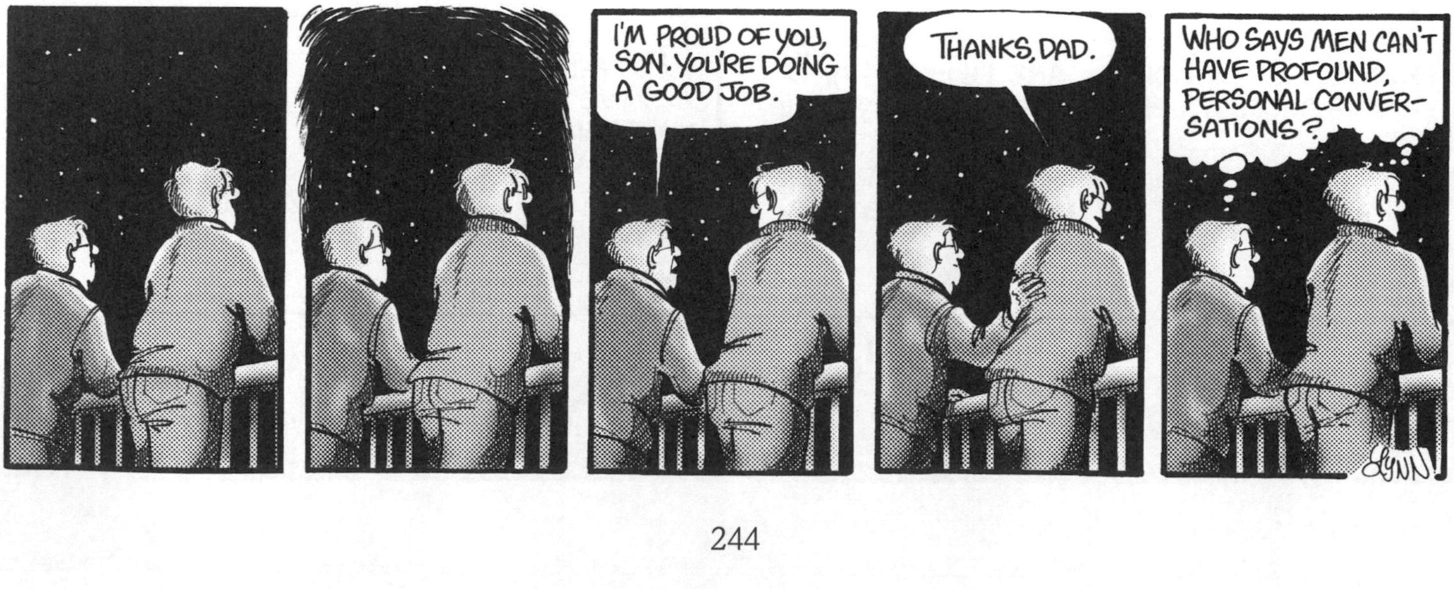
I'M PROUD OF YOU, SON. YOU'RE DOING A GOOD JOB.
THANKS, DAD.
WHO SAYS MEN CAN'T HAVE PROFOUND, PERSONAL CONVER-SATIONS?
LYNN

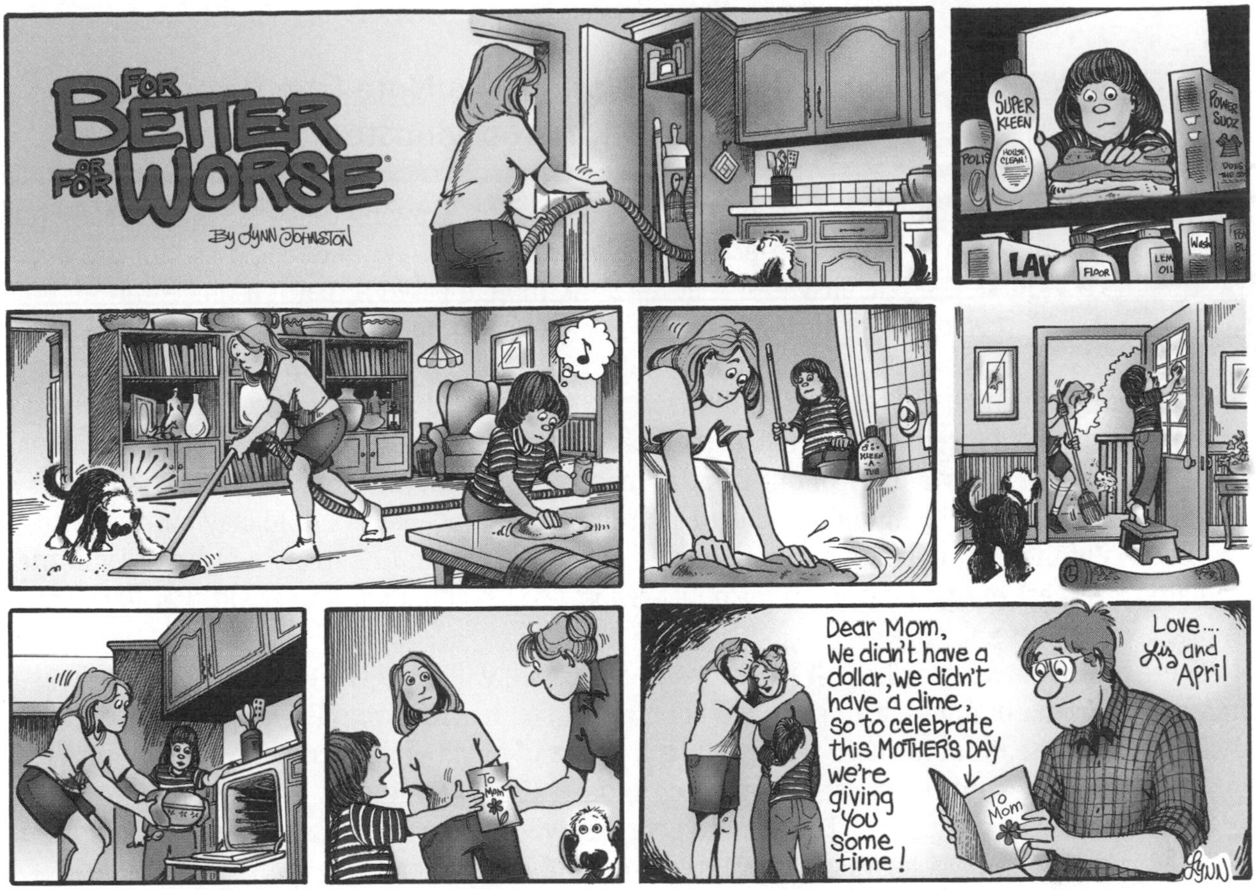
FOR BETTER OR FOR WORSE
By Lynn Johnston
SUPER KLEEN
HOUSE CLEAN!
POWER SUDZ
KLEEN-A-TUB
To Mom
Dear Mom, We didn't have a dollar, we didn't have a dime, so to celebrate this MOTHER'S DAY we're giving you some time!
Love.... Liz and April
To Mom
Lynn

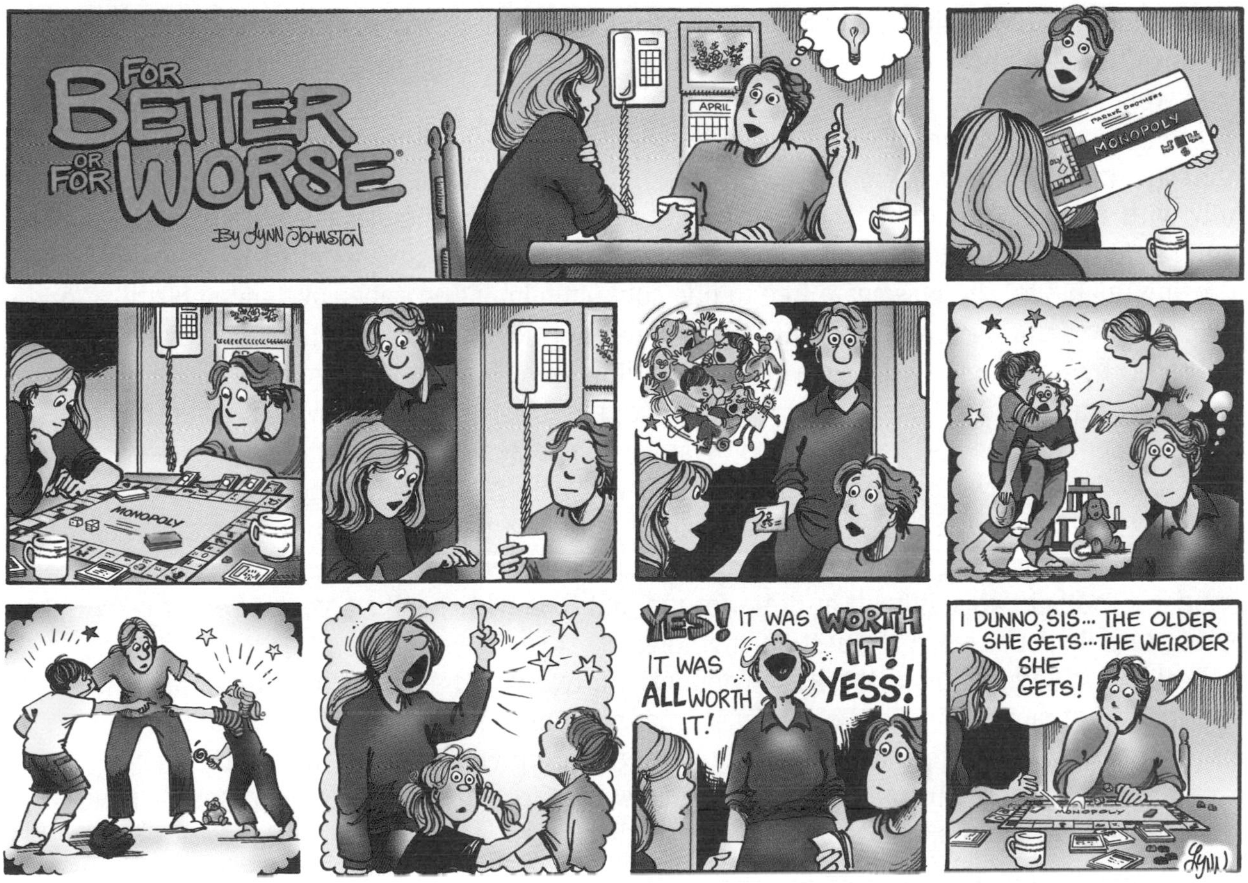
FOR BETTER OR FOR WORSE
By Lynn Johnston
APRIL
MONOPOLY
MONOPOLY
YES! IT WAS WORTH IT! YESS!
IT WAS ALL WORTH IT!
I DUNNO, SIS... THE OLDER SHE GETS... THE WEIRDER SHE GETS!
Lynn

A Window into Two Worlds — a Note from Lynn and Rod's Son, Aaron Johnston

I think the question I got asked the most growing up was, "Is that really you in the comic strip?" and the answer has always been "Sort of, but not really." The real answer is that the strip, though based in part on our family and our personalities during the early years, mostly comes from Lynn's own imagination. Of course, some events are taken from reality, but as a whole it is Lynn's imaginary "second" family that is presented to the world every day. Bits and pieces from us, our friends, and sometimes neighbors, and other family members are certainly reflected from time to time, but the strip is not necessarily a diary of our lives, as many people believe. More so, I think Katie and I played an important role being the backboard Lynn used to bounce ideas off, to stay current with how the kids of the day spoke, or to offer a general opinion through the creative process. Lynn tried very hard to respect our privacy and remain just "Mom" to us, although, I do admit that John and our dad bear a strong resemblance . . .

There are two examples I recall where instances from my life entered the strip. The first was when a good friend of mine, just before the big high school dance, developed what I called a "nuclear zit" on the tip of his nose which was the object of much embarrassment—this in turn happened to Michael during one series of strips. Another time, I remember Lynn asking if it would be OK for Michael to get glasses. This was a very sensitive issue because I myself wore glasses and at the time loathed them. Michael's getting glasses would only heighten the esteem issues I already faced as a teenager as well as further fuel the impression by others that we were one and the same. I remember dreading the notion and asking if Elizabeth could instead go through the story line, which is what ended up happening. I think this is a great example of how we, as a family, were respected and consulted—and how Lynn was sensitive to the impact that the strip had on us, yet at times our stories were still told when needed.

I think that in the late '80s and early '90s there was a real split in the direction of the Pattersons. Instead of being a reflection of our family, they truly became Lynn's own imaginary family with a life all their own. The passing of her parents was difficult for Lynn, and she was able to use the strip to keep the loving memory of her father alive. Later, after wanting to have another child and being unable to, she was again free to find some fulfillment on paper by "giving birth" and raising April. It was during those years that I left home and moved west. Shortly after leaving, I was encouraged by my mom to take up a career in writing, which did not interest me. Soon after, Michael became a writer instead, and his alter ego, the disheveled hippy "Weed" character entered the strip. I believe Weed—like me, a photographer in conflict with his family's success—was Lynn's way of injecting my own personality into the strip as Michael became an independent imaginary son joining April and Grandpa Jim. A few years later, Lynn encouraged Katie to become a teacher. When it became clear that wasn't going to happen, Elizabeth fulfilled that desire in the story lines. Growing up under a spotlight was difficult at times for me, but today, Michael is a very different person than I am, and I rarely get asked that question anymore.

Really, *For Better or For Worse* is a window into two worlds—it is a mixture of fantasy, reality, and humor all wrapped into four daily panels that millions of people have grown to love and consider a part of their lives. We as a family have grown up with the Pattersons, and they are very much a part of our own lives. Almost anywhere in the world I go, I can open a newspaper and feel a sense of "home." Of this and of my mother, I am very proud.

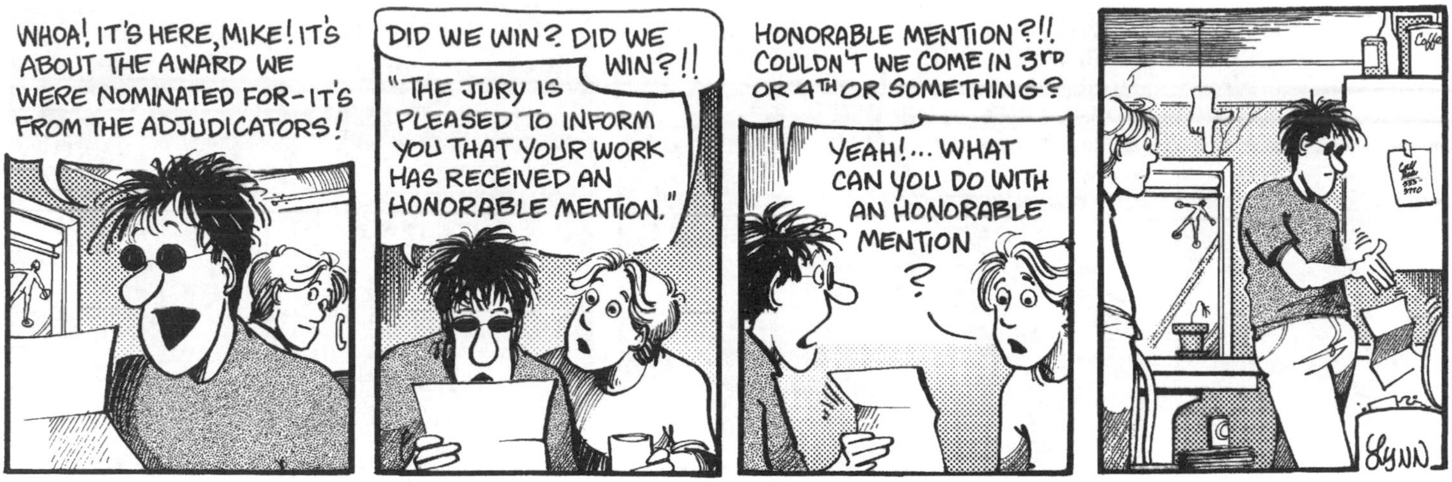
WHOA! IT'S HERE, MIKE! IT'S ABOUT THE AWARD WE WERE NOMINATED FOR - IT'S FROM THE ADJUDICATORS!
DID WE WIN? DID WE WIN?!!
"THE JURY IS PLEASED TO INFORM YOU THAT YOUR WORK HAS RECEIVED AN HONORABLE MENTION."
HONORABLE MENTION?!! COULDN'T WE COME IN 3RD OR 4TH OR SOMETHING?
YEAH!... WHAT CAN YOU DO WITH AN HONORABLE MENTION?
LYNN

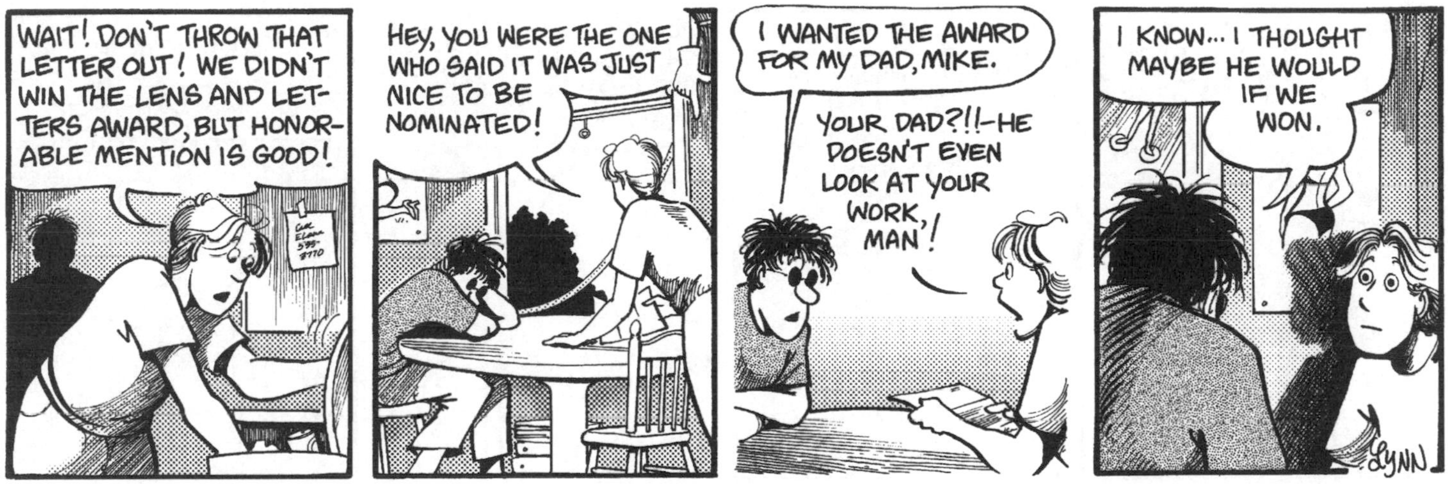
WAIT! DON'T THROW THAT LETTER OUT! WE DIDN'T WIN THE LENS AND LETTERS AWARD, BUT HONORABLE MENTION IS GOOD!
HEY, YOU WERE THE ONE WHO SAID IT WAS JUST NICE TO BE NOMINATED!
I WANTED THE AWARD FOR MY DAD, MIKE.
YOUR DAD?!!-HE DOESN'T EVEN LOOK AT YOUR WORK, MAN!
I KNOW... I THOUGHT MAYBE HE WOULD IF WE WON.
LYNN

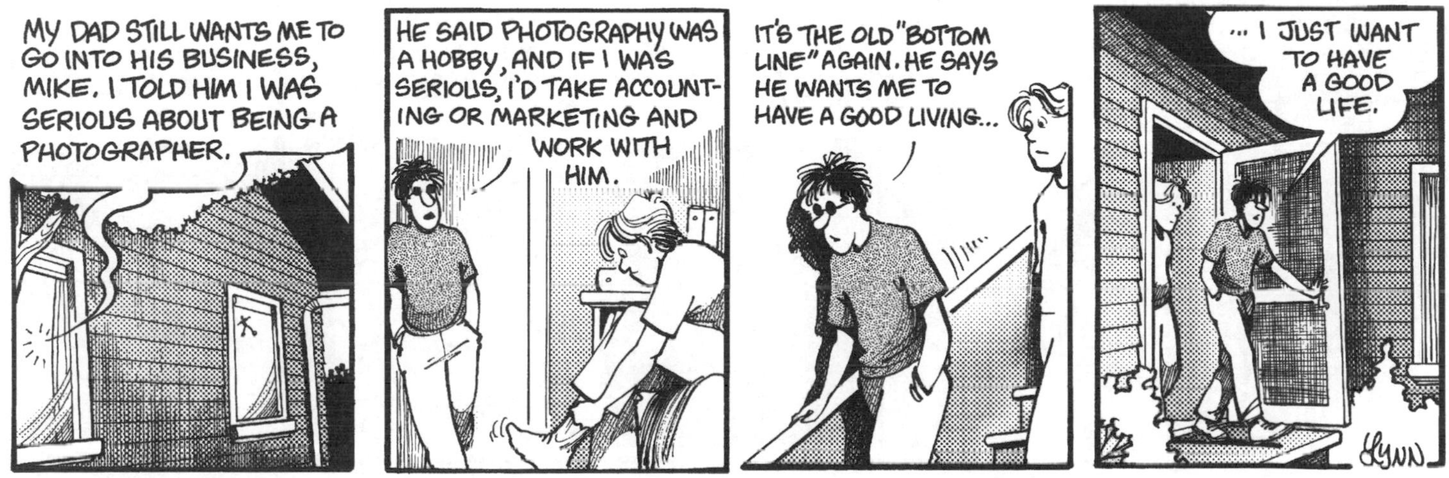
MY DAD STILL WANTS ME TO GO INTO HIS BUSINESS, MIKE. I TOLD HIM I WAS SERIOUS ABOUT BEING A PHOTOGRAPHER.
HE SAID PHOTOGRAPHY WAS A HOBBY, AND IF I WAS SERIOUS, I'D TAKE ACCOUNTING OR MARKETING AND WORK WITH HIM.
IT'S THE OLD "BOTTOM LINE" AGAIN. HE SAYS HE WANTS ME TO HAVE A GOOD LIVING...
... I JUST WANT TO HAVE A GOOD LIFE.
LYNN

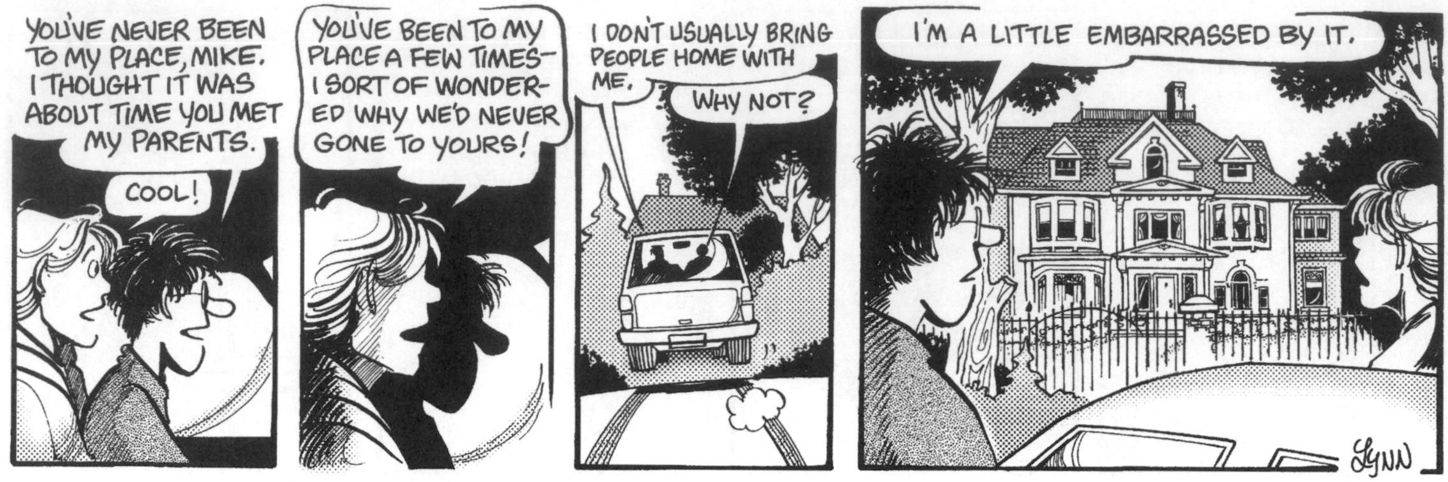
YOU'VE NEVER BEEN TO MY PLACE, MIKE. I THOUGHT IT WAS ABOUT TIME YOU MET MY PARENTS.
COOL!
YOU'VE BEEN TO MY PLACE A FEW TIMES- I SORT OF WONDER-ED WHY WE'D NEVER GONE TO YOURS!
I DON'T USUALLY BRING PEOPLE HOME WITH ME.
WHY NOT?
I'M A LITTLE EMBARRASSED BY IT.
LYNN

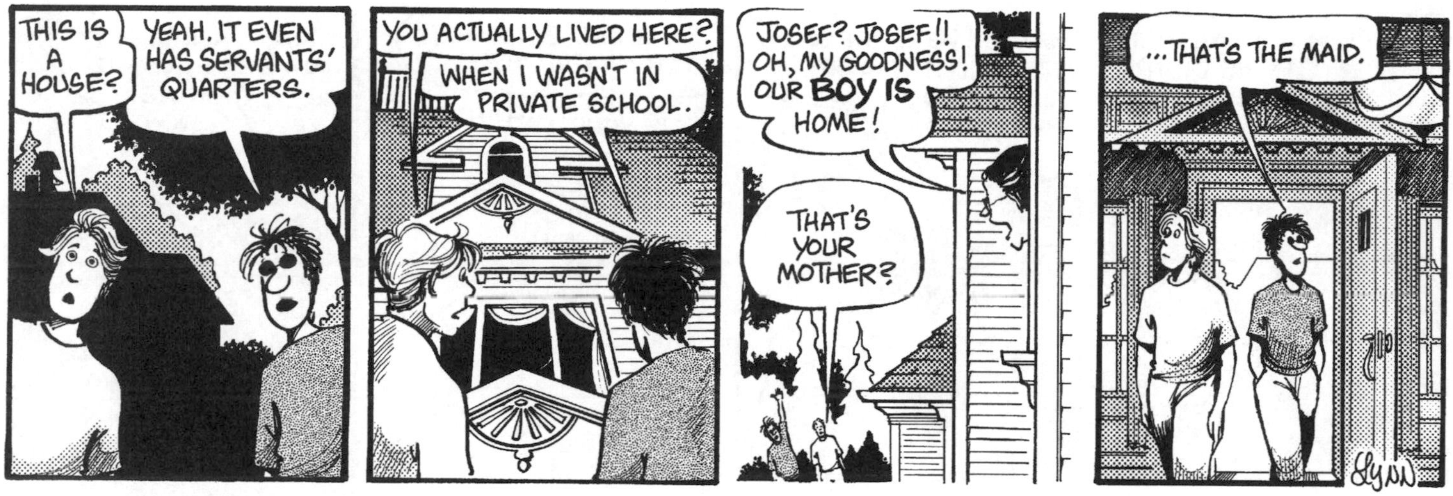
THIS IS A HOUSE?
YEAH. IT EVEN HAS SERVANTS' QUARTERS.
YOU ACTUALLY LIVED HERE?
WHEN I WASN'T IN PRIVATE SCHOOL.
JOSEF? JOSEF!! OH, MY GOODNESS! OUR BOY IS HOME!
THAT'S YOUR MOTHER?
...THAT'S THE MAID.
LYNN

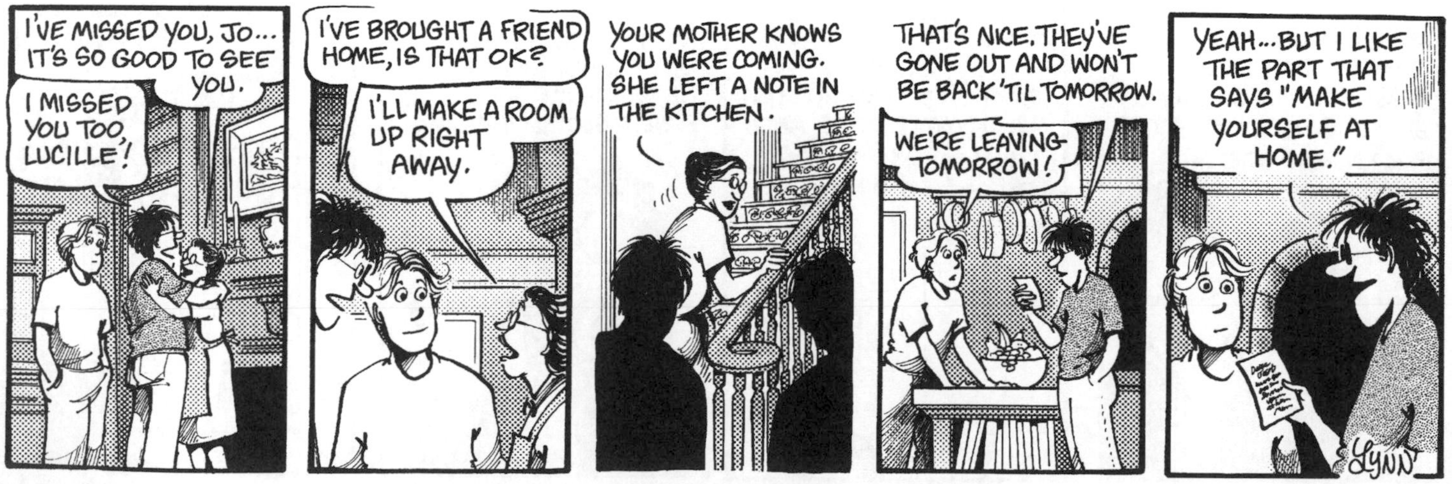
I'VE MISSED YOU, JO... IT'S SO GOOD TO SEE YOU.
I MISSED YOU TOO, LUCILLE!
I'VE BROUGHT A FRIEND HOME, IS THAT OK?
I'LL MAKE A ROOM UP RIGHT AWAY.
YOUR MOTHER KNOWS YOU WERE COMING. SHE LEFT A NOTE IN THE KITCHEN.
THAT'S NICE. THEY'VE GONE OUT AND WON'T BE BACK 'TIL TOMORROW.
WE'RE LEAVING TOMORROW!
YEAH... BUT I LIKE THE PART THAT SAYS "MAKE YOURSELF AT HOME."
LYNN

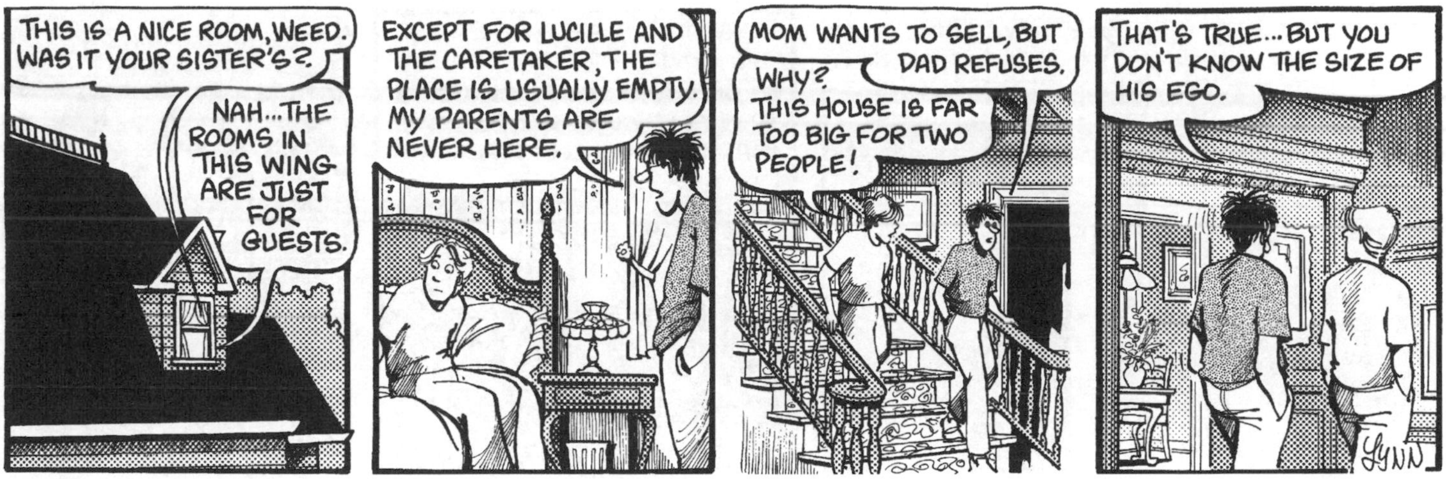
THIS IS A NICE ROOM, WEED. WAS IT YOUR SISTER'S?
NAH...THE ROOMS IN THIS WING ARE JUST FOR GUESTS.
EXCEPT FOR LUCILLE AND THE CARETAKER, THE PLACE IS USUALLY EMPTY. MY PARENTS ARE NEVER HERE.
MOM WANTS TO SELL, BUT DAD REFUSES.
WHY? THIS HOUSE IS FAR TOO BIG FOR TWO PEOPLE!
THAT'S TRUE...BUT YOU DON'T KNOW THE SIZE OF HIS EGO.
LYNN

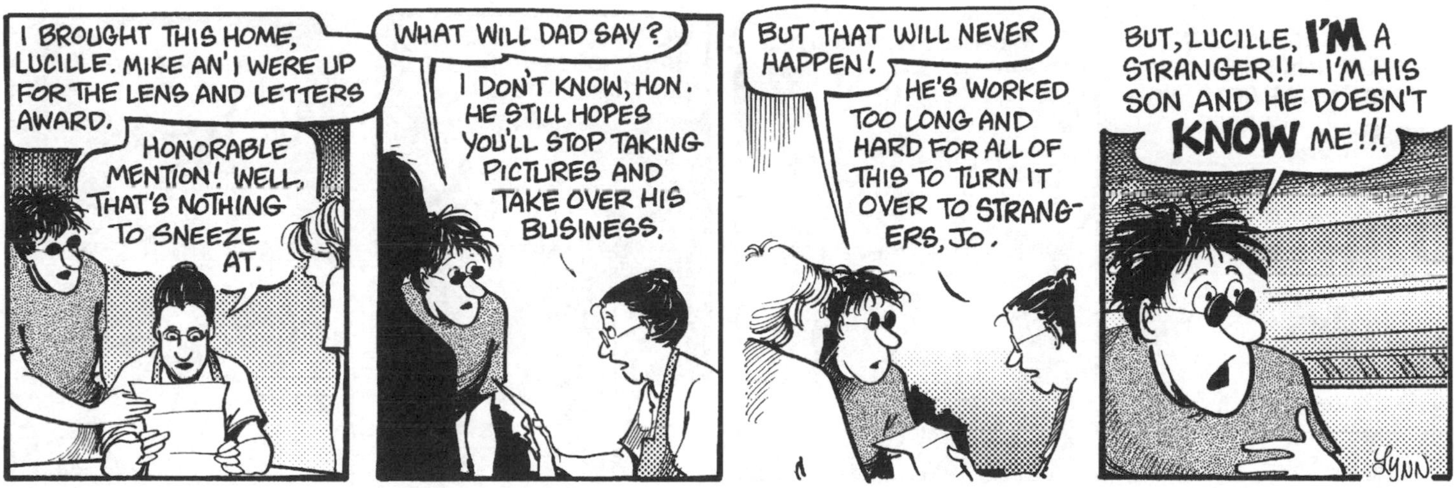
I BROUGHT THIS HOME, LUCILLE. MIKE AN' I WERE UP FOR THE LENS AND LETTERS AWARD.
HONORABLE MENTION! WELL, THAT'S NOTHING TO SNEEZE AT.
WHAT WILL DAD SAY?
I DON'T KNOW, HON. HE STILL HOPES YOU'LL STOP TAKING PICTURES AND TAKE OVER HIS BUSINESS.
BUT THAT WILL NEVER HAPPEN!
HE'S WORKED TOO LONG AND HARD FOR ALL OF THIS TO TURN IT OVER TO STRANGERS, JO.
BUT, LUCILLE, I'M A STRANGER!! – I'M HIS SON AND HE DOESN'T KNOW ME!!!
LYNN

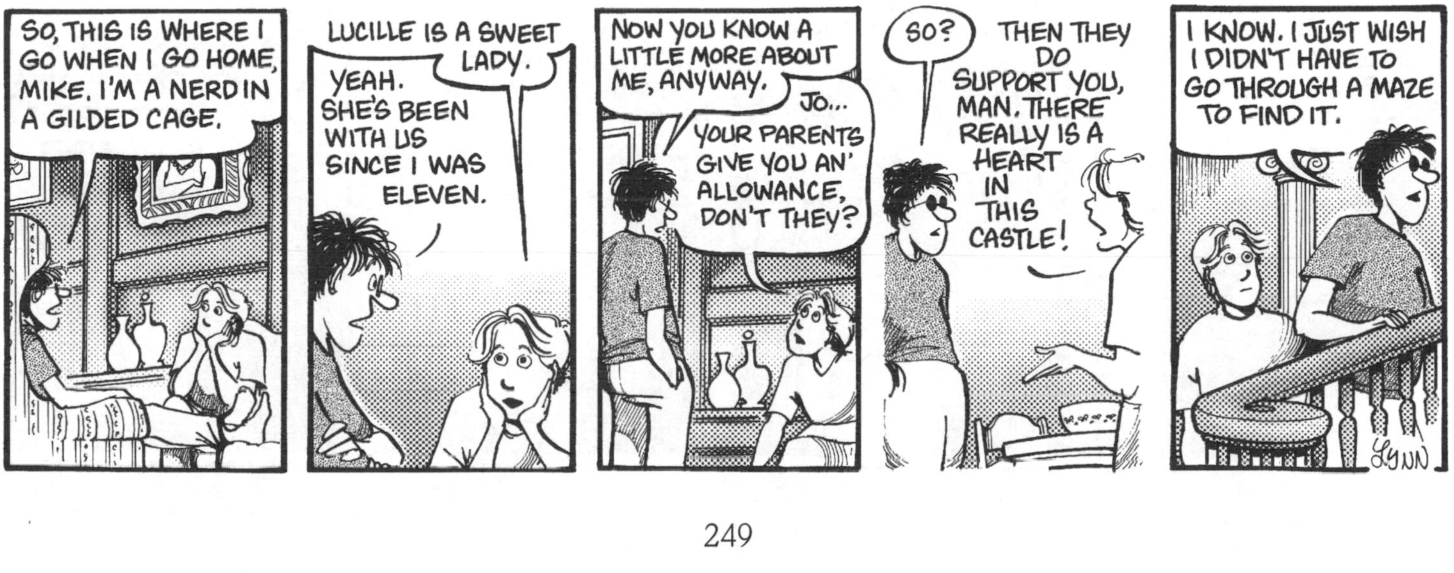
SO, THIS IS WHERE I GO WHEN I GO HOME, MIKE. I'M A NERD IN A GILDED CAGE.
LUCILLE IS A SWEET LADY.
YEAH. SHE'S BEEN WITH US SINCE I WAS ELEVEN.
NOW YOU KNOW A LITTLE MORE ABOUT ME, ANYWAY.
JO... YOUR PARENTS GIVE YOU AN' ALLOWANCE, DON'T THEY?
SO?
THEN THEY DO SUPPORT YOU, MAN. THERE REALLY IS A HEART IN THIS CASTLE!
I KNOW. I JUST WISH I DIDN'T HAVE TO GO THROUGH A MAZE TO FIND IT.
LYNN

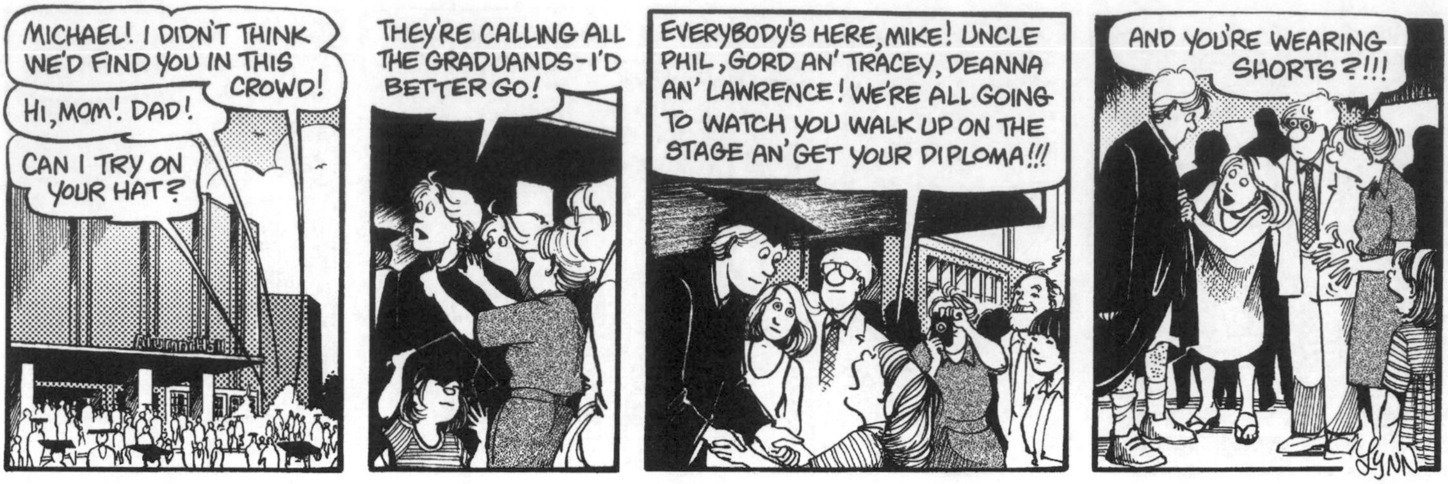
MICHAEL! I DIDN'T THINK WE'D FIND YOU IN THIS CROWD!
HI, MOM! DAD!
CAN I TRY ON YOUR HAT?
THEY'RE CALLING ALL THE GRADUANDS - I'D BETTER GO!
EVERYBODY'S HERE, MIKE! UNCLE PHIL, GORD AN' TRACEY, DEANNA AN' LAWRENCE! WE'RE ALL GOING TO WATCH YOU WALK UP ON THE STAGE AN' GET YOUR DIPLOMA!!!
AND YOU'RE WEARING SHORTS?!!!

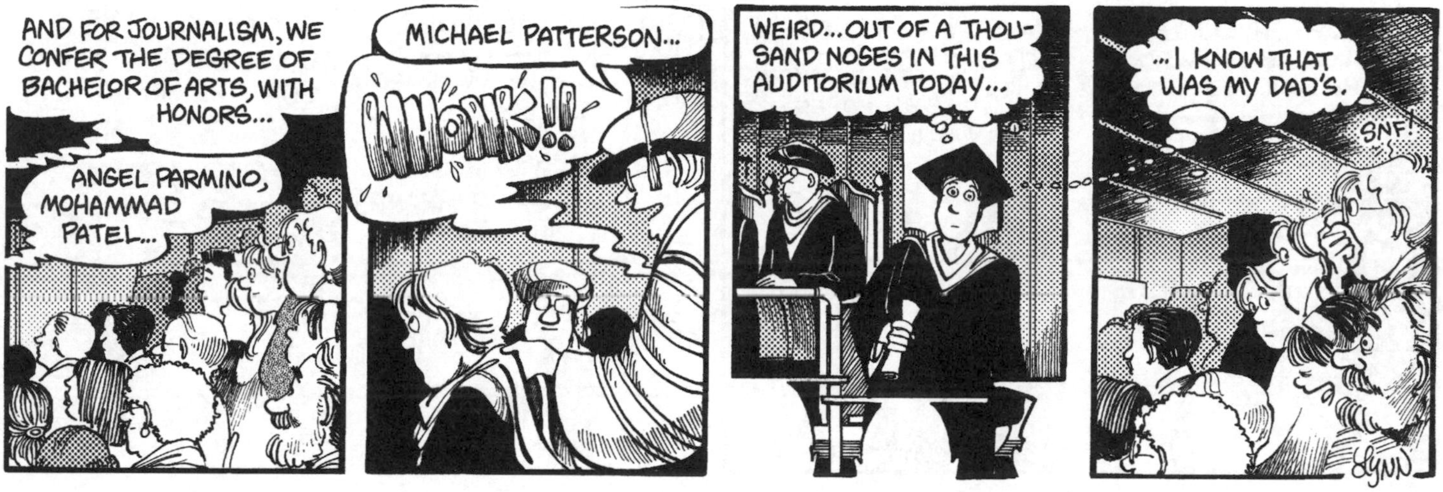
AND FOR JOURNALISM, WE CONFER THE DEGREE OF BACHELOR OF ARTS, WITH HONORS...
ANGEL PARMINO, MOHAMMAD PATEL...
MICHAEL PATTERSON...
WHONK!!
WEIRD... OUT OF A THOUSAND NOSES IN THIS AUDITORIUM TODAY...
...I KNOW THAT WAS MY DAD'S.
SNF!

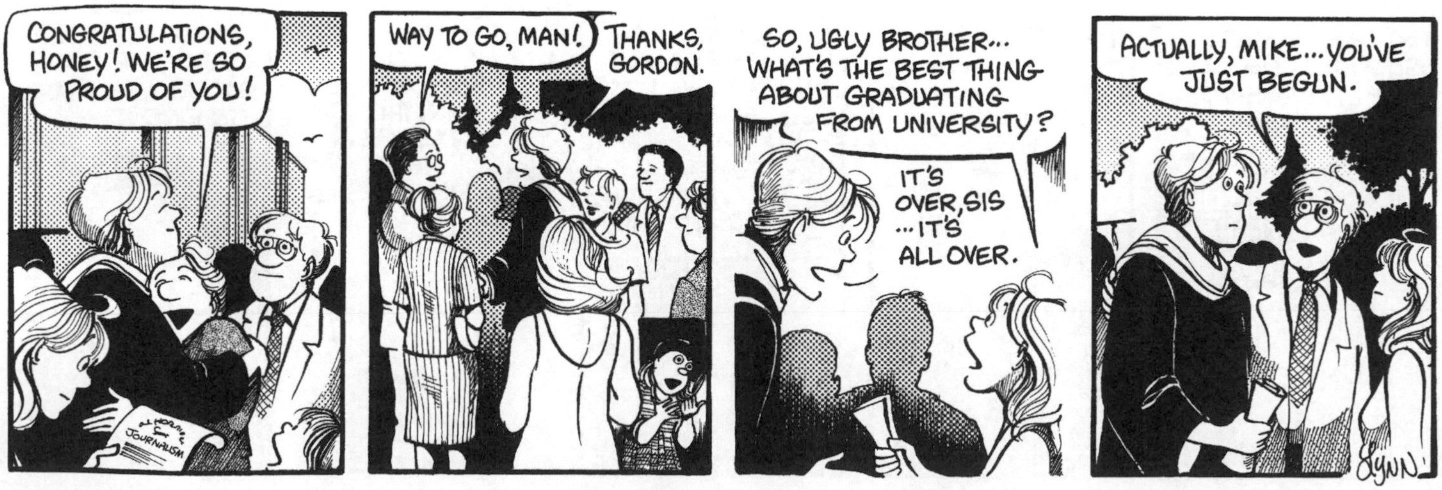
CONGRATULATIONS, HONEY! WE'RE SO PROUD OF YOU!
WAY TO GO, MAN!
THANKS, GORDON.
SO, UGLY BROTHER... WHAT'S THE BEST THING ABOUT GRADUATING FROM UNIVERSITY?
IT'S OVER, SIS ...IT'S ALL OVER.
ACTUALLY, MIKE... YOU'VE JUST BEGUN.

WE'RE MEETING MICHAEL AT THE AIRPORT FIRST, AN' THEN WE'RE GOING TO THE TRAIN STATION TO SAY GOODBYE TO ELIZABETH?

UH-HUH

ELIZABETH PATTERSON NORTH BAY

WE DIDN'T EXPECT ALL THIS EXCITEMENT IN ONE DAY, BUT THAT'S LIFE!

LOOK AT ALL THE BAGS AND BOXES! WE'LL HAVE TO CHECK THESE AT THE TRAIN BEFORE WE GO TO THE AIRPORT!

I'M SORRY, MOM—I DIDN'T THINK MOVING WOULD BE SO MUCH WORK!

DON'T WORRY, HONEY. I DON'T MIND THE CHAOS!

ELIZABETH PATTERSON NORTH BAY

...IT KEEPS ME FROM CRYING.

LOOK AT THIS, MIKE—WE HAVE A WELCOMING COMMITTEE!

ARRIVALS

HEY, BIG BROTHER, YOU'RE JUST IN TIME TO SAY GOODBYE TO ME. IN 3 HOURS I'LL BE ON THE TRAIN TO NORTH BAY!

HOW WAS IRELAND?

DID YOU GET A GOOD STORY?

OH, MAN, WE'VE GOT SO MUCH TO TELL YOU!

CANADIAN CUSTOMS

SOME DAY, WHEN I'M BIG, I'M GOING TO REMEMBER TO TALK TO SHORT PEOPLE.

I'D LIKE TO SPEND MORE TIME WITH YOUR FAMILY, MIKE, BUT I HAVE TO GET HOME.

HONEY, WE KNOW YOU'RE TIRED. MAYBE YOU SHOULD GO WITH JOSEF.

ARE YOU KIDDING? I WANT TO SEE LIZARD-BREATH TAKE OFF FOR UNIVERSITY!

I WANT TO SEE MY LITTLE SISTER STEP INTO THE REAL WORLD!

TRACK 2

THE FIRST STEP SEEMS LIKE SUCH A BIG ONE!

NR

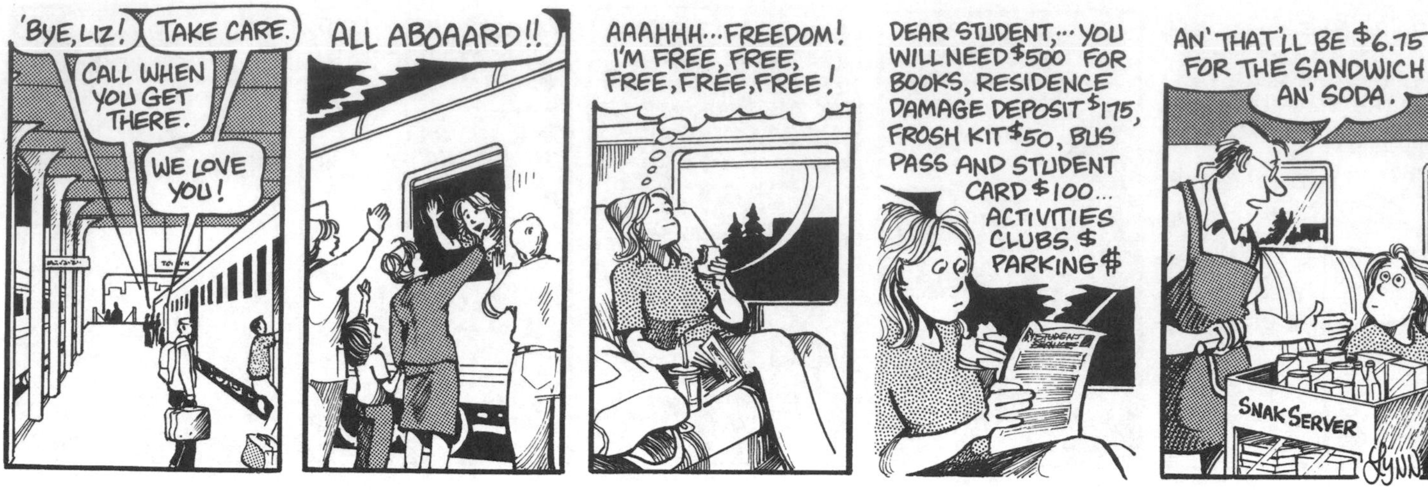
'BYE, LIZ!
TAKE CARE.
CALL WHEN YOU GET THERE.
WE LOVE YOU!
ALL ABOAARD!!
AAAHHH... FREEDOM! I'M FREE, FREE, FREE, FREE, FREE!
DEAR STUDENT,... YOU WILL NEED $500 FOR BOOKS, RESIDENCE DAMAGE DEPOSIT $175, FROSH KIT $50, BUS PASS AND STUDENT CARD $100... ACTIVITIES CLUBS, $ PARKING $
AN' THAT'LL BE $6.75 FOR THE SANDWICH AN' SODA.
SNAK SERVER
LYNN

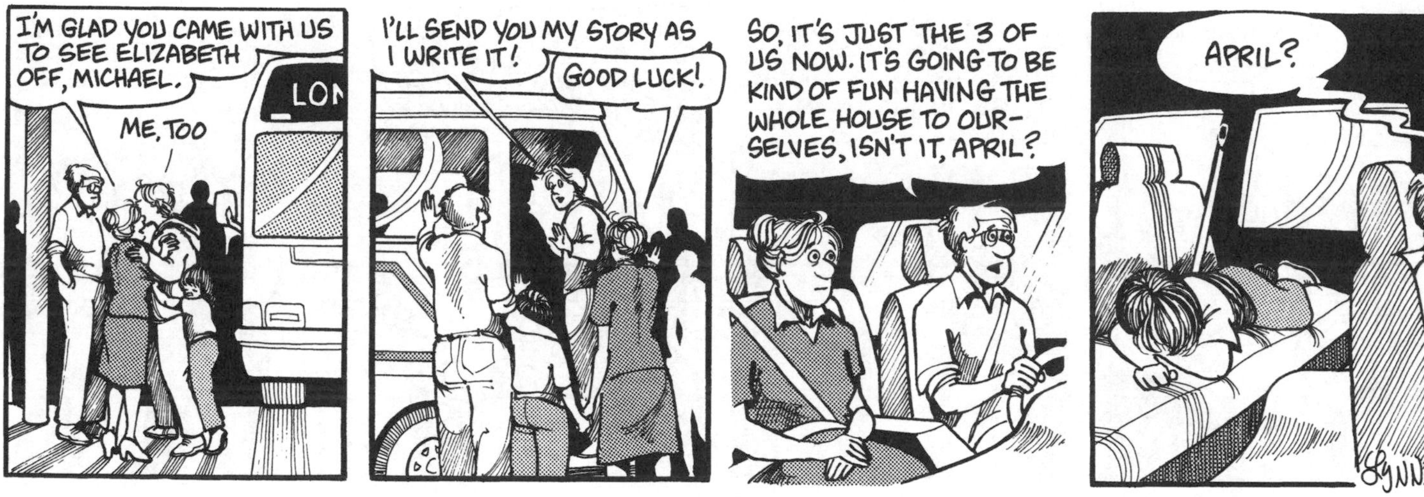
I'M GLAD YOU CAME WITH US TO SEE ELIZABETH OFF, MICHAEL.
ME, TOO
I'LL SEND YOU MY STORY AS I WRITE IT!
GOOD LUCK!
SO, IT'S JUST THE 3 OF US NOW. IT'S GOING TO BE KIND OF FUN HAVING THE WHOLE HOUSE TO OURSELVES, ISN'T IT, APRIL?
APRIL?
LYNN

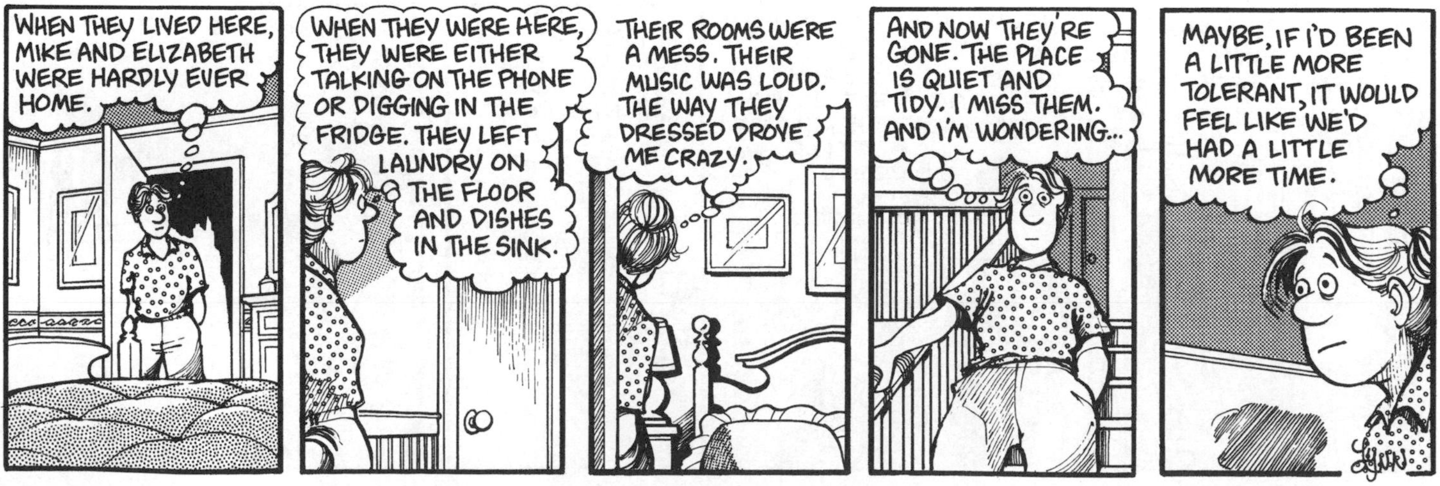
WHEN THEY LIVED HERE, MIKE AND ELIZABETH WERE HARDLY EVER HOME.
WHEN THEY WERE HERE, THEY WERE EITHER TALKING ON THE PHONE OR DIGGING IN THE FRIDGE. THEY LEFT LAUNDRY ON THE FLOOR AND DISHES IN THE SINK.
THEIR ROOMS WERE A MESS. THEIR MUSIC WAS LOUD. THE WAY THEY DRESSED DROVE ME CRAZY.
AND NOW THEY'RE GONE. THE PLACE IS QUIET AND TIDY. I MISS THEM. AND I'M WONDERING...
MAYBE, IF I'D BEEN A LITTLE MORE TOLERANT, IT WOULD FEEL LIKE WE'D HAD A LITTLE MORE TIME.
LYNN

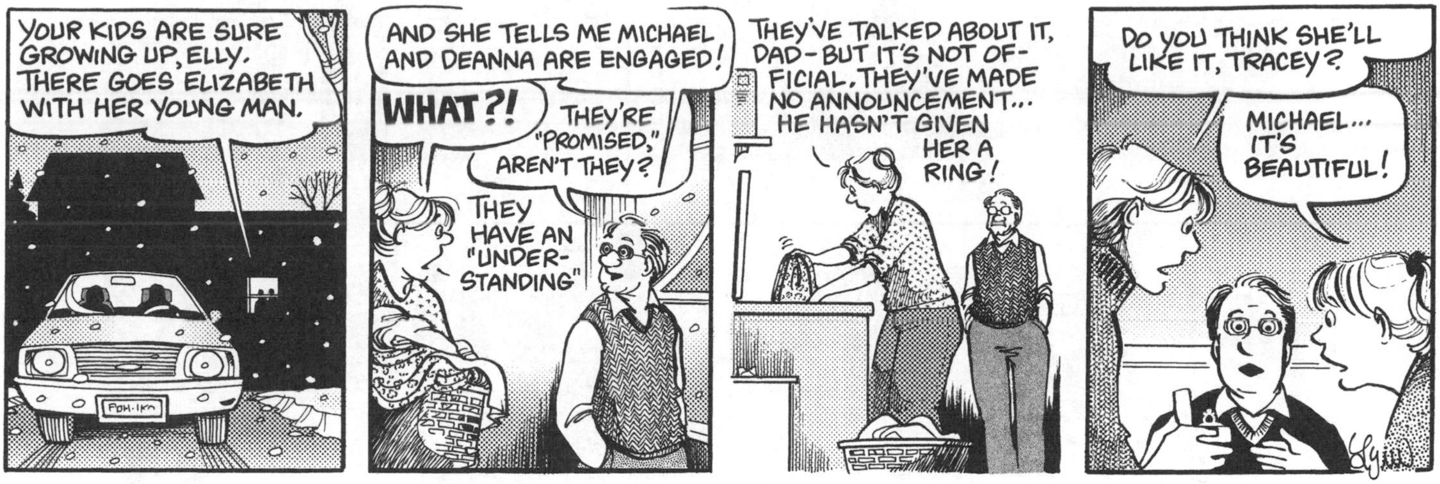
YOUR KIDS ARE SURE GROWING UP, ELLY. THERE GOES ELIZABETH WITH HER YOUNG MAN.
AND SHE TELLS ME MICHAEL AND DEANNA ARE ENGAGED!
WHAT?!
THEY'RE "PROMISED," AREN'T THEY?
THEY HAVE AN "UNDER-STANDING"
THEY'VE TALKED ABOUT IT, DAD - BUT IT'S NOT OF-FICIAL. THEY'VE MADE NO ANNOUNCEMENT... HE HASN'T GIVEN
HER A RING!
DO YOU THINK SHE'LL LIKE IT, TRACEY?
MICHAEL... IT'S BEAUTIFUL!

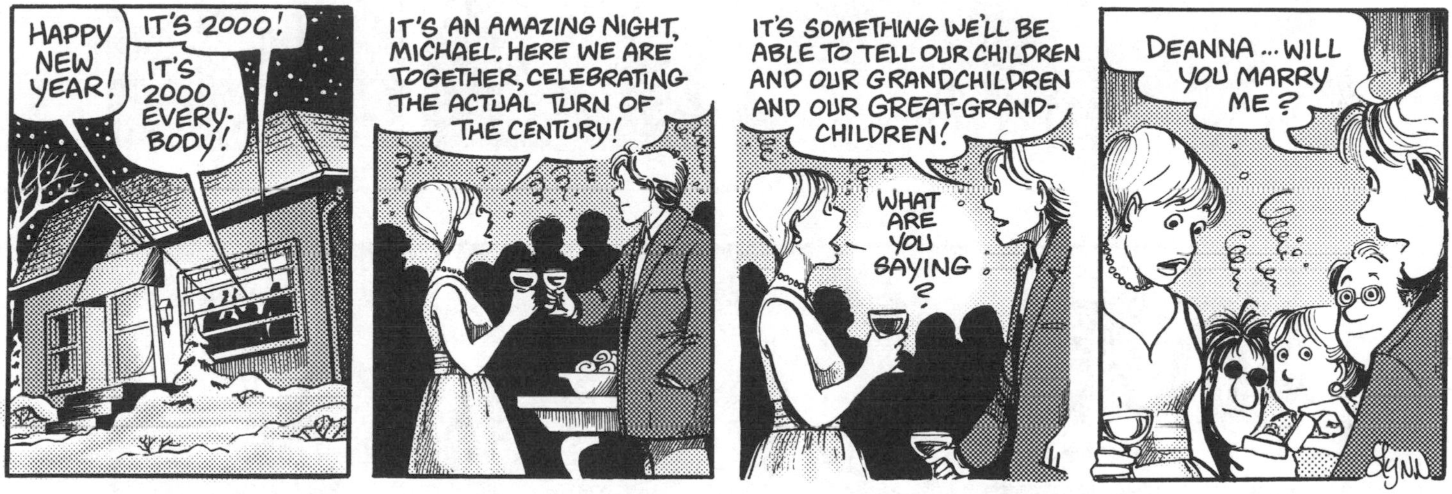
HAPPY NEW YEAR!
IT'S 2000!
IT'S 2000 EVERY-BODY!
IT'S AN AMAZING NIGHT, MICHAEL. HERE WE ARE TOGETHER, CELEBRATING THE ACTUAL TURN OF THE CENTURY!
IT'S SOMETHING WE'LL BE ABLE TO TELL OUR CHILDREN AND OUR GRANDCHILDREN AND OUR GREAT-GRAND-CHILDREN!
WHAT ARE YOU SAYING?
DEANNA... WILL YOU MARRY ME?

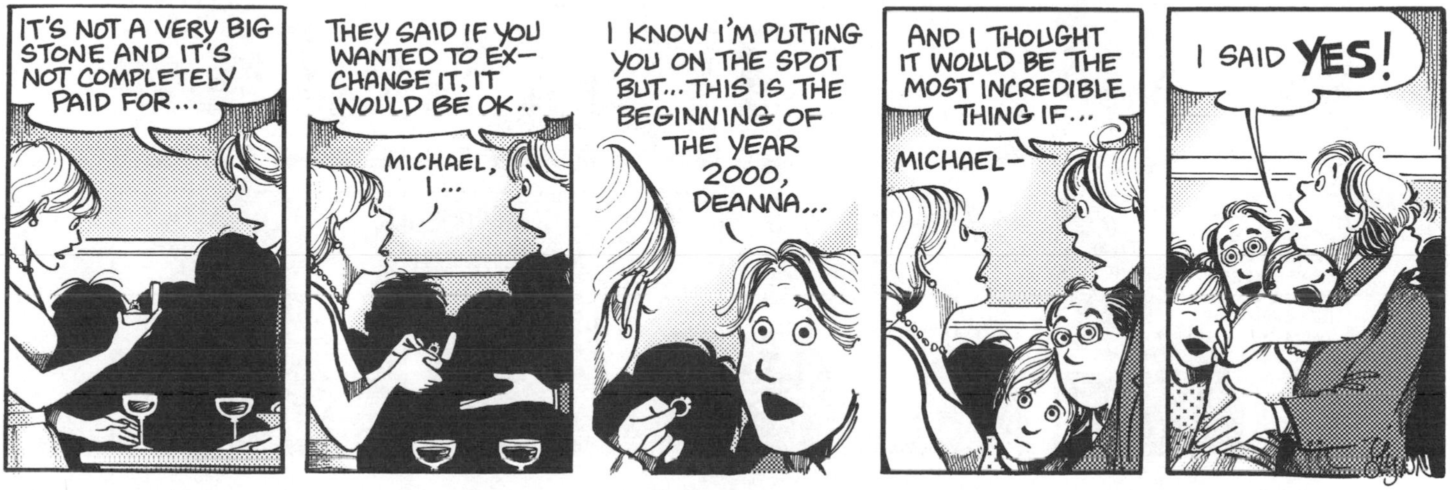
IT'S NOT A VERY BIG STONE AND IT'S NOT COMPLETELY PAID FOR...
THEY SAID IF YOU WANTED TO EX-CHANGE IT, IT WOULD BE OK...
MICHAEL, I...
I KNOW I'M PUTTING YOU ON THE SPOT BUT... THIS IS THE BEGINNING OF THE YEAR 2000, DEANNA...
AND I THOUGHT IT WOULD BE THE MOST INCREDIBLE THING IF...
MICHAEL-
I SAID YES!

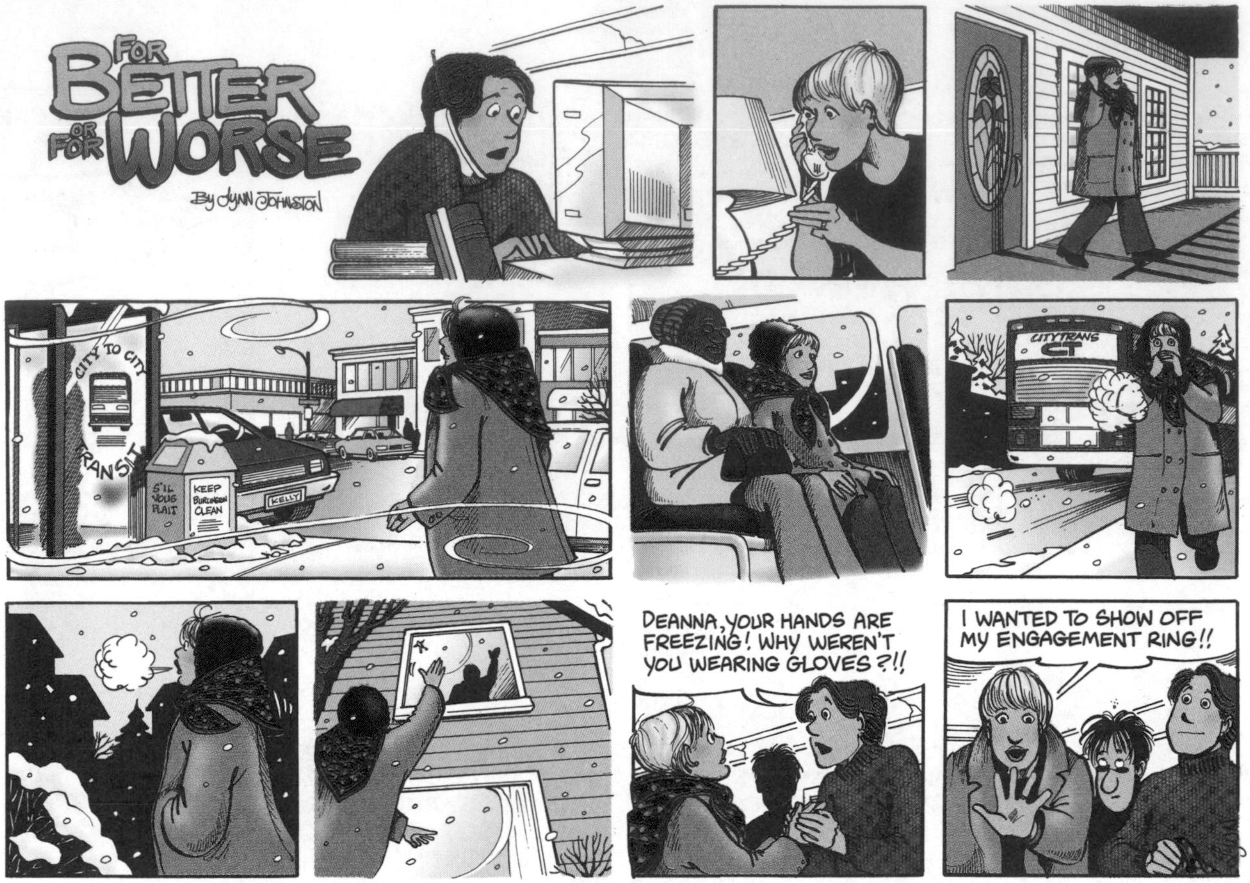
FOR BETTER OR FOR WORSE
By Lynn Johnston
CITY TO CITY TRANSIT
S'IL VOUS PLAIT
KEEP BURLINGTON CLEAN
CITYTRANS CT
DEANNA, YOUR HANDS ARE FREEZING! WHY WEREN'T YOU WEARING GLOVES?!!
I WANTED TO SHOW OFF MY ENGAGEMENT RING!!

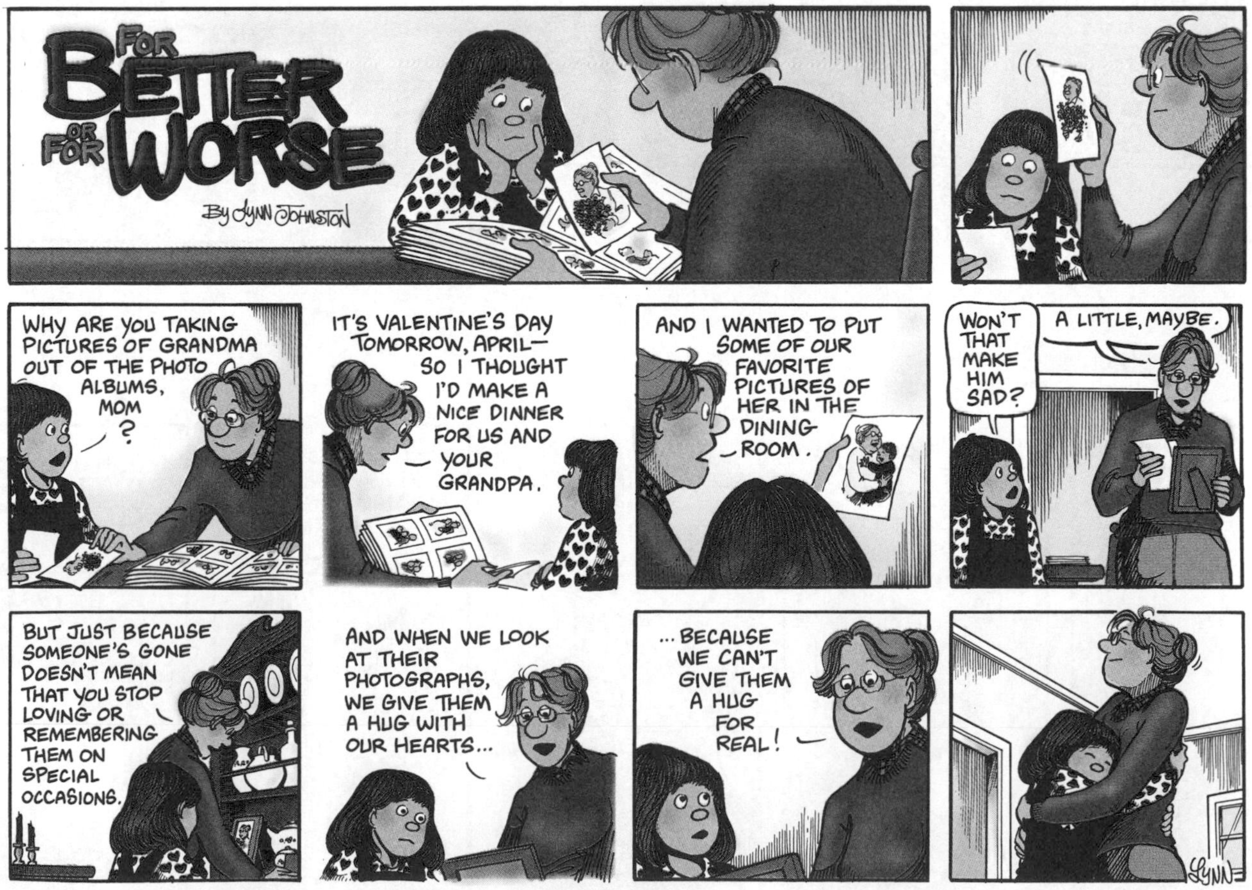
FOR BETTER OR FOR WORSE
By Lynn Johnston
WHY ARE YOU TAKING PICTURES OF GRANDMA OUT OF THE PHOTO ALBUMS, MOM?
IT'S VALENTINE'S DAY TOMORROW, APRIL— SO I THOUGHT I'D MAKE A NICE DINNER FOR US AND YOUR GRANDPA.
AND I WANTED TO PUT SOME OF OUR FAVORITE PICTURES OF HER IN THE DINING ROOM.
WON'T THAT MAKE HIM SAD?
A LITTLE, MAYBE.
BUT JUST BECAUSE SOMEONE'S GONE DOESN'T MEAN THAT YOU STOP LOVING OR REMEMBERING THEM ON SPECIAL OCCASIONS.
AND WHEN WE LOOK AT THEIR PHOTOGRAPHS, WE GIVE THEM A HUG WITH OUR HEARTS...
...BECAUSE WE CAN'T GIVE THEM A HUG FOR REAL!
LYNN

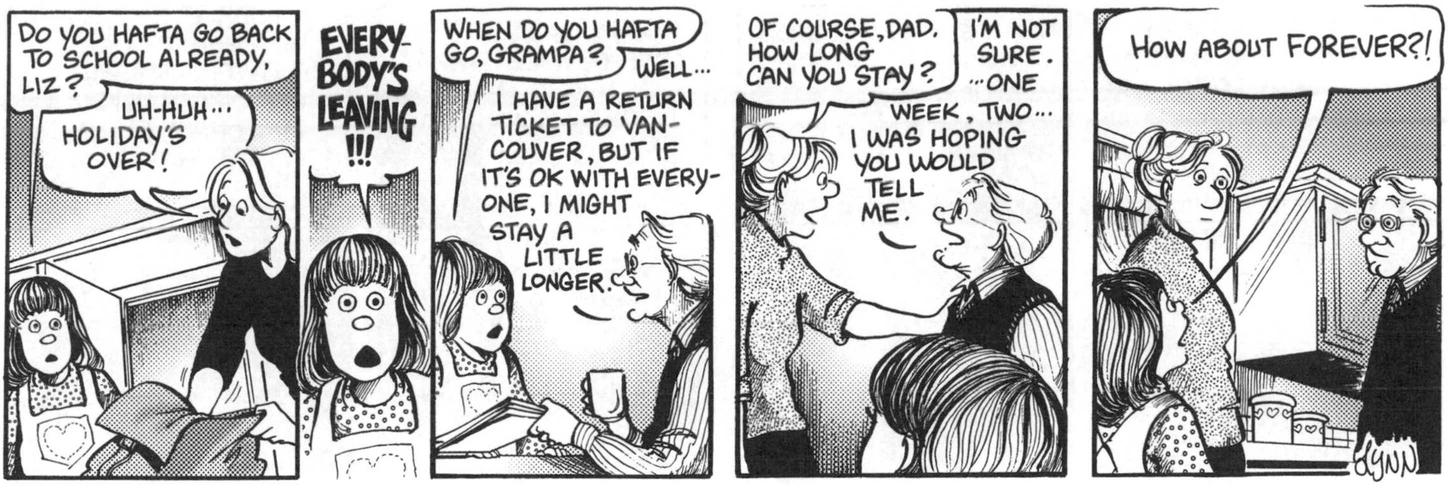
DO YOU HAFTA GO BACK TO SCHOOL ALREADY, LIZ?
UH-HUH... HOLIDAY'S OVER!
EVERY-BODY'S LEAVING!!!
WHEN DO YOU HAFTA GO, GRAMPA?
WELL...
I HAVE A RETURN TICKET TO VAN-COUVER, BUT IF IT'S OK WITH EVERY-ONE, I MIGHT STAY A LITTLE LONGER.
OF COURSE, DAD. HOW LONG CAN YOU STAY?
I'M NOT SURE. ...ONE WEEK, TWO... I WAS HOPING YOU WOULD TELL ME.
HOW ABOUT FOREVER?!

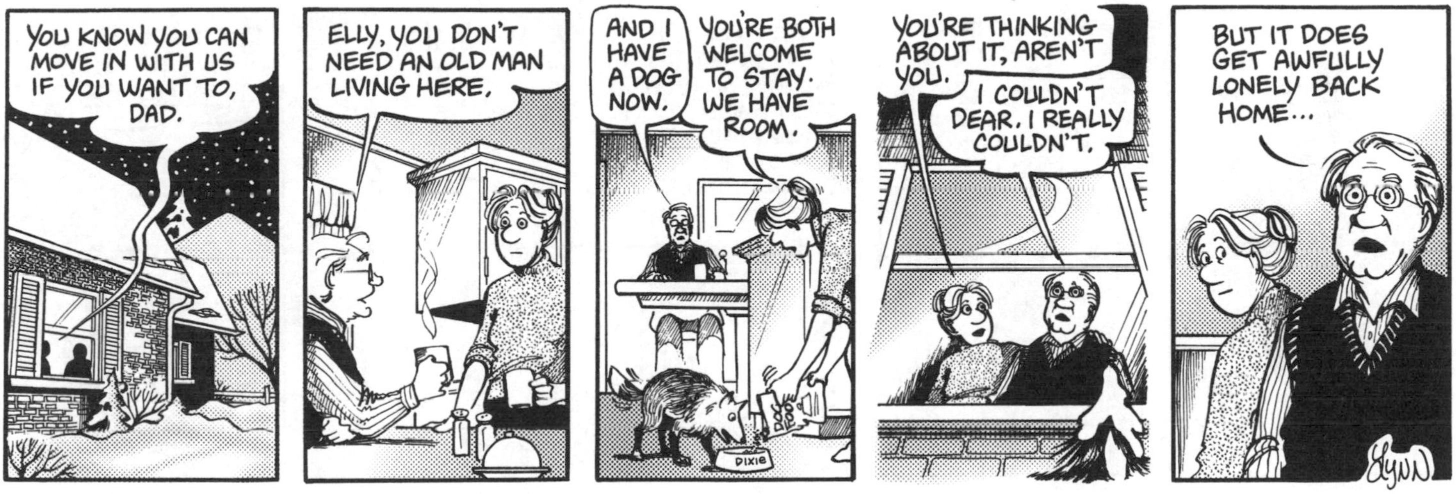
YOU KNOW YOU CAN MOVE IN WITH US IF YOU WANT TO, DAD.
ELLY, YOU DON'T NEED AN OLD MAN LIVING HERE.
AND I HAVE A DOG NOW.
YOU'RE BOTH WELCOME TO STAY. WE HAVE ROOM.
DIXIE
YOU'RE THINKING ABOUT IT, AREN'T YOU.
I COULDN'T DEAR. I REALLY COULDN'T.
BUT IT DOES GET AWFULLY LONELY BACK HOME...

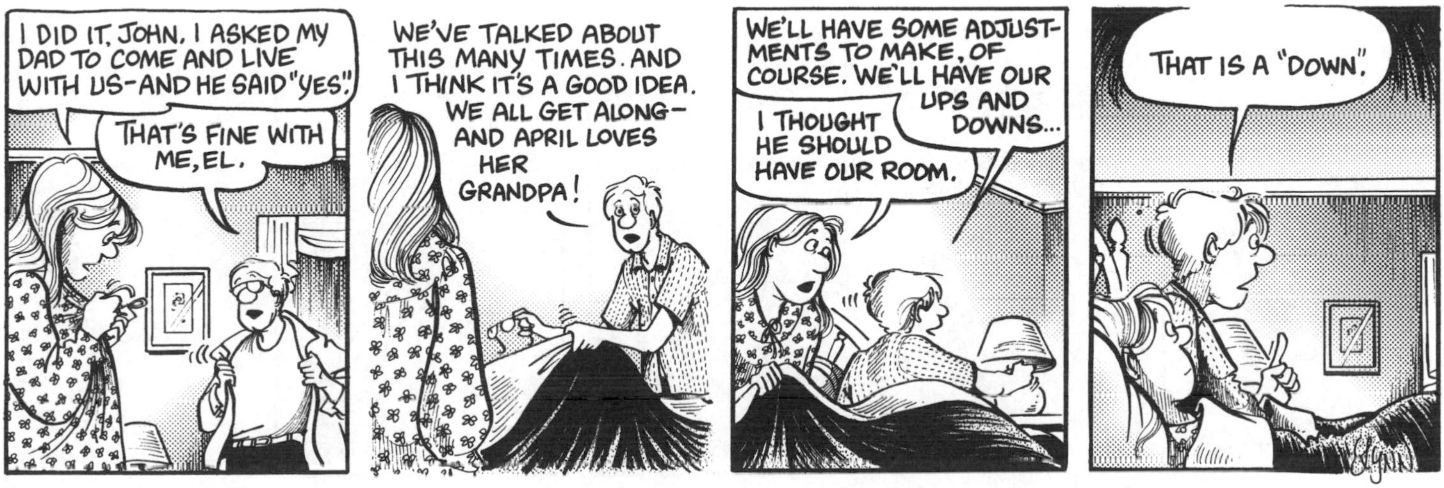
I DID IT, JOHN. I ASKED MY DAD TO COME AND LIVE WITH US-AND HE SAID "YES"!
THAT'S FINE WITH ME, EL.
WE'VE TALKED ABOUT THIS MANY TIMES. AND I THINK IT'S A GOOD IDEA. WE ALL GET ALONG-AND APRIL LOVES HER GRANDPA!
WE'LL HAVE SOME ADJUST-MENTS TO MAKE, OF COURSE. WE'LL HAVE OUR UPS AND DOWNS...
I THOUGHT HE SHOULD HAVE OUR ROOM.
THAT IS A "DOWN".

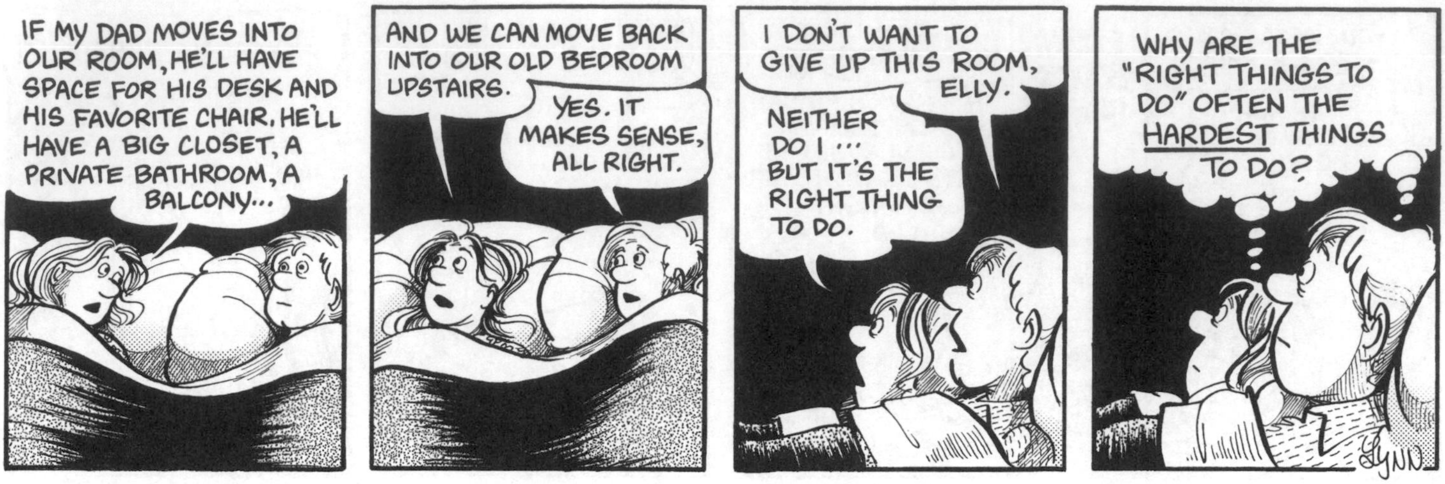
IF MY DAD MOVES INTO OUR ROOM, HE'LL HAVE SPACE FOR HIS DESK AND HIS FAVORITE CHAIR. HE'LL HAVE A BIG CLOSET, A PRIVATE BATHROOM, A BALCONY...
AND WE CAN MOVE BACK INTO OUR OLD BEDROOM UPSTAIRS.
YES. IT MAKES SENSE, ALL RIGHT.
I DON'T WANT TO GIVE UP THIS ROOM, ELLY.
NEITHER DO I ... BUT IT'S THE RIGHT THING TO DO.
WHY ARE THE "RIGHT THINGS TO DO" OFTEN THE HARDEST THINGS TO DO?
LYNN

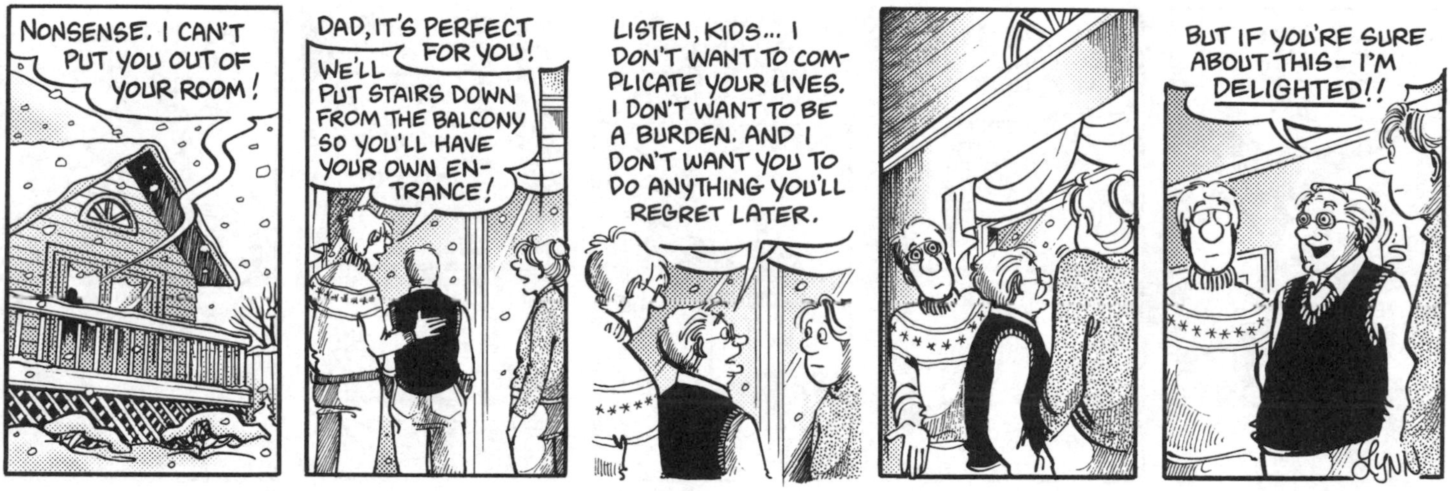
NONSENSE. I CAN'T PUT YOU OUT OF YOUR ROOM!
DAD, IT'S PERFECT FOR YOU!
WE'LL PUT STAIRS DOWN FROM THE BALCONY SO YOU'LL HAVE YOUR OWN EN-TRANCE!
LISTEN, KIDS... I DON'T WANT TO COM-PLICATE YOUR LIVES. I DON'T WANT TO BE A BURDEN. AND I DON'T WANT YOU TO DO ANYTHING YOU'LL REGRET LATER.
BUT IF YOU'RE SURE ABOUT THIS— I'M DELIGHTED!!
LYNN

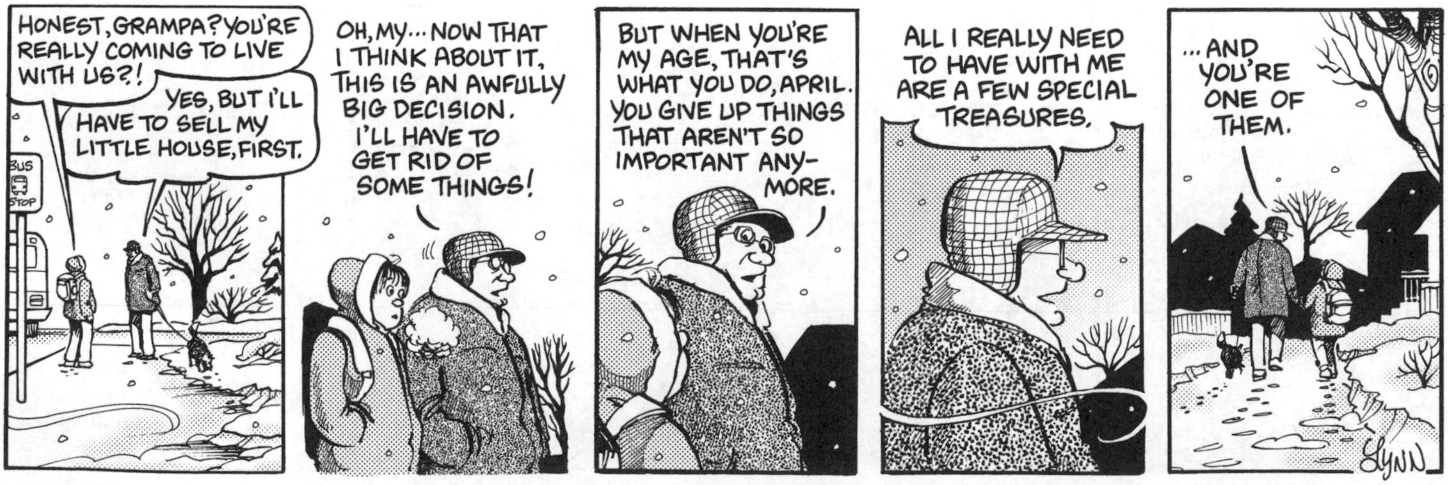
HONEST, GRAMPA? YOU'RE REALLY COMING TO LIVE WITH US?!
YES, BUT I'LL HAVE TO SELL MY LITTLE HOUSE, FIRST.
BUS STOP
OH, MY... NOW THAT I THINK ABOUT IT, THIS IS AN AWFULLY BIG DECISION. I'LL HAVE TO GET RID OF SOME THINGS!
BUT WHEN YOU'RE MY AGE, THAT'S WHAT YOU DO, APRIL. YOU GIVE UP THINGS THAT AREN'T SO IMPORTANT ANY-MORE.
ALL I REALLY NEED TO HAVE WITH ME ARE A FEW SPECIAL TREASURES.
...AND YOU'RE ONE OF THEM.
LYNN

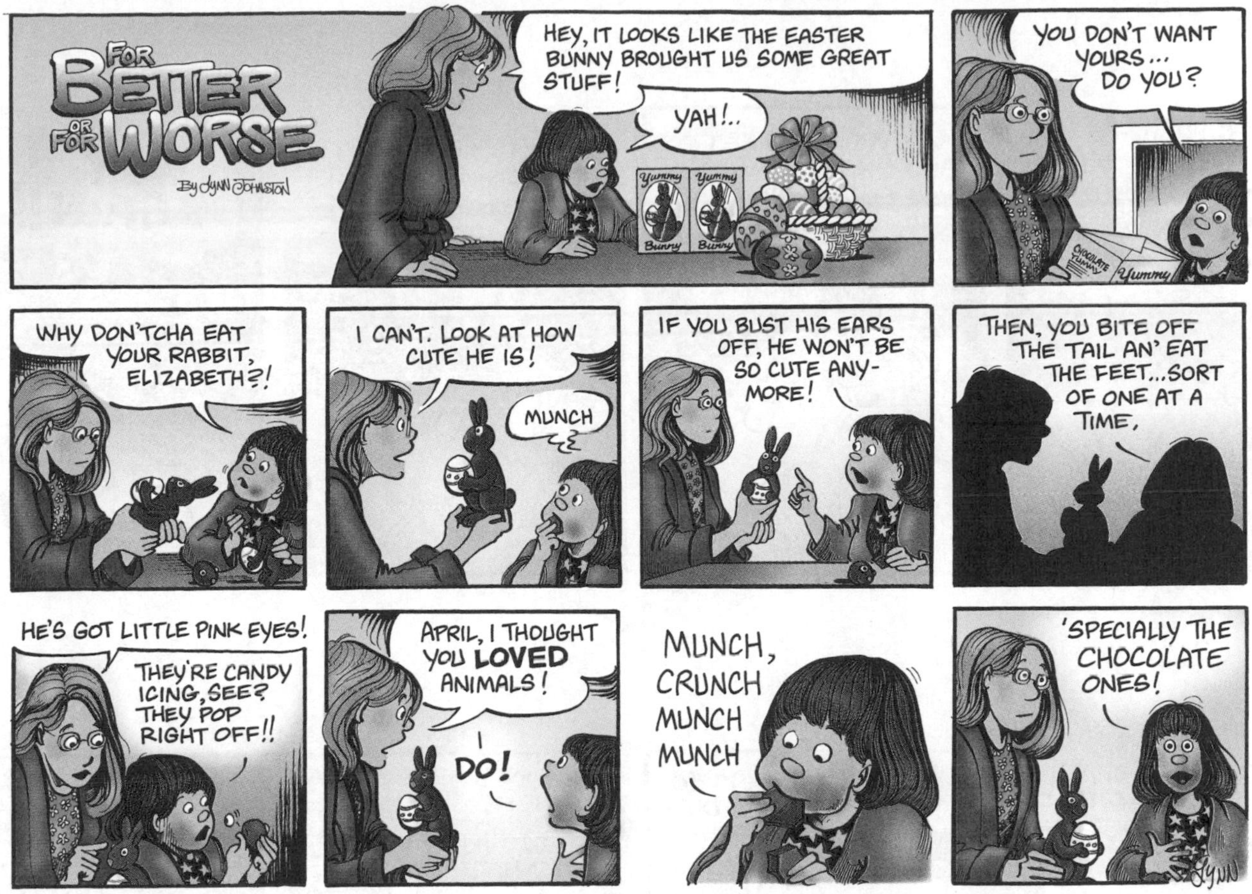
FOR BETTER OR FOR WORSE
BY LYNN JOHNSTON
HEY, IT LOOKS LIKE THE EASTER BUNNY BROUGHT US SOME GREAT STUFF!
YAH!..
Yummy Bunny
Yummy Bunny
YOU DON'T WANT YOURS... DO YOU?
CHOCOLATE YUMMY
Yummy
WHY DON'TCHA EAT YOUR RABBIT, ELIZABETH?!
I CAN'T. LOOK AT HOW CUTE HE IS!
MUNCH
IF YOU BUST HIS EARS OFF, HE WON'T BE SO CUTE ANY-MORE!
THEN, YOU BITE OFF THE TAIL AN' EAT THE FEET...SORT OF ONE AT A TIME.
HE'S GOT LITTLE PINK EYES!
THEY'RE CANDY ICING, SEE? THEY POP RIGHT OFF!!
APRIL, I THOUGHT YOU **LOVED** ANIMALS!
I **DO!**
MUNCH, CRUNCH MUNCH MUNCH
'SPECIALLY THE CHOCOLATE ONES!
LYNN

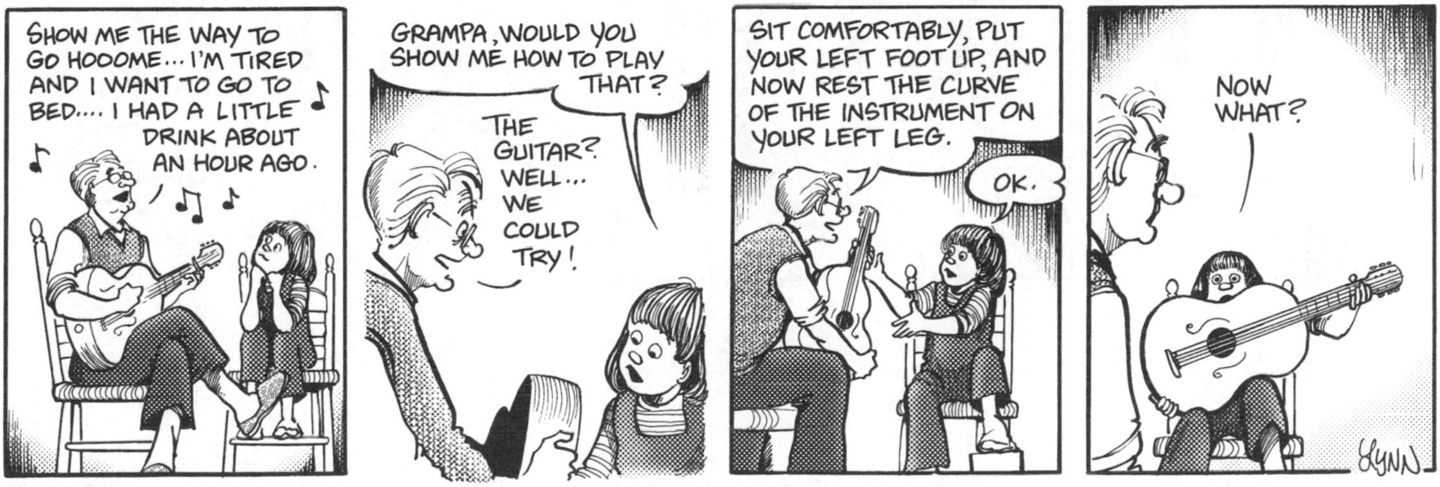
SHOW ME THE WAY TO GO HOOOME... I'M TIRED AND I WANT TO GO TO BED.... I HAD A LITTLE DRINK ABOUT AN HOUR AGO.
GRAMPA, WOULD YOU SHOW ME HOW TO PLAY THAT?
THE GUITAR? WELL... WE COULD TRY!
SIT COMFORTABLY, PUT YOUR LEFT FOOT UP, AND NOW REST THE CURVE OF THE INSTRUMENT ON YOUR LEFT LEG.
OK.
NOW WHAT?
LYNN

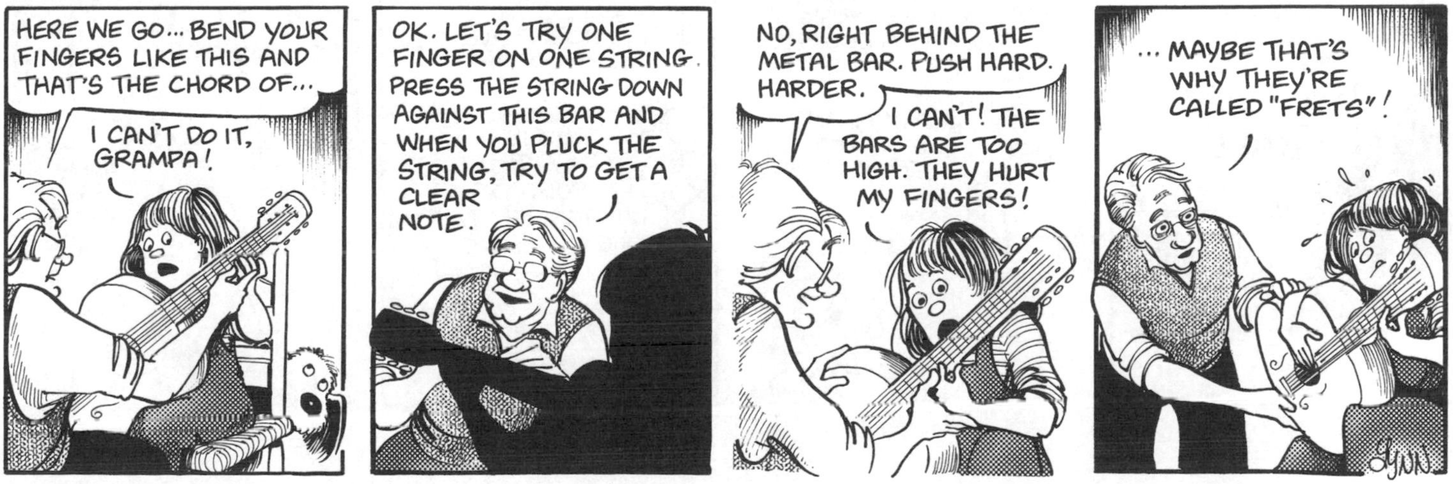
HERE WE GO... BEND YOUR FINGERS LIKE THIS AND THAT'S THE CHORD OF...
I CAN'T DO IT, GRAMPA!
OK. LET'S TRY ONE FINGER ON ONE STRING. PRESS THE STRING DOWN AGAINST THIS BAR AND WHEN YOU PLUCK THE STRING, TRY TO GET A CLEAR NOTE.
NO, RIGHT BEHIND THE METAL BAR. PUSH HARD. HARDER.
I CAN'T! THE BARS ARE TOO HIGH. THEY HURT MY FINGERS!
... MAYBE THAT'S WHY THEY'RE CALLED "FRETS"!
LYNN

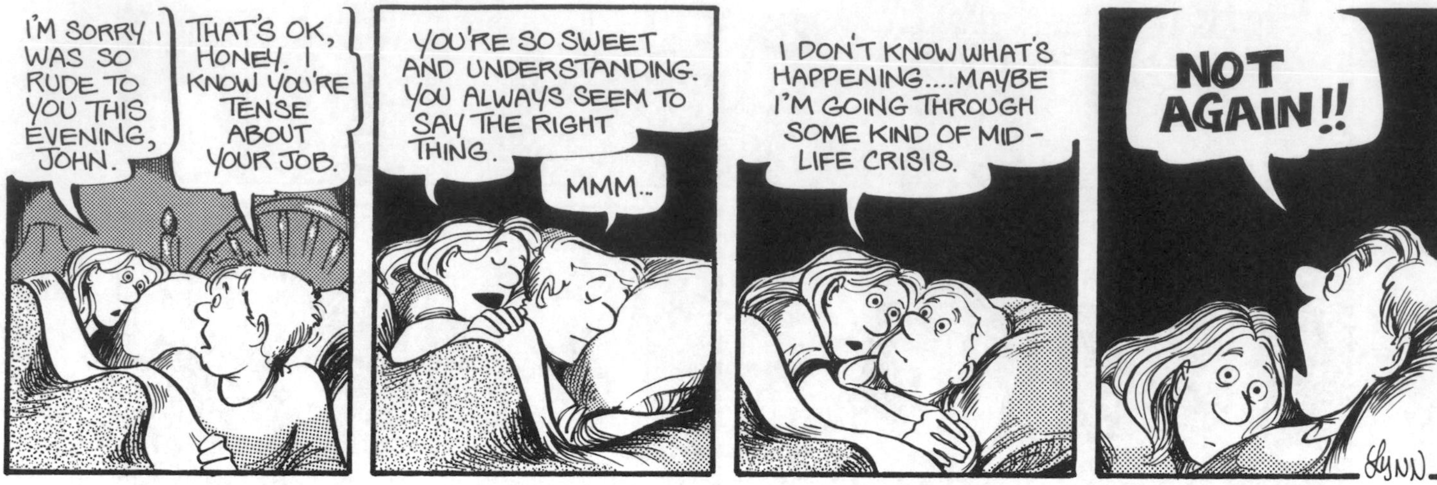
I'M SORRY I WAS SO RUDE TO YOU THIS EVENING, JOHN.
THAT'S OK, HONEY. I KNOW YOU'RE TENSE ABOUT YOUR JOB.
YOU'RE SO SWEET AND UNDERSTANDING. YOU ALWAYS SEEM TO SAY THE RIGHT THING.
MMM...
I DON'T KNOW WHAT'S HAPPENING....MAYBE I'M GOING THROUGH SOME KIND OF MID-LIFE CRISIS.
NOT AGAIN!!
LYNN

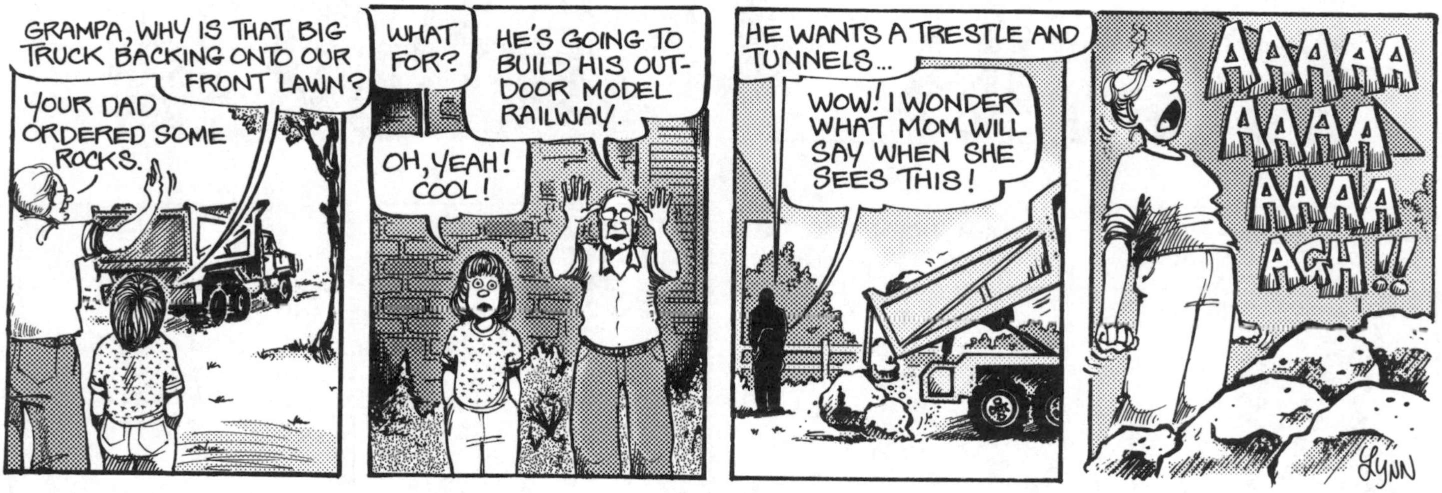
GRAMPA, WHY IS THAT BIG TRUCK BACKING ONTO OUR FRONT LAWN?
YOUR DAD ORDERED SOME ROCKS.
WHAT FOR?
HE'S GOING TO BUILD HIS OUT-DOOR MODEL RAILWAY.
OH, YEAH! COOL!
HE WANTS A TRESTLE AND TUNNELS...
WOW! I WONDER WHAT MOM WILL SAY WHEN SHE SEES THIS!
AAAAA AAAA AAAA AGH!!
LYNN

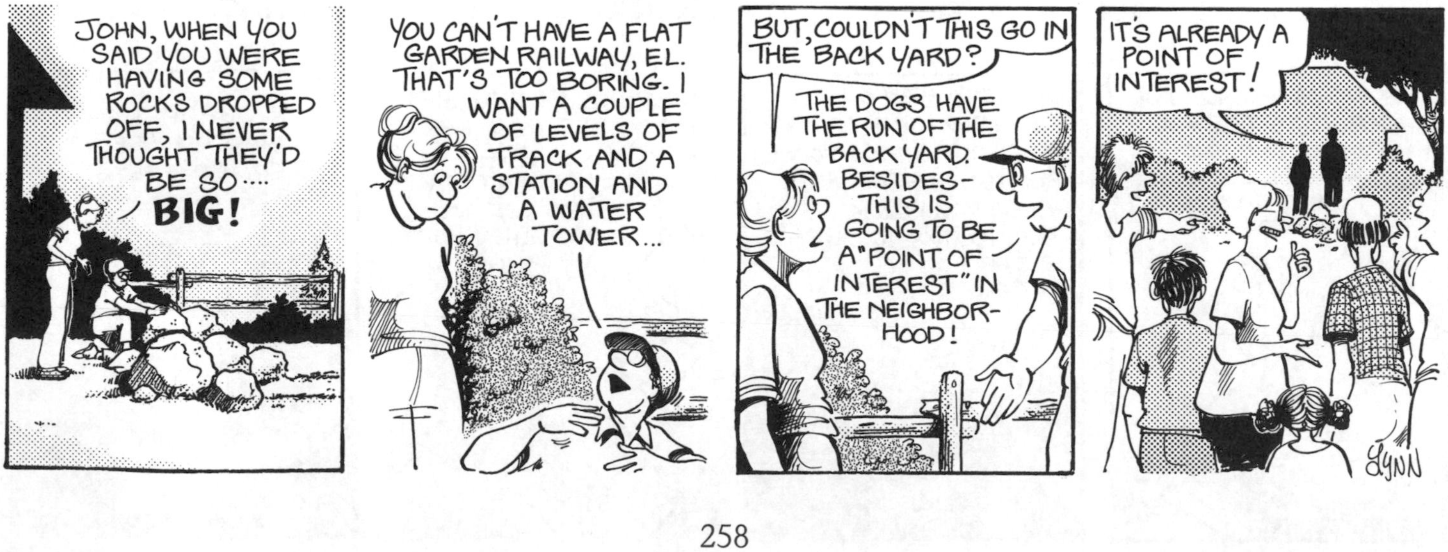
JOHN, WHEN YOU SAID YOU WERE HAVING SOME ROCKS DROPPED OFF, I NEVER THOUGHT THEY'D BE SO.... BIG!
YOU CAN'T HAVE A FLAT GARDEN RAILWAY, EL. THAT'S TOO BORING. I WANT A COUPLE OF LEVELS OF TRACK AND A STATION AND A WATER TOWER...
BUT, COULDN'T THIS GO IN THE BACK YARD?
THE DOGS HAVE THE RUN OF THE BACK YARD. BESIDES-THIS IS GOING TO BE A "POINT OF INTEREST" IN THE NEIGHBOR-HOOD!
IT'S ALREADY A POINT OF INTEREST!
LYNN

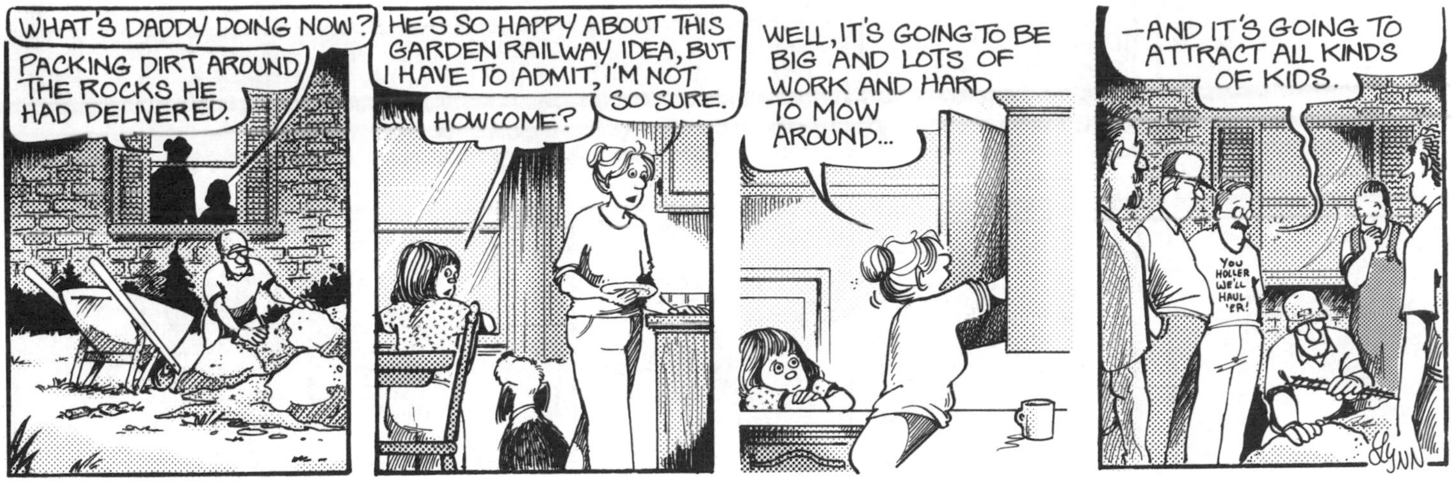
WHAT'S DADDY DOING NOW?
PACKING DIRT AROUND THE ROCKS HE HAD DELIVERED.
HE'S SO HAPPY ABOUT THIS GARDEN RAILWAY IDEA, BUT I HAVE TO ADMIT, I'M NOT SO SURE.
HOW COME?
WELL, IT'S GOING TO BE BIG AND LOTS OF WORK AND HARD TO MOW AROUND...
—AND IT'S GOING TO ATTRACT ALL KINDS OF KIDS.
YOU HOLLER WE'LL HAUL 'ER!
LYNN

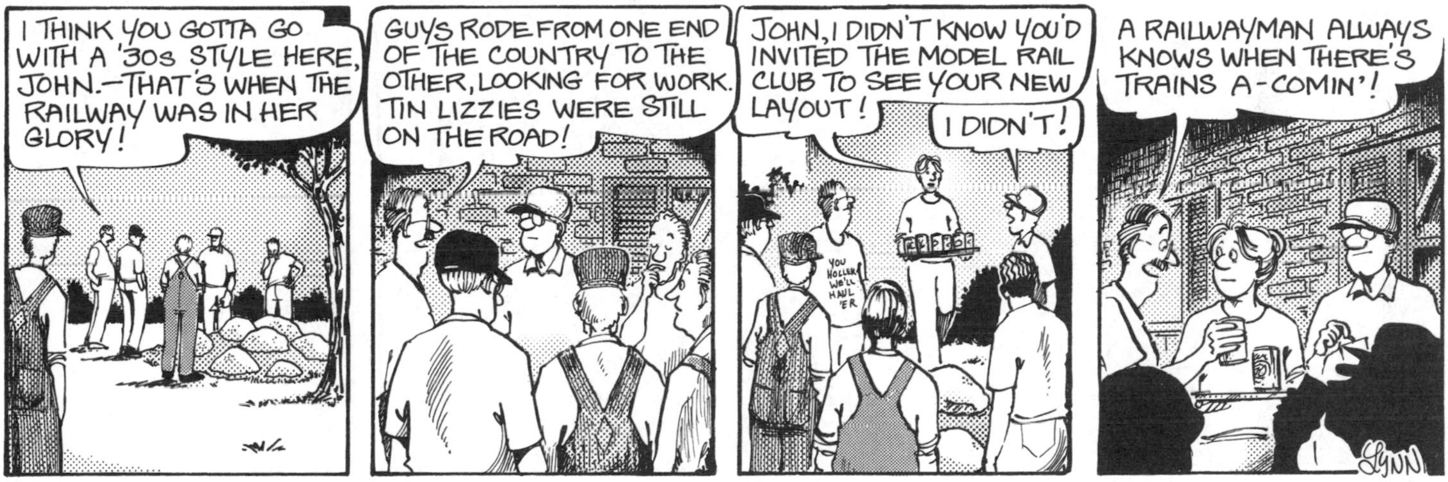
I THINK YOU GOTTA GO WITH A '30s STYLE HERE, JOHN.—THAT'S WHEN THE RAILWAY WAS IN HER GLORY!
GUYS RODE FROM ONE END OF THE COUNTRY TO THE OTHER, LOOKING FOR WORK. TIN LIZZIES WERE STILL ON THE ROAD!
JOHN, I DIDN'T KNOW YOU'D INVITED THE MODEL RAIL CLUB TO SEE YOUR NEW LAYOUT!
I DIDN'T!
YOU HOLLER WE'LL HAUL 'ER
A RAILWAYMAN ALWAYS KNOWS WHEN THERE'S TRAINS A-COMIN'!
LYNN

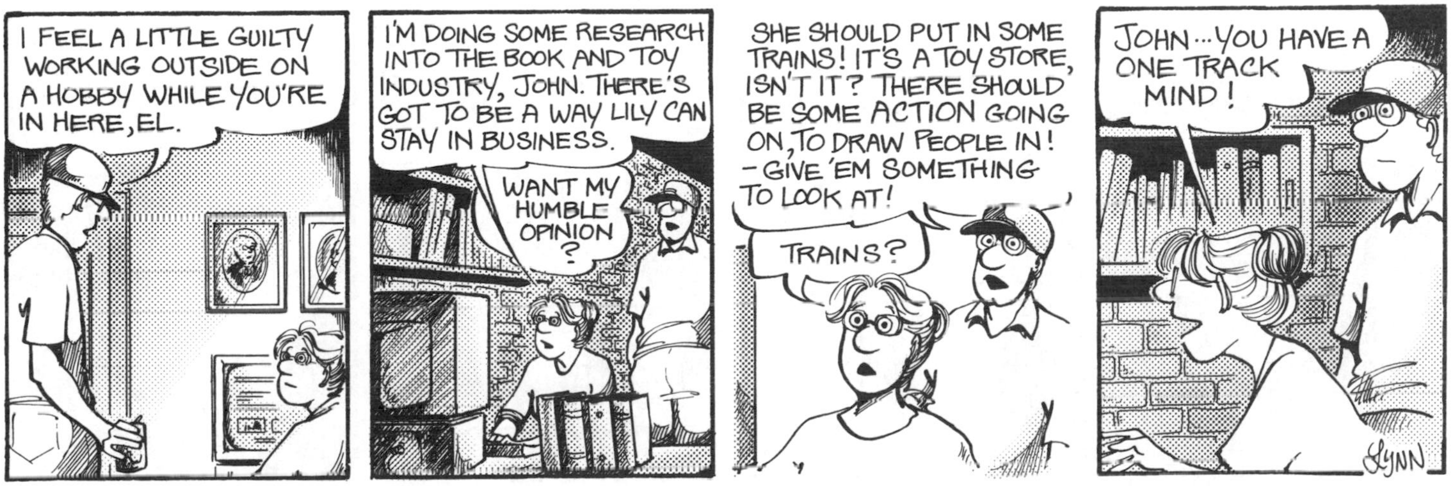
I FEEL A LITTLE GUILTY WORKING OUTSIDE ON A HOBBY WHILE YOU'RE IN HERE, EL.
I'M DOING SOME RESEARCH INTO THE BOOK AND TOY INDUSTRY, JOHN. THERE'S GOT TO BE A WAY LILY CAN STAY IN BUSINESS.
WANT MY HUMBLE OPINION?
SHE SHOULD PUT IN SOME TRAINS! IT'S A TOY STORE, ISN'T IT? THERE SHOULD BE SOME ACTION GOING ON, TO DRAW PEOPLE IN! - GIVE 'EM SOMETHING TO LOOK AT!
TRAINS?
JOHN ... YOU HAVE A ONE TRACK MIND!
LYNN

Panel 1: THIS IS A GOOD ARTI-CLE, MICHAEL! YOUR FOLKS WILL BE GET-TING CALLS FROM ANTIQUE DEALERS SOON! — THE CALLS HAVE STARTED ALREADY.

Panel 2: THEY DON'T KNOW WHAT TO DO WITH THE TOYS, DEANNA; HOW MANY TO SELL, WHOM TO TRUST...

Panel 3: IT'S AMAZING HOW SOMETHING UN-EXPECTED CAN SUDDENLY SET YOUR HEAD SPINNING! — UM....

Panel 4: I MIGHT HAVE A JOB IN TORONTO. IF I GET IT... AND IF IT'S FULL TIME —WE COULD GET MARRIED.

Panel 5: MICHAEL?

Panel 6: DEANNA, DID YOU SAY YOU WANTED TO GET MARRIED? — I SAID WE COULD GET MARRIED IF I GET THIS JOB!

Panel 7: SOMEONE I KNOW IS TAKING A MATERNITY LEAVE FROM THE PHAR-MACY AT SICK CHILDREN'S HOSPITAL IN TORONTO. THEY'LL NEED A REPLACEMENT PHARMACIST, AND I'VE GOT A PRETTY GOOD CHANCE!

Panel 8: SHE MAY NOT WANT TO GO BACK FULL TIME, WHICH MEANS I COULD TAKE THAT POSITION! MICHAEL, THIS IS EXACTLY WHAT I'VE BEEN WAITING FOR.

Panel 9: NOW, ARE YOU LISTENING TO ME, OR ARE YOU DAYDREAMING? — BOTH.

Panel 10: SO, BESIDES ME... WHAT'S CHANGED AROUND HERE?

Panel 11: I MIGHT HAVE A JOB IN TORONTO! — THAT MEANS WE COULD GET MARRIED, WEED-O!

Panel 12: ISN'T THAT INCREDIBLE NEWS?! — I DUNNO...

Panel 13: WOULD I BE INVITED AS A FRIEND OR A PHOTO-GRAPHER?

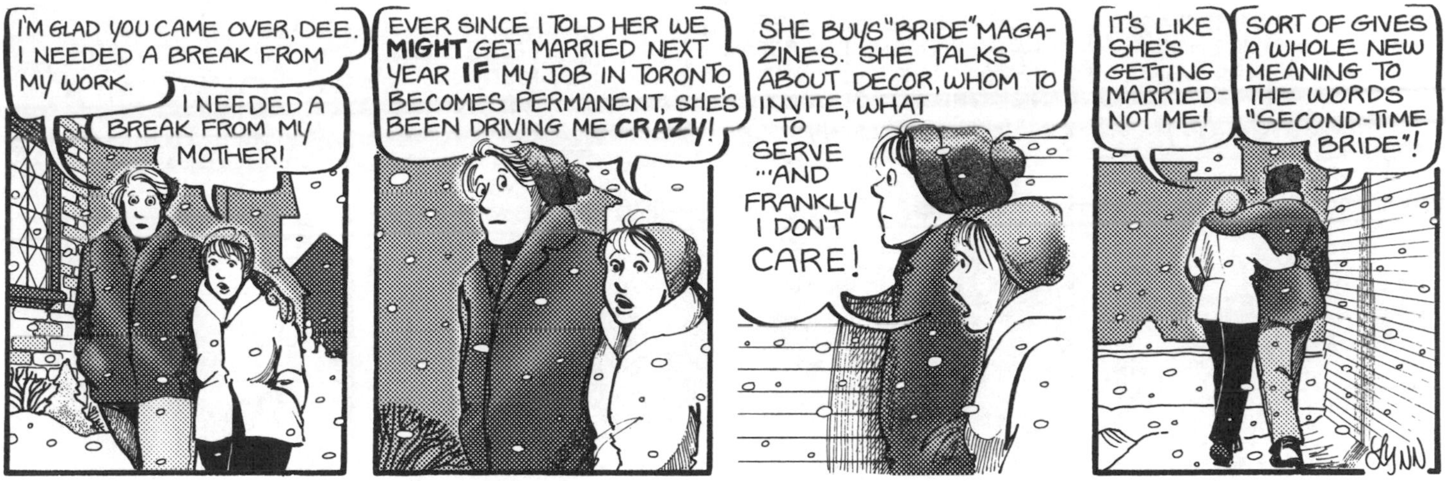
I'M GLAD YOU CAME OVER, DEE. I NEEDED A BREAK FROM MY WORK.
I NEEDED A BREAK FROM MY MOTHER!
EVER SINCE I TOLD HER WE **MIGHT** GET MARRIED NEXT YEAR **IF** MY JOB IN TORONTO BECOMES PERMANENT, SHE'S BEEN DRIVING ME **CRAZY**!
SHE BUYS "BRIDE" MAGAZINES. SHE TALKS ABOUT DECOR, WHOM TO INVITE, WHAT TO SERVE ...AND FRANKLY I DON'T CARE!
IT'S LIKE SHE'S GETTING MARRIED- NOT ME!
SORT OF GIVES A WHOLE NEW MEANING TO THE WORDS "SECOND-TIME BRIDE"!
LYNN

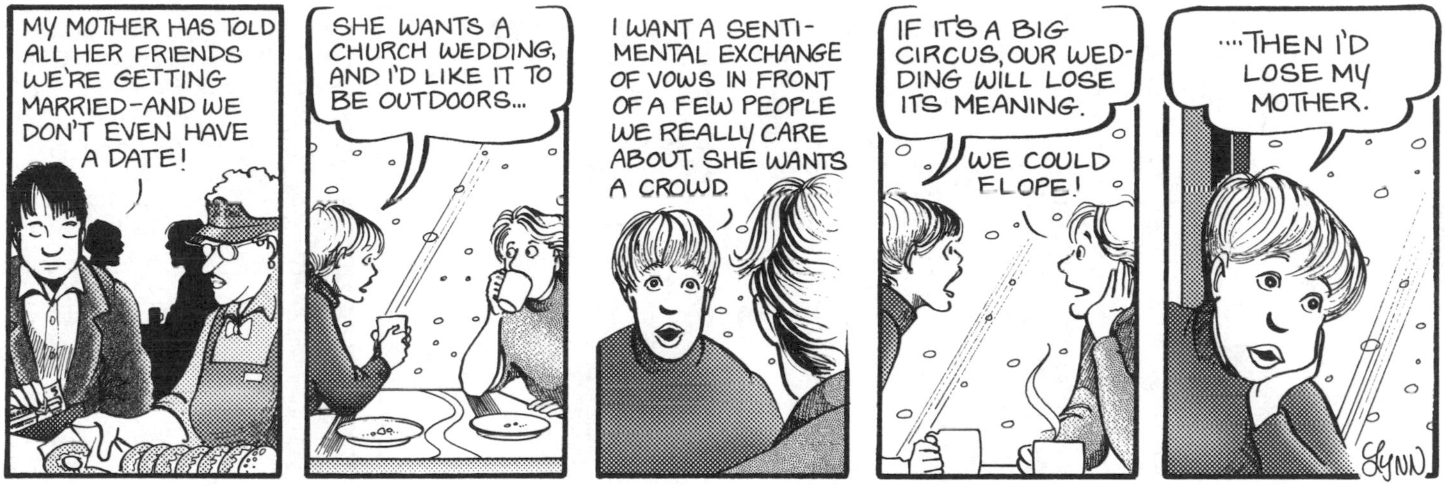
MY MOTHER HAS TOLD ALL HER FRIENDS WE'RE GETTING MARRIED–AND WE DON'T EVEN HAVE A DATE!
SHE WANTS A CHURCH WEDDING, AND I'D LIKE IT TO BE OUTDOORS...
I WANT A SENTIMENTAL EXCHANGE OF VOWS IN FRONT OF A FEW PEOPLE WE REALLY CARE ABOUT. SHE WANTS A CROWD.
IF IT'S A BIG CIRCUS, OUR WEDDING WILL LOSE ITS MEANING.
WE COULD ELOPE!
...THEN I'D LOSE MY MOTHER.
LYNN

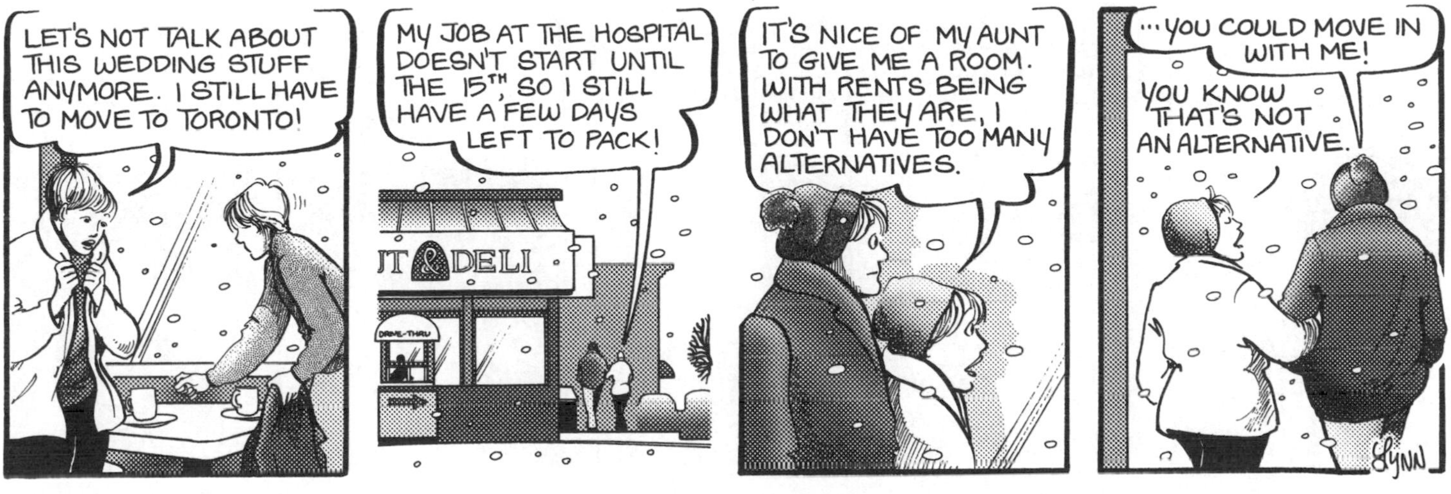
LET'S NOT TALK ABOUT THIS WEDDING STUFF ANYMORE. I STILL HAVE TO MOVE TO TORONTO!
MY JOB AT THE HOSPITAL DOESN'T START UNTIL THE 15TH, SO I STILL HAVE A FEW DAYS LEFT TO PACK!
UT & DELI
DRIVE-THRU
IT'S NICE OF MY AUNT TO GIVE ME A ROOM. WITH RENTS BEING WHAT THEY ARE, I DON'T HAVE TOO MANY ALTERNATIVES.
...YOU COULD MOVE IN WITH ME!
YOU KNOW THAT'S NOT AN ALTERNATIVE.
LYNN

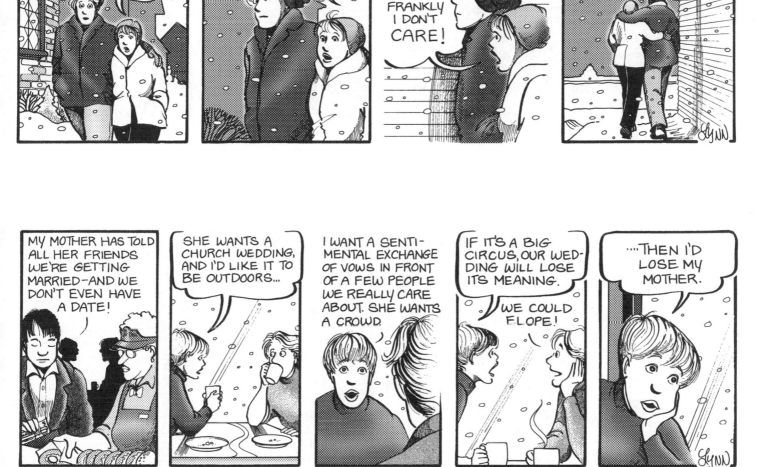

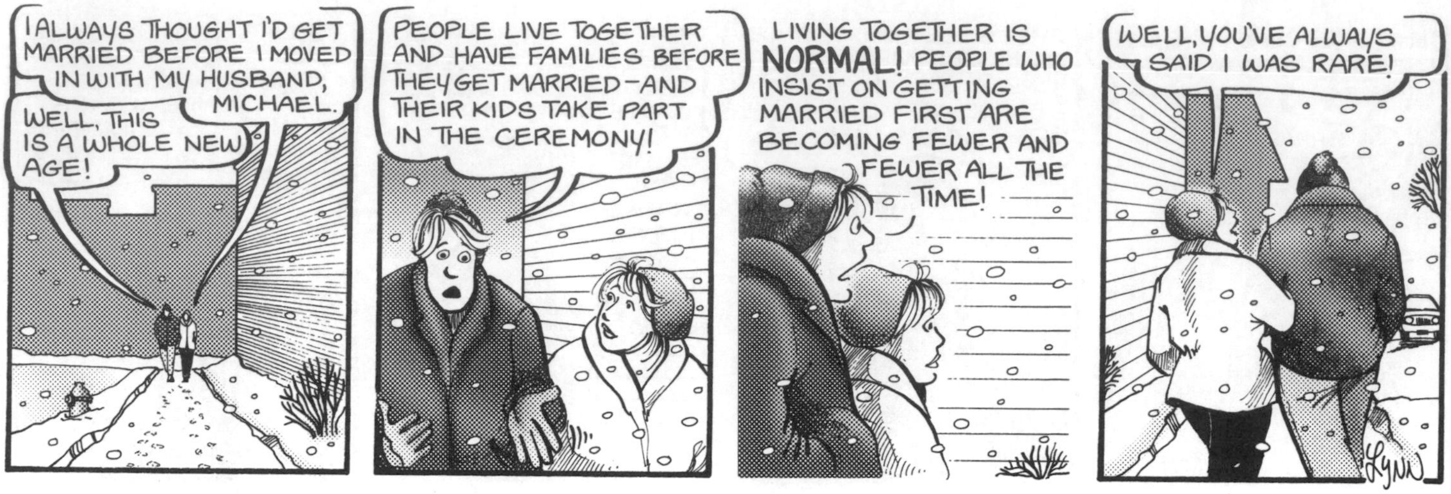
I ALWAYS THOUGHT I'D GET MARRIED BEFORE I MOVED IN WITH MY HUSBAND, MICHAEL.
WELL, THIS IS A WHOLE NEW AGE!
PEOPLE LIVE TOGETHER AND HAVE FAMILIES BEFORE THEY GET MARRIED-AND THEIR KIDS TAKE PART IN THE CEREMONY!
LIVING TOGETHER IS NORMAL! PEOPLE WHO INSIST ON GETTING MARRIED FIRST ARE BECOMING FEWER AND FEWER ALL THE TIME!
WELL, YOU'VE ALWAYS SAID I WAS RARE!
LYNN

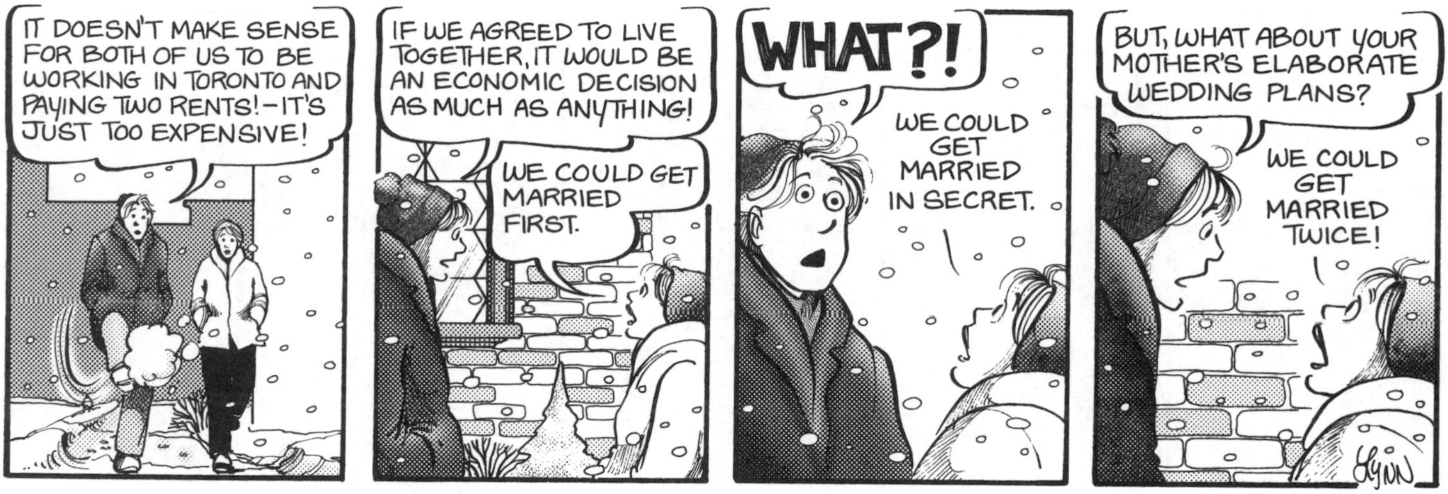
IT DOESN'T MAKE SENSE FOR BOTH OF US TO BE WORKING IN TORONTO AND PAYING TWO RENTS!-IT'S JUST TOO EXPENSIVE!
IF WE AGREED TO LIVE TOGETHER, IT WOULD BE AN ECONOMIC DECISION AS MUCH AS ANYTHING!
WE COULD GET MARRIED FIRST.
WHAT?!
WE COULD GET MARRIED IN SECRET.
BUT, WHAT ABOUT YOUR MOTHER'S ELABORATE WEDDING PLANS?
WE COULD GET MARRIED TWICE!
LYNN

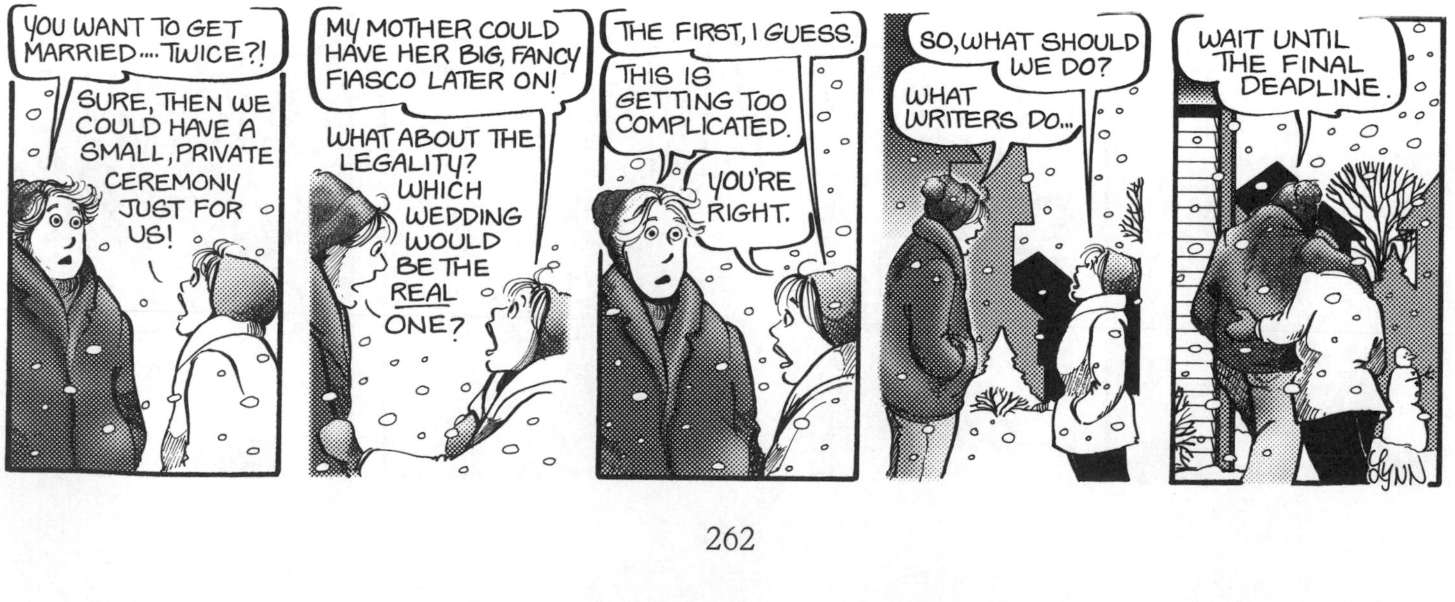
YOU WANT TO GET MARRIED.... TWICE?!
SURE, THEN WE COULD HAVE A SMALL, PRIVATE CEREMONY JUST FOR US!
MY MOTHER COULD HAVE HER BIG, FANCY FIASCO LATER ON!
WHAT ABOUT THE LEGALITY? WHICH WEDDING WOULD BE THE REAL ONE?
THE FIRST, I GUESS.
THIS IS GETTING TOO COMPLICATED.
YOU'RE RIGHT.
SO, WHAT SHOULD WE DO?
WHAT WRITERS DO...
WAIT UNTIL THE FINAL DEADLINE.
LYNN

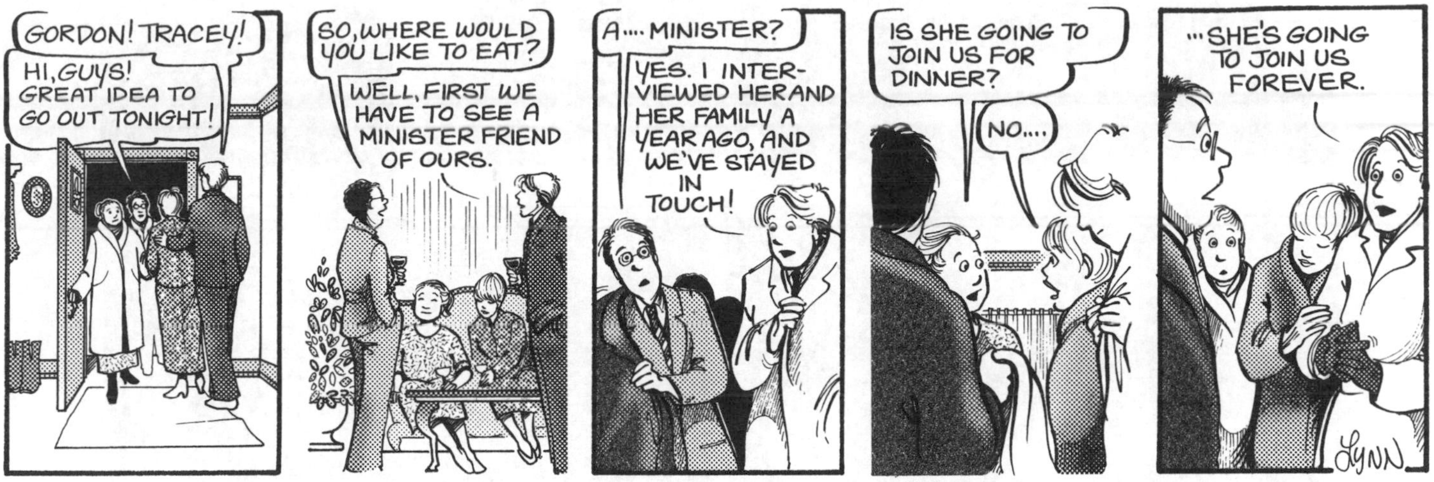
GORDON! TRACEY!
HI, GUYS! GREAT IDEA TO GO OUT TONIGHT!
SO, WHERE WOULD YOU LIKE TO EAT?
WELL, FIRST WE HAVE TO SEE A MINISTER FRIEND OF OURS.
A.... MINISTER?
YES. I INTERVIEWED HER AND HER FAMILY A YEAR AGO, AND WE'VE STAYED IN TOUCH!
IS SHE GOING TO JOIN US FOR DINNER?
NO....
...SHE'S GOING TO JOIN US FOREVER.
LYNN

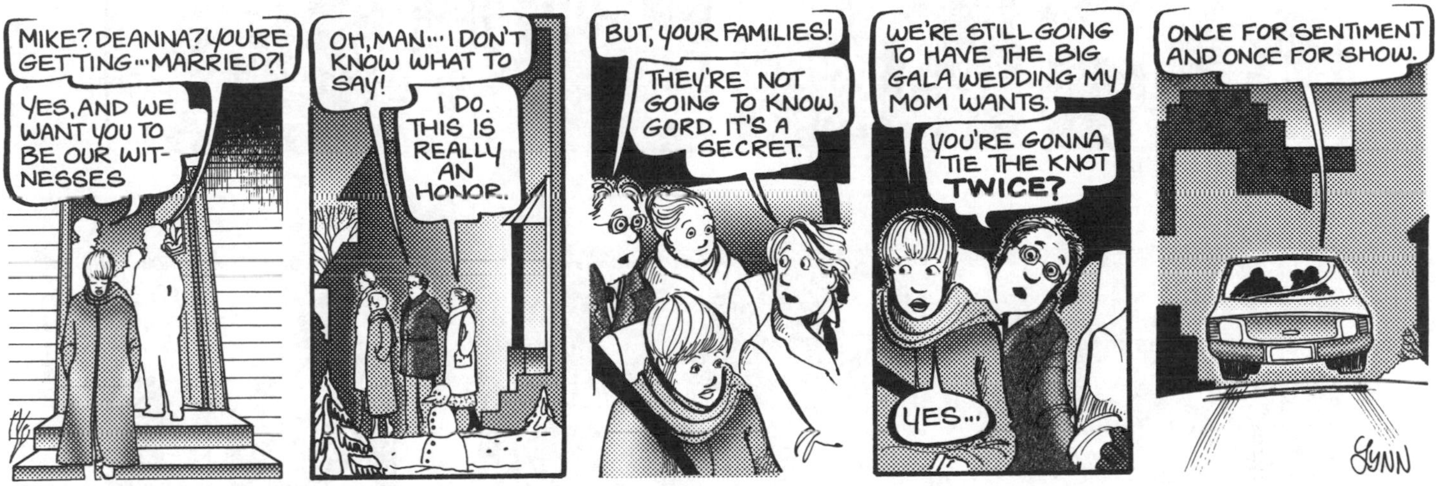
MIKE? DEANNA? YOU'RE GETTING...MARRIED?!
YES, AND WE WANT YOU TO BE OUR WITNESSES
OH, MAN... I DON'T KNOW WHAT TO SAY!
I DO. THIS IS REALLY AN HONOR.
BUT, YOUR FAMILIES!
THEY'RE NOT GOING TO KNOW, GORD. IT'S A SECRET.
WE'RE STILL GOING TO HAVE THE BIG GALA WEDDING MY MOM WANTS.
YOU'RE GONNA TIE THE KNOT TWICE?
YES...
ONCE FOR SENTIMENT AND ONCE FOR SHOW.
LYNN

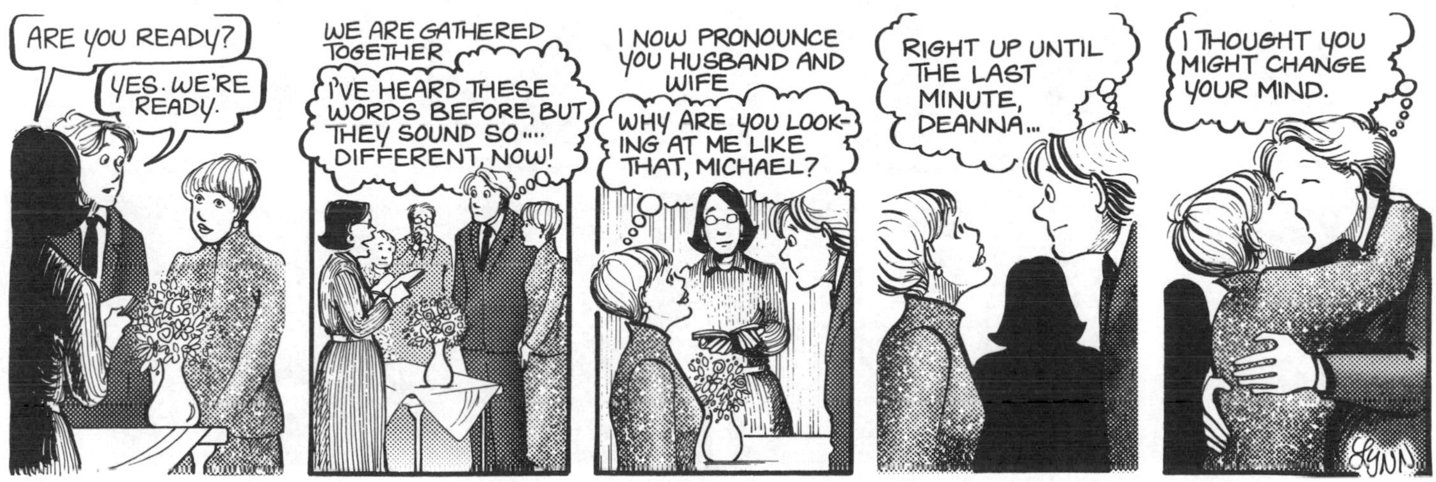
ARE YOU READY?
YES. WE'RE READY.
WE ARE GATHERED TOGETHER
I'VE HEARD THESE WORDS BEFORE, BUT THEY SOUND SO.... DIFFERENT, NOW!
I NOW PRONOUNCE YOU HUSBAND AND WIFE
WHY ARE YOU LOOKING AT ME LIKE THAT, MICHAEL?
RIGHT UP UNTIL THE LAST MINUTE, DEANNA...
I THOUGHT YOU MIGHT CHANGE YOUR MIND.
LYNN

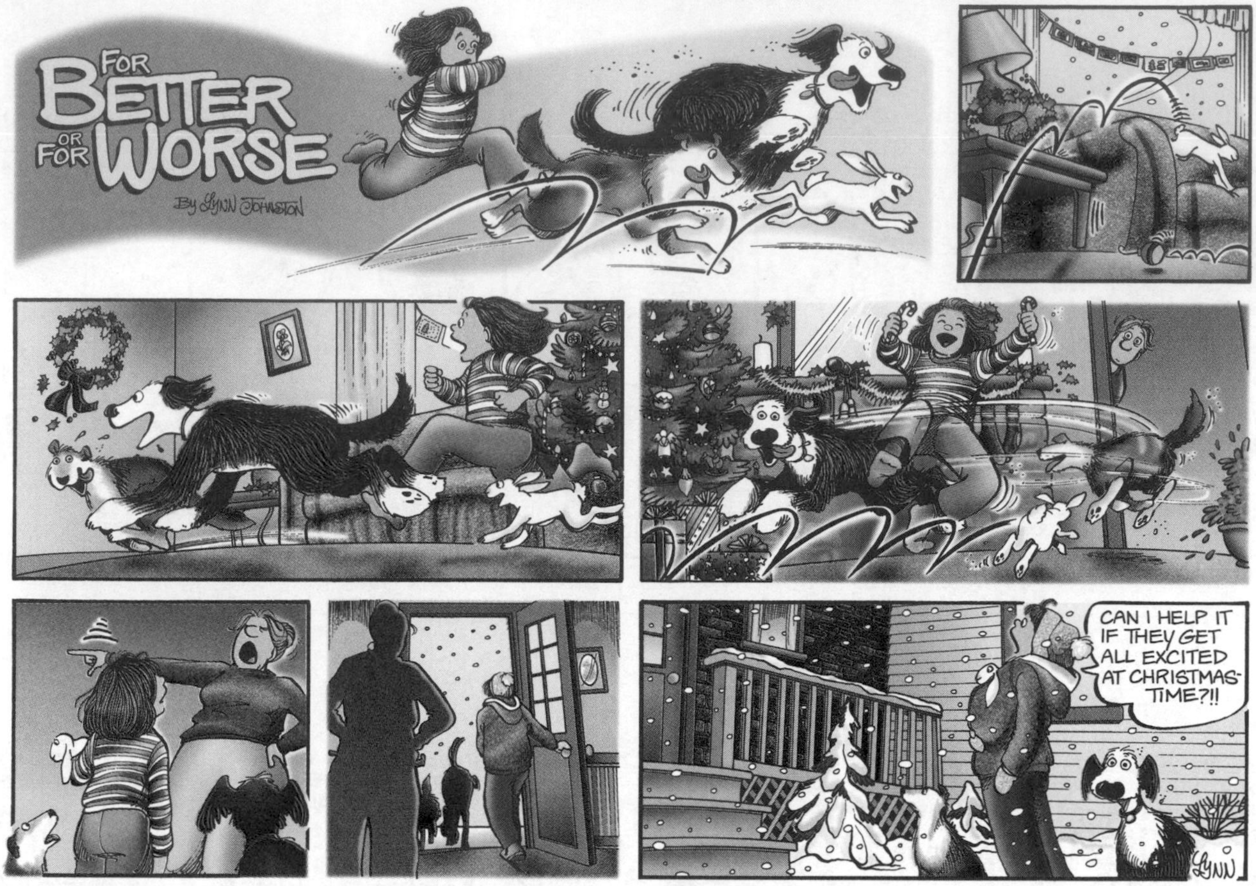
FOR BETTER OR FOR WORSE
BY LYNN JOHNSTON
CAN I HELP IT IF THEY GET ALL EXCITED AT CHRISTMAS-TIME?!!
LYNN

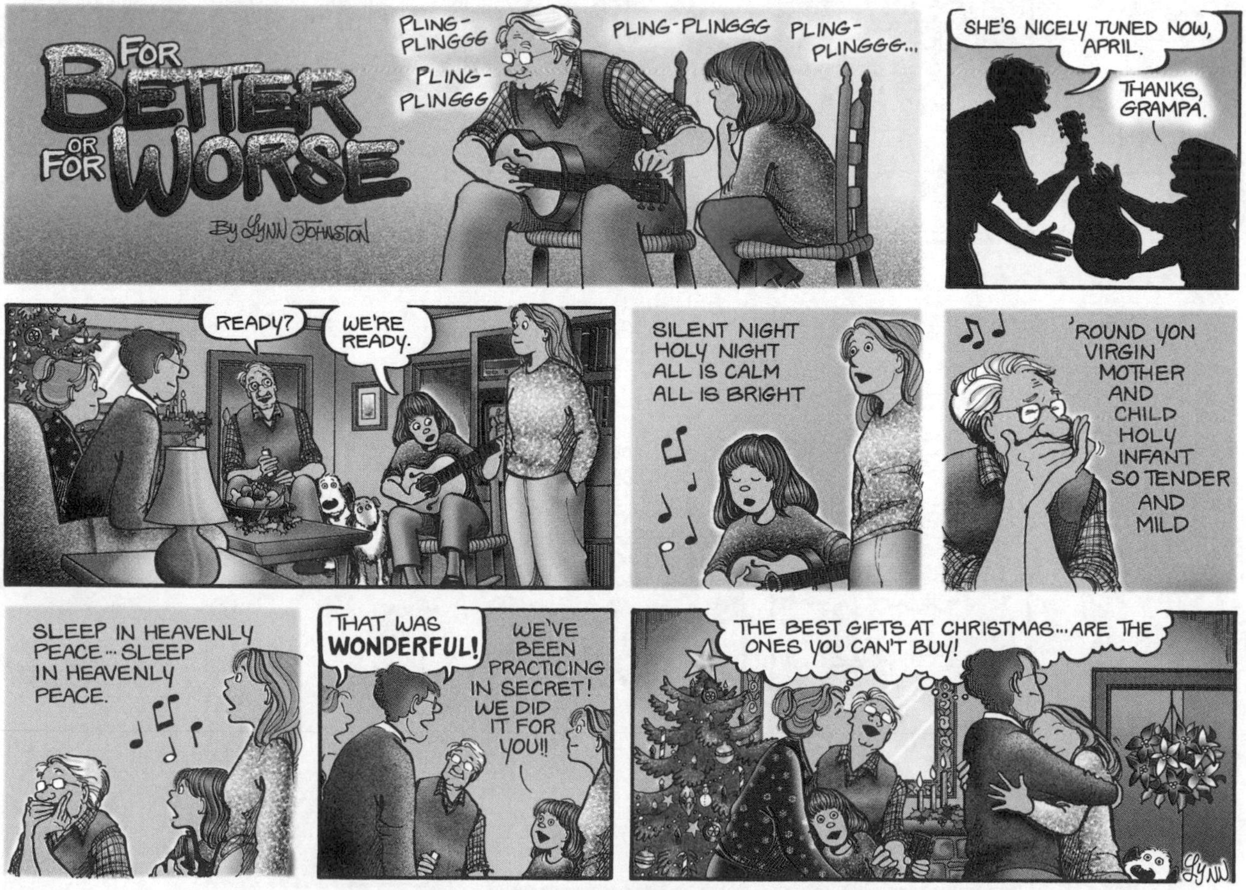
FOR BETTER OR FOR WORSE
BY LYNN JOHNSTON
PLING-PLINGGG
PLING-PLINGGG
PLING-PLINGGG
PLING-PLINGGG...
SHE'S NICELY TUNED NOW, APRIL.
THANKS, GRAMPA.
READY?
WE'RE READY.
SILENT NIGHT HOLY NIGHT ALL IS CALM ALL IS BRIGHT
'ROUND YON VIRGIN MOTHER AND CHILD HOLY INFANT SO TENDER AND MILD
SLEEP IN HEAVENLY PEACE... SLEEP IN HEAVENLY PEACE.
THAT WAS WONDERFUL!
WE'VE BEEN PRACTICING IN SECRET! WE DID IT FOR YOU!!
THE BEST GIFTS AT CHRISTMAS... ARE THE ONES YOU CAN'T BUY!
LYNN

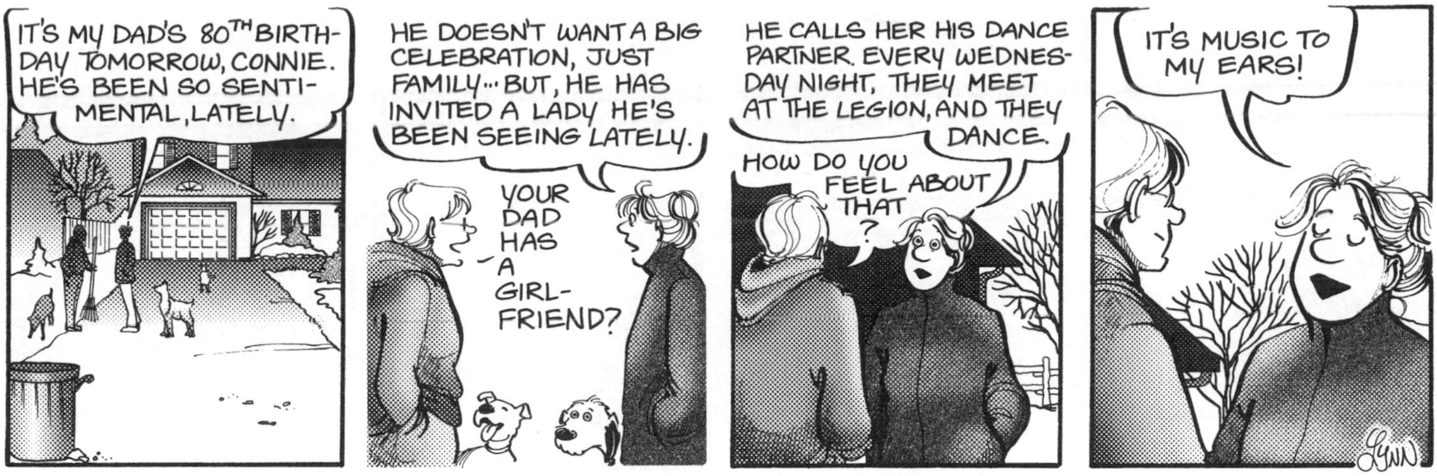
IT'S MY DAD'S 80TH BIRTHDAY TOMORROW, CONNIE. HE'S BEEN SO SENTIMENTAL, LATELY.
HE DOESN'T WANT A BIG CELEBRATION, JUST FAMILY... BUT, HE HAS INVITED A LADY HE'S BEEN SEEING LATELY.
YOUR DAD HAS A GIRL-FRIEND?
HE CALLS HER HIS DANCE PARTNER. EVERY WEDNESDAY NIGHT, THEY MEET AT THE LEGION, AND THEY DANCE.
HOW DO YOU FEEL ABOUT THAT?
IT'S MUSIC TO MY EARS!
LYNN

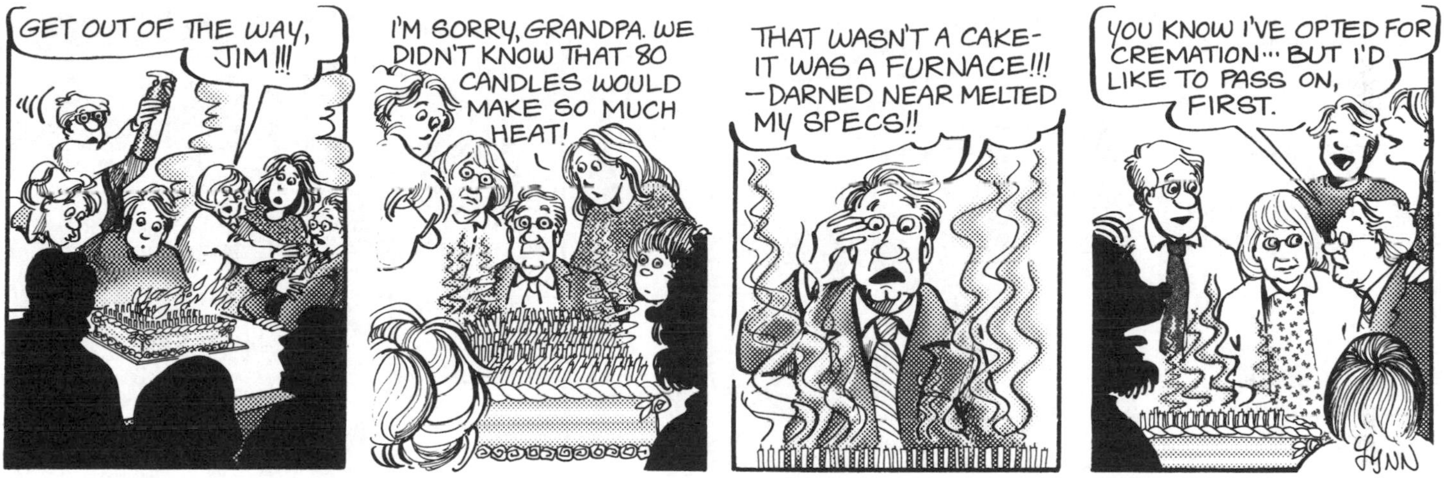
GET OUT OF THE WAY, JIM!!!
I'M SORRY, GRANDPA. WE DIDN'T KNOW THAT 80 CANDLES WOULD MAKE SO MUCH HEAT!
THAT WASN'T A CAKE- IT WAS A FURNACE!!! —DARNED NEAR MELTED MY SPECS!!
YOU KNOW I'VE OPTED FOR CREMATION... BUT I'D LIKE TO PASS ON, FIRST.
LYNN

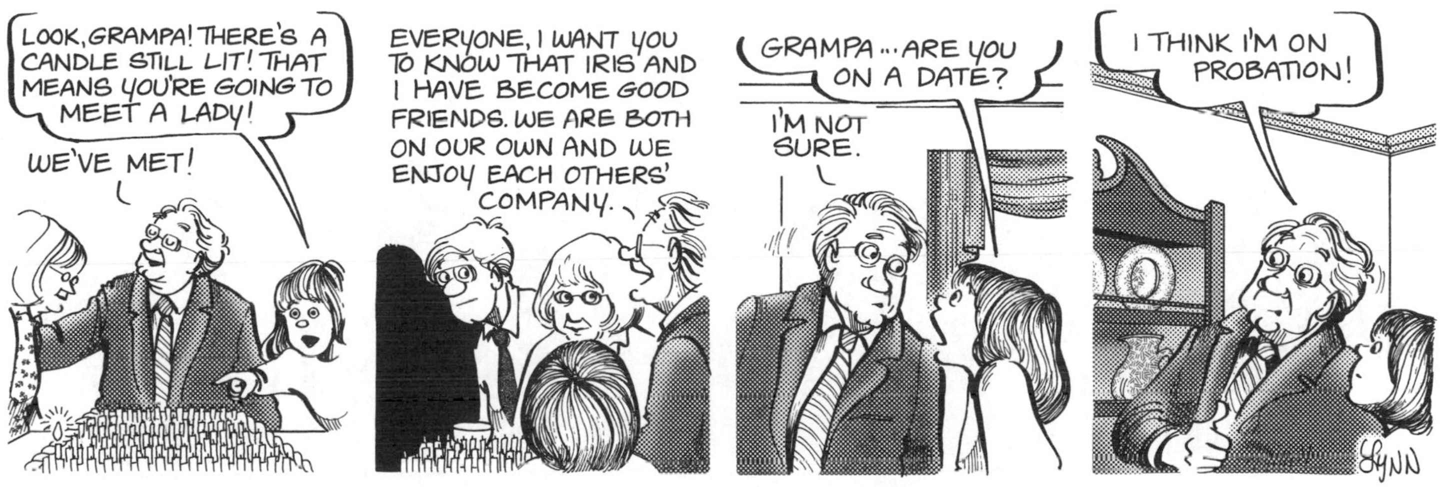
LOOK, GRAMPA! THERE'S A CANDLE STILL LIT! THAT MEANS YOU'RE GOING TO MEET A LADY!
WE'VE MET!
EVERYONE, I WANT YOU TO KNOW THAT IRIS AND I HAVE BECOME GOOD FRIENDS. WE ARE BOTH ON OUR OWN AND WE ENJOY EACH OTHERS' COMPANY.
GRAMPA... ARE YOU ON A DATE?
I'M NOT SURE.
I THINK I'M ON PROBATION!
LYNN

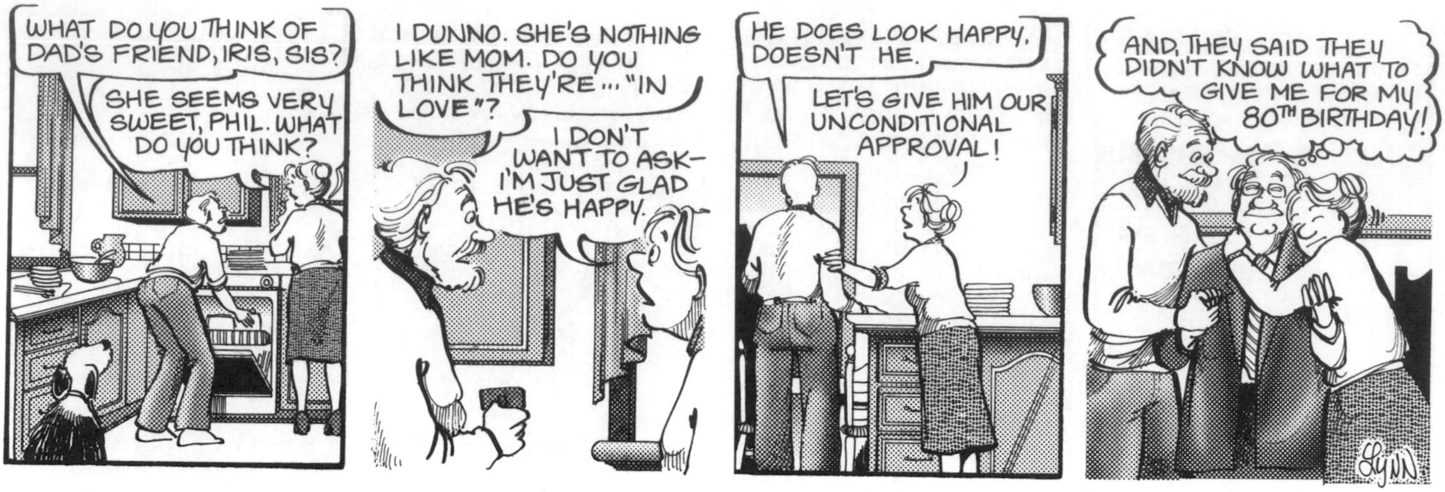
WHAT DO YOU THINK OF DAD'S FRIEND, IRIS, SIS?
SHE SEEMS VERY SWEET, PHIL. WHAT DO YOU THINK?
I DUNNO. SHE'S NOTHING LIKE MOM. DO YOU THINK THEY'RE... "IN LOVE"?
I DON'T WANT TO ASK- I'M JUST GLAD HE'S HAPPY.
HE DOES LOOK HAPPY, DOESN'T HE.
LET'S GIVE HIM OUR UNCONDITIONAL APPROVAL!
AND, THEY SAID THEY DIDN'T KNOW WHAT TO GIVE ME FOR MY 80TH BIRTHDAY!
LYNN

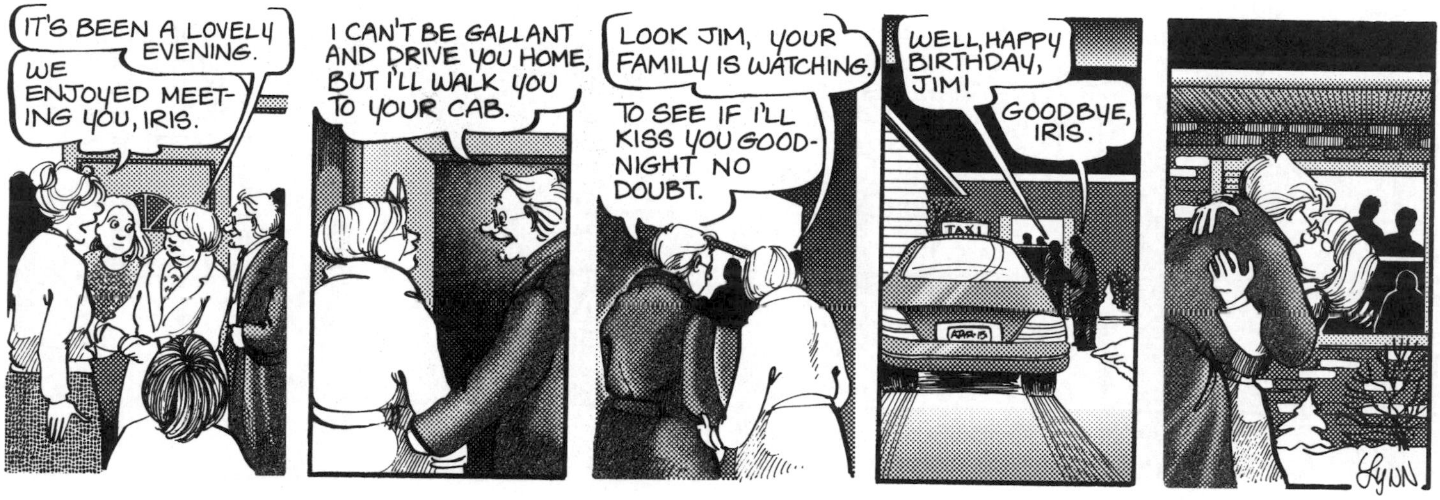
IT'S BEEN A LOVELY EVENING.
WE ENJOYED MEETING YOU, IRIS.
I CAN'T BE GALLANT AND DRIVE YOU HOME, BUT I'LL WALK YOU TO YOUR CAB.
LOOK JIM, YOUR FAMILY IS WATCHING.
TO SEE IF I'LL KISS YOU GOOD-NIGHT NO DOUBT.
WELL, HAPPY BIRTHDAY, JIM!
GOODBYE, IRIS.
TAXI
LYNN

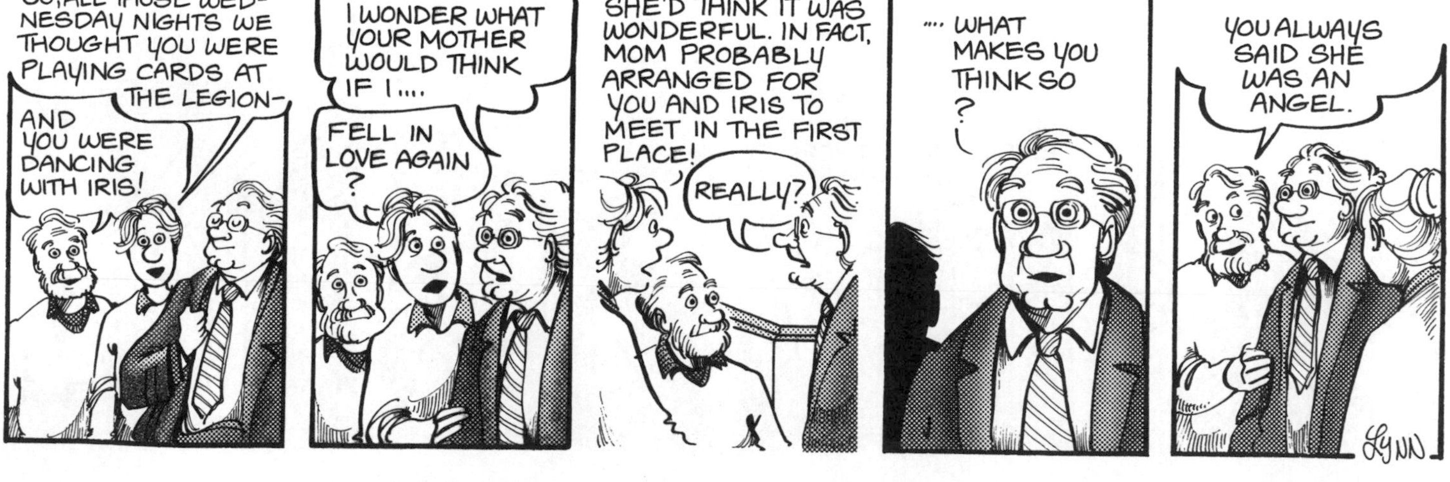
SO, ALL THOSE WEDNESDAY NIGHTS WE THOUGHT YOU WERE PLAYING CARDS AT THE LEGION-
AND YOU WERE DANCING WITH IRIS!
I WONDER WHAT YOUR MOTHER WOULD THINK IF I....
FELL IN LOVE AGAIN?
SHE'D THINK IT WAS WONDERFUL. IN FACT, MOM PROBABLY ARRANGED FOR YOU AND IRIS TO MEET IN THE FIRST PLACE!
REALLY?
.... WHAT MAKES YOU THINK SO?
YOU ALWAYS SAID SHE WAS AN ANGEL.
LYNN

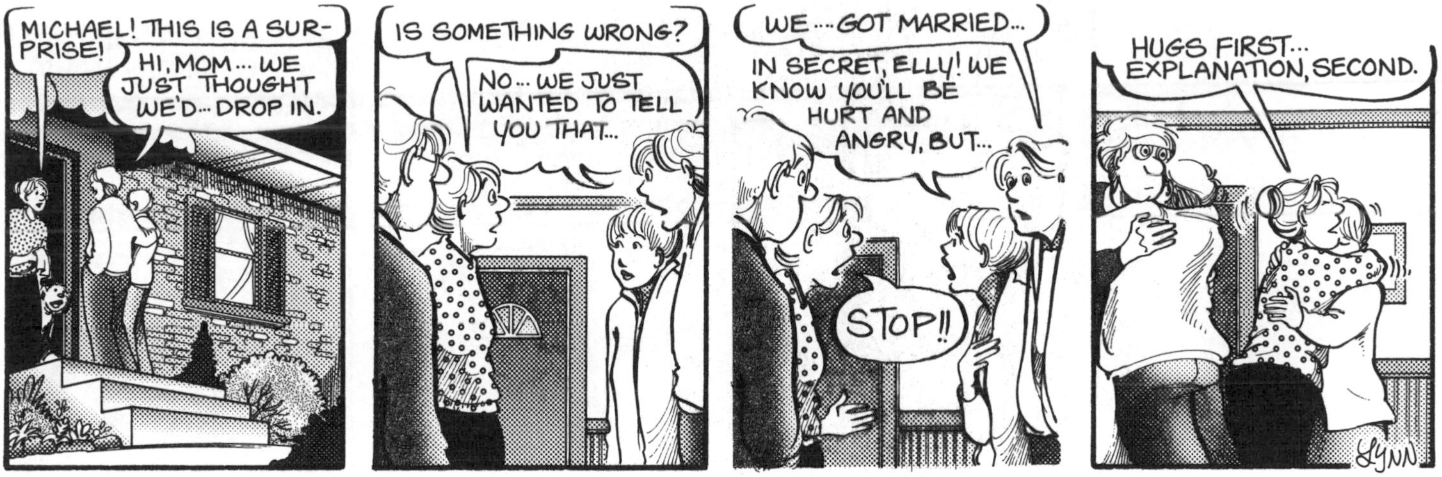
MICHAEL! THIS IS A SURPRISE!
HI, MOM... WE JUST THOUGHT WE'D... DROP IN.
IS SOMETHING WRONG?
NO... WE JUST WANTED TO TELL YOU THAT...
WE.... GOT MARRIED...
IN SECRET, ELLY! WE KNOW YOU'LL BE HURT AND ANGRY, BUT...
STOP!!
HUGS FIRST... EXPLANATION, SECOND.
LYNN

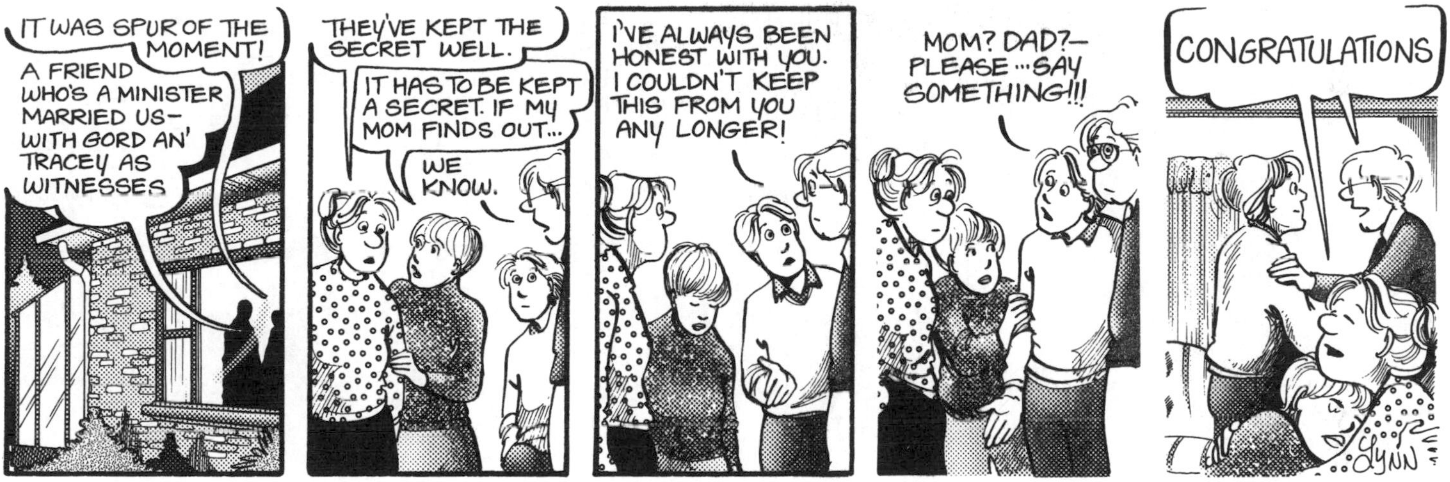
IT WAS SPUR OF THE MOMENT!
A FRIEND WHO'S A MINISTER MARRIED US- WITH GORD AN' TRACEY AS WITNESSES
THEY'VE KEPT THE SECRET WELL.
IT HAS TO BE KEPT A SECRET. IF MY MOM FINDS OUT...
WE KNOW.
I'VE ALWAYS BEEN HONEST WITH YOU. I COULDN'T KEEP THIS FROM YOU ANY LONGER!
MOM? DAD?— PLEASE ... SAY SOMETHING!!!
CONGRATULATIONS
LYNN

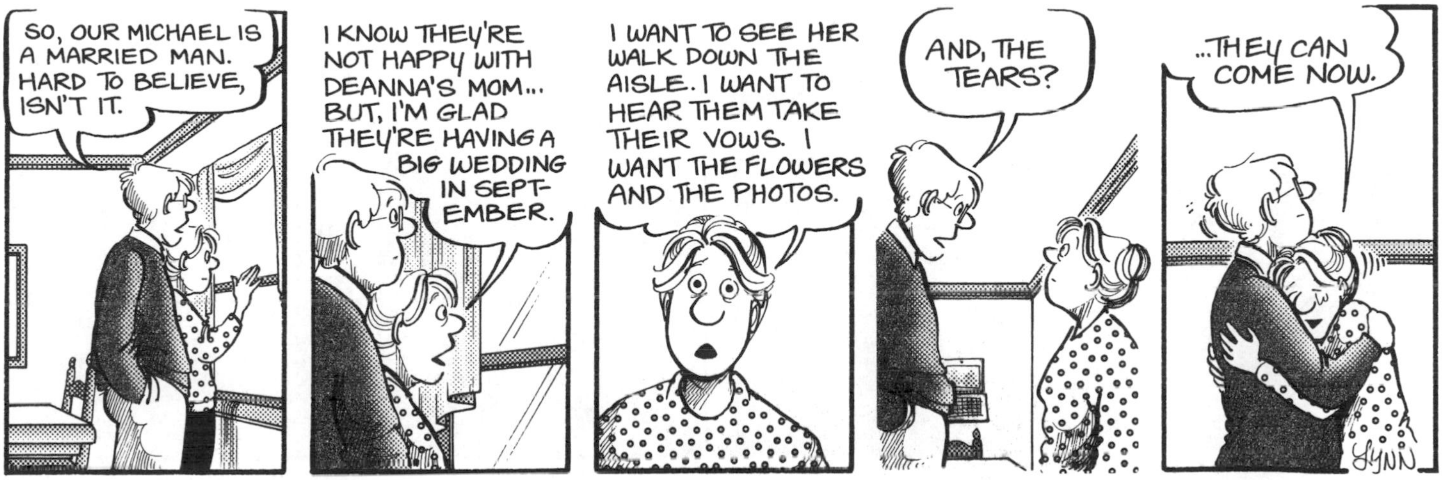
SO, OUR MICHAEL IS A MARRIED MAN. HARD TO BELIEVE, ISN'T IT.
I KNOW THEY'RE NOT HAPPY WITH DEANNA'S MOM... BUT, I'M GLAD THEY'RE HAVING A BIG WEDDING IN SEPTEMBER.
I WANT TO SEE HER WALK DOWN THE AISLE. I WANT TO HEAR THEM TAKE THEIR VOWS. I WANT THE FLOWERS AND THE PHOTOS.
AND, THE TEARS?
...THEY CAN COME NOW.
LYNN

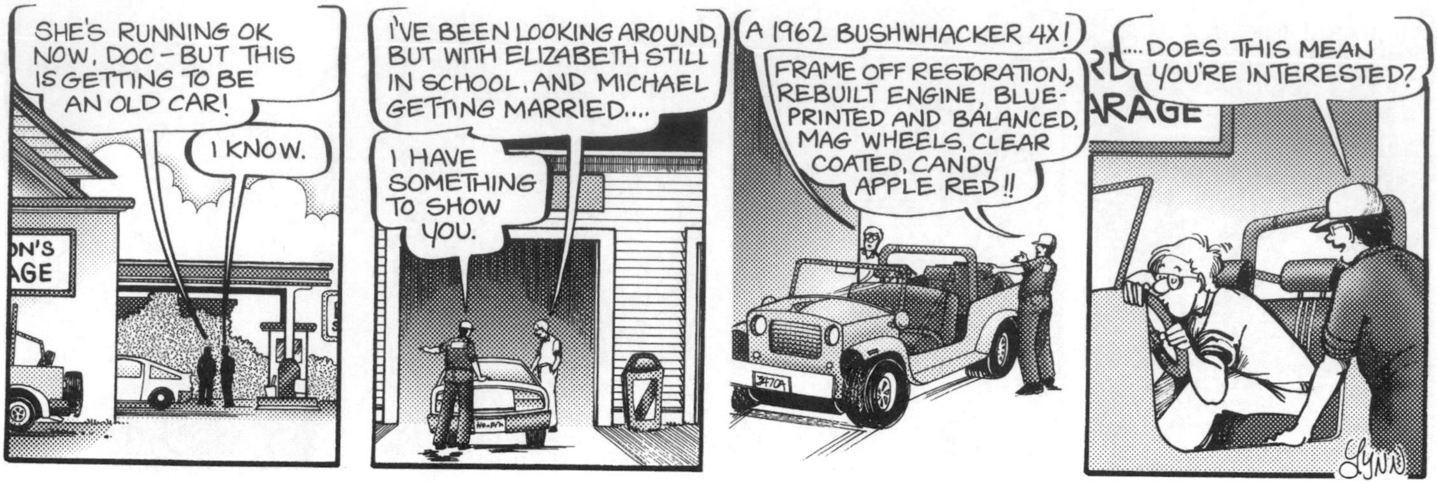
SHE'S RUNNING OK NOW, DOC - BUT THIS IS GETTING TO BE AN OLD CAR!
I KNOW.
I'VE BEEN LOOKING AROUND, BUT WITH ELIZABETH STILL IN SCHOOL, AND MICHAEL GETTING MARRIED....
I HAVE SOMETHING TO SHOW YOU.
A 1962 BUSHWHACKER 4X!
FRAME OFF RESTORATION, REBUILT ENGINE, BLUE-PRINTED AND BALANCED, MAG WHEELS, CLEAR COATED, CANDY APPLE RED!!
....DOES THIS MEAN YOU'RE INTERESTED?
Lynn

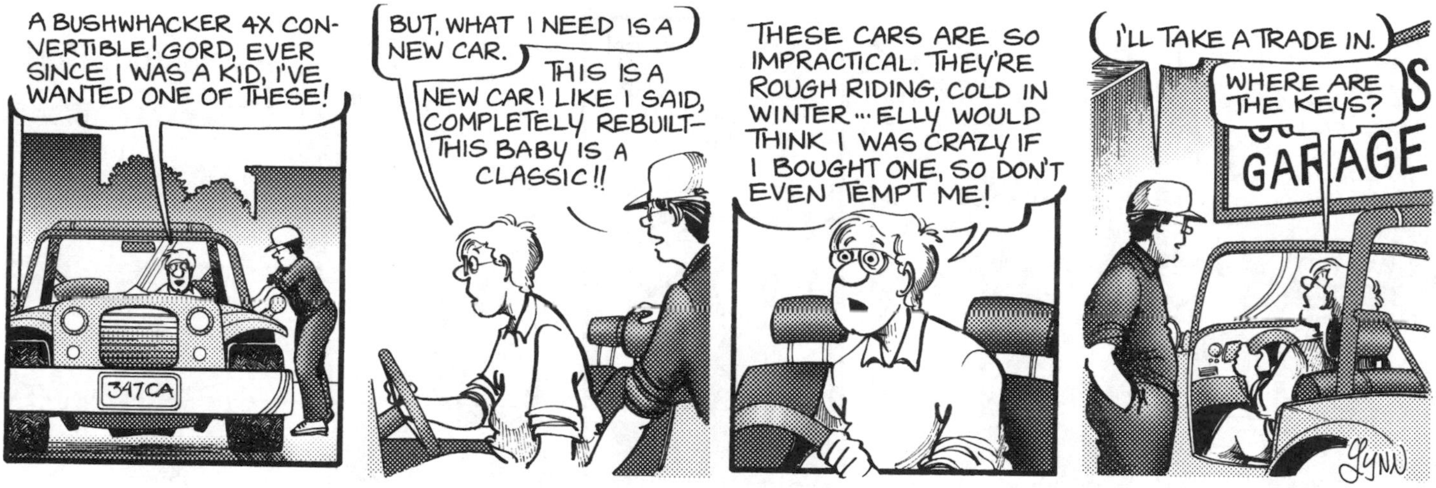
A BUSHWHACKER 4X CONVERTIBLE! GORD, EVER SINCE I WAS A KID, I'VE WANTED ONE OF THESE!
347CA
BUT, WHAT I NEED IS A NEW CAR.
THIS IS A NEW CAR! LIKE I SAID, COMPLETELY REBUILT- THIS BABY IS A CLASSIC!!
THESE CARS ARE SO IMPRACTICAL. THEY'RE ROUGH RIDING, COLD IN WINTER... ELLY WOULD THINK I WAS CRAZY IF I BOUGHT ONE, SO DON'T EVEN TEMPT ME!
I'LL TAKE A TRADE IN.
WHERE ARE THE KEYS?
GARAGE
Lynn

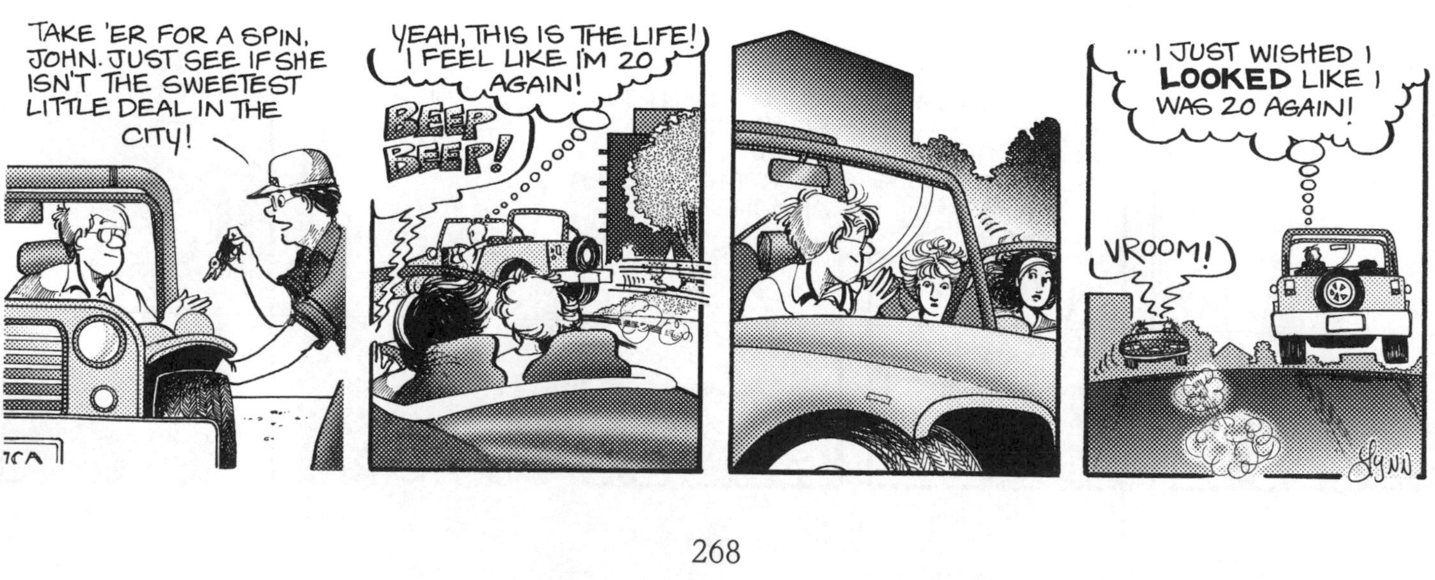
TAKE 'ER FOR A SPIN, JOHN. JUST SEE IF SHE ISN'T THE SWEETEST LITTLE DEAL IN THE CITY!
YEAH, THIS IS THE LIFE! I FEEL LIKE I'M 20 AGAIN!
BEEP BEEP!
... I JUST WISHED I **LOOKED** LIKE I WAS 20 AGAIN!
VROOM!
Lynn

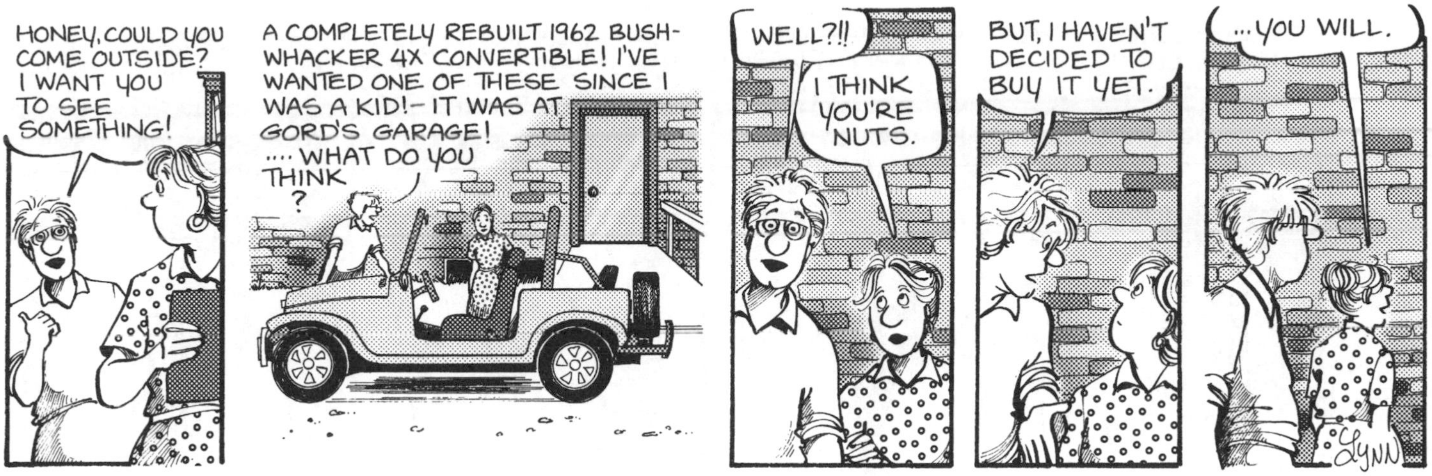
HONEY, COULD YOU COME OUTSIDE? I WANT YOU TO SEE SOMETHING!
A COMPLETELY REBUILT 1962 BUSHWHACKER 4X CONVERTIBLE! I'VE WANTED ONE OF THESE SINCE I WAS A KID!– IT WAS AT GORD'S GARAGE! .... WHAT DO YOU THINK
?
WELL?!!
I THINK YOU'RE NUTS.
BUT, I HAVEN'T DECIDED TO BUY IT YET.
...YOU WILL.
LYNN

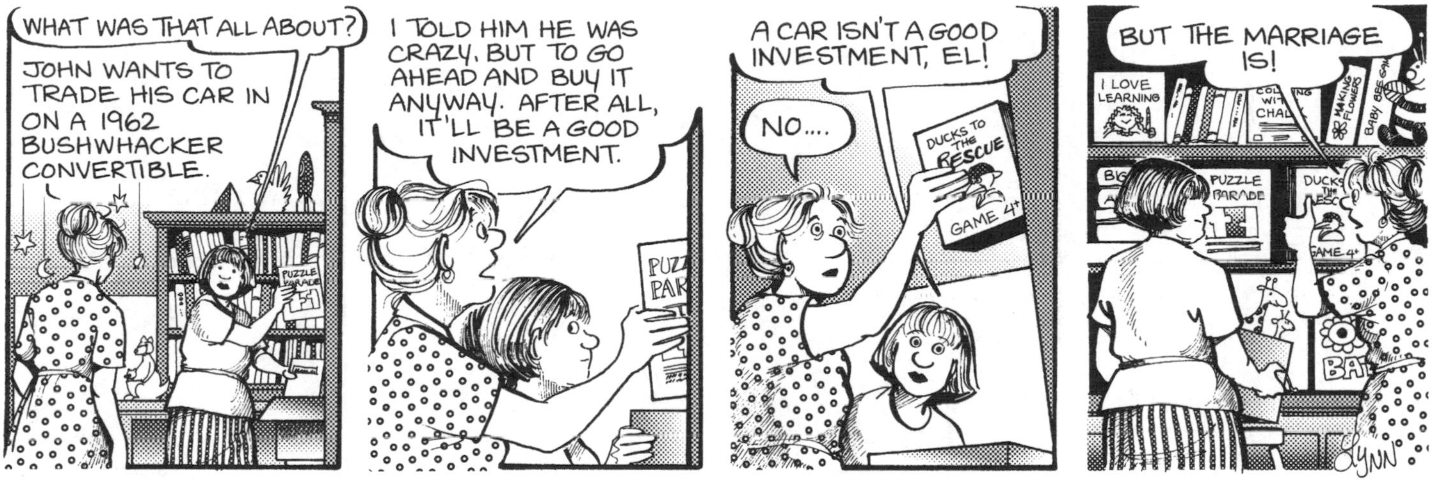
WHAT WAS THAT ALL ABOUT?
JOHN WANTS TO TRADE HIS CAR IN ON A 1962 BUSHWHACKER CONVERTIBLE.
PUZZLE PARADE
I TOLD HIM HE WAS CRAZY, BUT TO GO AHEAD AND BUY IT ANYWAY. AFTER ALL, IT'LL BE A GOOD INVESTMENT.
A CAR ISN'T A GOOD INVESTMENT, EL!
NO....
DUCKS TO THE RESCUE
GAME 4+
BUT THE MARRIAGE IS!
I LOVE LEARNING
MAKING FLOWERS
LYNN

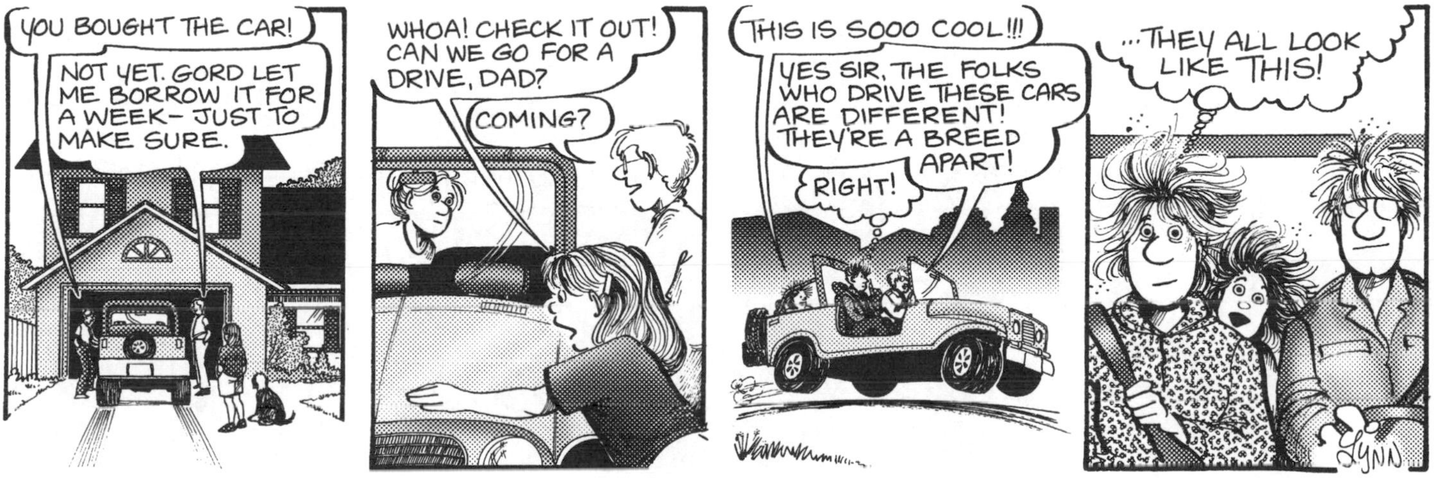
YOU BOUGHT THE CAR!
NOT YET. GORD LET ME BORROW IT FOR A WEEK– JUST TO MAKE SURE.
WHOA! CHECK IT OUT! CAN WE GO FOR A DRIVE, DAD?
COMING?
THIS IS SOOO COOL!!!
YES SIR, THE FOLKS WHO DRIVE THESE CARS ARE DIFFERENT! THEY'RE A BREED APART!
RIGHT!
...THEY ALL LOOK LIKE THIS!
LYNN

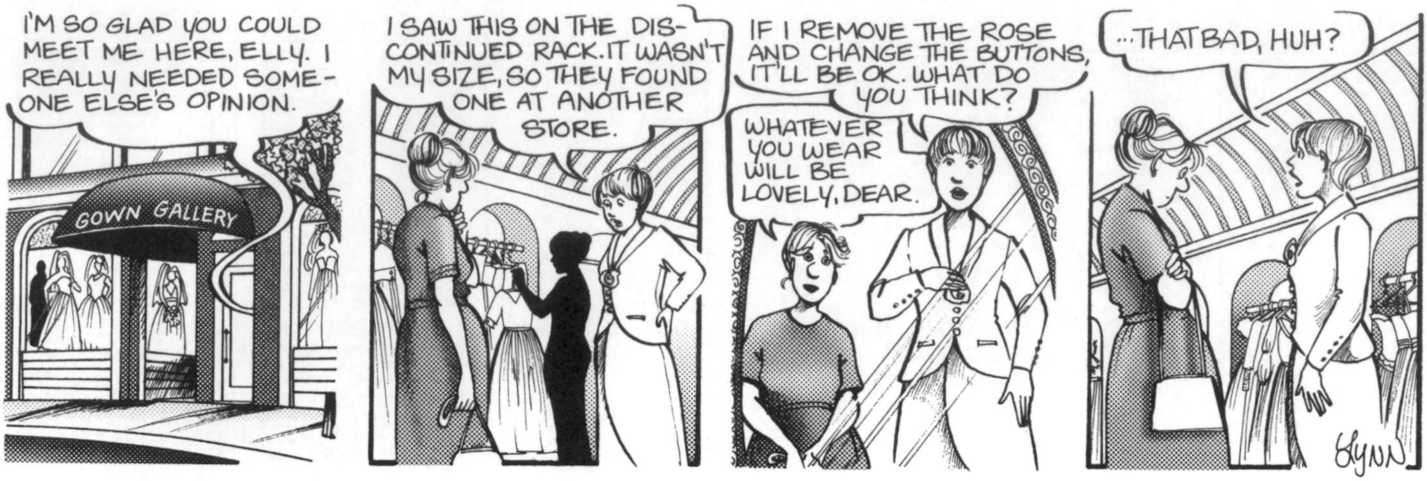
I'M SO GLAD YOU COULD MEET ME HERE, ELLY. I REALLY NEEDED SOME-ONE ELSE'S OPINION.
GOWN GALLERY
I SAW THIS ON THE DIS-CONTINUED RACK. IT WASN'T MY SIZE, SO THEY FOUND ONE AT ANOTHER STORE.
IF I REMOVE THE ROSE AND CHANGE THE BUTTONS, IT'LL BE OK. WHAT DO YOU THINK?
WHATEVER YOU WEAR WILL BE LOVELY, DEAR.
...THAT BAD, HUH?
LYNN

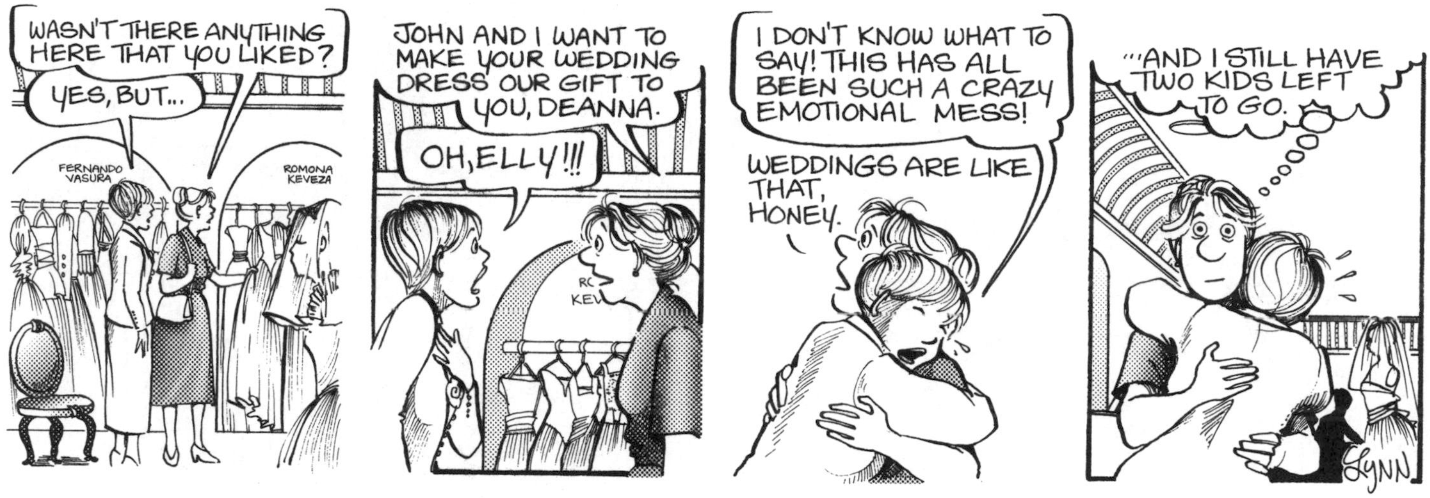
WASN'T THERE ANYTHING HERE THAT YOU LIKED?
YES, BUT...
FERNANDO VASURA
ROMONA KEVEZA
JOHN AND I WANT TO MAKE YOUR WEDDING DRESS OUR GIFT TO YOU, DEANNA.
OH, ELLY!!!
I DON'T KNOW WHAT TO SAY! THIS HAS ALL BEEN SUCH A CRAZY EMOTIONAL MESS!
WEDDINGS ARE LIKE THAT, HONEY.
...AND I STILL HAVE TWO KIDS LEFT TO GO.
LYNN

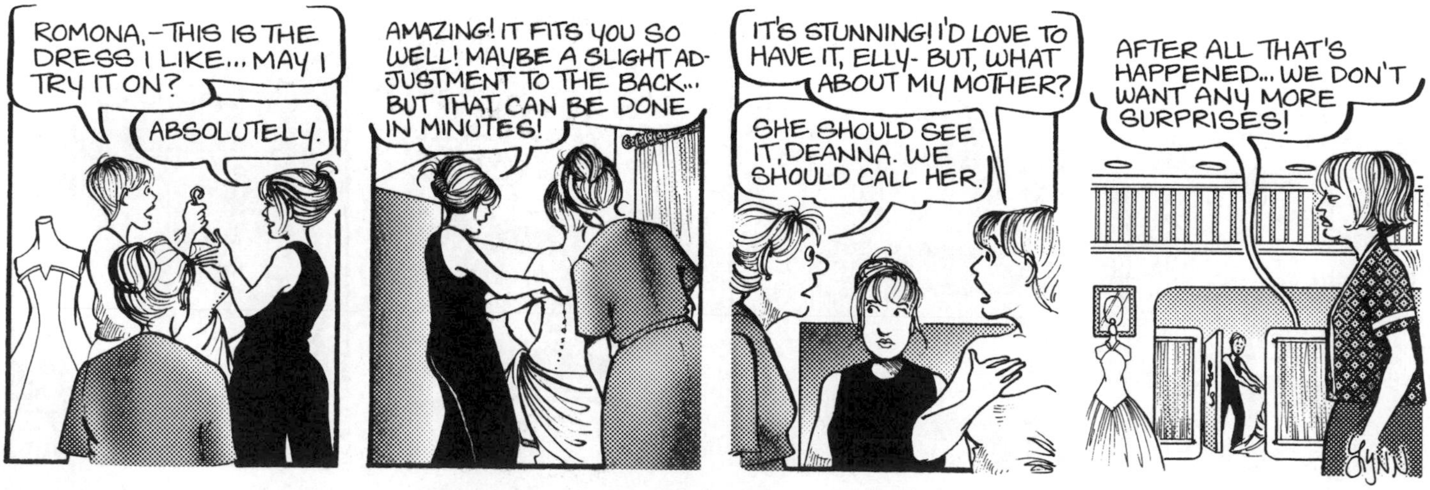
ROMONA, - THIS IS THE DRESS I LIKE... MAY I TRY IT ON?
ABSOLUTELY.
AMAZING! IT FITS YOU SO WELL! MAYBE A SLIGHT AD-JUSTMENT TO THE BACK... BUT THAT CAN BE DONE IN MINUTES!
IT'S STUNNING! I'D LOVE TO HAVE IT, ELLY- BUT, WHAT ABOUT MY MOTHER?
SHE SHOULD SEE IT, DEANNA. WE SHOULD CALL HER.
AFTER ALL THAT'S HAPPENED... WE DON'T WANT ANY MORE SURPRISES!
LYNN

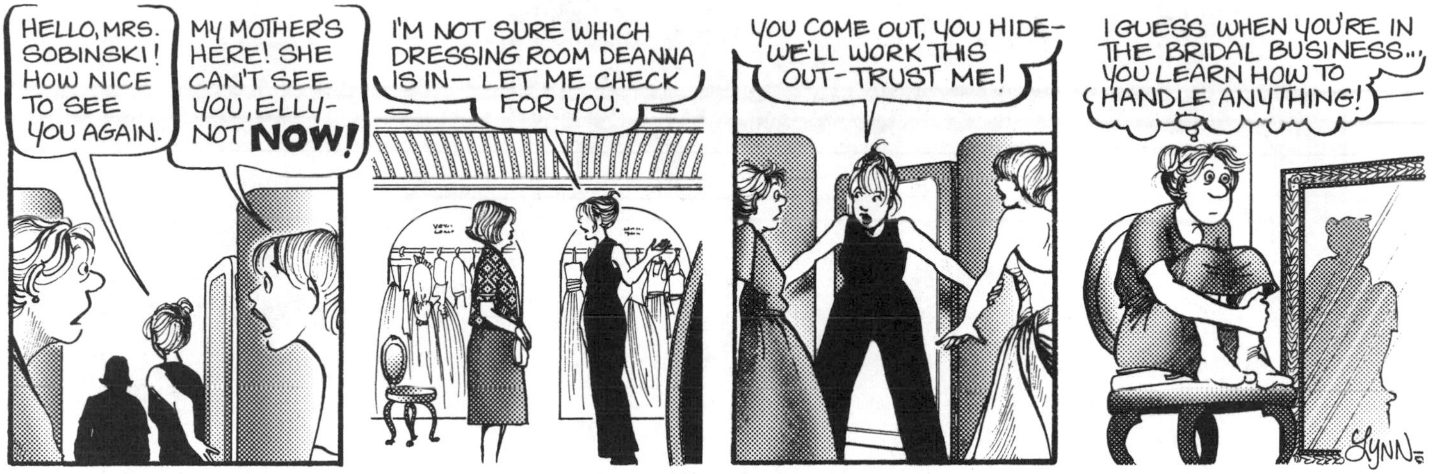
HELLO, MRS. SOBINSKI! HOW NICE TO SEE YOU AGAIN.
MY MOTHER'S HERE! SHE CAN'T SEE YOU, ELLY- NOT NOW!
I'M NOT SURE WHICH DRESSING ROOM DEANNA IS IN— LET ME CHECK FOR YOU.
YOU COME OUT, YOU HIDE- WE'LL WORK THIS OUT- TRUST ME!
I GUESS WHEN YOU'RE IN THE BRIDAL BUSINESS... YOU LEARN HOW TO HANDLE ANYTHING!

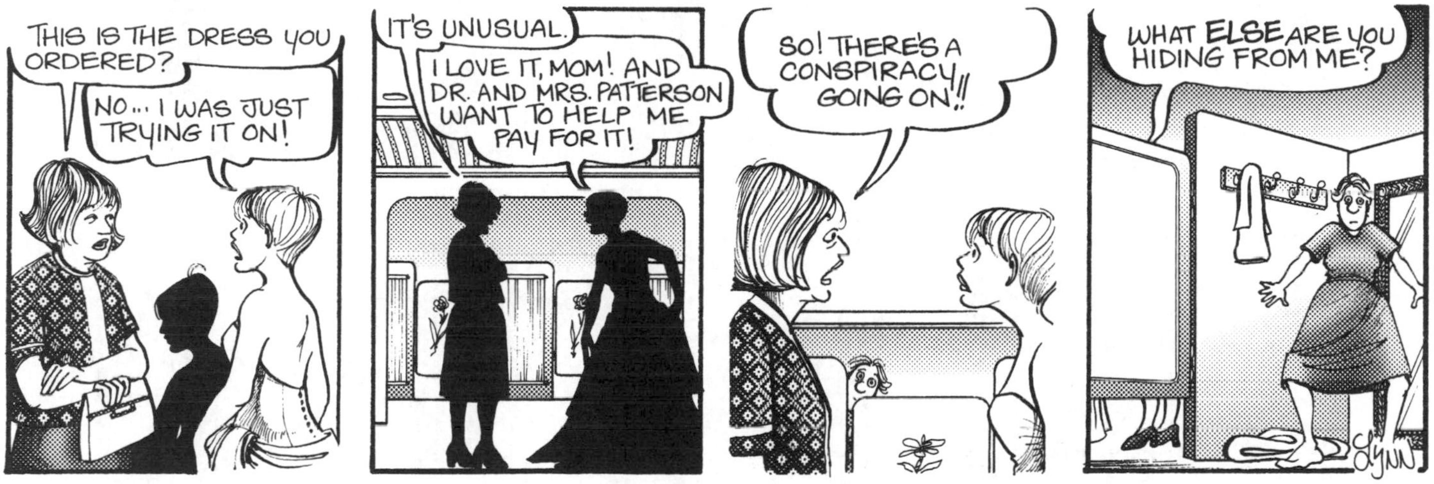
THIS IS THE DRESS YOU ORDERED?
NO... I WAS JUST TRYING IT ON!
IT'S UNUSUAL.
I LOVE IT, MOM! AND DR. AND MRS. PATTERSON WANT TO HELP ME PAY FOR IT!
SO! THERE'S A CONSPIRACY GOING ON!!
WHAT ELSE ARE YOU HIDING FROM ME?

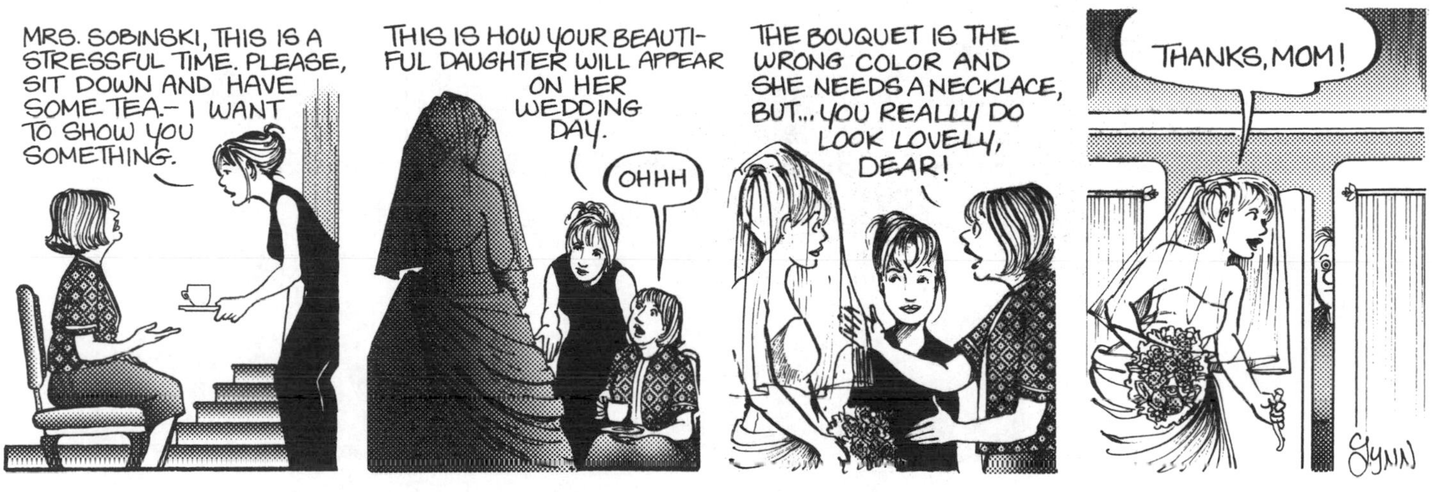
MRS. SOBINSKI, THIS IS A STRESSFUL TIME. PLEASE, SIT DOWN AND HAVE SOME TEA.- I WANT TO SHOW YOU SOMETHING.
THIS IS HOW YOUR BEAUTIFUL DAUGHTER WILL APPEAR ON HER WEDDING DAY.
OHHH
THE BOUQUET IS THE WRONG COLOR AND SHE NEEDS A NECKLACE, BUT... YOU REALLY DO LOOK LOVELY, DEAR!
THANKS, MOM!

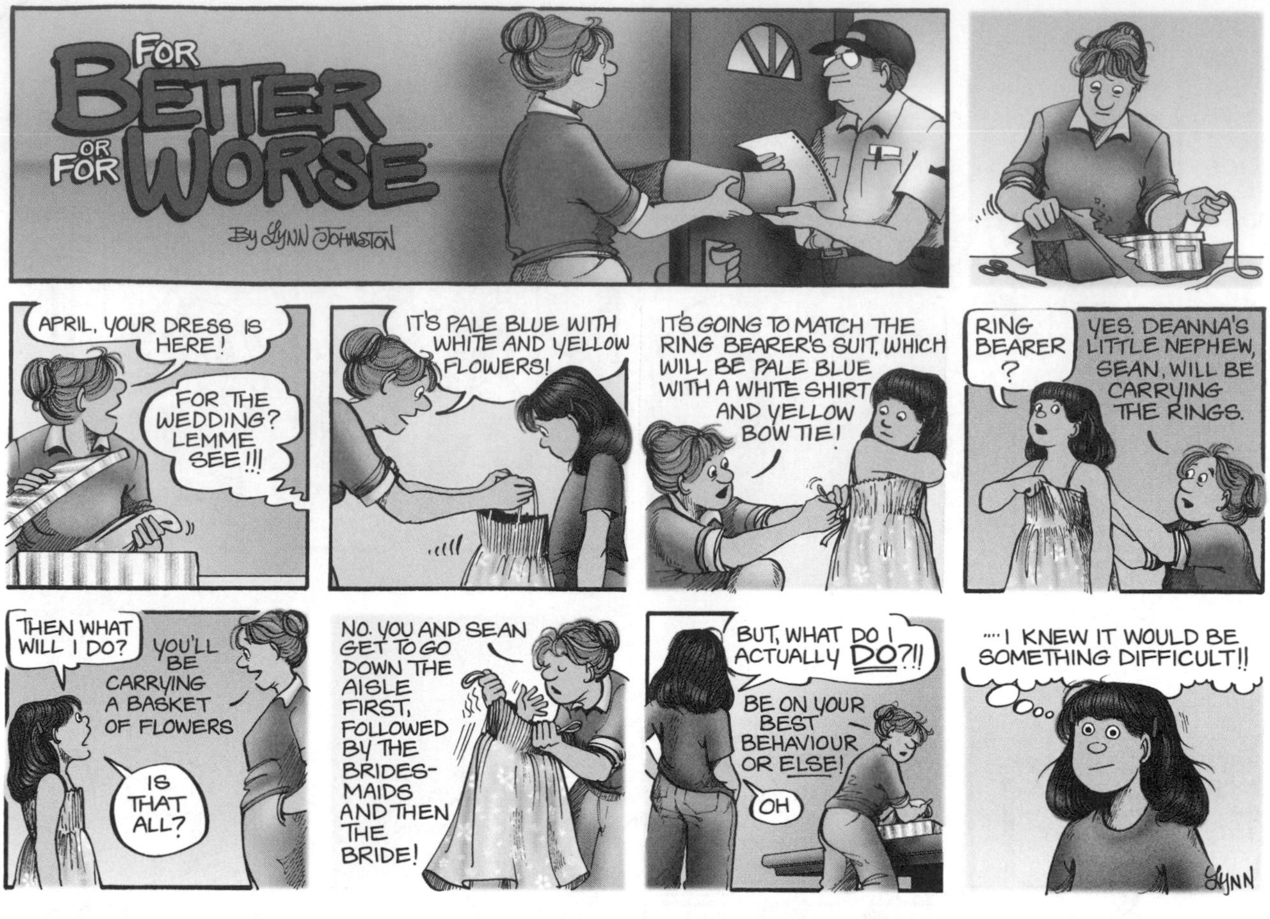
FOR BETTER OR FOR WORSE
By Lynn Johnston
APRIL, YOUR DRESS IS HERE!
FOR THE WEDDING? LEMME SEE!!!
IT'S PALE BLUE WITH WHITE AND YELLOW FLOWERS!
IT'S GOING TO MATCH THE RING BEARER'S SUIT, WHICH WILL BE PALE BLUE WITH A WHITE SHIRT AND YELLOW BOW TIE!
RING BEARER?
YES. DEANNA'S LITTLE NEPHEW, SEAN, WILL BE CARRYING THE RINGS.
THEN WHAT WILL I DO?
YOU'LL BE CARRYING A BASKET OF FLOWERS
IS THAT ALL?
NO. YOU AND SEAN GET TO GO DOWN THE AISLE FIRST, FOLLOWED BY THE BRIDES-MAIDS AND THEN THE BRIDE!
BUT, WHAT DO I ACTUALLY DO?!!
BE ON YOUR BEST BEHAVIOUR OR ELSE!
OH
....I KNEW IT WOULD BE SOMETHING DIFFICULT!!
Lynn

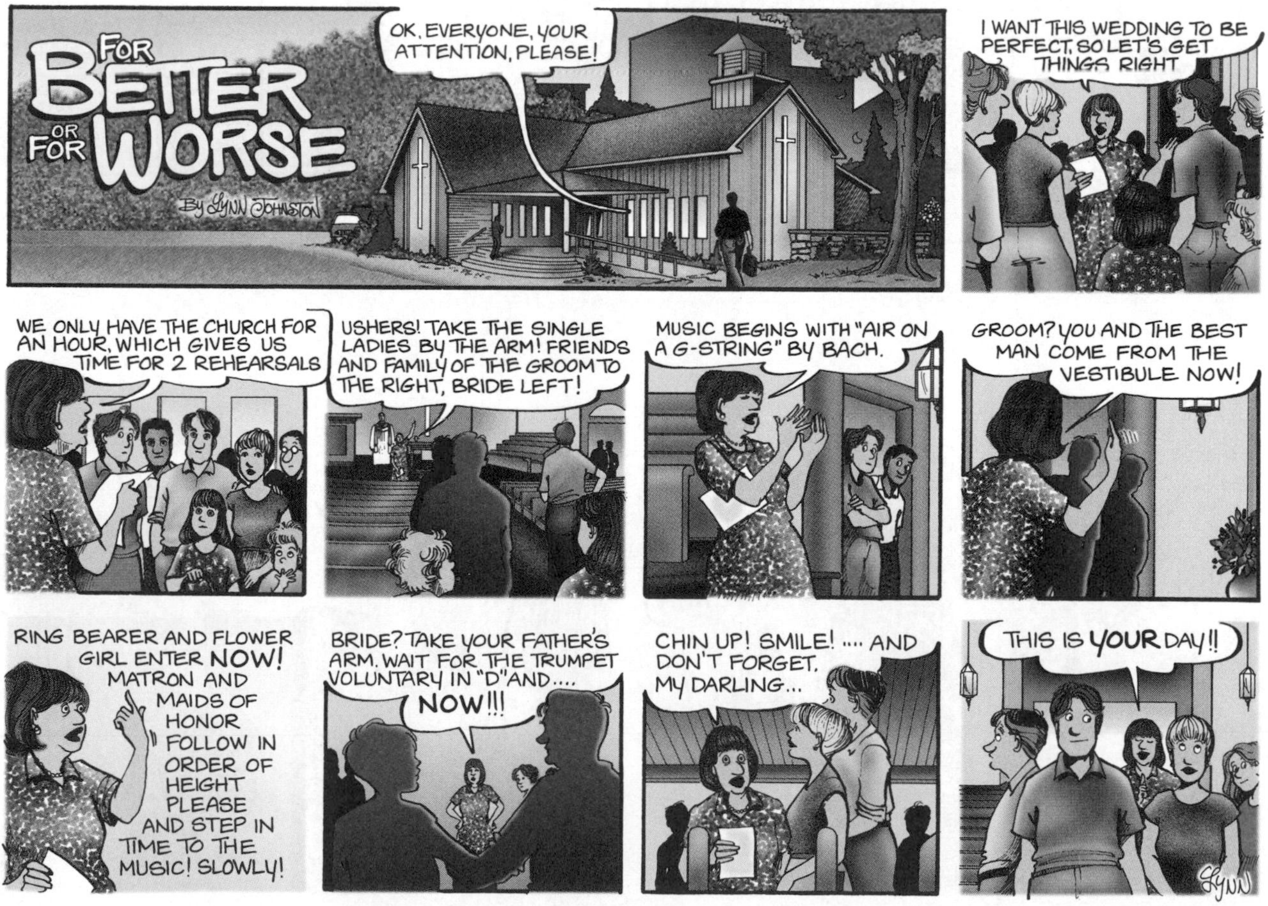
FOR BETTER OR FOR WORSE
By Lynn Johnston
OK, EVERYONE, YOUR ATTENTION, PLEASE!
I WANT THIS WEDDING TO BE PERFECT, SO LET'S GET THINGS RIGHT
WE ONLY HAVE THE CHURCH FOR AN HOUR, WHICH GIVES US TIME FOR 2 REHEARSALS
USHERS! TAKE THE SINGLE LADIES BY THE ARM! FRIENDS AND FAMILY OF THE GROOM TO THE RIGHT, BRIDE LEFT!
MUSIC BEGINS WITH "AIR ON A G-STRING" BY BACH.
GROOM? YOU AND THE BEST MAN COME FROM THE VESTIBULE NOW!
RING BEARER AND FLOWER GIRL ENTER NOW! MATRON AND MAIDS OF HONOR FOLLOW IN ORDER OF HEIGHT PLEASE AND STEP IN TIME TO THE MUSIC! SLOWLY!
BRIDE? TAKE YOUR FATHER'S ARM. WAIT FOR THE TRUMPET VOLUNTARY IN "D" AND....
NOW!!!
CHIN UP! SMILE! .... AND DON'T FORGET, MY DARLING...
THIS IS YOUR DAY!!
Lynn

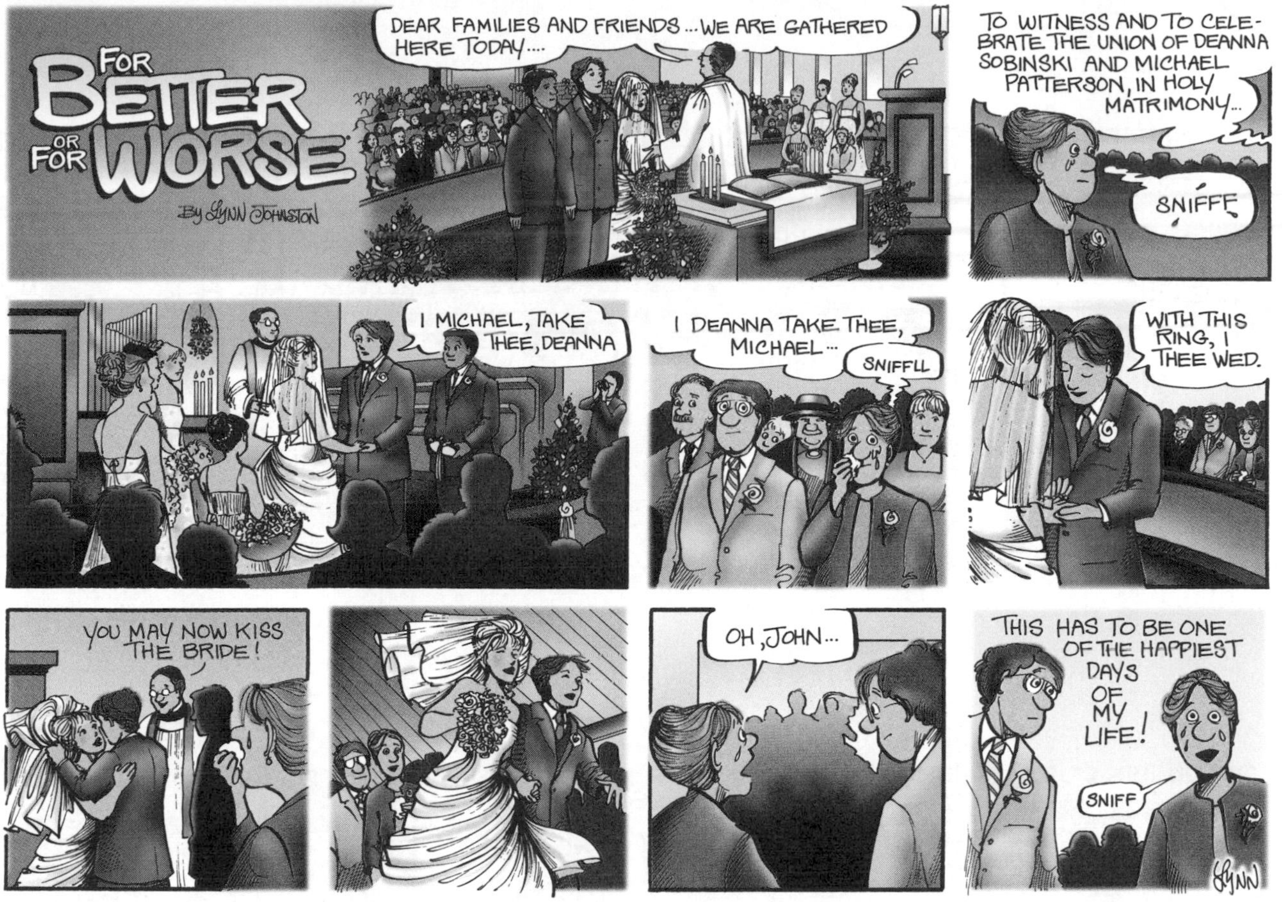
FOR BETTER OR FOR WORSE
By LYNN JOHNSTON
DEAR FAMILIES AND FRIENDS ... WE ARE GATHERED HERE TODAY....
TO WITNESS AND TO CELEBRATE THE UNION OF DEANNA SOBINSKI AND MICHAEL PATTERSON, IN HOLY MATRIMONY...
SNIFFF
I MICHAEL, TAKE THEE, DEANNA
I DEANNA TAKE THEE, MICHAEL...
SNIFFLL
WITH THIS RING, I THEE WED.
YOU MAY NOW KISS THE BRIDE!
OH, JOHN...
THIS HAS TO BE ONE OF THE HAPPIEST DAYS OF MY LIFE!
SNIFF
LYNN

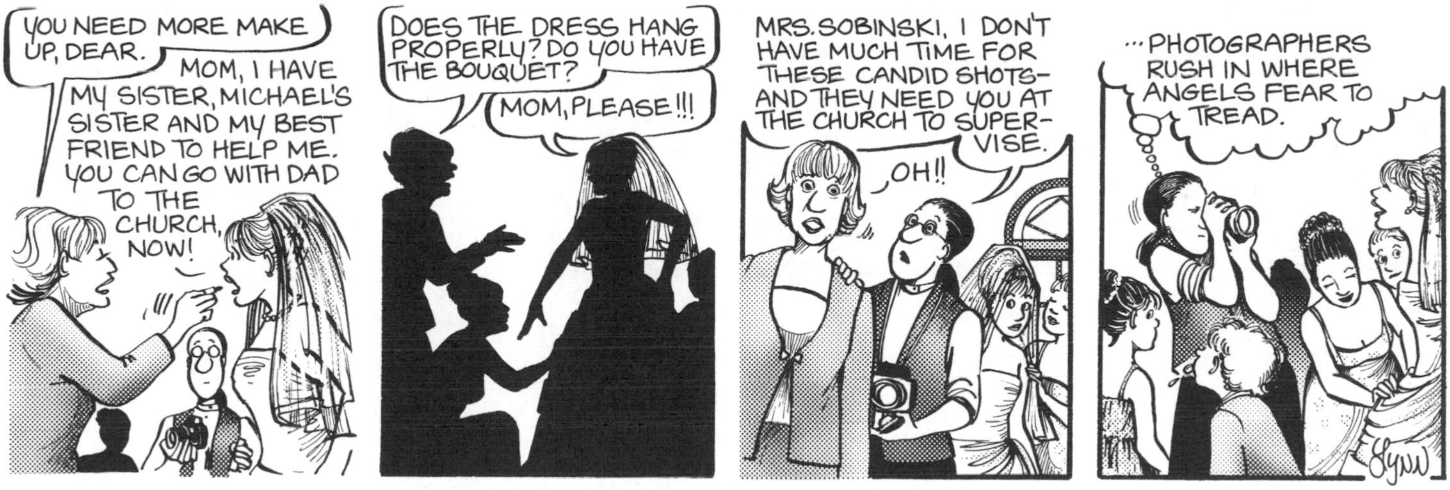
YOU NEED MORE MAKE UP, DEAR.
MOM, I HAVE MY SISTER, MICHAEL'S SISTER AND MY BEST FRIEND TO HELP ME. YOU CAN GO WITH DAD TO THE CHURCH, NOW!
DOES THE DRESS HANG PROPERLY? DO YOU HAVE THE BOUQUET?
MOM, PLEASE!!!
MRS. SOBINSKI, I DON'T HAVE MUCH TIME FOR THESE CANDID SHOTS- AND THEY NEED YOU AT THE CHURCH TO SUPERVISE.
OH!!
...PHOTOGRAPHERS RUSH IN WHERE ANGELS FEAR TO TREAD.
LYNN

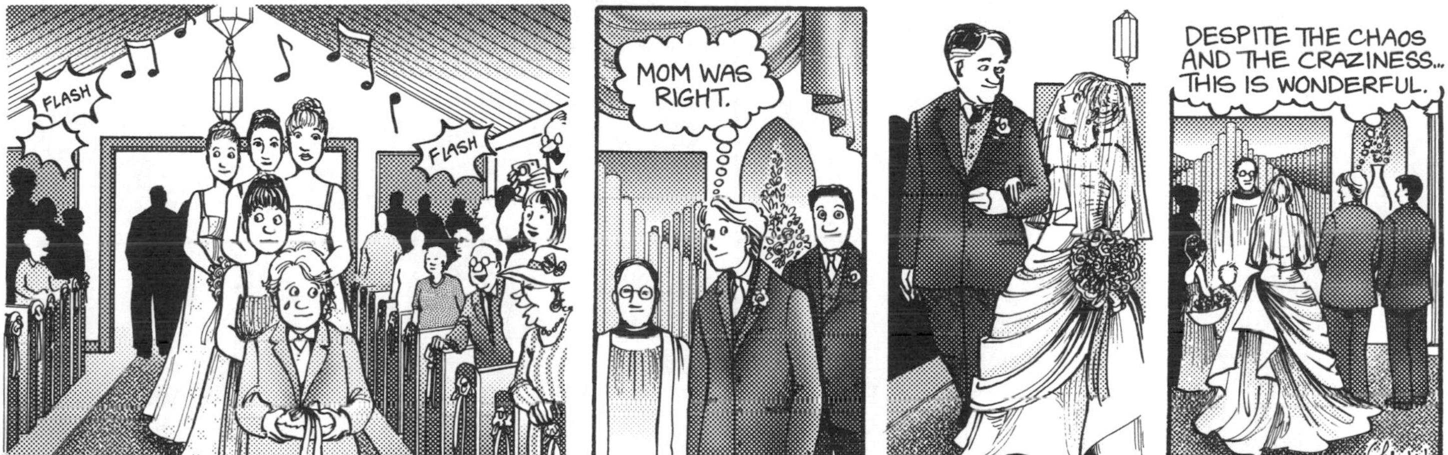
FLASH
FLASH
MOM WAS RIGHT.
DESPITE THE CHAOS AND THE CRAZINESS... THIS IS WONDERFUL.
LYNN

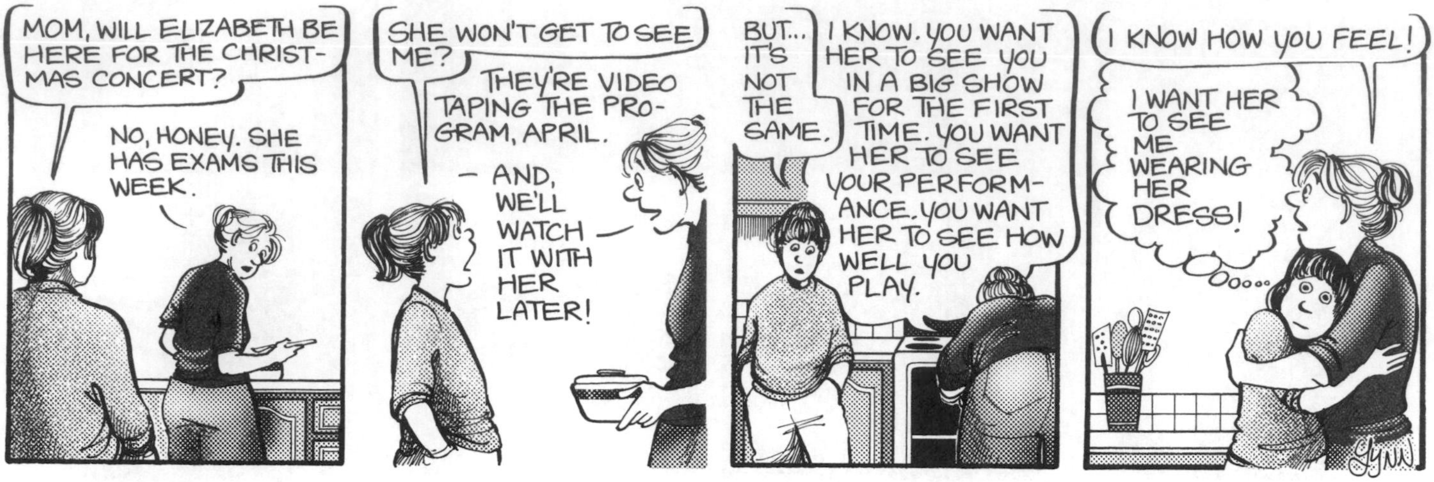
MOM, WILL ELIZABETH BE HERE FOR THE CHRISTMAS CONCERT?
NO, HONEY. SHE HAS EXAMS THIS WEEK.
SHE WON'T GET TO SEE ME?
THEY'RE VIDEO TAPING THE PROGRAM, APRIL.
– AND, WE'LL WATCH IT WITH HER LATER!
BUT... IT'S NOT THE SAME.
I KNOW. YOU WANT HER TO SEE YOU IN A BIG SHOW FOR THE FIRST TIME. YOU WANT HER TO SEE YOUR PERFORMANCE. YOU WANT HER TO SEE HOW WELL YOU PLAY.
I KNOW HOW YOU FEEL!
I WANT HER TO SEE ME WEARING HER DRESS!
LYNN

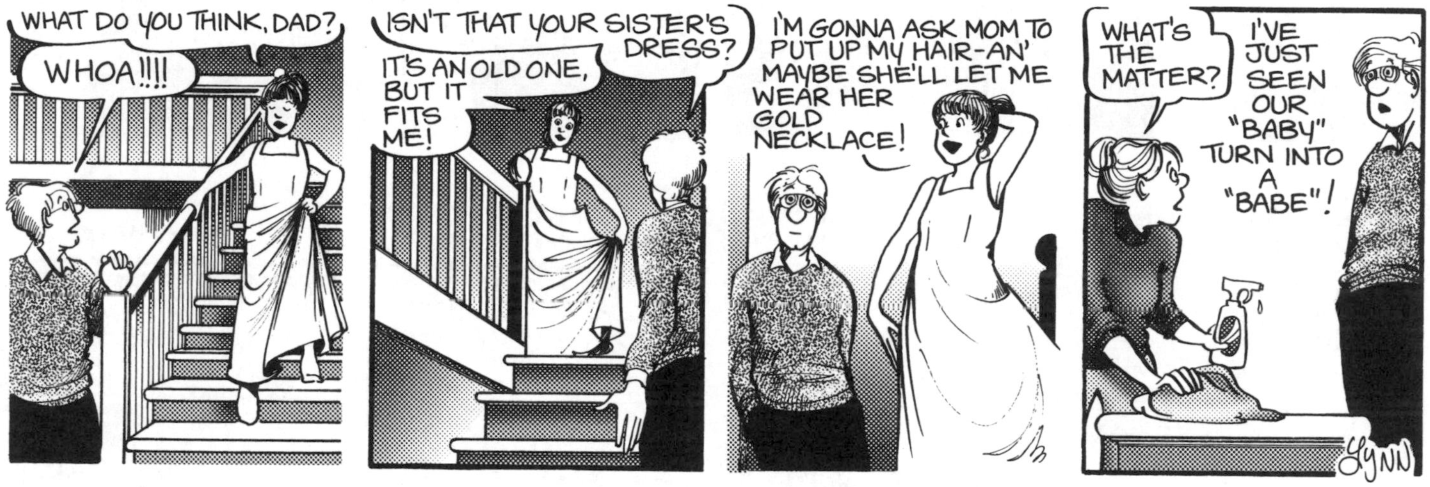
WHAT DO YOU THINK, DAD?
WHOA!!!!
ISN'T THAT YOUR SISTER'S DRESS?
IT'S AN OLD ONE, BUT IT FITS ME!
I'M GONNA ASK MOM TO PUT UP MY HAIR-AN' MAYBE SHE'LL LET ME WEAR HER GOLD NECKLACE!
WHAT'S THE MATTER?
I'VE JUST SEEN OUR "BABY" TURN INTO A "BABE"!
LYNN

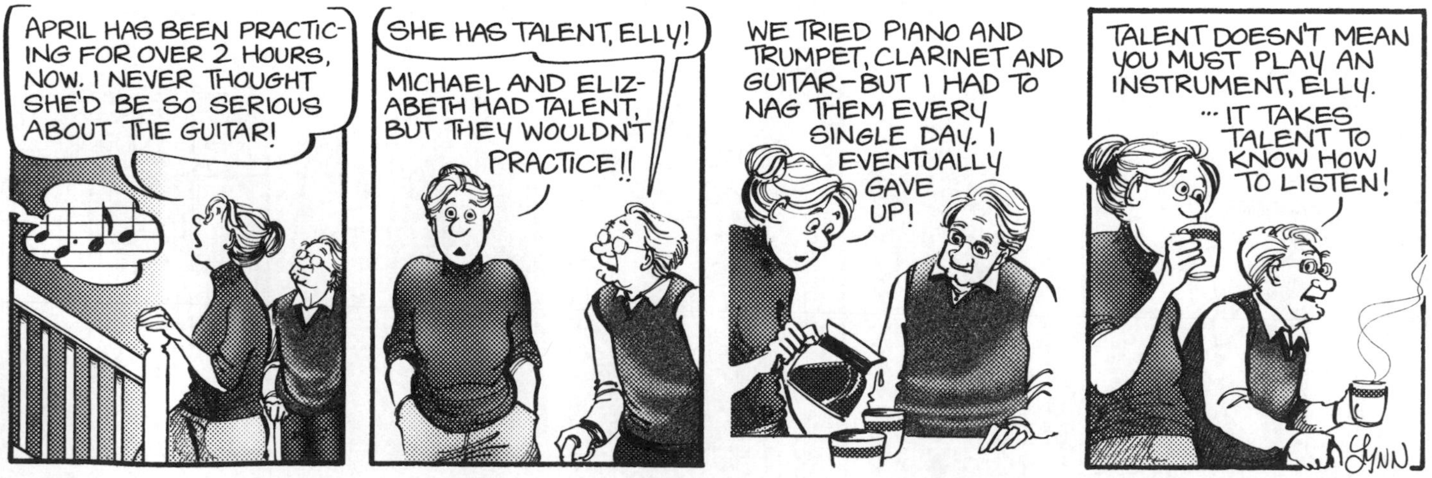
APRIL HAS BEEN PRACTICING FOR OVER 2 HOURS, NOW. I NEVER THOUGHT SHE'D BE SO SERIOUS ABOUT THE GUITAR!
SHE HAS TALENT, ELLY!
MICHAEL AND ELIZABETH HAD TALENT, BUT THEY WOULDN'T PRACTICE!!
WE TRIED PIANO AND TRUMPET, CLARINET AND GUITAR–BUT I HAD TO NAG THEM EVERY SINGLE DAY. I EVENTUALLY GAVE UP!
TALENT DOESN'T MEAN YOU MUST PLAY AN INSTRUMENT, ELLY.
...IT TAKES TALENT TO KNOW HOW TO LISTEN!
LYNN

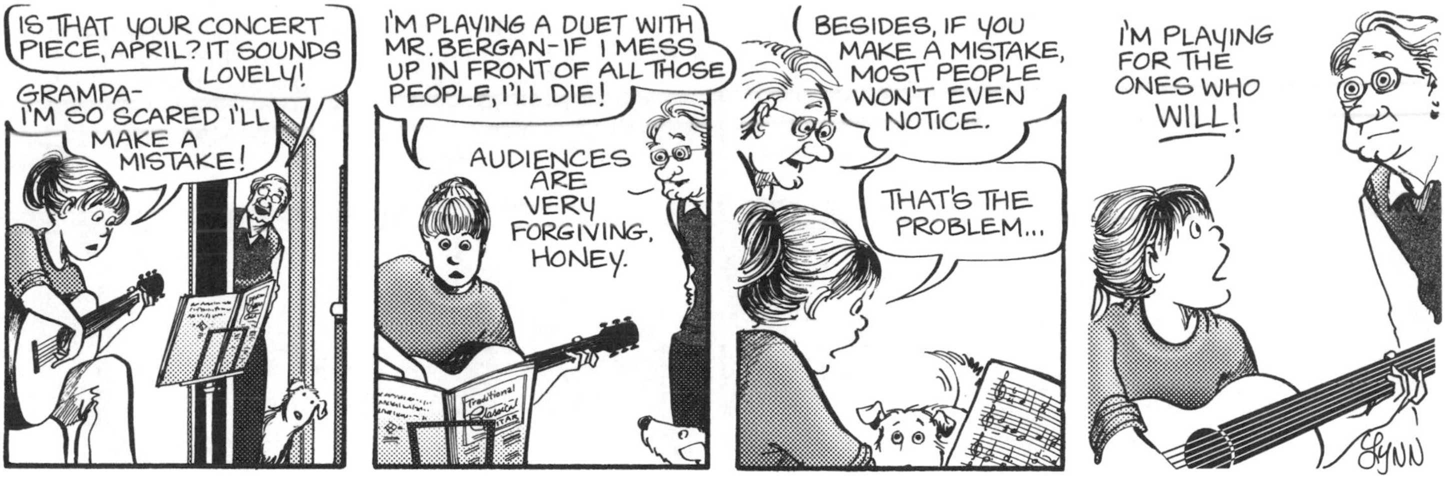
IS THAT YOUR CONCERT PIECE, APRIL? IT SOUNDS LOVELY!
GRAMPA- I'M SO SCARED I'LL MAKE A MISTAKE!
I'M PLAYING A DUET WITH MR. BERGAN- IF I MESS UP IN FRONT OF ALL THOSE PEOPLE, I'LL DIE!
AUDIENCES ARE VERY FORGIVING, HONEY.
BESIDES, IF YOU MAKE A MISTAKE, MOST PEOPLE WON'T EVEN NOTICE.
THAT'S THE PROBLEM...
I'M PLAYING FOR THE ONES WHO WILL!
LYNN

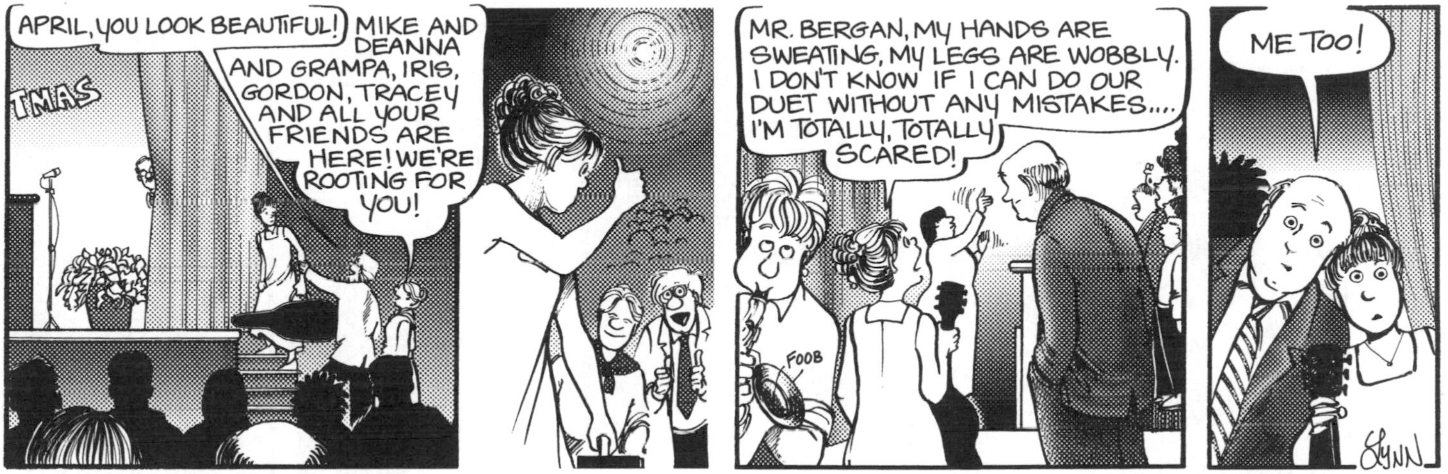
APRIL, YOU LOOK BEAUTIFUL!
MIKE AND DEANNA AND GRAMPA, IRIS, GORDON, TRACEY AND ALL YOUR FRIENDS ARE HERE! WE'RE ROOTING FOR YOU!
TMAS
MR. BERGAN, MY HANDS ARE SWEATING, MY LEGS ARE WOBBLY. I DON'T KNOW IF I CAN DO OUR DUET WITHOUT ANY MISTAKES.... I'M TOTALLY, TOTALLY SCARED!
FOOB
ME TOO!
LYNN

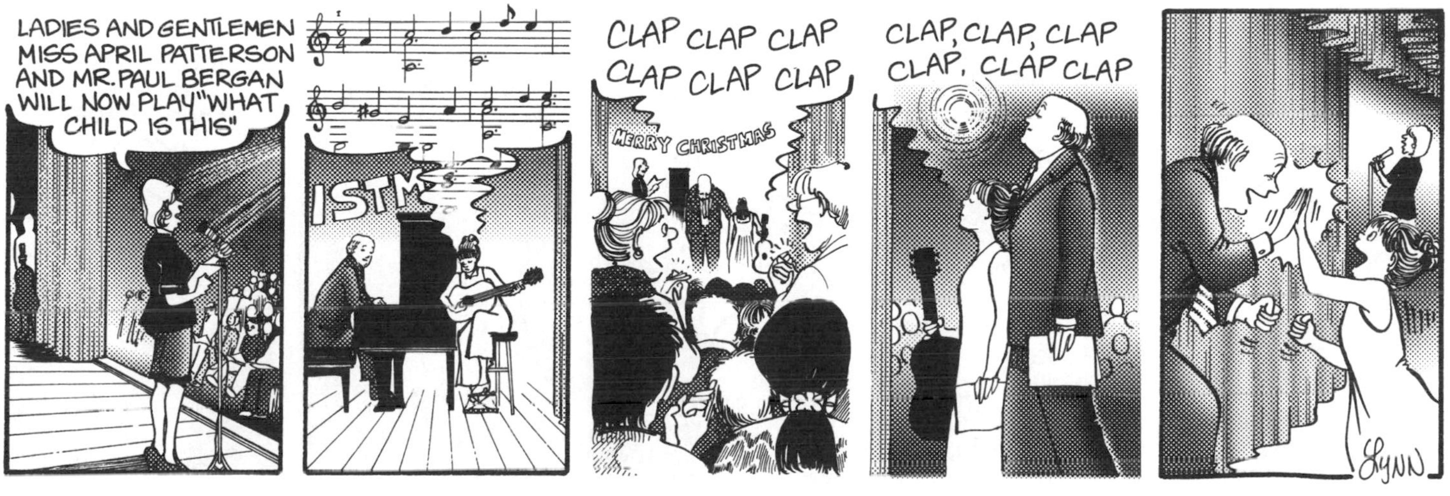
LADIES AND GENTLEMEN MISS APRIL PATTERSON AND MR. PAUL BERGAN WILL NOW PLAY "WHAT CHILD IS THIS"
ISTM
CLAP CLAP CLAP CLAP CLAP CLAP
MERRY CHRISTMAS
CLAP, CLAP, CLAP CLAP, CLAP CLAP
LYNN

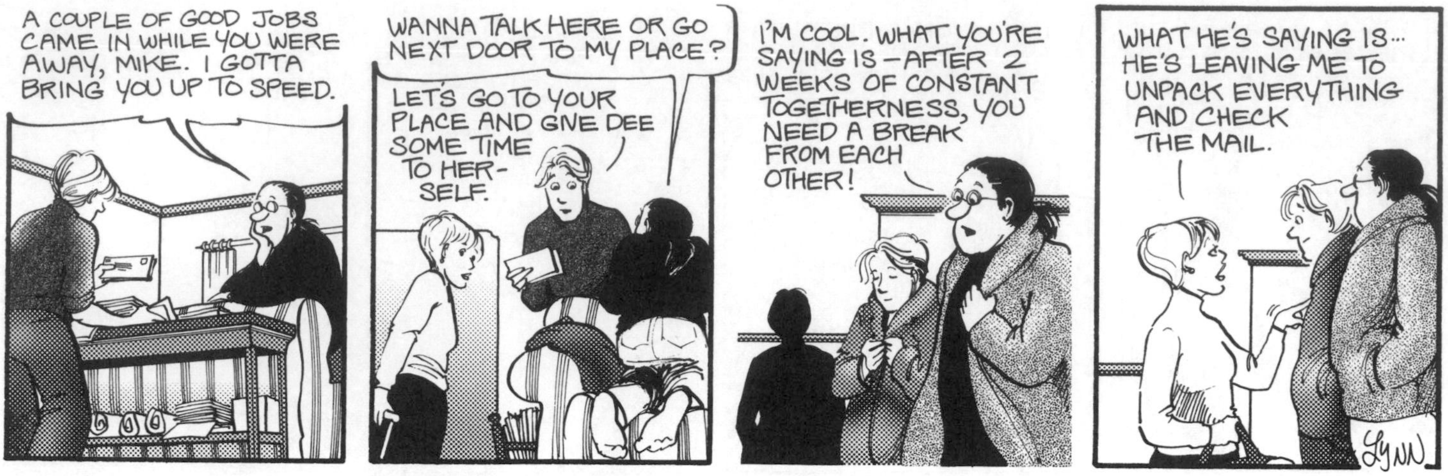
A COUPLE OF GOOD JOBS CAME IN WHILE YOU WERE AWAY, MIKE. I GOTTA BRING YOU UP TO SPEED.
WANNA TALK HERE OR GO NEXT DOOR TO MY PLACE?
LET'S GO TO YOUR PLACE AND GIVE DEE SOME TIME TO HER-SELF.
I'M COOL. WHAT YOU'RE SAYING IS – AFTER 2 WEEKS OF CONSTANT TOGETHERNESS, YOU NEED A BREAK FROM EACH OTHER!
WHAT HE'S SAYING IS... HE'S LEAVING ME TO UNPACK EVERYTHING AND CHECK THE MAIL.
LYNN

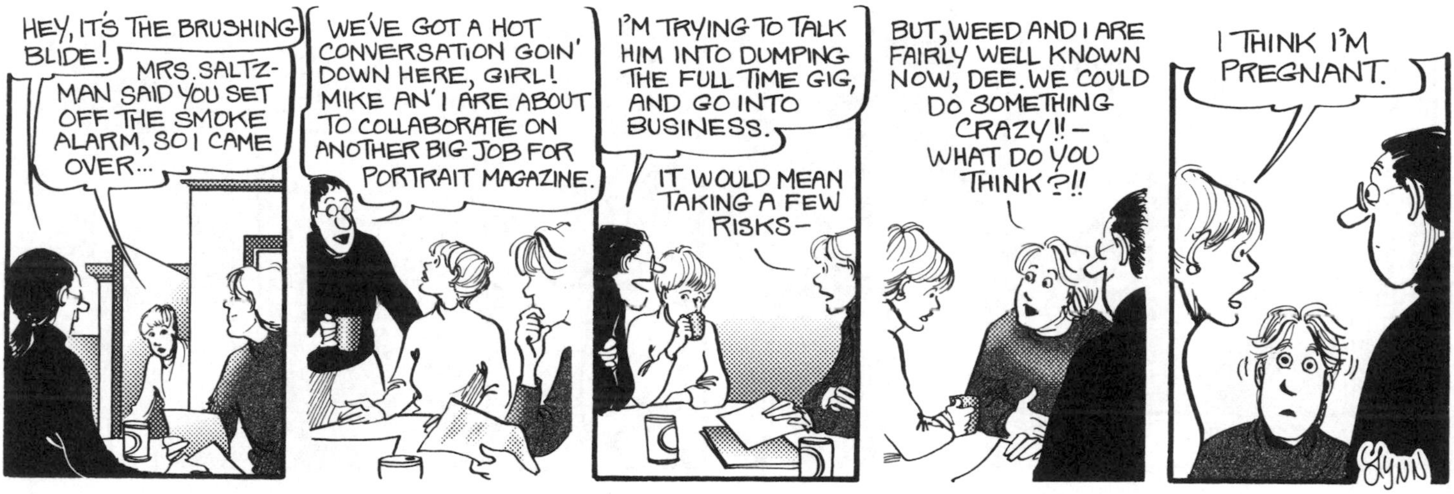
HEY, IT'S THE BRUSHING BLIDE!
MRS. SALTZ-MAN SAID YOU SET OFF THE SMOKE ALARM, SO I CAME OVER...
WE'VE GOT A HOT CONVERSATION GOIN' DOWN HERE, GIRL! MIKE AN' I ARE ABOUT TO COLLABORATE ON ANOTHER BIG JOB FOR PORTRAIT MAGAZINE.
I'M TRYING TO TALK HIM INTO DUMPING THE FULL TIME GIG, AND GO INTO BUSINESS.
IT WOULD MEAN TAKING A FEW RISKS –
BUT, WEED AND I ARE FAIRLY WELL KNOWN NOW, DEE. WE COULD DO SOMETHING CRAZY!! – WHAT DO YOU THINK?!!
I THINK I'M PREGNANT.
LYNN

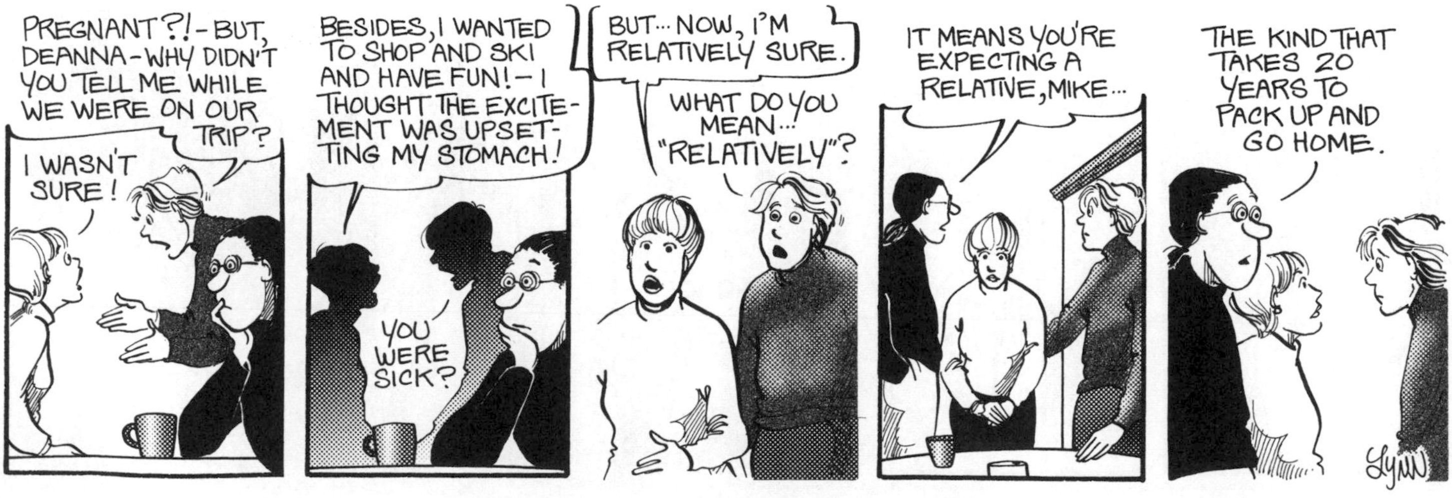
PREGNANT?! – BUT, DEANNA – WHY DIDN'T YOU TELL ME WHILE WE WERE ON OUR TRIP?
I WASN'T SURE!
BESIDES, I WANTED TO SHOP AND SKI AND HAVE FUN! – I THOUGHT THE EXCITE-MENT WAS UPSET-TING MY STOMACH!
YOU WERE SICK?
BUT... NOW, I'M RELATIVELY SURE.
WHAT DO YOU MEAN... "RELATIVELY"?
IT MEANS YOU'RE EXPECTING A RELATIVE, MIKE...
THE KIND THAT TAKES 20 YEARS TO PACK UP AND GO HOME.
LYNN

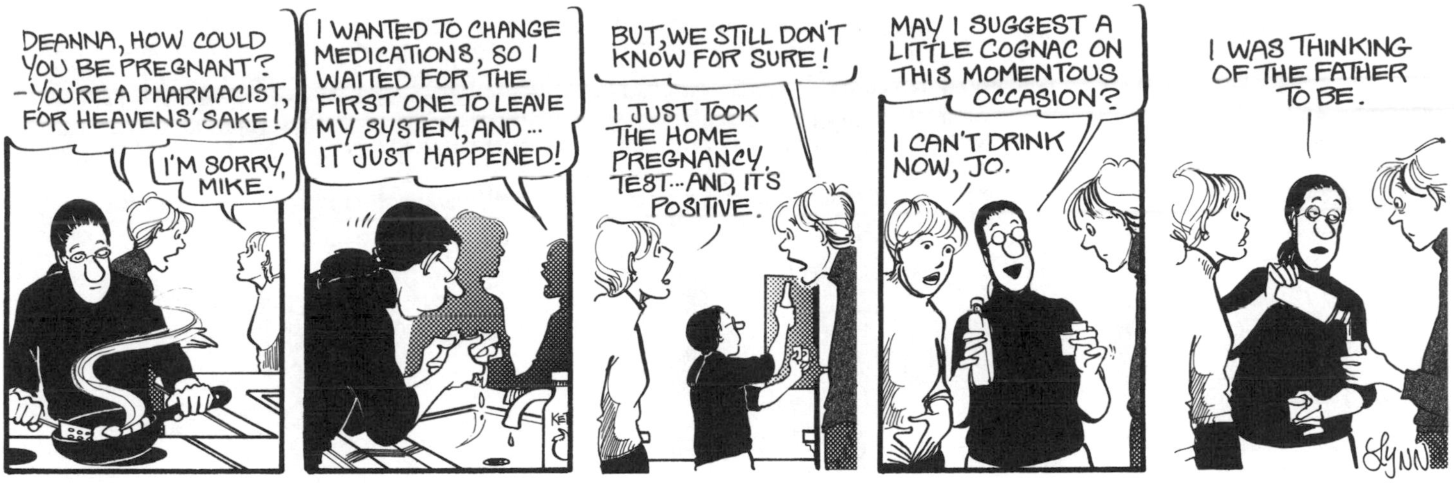
DEANNA, HOW COULD YOU BE PREGNANT? -YOU'RE A PHARMACIST, FOR HEAVENS' SAKE!
I'M SORRY, MIKE.
I WANTED TO CHANGE MEDICATIONS, SO I WAITED FOR THE FIRST ONE TO LEAVE MY SYSTEM, AND... IT JUST HAPPENED!
BUT, WE STILL DON'T KNOW FOR SURE!
I JUST TOOK THE HOME PREGNANCY TEST... AND, IT'S POSITIVE.
MAY I SUGGEST A LITTLE COGNAC ON THIS MOMENTOUS OCCASION?
I CAN'T DRINK NOW, JO.
I WAS THINKING OF THE FATHER TO BE.
LYNN

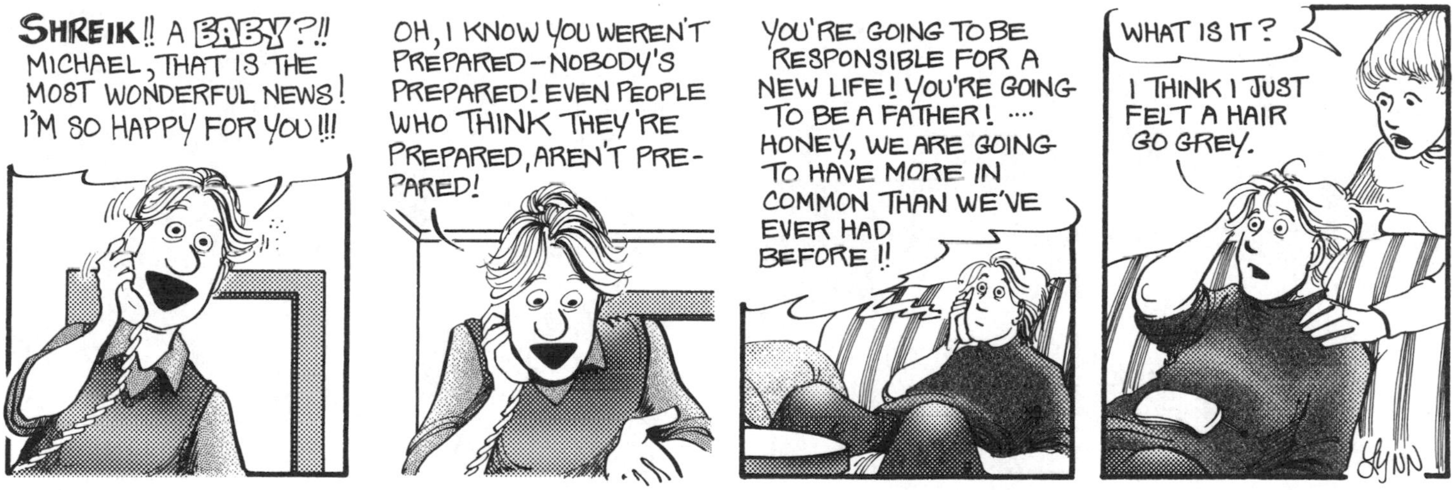
SHREIK!! A BABY?!! MICHAEL, THAT IS THE MOST WONDERFUL NEWS! I'M SO HAPPY FOR YOU!!!
OH, I KNOW YOU WEREN'T PREPARED - NOBODY'S PREPARED! EVEN PEOPLE WHO THINK THEY'RE PREPARED, AREN'T PREPARED!
YOU'RE GOING TO BE RESPONSIBLE FOR A NEW LIFE! YOU'RE GOING TO BE A FATHER! .... HONEY, WE ARE GOING TO HAVE MORE IN COMMON THAN WE'VE EVER HAD BEFORE!!
WHAT IS IT?
I THINK I JUST FELT A HAIR GO GREY.
LYNN

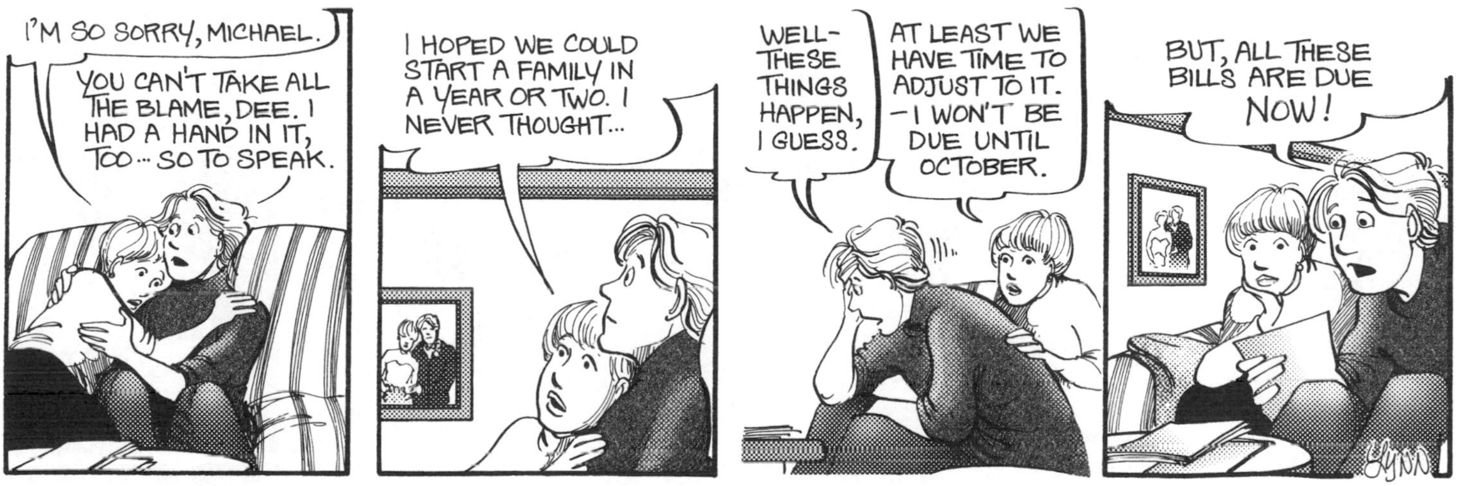
I'M SO SORRY, MICHAEL.
YOU CAN'T TAKE ALL THE BLAME, DEE. I HAD A HAND IN IT, TOO... SO TO SPEAK.
I HOPED WE COULD START A FAMILY IN A YEAR OR TWO. I NEVER THOUGHT...
WELL- THESE THINGS HAPPEN, I GUESS.
AT LEAST WE HAVE TIME TO ADJUST TO IT. - I WON'T BE DUE UNTIL OCTOBER.
BUT, ALL THESE BILLS ARE DUE NOW!
LYNN

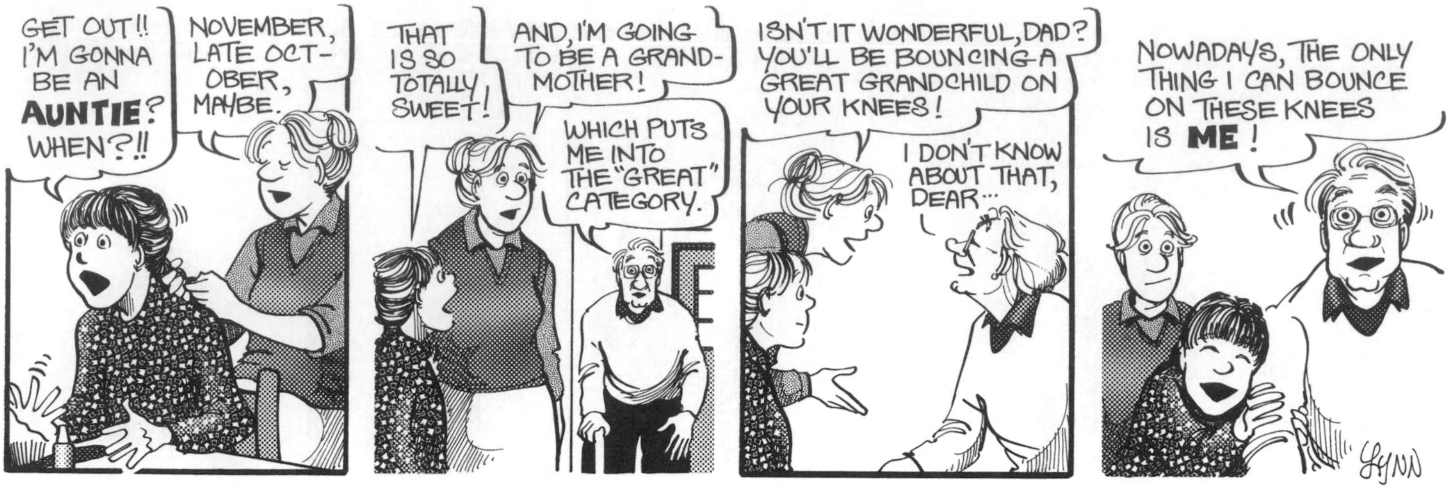
GET OUT!! I'M GONNA BE AN AUNTIE? WHEN?!!
NOVEMBER, LATE OCTOBER, MAYBE.
THAT IS SO TOTALLY SWEET!
AND, I'M GOING TO BE A GRANDMOTHER!
WHICH PUTS ME INTO THE "GREAT" CATEGORY.
ISN'T IT WONDERFUL, DAD? YOU'LL BE BOUNCING A GREAT GRANDCHILD ON YOUR KNEES!
I DON'T KNOW ABOUT THAT, DEAR...
NOWADAYS, THE ONLY THING I CAN BOUNCE ON THESE KNEES IS ME!
LYNN

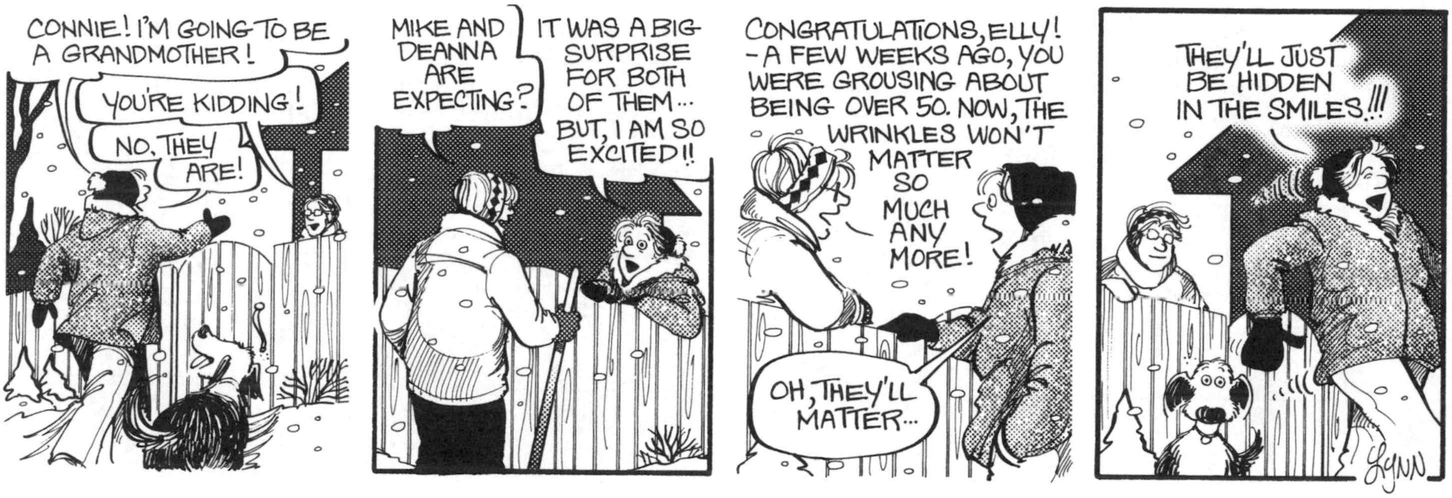
CONNIE! I'M GOING TO BE A GRANDMOTHER!
YOU'RE KIDDING!
NO, THEY ARE!
MIKE AND DEANNA ARE EXPECTING?
IT WAS A BIG SURPRISE FOR BOTH OF THEM... BUT, I AM SO EXCITED!!
CONGRATULATIONS, ELLY! - A FEW WEEKS AGO, YOU WERE GROUSING ABOUT BEING OVER 50. NOW, THE WRINKLES WON'T MATTER SO MUCH ANY MORE!
OH, THEY'LL MATTER...
THEY'LL JUST BE HIDDEN IN THE SMILES!!!
LYNN

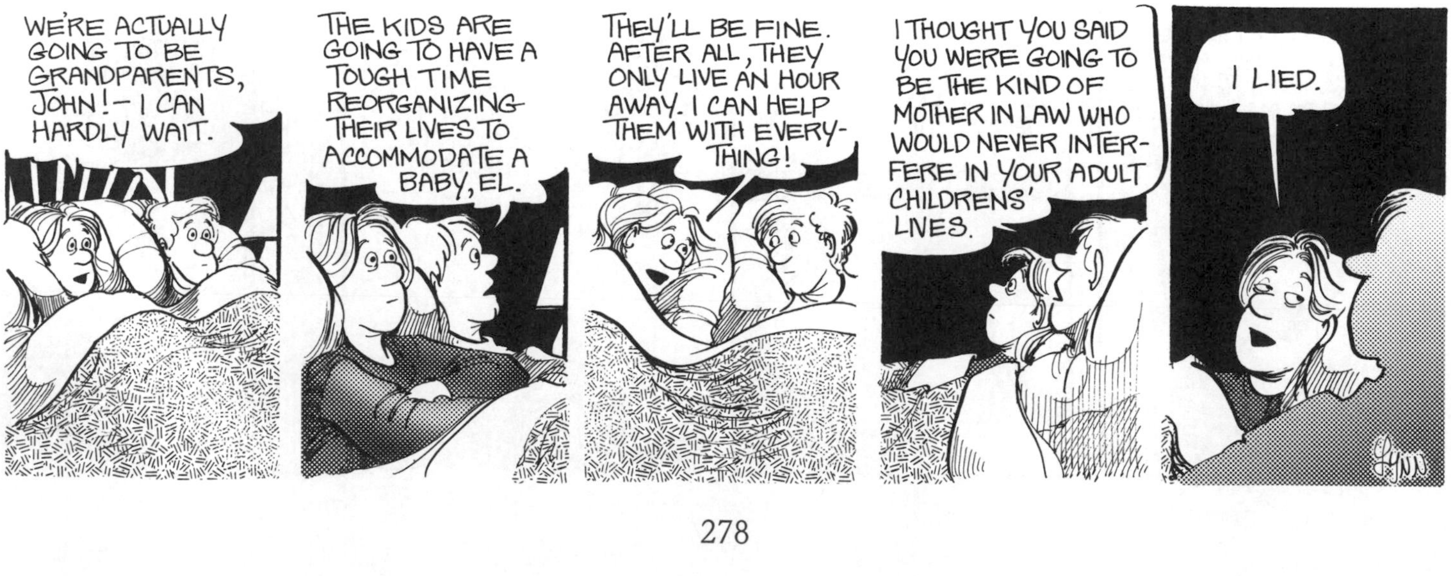
WE'RE ACTUALLY GOING TO BE GRANDPARENTS, JOHN! - I CAN HARDLY WAIT.
THE KIDS ARE GOING TO HAVE A TOUGH TIME REORGANIZING THEIR LIVES TO ACCOMMODATE A BABY, EL.
THEY'LL BE FINE. AFTER ALL, THEY ONLY LIVE AN HOUR AWAY. I CAN HELP THEM WITH EVERYTHING!
I THOUGHT YOU SAID YOU WERE GOING TO BE THE KIND OF MOTHER IN LAW WHO WOULD NEVER INTERFERE IN YOUR ADULT CHILDRENS' LIVES.
I LIED.
LYNN

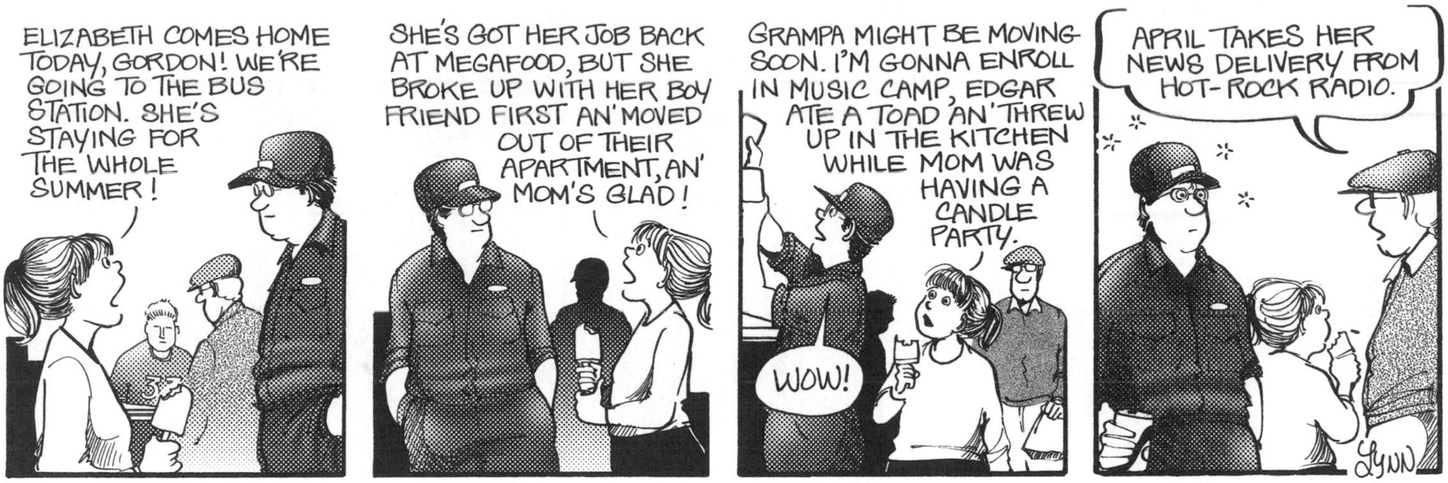
ELIZABETH COMES HOME TODAY, GORDON! WE'RE GOING TO THE BUS STATION. SHE'S STAYING FOR THE WHOLE SUMMER!
SHE'S GOT HER JOB BACK AT MEGAFOOD, BUT SHE BROKE UP WITH HER BOY FRIEND FIRST AN' MOVED OUT OF THEIR APARTMENT, AN' MOM'S GLAD!
GRAMPA MIGHT BE MOVING SOON. I'M GONNA ENROLL IN MUSIC CAMP, EDGAR ATE A TOAD AN' THREW UP IN THE KITCHEN WHILE MOM WAS HAVING A CANDLE PARTY.
WOW!
APRIL TAKES HER NEWS DELIVERY FROM HOT-ROCK RADIO.
LYNN

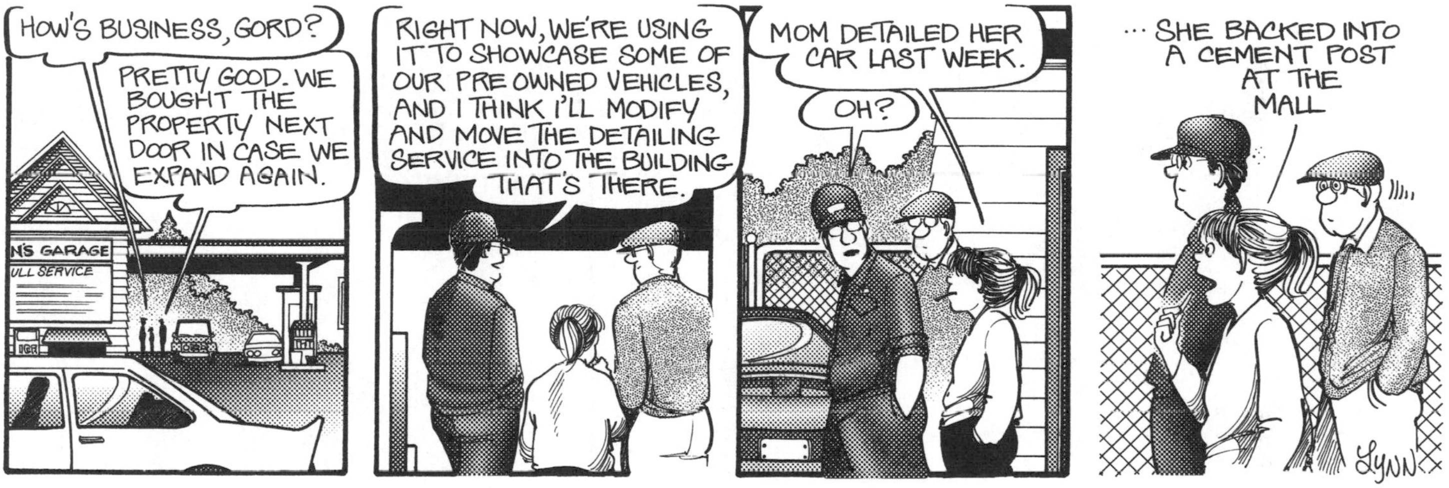
HOW'S BUSINESS, GORD?
PRETTY GOOD. WE BOUGHT THE PROPERTY NEXT DOOR IN CASE WE EXPAND AGAIN.
N'S GARAGE
ULL SERVICE
RIGHT NOW, WE'RE USING IT TO SHOWCASE SOME OF OUR PRE OWNED VEHICLES, AND I THINK I'LL MODIFY AND MOVE THE DETAILING SERVICE INTO THE BUILDING THAT'S THERE.
MOM DETAILED HER CAR LAST WEEK.
OH?
... SHE BACKED INTO A CEMENT POST AT THE MALL
LYNN

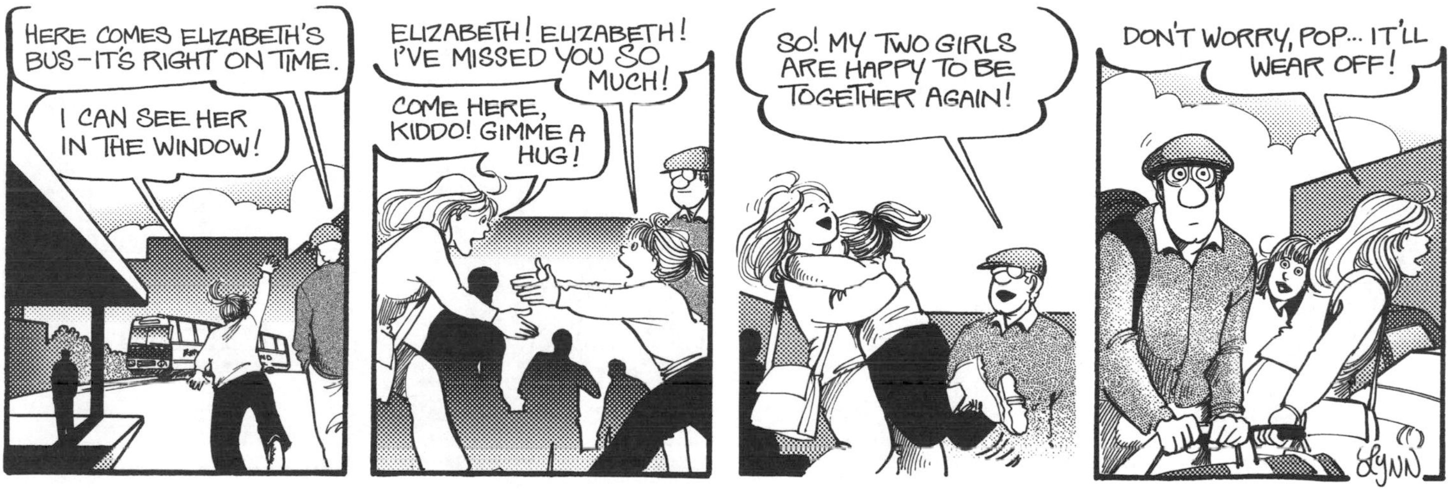
HERE COMES ELIZABETH'S BUS - IT'S RIGHT ON TIME.
I CAN SEE HER IN THE WINDOW!
ELIZABETH! ELIZABETH! I'VE MISSED YOU SO MUCH!
COME HERE, KIDDO! GIMME A HUG!
SO! MY TWO GIRLS ARE HAPPY TO BE TOGETHER AGAIN!
DON'T WORRY, POP... IT'LL WEAR OFF!
LYNN

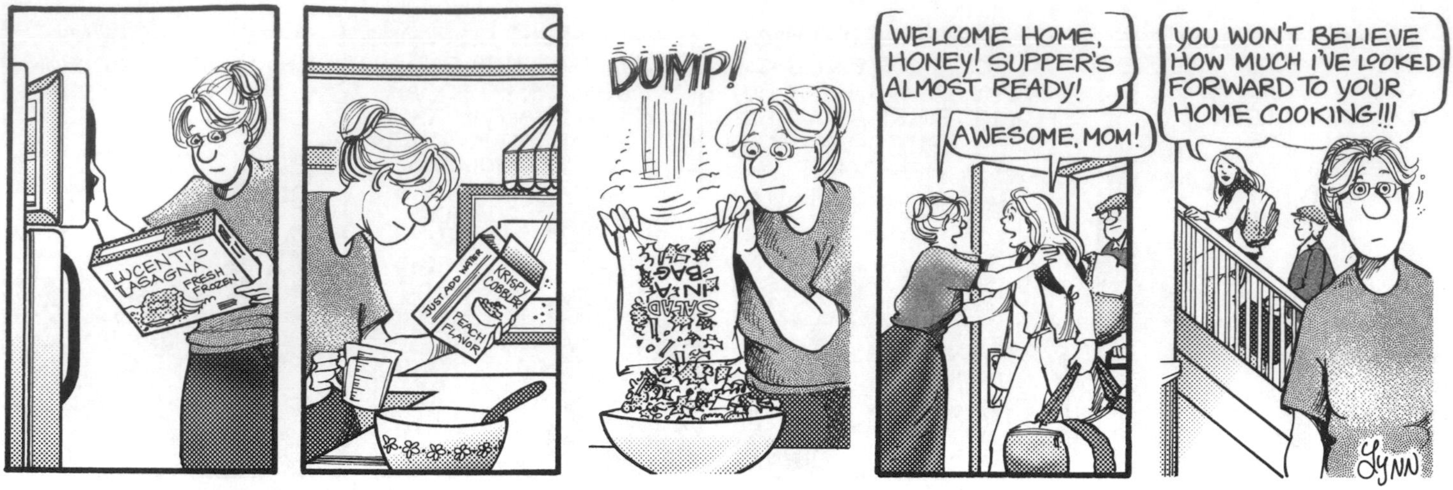
LUCENTI'S LASAGNA FRESH FROZEN
JUST ADD WATER KRISPY COBBLER PEACH FLAVOR
DUMP!
WELCOME HOME, HONEY! SUPPER'S ALMOST READY!
AWESOME, MOM!
YOU WON'T BELIEVE HOW MUCH I'VE LOOKED FORWARD TO YOUR HOME COOKING!!!
Lynn

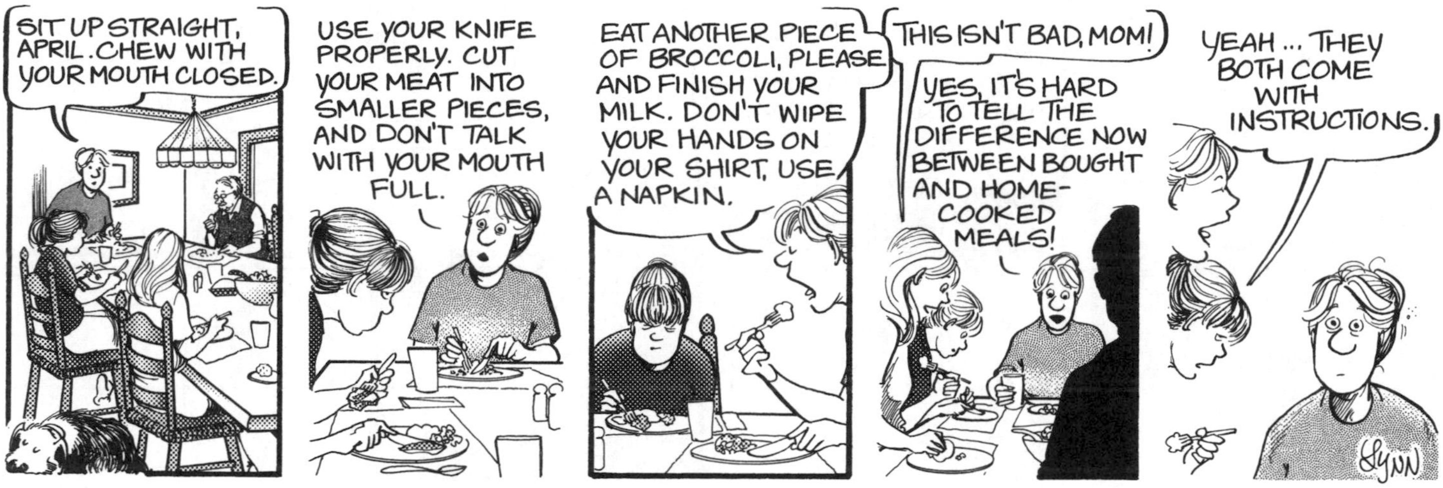
SIT UP STRAIGHT, APRIL. CHEW WITH YOUR MOUTH CLOSED.
USE YOUR KNIFE PROPERLY. CUT YOUR MEAT INTO SMALLER PIECES, AND DON'T TALK WITH YOUR MOUTH FULL.
EAT ANOTHER PIECE OF BROCCOLI, PLEASE AND FINISH YOUR MILK. DON'T WIPE YOUR HANDS ON YOUR SHIRT, USE A NAPKIN.
THIS ISN'T BAD, MOM!
YES, IT'S HARD TO TELL THE DIFFERENCE NOW BETWEEN BOUGHT AND HOME-COOKED MEALS!
YEAH ... THEY BOTH COME WITH INSTRUCTIONS.
Lynn

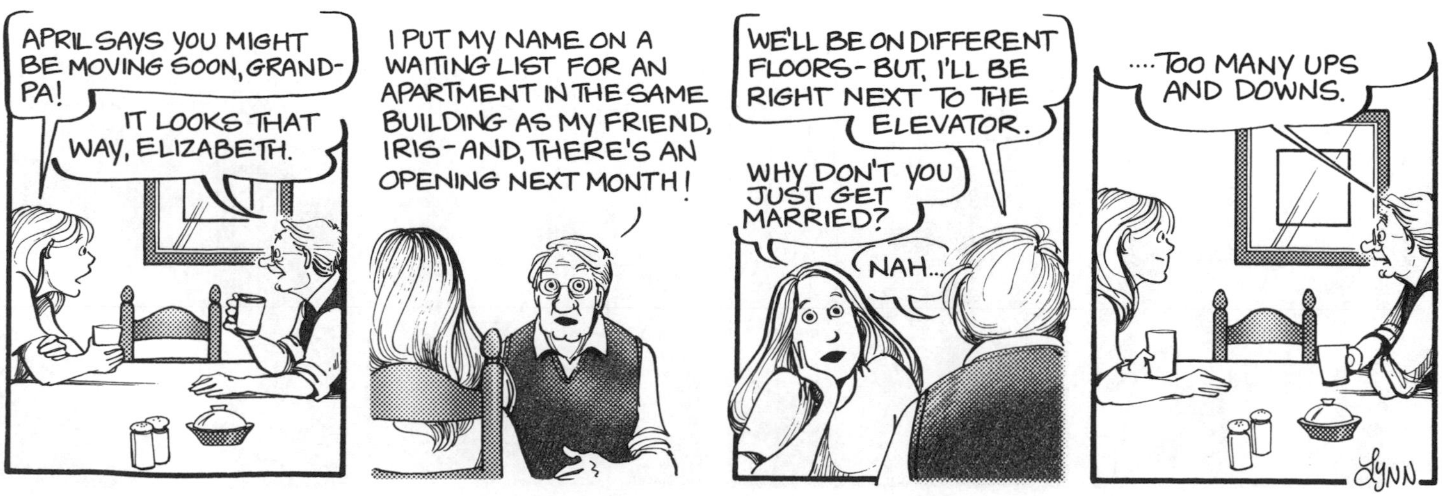
APRIL SAYS YOU MIGHT BE MOVING SOON, GRAND-PA!
IT LOOKS THAT WAY, ELIZABETH.
I PUT MY NAME ON A WAITING LIST FOR AN APARTMENT IN THE SAME BUILDING AS MY FRIEND, IRIS - AND, THERE'S AN OPENING NEXT MONTH!
WE'LL BE ON DIFFERENT FLOORS - BUT, I'LL BE RIGHT NEXT TO THE ELEVATOR.
WHY DON'T YOU JUST GET MARRIED?
NAH...
....TOO MANY UPS AND DOWNS.
Lynn

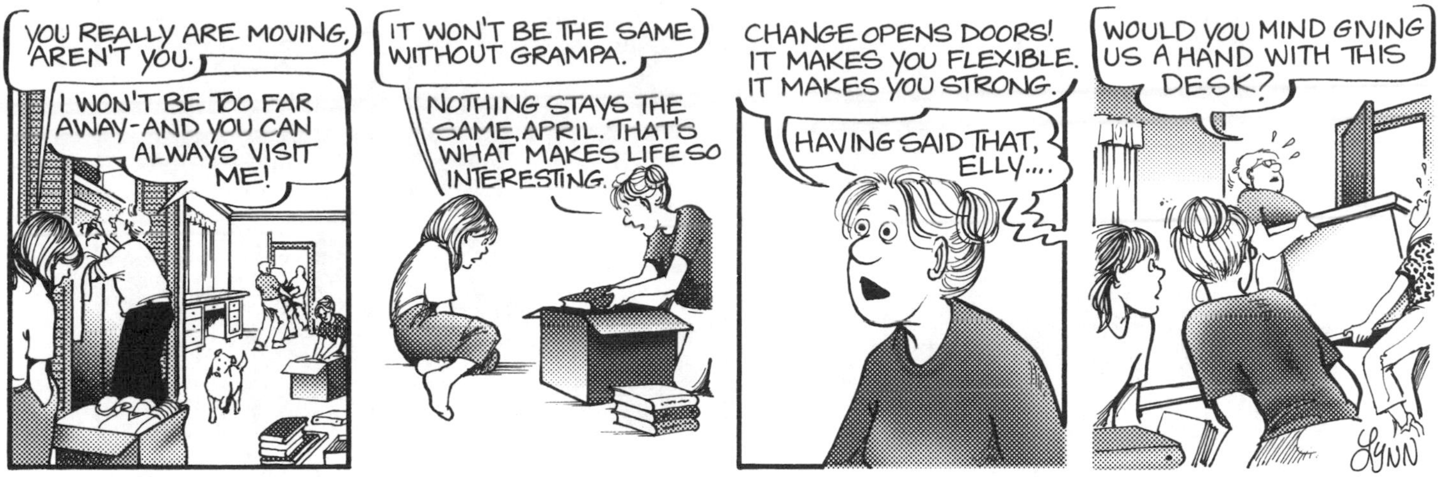
YOU REALLY ARE MOVING, AREN'T YOU.
I WON'T BE TOO FAR AWAY-AND YOU CAN ALWAYS VISIT ME!
IT WON'T BE THE SAME WITHOUT GRAMPA.
NOTHING STAYS THE SAME, APRIL. THAT'S WHAT MAKES LIFE SO INTERESTING.
CHANGE OPENS DOORS! IT MAKES YOU FLEXIBLE. IT MAKES YOU STRONG.
HAVING SAID THAT, ELLY....
WOULD YOU MIND GIVING US A HAND WITH THIS DESK?
LYNN

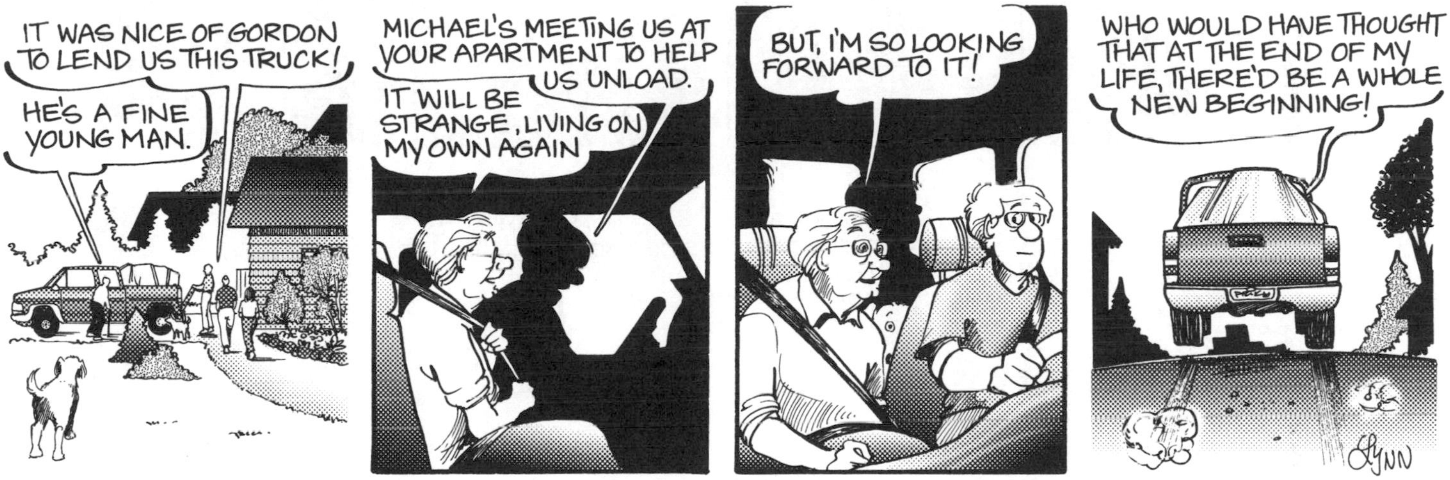
IT WAS NICE OF GORDON TO LEND US THIS TRUCK!
HE'S A FINE YOUNG MAN.
MICHAEL'S MEETING US AT YOUR APARTMENT TO HELP US UNLOAD.
IT WILL BE STRANGE, LIVING ON MY OWN AGAIN
BUT, I'M SO LOOKING FORWARD TO IT!
WHO WOULD HAVE THOUGHT THAT AT THE END OF MY LIFE, THERE'D BE A WHOLE NEW BEGINNING!
LYNN

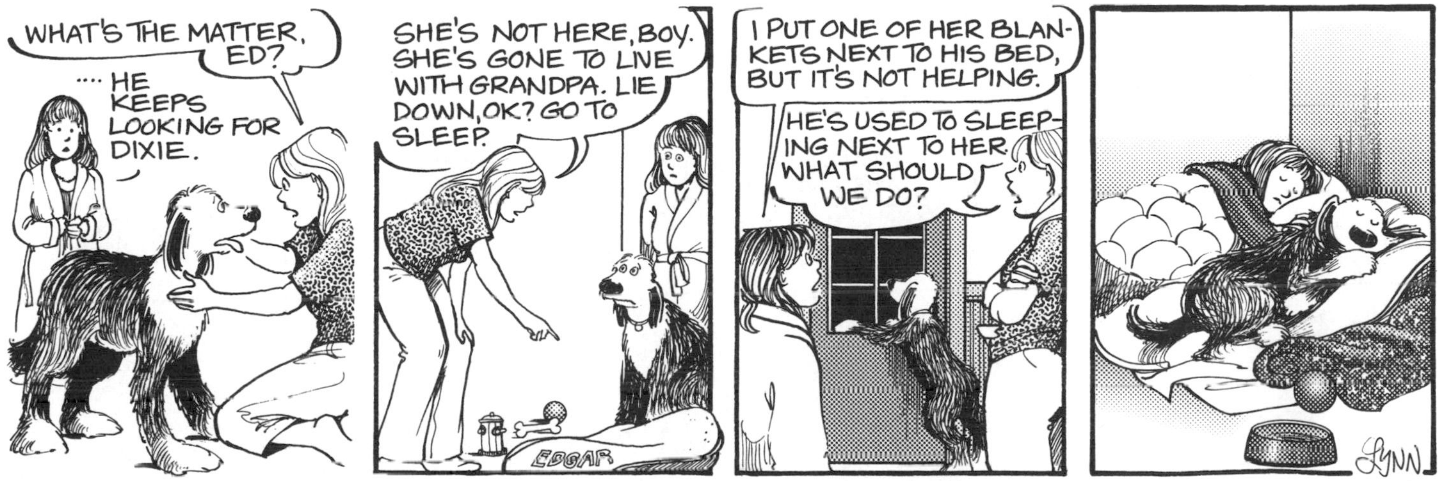
WHAT'S THE MATTER, ED?
.... HE KEEPS LOOKING FOR DIXIE.
SHE'S NOT HERE, BOY. SHE'S GONE TO LIVE WITH GRANDPA. LIE DOWN, OK? GO TO SLEEP.
EDGAR
I PUT ONE OF HER BLANKETS NEXT TO HIS BED, BUT IT'S NOT HELPING.
HE'S USED TO SLEEPING NEXT TO HER WHAT SHOULD WE DO?
LYNN

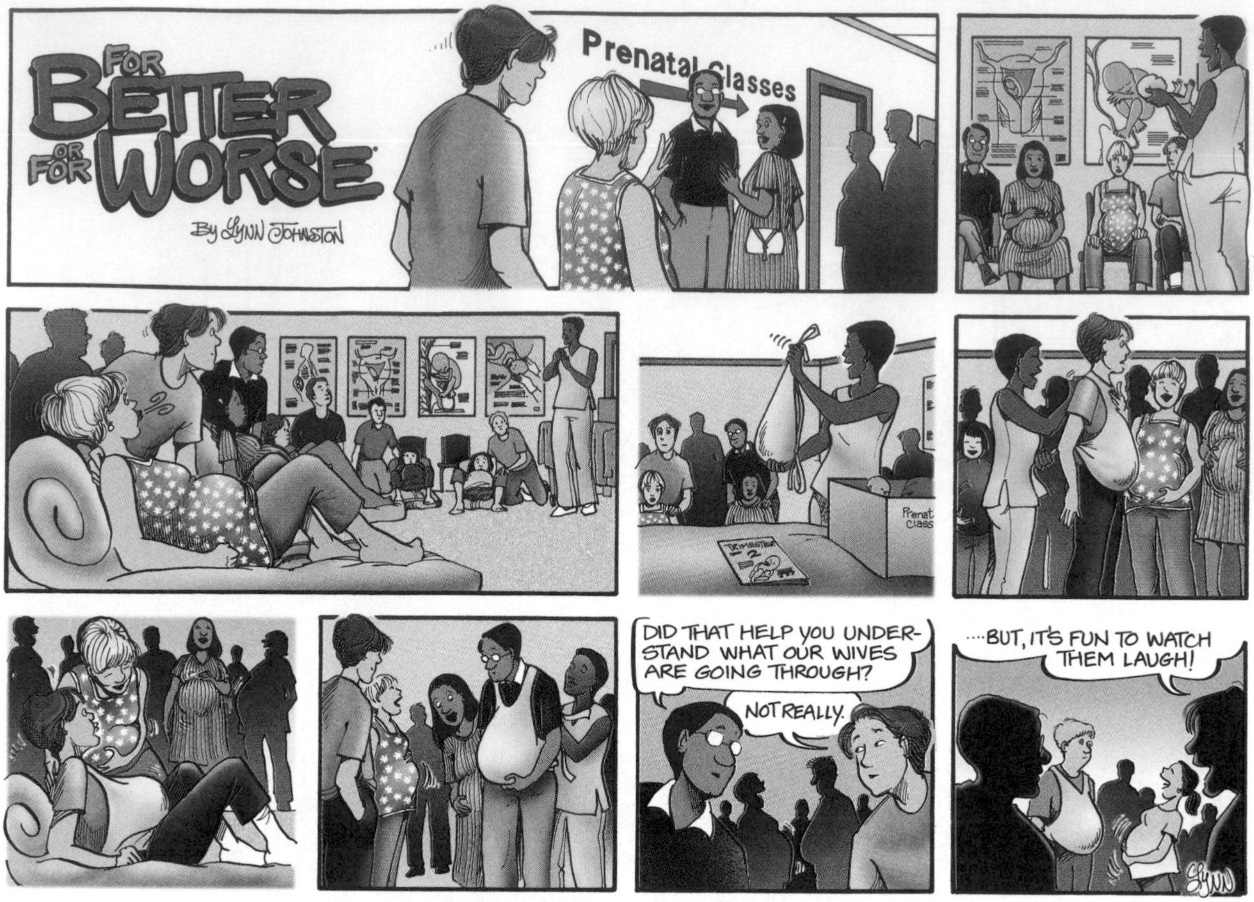
FOR BETTER OR FOR WORSE
BY LYNN JOHNSTON
Prenatal Classes
Trimester 2
Prenatal Class
DID THAT HELP YOU UNDERSTAND WHAT OUR WIVES ARE GOING THROUGH?
NOT REALLY.
....BUT, IT'S FUN TO WATCH THEM LAUGH!
LYNN

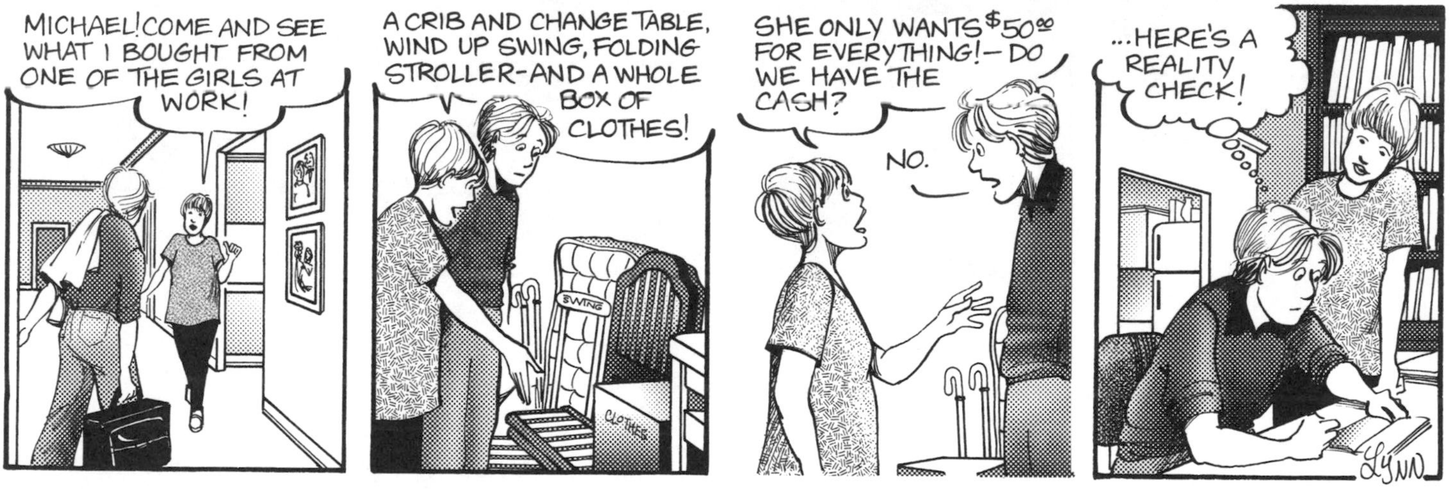
MICHAEL! COME AND SEE WHAT I BOUGHT FROM ONE OF THE GIRLS AT WORK!
A CRIB AND CHANGE TABLE, WIND UP SWING, FOLDING STROLLER- AND A WHOLE BOX OF CLOTHES!
SWING
CLOTHES
SHE ONLY WANTS $50.00 FOR EVERYTHING!- DO WE HAVE THE CASH?
NO.
...HERE'S A REALITY CHECK!
LYNN

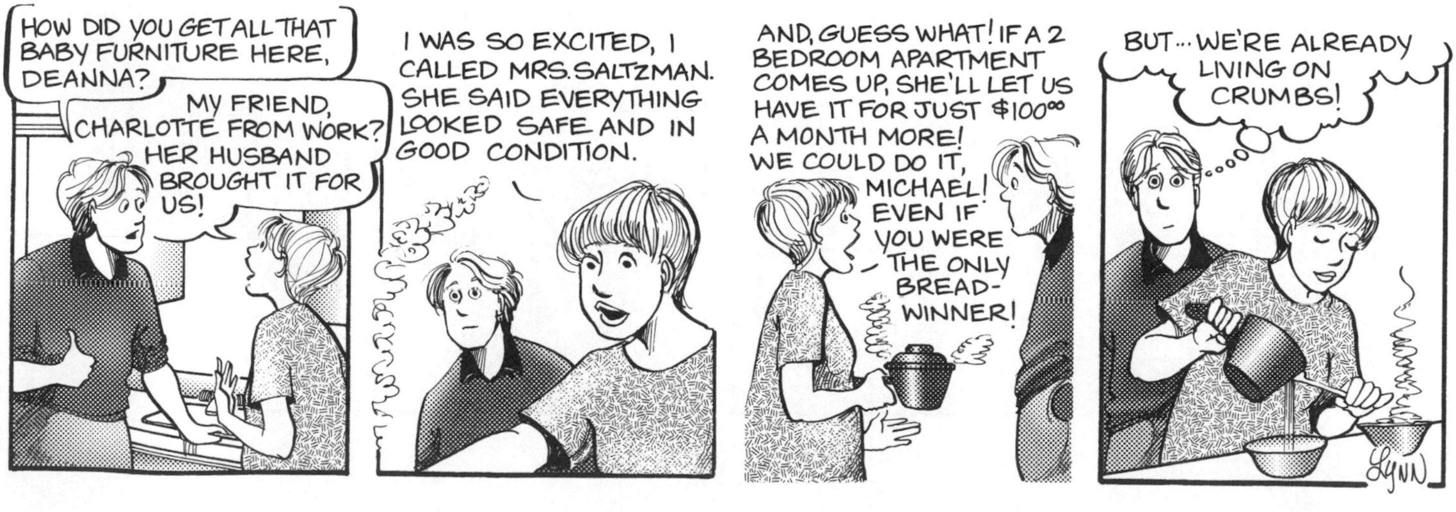
HOW DID YOU GET ALL THAT BABY FURNITURE HERE, DEANNA?
MY FRIEND, CHARLOTTE FROM WORK? HER HUSBAND BROUGHT IT FOR US!
I WAS SO EXCITED, I CALLED MRS. SALTZMAN. SHE SAID EVERYTHING LOOKED SAFE AND IN GOOD CONDITION.
AND, GUESS WHAT! IF A 2 BEDROOM APARTMENT COMES UP, SHE'LL LET US HAVE IT FOR JUST $100.00 A MONTH MORE! WE COULD DO IT, MICHAEL! EVEN IF YOU WERE THE ONLY BREAD-WINNER!
BUT... WE'RE ALREADY LIVING ON CRUMBS!
LYNN

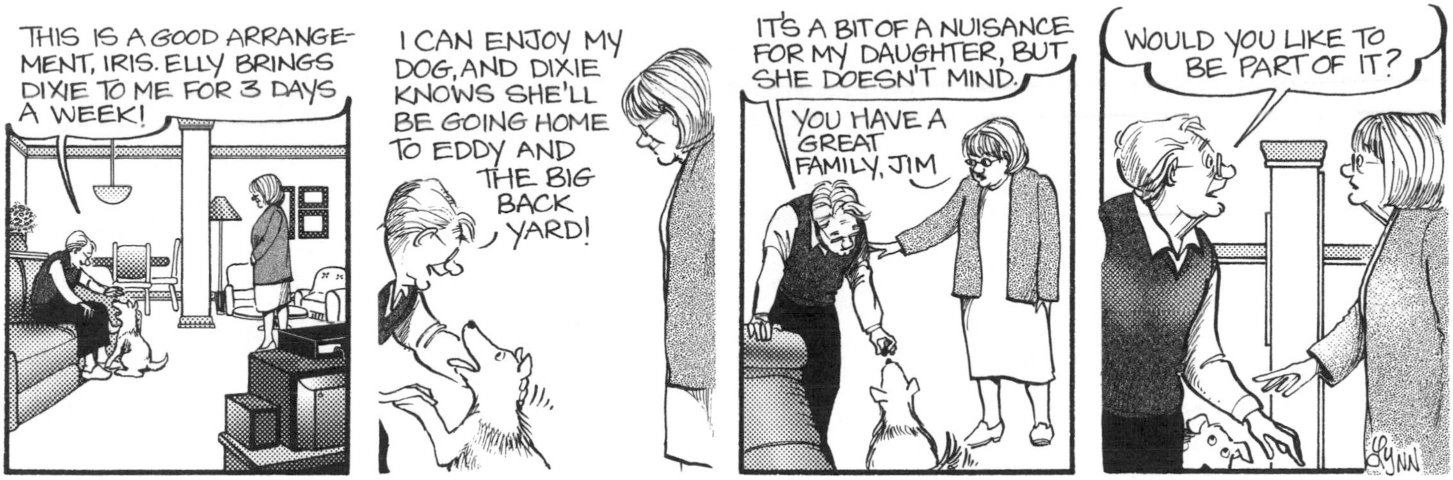
THIS IS A GOOD ARRANGE-MENT, IRIS. ELLY BRINGS DIXIE TO ME FOR 3 DAYS A WEEK!
I CAN ENJOY MY DOG, AND DIXIE KNOWS SHE'LL BE GOING HOME TO EDDY AND THE BIG BACK YARD!
IT'S A BIT OF A NUISANCE FOR MY DAUGHTER, BUT SHE DOESN'T MIND.
YOU HAVE A GREAT FAMILY, JIM
WOULD YOU LIKE TO BE PART OF IT?
LYNN

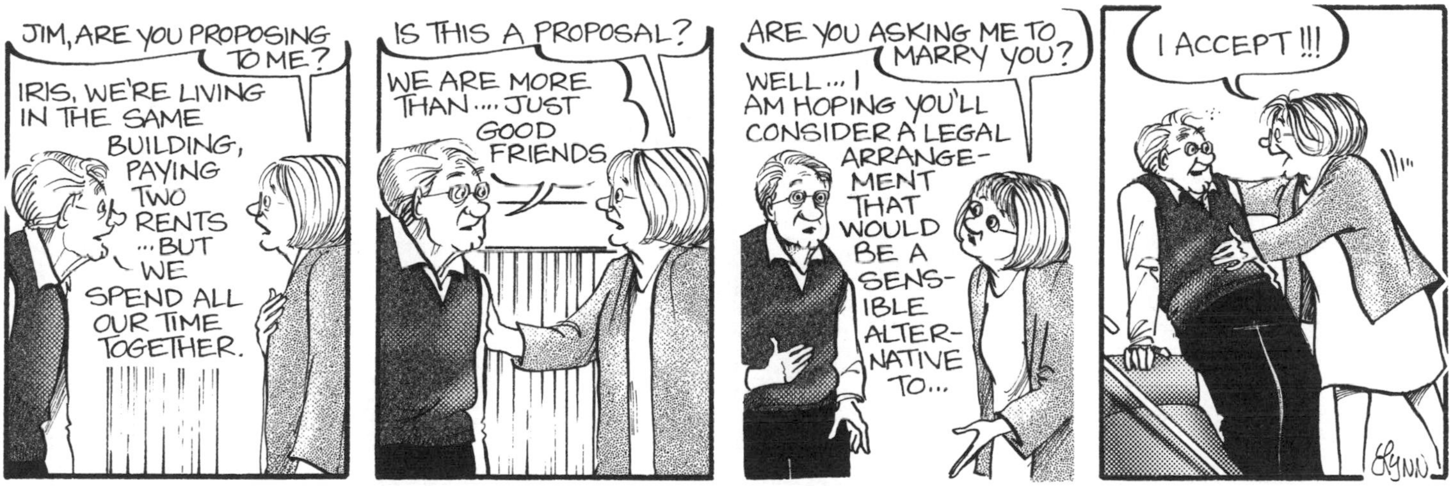
JIM, ARE YOU PROPOSING TO ME?
IRIS, WE'RE LIVING IN THE SAME BUILDING, PAYING TWO RENTS ...BUT WE SPEND ALL OUR TIME TOGETHER.
IS THIS A PROPOSAL?
WE ARE MORE THAN.... JUST GOOD FRIENDS
ARE YOU ASKING ME TO MARRY YOU?
WELL... I AM HOPING YOU'LL CONSIDER A LEGAL ARRANGE-MENT THAT WOULD BE A SENS-IBLE ALTER-NATIVE TO...
I ACCEPT !!!
LYNN

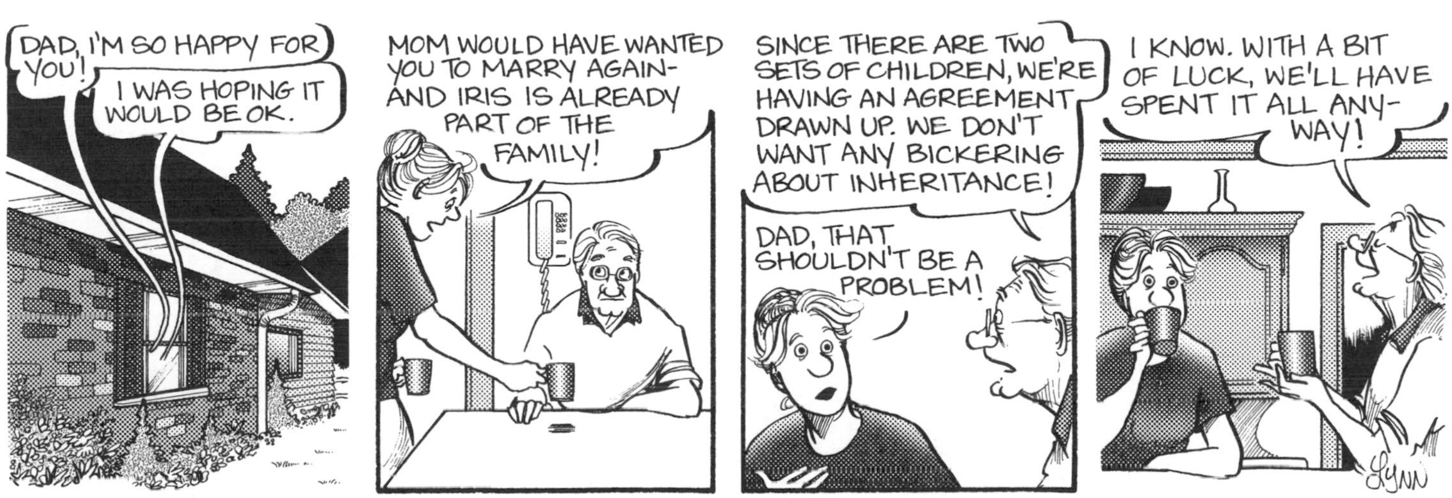
DAD, I'M SO HAPPY FOR YOU!
I WAS HOPING IT WOULD BE OK.
MOM WOULD HAVE WANTED YOU TO MARRY AGAIN- AND IRIS IS ALREADY PART OF THE FAMILY!
SINCE THERE ARE TWO SETS OF CHILDREN, WE'RE HAVING AN AGREEMENT DRAWN UP. WE DON'T WANT ANY BICKERING ABOUT INHERITANCE!
DAD, THAT SHOULDN'T BE A PROBLEM!
I KNOW. WITH A BIT OF LUCK, WE'LL HAVE SPENT IT ALL ANY-WAY!
LYNN

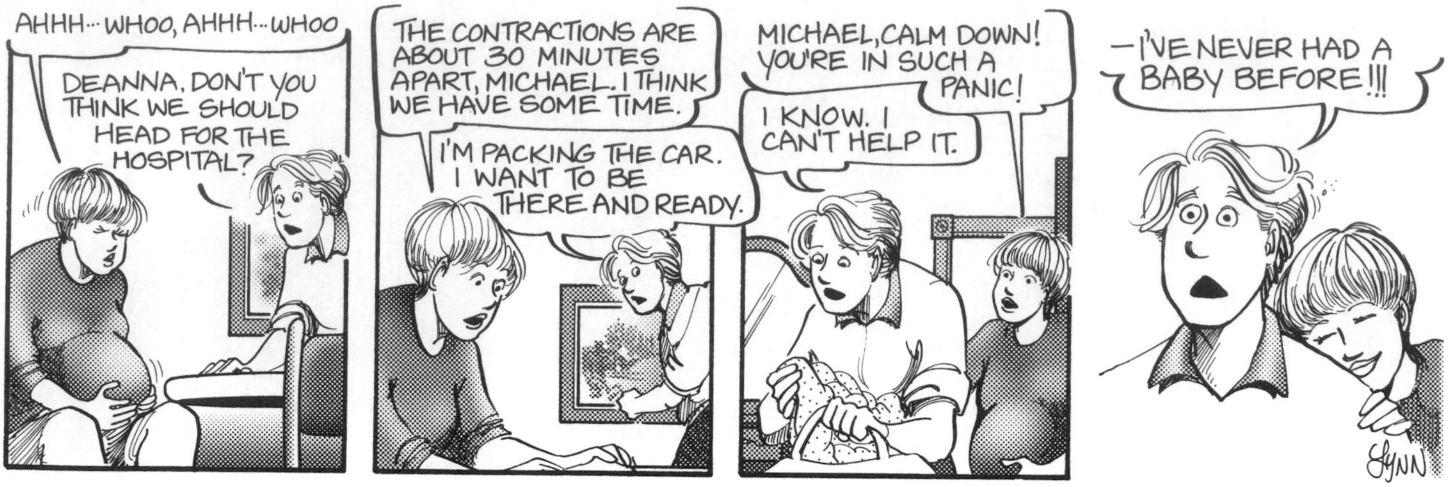
AHHH... WHOO, AHHH... WHOO
DEANNA, DON'T YOU THINK WE SHOULD HEAD FOR THE HOSPITAL?
THE CONTRACTIONS ARE ABOUT 30 MINUTES APART, MICHAEL. I THINK WE HAVE SOME TIME.
I'M PACKING THE CAR. I WANT TO BE THERE AND READY.
MICHAEL, CALM DOWN! YOU'RE IN SUCH A PANIC!
I KNOW. I CAN'T HELP IT.
–I'VE NEVER HAD A BABY BEFORE!!!
LYNN

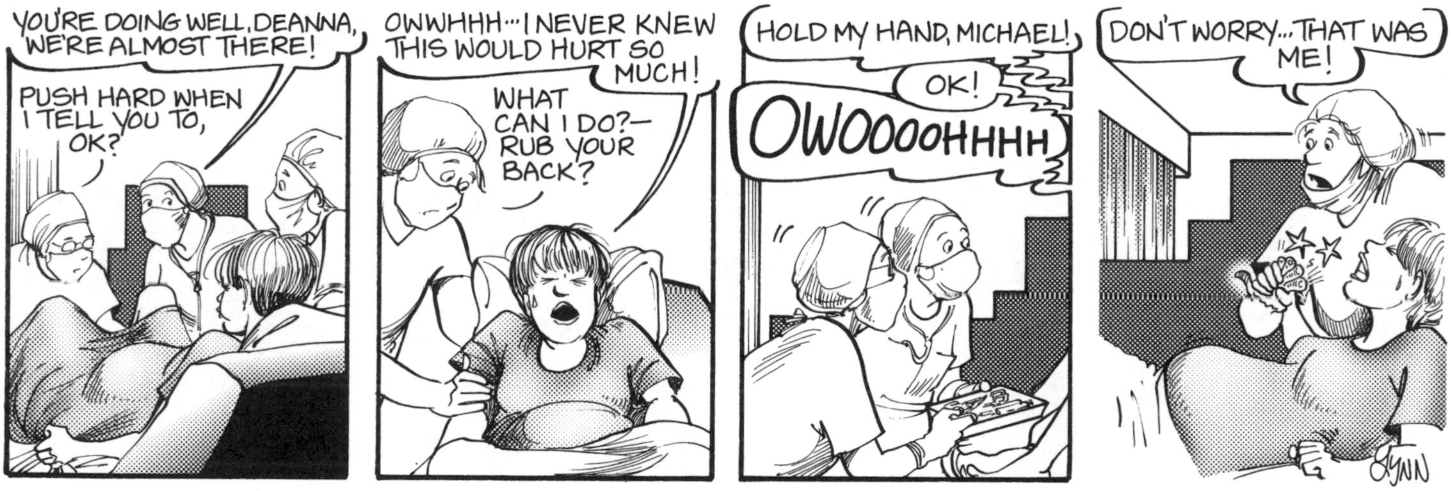
YOU'RE DOING WELL, DEANNA, WE'RE ALMOST THERE!
PUSH HARD WHEN I TELL YOU TO, OK?
OWWHHH... I NEVER KNEW THIS WOULD HURT SO MUCH!
WHAT CAN I DO?– RUB YOUR BACK?
HOLD MY HAND, MICHAEL!
OK!
OWOOOOHHHH
DON'T WORRY... THAT WAS ME!
LYNN

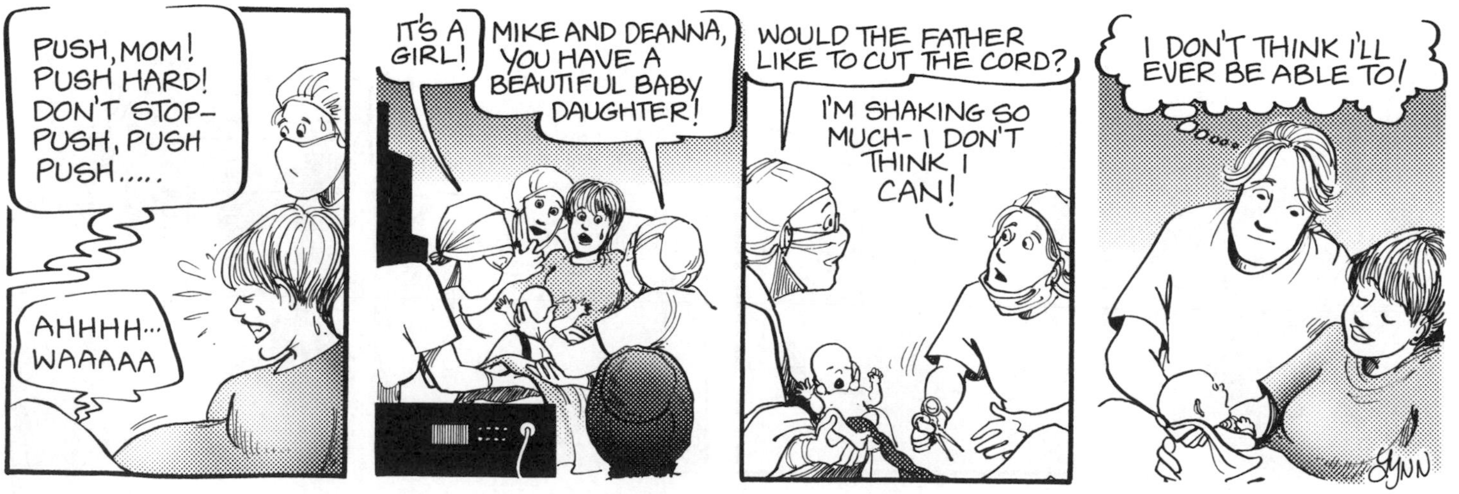
PUSH, MOM! PUSH HARD! DON'T STOP- PUSH, PUSH PUSH.....
AHHHH... WAAAAA
IT'S A GIRL!
MIKE AND DEANNA, YOU HAVE A BEAUTIFUL BABY DAUGHTER!
WOULD THE FATHER LIKE TO CUT THE CORD?
I'M SHAKING SO MUCH- I DON'T THINK I CAN!
I DON'T THINK I'LL EVER BE ABLE TO!
LYNN

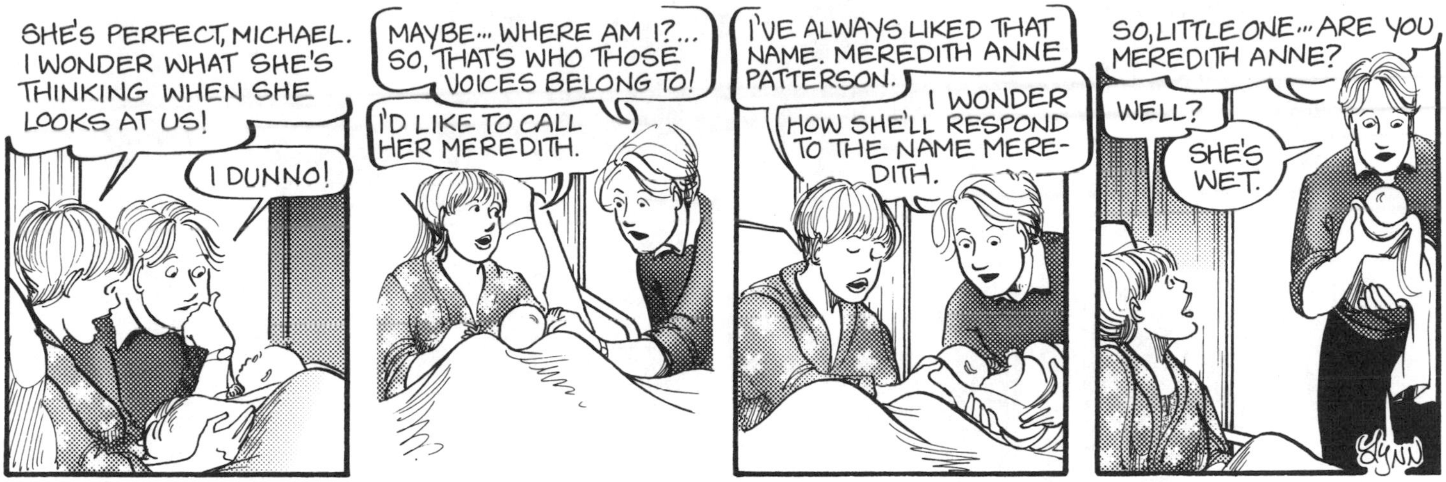
SHE'S PERFECT, MICHAEL. I WONDER WHAT SHE'S THINKING WHEN SHE LOOKS AT US!
I DUNNO!
MAYBE... WHERE AM I?... SO, THAT'S WHO THOSE VOICES BELONG TO!
I'D LIKE TO CALL HER MEREDITH.
I'VE ALWAYS LIKED THAT NAME. MEREDITH ANNE PATTERSON.
I WONDER HOW SHE'LL RESPOND TO THE NAME MERE-DITH.
SO, LITTLE ONE... ARE YOU MEREDITH ANNE?
WELL?
SHE'S WET.
LYNN

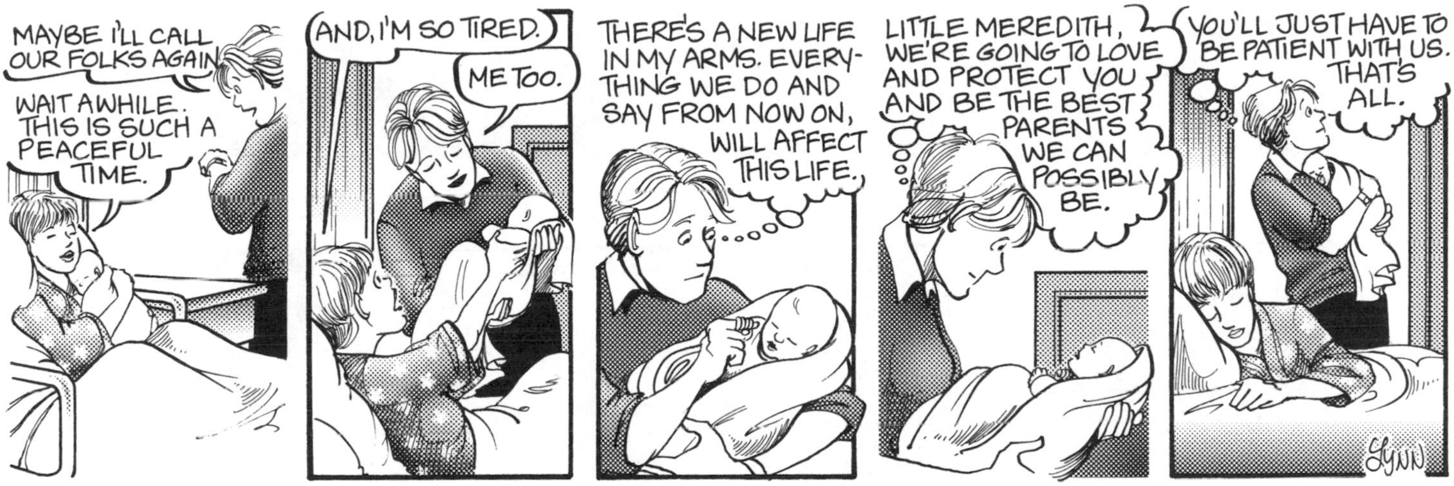
MAYBE I'LL CALL OUR FOLKS AGAIN.
WAIT AWHILE. THIS IS SUCH A PEACEFUL TIME.
AND, I'M SO TIRED.
ME TOO.
THERE'S A NEW LIFE IN MY ARMS. EVERY-THING WE DO AND SAY FROM NOW ON, WILL AFFECT THIS LIFE.
LITTLE MEREDITH, WE'RE GOING TO LOVE AND PROTECT YOU AND BE THE BEST PARENTS WE CAN POSSIBLY BE.
YOU'LL JUST HAVE TO BE PATIENT WITH US. THAT'S ALL.
LYNN

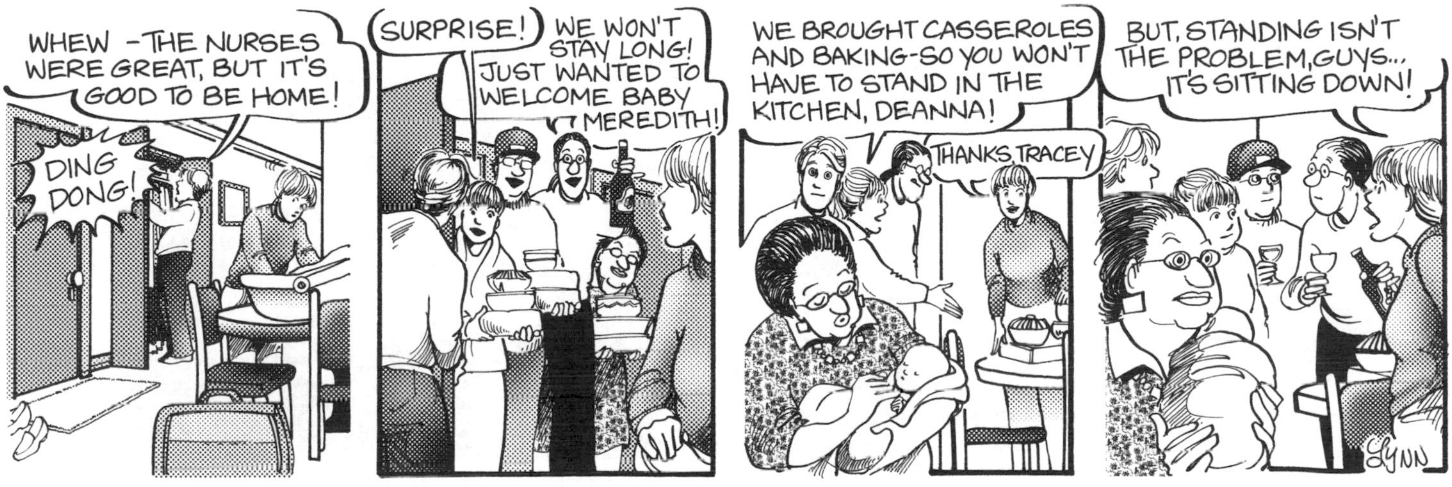
WHEW - THE NURSES WERE GREAT, BUT IT'S GOOD TO BE HOME!
DING DONG!
SURPRISE!
WE WON'T STAY LONG! JUST WANTED TO WELCOME BABY MEREDITH!
WE BROUGHT CASSEROLES AND BAKING-SO YOU WON'T HAVE TO STAND IN THE KITCHEN, DEANNA!
THANKS, TRACEY
BUT, STANDING ISN'T THE PROBLEM, GUYS... IT'S SITTING DOWN!
LYNN

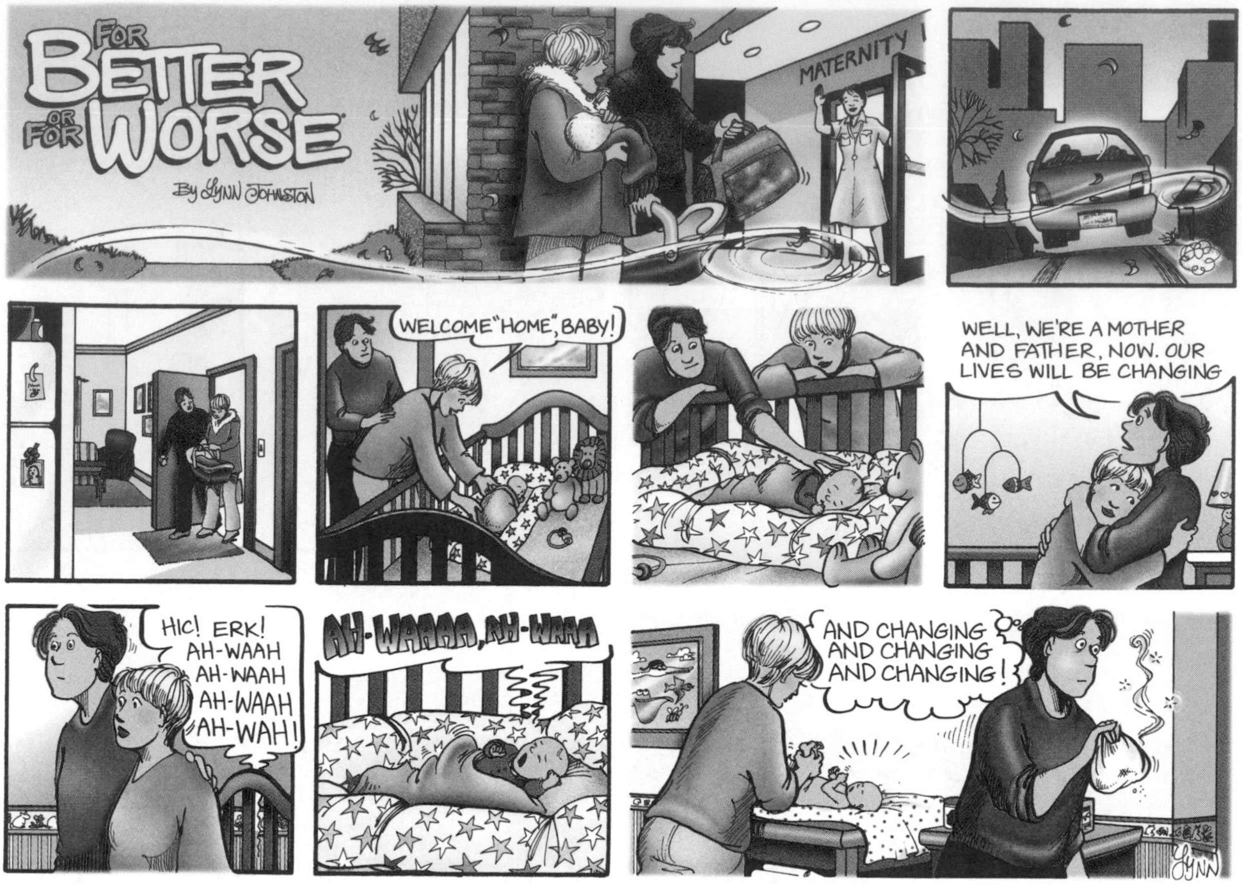
FOR BETTER OR FOR WORSE
By Lynn Johnston
MATERNITY
WELCOME "HOME", BABY!
WELL, WE'RE A MOTHER AND FATHER, NOW. OUR LIVES WILL BE CHANGING
HIC! ERK! AH-WAAH AH-WAAH AH-WAAH AH-WAH!
AH-WAAAA, AH-WAA
AND CHANGING AND CHANGING AND CHANGING!
Lynn

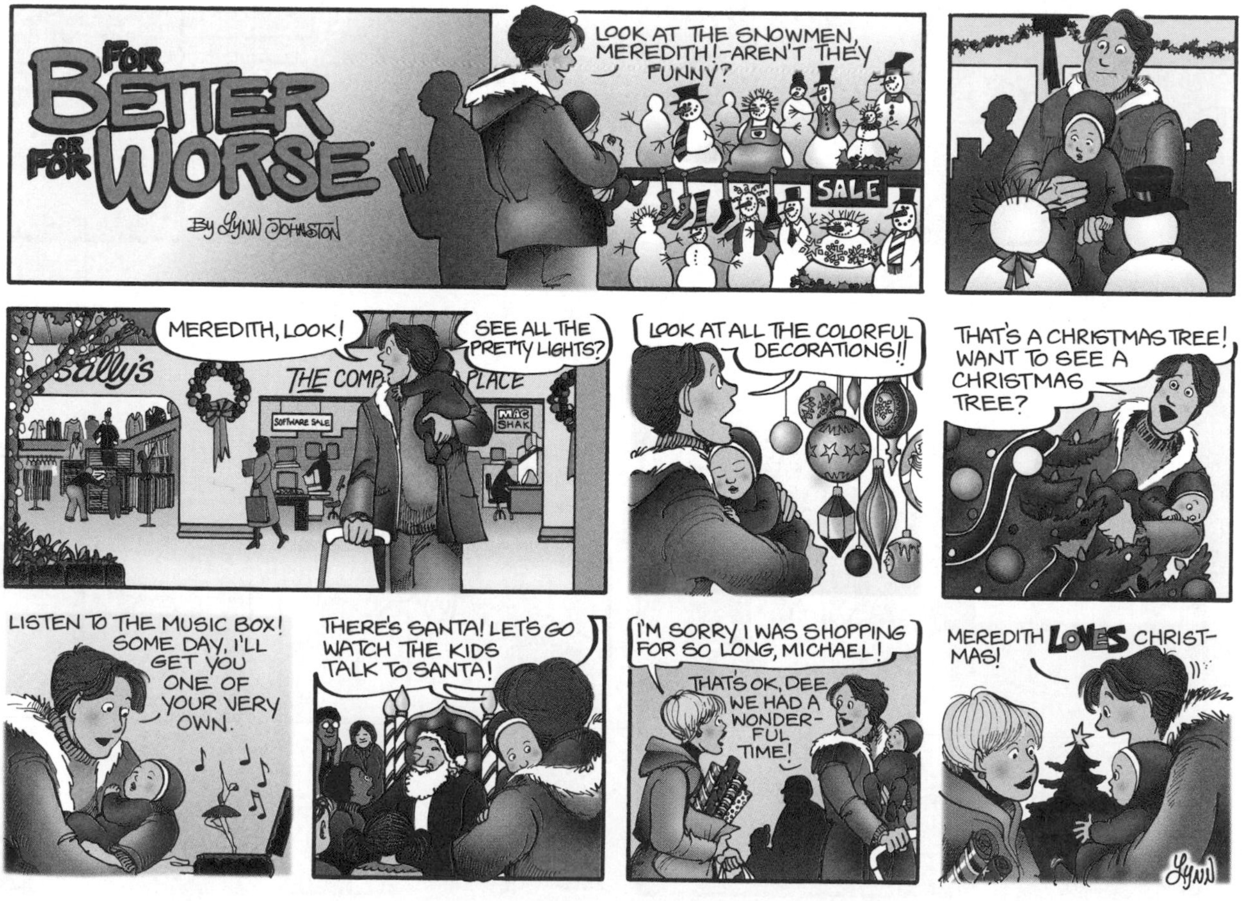
FOR BETTER OR FOR WORSE
By Lynn Johnston
LOOK AT THE SNOWMEN, MEREDITH! –AREN'T THEY FUNNY?
SALE
MEREDITH, LOOK!
SEE ALL THE PRETTY LIGHTS?
Sally's
THE COMPUTER PLACE
SOFTWARE SALE
MAC SHAK
LOOK AT ALL THE COLORFUL DECORATIONS!!
THAT'S A CHRISTMAS TREE! WANT TO SEE A CHRISTMAS TREE?
LISTEN TO THE MUSIC BOX! SOME DAY, I'LL GET YOU ONE OF YOUR VERY OWN.
THERE'S SANTA! LET'S GO WATCH THE KIDS TALK TO SANTA!
I'M SORRY I WAS SHOPPING FOR SO LONG, MICHAEL!
THAT'S OK, DEE. WE HAD A WONDERFUL TIME!
MEREDITH LOVES CHRISTMAS!
Lynn

Panel 1: MY MOM SAID YES! — SHE SAID WE COULD PRACTICE DOWNSTAIRS!
TOUCHDOWN, DUDES!
OK!
EXCELLENT!

Panel 2: WE COULD BECOME AN ACTUAL GROUP, GUYS!
WE COULD TOUR!
WHAT SHOULD WE CALL OURSELVES?
WE NEED A GOOD NAME!

Panel 3: WHAT ABOUT "PHATCHANCE"?
NAH. I LIKE "VENOMOUS" — IT'S GOTTA BE VENOMOUS SOMETHING.
I LIKE "PEACEBEINGS"
UH, GUYS...

Panel 4: SHOULDN'T WE LEARN HOW TO PLAY SOMETHING, FIRST?

Panel 5: THIS IS AWESOME! WE'RE SET UP LIKE AN ACTUAL BAND!

Panel 6: I TOLD MR. BERGAN WHAT WE WERE DOING, AN' HE GAVE ME SOME SIMPLE PIECES TO HELP US GET USED TO PLAYING TOGETHER.

Panel 7: WHAKKITA BAM BOP, WHAKKITA BAM BOP
POINK
TWANGG
FOOM

Panel 8: BOOMPAWAP FWOINGGGABLANGG FOOM-FOOM BLAM
ARE YOU SURE YOU DON'T MIND HAVING THE GROUP HERE, ELLY?
WHAT?

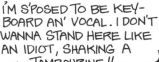

Panel 9: COME ON, GUYS. EVERYONE'S PLAYIN' THEIR OWN THING! IF WE'RE GONNA BE SERIOUS, WE HAFTA TAKE ONE PIECE OF MUSIC, AN' WORK ON IT!

Panel 10: WHEN DO I GET TO SING?
LATER, OK?
JUST KEEP A RHYTHM WITH THE TAMBOURINE FOR AWHILE.

Panel 11: I'M S'POSED TO BE KEYBOARD AN' VOCAL. I DON'T WANNA STAND HERE LIKE AN IDIOT, SHAKING A TAMBOURINE!!

Panel 12: NO PROBLEM, BECKY — YOU CAN JUST STAND THERE LIKE AN IDIOT **WITHOUT** ONE!
JINGLE CHINKA JINGG!

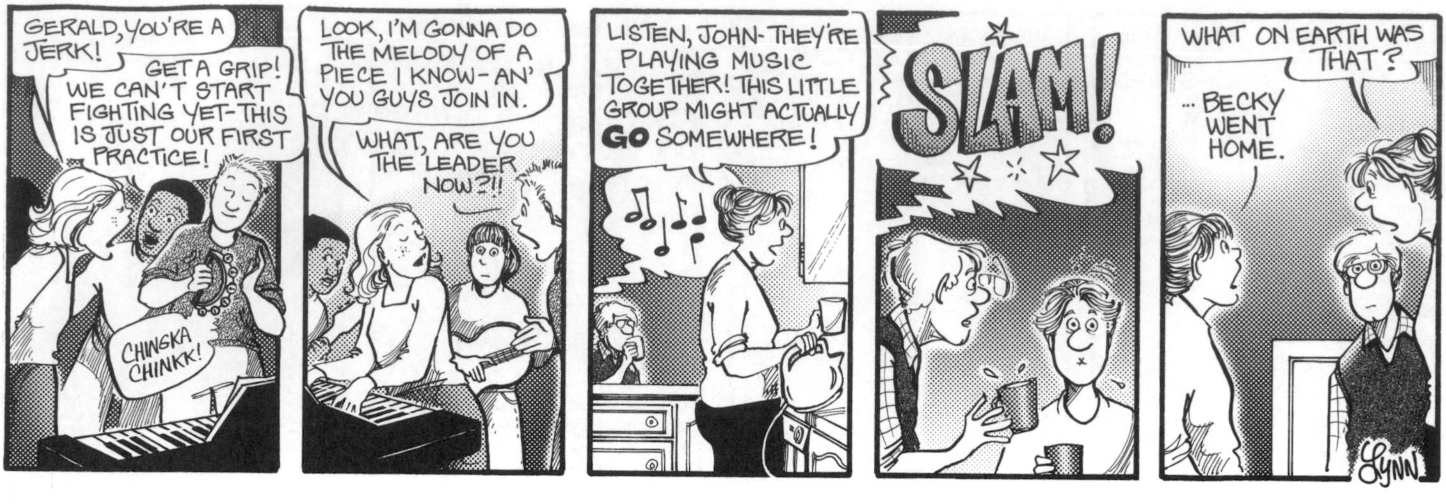
GERALD, YOU'RE A JERK!
GET A GRIP! WE CAN'T START FIGHTING YET- THIS IS JUST OUR FIRST PRACTICE!
CHINGKA CHINKK!
LOOK, I'M GONNA DO THE MELODY OF A PIECE I KNOW- AN' YOU GUYS JOIN IN.
WHAT, ARE YOU THE LEADER NOW?!!
LISTEN, JOHN- THEY'RE PLAYING MUSIC TOGETHER! THIS LITTLE GROUP MIGHT ACTUALLY GO SOMEWHERE!
SLAM!
WHAT ON EARTH WAS THAT?
... BECKY WENT HOME.
LYNN

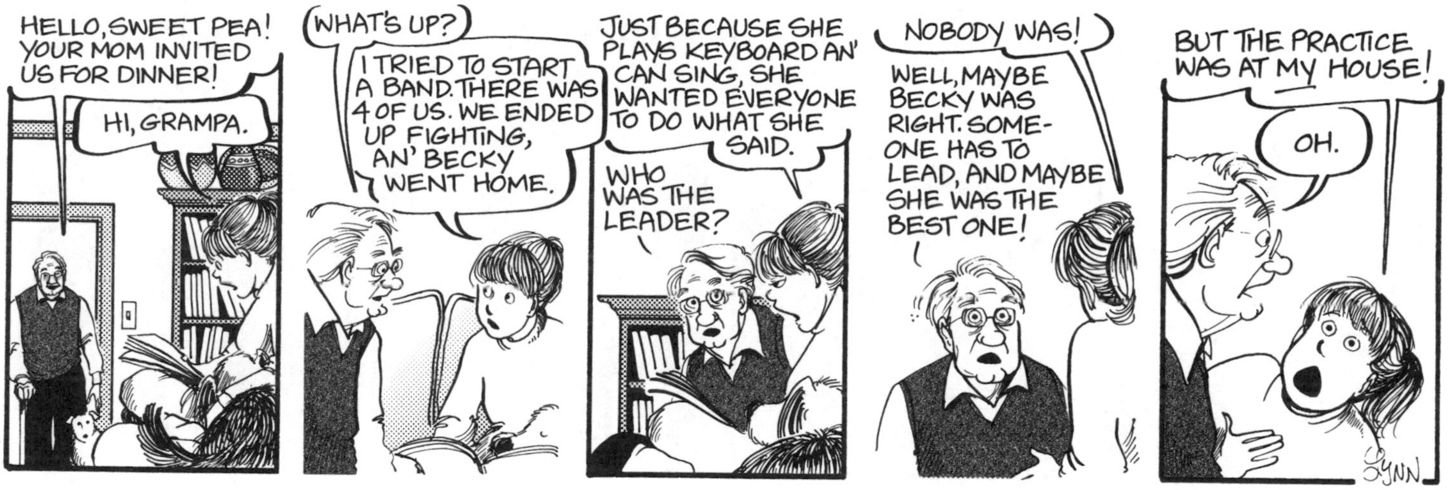
HELLO, SWEET PEA! YOUR MOM INVITED US FOR DINNER!
HI, GRAMPA.
WHAT'S UP?
I TRIED TO START A BAND. THERE WAS 4 OF US. WE ENDED UP FIGHTING, AN' BECKY WENT HOME.
JUST BECAUSE SHE PLAYS KEYBOARD AN' CAN SING, SHE WANTED EVERYONE TO DO WHAT SHE SAID.
WHO WAS THE LEADER?
NOBODY WAS!
WELL, MAYBE BECKY WAS RIGHT. SOMEONE HAS TO LEAD, AND MAYBE SHE WAS THE BEST ONE!
BUT THE PRACTICE WAS AT MY HOUSE!
OH.
LYNN

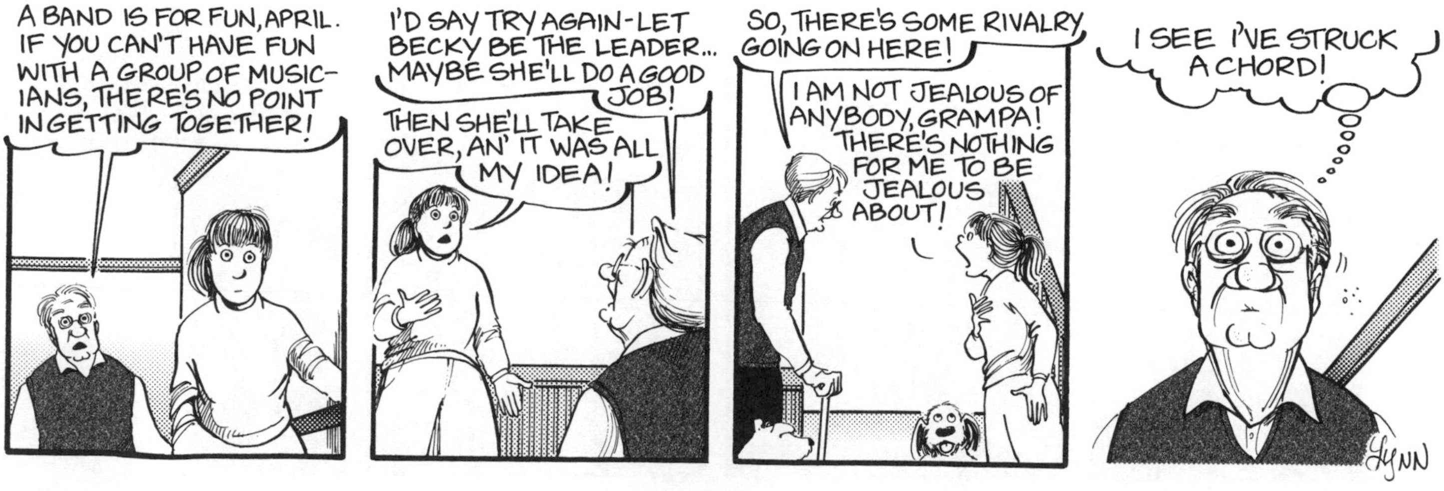
A BAND IS FOR FUN, APRIL. IF YOU CAN'T HAVE FUN WITH A GROUP OF MUSICIANS, THERE'S NO POINT IN GETTING TOGETHER!
I'D SAY TRY AGAIN- LET BECKY BE THE LEADER... MAYBE SHE'LL DO A GOOD JOB!
THEN SHE'LL TAKE OVER, AN' IT WAS ALL MY IDEA!
SO, THERE'S SOME RIVALRY GOING ON HERE!
I AM NOT JEALOUS OF ANYBODY, GRAMPA! THERE'S NOTHING FOR ME TO BE JEALOUS ABOUT!
I SEE I'VE STRUCK A CHORD!
LYNN

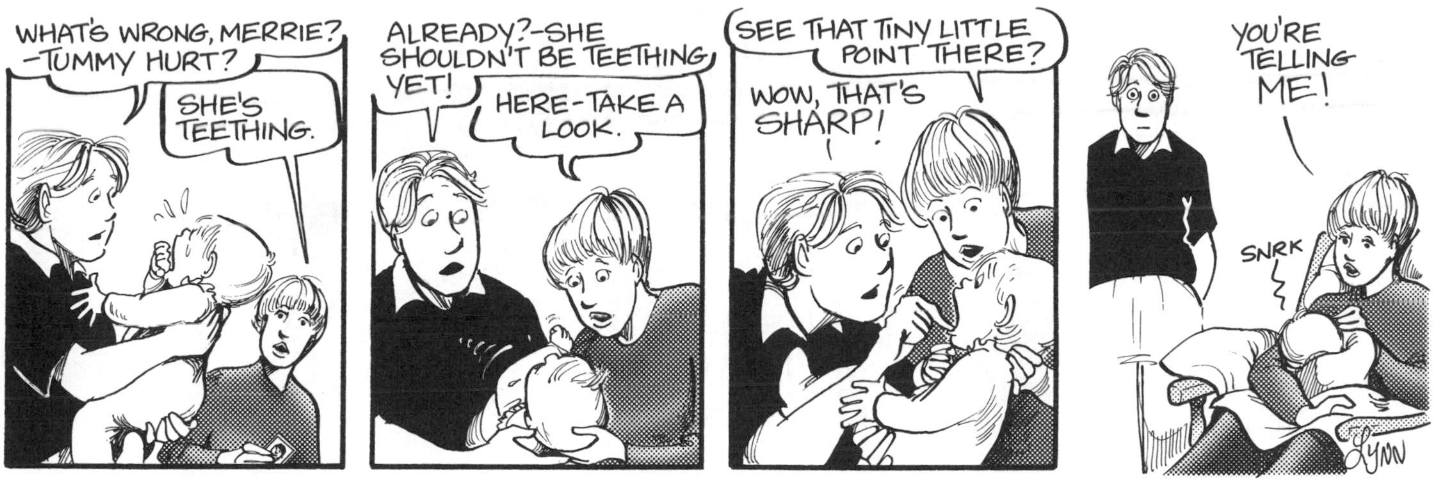
WHAT'S WRONG, MERRIE? -TUMMY HURT?
SHE'S TEETHING.
ALREADY?-SHE SHOULDN'T BE TEETHING YET!
HERE-TAKE A LOOK.
SEE THAT TINY LITTLE POINT THERE?
WOW, THAT'S SHARP!
YOU'RE TELLING ME!
SNRK
LYNN

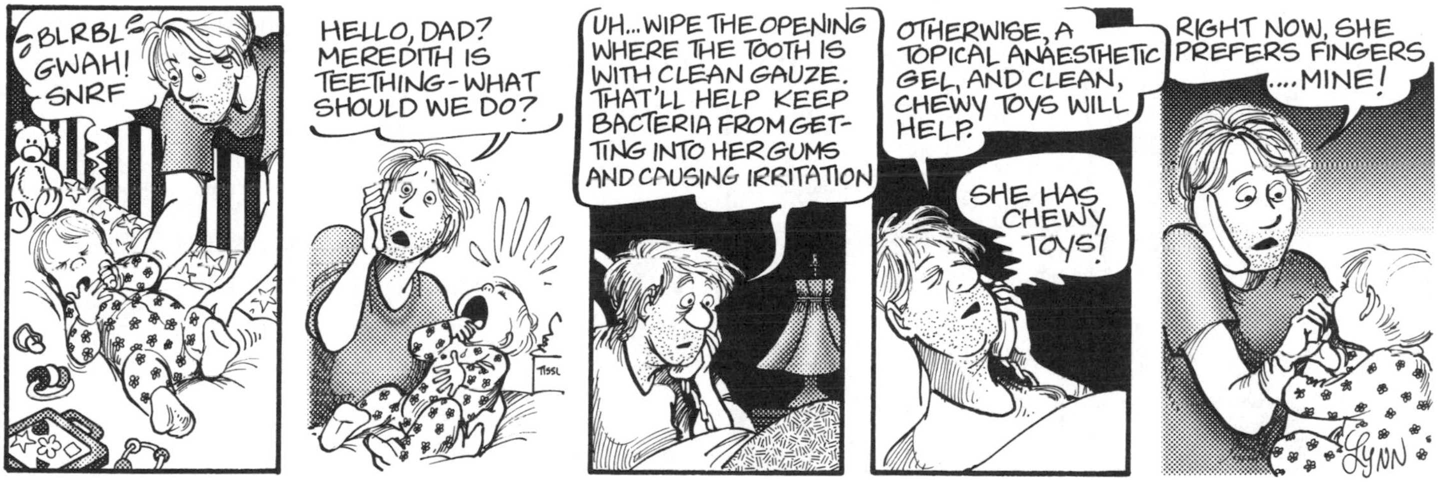
BLRBL GWAH! SNRF
HELLO, DAD? MEREDITH IS TEETHING-WHAT SHOULD WE DO?
UH...WIPE THE OPENING WHERE THE TOOTH IS WITH CLEAN GAUZE. THAT'LL HELP KEEP BACTERIA FROM GETTING INTO HER GUMS AND CAUSING IRRITATION
OTHERWISE, A TOPICAL ANAESTHETIC GEL, AND CLEAN, CHEWY TOYS WILL HELP.
SHE HAS CHEWY TOYS!
RIGHT NOW, SHE PREFERS FINGERS ....MINE!
LYNN

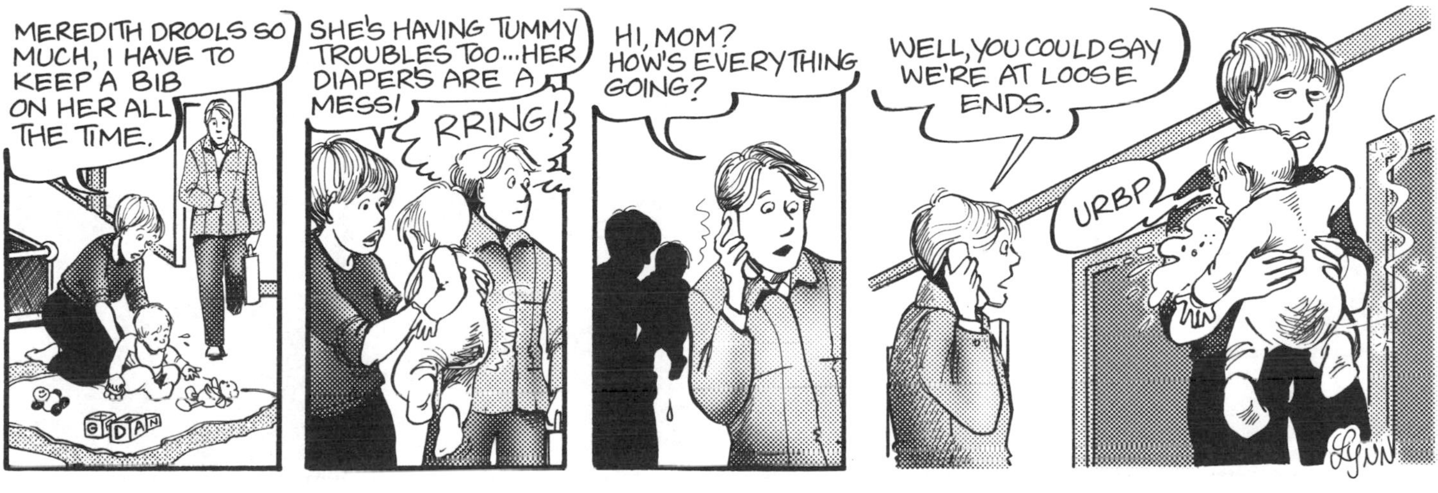
MEREDITH DROOLS SO MUCH, I HAVE TO KEEP A BIB ON HER ALL THE TIME.
SHE'S HAVING TUMMY TROUBLES TOO...HER DIAPER'S ARE A MESS!
RRING!
HI, MOM? HOW'S EVERYTHING GOING?
WELL, YOU COULD SAY WE'RE AT LOOSE ENDS.
URBP
LYNN

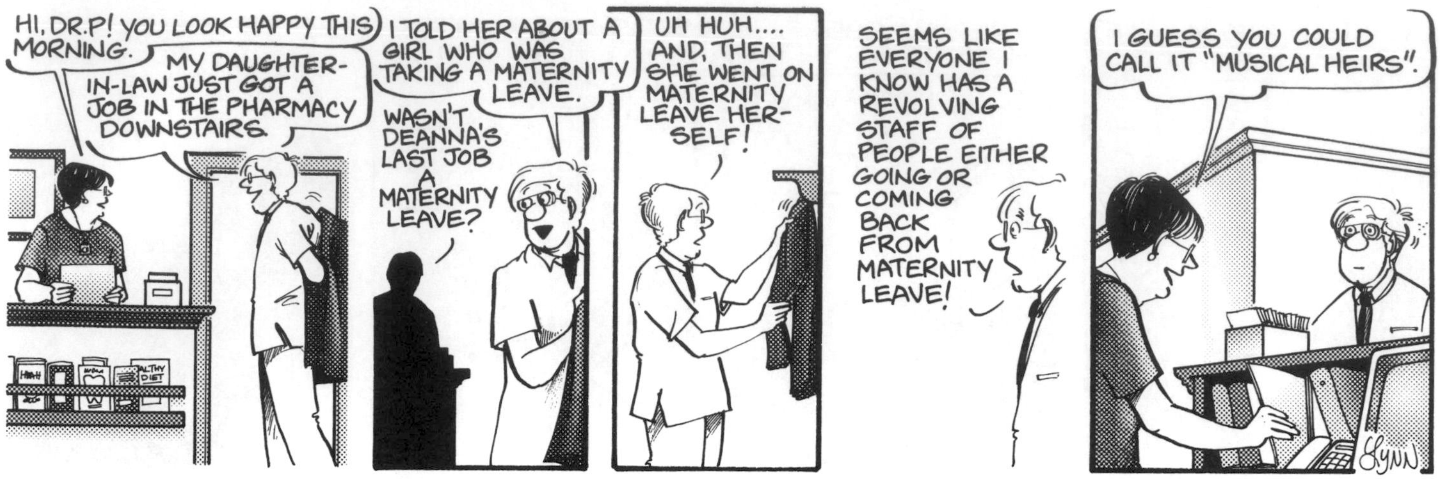
HI, DR.P! YOU LOOK HAPPY THIS MORNING.
MY DAUGHTER-IN-LAW JUST GOT A JOB IN THE PHARMACY DOWNSTAIRS.
I TOLD HER ABOUT A GIRL WHO WAS TAKING A MATERNITY LEAVE.
WASN'T DEANNA'S LAST JOB A MATERNITY LEAVE?
UH HUH.... AND, THEN SHE WENT ON MATERNITY LEAVE HERSELF!
SEEMS LIKE EVERYONE I KNOW HAS A REVOLVING STAFF OF PEOPLE EITHER GOING OR COMING BACK FROM MATERNITY LEAVE!
I GUESS YOU COULD CALL IT "MUSICAL HEIRS".
LYNN

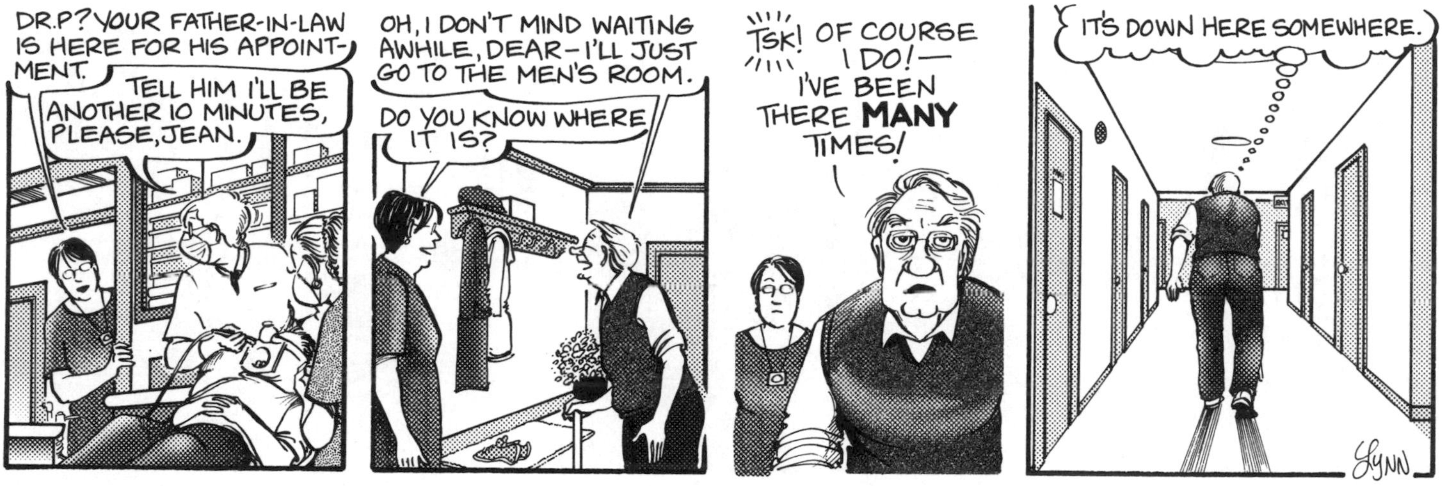
DR.P? YOUR FATHER-IN-LAW IS HERE FOR HIS APPOINTMENT.
TELL HIM I'LL BE ANOTHER 10 MINUTES, PLEASE, JEAN.
OH, I DON'T MIND WAITING AWHILE, DEAR – I'LL JUST GO TO THE MEN'S ROOM.
DO YOU KNOW WHERE IT IS?
TSK! OF COURSE I DO! — I'VE BEEN THERE MANY TIMES!
IT'S DOWN HERE SOMEWHERE.
LYNN

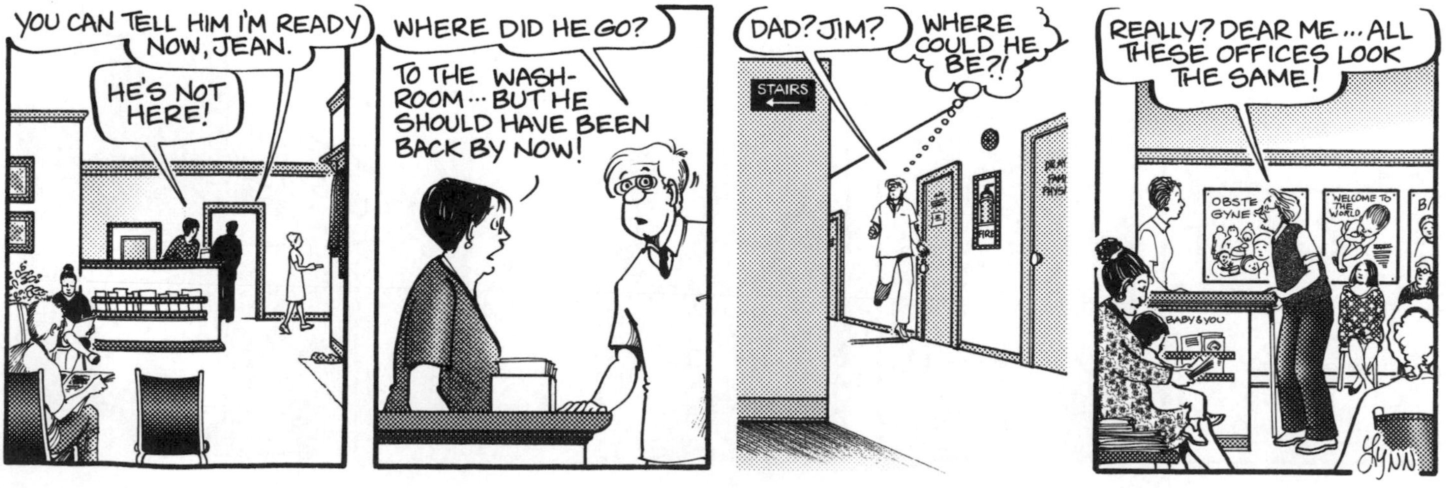
YOU CAN TELL HIM I'M READY NOW, JEAN.
HE'S NOT HERE!
WHERE DID HE GO?
TO THE WASHROOM... BUT HE SHOULD HAVE BEEN BACK BY NOW!
DAD? JIM?
WHERE COULD HE BE?!
STAIRS
REALLY? DEAR ME... ALL THESE OFFICES LOOK THE SAME!
LYNN

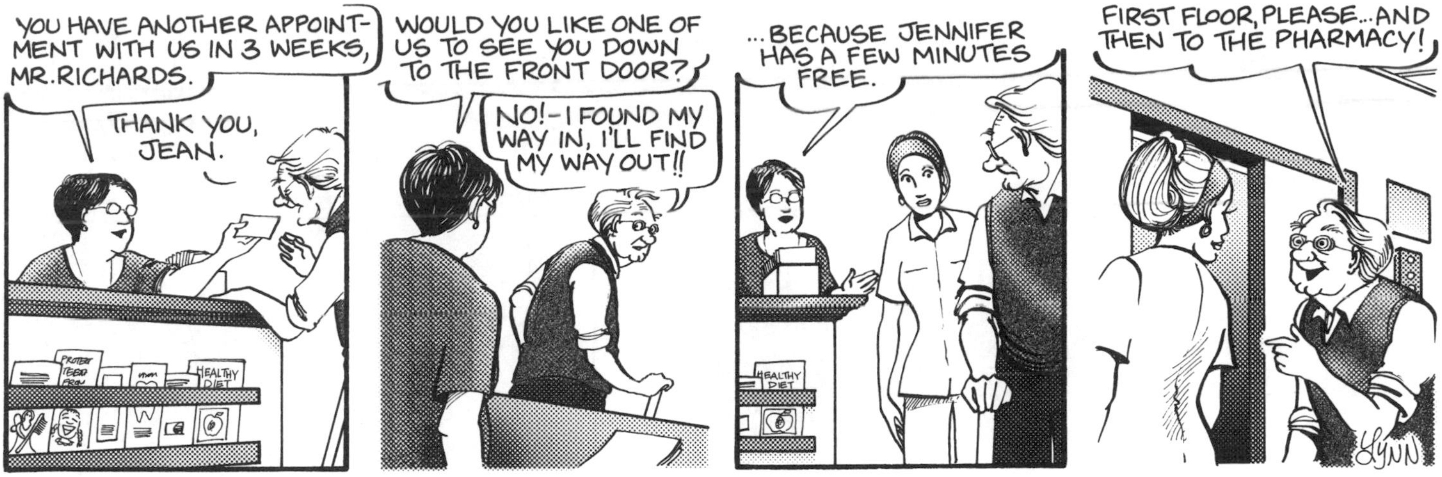
YOU HAVE ANOTHER APPOINTMENT WITH US IN 3 WEEKS, MR. RICHARDS.
THANK YOU, JEAN.
HEALTHY DIET
WOULD YOU LIKE ONE OF US TO SEE YOU DOWN TO THE FRONT DOOR?
NO! - I FOUND MY WAY IN, I'LL FIND MY WAY OUT!!
...BECAUSE JENNIFER HAS A FEW MINUTES FREE.
HEALTHY DIET
FIRST FLOOR, PLEASE... AND THEN TO THE PHARMACY!
LYNN

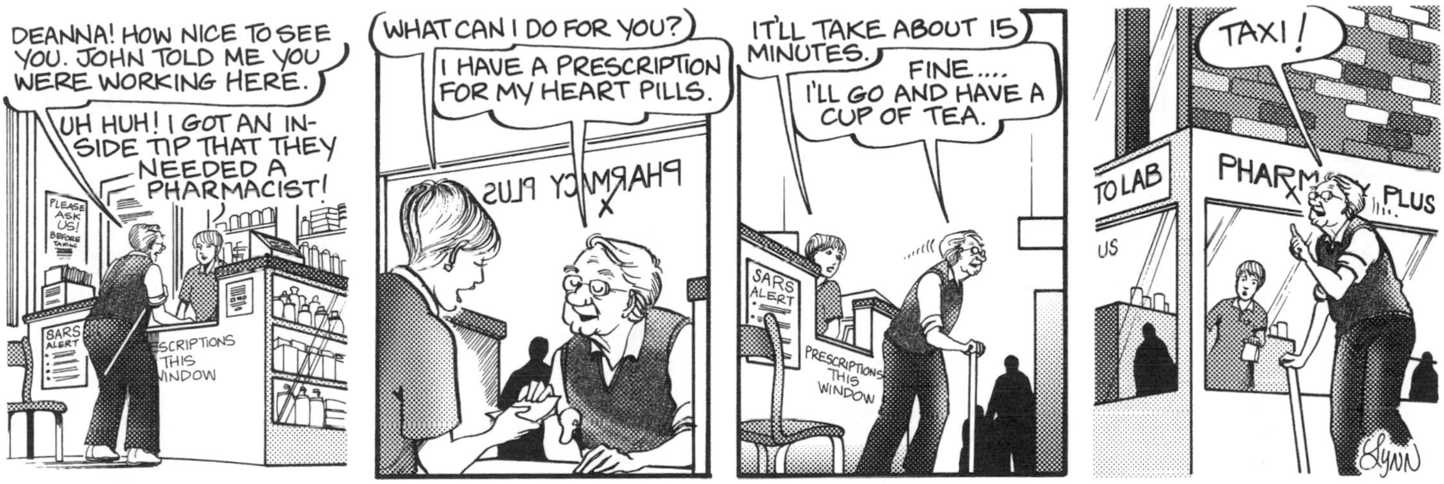
DEANNA! HOW NICE TO SEE YOU. JOHN TOLD ME YOU WERE WORKING HERE.
UH HUH! I GOT AN INSIDE TIP THAT THEY NEEDED A PHARMACIST!
PLEASE ASK US! BEFORE TAKING
SARS ALERT
PRESCRIPTIONS THIS WINDOW
WHAT CAN I DO FOR YOU?
I HAVE A PRESCRIPTION FOR MY HEART PILLS.
IT'LL TAKE ABOUT 15 MINUTES.
FINE.... I'LL GO AND HAVE A CUP OF TEA.
SARS ALERT
PRESCRIPTIONS THIS WINDOW
TAXI!
TO LAB
PHARM PLUS
LYNN

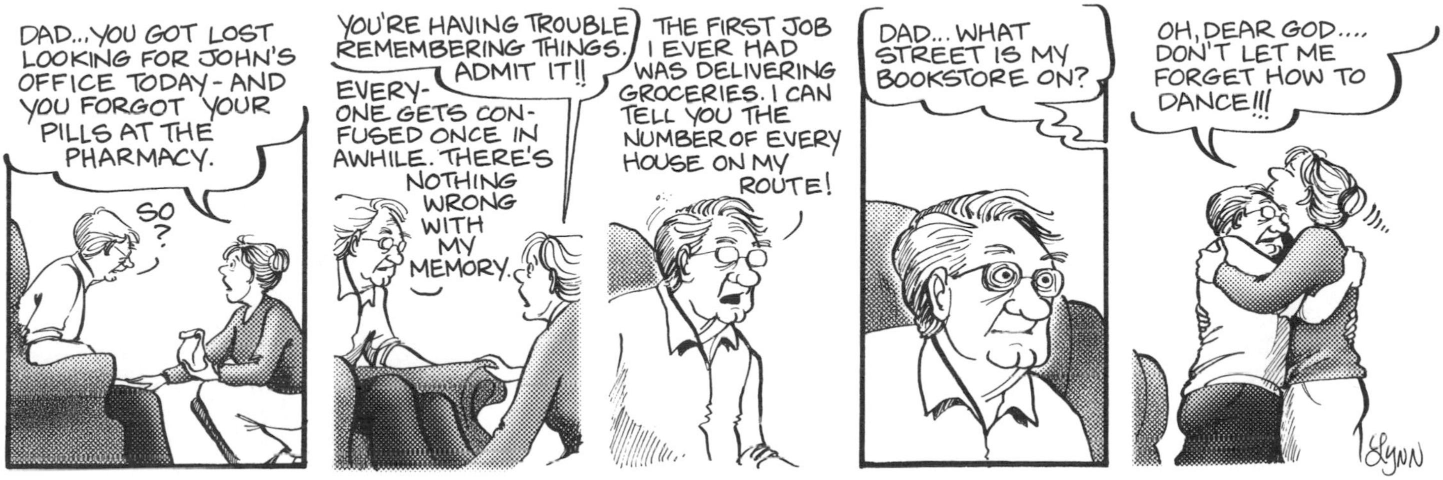
DAD... YOU GOT LOST LOOKING FOR JOHN'S OFFICE TODAY - AND YOU FORGOT YOUR PILLS AT THE PHARMACY.
SO ?
YOU'RE HAVING TROUBLE REMEMBERING THINGS. ADMIT IT!!
EVERYONE GETS CONFUSED ONCE IN AWHILE. THERE'S NOTHING WRONG WITH MY MEMORY.
THE FIRST JOB I EVER HAD WAS DELIVERING GROCERIES. I CAN TELL YOU THE NUMBER OF EVERY HOUSE ON MY ROUTE!
DAD... WHAT STREET IS MY BOOKSTORE ON?
OH, DEAR GOD.... DON'T LET ME FORGET HOW TO DANCE!!!
LYNN

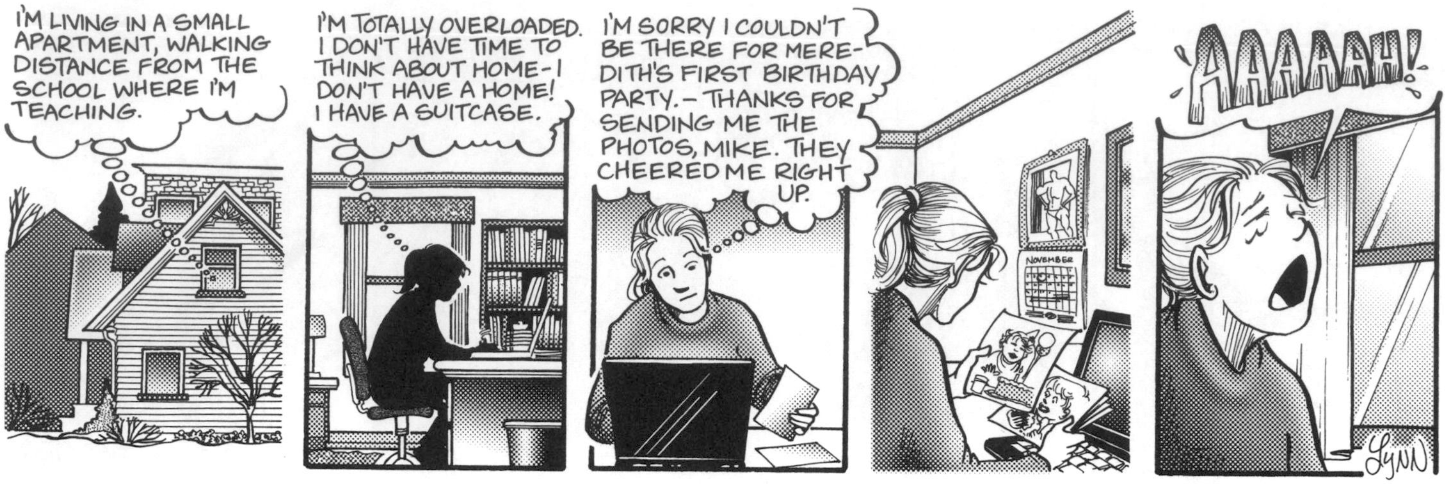
I'M LIVING IN A SMALL APARTMENT, WALKING DISTANCE FROM THE SCHOOL WHERE I'M TEACHING.
I'M TOTALLY OVERLOADED. I DON'T HAVE TIME TO THINK ABOUT HOME - I DON'T HAVE A HOME! I HAVE A SUITCASE.
I'M SORRY I COULDN'T BE THERE FOR MEREDITH'S FIRST BIRTHDAY PARTY. - THANKS FOR SENDING ME THE PHOTOS, MIKE. THEY CHEERED ME RIGHT UP.
NOVEMBER
AAAAAH!
LYNN

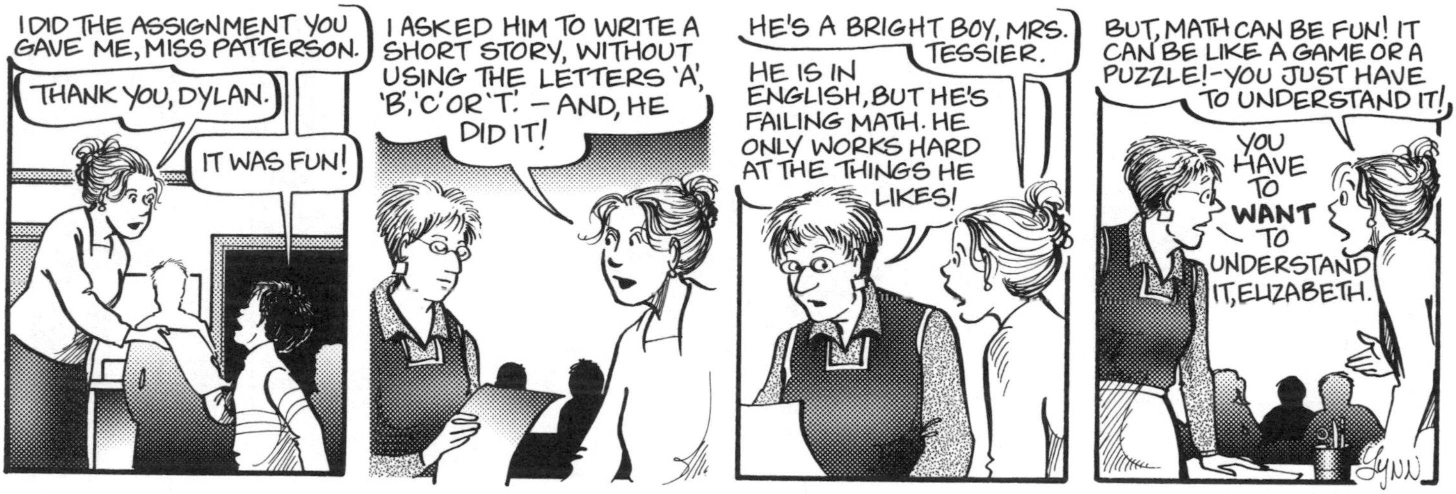
I DID THE ASSIGNMENT YOU GAVE ME, MISS PATTERSON.
THANK YOU, DYLAN.
IT WAS FUN!
I ASKED HIM TO WRITE A SHORT STORY, WITHOUT USING THE LETTERS 'A', 'B', 'C' OR 'T'. - AND, HE DID IT!
HE'S A BRIGHT BOY, MRS. TESSIER.
HE IS IN ENGLISH, BUT HE'S FAILING MATH. HE ONLY WORKS HARD AT THE THINGS HE LIKES!
BUT, MATH CAN BE FUN! IT CAN BE LIKE A GAME OR A PUZZLE! - YOU JUST HAVE TO UNDERSTAND IT!
YOU HAVE TO **WANT** TO UNDERSTAND IT, ELIZABETH.
LYNN

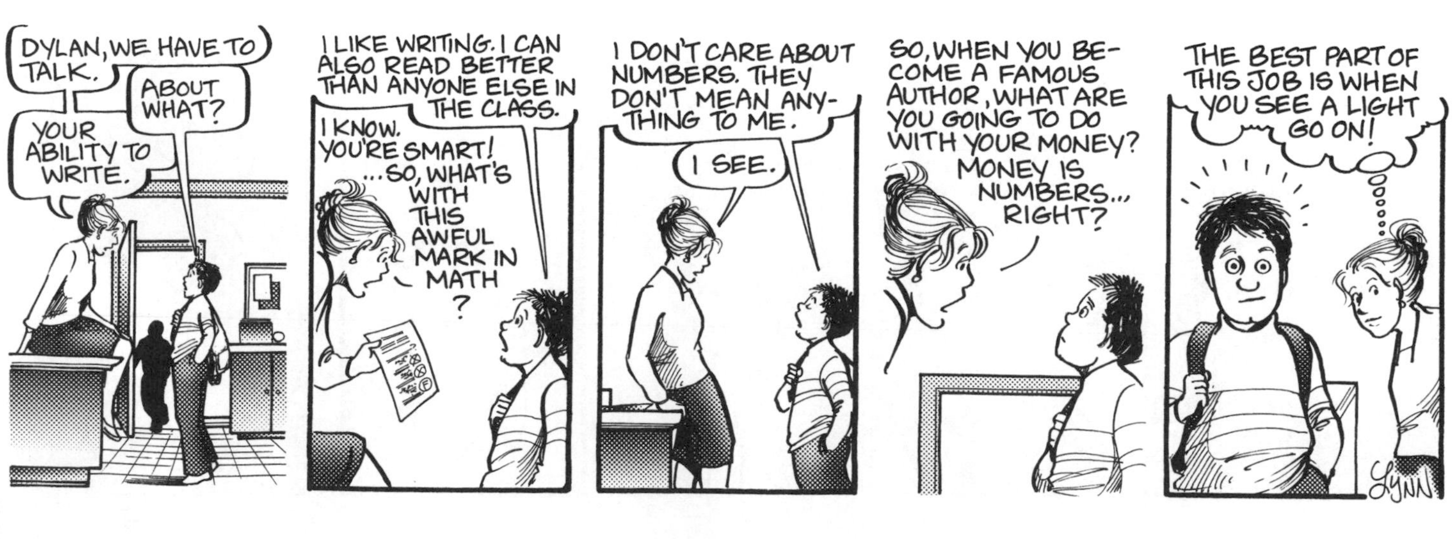
DYLAN, WE HAVE TO TALK.
ABOUT WHAT?
YOUR ABILITY TO WRITE.
I LIKE WRITING. I CAN ALSO READ BETTER THAN ANYONE ELSE IN THE CLASS.
I KNOW. YOU'RE SMART! ...SO, WHAT'S WITH THIS AWFUL MARK IN MATH?
I DON'T CARE ABOUT NUMBERS. THEY DON'T MEAN ANYTHING TO ME.
I SEE.
SO, WHEN YOU BECOME A FAMOUS AUTHOR, WHAT ARE YOU GOING TO DO WITH YOUR MONEY?
MONEY IS NUMBERS.., RIGHT?
THE BEST PART OF THIS JOB IS WHEN YOU SEE A LIGHT GO ON!
LYNN

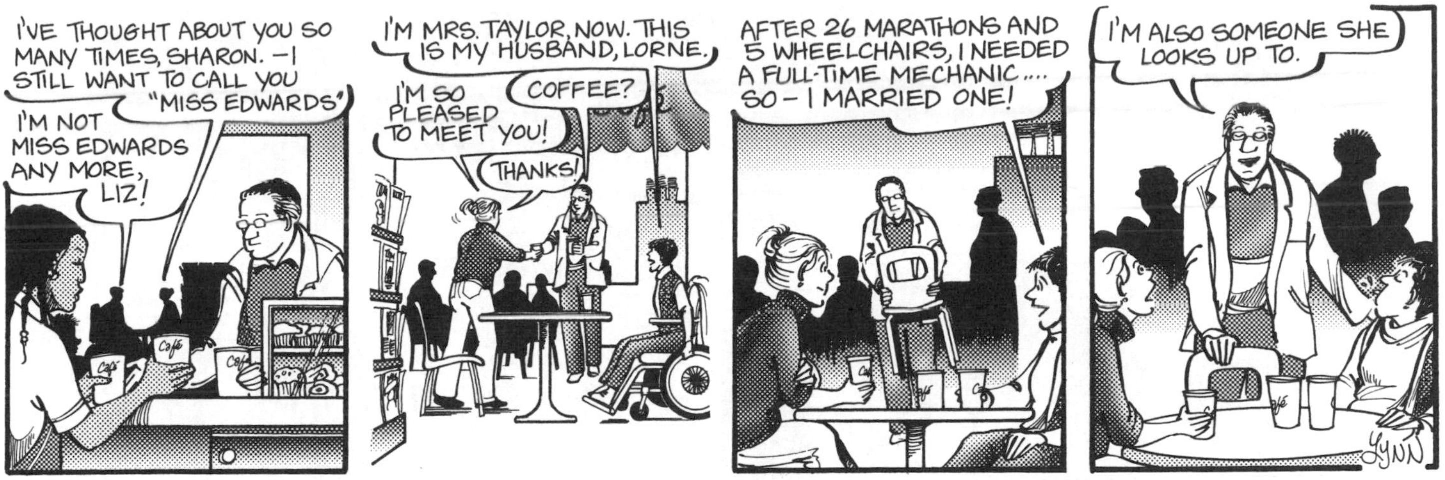
I'VE THOUGHT ABOUT YOU SO MANY TIMES, SHARON. —I STILL WANT TO CALL YOU "MISS EDWARDS"
I'M NOT MISS EDWARDS ANY MORE, LIZ!
I'M MRS. TAYLOR, NOW. THIS IS MY HUSBAND, LORNE.
I'M SO PLEASED TO MEET YOU!
COFFEE?
THANKS!
AFTER 26 MARATHONS AND 5 WHEELCHAIRS, I NEEDED A FULL-TIME MECHANIC.... SO – I MARRIED ONE!
I'M ALSO SOMEONE SHE LOOKS UP TO.
LYNN

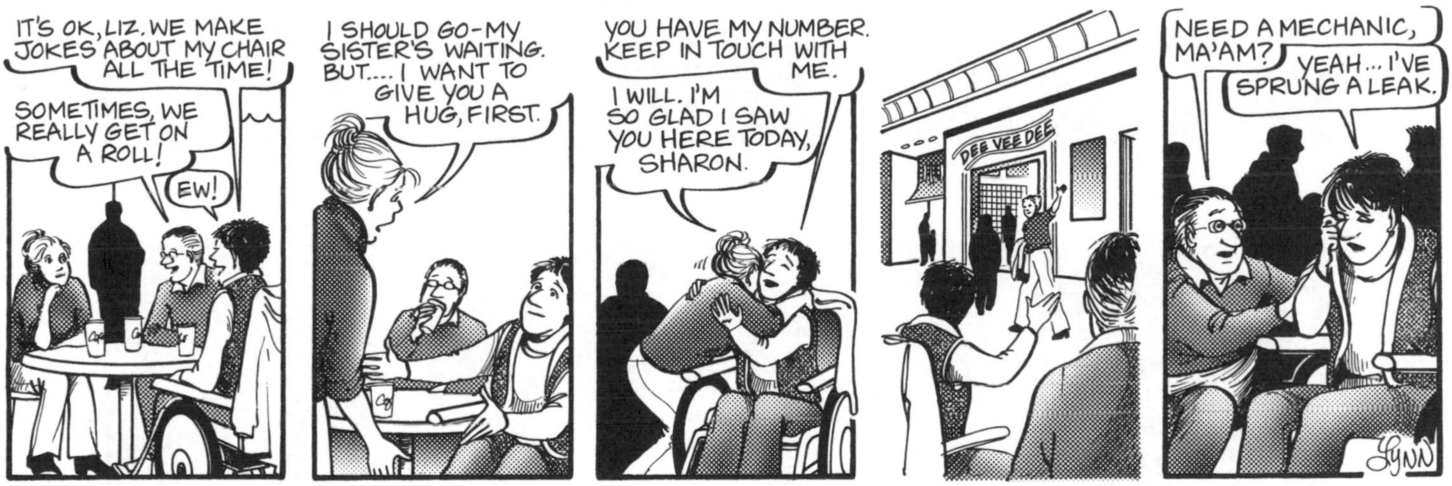
IT'S OK, LIZ. WE MAKE JOKES ABOUT MY CHAIR ALL THE TIME!
SOMETIMES, WE REALLY GET ON A ROLL!
EW!
I SHOULD GO—MY SISTER'S WAITING. BUT.... I WANT TO GIVE YOU A HUG, FIRST.
YOU HAVE MY NUMBER. KEEP IN TOUCH WITH ME.
I WILL. I'M SO GLAD I SAW YOU HERE TODAY, SHARON.
DEE VEE DEE
NEED A MECHANIC, MA'AM?
YEAH... I'VE SPRUNG A LEAK.
LYNN

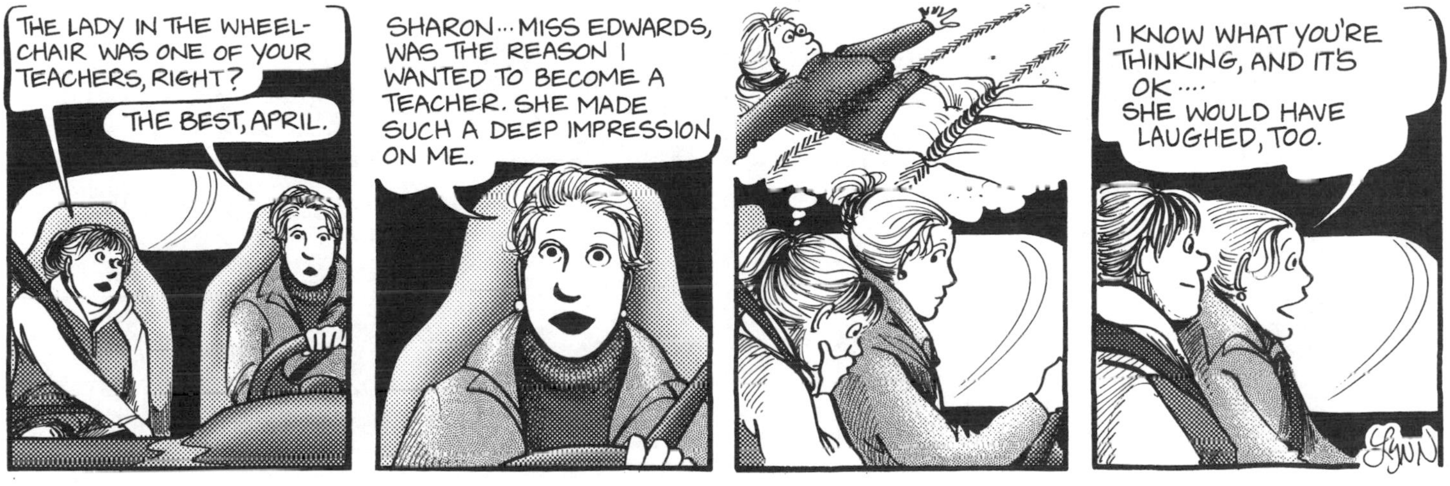
THE LADY IN THE WHEEL-CHAIR WAS ONE OF YOUR TEACHERS, RIGHT?
THE BEST, APRIL.
SHARON... MISS EDWARDS, WAS THE REASON I WANTED TO BECOME A TEACHER. SHE MADE SUCH A DEEP IMPRESSION ON ME.
I KNOW WHAT YOU'RE THINKING, AND IT'S OK.... SHE WOULD HAVE LAUGHED, TOO.
LYNN

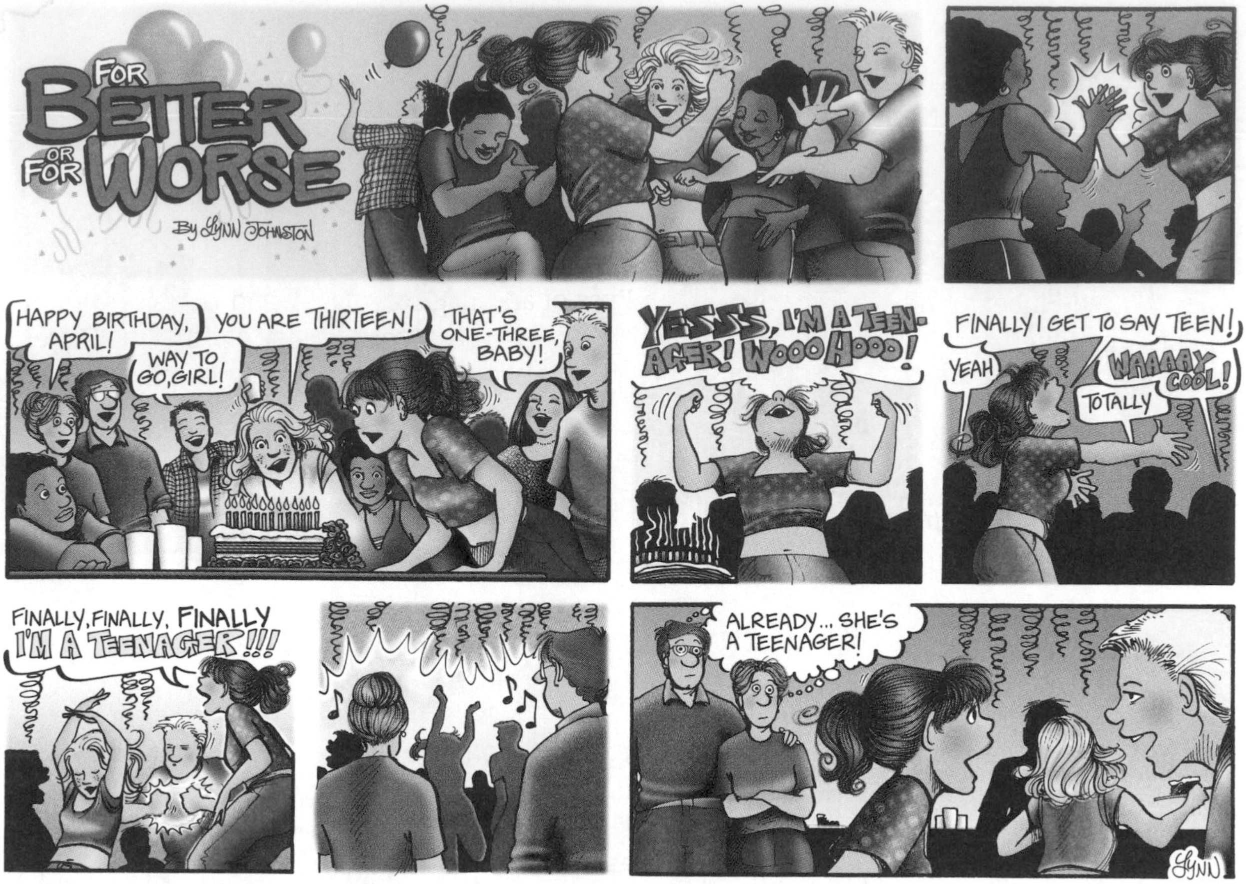
FOR BETTER OR FOR WORSE
By Lynn Johnston
HAPPY BIRTHDAY, APRIL!
YOU ARE THIRTEEN!
WAY TO GO, GIRL!
THAT'S ONE-THREE, BABY!
YESSS, I'M A TEEN-AGER! WOOO HOOO!
FINALLY I GET TO SAY TEEN!
YEAH
TOTALLY
WAAAAY COOL!
FINALLY, FINALLY, FINALLY
I'M A TEENAGER!!!
ALREADY... SHE'S A TEENAGER!
LYNN

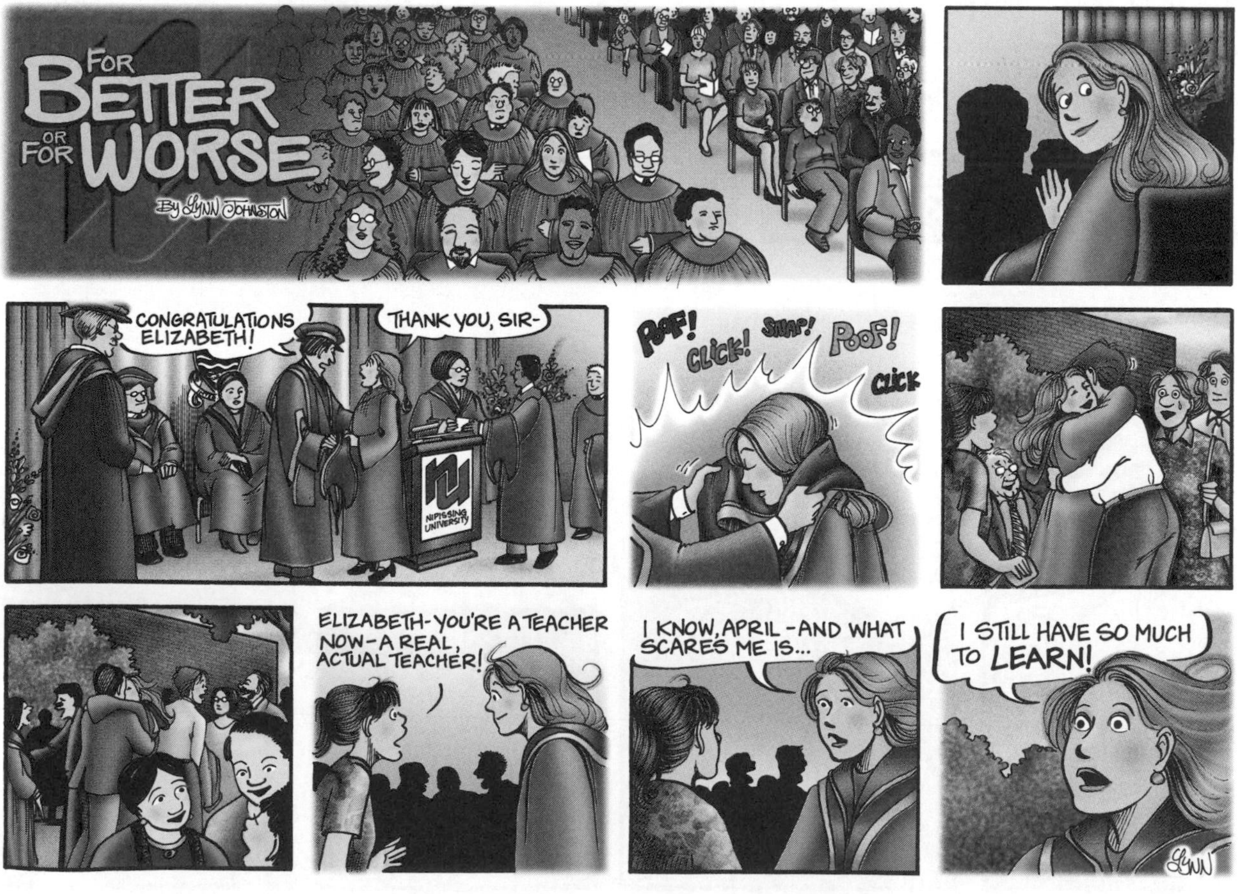
FOR BETTER OR FOR WORSE
By Lynn Johnston
CONGRATULATIONS ELIZABETH!
THANK YOU, SIR-
NIPISSING UNIVERSITY
POOF!
CLICK!
SNAP!
POOF!
CLICK
ELIZABETH- YOU'RE A TEACHER NOW- A REAL, ACTUAL TEACHER!
I KNOW, APRIL - AND WHAT SCARES ME IS...
I STILL HAVE SO MUCH TO LEARN!
LYNN

Afterword

Come September, I will have chronicled the lives of an imaginary family and their friends for 25 years. The time has gone by so fast! Rod and I look at photographs of ourselves then and are surprised by how young we looked! His hair has suddenly started to turn silver, and mine, too, is graying in the same pattern as my mother's did. Our children are adults with whom we have a loving and mature relationship. It feels good to see that when they left the nest, we really had taught them how to fly.

We have shared my unusual job together. It has sometimes hurt, but it has also been a blessing. We have met some of our heroes. Financially, we have enough to share. We have had the opportunity to work with and become close to wonderful, talented people, and we have had a very personal relationship with millions more! It's my syndicate who gave me a chance of a lifetime and the readers who accepted my work that I must thank. It has not been a job but a privilege to have been able to let this parallel world flow through me into newsprint. The best part is knowing so many people have shared this comic strip saga with us for so long! It has been a pleasure to work for and with you.

Sincerely,

Lynn

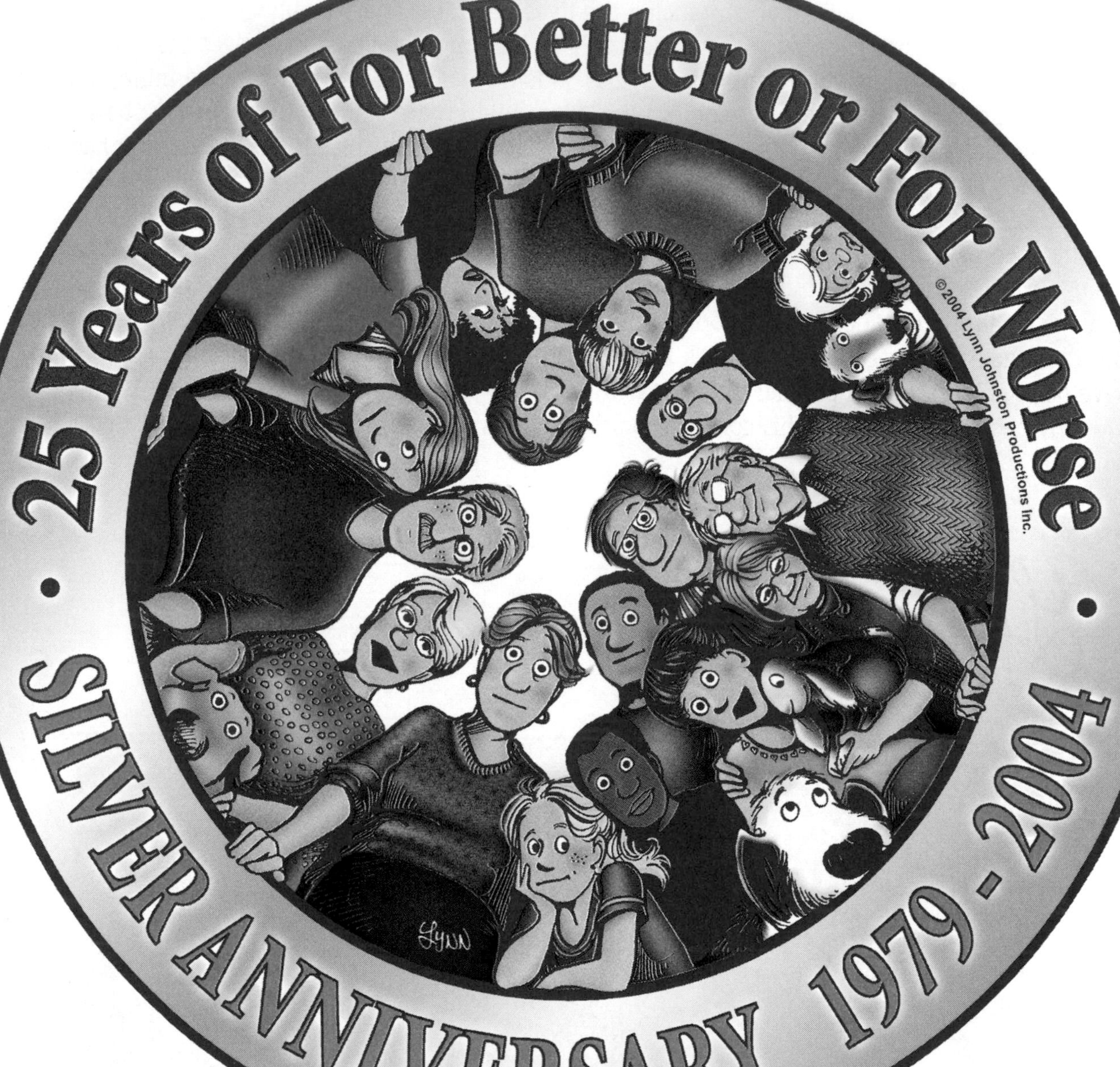

25 Years of For Better or For Worse
SILVER ANNIVERSARY 1979 - 2004
©2004 Lynn Johnston Productions Inc.
LYNN